Baseball Prospectus

2000

Jeff Bower
Clay Davenport
Jeff Hildebrand
Rany Jazayerli
Chris Kahrl
Keith Law
Dave Pease
Steven Rubio
Joseph S. Sheehan
Greg Spira
Michael Wolverton
Keith Woolner

Brassey's Sports

Brassey's

WASHINGTON, D.C.

Editorial Offices:
22841 Quicksilver Drive
Dulles, VA 20166

Order Department:
P.O. Box 960
Herndon, VA 20172

Brassey's books are available at special discounts for bulk purchases for sales promotions, premiums, fund-raising, or educational use.

Designed by Pen & Palette Unlimited

First Edition

10 9 8 7 6 5 4 3 2 1

Printed in the United States of America

Contents

Fungoes

Acknowledgments

We *Prospectus* types need to thank a lot of the people who help make this book possible, either through their contributions or suggestions or because they're major- and minor-league baseball personnel who have taken the time to answer our questions, bring us into the press box and give us insight into their organizations.

As always, we're grateful to our publisher, Brassey's, and especially Julie Kuzneski, who managed not to lose her cool no matter how many times we stretched our deadlines; Don McKeon for his input; Don Rodgers of Pen & Palette for his work on layout; and Deborah Way and Will Allison for their work on copyediting this year's manuscript.

Among people in the commentator community, we're grateful to Rob Neyer of ESPN.com for his support as well as his constructive criticism; *BP* alum Gary Huckabay for his direct and occasionally brutal recommendations; Harold Brooks for his willingness to review our work from time to time for statistical accuracy; Mat Olkin of STATS, Inc. and now *Baseball Weekly* for a few kind words and probably even a shared dream; and prospect mavens John Sickels of STATS, Inc. and David Rawnsley of *Baseball America* for occasionally sharing their points of view. In an industry filled with interesting and good-natured folks, these are the ones who stand out.

Within the professional baseball community, several people have been extremely helpful. Jeff Bower would like to thank Tim Hevly, formerly of the Seattle Mariners (Media Relations), Tampa Bay Devil Rays' Carmen Molina (Media Relations), the Tacoma Rainiers' Kevin Kalal (Media Relations) and Mike Curto (announcer), the Everett AquaSox's Robb Stanton (you name it, he does it). I'd like to thank the White Sox's Kenny Williams, the Twins' Rob Antony, the A's Billy Beane and Grady Fuson, the Cubs' Ed Lynch and Sharon Pannozzo, the Astros' Tim Purpura, and the Expos' Monique Giroux. I'd like to really express my heartfelt appreciation to Scott Reifert, Jennifer Sloan and the rest of the crew in the White Sox's Public Relations department for going above and beyond the call of duty.

Dave Pease wants to say thanks to Andres Phippard, Woody Farmer, Dan DuPont, Kristy Thompson and Debbie Arellano for their help on this year's book. Massive props to Felix Wisgo for his help with Web page administration, and thanks to Jeff Pease, who took time out of his busy schedule to help with the cover art and the Web page. Keith Woolner wants to thank Ted "Valentine" Fischer, Kevin Vahey, Mike Koblish, Tom Fontaine, Nate Calvin and the Red Sox mailing list. Keith Law would like to thank Paul Tinnell, Cam Bonifay and Jim Trdnich of the Pittsburgh Pirates, Robin Wentz of the Altoona Curve, and a long list of minor-league personnel who helped him craft this year's Pirates chapter. Steven Rubio would like to thank Brian Sabean for always giving him something to write about. Jeff Hildebrand would like to thank Hank Davis, David Fynan, Pat Hildebrand, Sue Leopold and the Phillies mailing list. Michael Wolverton would like to thank Jamey Newberg. Jeff Bower would especially like to thank *Baseball America*'s Lacy Lusk (Associate Editor).

My thanks go to James Kushner for his occasional contributions to *Baseball Prospectus Online*, even the ones we don't use because they're just fun letters about something he saw in the California League; and to reader Brett Bonfield for a months-long argument on the merits of Jim Fregosi which, frankly, he won.

Lastly, I'd like to thank two men in particular for their willingness to give me my first breaks in Chicago radio and television, respectively: Mike Murphy of WSCR-AM, and Rob Goldman, the sports director at CLTV. Working on the book gave me the opportunity to work with each of these engaging, funny and intelligent men, an unexpected bonus in a project that's generally a bundle of fun from beginning to end.

Finally, to everyone who ought to be here—and there are a lot of you—we're sorry that as this list is thrown together, we've forgotten to give you the credit you're entitled to. Just send us a reminder, and the pleasure will be all ours making it up to you.

Chris Kahrl
Chicago
December 20, 1999

Foreword:
Fighting the Good Fight

by Rob Neyer,
ESPN.Com

In *The Intuitionist*, Colson Whitehead's 1999 novel, a battle is joined between two opposing schools of New York elevator inspectors, the Intuitionists and the Empiricists. The Empiricists, in this case, are the staid, conservative old guard, while the Intuitionists are the trod-upon, misunderstood upstarts.

In baseball, the situation is reversed. With the possible exception of Branch Rickey, the Intuitionists have ruled the game since Abner Doubleday was a cadet at West Point. The Empiricists, on the rare occasions they've dared to raise their hands, have generally been shouted down.

But as I write this on December 7, 1999, it strikes me that just as World War II essentially ended on the day the Japanese bombed Pearl Harbor, the battle between baseball's Intuitionists and Empiricists turned in the spring of 1982, when the first of Bill James's mass-market *Baseball Abstracts* landed in bookstores.

James wrote seven nationally distributed *Baseball Abstracts*, each containing hundreds of nuggets—hundreds of *truths*—about the game, and in the process, he attracted a significant following among free-thinking baseball fans. As the 1980s turned into the 1990s, however, we saw little progress in the thought processes of the baseball world. Sure, nontraditional statistics finally began to appear in national media coverage, but the majority of the big boys—the men on TV, the men who make the personnel decisions for the clubs and the men who write the newspaper columns—never got the message.

This eventually became discouraging to those of us who grew up reading the *Baseball Abstract*. Did I say discouraging? How about frustrating. Confounding. Occasionally infuriating. How could so many men who make such a wonderful living from the game, *our* game, utterly ignore such obvious truths?

This is perhaps a gross generalization, but I suspect that those men were too entrenched in their thinking, too comfortable in their jobs—too *old*, to put it bluntly—to bother with this Bill James fellow, or that Pete Palmer guy, or that Craig Wright character.

If we had been wiser, we who grew up reading the *Abstracts*, we would have recognized a simple fact of life. The men who rule the world aren't young men. They're men in their thirties and forties and fifties. And wouldn't you know it, now *we're* in our thirties (or getting awfully close).

And look at us. I picked up my first *Baseball Abstract* in 1984. Five years later I found myself working for Bill James himself, and now I write a daily baseball column for ESPN.com, the Internet's top sports website.

David Schoenfield (*Baseball Abstract* Class of '82), my editor, oversees ESPN.com's baseball coverage, where the influence of Bill James can be seen every day in many ways. Schoenfield was 12 years old in 1982, and almost certainly qualifies as one of the all-time youngest *Abstract* readers.

Steve Moyer (Class of '83) has carved an Internet niche for himself, combining intelligence and irreverence in his work for *My Baseball Daily*.

Mat Olkin (Class of '84) recently signed on with *Baseball Weekly*, and he immediately added a caliber of thoughtful analysis the publication had previously been missing.

David Rawnsley (Class of '81), a combination scout/sabermetrician, has become a star at *Baseball America*. We can only hope that no major-league team is smart enough to steal him from the public domain.

John Sickels (Class of '83) is all over the place, perhaps most notably in his own annual—and indispensable—book, the *STATS Minor League Scouting Notebook*.

It seems we have somehow found a national audience for our ramblings. I suspect we shall see our audience grow and grow, and grow some more. There are baseball fans currently in their teens who read ESPN.com and *Baseball Weekly*, and some of them will eventually take our jobs. Just as Barry Bonds is stronger and faster than Stan Musial, the next generation will be smarter and more clever than we are. And the world of baseball analysis will be better for it.

But although we know we're going to win the war, we also know that there are many years of tough battles ahead. And to be frank, those of us in the mainstream media don't really have the stomach for the work, the storming of the beaches and the parachute drops behind enemy lines. We're fat and happy, and we enjoy our steady jobs and our generous paychecks. What's more, the men who sign those paychecks, while often sympathetic (or at least tolerant), are not interested in revolution. All you have to do is read *USA Today* or watch *Baseball Tonight,* and you'll know exactly what I'm talking about.

Fortunately, there is a group of more selfless fellows, fellows who don't have jobs with big media conglomerates to protect. They're the type of fellows who wrote the book you hold in your hands.

Back in about 1980, Bill James invented the word "sabermetrics," which might best be defined as "the scientific pursuit of baseball knowledge." Twenty years later, the authors of this book represent the best ideals of that pursuit. For them, it's not about money, nor is it about fame. It's about baseball and it's about science. The authors of *Baseball Prospectus* are doing the work I like to think I would be doing, were I younger and braver. And I am grateful to them for it.

Be patient, my friends: the Empiricists shall prevail. Turn this page and watch it happen.

In addition to his regular gig with ESPN.com, Rob Neyer maintains his own website, robneyer.com, *where he and* Baseball Prospectus *co-author Rany Jazayerli (Class of '88) regularly commiserate about "their" Kansas City Royals. Rob's book,* Baseball Dynasties, *co-written with Eddie Epstein (Class of '83), will be published in March 2000.*

Reshaping the Debate:
Performance Analysis vs. Skills Analysis

by Joseph S. Sheehan

"Stathead."

"Stat-drunk computer nerd."

"Rotisserie geek."

You can earn a lot of derision when you look at things in a new way, and the people who have applied statistical tools to evaluate baseball players and teams have heard the above epithets and more. The work of people such as Bill James, Craig Wright and Clay Davenport has often been dismissed as the mind-numbing analysis of people who need to put their slide rules away and get out and watch a game once in a while. Their efforts, which have been dubbed "statistical analysis," have expanded and improved the body of objective baseball knowledge, and their work is even beginning to penetrate the insular world of baseball front offices.

But the term "statistical analysis," as applied to baseball, isn't descriptive enough. Actuaries analyze statistics, and while the work pays well, it is pretty dry stuff. Life-expectancy tables and risk/benefit workups aren't going to get your average Red Sox fan excited, nor should they: baseball fans care about their teams, and the players on them, not a series of numbers.

But baseball statistics are not numbers generated for their own sake. *Statistics are a record of the performance of players and teams.* Period. Benjamin Disraeli's oft-quoted line—"There are three types of lies: lies, damned lies and statistics."—just doesn't apply.

Looking at statistics—looking at the record of player and team performance—helps analysts reach conclusions about players. So when Rany Jazayerli writes that Jose Rosado is one of the 10 best starting pitchers in the American League, that's not an analysis of statistics, that's an analysis of performance. In the same way that a scout watches a player run and decides whether he's fast or slow, analysts look at a player's EQA and determine how good a year he had. That's performance analysis, a more descriptive term for the work we do.

The distinction is critical in moving this type of baseball analysis from an outsider view to the mainstream, so that in the front office of a major-league team it can be as acceptable to look at a player's on-base percentage as to look at a scout's opinion of his foot speed. Organizations need to credit a pitcher for his consistently good Triple-A performance in the same way that they mark him down for his below-average fastball.

Reshaping the debate between traditional baseball people and the analyst community will give a significant push to what is currently a creeping movement. If you look at the success of the New York Yankees of the late 1990s or the 1999 Oakland A's, it's clear that some teams have embraced one of the fundamental tenets of baseball analysis: the importance of on-base percentage in scoring runs. In fact, the A's have become the first organization to emphasize plate discipline in their player-development program.

We have seen the work of Wright and Rany Jazayerli on pitcher usage, particularly young-pitcher usage, start to make inroads within the game. Teams have become increasingly aware of the workloads they put on their best pitching prospects, recognizing relationships between workload and injury and workload and ineffectiveness. Given the significant investments that organizations make in their top talent, this is a prime area in which baseball analysis can make a financial impact as well as an on-field impact.

Performance analysis does not, and should not, exist in a vacuum. First of all, it is important to understand the context of statistics, and the Davenport Translations you see in this book are prima facie evidence of this. The line ".280/.350/.450" is about as informative as a George W. Bush campaign speech. At what level was this performance? How old is the player? In what park and what league does he play? What position?

And once you have all those answers, you still have only half the picture. Every player has a skill set, abilities that make him the player he is. Each player has certain strengths and weaknesses. Skills analysis—the province of scouts, managers and coaches—isn't made obsolete by performance analysis. It's enhanced by it.

Knowing that a 23-year-old right-hander has a live fastball, a middling curve and a change-up he can spot at will is essential. A pitcher's repertoire, a hitter's bat speed, a shortstop's arm . . . if you're going to develop a complete, accurate picture of any player, you must know these things. But you also want to know if the pitcher has an acceptable strikeout rate, because that's the best predictor of career length. You want to know if the player can drive the ball, as measured by his slugging percentage and isolated power. And if that shortstop is among the league leaders in assists and double plays, it's an excellent indication that he is great at using his arm to get outs. Isn't that what fans and general managers really want to know?

Performance analysis has limitations. Amateur baseball players, with aluminum bats, shorter schedules and widely variable levels of competition, are best analyzed by their skills. Performance analysis of players in short-season leagues is also unreliable, both because of limited sample sizes and the adjustments that the players, usually new to professional baseball, are making. Given a choice between a scouting report and a Davenport Translation on an 18-year-old with 200 plate appearances in the Gulf Coast League, the scouting report will be a better tool.

Performance analysis paired with skills analysis is how successful teams are going to be built in the 21st century.

Good organizations will accept that there's as much to be gained from looking seriously at a player's track record as there is from looking at the scouting reports on him. Successful teams will be built on principles that have developed from performance analysis. Ideas that were radical just 10 years ago will become conventional wisdom, as people like Billy Beane have success, and as other organizations imitate what made the A's successful.

Reshaping the debate continues a cycle that began with Branch Rickey's conclusions about on-base percentage and continued through Bill James's work in popularizing sabermetrics. It provides a means for the baseball mainstream to embrace the concepts of performance analysis while maintaining their established, valuable methods of skills analysis. Eventually, there will be no debate, as both will be used routinely in evaluating talent and building baseball teams. A better brand of baseball for everyone will be the ultimate legacy of performance analysis.

Davenport Translations Q&A

by Clay Davenport

Mike Piazza				C				**Bats R**	**Age 31**										
YEAR	TEAM	LGE	AB	H	DB	TP	HR	BB/SO	R	RBI	SB	CS	OUT	BA	OBP	SLG	EQA	EQR	DEFENSE
1997	LosAngls	NL	573	213	32	1	45	70/76	109	131	4	1	361	.372	.443	.667	.354	135	
1998	LosAngls	NL	152	46	5	0	10	11/26	21	32	0	0	106	.303	.350	.533	.288	23	35-C 94
1998	NY Mets	NL	403	146	28	1	27	47/52	70	81	1	0	257	.362	.432	.638	.344	89	99-C 97
1999	NY Mets	NL	538	166	22	0	41	44/69	96	120	2	2	374	.309	.362	.578	.301	93	129-C 96
2000	NY Mets	NL	502	156	17	0	36	62/68	86	121	2	1	347	.311	.387	.560	.312	94	

Q: Didn't Mike Piazza have 40 homers, not 41? He had a different batting average, too.

A: Yes, he did. *Baseball Prospectus* isn't a statistical encyclopedia, but a performance-analysis notebook. Rather than run a player's actual stat line—data that is available from dozens of other sources—we present context-adjusted information that shows what his performance was worth.

Q: Isn't the player's actual stat line a good measure of his worth?

A: No, not necessarily, because not everybody is playing on the same field. A hitter on the High Desert Mavericks has certain advantages over a hitter on the Mets, and these advantages show up in the stats. He's playing against a lower quality of pitchers and fielders, he's in a league full of good hitters' parks and he plays half his games in the best hitters' park in the league. Piazza played against major leaguers in a park that generally hurts hitters. The standards for a good performance are slightly different in every park in a given league, and can be wildly different between leagues.

What we do is measure how much those standards differ, and compensate for them. Everybody, from the American to the Appalachian Leagues, goes through the filter. Everybody is compared to the level of performance that we would expect from an average major-league hitter in that league and park. In the end, when we've rated a player as hitting X% more singles than an average hitter, and Y% more doubles, and Z% fewer home runs, and so on, we turn it back into a statistical line based on a single standard instead of 192 different standards, as would be the case with the player's raw stats.

If you think of the different leagues as countries with their own languages, the parks as different tribes with their own dialects, and the stats within those parks as words in those dialects, then what we are doing is translating all of these different languages into a common tongue, so we can understand what everybody is saying. That's why this entire system goes by the name of Davenport Translations, or DTs.

Q: So what is that common standard?

A: We've tried to match the offensive levels of the late 1990s, which are pretty high by historical standards. A .270 batting average, .340 on-base percentage, .430 slugging average and .260 Equivalent Average are considered normal for hitters.

In full, the standard is shown in Figure 1.

The difference in the slugging average (the numbers above produce .432, not .430) is due to rounding. For instance, it's really 15.8 home runs per 500 at-bats, not 16. The difference in the OBP is in part a rounding effect, but also reflects the five times the average hitter is hit by pitches. We don't have the space to show HBP, but they are included in everyone's OBP and EqA.

Q: Back up a second. What was that "Equivalent Average" thing?

A: EqA is similar to metrics like Runs Created or Linear Weights. It evaluates a player's statistical line to estimate how many runs the performance was worth to the league

Figure 1

	AB	H	DB	TP	HR	BB/SO	R	RBI	SB	CS	OUT	BA	OBP	SLG	EQA	EQR	DEFENSE
Hitters	500	135	27	3	16	48/94	69	66	9	5	370	.270	.340	.430	.260	64	162-OF 100

as a whole. In the case of a very bad hitter, the performance might even be worth negative runs. This is the player's Equivalent Runs, or EqR. EqA is basically EqR per out, although there's some extra math thrown in.

Q: And the extra math is there because...?

A: Because I want the final answer to look like a batting average. The problem with many new metrics is that people don't know, just by looking at how the player scores, whether it is a performance that should lead the league or get him sent down to Triple-A. There is little to no sense of context for on-base-plus-slugging (OPS) or Runs Created per 27 outs (RC/27).

Despite its many flaws as an evaluation tool, batting average has the best-known scale of any statistic in sports: .225 stinks, .300 is a recognized achievement, .350 puts you at or near the top of the league and .400 is almost mythic. EqA shamelessly copies that. Think of how good .330 is as a batting average; that's almost exactly how good a .330 EqA is. Pick any achievement: the BA and EqA numbers that correspond to that achievement are generally very similar, as Table 1 shows.

Q: I thought I read somewhere that EqA wasn't nearly as good as some of the other available metrics.

A: Don't believe everything you read. (That goes for what you see in this book, too; infallibility is an issue for the papacy, not *Baseball Prospectus*.) Pretty much everyone who has developed a metric will tell you why theirs is the best and the others are screwed up. But there are many ways to fudge the comparisons.

One classic method is to provide extra data in calculating your metric—such as the number of times grounded into double plays—without providing it for the other metrics you're testing. Another method is to pick a narrow time period during which your metric happens to come out ahead, or to tune the calculations to that period

to make sure that it does. Yet another is to subtly vary the testing; while the main studies I've seen in print compare rate statistics to runs per out, virtually all do considerably better with a per-plate-appearance comparison. By using per-out tests, the experimenter fails to use the metric to its greatest potential.

It's also possible to simply botch the tests. Some people treat a regression analysis like a papal decree, but if the regression isn't applied at the right point, it doesn't tell you a blessed thing. You cannot, under any circumstances, turn a rate statistic (batting, slugging, Total and Equivalent averages) into runs by simply saying, "Ten percent better than league average equals 10% more runs per plate appearance." Figuring out what a 10% advantage in BA means in terms of runs is the whole point of doing a regression. Assuming you know the relationship means you are testing nothing more than your assumptions.

Indeed, most statistics have steeper relationships than 1-to-1. A 10% advantage in EqA means a team will score 20% more runs, not 10%. For batting average, a 10% advantage gives you 19% more runs; the same advantage in slugging average gets you 14% more; for OBP it is 21%; for Total Average, 13%; for OPS, 19%; only on-base-times-slugging (OTS) generates a 10% advantage in runs.

What you get by doing it wrong is a combination of the statistic's genuine error, plus something more that depends on how far from 1-to-1 the relationship really is. It is easy to tell if someone has made this mistake. Just look to see if they have slugging average, by itself, rated higher than on-base-plus-slugging. If they do, ignore their work; their test was so flawed that it is useless.

Q: So EqA is accurate?

A: The best way to measure accuracy is with a score called the root-mean-square error. You take the actual runs scored (1,009 for the 1999 Indians), subtract the predicted

Table 1

	Batting Average	Equivalent Average
Single-season record	Rogers Hornsby, 1924, .424	Babe Ruth, 1920, .423
Career record	Ty Cobb, .367	Babe Ruth, .378
Career #5	Tris Speaker, .345	Frank Thomas, .347
Career #10	Harry Heilmann, .342	Jimmie Foxx, .337
Career #100	Richie Ashburn, .308	Darryl Strawberry, .306
Career #250	Cy Williams, .292	Andy Van Slyke, .291
Career #500	Joey Cora, .277	Jimmy Collins, .278
Career #1000	Ed Sprague, .246	Hobe Ferris, .242
1999 AL Leader	Nomar Garciaparra, .357	Manny Ramirez, .349
1999 NL Leader	Larry Walker, .379	Chipper Jones, .355

runs (989 for EqA, an error of 20) and square it (to get 400). Add up all the squared errors, divide by the number of teams, take the square root and you've got the RMSE.

No statistic does better than EqA over the entire 20th century, when all methods have access to the same data and advantages. Some do better within individual years or decades, but not over the long haul. That said, 1999 wasn't one of the system's best years, as you can see in Table 2, which ranks the methods.

Table 2

| | Root Mean Square Errors | | |
	1901-99	1990-99	1999
Equivalent Average	22.93	22.53	18.96
Linear Weights (Palmer)	23.39	22.30	17.71
Extrapolated Runs (Furtado)	23.54	22.38	17.74
Total Average (Boswell)	24.04	24.03	22.31
On-base-times-slugging (OTS)	24.26	23.61	18.68
On-base-plus-slugging (OPS)	24.39	23.74	19.31
Runs Created (SB version, James)	24.94	23.44	19.27
Slugging Average	30.60	28.28	28.75
On-base Percentage	34.09	36.64	38.37
Batting Average	39.74	40.46	44.85

Q: What about the numbers under "Defense"?

A: Those show how the player's defensive performance rates. The number before the position shows you how often he played that position; it represents not actual games as recorded in the usual fielding statistics, but full nine-inning games, based on actual innings played (for major leaguers) and estimated innings played (for minor leaguers). The number after the position is a rating of how well the player played. An average major-league fielder scores 100. Eighty-five is about as bad as any major-league regular can be without becoming a full-time DH. Anything above 110 is a legitimate Gold Glove performance. The numbers needed for catcher's defense weren't available in 1997, which is why Piazza's 1997 is blank.

The defensive rating is based primarily on plays made. The primary ingredients are putouts for outfielders,

assists for infielders and stolen base/caught stealing information for catchers, but errors are also counted. In each case, a player's statistics have been compared to those of the other members of his team; this offers clues as to whether the team's pitching staff skewed the chances towards either fly balls or ground balls, or towards the left or right side of the field. That gives a better estimate of how many plays an average fielder should have made on this team, which we compare to how many plays the player in question really did make. The scores have also been adjusted for the skill level of the league; just because you're an above-average shortstop in the Sally League doesn't mean you'll be even average in the majors.

Q: You've got stats for 2000 in the chart. What are you, psychic?

A: No, but I knew you were going to ask that. The 2000 numbers are the guesses made by a computer program called "Wilton," which is akin to another program we've used which was called "Vladimir." The Wiltons are a guess at the player's actual 2000 statistics, not his translated numbers, so the projection for a Colorado player will already have the altitude effect built in. The projection is made by looking at players throughout history with similar statistical profiles over a multi-year period, and seeing how they performed in the following year.

Q: I assume you rate pitchers, too.

A: Of course. A pitcher's statistics are translated exactly the same way that a hitter's numbers are, and the same factors (league offense, home park, competitive level and relative age) go into the equation, along with one more: the quality of the defense behind him, as rated by the system mentioned above. A pitcher's translation is shown in Figure 2.

The ERA figure is actually based on total runs allowed, not simply earned runs; the defensive adjustments should, we hope, control for the poor defensive play that leads to unearned runs. The won/lost record assumes the pitcher had average run support, and is calculated using a modified Pythagorean equation. This modification is especially important for pitchers, because the exponent in the Pythagorean equation actually depends on the

Figure 2

Pedro Martinez						**Throws R Age 28**											
YEAR	TEAM	LGE	IP	H	ER	HR	BB	K	ERA	W	L	H/9	HR/9	BB/9	K/9	KWH	PERA
1997	Montreal	NL	241.3	160	63	16	70	284	2.35	21	6	5.97	0.60	2.61	10.59	5.38	2.27
1998	Boston	AL	234.0	185	76	24	70	254	2.92	18	8	7.12	0.92	2.69	9.77	3.72	3.12
1999	Boston	AL	217.7	145	44	8	36	323	1.82	21	3	6.00	0.33	1.49	13.36	14.93	1.74

level of run scoring, which the pitcher himself partly controls. The standard line for a pitcher is shown in Figure 3.

The advantage with pitchers is that we know how many runs they actually gave up, and we can use that information. Sometimes, though, the number of runs they actually gave up has a strong luck component, for good or bad. That's why we also include two measures of a pitcher's performance that are independent of his runs allowed.

Peripheral ERA, or PERA, is the ERA you would expect from a pitcher who gave up this many hits, home runs and walks in this many innings; it is essentially the equivalent average, calculated from the known pitching components (H, HR, BB) and assuming more or less average values for the rest. It is as good a predictor of next year's ERA as this year's ERA, meaning if a pitcher's PERA is a lot better than his ERA, he's a good bet to improve the following year. The reverse is also true.

KWH compares strikeouts, not just to walks, but also to hits allowed. It is scaled so that 1.00 is the major-league average, with higher numbers being better. Roughly speaking, KWH serves as an indicator of continuing success; pitchers with poor KWH scores may have a good ERA one year, but they aren't as likely to keep it up the following season. Nor do they last as long; pitchers with low KWHs drop out of the league sooner than pitchers the same age, with the same ERA, but a higher KWH.

Figure 3

	IP	H	ER	HR	BB	K	ERA	W	L	H/9	HR/9	BB/9	K/9	KWH	PERA
Average	200.0	200	100	22	78	144	4.50	11	11	9.00	1.00	3.50	6.50	1.00	4.50

Q: In last year's book, you guys had an "Extra Players" section for everyone you didn't have player comments on. Where is that?

A: This year, although this is our biggest edition ever, we ran out of space. However, you'll be able to find all of these players on our website (www.baseballprospectus.com). In addition, we invite our readers to ask for Wilton projections for any player who changes teams before or during spring training. Just email us with a request through our site, and we'll fire back a projection. In the near future, the website will also be featuring more information about historical translations, and about comparing players across eras. We also expect to be unveiling a database of all major league players' statistics, listing both their regular season stats and their DTs. So please enjoy all of that stuff, and feel free to write in with any comments or criticisms you may have.

Support-Neutral Records

by Michael Wolverton

The Support-Neutral system measures the value of individual starts and their contribution to winning. By looking at a pitcher's performance start by start, we learn about his consistency throughout the year and how it impacted his team. We can't see that by looking at average or cumulative run prevention. This data can help us answer interesting questions: given equal ERAs, do some pitchers pitch in a way that will tend to win more games than other pitchers? In particular, is it better for a starter to be either very good or very bad on a given day, or consistently average? Does the park have a smaller influence on the value of the start when the start is very good or very bad? The key, of course, is developing metrics that measure the start's impact on winning the game.

Support-Neutral metrics evaluate a starter's contribution to winning and losing irrespective of the support he receives from his team's offense and relief staff. A starter's Support-Neutral Win/Loss record (SNWL) is how many games he would be expected to win and lose given his pitching performances, assuming he had a league-average offense and bullpen behind him. A starter's Support-Neutral Value Added (SNVA) measures the extra games his team would be expected to win with his pitching performances instead of an average pitcher's. The game-by-game perspective of the SN stats removes distortions that can be introduced in cumulative run prevention stats like ERA and *Total Baseball's* Adjusted Pitching Wins (APW). As a result, I think the SN stats give a more accurate picture of a starter's value than APW.

How Support-Neutral Measures are Calculated

A starter's SNW total is calculated by determining, for each start he makes, the probability that he would get the win given the way he pitched in that game, then summing up the individual probabilities over all of his starts. The sum gives you the number of wins a pitcher could expect to get for an average team, given his performances. A performance consists only of the number of innings pitched, the number of runs given up while the starter was in the game, the number of outs and location of any runners when the starter left the game, the park in which the game was played and whether the pitcher was at home or on the road. The Support-Neutral system assumes that these are the only things that influence whether the pitcher wins or loses.

Getting these probabilities is a little complicated. A starting pitcher normally gets a win when two things happen: he leaves the game with the lead and his team holds it without ever giving it up. To calculate the probability of a pitcher's getting a win for an average team, I look at every possible sequence of innings that could lead to a win.

For example, consider David Cone's start in the famous "Knoblauch's Boner" Game 2 of the 1998 ALCS (eight innings pitched, one run allowed at home). Such a start would result in a W if:

- His team scored two runs in the first eight innings and his relievers gave up none in the ninth, or
- His team scored three runs in the first eight innings and his relievers gave up one in the ninth, or
- His team scored three runs in the first eight innings and his relievers gave up two in the ninth, or
- Etc., etc., etc....

I figure out each of the individual probabilities above, substituting "league average" for "his," then combine them. The individual inning probabilities (e.g., the probability of "average relievers gave up one run in the ninth") come from the league single-inning scoring distribution for that year. For example, in 1997, major-league teams scored zero runs in about 71% of the innings, one run in 15% of the innings, two runs in 7% of the innings, etc. Park effects are figured in by changing the definition of "average team." For example, an average team will score more runs at Coors Field and fewer in Dodger Stadium, and the run-scoring distribution is altered to reflect that.

The end results are three probabilities: the start resulting in a win for the pitcher (SNW), the start resulting in a loss for the pitcher (SNL) and the start resulting in a win for an average team (SNVA). Cone's start calculates to a 0.74 SNW and a 0.05 SNL. The start will result in a team win 84% of the time; since SNVA is concerned with comparing a starter to a league-average pitcher, and since an average pitcher's starts will result in 50% wins, Cone's start gets an SNVA rating of 0.84 – 0.5 = 0.34 games above average.

Support-Neutral stats remove bullpen support from a starter's numbers. The input used to calculate SNW, SNL and SNVA includes the state of the bases when the starter leaves the game. So, for example, if a starter gets yanked with two outs and runners on first and third in the seventh inning after three runs have scored, and his reliever allows both runners to score, the SN stats will be calculated based on six full innings, three runs in, runners on first and third with two outs. A box score would only indicate six full innings, two outs and five runs allowed.

Why Support-Neutral Measures Are Good

Do the Support-Neutral stats tell us anything that Thorn and Palmer's Adjusted Pitching Wins (APW) weren't already telling us? Consider the following two pitchers:

	Pitcher A				Pitcher B	
Start	IP	R		Start	IP	R
Game 1	4	8		Game 1	0	14
Game 2	4	8		Game 2	8	2
TOTAL	8	16		TOTAL	8	16

Any statistic measuring cumulative run prevention will rate these two pitchers even. Pitcher B has helped his team more, though. An average team is very likely to go 0-2 behind Pitcher A's two starts, but that same average team has a pretty good shot at winning Pitcher B's second game. The Support-Neutral stats accurately measure this: Pitcher A's SNW/L record is right around 0-2, while Pitcher B's SNW/L record is closer to 1-1. Pitcher A's SNVA mark shows him 0.86 games below average, while Pitcher B's SNVA is a much more tolerable 0.27 games below average.

All runs are not created equal. Pitcher B's Game 1 isn't a whole lot worse than Pitcher A's Game 1, even though he gave up many more runs in fewer innings. Cumulative run prevention stats (ERA, APW) treat run number 14 in that game as equal to the first run, and that's where they go wrong. In fact, APW concludes that Pitcher B's start in Game 1 cost his team well over a full game in the standings, an absolute impossibility. SNVA's conclusion is a much more reasonable half-game cost. He guaranteed them a single loss, and that's all.

Guide to Support-Neutral Tables

The tables and discussions of Support-Neutral stats in this book include the following measures:

- A pitcher's Support-Neutral W/L record (SNW, SNL).
- His Support-Neutral Winning Percentage (SNPct): SNW/(SNW+SNL). This is the Support-Neutral rate statistic, analogous to RA, and is referred to extensively in the team discussions.
- His actual W/L record (W, L).
- His runs allowed per 9 innings (RA).
- His Adjusted Pitching Wins (APW), a measure of the number of wins a pitcher is worth, computed from the number of runs he prevented that a league-average pitcher would have allowed. This is a modified version of the Total Baseball measure using runs rather than earned runs. It is included in the tables for comparison with SNVA.
- His Support-Neutral Value Added (SNVA).
- His Support-Neutral Wins Above Replacement (SNWAR), the number of SNWs a pitcher has above what a .425 pitcher would get in the same number of Support-Neutral decisions.

The park-effect numbers in the Support-Neutral team sections are two-year averages of one-year park factors from 1998 and 1999. The exceptions, for which one-year factors were used, are the ballparks that changed significantly between 1998 and 1999: Olympic Stadium in Montreal and the Kingdome/Safeco Field in Seattle. The DH is accounted for by treating it as a "ground rule" of the park and incorporating it into the park effect. As a result, the park effects used for the calculation of the SN numbers are adjusted so that the difference between AL and NL scoring in 1999 was added to or subtracted from each park, depending on which league it was in. Each AL park inflated run scoring by an additional 3% over the raw park factor, and each NL park deflated run scoring by an additional 3%.

1999 SNW/L Leader Boards

Top 30 Major-League Starters (ranked by SNWAR):

Pitcher	Team	SNW	SNL	SNPct	W	L	RA	APW	SNVA	SNWAR
Randy Johnson	ARI	21.0	7.2	.745	17	9	2.85	6.52	6.65	9.03
Pedro Martinez	BOS	18.3	3.8	.828	22	4	2.38	6.47	6.91	8.88
Mike Hampton	HOU	17.1	8.2	.676	22	4	3.24	3.93	4.20	6.34
Kevin Brown	LAD	17.7	9.5	.651	18	9	3.53	3.31	3.84	6.14
Kevin Millwood	ATL	16.0	7.9	.670	18	7	3.16	4.06	3.74	5.85
Jamie Moyer	SEA	15.7	8.8	.642	14	8	4.26	2.72	3.35	5.31
Brad Radke	MIN	15.2	9.1	.625	12	14	3.99	2.69	2.80	4.87
Omar Daal	ARI	14.4	8.3	.633	16	9	3.86	2.91	2.95	4.74
Mike Mussina	BAL	14.2	8.1	.637	18	7	3.90	2.52	2.83	4.74
John Smoltz	ATL	13.4	7.1	.653	11	8	3.38	2.87	2.79	4.69
Bartolo Colon	CLE	14.3	8.3	.632	18	5	4.26	2.68	2.86	4.68
Freddy Garcia	SEA	14.0	8.7	.618	17	8	4.29	2.34	2.58	4.37
Curt Schilling	PHI	12.2	6.5	.654	15	6	3.69	2.92	2.86	4.25
Pete Harnisch	CIN	13.9	8.8	.612	16	10	3.90	2.45	2.32	4.25
Jose Lima	HOU	15.5	11.2	.582	21	10	3.95	2.17	2.00	4.18
Jose Rosado	KCR	13.8	9.1	.604	10	14	4.46	1.94	2.09	4.10
Bret Saberhagen	BOS	9.6	4.3	.690	10	6	3.25	2.64	2.42	3.67
Tim Hudson	OAK	10.0	5.0	.665	11	2	3.70	2.24	2.26	3.60
Shane Reynolds	HOU	14.8	11.6	.561	16	14	4.20	1.41	1.45	3.58
Dave Burba	CLE	13.6	10.1	.575	15	9	4.62	2.08	1.76	3.55
David Cone	NYY	12.6	8.7	.591	12	9	3.91	2.24	1.84	3.53
Pedro Astacio	COL	14.8	11.7	.558	17	11	5.43	2.05	1.39	3.52
Greg Maddux	ATL	14.0	10.9	.563	19	9	4.23	1.39	1.42	3.42
Orlando Hernandez	NYY	13.5	10.4	.566	17	9	4.53	1.07	1.43	3.36
Juan Guzman	B/C	12.9	9.7	.572	11	12	4.32	1.60	1.45	3.32
Mike Sirotka	CHW	13.2	10.3	.562	11	13	4.65	1.17	1.33	3.21
Masato Yoshii	NYM	11.8	8.5	.580	12	8	4.29	1.10	1.48	3.15
Todd Ritchie	PIT	11.0	7.6	.592	15	8	4.11	1.78	1.58	3.11
Darren Oliver	STL	12.2	9.2	.569	9	9	4.40	1.09	1.27	3.09
Jeff Suppan	KCR	12.9	10.2	.557	10	12	4.87	1.06	1.29	3.04

It's rare for a season to produce two starting-pitching performances of this caliber. Randy Johnson's season was the second-best since we started tracking the Support-Neutral stats in 1992, and Pedro Martinez's season was right behind at number three. The top five: Roger Clemens in 1997, Johnson in 1999, Martinez in 1999, Greg Maddux in 1995, Maddux in 1997.

Martinez missed a few starts due to injury and therefore finished below Johnson in value above replacement level, but his Support-Neutral Winning Percentage of .828 is the second-best since 1992, behind Maddux's .836 in 1995. Five pitchers account for all of the top 10 seasons in SNWAR since 1992—the four already mentioned plus Kevin Appier, whose 1993 is the eighth-best season in that period.

Bottom 10 Major-League Starters, ranked by SNWAR:

Pitcher	Team	SNW	SNL	SNPct	W	L	RA	APW	SNVA	SNWAR
Micah Bowie	CHC	1.2	6.4	.158	2	6	10.34	-2.63	-2.43	-2.04
Jose Silva	PIT	1.8	6.7	.207	1	8	8.72	-2.45	-2.38	-1.85
Willie Blair	DET	3.1	8.4	.267	3	8	8.74	-2.87	-2.59	-1.81
Dan Perkins	MIN	1.6	6.1	.209	1	7	9.06	-2.16	-2.10	-1.65
Paul Spoljaric	P/T	0.1	4.0	.026	0	5	19.36	-2.54	-1.91	-1.64
Carlos Perez	LAD	3.2	8.3	.282	2	10	8.02	-3.02	-2.44	-1.64
LaTroy Hawkins	MIN	8.1	14.8	.355	10	14	7.02	-3.33	-3.21	-1.61
Brian Meadows	FLA	7.4	13.6	.353	11	15	5.90	-2.58	-3.00	-1.52
Tom Candiotti	O/C	2.4	6.7	.265	3	5	8.56	-2.01	-1.93	-1.45
Tim Belcher	ANA	5.8	11.2	.341	6	8	7.07	-2.63	-2.54	-1.42

1999 featured stiff competition for the title of worst starting pitcher in baseball, but Micah Bowie claimed the title with a strong showing down the stretch. Bowie gave up five or more runs in seven of his 11 starts, and he failed to complete five innings in six of those. LaTroy Hawkins showed a level of durability that's rare among bad pitchers. The Twins weren't bothered enough by his bad performance to yank him from the rotation, and as a result he was able to accumulate one of the highest Support-Neutral Loss totals of the past eight years. Hawkins's 14.8 SNLs rank behind only Mike Moore's 15.9 in 1993, Jaime Navarro's 15.7 in 1997, Livan Hernandez's 15.0 in 1998 and Mark Leiter's 14.9 in 1997.

Luckiest 10 Major-League Starters, ranked by
$[W - E(W)] + [E(L) - L]$:

Pitcher	Team	E(W)	E(L)	W	L	Diff.
Kent Bottenfield	STL	11.1	9.8	18	7	9.8
Mike Hampton	HOU	17.0	8.2	22	4	9.2
Russ Ortiz	SFG	11.8	11.8	18	9	9.1
Mike Morgan	TEX	5.3	10.7	11	8	8.4
Kirk Rueter	SFG	10.1	13.2	15	10	8.0
Aaron Sele	TEX	11.9	10.9	18	9	8.0
Bartolo Colon	CLE	14.2	8.3	18	5	7.1
Jason Bere	C/M	3.1	5.1	5	0	7.0
Greg Maddux	ATL	13.9	10.9	19	9	6.9
Jose Lima	HOU	15.5	11.2	21	10	6.7

In the past, we've referred to the award for finishing at the top of this list as the Catfish Hunter Trophy. This year, we're officially changing the name to the Lew Burdette Trophy. See the Red Sox SNWL comment for the explanation. The 1999 Lew Burdette winner is Kent Bottenfield, who was only a little better than average in run prevention but rode good offensive support to an All-Star appearance and some token Cy Young support. Mike Hampton's luck was almost as good, although in his case the "luck" was due in part to his fantastic year at the plate.

Unluckiest 10 Major-League Starters, ranked by
$[W - E(W)] + [E(L) - L]$:

Pitcher	Team	E(W)	E(L)	W	L	Diff.
Steve Trachsel	CHC	11.5	13.1	8	18	-8.3
Jose Rosado	KCR	13.2	9.1	10	14	-8.1
Brad Radke	MIN	15.2	9.1	12	14	-8.0
Dustin Hermanson	MON	12.8	11.0	9	14	-6.9
Ismael Valdes	LAD	12.1	10.3	9	14	-6.8
Ken Hill	ANA	6.7	7.1	4	11	-6.6
Chris Holt	HOU	8.0	9.6	5	13	-6.4
Randy Johnson	ARI	21.0	7.2	17	9	-5.8
Brian Moehler	DET	11.2	11.7	10	16	-5.5
Eric Milton	MIN	12.6	11.1	7	11	-5.5

A number of the league's top starters pitched in bad luck in 1999, including the very best of the bunch, Randy Johnson. Johnson's bad luck was concentrated in a single five-start stretch during which his SNWL record was 3.9-0.3 but his actual record was 0-4. Outside of that stretch, his record was actually a little on the lucky side.

Two other top pitchers who didn't get the recognition they deserved were Jose Rosado and Brad Radke. Radke is no stranger to this list, having had the majors' fourth-unluckiest record in 1996. Both he and Rosado are among the unluckiest starters of the decade. Each has a career record below .500 despite better-than-average career run prevention.

Pitcher Abuse Points

by Rany Jazayerli and Keith Woolner

Kerry Wood needs no introduction. A year ago, he teased us with the limitless potential of his arm; this year, the name only reminds us of the fragility of that arm. Last year, we used his brilliance as incentive to make a case for protecting young pitchers from overuse. Now, he serves as a warning of what may happen when they aren't protected.

Wood's injury brought the baseball establishment one step closer to accepting that the most precocious of the game's pitchers are the ones most in danger of having their careers ruined. In a less sophisticated time, we could watch the craftiness of Fernando Valenzuela, the zaniness of Mark Fidrych or the sheer power of Dwight Gooden, and wonder what these prodigies would do once they were armed with maturity and experience. Our understanding developed by watching their ruin, sometimes quick and sometimes, as with Gooden, painfully slow. But Wood fell from the pantheon of pitching greats almost as quickly as he arrived, and for maybe the first time, organizations didn't just accept his passing as the result of some kind of curse on young pitchers. They looked for an explanation.

It's simple, really. Throwing overhand is not a natural act. Throwing overhand repeatedly can be damaging to the arm. And throwing overhand repeatedly before the shoulder and elbow have completely matured—the plight of the young star—can rob a pitcher of his gift, completely and irrevocably.

Consider that since the live-ball era began in 1920, 17 pitchers have won at least 150 games by their 30th birthday. Not a single one went on to finish his career with at least 300 wins. Hal Newhouser, who led the pack with 188 wins before he turned 30, won just 19 afterwards. If you want to disregard Prince Hal because he beat up on wartime hitters, next on the list is Catfish Hunter, who won 184 games before and 40 after. Some of these pitchers were washed up well before their 30th birthday, like Dizzy Dean, who won just 16 games after he turned 28. Gooden became just an average pitcher after he tore his rotator cuff at age 24, and hasn't been even average since he turned 29.

This is fairly astonishing when you consider how success as a young hitter generally translates into a long, productive career. Among the 10 players with the most hits by age 30 are Ty Cobb, Hank Aaron, Robin Yount and Al Kaline. Of this group, only Jimmie Foxx and Joe Medwick retired short of 2,700 hits. Of the 10 most prolific home run hitters at age 30, only Ralph Kiner and Johnny Bench failed to reach 500 for their careers.

The Learning Process

Still, even as baseball has grown to accept the fragility of young pitchers, many in the business still cling to outdated, counterproductive theories on how to prevent these injuries. But this isn't a baseball issue: it's a medical issue. No one asks Dr. Frank Jobe about the best way to hold Tony Womack on first base, and no one should ask Jim Leyland or Ray Miller how to read an MRI or where to make the first incision. Still, baseball insiders act as if they know best how to keep a pitcher healthy, often espousing ideas such as having a young pitcher throw *more* pitches in an effort to build up his stamina and teach him how to pitch while tired. This makes as much sense as beating your head against a wall to handle migraine headaches.

Now, however, enough light has been shined on this issue that some teams are finally breaking free of conventional wisdom and exercising caution. In Detroit, where they still wistfully remember Mark Fidrych's rookie season, a chance for absolution arrived with Jeff Weaver. The Tigers did their best to atone for the past, faithfully keeping Weaver on a 110-pitch limit all season. Not everyone is so enlightened. In Seattle, Lou Piniella subjected his outstanding rookie pitcher, Freddy Garcia, to a workload normally reserved for a thirtysomething pitcher with years of experience.

The word is out. It may only be a whisper now, but it is growing louder, protecting more and more pitchers. It makes possible a future in which the Goodens and Woods and even the Edwin Correas are not forced to grow up too fast, and are able to make their contributions to baseball over 10 or 15 or 20 years. We could have a future in which our brightest mound stars don't leave us too soon, elevating the quality of pitching throughout baseball. And in elevating the quality of play on the field, the game itself will be elevated.

Measuring the Damage

How does the system of Pitcher Abuse Points (PAP, for short) fit into this? By measuring the burden that each pitcher bears: the number of pitches thrown. We can do this because the information revolution has finally given us pitch counts for every pitcher and every game. We now know that all innings are not created equal, and that pitchers who work efficiently, like Greg Maddux, are not evaluated accurately by looking at their inning totals. Conversely, neither are pitchers like Russ Ortiz, who labor through every inning with a series of walks and full counts.

But PAP isn't strictly a measure of pitch counts, because it is also based on the premise that all pitches are not created equal. The medical theory behind the most common and worrisome injuries to pitchers—to the muscles of the shoulder that make up the rotator cuff, and to the ligaments that hold the elbow in place—is that they are caused not merely by overuse, but by overuse of an already fatigued arm. A pitcher can throw 10 pitches a day, 365 days a year, and do less damage to his arm than he would in a single 180-pitch outing. In fact, small amounts of work on a frequent schedule can help keep the arm limber, which is why pitchers throw on the side between starts. It's also why Leo Mazzone can have his pitchers throw twice between starts (sometimes, as we saw in October, during games) without increasing the risk of injury.

So rather than measure the number of pitches thrown that are not damaging, PAP focuses only on those pitches thrown at the brink of fatigue, the ones that can progressively cause inflammation, swelling or trauma to occur. Specifically, the "Abuse Points" of PAP are awarded to a starting pitcher after he has thrown 100 pitches in a start. At first, one Abuse Point is awarded for each pitch, but at each successive plateau of 10 pitches, the penalty for each extra pitch rises by one. In other words:

- Pitches 1-100: no PAPs awarded.
- Pitches 101-110: 1 PAP per pitch.
- Pitches 111-120: 2 PAPs per pitch.
- Pitches 121-130: 3 PAPs per pitch.
- Pitches 131-140: 4 PAPs per pitch.
- Pitches 141-150: 5 PAPs per pitch, and so on, until the outing is over.

Why is 100 used as the threshold? It's certainly not because every pitcher should come out after 100 pitches, or that outings longer than that are foolish and reckless. But repeated outings that go beyond 100 pitches can, over time, cause the kind of chronic overuse injury which may render the pitcher incapacitated or ineffective. By awarding penalties only to outings beyond 100 pitches, PAP effectively rewards a pitcher for having a shorter outing. There is little doubt that interspersing the occasional 87-pitch effort helps a pitcher stay healthy.

As important as a pitcher's overall workload is the pace at which he is worked, so along with PAP we list PAP per start (PAP/S), making it easier to identify the veteran pitcher who was overworked so intensely that he spent the second half of the season on the disabled list, or the rookie phenom who was worked to the bone after being called up in August.

Medical research shows that a pitcher's arm does not reach full maturity until his mid-20s, which is entirely consistent with the research done by Craig Wright more than a decade ago. His work demonstrated that the pitchers who pitched the most innings before the age of 25 were most likely to see their careers end prematurely. So along with reporting PAP and PAP/S, we have also made an age-dependent adjustment to each pitcher's PAP score. No adjustment is made for pitchers aged 32 or older, but for every year under 32, the PAP score is increased by one-sixth the original total, so that:

- A 29-year-old has his PAP score multiplied by 1.5.
- A 26-year-old has his PAP score multiplied by 2.
- A 23-year-old has his PAP score multiplied by 2.5.
- A 20-year-old has his PAP score multiplied by 3.

This is recorded as Age-Adjusted PAP, with the total per start known as Age-Adjusted Workload, or simply Workload. This final measure is the one we will use as the ultimate evaluation of how much wisdom, or lack of it, was used in the handling of each pitcher. When reading the commentary on PAP at the end of each chapter, "workload" is used as a general term, but "Workload" refers to this specific measurement.

A Look Back

What can PAP tell us about a pitcher's future? Let's look at the 12 highest workloads of 1998:

1. Livan Hernandez: Hernandez, who had a Workload more than 50% higher than any other pitcher, managed to survive the season without being disabled. He also had another disappointing year, especially for Giant fans who expected more from him after he was acquired for the Giants' two best pitching prospects. He may be "healthy" in the sense that he can take the mound every five days, but in light of his excellent rookie performance, it's hard to imagine that he hasn't been pitching hurt the last two years.

2. Kelvim Escobar: Escobar made this list with only 10 starts in 1998. That concentrated stress may have helped to send his ERA soaring to 5.69 last year, after he entered the season with a career ERA of 3.50. He has to be considered potentially damaged goods.

3. Pedro Martinez: He won the Cy Young Award with one of the great pitching seasons in history. He also missed nearly an entire month in the middle of the season, and an uncooperative muscle in his back kept all of New England on antacids in October.

4. Kerry Wood: Out for the year after elbow ligament transplant surgery.

5. Rafael Medina: Another pitcher who made the list in just a handful of starts—12 in 1998—Medina was pushed to the bullpen last season and showed only a fraction of the promise the Marlins saw when they asked for him in the Kevin Brown trade.

6. Randy Johnson: As we said last year, the normal rules don't seem to apply to Johnson, not only because of his physique, but because he was a late bloomer and wasn't worked very hard in his early 20s. He's on the list again this year, and once again I wouldn't bat an eye.

7. Bartolo Colon: Colon went 18-5 with a 3.95 ERA but struggled in the first half of the season, continuing the poor pitching that had plagued him in the second half of 1998. His workload decreased in 1999, and he was the league's best non-Martinez pitcher after the All-Star break.

8. Curt Schilling: Despite his advanced age, Schilling's history of arm troubles, combined with his Workload, made us very concerned about his future. The Phillies didn't show similar concern, and Schilling missed six weeks with arm trouble. He's unlikely to ever again be the pitcher he was from 1996 to 1998.

9. Orlando Hernandez: Livan's brother had a good year, but now that we know he's four years older than he claimed to be, it's clear he didn't belong on this list.

10. Jason Schmidt: Schmidt has been touted as a future ace since before the Braves traded him to Pittsburgh in 1996. His workloads have consistently been high, and for the second straight year, Schmidt got off to a hot start (3-1, 2.86 ERA in April) before tailing off to an uninspiring season.

11. Andy Pettitte: He stayed healthy but had a second straight disappointing season after being a Cy Young candidate in both 1996 and 1997.

12. Tony Saunders: He cracked his humerus bone while pitching in May, an injury you wouldn't wish on your worst enemy. And he wasn't pitching all that well (6.43 ERA) before his season ended.

This list demonstrates the uses and limitations of the PAP system. It can't claim to predict injury with any degree of certainty. It can't even predict that a pitcher is definitely headed towards a decline, as Colon shows. But very few pitchers with high Workloads are going to avoid the disabled list for long. And even in the absence of a defined injury, the disappointing performances of Livan Hernandez and Escobar and Medina and even Pettitte and Schmidt show that many youngsters, while able to continue pitching, have

been robbed of some of the talent that made them so special in the first place.

Looking Further Back

Since we introduced the PAP system in 1998, we have been able to recover pitch-count data for more than 95% of the games played since 1988, providing a vital historical perspective on the value of the approach. It is important to keep in mind that pitch counts are not an official statistic, and the sources that keep them—STATS, Inc. and The Baseball Workshop—don't always agree on the number of pitches thrown, sometimes differing by as many as four or five pitches. Some of that may stem from different methods of counting the pitches thrown on intentional walks, while some appears to be simply the result of missing a pitch here and there. So while the numbers we present here cannot be considered definitive, they're as accurate as we are likely to get.

Table 1 lists the winners of the Most-Abused Pitcher Award for each year from 1988-98.

Table 1

Year	Pitcher	PAP/S	Age	Workload
1988	Bobby Witt	57.8	24	134.9
1989	Roger Clemens	51.1	26	102.3
1990	Pedro Martinez	39.3	22	104.8
1991	Jose DeJesus	26.0	26	52.0
1992	Randy Johnson	55.3	28	92.2
1993	Cal Eldred	40.7	25	88.2
1994	Randy Johnson	54.9	30	73.2
1995	Alex Fernandez	28.9	25	62.6
1996	Alex Fernandez	28.6	26	57.2
1997	Pedro Martinez	29.5	25	63.9
1998	Livan Hernandez	46.1	23	115.2

Bobby Witt arrived in the major leagues in 1986 with one of the liveliest and wildest arms baseball had seen in a very long time. In his first two seasons, he walked 283 men while striking out 334 in 301 innings, an absurd display of untamed power.

In 1988, Witt began to harness his control. He made only 22 starts, but had 13 complete games and threw 174 innings—nearly eight per start—while averaging 5.2 walks and 7.6 strikeouts per nine innings. Bobby Valentine's ridiculous expectations hurt Witt, and his ERA climbed back over 5.00 in 1989. In 1990, Witt finally arrived, going 13-2 with a 2.46 ERA from July 1 to the end of the season, and he was being hailed as baseball's next great pitcher. After leading the majors in Workload in 1988, he ranked third in 1989 and second in 1990.

In 1991, he blew out his arm and has never been the same. Witt never struck out fewer than 7.6 batters per nine innings before the injury; he hasn't struck out more than 7.4 batters per nine innings since. After never giving up more than a hit per inning before the injury, Witt has now given up more than a hit per inning for eight straight seasons.

Witt isn't the only spectacular flameout on the list. Jose DeJesus had an arm almost as lively—and just as wild—as Witt's, and it didn't take even three years of abuse to destroy it. After the 1991 season, DeJesus underwent major arm surgery, and the rest of his career consisted of five appearances with the Royals in 1994. Cal Eldred, who had a 1.79 ERA as a rookie, wore out in 1993 and hasn't been the same since. He missed most of 1995 and 1996 with arm trouble. Ramon Martinez never had another season like 1990, when he went 20-6 with a 2.92 ERA, and became progressively less durable before finally blowing out his shoulder in 1998. Alex Fernandez, of course, went under the knife in 1997.

The only pitchers on the list who showed no ill effects from the burden they carried are Roger Clemens, who is well-known for his strenuous conditioning, and Randy Johnson, who is Randy Johnson and not subject to the rules of biomechanics that restrict the rest of us.

There's more to PAP than these horror stories. Looking back at the data, we discovered some good news: a definite, positive trend of decreasing starting pitcher workloads, summarized in Table 2.

Table 2

Year	Pitches/S	PAP/S	Workload	(per thousand starts)		
				121-130	131-140	141+
1988	95.5	11.98	20.88	79	35	14
1989	93.7	10.77	18.30	75	30	12
1990	92.9	9.84	17.39	72	28	11
1991	93.6	8.96	15.55	68	24	4
1992	94.5	9.61	16.22	71	25	7
1993	94.9	9.70	17.10	72	24	7
1994	96.7	10.88	18.22	87	30	6
1995	94.0	9.06	15.08	70	12	6
1996	95.4	9.18	14.99	76	19	3
1997	95.3	7.89	12.73	62	11	2
1998	95.9	8.62	14.19	66	19	4
1999	96.2	8.37	13.74	66	16	2

Even as the average number of pitches thrown has remained steady over the last 12 years, PAP scores and Workloads have decreased nearly 30% from 1988. Why? Because the far right end of the spectrum—the 130-pitch outings—are well on their way to being eliminated. An outing of more than 140 pitches, which might have happened in one of 50 games a decade ago, is more on the order of one in 200 games today. Put another way, you'd see two of these a week in 1988. Now it's one every two weeks. The 130-pitch outing is less than half as frequent now as in the late 1980s.

Just having the pitch counts available, forcing managers to be aware of them, has helped eliminate the most egregious excesses. We're looking forward to an era in which we won't need to devote an entire chapter of *Baseball Prospectus* to the issue of pitcher abuse.

We leave you with the Danger Dozen—the 12 Most-Abused Pitchers of 1999:

Pitcher	Team	Age	PAP	GS	PAP/S	AAW
Livan Hernandez	F/S	24	924	30	30.8	71.9
Russ Ortiz	SFG	25	932	33	28.2	61.2
Freddy Garcia	SEA	22	656	33	19.9	53.0
Pedro Martinez	BOS	27	791	29	27.3	50.0
Jose Rosado	KCR	24	603	33	18.3	42.6
Randy Wolf	PHI	22	332	21	15.8	42.2
Randy Johnson	ARZ	35	1358	35	38.8	38.8
Bartolo Colon	CLE	24	529	32	16.5	38.6
Pedro Astacio	COL	29	816	34	24.0	36.0
Jason Schmidt	PIT	26	582	33	17.6	35.3
Jamey Wright	COL	24	228	16	14.3	33.3
Shawn Estes	SFG	26	496	32	15.5	31.0

Withstanding a furious charge from Russ Ortiz, new teammate Livan Hernandez holds onto his title of Most-Abused Pitcher for another year. The last pitcher to win back-to-back MAP awards was Alex Fernandez. If Hernandez follows the same timetable, we can expect him to be in an operating room this October.

Anaheim Angels

The Angels began 1999 as the popular favorite in the AL West, with a wealth of outfield talent and a few good young hitters with upside. In addition to the core carried over from 1998, they had signed a shiny new first baseman guaranteed to give them a .300/.400/.550 season and push them past the Texas Rangers into the playoffs.

By the end of the season, the Angels were the worst team in the AL West. Those good young hitters had put together years ranging from unimpressive to downright brutal. That shiny new first baseman spent most of the year at DH and was below average at the position. The postseason hadn't even been discussed since July 25.

The popular excuse was injuries, and the Angels certainly had their fair share. Center fielder Jim Edmonds missed four months after shoulder surgery. Right fielder Tim Salmon missed two months after injuring his wrist in May—this following a torrid April. The first baseman, Mo Vaughn, sprained his ankle four innings into the season and missed six weeks, returning as a .270-hitting DH with middling power. Starting shortstop Gary DiSarcina suffered a broken wrist in spring training and missed the first half of the season.

That's the middle of the lineup and a bonus injury—all part of why the Angels were done by the time football training camps opened. The team would finish the year 13th in the league in runs scored and EqA. Their pitching was actually decent, led by a great performance from a no-name bullpen. The team ERA, 4.79, was good for fifth in the league. Even accounting for the slight benefit of Edison Field, that's an average staff.

The Angels faced some major issues in the offseason. Having fired Manager Terry Collins and forced GM Bill Bavasi to resign, they went into the winter with a new braintrust of Manager Mike Scioscia and GM Bill Stoneman. Stoneman spent a number of years with the Montreal Expos, helping them build competitive teams on below-average budgets. Scioscia has managed at the Triple-A level, but this will be his first major-league stint.

The Scioscia hiring was a mixed bag. While it was good to see the Angels avoid the trap of hiring for experience, even when it's experience at losing, there may have been better candidates—in particular, good minority candidates like Chris Chambliss. Additionally, the team was determined to hire a former major-league player, after Collins's lack of playing experience became an issue in the clubhouse in 1999. The hiring of Scioscia generated a lot of positive press, thanks to a local media that fondly remembers him from his days with the Dodgers.

Stoneman's experience with the Expos has increased speculation that the Angels will cut salary and start over, in part to make the team more attractive to potential buyers. It's no secret that Disney wants out of baseball, having accomplished its goal of keeping the Angels in Anaheim to enhance the city's reputation as a tourist destination. Disney hasn't achieved the marketing synergy it had anticipated, and Disney upper management has occasionally chafed at working within the structure of Major League Baseball.

The new management team should be a good thing, because it really is time for the Angels to start over. This team, the Salmon/Edmonds/DiSarcina/Garret Anderson Angels, didn't win anything in its time, and its players are now either past their peak or at its tail end. The team has gone from a young one to a middling/old one; adding Vaughn didn't help, and adding Troy Glaus and a catcher younger than Matt Walbeck won't be enough to reverse the trend. There are no prospects in the development pipeline who can play second base or shortstop, the two positions where the Angels desperately need good young players.

The starting rotation needs to be completely revamped because it suffers from an even more serious age problem. One of the worst things the Bavasi management team did was bring in Ken Hill and Tim Belcher, two pitchers who had no business being given multi-year deals and being relied on for 200 quality innings each. In three seasons for the Angels, the two have combined for a 5.54 ERA in just 363⅔ innings, at a combined cost of about $14 million so far. Each pitcher is

Angels Prospectus

1999 record: 70-92; Fourth place, AL West

Pythagorean W/L: 70-92

Runs scored: 711 (13th in AL)

Runs allowed: 826 (4th in AL)

Team EQA: .237 (13th in AL)

1999 team age: 30.1 (4th-oldest in AL)

1999 park: Edison International Field; neutral park, decreased run scoring by less than 1%.

1999: Injuries made an overrated, aging, mediocre team look even worse.

2000: They should bottom out before reemerging in 2001.

under contract for 2000 as well, a significant problem for both the budget and the team on the field.

Longtime ace Chuck Finley is a free agent, after the team fumbled away a chance to trade him at last year's deadline. The Angels were unable to sign him before he hit the market, and once he did, his price shot through the roof. He signed with the Indians for three years and $26 million, when the Angels could have signed him during 1999 for two years and about half that. Finley has been a very consistent starter, but he is 35 and has thrown a lot of pitches. He's benefiting from the thin crop of free-agent pitchers this year. In the long term, not signing him is the best thing for the Angels, especially if it pushes them into a rebuilding process.

There's one unfortunate catch: the Angels won't get a draft pick in return. They had an agreement with Finley that prevented them from offering him arbitration, which is a required step in getting compensation. So the Angels, having lost their chance to cash in their biggest chip, ended up getting nothing in return.

Stoneman now has his decisions to make. Edmonds and Anderson are each one year away from free agency. It would seem certain that one of them will be traded, but the Angels have had four outfielders for three spots since 1997 without making a trade, so perhaps the streak will continue. Still, both players are cheap, both have significant trade value and the Angels simply have no need for both of them with Darin Erstad—whose trade value is at a low point after his brutal season—available to play left field.

While the Angels are talking, as they always do, about adding a starting pitcher to fix that perceived deficit, they'd be much better off trying to add a cheap, young middle infielder with on-base skills. The Angels' second-base prospects of late, Justin Baughman and Trent Durrington, are nearly identical in that they're fast, fair defensively and think a fourth ball is something you'd see at a freak show. The top shortstop prospect, Nelson Castro, was waived after the season, after his sixth year of not hitting, and is now Giants' property.

The Angels need to dial up the Yankees' Brian Cashman and try to turn one of their extra outfielders into D'Angelo Jimenez and a live arm or two with some upside. It would make them much younger, fill one of the middle infield holes and give them an OBP boost, all while reducing the payroll. Perhaps Cashman would balk, but given the Yankees' depth and their relative weakness in left field, it's certainly worth the phone call.

Trades will help, but the biggest improvements are going to have to come from within. The Angels' player development program has been a grave disappointment since the core of the current team reached the majors. With that in

mind, the team let a dozen scouts go at the end of the season.

We've been proponents of holding scouts accountable for the talent they sign, and on one level, it's good to see an organization recognize that the limitations of their talent base can be traced to poor scouting. That said, the firings didn't seem to be well thought out; rather, they had a punitive, housecleaning quality. While the Angels targeted the scouting department, they didn't target scouts based on the track records of their signings. It's a start, though, and may set a precedent of accountability.

The Angels' primary on-field problem is an offense that doesn't get enough runners on base, and that is mainly because the team doesn't walk enough, and hasn't for a number of years. In drafting, signing and developing offensive talent, the Angels could take a lesson from Oakland, which has emphasized plate discipline in the developmental process. Despite a credible job by the pitching staff in 1999, particularly by the bullpen, the Angels just didn't put enough runs on the board to win, for the same reason they've struggled to score in three of the past four years. Table 1 illustrates the problem.

Table 1

Year	Rank in OBP	Rank in Runs
1999	14th	13th
1998	10th	10th
1997	5th	5th
1996	11th	13th

You don't have to be Clay Davenport to see a correlation. The Angels have continued to build their offense—Tim Salmon excepted—around players with good batting averages and good power, but poor-to-fair walk rates. These lineups do not score enough runs to support a pitching staff that, more often than not, has been good enough to make them contenders.

It is virtually impossible to contend in the AL without a .350 OBP as a team. If the Angels want to move into the AL's elite, they're going to have to add players who get on base. Sometimes, it is that simple.

The Angels have almost no chance of being a factor in 2000. The offense should be better, if only because it can't be much worse. The lineup will feature scars at second base and shortstop, and only Salmon and Vaughn can be expected to be above average offensively for their positions. There is some upside in Troy Glaus, and if the team can work outfielder and OBP machine Mike Colangelo into the lineup, he could boost their run scoring.

The team is going to be working in some good young pitchers. The 2000 Angel rotation should feature Jarrod

Washburn, Ramon Ortiz and possibly Scott Schoeneweis. Collectively, they won't set the league on fire this year, but they should lay the groundwork to be the core of the next Angel contender in 2001 or 2002. Right now, they are the team's future, and the sooner the Angels break with the past and embrace that future, the better off they will be.

HITTERS (Averages: BA: .270 / OBP: .340 / SLG: .430 / EQA: .260)

Chuck Abbott   SS   Bats R   Age 25

YEAR	TEAM	LGE	AB	H	DB	TP	HR	BB/SO	R	RBI	SB	CS	OUT	BA	OBP	SLG	EQA	EQR	DEFENSE
1997	CedarRpd	Mid	529	108	21	3	7	45/183	59	42	12	6	427	.204	.269	.295	.191	34	111-2B 98
1998	Midland	Tex	518	114	18	6	1	28/154	51	44	8	5	409	.220	.264	.284	.181	29	131-SS 87
1999	Erie	Eas	449	95	13	1	4	33/156	55	36	4	5	359	.212	.268	.272	.177	24	123-SS 83
2000	*Anaheim*	*AL*	*444*	*91*	*14*	*2*	*3*	*36/147*	*36*	*26*	*10*	*5*	*358*	*.205*	*.265*	*.266*	*.176*	*23*	

Gary DiSarcina is no bargain, but he's got job security like you wouldn't believe: Abbott is the only shortstop prospect the Angels have above A ball. There's simply nothing Abbott does well, despite which he'll have a chance to move up to Triple-A in 2000. Non-prospect with extreme prejudice.

Garret Anderson   CF   Bats L   Age 28

YEAR	TEAM	LGE	AB	H	DB	TP	HR	BB/SO	R	RBI	SB	CS	OUT	BA	OBP	SLG	EQA	EQR	DEFENSE	
1997	Anaheim	AL	622	190	36	3	8	25/67	73	89	10	4	436	.305	.335	.412	.253	70	143-OF 102	
1998	Anaheim	AL	624	189	42	8	15	27/78	61	78	7	3	438	.303	.333	.468	.266	80	153-OF 98	
1999	Anaheim	AL	616	185	35	2	20	27/81	80	74	3	4	435	.300	.330	.461	.261	76	114-CF 104	31-LF 92
2000	*Anaheim*	*AL*	*585*	*175*	*32*	*2*	*17*	*38/73*	*85*	*97*	*5*	*3*	*413*	*.299*	*.342*	*.448*	*.265*	*75*		

His defensive numbers were much better in center field than they had been in the corners, and he did receive praise for his play in the wake of Jim Edmonds' injury. Offensively, he was the same as ever; of course, a .260 EqA from a good glove in center field is a positive, while the same performance by an indifferent left fielder is useless. The Angels have to move an outfielder, so it's hard to say what position or uniform Anderson will be occupying in 2000. He'll hit what he always hits, regardless.

Nelson Castro   SS   Bats R   Age 24

YEAR	TEAM	LGE	AB	H	DB	TP	HR	BB/SO	R	RBI	SB	CS	OUT	BA	OBP	SLG	EQA	EQR	DEFENSE
1997	Boise	Nwn	294	67	12	1	5	23/57	39	23	7	3	230	.228	.289	.327	.211	23	67-SS 94
1998	Lk Elsin	Cal	476	100	16	5	4	29/106	50	32	16	6	382	.210	.262	.290	.187	29	129-SS 85
1999	Lk Elsin	Cal	446	99	19	8	1	24/80	41	37	21	8	355	.222	.264	.307	.196	30	123-SS 96
2000	*San Fran*	*NL*	*423*	*94*	*17*	*4*	*4*	*31/84*	*45*	*32*	*19*	*8*	*337*	*.222*	*.275*	*.310*	*.206*	*32*	

Even an organization as desperate for a shortstop as the Angels can't wait forever. Castro now has almost 1,000 plate appearances in the California League that say he can't hit; he also can't field particularly well, which means he's a pinch-runner prospect. Castro was released after the season, and the Giants picked him up. He's no threat to Rich Aurilia.

Mike Colangelo   CF   Bats R   Age 23

YEAR	TEAM	LGE	AB	H	DB	TP	HR	BB/SO	R	RBI	SB	CS	OUT	BA	OBP	SLG	EQA	EQR	DEFENSE
1998	CedarRpd	Mid	85	21	6	0	4	10/16	10	6	2	1	65	.247	.335	.459	.265	12	
1998	Lk Elsin	Cal	146	46	11	2	4	10/24	25	15	1	3	103	.315	.376	.500	.285	22	34-OF 111
1999	Erie	Eas	109	33	9	2	1	12/23	20	10	2	2	78	.303	.386	.450	.281	16	24-OF 85
1999	Edmonton	PCL	102	33	5	1	0	11/18	10	7	1	1	70	.324	.398	.392	.275	14	21-OF 82
2000	*Anaheim*	*AL*	*160*	*47*	*11*	*1*	*4*	*18/35*	*28*	*27*	*2*	*1*	*114*	*.294*	*.365*	*.450*	*.277*	*23*	

Angel fans, and the media that feed them, are fond of yammering about the Angel "curse." It's bullfeathers, of course . . . but then Mike Colangelo comes along and puts that small bit of doubt in your mind. Colangelo, the team's best offensive prospect, flew though the system in just over a year and landed in Anaheim on June 13. In the seventh inning of his major-league debut, he collided with Reggie Williams while chasing a fly ball and tore ligaments in his thumb, ending his season.

    The Angels need another outfielder like they need to raise ticket prices, but Colangelo is the only thing that resembles a leadoff hitter in the system, so finding a place for him is mandatory. Unless they trade two outfielders, though, he'll start the year at Edmonton.

Jeff DaVanon　　OF　　Bats B　Age 26

YEAR	TEAM	LGE	AB	H	DB	TP	HR	BB/SO	R	RBI	SB	CS	OUT	BA	OBP	SLG	EQA	EQR	DEFENSE
1997	Visalia	Cal	412	83	13	2	4	60/108	45	26	9	6	334	.201	.303	.272	.202	31	105-OF 91
1998	Modesto	Cal	309	75	12	2	4	41/82	37	38	11	4	238	.243	.333	.333	.236	32	67-OF 86
1999	Midland	Tex	369	93	21	5	7	38/84	53	37	7	4	280	.252	.326	.393	.245	42	86-OF 90
1999	Edmonton	PCL	129	33	6	2	4	16/29	23	13	7	3	98	.256	.341	.426	.263	17	34-OF 102
2000	*Anaheim*	*AL*	*466*	*116*	*24*	*5*	*10*	*62/113*	*76*	*61*	*13*	*6*	*356*	*.249*	*.337*	*.386*	*.250*	*56*	

DaVanon is the least valuable of the three players the Angels scored in exchange for Randy Velarde and Omar Olivares. He had no chance to make headway in the A's chain, and isn't in much better shape with the Angels, given all their outfielders. He'll be in the mix for a utility job, trying to be the new Rex Hudler. A sane version.

Steve Decker　　C/3B　　Bats R　Age 34

YEAR	TEAM	LGE	AB	H	DB	TP	HR	BB/SO	R	RBI	SB	CS	OUT	BA	OBP	SLG	EQA	EQR	DEFENSE	
1997	Tacoma	PCL	341	83	17	1	7	15/42	29	35	0	0	258	.243	.277	.361	.212	27	22-3B 94	
1998	Norfolk	Int	353	92	13	0	10	42/55	42	46	0	1	262	.261	.345	.382	.249	41	70-1B 99	21-C 88
1999	Edmonton	PCL	222	50	14	1	10	36/41	35	34	0	0	172	.225	.339	.432	.261	30	38-3B 92	
1999	Anaheim	AL	62	14	6	0	0	13/9	5	4	0	0	48	.226	.368	.323	.249	7		
2000	*Anaheim*	*AL*	*248*	*58*	*8*	*0*	*8*	*38/40*	*34*	*34*	*0*	*0*	*190*	*.234*	*.336*	*.363*	*.243*	*28*		

Decker can be a useful bench player, thanks to his ability to catch, play third base and hit left-handed pitching. It's a fairly unique combination, and one that should keep him in the major leagues. Decker is in the NRI phase of his career; he would fit in Toronto.

Jason Dewey　　C　　Bats R　Age 23

YEAR	TEAM	LGE	AB	H	DB	TP	HR	BB/SO	R	RBI	SB	CS	OUT	BA	OBP	SLG	EQA	EQR	DEFENSE
1997	Boise	Nwn	272	66	12	1	9	25/75	32	37	1	1	207	.243	.309	.393	.236	28	
1998	Lk Elsin	Cal	399	100	23	2	14	52/120	48	50	4	4	303	.251	.337	.424	.256	50	84-C 87
1999	Lk Elsin	Cal	242	68	16	0	10	23/62	36	24	0	0	174	.281	.346	.471	.272	34	63-C 93
1999	Erie	Eas	140	29	6	0	4	14/51	15	12	0	1	112	.207	.279	.336	.205	11	39-C 92
2000	*Anaheim*	*AL*	*363*	*96*	*13*	*0*	*16*	*46/107*	*54*	*63*	*1*	*1*	*268*	*.264*	*.347*	*.433*	*.265*	*48*	

Dewey has been added to the 40-man roster, a good sign for him. The Angels have a collection of C+ catching prospects who can hit a little at the upper levels—guys like Bret Hemphill and Ben Molina. Dewey is that same type of player, but younger, and a marginally better catcher than those two. He's been moving through the system at a snail's pace; he needs to have a few big months to get noticed and make some time.

Gary DiSarcina　　SS　　Bats R　Age 32

YEAR	TEAM	LGE	AB	H	DB	TP	HR	BB/SO	R	RBI	SB	CS	OUT	BA	OBP	SLG	EQA	EQR	DEFENSE
1997	Anaheim	AL	548	135	28	2	4	14/28	50	45	7	8	421	.246	.271	.327	.196	36	149-SS 103
1998	Anaheim	AL	552	161	40	3	3	20/50	71	55	10	7	398	.292	.326	.391	.242	57	156-SS 99
1999	Anaheim	AL	271	61	7	1	1	12/32	29	27	2	2	212	.225	.263	.269	.172	13	79-SS 99
2000	*Anaheim*	*AL*	*355*	*91*	*18*	*1*	*2*	*22/34*	*38*	*33*	*4*	*3*	*267*	*.256*	*.300*	*.330*	*.212*	*28*	

The end of the Bill Bavasi era will also mark the end of the Salmon/Edmonds/DiSarcina Angels, a team that never won anything despite being in three division races. DiSarcina's broken wrist shouldn't have hurt the Angels much, but with Andy Sheets and Jeff Huson getting his playing time, it did. He'll have the shortstop job unless the Angels can convince Herk Robinson to take him.

Trent Durrington　　2B　　Bats R　Age 24

YEAR	TEAM	LGE	AB	H	DB	TP	HR	BB/SO	R	RBI	SB	CS	OUT	BA	OBP	SLG	EQA	EQR	DEFENSE	
1997	Lk Elsin	Cal	414	96	19	2	3	40/88	40	30	25	9	327	.232	.311	.309	.222	38	111-2B 92	
1998	Midland	Tex	349	67	6	1	1	40/82	42	23	13	7	289	.192	.297	.223	.186	22	74-2B 96	25-OF 94
1999	Erie	Eas	399	104	23	1	3	41/70	59	28	30	10	305	.261	.339	.346	.245	45	106-2B 98	
1999	Anaheim	AL	122	22	1	0	0	8/28	12	3	4	3	103	.180	.231	.189	.117	2	34-2B 98	
2000	*Anaheim*	*AL*	*463*	*110*	*17*	*1*	*2*	*57/93*	*74*	*34*	*33*	*11*	*364*	*.238*	*.321*	*.292*	*.223*	*43*		

Justin Baughman with an accent. Durrington is a fast second baseman from Australia who doesn't hit but doesn't field well enough to make up for it. Right now, he's the only candidate to play second base for the Angels in 2000, especially after his good Arizona Fall League performance. A double-play combination of DiSarcina and Durrington would be the worst in the league by far.

Jim Edmonds   CF   Bats L   Age 30

YEAR	TEAM	LGE	AB	H	DB	TP	HR	BB/SO	R	RBI	SB	CS	OUT	BA	OBP	SLG	EQA	EQR	DEFENSE
1997	Anaheim	AL	499	145	23	0	27	57/77	78	77	5	7	361	.291	.369	.499	.285	78	115-OF 108
1998	Anaheim	AL	601	190	37	2	27	55/111	112	91	6	5	416	.316	.374	.519	.293	97	144-OF 110
1999	Anaheim	AL	203	50	15	2	5	25/45	30	21	5	4	157	.246	.329	.414	.250	24	42-CF 101
2000	*Anaheim*	*AL*	*355*	*105*	*21*	*1*	*15*	*45/66*	*66*	*69*	*5*	*4*	*254*	*.296*	*.375*	*.487*	*.288*	*57*	

His decision to try and avoid surgery on his left shoulder blew up when the injury flared up right before Opening Day. After four months of rehabilitation, he came back to a team playing out the string. He's the pivotal player for the Angels in terms of which direction they take in 2000: if they trade him, it's a white flag. Just before Christmas, the Angels seemed ready to trade Edmonds to Oakland. No matter who he's with, Edmonds will play more than the projection indicates.

Darin Erstad   1B/LF   Bats L   Age 26

YEAR	TEAM	LGE	AB	H	DB	TP	HR	BB/SO	R	RBI	SB	CS	OUT	BA	OBP	SLG	EQA	EQR	DEFENSE	
1997	Anaheim	AL	536	160	34	4	16	47/83	95	74	23	8	384	.299	.360	.466	.279	79	122-1B 93	
1998	Anaheim	AL	538	163	41	3	19	42/75	82	80	18	6	381	.303	.360	.496	.285	83	57-1B 101	69-OF 89
1999	Anaheim	AL	583	145	23	5	12	40/101	77	49	13	7	445	.249	.298	.367	.225	54	72-1B 97	64-LF 118
2000	*Anaheim*	*AL*	*536*	*145*	*24*	*4*	*17*	*48/86*	*80*	*81*	*13*	*6*	*397*	*.271*	*.330*	*.425*	*.256*	*66*		

Erstad made the 1998 AL All-Star team off a dominant first half; he's hit an empty .250 since. His poor second half in '98 was due to a damaged hamstring. His 1999 had more to do with forgetting how to drive the ball. He then got frustrated and watched his plate discipline fall apart. It's hard not to adjust expectations downward at this point, but Erstad's basic skill set is still there, and I think he's going to get back to the .285 EqA level. I'll say it again: the Angels need to stick him in the outfield and leave him alone.

Troy Glaus   3B   Bats R   Age 23

YEAR	TEAM	LGE	AB	H	DB	TP	HR	BB/SO	R	RBI	SB	CS	OUT	BA	OBP	SLG	EQA	EQR	DEFENSE
1998	Midland	Tex	185	46	8	1	14	31/45	35	34	2	1	140	.249	.361	.530	.291	32	48-3B 105
1998	Vancouvr	PCL	220	65	13	0	15	19/55	28	37	3	2	157	.295	.358	.559	.295	37	58-3B 110
1998	Anaheim	AL	165	37	6	0	2	15/50	18	24	1	0	128	.224	.289	.297	.200	11	46-3B 104
1999	Anaheim	AL	548	130	25	0	29	64/144	77	73	5	1	419	.237	.324	.442	.257	70	152-3B 103
2000	*Anaheim*	*AL*	*429*	*112*	*18*	*0*	*32*	*57/122*	*74*	*94*	*4*	*1*	*318*	*.261*	*.348*	*.527*	*.288*	*71*	

The value of starting out hot and going cold, versus the opposite, was demonstrated by Glaus in 1999. He posted an 1121 OPS in April, leading the league in doubles. So when he hit .130 with a 365 OPS in May, his overall numbers looked halfway decent, making it easier for the Angels to stick with him. He was close to a demotion a few times, but was never sent down, so give them credit for that. Glaus's walk rate and strikeout-to-walk ratio improved considerably in the second half, so I think that projection looks about right.

Todd Greene   RF/DH/C   Bats R   Age 29

YEAR	TEAM	LGE	AB	H	DB	TP	HR	BB/SO	R	RBI	SB	CS	OUT	BA	OBP	SLG	EQA	EQR	DEFENSE
1997	Vancouvr	PCL	254	75	14	1	18	14/35	34	51	3	1	180	.295	.342	.571	.293	42	
1997	Anaheim	AL	124	36	4	0	10	6/24	23	24	2	0	88	.290	.323	.565	.286	19	
1998	Vancouvr	PCL	109	27	8	0	6	10/19	12	16	1	0	82	.248	.323	.486	.268	15	
1999	Edmonton	PCL	72	15	6	0	3	0/13	7	9	0	0	57	.208	.216	.417	.201	5	
1999	Anaheim	AL	321	77	16	1	14	8/63	32	39	1	4	248	.240	.265	.427	.223	29	21-RF 83
2000	*Anaheim*	*AL*	*303*	*77*	*12*	*0*	*18*	*15/56*	*34*	*52*	*1*	*2*	*228*	*.254*	*.289*	*.472*	*.248*	*35*	

Greene's major-league career: .247/.281/.430 in about a season's worth of playing time. He's actually getting worse instead of better, suffering from shoulder damage that makes it difficult for him to catch and stagnating as a hitter. Greene could help a team as a platoon DH and third catcher; the Angels have such a logjam at DH that he'll need to go elsewhere to get that opportunity.

Nathan Haynes   CF   Bats L   Age 20

YEAR	TEAM	LGE	AB	H	DB	TP	HR	BB/SO	R	RBI	SB	CS	OUT	BA	OBP	SLG	EQA	EQR	DEFENSE
1997	So Oregn	Nwn	83	18	0	1	0	18/22	8	6	5	2	67	.217	.363	.241	.231	9	20-OF 100
1998	Modesto	Cal	515	120	15	5	1	41/141	62	33	20	9	404	.233	.293	.287	.202	37	120-OF 92
1999	Visalia	Cal	144	39	5	1	1	13/26	19	10	6	4	109	.271	.339	.340	.235	15	31-OF 107
1999	Lk Elsin	Cal	110	32	6	4	1	9/18	13	12	4	2	80	.291	.348	.445	.267	15	26-OF 105
2000	Anaheim	AL	350	93	13	4	1	40/79	57	35	14	5	262	.266	.341	.334	.240	37	

The main player the Angels received in the Velarde/Olivares trade, Haynes is a toolsy outfielder who improved considerably in his second year in the California League. Haynes can run better than this: his season began with groin surgery that slowed him down. His time with the A's has instilled in him the value of plate discipline, so if he can avoid being deprogrammed by the Angels, he's on track to be their center fielder and leadoff hitter by midseason 2001.

Bret Hemphill   C   Bats B   Age 28

YEAR	TEAM	LGE	AB	H	DB	TP	HR	BB/SO	R	RBI	SB	CS	OUT	BA	OBP	SLG	EQA	EQR	DEFENSE
1997	Midland	Tex	260	57	12	1	6	33/71	28	36	0	1	204	.219	.318	.342	.227	25	
1998	Vancouvr	PCL	156	35	8	2	3	10/36	13	10	0	1	122	.224	.271	.359	.207	12	36-C 90
1999	Edmonton	PCL	241	60	13	1	4	25/63	20	21	1	0	181	.249	.327	.361	.237	25	56-C 99
2000	Anaheim	AL	218	48	10	1	4	26/55	25	23	0	0	170	.220	.303	.330	.217	19	

Hemphill missed most of 1998 after shoulder surgery, yet returned as pretty much the same player. His chance to have a significant slice of the Angel catching job may be gone, though. As a switch-hitter who can play defense, he's the same type of player as Matt Walbeck, but cheaper and better. He would make a good backup for Ben Molina.

Jeff Huson   IF   Bats L   Age 35

YEAR	TEAM	LGE	AB	H	DB	TP	HR	BB/SO	R	RBI	SB	CS	OUT	BA	OBP	SLG	EQA	EQR	DEFENSE	
1997	Milwauke	AL	143	29	4	0	0	4/14	12	11	3	0	114	.203	.237	.231	.145	5	19-2B 97	11-1B 76
1998	Tucson	PCL	80	19	2	1	1	4/15	5	9	0	1	62	.237	.280	.325	.198	5		
1999	Anaheim	AL	224	58	5	2	0	13/27	19	17	10	1	167	.259	.300	.299	.212	17	29-2B 106	
2000	Anaheim	AL	109	24	4	0	0	8/14	9	6	2	0	85	.220	.274	.257	.178	6		

A few years back, Huson was a good use of a roster spot, a left-handed hitter with some speed and some pop who could play three infield positions. In 1999, the Angels were forced to use him as the starting second baseman, which worked as well as you'd expect. Huson has lost his pop, yet is still a reasonable 25th man.

Norm Hutchins   OF   Bats B   Age 24

YEAR	TEAM	LGE	AB	H	DB	TP	HR	BB/SO	R	RBI	SB	CS	OUT	BA	OBP	SLG	EQA	EQR	DEFENSE
1997	Lk Elsin	Cal	567	149	28	8	14	13/143	59	55	19	8	426	.263	.284	.414	.233	56	132-OF 101
1998	Midland	Tex	386	102	18	6	8	9/93	49	36	16	6	290	.264	.286	.404	.232	38	89-OF 101
1999	Edmonton	PCL	514	112	23	5	5	34/125	60	39	18	12	414	.218	.275	.311	.198	36	128-OF 101
2000	Anaheim	AL	502	127	19	5	12	29/122	64	58	20	9	384	.253	.294	.382	.229	48	

His prospect status has gone the way of so many other tools outfielders who don't walk. Most of these guys can salvage a career as a fourth outfielder—also known as the Gerald Williams career path. Hutchins is in the wrong organization for this, so he'll have to wait for free agency next winter.

Brooks Kieschnick   DH/1B   Bats L   Age 28

YEAR	TEAM	LGE	AB	H	DB	TP	HR	BB/SO	R	RBI	SB	CS	OUT	BA	OBP	SLG	EQA	EQR	DEFENSE
1997	ChiCubs	NL	90	17	3	0	4	12/21	9	12	1	0	73	.189	.284	.356	.219	8	16-OF 105
1997	Iowa	AA	366	86	18	0	17	30/100	48	56	0	1	281	.235	.295	.423	.238	39	63-1B 89
1998	St Pete	Fla	107	21	4	0	4	7/23	11	12	0	0	86	.196	.246	.346	.193	7	18-OF 72
1999	Durham	Int	75	14	3	0	1	4/15	5	4	0	0	61	.187	.228	.267	.150	3	
1999	Edmonton	PCL	289	74	16	2	15	15/65	37	49	0	1	216	.256	.296	.481	.252	35	28-1B 100
2000	Cincnnti	NL	297	70	12	0	15	25/69	33	44	0	0	227	.236	.295	.428	.238	31	

Kieschnick wasn't actually Angel property in 1999. He spent most of the season on loan to Edmonton from the Tampa Bay organization, mostly playing DH and hitting moon shots. He could still help a team needing left-handed power off the bench. He's been signed to a minor-league deal by the Reds, but they couldn't make room for Mark Sweeney last year, so it doesn't look good for Kieschnick.

Adam Leggett 2B Bats B Age 24

YEAR	TEAM	LGE	AB	H	DB	TP	HR	BB/SO	R	RBI	SB	CS	OUT	BA	OBP	SLG	EQA	EQR	DEFENSE
1997	Boise	Nwn	223	41	15	1	1	21/58	29	22	2	1	183	.184	.264	.274	.180	13	57-2B 92
1998	CedarRpd	Mid	457	105	22	2	11	64/88	61	39	8	6	358	.230	.330	.359	.238	50	122-2B 104
1999	Lk Elsin	Cal	187	39	8	0	4	14/32	13	20	2	1	149	.209	.268	.316	.195	13	41-2B 98
1999	Erie	Eas	74	12	0	0	1	17/15	7	5	1	2	64	.162	.319	.203	.187	5	19-2B 110
2000	*Anaheim*	*AL*	*294*	*60*	*14*	*1*	*5*	*41/57*	*35*	*27*	*4*	*3*	*237*	*.204*	*.301*	*.310*	*.211*	*24*	

The injury to Justin Baughman and the trade of Randy Velarde increased Leggett's opportunity just in time for him to stop hitting. The organization is desperate for help at second base, and Leggett can get on base and field the position. He has no realistic chance to start the year in Anaheim; he needs to go to Erie or Edmonton and have two good months to give the Angels an option when Durrington flops.

Keith Luuloa IF Bats R Age 25

YEAR	TEAM	LGE	AB	H	DB	TP	HR	BB/SO	R	RBI	SB	CS	OUT	BA	OBP	SLG	EQA	EQR	DEFENSE	
1997	Midland	Tex	411	92	24	4	7	28/66	47	41	4	2	321	.224	.280	.353	.213	33	92-2B 88	27-SS 88
1998	Midland	Tex	469	124	33	6	11	58/62	57	66	3	2	347	.264	.351	.431	.265	63	57-2B 95	30-3B 117
1999	Edmonton	PCL	389	94	18	1	3	37/54	40	35	5	5	300	.242	.314	.316	.216	33	62-2B 103	37-3B 99
2000	*Anaheim*	*AL*	*471*	*117*	*25*	*3*	*9*	*51/66*	*64*	*58*	*4*	*3*	*357*	*.248*	*.322*	*.372*	*.237*	*49*		

Luuloa wasn't able to match his breakout 1998, succumbing to fatigue after playing in both the Arizona Fall League and the Venezuelan League after the season. He goes into the spring battling DaVanon and Huson for a bench job; if he makes the team, he'll be the starting second baseman by the All-Star break. He is the best internal candidate for the job.

Ben Molina C Bats R Age 25

YEAR	TEAM	LGE	AB	H	DB	TP	HR	BB/SO	R	RBI	SB	CS	OUT	BA	OBP	SLG	EQA	EQR	DEFENSE
1997	Lk Elsin	Cal	150	37	9	2	3	4/9	14	25	0	0	113	.247	.266	.393	.216	12	
1997	Midland	Tex	103	28	6	0	5	7/8	13	21	0	0	75	.272	.318	.476	.261	13	
1998	Midland	Tex	150	43	6	0	6	10/8	19	26	0	0	107	.287	.340	.447	.263	19	33-C 92
1998	Vancouvr	PCL	184	52	8	1	1	4/14	11	20	1	1	133	.283	.298	.353	.217	15	44-C 97
1999	Edmonton	PCL	237	58	8	0	7	12/17	21	32	1	1	180	.245	.294	.367	.222	21	55-C 108
1999	Anaheim	AL	101	26	2	0	2	4/6	7	10	0	1	76	.257	.299	.337	.211	8	29-C 103
2000	*Anaheim*	*AL*	*354*	*98*	*12*	*1*	*9*	*22/24*	*42*	*49*	*1*	*1*	*257*	*.277*	*.319*	*.393*	*.240*	*36*	

A few years ago, Molina spent as much time at other positions as behind the plate, due to questions about his defense. He's turned himself into a fair catcher; he hasn't hit since Double-A, though, and the last thing the Angels need is another offensive problem in the lineup. The team was very impressed with him in September, particularly his glove. He'll have at least a share of the catching job.

Orlando Palmeiro OF Bats L Age 31

YEAR	TEAM	LGE	AB	H	DB	TP	HR	BB/SO	R	RBI	SB	CS	OUT	BA	OBP	SLG	EQA	EQR	DEFENSE	
1997	Anaheim	AL	134	29	2	2	0	16/11	18	8	2	2	107	.216	.305	.261	.196	9	43-OF 88	
1998	Vancouvr	PCL	141	37	11	2	1	13/11	16	23	2	1	105	.262	.325	.390	.243	15	37-OF 98	
1998	Anaheim	AL	165	54	7	2	0	20/11	27	20	4	4	115	.327	.400	.394	.273	22	39-OF 102	
1999	Anaheim	AL	314	85	11	1	1	36/30	42	21	5	5	234	.271	.357	.322	.238	32	49-LF 100	24-RF 100
2000	*Anaheim*	*AL*	*259*	*69*	*9*	*3*	*0*	*34/22*	*38*	*28*	*3*	*4*	*194*	*.266*	*.352*	*.324*	*.236*	*26*		

The slap-hitting style that serves him well as a fourth outfielder and pinch-hitter wore thin when he was forced into a regular role in the first half. Like Chad Curtis, Palmeiro is an excellent player in his role, and a poor one if pushed beyond that. Look for him to bounce back in 2000.

Tim Salmon RF Bats R Age 31

YEAR	TEAM	LGE	AB	H	DB	TP	HR	BB/SO	R	RBI	SB	CS	OUT	BA	OBP	SLG	EQA	EQR	DEFENSE
1997	Anaheim	AL	577	169	26	1	33	91/136	90	123	9	12	420	.293	.397	.513	.298	102	148-OF 101
1998	Anaheim	AL	464	143	26	1	28	89/98	83	88	0	1	322	.308	.423	.550	.321	94	
1999	Anaheim	AL	349	92	23	2	16	59/82	54	63	4	1	258	.264	.370	.479	.285	56	89-RF 101
2000	Anaheim	AL	357	99	16	1	21	67/80	72	79	2	2	260	.277	.392	.504	.300	64	

The best April of his career was followed by a sprained left wrist that kept him out until the All-Star break. He came back about three weeks too soon, and his presence in the lineup did more harm than good. Once healthy, he was Tim Salmon. The good news is that he was over the foot injury that made him a DH in 1998 and was back to his old nimble self in right field. His 1998 level is within reach.

Andy Sheets IF Bats R Age 28

YEAR	TEAM	LGE	AB	H	DB	TP	HR	BB/SO	R	RBI	SB	CS	OUT	BA	OBP	SLG	EQA	EQR	DEFENSE
1997	Tacoma	PCL	394	83	14	0	11	34/109	37	36	4	2	313	.211	.276	.330	.204	30	107-SS 93
1997	Seattle	AL	89	23	3	0	4	6/33	17	9	2	0	66	.258	.305	.427	.248	10	15-3B 100
1998	San Dieg	NL	199	53	7	3	8	21/60	34	32	8	2	148	.266	.340	.452	.268	28	28-SS 107
1999	Anaheim	AL	244	47	7	0	4	11/59	20	28	1	2	199	.193	.227	.270	.151	9	68-SS 89
2000	Anaheim	AL	258	56	8	1	6	23/69	25	25	3	1	203	.217	.281	.326	.205	19	

Like Huson and Palmeiro, Sheets is a decent bench player who was in over his head as a regular. Sheets was picked up from the Padres in the spring after the DiSarcina injury, and his inability to even match DiSarcina's meager production further hampered an offense missing two good hitters. Among the stiffs fighting for jobs in the Angels' middle infield, Sheets is the player I'd most like to have as the fifth infielder.

Mo Vaughn 1B/DH Bats L Age 32

YEAR	TEAM	LGE	AB	H	DB	TP	HR	BB/SO	R	RBI	SB	CS	OUT	BA	OBP	SLG	EQA	EQR	DEFENSE
1997	Boston	AL	524	167	20	0	37	83/148	88	95	2	2	359	.319	.425	.569	.326	109	127-1B 90
1998	Boston	AL	606	206	30	2	40	59/141	103	110	0	0	400	.340	.406	.594	.324	119	142-1B 97
1999	Anaheim	AL	520	145	19	0	32	48/127	57	100	0	0	375	.279	.352	.500	.281	79	68-1B 93
2000	Anaheim	AL	559	167	19	0	38	75/135	101	133	0	0	392	.299	.382	.537	.304	100	

The ankle he sprained in April made it difficult for him to generate power or play the field. He wasn't really healthy until the Angels' season was long over, finishing the year on a hot streak. The power will be back; of greater concern is his walk rate, which slipped precipitously in 1998 and didn't recover in 1999. Vaughn is being paid as one of the best hitters in baseball, a .320 EqA guy, which is a level I don't expect him to reach again.

Matt Walbeck C Bats B Age 30

YEAR	TEAM	LGE	AB	H	DB	TP	HR	BB/SO	R	RBI	SB	CS	OUT	BA	OBP	SLG	EQA	EQR	DEFENSE
1997	Detroit	AL	137	38	3	0	3	11/18	17	10	3	3	102	.277	.331	.365	.236	14	
1998	Anaheim	AL	339	90	15	2	6	29/66	40	45	1	1	250	.265	.327	.375	.239	35	96-C 98
1999	Anaheim	AL	287	67	8	1	3	23/46	24	20	2	3	223	.233	.297	.300	.202	20	81-C 101
2000	Anaheim	AL	241	56	8	1	5	23/41	25	26	2	2	187	.232	.299	.336	.215	20	

The Angels finally tired of him in August, more or less handing the catching job to Ben Molina. As an Established Major Leaguer, he'll begin bouncing around the league, grabbing 100 to 200 at-bats a year as a backup catcher. He's a borderline player at best.

PITCHERS (Averages: ERA: 4.50 / H/9: 9.00 / HR/9: 1.00 / BB/9: 3.50 / K/9: 6.50 / KWH: 1.00)

Juan Alvarez Throws L Age 26

YEAR	TEAM	LGE	IP	H	ER	HR	BB	K	ERA	W	L	H/9	HR/9	BB/9	K/9	KWH	PERA
1997	Lk Elsin	Cal	48.0	41	11	2	16	30	2.06	4	1	7.69	0.38	3.00	5.63	1.03	3.00
1997	Midland	Tex	36.3	66	40	5	26	23	9.91	1	3	16.35	1.24	6.44	5.70	0.23	10.90
1998	Midland	Tex	43.0	46	29	5	26	32	6.07	2	3	9.63	1.05	5.44	6.70	0.64	5.65
1999	Erie	Eas	28.7	26	18	4	8	16	5.65	1	2	8.16	1.26	2.51	5.02	0.92	3.77
1999	Edmonton	PCL	27.0	32	13	2	9	20	4.33	2	1	10.67	0.67	3.00	6.67	1.04	5.00

Alvarez is a left-handed specialist who throws hard and was impressive in a handful of outings with Anaheim late in the year. How Mike Scioscia will handle the bullpen is an unknown, but Alvarez gives him one piece of the puzzle should he have LaRussa/Riggleman tendencies.

Tim Belcher Throws R Age 38

YEAR	TEAM	LGE	IP	H	ER	HR	BB	K	ERA	W	L	H/9	HR/9	BB/9	K/9	KWH	PERA
1997	KansasCy	AL	216.3	236	118	28	71	115	4.91	11	13	9.82	1.16	2.95	4.78	0.59	4.91
1998	KansasCy	AL	242.0	228	107	33	77	133	3.98	15	12	8.48	1.23	2.86	4.95	0.75	4.20
1999	Anaheim	AL	130.3	168	97	24	45	53	6.70	4	10	11.60	1.66	3.11	3.66	0.28	6.63

Wow. A pitcher approaching 40 with a lot of miles on him and a poor strikeout rate gets hammered and is unable to get through the year without being injured. Stunning. Belcher's signing, on the heels of 1998's Ken Hill fiasco, is a clear sign that Disney doesn't apply the same due diligence in its baseball operation as it does in the rest of its business. Worse still, the money the Angels are paying Belcher and Hill kept them from signing Chuck Finley, lifelong Angel and better pitcher. Elbow surgery will keep him out until late in spring training. It doesn't really matter: Belcher is done.

Brian Cooper Throws R Age 25

YEAR	TEAM	LGE	IP	H	ER	HR	BB	K	ERA	W	L	H/9	HR/9	BB/9	K/9	KWH	PERA
1997	Lk Elsin	Cal	109.3	131	65	8	31	72	5.35	5	7	10.78	0.66	2.55	5.93	0.95	4.77
1998	Midland	Tex	154.3	235	138	33	71	115	8.05	4	13	13.70	1.92	4.14	6.71	0.59	8.86
1999	Erie	Eas	146.3	186	79	17	34	109	4.86	7	9	11.44	1.05	2.09	6.70	1.40	5.41
1999	Edmonton	PCL	30.0	30	17	0	12	26	5.10	1	2	9.00	0.00	3.60	7.80	1.40	3.60
1999	Anaheim	AL	27.3	23	14	3	17	15	4.61	1	2	7.57	0.99	5.60	4.94	0.43	4.61

As expected, Cooper was able to reestablish himself as a prospect in the Eastern League. Pitchers who don't overpower hitters need more help than others, and Cooper relies more on a change-up and command than a big heater. With Finley expected to leave, Cooper will battle Scott Schoeneweis for the #5 starter spot in the spring. There's an adjustment period coming; while Cooper may eventually be a major-league starter, he's a bad bet in 2000.

Seth Etherton Throws R Age 23

YEAR	TEAM	LGE	IP	H	ER	HR	BB	K	ERA	W	L	H/9	HR/9	BB/9	K/9	KWH	PERA
1998	Midland	Tex	46.3	62	36	9	14	29	6.99	1	4	12.04	1.75	2.72	5.63	0.72	6.80
1999	Erie	Eas	159.7	181	83	14	47	126	4.68	9	9	10.20	0.79	2.65	7.10	1.39	4.62
1999	Edmonton	PCL	20.3	26	12	6	7	16	5.31	1	1	11.51	2.66	3.10	7.08	1.05	7.97

Etherton was also helped by Erie, although he's more a classic pitching prospect than Cooper, throwing in the low 90s. With two fragile veterans fronting a lot of kids, the Angels are likely to use 10 to 12 starters in 2000, so Etherton should be up during the year. Like Cooper, he won't be ready to contribute this year, but, along with Washburn and Ortiz, will be part of a very good Angel rotation in 2002.

Chuck Finley Throws L Age 37

YEAR	TEAM	LGE	IP	H	ER	HR	BB	K	ERA	W	L	H/9	HR/9	BB/9	K/9	KWH	PERA
1997	Anaheim	AL	166.7	145	71	18	66	157	3.83	11	8	7.83	0.97	3.56	8.48	1.92	3.83
1998	Anaheim	AL	222.0	207	91	18	113	214	3.69	15	10	8.39	0.73	4.58	8.68	1.46	4.30
1999	Anaheim	AL	211.3	197	108	20	91	205	4.60	11	12	8.39	0.85	3.88	8.73	1.75	4.17

The Angels' decision to hold on to Finley at the trade deadline was inexplicable, predicated on the idea that they would sign him before he went on the market. They didn't, he did and now the Angels don't even have Enrique Wilson to show for him. Remember, these guys are the professionals. Finley has never had a major arm injury and his peripherals are the same year-in and year-out. He's a good signing for the Indians for 2000. Beyond that, he's a question mark.

Mike Fyhrie Throws R Age 30

YEAR	TEAM	LGE	IP	H	ER	HR	BB	K	ERA	W	L	H/9	HR/9	BB/9	K/9	KWH	PERA
1998	Norfolk	Int	97.7	122	85	11	50	51	7.83	3	8	11.24	1.01	4.61	4.70	0.32	6.27
1999	Edmonton	PCL	109.7	93	48	7	48	89	3.94	7	5	7.63	0.57	3.94	7.30	1.33	3.53
1999	Anaheim	AL	51.0	61	30	7	20	27	5.29	3	3	10.76	1.24	3.53	4.76	0.45	5.82

(Mike Fyhrie *continued*)

Fyhrie had his best season in the right organization, earning a call-up to Anaheim during the team's July collapse. His stuff isn't impressive at all, and his performance at Edmonton screams "fluke." After a good first start with the Angels, Fyhrie pitched poorly. It's unlikely that he'll ever spend three months in the major leagues again.

Steve Green   Throws R   Age 22

YEAR	TEAM	LGE	IP	H	ER	HR	BB	K	ERA	W	L	H/9	HR/9	BB/9	K/9	KWH	PERA
1998	CedarRpd	Mid	75.7	117	67	13	33	43	7.97	2	6	13.92	1.55	3.93	5.11	0.36	8.44
1999	Lk Elsin	Cal	112.0	145	74	11	40	67	5.95	4	8	11.65	0.88	3.21	5.38	0.58	5.79
1999	Erie	Eas	39.0	40	28	5	21	26	6.46	1	3	9.23	1.15	4.85	6.00	0.60	5.31

The organization likes this Canadian right-hander, who reached Double-A in just his second professional season. Despite his youth, Green has completed one of every six starts he's made over two years, including five complete games in 1999. You can guess what we think of that. Pitchers in the Angel organization accounted for six of the 12 highest innings totals by minor-league pitchers, including three of the top four slots. The only thing you develop that way is surgical scars.

Shigetoshi Hasegawa   Throws R   Age 31

YEAR	TEAM	LGE	IP	H	ER	HR	BB	K	ERA	W	L	H/9	HR/9	BB/9	K/9	KWH	PERA
1997	Anaheim	AL	119.0	112	53	13	46	84	4.01	7	6	8.47	0.98	3.48	6.35	1.02	4.16
1998	Anaheim	AL	96.3	86	35	13	33	74	3.27	7	4	8.03	1.21	3.08	6.91	1.44	4.02
1999	Anaheim	AL	76.0	80	42	12	33	45	4.97	4	4	9.47	1.42	3.91	5.33	0.57	5.45

His usage changed in 1999, as Terry Collins got away from using him for three innings at a time, instead making him a more conventional setup man. Hasegawa didn't take well to the change; more accurately, his breaking stuff didn't, leading to more fly balls, extra-base hits and runs. What should be a tough year for the Angel rotation will create more long-relief opportunities for Hasegawa. The team won't be good, but he will.

Ken Hill   Throws R   Age 34

YEAR	TEAM	LGE	IP	H	ER	HR	BB	K	ERA	W	L	H/9	HR/9	BB/9	K/9	KWH	PERA
1997	Texas	AL	114.0	121	61	10	57	69	4.82	6	7	9.55	0.79	4.50	5.45	0.52	4.97
1997	Anaheim	AL	80.0	62	30	7	39	38	3.38	6	3	6.98	0.79	4.39	4.28	0.45	3.49
1998	Anaheim	AL	102.3	122	58	6	49	57	5.10	5	6	10.73	0.53	4.31	5.01	0.41	5.28
1999	Anaheim	AL	127.0	129	68	12	74	78	4.82	7	7	9.14	0.85	5.24	5.53	0.48	5.10

The good news is that once he let his elbow heal, he pitched very well, posting a 2.84 ERA after a month-long DL stint. If he can hold it together for three months, the Angels should be able to get a prospect or two for him at the trade deadline, which is about the happiest ending they can hope for here.

Mike Holtz   Throws L   Age 27

YEAR	TEAM	LGE	IP	H	ER	HR	BB	K	ERA	W	L	H/9	HR/9	BB/9	K/9	KWH	PERA
1997	Anaheim	AL	44.0	36	19	7	15	40	3.89	3	2	7.36	1.43	3.07	8.18	2.21	3.89
1998	Anaheim	AL	30.3	37	15	0	16	29	4.45	2	1	10.98	0.00	4.75	8.60	1.06	5.04
1999	Edmonton	PCL	26.3	21	7	4	13	31	2.39	2	1	7.18	1.37	4.44	10.59	2.63	4.10
1999	Anaheim	AL	22.0	26	19	3	15	18	7.77	1	1	10.64	1.23	6.14	7.36	0.62	6.95

Juan Alvarez has his job now, so Holtz will have to move elsewhere. He still has the sweeping curve that made him so nasty in 1996 and 1997, and will be back in the major leagues soon enough. His biggest problem is that he needs work to keep the curve sharp, but he can't face right-handed hitters, who treat him like music critics treat a Celine Dion record.

Mike James   Throws R   Age 32

YEAR	TEAM	LGE	IP	H	ER	HR	BB	K	ERA	W	L	H/9	HR/9	BB/9	K/9	KWH	PERA
1997	Anaheim	AL	64.0	66	29	3	28	58	4.08	4	3	9.28	0.42	3.94	8.16	1.36	4.22
1998	Anaheim	AL	14.0	10	3	0	7	12	1.93	2	0	6.43	0.00	4.50	7.71	1.54	2.57

Formerly known as a dominant setup man, James has missed almost all of the past two seasons with forearm, shoulder and elbow injuries. The Cardinals signed him to a minor-league deal with an invitation to camp. When healthy, James has been effective, and the Cardinals don't exactly have the Braves' bullpen, so there's some opportunity for him.

Al Levine — Throws R — Age 32

YEAR	TEAM	LGE	IP	H	ER	HR	BB	K	ERA	W	L	H/9	HR/9	BB/9	K/9	KWH	PERA
1997	Nashvill	AmA	34.7	65	36	3	13	25	9.35	1	3	16.88	0.78	3.38	6.49	0.55	9.09
1997	ChiSox	AL	27.7	33	20	4	17	22	6.51	1	2	10.73	1.30	5.53	7.16	0.64	6.83
1998	Oklahoma	PCL	48.7	59	37	6	20	24	6.84	2	3	10.91	1.11	3.70	4.44	0.36	5.73
1998	Texas	AL	60.7	63	25	5	17	19	3.71	4	3	9.35	0.74	2.52	2.82	0.25	4.01
1999	Anaheim	AL	83.7	77	38	11	28	38	4.09	5	4	8.28	1.18	3.01	4.09	0.50	4.09

Levine was the most anonymous member of the deep and effective Angel bullpen in 1999. He does the little things: getting ground balls, controlling the running game and stranding inherited runners. He doesn't do the big things, so expanding his role beyond middle relief would be a mistake.

Mike Magnante — Throws L — Age 35

YEAR	TEAM	LGE	IP	H	ER	HR	BB	K	ERA	W	L	H/9	HR/9	BB/9	K/9	KWH	PERA
1997	New Orln	AmA	22.3	36	18	0	6	19	7.25	1	1	14.51	0.00	2.42	7.66	1.25	6.04
1997	Houston	NL	47.0	41	16	2	11	40	3.06	3	2	7.85	0.38	2.11	7.66	2.65	2.87
1998	Houston	NL	51.7	58	28	2	28	37	4.88	3	3	10.10	0.35	4.88	6.45	0.63	5.05
1999	Anaheim	AL	68.7	68	29	2	28	45	3.80	5	3	8.91	0.26	3.67	5.90	0.79	3.80

He's 35, so he's got about 10 years left as a left-handed relief specialist. Magnante doesn't throw hard enough to justify the use of a catcher's mitt, despite which he's pretty good at what he does: he held left-handed hitters to a 598 OPS in 1999. The A's signed him to a two-year deal.

Elvin Nina — Throws R — Age 24

YEAR	TEAM	LGE	IP	H	ER	HR	BB	K	ERA	W	L	H/9	HR/9	BB/9	K/9	KWH	PERA
1997	So Oregn	Nwn	27.3	47	28	5	22	15	9.22	1	2	15.48	1.65	7.24	4.94	0.16	11.20
1998	Visalia	Cal	122.0	162	90	11	79	88	6.64	4	10	11.95	0.81	5.83	6.49	0.45	7.01
1999	Modesto	Cal	67.7	69	35	2	48	51	4.66	4	4	9.18	0.27	6.38	6.78	0.59	4.92
1999	Midland	Tex	29.7	37	22	0	23	14	6.67	1	2	11.22	0.00	6.98	4.25	0.17	6.07
1999	Erie	Eas	23.0	25	14	2	16	15	5.48	1	2	9.78	0.78	6.26	5.87	0.42	5.87

Nina, the third player picked up in the Velarde/Olivares trade, pitched well as a California League repeater. He's not a prospect in this organization on merit. He might end up with a career if he's the last man standing after the Angels kill off their real pitching prospects.

Ramon Ortiz — Throws R — Age 24

YEAR	TEAM	LGE	IP	H	ER	HR	BB	K	ERA	W	L	H/9	HR/9	BB/9	K/9	KWH	PERA
1997	CedarRpd	Mid	167.0	210	102	27	65	158	5.50	8	11	11.32	1.46	3.50	8.51	1.37	6.41
1998	Midland	Tex	45.3	54	30	9	19	44	5.96	2	3	10.72	1.79	3.77	8.74	1.41	6.55
1999	Erie	Eas	96.3	107	46	12	45	69	4.30	6	5	10.00	1.12	4.20	6.45	0.74	5.51
1999	Edmonton	PCL	52.0	46	24	6	22	53	4.15	3	3	7.96	1.04	3.81	9.17	2.07	4.15
1999	Anaheim	AL	48.0	50	32	6	24	45	6.00	2	3	9.38	1.13	4.50	8.44	1.26	5.25

You would think that after the Angels burnt him out in 1997, they'd have learned their lesson about monitoring pitcher workloads in the minor leagues. Ortiz had minor elbow surgery in 1998 following his seven-complete-game second half at Cedar Rapids. He was one of the lucky ones: his fastball and command returned after surgery, and he shot to the majors in 1999 having added a change-up. You can't breathe for the comparisons to another vertically-challenged, hard-throwing Dominican right-hander. Ortiz isn't that good, but he will be the Angel ace a year from now.

Troy Percival — Throws R — Age 30

YEAR	TEAM	LGE	IP	H	ER	HR	BB	K	ERA	W	L	H/9	HR/9	BB/9	K/9	KWH	PERA
1997	Anaheim	AL	53.0	38	18	6	22	73	3.06	4	2	6.45	1.02	3.74	12.40	4.76	3.23
1998	Anaheim	AL	66.0	45	29	5	38	88	3.95	4	3	6.14	0.68	5.18	12.00	3.38	3.27
1999	Anaheim	AL	56.3	38	22	8	22	60	3.51	4	2	6.07	1.28	3.51	9.59	3.22	3.20

(Troy Percival *continued*)

High-profile closers are overrated as a species, and on a team going nowhere their primary value is as trade bait. Percival is worth a lot more on the market than on the field, as his save totals have masked the fact that he's slipped at least a notch. I'll be surprised if he finishes the year as an Angel.

Mark Petkovsek · Throws R · Age 34

YEAR	TEAM	LGE	IP	H	ER	HR	BB	K	ERA	W	L	H/9	HR/9	BB/9	K/9	KWH	PERA
1997	St Louis	NL	95.3	111	61	15	32	47	5.76	4	7	10.48	1.42	3.02	4.44	0.46	5.66
1998	St Louis	NL	107.3	132	61	9	39	53	5.11	5	7	11.07	0.75	3.27	4.44	0.41	5.37
1999	Anaheim	AL	81.7	86	36	5	20	44	3.97	5	4	9.48	0.55	2.20	4.85	0.84	3.86

While his innings pitched were down, Petkovsek made the most appearances of his career. The extra work fatigued him, leading to a "dead arm" period after the All-Star break that damaged his stat line. For most of the season, he was an excellent setup man for Percival, and more proof that relievers are interchangeable.

Lou Pote · Throws R · Age 28

YEAR	TEAM	LGE	IP	H	ER	HR	BB	K	ERA	W	L	H/9	HR/9	BB/9	K/9	KWH	PERA
1997	Arkansas	Tex	20.7	20	14	1	10	16	6.10	1	1	8.71	0.44	4.35	6.97	0.96	3.92
1998	Midland	Tex	143.7	223	123	17	70	88	7.71	4	12	13.97	1.06	4.39	5.51	0.37	8.02
1999	Edmonton	PCL	143.3	179	80	17	50	93	5.02	7	9	11.24	1.07	3.14	5.84	0.72	5.71
1999	Anaheim	AL	28.7	24	9	1	11	20	2.83	2	1	7.53	0.31	3.45	6.28	1.13	3.14

Pote is a good story, a professional since 1991 who finally made the major leagues last summer. He has some surface similarities to Levine and goes into the spring trying to take his job. While the Angel bullpen was effective in 1999, almost all of the contributors had below-average strikeout rates, so some decline is inevitable.

Scott Schoeneweis · Throws L · Age 26

YEAR	TEAM	LGE	IP	H	ER	HR	BB	K	ERA	W	L	H/9	HR/9	BB/9	K/9	KWH	PERA
1997	Midland	Tex	111.7	150	81	8	47	81	6.53	4	8	12.09	0.64	3.79	6.53	0.70	6.04
1998	Vancouvr	PCL	165.0	209	114	17	67	109	6.22	6	12	11.40	0.93	3.65	5.95	0.63	5.89
1999	Edmonton	PCL	33.0	62	35	5	14	23	9.55	1	3	16.91	1.36	3.82	6.27	0.46	10.09
1999	Anaheim	AL	38.7	47	25	3	14	23	5.82	1	3	10.94	0.70	3.26	5.35	0.60	5.12

Schoeneweis pitched junk relief for the Angels in the first half and was nothing special, then got bludgeoned on his return to Edmonton. He's fallen behind Ortiz and Cooper in the organization's view, and needs a good spring to reestablish himself. In almost 40 innings, no one stole a base on him.

Scot Shields · Throws R · Age 24

YEAR	TEAM	LGE	IP	H	ER	HR	BB	K	ERA	W	L	H/9	HR/9	BB/9	K/9	KWH	PERA
1997	Boise	Nwn	47.3	59	25	2	30	34	4.75	2	3	11.22	0.38	5.70	6.46	0.49	6.08
1998	CedarRpd	Mid	67.3	87	47	7	39	55	6.28	2	5	11.63	0.94	5.21	7.35	0.67	6.68
1999	Lk Elsin	Cal	98.3	107	44	2	46	77	4.03	6	5	9.79	0.18	4.21	7.05	0.90	4.39
1999	Erie	Eas	71.0	70	31	10	29	65	3.93	5	3	8.87	1.27	3.68	8.24	1.56	4.82

The converted reliever moved into the rotation at midseason and still finished 12th among minor leaguers in innings pitched, averaging a whopping 7½ innings per start at Erie. Then he went to the Arizona Fall League and got hammered in 26 more innings. He's 24, and hadn't been worked particularly hard prior to 1999, so he may survive. That doesn't mean it isn't reckless. Shields has good command of two pitches, and would be better served moving back to the bullpen.

Steve Sparks · Throws R · Age 34

YEAR	TEAM	LGE	IP	H	ER	HR	BB	K	ERA	W	L	H/9	HR/9	BB/9	K/9	KWH	PERA
1998	Midland	Tex	38.3	55	43	3	20	26	10.10	1	3	12.91	0.70	4.70	6.10	0.46	7.04
1998	Vancouvr	PCL	25.7	27	13	2	7	15	4.56	1	2	9.47	0.70	2.45	5.26	0.89	4.21
1998	Anaheim	AL	127.7	129	63	13	60	91	4.44	7	7	9.09	0.92	4.23	6.42	0.80	4.72
1999	Anaheim	AL	146.0	165	95	18	80	75	5.86	6	10	10.17	1.11	4.93	4.62	0.32	5.86

If knuckleball-only pitchers really are dying out, Sparks may be the last one to go. With the apparent end of Tom Candiotti's career, we're left with him, Tim Wakefield and Dennis Springer. Sparks's command of his knuckler isn't great, and he has no effective second pitch to use when he falls behind, so it's hard for me to see him getting better than this.

Jarrod Washburn　　Throws L　　Age 25

YEAR	TEAM	LGE	IP	H	ER	HR	BB	K	ERA	W	L	H/9	HR/9	BB/9	K/9	KWH	PERA
1997	Midland	Tex	186.7	216	106	23	77	128	5.11	9	12	10.41	1.11	3.71	6.17	0.74	5.54
1998	Vancouvr	PCL	84.3	99	48	7	47	55	5.12	4	5	10.57	0.75	5.02	5.87	0.49	5.76
1998	Anaheim	AL	73.0	70	38	10	29	48	4.68	4	4	8.63	1.23	3.58	5.92	0.85	4.56
1999	Edmonton	PCL	56.7	52	30	5	20	45	4.76	3	3	8.26	0.79	3.18	7.15	1.45	3.81
1999	Anaheim	AL	60.7	62	34	5	25	40	5.04	3	4	9.20	0.74	3.71	5.93	0.77	4.45

Washburn pitched well when placed in the rotation down the stretch, and should be the Angels #3 starter in 2000. He's reminiscent of Denny Neagle, who didn't become a top starting pitcher until he was 26; they're both flyball pitchers who aren't overpowering. The Angels should leave Washburn alone and let him get 32 starts in 2000; he'll be a very good pitcher in 2001 and beyond.

Matt Wise　　Throws R　　Age 24

YEAR	TEAM	LGE	IP	H	ER	HR	BB	K	ERA	W	L	H/9	HR/9	BB/9	K/9	KWH	PERA
1997	Boise	Nwn	76.3	83	47	7	41	48	5.54	3	5	9.79	0.83	4.83	5.66	0.51	5.31
1998	Midland	Tex	163.0	207	108	22	54	109	5.96	7	11	11.43	1.21	2.98	6.02	0.79	5.96
1999	Erie	Eas	92.0	123	58	11	27	58	5.67	4	6	12.03	1.08	2.64	5.67	0.76	6.07

Elbow surgery cut his season short; before it, he wasn't pitching well, especially in comparison to fellow Seawolves Cooper and Etherton. The Angels let Wise throw a few innings in the Arizona Fall League, so they haven't forgotten about him. He'll go back to the Eastern League this year; I expect we'll see him at Edison Field at some point during the season.

| Support-Neutral Records | | | | ANAHEIM ANGELS | | | | | | | Park Effect: -2.5% | |
PITCHER	GS	IP	R	SNW	SNL	SNPCT	W	L	RA	APW	SNVA	SNWAR
Tim Belcher	24	132.3	104	5.8	11.2	.341	6	8	7.07	-2.63	-2.54	-1.42
Brian Cooper	5	27.7	15	1.5	1.7	.469	1	1	4.88	0.08	-0.06	0.14
Chuck Finley	33	213.3	117	13.2	11.2	.541	12	11	4.94	0.49	0.94	2.83
Mike Fyhrie	7	33.7	25	1.7	2.7	.392	0	4	6.68	-0.53	-0.41	-0.15
Shigetoshi Hasegawa	1	2.3	4	0.0	0.7	.022	0	1	15.43	-0.25	-0.28	-0.27
Ken Hill	22	123.7	70	7.3	7.1	.508	4	11	5.09	0.08	0.20	1.20
Al Levine	1	4.0	0	0.5	0.0	1.000	0	0	0.00	0.21	0.21	0.26
Jack McDowell	4	19.0	17	1.1	1.8	.386	0	4	8.05	-0.57	-0.34	-0.11
Omar Olivares	20	131.0	62	9.2	5.9	.608	8	9	4.26	1.22	1.53	2.78
Ramon Ortiz	9	48.3	35	2.4	4.0	.373	2	3	6.52	-0.68	-0.81	-0.33
Steve Sparks	26	145.0	98	7.7	10.6	.420	5	11	6.08	-1.39	-1.47	-0.09
Jarrod Washburn	10	54.7	30	3.4	3.4	.493	4	5	4.94	0.12	0.08	0.46
TOTALS	162	935.0	577	53.7	60.2	.471	42	68	5.55	-3.84	-2.97	5.30

What about Chuck Finley's Hall of Fame chances? OK, stop laughing. I know as well as anybody that if his career ended today, Finley would have as much chance of being voted in as the guy who came up with the idea of putting a rock quarry behind the Edison Field outfield. Then again, Finley's career isn't ending today. At the end of July, sporting a 6.9-9.3 (.426) SNW/L record, he might have looked like he was winding down. But he served notice, with a fantastic 6.3-1.9 (.770) record over the last two months, that he intends to be around for a few more years. Additionally, his longevity and run-prevention numbers, adjusted for league scoring levels, are similar to those of Bob Lemon and Lefty Gomez, among others. At the least, he's made a persuasive case for being the greatest Angel pitcher ever, surpassing what Nolan Ryan did in Southern California.... Knuckleballers are trendy in certain analyst circles. Some of the more thoughtful baseball writers often wonder aloud why there aren't more of them and whether they're being discriminated against. After last year, we might start wondering why there are so many of them. In 1999, baseball's four knuckleballers—Tom Candiotti, Steve Sparks, Dennis Springer and Tim Wakefield—combined for a 22.7-35.9 (.387) SNW/L record. Sparks was the best of the four, and that's damning with faint praise.

Pitcher Abuse Points

PITCHER	AGE	GS	PAP	PAP/S	WKLD	MAX	1-90	91-100	101-110	111-120	121-130	131-140	141+
Tim Belcher	37	24	30	1.3	1.3	117	14	7	2	1	0	0	0
Brian Cooper	24	5	26	5.2	12.1	115	2	1	1	1	0	0	0
Chuck Finley	36	33	591	17.9	17.9	136	2	8	8	8	5	2	0
Mike Fyhrie	29	7	39	5.6	8.4	121	3	2	1	0	1	0	0
Shigetoshi Hasegawa	30	1	0	0.0	0.0	57	1	0	0	0	0	0	0
Ken Hill	33	22	151	6.9	6.9	123	7	4	7	2	2	0	0
Al Levine	31	1	0	0.0	0.0	68	1	0	0	0	0	0	0
Jack McDowell	33	4	1	0.3	0.3	101	3	0	1	0	0	0	0
Omar Olivares	31	20	120	6.0	7.0	123	4	9	3	3	1	0	0
Ramon Ortiz	23	9	17	1.9	4.7	109	4	3	2	0	0	0	0
Steve Sparks	33	26	275	10.6	10.6	134	7	6	8	2	1	2	0
Jarrod Washburn	24	10	21	2.1	4.9	112	4	2	3	1	0	0	0
ANAHEIM		162	1271	7.8	8.6	136	52	42	36	18	10	4	0
Ranking (AL)				9	13								

The Angels dropped from sixth in the AL in Workload in 1998 to 13th last year. Determining whether that was because Terry Collins became a kinder, gentler manager or because the Angels simply didn't have any pitchers worth riding is an exercise left to the reader.... At least they took better care of Chuck Finley, whose PAPs dropped from 907 a year ago. Finley was arguably the league's best pitcher (7-1, 2.49 ERA) after trade deadline day. On a largely veteran staff, it is worth mentioning that the few young pitchers were treated with care. Ramon Ortiz picked up just 17 PAPs; he had already missed most of 1998 with arm troubles after the Angels had him throw eight complete games as a 21-year-old in A ball.

Baltimore Orioles

"Baltimore? It's like being hit in the head over and over with a crowbar. What's the difference?"

— *Twelve Angry Men,* by Reginald Rose

The story of baseball in Baltimore has made the unfortunate transition to soap opera. The cast is full of aging stars who can't handle the roles they once played and now go through the motions. The plot lines include a meddling, power-mad family, vindictive and nepotistic, with constant petty squabbling among the staff.

<whack>

First comes the continuing saga of the Orioles' front office, which has generated new employment for Kremlin-watchers. You remember them, no? Those bland academics who analyzed words and photographs in excruciating detail to find out who was in or out of favor in Moscow during the Cold War? The question "Who's running this team?" echoed through Charm City all season, without ever being resolved.

Three months into the offseason, we may finally have an answer. Sure, Peter Angelos has the final say, but that's not the same thing, is it? We know that Ray Miller received a public denunciation when GM Frank Wren openly recommended his firing; we know that Wren was subsequently humiliated when the Boss didn't go along. At season's end, both were fired, Wren receiving a free character assassination as his parting gift. The statement announcing his firing said nothing about his baseball acumen, dwelling instead on "insults" that had been leveled at members of the team and the front office.

The actions of the mid-level managers, long-rumored but veiled, really came into the open after the season. The attack on Wren was led by Joe Foss, the club vice-chairman and an old friend of Angelos. In the wake of the Wren firing the Orioles proceeded with a five-headed "GM by committee." John and Louis Angelos are sons of the owner; their qualifications, relative to their father, are that they, at least, are genuine baseball fans. Tom Trebelhorn is the farm director and seems to favor athletes and established, if mediocre,

major leaguers. Trebelhorn was mentioned frequently as the man who would step into the manager's office if Miller had been fired during the season. Tony DeMacio is the scouting director and had a lead role in the Orioles' draft last year. He appears be the low man in the power structure.

Until December, Syd Thrift was the director of player personnel. He was the group's voice, and appears to have a direct line to Peter Angelos. He's had his hands in everything over the past few years; it will be interesting to see what happens now that he has been made vice president of baseball operations, replacing Wren and left to bear responsibility for his own actions.

<whack>

By any standard, Wren got off to a horrible first month in the GM's seat. He was hired in November, by which time the Orioles who would be lost (Rafael Palmeiro, Roberto Alomar, Alan Mills) were already gone. His trade of Armando Benitez for Charles Johnson, a politically necessary move, turned out well when Chris Hoiles's arthritis forced him out of spring training and into retirement. The move further weakened the bullpen, though, and Wren's attempts to remedy that were disastrous. He botched the Xavier Hernandez signing and cost the Orioles a million bucks in doing so, and he made the curious decision of trying to build Baltimore's bullpen by raiding Seattle's.

Will Clark and Delino DeShields were brought in, despite the presence of Calvin Pickering and Jerry Hairston at their positions, about the only two near-ready prospects the O's had. Albert Belle's signing was a move driven through by Angelos, a pre-emptive strike designed to keep the slugger out of the Yankees' lineup.

Wren's performance improved after the initial shakiness, although he let the organization be fooled once again by a July winning streak. For the second year in a row, the belief that they had a chance at the wild card curtailed their efforts to trade for prospects. As a result, their trading forays were

---

Orioles Prospectus

1999 record: 78-84; Fourth place, AL East

Pythagorean W/L: 84-78

Runs scored: 851 (8th in AL)

Runs allowed: 815 (3rd in AL)

Team EQA: .265 (4th in AL)

1999 team age: 30.9 (oldest in AL)

1999 park: Oriole Park at Camden Yards; slight pitchers' park, decreased run scoring by 2%.

1999: An old team got older without getting better. Again.

2000: They've signed Harold Baines, so they still have no clue.

---

limited (Juan Guzman to the Reds for two young pitchers and Harold Baines to the Indians for the same), and primarily served to add a little depth to the minor-league system.

<whack>

The high point for Wren, and potentially for the Orioles' future, was the 1999 draft. Thanks to the free-agent losses, the Orioles had an unprecedented seven of the top 50 picks: their own #1, plus first-round and supplemental picks for Alomar, Palmeiro and Eric Davis. They turned that into a polished college pitcher (Mike Paradis), three high-school left-handers (Richard Stahl, Josh Cenate and Scott Rice) and three college players (shortstop Brian Roberts and outfielders Keith Reed and Larry Bigbie). Significantly, the Orioles signed them all; in fact, they signed every one of their picks from the first 10 rounds. All of the collegians played at Delmarva last year. The hope is that they'll advance quickly through the system.

On the field, the Orioles were directionless. The decision to fire Ray Miller was undoubtedly correct, irrespective of the Byzantine process needed to reach it. In its preseason issue, *Baseball America* rated Miller 14th among AL managers, and he spent the year living down to that rating. He was whiny, incapable of admitting any personal failing. He was obsessed by physical fitness, as opposed to baseball skill, in evaluating players and prospects. He criticized players to the media, eventually losing the respect of his troops.

Even the pitchers, who could most be expected to support a pitching-coach-turned-manager, deserted Miller in a litany of complaints about overuse in warmups and ill-defined roles. In fact, Miller had an appalling record with pitchers as Orioles manager. As Table 1 shows, pretty much everyone who came to Baltimore under Miller performed worse with him, while those who left did better.

The "Wt. by min." line means that the ERAs are weighted equally in each set by whichever set had fewer innings pitched; Slocumb's 11.42 and 3.97 are both counted as occurring in 8⅔ innings. Only three pitchers (Jim Corsi, Juan Guzman and Alan Mills) out of 19 did better under Miller; if they all had a 50/50 chance of doing better or worse, the odds against a ³⁄₁₆ split are about 450-to-1. Clearly, this is something more than a coincidence.

<whack>

The hitters who came to Baltimore didn't tail off the way pitchers did, but they underachieved nonetheless. The Orioles scored 27 fewer runs than their statistics suggested; that was easily the worst in the AL, and only the Mets surpassed it among NL teams. That was primarily the result of an old team limited to station-to-station baserunning, plus poor clutch hitting throughout the season.

As if it weren't bad enough to score fewer runs than they should have, the Orioles didn't win as often as they should have given the runs they did score. The Orioles outscored their opponents by 36 runs in 1999, and could have been expected to win 84 games. They won 78; Kansas City was the only team in either league further off their projected wins. The salt in the wound was that the Orioles did post a winning record, a solid 63-50, outside of their own division, but were incapable of beating the teams they were actually competing against.

<whack>

After a dreadful 1995 season, the Orioles replaced Phil Regan, a respected pitching coach but horrible manager, with Davey Johnson, who had a proven record of winning with the Mets and Reds. They immediately went from below .500 to the playoffs. In replacing Miller with Mike Hargrove, they'll hope history repeats itself.

The main drawback is that the cast is pretty much the same, only older, and the chaos in the front office shows no signs of dissipating. The Orioles are much closer to last place in the AL East than they are to challenging the Yankees—or the Red Sox, for that matter—and are likely to get worse before they get better.

Table 1

1997-1999	For Miller		For Anyone Else	
	Innings	DT-ERA	Innings	DT-ERA
Armando Benitez	67.2	3.59	150.2	2.21
Ricky Bones	43.2	5.36	134.2	4.61
Norm Charlton	34.7	6.49	123.1	5.62
Rocky Coppinger	21.3	8.02	37.3	3.38
Jim Corsi	13.0	2.77	150.0	3.36
Scott Erickson	478.0	4.44	221.1	3.90
Mike Fetters	31.0	6.10	118.3	3.88
Juan Guzman	187.0	4.38	282.0	4.72
Jason Johnson	114.3	5.35	60.2	5.34
Scott Kamieniecki	110.0	5.65	179.1	3.96
Terry Mathews	20.0	6.30	102.0	4.59
Alan Mills	76.0	3.55	110.2	4.31
Mike Mussina	406.2	3.56	224.1	3.29
Jesse Orosco	88.1	3.87	50.1	2.15
Al Reyes	29.1	4.30	125.0	4.03
Arthur Rhodes	128.2	4.27	95.3	2.83
Heathcliff Slocumb	8.2	11.42	199.2	3.97
Pete Smith	44.2	5.84	157.1	5.32
Mike Timlin	62.1	4.04	128.0	2.60
TOTAL	1965.1	4.45	2650.1	3.96
Wt. by min.	1401.1	4.55	1401.1	3.83

HITTERS (Averages: BA: .270 / OBP: .340 / SLG: .430 / EQA: .260)

Charles Alley   C   Bats B   Age 23

YEAR	TEAM	LGE	AB	H	DB	TP	HR	BB/SO	R	RBI	SB	CS	OUT	BA	OBP	SLG	EQA	EQR	DEFENSE
1997	Delmarva	SAL	259	57	18	1	3	29/46	16	28	3	1	203	.220	.312	.332	.224	24	
1998	Frederck	Car	354	87	21	1	10	55/58	41	44	0	1	268	.246	.351	.395	.256	45	92-C 95
1999	Frederck	Car	137	30	4	0	2	19/27	19	11	0	1	108	.219	.317	.292	.211	11	41-C 98
2000	*Baltimor*	*AL*	*216*	*52*	*9*	*0*	*6*	*33/39*	*31*	*29*	*0*	*1*	*165*	*.241*	*.341*	*.366*	*.247*	*25*	

He was listed as "Chip" in previous editions, though he despises the name; he was just too shy to challenge it before. His foot was seriously injured in a home-plate collision during Bowie's first week; he came back at Frederick, but played in pain.

Wady Almonte   OF   Bats R   Age 25

YEAR	TEAM	LGE	AB	H	DB	TP	HR	BB/SO	R	RBI	SB	CS	OUT	BA	OBP	SLG	EQA	EQR	DEFENSE
1997	Frederck	Car	206	48	11	1	9	11/61	27	29	2	1	159	.233	.281	.427	.234	21	41-OF 100
1997	Bowie	Eas	226	45	8	2	5	21/66	21	21	2	2	183	.199	.278	.319	.201	17	62-OF 87
1999	Bowie	Eas	486	122	24	3	13	20/81	52	62	5	5	369	.251	.287	.393	.225	44	103-OF 91
2000	*Baltimor*	*AL*	*361*	*89*	*14*	*2*	*13*	*26/106*	*41*	*50*	*4*	*3*	*275*	*.247*	*.297*	*.404*	*.236*	*37*	

Almonte is a toolsy right fielder with a fine arm and reasonable power who can't get on base. He's comparable to Alex Ochoa, although he hasn't been hyped as much.

Rich Amaral   OF/DH   Bats R   Age 38

YEAR	TEAM	LGE	AB	H	DB	TP	HR	BB/SO	R	RBI	SB	CS	OUT	BA	OBP	SLG	EQA	EQR	DEFENSE
1997	Seattle	AL	190	53	2	0	2	9/33	32	21	12	8	145	.279	.323	.321	.222	17	36-OF 90
1998	Seattle	AL	134	38	3	0	2	12/23	24	7	11	1	97	.284	.347	.351	.256	16	30-OF 94
1999	Baltimor	AL	136	36	8	1	0	14/20	19	10	9	6	106	.265	.338	.338	.235	14	
2000	*Baltimor*	*AL*	*123*	*29*	*3*	*0*	*1*	*13/19*	*16*	*9*	*6*	*4*	*98*	*.236*	*.309*	*.285*	*.208*	*10*	

Most teams would use the utility man/fourth outfielder role to break in a youngster. The Orioles are not most teams. Amaral's offensive value has just about disappeared, reducing him to a pinch-runner and defensive replacement. There are better uses for a roster spot.

Brady Anderson   CF   Bats L   Age 36

YEAR	TEAM	LGE	AB	H	DB	TP	HR	BB/SO	R	RBI	SB	CS	OUT	BA	OBP	SLG	EQA	EQR	DEFENSE
1997	Baltimor	AL	589	171	38	8	18	80/101	94	71	18	13	431	.290	.395	.474	.291	99	121-OF 104
1998	Baltimor	AL	481	117	31	3	18	74/76	82	50	19	7	371	.243	.362	.432	.273	72	120-OF 105
1999	Baltimor	AL	559	156	30	5	22	89/105	100	74	36	8	411	.279	.400	.469	.300	101	124-CF 96
2000	*Baltimor*	*AL*	*437*	*105*	*16*	*3*	*13*	*70/77*	*75*	*59*	*15*	*6*	*338*	*.240*	*.345*	*.380*	*.256*	*56*	

His defense was one of the Orioles pitching staff's biggest problems. Anderson's ability to cut off balls in the gaps has seriously diminished, yet he complained loudly when asked to play left field in September. He isn't going to be moved from center field without a fight. Anderson is still a fine hitter, but his defense looks like it will haunt the O's for at least another season.

Albert Belle   RF   Bats R   Age 33

YEAR	TEAM	LGE	AB	H	DB	TP	HR	BB/SO	R	RBI	SB	CS	OUT	BA	OBP	SLG	EQA	EQR	DEFENSE
1997	ChiSox	AL	635	180	40	2	33	49/101	89	118	4	4	459	.283	.342	.509	.278	93	145-OF 94
1998	ChiSox	AL	607	201	45	2	50	79/82	108	147	5	4	410	.331	.409	.659	.336	134	153-OF 94
1999	Baltimor	AL	604	178	32	1	37	94/82	100	109	18	3	429	.295	.396	.535	.309	114	151-RF 98
2000	*Baltimor*	*AL*	*592*	*168*	*29*	*1*	*37*	*87/82*	*113*	*131*	*7*	*3*	*427*	*.284*	*.376*	*.524*	*.301*	*106*	

Last spring the talk was that Belle would hit 60 home runs in the "cozy confines of Camden Yards." Of course that was ridiculous, since OP@CY continues to be a pitchers' park and gives only a modest boost to home runs for right-handed hitters. Belle had a poor year by his standards, and started especially slow; by the time he began hitting, the Orioles were completely out of it and the usual talk of his not being "clutch" had returned. He had a few behavioral run-ins—about par for him—but he accommodated the team by moving to right field and surprised AL baserunners by notching 17 assists.

Mike Bordick   SS   Bats R   Age 34

YEAR	TEAM	LGE	AB	H	DB	TP	HR	BB/SO	R	RBI	SB	CS	OUT	BA	OBP	SLG	EQA	EQR	DEFENSE
1997	Baltimor	AL	510	123	21	1	7	30/63	54	46	0	2	389	.241	.286	.327	.205	37	147-SS 97
1998	Baltimor	AL	467	125	29	1	14	37/64	58	51	5	7	349	.268	.335	.424	.253	56	143-SS 105
1999	Baltimor	AL	628	173	36	7	9	47/102	86	71	14	4	459	.275	.331	.398	.250	71	153-SS 107
2000	*Baltimor*	*AL*	*391*	*100*	*16*	*1*	*10*	*35/59*	*49*	*51*	*3*	*2*	*293*	*.256*	*.317*	*.379*	*.238*	*41*	

I've said plenty of negative things about Mike Bordick in the past, especially after he played so poorly in 1996 and 1997. His last two years, though, have been exactly what most teams say they want from their shortstop: a good glove with an average bat. Of course, that's no reason to bat him second in the lineup, especially against right-handed pitchers, off whom he hit .252/.304/.368.

Howie Clark   UT   Bats L   Age 26

YEAR	TEAM	LGE	AB	H	DB	TP	HR	BB/SO	R	RBI	SB	CS	OUT	BA	OBP	SLG	EQA	EQR	DEFENSE	
1997	Bowie	Eas	318	83	10	0	9	24/41	30	31	1	1	236	.261	.314	.377	.234	31	61-3B 82	10-2B 94
1998	Bowie	Eas	277	68	9	0	9	22/45	29	37	1	1	210	.245	.306	.375	.230	27	51-OF 85	
1998	Rochestr	Int	96	21	5	1	2	7/12	12	7	1	1	76	.219	.272	.354	.208	7		
1999	Bowie	Eas	127	32	3	0	2	7/14	13	9	1	0	95	.252	.301	.323	.213	10		
1999	Rochestr	Int	280	72	17	3	4	26/26	26	21	1	1	209	.257	.322	.382	.239	29	68-OF 91	
2000	*Baltimor*	*AL*	*377*	*98*	*15*	*1*	*12*	*34/44*	*47*	*55*	*1*	*1*	*280*	*.260*	*.321*	*.401*	*.246*	*42*		

Clark can, and has, played all nine positions. He's also very popular with his fellow minor leaguers. In midsummer, when Will the Thrill again became Will the DL, Orioles farmhands were plenty upset that this Clark didn't replace him on the major-league roster, while journeyman Derrick May, who hasn't busted his butt for the Orioles organization for the past eight years, did.

That's not to say that Clark is a legitimate prospect. It's just that it would have been a welcome nod of appreciation, to him and to the minor-league system as a whole, an acknowledgement that they aren't invisible men. It was a chance to let them know that hard work will be rewarded, and that they have some chance of playing in Baltimore instead of being blocked by the free agent of the month.

Will Clark   1B   Bats L   Age 36

YEAR	TEAM	LGE	AB	H	DB	TP	HR	BB/SO	R	RBI	SB	CS	OUT	BA	OBP	SLG	EQA	EQR	DEFENSE
1997	Texas	AL	390	128	27	1	13	46/60	54	50	0	0	262	.328	.404	.503	.304	67	98-1B 99
1998	Texas	AL	546	162	34	2	23	69/95	90	95	1	0	384	.297	.379	.493	.291	88	131-1B 92
1999	Baltimor	AL	249	75	11	0	11	35/42	36	28	2	2	176	.301	.392	.478	.292	40	60-1B 101
2000	*Baltimor*	*AL*	*242*	*65*	*10*	*0*	*11*	*39/41*	*42*	*45*	*0*	*0*	*177*	*.269*	*.370*	*.446*	*.281*	*37*	

For the second time in his career, he replaced Rafael Palmeiro as a team's primary first baseman, and once again he suffered badly by comparison. Clark drove in 29 runs in 1999; Palmeiro beat that just in June, then did it again in August. Clark was absolutely helpless against left-handers this year, and I think it's the first sign that he's about to fall right off the table.

Ivanon Coffie   3B   Bats L   Age 23

YEAR	TEAM	LGE	AB	H	DB	TP	HR	BB/SO	R	RBI	SB	CS	OUT	BA	OBP	SLG	EQA	EQR	DEFENSE	
1997	Delmarva	SAL	313	79	15	4	3	20/46	32	40	7	5	239	.252	.303	.355	.223	28	74-SS 95	
1998	Frederck	Car	486	117	17	1	17	45/105	56	69	8	5	374	.241	.308	.385	.234	50	52-3B 73	50-SS 100
1999	Bowie	Eas	198	36	11	2	3	16/47	19	21	1	1	163	.182	.245	.303	.179	11	50-3B 96	
1999	Frederck	Car	284	74	17	3	11	22/62	29	44	3	2	212	.261	.320	.458	.257	36	53-3B 104	
2000	*Baltimor*	*AL*	*459*	*117*	*22*	*2*	*15*	*47/99*	*64*	*67*	*6*	*5*	*347*	*.255*	*.324*	*.410*	*.250*	*54*		

He was overmatched at Bowie before going on a tear in a return visit to Frederick. Coffie was one of many Orioles minor leaguers who prospered under the tutelage of Frederick's manager, Andy Etchebarren, and hitting coach, Floyd Rayford, only to flounder elsewhere. Several players were sent to Frederick specifically for hitting instruction. 1999 was Coffie's first full season at third base, and his defense was much improved over '98.

Jeff Conine   1B   Bats R   Age 34

YEAR	TEAM	LGE	AB	H	DB	TP	HR	BB/SO	R	RBI	SB	CS	OUT	BA	OBP	SLG	EQA	EQR	DEFENSE
1997	Florida	NL	411	102	14	1	18	57/88	47	62	2	0	309	.248	.343	.418	.260	53	117-1B 107
1998	KansasCy	AL	307	77	19	0	10	24/66	28	42	3	0	230	.251	.309	.410	.243	34	72-OF 90
1999	Baltimor	AL	442	128	29	1	13	25/40	49	70	0	3	317	.290	.332	.448	.258	54	93-1B 95
2000	*Baltimor*	*AL*	*353*	*95*	*14*	*0*	*14*	*37/48*	*50*	*58*	*1*	*1*	*259*	*.269*	*.338*	*.428*	*.261*	*45*	

Conine was the beneficiary of an almost unbelieveable hype job by the media covering the Orioles in 1999. Nobody seemed to notice that he was a below-average hitter—not just for a first baseman, but for an American Leaguer. He doesn't do a thing for the team except to supply Veteran Presence, not exactly in short supply here.

Craig Daedelow   UT   Bats R   Age 24

YEAR	TEAM	LGE	AB	H	DB	TP	HR	BB/SO	R	RBI	SB	CS	OUT	BA	OBP	SLG	EQA	EQR	DEFENSE
1997	Delmarva	SAL	285	71	17	1	1	21/47	30	30	4	2	216	.249	.301	.326	.214	23	23-SS 111
1998	Frederck	Car	126	32	1	0	2	14/18	11	15	1	0	94	.254	.332	.310	.226	11	
1999	Delmarva	SAL	169	42	3	1	0	28/29	21	15	0	1	128	.249	.361	.278	.230	16	18-2B 101
1999	Frederck	Car	51	7	1	0	0	3/7	5	2	0	0	44	.137	.185	.157	—	0	
2000	*Baltimor*	*AL*	*187*	*45*	*4*	*0*	*2*	*25/30*	*23*	*18*	*1*	*1*	*143*	*.241*	*.330*	*.294*	*.221*	*16*	

Like Howie Clark, he can play all nine positions, so the Orioles have moved him all over the organization to cover for disabled players. Unfortunately for him, he's spent too much time on the DL himself. His 1998 season ended when he got his left arm stuck between two billboards on the outfield fence and had to have Tommy John surgery. Last season ended when he blew out his elbow pitching mopup relief, sending him for another Tommy John operation.

Tommy Davis   C   Bats R   Age 27

YEAR	TEAM	LGE	AB	H	DB	TP	HR	BB/SO	R	RBI	SB	CS	OUT	BA	OBP	SLG	EQA	EQR	DEFENSE
1997	Rochestr	Int	440	125	20	2	13	34/90	62	53	4	1	316	.284	.338	.427	.259	54	117-1B 108
1998	Bowie	Eas	133	31	6	0	2	10/30	9	13	0	0	102	.233	.298	.323	.211	10	21-C 81
1999	Rochestr	Int	413	95	10	0	10	17/71	37	45	1	3	321	.230	.260	.327	.191	26	59-C 94
2000	*Baltimor*	*AL*	*307*	*76*	*9*	*0*	*11*	*23/57*	*33*	*41*	*1*	*1*	*232*	*.248*	*.300*	*.384*	*.232*	*30*	

Davis plays catcher like the converted first baseman he is; since he hits like a converted catcher, he's not going anywhere. Jayson Werth is about to make him obsolete.

Delino DeShields   2B   Bats L   Age 31

YEAR	TEAM	LGE	AB	H	DB	TP	HR	BB/SO	R	RBI	SB	CS	OUT	BA	OBP	SLG	EQA	EQR	DEFENSE
1997	St Louis	NL	581	174	30	14	12	54/71	89	59	45	14	421	.299	.362	.461	.281	88	136-2B 98
1998	St Louis	NL	424	123	24	8	7	56/59	75	44	27	11	312	.290	.373	.434	.277	63	101-2B 96
1999	Baltimor	AL	329	85	13	2	5	33/52	42	31	11	8	252	.258	.328	.356	.234	33	85-2B 95
2000	*Baltimor*	*AL*	*325*	*86*	*14*	*5*	*6*	*44/47*	*60*	*43*	*15*	*6*	*245*	*.265*	*.352*	*.394*	*.262*	*43*	

From a spring-training broken thumb to a season-ending quadriceps injury that required offseason surgery, DeShields was almost never healthy in 1999. It showed in his performance. He'll be hard-pressed to keep his job away from Jerry Hairston in 2000.

Rick Elder   1B   Bats L   Age 20

YEAR	TEAM	LGE	AB	H	DB	TP	HR	BB/SO	R	RBI	SB	CS	OUT	BA	OBP	SLG	EQA	EQR	DEFENSE
1999	Bluefld	App	157	36	6	1	6	19/62	18	20	0	0	121	.229	.317	.395	.242	17	22-1B 71
1999	Delmarva	SAL	38	4	0	0	2	8/15	6	4	0	0	34	.105	.261	.263	.180	2	
2000	*Baltimor*	*AL*	*87*	*17*	*2*	*1*	*6*	*16/62*	*13*	*16*	*0*	*0*	*70*	*.195*	*.320*	*.448*	*.260*	*12*	

Elder is a big (6′6″, 230 pounds) 1998 first-round pick—primarily a first baseman, though he can manage in the outfield. Last year he was forced into a lot of DH time by shoulder and elbow problems. To date, he's shown a huge, all-or-nothing swing, which he'll have to cut down on to progress.

Mike Figga   C   Bats R   Age 29

YEAR	TEAM	LGE	AB	H	DB	TP	HR	BB/SO	R	RBI	SB	CS	OUT	BA	OBP	SLG	EQA	EQR	DEFENSE
1997	Columbus	Int	394	89	14	3	10	10/111	40	45	2	2	307	.226	.248	.353	.195	26	
1998	Columbus	Int	459	109	27	2	18	25/121	43	69	1	1	351	.237	.279	.423	.231	45	100-C 89
1999	Baltimor	AL	86	19	3	0	1	1/27	10	5	0	2	69	.221	.230	.291	.151	3	28-C 92
2000	*Baltimor*	*AL*	*234*	*55*	*12*	*1*	*7*	*12/65*	*22*	*28*	*0*	*1*	*180*	*.235*	*.272*	*.385*	*.217*	*20*	

Figga spent nearly two months on the Yankees' roster without ever getting up to bat. The Orioles had a catcher problem behind Charles Johnson in June (due to Chris Hoiles's retirement, Lenny Webster's sprained ankle and Tommy Davis's not being very good), so they grabbed Figga off waivers. He was overmatched by even this limited role. He was waived after the season and picked up by Tampa Bay, giving the Devil Rays three lousy right-handed-hitting catchers. Is that a record?

Jesse Garcia   SS/2B   Bats R   Age 26

YEAR	TEAM	LGE	AB	H	DB	TP	HR	BB/SO	R	RBI	SB	CS	OUT	BA	OBP	SLG	EQA	EQR	DEFENSE	
1997	Bowie	Eas	444	98	18	1	4	27/76	42	35	5	4	350	.221	.272	.293	.188	27	124-2B 102	
1998	Bowie	Eas	260	64	13	1	1	27/40	35	16	6	2	198	.246	.319	.315	.222	23	78-2B 99	
1998	Rochestr	Int	161	44	7	3	0	4/23	16	16	4	3	120	.273	.302	.354	.220	14	43-2B 110	
1999	Rochestr	Int	220	50	11	1	1	8/23	19	18	5	4	174	.227	.254	.300	.180	12	39-SS 91	18-2B 95
1999	Baltimor	AL	29	6	0	0	2	2/3	6	2	0	0	23	.207	.258	.414	.220	3		
2000	*Baltimor*	*AL*	*275*	*64*	*12*	*1*	*2*	*19/37*	*27*	*22*	*5*	*3*	*214*	*.233*	*.282*	*.305*	*.199*	*19*		

An outstanding defensive second baseman, Garcia played shortstop this year to make room for Hairston, a converted shortstop. Go figure. Injuries cut into his playing time, and there is no reason to believe his bat will ever be adequate for even a utility role in the majors.

Jerry Hairston   2B   Bats R   Age 24

YEAR	TEAM	LGE	AB	H	DB	TP	HR	BB/SO	R	RBI	SB	CS	OUT	BA	OBP	SLG	EQA	EQR	DEFENSE
1997	Bluefld	App	219	53	11	2	1	13/31	22	20	3	3	169	.242	.298	.324	.210	17	55-SS 113
1998	Frederck	Car	302	79	22	2	5	25/32	48	29	5	3	226	.262	.333	.397	.249	35	65-SS 115
1998	Bowie	Eas	222	66	13	2	5	16/24	37	33	4	2	158	.297	.356	.441	.269	30	52-2B 103
1999	Rochestr	Int	413	114	24	4	6	24/50	54	41	14	8	307	.276	.341	.397	.252	49	88-2B 99
1999	Baltimor	AL	175	46	12	1	4	9/24	24	16	9	4	133	.263	.310	.411	.244	20	49-2B 100
2000	*Baltimor*	*AL*	*534*	*146*	*30*	*4*	*13*	*43/65*	*80*	*75*	*16*	*9*	*397*	*.273*	*.328*	*.418*	*.254*	*65*	

DeShields's injuries allowed Hairston to get an extended audition with the big club last year, and he took full advantage. The numbers don't do justice to his play, even if they are an accurate assessment of value. He was fun to watch on the field; he played with an energy that was rarely seen on the aging, lackluster Orioles.

Charles Johnson   C   Bats R   Age 28

YEAR	TEAM	LGE	AB	H	DB	TP	HR	BB/SO	R	RBI	SB	CS	OUT	BA	OBP	SLG	EQA	EQR	DEFENSE
1997	Florida	NL	423	109	26	1	21	59/108	44	65	0	2	316	.258	.353	.473	.274	62	
1998	Florida	NL	115	27	4	0	8	16/29	13	25	0	1	89	.235	.328	.478	.264	16	30-C 100
1998	LosAngls	NL	352	82	10	0	15	29/96	33	39	0	1	271	.233	.293	.389	.228	34	100-C 107
1999	Baltimor	AL	424	106	21	1	15	50/107	54	50	0	0	318	.250	.335	.410	.253	51	123-C 104
2000	*Baltimor*	*AL*	*449*	*108*	*17*	*0*	*23*	*61/115*	*64*	*76*	*0*	*1*	*342*	*.241*	*.331*	*.432*	*.259*	*59*	

For several years, the Orioles complained long and loud about the state of their defense behind the plate. So last year they finally did something about it, at a cost of Armando Benitez. Johnson did exactly what should have been expected of him, no more, no less. The slight decline in his hitting stats can be explained by the lack of left-handers in the AL, because he murders them.

Gene Kingsale   CF   Bats B   Age 23

YEAR	TEAM	LGE	AB	H	DB	TP	HR	BB/SO	R	RBI	SB	CS	OUT	BA	OBP	SLG	EQA	EQR	DEFENSE
1998	Bowie	Eas	430	107	12	4	1	41/77	57	31	19	8	331	.249	.328	.302	.225	40	112-OF 112
1999	Bowie	Eas	272	60	12	3	3	27/47	36	20	8	6	218	.221	.293	.320	.209	22	67-OF 108
1999	Rochestr	Int	191	55	5	0	3	10/23	24	18	7	7	143	.288	.332	.361	.233	19	47-OF 108
1999	Baltimor	AL	85	21	1	0	0	4/13	8	6	1	3	67	.247	.297	.259	.179	5	23-CF 90
2000	*Baltimor*	*AL*	*352*	*90*	*10*	*2*	*4*	*35/66*	*47*	*36*	*12*	*7*	*269*	*.256*	*.323*	*.330*	*.229*	*34*	

One look at him and it's easy to see where his problem lies: his wrists and arms are no bigger around than the narrow part of his bat. Kingsale has the build of a runner or high jumper. That's great when he's in the field—he is extremely fast and a great center fielder—but he just doesn't have enough strength to swing a bat at the major-league level.

Eddy Martinez   SS   Bats R   Age 22

YEAR	TEAM	LGE	AB	H	DB	TP	HR	BB/SO	R	RBI	SB	CS	OUT	BA	OBP	SLG	EQA	EQR	DEFENSE
1997	Frederck	Car	178	41	2	0	2	14/43	11	13	3	4	141	.230	.292	.275	.190	11	52-SS 78
1998	Delmarva	SAL	367	87	15	1	2	27/67	33	32	8	3	283	.237	.292	.300	.203	26	110-SS 97
1999	Frederck	Car	429	121	20	1	3	43/96	60	49	4	2	310	.282	.359	.354	.250	48	124-SS 95
2000	Baltimor	AL	382	103	13	1	3	38/81	50	42	5	3	282	.270	.336	.332	.234	38	

He made it to Rochester two years ago, although that was due more to the team's desperately needing a shortstop than to his being good enough for Triple-A. He was sent back to Delmarva in 1998, essentially to start his minor-league journey again, and was still young enough to be a prospect in spite of it. That said, I'm leery of reading too much into his improvement last year, as I am of all improvements that occur when repeating a level.

Luis Matos   CF   Bats R   Age 21

YEAR	TEAM	LGE	AB	H	DB	TP	HR	BB/SO	R	RBI	SB	CS	OUT	BA	OBP	SLG	EQA	EQR	DEFENSE
1997	Bluefld	App	239	52	7	2	1	12/39	17	22	7	2	189	.218	.260	.276	.181	13	61-OF 114
1997	Delmarva	SAL	122	26	2	2	0	7/21	8	12	3	2	98	.213	.264	.262	.174	6	29-OF 112
1998	Delmarva	SAL	510	124	25	5	6	31/91	50	49	16	7	393	.243	.292	.347	.218	44	132-OF 103
1999	Frederck	Car	280	81	14	1	8	15/34	32	37	14	4	203	.289	.328	.432	.259	35	66-OF 103
1999	Bowie	Eas	286	66	12	1	8	10/40	34	31	8	3	223	.231	.259	.364	.208	22	63-OF 106
2000	Baltimor	AL	561	146	22	3	14	37/83	73	69	17	7	422	.260	.306	.385	.237	58	

A bright light in a dark system, Matos leapt out of obscurity with a sensational performance at Frederick. His power has developed nicely as he's aged, he has exceptional range in the field and he put a healthy dent in his strikeout rate last year. He could stand to take a few more walks, but his primary need is to get the average up. Keep a close watch on him.

Derrick May   PH   Bats L   Age 31

YEAR	TEAM	LGE	AB	H	DB	TP	HR	BB/SO	R	RBI	SB	CS	OUT	BA	OBP	SLG	EQA	EQR	DEFENSE
1997	Philadel	NL	150	35	6	1	1	8/26	8	13	3	1	116	.233	.272	.307	.195	10	37-OF 93
1998	Ottawa	Int	68	22	5	0	4	10/8	12	15	0	1	47	.324	.416	.574	.318	13	
1998	Montreal	NL	184	48	8	0	6	10/23	14	17	0	0	136	.261	.299	.402	.234	18	36-OF 88
1999	Rochestr	Int	295	73	18	2	3	16/31	30	32	2	1	223	.247	.288	.353	.215	24	66-OF 90
1999	Baltimor	AL	49	13	0	0	4	3/6	5	11	0	0	36	.265	.308	.510	.265	7	
2000	Baltimor	AL	233	61	11	1	6	19/27	29	32	1	1	173	.262	.317	.395	.243	25	

The Orioles signed May as an insurance policy in case of injury, since they have no faith in any of their minor leaguers. He got his chance in August when Will Clark went down, and performed surprisingly well as a pinch-hitter, occasional DH and outfielder. He did all of this in a strict platoon role: May didn't face a single left-handed pitcher in 1999.

Darnell McDonald   OF   Bats R   Age 21

YEAR	TEAM	LGE	AB	H	DB	TP	HR	BB/SO	R	RBI	SB	CS	OUT	BA	OBP	SLG	EQA	EQR	DEFENSE
1998	Delmarva	SAL	535	126	24	4	5	26/118	61	35	13	5	414	.236	.275	.323	.202	38	117-OF 87
1999	Frederck	Car	523	136	24	5	7	49/89	68	66	13	5	392	.260	.327	.365	.239	55	108-OF 95
2000	Baltimor	AL	404	107	22	2	6	38/78	59	49	10	3	300	.265	.328	.374	.245	45	

McDonald is probably the best all-around athlete in the Orioles system. Their #1 pick in 1997, he improved noticeably in his second professional season. The improvement in his strikeout-to-walk ratio is key, and should translate into improved offensive performance in the future. He still isn't playing like the mega-prospect his tools suggest, but he's showing progress that past tools prospects didn't.

Ryan Minor   3B   Bats R   Age 26

YEAR	TEAM	LGE	AB	H	DB	TP	HR	BB/SO	R	RBI	SB	CS	OUT	BA	OBP	SLG	EQA	EQR	DEFENSE
1997	Delmarva	SAL	505	127	28	1	20	40/113	61	70	2	1	379	.251	.319	.430	.251	60	111-3B 92
1998	Bowie	Eas	523	115	18	2	14	25/163	59	57	1	2	410	.220	.269	.342	.202	38	133-3B 94
1999	Rochestr	Int	384	87	19	1	16	29/131	42	50	2	1	298	.227	.288	.406	.231	38	81-3B 96
1999	Baltimor	AL	124	24	6	0	3	7/43	12	9	1	0	100	.194	.237	.315	.179	7	37-3B 98
2000	*Baltimor*	*AL*	*478*	*111*	*21*	*1*	*17*	*37/151*	*51*	*61*	*1*	*1*	*368*	*.232*	*.287*	*.387*	*.227*	*45*	

Minor's performance while replacing Ripken—which wasn't all that far out of line with his minor-league performance—may have finally convinced the Orioles that there's more to being a baseball player than looking good in the uniform. On the bright side, he's better than Josh Booty.

Ntema Ndungidi   OF   Bats L   Age 21

YEAR	TEAM	LGE	AB	H	DB	TP	HR	BB/SO	R	RBI	SB	CS	OUT	BA	OBP	SLG	EQA	EQR	DEFENSE
1998	Bluefld	App	210	46	9	2	5	24/57	15	20	1	2	166	.219	.301	.352	.221	19	46-OF 79
1999	Delmarva	SAL	228	44	8	2	0	41/55	24	22	7	1	185	.193	.320	.246	.209	19	58-OF 80
1999	Frederck	Car	200	52	13	2	0	33/42	36	16	2	1	149	.260	.370	.345	.254	24	52-OF 98
2000	*Baltimor*	*AL*	*234*	*50*	*10*	*2*	*1*	*45/62*	*38*	*20*	*4*	*1*	*185*	*.214*	*.341*	*.286*	*.230*	*23*	

Born in Zaire, raised in Montreal and schooled at a high school with no baseball team, "Papy" is an extremely raw player, prone to horrific mistakes, especially in the field. Curiously, his chief offensive skill is his outstanding batting eye, odd for someone with his limited experience. He was promoted from Delmarva solely to get him under Etchebarren's wing.

Augie Ojeda   SS   Bats B   Age 25

YEAR	TEAM	LGE	AB	H	DB	TP	HR	BB/SO	R	RBI	SB	CS	OUT	BA	OBP	SLG	EQA	EQR	DEFENSE
1997	Frederck	Car	131	39	8	1	1	13/18	20	16	1	2	94	.298	.364	.397	.258	16	33-SS 102
1997	Bowie	Eas	207	58	7	1	2	25/18	26	20	5	0	149	.280	.364	.353	.256	25	57-SS 103
1998	Bowie	Eas	256	60	8	2	1	31/30	31	17	0	2	198	.234	.323	.293	.213	21	69-SS 102
1999	Bowie	Eas	468	110	17	3	8	41/53	58	47	3	1	359	.235	.306	.335	.220	41	133-SS 102
2000	*ChiCubs*	*NL*	*418*	*106*	*16*	*2*	*7*	*44/47*	*51*	*48*	*4*	*2*	*314*	*.254*	*.325*	*.352*	*.228*	*39*	

Stuck at Bowie despite a string of injuries to Rochester shortstops, he's never been able to replicate his initial professional success. Considering that his glovework, little-ball skills and attitude all come highly praised by his managers, it surprises me that he gets so little consideration from the organization. He could still manage a Reboulet-like career.

Richard Paz   3B   Bats R   Age 22

YEAR	TEAM	LGE	AB	H	DB	TP	HR	BB/SO	R	RBI	SB	CS	OUT	BA	OBP	SLG	EQA	EQR	DEFENSE	
1997	Delmarva	SAL	400	92	17	3	2	33/61	50	42	6	2	310	.230	.294	.303	.205	30	43-SS 94	20-3B 100
1998	Delmarva	SAL	337	91	11	3	4	63/42	39	43	8	3	249	.270	.393	.356	.269	47	88-3B 97	
1998	Frederck	Car	148	35	7	0	4	19/21	27	8	3	1	114	.236	.334	.365	.243	17	28-3B 82	
1999	Frederck	Car	171	43	9	0	0	41/26	22	16	8	4	132	.251	.400	.304	.261	23	49-3B 107	
1999	Bowie	Eas	278	76	13	1	2	42/36	33	18	6	2	204	.273	.377	.349	.259	35	67-3B 95	
2000	*Baltimor*	*AL*	*490*	*130*	*26*	*2*	*4*	*80/67*	*93*	*57*	*15*	*4*	*364*	*.265*	*.368*	*.351*	*.260*	*63*		

The little Venezuelan (5'8", 170 pounds) continues to get no consideration as a prospect despite posting impressive DTs. He's a slap hitter with no power at all, but is one of the best walkers in the minor leagues. The profile is similar to Dave Magadan's minor league career.

Calvin Pickering   1B   Bats L   Age 23

YEAR	TEAM	LGE	AB	H	DB	TP	HR	BB/SO	R	RBI	SB	CS	OUT	BA	OBP	SLG	EQA	EQR	DEFENSE
1997	Delmarva	SAL	461	127	24	1	24	46/141	74	64	2	1	335	.275	.349	.488	.277	68	114-1B 84
1998	Bowie	Eas	492	139	25	1	29	86/116	82	99	3	4	357	.283	.399	.514	.302	90	126-1B 79
1999	Rochestr	Int	372	100	14	1	15	53/99	53	54	1	2	274	.269	.374	.433	.275	54	96-1B 83
1999	Baltimor	AL	40	5	1	0	1	10/16	4	5	0	0	35	.125	.300	.225	.190	3	
2000	*Baltimor*	*AL*	*389*	*107*	*15*	*1*	*23*	*67/104*	*74*	*84*	*2*	*1*	*283*	*.275*	*.382*	*.496*	*.297*	*68*	

Big Cal suffered through a disappointing year. He hurt his shoulder in the spring, and it bothered him throughout the first half. He finally got going just before Will Clark went down for the season, but sulked when he was passed over in favor of Derrick May. He carries a lot of weight, something Ray Miller couldn't stand.

Jeff Reboulet   UT   Bats R   Age 36

YEAR	TEAM	LGE	AB	H	DB	TP	HR	BB/SO	R	RBI	SB	CS	OUT	BA	OBP	SLG	EQA	EQR	DEFENSE	
1997	Baltimor	AL	228	55	7	0	5	22/42	25	28	3	0	173	.241	.311	.338	.225	21	45-2B 99	12-SS 88
1998	Baltimor	AL	127	33	3	0	2	18/33	19	9	0	1	95	.260	.361	.331	.243	14		
1999	Baltimor	AL	153	24	4	0	0	32/29	23	4	1	0	129	.157	.310	.183	.181	9	24-2B 104	23-3B 107
2000	KansasCy	AL	102	20	0	0	2	16/21	10	8	1	0	82	.196	.305	.255	.193	7		

It's about time for him to retire, since his bat speed has dropped off to the point that all he can really do is try to foul off pitches and draw a walk. His defense is still good; having him and Amaral on the bench gave Ray Miller flexibility but no punch.

Cal Ripken   3B   Bats R   Age 39

YEAR	TEAM	LGE	AB	H	DB	TP	HR	BB/SO	R	RBI	SB	CS	OUT	BA	OBP	SLG	EQA	EQR	DEFENSE
1997	Baltimor	AL	615	170	23	0	20	52/70	76	85	1	0	445	.276	.339	.411	.255	73	150-3B 107
1998	Baltimor	AL	603	168	27	1	15	50/66	64	61	0	2	437	.279	.338	.401	.250	68	157-3B 96
1999	Baltimor	AL	330	112	23	0	19	9/31	47	54	0	1	219	.339	.363	.582	.303	55	79-3B 88
2000	Baltimor	AL	271	67	9	0	9	22/28	30	36	0	0	204	.247	.304	.380	.233	27	

Did pursuit of The Streak cost us this? After a horrendous start afield, aplate and ahome—his father died during spring training—Ripken went on the disabled list for the first time ever, courtesy of a stiff back. When he returned, he started stroking the ball and kept going at a torrid pace, including a league-record six-hit game. He hit his 400th home run, and his 3,000th hit seemed a foregone conclusion. Then the back forced him out a second time, requiring surgery. He's expected to be fully healthy in April to get those last nine hits.

B.J. Surhoff   LF   Bats L   Age 35

YEAR	TEAM	LGE	AB	H	DB	TP	HR	BB/SO	R	RBI	SB	CS	OUT	BA	OBP	SLG	EQA	EQR	DEFENSE
1997	Baltimor	AL	528	153	32	5	18	45/58	79	87	1	1	376	.290	.352	.472	.274	74	123-OF 99
1998	Baltimor	AL	575	165	33	2	23	48/79	78	92	8	7	417	.287	.343	.471	.269	78	150-OF 93
1999	Baltimor	AL	670	206	33	2	28	35/78	95	101	5	1	465	.307	.344	.488	.276	93	143-LF 110
2000	Baltimor	AL	568	157	22	0	23	49/69	77	95	2	2	413	.276	.334	.437	.261	72	

Surhoff set personal highs in almost every category, with the most significant one being at-bats. The counting stats are elevated simply because of the playing time, nothing more; his rate stats show you this was a typical Surhoff season, only longer. He's been one of the most consistent hitters over the last four years, and there's no reason to expect radical changes.

Jayson Werth   C   Bats R   Age 21

YEAR	TEAM	LGE	AB	H	DB	TP	HR	BB/SO	R	RBI	SB	CS	OUT	BA	OBP	SLG	EQA	EQR	DEFENSE
1998	Delmarva	SAL	417	98	20	2	7	41/93	51	42	8	3	322	.235	.318	.343	.230	41	107-C 102
1999	Frederck	Car	245	73	12	1	3	30/36	34	27	8	2	174	.298	.379	.392	.271	33	62-C 98
1999	Bowie	Eas	123	32	5	1	1	14/27	15	10	4	1	92	.260	.342	.341	.243	13	23-C 95
2000	Baltimor	AL	276	75	11	1	4	33/58	45	34	8	2	203	.272	.350	.362	.253	33	

A tall, athletic catcher who's drawn comparisons to Jason Kendall and Dale Murphy, Werth comes from a family of major leaguers. He's a line-drive hitter who hasn't yet shown power, but everybody assumes that will come before long. The statistical decline at Double-A is deceptive; he was tearing the league apart until a baserunning injury left him with a hairline fracture of his wrist, and he hit just .171 while playing through it. The biggest question is whether the Orioles will allow him to remain at catcher or move him to the outfield.

PITCHERS (Averages: ERA: 4.50 / H/9: 9.00 / HR/9: 1.00 / BB/9: 3.50 / K/9: 6.50 / KWH: 1.00)

Ricky Bones — Throws R — Age 31

YEAR	TEAM	LGE	IP	H	ER	HR	BB	K	ERA	W	L	H/9	HR/9	BB/9	K/9	KWH	PERA
1997	Tucson	PCL	39.7	41	18	2	9	18	4.08	2	2	9.30	0.45	2.04	4.08	0.66	3.63
1997	Cincnnti	NL	18.0	32	22	2	12	8	11.00	0	2	16.00	1.00	6.00	4.00	0.12	10.00
1997	KansasCy	AL	79.7	99	54	9	26	37	6.10	3	6	11.18	1.02	2.94	4.18	0.40	5.54
1998	SaltLake	PCL	47.3	40	18	5	23	34	3.42	3	2	7.61	0.95	4.37	6.46	0.94	3.99
1998	Omaha	PCL	13.3	21	16	5	11	6	10.80	0	1	14.18	3.38	7.43	4.05	0.12	12.82
1998	KansasCy	AL	55.0	44	15	4	26	39	2.45	5	1	7.20	0.65	4.25	6.38	0.99	3.44
1999	Baltimor	AL	43.7	57	26	6	19	27	5.36	2	3	11.75	1.24	3.92	5.56	0.50	6.60

After a sensational year with the Royals, Bones turned back into the soft-tossing, hit-yielding, run-producing machine he's been for his entire career. Even with all the problems the Orioles were having in the bullpen, they saw fit to release him in August.

Jim Corsi — Throws R — Age 38

YEAR	TEAM	LGE	IP	H	ER	HR	BB	K	ERA	W	L	H/9	HR/9	BB/9	K/9	KWH	PERA
1997	Boston	AL	59.0	52	22	1	21	40	3.36	4	3	7.93	0.15	3.20	6.10	1.09	3.05
1998	Boston	AL	66.0	57	22	5	25	50	3.00	5	2	7.77	0.68	3.41	6.82	1.31	3.55
1999	Boston	AL	25.0	22	12	4	19	14	4.32	2	1	7.92	1.44	6.84	5.04	0.35	5.76
1999	Rochestr	Int	10.0	13	4	0	3	6	3.60	1	0	11.70	0.00	2.70	5.40	0.69	4.50
1999	Baltimor	AL	13.0	15	4	2	1	8	2.77	1	0	10.38	1.38	0.69	5.54	3.19	4.85

And into Bones's place, they called up this fellow from Rochester. Not a pitcher who could use some experience now and might be a contributor if the Orioles get themselves straightened out, but a rent-a-player with no ties to the organization who became a free agent after the season. It's not as if Corsi pitched in meaningful games; they should have been used to give young pitchers game experience, not to give experienced pitchers games.

Javier de la Hoya — Throws R — Age 30

YEAR	TEAM	LGE	IP	H	ER	HR	BB	K	ERA	W	L	H/9	HR/9	BB/9	K/9	KWH	PERA
1998	Bowie	Eas	28.7	40	16	4	9	24	5.02	1	2	12.56	1.26	2.83	7.53	1.20	6.59
1999	Bowie	Eas	70.7	85	39	12	21	50	4.97	4	4	10.83	1.53	2.67	6.37	1.05	5.86
1999	Rochestr	Int	77.7	96	50	13	29	50	5.79	3	6	11.12	1.51	3.36	5.79	0.67	6.26

He's not a prospect at his age, but I really wanted to salute a guy who dropped out of Double-A six years ago. Since then, he's survived two arm surgeries, knocked around the Taiwanese and Mexican leagues and finally, after 10 years as a professional player, made it to Triple-A and pitched for Mexico in the Pan Am games. Here's to the next step, Javier, whoever you're playing for this year.

Radhames Dykhoff — Throws L — Age 25

YEAR	TEAM	LGE	IP	H	ER	HR	BB	K	ERA	W	L	H/9	HR/9	BB/9	K/9	KWH	PERA
1997	Frederck	Car	64.0	60	22	5	44	71	3.09	5	2	8.44	0.70	6.19	9.98	1.43	4.92
1998	Bowie	Eas	90.7	95	58	10	61	78	5.76	4	6	9.43	0.99	6.06	7.74	0.78	5.76
1999	Rochestr	Int	80.0	73	41	10	33	50	4.61	4	5	8.21	1.13	3.71	5.63	0.78	4.27

Part of the Orioles' Aruban Army, Dykhoff has been groomed as a left-handed specialist. He's an extreme flyball pitcher, and that won't work too well with the current Orioles outfield.

Scott Erickson — Throws R — Age 32

YEAR	TEAM	LGE	IP	H	ER	HR	BB	K	ERA	W	L	H/9	HR/9	BB/9	K/9	KWH	PERA
1997	Baltimor	AL	221.3	216	96	15	61	132	3.90	14	11	8.78	0.61	2.48	5.37	0.99	3.62
1998	Baltimor	AL	250.0	280	117	21	72	187	4.21	15	13	10.08	0.76	2.59	6.73	1.30	4.50
1999	Baltimor	AL	228.0	241	119	24	96	109	4.70	12	13	9.51	0.95	3.79	4.30	0.38	4.86

A tale of two seasons. In early June, he was 1-8 with an ERA over 7.00 and was being pasted every time out. His fastball had no zip and his sinker was sailing. He was unimpressive from there to the All-Star break, though he didn't lose any more games, then started rolling through the second half. After June 4, he was 14-4 with a 3.81 ERA and had made it clear he should still be in the Orioles' plans.

Brian Falkenborg   Throws R   Age 22

YEAR	TEAM	LGE	IP	H	ER	HR	BB	K	ERA	W	L	H/9	HR/9	BB/9	K/9	KWH	PERA
1997	Delmarva	SAL	115.7	166	101	8	66	74	7.86	3	10	12.92	0.62	5.14	5.76	0.37	7.08
1998	Frederck	Car	73.3	104	54	8	25	51	6.63	3	5	12.76	0.98	3.07	6.26	0.75	6.50
1999	Bowie	Eas	79.0	90	45	11	40	63	5.13	4	5	10.25	1.25	4.56	7.18	0.82	5.92

Falkenborg added 30 pounds to his body and an extra 4 mph to his fastball. His Bowie record is deceptive; he went 3-6, getting just six runs of support in the losses. He also suffered an inflamed nerve in his elbow for the second straight year, and the thinking is that he may not have the durability to continue starting.

Mike Fetters   Throws R   Age 35

YEAR	TEAM	LGE	IP	H	ER	HR	BB	K	ERA	W	L	H/9	HR/9	BB/9	K/9	KWH	PERA
1997	Milwauke	AL	71.0	59	27	4	34	63	3.42	5	3	7.48	0.51	4.31	7.99	1.48	3.55
1998	Oakland	AL	47.3	46	24	3	22	34	4.56	2	3	8.75	0.57	4.18	6.46	0.85	4.18
1998	Anaheim	AL	11.3	14	8	2	4	9	6.35	0	1	11.12	1.59	3.18	7.15	1.08	6.35
1999	Baltimor	AL	31.0	34	21	5	21	22	6.10	1	2	9.87	1.45	6.10	6.39	0.51	6.68

He had two good stretches for the Orioles: six hitless appearances in May and the three months he spent on the disabled list with a strained elbow. Fetters gets hurt more frequently than Ally McBeal's feelings and can't be counted on for anything other than carbon dioxide.

Doug Johns   Throws L   Age 32

YEAR	TEAM	LGE	IP	H	ER	HR	BB	K	ERA	W	L	H/9	HR/9	BB/9	K/9	KWH	PERA
1997	Omaha	AmA	43.0	62	37	7	13	21	7.74	1	4	12.98	1.47	2.72	4.40	0.41	7.12
1997	Rochestr	Int	53.3	64	27	5	14	34	4.56	3	3	10.80	0.84	2.36	5.74	0.96	4.89
1998	Rochestr	Int	10.0	9	4	2	6	3	3.60	1	0	8.10	1.80	5.40	2.70	0.12	5.40
1998	Baltimor	AL	86.0	107	43	8	33	34	4.50	5	5	11.20	0.84	3.45	3.56	0.24	5.55
1999	Rochestr	Int	28.7	37	21	3	6	15	6.59	1	2	11.62	0.94	1.88	4.71	0.76	5.34
1999	Baltimor	AL	86.0	80	41	8	24	51	4.29	5	5	8.37	0.84	2.51	5.34	1.01	3.66

Johns continues to perform adequately despite having nothing that would impress a scout. His usage will likely be long relief or spot starting once again, providing another usage doesn't catch up with him—he was arrested twice last year on marijuana charges.

Jason Johnson   Throws R   Age 26

YEAR	TEAM	LGE	IP	H	ER	HR	BB	K	ERA	W	L	H/9	HR/9	BB/9	K/9	KWH	PERA
1997	Lynchbrg	Car	91.3	128	57	5	36	63	5.62	4	6	12.61	0.49	3.55	6.21	0.64	6.11
1997	Carolina	Sou	55.7	60	30	6	18	50	4.85	3	3	9.70	0.97	2.91	8.08	1.73	4.69
1998	TampaBay	AL	60.7	74	36	8	28	37	5.34	3	4	10.98	1.19	4.15	5.49	0.49	6.08
1999	Rochestr	Int	42.7	38	19	6	29	40	4.01	3	2	8.02	1.27	6.12	8.44	1.08	5.27
1999	Baltimor	AL	114.3	118	68	14	54	73	5.35	5	8	9.29	1.10	4.25	5.75	0.62	5.04

He was traded for Danny Clyburn in the spring, and the O's got the better of the deal. Johnson is a late bloomer, toiling for five years in the minors before suddenly catapulting from A ball to the majors in 1997, and he still looks like he's learning how to pitch. He finished the season strong, winning his last five decisions to finish above .500. I'm not sure why, but I've got a good feeling about him going into 2000.

Scott Kamieniecki   Throws R   Age 36

YEAR	TEAM	LGE	IP	H	ER	HR	BB	K	ERA	W	L	H/9	HR/9	BB/9	K/9	KWH	PERA
1997	Baltimor	AL	179.3	176	79	18	68	110	3.96	11	9	8.83	0.90	3.41	5.52	0.76	4.27
1998	Baltimor	AL	54.3	66	39	7	27	25	6.46	2	4	10.93	1.16	4.47	4.14	0.26	6.29
1999	Rochestr	Int	22.0	26	14	5	6	12	5.73	1	1	10.64	2.05	2.45	4.91	0.69	6.14
1999	Baltimor	AL	55.7	51	30	3	28	40	4.85	3	3	8.25	0.49	4.53	6.47	0.84	4.04

After offseason neck surgery and a spring-training hamstring pull, Kammie was thrown into the fifth-starter slot and blasted twice, earning a ticket to Rochester. He was blasted again in his first game back, at which point he'd given up 16 runs in six innings—as many runs as he would allow in his next 50 innings out of the bullpen. The Indians signed him to a two-year deal and plan to use him solely as a reliever.

Ryan Kohlmeier — Throws R — Age 23

YEAR	TEAM	LGE	IP	H	ER	HR	BB	K	ERA	W	L	H/9	HR/9	BB/9	K/9	KWH	PERA
1997	Delmarva	SAL	69.7	67	31	10	24	67	4.00	4	4	8.66	1.29	3.10	8.66	2.09	4.39
1998	Bowie	Eas	48.3	60	41	13	19	46	7.63	1	4	11.17	2.42	3.54	8.57	1.39	7.45
1999	Bowie	Eas	58.7	55	28	11	32	64	4.30	4	3	8.44	1.69	4.91	9.82	1.74	5.52

Bowie's closer and all-time saves leader was very tough on right-handed hitters but struggled with lefties. Another extreme flyball pitcher, he should turn into a major-league reliever in 2001.

Doug Linton — Throws R — Age 34

YEAR	TEAM	LGE	IP	H	ER	HR	BB	K	ERA	W	L	H/9	HR/9	BB/9	K/9	KWH	PERA
1998	SaltLake	PCL	79.3	111	53	17	16	50	6.01	3	6	12.59	1.93	1.82	5.67	1.05	7.03
1999	Rochestr	Int	114.0	130	59	12	30	83	4.66	6	7	10.26	0.95	2.37	6.55	1.32	4.74
1999	Baltimor	AL	58.0	69	38	12	24	32	5.90	2	4	10.71	1.86	3.72	4.97	0.46	6.52

It's one thing to have the team age propped up by players like Harold Baines or Cal Ripken, and another to rely on scrap heapers like Linton to get through the season.

Calvin Maduro — Throws R — Age 25

YEAR	TEAM	LGE	IP	H	ER	HR	BB	K	ERA	W	L	H/9	HR/9	BB/9	K/9	KWH	PERA
1997	Scran-WB	Int	76.3	79	50	10	58	45	5.90	3	5	9.31	1.18	6.84	5.31	0.33	6.25
1997	Philadel	NL	70.3	85	60	13	43	29	7.68	2	6	10.88	1.66	5.50	3.71	0.17	7.29
1998	Scran-WB	Int	167.7	230	130	27	71	105	6.98	6	13	12.35	1.45	3.81	5.64	0.50	7.19
1999	Rochestr	Int	163.7	190	86	21	64	130	4.73	9	9	10.45	1.15	3.52	7.15	1.04	5.50

Back in his original organization—the Orioles traded him to Philadelphia for Todd Zeile and Pete Incaviglia in 1996—he had by far his best season since he left. While the Orioles never called him up, they did add him to the 40-man roster in October.

Sean Maloney — Throws R — Age 29

YEAR	TEAM	LGE	IP	H	ER	HR	BB	K	ERA	W	L	H/9	HR/9	BB/9	K/9	KWH	PERA
1997	Tucson	PCL	17.3	25	10	3	3	17	5.19	1	1	12.98	1.56	1.56	8.83	2.88	6.75
1998	Albuquer	PCL	34.7	39	19	5	10	31	4.93	2	2	10.13	1.30	2.60	8.05	1.84	5.19
1999	Frederck	Car	22.7	30	15	3	13	14	5.96	1	2	11.91	1.19	5.16	5.56	0.38	7.15
1999	Bowie	Eas	9.7	13	5	1	4	13	4.66	0	1	12.10	0.93	3.72	12.10	2.43	6.52

The former major leaguer found himself all the way back in A ball as he tried to recover from multiple arm surgeries that had derailed his career. He still has an exceptional splitter, but not enough velocity to make it effective.

Gabe Molina — Throws R — Age 25

YEAR	TEAM	LGE	IP	H	ER	HR	BB	K	ERA	W	L	H/9	HR/9	BB/9	K/9	KWH	PERA
1997	Delmarva	SAL	84.3	82	36	4	46	79	3.84	5	4	8.75	0.43	4.91	8.43	1.24	4.38
1998	Bowie	Eas	59.7	56	28	5	31	60	4.22	4	3	8.45	0.75	4.68	9.05	1.55	4.37
1999	Rochestr	Int	56.0	47	22	3	25	51	3.54	4	2	7.55	0.48	4.02	8.20	1.65	3.37
1999	Baltimor	AL	23.0	22	18	4	15	14	7.04	1	2	8.61	1.57	5.87	5.48	0.44	5.87

The stocky right-hander made three trips to Baltimore last season, and until the final week against the Yankees and Red Sox, he performed well. In Rochester he closed, riding a tough slider to 18 saves; he won't be a closer in the majors, even if he did get a few cracks at it during the Orioles' great summer bullpen meltdown.

Mike Mussina — Throws R — Age 31

YEAR	TEAM	LGE	IP	H	ER	HR	BB	K	ERA	W	L	H/9	HR/9	BB/9	K/9	KWH	PERA
1997	Baltimor	AL	224.3	195	82	25	55	220	3.29	16	9	7.82	1.00	2.21	8.83	3.37	3.37
1998	Baltimor	AL	205.3	186	79	21	43	176	3.46	14	9	8.15	0.92	1.88	7.71	2.89	3.37
1999	Baltimor	AL	201.3	205	82	14	50	176	3.67	13	9	9.16	0.63	2.24	7.87	2.26	3.75

He's the staff ace and a Gold Glover who finished second in the Cy Young voting. He's a reasonable candidate for the third-best pitcher of the 1990s. It's just that he can't seem to get through an entire season without being hit by a line drive.

Jesse Orosco   Throws L   Age 43

YEAR	TEAM	LGE	IP	H	ER	HR	BB	K	ERA	W	L	H/9	HR/9	BB/9	K/9	KWH	PERA
1997	Baltimor	AL	50.3	28	12	6	30	46	2.15	5	1	5.01	1.07	5.36	8.23	1.88	3.22
1998	Baltimor	AL	56.3	45	19	6	29	50	3.04	4	2	7.19	0.96	4.63	7.99	1.43	3.83
1999	Baltimor	AL	32.0	27	19	5	19	36	5.34	2	2	7.59	1.41	5.34	10.13	1.89	4.78

The race to the all-time appearances record turned into a crawl as Orosco was mauled repeatedly in the first three months of 1999. From July on he was kept on a very short leash, facing one batter in 19 of his last 33 appearances, and just two in 10 of the others. He allowed just seven hits and three runs in that span, so maybe the ol' boy's not washed up yet.

Sidney Ponson   Throws R   Age 23

YEAR	TEAM	LGE	IP	H	ER	HR	BB	K	ERA	W	L	H/9	HR/9	BB/9	K/9	KWH	PERA
1997	Bowie	Eas	68.7	91	58	10	34	45	7.60	2	6	11.93	1.31	4.46	5.90	0.49	7.08
1998	Baltimor	AL	134.3	155	77	18	43	86	5.16	6	9	10.38	1.21	2.88	5.76	0.83	5.29
1999	Baltimor	AL	207.7	225	110	31	78	115	4.77	11	12	9.75	1.34	3.38	4.98	0.56	5.24

Ponson's season looked a lot better before he ran into a dead arm in September, and a look at the PAP data for the Orioles will show you why he had one. There isn't much excuse for a 22-year-old to lead the league in complete games, as Ponson did for much of the season before being passed by David Wells in September. I'm pessimistic about his 2000 performance.

Al Reyes   Throws R   Age 29

YEAR	TEAM	LGE	IP	H	ER	HR	BB	K	ERA	W	L	H/9	HR/9	BB/9	K/9	KWH	PERA
1997	Tucson	PCL	53.3	54	38	11	36	57	6.41	2	4	9.11	1.86	6.08	9.62	1.25	6.58
1997	Milwauke	AL	30.0	31	17	4	9	28	5.10	1	2	9.30	1.20	2.70	8.40	2.10	4.50
1998	Milwauke	NL	58.3	54	24	9	33	56	3.70	4	2	8.33	1.39	5.09	8.64	1.31	5.09
1999	Milwauke	NL	36.7	26	15	5	24	38	3.68	2	2	6.38	1.23	5.89	9.33	1.73	4.17
1999	Baltimor	AL	29.3	23	14	3	16	29	4.30	2	1	7.06	0.92	4.91	8.90	1.71	3.99

Picked up from the Brewers for Rocky Coppinger, he endeared himself to Ray Miller simply by not being overweight. His career ERA is 4.23 and he has struck out a batter per inning, so clearly he can help someone.

Arthur Rhodes   Throws L   Age 30

YEAR	TEAM	LGE	IP	H	ER	HR	BB	K	ERA	W	L	H/9	HR/9	BB/9	K/9	KWH	PERA
1997	Baltimor	AL	95.3	74	30	8	26	103	2.83	8	3	6.99	0.76	2.45	9.72	4.12	2.83
1998	Baltimor	AL	76.3	65	28	7	35	84	3.30	5	3	7.66	0.83	4.13	9.90	2.32	3.89
1999	Baltimor	AL	52.3	43	33	8	44	60	5.68	2	4	7.39	1.38	7.57	10.32	1.42	5.68

Miller tried to use him as a closer for a few games when Timlin's stuggles were at their peak. Rhodes pitched badly and complained that he preferred to be used in the middle of the game, not the end. He also complained about not getting paid like a closer. The whining about his salary was abated when he signed a four-year, $13 million deal with the Mariners. He's the best reliever Mt. Piniella has had in quite some time, so this should be interesting. There's another 1997 in him.

Matt Riley   Throws L   Age 20

YEAR	TEAM	LGE	IP	H	ER	HR	BB	K	ERA	W	L	H/9	HR/9	BB/9	K/9	KWH	PERA
1998	Delmarva	SAL	77.3	57	27	0	59	87	3.14	6	3	6.63	0.00	6.87	10.13	1.68	3.49
1999	Frederck	Car	49.3	43	23	6	16	42	4.20	3	2	7.84	1.09	2.92	7.66	1.92	3.65
1999	Bowie	Eas	119.3	133	61	14	46	107	4.60	6	7	10.03	1.06	3.47	8.07	1.40	5.13
1999	Baltimor	AL	11.0	17	8	4	12	6	6.55	0	1	13.91	3.27	9.82	4.91	0.13	13.91

Riley has a chance to be the Spaceman Lee of the '00s. As we said in the '90s, he's edgy—tattooed, pierced, dyed, brash and outspoken. He also wore down as the season went on, and his cup of coffee in Baltimore didn't approach his performance earlier in the year. He's been so heavily hyped so far, for his talent and personality, that I worry about him living up to it—or going the Fidrych direction if he does live up to it.

B.J. Ryan   Throws L   Age 24

YEAR	TEAM	LGE	IP	H	ER	HR	BB	K	ERA	W	L	H/9	HR/9	BB/9	K/9	KWH	PERA
1998	Billings	Pio	15.3	19	4	0	5	16	2.35	2	0	11.15	0.00	2.93	9.39	2.01	4.70
1998	Chattang	Sou	16.0	14	4	0	6	17	2.25	2	0	7.88	0.00	3.38	9.56	2.57	2.81
1999	Chattang	Sou	40.7	37	14	1	19	37	3.10	3	2	8.19	0.22	4.20	8.19	1.46	3.54
1999	Rochestr	Int	14.3	8	4	2	4	18	2.51	2	0	5.02	1.26	2.51	11.30	7.57	2.51
1999	Baltimor	AL	18.3	9	5	0	11	29	2.45	2	0	4.42	0.00	5.40	14.24	6.35	1.96

Acquired in the Juan Guzman trade, Ryan's ascent from the Pioneer League to the majors has been meteoric. He's a tall, sidearming left-hander who hides the ball well. While it will be tempting to use him as a specialist, he's been equally tough on right-handed hitters so far.

Jacobo Sequea   Throws R   Age 18

YEAR	TEAM	LGE	IP	H	ER	HR	BB	K	ERA	W	L	H/9	HR/9	BB/9	K/9	KWH	PERA
1998	Charl-WV	SAL	50.3	83	51	4	46	22	9.12	1	5	14.84	0.72	8.23	3.93	0.09	9.83
1999	Rockford	Mid	83.0	108	60	8	50	48	6.51	3	6	11.71	0.87	5.42	5.20	0.32	6.72
1999	Delmarva	SAL	27.3	45	25	5	23	16	8.23	1	2	14.82	1.65	7.57	5.27	0.18	10.87

Sequea was also acquired in the Guzman deal. If he were American instead of Venezuelan, he'd be touted as one of the top high-school pitchers in the country and a possible #1 overall draft pick. Instead, he already has two years of A-ball experience under his belt. Sequea throws in the 90s; as yet, though, he doesn't really know where the ball is going.

John Stephens   Throws R   Age 20

YEAR	TEAM	LGE	IP	H	ER	HR	BB	K	ERA	W	L	H/9	HR/9	BB/9	K/9	KWH	PERA
1997	Bluefld	App	22.0	25	8	4	7	18	3.27	1	1	10.23	1.64	2.86	7.36	1.38	5.73
1998	Delmarva	SAL	31.7	35	16	4	17	26	4.55	2	2	9.95	1.14	4.83	7.39	0.85	5.68
1999	Delmarva	SAL	160.3	195	99	12	51	140	5.56	7	11	10.95	0.67	2.86	7.86	1.47	5.00

There was some concern that the Aussie's career was over in 1998, after he hurt his neck fielding a bunt. That seemed more likely last spring when he could get up to only 83 mph on the radar gun, down from 90 mph before the injury. And yet, with control and an outrageously slow curve ball that breaks across two counties, he led the Sally League in strikeouts. That pitch won't dominate at higher levels the way it did at Delmarva; he'll have to recover some of his velocity.

Mike Timlin   Throws R   Age 34

YEAR	TEAM	LGE	IP	H	ER	HR	BB	K	ERA	W	L	H/9	HR/9	BB/9	K/9	KWH	PERA
1997	Toronto	AL	47.0	40	16	6	15	36	3.06	3	2	7.66	1.15	2.87	6.89	1.61	3.64
1997	Seattle	AL	26.3	26	11	2	5	9	3.76	2	1	8.89	0.68	1.71	3.08	0.47	3.42
1998	Seattle	AL	81.0	72	21	5	17	61	2.33	7	2	8.00	0.56	1.89	6.78	2.27	3.00
1999	Baltimor	AL	62.3	51	28	8	22	51	4.04	4	3	7.36	1.16	3.18	7.36	1.73	3.61

Timlin was a big part of the Orioles' disappointing season, as he took until the All-Star break to find a decent pitching rhythm. He claims the problems started when at times he was asked to pitch in the eighth inning. After the break, he never pitched more than one inning, converted 18 of 19 save opportunities and had a 1.40 ERA. Perhaps the Orioles should listen to what he says.

Josh Towers   Throws R   Age 23

YEAR	TEAM	LGE	IP	H	ER	HR	BB	K	ERA	W	L	H/9	HR/9	BB/9	K/9	KWH	PERA
1997	Delmarva	SAL	17.0	25	12	2	3	11	6.35	1	1	13.24	1.06	1.59	5.82	1.21	6.35
1997	Frederck	Car	51.0	89	41	5	21	48	7.24	2	4	15.71	0.88	3.71	8.47	0.92	8.65
1998	Frederck	Car	138.0	173	75	15	13	87	4.89	7	8	11.28	0.98	0.85	5.67	2.51	4.70
1999	Bowie	Eas	178.0	239	100	28	28	87	5.06	9	11	12.08	1.42	1.42	4.40	0.85	5.92

Freak stats are fun, if not especially meaningful. Towers is known as a control guy—"Be a man, make them hit it," he says—and is capable of doing things like throwing a nine-inning, 79-pitch complete game. The freak stat: he was 9-2 when he walked at least one batter and 3-5 when he didn't.

Support-Neutral Records — BALTIMORE ORIOLES — Park Effect: -5.5%

PITCHER	GS	IP	R	SNW	SNL	SNPCT	W	L	RA	APW	SNVA	SNWAR
Ricky Bones	2	6.3	6	0.2	0.8	.174	0	1	8.53	-0.23	-0.27	-0.25
Rocky Coppinger	2	6.7	10	0.1	1.2	.064	0	1	13.50	-0.59	-0.48	-0.46
Scott Erickson	34	230.3	127	13.5	12.9	.511	15	12	4.96	0.28	0.13	2.27
Juan Guzman	21	122.7	63	7.7	6.4	.546	5	9	4.62	0.59	0.53	1.70
Doug Johns	5	33.0	14	2.0	1.3	.604	2	2	3.82	0.44	0.38	0.58
Jason Johnson	21	114.7	73	6.1	7.7	.444	8	7	5.73	-0.78	-0.88	0.26
Scott Kamieniecki	3	8.3	14	0.4	1.5	.201	0	2	15.12	-0.87	-0.56	-0.43
Doug Linton	8	47.0	30	2.1	3.1	.399	1	4	5.74	-0.33	-0.49	-0.13
Mike Mussina	31	203.3	88	14.2	8.1	.637	18	7	3.90	2.52	2.83	4.74
Sidney Ponson	32	210.0	118	12.5	11.6	.519	12	12	5.06	0.05	0.46	2.27
Matt Riley	3	11.0	9	0.3	1.3	.168	0	0	7.36	-0.26	-0.43	-0.40
TOTALS	162	993.3	552	59.0	56.0	.513	61	57	5.00	0.82	1.21	10.14

Quick, name the only AL team in 1999 with four above-average starters (minimum 20 starts). No, it wasn't the Yankees. According to the Support-Neutral measures, it was the Orioles, with Mike Mussina, Juan Guzman, Sidney Ponson and Scott Erickson all having a Support-Neutral Winning Percentage better than .500. (Admittedly, the Yankees came about as close as humanly possible, with Andy Pettitte missing by .001.) Despite the impressive record of their top four starters, Baltimore's overall performance was brought down by the various fifth and spot starters they used. The cumulative Support-Neutral W/L record of their top four pitchers above 48-39 (.551); everyone else posted an 11-17 (.399) record. As a result, the Orioles had only the 10th-best rotation in the majors, worth a little more than a win above average.... You're facing an uphill battle if you want to make Orioles fans forget Jim Palmer, but if anyone has a chance to do it, it's Mike Mussina. Through his first nine years, Mussina has pitched 1,772 innings and posted a park-adjusted ERA 32% better than the league. Through his first nine years, Palmer had pitched 1,866⅔ innings and owned an ERA 27% better than the league. Mussina still has a long way to go to be considered the greatest pitcher in Orioles history—Palmer's best season was in the 10th year of his career, and he had three terrific years after that—but Moose is off to a good start.

Pitcher Abuse Points

PITCHER	AGE	GS	PAP	PAP/S	WKLD	MAX	1-90	91-100	101-110	111-120	121-130	131-140	141+
Ricky Bones	30	2	0	0.0	0.0	60	2	0	0	0	0	0	0
Rocky Coppinger	25	2	0	0.0	0.0	90	2	0	0	0	0	0	0
Scott Erickson	31	34	613	18.0	21.0	131	4	3	10	8	8	1	0
Juan Guzman	32	21	263	12.5	12.5	125	5	2	7	3	4	0	0
Doug Johns	31	5	2	0.4	0.5	102	2	2	1	0	0	0	0
Jason Johnson	25	21	166	7.9	17.1	120	7	4	4	6	0	0	0
Scott Kamieniecki	35	3	0	0.0	0.0	77	3	0	0	0	0	0	0
Doug Linton	34	8	17	2.1	2.1	111	3	2	2	1	0	0	0
Mike Mussina	30	31	386	12.5	16.6	133	11	5	5	5	4	1	0
Sidney Ponson	22	32	345	10.8	28.8	129	5	8	8	8	3	0	0
Matt Riley	19	3	14	4.7	14.8	112	2	0	0	1	0	0	0
BALTIMORE		162	1806	11.1	17.5	133	46	26	37	32	19	2	0
Ranking (AL)			3	4									

We all have limitations. I can't sing. Joe Sheehan can't dunk. And Ray Miller can't manage. If he had known his limitations, or if he could have remembered back to his unsuccessful stint with the Twins in the mid-1980s, he might have remained one of the most respected pitching coaches in the game. Instead, he was unable to keep the Orioles' bullpen from imploding in the first half of the year, and while he had three veteran starters in Mike Mussina, Scott Erickson and Juan Guzman to work deep into games, he made the mistake of making Sidney Ponson do the same. Ponson, at midseason, had developed into one of the most promising young starters in baseball. His disintegration in the second half, culminating in an 8.44 ERA in September, makes a lost season for the Orioles even worse, as they've damaged one of the cornerstones of their rebuilding.... Mussina posted his lowest Workload in years and had a fine season. But given the load that was placed on him from the moment he arrived in the majors, I don't expect him to have an effective season after the age of 35 unless he reinvents himself as a finesse pitcher.

Boston Red Sox

Last year, for the first time in 13 years, Red Sox fans had reason to be happy during the postseason. With a record-setting romp over the Indians in the Division Series, they won their first October series since the 1986 ALCS. It was only their third postseason series win since 1918, the other being the 1975 ALCS.

The pinnacle of glee came during the over-hyped ALCS confrontation between Boston's greatest pitcher ever, Roger Clemens, and 1999 Cy Young winner Pedro Martinez. Martinez won the battle, dominating New York as the Sox thumped Clemens. But it was the Yankees—assisted by some terrible umpiring—who would win the ALCS and later the World Series. More cries of "wait 'til next year" went up from frustrated Boston fans.

The popular image of the 1999 Red Sox was one of a team consisting of two giants and 23 midgets. While it's true that a tremendous amount of the team's value is in its two superstars—Martinez and shortstop Nomar Garciaparra—the characterization fails to account for the team's genuinely excellent pitching. The Sox had the fourth-best record in the league at 94-68, while allowing the fewest runs in the league. Take away Pedro Martinez, and you still have the second-best pitching staff in the league; take away Garciaparra, and you have the 11th-best offense.

That pitching staff was fascinating. Boston led the AL in ERA for the first time since before women could vote, yet had only one pitcher with enough innings to qualify for the ERA title. No team had ever won 90 or more games with as many pitchers contributing as Boston sent to the mound, nor had any team ever done so without having at least two pitchers notch more than 10 wins—a feat the Sox accomplished. Pedro Martinez was the best pitcher in the league, setting a major-league record for strikeout rate. He was the second pitcher since World War II to win the AL's pitching Triple Crown outright, joining the aforementioned Clemens. He capped his season with two electrifying performances in the playoffs. Martinez was the unanimous Cy Young Award winner and runner-up in the AL MVP voting. He was even named the All-Star Game MVP.

Behind Martinez, the Boston rotation was managed masterfully amidst injuries and near-retirements. The starters averaged 88 pitches per start, the lowest in the majors, and ranked ninth in the league in number of 120-pitch starts. And the latter statistic is slightly deceiving, as all but two of the longer starts were by Martinez. Disregarding the top workhorse for each team, no team had fewer long starts than Boston. Given the surgically rebuilt arm of Bret Saberhagen and the emergence of young pitchers like Brian Rose and Juan Pena, a light workload is exactly what the Boston rotation needed.

As a result of the limitations placed on the starters, the bullpen was ridden hard. The average relief stint for a Boston pitcher was 21 pitches, and the pen threw more than 53 pitches per game—both figures sixth in the majors. Yet the pen did not wilt under this workload, despite the loss of closer Tom Gordon early in the year. Indeed, the bullpen was particularly sharp down the stretch, with a composite ERA more than a full run better in August, September and October (3.09) than in the four previous months (4.45). Derek Lowe, Rich Garces and Rheal Cormier anchored the pen, aided by surprise closer Tim Wakefield during the summer.

Boston's not-so-secret weapon is pitching coach Joe Kerrigan, who has duplicated his developmental and rehabilitative successes with Montreal in Boston, and has earned a mention alongside Leo Mazzone among the game's top pitching coaches. At this writing, Kerrigan is apparently frustrated at the paltry terms of the contract that the Red Sox are offering. A team that leans as heavily on its pitching as the Sox do needs a top-notch pitching coach in place to support that strength. The Sox should do everything to keep Kerrigan in the fold.

Pitching, though, is only half the story. You still have to put runs on the board. The problem for the Red Sox offense

Red Sox Prospectus

1999 record: 94-68; Second place, AL East; AL wild card; Lost to Yankees in ALCS, 4-1

Pythagorean W/L: 92-70

Runs scored: 836 (9th in AL)

Runs allowed: 718 (1st in AL)

Team EQA: .258 (8th in AL)

1999 team age: 29.4 (8th-oldest in AL)

1999 park: Fenway Park; good hitters' park, increased run scoring by 10%.

1999: Two great players and an excellent managing job pushed them into October.

2000: Their basic problems, rotation depth and a mediocre lineup, haven't been solved.

is that, with the exception of center field, there are no gaping holes on the team, making any significant improvement costly. Only Garciaparra, Jose Offerman and Jason Varitek were substantially above average for their positions in 1999. Brian Daubach, Troy O'Leary, Mike Stanley and Trot Nixon were solid individually, but combined, they gave the Red Sox nothing beyond what the typical AL team was getting at their positions. At third base, John Valentin was well below average but can be expected to return to league-average in 2000.

The exception, the Darren Lewis/Damon Buford platoon in center field, was among the least productive positions in the majors, combining for around 40 runs fewer than the league's average center fielder. Not even Lewis's outstanding defense is going to make up that difference. The situation should improve in 2000 with the addition of Carl Everett. Everett is unlikely to match his breakout 1999, but even a regression to his 1998 level will generate a lot of extra runs for the Sox.

Overseeing this peculiar collection of talent is ringmaster Jimy Williams, the 1999 AL Manager of the Year. While the award had as much to do with low media expectations for the team as with Williams's performance, he did many things right in '99. He has a knack for getting playing time for all of his position players, and he had the good sense to leverage Kerrigan's talents in handling the pitching staff. Perhaps more importantly, the players like and respect Williams, who has turned out to be the best antidote to the intelligent but impersonal Dan Duquette.

Yet at the same time, Williams's in-game management can be frustrating, as he misses obvious pinch-hit and platoon opportunities and fails to make pitching changes at critical junctures. These shortcomings are magnified in a short playoff series, and Williams was clearly outfoxed by Joe Torre in the late-inning chess games of the ALCS.

Given the tendency for managers such as Williams and Bobby Cox to be outmanaged in the playoffs, one wonders whether the next evolution in field management will be a position of "strategy coach," to go along with pitching, batting, base and bullpen coaches. Such a development wouldn't force managers to abdicate responsibility for in-game strategy. Rather, it would ensure that someone on the staff would be focused on staying three steps ahead of the opponent and ready to advise the manager in the same way that coaching specialists do.

On the other hand, a strategy coach would probably cut too close to the authority and ego of a manager, infringing on what has traditionally been his domain. The idea would no doubt meet with fierce resistance, so it will probably be a number of years before we see it attempted, if ever.

For the 2000 season, several of the team's better players, such as Garciaparra, Nixon, Varitek and Daubach, are already locked in at below-market rates and represent good value. The expensive, average players like Valentin, Stanley and O'Leary will be hard to move because they aren't good enough to demand much talent in return, and the Sox don't really need to dump their salaries as much as they need an infusion of superior position players. Precisely because so many of their players are average, getting a significant upgrade will come at a steep cost. The Sox will have to take on more salary than they care to, take a chance on someone else's headache or part with some of the jewels of their farm system to improve the offense in 2000.

Given the organizational pitching depth, their best trade bait might be Bret Saberhagen. He's still effective, and, when managed carefully, is almost as good as he was at his peak. A team in search of veteran pitching could be willing to give the Red Sox what they need. That would leave the Sox with a rotation of Pedro and Ramon Martinez as the top two starters, and the group of Lowe, Rose, Pena, Wakefield, Tomokazu Ohka and Jin Ho Cho vying for the other three slots. One or more of the young pitchers will probably be moved as well. A Martinez times two/Lowe/Rose/Pena rotation would be effective and affordable, even with Pedro's salary in the mix.

The key question for the Red Sox is simple: Is 2000 "next year"? For all their offensive shortcomings, the team still won 94 games in 1999, and had Bernie Williams chosen Boston over New York prior to the season, it could have been the Yankees fighting to hold off Oakland for the wild-card spot.

In Pedro Martinez, Garciaparra, Varitek and Nixon, the team has a core of players who will be peaking in the coming seasons. The farm system has a glut of talent that will arrive in the next two years. Both superstars are under contract at reasonable rates until 2004. That gives Duquette five seasons to leverage the farm system and find the pieces needed to assemble a championship team. Not a salary-efficient, waiver-wire contender, but an honest-to-goodness dominant force in the AL.

Five rolls of the dice, starting in 2000. As the luster of hosting the All-Star Game fades, and as the team faces the prospect of luring the faithful to a new Fenway, there would be no better incentive for fans to come out than a World Series winner.

HITTERS (Averages: BA: .270 / OBP: .340 / SLG: .430 / EQA: .260)

Israel Alcantara — OF — Bats R — Age 27

YEAR	TEAM	LGE	AB	H	DB	TP	HR	BB/SO	R	RBI	SB	CS	OUT	BA	OBP	SLG	EQA	EQR	DEFENSE	
1997	Harrisbg	Eas	302	70	11	2	17	19/95	33	44	2	2	234	.232	.282	.450	.239	33	38-3B 94	28-1B 89
1998	St Pete	Fla	143	35	3	0	7	15/37	14	16	0	0	108	.245	.322	.413	.248	16	22-3B 92	
1998	Reading	Eas	204	52	11	1	11	13/41	28	32	0	0	153	.255	.304	.480	.256	25		
1999	Trenton	Eas	296	72	17	0	15	19/91	35	42	2	1	225	.243	.295	.453	.246	34	45-OF 103	
1999	Pawtuckt	Int	81	19	4	0	6	7/32	10	16	0	0	62	.235	.315	.506	.267	11		
2000	Boston	AL	374	95	17	1	21	34/110	52	67	1	1	280	.254	.316	.473	.259	48		

Alcantara beat up Double-A pitching for most of the year, getting himself named to the Eastern League All-Star team. He got a brief trial at Pawtucket and continued to hit well, with more than half of his hits going for extra bases. Previously a poor defensive infielder, he moved to the outfield last year and did not embarrass himself. He's old for his level and has been considered a head case, which has held him back. He deserves a chance to be fourth outfielder in the majors.

Damon Buford — CF — Bats R — Age 30

YEAR	TEAM	LGE	AB	H	DB	TP	HR	BB/SO	R	RBI	SB	CS	OUT	BA	OBP	SLG	EQA	EQR	DEFENSE
1997	Texas	AL	365	81	13	0	10	28/80	47	39	18	7	291	.222	.284	.340	.216	31	117-OF 100
1998	Boston	AL	215	60	14	4	10	22/42	35	40	4	5	160	.279	.349	.521	.279	33	54-OF 108
1999	Boston	AL	295	69	16	2	5	18/74	35	34	9	2	228	.234	.283	.353	.218	25	72-CF 106
2000	ChiCubs	NL	253	63	12	2	9	24/60	36	35	9	3	193	.249	.314	.419	.244	28	

Buford returned to earth after one year of usefulness. He's still good defensively, but the entire package isn't worth more than the major-league minimum. He's been traded to the Cubs for Manny Alexander, and is expected to be the everyday center fielder for them, so the projected playing time above—while what he deserves—may be light.

Morgan Burkhart — 1B — Bats B — Age 28

YEAR	TEAM	LGE	AB	H	DB	TP	HR	BB/SO	R	RBI	SB	CS	OUT	BA	OBP	SLG	EQA	EQR	DEFENSE
1999	Sarasota	Fla	251	69	11	0	17	27/42	37	43	2	1	183	.275	.353	.522	.286	40	56-1B 97
1999	Trenton	Eas	244	48	12	1	9	22/50	30	30	1	0	196	.197	.281	.365	.218	22	18-1B 72
2000	Boston	AL	249	61	10	0	21	32/59	40	56	1	0	188	.245	.331	.538	.281	39	

Burkhart spent four years in the Frontier League, winning the Triple Crown in 1998 and setting several league records in the process. *Baseball America* named him the best first baseman in A ball in 1999, and he was promoted to Trenton in late June. He tore up the Mexican Fall League, batting over .400 and leading the league in most offensive categories. Best-case scenario? He could be the next Erubiel Durazo. If he gets called up, he would be the first Frontier League alumnus to reach the majors.

James Chamblee — 2B/OF — Bats R — Age 25

YEAR	TEAM	LGE	AB	H	DB	TP	HR	BB/SO	R	RBI	SB	CS	OUT	BA	OBP	SLG	EQA	EQR	DEFENSE	
1997	Michigan	Mid	498	128	26	3	19	39/115	81	54	7	2	372	.257	.327	.436	.257	62	103-2B 96	22-SS 105
1998	Trenton	Eas	497	112	32	2	16	52/145	62	58	6	3	388	.225	.315	.394	.241	55	131-2B 97	
1999	Pawtuckt	Int	461	114	18	2	20	35/130	66	69	3	2	349	.247	.316	.425	.248	53	101-2B 98	21-3B 80
2000	Boston	AL	530	137	26	2	21	56/145	77	86	4	2	395	.258	.329	.434	.255	65		

Chamblee had been removed from the 40-man roster, which probably cost him the promotion to Boston that went to Wilton Veras instead. An International League All-Star in 1999, he could make a nice Rule 5 draft pick. He's got a strong arm, good size (6'4" and lanky) and good power for a middle infielder. If he makes more consistent contact—strikeouts are a problem— he's a solid major leaguer. Among Chamblee, Jose Offerman, David Eckstein and Adam Everett, there's enough organizational depth at second base to make one or more expendable via trade. Management seems to recognize this, and a position shift may be in the works for Chamblee, as he's being used as an outfielder in the Mexican Fall League.

Michael Coleman   CF   Bats R   Age 24

YEAR	TEAM	LGE	AB	H	DB	TP	HR	BB/SO	R	RBI	SB	CS	OUT	BA	OBP	SLG	EQA	EQR	DEFENSE
1997	Trenton	Eas	390	109	17	7	12	31/92	44	48	13	4	285	.279	.338	.451	.266	52	102-OF 106
1997	Pawtuckt	Int	113	33	9	2	6	10/26	23	16	3	1	81	.292	.359	.566	.299	20	27-OF 96
1998	Pawtuckt	Int	340	80	9	0	13	21/93	39	32	8	6	266	.235	.294	.376	.225	32	87-OF 100
1999	Pawtuckt	Int	464	115	26	3	25	43/128	77	60	10	5	354	.248	.315	.478	.261	62	109-OF 108
2000	*Boston*	*AL*	*455*	*124*	*23*	*2*	*25*	*48/120*	*78*	*87*	*11*	*4*	*335*	*.273*	*.342*	*.497*	*.277*	*67*	

Coleman reestablished himself as one of the top prospects in the system after a disappointing 1998. As an excellent defensive outfielder with power, he deserves at least a platoon job in center field for Boston in 2000, especially considering Carl Everett's large platoon split. There is still an occasional attitude problem that could keep the organization from embracing him.

Brian Daubach   1B   Bats L   Age 28

YEAR	TEAM	LGE	AB	H	DB	TP	HR	BB/SO	R	RBI	SB	CS	OUT	BA	OBP	SLG	EQA	EQR	DEFENSE	
1997	Charlott	Int	463	109	30	2	16	50/134	51	70	1	5	359	.235	.317	.413	.243	52	97-1B 97	
1998	Charlott	Int	496	130	38	3	24	62/127	76	89	5	2	368	.262	.358	.496	.283	78	101-OF 82	21-1B 109
1999	Boston	AL	376	108	33	3	19	32/92	55	65	0	1	269	.287	.348	.543	.288	60	54-1B 107	
2000	*Boston*	*AL*	*441*	*116*	*34*	*2*	*20*	*55/112*	*75*	*82*	*1*	*1*	*326*	*.263*	*.345*	*.485*	*.274*	*64*		

Daubach was one of the great stories of 1999. A 27-year-old hitter who was released by the Marlins after a great 1998, he replaced Mo Vaughn at first base and out-hit him for most of the year. He's probably not going to get better than this, and the way he looked in September (.173/.246/.327) makes you wonder if the league has figured him out. He's very patient at the plate, leading the team in pitches seen per plate appearance.

Joe DePastino   C   Bats R   Age 26

YEAR	TEAM	LGE	AB	H	DB	TP	HR	BB/SO	R	RBI	SB	CS	OUT	BA	OBP	SLG	EQA	EQR	DEFENSE
1997	Trenton	Eas	281	66	15	1	13	23/67	40	43	1	1	216	.235	.304	.434	.245	32	
1998	Trenton	Eas	279	72	12	0	9	22/55	28	36	2	0	207	.258	.314	.398	.241	30	56-C 103
1999	Trenton	Eas	23	4	2	0	1	3/3	3	3	0	0	19	.174	.286	.391	.228	2	
1999	Pawtuckt	Int	256	56	9	0	10	21/44	26	38	1	1	201	.219	.280	.371	.217	22	72-C 102
2000	*Boston*	*AL*	*255*	*61*	*10*	*0*	*12*	*26/47*	*33*	*39*	*1*	*0*	*194*	*.239*	*.310*	*.420*	*.244*	*28*	

DePastino won the Pawtucket catching job over Mandy Romero, who was later dealt to the Mets. He has a good arm and pitchers seem to like throwing to him. His future with Boston is uncertain, as he's blocked by Jason Varitek and Scott Hatteberg and getting pushed by Steve Lomasney. His best chance of making the majors is if Hatteberg is traded.

David Eckstein   2B   Bats R   Age 25

YEAR	TEAM	LGE	AB	H	DB	TP	HR	BB/SO	R	RBI	SB	CS	OUT	BA	OBP	SLG	EQA	EQR	DEFENSE
1997	Lowell	NYP	256	61	10	2	4	25/34	26	27	7	2	197	.238	.321	.340	.232	25	64-2B 98
1998	Sarasota	Fla	509	121	26	2	2	65/62	60	39	14	7	395	.238	.340	.308	.231	51	115-2B 102
1999	Trenton	Eas	492	131	22	3	4	69/54	78	39	14	7	368	.266	.375	.348	.257	62	126-2B 99
2000	*Boston*	*AL*	*430*	*110*	*21*	*2*	*3*	*67/49*	*75*	*46*	*12*	*5*	*325*	*.256*	*.356*	*.335*	*.245*	*48*	

Baseball America named him the best second baseman in Double-A, and Eastern League managers named him the league's best defensive second baseman, despite a below-average arm. He embraces his role as a leadoff hitter, and his .440 OBP was second in the league. A big area of improvement was staying strong the whole year, due in part to a regimen of lifting weights after every game. Eckstein is a B+ second-base prospect with an offensive upside comparable to Jose Offerman.

Adam Everett   SS   Bats R   Age 23

YEAR	TEAM	LGE	AB	H	DB	TP	HR	BB/SO	R	RBI	SB	CS	OUT	BA	OBP	SLG	EQA	EQR	DEFENSE
1998	Lowell	NYP	73	18	7	1	0	9/13	8	6	1	0	55	.247	.342	.370	.249	9	20-SS 96
1999	Trenton	Eas	343	87	9	0	10	33/66	45	39	12	3	259	.254	.332	.367	.244	38	97-SS 95
2000	*Houston*	*NL*	*186*	*47*	*5*	*0*	*8*	*22/48*	*28*	*27*	*7*	*1*	*140*	*.253*	*.332*	*.409*	*.258*	*24*	

(Adam Everett *continued*)

One of the jewels of the system. He jumped straight to Double-A after just a month of rookie ball in 1998. He's strong-armed, sure-handed and can go deep into the hole; some consider Everett to be the best middle-infield glove ever to play at Trenton. Listed at 6' and 156 pounds, his size raises concerns about his endurance and stamina, and he might benefit by bulking up a bit. Everett was often compared to Nomar Garciaparra early on, and that may have put too much pressure on him. He was hitting .207/.319/.233 after 116 at-bats, then was dropped from #2 to #9 in the lineup and hit .293/.375/.464 the rest of the way.

Everett was traded to the Astros for center fielder Carl Everett. With the loss of Ricky Gutierrez, the Houston shortstop job is wide open, and Everett goes into the spring with a chance at it. The organization will be under some pressure to justify trading Carl Everett, so he may have a slight advantage over Julio Lugo.

Chad Fonville   IF   Bats B   Age 29

YEAR	TEAM	LGE	AB	H	DB	TP	HR	BB/SO	R	RBI	SB	CS	OUT	BA	OBP	SLG	EQA	EQR	DEFENSE	
1997	Albuquer	PCL	363	64	3	2	0	20/44	31	16	14	7	306	.176	.224	.196	.123	8	47-OF 92	25-2B 97
1998	New Havn	Eas	193	45	1	0	0	18/26	19	8	9	3	151	.233	.301	.238	.193	12	29-OF 93	
1999	Pawtuckt	Int	256	57	3	1	1	15/34	24	11	4	3	202	.223	.270	.254	.172	12	18-SS 97	17-2B 96
2000	*Boston*	*AL*	*224*	*47*	*4*	*0*	*0*	*16/29*	*15*	*9*	*6*	*3*	*180*	*.210*	*.262*	*.228*	*.155*	*9*		

Fonville plays multiple positions but doesn't hit well enough to start at any of them. He's a waste of a roster spot in Pawtucket, taking playing time from more worthy players.

Jeff Frye   2B   Bats R   Age 33

YEAR	TEAM	LGE	AB	H	DB	TP	HR	BB/SO	R	RBI	SB	CS	OUT	BA	OBP	SLG	EQA	EQR	DEFENSE
1997	Boston	AL	403	126	36	2	3	25/42	54	49	19	8	285	.313	.356	.434	.269	53	79-2B 102
1999	Pawtuckt	Int	9	2	0	0	0	2/1	0	1	0	0	7	.222	.364	.222	.220	1	
1999	Boston	AL	113	31	2	0	1	12/11	12	11	2	2	84	.274	.349	.319	.233	11	23-2B 92
2000	*Boston*	*AL*	*95*	*27*	*3*	*0*	*2*	*10/20*	*14*	*13*	*2*	*2*	*70*	*.284*	*.352*	*.379*	*.248*	*11*	

Frye is a great example of a player who shouldn't get a three-year contract. At the time of the deal, he was 30 years old and injury-prone, and his production wasn't all that great. The $2.5 million he's making in 2000 is an awful lot to spend on a sixth infielder, and I can't imagine that there are many takers for Frye on the trade front.

Nomar Garciaparra   SS   Bats R   Age 26

YEAR	TEAM	LGE	AB	H	DB	TP	HR	BB/SO	R	RBI	SB	CS	OUT	BA	OBP	SLG	EQA	EQR	DEFENSE
1997	Boston	AL	683	210	45	12	30	31/88	119	96	22	9	482	.307	.344	.540	.287	107	151-SS 99
1998	Boston	AL	602	195	38	9	34	31/61	106	117	10	6	413	.324	.365	.586	.304	105	143-SS 94
1999	Boston	AL	522	183	44	4	24	44/39	93	93	14	3	342	.351	.409	.588	.326	103	132-SS 100
2000	*Boston*	*AL*	*582*	*193*	*39*	*7*	*33*	*48/53*	*120*	*140*	*14*	*4*	*393*	*.332*	*.383*	*.593*	*.315*	*110*	

Batting champion, cornerstone of the offense, one of the best players in the league . . . and still getting better. He's a marvel to watch: fidgety in the batters box, smooth grace in the field. Garciaparra is an Extremely Aggressive Hitter; he saw fewer pitches per plate appearance than anyone on the team with significant playing time, but you can't argue with the results. His defensive reputation is seriously inflated in Boston, but he's still neck-and-neck with Derek Jeter and Alex Rodriguez for the title of best shortstop in baseball heading into 2000.

David Gibralter   1B   Bats R   Age 25

YEAR	TEAM	LGE	AB	H	DB	TP	HR	BB/SO	R	RBI	SB	CS	OUT	BA	OBP	SLG	EQA	EQR	DEFENSE
1997	Trenton	Eas	485	125	25	1	12	32/107	58	72	2	3	363	.258	.312	.388	.235	49	114-1B 98
1998	Trenton	Eas	389	95	12	0	15	20/92	42	55	1	2	296	.244	.291	.391	.226	36	90-1B 85
1999	Trenton	Eas	452	116	17	1	19	21/77	58	73	2	2	338	.257	.302	.425	.241	48	99-1B 84
2000	*Boston*	*AL*	*437*	*118*	*17*	*1*	*21*	*30/85*	*55*	*76*	*1*	*1*	*320*	*.270*	*.317*	*.458*	*.255*	*53*	

Gibralter refused to play in Mexico when he was asked to go there after 1998, but responded with a career high in home runs in his third season at Double-A. He's a six-year minor-league free agent, blocked by Daubach and Dernell Stenson, and will probably move to another organization.

Raul Gonzalez   OF   Bats R   Age 26

YEAR	TEAM	LGE	AB	H	DB	TP	HR	BB/SO	R	RBI	SB	CS	OUT	BA	OBP	SLG	EQA	EQR	DEFENSE
1997	Wichita	Tex	448	108	27	2	11	27/60	47	53	7	4	344	.241	.287	.384	.224	41	99-OF 88
1998	Wichita	Tex	445	109	18	1	11	42/64	51	54	5	4	340	.245	.312	.364	.230	43	101-OF 90
1999	Trenton	Eas	510	140	30	2	13	35/83	59	74	5	2	372	.275	.323	.418	.250	58	119-OF 101
2000	Boston	AL	482	129	20	1	16	46/74	66	74	3	2	355	.268	.331	.413	.250	56	

Gonzalez made the Eastern League All-Star team, hit .335 and set club records for hits and RBIs. He dropped 15 pounds before 1999 and worked on his defense to the point where he can play any of the outfield spots. This was his fourth year at Double-A, which at age 26 doesn't bode well—he's just beating up on younger competition with that compact, line-drive stroke.

Creighton Gubanich   C   Bats R   Age 28

YEAR	TEAM	LGE	AB	H	DB	TP	HR	BB/SO	R	RBI	SB	CS	OUT	BA	OBP	SLG	EQA	EQR	DEFENSE
1997	Edmonton	PCL	139	35	8	0	5	10/47	14	21	0	1	105	.252	.309	.417	.241	15	
1997	Tucson	PCL	82	23	2	0	4	0/21	9	12	1	0	59	.280	.287	.451	.244	9	
1998	LasVegas	PCL	288	69	14	0	14	23/93	33	49	1	1	220	.240	.301	.434	.243	32	67-C 89
1999	Pawtuckt	Int	91	22	1	0	4	5/25	9	7	0	0	69	.242	.281	.385	.221	8	19-C 98
1999	Boston	AL	47	13	1	1	1	2/13	3	10	0	0	34	.277	.333	.404	.250	5	
2000	Milwauke	NL	177	43	5	0	9	14/55	18	27	0	0	134	.243	.298	.424	.238	19	

Gubanich provides a little pop out of the backup catcher slot, which isn't bad for the major-league minimum. He beats out Nomar Garciaparra for the coveted "most unusual name" award. The competition in Milwaukee is Henry Blanco and Bobby Hughes, so this will be his last best chance to carve out a career.

Scott Hatteberg   C   Bats L   Age 30

YEAR	TEAM	LGE	AB	H	DB	TP	HR	BB/SO	R	RBI	SB	CS	OUT	BA	OBP	SLG	EQA	EQR	DEFENSE
1997	Boston	AL	349	98	22	1	11	38/67	45	44	0	1	252	.281	.355	.444	.269	47	
1998	Boston	AL	358	99	21	1	13	42/57	44	42	0	0	259	.277	.361	.450	.274	51	103-C 100
1999	Boston	AL	81	22	4	0	1	17/14	11	10	0	0	59	.272	.404	.358	.274	12	
1999	Pawtuckt	Int	35	6	1	0	0	3/7	2	3	0	0	29	.171	.237	.200	.123	1	
2000	Boston	AL	162	44	7	0	6	24/28	27	28	0	0	118	.272	.366	.426	.270	22	

Hatteberg lost his starting catcher job to Jason Varitek after an elbow injury sidelined him for most of the first half. He's still an above-average offensive catcher and is considered prime trade bait for a team in need of a receiver who can hit a little. He has trouble with left-handed pitchers and probably needs to be platooned.

Butch Huskey   OF/1B/3B Bats R   Age 28

YEAR	TEAM	LGE	AB	H	DB	TP	HR	BB/SO	R	RBI	SB	CS	OUT	BA	OBP	SLG	EQA	EQR	DEFENSE	
1997	NY Mets	NL	476	137	27	2	25	25/83	61	81	6	5	344	.288	.325	.511	.271	66	79-OF 102	14-1B 96
1998	NY Mets	NL	375	100	15	1	15	25/64	45	63	8	7	282	.267	.314	.432	.247	43	90-OF 99	
1999	Seattle	AL	259	73	7	0	15	23/45	39	45	3	1	187	.282	.340	.483	.273	36	26-LF 106	20-RF 103
1999	Boston	AL	123	32	4	0	7	6/20	16	26	0	0	91	.260	.295	.463	.248	14		
2000	Boston	AL	338	96	10	0	21	31/57	52	69	4	2	244	.284	.344	.500	.277	49		

The closest thing to a big trade for the stretch drive Duquette made was acquiring Huskey from Seattle. He provided some needed power against left-handers but overall wasn't noticeably more productive than O'Leary, Nixon, Stanley or Daubach—whose at-bats he was getting. He was non-tendered and was a free agent in late December.

Reggie Jefferson   DH   Bats L   Age 31

YEAR	TEAM	LGE	AB	H	DB	TP	HR	BB/SO	R	RBI	SB	CS	OUT	BA	OBP	SLG	EQA	EQR	DEFENSE
1997	Boston	AL	488	158	29	2	14	21/89	71	66	1	2	332	.324	.362	.477	.279	68	
1998	Boston	AL	195	60	16	1	8	21/39	23	30	0	0	135	.308	.378	.523	.297	32	
1999	Boston	AL	204	55	12	1	5	14/54	19	16	0	0	149	.270	.323	.412	.247	23	
2000	Boston	AL	168	49	8	0	5	16/38	25	28	0	0	119	.292	.353	.429	.264	21	

(Reggie Jefferson *continued*)

He stopped hitting last year, losing the only skill that made him remotely valuable. Jefferson stormed off the team after being left off the playoff roster in the first round, which didn't endear him to management or his teammates. It's too bad, because the Red Sox could have used his bat against the Yankees in the ALCS. Jefferson is not a Team Player™.

Darren Lewis   CF   Bats R   Age 32

YEAR	TEAM	LGE	AB	H	DB	TP	HR	BB/SO	R	RBI	SB	CS	OUT	BA	OBP	SLG	EQA	EQR	DEFENSE	
1997	ChiSox	AL	77	18	1	0	0	11/13	15	5	11	4	63	.234	.330	.247	.222	7	45-OF 87	
1997	LosAngls	NL	79	25	3	1	1	6/17	7	10	3	2	56	.316	.365	.418	.265	10	17-OF 117	
1998	Boston	AL	583	156	25	3	8	68/92	89	60	26	12	439	.268	.352	.362	.250	69	147-OF 111	
1999	Boston	AL	466	107	12	6	2	40/52	56	36	16	10	369	.230	.297	.294	.204	35	83-CF 109	43-RF 106
2000	*Boston*	*AL*	*394*	*100*	*15*	*2*	*3*	*46/52*	*57*	*39*	*14*	*9*	*303*	*.254*	*.332*	*.325*	*.227*	*37*		

Lewis is less powerful than the League of Nations. He tied Brian L. Hunter for the second-lowest isolated power in the league, behind shortstop Mike Caruso of the White Sox. His glove is fantastic, and on a staff like Boston's, you have to give him some additional credit for keeping the Bret Saberhagens and Juan Penas from having to throw to an extra batter here or there. On the other hand, a real hitter would have produced some extra runs, allowing the Sox to turn the game over to middle relief without worrying. He's signed for 2000, so he will be back in a defensive-replacement role.

Steve Lomasney   C   Bats R   Age 22

YEAR	TEAM	LGE	AB	H	DB	TP	HR	BB/SO	R	RBI	SB	CS	OUT	BA	OBP	SLG	EQA	EQR	DEFENSE
1997	Michigan	Mid	331	81	23	2	11	24/102	39	39	1	2	252	.245	.310	.426	.244	37	
1998	Sarasota	Fla	446	93	16	1	20	48/159	55	49	5	2	355	.209	.301	.383	.233	46	83-C 99
1999	Sarasota	Fla	193	48	8	0	9	22/63	29	25	2	1	146	.249	.340	.430	.260	25	47-C 104
1999	Trenton	Eas	154	35	4	0	11	26/45	19	26	4	3	122	.227	.361	.468	.276	24	46-C 95
2000	*Boston*	*AL*	*397*	*98*	*16*	*1*	*21*	*54/130*	*63*	*70*	*6*	*3*	*302*	*.247*	*.337*	*.451*	*.263*	*54*	

He's the top catching prospect in the organization, and the second-best positional prospect behind Dernell Stenson. Boston hasn't developed a good starting catcher since Rich Gedman, but Lomasney should peak somewhere between him and Carlton Fisk. Scouts think he has 30-home-run potential. His batting average is low, but it's not due to a long swing. He may take too many strikes. Defensively, he has a good arm and is agile behind the plate. The ERAs of four Thunder pitchers dropped by an average of 1.2 runs after he starting catching at Trenton. Coincidence? Probably. All-Star potential? Definitely.

Lou Merloni   IF   Bats R   Age 29

YEAR	TEAM	LGE	AB	H	DB	TP	HR	BB/SO	R	RBI	SB	CS	OUT	BA	OBP	SLG	EQA	EQR	DEFENSE	
1997	Trenton	Eas	259	66	15	3	3	20/50	35	26	2	1	194	.255	.327	.371	.239	27	53-3B 101	
1997	Pawtuckt	Int	166	43	5	0	5	10/21	18	20	0	1	124	.259	.315	.380	.233	16	33-2B 96	
1998	Pawtuckt	Int	87	28	4	1	5	13/14	13	15	1	1	60	.322	.446	.563	.331	19		
1998	Boston	AL	96	27	4	0	2	6/20	10	16	1	0	69	.281	.337	.385	.249	11	24-2B 98	
1999	Boston	AL	125	31	3	0	2	7/16	15	13	0	0	94	.248	.298	.320	.209	9		
1999	Pawtuckt	Int	228	54	10	1	5	24/42	33	26	1	1	175	.237	.329	.355	.236	24	28-SS 95	24-3B 110

When you're an adequate but unremarkable bench player, the best job security comes from being a local hero and a close personal friend of the team's best player. Merloni will play in Japan in 2000.

Trot Nixon   RF   Bats L   Age 26

YEAR	TEAM	LGE	AB	H	DB	TP	HR	BB/SO	R	RBI	SB	CS	OUT	BA	OBP	SLG	EQA	EQR	DEFENSE
1997	Pawtuckt	Int	478	111	18	2	19	53/84	69	54	8	3	370	.232	.310	.397	.240	52	130-OF 101
1998	Pawtuckt	Int	507	140	24	3	18	63/85	76	59	15	9	376	.276	.361	.442	.271	72	125-OF 94
1999	Boston	AL	376	99	23	5	13	48/75	60	46	3	1	278	.263	.351	.455	.271	53	115-RF 97
2000	*Boston*	*AL*	*447*	*118*	*22*	*4*	*18*	*60/82*	*78*	*77*	*8*	*4*	*333*	*.264*	*.351*	*.452*	*.270*	*63*	

If a player could win Comeback Player of the Year as a rookie, Nixon might have done it. He started the year in a horrible funk, hitting .105/.209/.263 in April, but rebounded to hit .296/.389/.587 after the All-Star break. Nixon needs to start hitting left-handers, but didn't get much of a chance in 1999: just 43 at-bats. It will be interesting to see what Nixon, having made the adjustment to the majors, can do in 2000.

Jon Nunnally   OF   Bats L   Age 28

YEAR	TEAM	LGE	AB	H	DB	TP	HR	BB/SO	R	RBI	SB	CS	OUT	BA	OBP	SLG	EQA	EQR	DEFENSE
1997	Omaha	AA	229	51	10	1	10	32/75	26	24	5	2	180	.223	.326	.406	.250	28	67-OF 109
1997	Cincnnti	NL	202	63	13	3	13	26/50	37	34	5	3	142	.312	.396	.599	.317	40	51-OF 106
1998	Cincnnti	NL	176	38	7	0	8	34/37	29	21	3	5	143	.216	.346	.392	.250	22	51-OF 108
1998	Indianap	Int	293	64	17	1	8	37/79	41	41	4	3	232	.218	.310	.365	.230	30	77-OF 96
1999	Pawtuckt	Int	493	110	21	2	16	69/113	64	54	16	3	386	.223	.321	.371	.242	56	119-OF 98
2000	*NY Mets*	*NL*	*465*	*108*	*19*	*0*	*20*	*70/116*	*68*	*68*	*9*	*4*	*361*	*.232*	*.333*	*.402*	*.254*	*59*	

Knowledgeable fans were clamoring for his promotion as he tore apart Triple-A pitching early in the year, but he faded in the second half to post merely respectable numbers. Nunnally still would have been better to have in Boston than Buford, without sacrificing much defensively, but he was ignored by management. He doesn't have anything to prove in the minors. Traded to the Mets, he'll battle for the fifth outfielder job.

Jose Offerman   2B   Bats B   Age 31

YEAR	TEAM	LGE	AB	H	DB	TP	HR	BB/SO	R	RBI	SB	CS	OUT	BA	OBP	SLG	EQA	EQR	DEFENSE
1997	KansasCy	AL	421	123	23	6	2	38/61	56	37	9	10	308	.292	.351	.390	.250	48	99-2B 88
1998	KansasCy	AL	599	184	26	13	7	86/94	93	61	39	12	427	.307	.399	.429	.289	96	153-2B 97
1999	Boston	AL	576	163	34	11	7	88/79	95	61	18	13	425	.283	.380	.417	.273	82	123-2B 94
2000	*Boston*	*AL*	*500*	*143*	*29*	*9*	*5*	*78/71*	*101*	*73*	*14*	*10*	*367*	*.286*	*.382*	*.410*	*.272*	*71*	

Hired to be a first-class leadoff hitter and not a Mo Vaughn replacement, Offerman did his job quite well, earning a spot on the All-Star team in the process. His defensive skills are widely derided, but the talk is overblown. He's slightly below average, with above-average range offsetting some problems turning the double play. There's been some talk of moving him to center field, as the Sox have several second-base prospects nearing the majors.

Troy O'Leary   LF   Bats L   Age 30

YEAR	TEAM	LGE	AB	H	DB	TP	HR	BB/SO	R	RBI	SB	CS	OUT	BA	OBP	SLG	EQA	EQR	DEFENSE
1997	Boston	AL	498	156	33	4	15	36/67	63	78	0	5	347	.313	.362	.486	.279	71	131-OF 94
1998	Boston	AL	610	166	36	9	22	34/106	92	79	2	2	446	.272	.316	.469	.258	76	153-OF 97
1999	Boston	AL	589	161	38	4	25	49/91	76	92	1	2	430	.273	.333	.479	.268	80	153-LF 104
2000	*Boston*	*AL*	*498*	*141*	*32*	*3*	*18*	*51/78*	*81*	*89*	*1*	*2*	*359*	*.283*	*.350*	*.468*	*.271*	*69*	

O'Leary set career highs in hits, home runs and RBIs—largely due to appearing in 157 games. He'll deserve all the credit if Garciaparra sees his intentional-walk totals drop dramatically (following O'Leary's Division Series Game 4 performance). He continues to improve defensively, as well.

    O'Leary is nonetheless emblematic of the dilemma the Sox face in trying to improve their offense. He's a league-average left fielder, which is fairly valuable, and is making significant but not outrageous money ($4 million for 2000). He's not a gaping hole, but the cost to improve the position will be high, either in prospects or salary. The choices are overpaying to get better production or coasting along with a mediocre offensive team.

Donnie Sadler   UT   Bats R   Age 25

YEAR	TEAM	LGE	AB	H	DB	TP	HR	BB/SO	R	RBI	SB	CS	OUT	BA	OBP	SLG	EQA	EQR	DEFENSE	
1997	Pawtuckt	Int	485	99	18	2	10	47/118	64	32	15	10	396	.204	.277	.311	.200	36	79-2B 99	46-SS 96
1998	Pawtuckt	Int	131	27	4	1	2	23/23	20	9	7	1	105	.206	.325	.298	.229	13	32-2B 100	
1998	Boston	AL	124	28	5	4	3	5/27	20	15	3	0	96	.226	.273	.403	.229	12	37-2B 95	
1999	Pawtuckt	Int	171	45	10	3	1	13/37	18	14	3	2	128	.263	.325	.374	.238	18	36-SS 97	
1999	Boston	AL	106	29	4	1	0	4/20	16	4	2	1	78	.274	.300	.330	.213	8		
2000	*Boston*	*AL*	*330*	*84*	*12*	*4*	*7*	*30/70*	*46*	*41*	*11*	*5*	*251*	*.255*	*.317*	*.379*	*.237*	*34*		

Boston's answer to Herb Washington. OK, that's too harsh. Sadler is fast and a good defender, capable of playing shortstop, second base or even the outfield in a pinch. He still hasn't shown he can hit major-league pitching.

Mike Stanley   1B/DH   Bats R   Age 37

YEAR	TEAM	LGE	AB	H	DB	TP	HR	BB/SO	R	RBI	SB	CS	OUT	BA	OBP	SLG	EQA	EQR	DEFENSE	
1997	Boston	AL	259	79	15	0	14	37/48	44	53	0	1	181	.305	.406	.525	.308	48	23-1B 97	
1997	NY Yanks	AL	87	26	6	0	4	15/21	16	13	0	0	61	.299	.402	.506	.304	16		
1998	Toronto	AL	340	82	11	0	23	54/84	47	46	2	1	259	.241	.354	.476	.277	52	20-1B 95	
1998	Boston	AL	155	45	8	0	8	26/42	23	31	1	0	110	.290	.399	.497	.302	27		
1999	Boston	AL	420	115	18	0	19	64/94	53	66	0	0	305	.274	.384	.452	.285	66	100-1B 106	
2000	*Boston*	*AL*	*341*	*87*	*10*	*0*	*16*	*65/78*	*60*	*63*	*0*	*0*	*254*	*.255*	*.374*	*.425*	*.274*	*50*		

Stanley defied the aging process for another year, putting up a fine season at first base. He has a decent shot at reaching 200 career home runs—pretty remarkable since he had just 24 in 1,160 at-bats through age 30. With enough 1999 plate appearances to automatically trigger an option for 2000, he'll get plenty of time at first base and DH for the Sox.

Dernell Stenson   1B   Bats L   Age 22

YEAR	TEAM	LGE	AB	H	DB	TP	HR	BB/SO	R	RBI	SB	CS	OUT	BA	OBP	SLG	EQA	EQR	DEFENSE
1997	Michigan	Mid	485	124	29	1	15	56/110	62	63	3	2	363	.256	.351	.412	.261	63	105-OF 83
1998	Trenton	Eas	514	127	18	1	24	74/132	81	66	3	2	389	.247	.355	.426	.266	71	132-OF 93
1999	Pawtuckt	Int	437	110	26	2	15	47/119	53	67	1	1	328	.252	.332	.423	.254	54	113-1B 71
2000	*Boston*	*AL*	*477*	*128*	*21*	*1*	*23*	*70/123*	*81*	*91*	*2*	*1*	*350*	*.268*	*.362*	*.461*	*.277*	*70*	

Stenson declined offensively as he struggled with the transition from the outfield to first base, where he was brutal defensively. A smart batter with an even temperament, he's projected to be a franchise hitter. He still has trouble with breaking balls but is willing to take outside pitches the other way and has no fear of left-handers. His ETA in Boston is 2001, but he could be up late this year.

John Valentin   3B   Bats R   Age 33

YEAR	TEAM	LGE	AB	H	DB	TP	HR	BB/SO	R	RBI	SB	CS	OUT	BA	OBP	SLG	EQA	EQR	DEFENSE	
1997	Boston	AL	573	177	48	6	18	55/63	93	75	7	4	400	.309	.375	.508	.292	92	78-2B 108	63-3B 98
1998	Boston	AL	587	146	38	2	24	74/80	107	71	3	5	446	.249	.342	.443	.262	79	152-3B 109	
1999	Boston	AL	446	110	26	1	11	35/68	52	63	0	1	337	.247	.307	.383	.232	44	107-3B 110	
2000	*Boston*	*AL*	*467*	*119*	*25*	*1*	*16*	*56/65*	*68*	*72*	*1*	*2*	*350*	*.255*	*.335*	*.415*	*.252*	*56*		

Last year was dismal for Valentin. Hampered by injuries, he was unable to bounce back from a substandard 1998, and now hears Wilton Veras's footsteps behind him. His performance in the postseason was a pleasant reminder of what he can do when healthy, and he remains a fine defensive third baseman. His contract is a lodestone in any potential trade, so chances are he'll be back with the Sox.

Jason Varitek   C   Bats B   Age 28

YEAR	TEAM	LGE	AB	H	DB	TP	HR	BB/SO	R	RBI	SB	CS	OUT	BA	OBP	SLG	EQA	EQR	DEFENSE
1997	Tacoma	PCL	302	63	8	0	11	25/80	36	32	0	1	240	.209	.273	.344	.205	23	
1998	Boston	AL	222	56	11	0	8	16/44	30	33	2	2	168	.252	.309	.410	.240	24	57-C 93
1999	Boston	AL	488	128	38	2	19	41/85	64	70	1	2	362	.262	.322	.465	.260	62	130-C 92
2000	*Boston*	*AL*	*407*	*103*	*23*	*1*	*17*	*37/76*	*55*	*65*	*1*	*1*	*305*	*.253*	*.315*	*.440*	*.250*	*48*	

Varitek took advantage of Hatteberg's injury to become the second-best offensive catcher in the AL. He hit equally well from both sides of the plate last year and is good defensively—his high passed-ball total comes from catching Tim Wakefield's knuckler. The deal that brought Varitek and Derek Lowe to Boston for Heathcliff Slocumb is starting to look like Jeff Bagwell for Larry Andersen in reverse.

Wilton Veras   3B   Bats R   Age 22

YEAR	TEAM	LGE	AB	H	DB	TP	HR	BB/SO	R	RBI	SB	CS	OUT	BA	OBP	SLG	EQA	EQR	DEFENSE
1997	Michigan	Mid	498	131	20	2	8	20/53	41	55	1	1	368	.263	.298	.359	.221	42	128-3B 95
1998	Trenton	Eas	474	132	28	3	16	10/64	64	62	3	3	345	.278	.301	.451	.247	52	126-3B 99
1999	Trenton	Eas	479	127	22	1	11	14/57	57	65	4	3	355	.265	.291	.384	.225	42	115-3B 109
1999	Boston	AL	117	32	5	1	2	4/14	13	12	0	2	87	.274	.309	.385	.227	11	33-3B 101
2000	*Boston*	*AL*	*491*	*142*	*19*	*1*	*14*	*23/59*	*58*	*74*	*2*	*2*	*351*	*.289*	*.321*	*.418*	*.246*	*52*	

He blew past Cole Liniak to become the organization's top third-base prospect, making Liniak trade bait for Rod Beck in the process. Veras shows signs of brilliance as a hitter but hasn't yet shown the patience that could make him a superstar. Of course, Garciaparra doesn't walk a great deal either, but projecting that kind of development, even with Veras being younger than Garciaparra was at the same stage, is speculative.

PITCHERS (Averages: ERA: 4.50 / H/9: 9.00 / HR/9: 1.00 / BB/9: 3.50 / K/9: 6.50 / KWH: 1.00)

Rod Beck — Throws R — Age 31

YEAR	TEAM	LGE	IP	H	ER	HR	BB	K	ERA	W	L	H/9	HR/9	BB/9	K/9	KWH	PERA
1997	San Fran	NL	69.7	68	30	8	8	49	3.88	5	3	8.78	1.03	1.03	6.33	3.30	3.49
1998	ChiCubs	NL	80.7	88	33	11	22	78	3.68	5	4	9.82	1.23	2.45	8.70	2.35	4.80
1999	ChiCubs	NL	30.7	40	23	5	12	13	6.75	1	2	11.74	1.47	3.52	3.82	0.26	6.75
1999	Boston	AL	14.3	8	2	0	5	12	1.26	2	0	5.02	0.00	3.14	7.53	2.69	1.88

Beck's taterrific postseason may finally dispel the notion that he's an effective major-league closer. He lost his velocity years ago and started to lose his control last year. He stands a good chance of being in the pen this year, but won't be closing except in emergencies.

Kirk Bullinger — Throws R — Age 30

YEAR	TEAM	LGE	IP	H	ER	HR	BB	K	ERA	W	L	H/9	HR/9	BB/9	K/9	KWH	PERA
1997	Harrisbg	Eas	25.3	27	11	4	7	15	3.91	2	1	9.59	1.42	2.49	5.33	0.89	4.97
1997	Ottawa	Int	30.7	19	8	0	11	12	2.35	2	1	5.58	0.00	3.23	3.52	0.51	1.76
1998	Ottawa	Int	16.7	17	2	0	7	6	1.08	2	0	9.18	0.00	3.78	3.24	0.23	3.78
1999	Trenton	Eas	15.7	9	3	1	6	12	1.72	2	0	5.17	0.57	3.45	6.89	1.99	2.30
1999	Pawtuckt	Int	37.3	38	13	3	15	23	3.13	3	1	9.16	0.72	3.62	5.54	0.69	4.34

Jim's brother is a career minor leaguer who lucked into a very brief fill-in role with Boston. He's not a prospect, just a warm body with a moderately good track record in the minors.

Jin Ho Cho — Throws R — Age 24

YEAR	TEAM	LGE	IP	H	ER	HR	BB	K	ERA	W	L	H/9	HR/9	BB/9	K/9	KWH	PERA
1998	Sarasota	Fla	30.0	41	17	2	6	23	5.10	1	2	12.30	0.60	1.80	6.90	1.61	5.40
1998	Trenton	Eas	71.7	66	24	5	22	50	3.01	6	2	8.29	0.63	2.76	6.28	1.29	3.52
1998	Boston	AL	19.0	28	16	4	3	15	7.58	1	1	13.26	1.89	1.42	7.11	2.00	7.11
1999	Pawtuckt	Int	109.7	99	41	11	30	72	3.36	8	4	8.12	0.90	2.46	5.91	1.30	3.53
1999	Boston	AL	40.0	42	21	6	8	16	4.72	2	2	9.45	1.35	1.80	3.60	0.57	4.50

Still the most promising prospect to emerge from the organization's efforts in Korea, Cho flourished in Triple-A after dominating Double-A in 1998. He's not quite ready for Fenway, as his brief stint demonstrated, but he will be soon. Cho has excellent control and solid strikeout rates, but ranks behind Rose, Pena and maybe Ohka among Boston pitching prospects. He's a prime trade candidate if the Sox pursue a big outfield bat.

Rheal Cormier — Throws L — Age 33

YEAR	TEAM	LGE	IP	H	ER	HR	BB	K	ERA	W	L	H/9	HR/9	BB/9	K/9	KWH	PERA
1996	Montreal	NL	161.3	170	78	16	45	95	4.35	9	9	9.48	0.89	2.51	5.30	0.88	4.30
1999	Boston	AL	64.7	56	28	3	17	40	3.90	4	3	7.79	0.42	2.37	5.57	1.26	2.92

After surgery wiped out two years, Cormier came back as both a specialist (29 appearances of less than an inning) and a middle reliever (31 appearances of one to three innings), which made him more valuable than as either alone. He held left-handed hitters to a .198 average and a 547 OPS. The Red Sox have picked up a $2 million option for 2000, and he's expected to be an important part of the pen.

Jared Fernandez   Throws R   Age 28

YEAR	TEAM	LGE	IP	H	ER	HR	BB	K	ERA	W	L	H/9	HR/9	BB/9	K/9	KWH	PERA
1997	Pawtuckt	Int	58.0	87	50	7	31	27	7.76	2	4	13.50	1.09	4.81	4.19	0.20	7.91
1997	Trenton	Eas	105.0	175	117	11	78	53	10.03	2	10	15.00	0.94	6.69	4.54	0.15	9.60
1998	Trenton	Eas	108.0	162	104	9	64	52	8.67	3	9	13.50	0.75	5.33	4.33	0.19	7.75
1998	Pawtuckt	Int	24.0	28	17	5	8	13	6.38	1	2	10.50	1.88	3.00	4.88	0.56	6.00
1999	Trenton	Eas	16.3	25	12	4	9	7	6.61	1	1	13.78	2.20	4.96	3.86	0.16	9.92
1999	Pawtuckt	Int	160.3	181	86	18	44	65	4.83	8	10	10.16	1.01	2.47	3.65	0.40	4.77

One Pawtucket observer said of Fernandez, listed at 6′2″ and 223 pounds, "No player I know in the system looks less like an athlete than he does." Strong words, considering Rich Garces is in the organization. Used more in relief in the past, he started 17 games at Pawtucket last year, pitched well and ate innings (hmmm . . . poor choice of words). While he's already 28, he is a knuckleballer, so the usual age issues don't apply. Fernandez could be a cheap Wakefield replacement, and his being in an organization that has had experience and success with a knuckleballer can't hurt.

Bryce Florie   Throws R   Age 30

YEAR	TEAM	LGE	IP	H	ER	HR	BB	K	ERA	W	L	H/9	HR/9	BB/9	K/9	KWH	PERA
1997	Milwauke	AL	76.3	70	39	4	42	54	4.60	4	4	8.25	0.47	4.95	6.37	0.74	4.13
1998	Detroit	AL	134.3	137	74	15	62	99	4.96	7	8	9.18	1.00	4.15	6.63	0.86	4.89
1999	Detroit	AL	52.0	58	27	5	20	41	4.67	3	3	10.04	0.87	3.46	7.10	1.08	5.02
1999	Boston	AL	30.7	30	16	2	15	26	4.70	1	2	8.80	0.59	4.40	7.63	1.12	4.40

Acquired from Detroit for minor leaguer Mike Maroth, Florie is a serviceable middle reliever who is now with his fourth major-league team since 1995. He had a fine rookie season in relief with the Padres in '95, but hasn't matched that success. Florie is a groundball pitcher, which is a good thing in Fenway. I think working with Kerrigan could be a big break for him, and I expect him to be a solid contributor to the 2000 bullpen.

Rich Garces   Throws R   Age 29

YEAR	TEAM	LGE	IP	H	ER	HR	BB	K	ERA	W	L	H/9	HR/9	BB/9	K/9	KWH	PERA
1997	Pawtuckt	Int	30.3	27	6	0	14	34	1.78	3	0	8.01	0.00	4.15	10.09	2.29	3.26
1997	Boston	AL	14.0	13	8	2	9	12	5.14	1	1	8.36	1.29	5.79	7.71	0.92	5.14
1998	Boston	AL	46.0	35	18	6	29	35	3.52	3	2	6.85	1.17	5.67	6.85	0.90	4.30
1999	Pawtuckt	Int	27.0	26	11	5	11	21	3.67	2	1	8.67	1.67	3.67	7.00	1.15	5.00
1999	Boston	AL	41.7	22	7	1	17	34	1.51	4	1	4.75	0.22	3.67	7.34	2.31	1.73

A dominant reliever trapped in Paul Prudhomme's body. The Red Sox media guide lists him at 6′2″ and 223 pounds, which is accurate only if the scale is on Mars. Garces's health has always been a problem, but when he's sound, he's tough to hit. Held opposing hitters to a .171/.262/.233 performance and had no significant platoon split. Losing 30 pounds could add a decade to his career and make him several million dollars richer, both in salary and in savings on groceries.

Tom Gordon   Throws R   Age 32

YEAR	TEAM	LGE	IP	H	ER	HR	BB	K	ERA	W	L	H/9	HR/9	BB/9	K/9	KWH	PERA
1997	Boston	AL	186.0	144	74	9	78	161	3.58	13	8	6.97	0.44	3.77	7.79	1.72	3.00
1998	Boston	AL	79.3	54	22	2	26	79	2.50	7	2	6.13	0.23	2.95	8.96	3.32	2.16
1999	Boston	AL	18.3	15	9	2	12	25	4.42	1	1	7.36	0.98	5.89	12.27	2.59	4.42

Gordon was the top closer in the league in 1998, but was overworked and paid for it in 1999, as he was injured most of the year. This threw the bullpen, which had been considered a strength, into turmoil. But Wakefield and Lowe picked up the "closer" role pretty well, and Garces, Cormier, Beck and John Wasdin all contributed. The vulnerability of individual pitchers is another reason the closer strategy is overrated. If you have several pitchers, each of whom is effective and called upon to close out games over the course of a season, you won't run into situations in which you lose a designated "closer" and force a pitcher into an unfamiliar situation during a pennant race. Gordon is expected to miss 2000 after elbow surgery.

Sun Kim — Throws R — Age 22

YEAR	TEAM	LGE	IP	H	ER	HR	BB	K	ERA	W	L	H/9	HR/9	BB/9	K/9	KWH	PERA
1998	Sarasota	Fla	144.0	193	104	21	52	102	6.50	5	11	12.06	1.31	3.25	6.38	0.77	6.56
1999	Trenton	Eas	138.0	194	103	17	48	107	6.72	5	10	12.65	1.11	3.13	6.98	0.92	6.65

Kim had several strong starts in June, then appeared in and won the Futures Game, which caused him to miss his turn in the rotation at Trenton. He was out of sync after his return, and erratic thereafter. Kim has good stuff and doesn't walk many hitters, but allowed a club-high 16 home runs. His big problem is consistency; he'd give up runs in his first and last innings, but mow down 12 out of 13 in the interim. Fellow Korean import Cho worked with him, stressing the importance of keeping the ball down. He's a great fielder, has worked on controlling the running game, continues to learn how to pitch and is still a fine prospect.

Derek Lowe — Throws R — Age 27

YEAR	TEAM	LGE	IP	H	ER	HR	BB	K	ERA	W	L	H/9	HR/9	BB/9	K/9	KWH	PERA
1997	Tacoma	PCL	54.3	53	25	3	21	41	4.14	3	3	8.78	0.50	3.48	6.79	1.13	3.81
1997	Seattle	AL	54.3	55	37	10	20	39	6.13	2	4	9.11	1.66	3.31	6.46	1.03	5.13
1997	Pawtuckt	Int	29.3	26	9	3	12	18	2.76	2	1	7.98	0.92	3.68	5.52	0.78	3.99
1998	Boston	AL	123.3	124	61	5	44	78	4.45	7	7	9.05	0.36	3.21	5.69	0.83	3.79
1999	Boston	AL	111.7	76	28	6	24	83	2.26	10	2	6.13	0.48	1.93	6.69	2.82	2.01

The key man in the bullpen, Lowe was nearly as good as Pedro in half as many innings. Recently, four relievers have put up as dominant a season in middle relief as Lowe did, after which their paths diverged. Some stayed in middle relief, others moved to closer, while others started. Their performances:

			W	L	G	SV	IP	H	HR	BB	SO	ERA
Xavier Hernandez	1992	HOU	9	1	77	7	111	81	5	42	96	2.11
Duane Ward	1992	TOR	7	4	79	12	101⅓	76	5	39	103	1.95
Pedro J. Martinez	1993	LA	10	5	65	2	107	76	5	57	119	2.61
Mariano Rivera	1996	NY	8	3	61	5	107⅔	73	1	34	130	2.09
Derek Lowe	1999	BOS	6	3	74	15	109⅓	84	7	25	80	2.63

The contrasts are striking. Duane Ward's 1992 was his fifth straight 100-inning season. He managed to pitch 71 innings and log 45 saves in 1993 before his arm fell off, ending his career. Xavier Hernandez carried a heavy load again in 1993 and put up an excellent campaign. He developed arm problems in 1994, and while he never got close to that level again, he had a few decent years as a middle reliever. Mariano Rivera became a closer, his workload dropped by a third and he went on to be a World Series MVP. Pedro Martinez was moved into the rotation in 1994 and, well, we all know the story there.

The bad sign for Lowe is that the two pitchers who were worked hard in multiple years were the ones who broke down. Lowe threw 126 innings in 63 games in 1998. He's too good a pitcher to jeopardize by asking him for another 100 innings in relief. He ought to move into the rotation or have his relief workload reduced slightly (while being restricted to high-leverage situations). Whether Lowe becomes Mariano Rivera or Pedro Martinez remains to be seen; his interest in starting may tip the scales.

Pedro Martinez — Throws R — Age 28

YEAR	TEAM	LGE	IP	H	ER	HR	BB	K	ERA	W	L	H/9	HR/9	BB/9	K/9	KWH	PERA
1997	Montreal	NL	241.3	160	63	16	70	284	2.35	21	6	5.97	0.60	2.61	10.59	5.38	2.27
1998	Boston	AL	234.0	185	76	24	70	254	2.92	18	8	7.12	0.92	2.69	9.77	3.72	3.12
1999	Boston	AL	217.7	145	44	8	36	323	1.82	21	3	6.00	0.33	1.49	13.36	14.93	1.74

What more can be said about his outstanding season? Well, Martinez posted the third-best translated ERA in history, behind Greg Maddux's 1995 and Walter Johnson's 1913. He had the best strikeout-to-walk ratio of any pitcher ever with more than 200 strikeouts, and the best baserunners-to-innings-pitched ratio ever in a DH league. Martinez has now placed first or second in Cy Young voting three years in a row—a feat matched only by Sandy Koufax, Jim Palmer and Maddux. He's gregarious, enthusiastic and immensely popular in Boston. The best part? He's signed through 2004. Roger who?

Ramon Martinez Throws R Age 32

YEAR	TEAM	LGE	IP	H	ER	HR	BB	K	ERA	W	L	H/9	HR/9	BB/9	K/9	KWH	PERA
1997	LosAngls	NL	128.3	134	70	15	71	111	4.91	6	8	9.40	1.05	4.98	7.78	0.97	5.40
1998	LosAngls	NL	99.7	80	43	9	43	86	3.88	6	5	7.22	0.81	3.88	7.77	1.61	3.52
1999	Boston	AL	21.3	12	6	2	8	16	2.53	2	0	5.06	0.84	3.38	6.75	1.99	2.11

Clipped from that DT are more rehab stints than you'll find in a Robert Downey Jr. travelogue. The other Martinez showed signs of a Saberhagen-like renaissance with a couple of strong late-season starts and solid playoff turns against the Indians and Yankees. The combination of pitching with his brother and rehabbing with Joe Kerrigan is ideal for Ramon. He's penciled in as the #2 starter this year.

Kent Mercker Throws L Age 32

YEAR	TEAM	LGE	IP	H	ER	HR	BB	K	ERA	W	L	H/9	HR/9	BB/9	K/9	KWH	PERA
1997	Cincnnti	NL	146.7	133	61	16	65	70	3.74	9	7	8.16	0.98	3.99	4.30	0.42	4.23
1998	St Louis	NL	164.0	201	97	11	57	69	5.32	8	10	11.03	0.60	3.13	3.79	0.31	5.10
1999	St Louis	NL	104.0	123	67	15	49	62	5.80	5	7	10.64	1.30	4.24	5.37	0.48	6.14
1999	Boston	AL	26.3	21	10	0	13	18	3.42	2	1	7.18	0.00	4.44	6.15	0.89	3.08

Expected to bolster the staff with some left-handed experience, Mercker got three starts in the postseason and wasn't effective in any of them. He did, however, pitch well down the stretch. He declined a $1.8 million option for 2000 to test the market, making him the early favorite for this winter's Jody Reed Award.

Tomokazu Ohka Throws R Age 24

YEAR	TEAM	LGE	IP	H	ER	HR	BB	K	ERA	W	L	H/9	HR/9	BB/9	K/9	KWH	PERA
1999	Trenton	Eas	66.3	79	33	9	28	42	4.48	4	3	10.72	1.22	3.80	5.70	0.60	5.83
1999	Pawtuckt	Int	68.3	60	15	5	12	57	1.98	7	1	7.90	0.66	1.58	7.51	3.37	2.90
1999	Boston	AL	13.7	19	10	2	6	8	6.59	1	1	12.51	1.32	3.95	5.27	0.42	7.24

Boston was allowed to purchase Ohka as a favor for helping the Yokohama club in Japan sign a Korean reliever. After an undistinguished career in Japan, Ohka went undefeated in the American minors, posting a 3.00 ERA in Double-A and a 1.58 ERA in Triple-A. He throws five pitches, including a forkball that nobody in Japan could catch, which made him reluctant to use it. He has a typical Japanese aversion to pitching inside to left-handed hitters, which he's working to overcome. While it's hard to base anything on a single year, Ohka's future looks very bright.

Juan Pena Throws R Age 23

YEAR	TEAM	LGE	IP	H	ER	HR	BB	K	ERA	W	L	H/9	HR/9	BB/9	K/9	KWH	PERA
1997	Sarasota	Fla	87.3	83	48	10	30	69	4.95	5	5	8.55	1.03	3.09	7.11	1.43	4.12
1997	Trenton	Eas	89.3	117	64	12	33	63	6.45	3	7	11.79	1.21	3.32	6.35	0.77	6.35
1998	Pawtuckt	Int	138.3	146	71	16	54	129	4.62	7	8	9.50	1.04	3.51	8.39	1.58	4.81
1999	Pawtuckt	Int	48.0	45	25	8	13	55	4.69	2	3	8.44	1.50	2.44	10.31	3.86	4.31
1999	Boston	AL	13.3	8	1	0	3	15	0.68	1	0	5.40	0.00	2.03	10.13	7.01	1.35

Perhaps the best pitching prospect in the system, Pena pitched two sensational games for the Sox before succumbing to shoulder stiffness that sidelined him for the season. He was worked hard in the minors at a very young age, and the Red Sox may be paying for it now. When healthy, Pena didn't dominate with heat, but still racked up impressive strikeout rates, which bodes well for future success if he recovers. Ultra-trivia: Pena had the third-best ERA of any pitcher since 1920 who made at least two starts without any relief appearances.

Mark Portugal Throws R Age 37

YEAR	TEAM	LGE	IP	H	ER	HR	BB	K	ERA	W	L	H/9	HR/9	BB/9	K/9	KWH	PERA
1997	Philadel	NL	13.7	18	8	0	5	2	5.27	1	1	11.85	0.00	3.29	1.32	0.03	5.27
1998	Philadel	NL	168.3	190	86	26	34	100	4.60	9	10	10.16	1.39	1.82	5.35	1.16	4.92
1999	Boston	AL	154.7	164	83	24	40	82	4.83	8	9	9.54	1.40	2.33	4.77	0.77	4.77

He was never a great pitcher, but his excellent control always had him turning in seasons a little better than you thought he would. Portugal came close to retiring in early June, and given how he pitched after the All-Star break (the league hit

.327/.355/.555 off him) it probably would have been for the best. He was abruptly released right before the end of the season, upsetting some players and focusing attention once again on the interpersonal skills of Dan Duquette. It was the right move for the team at the time.

Pat Rapp   Throws R   Age 32

YEAR	TEAM	LGE	IP	H	ER	HR	BB	K	ERA	W	L	H/9	HR/9	BB/9	K/9	KWH	PERA
1997	Florida	NL	107.7	123	59	11	54	60	4.93	5	7	10.28	0.92	4.51	5.02	0.40	5.60
1997	San Fran	NL	32.7	38	24	5	22	26	6.61	1	3	10.47	1.38	6.06	7.16	0.60	6.89
1998	KansasCy	AL	195.3	192	101	22	113	135	4.65	11	11	8.85	1.01	5.21	6.22	0.63	5.11
1999	Boston	AL	150.7	133	64	11	68	93	3.82	10	7	7.94	0.66	4.06	5.56	0.71	3.82

A signing that was derided at the time, Rapp surprised critics by turning in his best season. He was Boston's #3 starter for much of the summer, yet was left off the Division Series roster in favor of Ramon Martinez, Mercker and Wasdin. He's a replacement-level free agent who should end up as the #4 starter on a bad team like the Cubs or Angels.

Brian Rose   Throws R   Age 24

YEAR	TEAM	LGE	IP	H	ER	HR	BB	K	ERA	W	L	H/9	HR/9	BB/9	K/9	KWH	PERA
1997	Pawtuckt	Int	186.0	205	77	21	48	99	3.73	12	9	9.92	1.02	2.32	4.79	0.74	4.60
1998	Pawtuckt	Int	17.3	25	18	5	4	15	9.35	0	2	12.98	2.60	2.08	7.79	1.68	8.31
1998	Boston	AL	37.3	44	30	8	14	18	7.23	1	3	10.61	1.93	3.38	4.34	0.39	6.51
1999	Pawtuckt	Int	28.0	28	9	6	9	27	2.89	2	1	9.00	1.93	2.89	8.68	2.16	5.14
1999	Boston	AL	101.0	102	49	17	29	53	4.37	6	5	9.09	1.51	2.58	4.72	0.71	4.72

When Rose and Pena came up and had two terrific starts each in May, fans felt a sense of magic. Were they going to be the pitching equivalent of Jim Rice and Fred Lynn? Sadly, both pitchers came down with sore arms, which not only shattered the illusion but called into question the organization's pitching-development program. Rose was so ineffective thereafter that he was sent back to Triple-A in August. He's still expected to compete for a rotation spot in the spring.

Bret Saberhagen   Throws R   Age 36

YEAR	TEAM	LGE	IP	H	ER	HR	BB	K	ERA	W	L	H/9	HR/9	BB/9	K/9	KWH	PERA
1997	Boston	AL	26.3	29	18	5	10	14	6.15	1	2	9.91	1.71	3.42	4.78	0.51	5.81
1998	Boston	AL	175.3	179	77	20	30	101	3.95	11	8	9.19	1.03	1.54	5.18	1.42	3.85
1999	Boston	AL	122.3	110	34	9	11	84	2.50	11	3	8.09	0.66	0.81	6.18	4.36	2.72

Williams and Kerrigan coaxed another 120 quality innings out of his tender arm, but once again Saberhagen could not stay healthy for an entire season. His 2.95 ERA would have ranked second in the league had he thrown enough innings. He still ranks as one of the greatest control pitchers in history and missed having as many wins as walks—a feat he managed in 1994—by one. He's slated to have surgery in the offseason and be back as the Sox #3 starter, behind the Martinez brothers.

Julio Santana   Throws R   Age 27

YEAR	TEAM	LGE	IP	H	ER	HR	BB	K	ERA	W	L	H/9	HR/9	BB/9	K/9	KWH	PERA
1997	Texas	AL	107.0	134	77	15	49	65	6.48	4	8	11.27	1.26	4.12	5.47	0.48	6.39
1998	TampaBay	AL	141.0	144	69	16	61	61	4.40	8	8	9.19	1.02	3.89	3.89	0.32	4.79
1999	TampaBay	AL	56.0	62	43	9	32	35	6.91	2	4	9.96	1.45	5.14	5.63	0.46	6.27

Picked up from the Devil Rays in July, Santana had a stretch of moderate effectiveness in 1998, but hasn't really shown much else. He's prone to the long ball and walks too many hitters. He was injured at the time of the trade and never actually pitched for Boston. He's just another spare arm in the bullpen mix for 2000.

Marino Santana   Throws R   Age 28

YEAR	TEAM	LGE	IP	H	ER	HR	BB	K	ERA	W	L	H/9	HR/9	BB/9	K/9	KWH	PERA
1997	Jacksnvl	Sou	65.7	72	37	8	51	72	5.07	3	4	9.87	1.10	6.99	9.87	1.05	6.58
1998	Toledo	Int	65.3	51	34	10	37	79	4.68	3	4	7.03	1.38	5.10	10.88	2.47	4.41
1999	Pawtuckt	Int	39.0	29	14	5	19	39	3.23	3	1	6.69	1.15	4.38	9.00	2.06	3.69
1999	Boston	AL	4.3	7	6	3	3	4	12.46	0	0	14.54	6.23	6.23	8.31	0.57	16.61

This was another of Duquette's patented low-risk turnaround pitching projects. Santana is too wild to be effective in the majors, but he didn't cost the team much. The success rate necessary for this strategy to break even is low.

Tim Wakefield   Throws R   Age 33

YEAR	TEAM	LGE	IP	H	ER	HR	BB	K	ERA	W	L	H/9	HR/9	BB/9	K/9	KWH	PERA
1997	Boston	AL	205.3	180	96	22	88	153	4.21	12	11	7.89	0.96	3.86	6.71	1.10	3.99
1998	Boston	AL	216.3	208	115	28	83	148	4.78	11	13	8.65	1.16	3.45	6.16	0.95	4.45
1999	Boston	AL	144.3	133	77	16	70	107	4.80	7	9	8.29	1.00	4.36	6.67	0.92	4.43

The knuckleball has given him a reputation for inconsistency, but look at those translated ERAs: he's been the model of consistency on a seasonal basis. His stint as a closer when Tom Gordon went down called to mind a time when just about all knuckleballers were relievers. Wakefield will make $4.5 million in 2000, and would be tradable if other teams realized the value of an average inning-eater who just happens not to be able to hit 80 mph on the fast gun.

John Wasdin   Throws R   Age 27

YEAR	TEAM	LGE	IP	H	ER	HR	BB	K	ERA	W	L	H/9	HR/9	BB/9	K/9	KWH	PERA
1997	Boston	AL	127.0	114	60	17	38	85	4.25	7	7	8.08	1.20	2.69	6.02	1.25	3.90
1998	Boston	AL	96.3	110	53	13	28	60	4.95	5	6	10.28	1.21	2.62	5.61	0.87	5.14
1999	Boston	AL	75.7	61	31	12	17	59	3.69	5	3	7.26	1.43	2.02	7.02	2.51	3.45
1999	Pawtuckt	Int	29.3	20	9	1	7	24	2.76	2	1	6.14	0.31	2.15	7.36	3.07	1.84

The moral to Wasdin's 1999 season is this: never, ever, EVER bring him into a game with runners on base. Only three of the 14 home runs he allowed were solo shots. Batters hit just .216/.258/.318 with the bases empty, but improved to .269/.321/.625 with runners on base and jumped all over him to the tune of .321/.345/.750 with runners in scoring position. Despite the splits, he's still improving and will be in the bullpen mix.

Bob Wolcott   Throws R   Age 26

YEAR	TEAM	LGE	IP	H	ER	HR	BB	K	ERA	W	L	H/9	HR/9	BB/9	K/9	KWH	PERA
1997	Tacoma	PCL	34.7	41	21	3	7	25	5.45	2	2	10.64	0.78	1.82	6.49	1.63	4.41
1997	Seattle	AL	103.0	121	62	20	29	59	5.42	4	7	10.57	1.75	2.53	5.16	0.74	5.85
1998	Tucson	PCL	131.7	150	68	12	30	84	4.65	7	8	10.25	0.82	2.05	5.74	1.17	4.44
1998	Arizona	NL	32.3	35	28	7	14	20	7.79	1	3	9.74	1.95	3.90	5.57	0.61	6.12
1999	Pawtuckt	Int	123.0	139	65	15	31	59	4.76	7	7	10.17	1.10	2.27	4.32	0.60	4.76

It seems like he's been around forever, thanks to his 1995 postseason heroics with Seattle, but he's still just 26. Wolcott was leading the International League in ERA in August before getting pounded for nine earned runs in 4⅓ innings, which caused his ERA to jump from 2.96 to 3.67. He's not likely to have much of a future in Boston, other than an outside chance at a long relief role.

Support-Neutral Records — BOSTON RED SOX — Park Effect: +8.5%

PITCHER	GS	IP	R	SNW	SNL	SNPCT	W	L	RA	APW	SNVA	SNWAR
Jin Ho Cho	7	36.0	23	1.8	2.3	.441	2	3	5.75	-0.11	-0.16	0.07
Bryce Florie	2	7.7	2	0.7	0.2	.771	0	0	2.35	0.24	0.22	0.29
Kip Gross	1	3.0	5	0.1	0.6	.091	0	0	15.00	-0.29	-0.26	-0.21
Pedro Martinez	29	208.3	55	18.3	3.8	.828	22	4	2.38	6.47	6.91	8.88
Ramon Martinez	4	20.7	8	1.7	0.9	.650	2	1	3.48	0.41	0.37	0.58
Kent Mercker	5	25.7	12	1.7	1.1	.608	2	0	4.21	0.32	0.31	0.51
Tomokazu Ohka	2	5.7	12	0.0	1.5	.024	0	2	19.06	-0.78	-0.69	-0.61
Juan Pena	2	13.0	1	1.4	0.0	.969	2	0	0.69	0.62	0.65	0.79
Mark Portugal	27	143.7	94	8.3	9.8	.460	7	11	5.89	-0.64	-0.77	0.63
Pat Rapp	26	126.0	71	9.0	7.6	.542	6	7	5.07	0.48	0.63	1.95
Brian Rose	18	92.0	56	5.4	6.2	.466	6	5	5.48	-0.03	-0.37	0.48
Bret Saberhagen	22	119.0	43	9.6	4.3	.690	10	6	3.25	2.64	2.42	3.67
Tim Wakefield	17	93.7	71	4.3	7.3	.373	5	9	6.82	-1.30	-1.46	-0.61
TOTALS	162	894.3	453	62.2	45.5	.577	64	48	4.56	8.05	7.78	16.41

Despite missing almost all of the past two years, Ramon Martinez finished the 1990s as the luckiest starter of the decade. That is, his actual record during the decade exceeded his Support-Neutral record to a greater extent than any other starter's. We don't have the Support-Neutral numbers for decades before this one, but some quick number-crunching with Bill James's Pythagorean formula reveals likely candidates for past titles: Ron Darling for the 1980s, Catfish Hunter for the 1970s, Denny McLain for the 1960s, Vic Raschi for the 1950s, Raschi again for the 1940s, Johnny Allen for the 1930s, Art Nehf for the 1920s, Jack Coombs for the 1910s and Sam Leever for the 1900s. The century's luckiest pitcher was probably Lew Burdette, who compiled a lifetime 203-144 record despite having a below-average career ERA. See the Kansas City SNW/L comment for these pitchers' unlucky counterparts.

Pitcher Abuse Points

PITCHER	AGE	GS	PAP	PAP/S	WKLD	MAX	1-90	91-100	101-110	111-120	121-130	131-140	141+
Jin Ho Cho	23	7	0	0.0	0.0	91	6	1	0	0	0	0	0
Bryce Florie	29	2	0	0.0	0.0	85	2	0	0	0	0	0	0
Kip Gross	34	1	0	0.0	0.0	76	1	0	0	0	0	0	0
Pedro Martinez	27	29	791	27.3	50.0	137	3	4	6	5	7	4	0
Ramon Martinez	31	4	0	0.0	0.0	98	1	3	0	0	0	0	0
Kent Mercker	31	5	9	1.8	2.1	107	3	0	2	0	0	0	0
Tomokazu Ohka	23	2	0	0.0	0.0	89	2	0	0	0	0	0	0
Juan Pena	22	2	20	10.0	26.7	115	1	0	0	1	0	0	0
Mark Portugal	36	27	50	1.9	1.9	119	19	6	0	2	0	0	0
Pat Rapp	31	26	34	1.3	1.5	111	15	6	4	1	0	0	0
Brian Rose	23	18	9	0.5	1.3	105	12	4	2	0	0	0	0
Bret Saberhagen	35	22	9	0.4	0.4	106	15	5	2	0	0	0	0
Tim Wakefield	32	17	113	6.6	6.6	122	9	2	3	1	2	0	0
BOSTON		162	1035	6.4	10.8	137	89	31	19	10	9	4	0
Ranking (AL)				11	12								

Over the last two years, Jimy Williams's formula has been to ride Pedro Martinez as much as he can, protect his other starters to the hilt and use Tim Wakefield to fill in the gaps. Red Sox starters other than Martinez and Wakefield had just 131 PAPs last year, and in 1998 they had only 28! The formula is undeniably successful, in large part because Williams has managed to keep Bret Saberhagen effective and semi-healthy. You can count on one hand—maybe only one finger—the managers who would have kept Saberhagen on such a tight leash for so long. How many people realize that Saberhagen had the second-best ERA in the league of anyone with at least 110 innings pitched? Remember the odd-year/even-year quirk that Saberhagen had in the 1980s? The explanation was simple: Saberhagen would have a great year during which his manager would burn him out, he would be hurt the next year, regain his strength and be great again the year after that. It took Jimy Williams to figure out how to end that cycle. Given Williams's success with Saberhagen, I think Ramon Martinez is in the best possible hands to become a great pitcher again.

Chicago White Sox

For a classic "half-empty or half-full" debate, let's turn to the White Sox. Coming into the 1999 season, the AL Central was expected to be extremely weak. The Twins and Royals were going to lean heavily on rookies. Randy Smith was busy spending money in Detroit but wasn't building a team capable of much more than recent Twins teams built with Otis Nixon and Terry Steinbach, or recent Royals teams built around Jeff King and Jay Bell. Beyond the Indians, the only team in the division that posted a winning record against the East, West or National League was the last-place Twins, who had a 10-7 interleague mark.

Despite the departures of Robin Ventura and Albert Belle, this level of competition meant that the low pre-season expectations for the Sox were inappropriately low—even if the team was entering the second year of a rebuilding program. While plenty of pundits spent their time talking about "improved" teams like the Tigers—teams that spent money on stiffs like Gregg Jefferies—the Sox finished second by default. Even at that, things did not work out as planned. So did the Sox make progress?

At the All-Star break the Sox were 42-43, pretending to be on the fringe of the wild-card race. At that point the team suffered simultaneous collapses of the rotation and the offense, which killed off wild-card talk pretty quickly. The organization is sensible enough to realize it isn't poised on the brink of greatness. In the short term, how much progress the Sox make depends on how much more mileage they can get out of those already on board. That, in turn, depends on manager Jerry Manuel and the job he does both in creating opportunities for players to succeed and in selecting the right players with which to build an eventual contender.

In a high-offense era like the one we're in, running a pitching staff well is the most critical aspect of a manager's job. On that score, there are a few reasons to like Manuel. The Sox rotation featured an improved Mike Sirotka, and both Jim Parque and John Snyder jumped out to good starts before terrible second-half fades. For a brief period of time,

even Jaime Navarro looked almost useful. Amidst all of the ups and downs, Manuel and the Sox were the best in the league at not blowing a quality start: only once all season did a Sox starter give up three runs or fewer in six innings only to subsequently allow a fourth run. Manuel also did a good job of not putting too heavy a workload on any of his starters— never skipping a turn in the rotation and allowing all of his starters to benefit from extra rest days.

There are a few nagging considerations as to whether or not Manuel runs his rotation better than most managers. To his credit, a strong bullpen encouraged him to trust leads to it rather than to a tiring starter. But the performances of his starting pitchers weren't the kind that forced Manuel to choose often between a tiring starter in the middle of a good outing or that bullpen.

After May 15, Snyder had a hard time giving up fewer than three runs in the first inning, let alone getting as far as the sixth. Parque was similarly awful after a thumb injury at the end of July, while James Baldwin was the opposite, pitching so badly in the first half that Manuel was never faced with critical seventh-inning decisions involving him. Navarro slipped from near-mediocrity in the first half to the kind of performances Sox fans have come to know and abhor. So whether Manuel really managed his rotation well is an open question. He didn't ask too much of his young starters, and generally they didn't give him much. Perhaps the best reason to be optimistic was that he didn't push Kip Wells hard.

Manuel also built a strong bullpen. While Jack McKeon's Reds highlighted the value of a bullpen structured around relievers who pitch multiple innings, Manuel was making a similar point with his pen. Keith Foulke might still be more valuable as a starting pitcher, but after having the best relief season in baseball, it isn't as though he's being wasted. Pitching in Foulke's shadow, Sean Lowe was one of the league's 10 best relievers, giving the Sox more than 90 quality innings. The absence of a useful left-handed reliever was a season-long problem, but Manuel was on Felipe Alou's staff

> ## White Sox Prospectus
>
> **1999 record:** 75-86; Second place, AL Central
> **Pythagorean W/L:** 73-89
> **Runs scored:** 777 (10th in AL)
> **Runs allowed:** 870 (10th in AL)
> **Team EQA:** .256 (10th in AL)
> **1999 team age:** 26.1 (youngest in AL)
> **1999 park:** Comiskey Park; slight pitchers' park, decreased run scoring by 6%.
> **1999:** A lot of positives as young players established themselves.
> **2000:** The rebuilding continues as a flood of talent arrives; they could surprise.

back in the years when the Expos were winning games without one. If you don't have someone like Steve Kline lying around, and you don't want to buy Dan Plesac, why give innings and critical situations to a marginal pitcher who just happens to be left-handed? If the Sox can't find a good left-handed reliever, they're better off going without one than relying on pyromaniacs like Bryan Ward or Scott Eyre.

Manuel had some success developing hitters. Though there were definite disappointments—like Mike Caruso, and Frank Thomas, and Ray Durham settling for a merely good season instead of building on his great 1998—they were outweighed by positives. In their sophomore campaigns, both Magglio Ordonez and Paul Konerko became the power sources the Sox had hoped they would be. Ordonez, in particular, took a big step towards becoming a star, and looks primed to enjoy a good four- or five-year run. After Jeff Abbott blew his chance at the left-field job, Carlos Lee proved he can hit a little. Chris Singleton came out of Triple-A to have a nifty little year.

The problem is not whether these players can contribute to a good team, but where they'll play and who will stay, because none of them does a great job of getting on base. The Sox were 10th in the league in scoring, thanks to finishing 11th in on-base percentage and 13th in walks. They have to do better than that if they're serious about improving, which means making some difficult decisions about who to cash in and who to keep.

From a player-development perspective, it was a great year for the Sox. While the rebuilding program is in progress at the major-league level, it won't be a set piece featuring only the players already in the pipeline. The Sox used some of the money saved by Albert Belle's defection on the draft, spending $5 million just to sign last year's top picks. Taking compensation of their draft picks a bit more seriously is progress: the foul-up that let 1996 first-rounder Bobby Seay sign with the Devil Rays is now a distant memory.

What's interesting is that the Sox have been stocking up on pitching in the draft and in almost every deal they've made. While the Cubs spend their time talking about how they're focused on developing pitching, the White Sox are actually doing things to make sure they produce it. There isn't a particular focus on high-school or college pitchers, on guys who throw hard or guys with great command, on guys from top college programs or small schools. The Sox pick pitchers of every stripe, giving them a diverse group of prospects—from highly-touted college stars like Kip Wells to high-school phenoms like Jon Garland, from juco surprises like Aaron Myette to college veterans like Josh Fogg or Matt Ginter or even Pat Daneker.

Developmentally, quantity is a good way to produce some quality pitching. After the bitter experiences with Kirk McCaskill and Jaime Navarro, the Sox are determined to avoid long-term contracts for free-agent pitching.

Developing pitching is more than just the most cost-effective way to get it, it's also the best way to have something attractive to offer for other teams' top-tier players. Mark McGwire was landed for some guys called pitching prospects, and if you have enough of them around, you can toss a handful to a desperate team that's looking to unload a star. Being able to trade pitching talent for a great offensive player in his prime should be a critical advantage for the Sox once they get into near-contention, but as general manager Ron Schueler knows, that time hasn't come yet. The Sox are lying in wait for their window of opportunity, and through patience with young talent, they will continue to get better.

Assuming they only want to pick up one great offensive player, the Sox will have to come to a decision about Frank Thomas's future. The antagonism between Thomas and Manuel is pretty straightforward and does neither man credit. Thomas is convinced he should never take the field again, and it's easy to see why. Although he's always been a good athlete, the Big Hurt was never a good defensive player, and not for lack of effort, even now after years of humiliating failures. Thomas's problem in the field is that he tries to play the position, while most people would be happy if he just stood still. A decade of struggle has left a proud athlete unwilling to accept further embarrassment.

After a particularly brutal play against Oakland in early August, Thomas went into a tirade over his shortcomings and explained that his manager was foolish for putting him out there. Manuel has never been afraid to talk to the press about a player's failings, but once the shoe was on the other foot, he took the gloves off. Thomas was accused of jaking, and rumors swirled that Manuel refused to play him or Thomas refused to play for him. Thomas was then sent away for surgery on a bone spur to Manuel's derisive "he can't do anything, anyway." This is sillier still because it isn't as if we're talking about Billy Martin and Reggie Jackson here. While Manuel may win his fight, if Thomas is dumped to suit either of them, it's hard to see how the Sox will get appropriate value, let alone replace Thomas's on-base skills.

The Sox can expect good things from rookies like Kip Wells, Aaron Myette and Joe Crede in 2000. But what happens if the window opens? Say the Indians finally collapse under the weight of too many ill-advised long-term contracts to the over-30 set, and it's the Twins or Royals who go through first? This Sox team isn't strong enough to contend in the AL right now and may not be good enough to stay ahead of the Royals or Twins three years down the road. This season should be a third year of consolidation. If the Tribe falters, the Sox can put some pressure on them, but better things await the Sox in 2001 and 2002 if they're prepared to enter the coming winter as major players in the free-agent market.

If Crede or Konerko claims the third-base job, the Sox will need only a shortstop. The Sox would have to set aside their differences with Scott Boras over Bobby Seay and

Bobby Hill to bring Alex Rodriguez to the South Side, but there are bigger stakes here. Owner Jerry Reinsdorf made a good chunk of change by employing Michael Jordan, so he probably knows a thing or two about the going rate for superstars. Signing A-Rod could be the only way he's going to have a product that will not only compete with the Indians in the division, but get the attention of Sammycentric Chicago.

HITTERS (Averages: BA: .270 / OBP: .340 / SLG: .430 / EQA: .260)

Jeff Abbott — OF — Bats R — Age 27

YEAR	TEAM	LGE	AB	H	DB	TP	HR	BB/SO	R	RBI	SB	CS	OUT	BA	OBP	SLG	EQA	EQR	DEFENSE
1997	Nashvill	AA	466	139	33	3	8	35/55	76	54	9	5	332	.298	.354	.433	.266	61	114-OF 98
1998	ChiSox	AL	244	69	14	1	12	8/27	32	40	3	3	178	.283	.306	.496	.259	30	57-OF 98
1999	ChiSox	AL	57	9	0	0	2	5/12	5	6	1	1	49	.158	.226	.263	.152	2	
1999	Charlott	Int	273	73	18	2	6	11/30	30	27	1	2	202	.267	.296	.414	.234	27	68-OF 93
2000	ChiSox	AL	311	85	17	1	10	25/38	44	48	3	2	228	.273	.327	.431	.256	38	

Abbott makes for a good cautionary tale. Outfield prospects without great power who don't play center field can't afford a bad month, especially in an organization as loaded with outfield prospects as the White Sox. Benched and then demoted after a miserable April, he dislocated his shoulder at the end of May. Abbott has a lot in common with Bruce Aven: he's got decent power, he knows how to hit and he's good in either outfield corner. He'll make a good fourth outfielder—just not for the White Sox.

Eric Battersby — 1B — Bats R — Age 24

YEAR	TEAM	LGE	AB	H	DB	TP	HR	BB/SO	R	RBI	SB	CS	OUT	BA	OBP	SLG	EQA	EQR	DEFENSE	
1999	Burlingt	Mid	474	104	19	1	13	57/103	48	57	4	1	371	.219	.306	.346	.225	44	92-1B 95	38-OF 88
2000	ChiSox	AL	218	50	7	0	7	32/65	31	28	2	0	168	.229	.328	.358	.241	24		

Battersby was drafted out of St. Mary's of Texas in the NAIA after starring as a left-handed pitcher and outfielder. He was old for his league but worthy of a mention because of some playoff hijinks: a four-home-run game to clinch the Midwest League semifinals and four RBIs in the league championship game. Not really a prospect, but he may jump up to Birmingham.

Tilson Brito — IF — Bats R — Age 28

YEAR	TEAM	LGE	AB	H	DB	TP	HR	BB/SO	R	RBI	SB	CS	OUT	BA	OBP	SLG	EQA	EQR	DEFENSE
1997	Toronto	AL	126	28	4	0	0	9/27	9	8	1	0	98	.222	.286	.254	.184	7	20-2B 117
1998	Tacoma	PCL	143	33	11	1	1	6/32	16	9	0	1	111	.231	.269	.343	.200	10	22-2B 96
1999	Charlott	Int	400	107	24	4	7	25/73	43	41	3	3	296	.268	.326	.400	.245	44	93-2B 99
2000	ChiSox	AL	320	85	17	1	7	23/61	39	42	2	2	237	.266	.315	.391	.239	33	

Jerry Manuel spent most of the season complaining that he didn't have a veteran utility infielder, but the organization did. The Sox simply didn't like Brito enough to bring him up. He can play shortstop or third base, and he's a better hitter than Craig Wilson. They were probably hamstrung because Brito was supposed to star on the Dominican Republic's Pan American Games team.

Mike Caruso — SS — Bats L — Age 23

YEAR	TEAM	LGE	AB	H	DB	TP	HR	BB/SO	R	RBI	SB	CS	OUT	BA	OBP	SLG	EQA	EQR	DEFENSE
1997	San Jose	Cal	445	132	24	7	2	27/19	59	39	6	7	320	.297	.343	.396	.249	49	106-SS 95
1997	WnstnSlm	Car	121	28	2	2	0	1/8	10	13	2	0	93	.231	.247	.281	.171	6	26-SS 92
1998	ChiSox	AL	522	160	16	7	5	13/37	77	53	20	6	368	.307	.332	.393	.249	57	128-SS 91
1999	ChiSox	AL	529	131	10	4	2	15/36	54	33	12	15	413	.248	.272	.293	.183	30	125-SS 96
2000	ChiSox	AL	554	159	16	5	3	25/36	66	59	16	12	407	.287	.318	.350	.228	50	

He's a spectacularly unproductive player, playing as if Dr. Frankenstein put him together using Rafael Ramirez's glove, Chet Lemon's baserunning and Mark Belanger's bat—spare parts no one should even have had lying around.

There are a lot of problems here. First, Caruso clearly doesn't know the game well enough. That's a product of skipping Double- and Triple-A and not having a lot of game experience to draw on. If there's a mistake to make, Caruso makes it, such as blowing a game by forgetting he's the cutoff man or regularly getting thrown out at third. He didn't know how to adjust once teams decided to defense his attempts to bunt for a hit. I wouldn't say it's just bad coaching: Jerry Manuel worked with him in camp on his defense, and Caruso's throwing definitely improved. He just has no idea what pitches to take or when, and he didn't improve once he was removed from the top of the order in July.

It didn't help that Manuel started trashing Caruso in camp before anything had gone wrong, saying he could lose his job to a scrub like Gabby Martinez. Once the season started and Caruso struggled, nary a week passed without Manuel emptying both barrels into him. Did Caruso earn it? Obviously. But you'll never see Bobby Cox or Jimy Williams running their players down, in good times or bad. Good managers don't do it, because they don't need to cultivate the local media to win respect or approval. Caruso could use a season at Triple-A just to learn without being held up for ridicule after every mistake.

McKay Christensen   CF   Bats L   Age 24

YEAR	TEAM	LGE	AB	H	DB	TP	HR	BB/SO	R	RBI	SB	CS	OUT	BA	OBP	SLG	EQA	EQR	DEFENSE
1997	Hickory	SAL	519	132	13	9	6	45/62	74	39	10	9	396	.254	.323	.349	.230	50	125-OF 103
1998	WnstnSlm	Car	374	97	17	5	4	47/54	57	28	8	4	281	.259	.353	.364	.250	44	96-OF 106
1999	ChiSox	AL	53	12	1	0	1	3/7	9	6	2	1	42	.226	.268	.302	.192	3	
1999	Birmnghm	Sou	296	79	6	5	3	23/49	40	23	10	3	220	.267	.331	.351	.239	31	74-OF 113
2000	*ChiSox*	*AL*	*338*	*90*	*11*	*4*	*4*	*39/50*	*51*	*41*	*9*	*5*	*253*	*.266*	*.342*	*.358*	*.245*	*38*	

He surprised everyone by making the team out of camp, in part due to Brian Simmons's injury. He was clearly not ready. Christensen is another player at loggerheads with Sox coaching, because instead of following batting coach Von Joshua's advice and spraying the ball around, he prefers to pull the ball. He's a flyer in center field and willing to take a walk, but he isn't going to grow up to be Brett Butler.

Joe Crede   3B   Bats R   Age 22

YEAR	TEAM	LGE	AB	H	DB	TP	HR	BB/SO	R	RBI	SB	CS	OUT	BA	OBP	SLG	EQA	EQR	DEFENSE
1997	Hickory	SAL	411	103	16	0	8	21/84	39	56	1	1	309	.251	.293	.348	.215	33	112-3B 98
1998	WnstnSlm	Car	507	146	28	2	21	49/95	84	79	4	3	364	.288	.359	.475	.278	74	128-3B 112
1999	Birmnghm	Sou	294	69	13	1	4	16/48	32	36	1	3	228	.235	.276	.327	.198	20	71-3B 91
2000	*ChiSox*	*AL*	*323*	*88*	*9*	*0*	*12*	*29/58*	*42*	*51*	*1*	*1*	*236*	*.272*	*.332*	*.412*	*.254*	*38*	

His bad second half in 1998 and his miserable 1999 are being written off because he was playing through a broken toe that he thought would go away if he left it alone. He's expected to heal completely after having had surgery last July, and he will challenge for the third-base job in camp. He's got a great glove and line-drive power, and the organization is ecstatic about his playing hurt. I'd call it foolish or irresponsible, but fortunately he didn't damage his future.

Jason Dellaero   SS   Bats B   Age 23

YEAR	TEAM	LGE	AB	H	DB	TP	HR	BB/SO	R	RBI	SB	CS	OUT	BA	OBP	SLG	EQA	EQR	DEFENSE
1997	Hickory	SAL	197	50	10	2	6	14/50	32	24	1	0	147	.254	.310	.416	.244	22	53-SS 92
1998	WnstnSlm	Car	434	88	23	2	11	24/142	42	46	6	2	348	.203	.250	.341	.196	30	120-SS 79
1999	WnstnSlm	Car	188	40	10	0	3	13/59	17	17	4	2	150	.213	.271	.314	.197	13	52-SS 99
1999	Birmnghm	Sou	274	68	14	2	9	9/78	33	36	3	4	210	.248	.278	.412	.225	25	80-SS 97
2000	*ChiSox*	*AL*	*366*	*83*	*14*	*1*	*11*	*23/112*	*35*	*40*	*4*	*2*	*285*	*.227*	*.272*	*.361*	*.212*	*30*	

Dellaero claims he had an awful season in 1998 because he was moping over not beating out Caruso for the shortstop job in camp, but so far he hasn't hit anywhere. He did improve at Birmingham when he learned to stop strangling the bat; it just wasn't enough. He has a great arm and he may win the starting shortstop job, if only to punish Caruso. The limitations of both players serve as ample explanation for why the Sox drafted Miami shortstop Bobby Hill, a Scott Boras client who remained unsigned in December.

Ray Durham   2B   Bats B   Age 28

YEAR	TEAM	LGE	AB	H	DB	TP	HR	BB/SO	R	RBI	SB	CS	OUT	BA	OBP	SLG	EQA	EQR	DEFENSE
1997	ChiSox	AL	635	175	27	6	11	57/92	103	52	33	17	477	.276	.342	.389	.251	75	153-2B 104
1998	ChiSox	AL	634	182	34	9	19	70/103	119	65	32	9	461	.287	.364	.459	.280	96	155-2B 99
1999	ChiSox	AL	609	179	30	8	12	66/105	100	55	34	12	442	.294	.367	.429	.274	87	142-2B 100
2000	*ChiSox*	*AL*	*510*	*139*	*21*	*6*	*11*	*58/84*	*89*	*70*	*23*	*9*	*380*	*.273*	*.347*	*.402*	*.261*	*66*	

While the Sox keep kicking around the idea of moving Durham to center field, Manuel does seem to understand that it won't help unless the team finds somebody who can hit well enough to take his place at second base. He's beginning to remind me of Bill Doran or Bobby Grich or Willie Randolph, in that he's his generation's great unsung second baseman. It looks like he's never going to surpass Roberto Alomar, any more than Doran surpassed Ryne Sandberg or Grich surpassed Joe Morgan.

Brook Fordyce   C   Bats R   Age 30

YEAR	TEAM	LGE	AB	H	DB	TP	HR	BB/SO	R	RBI	SB	CS	OUT	BA	OBP	SLG	EQA	EQR	DEFENSE
1997	Cincnnti	NL	96	20	2	0	2	8/15	7	9	2	0	76	.208	.269	.292	.192	6	
1998	Cincnnti	NL	147	38	7	0	4	11/27	8	15	0	1	110	.259	.310	.388	.233	14	41-C 102
1999	ChiSox	AL	332	99	25	1	9	17/48	33	46	2	0	233	.298	.338	.461	.267	43	91-C 99
2000	ChiSox	AL	231	64	10	0	9	17/35	31	38	1	0	167	.277	.327	.437	.259	28	

Fordyce was stolen from the Reds for a minor-league reliever. The Sox say they want a strong-armed catcher, but they already have two. Fordyce was awful trying to stop the running game in the first two months, throwing out only two of 27 basestealers. Coaches Mark Salas and Art Kusyner found he was crouching too low with his feet too far apart. After correcting his positioning, he threw out 41% of those who tried to run over the last four months. Add the fact Fordyce can hit a little, and you've got a great catching situation. He's been signed to a two-year extension, nipping trade rumors in the bud.

Dave Hollins   3B   Bats B   Age 34

YEAR	TEAM	LGE	AB	H	DB	TP	HR	BB/SO	R	RBI	SB	CS	OUT	BA	OBP	SLG	EQA	EQR	DEFENSE
1997	Anaheim	AL	569	164	29	2	16	58/119	97	82	16	6	411	.288	.363	.431	.271	79	129-3B 95
1998	Anaheim	AL	364	91	17	2	11	43/67	58	38	10	3	276	.250	.341	.398	.255	45	86-3B 98
1999	Toronto	AL	99	22	4	0	2	4/22	11	6	0	0	77	.222	.252	.323	.187	6	
1999	Charlott	Int	196	51	11	0	6	27/41	34	23	3	1	146	.260	.379	.408	.274	29	42-3B 76
2000	ChiSox	AL	307	75	11	1	11	43/63	47	45	6	2	234	.244	.337	.394	.254	38	

He doesn't have a position, and he hasn't hit well enough to DH since 1993. When even ex-Phillie friend Jim Fregosi won't keep him around as a crony, the end is nigh. Hollins is now a backup infielder who doesn't hit much and doesn't play the middle infield. Dave, the password is . . . "Amway."

Jeff Inglin   RF   Bats R   Age 24

YEAR	TEAM	LGE	AB	H	DB	TP	HR	BB/SO	R	RBI	SB	CS	OUT	BA	OBP	SLG	EQA	EQR	DEFENSE
1997	Hickory	SAL	554	164	33	4	16	43/88	79	84	12	4	394	.296	.350	.457	.271	76	84-OF 88
1998	Birmnghm	Sou	497	112	20	4	22	59/104	59	77	2	1	386	.225	.312	.414	.244	57	114-OF 93
1999	Birmnghm	Sou	437	116	24	3	13	45/66	49	50	10	1	322	.265	.340	.423	.261	56	102-OF 91
2000	ChiSox	AL	537	148	27	3	24	66/92	95	98	10	3	392	.276	.355	.471	.280	82	

Another example of a player improving in his second season in a league. Inglin has the arm for right field, but Ordonez isn't going anywhere, and the Sox are already loaded with right-handed power. When Carlos Lee was moved to the outfield, Inglin's shot at making the team in the foreseeable future started to take on water. He has value, just no star power.

Darrin Jackson   OF   Bats R   Age 36

YEAR	TEAM	LGE	AB	H	DB	TP	HR	BB/SO	R	RBI	SB	CS	OUT	BA	OBP	SLG	EQA	EQR	DEFENSE
1997	Minnesot	AL	130	34	2	1	3	3/20	18	21	2	0	96	.262	.278	.362	.215	10	34-OF 109
1997	Milwauke	AL	81	22	4	0	3	2/10	7	16	2	1	60	.272	.289	.432	.238	8	20-OF 118
1998	Milwauke	NL	205	50	14	1	4	9/36	20	20	1	1	156	.244	.279	.380	.218	17	51-OF 100
1999	ChiSox	AL	149	41	9	1	4	1/20	20	15	4	1	109	.275	.280	.430	.236	15	

Now that he's retired, Jackson will make a great coach. The White Sox wanted him to come back, but he isn't worth the roster spot. He's a good guy and a role model for other cancer survivors.

Mark Johnson   C   Bats L   Age 24

YEAR	TEAM	LGE	AB	H	DB	TP	HR	BB/SO	R	RBI	SB	CS	OUT	BA	OBP	SLG	EQA	EQR	DEFENSE
1997	WnstnSlm	Car	386	88	23	3	4	90/85	49	38	2	1	299	.228	.379	.334	.257	50	
1998	Birmnghm	Sou	382	98	17	2	8	85/74	54	45	0	1	285	.257	.398	.374	.274	56	103-C 92
1999	ChiSox	AL	206	47	7	0	5	34/58	24	16	3	1	160	.228	.343	.335	.240	23	65-C 100
2000	ChiSox	AL	284	69	14	1	6	57/67	52	39	2	1	216	.243	.370	.363	.261	38	

Johnson is already one of the best defensive catchers in the game, good at framing and receiving pitches. He's also one of the most nimble catchers, making it look easy when he pushes off his back leg from the crouch to put himself squarely in front of an errant pitch. Beyond that, he contributes to the offense by working pitchers and taking walks. He's comparable to Mike LaValliere, and potentially better.

Paul Konerko   1B   Bats R   Age 24

YEAR	TEAM	LGE	AB	H	DB	TP	HR	BB/SO	R	RBI	SB	CS	OUT	BA	OBP	SLG	EQA	EQR	DEFENSE	
1997	Albuquer	PCL	459	121	19	1	28	51/63	65	85	1	2	340	.264	.346	.492	.276	68	102-3B 89	23-1B 94
1998	LosAngls	NL	146	34	3	0	4	10/29	15	17	0	1	113	.233	.292	.336	.210	11		
1998	Cincnnti	NL	74	17	3	0	3	6/10	7	13	0	0	57	.230	.297	.392	.231	7		
1998	Indianap	Int	150	46	5	0	8	16/18	22	35	1	0	104	.307	.380	.500	.294	24	35-3B 93	
1999	ChiSox	AL	511	151	33	4	23	39/68	66	76	1	0	360	.295	.348	.511	.282	76	88-1B 108	
2000	*ChiSox*	*AL*	*494*	*146*	*25*	*1*	*29*	*53/68*	*85*	*108*	*1*	*1*	*349*	*.296*	*.364*	*.526*	*.295*	*83*		

Konerko finally got the playing time and the position that the Dodgers wouldn't give him. After a sluggish start, he proved he was the hitter everyone expected him to be. Slower than a three-toed sloth caught in a bear trap set in cement, he says he's going to work on his quickness over the winter. That should be enough to shed the cement. He's still willing to go back to third base, but that will happen only if Crede isn't ready and Manuel decides to demonize Greg Norton. Konerko was targeted by an embarrassed Tommy Lasorda for some false claims about a hip condition that the Pastaman said would ruin his career, an issue that came up only after Lasorda was ridiculed for trading Konerko. The projection above is a low starting point.

Carlos Lee   LF   Bats R   Age 24

YEAR	TEAM	LGE	AB	H	DB	TP	HR	BB/SO	R	RBI	SB	CS	OUT	BA	OBP	SLG	EQA	EQR	DEFENSE
1997	WnstnSlm	Car	553	159	45	3	15	24/65	66	66	5	3	397	.288	.319	.461	.258	67	133-3B 95
1998	Birmnghm	Sou	550	153	27	1	21	21/57	59	84	6	3	400	.278	.307	.445	.249	62	126-3B 89
1999	Charlott	Int	92	29	3	0	4	7/14	12	17	1	1	64	.315	.369	.478	.281	13	
1999	ChiSox	AL	492	145	34	2	15	7/72	61	79	4	2	349	.295	.310	.463	.255	57	97-LF 92
2000	*ChiSox*	*AL*	*580*	*174*	*29*	*1*	*24*	*29/76*	*83*	*104*	*7*	*2*	*408*	*.300*	*.333*	*.478*	*.272*	*79*	

Lee is interesting, because he hasn't really learned to hit yet. He's still at the "see ball, hit ball hard" stage, and hasn't learned to wait on his pitch, work a pitcher to get that pitch or turn on a pitch and jerk it to left field. Manuel wants to see him become more selective, but he's less likely to make progress in that area than in learning how to work for a pitch to hammer. He has a lot of work to do in left field; he's willing to try, but the Sox may move him to first base if they send Konerko to third.

Jeff Liefer   1B/LF   Bats L   Age 25

YEAR	TEAM	LGE	AB	H	DB	TP	HR	BB/SO	R	RBI	SB	CS	OUT	BA	OBP	SLG	EQA	EQR	DEFENSE	
1997	Birmnghm	Sou	477	105	23	6	14	27/123	52	57	1	0	372	.220	.270	.382	.216	40	105-OF 85	
1998	Birmnghm	Sou	472	121	30	4	18	41/133	64	65	1	1	352	.256	.325	.451	.258	60	99-1B 94	
1999	ChiSox	AL	113	28	7	1	0	7/28	7	13	2	0	85	.248	.292	.327	.213	9		
1999	Charlott	Int	168	51	14	1	7	17/27	28	26	1	1	118	.304	.370	.524	.293	27	24-1B 106	17-OF 78
2000	*ChiSox*	*AL*	*398*	*103*	*22*	*3*	*14*	*40/95*	*57*	*63*	*2*	*1*	*296*	*.259*	*.326*	*.435*	*.258*	*50*		

He made the team out of spring training when everyone belatedly noticed that the Sox didn't have any left-handed power. Between injuries and his defensive limitations—there will be no return to third base or left field in anything other than an emergency—he can go only as far as his bat takes him. Dumping Mario Valdez makes it pretty clear who the organization prefers, so Liefer has an opportunity to win playing time at first base if Konerko is moved to third. If you haven't figured it out yet, the Sox have a lot of options for the infield corners.

Terrell Merriman   OF   Bats L   Age 22

YEAR	TEAM	LGE	AB	H	DB	TP	HR	BB/SO	R	RBI	SB	CS	OUT	BA	OBP	SLG	EQA	EQR	DEFENSE
1998	Bristol	App	130	26	4	0	2	11/36	13	11	3	1	105	.200	.262	.277	.182	7	35-OF 102
1999	Burlingt	Mid	381	95	14	6	13	53/88	50	58	11	2	288	.249	.343	.420	.262	51	103-OF 90
2000	*ChiSox*	*AL*	*178*	*43*	*7*	*1*	*7*	*28/49*	*31*	*27*	*5*	*1*	*136*	*.242*	*.345*	*.410*	*.264*	*24*	

Merriman is an athletic outfielder who was nabbed out of a small college in the 34th round, a nice piece of scouting. He might have been the best hitting prospect on a good Burlington team; Battersby and third baseman Ryan Hankins were a bit old for the league, while Merriman out-hit outfielders Mario Valenzuela and Jason Fennell. Center-field prospect J.R. Mounts struggled badly, and may have to repeat the Midwest League.

Chad Mottola CF Bats R Age 28

YEAR	TEAM	LGE	AB	H	DB	TP	HR	BB/SO	R	RBI	SB	CS	OUT	BA	OBP	SLG	EQA	EQR	DEFENSE
1997	Chattang	Sou	170	47	8	2	3	10/28	21	20	3	1	124	.276	.319	.400	.244	18	41-OF 89
1997	Indianap	AA	288	76	11	5	5	12/48	27	39	8	3	215	.264	.303	.389	.234	29	70-OF 94
1998	Oklahoma	PCL	257	60	12	1	1	14/54	22	17	5	2	199	.233	.275	.300	.193	16	67-OF 92
1999	Charlott	Int	504	136	25	3	14	46/91	67	67	11	4	372	.270	.334	.415	.255	61	139-OF 97
2000	Toronto	AL	461	121	20	3	12	41/84	64	63	9	4	344	.262	.323	.397	.245	51	

This year's Charlotte team got to the Triple-A World Series on the strength of a good combination of minor-league veterans and borderline prospects. Mottola is both, and had an All-Star season after signing as a minor-league free agent. He's got some pop and a strong arm, but he doesn't have the range to play center field every day. He would still make a nice fourth outfielder for some teams.

Greg Norton 3B Bats B Age 27

YEAR	TEAM	LGE	AB	H	DB	TP	HR	BB/SO	R	RBI	SB	CS	OUT	BA	OBP	SLG	EQA	EQR	DEFENSE
1997	Nashvill	AA	417	104	25	1	21	50/106	71	64	3	3	316	.249	.336	.465	.265	57	93-3B 90
1998	ChiSox	AL	299	72	17	2	9	25/75	37	35	3	3	230	.241	.304	.401	.236	31	71-1B 88
1999	ChiSox	AL	434	110	22	0	17	64/93	57	48	4	4	328	.253	.352	.422	.262	58	110-3B 105
2000	ChiSox	AL	420	104	19	0	19	54/96	62	69	3	3	319	.248	.333	.429	.258	54	

Norton gets flogged for his errors, but the criticism of his defense is overstated. He does a good job of guarding the line and has good range. His arm is scattershot, so he makes errors in bunches. The criticism of his glovework may mean he never gets to be a regular at third base again, but he has experience at all four infield positions. He had a good run while batting second in September after Thomas's injury exacerbated the lineup's on-base problems enough to make them desperate for baserunners. The Sox should have thought of it sooner. He's a much better option at the top of the order than Caruso, but he does need to be platooned, as he simply can't bat right-handed. Give him 300 at-bats and use him in the field as needed, and you've got a great part-time player.

Magglio Ordonez RF Bats R Age 26

YEAR	TEAM	LGE	AB	H	DB	TP	HR	BB/SO	R	RBI	SB	CS	OUT	BA	OBP	SLG	EQA	EQR	DEFENSE
1997	Nashvill	AA	524	161	28	3	12	27/62	58	81	11	7	370	.307	.344	.441	.263	65	122-OF 103
1998	ChiSox	AL	534	151	25	2	14	27/52	67	62	8	7	390	.283	.328	.416	.249	60	138-OF 101
1999	ChiSox	AL	622	187	35	3	29	40/64	93	109	13	6	441	.301	.344	.506	.279	91	151-RF 99
2000	ChiSox	AL	573	166	29	2	22	46/59	89	99	9	4	411	.290	.342	.462	.272	79	

He's probably the most fun player to watch in Chicago today. He has tremendous bat speed and a great arm, and he can field caroms in the corner with the grace of a jai alai player. The good news is, he broke through for an All-Star season; the bad news is, he wore down in the second half. Among the reasons offered were that he was tired after playing a full season of winter ball, that he'd lost 13 pounds and that he was trying too hard to reach 30 home runs. He was supposed to cut back on winter ball in the offseason. Regardless, he'll come down from last year's high, so that projection looks about right.

Josh Paul C Bats R Age 25

YEAR	TEAM	LGE	AB	H	DB	TP	HR	BB/SO	R	RBI	SB	CS	OUT	BA	OBP	SLG	EQA	EQR	DEFENSE
1997	Birmnghm	Sou	115	31	4	0	1	9/27	13	13	4	1	85	.270	.327	.330	.231	11	
1998	WnstnSlm	Car	454	101	17	5	10	32/96	52	51	8	3	356	.222	.278	.348	.212	37	108-C 99
1999	Birmnghm	Sou	322	78	17	2	3	20/77	36	32	3	3	247	.242	.293	.335	.212	25	83-C 101
2000	ChiSox	AL	279	64	11	2	4	23/64	29	26	3	2	217	.229	.288	.326	.208	22	

Sometimes an organization remains devoted to a prospect the way some people remain devoted to bad ideas, like new math, supply-side economics or czarism. Paul has never hit well, but he carries a nice defensive reputation—he threw out 40% of attempted basestealers—and he was once a high draft pick. He gets good marks for leadership skills. Still, he hasn't hit and doesn't seem likely to start.

Luis Raven DH Bats R Age 31

YEAR	TEAM	LGE	AB	H	DB	TP	HR	BB/SO	R	RBI	SB	CS	OUT	BA	OBP	SLG	EQA	EQR	DEFENSE
1997	Birmnghm	Sou	455	122	25	2	19	30/152	57	71	2	1	334	.268	.318	.457	.257	56	37-3B 78
1999	Charlott	Int	527	125	28	3	23	37/140	70	88	3	0	402	.237	.290	.433	.240	57	
2000	ChiSox	AL	388	96	18	1	18	32/116	50	61	2	0	292	.247	.305	.438	.250	46	

A professional hitter who has bat and will travel, Raven is similar to Jeff Manto, just not as good. He spent 1998 in the Mexican League, then came back to set International League records in home runs (33) and RBIs (125). Scouts will tell you he can't handle inside heat or breaking pitches outside, but an NL team that needs a deluxe right-handed pinch-hitter could do worse than carry Raven.

Liu Rodriguez 2B/SS Bats B Age 23

YEAR	TEAM	LGE	AB	H	DB	TP	HR	BB/SO	R	RBI	SB	CS	OUT	BA	OBP	SLG	EQA	EQR	DEFENSE	
1997	Hickory	SAL	468	121	22	5	1	57/57	60	51	4	6	353	.259	.343	.333	.235	47	124-2B 100	
1998	WnstnSlm	Car	431	112	29	2	2	42/39	56	39	7	4	323	.260	.334	.350	.237	44	93-2B 98	
1999	Birmnghm	Sou	246	67	10	1	3	17/36	35	31	3	2	181	.272	.325	.358	.233	24	33-2B 89	23-SS 103
1999	ChiSox	AL	93	22	2	2	1	11/11	7	11	0	0	71	.237	.337	.333	.235	9		
2000	ChiSox	AL	324	87	16	2	3	35/39	46	39	4	3	240	.269	.340	.358	.243	35		

This is the second-best second baseman in the Windy City. He can get on base and hangs tough turning the deuce. Even so, he's not good enough to encourage the Sox to move Durham to the outfield. Like a lot of good minor-league second basemen, if he proves he can play shortstop, he'll eventually be a major-league utility infielder. If he doesn't, he won't make it.

Aaron Rowand OF Bats R Age 22

YEAR	TEAM	LGE	AB	H	DB	TP	HR	BB/SO	R	RBI	SB	CS	OUT	BA	OBP	SLG	EQA	EQR	DEFENSE
1998	Hickory	SAL	222	65	13	2	4	17/35	31	24	3	1	158	.293	.353	.423	.265	28	45-OF 98
1999	WnstnSlm	Car	520	134	30	2	25	23/91	79	74	7	5	391	.258	.300	.467	.251	62	98-OF 99
2000	ChiSox	AL	312	85	14	1	18	23/63	45	59	4	2	229	.272	.322	.497	.271	44	

Rowand took the step in 1999 that Carlos Lee needs to take: he learned which pitches he can hammer. For his trouble, he was named the Carolina League's best hitting prospect by *Baseball America*. He needs to improve his command of the strike zone, because a Sox lineup that includes Lee, Ordonez, Konerko and Caruso will have on-base problems. I'm not talking 60 walks, just improvement. While Lee's move to the outfield doesn't make things any easier for Rowand, if he survives the jump to Double-A, he'll be ready by 2001.

Brian Simmons CF Bats B Age 26

YEAR	TEAM	LGE	AB	H	DB	TP	HR	BB/SO	R	RBI	SB	CS	OUT	BA	OBP	SLG	EQA	EQR	DEFENSE
1997	Birmnghm	Sou	551	126	27	8	12	68/137	79	53	10	7	432	.229	.315	.372	.234	57	136-OF 104
1998	Calgary	PCL	348	85	19	3	9	34/84	53	37	7	4	267	.244	.313	.394	.239	37	92-OF 98
1999	Charlott	Int	283	64	9	0	8	29/66	38	32	5	2	221	.226	.307	.343	.224	26	79-OF 97
1999	ChiSox	AL	126	29	3	3	4	8/30	13	16	4	0	97	.230	.276	.397	.230	12	
2000	ChiSox	AL	381	84	13	3	12	43/91	48	46	8	3	300	.220	.300	.365	.229	38	

Simmons had the center-field job won last spring before getting his hand gashed during a slide into second base. He wouldn't have hit enough to keep it, and this was probably his only shot at winning a starting job. He can hit right-handers well enough, and he's got good range and a strong arm. As long as Lee plays left field, the Sox will need a defensive replacement: here he is.

Mitch Simons IF Bats R Age 31

YEAR	TEAM	LGE	AB	H	DB	TP	HR	BB/SO	R	RBI	SB	CS	OUT	BA	OBP	SLG	EQA	EQR	DEFENSE	
1997	SaltLake	PCL	448	105	26	6	3	33/54	54	38	15	4	347	.234	.293	.339	.219	39	74-2B 101	
1998	Rochestr	Int	192	38	8	1	1	16/18	17	14	4	1	155	.198	.263	.266	.178	10	45-SS 93	
1998	Tacoma	PCL	180	38	8	1	1	12/25	20	16	6	1	143	.211	.271	.283	.192	12	26-SS 87	
1999	Charlott	Int	469	115	24	1	5	34/74	60	38	13	5	358	.245	.309	.333	.223	42	44-2B 99	39-3B 93
2000	ChiSox	AL	390	88	18	2	3	36/56	43	32	9	3	305	.226	.291	.305	.207	30		

(Mitch Simons *continued*)

He was an offensive machine in the International League championship series and the Triple-A World Series. Simons is not a prospect by any stretch of the imagination, but he is somebody who could turn up as a team's utility infielder off his moment of postseason greatness.

Chris Singleton   CF   Bats L   Age 27

YEAR	TEAM	LGE	AB	H	DB	TP	HR	BB/SO	R	RBI	SB	CS	OUT	BA	OBP	SLG	EQA	EQR	DEFENSE
1997	Shrevprt	Tex	459	120	22	6	8	15/62	55	43	13	6	345	.261	.286	.388	.226	42	118-OF 102
1998	Columbus	Int	412	91	16	8	4	18/87	42	35	5	2	323	.221	.259	.328	.195	27	117-OF 102
1999	ChiSox	AL	495	149	32	6	16	16/45	67	67	20	5	351	.301	.324	.487	.270	66	116-CF 107
2000	*ChiSox*	*AL*	*466*	*127*	*23*	*6*	*12*	*25/59*	*65*	*65*	*14*	*4*	*343*	*.273*	*.310*	*.425*	*.250*	*54*	

While I'm not really optimistic about his future, you can't help but love what he did. He's an exaggerated example of a claim we'll make for several players throughout this book: there are minor leaguers who can play this game if they get the chance. Singleton is probably the ultimate Manuel player—quiet, Christian, a good glove man and situational hitter, but not great at playing baseball.

Jim Terrell   3B   Bats L   Age 22

YEAR	TEAM	LGE	AB	H	DB	TP	HR	BB/SO	R	RBI	SB	CS	OUT	BA	OBP	SLG	EQA	EQR	DEFENSE	
1997	Bristol	App	178	33	2	1	1	11/43	18	15	2	0	145	.185	.235	.225	.139	5	47-2B 85	
1998	Hickory	SAL	510	147	20	3	11	43/91	60	49	9	4	367	.288	.347	.404	.257	61	84-3B 89	19-2B 97
1999	WnstnSlm	Car	445	114	33	4	3	41/76	62	40	8	3	334	.256	.325	.369	.239	47	112-3B 83	
2000	*ChiSox*	*AL*	*468*	*130*	*24*	*2*	*10*	*50/83*	*74*	*67*	*7*	*2*	*340*	*.278*	*.347*	*.402*	*.260*	*59*		

The son of ex-major-leaguer Jerry Terrell, who just happened to be Jim's manager at Winston-Salem. The Sox have a few family members playing for them: Jerry Manuel's nephew Marcellous and Hawk Harrelson's son Casey were both puttering around the system in 1999. Unlike them, Terrell is a ballplayer. What position he's going to end up playing is an open question; he has experience at all four infield spots as well as the outfield. The best case is that he turns into a better version of Lenny Harris.

Frank Thomas   DH/1B   Bats R   Age 32

YEAR	TEAM	LGE	AB	H	DB	TP	HR	BB/SO	R	RBI	SB	CS	OUT	BA	OBP	SLG	EQA	EQR	DEFENSE
1997	ChiSox	AL	529	189	31	0	38	106/66	108	126	1	1	341	.357	.467	.631	.357	130	92-1B 91
1998	ChiSox	AL	584	157	37	2	29	107/91	106	106	6	0	427	.269	.388	.488	.295	101	
1999	ChiSox	AL	482	147	28	0	17	81/66	67	74	3	3	338	.305	.414	.469	.301	84	47-1B 92
2000	*ChiSox*	*AL*	*480*	*141*	*19*	*0*	*28*	*95/67*	*103*	*110*	*3*	*1*	*340*	*.294*	*.410*	*.508*	*.312*	*93*	

He's the best bat in the division not wearing an Indians uniform, and for all of the grief he takes, you'd think he hit like Ozzie Guillen. He came into the year reportedly obsessed with hitting over .300, and during the season focused on that at the expense of his power. A few ill-considered run-ins with umpires on the subject of the strike zone haven't helped him catch any breaks. While everyone in Chicago is talking about trading him, doing so guarantees his contract through 2006 and activates a no-trade clause. There might be a team dumb enough to make that trade, but the Orioles are already paying Will Clark plenty.

Craig Wilson   IF   Bats R   Age 29

YEAR	TEAM	LGE	AB	H	DB	TP	HR	BB/SO	R	RBI	SB	CS	OUT	BA	OBP	SLG	EQA	EQR	DEFENSE	
1997	Nashvill	AA	456	109	17	2	4	39/35	59	35	3	2	349	.239	.300	.311	.209	35	113-SS 96	
1998	Calgary	PCL	422	104	16	1	9	29/45	46	48	2	1	319	.246	.298	.353	.220	36	49-2B 90	27-SS 102
1999	ChiSox	AL	252	60	8	1	4	20/22	26	25	1	1	193	.238	.294	.325	.209	19	50-3B 118	
2000	*ChiSox*	*AL*	*279*	*68*	*11*	*1*	*4*	*26/26*	*30*	*30*	*1*	*1*	*212*	*.244*	*.308*	*.333*	*.220*	*24*		

Scrappy, a gamer, heady… you've heard all of the code words for "hard-working white guy." He can pick it wherever he's playing, but his chief value is as a platoon mate and defensive caddy for Norton. That means he's out of a job when Crede's ready, the same as Norton. Keeping both as utilitymen would make for a strong bench.

PITCHERS (Averages: ERA: 4.50 / H/9: 9.00 / HR/9: 1.00 / BB/9: 3.50 / K/9: 6.50 / KWH: 1.00)

Luis Andujar   Throws R   Age 27

YEAR	TEAM	LGE	IP	H	ER	HR	BB	K	ERA	W	L	H/9	HR/9	BB/9	K/9	KWH	PERA
1997	Syracuse	Int	37.3	42	27	6	15	24	6.51	1	3	10.13	1.45	3.62	5.79	0.68	5.79
1997	Toronto	AL	50.3	74	42	8	21	28	7.51	2	4	13.23	1.43	3.75	5.01	0.38	7.69
1998	Syracuse	Int	32.0	28	12	5	7	20	3.38	3	1	7.88	1.41	1.97	5.63	1.52	3.66
1998	Calgary	PCL	49.0	66	38	7	18	38	6.98	1	4	12.12	1.29	3.31	6.98	0.91	6.61
1999	Charlott	Int	60.3	63	19	3	15	51	2.83	5	2	9.40	0.45	2.24	7.61	2.06	3.73

He's still going, and still capable of being a solid major-league reliever if he has a good camp. Andujar was finally left alone to close for Charlotte after losing two years to attempts to keep him starting, despite his wonky elbow. The two good lines up there are his two relief-only seasons or partial seasons. The Sox are loaded in the pen, but Andujar could join any club as a minor-league free agent this winter.

James Baldwin   Throws R   Age 28

YEAR	TEAM	LGE	IP	H	ER	HR	BB	K	ERA	W	L	H/9	HR/9	BB/9	K/9	KWH	PERA
1997	ChiSox	AL	202.3	195	116	18	83	141	5.16	10	12	8.67	0.80	3.69	6.27	0.92	4.18
1998	ChiSox	AL	160.0	172	95	16	63	109	5.34	7	11	9.68	0.90	3.54	6.13	0.82	4.78
1999	ChiSox	AL	200.0	208	104	30	78	126	4.68	11	11	9.36	1.35	3.51	5.67	0.73	5.08

Baldwin's second-half-resurrection act has just about worn out its welcome. At the All-Star break he had a 6.62 ERA, and Jerry Manuel was grumping about his lack of concentration. He still keeps falling in love with his curve, only to see it flatten out from overuse and get hammered. Baldwin rattled off seven quality starts in his last 11, posting an ERA of 3.56 after the break. I'm not convinced he's fixed the problem: the peripheral numbers are all headed the wrong way. The talent is there for him to turn into a solid third starter, but no organization can wait forever.

Lorenzo Barcelo   Throws R   Age 22

YEAR	TEAM	LGE	IP	H	ER	HR	BB	K	ERA	W	L	H/9	HR/9	BB/9	K/9	KWH	PERA
1997	San Jose	Cal	83.0	105	48	14	34	63	5.20	4	5	11.39	1.52	3.69	6.83	0.83	6.61
1997	Shrevprt	Tex	28.7	35	22	5	9	17	6.91	1	2	10.99	1.57	2.83	5.34	0.69	5.97
1997	Birmnghm	Sou	31.0	41	22	3	10	24	6.39	1	2	11.90	0.87	2.90	6.97	1.05	5.81
1999	Birmnghm	Sou	19.0	17	10	0	6	12	4.74	1	1	8.05	0.00	2.84	5.68	1.05	2.84

After missing 1998 with reconstructive elbow surgery, the man who was supposed to be the key player in the 1997 trade with the Giants came back with mid-90s heat. His curveball hasn't returned from the operating room, but he's working on a slurve and was trying to add a change-up in the Arizona Fall League. He's young enough to recover a brilliant career.

Kevin Beirne   Throws R   Age 26

YEAR	TEAM	LGE	IP	H	ER	HR	BB	K	ERA	W	L	H/9	HR/9	BB/9	K/9	KWH	PERA
1997	WnstnSlm	Car	76.7	88	51	8	35	52	5.99	3	6	10.33	0.94	4.11	6.10	0.66	5.40
1997	Birmnghm	Sou	69.3	85	56	4	46	39	7.27	2	6	11.03	0.52	5.97	5.06	0.29	6.23
1998	Birmnghm	Sou	157.7	165	83	13	90	117	4.74	9	9	9.42	0.74	5.14	6.68	0.69	5.14
1999	Charlott	Int	112.7	138	70	12	40	55	5.59	5	8	11.02	0.96	3.20	4.39	0.41	5.51

Beirne started the year a good half-season away from getting a crack at the major-league rotation. He couldn't do it. A strained arm left him pitching in pain with reduced velocity until he was diagnosed with a deep chest muscle strain and shut down. When healthy, he has velocity in the low 90s, a nasty overhand curve and a decent change-up and slider. With so many other good arms moving up in the organization, he's going to have impress people quickly to get a shot.

Chad Bradford   Throws R   Age 25

YEAR	TEAM	LGE	IP	H	ER	HR	BB	K	ERA	W	L	H/9	HR/9	BB/9	K/9	KWH	PERA
1997	WnstnSlm	Car	51.3	65	38	3	29	31	6.66	2	4	11.40	0.53	5.08	5.44	0.38	5.96
1998	Birmnghm	Sou	16.7	15	6	2	8	11	3.24	1	1	8.10	1.08	4.32	5.94	0.75	4.32
1998	Calgary	PCL	51.0	50	11	3	12	23	1.94	5	1	8.82	0.53	2.12	4.06	0.66	3.35
1998	ChiSox	AL	30.7	26	15	0	8	11	4.40	2	1	7.63	0.00	2.35	3.23	0.43	2.35
1999	Charlott	Int	75.0	62	16	2	16	49	1.92	7	1	7.44	0.24	1.92	5.88	1.81	2.40

(Chad Bradford *continued*)

Bradford is a big submariner who can toss four pitches for strikes, the best a circle change. He generates a ton of groundball outs, nearly four times as many as the number of flyball outs. The White Sox already have a good pen, so it won't be easy for him to earn a job, but he's more than ready right now.

Carlos Castillo   Throws R   Age 25

YEAR	TEAM	LGE	IP	H	ER	HR	BB	K	ERA	W	L	H/9	HR/9	BB/9	K/9	KWH	PERA
1997	ChiSox	AL	66.7	65	31	8	33	43	4.18	4	3	8.78	1.08	4.46	5.81	0.64	4.86
1998	ChiSox	AL	100.7	92	56	16	36	65	5.01	5	6	8.23	1.43	3.22	5.81	0.95	4.38
1999	Charlott	Int	136.7	152	79	25	33	93	5.20	6	9	10.01	1.65	2.17	6.12	1.29	5.27
1999	ChiSox	AL	41.0	44	23	9	13	24	5.05	2	3	9.66	1.98	2.85	5.27	0.75	5.71

Castillo is a target for boo birds. Whether it's another taterrific day at the office or his frequent flirtations with 300 pounds, he's hard to miss. In August, everyone got a drive-through-window peek into Castillo's experiences with the workaday world: after another bad game, he pointed out that he doesn't boo fry cooks at McDonald's when they let him down. While he shows flashes of talent, changing speeds on his curve, he has to give up his love affair with Joe Sheehan's favorite food groups, like starch, lard and hops.

Carlos Chantres   Throws R   Age 24

YEAR	TEAM	LGE	IP	H	ER	HR	BB	K	ERA	W	L	H/9	HR/9	BB/9	K/9	KWH	PERA
1997	WnstnSlm	Car	155.7	192	112	23	80	117	6.48	6	11	11.10	1.33	4.63	6.76	0.67	6.59
1998	WnstnSlm	Car	82.0	92	58	12	57	61	6.37	3	6	10.10	1.32	6.26	6.70	0.53	6.70
1998	Birmnghm	Sou	50.3	64	34	6	40	40	6.08	2	4	11.44	1.07	7.15	7.15	0.47	7.69
1999	Birmnghm	Sou	130.3	150	78	14	67	85	5.39	6	8	10.36	0.97	4.63	5.87	0.54	5.73

Nobody thinks he has great stuff, yet he still managed to be a Double-A All-Star. Because the Sox have done such a good job drafting and developing pitching talent, he's just one arm among many in the system. Under those circumstances, he's someone who may get bumped into the bullpen and thrive.

Pat Daneker   Throws R   Age 24

YEAR	TEAM	LGE	IP	H	ER	HR	BB	K	ERA	W	L	H/9	HR/9	BB/9	K/9	KWH	PERA
1997	Bristol	App	53.7	118	72	5	29	29	12.07	1	5	19.79	0.84	4.86	4.86	0.18	11.91
1998	Hickory	SAL	106.3	155	66	16	23	60	5.59	5	7	13.12	1.35	1.95	5.08	0.75	6.77
1998	WnstnSlm	Car	50.0	66	18	4	7	30	3.24	4	2	11.88	0.72	1.26	5.40	1.46	5.04
1999	Birmnghm	Sou	101.0	128	56	7	33	57	4.99	5	6	11.41	0.62	2.94	5.08	0.57	5.26
1999	Charlott	Int	50.0	64	32	9	17	33	5.76	2	4	11.52	1.62	3.06	5.94	0.75	6.48

As you'd expect from a college pitcher from a top program (Virginia), Daneker moved up quickly. He's a sinker/slider type who doesn't throw especially hard. He's still refining a change-up and knows he has to hit his spots to succeed. Because he's got a jowly square head, or because he doesn't get rattled, he's got a bulldog reputation. Daneker was rushed up to take Snyder's spot in the rotation in July, but didn't stick because Kip Wells and Aaron Myette are better prospects. He'll win a rotation spot only if he has a good camp while others fail.

Scott Eyre   Throws L   Age 28

YEAR	TEAM	LGE	IP	H	ER	HR	BB	K	ERA	W	L	H/9	HR/9	BB/9	K/9	KWH	PERA
1997	Birmnghm	Sou	114.7	135	74	14	65	94	5.81	5	8	10.60	1.10	5.10	7.38	0.75	6.20
1997	ChiSox	AL	61.0	60	32	10	31	36	4.72	3	4	8.85	1.48	4.57	5.31	0.52	5.31
1998	ChiSox	AL	107.0	112	72	22	67	74	6.06	4	8	9.42	1.85	5.64	6.22	0.55	6.56
1999	Charlott	Int	68.7	76	29	3	25	54	3.80	5	3	9.96	0.39	3.28	7.08	1.15	4.33
1999	ChiSox	AL	25.3	36	19	6	14	17	6.75	1	2	12.79	2.13	4.97	6.04	0.43	8.88

Eyre has good velocity for a left-hander, but his control has never been good enough for him to be a one-out specialist. If the Sox don't pick up a veteran, he has a shot to be the second left-hander behind Jesus Pena. He would be valuable if used in long relief.

Juan Figueroa   Throws R   Age 21

YEAR	TEAM	LGE	IP	H	ER	HR	BB	K	ERA	W	L	H/9	HR/9	BB/9	K/9	KWH	PERA
1998	Bristol	App	71.7	114	68	15	29	62	8.54	2	6	14.32	1.88	3.64	7.79	0.87	9.04
1999	Burlingt	Mid	112.7	116	53	10	51	100	4.23	7	6	9.27	0.80	4.07	7.99	1.26	4.63
1999	WnstnSlm	Car	55.3	78	52	2	22	37	8.46	1	5	12.69	0.33	3.58	6.02	0.60	6.02

Figueroa is a gangly Dominican (6'3", 150 pounds) with a maximum-effort delivery. He's moving up quickly, as the Sox think he's a good learner with pitching savvy, and the expectation is that he'll pick up velocity as he fills out. Like most A-ball pitchers, he's a risk, but one with a high ceiling.

Joshua Fogg   Throws R   Age 23

YEAR	TEAM	LGE	IP	H	ER	HR	BB	K	ERA	W	L	H/9	HR/9	BB/9	K/9	KWH	PERA
1998	Hickory	SAL	37.7	47	22	5	18	19	5.26	2	2	11.23	1.19	4.30	4.54	0.32	6.45
1999	WnstnSlm	Car	101.0	109	49	4	39	78	4.37	6	5	9.71	0.36	3.48	6.95	1.07	4.28
1999	Birmnghm	Sou	50.7	78	42	8	20	33	7.46	2	4	13.86	1.42	3.55	5.86	0.52	7.99

He was the first-team All-American closer at the University of Florida in 1998. So what did the Sox do? Converted him to starting to give him the innings he needs to improve command of his pitches other than a good fastball. You see a lot of this, and it's the difference between a usage pattern that's development-oriented and one that apes the major-league closer-driven "way to win."

What's important to realize is that not only does this make Fogg a better pitcher, it doesn't make a difference in terms of wins and losses for an A-ball team. It also reflects a sensible choice for major-league organizations: if college coaches want to use their best pitchers as closers in a knee-jerk response to the way things are done in the major leagues, fine. The kid who closed isn't going to have serious mileage on his arm before he's 22. That's great for player development, because you don't want kids slagged for the greater glory of the alma mater. It also reflects a deeper problem, which is how the creation of a statistic, the save, has corrupted the way people use talent.

Tom Fordham   Throws L   Age 26

YEAR	TEAM	LGE	IP	H	ER	HR	BB	K	ERA	W	L	H/9	HR/9	BB/9	K/9	KWH	PERA
1997	Nashvill	AmA	113.3	121	67	13	60	81	5.32	5	8	9.61	1.03	4.76	6.43	0.68	5.40
1998	Calgary	PCL	55.3	39	20	5	30	33	3.25	4	2	6.34	0.81	4.88	5.37	0.70	3.42
1998	ChiSox	AL	48.3	49	33	7	44	23	6.14	2	3	9.12	1.30	8.19	4.28	0.18	6.89
1999	Charlott	Int	111.3	149	94	22	73	88	7.60	3	9	12.04	1.78	5.90	7.11	0.53	8.33

Sometimes you eat the bear, sometimes the bear eats you, and sometimes the bear eats you one limb at a time over six months because he's a mean bastard. Working high in the strike zone with no great out pitch is a tough way for anyone to make a living. Fordham is now descending from prospectdom and could use a change of organizations.

Keith Foulke   Throws R   Age 27

YEAR	TEAM	LGE	IP	H	ER	HR	BB	K	ERA	W	L	H/9	HR/9	BB/9	K/9	KWH	PERA
1997	Phoenix	PCL	71.3	83	38	10	16	46	4.79	4	4	10.47	1.26	2.02	5.80	1.19	5.05
1997	San Fran	NL	44.7	61	41	10	19	31	8.26	1	4	12.29	2.01	3.83	6.25	0.62	7.86
1997	ChiSox	AL	28.7	27	10	4	5	21	3.14	2	1	8.48	1.26	1.57	6.59	2.44	3.77
1998	ChiSox	AL	65.3	50	29	9	21	58	3.99	4	3	6.89	1.24	2.89	7.99	2.39	3.31
1999	ChiSox	AL	105.7	68	24	10	20	126	2.04	10	2	5.79	0.85	1.70	10.73	8.72	2.13

Foulke clearly has come to relish his role as the guy who enters the tight game. Interestingly, he wasn't the guy brought in with runners aboard; usually, those situations went to Sean Lowe or Bill Simas. Instead, Foulke would come in to pitch whole innings before the ninth. His palmball is dynamite, but it isn't as though he doesn't have a full repertoire. It's sort of a shame: he's so good in middle relief that he's probably never going to move back into the rotation, even though he'd be a good starter.

Jon Garland   Throws R   Age 20

YEAR	TEAM	LGE	IP	H	ER	HR	BB	K	ERA	W	L	H/9	HR/9	BB/9	K/9	KWH	PERA
1998	Rockford	Mid	95.7	168	94	16	59	49	8.84	2	9	15.80	1.51	5.55	4.61	0.18	10.44
1998	Hickory	SAL	24.0	46	26	3	18	13	9.75	1	2	17.25	1.13	6.75	4.88	0.15	11.62
1999	WnstnSlm	Car	116.7	126	61	9	44	62	4.71	6	7	9.72	0.69	3.39	4.78	0.52	4.55
1999	Birmnghm	Sou	36.3	46	25	4	20	22	6.19	1	3	11.39	0.99	4.95	5.45	0.39	6.44

(Jon Garland *continued*)

How could a trade turn out much better? As he grows up, Garland's fastball is inching into the mid-90s, and its great sinking action generates lots of ground balls. He's also starting to throw his curve and change-up for strikes and is learning to throw a cutter and use both sides of the plate. The Sox decided to promote almost everyone in the organization with talent to Charlotte to give all of them a look during the Triple-A World Series. Garland was the guy who made Vancouver look so bad that Ron Schueler was buzzing about his chances of winning a spot in the 2000 rotation. That's a reach, but he could be ready by August. Cub fans can take heart, though: Matt Karchner is going to pitch next year, right?

Bobby Howry   Throws R   Age 26

YEAR	TEAM	LGE	IP	H	ER	HR	BB	K	ERA	W	L	H/9	HR/9	BB/9	K/9	KWH	PERA
1997	Shrevprt	Tex	48.7	69	41	7	25	36	7.58	1	4	12.76	1.29	4.62	6.66	0.56	7.58
1997	Birmnghm	Sou	11.7	18	4	1	3	2	3.09	1	0	13.89	0.77	2.31	1.54	0.06	6.94
1998	Calgary	PCL	31.3	25	11	2	12	19	3.16	2	1	7.18	0.57	3.45	5.46	0.90	3.16
1998	ChiSox	AL	54.0	37	18	7	19	51	3.00	4	2	6.17	1.17	3.17	8.50	2.76	3.00
1999	ChiSox	AL	68.0	55	29	7	37	82	3.84	5	3	7.28	0.93	4.90	10.85	2.47	3.97

Howry has the chance to be more than your run-of-the-mill flamethrowing closer. Like Roberto Hernandez before him, he's also got a slider and a curve, and he's working on a change-up. He'd get into ruts by relying on just his fastball, which led to a couple of ugly blown saves against the Rangers. How much of that is getting into bad habits because closers are supposed to blow people away? He's a closer with a chance to get much better on a team that will get better.

Jason Lakman   Throws R   Age 23

YEAR	TEAM	LGE	IP	H	ER	HR	BB	K	ERA	W	L	H/9	HR/9	BB/9	K/9	KWH	PERA
1997	Hickory	SAL	142.3	185	110	14	99	116	6.96	5	11	11.70	0.89	6.26	7.33	0.55	7.15
1998	WnstnSlm	Car	82.7	76	47	1	40	71	5.12	4	5	8.27	0.11	4.35	7.73	1.24	3.59
1998	Birmnghm	Sou	68.7	98	69	16	38	65	9.04	2	6	12.84	2.10	4.98	8.52	0.85	8.91
1999	WnstnSlm	Car	116.7	127	79	6	65	79	6.09	5	8	9.80	0.46	5.01	6.09	0.56	5.01

Despite a great fastball, Lakman couldn't crack Birmingham's rotation and scuffled during his return engagement with the Carolina League. It probably wasn't a coincidence when he earned a suspension for violating the organization's alcohol policy. Anybody with a 95-mph fastball gets a chance someday, but Lakman's is far away.

Sean Lowe   Throws R   Age 29

YEAR	TEAM	LGE	IP	H	ER	HR	BB	K	ERA	W	L	H/9	HR/9	BB/9	K/9	KWH	PERA
1997	Louisvil	AmA	127.3	160	85	12	64	100	6.01	5	9	11.31	0.85	4.52	7.07	0.73	6.08
1997	St Louis	NL	17.0	28	22	2	11	8	11.65	0	2	14.82	1.06	5.82	4.24	0.16	9.00
1998	Memphis	PCL	140.7	166	66	16	72	92	4.22	9	7	10.62	1.02	4.61	5.89	0.53	5.95
1999	ChiSox	AL	96.0	85	34	9	45	63	3.19	7	4	7.97	0.84	4.22	5.91	0.78	4.03

The Cardinals were never satisfied with Lowe's velocity, asking for and apparently expecting the impossible 110%. They could have settled for a great sinker, like the Sox did by swiping him for tall goof John Ambrose. He's another good reliever who came out of the woodwork. All it takes is a manager, pitching coach or GM to identify a player's skills and let him use them to best advantage, which is exactly what the Sox did.

Aaron Myette   Throws R   Age 22

YEAR	TEAM	LGE	IP	H	ER	HR	BB	K	ERA	W	L	H/9	HR/9	BB/9	K/9	KWH	PERA
1997	Bristol	App	40.3	59	38	9	28	27	8.48	1	3	13.17	2.01	6.25	6.02	0.33	9.60
1997	Hickory	SAL	30.0	25	8	2	15	18	2.40	2	1	7.50	0.60	4.50	5.40	0.65	3.60
1998	Hickory	SAL	94.7	108	56	5	41	66	5.32	5	6	10.27	0.48	3.90	6.27	0.74	4.85
1998	WnstnSlm	Car	42.7	40	18	5	19	39	3.80	3	2	8.44	1.05	4.01	8.23	1.50	4.43
1999	Birmnghm	Sou	153.7	167	89	20	82	112	5.21	7	10	9.78	1.17	4.80	6.56	0.68	5.68

Myette is further proof that Canadians just aren't like the rest of us. He'll do silly things like wear eye black, or tell his manager that he couldn't swallow because pitching in the majors for the first time is pretty intense. That's way too honest. He has good command and velocity with two-seam and four-seam fastballs, and his slider has been called the organization's best breaking pitch, albeit before Kip Wells arrived. He spent most of 1999 trying to get a good feel for a change-up. I like his future; he'll probably be a midseason call-up.

Jaime Navarro   Serves it Up R   Age 33

YEAR	TEAM	LGE	IP	H	ER	HR	BB	K	ERA	W	L	H/9	HR/9	BB/9	K/9	KWH	PERA
1997	ChiSox	AL	212.7	255	140	20	73	143	5.92	9	15	10.79	0.85	3.09	6.05	0.82	5.21
1998	ChiSox	AL	173.3	220	127	28	80	72	6.59	6	13	11.42	1.45	4.15	3.74	0.22	6.75
1999	ChiSox	AL	160.7	195	111	26	69	76	6.22	6	12	10.92	1.46	3.87	4.26	0.32	6.27

Only one more year to go, Sox fans, but what do you do if you're Navarro? Can't get anyone out? Tell everyone your old man told you to throw sidearm, and then do it! Everyone thinks you're a head case? Tell everyone you won't criticize your team-mates, then pick a fight with Jeff Abbott! Prove you're a leader by announcing at the All-Star break that you're going to lead the Sox to the wild card! Navarro's gift is that he has all the depth of your basic James Bond villain, right down to the fiendish plans that always blow up in his face because he's too busy talking about them. He needs an appropriate super villain secret identity, like "Captain Destructo" or "The Money Pit."

Jim Parque   Throws L   Age 24

YEAR	TEAM	LGE	IP	H	ER	HR	BB	K	ERA	W	L	H/9	HR/9	BB/9	K/9	KWH	PERA
1997	WnstnSlm	Car	59.7	37	23	4	26	56	3.47	4	3	5.58	0.60	3.92	8.45	2.44	2.56
1998	Calgary	PCL	47.7	49	24	6	28	27	4.53	2	3	9.25	1.13	5.29	5.10	0.40	5.48
1998	ChiSox	AL	113.3	133	67	13	51	78	5.32	5	8	10.56	1.03	4.05	6.19	0.67	5.64
1999	ChiSox	AL	174.7	199	97	20	76	113	5.00	9	10	10.25	1.03	3.92	5.82	0.63	5.41

Parque was enjoying a great first half and credited ex-pitching coach Mike Pazik's absence for some of it. Once Pazik was canned, Parque resurrected a change-up that Pazik thought was too slow, and it helped Parque become that much more effective changing speeds. After suffering a bruised left thumb thanks to a line drive at the end of July, he gave up 51 runs in 52 innings over his last ten starts, while failing to log a single quality start. This being the Sox, they blamed the bad finish on a selfish drive for the 10th win he never got, but who decided he could pitch through it? Parque is better than these numbers indicate, and capable of breaking through in 2000.

Jesus Pena   Throws L   Age 25

YEAR	TEAM	LGE	IP	H	ER	HR	BB	K	ERA	W	L	H/9	HR/9	BB/9	K/9	KWH	PERA
1997	Hickory	SAL	60.7	73	33	4	27	38	4.90	3	4	10.83	0.59	4.01	5.64	0.55	5.34
1998	WnstnSlm	Car	29.0	28	17	3	17	25	5.28	1	2	8.69	0.93	5.28	7.76	0.98	4.97
1998	Birmnghm	Sou	22.3	22	13	4	10	22	5.24	1	1	8.87	1.61	4.03	8.87	1.64	5.24
1999	Birmnghm	Sou	42.0	41	16	2	20	37	3.43	3	2	8.79	0.43	4.29	7.93	1.25	4.07
1999	ChiSox	AL	20.7	19	13	3	23	20	5.66	1	1	8.27	1.31	10.02	8.71	0.68	6.97

A nice snag from the Pirates in the minor-league portion of the Rule 5 draft in 1996, Pena has a bit of the hot dog in him. He's your basic Eck-style pistollero, which would probably get him arrested for carrying a concealed weapon in today's easily frightened society. He throws hard, is working on a slider and is likely to hold the left-handed specialist role for the foresee-able future.

Mark Roberts   Throws R   Age 24

YEAR	TEAM	LGE	IP	H	ER	HR	BB	K	ERA	W	L	H/9	HR/9	BB/9	K/9	KWH	PERA
1997	Princetn	App	16.3	28	13	2	5	8	7.16	1	1	15.43	1.10	2.76	4.41	0.34	8.27
1997	Hickory	SAL	19.7	31	16	4	13	10	7.32	1	1	14.19	1.83	5.95	4.58	0.19	10.07
1997	WnstnSlm	Car	87.0	97	57	11	51	48	5.90	4	6	10.03	1.14	5.28	4.97	0.35	6.00
1998	WnstnSlm	Car	154.3	212	117	20	71	101	6.82	5	12	12.36	1.17	4.14	5.89	0.51	7.00
1999	Birmnghm	Sou	114.7	133	78	12	45	68	6.12	5	8	10.44	0.94	3.53	5.34	0.58	5.26

Roberts was drafted out of the University of Southern Florida in 1996. Your basic polished college pitcher, Roberts has been old for his leagues and works high in the strike zone. His command is good, but not as good as Daneker's. When Garland and Wells moved through, Roberts was bumped into the pen. His future is as a swingman.

Jason Secoda   Throws R   Age 25

YEAR	TEAM	LGE	IP	H	ER	HR	BB	K	ERA	W	L	H/9	HR/9	BB/9	K/9	KWH	PERA
1997	WnstnSlm	Car	111.7	151	83	12	67	62	6.69	4	8	12.17	0.97	5.40	5.00	0.28	7.17
1998	WnstnSlm	Car	10.7	11	3	0	3	5	2.53	1	0	9.28	0.00	2.53	4.22	0.57	3.37
1998	Birmnghm	Sou	61.7	87	52	7	38	36	7.59	2	5	12.70	1.02	5.55	5.25	0.29	7.59
1999	Birmnghm	Sou	104.7	128	64	7	45	72	5.50	5	7	11.01	0.60	3.87	6.19	0.67	5.42
1999	Charlott	Int	44.3	55	31	9	11	29	6.29	2	3	11.17	1.83	2.23	5.89	1.04	6.09

The pitching prospect nobody talks about, Secoda's fastball has inched up into the 90s, and he complements it with a good splitter. He used to be wilder than Hunter S. Thompson at a prayer breakfast, but his control improved greatly in 1999. I don't have an explanation for why he pitched 1998 exclusively in relief; he wasn't injured. He's someone who could sneak into the major league rotation once the veterans falter and if the better-known prospects struggle.

Bill Simas   Throws R   Age 28

YEAR	TEAM	LGE	IP	H	ER	HR	BB	K	ERA	W	L	H/9	HR/9	BB/9	K/9	KWH	PERA
1997	ChiSox	AL	42.0	44	21	6	24	38	4.50	3	2	9.43	1.29	5.14	8.14	1.02	5.79
1998	ChiSox	AL	70.7	53	27	11	23	57	3.44	5	3	6.75	1.40	2.93	7.26	1.99	3.44
1999	ChiSox	AL	72.3	69	31	5	31	42	3.86	5	3	8.59	0.62	3.86	5.23	0.62	3.98

Something was definitely wrong in 1999. Manuel liked to bring him into situations with runners on base and in scoring position, but Simas was gas on the fire, allowing an 807 OPS with runners on and a 942 OPS with runners in scoring position. Although he wasn't close to being the worst in the league at allowing inherited runners to score, the Sox weren't a good enough offensive team to survive this kind of performance. His fastball lacked the movement it had in previous seasons. Assuming he's healthy, he'll be better off if he isn't brought in mid-inning.

Mike Sirotka   Throws L   Age 29

YEAR	TEAM	LGE	IP	H	ER	HR	BB	K	ERA	W	L	H/9	HR/9	BB/9	K/9	KWH	PERA
1997	Nashvill	AmA	110.3	129	54	12	26	79	4.40	6	6	10.52	0.98	2.12	6.44	1.39	4.81
1997	ChiSox	AL	32.3	35	8	4	5	24	2.23	3	1	9.74	1.11	1.39	6.68	2.46	4.18
1998	ChiSox	AL	212.7	251	128	28	50	130	5.42	10	14	10.62	1.18	2.12	5.50	1.01	5.08
1999	ChiSox	AL	209.7	224	94	21	55	128	4.03	13	10	9.62	0.90	2.36	5.49	0.99	4.29

Although he's turned into a solid major-league starter, he's one of the guys I'm worried about. His best pitch is a cut fastball, which puts him in the company of left-handers like Jim Abbott and Scott Karl, both of whose careers started off well only to lose ground year after year. Sirotka is different from Karl or Abbott in that he works high in the strike zone and isn't a ground-ball pitcher. I don't expect him to collapse; despite a rough spot during late July and August, he finished strong. It's just something to think about if he declines but remains effective in 2000.

John Snyder   Throws R   Age 25

YEAR	TEAM	LGE	IP	H	ER	HR	BB	K	ERA	W	L	H/9	HR/9	BB/9	K/9	KWH	PERA
1997	Birmnghm	Sou	106.7	144	80	9	46	73	6.75	4	8	12.15	0.76	3.88	6.16	0.60	6.24
1998	Calgary	PCL	96.7	112	46	10	39	55	4.28	6	5	10.43	0.93	3.63	5.12	0.52	5.31
1998	ChiSox	AL	86.7	95	46	13	24	53	4.78	5	5	9.87	1.35	2.49	5.50	0.92	4.98
1999	ChiSox	AL	129.7	159	91	24	47	68	6.32	5	9	11.04	1.67	3.26	4.72	0.46	6.39
1999	Charlott	Int	17.0	17	8	2	6	8	4.24	1	1	9.00	1.06	3.18	4.24	0.47	4.24

For the season's first six weeks, Snyder was one of the league's best starters, tossing seven consecutive quality starts. Then he gave up five or more runs in seven of his next eight starts. His ERA after the All-Star break was 8.05. Numerous excuses were sorted through: pitching coach Nardi Contreras tried to correct his delivery, then he couldn't throw his curve for strikes. He was demoted with a dead arm and finally had surgery to remove bone chips in his elbow. He's always had a bad delivery, but basically he didn't adapt when the league adjusted to him. He's not a good bet to win a rotation spot with Wells and Myette coming up.

Tanyon Sturtze   Throws R   Age 29

YEAR	TEAM	LGE	IP	H	ER	HR	BB	K	ERA	W	L	H/9	HR/9	BB/9	K/9	KWH	PERA
1997	Oklahoma	AmA	113.0	148	85	9	56	68	6.77	4	9	11.79	0.72	4.46	5.42	0.42	6.21
1997	Texas	AL	34.0	42	27	6	18	18	7.15	1	3	11.12	1.59	4.76	4.76	0.32	6.88
1998	Oklahoma	PCL	32.3	37	15	3	21	25	4.18	2	2	10.30	0.84	5.85	6.96	0.60	6.12
1999	Charlott	Int	104.3	84	49	6	45	92	4.23	6	6	7.25	0.52	3.88	7.94	1.67	3.28

A minor-league journeyman who was pulled off the mound while blowing the final game of the Triple-A World Series to be given the news he was being promoted. Purchasing his contract cost the Sox Mario Valdez, since the first team eligible (the Twins) didn't let him pass through waivers. Sturtze's straight fastball makes a nice offering for people looking to pad salary arbitration cases or get that first major league hit. It's been tasty.

Bryan Ward   Throws L   Age 28

YEAR	TEAM	LGE	IP	H	ER	HR	BB	K	ERA	W	L	H/9	HR/9	BB/9	K/9	KWH	PERA
1997	Portland	Eas	71.0	88	45	15	23	51	5.70	3	5	11.15	1.90	2.92	6.46	0.96	6.59
1997	Charlott	Int	73.0	114	65	17	33	40	8.01	2	6	14.05	2.10	4.07	4.93	0.32	9.25
1998	Birmnghm	Sou	39.3	39	22	0	27	30	5.03	2	2	8.92	0.00	6.18	6.86	0.64	4.58
1998	ChiSox	AL	27.0	30	12	4	7	17	4.00	2	1	10.00	1.33	2.33	5.67	1.03	5.00
1999	ChiSox	AL	39.3	60	32	9	11	36	7.32	1	3	13.73	2.06	2.52	8.24	1.47	8.24
1999	Charlott	Int	15.0	16	7	2	3	13	4.20	1	1	9.60	1.20	1.80	7.80	2.63	4.20

It isn't every pitcher with extreme longball problems that you can say something nice about. Ward throws hard and just doesn't seem suited for the situational left-hander role. If a desperate team gives him a shot as a fifth starter, he could surprise people. Tragically, he got rid of his amazing facial hair in a fit of pique after another bad day at the office.

Kip Wells   Throws R   Age 23

YEAR	TEAM	LGE	IP	H	ER	HR	BB	K	ERA	W	L	H/9	HR/9	BB/9	K/9	KWH	PERA
1999	WnstnSlm	Car	83.3	93	44	5	40	68	4.75	4	5	10.04	0.54	4.32	7.34	0.93	4.97
1999	Birmnghm	Sou	66.0	60	29	5	33	36	3.95	4	3	8.18	0.68	4.50	4.91	0.49	4.09
1999	ChiSox	AL	35.7	32	15	2	14	30	3.79	2	2	8.07	0.50	3.53	7.57	1.50	3.53

The team's first-round pick in 1998, who signed for a $1.5 million bonus after a protracted holdout, is already one of the best pitching prospects in the game. *Baseball America*'s polling named him the best prospect in the Carolina League and third-best in the Southern League, after only 14 starts in the former and 11 starts in the latter. Unlike a lot of top college pitchers, Wells has great velocity, better than most pitchers anywhere. He also has an off-the-table curve and a slider he can throw at any point in the count. Rookie pitchers are always tough to predict—witness Jeff Weaver—but Wells will be in the Sox rotation, and has a great shot to be the 2000 AL Rookie of the Year.

Support-Neutral Records — CHICAGO WHITE SOX — Park Effect: -1.2%

PITCHER	GS	IP	R	SNW	SNL	SNPCT	W	L	RA	APW	SNVA	SNWAR
James Baldwin	33	196.7	116	11.5	11.8	.494	12	13	5.31	-0.24	-0.19	1.60
Carlos Castillo	2	8.3	9	0.4	0.9	.333	0	1	9.72	-0.39	-0.24	-0.12
Pat Daneker	2	12.0	8	0.5	0.8	.386	0	0	6.00	-0.10	-0.15	-0.05
Aaron Myette	3	13.7	10	0.5	1.2	.306	0	2	6.59	-0.20	-0.30	-0.21
Jaime Navarro	27	151.3	123	6.8	12.4	.353	7	12	7.31	-3.32	-2.77	-1.38
Jim Parque	30	170.7	110	8.5	11.6	.421	9	15	5.80	-1.07	-1.50	-0.07
Mike Sirotka	32	209.0	108	13.2	10.3	.562	11	13	4.65	1.17	1.33	3.21
John Snyder	25	129.3	103	6.7	11.1	.375	9	12	7.17	-2.64	-2.15	-0.90
Tanyon Sturtze	1	6.0	0	0.7	0.0	1.000	0	0	0.00	0.32	0.33	0.39
Kip Wells	7	35.7	17	2.6	1.6	.627	4	1	4.29	0.33	0.43	0.84
TOTALS	162	932.7	604	51.3	61.7	.454	52	69	5.83	-6.14	-5.20	3.31

John Snyder had the most extreme Jekyll-and-Hyde season you'll ever see. Through his first seven starts, he was one of the top starters in the majors with a 4.1-0.7 (.847) Support-Neutral W/L record. From there to the end of the season, he put together what has to be one of the worst extended runs of pitching of all time: a 2.6-10.4 (.198) SNW/L record, allowing 93 runs in 84⅓ innings over 18 starts. Those numbers are reminiscent of Steve Blass's famous 1973 season, the worst of the 20th century: 18 starts, 88⅔ innings, 98 runs allowed, a 2.0-11.2 (.153) SNW/L record. Don't look for the so-called "Steve Blass Disease" in Snyder's situation, though; Blass is well known for having suddenly lost the ability to throw strikes, while Snyder's problems stemmed mostly from being hit hard. . . . The White Sox need to learn something about sunk costs. It's hard to fault them for signing Jaime Navarro back in 1996. He was coming off two above-average workhorse seasons with the team across town. But couldn't they have dropped him from the rotation after one horrendous season? Two? They were going to have to pay him no matter what; why compound the mistake by letting him continue to do on-field damage as well? Navarro has been, by far, the worst starter in the majors over the last three seasons, with a 24-41 SNW/L record. Despite poor performance month after month and year after year, the White Sox kept sending him out there, for a total of 87 starts. Navarro isn't the only reason the White Sox have had one of the bottom six rotations in the majors in each of the last three years, but he's the biggest.

Pitcher Abuse Points

PITCHER	AGE	GS	PAP	PAP/S	WKLD	MAX	1-90	91-100	101-110	111-120	121-130	131-140	141+
James Baldwin	27	33	206	6.2	11.4	120	9	9	8	7	0	0	0
Carlos Castillo	24	2	0	0.0	0.0	83	2	0	0	0	0	0	0
Pat Daneker	23	2	0	0.0	0.0	87	2	0	0	0	0	0	0
Aaron Myette	21	3	0	0.0	0.0	89	3	0	0	0	0	0	0
Jaime Navarro	31	27	246	9.1	10.6	126	6	8	8	1	4	0	0
Jim Parque	24	30	272	9.1	21.2	124	6	7	8	7	2	0	0
Mike Sirotka	28	32	393	12.3	20.5	132	4	7	10	8	2	1	0
John Snyder	24	25	32	1.3	3.0	109	11	8	6	0	0	0	0
Tanyon Sturtze	28	1	0	0.0	0.0	86	1	0	0	0	0	0	0
Kip Wells	22	7	0	0.0	0.0	89	7	0	0	0	0	0	0
CHICAGO		162	1149	7.1	12.5	132	51	39	40	23	8	1	0
Ranking (AL)				10	9								

In 1998, Jerry Manuel's boys ranked dead last in the AL in PAPs, and we speculated that such delicate handling of a very young staff would pay dividends last year. At the All-Star break, Jim Parque had a 3.94 ERA and Mike Sirotka a 3.20 ERA. That Sirotka subsequently tailed off (4.93) and Parque completely went to pot (6.95) might have been a reflection of having Workloads of over 20, though in fairness it must be said that Parque was pitching with a severely bruised thumb for much of the second half. John Snyder also drove off the cliff after a promising start. In his case it had nothing to do with his pitch counts and everything to do with the fact that he had just been lucky for six weeks and was unable to adjust once the hitters did. . . . The second-half slides of Parque and Sirotka aside, Manuel seems to be the right man to break in the Pale Hose's many young pitchers. Pat Daneker, Aaron Myette and Kip Wells, all 23 or younger last year, made 12 starts combined, and not once did they throw even 90 pitches.

Cleveland Indians

If there's one lesson that the 1999 season should hold for every baseball fan, it's that 1,009 runs cannot overcome the impact of the decisions made by a team's power brokers. After slogging through nearly eight months of action to get their fifth straight division title, after scoring those thousand runs, the Indians weren't good enough to overcome the choices made by General Manager John Hart and Manager Mike Hargrove.

How do you score a thousand runs? More importantly, how do you blow it if you've got the kind of team that can score a thousand runs?

Scoring a thousand runs isn't very common; the last team to do it was the 1950 Red Sox, who managed to finish third behind the Yankees and Tigers despite scoring 1,027 runs. The feat was probably easier for the Red Sox back then than it was for the Indians in 1999. The 1950 AL was heavily unbalanced, featuring four awful teams in a field of eight: the ever-present Senators, A's and Browns, plus a bad White Sox team waiting for Paul Richards—and later Al Lopez—to get them into contention.

Remember that plenty of things went wrong for the Indians' lineup in 1999. Travis Fryman missed half the year, and wasn't nearly as productive as he had been in 1998 when he was playing. Enrique Wilson did not fill Fryman's shoes offensively. Sandy Alomar was hurt most of the year, and his stand-in, Einar Diaz, didn't put many runs on the board. Jim Thome didn't have an especially great year by his own standards, and while Richie Sexson had a nice season, it wasn't one in which he helped his teammates much by getting on base. Still, the Indians' offense improved by 159 runs over 1998. So how did they do this?

First off, John Hart built a top of the order that became a perpetual offense machine. The front six batters in the order were usually Kenny Lofton, Omar Vizquel, Roberto Alomar, Manny Ramirez, David Justice and Thome. The lowest OBP in that front six was Vizquel's .397. For some perspective, that "low" OBP would have been fourth among AL leadoff hitters.

Is it any wonder Richie Sexson had 116 RBIs batting behind them?

While Ramirez's big year could be anticipated because he was entering his age-27 season, there was no way to anticipate the years Lofton, Vizquel and Alomar had in front of him. All three raised their on-base percentages over 1998, from Lofton's 34-point improvement to Alomar's whopping 75-point jump. Even with Lofton's injury costing him most of the last two months of the season, the three players most responsible for creating a team's scoring chances all managed to improve their performance significantly, despite all of them being on the wrong side of 30.

How likely was that? Alomar enjoyed one of the best single-season improvements ever for a player his age. Since 1960, only six players who were Alomar's age and had 500 or more plate appearances have had bigger jumps in Equivalent Average from the previous season: Willie Stargell in 1971, Manny Sanguillen in 1975, Rickey Henderson in 1990, Paul O'Neill in 1994 and Scott Brosius and Albert Belle in 1998. As Clay Davenport explains it, since 1960 there have been 529 players who had at least 250 at-bats at ages 30 and 31. Only 15 of them improved by more than Alomar's 49-point gain in Equivalent Average (EqA), so we could say that the chance of Alomar's having that large an improvement was 15/529, or about 3%.

Likewise, there were 439 players who met the criteria for ages 31-32 (Lofton's and Vizquel's ages in 1998 and 1999). Of that group, 116 of them did better than Lofton's +15 in EqA (26.4%), and 41 did better than Vizquel's +34 (9.3%). The chance that all three would have the seasons they did comes out to 0.44%, or about 1 in 226.

What all this math tells us is that it was pretty unlikely that Lofton, Vizquel and Alomar were all going to improve as much as they did in 1999. But were there other factors that might have contributed, not just to these three having good years, but to how the team scored a thousand runs? Consider some of the other players who fueled the Indians' offense.

Indians Prospectus

1999 record: 97-65; First place, AL Central; Lost to Red Sox in Division Series, 3-2

Pythagorean W/L: 93-69

Runs scored: 1,009 (1st in AL)

Runs allowed: 860 (8th in AL)

Team EQA: .276 (2nd in AL)

1999 team age: 29.4 (8th-oldest in AL)

1999 park: Jacobs Field; slight hitters' park, increased run scoring by 6%.

1999: 1,009 runs don't buy what they used to; Hargrove takes the fall.

2000: The same cast returns. Without adding some pitching, they'll decline.

Justice set a career high in walks, although his other numbers didn't shift significantly. Jim Thome's OBP went up, but he didn't have one of his better power seasons. What Thome did do was give the team almost 100 more plate appearances than he had in 1998, so even though he didn't hit for as much power, he gave the team more quality playing time overall by reaching base 46 more times in 23 more games played. So, the easy answer is that the Indians scored a lot of runs because everybody was getting on base.

Think of what that means for the team that's trying to stop the Indians. Walks mean pitches, lots of them. They mean more pitches from the stretch, which take more effort while being less effective. It takes more pitches to get through an inning, which means your starter is likely to get fatigued earlier in the game.

Concepts like lineup protection—one batter improving because of who bats behind him—and clutch hitting—some players being consistently better in whatever you choose to call a key situation—have been pretty well debunked by serious research. But what if this is an example of a lineup where all the hitters getting on base does make everyone in the lineup better? The 1999 Indians would be one of the finest examples of offensive synergy possible, a lineup in which players end up hitting better because of what their teammates have done. The Indians' success was the product of hammering away inning after inning, where the cumulative effect of fouling off and taking pitches meant just as much as racking up hits, until finally the starting pitcher had to either give in or get out.

That's mostly conjecture, obviously. But if an offense structured to put people on base is the best way not just to score runs, but to beat the bejesus out of the opposition, you'd expect that team to see a lot of relievers, and not the good ones. If you get to your opponent's starter early, you're not seeing the great closers or the specialized setup men. You're seeing Terry Mathews or Tim Worrell, the other team's 10th or 11th man. That gives a good offense the opportunity to turn a beating into a rout.

Courtesy of Keith Woolner, Table 1 breaks down how teams scored off starters and relievers in the AL last year. The teams are listed by total runs scored.

The numbers to be impressed with here are how few starter innings were thrown against the Indians, how many relief innings were thrown against them and how the Indians did a better job scoring runs off relievers than most teams did against starting pitchers. There's no shame in beating the crap out of people like Terry Mathews. It's his job, just as it's the job of a good offense to put its opponents in a vulnerable situation, where it can apply a killing blow.

This isn't a recent development, but it is the way an offense whose chief strengths are patience and power can run rampant and win games in the sixth or seventh innings while managers and general managers fret over closers and the ninth inning. Some teams have adapted. The White Sox have Keith Foulke as a middle-innings closer, shutting down the really dangerous fires in the sixth and seventh. Texas got that kind of work out of Jeff Zimmerman last year, and the Tigers have Doug Brocail. Whether teams learn from these examples and change their reliever usage patterns, and whether guys like Foulke or Brocail or Zimmerman will get the benefit of a better metric than the "hold," remains to be seen. Ideally, "closers" would be the term applied to the guys who keep offensive killing machines like the 1999 Indians from bludgeoning their teams, and not to the high-priced dandies who get to rack up saves.

Mike Hargrove, Phil Regan and John Hart all deserve blame for taking a great offensive team and flubbing another shot at the World Series. One of the problems in having all

Table 1

	Runs Scored off Starters	Opp. Starter IP	R/9 IP	Runs Scored off Relievers	Opposing Reliever IP	R/9 IP
Indians	645	892.0	6.5	364	545.0	6.0
Rangers	625	901.0	6.2	320	521.2	5.5
Yankees	592	889.0	6.0	308	535.0	5.2
Athletics	625	888.0	6.3	268	546.1	4.4
Blue Jays	587	972.2	5.4	296	464.0	5.7
Mariners	580	923.2	5.7	279	511.0	4.9
Royals	603	929.0	5.8	253	505.2	4.5
Orioles	585	961.0	5.5	271	493.0	4.9
Red Sox	579	958.1	5.4	257	465.2	5.0
White Sox	537	958.1	5.0	240	485.0	4.5
Devil Rays	551	941	5.3	221	502.2	4.0
Tigers	536	986.2	4.9	211	442.2	4.3
Angels	501	1014.0	4.5	210	427.1	4.4
Twins	469	967.1	4.4	217	472.2	4.1

those runs is that it led to some pretty lazy management of the pitching staff. Coming out of spring training, the Indians casually discarded both Orel Hershiser and Ron Villone, guys they'd be begging to get back by May.

All those runs helped the Indians claim a dubious place in major-league history: thanks to the "contributions" of Dwight Gooden and Jaret Wright, Cleveland was the first winning team ever to have two starters with ERAs higher than 6.00 start 20 or more games. While the Indians were busy having fun outscoring everyone, they didn't notice that no other team would live with a done Gooden or an injured Wright or beat-up old men like Mark Langston and Tom Candiotti.

You have to wonder why the Indians even employ pitchers at Buffalo: could someone like Jason Rakers really have been any worse? Armed with run support and some famous infield defense, any of the Bisons' starters would have been better, and they certainly would have been healthier. By the time Hart noticed that his starting pitching was a problem, the solution was to try the ultimate fragile pitcher, Steve Karsay. After that experiment cost them their middle relief ace, their fallback was an injured Jaret Wright, who stayed hurt and pitched like it.

Hart deserves most of the responsibility for these failures, not just for what he did during the summer and for tossing Hershiser and Villone, but for failing to get available starters like Jon Lieber the previous winter, or turning Chad Ogea into Jerry Spradlin into Dan McKinley, a minor-league outfielder the Tribe didn't need.

Maybe the shock of losing to the Marlins had Hart overly pen-obsessed, but that wouldn't explain what pitching coach Phil Regan was up to all summer. Gooden, Wright, Paul Shuey, Steve Reed and Ricky Rincon all pitched hurt down the stretch, and in each case, the Indians said they had been pitching hurt without telling Regan. Whether the mound guru who couldn't get good work out of Kevin Brown and Jamie Moyer when he managed the Orioles in 1995, and who presided over Kerry Wood's big elbow blowout in 1998 was the kind of magician the Indians needed in 1999 is an open question. But comments from Indians pitchers all spring and into summer made it clear there was a communication problem, something no team with postseason ambitions can afford.

The pitching problem was highlighted by the Indians' record against good teams. Following Lou Boudreau's advice about hammering the bad teams is fine, but the Tribe managed to go only 10-22 against the other playoff teams during the regular season. So while they were entertaining their fans all summer, Hart hadn't built a team that could beat the Red Sox, let alone win the World Series. The Division Series brought to the fore the sloppy management of the pitching staff, as one injured or struggling pitcher after another got his head handed to him by the Red Sox. Mike Hargrove earned a share of the blame: the man didn't try to bring a useful pitching staff into the postseason, and that killed the Indians more than the decision to use Jaret Wright in relief in Game 3.

The issue now is whether there's still time to get that championship ring with the team in place. It isn't impossible. Charlie Manuel is more than just a fine hitting coach; he's also been a very successful manager in the minors. I can envision a scenario similar to the one where the 1983 Orioles won with Joe Altobelli managing them, the year after the great Earl Weaver had retired. But the Indians are going to need more than an expensive Cuban enigma like Danys Baez to solve their pitching problems, and the offense is old. While none of the rebuilding programs in the division has come far enough fast enough to make 2000 look like a dogfight, the Indians' offense is old and has nowhere to go but down. The Tribe won't have the luxury of a 20-game lead this year. Can this team have one last hurrah before the rot really seeps in?

HITTERS (Averages: BA: .270 / OBP: .340 / SLG: .430 / EQA: .260)

Roberto Alomar 2B Bats B Age 32

YEAR	TEAM	LGE	AB	H	DB	TP	HR	BB/SO	R	RBI	SB	CS	OUT	BA	OBP	SLG	EQA	EQR	DEFENSE
1997	Baltimor	AL	411	139	25	2	14	38/41	63	59	9	3	275	.338	.399	.511	.304	70	102-2B 99
1998	Baltimor	AL	591	173	35	2	15	57/68	85	57	17	5	423	.293	.357	.435	.270	80	142-2B 102
1999	Clevelnd	AL	553	175	40	3	22	91/96	125	108	37	6	384	.316	.419	.519	.319	110	146-2B 100
2000	Clevelnd	AL	523	163	31	2	18	77/76	119	99	21	4	364	.312	.400	.482	.301	90	

Last year, we wrote that Alomar was a player the Indians didn't need, which turned out to be just a wee bit wide of the mark. While he wasn't as handy as Kevin Brown might have been, the question now isn't whether he's going to be a Hall of Famer, but whether or not he deserves to be mentioned in the same breath as Joe Morgan. This sounds like sour grapes, but he won't have another season this good during the contract's last three years.

Sandy Alomar   C   Bats R   Age 34

YEAR	TEAM	LGE	AB	H	DB	TP	HR	BB/SO	R	RBI	SB	CS	OUT	BA	OBP	SLG	EQA	EQR	DEFENSE
1997	Clevelnd	AL	453	152	29	0	25	16/46	62	86	0	2	303	.336	.363	.565	.299	74	
1998	Clevelnd	AL	406	92	24	2	6	16/44	41	41	0	3	317	.227	.261	.340	.195	27	106-C 100
1999	Clevelnd	AL	136	41	9	0	7	2/23	17	24	0	1	96	.301	.312	.522	.267	18	33-C 86
2000	Clevelnd	AL	287	76	11	0	11	16/34	31	43	0	1	212	.265	.304	.418	.237	29	

While we're all convinced that medicine can fix anything these days, Sandy may finally be reaching the point where nothing can be done for his knees. Repeated hyalgan lubricant injections and painkillers didn't help. He tried to change his throwing mechanics, but he still couldn't help the Indians behind the plate. By season's end, he was talking about experimental cartilage regrowth. The hope for a World Series ring may keep him out there, but retirement isn't far off.

Carlos Baerga   IF   Bats B   Age 31

YEAR	TEAM	LGE	AB	H	DB	TP	HR	BB/SO	R	RBI	SB	CS	OUT	BA	OBP	SLG	EQA	EQR	DEFENSE
1997	NY Mets	NL	472	134	25	1	10	19/53	53	53	1	6	344	.284	.316	.405	.238	47	115-2B 98
1998	NY Mets	NL	519	145	29	1	8	23/54	48	56	0	1	375	.279	.318	.385	.237	51	130-2B 96
1999	Indianap	Int	222	59	6	0	3	6/20	24	22	1	1	164	.266	.288	.333	.206	16	31-3B 100
1999	LasVegas	PCL	89	20	4	0	2	7/5	10	7	0	0	69	.225	.287	.337	.210	7	
1999	San Dieg	NL	81	20	2	0	2	5/14	6	5	1	0	61	.247	.309	.346	.226	7	
1999	Clevelnd	AL	57	13	0	0	1	3/10	4	5	1	1	45	.228	.267	.281	.178	3	
2000	Clevelnd	AL	416	112	11	0	9	25/45	43	51	1	2	306	.269	.311	.361	.223	36	

The Beeg Belly came back to Cleveland in an overtly feel-good, prodigal-son scenario that did absolutely nothing to help the Indians win a single game. When those are the kinds of things that dictate who gets brought in and why, the organization has moved beyond performance-oriented player evaluation into the "who gets to be dugout cheerleader?" irrelevancy that wastes time and at-bats better devoted to Russ Branyan.

Harold Baines   DH   Bats L   Age 41

YEAR	TEAM	LGE	AB	H	DB	TP	HR	BB/SO	R	RBI	SB	CS	OUT	BA	OBP	SLG	EQA	EQR	DEFENSE
1997	ChiSox	AL	318	101	14	0	14	39/45	39	53	0	1	218	.318	.392	.494	.296	52	
1997	Baltimor	AL	134	40	3	0	5	13/14	15	16	0	0	94	.299	.361	.433	.269	18	
1998	Baltimor	AL	294	91	13	0	11	31/39	39	58	0	0	203	.310	.377	.466	.284	44	
1999	Baltimor	AL	342	110	16	1	23	39/38	52	75	1	2	234	.322	.391	.576	.312	64	
1999	Clevelnd	AL	84	22	2	0	1	10/10	5	15	0	0	62	.262	.340	.321	.232	8	
2000	Baltimor	AL	340	88	9	0	13	46/41	49	54	0	1	253	.259	.347	.400	.258	43	

It will take two years for him to get the 27 home runs he needs to reach 400, but would even that be enough to create a case for the Hall of Fame? As Clay Davenport points out, Harold Baines has a .290 career EqA with 1,542 EqR, or 679 more than a replacement hitter would have generated (Runs Above Replacement, or RAR). The EqA is around 280th all-time, tied with guys like Kirby Puckett, Mickey Tettleton, Jay Buhner, Ron Fairly and Rudy York. The 1,542 EqR are 54th all-time, and his 679 RAR are 71st. How does Baines's career compare to some other noted designated hitters and corner outfielders?

Player	EQA	EQR	RAR
Harold Baines	.290	1542 (54)	679 (71)
Andre Dawson	.285	1573	654
Joe Carter	.268	1170	371
Dave Kingman	.275	1025	373
Don Baylor	.288	1372	588
Hal McRae	.289	1173	512
Tony Perez	.289	1594	698
Rusty Staub	.294	1656	762

Man, Joe Carter was overrated. In that group, the strongest comparison to Baines in terms of skill set, production and career length is Rusty Staub, and nobody takes Staub's Hall chances seriously. Like Staub or Don Baylor or Hal McRae, Baines started off not as a DH, but as a great ballplayer who could do everything on the field, and that was taken away from him. He hasn't used the DH to improve his career totals, like Andre Dawson did. Without the DH, he would have been Joe Hauser, a great might-have-been who lost a career to injury. While Harold Baines has been the most productive DH over the rule's lifetime, he won't get much consideration from the Hall.

Russ Branyan 3B Bats L Age 24

YEAR	TEAM	LGE	AB	H	DB	TP	HR	BB/SO	R	RBI	SB	CS	OUT	BA	OBP	SLG	EQA	EQR	DEFENSE
1997	Kinston	Car	308	84	23	2	24	43/94	51	62	2	1	225	.273	.369	.594	.307	59	69-3B 82
1997	Akron	Eas	139	30	4	0	10	23/58	21	24	0	0	109	.216	.333	.460	.265	20	39-3B 104
1998	Akron	Eas	164	44	9	2	15	31/57	30	40	1	1	121	.268	.385	.622	.317	34	39-3B 92
1999	Buffalo	Int	396	78	10	1	27	45/188	43	56	6	2	320	.197	.285	.432	.238	44	107-3B 98
1999	Clevelnd	AL	38	8	2	0	1	2/19	4	6	0	0	30	.211	.268	.342	.203	3	
2000	*Clevelnd*	*AL*	*325*	*77*	*15*	*1*	*25*	*43/139*	*53*	*68*	*3*	*2*	*250*	*.237*	*.326*	*.520*	*.273*	*49*	

Branyan is the ultimate high-stakes batter. Situational hitting? That's for people who aren't in scoring position when they come to the plate. Call it nostalgia for Rob Deer, but I really want to see what happens if Branyan gets 500 plate appearances. Sure, he could set a major-league record for strikeouts while struggling to stay above the Mendoza line. He could still pop 30 home runs while playing a solid third base.

Mark Budzinski CF Bats L Age 26

YEAR	TEAM	LGE	AB	H	DB	TP	HR	BB/SO	R	RBI	SB	CS	OUT	BA	OBP	SLG	EQA	EQR	DEFENSE
1997	Kinston	Car	252	61	13	2	5	37/66	33	29	3	2	193	.242	.341	.369	.246	29	63-OF 100
1998	Akron	Eas	482	109	19	4	8	38/134	54	50	7	4	377	.226	.284	.332	.208	37	127-OF 100
1999	Akron	Eas	304	72	17	4	4	35/73	43	34	4	2	234	.237	.322	.359	.235	31	82-OF 95
1999	Buffalo	Int	133	33	7	2	1	18/40	18	12	2	1	101	.248	.338	.353	.241	14	44-OF 103
2000	*Clevelnd*	*AL*	*437*	*105*	*21*	*4*	*8*	*55/115*	*62*	*53*	*6*	*3*	*335*	*.240*	*.325*	*.362*	*.235*	*45*	

He's considered great on defense, not surprising for a guy who used to be Jimmy Carter's national security advisor. Budzinski moved up to play center field for Buffalo after Dave Roberts got called up to Cleveland. He has hidden value because he can't handle left-handers, so in a platoon role or as a fourth or fifth outfielder, he'd be useful.

Jolbert Cabrera UT Bats R Age 27

YEAR	TEAM	LGE	AB	H	DB	TP	HR	BB/SO	R	RBI	SB	CS	OUT	BA	OBP	SLG	EQA	EQR	DEFENSE	
1997	Harrisbg	Eas	173	36	6	0	2	20/32	20	8	3	2	139	.208	.293	.277	.197	12	25-2B 84	
1997	Ottawa	Int	193	52	11	3	0	7/31	23	11	10	4	145	.269	.295	.358	.224	17	42-3B 107	
1998	Buffalo	Int	497	135	18	1	8	53/79	70	36	13	9	371	.272	.355	.360	.248	57	121-SS 93	
1999	Clevelnd	AL	37	6	1	0	0	1/8	5	1	3	0	31	.162	.205	.189	.131	1		
1999	Buffalo	Int	279	66	11	3	0	20/47	32	21	12	3	216	.237	.292	.297	.207	21	39-OF 107	20-SS 94
2000	*Clevelnd*	*AL*	*363*	*90*	*16*	*2*	*4*	*37/61*	*51*	*36*	*14*	*6*	*279*	*.248*	*.317*	*.336*	*.225*	*34*		

Cabrera made the roster on Opening Day and had only 20 at-bats when he was demoted almost 10 weeks later. When the Indians decided to carry twelve pitchers, he should have been the kind of utilityman to keep and use. He's been an All-Star at shortstop in the minors, and he picked up the outfield easily enough. He'll be a useful reserve on a team that isn't afraid to use him.

Wil Cordero OF Bats R Age 28

YEAR	TEAM	LGE	AB	H	DB	TP	HR	BB/SO	R	RBI	SB	CS	OUT	BA	OBP	SLG	EQA	EQR	DEFENSE
1997	Boston	AL	570	163	28	3	18	27/117	80	71	1	3	410	.286	.324	.440	.253	66	125-OF 93
1998	ChiSox	AL	341	92	19	2	13	20/65	56	48	2	1	250	.270	.316	.452	.255	41	78-1B 104
1999	Clevelnd	AL	192	56	11	0	9	13/37	31	30	2	0	136	.292	.355	.490	.282	29	28-LF 96
2000	*Pittsbrg*	*NL*	*307*	*90*	*17*	*1*	*15*	*22/62*	*44*	*58*	*1*	*1*	*218*	*.293*	*.340*	*.502*	*.275*	*43*	

Success breeds imitation? The Yankees sign and carry a veteran player or two more than they really need but send Darryl Strawberry and Jeff Nelson to Tampa to hang out until it's time to tune up for the postseason. Cordero essentially got to do the same thing by breaking his wrist in early June, fattening up on a rehab assignment before coming back for postseason chores. Meanwhile, the regular season experience can go to people who need to develop by playing, whether it's Ricky Ledee or Richie Sexson. Pittsburgh signed Cordero to a three-year deal, a silly move unless they're planning to move him back to shortstop. There's been speculation he'll play third.

Jacob Cruz   OF   Bats L   Age 27

YEAR	TEAM	LGE	AB	H	DB	TP	HR	BB/SO	R	RBI	SB	CS	OUT	BA	OBP	SLG	EQA	EQR	DEFENSE
1997	Phoenix	PCL	471	142	33	2	9	49/68	66	65	12	2	331	.301	.370	.437	.277	67	113-OF 101
1998	Fresno	PCL	338	83	13	3	12	37/62	42	43	8	3	258	.246	.330	.408	.252	41	84-OF 92
1998	Buffalo	Int	169	48	7	1	10	9/29	24	27	1	2	123	.284	.323	.515	.270	23	41-OF 86
1999	Buffalo	Int	202	48	6	2	5	16/43	22	23	2	1	155	.238	.301	.361	.225	19	38-OF 91
1999	Clevelnd	AL	87	28	3	1	3	4/13	12	15	0	2	61	.322	.359	.483	.272	12	
2000	*Clevelnd*	*AL*	*365*	*102*	*14*	*2*	*13*	*38/65*	*56*	*61*	*5*	*3*	*266*	*.279*	*.347*	*.436*	*.262*	*47*	

Cruz opened the year with bone chips in his elbow, started the season with a strained ribcage and was finished off by a thumb injury in August. Amidst all of that, he reminded people that he can hit. He can be an adequate fill-in as a left fielder. Sometimes, guys like that squeeze out a career as Luis Gonzalez, but mostly they end up playing for the Reds for about four months before rotting in Pawtucket. It's the Jon Nunnally career path.

Einar Diaz   C   Bats R   Age 27

YEAR	TEAM	LGE	AB	H	DB	TP	HR	BB/SO	R	RBI	SB	CS	OUT	BA	OBP	SLG	EQA	EQR	DEFENSE
1997	Buffalo	AA	342	87	19	2	2	15/36	39	30	2	4	259	.254	.296	.339	.212	27	
1998	Buffalo	Int	415	114	19	3	5	13/37	49	49	2	2	303	.275	.305	.371	.227	37	111-C 100
1999	Clevelnd	AL	389	106	20	1	3	19/41	39	29	11	4	287	.272	.315	.352	.230	36	109-C 102
2000	*Clevelnd*	*AL*	*370*	*99*	*19*	*1*	*6*	*21/37*	*43*	*44*	*5*	*3*	*274*	*.268*	*.307*	*.373*	*.227*	*34*	

Even though he's right-handed, he's sort of like Jorge Fabregas, because the only pitch he can kill is the chest-high fastball. Everything else gives him trouble. He's a nice backup because he can field the position, but if Alomar's knees are shot, the Indians need to get somebody who can contribute offensively.

Mike Edwards   3B   Bats R   Age 23

YEAR	TEAM	LGE	AB	H	DB	TP	HR	BB/SO	R	RBI	SB	CS	OUT	BA	OBP	SLG	EQA	EQR	DEFENSE
1997	BlngtnNC	App	239	52	13	1	2	26/57	27	23	3	2	189	.218	.296	.305	.206	18	46-3B 109
1998	Columbus	SAL	505	125	33	3	6	53/96	60	60	6	3	383	.248	.321	.360	.234	51	115-3B 95
1999	Kinston	Car	471	123	23	3	16	77/117	64	73	4	2	350	.261	.372	.425	.273	68	127-3B 89
2000	*Clevelnd*	*AL*	*439*	*113*	*21*	*1*	*11*	*67/100*	*73*	*63*	*5*	*2*	*328*	*.257*	*.356*	*.385*	*.255*	*54*	

Edwards was picked out of high school in 1995 and is slowly developing into a pretty good prospect. An ex-shortstop, he's got a good defensive reputation. If Branyan doesn't develop, Edwards is the guy with the best shot at inheriting the job from Fryman.

   The 1999 Kinston Indians were a sort of experiment in making an organizational approach take shape on the field. Edwards, Jon Hamilton, Zach Sorensen and Scott Pratt together represent a nifty core for the kind of baseball the Indians say they want to play: getting on base, hitting for power and playing good defense. None of them look like they have star potential, but all of them are better prospects than guys like David Miller or Danny Peoples. It will be interesting to see how well it carries over to Double-A.

Travis Fryman   3B   Bats R   Age 31

YEAR	TEAM	LGE	AB	H	DB	TP	HR	BB/SO	R	RBI	SB	CS	OUT	BA	OBP	SLG	EQA	EQR	DEFENSE
1997	Detroit	AL	593	163	29	3	22	43/109	88	99	16	3	433	.275	.330	.445	.262	76	152-3B 105
1998	Clevelnd	AL	550	153	32	2	26	42/122	67	87	8	8	405	.278	.333	.485	.267	75	145-3B 94
1999	Clevelnd	AL	320	80	17	2	9	21/57	41	43	2	1	241	.250	.298	.400	.234	32	81-3B 106
2000	*Clevelnd*	*AL*	*395*	*101*	*16*	*1*	*17*	*33/78*	*52*	*62*	*5*	*2*	*296*	*.256*	*.313*	*.430*	*.247*	*45*	

The Indians had already gotten the best year out of him that they were going to get. This is what happens to players who hit 30 without ever starring. They get old, they get injury-prone and they cash checks. Sort of like Gerald Ford. Fryman missed time with a bad back and a knee injury. He's still a solid fielder, and a good guy to share time with Branyan for platooning, defense and days that Charlie Manuel wants to pull Branyan aside and work with him.

Jon Hamilton   OF   Bats L   Age 22

YEAR	TEAM	LGE	AB	H	DB	TP	HR	BB/SO	R	RBI	SB	CS	OUT	BA	OBP	SLG	EQA	EQR	DEFENSE
1997	BlngtnNC	App	253	48	9	3	2	36/74	25	12	7	2	207	.190	.296	.273	.203	19	64-OF 107
1998	Columbus	SAL	497	109	20	7	13	64/131	62	53	8	4	392	.219	.314	.366	.234	52	132-OF 100
1999	Kinston	Car	485	127	30	3	14	49/110	65	56	4	2	360	.262	.330	.423	.254	59	128-OF 100
2000	Clevelnd	AL	540	142	27	4	17	66/131	87	84	9	4	402	.263	.343	.422	.258	68	

The Indians have a number of high-draft-choice outfielders ahead of Hamilton, but most of them are already 25 or 26 and can only look forward to the Akron/Buffalo shuttle. By contrast, Hamilton can run, play the field and has shown good power early. He needs to improve across the board to really have a chance at the majors with the Tribe, but he's the one outfielder in the organization young enough to do it.

Heath Hayes   C   Bats R   Age 28

YEAR	TEAM	LGE	AB	H	DB	TP	HR	BB/SO	R	RBI	SB	CS	OUT	BA	OBP	SLG	EQA	EQR	DEFENSE
1997	Kinston	Car	390	83	15	1	17	26/124	39	41	1	1	308	.213	.264	.387	.215	33	
1998	Akron	Eas	332	62	14	1	8	17/105	29	37	1	2	272	.187	.230	.307	.170	16	85-C 93
1999	Akron	Eas	425	96	16	1	12	28/129	40	51	1	0	329	.226	.281	.353	.213	34	88-C 91
2000	Clevelnd	AL	379	82	10	0	15	29/117	33	44	1	1	298	.216	.272	.361	.207	29	

A strong-armed ex-infielder who still hasn't mastered footwork behind the plate to help his throwing. Not really a prospect, but if the Indians forget to bring in another catcher, he's somebody who might get to caddy for Diaz.

Tyler Houston   C/E5   Bats L   Age 29

YEAR	TEAM	LGE	AB	H	DB	TP	HR	BB/SO	R	RBI	SB	CS	OUT	BA	OBP	SLG	EQA	EQR	DEFENSE
1997	ChiCubs	NL	196	50	7	0	3	9/35	14	28	1	0	146	.255	.288	.337	.210	15	
1998	ChiCubs	NL	257	67	6	1	10	13/52	26	34	2	2	192	.261	.296	.409	.234	25	52-C 95
1999	ChiCubs	NL	248	56	9	1	8	25/66	24	24	1	1	193	.226	.297	.367	.224	23	49-3B 84
2000	Clevelnd	AL	238	56	7	1	8	21/59	26	30	1	1	183	.235	.297	.374	.223	21	

One of the season's more notable absurdities was the *Chicago Tribune* naming a midseason Chicago-only All-Star team. Houston was named Chicago's best third baseman. You might forgive journalists for naming a no-tools zero because Greg Norton's E5s made them squeamish. That doesn't excuse the Cubs for playing him.

Maicer Isturiz   SS   Bats B   Age 19

YEAR	TEAM	LGE	AB	H	DB	TP	HR	BB/SO	R	RBI	SB	CS	OUT	BA	OBP	SLG	EQA	EQR	DEFENSE
1998	BlngtnNC	App	217	52	9	1	1	11/35	19	21	5	3	168	.240	.276	.304	.194	14	55-SS 100
1999	Columbus	SAL	224	59	4	2	4	17/28	33	19	5	1	166	.263	.317	.353	.232	21	44-SS 89
2000	Clevelnd	AL	162	44	4	1	2	12/38	21	18	4	1	119	.272	.322	.346	.229	15	

The Indians expect this young Venezuelan to inherit the shortstop job from Omar Vizquel someday. He missed the start of the year with shoulder surgery, but he still made progress at the plate. Isturiz could be ready by 2002, the last year of Vizquel's contract, but keep in mind that he is following in the wake of Zach Sorensen from the Kinston class of '99.

Dave Justice   LF   Bats L   Age 34

YEAR	TEAM	LGE	AB	H	DB	TP	HR	BB/SO	R	RBI	SB	CS	OUT	BA	OBP	SLG	EQA	EQR	DEFENSE
1997	Clevelnd	AL	496	170	30	1	36	78/76	84	103	3	5	331	.343	.432	.625	.337	109	67-OF 92
1998	Clevelnd	AL	532	144	38	2	20	73/96	87	81	8	3	391	.271	.359	.462	.276	78	
1999	Clevelnd	AL	422	119	16	0	20	87/90	67	80	1	3	306	.282	.407	.462	.295	72	75-LF 94
2000	Clevelnd	AL	439	124	14	0	27	82/84	88	99	3	2	317	.282	.395	.499	.298	77	

Justice is a great second banana behind real stars like Roberto Alomar, Manny Ramirez and Jim Thome. Because of those guys, the Indians can afford watching Justice miss 30 or more games, but not every team can. Maybe he'd be less fragile if he became a regular DH, and maybe not. Doing it would make him less valuable, and he still flashes better leather in left field than Cordero or Sexson.

Kenny Lofton			**CF**				**Bats L**	**Age 33**										
YEAR	TEAM	LGE	AB	H	DB	TP	HR	BB/SO	R	RBI	SB	CS	OUT	BA	OBP	SLG	EQA	EQR	DEFENSE
1997	Atlanta	NL	502	167	22	6	5	63/82	86	48	21	20	355	.333	.409	.430	.283	76	110-OF 110
1998	Clevelnd	AL	591	161	31	6	11	84/78	91	58	47	10	440	.272	.365	.401	.272	85	144-OF 104
1999	Clevelnd	AL	458	134	28	6	6	72/84	100	35	25	6	330	.293	.395	.419	.287	73	110-CF 99
2000	*Clevelnd*	*AL*	*469*	*138*	*24*	*4*	*8*	*75/75*	*102*	*70*	*20*	*8*	*339*	*.294*	*.392*	*.414*	*.279*	*70*	

One of the time-honored sabermetric observations is that speed players age better than players with old players' skills like power and patience. Lofton seems a good example of that, although he's entering a phase of his career in which, like Rickey Henderson before him, his hamstrings seem to keep giving out. He may not be up to playing center field every day anymore. It's doubtful that the Indians can afford to keep both Justice and Lofton if each is good for just 120 games a year. Lofton will miss at least the first three months of the 2000 season after shoulder surgery in December.

Jeff Manto			**1B/3B**				**Bats R**	**Age 35**										
YEAR	TEAM	LGE	AB	H	DB	TP	HR	BB/SO	R	RBI	SB	CS	OUT	BA	OBP	SLG	EQA	EQR	DEFENSE
1997	Buffalo	AA	194	56	10	0	16	26/48	31	45	0	1	139	.289	.379	.588	.308	37	26-3B 94
1997	Syracuse	Int	135	26	5	1	2	17/32	15	9	1	1	110	.193	.287	.289	.197	9	
1998	Buffalo	Int	212	56	10	0	17	47/53	35	47	2	1	157	.264	.400	.552	.311	42	33-1B 107
1999	Buffalo	Int	205	51	7	0	17	55/52	35	31	2	1	155	.249	.413	.532	.313	42	50-1B 84
2000	*Colorado*	*NL*	*221*	*63*	*10*	*0*	*19*	*57/58*	*54*	*63*	*1*	*1*	*159*	*.285*	*.432*	*.588*	*.307*	*42*	

He keeps plugging away, still looking like the kind of guy who's going to make a great hitting coach. He's signed a minor-league deal with the Rockies, where he'll have a brilliant opportunity to get some well-deserved major-league playing time for the Cleveland West squad. If he gets 300 plate appearances, he'll make Dante Bichette look like a piker.

John McDonald			**SS**				**Bats R**	**Age 25**										
YEAR	TEAM	LGE	AB	H	DB	TP	HR	BB/SO	R	RBI	SB	CS	OUT	BA	OBP	SLG	EQA	EQR	DEFENSE
1997	Kinston	Car	557	137	26	3	4	37/77	66	45	3	3	423	.246	.295	.325	.209	42	129-SS 104
1998	Akron	Eas	517	113	17	2	2	35/61	58	39	11	4	408	.219	.275	.271	.185	30	133-SS 104
1999	Akron	Eas	229	60	4	0	3	13/29	23	23	3	2	171	.262	.305	.319	.212	18	55-SS 97
1999	Buffalo	Int	236	69	8	2	0	8/24	24	21	4	2	169	.292	.320	.343	.227	21	60-SS 98
2000	*Clevelnd*	*AL*	*468*	*121*	*16*	*1*	*2*	*31/56*	*48*	*42*	*6*	*3*	*350*	*.259*	*.305*	*.310*	*.207*	*34*	

While maintaining his great defensive reputation, McDonald changed his approach at the plate, concentrating on making contact and raising his batting average. That doesn't make him a good prospect, but it is enough to make some people think he could become Rey Sanchez.

David Miller			**OF/1B**				**Bats L**	**Age 26**											
YEAR	TEAM	LGE	AB	H	DB	TP	HR	BB/SO	R	RBI	SB	CS	OUT	BA	OBP	SLG	EQA	EQR	DEFENSE	
1997	Akron	Eas	512	137	25	7	3	34/82	63	48	14	6	381	.268	.315	.361	.232	49	132-OF 90	
1998	Buffalo	Int	418	102	18	1	8	51/75	47	46	3	5	321	.244	.329	.349	.232	42	116-OF 98	
1999	Buffalo	Int	326	70	19	2	1	26/63	28	29	7	4	260	.215	.273	.294	.191	21	52-OF 88	24-1B 88
2000	*Clevelnd*	*AL*	*308*	*75*	*18*	*2*	*3*	*30/56*	*40*	*31*	*6*	*4*	*237*	*.244*	*.311*	*.344*	*.221*	*27*		

If there was any doubt that he's a first-round flop, the jury's in and handing the judge a rope. At the time the Indians picked him out of Clemson, he could have been a left-handed pitcher or a hitter, so putting him on the Ron Mahay career path may be the only way to salvage something.

Scott Morgan			**OF**				**Bats R**	**Age 26**										
YEAR	TEAM	LGE	AB	H	DB	TP	HR	BB/SO	R	RBI	SB	CS	OUT	BA	OBP	SLG	EQA	EQR	DEFENSE
1997	Kinston	Car	381	103	27	2	17	33/95	65	48	2	1	279	.270	.334	.486	.270	53	84-OF 97
1998	Akron	Eas	459	114	29	3	18	44/133	75	67	2	3	348	.248	.322	.442	.254	57	109-OF 92
1999	Akron	Eas	350	83	23	1	18	26/112	53	49	3	1	268	.237	.292	.463	.248	41	81-OF 93
1999	Buffalo	Int	171	38	5	0	7	14/42	24	24	1	2	135	.222	.291	.374	.221	16	42-OF 98
2000	*Clevelnd*	*AL*	*504*	*127*	*25*	*0*	*26*	*53/144*	*73*	*87*	*3*	*2*	*379*	*.252*	*.323*	*.456*	*.257*	*64*	

Morgan was forced to repeat a year at Akron because the Indians wanted Buffalo to open with an outfield of Miller, David Roberts and Alex Ramirez. Because he's also 6'7" and has power, he gets compared to Richie Sexson, but he's older, has a history of back problems and hasn't mastered Triple-A. He's not a great bet to grow up to be Shane Spencer.

Danny Peoples — 1B — Bats R — Age 25

YEAR	TEAM	LGE	AB	H	DB	TP	HR	BB/SO	R	RBI	SB	CS	OUT	BA	OBP	SLG	EQA	EQR	DEFENSE
1997	Kinston	Car	426	98	16	1	30	69/149	67	68	4	1	329	.230	.343	.484	.275	65	72-OF 81
1998	Akron	Eas	224	56	12	0	9	24/61	25	29	1	1	169	.250	.325	.424	.251	27	41-OF 92
1999	Akron	Eas	503	111	21	2	17	40/160	60	60	1	1	393	.221	.282	.372	.218	44	92-1B 101
2000	*Clevelnd*	*AL*	*504*	*120*	*22*	*1*	*25*	*58/157*	*69*	*82*	*1*	*1*	*385*	*.238*	*.317*	*.435*	*.249*	*60*	

After battling back and knee problems in 1998, Peoples was finally healthy and had a miserable season at the plate. Peoples was the Indians' first-round pick in 1996, after Miller had been the first-round pick in 1995. And you wonder why John Hart discards scouting directors like unpopped kernels at the bottom of his popcorn?

Scott Pratt — 2B — Bats L — Age 23

YEAR	TEAM	LGE	AB	H	DB	TP	HR	BB/SO	R	RBI	SB	CS	OUT	BA	OBP	SLG	EQA	EQR	DEFENSE
1998	Watertwn	NYP	183	53	12	2	2	27/27	25	10	5	4	134	.290	.389	.410	.274	26	36-2B 99
1999	Kinston	Car	500	116	28	4	10	62/95	65	46	22	6	390	.232	.322	.364	.240	55	131-2B 82
2000	*Clevelnd*	*AL*	*303*	*79*	*17*	*2*	*7*	*45/69*	*58*	*42*	*13*	*4*	*228*	*.261*	*.356*	*.399*	*.262*	*40*	

An ex-shortstop picked out of Auburn in 1998 and moved over to second base to make way for fellow '98 draftee Zach Sorensen, he's already got a good reputation for being tough on the deuce. Like the rest of the Kinston cadre, he's got some power (42 extra-base hits), some speed (47 steals) and some patience (77 walks).

Alex Ramirez — OF — Bats R — Age 25

YEAR	TEAM	LGE	AB	H	DB	TP	HR	BB/SO	R	RBI	SB	CS	OUT	BA	OBP	SLG	EQA	EQR	DEFENSE
1997	Buffalo	AA	425	123	21	8	10	20/97	57	43	9	4	306	.289	.328	.447	.259	52	95-OF 90
1998	Buffalo	Int	522	149	20	6	31	9/103	82	90	4	3	376	.285	.303	.525	.266	69	110-OF 95
1999	Buffalo	Int	304	85	17	2	10	13/54	40	40	3	4	223	.280	.317	.447	.251	35	70-OF 99
1999	Clevelnd	AL	96	28	5	1	3	2/26	10	16	1	1	69	.292	.313	.458	.253	11	
2000	*Clevelnd*	*AL*	*514*	*154*	*25*	*4*	*24*	*25/103*	*75*	*98*	*6*	*5*	*365*	*.300*	*.332*	*.504*	*.271*	*70*	

Ramirez surpassed Tom Prince's Buffalo career record for RBIs in 1999, which probably wasn't one of the things his mama told him he'd grow up to accomplish. If given an opportunity, he could still turn in a Candy Maldonado career, filling in as a decent regular for a team that needs power. Maldonado didn't get his shot until he was 26 and had been dumped by a Dodger team thinking it needed to shake things up. Ramirez's situation is similar.

Manny Ramirez — RF — Bats R — Age 28

YEAR	TEAM	LGE	AB	H	DB	TP	HR	BB/SO	R	RBI	SB	CS	OUT	BA	OBP	SLG	EQA	EQR	DEFENSE
1997	Clevelnd	AL	563	191	34	0	30	76/110	98	90	2	3	375	.339	.425	.560	.324	112	139-OF 94
1998	Clevelnd	AL	563	161	34	2	43	72/118	100	133	4	3	405	.286	.373	.583	.306	105	147-OF 94
1999	Clevelnd	AL	512	168	34	3	41	88/131	118	148	2	4	348	.328	.439	.646	.344	121	137-RF 102
2000	*Clevelnd*	*AL*	*499*	*153*	*27*	*1*	*36*	*85/114*	*108*	*131*	*2*	*3*	*349*	*.307*	*.408*	*.581*	*.319*	*101*	

Ramirez is the player who gets picked on as the front man for Mike Hargrove's hands-off management style and the sloppiness it came to represent. That's similar to the things that used to be said about Davey Johnson and Darryl Strawberry in the 1980s. It's mostly another case of "tear down the star" for fun and headlines. Ramirez is one of the game's best hitters in his prime, and he's underrated in the field. The big question is whether new owner Larry Dolan will pay top dollar to keep him, because if there's someone the Indians ought to be paying, it isn't an Alomar or Jim Thome, it's Ramirez.

David Roberts — CF — Bats L — Age 28

YEAR	TEAM	LGE	AB	H	DB	TP	HR	BB/SO	R	RBI	SB	CS	OUT	BA	OBP	SLG	EQA	EQR	DEFENSE
1997	Jacksnvl	Sou	415	100	22	1	2	30/0	22	17	11	3	318	.241	.292	.313	.209	32	33-OF 103
1998	Jacksnvl	Sou	282	75	13	4	3	37/69	46	28	9	5	212	.266	.356	.372	.253	34	47-OF 98
1998	Akron	Eas	228	66	9	3	5	27/33	33	24	14	4	166	.289	.367	.421	.274	33	57-OF 101
1999	Buffalo	Int	351	84	12	7	1	34/57	46	30	25	3	270	.239	.309	.322	.230	34	87-OF 108
1999	Clevelnd	AL	142	32	4	0	2	8/16	24	11	11	3	113	.225	.267	.296	.200	10	32-CF 105
2000	*Clevelnd*	*AL*	*426*	*112*	*20*	*4*	*4*	*48/62*	*74*	*46*	*23*	*6*	*320*	*.263*	*.338*	*.357*	*.244*	*47*	

He bears an uncanny likeness to Ming the Merciless, but who would have thought the evil Ruler of the Universe was such a good baserunner? Normally, your average iron-fisted tyrant would relish raw power and hit like Russ Branyan. Instead, Flash Gordon's nemesis uses the little man's offensive game and makes a dandy spare part. Roberts will pick up a lot of playing time in center field in Lofton's absence.

Marcos Scutaro — 2B — Bats R — Age 24

YEAR	TEAM	LGE	AB	H	DB	TP	HR	BB/SO	R	RBI	SB	CS	OUT	BA	OBP	SLG	EQA	EQR	DEFENSE
1997	Kinston	Car	389	102	17	5	10	26/72	47	52	12	4	291	.262	.319	.409	.248	44	73-2B 96
1998	Akron	Eas	464	134	26	6	10	39/69	57	54	21	10	340	.289	.355	.435	.268	63	118-2B 97
1999	Buffalo	Int	462	120	21	2	7	53/69	63	43	16	5	347	.260	.343	.359	.247	52	122-2B 98
2000	*Clevelnd*	*AL*	*445*	*126*	*20*	*4*	*12*	*50/68*	*81*	*68*	*19*	*7*	*325*	*.283*	*.356*	*.427*	*.267*	*60*	

There are about a dozen major-league teams that wish they could boast a middle infield as good as Scutaro and Enrique Wilson. Both have been All-Stars at their positions in the minors, and Scutaro has some sock, good speed and a good glove. He also desperately needs to be traded before he has to start worrying about whether he'll have his Buffalo number retired during the same ceremony as Alex Ramirez and Tom Prince.

Richie Sexson — 1B/LF — Bats R — Age 25

YEAR	TEAM	LGE	AB	H	DB	TP	HR	BB/SO	R	RBI	SB	CS	OUT	BA	OBP	SLG	EQA	EQR	DEFENSE	
1997	Buffalo	AA	443	117	21	2	30	23/89	55	87	4	1	327	.264	.307	.524	.269	61	111-1B 97	
1998	Buffalo	Int	346	97	18	1	19	42/69	51	65	1	1	250	.280	.363	.503	.286	55	68-OF 94	20-1B 133
1998	Clevelnd	AL	172	52	15	1	10	5/41	26	32	1	1	121	.302	.334	.576	.289	27	39-1B 107	
1999	Clevelnd	AL	476	119	17	7	29	29/117	65	105	3	3	360	.250	.299	.498	.258	61	54-1B 117	41-LF 89
2000	*Clevelnd*	*AL*	*508*	*139*	*22*	*3*	*34*	*44/116*	*78*	*108*	*2*	*2*	*371*	*.274*	*.332*	*.530*	*.278*	*75*		

Yes, he's an extreme streak hitter, could learn to lay off a pitch or four and has a lot of work to do before he's going to be an adequate left fielder, but the power is impossible to overlook. It's probably symbolic of modern blandness that he isn't being compared to Babe Herman, the clumsy giant of the 1930s who also flashed excellent power and a great arm. Like Herman, Sexson can dive for a ball and hit the ground well short of where it lands. If Manny Ramirez does that, it's on "SportsCenter" for a month. Someone needs to give Richie a great nickname to get the ball rolling on his legend.

Zach Sorensen — SS — Bats B — Age 23

YEAR	TEAM	LGE	AB	H	DB	TP	HR	BB/SO	R	RBI	SB	CS	OUT	BA	OBP	SLG	EQA	EQR	DEFENSE
1998	Watertwn	NYP	210	54	8	5	5	27/36	27	20	5	2	158	.257	.342	.414	.258	27	52-SS 102
1999	Kinston	Car	521	117	17	5	8	48/126	64	51	11	6	410	.225	.292	.322	.210	42	130-SS 104
2000	*Clevelnd*	*AL*	*416*	*103*	*13*	*5*	*9*	*48/95*	*59*	*52*	*11*	*6*	*319*	*.248*	*.325*	*.368*	*.236*	*43*	

Sorenson played shortstop for Wichita State before getting nabbed in the 1998 draft. He's sort of the antithesis to John McDonald offensively, in that he does everything but hit for a nice average (read: he puts runs on the board) and he can steal a few bases. Like McDonald, he can pick it at shortstop. Among the Kinston class of 1999, he's the one who needs to do the most to improve and survive, because he's got Isturiz behind him.

Jim Thome — 1B — Bats L — Age 29

YEAR	TEAM	LGE	AB	H	DB	TP	HR	BB/SO	R	RBI	SB	CS	OUT	BA	OBP	SLG	EQA	EQR	DEFENSE
1997	Clevelnd	AL	497	149	23	0	43	118/140	104	104	1	1	349	.300	.437	.606	.338	116	143-1B 98
1998	Clevelnd	AL	432	123	34	2	28	86/138	83	77	1	0	309	.285	.408	.567	.319	89	116-1B 101
1999	Clevelnd	AL	485	132	28	2	30	119/172	91	96	0	0	353	.272	.419	.524	.315	98	106-1B 113
2000	*Clevelnd*	*AL*	*469*	*132*	*23*	*1*	*33*	*113/153*	*112*	*120*	*0*	*0*	*337*	*.281*	*.421*	*.546*	*.320*	*97*	

No sooner does Thome turn into a good first baseman than the team starts wondering if moving him off third base was such a good idea. While he volunteered to move back after Fryman went down, he's 20 or 30 pounds heavier than the last time he played over there. People tend to lose the skills they don't use, and in this case, the Indians wasted his when they didn't correct the mistake when they had the chance, after trading Matt Williams. Now, they've got Fryman for too much and too long.

Thome has stretches during which he'll struggle, like he did this year in May and June, when he pulls off of pitches and overswings. Constant maintenance and Charlie Manuel's close attention produce in-season corrections. He won't get back to where he was in 1997; he'll just settle for being one of the league's best first basemen.

Omar Vizquel SS Bats B Age 33

YEAR	TEAM	LGE	AB	H	DB	TP	HR	BB/SO	R	RBI	SB	CS	OUT	BA	OBP	SLG	EQA	EQR	DEFENSE
1997	Clevelnd	AL	567	165	23	7	5	54/56	89	49	45	13	415	.291	.355	.383	.261	72	149-SS 95
1998	Clevelnd	AL	568	158	28	6	2	59/63	77	46	32	11	421	.278	.350	.359	.251	66	150-SS 103
1999	Clevelnd	AL	566	184	35	4	4	57/50	101	59	42	10	391	.325	.388	.422	.285	85	135-SS 97
2000	*Clevelnd*	*AL*	*482*	*137*	*25*	*3*	*4*	*59/46*	*93*	*57*	*26*	*9*	*354*	*.284*	*.362*	*.373*	*.258*	*60*	

He made an ass of himself last spring by threatening to hold out, but showed up and had the best offensive season he's going to have. His value will never be higher than it is right now, and he's under contract for the next three years, so there's no better time than the present to ship him off to the Dodgers. Maybe we should leave well enough alone, but how does such a great defensive shortstop turn the deuce only 88 times while playing behind a pitching staff that put more than 1,500 men on first base during the season?

Enrique Wilson IF Bats B Age 24

YEAR	TEAM	LGE	AB	H	DB	TP	HR	BB/SO	R	RBI	SB	CS	OUT	BA	OBP	SLG	EQA	EQR	DEFENSE	
1997	Buffalo	AA	462	141	22	3	10	38/42	76	38	8	6	327	.305	.365	.431	.269	61	64-SS 97	50-2B 102
1998	Buffalo	Int	222	60	8	0	5	15/21	33	21	5	2	164	.270	.316	.374	.236	22	47-2B 92	
1998	Clevelnd	AL	89	28	5	0	2	3/8	12	11	2	4	65	.315	.344	.438	.252	10		
1999	Clevelnd	AL	330	84	21	1	2	21/41	37	22	5	4	250	.255	.301	.342	.217	28	48-3B 105	24-SS 87
2000	*Clevelnd*	*AL*	*368*	*107*	*20*	*1*	*9*	*30/40*	*56*	*56*	*7*	*4*	*265*	*.291*	*.344*	*.424*	*.258*	*45*		

On the subject of criminal waste, Enrique Wilson is a better shortstop than half of the guys starting in the AL. Unfortunately, he spends his time hoping Vizquel raises such a stink over his contract that the Indians finally trade Little O and hand him the job. His 1999 numbers look worse than they had to because he played through a jammed thumb that crippled him at the plate. He took one for the team: Fryman was already on the disabled list, and the Indians were afraid of letting Russ Branyan play.

PITCHERS (Averages: ERA: 4.50 / H/9: 9.00 / HR/9: 1.00 / BB/9: 3.50 / K/9: 6.50 / KWH: 1.00)

Paul Assenmacher Throws L Age 39

YEAR	TEAM	LGE	IP	H	ER	HR	BB	K	ERA	W	L	H/9	HR/9	BB/9	K/9	KWH	PERA
1997	Clevelnd	AL	49.0	42	15	5	15	53	2.76	4	1	7.71	0.92	2.76	9.73	3.33	3.49
1998	Clevelnd	AL	48.7	51	19	4	21	44	3.51	3	2	9.43	0.74	3.88	8.14	1.35	4.62
1999	Clevelnd	AL	33.7	48	28	6	16	30	7.49	1	3	12.83	1.60	4.28	8.02	0.88	8.02

He spent the year getting rocked harder than Tipper Gore at a Rammstein concert. At this point he should do everyone a favor and call it a career. The decision to put him on the postseason roster ranks among the worst of several 1999 postseason miscalculations.

Mike Bacsik Throws L Age 22

YEAR	TEAM	LGE	IP	H	ER	HR	BB	K	ERA	W	L	H/9	HR/9	BB/9	K/9	KWH	PERA
1997	Columbus	SAL	131.0	209	117	20	68	70	8.04	4	11	14.36	1.37	4.67	4.81	0.26	8.79
1998	Kinston	Car	151.0	195	90	22	51	91	5.36	7	10	11.62	1.31	3.04	5.42	0.62	6.20
1999	Akron	Eas	137.7	198	100	25	51	69	6.54	5	10	12.94	1.63	3.33	4.51	0.35	7.58

The Indians' minor league pitcher of the year in 1998, Bacsik isn't really a prospect yet. He spots his slow fastball well and mixes in a good changeup. He does not have a consistent breaking pitch, but his curve has promise. The key is that he's young for someone already pitching at Double-A. Because of that, if he fills out and picks up some velocity, he could turn into something.

Danys Baez   Throws R   Age 19, then 22, then . . .

Another Joe Cubas Cuban who fled to Costa Rica to become a free agent. The Tribe won the bidding by giving him a four-year, $14.5-million contract. He's big and he throws upwards of 98 mph, with an age that keeps moving up every time someone asks. While he isn't expected to walk into camp and claim a rotation spot, the possibility is there. It would be easy to forecast that he'll be in the rotation by midseason, like Livan Hernandez in 1997, but the Indians have a weaker rotation than the Marlins had. Baez will get every opportunity to win a job in the spring.

J.D. Brammer   Throws R   Age 25

YEAR	TEAM	LGE	IP	H	ER	HR	BB	K	ERA	W	L	H/9	HR/9	BB/9	K/9	KWH	PERA
1997	Columbus	SAL	109.0	171	132	14	74	72	10.90	2	10	14.12	1.16	6.11	5.94	0.31	9.00
1998	Kinston	Car	24.7	21	9	2	11	22	3.28	2	1	7.66	0.73	4.01	8.03	1.57	3.65
1998	Akron	Eas	19.7	26	14	3	11	18	6.41	1	1	11.90	1.37	5.03	8.24	0.85	7.32
1999	Akron	Eas	68.7	69	56	6	70	53	7.34	2	6	9.04	0.79	9.17	6.95	0.43	6.55

Picked in 1996 after a career at Stanford during which he was a back-of-the-bullpen type, Brammer has a solid fastball and a power curve that goes all over the place. Awful mechanics and inconsistent command are obviously a problem, but Brammer has the stuff to turn into a good major-league reliever. He already reminds me of Mark Clear, if only for the curveball.

Jamie Brown   Throws R   Age 23

YEAR	TEAM	LGE	IP	H	ER	HR	BB	K	ERA	W	L	H/9	HR/9	BB/9	K/9	KWH	PERA
1997	Watertwn	NYP	64.0	98	54	9	23	35	7.59	2	5	13.78	1.27	3.23	4.92	0.41	7.59
1998	Kinston	Car	157.3	213	127	17	60	106	7.26	5	12	12.18	0.97	3.43	6.06	0.66	6.35
1999	Akron	Eas	128.7	167	86	12	43	80	6.02	5	9	11.68	0.84	3.01	5.60	0.67	5.67

Brown mixes low-90s heat with an inconsistent but improving curve and a nice change-up. He's not an outstanding pitching prospect now; he is just young enough to turn into one. Brown survived his initial contact with Double-A and has stayed healthy so far. Survival and aptitude are the best qualities for people who don't have Rick Ankiel's talent, and Brown has both going for him so far.

Dave Burba   Throws R   Age 33

YEAR	TEAM	LGE	IP	H	ER	HR	BB	K	ERA	W	L	H/9	HR/9	BB/9	K/9	KWH	PERA
1997	Cincnnti	NL	162.0	156	83	22	77	123	4.61	9	9	8.67	1.22	4.28	6.83	0.94	4.83
1998	Clevelnd	AL	210.3	198	86	27	72	135	3.68	14	9	8.47	1.16	3.08	5.78	0.96	4.19
1999	Clevelnd	AL	222.3	200	98	26	94	179	3.97	14	11	8.10	1.05	3.81	7.25	1.27	4.17

A personal favorite for no really good reason. He's lost velocity steadily, but he'll dump two- and four-seam fastballs for strikes, as well as a forkball and circle change. He'll tease you with a curve that isn't a strike very often anymore. All of that adds up to a pitcher who's getting better as he gets older, the classic crafty right-hander. Strangely enough, Burba was much more effective on four days' rest than five or more, putting together 17 quality starts (one was subsequently blown) in 23 outings.

Jared Camp   Throws R   Age 25

YEAR	TEAM	LGE	IP	H	ER	HR	BB	K	ERA	W	L	H/9	HR/9	BB/9	K/9	KWH	PERA
1997	Kinston	Car	66.7	79	50	12	23	46	6.75	2	5	10.67	1.62	3.11	6.21	0.87	5.94
1997	Akron	Eas	61.3	85	49	12	28	31	7.19	2	5	12.47	1.76	4.11	4.55	0.30	7.78
1998	Akron	Eas	81.3	100	46	8	37	34	5.09	4	5	11.07	0.89	4.09	3.76	0.23	5.86
1999	Kinston	Car	49.0	68	23	3	22	37	4.22	3	2	12.49	0.55	4.04	6.80	0.68	6.24
1999	Akron	Eas	16.0	27	22	0	19	14	12.38	0	2	15.19	0.00	10.69	7.88	0.29	10.12
1999	Buffalo	Int	10.3	4	2	0	14	12	1.74	1	0	3.48	0.00	12.19	10.45	1.92	3.48

Camp, a hard thrower, was the first pick in the 1999 Rule 5 draft. The Twins then traded him to Florida, where he should make the Marlins as their last reliever. Camp has significant control issues and not much more than a great fastball, but he's a good gamble for a Marlins team that is stockpiling young arms.

Tom Candiotti   Throws R   Age 42

YEAR	TEAM	LGE	IP	H	ER	HR	BB	K	ERA	W	L	H/9	HR/9	BB/9	K/9	KWH	PERA
1997	LosAngls	NL	130.0	138	65	22	42	82	4.50	7	7	9.55	1.52	2.91	5.68	0.87	5.12
1998	Oakland	AL	200.7	215	115	28	65	98	5.16	10	12	9.64	1.26	2.92	4.40	0.51	4.89
1999	Oakland	AL	57.0	63	40	10	23	31	6.32	2	4	9.95	1.58	3.63	4.89	0.50	5.68
1999	Cleveland	AL	15.0	18	16	3	6	11	9.60	0	2	10.80	1.80	3.60	6.60	0.84	6.60

He's coming to the end of the road after losing his rotation spot in Oakland to Tim Hudson. It isn't his arm that's giving out as much as his knees, so he may yet sneak in another year with a team that wants a veteran fifth starter. He's still considering a standing offer to play the title role in "Ol' Google Eyes: The Life and Times of Ernest Borgnine."

Bartolo Colon   Throws R   Age 25

YEAR	TEAM	LGE	IP	H	ER	HR	BB	K	ERA	W	L	H/9	HR/9	BB/9	K/9	KWH	PERA
1997	Buffalo	AmA	53.3	53	19	4	26	48	3.21	4	2	8.94	0.68	4.39	8.10	1.25	4.56
1997	Cleveland	AL	94.0	104	61	11	45	66	5.84	4	6	9.96	1.05	4.31	6.32	0.70	5.46
1998	Cleveland	AL	210.7	192	78	13	83	162	3.33	15	8	8.20	0.56	3.55	6.92	1.23	3.63
1999	Cleveland	AL	207.0	175	84	21	74	166	3.65	14	9	7.61	0.91	3.22	7.22	1.59	3.57

He's as pure a power pitcher as you're going to find. When he's got the game's best sinking fastball working, Colon doesn't really need a second pitch because the movement is so devastating. His change-up has come along well, but his curveball is still only a sideshow. He came into camp heavy, and when Kerry Wood's elbow exploded, Colon got bum-rushed into a multi-year deal to insure himself against injury. After Colon's problems throwing on short rest in 1998, Hargrove was obviously tempting fate by having him pitch on short rest in the 1999 playoffs, especially when Colon had experienced tendinitis problems in September.

Sean DePaula   Throws R   Age 26

YEAR	TEAM	LGE	IP	H	ER	HR	BB	K	ERA	W	L	H/9	HR/9	BB/9	K/9	KWH	PERA
1997	Watertwn	NYP	15.3	32	10	2	13	10	5.87	1	1	18.78	1.17	7.63	5.87	0.18	12.91
1997	Columbus	SAL	64.7	95	78	5	65	49	10.86	1	6	13.22	0.70	9.05	6.82	0.29	9.19
1998	Kinston	Car	42.3	73	34	1	28	37	7.23	1	4	15.52	0.21	5.95	7.87	0.50	8.72
1998	Akron	Eas	15.7	20	13	0	18	13	7.47	1	1	11.49	0.00	10.34	7.47	0.35	7.47
1999	Kinston	Car	46.3	53	26	7	22	47	5.05	2	3	10.29	1.36	4.27	9.13	1.42	6.02
1999	Akron	Eas	25.7	26	15	3	20	23	5.26	1	2	9.12	1.05	7.01	8.06	0.76	5.96
1999	Cleveland	AL	11.7	8	5	0	3	19	3.86	1	0	6.17	0.00	2.31	14.66	11.24	1.54

He could have saved the Indians a lot of grief if he'd been trusted with greater responsibility a day or two earlier in the Division Series. DePaula is a great example of where a good major-league reliever can come from: almost anywhere. He was drafted in 1996 off a Wake Forest team that had Bret Wagner and Mark Seaver as its star pitchers. He throws a heavy sinker in the mid-90s that he complements with a forkball. All of that makes it difficult to get a hard-hit ball to the outfield off him.

Tim Drew   Throws R   Age 21

YEAR	TEAM	LGE	IP	H	ER	HR	BB	K	ERA	W	L	H/9	HR/9	BB/9	K/9	KWH	PERA
1998	Columbus	SAL	67.0	85	52	6	36	42	6.99	2	5	11.42	0.81	4.84	5.64	0.43	6.31
1998	Kinston	Car	80.7	138	80	12	42	48	8.93	2	7	15.40	1.34	4.69	5.36	0.30	9.48
1999	Kinston	Car	159.7	195	97	16	68	92	5.47	7	11	10.99	0.90	3.83	5.19	0.48	5.69

Most high-school pitchers don't work out, but J.D.'s kid brother looks like he's turning into one who will. Drew's fastball is picking up movement, he uses his change-up well and he's learning to turn his slider into a hammer he can drop anytime in the count. He's still working on his location, and he could move up quickly if it improves.

Dwight Gooden   Throws R   Age 35

YEAR	TEAM	LGE	IP	H	ER	HR	BB	K	ERA	W	L	H/9	HR/9	BB/9	K/9	KWH	PERA
1997	NY Yanks	AL	106.7	111	56	13	53	66	4.72	6	6	9.37	1.10	4.47	5.57	0.55	5.23
1998	Cleveland	AL	138.7	126	51	12	54	85	3.31	10	5	8.18	0.78	3.50	5.52	0.79	3.83
1999	Cleveland	AL	116.7	120	79	16	66	91	6.09	5	8	9.26	1.23	5.09	7.02	0.78	5.55

Is there still life in the Doctor? His fastball/slider repertoire is shot, so he's working on a change-up and a curveball. Not everyone has to pick up a new pitch at 34. The inconsistency was double-edged: Gooden would mix a good start with a bad month, giving the Indians just enough reason to hope he was about to put it all together.

Chris Haney　　　　　Throws L　　　Age 31

YEAR	TEAM	LGE	IP	H	ER	HR	BB	K	ERA	W	L	H/9	HR/9	BB/9	K/9	KWH	PERA
1997	Omaha	AmA	19.0	17	12	3	7	6	5.68	1	1	8.05	1.42	3.32	2.84	0.23	4.26
1997	KansasCy	AL	25.3	28	15	1	5	16	5.33	1	2	9.95	0.36	1.78	5.68	1.37	3.55
1998	KansasCy	AL	101.0	118	68	16	38	52	6.06	4	7	10.51	1.43	3.39	4.63	0.45	5.79
1999	Buffalo	Int	55.7	57	28	4	24	32	4.53	3	3	9.22	0.65	3.88	5.17	0.56	4.37
1999	Clevelnd	AL	41.0	41	19	3	15	23	4.17	3	2	9.00	0.66	3.29	5.05	0.64	4.17

Haney lost time in 1997 to non-arm injuries, including a strained hamstring and a broken ankle. He feels the Royals rushed him back in 1998, producing an ugly year. Considering that, he may earn another shot. The Indians certainly could have done worse than just putting him in the rotation every fifth day.

Mike Jackson　　　　Throws R　　　Age 35

YEAR	TEAM	LGE	IP	H	ER	HR	BB	K	ERA	W	L	H/9	HR/9	BB/9	K/9	KWH	PERA
1997	Clevelnd	AL	75.0	57	30	3	29	74	3.60	5	3	6.84	0.36	3.48	8.88	2.48	2.76
1998	Clevelnd	AL	65.3	40	9	4	13	56	1.24	7	0	5.51	0.55	1.79	7.71	4.51	1.79
1999	Clevelnd	AL	69.3	57	28	10	25	57	3.63	5	3	7.40	1.30	3.25	7.40	1.70	3.76

He's entering Jeff Reardon territory as far as effectiveness, and I don't mean that in the good way. Jackson had a dead arm by May, and also had to fight off a rib injury. He's turning into a one-inning pitcher with longball problems. Maybe the Tribe has to exorcise the ghost of Jose Mesa, because if there's a team that could afford to skip spending anything on a closer, it's the Indians. The Braves conjure up a new closer every year, because they understand that talent, not major league experience, wins games. The Tribe is already spending a good chunk of change on three veteran relievers (Steve Reed, Paul Shuey and Ricky Rincon), so why bother spending any more in the pen? Jackson signed with the Phillies, and will be the closer on an improved team.

Steve Karsay　　　　Throws R　　　Age 28

YEAR	TEAM	LGE	IP	H	ER	HR	BB	K	ERA	W	L	H/9	HR/9	BB/9	K/9	KWH	PERA
1997	Oakland	AL	138.3	151	77	18	48	93	5.01	7	8	9.82	1.17	3.12	6.05	0.89	5.01
1998	Buffalo	Int	76.0	97	42	5	17	53	4.97	4	4	11.49	0.59	2.01	6.28	1.27	4.86
1998	Clevelnd	AL	25.3	29	13	3	6	13	4.62	1	2	10.30	1.07	2.13	4.62	0.73	4.62
1999	Clevelnd	AL	79.7	67	25	5	29	70	2.82	6	3	7.57	0.56	3.28	7.91	1.88	3.28

So you have one of the game's most injury-prone pitchers, a guy whose elbow twitches just picking up a fork, and you finally find a role in which he can contribute, long relief. He's incredibly valuable to your team in this role, especially because you have only two starting pitchers you can count on.

So what do you do? You get greedy and put him into the rotation because you're deathly afraid of using anybody from Buffalo. Three starts later, you still have to find a way to avoid calling up anyone from Buffalo, and you no longer have your designated middle-innings stopper because you wanted to get five innings every five days instead of three innings every three or four.

You can almost sense the desperation the decision implied: it meant Hart and Hargrove were coming to terms with the fact that they hadn't gotten a starting pitcher over the winter, and their rotation wasn't good enough to go toe-to-toe with Boston or Texas, let alone the Yankees. So they were either desperate or criminally stupid.

Mark Langston　　　　Throws L　　　Age 39

YEAR	TEAM	LGE	IP	H	ER	HR	BB	K	ERA	W	L	H/9	HR/9	BB/9	K/9	KWH	PERA
1997	Anaheim	AL	49.0	58	30	7	30	31	5.51	2	3	10.65	1.29	5.51	5.69	0.41	6.61
1998	San Dieg	NL	77.7	114	60	12	43	53	6.95	3	6	13.21	1.39	4.98	6.14	0.43	8.23
1999	Buffalo	Int	17.7	18	10	4	9	9	5.09	1	1	9.17	2.04	4.58	4.58	0.37	6.11
1999	Clevelnd	AL	62.7	66	35	8	28	44	5.03	3	4	9.48	1.15	4.02	6.32	0.78	5.17

His "Night of the Living Dead" career keeps stumbling along in what has to be baseball's most extended farewell tour since Steve Carlton took almost four years before being told to get out and stay out. The Padres announced his retirement before asking him, which most people would take as a hint. If he's holding on until he reaches 200 wins, he's looking at about six or seven more years for the 21 victories he needs. The Indians gave him a minor-league contract primarily to suck up to Langston's friend Chuck Finley, a move that paid off when Finley signed with the Tribe.

Tom Martin — Throws L — Age 30

YEAR	TEAM	LGE	IP	H	ER	HR	BB	K	ERA	W	L	H/9	HR/9	BB/9	K/9	KWH	PERA
1997	Houston	NL	55.0	54	13	2	24	33	2.13	5	1	8.84	0.33	3.93	5.40	0.63	3.93
1998	Buffalo	Int	33.7	52	28	4	15	29	7.49	1	3	13.90	1.07	4.01	7.75	0.81	7.75
1998	Clevelnd	AL	15.3	28	19	3	13	9	11.15	0	2	16.43	1.76	7.63	5.28	0.17	12.33
1999	Clevelnd	AL	9.3	12	7	2	3	8	6.75	0	1	11.57	1.93	2.89	7.71	1.33	6.75

A torn labrum kept him out until the All-Star break, which means it isn't his fault that the team casually discarded Ron Villone. He still has better stuff than your average left-handed specialist, so the Indians' pen will be better if he and Rincon are healthy in 2000, with Paul Assenmacher sticking to modeling a new beard color in "Just For Men" commercials.

Willie Martinez — Throws R — Age 22

YEAR	TEAM	LGE	IP	H	ER	HR	BB	K	ERA	W	L	H/9	HR/9	BB/9	K/9	KWH	PERA
1997	Kinston	Car	124.7	165	81	15	47	88	5.85	5	9	11.91	1.08	3.39	6.35	0.75	6.28
1998	Akron	Eas	148.0	196	106	16	51	96	6.45	5	11	11.92	0.97	3.10	5.84	0.69	6.02
1999	Akron	Eas	136.3	195	98	21	49	75	6.47	5	10	12.87	1.39	3.23	4.95	0.44	7.20
1999	Buffalo	Int	21.0	31	17	3	7	11	7.29	1	1	13.29	1.29	3.00	4.71	0.42	7.29

Despite being named a Double-A All-Star, 1999 wasn't a good year for Martinez. In the past, we've been able to say injuries were keeping him from developing. This year, he didn't get hurt and was very hittable. Although he has good stuff—a hard curve and low-90s heat with good movement—his mechanics are inconsistent, and his mistakes within the zone go screaming into the gaps.

Charles Nagy — Throws R — Age 33

YEAR	TEAM	LGE	IP	H	ER	HR	BB	K	ERA	W	L	H/9	HR/9	BB/9	K/9	KWH	PERA
1997	Clevelnd	AL	227.3	245	106	25	77	150	4.20	13	12	9.70	0.99	3.05	5.94	0.89	4.71
1998	Clevelnd	AL	218.0	236	120	31	70	123	4.95	11	13	9.74	1.28	2.89	5.08	0.68	5.00
1999	Clevelnd	AL	204.7	226	104	22	57	130	4.57	11	12	9.94	0.97	2.51	5.72	0.98	4.62

He's lost a lot of velocity within the last year, compensating with improved command of his forkball. That's good news, because when it isn't forking, he's forked. Nagy is only two wins away from being the 10th-winningest pitcher in franchise history. That's not bad for a guy who has been just plodding along as a decent third starter since his last great season in 1996.

Robert Pugmire — Throws R — Age 21

YEAR	TEAM	LGE	IP	H	ER	HR	BB	K	ERA	W	L	H/9	HR/9	BB/9	K/9	KWH	PERA
1997	BlngtnNC	App	56.3	104	57	4	41	34	9.11	1	5	16.62	0.64	6.55	5.43	0.20	10.22
1999	Columbus	SAL	55.3	56	26	5	20	46	4.23	3	3	9.11	0.81	3.25	7.48	1.41	4.23
1999	Kinston	Car	91.0	107	54	10	29	65	5.34	4	6	10.58	0.99	2.87	6.43	1.02	5.14

Pugmire is another big kid from Washington state. What is it? The apples? Mount Rainier? Moisture in the bones? A new evil Windows application? He's being compared to Tim Drew for taking a big step forward this year, but that's flattering to Drew. This was his first full season in the pros, and he was 13-2 with 160 strikeouts and 39 walks in 152 innings. A 4-to-1 ratio of strikeouts to walks is outstanding at any level.

Jason Rakers — Throws R — Age 27

YEAR	TEAM	LGE	IP	H	ER	HR	BB	K	ERA	W	L	H/9	HR/9	BB/9	K/9	KWH	PERA
1997	Kinston	Car	88.3	139	67	11	24	66	6.83	3	7	14.16	1.12	2.45	6.72	0.98	7.34
1997	Akron	Eas	39.0	40	23	3	13	23	5.31	2	2	9.23	0.69	3.00	5.31	0.76	4.15
1998	Akron	Eas	28.7	45	14	2	9	20	4.40	2	1	14.13	0.63	2.83	6.28	0.74	6.91
1998	Buffalo	Int	120.0	148	76	12	42	75	5.70	5	8	11.10	0.90	3.15	5.63	0.68	5.47
1999	Buffalo	Int	123.7	172	91	15	35	73	6.62	4	10	12.52	1.09	2.55	5.31	0.66	6.33

His slow fastball and slider combo didn't work as well this year, so despite getting further than expected, it looks like he wasn't touted for a reason. His best hope was that the Indians would call him up after Wright and Gooden burned out, and Hart elected not to do that. His future is limited.

Steve Reed — Throws R — Age 34

YEAR	TEAM	LGE	IP	H	ER	HR	BB	K	ERA	W	L	H/9	HR/9	BB/9	K/9	KWH	PERA
1997	Colorado	NL	64.7	45	23	9	29	41	3.20	5	2	6.26	1.25	4.04	5.71	0.96	3.48
1998	San Fran	NL	53.7	33	11	4	20	47	1.84	5	1	5.53	0.67	3.35	7.88	2.50	2.35
1998	Clevelnd	AL	26.7	24	16	4	9	24	5.40	1	2	8.10	1.35	3.04	8.10	1.99	4.05
1999	Clevelnd	AL	62.3	66	29	9	19	45	4.19	4	3	9.53	1.30	2.74	6.50	1.21	4.76

He returned from Planet Coors with a hard-earned reputation as one of baseball's best relievers. Four months with the Giants only added to that reputation. Since coming over to the Tribe, though, the days on which his stuff is untouchable have been few and far between. At the end of 1998, he suffered a circulatory problem in his right arm, and in 1999 he hid an injury for almost a month. His elbow left him almost incapable of pitching in September, but as with their other injured pitchers, the Indians chose to go down with all hands on deck.

Paul Rigdon — Throws R — Age 24

YEAR	TEAM	LGE	IP	H	ER	HR	BB	K	ERA	W	L	H/9	HR/9	BB/9	K/9	KWH	PERA
1998	Kinston	Car	114.0	169	94	12	50	68	7.42	3	10	13.34	0.95	3.95	5.37	0.41	7.26
1999	Akron	Eas	47.3	26	8	3	11	20	1.52	4	1	4.94	0.57	2.09	3.80	1.05	1.71
1999	Buffalo	Int	99.0	124	61	10	29	54	5.55	4	7	11.27	0.91	2.64	4.91	0.61	5.36

Coming off Tommy John surgery on his elbow in 1997, he took a big step forward in 1999 after settling for staying healthy in 1998. Following a career as the closer at the University of Florida, he was considered a smart pitcher. In 1999, he came up with a sinker, which he locates well to go with a good slider and a change-up used to advantage. He's not a great prospect, just someone who could end up with a dozen starts after the veteran du jour burns out.

Ricky Rincon — Throws L — Age 30

YEAR	TEAM	LGE	IP	H	ER	HR	BB	K	ERA	W	L	H/9	HR/9	BB/9	K/9	KWH	PERA
1997	Pittsbrg	NL	61.7	47	23	5	26	66	3.36	4	3	6.86	0.73	3.79	9.63	2.66	3.21
1998	Pittsbrg	NL	65.3	51	30	6	30	61	4.13	4	3	7.03	0.83	4.13	8.40	1.82	3.44
1999	Clevelnd	AL	45.0	40	19	5	23	31	3.80	3	2	8.00	1.00	4.60	6.20	0.78	4.40

Last year's pickup of Rincon was a good reminder that quality hitters should fetch more than just a situational reliever. Trading Brian Giles for Jon Lieber would have made sense, since Lieber was as poised as Giles to break out and become a star. It didn't help that Mike Hargrove shoehorned Rincon, when he wasn't hurt, into a situational role he's overqualified for. If and when he's healthy, Rincon could step into the closer's role. That still won't even things up with the Bucs.

David Riske — Throws R — Age 23

YEAR	TEAM	LGE	IP	H	ER	HR	BB	K	ERA	W	L	H/9	HR/9	BB/9	K/9	KWH	PERA
1997	Kinston	Car	66.7	76	29	3	37	66	3.92	4	3	10.26	0.41	5.00	8.91	1.16	5.13
1998	Kinston	Car	50.3	61	21	6	21	48	3.75	4	2	10.91	1.07	3.75	8.58	1.34	5.72
1999	Akron	Eas	23.0	7	7	1	14	27	2.74	2	1	2.74	0.39	5.48	10.57	5.56	1.57
1999	Buffalo	Int	27.0	15	4	0	8	20	1.33	3	0	5.00	0.00	2.67	6.67	2.49	1.33
1999	Clevelnd	AL	14.3	19	13	2	6	16	8.16	0	2	11.93	1.26	3.77	10.05	1.68	6.91

Most solid minor-league relievers aren't really prospects, but Riske could be a rare exception. He's got a low-90s fastball, a solid forkball and a tumbling curve he uses to surprise people once in a while. Top it off with a deceptive three-quarters delivery that makes all of his pitches more effective, and you've got a guy who can pitch.

C.C. Sabathia — Throws L — Age 19

YEAR	TEAM	LGE	IP	H	ER	HR	BB	K	ERA	W	L	H/9	HR/9	BB/9	K/9	KWH	PERA
1998	BlngtnNC	App	16.0	27	17	1	10	22	9.56	0	2	15.19	0.56	5.63	12.38	1.34	9.00
1999	MahngVal	NYP	18.0	13	7	0	16	17	3.50	1	1	6.50	0.00	8.00	8.50	1.04	4.00
1999	Columbus	SAL	16.0	10	2	1	7	13	1.13	2	0	5.63	0.56	3.94	7.31	1.80	2.25
1999	Kinston	Car	30.3	38	26	4	22	22	7.71	1	2	11.27	1.19	6.53	6.53	0.43	7.42

Usually somebody with this little pro experience doesn't make the book, but Sabathia is extraordinary. At 19, he's only just beginning to grow into his 6'7" frame. His fastball already reaches 97 and his curve has promise. His elbow problems in 1999 weren't from pitching, but from a bone bruise caused by his rapid growth that could have become a stress fracture if he'd pitched through it. The Indians have been extremely careful with him, restricting his workload while trying to keep his weight down. Sabathia is not really a prospect yet, just a kid with some unique talents who needs to prove he can stay healthy while harnessing his ability.

Paul Shuey   Throws R   Age 29

YEAR	TEAM	LGE	IP	H	ER	HR	BB	K	ERA	W	L	H/9	HR/9	BB/9	K/9	KWH	PERA
1997	Clevelnd	AL	45.0	51	29	5	28	46	5.80	2	3	10.20	1.00	5.60	9.20	1.11	6.00
1998	Buffalo	Int	13.7	12	4	0	7	19	2.63	1	1	7.90	0.00	4.61	12.51	3.21	3.29
1998	Clevelnd	AL	53.0	40	16	6	26	59	2.72	4	2	6.79	1.02	4.42	10.02	2.50	3.74
1999	Clevelnd	AL	82.7	64	31	7	39	106	3.38	6	3	6.97	0.76	4.25	11.54	3.36	3.48

Shuey keeps teasing people by appearing to be on the cusp of a big breakthrough, if only he could avoid getting hurt. In 1999, he once again didn't escape the injury bug. Despite hamstring and back problems, Shuey still managed to pitch in 72 games without living up to his reputation for dominance. Nevertheless, if he's handed the closer's role, he'll get plenty of magazine-cover glory. His punchout of Nomar Garciaparra in the first game of the Division Series was my pick for the high-water mark of the Indians' season.

Jaret Wright   Throws R   Age 24

YEAR	TEAM	LGE	IP	H	ER	HR	BB	K	ERA	W	L	H/9	HR/9	BB/9	K/9	KWH	PERA
1997	Akron	Eas	52.7	45	25	4	25	47	4.27	3	3	7.69	0.68	4.27	8.03	1.47	3.76
1997	Buffalo	AmA	42.7	36	20	4	21	42	4.22	3	2	7.59	0.84	4.43	8.86	1.74	4.01
1997	Clevelnd	AL	90.7	78	41	8	35	63	4.07	6	4	7.74	0.79	3.47	6.25	1.09	3.57
1998	Clevelnd	AL	199.7	194	94	20	92	144	4.24	12	10	8.74	0.90	4.15	6.49	0.87	4.51
1999	Clevelnd	AL	135.7	137	86	16	74	94	5.71	6	9	9.09	1.06	4.91	6.24	0.65	5.17

What could go wrong, did. He butted heads with Phil Regan, fidgeted with his delivery, earned or was given a reputation as a headhunter, hurt his shoulder around the All-Star break, was rushed back in early August and never did put together any kind of consistency. The worst part of it was rushing him back: he clearly didn't have it in August, with none of his pitches working, and things didn't get better from there.

Support-Neutral Records					CLEVELAND INDIANS					Park Effect: +12.9%		
PITCHER	GS	IP	R	SNW	SNL	SNPCT	W	L	RA	APW	SNVA	SNWAR
Jim Brower	2	9.3	10	0.3	1.0	.231	1	0	9.64	-0.38	-0.34	-0.25
Dave Burba	34	220.0	113	13.6	10.1	.575	15	9	4.62	2.08	1.76	3.55
Tom Candiotti	2	4.3	12	0.0	1.4	.013	0	0	24.92	-0.84	-0.68	-0.60
Bartolo Colon	32	205.0	97	14.3	8.3	.632	18	5	4.26	2.68	2.86	4.68
Dwight Gooden	22	106.7	86	5.7	8.2	.409	3	4	7.26	-1.80	-1.05	-0.22
Chris Haney	4	21.3	16	0.9	1.7	.349	0	2	6.75	-0.25	-0.40	-0.19
Steve Karsay	3	13.0	6	1.1	0.7	.623	2	0	4.15	0.18	0.21	0.35
Mark Langston	5	24.3	22	1.4	2.2	.380	1	2	8.14	-0.62	-0.47	-0.16
Charles Nagy	32	201.0	117	12.3	10.7	.534	17	11	5.24	0.66	0.70	2.52
Jaret Wright	26	133.7	99	7.6	9.3	.450	8	10	6.67	-1.47	-0.94	0.42
TOTALS	162	938.7	578	57.2	53.7	.516	65	43	5.54	0.24	1.67	10.09

Even before Cleveland's collapse in the Division Series, it seemed to be accepted that the Indians were vulnerable because they couldn't pitch. It simply wasn't true. The 1999 Indians rotation was the ninth-best in baseball, worth about 1½ wins above average according to SNVA. That was just behind the eventual World Champion Yankees. What's more, many of those who were a drag on the Indians' rating—Jim Brower, Tom Candiotti, Dwight Gooden, Chris Haney and Mark Langston—were going to play no role in the playoffs. The average Support Neutral Winning Percentage of the Indians who would pitch in the playoffs—Bartolo Colon, Dave Burba, Charles Nagy and Jaret Wright—was .548, better than the .542 SNPct of the Yankees' four playoff starters. Given that the Yankees had plenty of success in the playoffs with their rotation, I don't see that the Indians' rotation made it impossible for them to win.

Pitcher Abuse Points

PITCHER	AGE	GS	PAP	PAP/S	WKLD	MAX	1-90	91-100	101-110	111-120	121-130	131-140	141+
Jim Brower	26	2	14	7.0	14.0	112	1	0	0	1	0	0	0
Dave Burba	32	34	474	13.9	13.9	128	6	3	11	9	5	0	0
Tom Candiotti	41	2	0	0.0	0.0	63	2	0	0	0	0	0	0
Bartolo Colon	24	32	529	16.5	38.6	128	4	3	7	12	6	0	0
Dwight Gooden	34	22	86	3.9	3.9	130	11	5	5	0	1	0	0
Chris Haney	30	4	7	1.8	2.3	107	2	1	1	0	0	0	0
Steve Karsay	27	3	0	0.0	0.0	93	2	1	0	0	0	0	0
Mark Langston	38	5	28	5.6	5.6	119	3	1	0	1	0	0	0
Charles Nagy	32	32	156	4.9	4.9	121	11	9	7	4	1	0	0
Jaret Wright	23	26	150	5.8	14.4	125	9	5	8	2	2	0	0
CLEVELAND		162	1444	8.9	14.8	130	51	28	39	29	15	0	0
Ranking (AL)			6	5									

Well, Mike Hargrove is gone, for better or for worse, and there's no sense kicking a man when he's down. I expected one of the Indians' duo of great pitching prospects, Bartolo Colon and Jaret Wright, to fizzle—I just didn't expect it to be Wright. But after putting up with a Workload of 37 in 1998, his decline was all-too-visible last season. He's only 24 and could bounce back, but what worries me is that the Tribe doesn't even have a diagnosis for what went wrong last year. If the doctors had found tendinitis or bone chips or leprosy, he could get treatment, go on rehab and come back. But when he can't throw strikes and his fastball has flattened out and the only thing wrong with his arm is that he can't throw strikes and his fastball has flattened out, how is he supposed to get better? . . . Colon surprised me. Despite a Workload of nearly 49 in 1998, and a similarly senseless amount of work last year, he pitched very well. He's still one player I think John Hart should wait on before offering him the Cleveland Special: a two-year contract extension with about nine option years.

Detroit Tigers

Losing is nothing to be ashamed of. Baseball, like all team sports, is a zero-sum game; every home run for a hitter is a home run allowed by a pitcher, every game won is a game lost. For every playoff contender, there has to be another team languishing at the bottom of the standings.

But every team on the wrong side of .500 is there for a reason, and whether it's an off-year for an otherwise solid franchise or yet another rebuilding year for a team that plays in a mausoleum in front of a few thousand francophones, the goal is to figure out how to stop losing. A team that loses year after year and has no idea why? *That's* a disgrace.

By that standard, the Tigers are one of the most disgraceful teams in baseball. Detroit is not a small market. It is not an apathetic sports town; on the contrary, there is as much four-sport passion in southeast Michigan as anywhere in America. Yet the Tigers continue to lose, year after year, and they have no idea why. They've tried building their team out of nothing but veteran experience; they've tried grabbing every young pitcher who can throw a lamb chop past a hungry wolf. Now they're pinning their hopes on a cash cow called Comerica Park.

Bad news, Mr. Ilitch. This idea isn't going to work, either.

The ballpark-construction craze that swept baseball in the 1990s was wildly successful: the bank vaults have opened with each new ballpark, with the laughable exception of New Comiskey. Any owner savvy enough or bold enough or just plain underhanded enough to get his city to build him a new park has been amply rewarded.

Increases in revenue should translate to increases in payroll, and increases in payroll should translate to a better team. That's the theory, anyway. Some franchises, such as the Indians, have used a new ballpark as the linchpin of their rebuilding strategy, and if there's one thing baseball teams can do well, it's imitate. These days, no plan for success is complete without a stipulation that the team must play in a brand-spanking-new high-tech ersatz-retro ballpark with more luxury boxes than you can count, more food than you'd find at The Cheesecake Factory and a retractable dome to protect against blizzards, acid rain and anything else Mother Nature has to offer.

That's how owners think. But how true is it? Is the equation as simple as new ballpark = playoff contender? Table 1 looks at the records of every team that has moved into a new stadium in the last 10 years, since SkyDome opened and the owners got their first glimpse of the possibilities.

The Blue Jays and Braves were good before, during and after the opening of their new ballparks, so there is little reason to credit their new digs for their success. The Rockies' playoff run coincided with the opening of Coors Field, but the succeeding years give us little reason to believe it was anything more than a fluke. Considering that the Rockies had already set all sorts of attendance records at Mile High Stadium, the fact that their playoff appearance came in 1995 was probably coincidental. The Rangers' rise to contention came several years after their new ballpark opened.

That leaves the Indians and the Orioles. Cleveland is, as it has been throughout the decade, the model for building a franchise, and one the Tigers are wise to emulate. But the Tigers are doing a poor job of imitation. Without understanding the fundamental aspects of John Hart's rebuilding job, they have confused the vital ingredients with the window dressing. Jacobs Field didn't help the Indians win. It helped the Indians keep winning after they already had a great team in place.

And this is why the Tigers are doomed to fail on the field even while succeeding at the gate. The Indians went into the Jake with an outstanding nucleus: Albert Belle, Carlos Baerga, Jim Thome, Manny Ramirez and Kenny Lofton—many of whom were already signed to long-term deals. The Indians had superstars who were not only the core of the great 1995 team, but the backbone of their ongoing success. The revenues generated by Jacobs Field have helped maintain that success, by allowing the Indians to keep their great players and sign others like Roberto Alomar. But the team developed its core of greatness on its own, before the new park was built.

Tigers Prospectus

1999 record: 69-92; Third place, AL Central

Pythagorean W/L: 69-93

Runs scored: 747 (12th in AL)

Runs allowed: 882 (11th in AL)

Team EQA: .247 (12th in AL)

1999 team age: 27.4 (4th-youngest in AL)

1999 park: Tiger Stadium; slight hitters' park, increased run scoring by 2%. Moving to Comerica Park for 2000 season.

1999: Another year on the treadmill for a franchise that has lost its way.

2000: They think they've improved; they haven't, and it will show.

Table 1

Team	New Park	Year -2	Year -1	Year 0	Year +1	Year +2	Year +3
Toronto	1989*	96-66	87-75	89-73#	86-76	91-71#	96-66#
Chicago(AL)	1991	69-92	94-68	87-75	86-76	94-68#	67-46
Baltimore	1992	76-85	67-95	89-73	85-77	63-49	71-73
Cleveland	1994	76-86	76-86	66-47	100-44#	99-62#	86-75#
Texas	1994	77-85	86-76	52-62	74-70	90-72#	77-85
Colorado	1995	67-95	53-64	77-67#	83-79	83-79	77-85
Atlanta	1997	90-54#	96-66#	101-61#	106-56#	103-59#	N/A
Seattle	1999*	90-72#	76-85	79-83	N/A	N/A	N/A

* Opened mid-season
\# Made playoffs

The hope for Tiger fans might be the 1992 Orioles. The Orioles limped through the 1991 season with a 67-95 record, and after their inspiring run in 1989, it looked like the franchise had fallen back in the crapper. But the opening of Camden Yards brought with it a 22-game improvement and the start of a six-year run of success. However, the keys to the Birds' improvement in 1992 were breakout seasons from Brady Anderson, Mike Mussina, Chris Hoiles and Leo Gomez. Anderson was acquired from the Red Sox midway through his rookie season; the others were all homegrown. In other words, even the Orioles' success was built on products of the team's own system—not only the four above, but Cal Ripken, Ben McDonald and Gregg Olson as well.

The Tigers, sad to say, have no superstars. They have no one likely to ever become a superstar. It's virtually impossible to win anything in baseball without at least one or two great players. Almost every 1999 playoff team had several: the Mets had Mike Piazza, Rickey Henderson and Edgardo Alfonzo; the Astros, Jeff Bagwell and Craig Biggio; the Rangers, Ivan Rodriguez and Rafael Palmeiro; the Red Sox, Pedro Martinez and Nomar Garciaparra. The Indians, Braves and Yankees are not worth going over. Only the Diamondbacks had no franchise hitters in their lineup, though Matt Williams, Jay Bell, Luis Gonzalez and Steve Finley did one hell of an impersonation, while Buck's boys had Randy Johnson pitching every fifth day.

The Tigers have tried to sell their fans on the notion that three or four dollar bills are worth more than a twenty. Damion Easley, Tony Clark and last year's big signing, Dean Palmer, are all good players. But none is good enough to be the best player on a playoff team. Having these kinds of players leaves the team with fewer avenues to improve. While you get as much production out of Clark and Easley as you would out of one Hall of Famer and one bum—Jeff Bagwell and Placido Polanco, Roberto Alomar and Doug Mientkiewicz—which combination would you rather have? Any GM with a dozen working neurons can find a first baseman who can out-hit Mientkiewicz in his sleep. But who is the weak link in the Clark/Easley tandem?

Detroit's inefficient talent distribution is paralleled by a wasteful allocation of financial resources. Baseball's economic structure is such that a player's salary does not always have a linear relationship to his value. The five-year player who gets $2 million in arbitration is often no better than the rookie making $200,000. Great players deserve $5 million and up, but no one else is so irreplaceable that he deserves seven figures. Yet on their Opening Day roster, the Tigers had 11 players making more than a million dollars, including Gregg Jefferies, Masao Kida, Bryce Florie, Todd Jones and Willie Blair. Does it make more sense to spread the wealth around to five journeymen, or give it all to someone like Roberto Alomar or Robin Ventura—someone whose contributions can't be matched by any number of average players?

The Palmer signing exposes another weakness in the Tigers' approach: good players decline in their early 30s, and giving one a long-term deal as a free agent usually means you'll be throwing money away by the end of the contract. The Giants broke the bank to sign Barry Bonds seven years ago, and he's still a bargain after all this time. But Palmer's defense is already starting to go; once his power starts to slip, he'll be close to useless.

So how do the Tigers get a superstar? The money flowing from Comerica Park would allow the Tigers to splurge for one in the free-agent market, except that superstars almost always re-sign with their old club or get traded before their contract expires. Randy Smith did try to open talks with the Mariners about Alex Rodriguez, but his embarrassing offer of Deivi Cruz, Justin Thompson and assorted flotsam and jetsam only underscores how little star potential the Tiger organization has. The Mariners aren't going to trade Rodriguez without getting solid assurances that the players they get in return are potential stars in their own right, as they did when they traded Randy Johnson. The Tigers may think that three good players are worth as much as one superstar, but the rest of the league is not so deluded.

To get a superstar, the Tigers elected to overpay, sending six players—four of them young and highly-regarded—to Texas for Juan Gonzalez. The move was almost universally derided, and rightly so. The Tigers have acquired just one year of Gonzalez's career, as he will be a free agent after 2000. For the privilege, they sent away their best starting pitcher in Justin Thompson, their best young player in Gabe Kapler and two excellent pitching prospects in Alan Webb and Francisco Cordero. It's another instance of the Tigers attempting to emulate better organizations but doing so in an inept, and ultimately losing, fashion.

Even with Comerica Park, the next few years look as bleak for the Tigers as the last 12 have been. The AL Central is the most rapidly improving division in baseball. The Indians still have another year or two left in their dynasty, and the White Sox, Royals and Twins are all feverishly rebuilding their teams around a core of great players. Even if Frank Thomas can't break out of his rut, the Pale Hose have Ray Durham and Magglio Ordonez, along with as much young pitching as anyone in the league. The Royals have Carlos Beltran, Carlos Febles, Mike Sweeney and a dozen other prospects who might develop into stars. Even the Twins, behind their star prospect troika of Michael Cuddyer, Michael Restovich and Matt LeCroy, have a lot to look forward to.

The Tigers? Jeff Weaver is their only potential ace on the mound. They have no position players with the upside of a Febles or a Cuddyer. In the minors, the only potential superstar is last year's #1 pick, Eric Munson, who could be the best-hitting catcher in baseball in five years if everything breaks just right. In a telling sign that the Tigers just don't get it, they are waffling over whether to leave Munson behind the plate at all. Munson's defensive skills are a little weak, in the way that Mike Piazza's defensive skills are a little weak. But if the Tigers don't let Munson prove that he can't catch, and sentence him instead to first base without any chance for appeal, they've wasted their best chance to develop the superstar they need.

The park may be new and fresh, but the organizational outlook is as old and stale as ever. And unless it changes, the Tigers of the new millennium are going to resemble Pez candy: a disappointing product in clever packaging.

HITTERS (Averages: BA: .270 / OBP: .340 / SLG: .430 / EQA: .260)

Kurt Airoso — OF — Bats R — Age 25

YEAR	TEAM	LGE	AB	H	DB	TP	HR	BB/SO	R	RBI	SB	CS	OUT	BA	OBP	SLG	EQA	EQR	DEFENSE	
1998	Lakeland	Fla	392	88	15	1	12	50/128	47	42	2	1	305	.224	.317	.360	.233	40	65-OF 88	
1999	Jacksnvl	Sou	545	128	25	4	8	68/128	72	54	5	2	419	.235	.323	.339	.230	53	134-OF 111	
2000	*Detroit*	*AL*	*334*	*76*	*11*	*1*	*11*	*49/93*	*45*	*45*	*2*	*1*	*259*	*.228*	*.326*	*.365*	*.239*	*36*		

A disciplined, intelligent hitter who is nevertheless about two years too old to be taken seriously as a prospect. He could make a fine fourth outfielder in the Chad Curtis mold, but it isn't likely to happen with the Tigers, who have enough fourth outfielders already. He's quietly waiting to become a minor-league free agent.

Gabe Alvarez — 3B — Bats R — Age 26

YEAR	TEAM	LGE	AB	H	DB	TP	HR	BB/SO	R	RBI	SB	CS	OUT	BA	OBP	SLG	EQA	EQR	DEFENSE	
1997	Mobile	Sou	425	109	25	1	11	38/71	52	57	1	1	317	.256	.323	.398	.244	46	108-3B 87	
1998	Toledo	Int	250	63	15	1	16	25/63	31	47	2	1	188	.252	.322	.512	.271	36	68-3B 105	
1998	Detroit	AL	198	45	7	0	6	18/64	15	28	1	3	156	.227	.298	.354	.218	17	51-3B 87	
1999	Toledo	Int	412	102	17	0	17	45/88	53	51	1	2	312	.248	.329	.413	.250	49	85-3B 86	17-OF 101
1999	Detroit	AL	53	11	3	0	2	2/9	5	4	0	0	42	.208	.236	.377	.198	4		
2000	*Detroit*	*AL*	*501*	*129*	*21*	*0*	*27*	*62/112*	*76*	*92*	*1*	*2*	*374*	*.257*	*.339*	*.461*	*.268*	*69*		

He can't really play third base, something even the Tigers realized after he committed five errors in a spring-training game. His bat can carry the position, but isn't good enough to warrant playing him at first base or in left field. We call this Prospect's Disease. Alvarez is 26 and unlikely to get much better. Barring a Phil Nevin-sized miracle, he's never going to be an everyday player.

Billy Ashley   LF/1B   Bats R   Age 29

YEAR	TEAM	LGE	AB	H	DB	TP	HR	BB/SO	R	RBI	SB	CS	OUT	BA	OBP	SLG	EQA	EQR	DEFENSE
1997	LosAngls	NL	133	34	6	0	7	8/46	12	20	0	0	99	.256	.303	.459	.251	16	19-OF 94
1998	Pawtuckt	Int	219	50	8	0	11	27/80	31	39	1	0	169	.228	.315	.416	.247	26	20-1B 93
1999	Toledo	Int	112	28	7	0	7	7/35	14	19	0	0	84	.250	.294	.500	.257	14	
2000	*Detroit*	*AL*	*164*	*40*	*7*	*0*	*10*	*18/55*	*23*	*30*	*0*	*0*	*124*	*.244*	*.319*	*.470*	*.262*	*22*	

He's still around at Triple-A, still has enough power to break the seat backs in the bleachers and still can't hit a major-league breaking ball. Even if he learns, he's 29, and organizations are skeptical of failed Dodger prospects. His ability to pummel left-handed pitching would justify the act of God needed to land him in the major leagues again.

Brad Ausmus   C   Bats R   Age 31

YEAR	TEAM	LGE	AB	H	DB	TP	HR	BB/SO	R	RBI	SB	CS	OUT	BA	OBP	SLG	EQA	EQR	DEFENSE
1997	Houston	NL	432	119	25	1	5	37/77	45	46	12	6	319	.275	.337	.373	.244	47	
1998	Houston	NL	418	117	9	4	7	52/58	64	47	11	3	304	.280	.364	.371	.259	52	118-C 104
1999	Detroit	AL	454	121	25	6	8	46/71	56	49	12	9	343	.267	.352	.401	.256	57	123-C 104
2000	*Detroit*	*AL*	*403*	*107*	*16*	*3*	*8*	*49/62*	*62*	*54*	*9*	*6*	*302*	*.266*	*.345*	*.380*	*.250*	*47*	

Randy Smith's obsession with ex-Padres and ex-Astros has become a real obstacle to the Tigers' getting the talent they really need. That said, Ausmus was a nice pickup, especially when Robert Fick went down for most of the year. Only Ivan Rodriguez and Charles Johnson are clearly better defensively in the AL, and Ausmus has learned to battle pitchers enough that he's not the automatic out he once was. Which is more frightening: that the Tigers were using Ausmus to lead off in September, or that, with a team-high .365 OBP, he was actually the right choice?

Kimera Bartee   OF   Bats B   Age 27

YEAR	TEAM	LGE	AB	H	DB	TP	HR	BB/SO	R	RBI	SB	CS	OUT	BA	OBP	SLG	EQA	EQR	DEFENSE
1997	Toledo	Int	511	113	15	6	3	42/155	58	31	24	7	405	.221	.285	.292	.203	38	137-OF 66
1998	Toledo	Int	216	48	4	0	3	12/47	18	11	3	2	170	.222	.268	.282	.182	12	47-OF 109
1998	Detroit	AL	98	19	5	1	3	5/34	17	14	7	5	84	.194	.233	.357	.194	7	
1999	Toledo	Int	417	105	11	7	9	28/84	47	33	13	7	319	.252	.299	.376	.228	40	104-OF 104
1999	Detroit	AL	77	15	0	3	0	8/20	10	3	3	3	65	.195	.271	.273	.181	5	23-CF 102
2000	*Detroit*	*AL*	*529*	*122*	*14*	*6*	*10*	*44/125*	*60*	*52*	*17*	*9*	*416*	*.231*	*.290*	*.336*	*.214*	*44*	

The poster boy for the ineptitude of the current Tigers regime, much the way Randy Winn is for the Devil Rays. As a rule, only poorly run organizations so lightly regard the ability to hit a baseball that they think it can be taught at the major-league level to anyone with a good set of legs. That he got at-bats in September reveals just how in denial the Tigers are.

Javier Cardona   C   Bats R   Age 24

YEAR	TEAM	LGE	AB	H	DB	TP	HR	BB/SO	R	RBI	SB	CS	OUT	BA	OBP	SLG	EQA	EQR	DEFENSE
1997	Lakeland	Fla	287	73	9	0	9	21/56	24	33	0	1	215	.254	.307	.380	.230	27	
1998	Jacksnvl	Sou	164	51	14	1	4	10/30	25	32	0	0	113	.311	.354	.482	.278	23	37-C 101
1998	Toledo	Int	163	31	2	0	5	7/32	11	15	0	0	132	.190	.228	.294	.163	7	47-C 100
1999	Jacksnvl	Sou	422	117	22	0	24	35/73	67	73	2	1	306	.277	.341	.500	.276	61	86-C 96
2000	*Detroit*	*AL*	*402*	*113*	*18*	*1*	*21*	*35/72*	*59*	*78*	*1*	*1*	*290*	*.281*	*.339*	*.488*	*.274*	*57*	

Once again Cardona had no difficulty with Double-A pitching, reaching double figures in home runs for the first time with 26 in just 108 games. With Ausmus in front of him and Eric Munson possibly behind him, Cardona figures to have little future with the Tigers. Still, they were impressed with his emergence this year and have moved him ahead of Robert Fick on the catching depth chart. In a world where Carlos Hernandez is worth millions of dollars, doling out the league minimum to Javier Cardona ought to look mighty attractive to some organizations.

Raul Casanova   C   Bats B   Age 27

YEAR	TEAM	LGE	AB	H	DB	TP	HR	BB/SO	R	RBI	SB	CS	OUT	BA	OBP	SLG	EQA	EQR	DEFENSE
1997	Detroit	AL	303	74	11	1	5	25/46	26	23	1	1	230	.244	.309	.337	.220	26	
1998	Toledo	Int	172	39	4	0	6	17/31	13	21	0	1	134	.227	.305	.355	.223	16	46-C 98
1999	Toledo	Int	161	31	7	0	5	4/31	16	18	0	0	130	.193	.216	.329	.170	8	27-C 98
2000	*Detroit*	*AL*	*192*	*43*	*7*	*0*	*6*	*16/34*	*18*	*22*	*0*	*0*	*149*	*.224*	*.284*	*.354*	*.214*	*16*	

Essentially finished as a prospect, Casanova best serves as a reminder of how pointless Randy Smith's obsession with his former team's players was. Free to go as a minor-league free agent, Casanova has to hope somebody remembers his big 1994 and gives him a shot.

Frank Catalanotto		IF					Bats L		Age 26									DEFENSE
YEAR	TEAM	LGE	AB	H	DB	TP	HR	BB/SO	R	RBI	SB	CS	OUT	BA	OBP	SLG	EQA	EQR	
1997	Toledo	Int	510	151	31	3	16	38/78	69	63	10	8	367	.296	.356	.463	.272	71	
1998	Toledo	Int	105	32	7	2	3	12/22	17	23	0	0	73	.305	.407	.495	.304	19	
1998	Detroit	AL	212	59	13	2	6	11/38	22	24	3	2	155	.278	.326	.443	.256	26	
1999	Detroit	AL	285	77	15	0	12	11/49	37	33	3	4	212	.270	.318	.449	.252	34	
2000	Texas	AL	350	101	17	1	14	27/60	52	62	4	3	252	.289	.340	.463	.262	44	

Our annual visit to an old BP friend finds Catalanotto playing well enough to force himself into the lineup on a half-time basis. Despite the hefty contracts given to Tony Clark, Damion Easley and Dean Palmer, the Cat played more than 20 games at each of their positions. He was part of the Gonzalez deal and is expected to be the platoon starter at second base for the Rangers. There is a cancer in this organization: Catalanotto, who was always a patient hitter in the minor leagues, has now drawn just 30 walks in 525 major-league at-bats.

Tony Clark		1B					Bats B		Age 28									DEFENSE
YEAR	TEAM	LGE	AB	H	DB	TP	HR	BB/SO	R	RBI	SB	CS	OUT	BA	OBP	SLG	EQA	EQR	
1997	Detroit	AL	577	161	29	3	32	89/138	102	113	1	3	419	.279	.379	.506	.292	97	154-1B 93
1998	Detroit	AL	599	174	30	0	36	60/125	80	100	3	3	428	.290	.358	.521	.287	95	142-1B 92
1999	Detroit	AL	531	147	24	0	31	57/133	67	92	2	1	385	.277	.354	.497	.281	81	130-1B 101
2000	Detroit	AL	554	151	19	0	34	76/130	92	116	1	1	404	.273	.360	.491	.284	87	

At 28, it's time to stop expecting more of Clark than he's already shown. He's capable of tremendous streaks, like the second-half binge that turned a horrible start (four home runs through May) into a respectable season. He's neither a problem nor a solution now, but is likely to be a problem by the time the Tigers surround him with the good hitters they need.

Deivi Cruz		SS					Bats R		Age 25									DEFENSE
YEAR	TEAM	LGE	AB	H	DB	TP	HR	BB/SO	R	RBI	SB	CS	OUT	BA	OBP	SLG	EQA	EQR	
1997	Detroit	AL	436	106	15	0	6	11/53	32	42	3	7	337	.243	.262	.319	.186	25	134-SS 100
1998	Detroit	AL	453	118	21	3	5	11/54	49	43	2	4	339	.260	.283	.353	.209	34	133-SS 103
1999	Detroit	AL	516	144	24	0	16	6/57	57	56	1	4	376	.279	.293	.419	.233	49	148-SS 107
2000	Detroit	AL	489	131	16	0	16	14/56	46	65	2	4	362	.268	.288	.399	.226	44	

He continues to be the most unappreciated defensive player in the game, and he continues to swing at anything that comes out of a pitcher's hand—baseballs, rosin bags, nail files . . . whatever. Still only 25, he's everything Rey Ordonez is supposed to be, and his second-half power (.485 slugging average) has people in Detroit predicting greatness. The only thing I predict is that his offensive skills will continue to be overrated. You want a sign of how deep the Tigers' problems run? Two of their everyday players, Cruz and Juan Encarnacion, had more home runs than walks.

Damion Easley		2B					Bats R		Age 30									DEFENSE	
YEAR	TEAM	LGE	AB	H	DB	TP	HR	BB/SO	R	RBI	SB	CS	OUT	BA	OBP	SLG	EQA	EQR		
1997	Detroit	AL	525	137	39	3	21	65/98	93	68	28	13	401	.261	.362	.467	.278	82	130-2B 100	9-SS 79
1998	Detroit	AL	592	160	36	2	27	37/110	79	95	13	5	437	.270	.331	.475	.267	81	135-2B 103	
1999	Detroit	AL	545	142	27	1	20	45/124	75	60	11	3	406	.261	.338	.424	.259	70	140-2B 102	
2000	Detroit	AL	466	119	23	1	20	51/97	72	75	10	4	351	.255	.329	.438	.259	60		

It's eerie how little there is to write about Tigers' players that wasn't written a year ago. Easley has the same skill package he had a year ago, hitting for a decent average and good power, running and turning the double play well. But he's a year closer to the end of his career, and the Tigers don't appear to be any closer to surrounding him with enough talent to make that career mean something.

Juan Encarnacion OF Bats R Age 24

YEAR	TEAM	LGE	AB	H	DB	TP	HR	BB/SO	R	RBI	SB	CS	OUT	BA	OBP	SLG	EQA	EQR	DEFENSE
1997	Jacksnvl	Sou	491	142	27	3	22	32/92	67	69	11	2	351	.289	.350	.491	.281	73	111-OF 96
1998	Toledo	Int	357	99	18	2	7	23/86	46	36	16	3	261	.277	.337	.398	.256	43	89-OF 94
1998	Detroit	AL	163	53	8	4	7	7/30	28	20	6	4	114	.325	.357	.552	.291	26	39-OF 86
1999	Detroit	AL	508	127	32	6	17	8/113	56	67	32	12	393	.250	.274	.437	.238	54	108-LF 100
2000	Detroit	AL	534	150	28	4	22	34/116	88	87	25	8	392	.281	.324	.472	.267	72	

Prior to last year, 17 players in major-league history had turned the ugly trick of having no more than 20 walks and at least 100 strikeouts. Five of them were 24 or younger: John Bateman (1963), David Green (1984), Cory Snyder (1986), Benito Santiago (1987) and Craig Paquette (1993). Santiago and Snyder were All-Star talents who never met the expectations that their rookie years generated. Green was a spectacular washout. Bateman, an everyday catcher at age 20, had exactly one good year in the majors, and Craig Paquette is still Craig Paquette. Encarnacion was also a disappointment defensively, and his once-limitless ceiling now appears as low as Pat Buchanan's presidential hopes.

Robert Fick C/1B Bats L Age 26

YEAR	TEAM	LGE	AB	H	DB	TP	HR	BB/SO	R	RBI	SB	CS	OUT	BA	OBP	SLG	EQA	EQR	DEFENSE
1997	W Michgn	Mid	479	131	37	2	13	54/85	69	62	5	2	350	.273	.348	.441	.266	64	100-1B 89
1998	Jacksnvl	Sou	520	142	40	4	14	47/94	73	80	4	2	380	.273	.339	.446	.263	67	79-C 93
1999	Toledo	Int	48	13	1	1	1	7/5	9	6	1	0	35	.271	.373	.396	.271	7	
1999	Detroit	AL	41	9	0	0	3	6/6	5	9	1	0	32	.220	.319	.439	.258	5	
2000	Detroit	AL	281	78	19	2	10	36/46	50	50	2	1	204	.278	.360	.466	.279	42	

A lost season. Fick had only 68 minor-league at-bats due to a chronically dislocated shoulder—an injury that couldn't have come at a worse point in his development. There were already questions regarding his ability to catch, and though he was back behind the plate a few times for the Tigers in September, he has to prove all over again that he has a catcher's throwing arm. I still like him; he's a left-handed hitter and showed he could still swing the bat when he played last year. His profile is very similar to Eric Munson's, and in the long run that's a fight he has little hope of winning.

Karim Garcia RF/LF Bats L Age 24

YEAR	TEAM	LGE	AB	H	DB	TP	HR	BB/SO	R	RBI	SB	CS	OUT	BA	OBP	SLG	EQA	EQR	DEFENSE	
1997	Albuquer	PCL	251	63	13	4	15	17/72	36	45	8	4	192	.251	.299	.514	.263	34	61-OF 87	
1998	Arizona	NL	336	76	11	8	10	17/76	40	44	5	4	264	.226	.263	.396	.216	29	87-OF 99	
1998	Tucson	PCL	103	28	4	1	8	13/24	16	20	4	1	76	.272	.353	.563	.297	18	24-OF 112	
1999	Detroit	AL	287	67	11	3	13	17/67	35	29	2	4	224	.233	.276	.429	.229	28	49-RF 95	26-LF 105
2000	Detroit	AL	340	81	12	4	17	27/80	42	54	5	4	263	.238	.294	.447	.244	39		

Garcia, like many a Dodgers prospect, was slotted into their Phenom program and rushed up the ladder. While his Triple-A debut in 1995 was extremely impressive for a 19-year-old, it created expectations that were almost as elevated as Albuquerque itself. His failure to live up to them over the ensuing three years should not damn him, and the Tigers admirably tried to buy low in getting him from Arizona. Of course, Luis Gonzalez promptly went nuts and made them look like idiots. Garcia had a strong second half; if he's really 24, and there's no reason to think otherwise, he's still likely to develop into the 30-homer man everyone thought he would be in the first place. A great fantasy bargain for just that reason.

Richard Gomez OF Bats R Age 22

YEAR	TEAM	LGE	AB	H	DB	TP	HR	BB/SO	R	RBI	SB	CS	OUT	BA	OBP	SLG	EQA	EQR	DEFENSE
1999	W Michgn	Mid	490	136	27	8	9	38/128	58	64	28	6	360	.278	.337	.420	.262	63	112-OF 90
2000	Detroit	AL	262	80	15	3	6	23/95	57	39	22	3	185	.305	.361	.454	.286	41	

Gomez led the organization with 66 steals, and for a speedster he's a surprisingly well-rounded hitter: he led West Michigan with a .303 average and 46 extra-base hits and was second on the team in walks. His speed will ensure that he rises quickly through the organization; his bat will give him the chance to take advantage of the opportunity.

Bill Haselman   C   Bats R   Age 34

YEAR	TEAM	LGE	AB	H	DB	TP	HR	BB/SO	R	RBI	SB	CS	OUT	BA	OBP	SLG	EQA	EQR	DEFENSE
1997	Boston	AL	212	51	12	0	7	14/42	21	26	0	2	163	.241	.295	.396	.228	20	
1998	Texas	AL	104	32	5	0	6	2/17	10	16	0	0	72	.308	.321	.529	.275	14	26-C 93
1999	Detroit	AL	142	38	5	0	5	8/26	12	14	2	0	104	.268	.307	.408	.242	15	35-C 99
2000	Texas	AL	132	35	4	0	6	10/24	16	22	0	0	97	.265	.317	.432	.245	14	

Haselman was justifiably angry after the Tigers told him he'd have a chance to start, then traded for Ausmus. He settled in and had another fine year as a second-stringer. Right now, you'd be hard-pressed to find a better backup catcher in the game. He was traded to Texas in the Gonzalez deal, and will back up Ivan Rodriguez in 2000.

Bob Higginson   RF   Bats L   Age 29

YEAR	TEAM	LGE	AB	H	DB	TP	HR	BB/SO	R	RBI	SB	CS	OUT	BA	OBP	SLG	EQA	EQR	DEFENSE
1997	Detroit	AL	543	162	31	5	27	67/82	91	97	12	7	388	.298	.379	.523	.296	93	138-OF 99
1998	Detroit	AL	609	173	39	4	24	60/99	88	80	2	3	439	.284	.354	.479	.276	88	153-OF 97
1999	Detroit	AL	374	87	15	0	12	59/66	46	42	4	6	293	.233	.340	.369	.243	43	86-RF 97
2000	Detroit	AL	397	108	22	1	17	58/66	70	73	3	4	293	.272	.365	.461	.278	60	

Higginson has been compared to Kirk Gibson so often that it's become burdensome for him, but the similarities, most notably in intensity, are there. What the two share is an utter disdain for anything that isn't about winning. When Gibson came up, his passion for winning was almost suffocating, making it difficult for him to motivate himself in losing seasons. Higginson is the same way, and while Gibson had the good fortune of breaking in with the young, brash, talented Tiger teams of the early 1980s, Higginson has suffered with one losing team after another. His patience, already worn thin, was rubbed completely raw last year. He needs a trade to a team with a winning atmosphere. Put him in a Yankee uniform, and he'll show us all what he can do.

Gregg Jefferies   DH   Bats B   Age 32

YEAR	TEAM	LGE	AB	H	DB	TP	HR	BB/SO	R	RBI	SB	CS	OUT	BA	OBP	SLG	EQA	EQR	DEFENSE
1997	Philadel	NL	482	125	26	3	12	53/27	68	49	10	6	363	.259	.335	.400	.250	57	124-OF 89
1998	Philadel	NL	486	143	25	3	8	28/26	65	48	11	3	346	.294	.334	.407	.253	56	108-OF 91
1999	Detroit	AL	205	40	5	0	7	10/11	20	17	3	4	169	.195	.247	.322	.184	12	
2000	Detroit	AL	266	66	11	1	6	24/15	33	32	4	2	202	.248	.310	.365	.230	26	

What an awful player he has become. The memory of the talent that made him the Minor League Player of the 1980s is as distant as the Viking spacecraft now, making you wonder how we all misjudged him so badly. The enduring images of Jefferies—the arrogant swagger that made him so lovable in 1988 and so despicable in 1989, his ceaseless and futile battles to conquer second base, then third base, then any position at all—make you wonder if maybe he thought being on top of the world at 20 meant that he had nothing more to achieve.

Gabe Kapler   CF   Bats R   Age 24

YEAR	TEAM	LGE	AB	H	DB	TP	HR	BB/SO	R	RBI	SB	CS	OUT	BA	OBP	SLG	EQA	EQR	DEFENSE
1997	Lakeland	Fla	526	137	34	4	19	46/75	72	71	3	3	392	.260	.324	.449	.257	65	136-OF 97
1998	Jacksnvl	Sou	552	165	42	4	27	46/96	91	116	4	2	389	.299	.357	.536	.291	89	138-OF 100
1999	Toledo	Int	54	16	4	2	3	8/10	9	12	0	1	39	.296	.387	.611	.311	11	
1999	Detroit	AL	414	99	22	4	17	37/74	55	45	11	5	320	.239	.305	.435	.247	48	104-CF 96
2000	Texas	AL	520	153	34	4	27	58/88	98	111	7	3	370	.294	.365	.531	.290	84	

There is no greater example of how overrated the concept of "tools" is. What, exactly, is a tool? Is it something inherent and fixed—like height—or can it be improved with hard work? Kapler, a 58th-round pick who has worked as hard at his craft as any man in baseball, made himself a great prospect . . . and suddenly the Tigers were raving about how he had improved his tools more than any player they had ever seen.

Supposedly, the whole value of rating players by "tools" is that it helps predict which players are likely to improve their performance. But how can you predict future performance using tools when you can't even predict what will happen to the tools themselves? Kapler has created for himself tools such as power and speed.

His rookie season was at times inconsistent, but like other late-draft finds such as Jeff Conine and Mike Piazza, Kapler is a self-made player, and I fully expect him to continue working until he's a star. He'll take Juan Gonzalez's place in Texas, and win the trade for the Rangers by himself.

Patrick Lennon   OF   Bats R   Age 32

YEAR	TEAM	LGE	AB	H	DB	TP	HR	BB/SO	R	RBI	SB	CS	OUT	BA	OBP	SLG	EQA	EQR	DEFENSE
1997	Edmonton	PCL	128	34	3	0	6	16/38	17	21	0	0	94	.266	.354	.430	.266	17	
1997	Oakland	AL	115	34	6	1	1	14/34	13	13	0	1	82	.296	.372	.391	.262	14	24-OF 94
1998	Syracuse	Int	440	108	20	4	19	70/135	66	71	6	3	335	.245	.351	.439	.267	62	80-OF 92
1999	Syracuse	Int	133	37	3	0	7	18/44	19	24	2	2	98	.278	.368	.459	.276	20	19-OF 97
1999	Toledo	Int	281	65	12	1	16	26/73	37	37	1	1	217	.231	.300	.452	.248	33	37-OF 92
2000	*Detroit*	*AL*	*360*	*86*	*12*	*1*	*18*	*50/106*	*53*	*60*	*2*	*1*	*275*	*.239*	*.332*	*.428*	*.257*	*46*	

He's in this chapter because he finished the season in the Tigers' chain, but the winds of fate that have tossed him like a tumbleweed could land him in any organization, in either hemisphere, by April. Every year we tell you he's a good hitter who could help any team courageous enough to take a chance on a career minor leaguer, and that's still true. Every year we tell you he won't get that chance, and that's also still true.

Jason Maxwell   SS   Bats R   Age 28

YEAR	TEAM	LGE	AB	H	DB	TP	HR	BB/SO	R	RBI	SB	CS	OUT	BA	OBP	SLG	EQA	EQR	DEFENSE	
1997	Orlando	Sou	415	92	18	4	9	60/87	57	38	6	4	327	.222	.324	.349	.233	43	114-SS 101	
1998	Iowa	PCL	480	121	33	3	10	41/102	63	44	5	1	360	.252	.318	.396	.243	52	102-2B 94	16-SS 96
1999	Toledo	Int	422	89	15	2	11	42/96	46	47	4	2	335	.211	.285	.334	.210	34	65-SS 94	37-2B 96
2000	*Detroit*	*AL*	*405*	*92*	*18*	*1*	*13*	*46/89*	*51*	*51*	*3*	*1*	*314*	*.227*	*.306*	*.373*	*.232*	*41*		

Maxwell was snagged from the Cubs before last season when he was inadvertently released in a waiver snafu. He looked like he could be a hell of a utility player, capable of playing all over the infield and contributing at the plate. Sadly, while his secondary skills were intact, his batting average dropped 60 points at Triple-A and he was passed over when it came time for September call-ups. I expect him to bounce back this year, but at 28, he's just as likely to just bounce around.

Dave McCarty   1B   Bats R   Age 30

YEAR	TEAM	LGE	AB	H	DB	TP	HR	BB/SO	R	RBI	SB	CS	OUT	BA	OBP	SLG	EQA	EQR	DEFENSE	
1997	Phoenix	PCL	416	115	21	3	14	35/84	54	57	5	3	304	.276	.335	.442	.260	52	70-1B 96	
1998	Tacoma	PCL	399	108	25	1	8	48/93	54	39	6	4	295	.271	.355	.398	.259	50	60-OF 101	36-1B 102
1999	Toledo	Int	469	109	22	2	23	56/121	64	56	4	4	364	.232	.319	.435	.251	57	115-1B 109	17-OF 96
2000	*Oakland*	*AL*	*436*	*113*	*22*	*1*	*17*	*54/106*	*67*	*71*	*4*	*4*	*327*	*.259*	*.341*	*.431*	*.262*	*57*		

At least among position players, McCarty was probably the most spectacular prospect flop of the 1990s. Why? For one, he had the benefit of hitting in some good minor-league ballparks, notably Salt Lake City. While his performance was impressive even after correcting for context, it's possible he took better advantage of those parks than the average hitter.

The simplest explanation for the flop is this: he regressed as a hitter. It happens all the time in the majors. Remember Ruben Sierra? Carlos Baerga? When it happens to a major leaguer, people blame the player. When it happens to a minor leaguer, people cast a suspicious eye on the notion that minor-league performance means something. McCarty still has fringe major-league skills, really no different from Pat Lennon, and about as unlikely to get an opportunity.

Eric Munson   1B/C   Bats L   Age 22

YEAR	TEAM	LGE	AB	H	DB	TP	HR	BB/SO	R	RBI	SB	CS	OUT	BA	OBP	SLG	EQA	EQR	DEFENSE
1999	W Michgn	Mid	259	63	12	1	13	28/49	32	34	1	1	197	.243	.330	.448	.260	34	31-1B 123
2000	*Detroit*	*AL*	*138*	*37*	*5*	*0*	*13*	*20/53*	*25*	*36*	*0*	*0*	*101*	*.268*	*.361*	*.587*	*.305*	*26*	

He certainly looks like he has a major-league bat, although his debut was not nearly as impressive as that of, say, Pat Burrell, the first collegian taken in 1998. But will he catch? He was used almost exclusively as a first baseman and DH in his debut, although Tiger officials blamed that on a nagging shoulder problem. If Munson is kept at first base, he's going to be no more than a modest improvement over the likes of Tony Clark. As a catcher, he has a chance to be the new Darren Daulton, the best-hitting catcher in the league.

Dean Palmer — 3B — Bats R — Age 31

YEAR	TEAM	LGE	AB	H	DB	TP	HR	BB/SO	R	RBI	SB	CS	OUT	BA	OBP	SLG	EQA	EQR	DEFENSE
1997	Texas	AL	354	88	18	0	15	24/81	45	54	1	0	266	.249	.298	.427	.241	38	92-3B 91
1997	KansasCy	AL	186	51	10	1	9	14/48	22	30	1	2	137	.274	.333	.484	.267	25	41-3B 99
1998	KansasCy	AL	567	155	26	2	33	46/131	79	111	7	2	414	.273	.335	.501	.275	82	127-3B 76
1999	Detroit	AL	556	144	25	2	36	50/154	83	91	3	3	415	.259	.331	.505	.273	81	138-3B 94
2000	*Detroit*	*AL*	*508*	*132*	*19*	*1*	*30*	*50/131*	*72*	*96*	*2*	*1*	*377*	*.260*	*.326*	*.478*	*.267*	*69*	

He did exactly what the Tigers wanted when they signed him, and exactly nothing to solve the problems that have plagued their lineup for five years. Palmer is one of the best power-hitting third basemen in baseball, but a table-clearer is only as valuable as his table-setters make him. Right now, the Tigers have a bunch of guys sitting down to eat but nobody bringing in plates from the kitchen. Never a great defender to begin with, Palmer is likely to move to first base before his contract ends, which would merely give the Tigers another mediocre bat at the easiest position to fill.

Luis Polonia — LF — Bats L — Age 35

YEAR	TEAM	LGE	AB	H	DB	TP	HR	BB/SO	R	RBI	SB	CS	OUT	BA	OBP	SLG	EQA	EQR	DEFENSE
1999	Toledo	Int	160	45	7	1	2	8/31	15	17	8	2	117	.281	.315	.375	.240	16	33-OF 94
1999	Detroit	AL	330	104	21	8	9	12/32	41	29	16	9	235	.315	.343	.509	.278	48	26-LF 101
2000	*Detroit*	*AL*	*239*	*74*	*16*	*4*	*6*	*13/39*	*44*	*39*	*12*	*5*	*170*	*.310*	*.345*	*.485*	*.278*	*35*	

Great. Polonia returned from a three-year absence and promptly set the world on fire, hitting over .400 for his first month and finishing at .324, the second-highest average of his career. Wonderful. But so freakin' what?! Every major-league team is either contending or rebuilding, whether they realize it or not. The Tigers clearly fall into the latter category, but giving a starting job to a 34-year-old Mexican League refugee is proof that they don't get it. Polonia has exactly zero chance of contributing to the next good Tigers team, and every at-bat he got was one fewer at-bat for Kapler or Encarnacion or Garcia. The best thing that could have happened was for Polonia to fall on his face and get benched after hitting .180 for a month. Unfortunately for the Tigers, he played so well that he'll be back this season, taking away even more development time for the players who might actually contribute to the team's revival.

Pedro Santana — 2B — Bats R — Age 23

YEAR	TEAM	LGE	AB	H	DB	TP	HR	BB/SO	R	RBI	SB	CS	OUT	BA	OBP	SLG	EQA	EQR	DEFENSE
1997	W Michgn	Mid	292	73	11	5	3	9/57	26	23	9	2	221	.250	.284	.353	.217	24	46-2B 97
1998	W Michgn	Mid	449	115	23	5	6	22/96	55	41	26	4	338	.256	.299	.370	.234	45	114-2B 93
1999	Jacksnvl	Sou	516	138	33	5	5	24/101	70	42	19	6	383	.267	.303	.380	.234	50	117-2B 98
2000	*Detroit*	*AL*	*505*	*141*	*29*	*5*	*8*	*31/101*	*79*	*63*	*22*	*5*	*369*	*.279*	*.321*	*.404*	*.250*	*58*	

Santana is a marginal prospect whose only above-average skill is his speed (98 steals the last two years). He's not a bad hitter, which may become a problem: he's just good enough with the stick to get an opportunity to play based on his legs. If he does, he's almost guaranteed to flop.

Chris Wakeland — OF — Bats L — Age 26

YEAR	TEAM	LGE	AB	H	DB	TP	HR	BB/SO	R	RBI	SB	CS	OUT	BA	OBP	SLG	EQA	EQR	DEFENSE
1997	W Michgn	Mid	425	102	29	1	7	29/137	43	56	7	3	326	.240	.293	.362	.222	38	114-OF 88
1998	Lakeland	Fla	492	109	21	3	12	46/143	51	55	5	5	388	.222	.292	.350	.217	42	122-OF 87
1999	Jacksnvl	Sou	215	55	13	2	9	26/62	30	24	3	2	162	.256	.343	.460	.268	30	52-OF 89
2000	*Detroit*	*AL*	*279*	*66*	*12*	*1*	*8*	*29/80*	*36*	*34*	*5*	*3*	*216*	*.237*	*.308*	*.373*	*.232*	*28*	

A fine hitter who impressed the Tigers as much with his defensive improvement as with his bat, Wakeland is, unfortunately, like many players in this organization, about two years too old to be taken seriously as a prospect. If Encarnacion continues to turn every pitcher into Bret Saberhagen, Wakeland has a chance to sneak into the Tigers' lineup as soon as this year.

Jason Wood   UT   Bats R   Age 30

YEAR	TEAM	LGE	AB	H	DB	TP	HR	BB/SO	R	RBI	SB	CS	OUT	BA	OBP	SLG	EQA	EQR	DEFENSE	
1997	Edmonton	PCL	486	121	26	4	12	31/83	52	54	1	2	367	.249	.302	.393	.233	48	115-3B 99	
1998	Edmonton	PCL	305	72	12	0	14	29/78	37	54	1	1	234	.236	.305	.413	.240	33	41-3B 93	20-2B 104
1998	Toledo	Int	170	41	6	0	6	12/33	19	23	0	0	129	.241	.294	.382	.227	16	27-3B 88	
1999	Toledo	Int	186	46	5	0	6	17/47	26	19	0	1	141	.247	.313	.371	.231	18	29-3B 91	
1999	Detroit	AL	44	7	0	0	1	2/13	4	6	0	0	37	.159	.196	.227	.100	1		
2000	*Detroit*	*AL*	*315*	*76*	*14*	*1*	*10*	*32/72*	*38*	*43*	*0*	*1*	*240*	*.241*	*.311*	*.387*	*.236*	*32*		

Wood had one last chance to establish himself as a bench player and blew it. He's on the wrong side of his 30th birthday now, and teams are too suspicious of offense-minded utility infielders to give him another chance. Wood has to hope to find work as an emergency backup who can fill in on a major-league roster for maybe two weeks a year, effectively doubling his Triple-A salary.

PITCHERS (Averages: ERA: 4.50 / H/9: 9.00 / HR/9: 1.00 / BB/9: 3.50 / K/9: 6.50 / KWH: 1.00)

Matt Anderson   Throws R   Age 23

YEAR	TEAM	LGE	IP	H	ER	HR	BB	K	ERA	W	L	H/9	HR/9	BB/9	K/9	KWH	PERA
1998	Lakeland	Fla	25.0	21	5	0	10	26	1.80	3	0	7.56	0.00	3.60	9.36	2.41	2.88
1998	Detroit	AL	44.3	37	15	3	32	45	3.05	3	2	7.51	0.61	6.50	9.14	1.28	4.47
1999	Detroit	AL	38.0	32	24	7	34	33	5.68	2	2	7.58	1.66	8.05	7.82	0.75	6.16
1999	Toledo	Int	36.3	35	27	9	32	31	6.69	1	3	8.67	2.23	7.93	7.68	0.64	7.68

Anderson throws as hard as any pitcher in the game, but needs to learn that major-league hitters are not intimidated by velocity that isn't accompanied by movement. As Whitey Herzog said, hitters could hit bullets out of a gun once they got the timing right. Right now, Anderson seems to be the intimidated one, to the point where he can't throw strikes with any consistency. The Tigers have him working on a split-finger fastball to add deception. I think he's at least a year away from any consistent success.

Willie Blair   Throws R   Age 34

YEAR	TEAM	LGE	IP	H	ER	HR	BB	K	ERA	W	L	H/9	HR/9	BB/9	K/9	KWH	PERA
1997	Detroit	AL	175.0	186	82	17	46	91	4.22	10	9	9.57	0.87	2.37	4.68	0.72	4.27
1998	Arizona	NL	145.3	175	95	27	54	68	5.88	6	10	10.84	1.67	3.34	4.21	0.37	6.25
1998	NY Mets	NL	28.3	24	10	4	10	20	3.18	2	1	7.62	1.27	3.18	6.35	1.25	3.81
1999	Detroit	AL	135.0	162	95	25	43	84	6.33	5	10	10.80	1.67	2.87	5.60	0.76	6.07

Just eat his contract already. And if anyone tells you the Diamondbacks are run by geniuses, remind him that they gave this tonic-to-slumps a four-year contract. Four months later, they were so desperate to dump him that they threw in Jeff Suppan. When Blair's sinker is working and he's hitting the corners of the strike zone, he can turn into John Burkett for a few innings. Lovely.

David Borkowski   Throws R   Age 23

YEAR	TEAM	LGE	IP	H	ER	HR	BB	K	ERA	W	L	H/9	HR/9	BB/9	K/9	KWH	PERA
1997	W Michgn	Mid	149.0	191	106	19	37	72	6.40	6	11	11.54	1.15	2.23	4.35	0.55	5.62
1998	Jacksnvl	Sou	159.3	245	115	27	52	79	6.50	6	12	13.84	1.53	2.94	4.46	0.37	7.85
1999	Toledo	Int	122.0	127	59	15	45	84	4.35	7	7	9.37	1.11	3.32	6.20	0.92	4.72
1999	Detroit	AL	77.3	82	51	9	39	51	5.94	3	6	9.54	1.05	4.54	5.94	0.61	5.24

The Tigers have been pumping Borkowski for years, in part because he's an area kid, but he does throw a good sinking fastball and is slowly gaining mastery of his other three pitches. He's been moved through the system quickly and probably could have used an entire season at Triple-A. He keeps his pitches down and his pitch count low and will probably make a nice #3 starter by next year.

Doug Brocail   Throws R   Age 33

YEAR	TEAM	LGE	IP	H	ER	HR	BB	K	ERA	W	L	H/9	HR/9	BB/9	K/9	KWH	PERA
1997	Detroit	AL	78.3	73	30	9	37	61	3.45	6	3	8.39	1.03	4.25	7.01	1.03	4.48
1998	Detroit	AL	63.0	46	21	2	19	56	3.00	5	2	6.57	0.29	2.71	8.00	2.68	2.29
1999	Detroit	AL	82.3	57	20	6	25	80	2.19	7	2	6.23	0.66	2.73	8.74	3.36	2.51

He's completely out of place on this team, because he's the sort of unsung player who helps a good team win. He doesn't have the fastball that managers look for in a closer, just the most underrated sinker in the game. Given the manner in which closers are used today, having Brocail pitch in high-leverage situations as a setup man may actually be better for the Tigers than using him to hold three-run leads in the ninth. Brocail is consistent, durable and, even at 33, very likely to still be pitching well when half the pitchers in this chapter are out of baseball.

Francisco Cordero   Throws R   Age 22

YEAR	TEAM	LGE	IP	H	ER	HR	BB	K	ERA	W	L	H/9	HR/9	BB/9	K/9	KWH	PERA
1997	W Michgn	Mid	50.0	49	18	3	18	46	3.24	4	2	8.82	0.54	3.24	8.28	1.79	3.78
1998	Jacksnvl	Sou	15.0	23	13	1	8	15	7.80	0	2	13.80	0.60	4.80	9.00	0.91	7.80
1999	Jacksnvl	Sou	49.7	42	11	4	24	48	1.99	5	1	7.61	0.72	4.35	8.70	1.71	3.81
1999	Detroit	AL	19.0	18	6	2	18	20	2.84	1	1	8.53	0.95	8.53	9.47	0.92	6.16

Cordero has been the Tigers' closer-in-waiting since 1997, but a pair of stress fractures just above the elbow stalled his development. He finally had definitive surgery to correct the problem, then had a breakthrough year. For someone who has had his name in bold print for so long, he's still very young, a full year younger than Matt Anderson. He throws nearly as hard, with more movement on his fastball, but unlike Anderson, he has already learned to adjust to failure. Included in the Gonzalez trade, he adds to the deep and nasty Texas pen.

Nate Cornejo   Throws R   Age 20

YEAR	TEAM	LGE	IP	H	ER	HR	BB	K	ERA	W	L	H/9	HR/9	BB/9	K/9	KWH	PERA
1999	W Michgn	Mid	157.7	219	109	6	76	89	6.22	6	12	12.50	0.34	4.34	5.08	0.36	6.16

Cornejo dropped from the first round into the supplemental portion of the 1998 draft after he tore both his ACLs in high school. While his dreams of running a 4.4 40 are over, he had no problems staying healthy and pitching well in the Midwest League. He's at least three years away from the majors, but with his performance so far and a heavy fastball in the low 90s, he's definitely a name to keep in mind.

Nelson Cruz   Throws R   Age 27

YEAR	TEAM	LGE	IP	H	ER	HR	BB	K	ERA	W	L	H/9	HR/9	BB/9	K/9	KWH	PERA
1997	Nashvill	AmA	122.0	152	81	19	37	82	5.98	5	9	11.21	1.40	2.73	6.05	0.89	5.90
1997	ChiSox	AL	26.7	28	17	6	9	23	5.74	1	2	9.45	2.03	3.04	7.76	1.57	5.74
1998	Calgary	PCL	124.0	167	84	16	48	83	6.10	5	9	12.12	1.16	3.48	6.02	0.64	6.53
1999	Toledo	Int	59.7	54	22	4	23	35	3.32	5	2	8.15	0.60	3.47	5.28	0.74	3.62
1999	Detroit	AL	67.3	70	38	9	23	47	5.08	3	4	9.36	1.20	3.07	6.28	1.03	4.81

This is what passes for a pitching prospect in the Tiger organization. Cruz washed out of the White Sox organization, but he has good control and throws reasonably hard, so he's got the Tigers hoping he can be somebody. Unless "somebody" means "middle reliever," their hopes are likely to be dashed.

Beiker Graterol   Throws R   Age 25

YEAR	TEAM	LGE	IP	H	ER	HR	BB	K	ERA	W	L	H/9	HR/9	BB/9	K/9	KWH	PERA
1997	Dunedin	Fla	76.7	105	56	11	35	42	6.57	3	6	12.33	1.29	4.11	4.93	0.36	7.04
1998	Knoxvill	Sou	64.7	83	45	8	22	42	6.26	2	5	11.55	1.11	3.06	5.85	0.72	5.98
1998	Syracuse	Int	91.0	116	61	9	34	55	6.03	4	6	11.47	0.89	3.36	5.44	0.57	5.74
1999	Toledo	Int	75.0	96	56	9	41	41	6.72	2	6	11.52	1.08	4.92	4.92	0.32	6.72

That injuries to Willie Blair and Bryce Florie would force Graterol into the Tigers' April rotation, after he was picked up for nothing from the Blue Jays in the offseason, is all you need to know about how out-of-whack the organization's expectations were. After getting pasted by the Yankees in his only start, Graterol was sent down in favor of Jeff Weaver.

Seth Greisinger — Throws R — Age 24

YEAR	TEAM	LGE	IP	H	ER	HR	BB	K	ERA	W	L	H/9	HR/9	BB/9	K/9	KWH	PERA
1997	Jacksnvl	Sou	143.7	229	116	29	58	86	7.27	4	12	14.35	1.82	3.63	5.39	0.42	8.90
1998	Toledo	Int	56.7	54	22	5	23	33	3.49	4	2	8.58	0.79	3.65	5.24	0.66	4.13
1998	Detroit	AL	131.3	139	73	16	50	67	5.00	7	8	9.53	1.10	3.43	4.59	0.48	4.87

He missed almost the entire season with a frayed ligament in his right elbow. The power of modern medicine is such that, given proper time to recover and rehabilitate, I think he'll return to the major leagues and eventually have some good years. As recently as 10 years ago, any pitcher who went under the knife was a longshot to ever regain his old form, so that is certainly progress. For 2000, Greisinger is unlikely to contribute anything more than some garbage innings in the second half.

Erik Hiljus — Throws R — Age 27

YEAR	TEAM	LGE	IP	H	ER	HR	BB	K	ERA	W	L	H/9	HR/9	BB/9	K/9	KWH	PERA
1998	Jacksnvl	Sou	58.0	67	41	8	37	63	6.36	2	4	10.40	1.24	5.74	9.78	1.20	6.52
1999	Jacksnvl	Sou	16.3	8	5	1	5	21	2.76	1	1	4.41	0.55	2.76	11.57	8.24	1.65
1999	Toledo	Int	56.7	55	34	5	18	62	5.40	2	4	8.74	0.79	2.86	9.85	2.90	3.97

Hiljus was a highly regarded Mets farmhand before missing a year and a half with arm woes. The Tigers picked him up as a reclamation project and put him in the bullpen, and he's beginning to justify their effort. He has a good repertoire for a reliever, breezed through Double-A and Triple-A last year, and showed enough in September that he's a good candidate for a relief spot this year. I like him, as much as one can like a middle-relief prospect.

Todd Jones — Throws R — Age 32

YEAR	TEAM	LGE	IP	H	ER	HR	BB	K	ERA	W	L	H/9	HR/9	BB/9	K/9	KWH	PERA
1997	Detroit	AL	70.0	60	28	3	35	71	3.60	5	3	7.71	0.39	4.50	9.13	1.79	3.60
1998	Detroit	AL	64.0	56	34	6	38	58	4.78	3	4	7.88	0.84	5.34	8.16	1.18	4.36
1999	Detroit	AL	67.0	61	26	6	34	66	3.49	4	3	8.19	0.81	4.57	8.87	1.57	4.30

He wasn't the best reliever on the team, but as we pointed out with Brocail, using your second-best reliever as your closer really isn't such a bad thing. In nearly half of his appearances, he came in to start the ninth inning with a two-run lead or better. Do you really need your best reliever in that spot? Even with a 3.80 ERA, he converted 30 of his 35 save opportunities. Jones is hopelessly overpaid because of his role; he's really no better than Turk Wendell or Tim Crabtree, and he's not likely to get any better.

Masao Kida — Throws R — Age 31

YEAR	TEAM	LGE	IP	H	ER	HR	BB	K	ERA	W	L	H/9	HR/9	BB/9	K/9	KWH	PERA
1999	Detroit	AL	65.3	70	42	5	29	51	5.79	3	4	9.64	0.69	3.99	7.03	0.96	4.68

Well, that gamble didn't pay off. The Tigers had higher expectations for Kida than paying $1.5 million to use him in meaningless mop-up situations, which proved to be all he was capable of handling. He's a good illustration of Randy Smith's preference for hard throwers over guys who actually know how to pitch. When he was signed, the Tigers were quick to point out that he had an ERA under 2.00 as a reliever in Japan in 1998. What they neglected to mention was that he was moved to the bullpen at midseason because he was ineffective in the rotation. I don't expect him to do anything this year to justify his salary.

Mike Maroth — Throws L — Age 22

YEAR	TEAM	LGE	IP	H	ER	HR	BB	K	ERA	W	L	H/9	HR/9	BB/9	K/9	KWH	PERA
1998	Lowell	NYP	30.3	26	15	2	18	21	4.45	2	1	7.71	0.59	5.34	6.23	0.70	4.15
1999	Lakeland	Fla	15.3	22	9	2	9	9	5.28	1	1	12.91	1.17	5.28	5.28	0.31	7.63
1999	Sarasota	Fla	102.7	148	79	4	44	52	6.93	3	8	12.97	0.35	3.86	4.56	0.31	6.31
1999	Jacksnvl	Sou	19.0	31	17	2	8	8	8.05	0	2	14.68	0.95	3.79	3.79	0.19	8.05

Acquired from the Red Sox for Bryce Florie, Maroth is the antithesis of the typical Tiger pitcher. He has marginal stuff but knows how to make the most of it. He's also left-handed, so his average repertoire won't be held against him. One of the better prospects in the system, but only because he's in this system.

Dave Mlicki — Throws R — Age 32

YEAR	TEAM	LGE	IP	H	ER	HR	BB	K	ERA	W	L	H/9	HR/9	BB/9	K/9	KWH	PERA
1997	NY Mets	NL	190.7	204	93	22	80	146	4.39	11	10	9.63	1.04	3.78	6.89	0.98	5.00
1998	NY Mets	NL	56.7	70	39	8	27	37	6.19	2	4	11.12	1.27	4.29	5.88	0.54	6.35
1998	LosAngls	NL	121.7	125	66	15	40	74	4.88	6	8	9.25	1.11	2.96	5.47	0.82	4.51
1999	Detroit	AL	192.7	201	96	21	68	122	4.48	11	10	9.39	0.98	3.18	5.70	0.81	4.58

He finally received some recognition after toiling in yeoman obscurity for years. Mlicki symbolizes the Tigers' need to scrap their pitching staff and start over, much as Easley and Clark do for the offense. Mlicki makes a good #4 starter; as an ace, which is what he was for the Tigers after Weaver imploded, he serves only as a bright neon sign blaring, "Warning: Team Under Construction. Expect Delays." He's been signed to a three-year deal for $15 million.

Brian Moehler — Throws R — Age 28

YEAR	TEAM	LGE	IP	H	ER	HR	BB	K	ERA	W	L	H/9	HR/9	BB/9	K/9	KWH	PERA
1997	Detroit	AL	175.3	198	93	20	61	98	4.77	9	10	10.16	1.03	3.13	5.03	0.59	5.03
1998	Detroit	AL	222.7	216	95	27	59	125	3.84	14	11	8.73	1.09	2.38	5.05	0.92	4.00
1999	Detroit	AL	197.7	219	103	19	58	109	4.69	11	11	9.97	0.87	2.64	4.96	0.70	4.55

You know, his success had been a mystery to us. But consider the case solved: he went 7-13 with a 5.24 ERA after getting caught scuffing the ball. He did pitch much better the last two months of the year, walking just 15 men in 73 innings. That doesn't mean he wasn't cheating again; Gaylord Perry was one heck of a control pitcher. Not to encourage such behavior, but if he wants to stay in the big leagues, he probably can't rely on his ability.

C.J. Nitkowski — Throws L — Age 27

YEAR	TEAM	LGE	IP	H	ER	HR	BB	K	ERA	W	L	H/9	HR/9	BB/9	K/9	KWH	PERA
1997	New Orln	AmA	163.3	212	100	10	64	122	5.51	7	11	11.68	0.55	3.53	6.72	0.82	5.57
1998	Houston	NL	59.3	51	27	4	24	42	4.10	4	3	7.74	0.61	3.64	6.37	1.08	3.49
1999	Detroit	AL	82.3	60	39	10	44	68	4.26	5	4	6.56	1.09	4.81	7.43	1.31	3.72

One of the more fiery players on the team, he ripped into Lance Parrish when he felt he wasn't getting an honest chance to show his skills. Nitkowski then made good on his word, pitching very well down the stretch when he was inserted into the rotation. He could very easily be this year's Ron Villone: he's also a former first-rounder, and is a left-hander with control problems entering his late 20s. It would not be surprising at all if he was the ace of the staff by the end of the year.

Adam Pettyjohn — Throws L — Age 23

YEAR	TEAM	LGE	IP	H	ER	HR	BB	K	ERA	W	L	H/9	HR/9	BB/9	K/9	KWH	PERA
1998	Jamestwn	NYP	20.7	28	13	0	5	15	5.66	1	1	12.19	0.00	2.18	6.53	1.20	4.79
1998	W Michgn	Mid	45.7	63	22	5	12	44	4.34	3	2	12.42	0.99	2.36	8.67	1.91	6.11
1999	Lakeland	Fla	56.7	76	42	3	14	41	6.67	2	4	12.07	0.48	2.22	6.51	1.18	5.24
1999	Jacksnvl	Sou	119.0	155	84	14	38	76	6.35	4	9	11.72	1.06	2.87	5.75	0.73	5.90

I don't know what's in the water at Fresno State, but Weaver's college teammate, who was drafted right after him in 1998, has moved nearly as quickly through the system, spending most of the year at Double-A. Pettyjohn has become one of the best left-handed pitching prospects in baseball, with outstanding control and instincts. If he gets a full year at Triple-A, he could make a serious contribution to the Tigers in 2001.

Brandon Reed — Throws R — Age 25

YEAR	TEAM	LGE	IP	H	ER	HR	BB	K	ERA	W	L	H/9	HR/9	BB/9	K/9	KWH	PERA
1997	Jacksnvl	Sou	159.7	227	115	25	58	73	6.48	6	12	12.80	1.41	3.27	4.11	0.30	7.16
1998	Toledo	Int	113.0	169	85	16	48	62	6.77	4	9	13.46	1.27	3.82	4.94	0.35	7.73
1999	Toledo	Int	87.3	110	55	6	28	52	5.67	4	6	11.34	0.62	2.89	5.36	0.66	5.15

After nearly making the big club out of spring training, Reed went back to Triple-A and was hit hard. An extreme finesse pitcher who relies on movement and different arm angles, he had trouble fooling anyone with his slider early on and was pasted, then finished strong. He has shown steady improvement over the last three years, but his best opportunity has probably come and gone.

Sean Runyan   Throws L   Age 26

YEAR	TEAM	LGE	IP	H	ER	HR	BB	K	ERA	W	L	H/9	HR/9	BB/9	K/9	KWH	PERA
1997	Mobile	Sou	58.7	60	26	4	31	42	3.99	4	3	9.20	0.61	4.76	6.44	0.71	4.76
1998	Detroit	AL	50.7	45	21	7	30	40	3.73	4	2	7.99	1.24	5.33	7.11	0.89	4.97
1999	Detroit	AL	10.7	9	4	2	3	6	3.38	1	0	7.59	1.69	2.53	5.06	1.00	4.22

After setting a record for most appearances (88) by a rookie, Runyan blew out his arm in May, forcing the Tigers to admit they screwed up badly. He's very well-liked by the organization and will be given every chance to make it back, but if they care so much about him, why don't they give him a chance to face more than two batters at a time? For his career, he's pitched in 100 games and thrown just 61 innings.

Victor Santos   Throws R   Age 23

YEAR	TEAM	LGE	IP	H	ER	HR	BB	K	ERA	W	L	H/9	HR/9	BB/9	K/9	KWH	PERA
1997	Lakeland	Fla	135.0	173	96	13	78	86	6.40	5	10	11.53	0.87	5.20	5.73	0.41	6.53
1998	Lakeland	Fla	95.0	106	45	11	31	57	4.26	6	5	10.04	1.04	2.94	5.40	0.74	4.93
1998	Jacksnvl	Sou	34.0	46	22	3	14	30	5.82	1	3	12.18	0.79	3.71	7.94	1.04	6.35
1999	Jacksnvl	Sou	163.7	175	97	17	62	120	5.33	7	11	9.62	0.93	3.41	6.60	0.99	4.73

A very good year at Double-A vaulted Santos from a marginal to a legitimate prospect. The Tigers' farm system suffers from the same problem as the major-league team: plenty of good prospects, nobody who qualifies as a phenom. Santos projects as a league-average pitcher in two or three years, a good #5 starter. Unless the Tigers get lucky and a couple of their prospects advance past their ceiling, they're looking at a lot of #5 starters and no one capable of handling a larger role.

Justin Thompson   Throws L   Age 27

YEAR	TEAM	LGE	IP	H	ER	HR	BB	K	ERA	W	L	H/9	HR/9	BB/9	K/9	KWH	PERA
1997	Detroit	AL	222.7	188	80	18	67	153	3.23	16	9	7.60	0.73	2.71	6.18	1.39	3.19
1998	Detroit	AL	224.0	222	105	18	83	151	4.22	13	12	8.92	0.72	3.33	6.07	0.92	4.10
1999	Detroit	AL	143.7	146	75	21	57	85	4.70	8	8	9.15	1.32	3.57	5.32	0.65	4.95

The pitcher we saw in 1997 may be gone for good. His career is already marred by severe elbow troubles that required Tommy John surgery, and though his workload wouldn't be unreasonable for a pitcher with no injury history, throwing 220 innings in back-to-back years was too much for him. The Tigers shut him down last year, mostly as a precaution. If put on the Alex Fernandez plan this year, I think he's good for 180 innings with a 3.50 ERA. Thompson was the big name in the Gonzalez trade and will be asked to carry a significant load for the Rangers, so he may be in trouble.

Jeff Weaver   Throws R   Age 23

YEAR	TEAM	LGE	IP	H	ER	HR	BB	K	ERA	W	L	H/9	HR/9	BB/9	K/9	KWH	PERA
1998	Jamestwn	NYP	11.7	8	6	0	1	7	4.63	0	1	6.17	0.00	0.77	5.40	4.58	1.54
1998	W Michgn	Mid	12.0	11	5	2	0	14	3.75	1	0	8.25	1.50	0.00	10.50	—	3.00
1999	Detroit	AL	164.7	169	92	24	54	117	5.03	8	10	9.24	1.31	2.95	6.39	1.12	4.76

Weaver looked like the superstar the Tigers needed, reaching the majors less than a year out of college and giving up two runs or fewer in 10 of his first 14 starts. He was hitting 94 mph on the gun with an effortless three-quarters motion, and it seemed like every pitch he threw was on the corner at the knees. In short, he looked every bit like the once-in-a-decade pitcher who arrives from a college campus with nothing to learn about getting major-league hitters out—a Mike Mussina for the '00s.

In the gutsiest and wisest decision made by an organization all year, the Tigers refused to let his success obscure the fact that 1999 was his first full year of professional baseball, and put him on a strict pitch limit: 100 pitches for his first six weeks and 110 after that. And they stuck by that rule, bending it for a total of one pitch all season.

And yet, a funny thing happened:

	W	L	ERA	IP	H	W	K	HR
Through June 22	6	3	2.93	86	65	25	51	9
After June 22	3	9	8.46	77.2	111	31	63	18

Weaver's descent into hell was quick and complete: he gave up six runs or more eight times in his last 14 starts as his overall numbers went from outstanding to just barely standing at all. He wasn't hurt. He wasn't missing the life on his pitches. And he wasn't able to turn things around, exasperating the team that had such high hopes for him.

The only chink in Weaver's armor early in the year was that his delivery, coming as close to sidearm as it did, appeared to make him vulnerable to left-handed hitters. And indeed, he did have a significant platoon split. Was it possible that his troubles in the second half of the year were the result of managers stacking their lineup with eight or nine left-handed hitters, leaving Weaver with no easy outs in the lineup?

Take a look. Weaver's June 27 start was filed under "July," in order to give a clearer picture of his decline and fall:

MONTH	%LH	AVG/OBP/SLG	OPS	%RH	AVG/OBP/SLG	OPS	DIFF.
April	61	.182/.280/.409	689	39	.100/.156/.167	323	366
May	59	.265/.315/.426	741	41	.156/.255/.200	455	286
June 1-22	50	.262/.328/.426	754	50	.220/.303/.339	642	112
July	65	.386/.443/.705	1148	35	.341/.420/.500	920	228
August	48	.293/.370/.561	931	52	.234/.280/.404	684	253
September	52	.386/.470/.737	1207	48	.340/.441/.560	1001	269

What's clear is that opposing managers were not altering their lineups to take advantage of Weaver's problems with left-handed hitters. Instead, it appears that Weaver simply lost it, and that's not the answer the Tigers want to hear. Left-handed hitters completely went to town in the second half, but right-handed hitters, whom he completely owned over the first three months, also improved their performance significantly. As the "Diff." column shows, his platoon differentials held steady at around 250 points of OPS all season.

The most plausible explanation is that since Weaver's fastball doesn't have much late movement, word got around that left-handers should just sit on one, and they began to torch him. Unlike Mussina, who has ice water in his veins, Weaver's blood tends to run a little closer to room temperature. He has a reputation for being a hothead and was unable or unwilling to adjust. He was also unsure how to handle his first taste of extended failure as a pro and lost confidence in himself. By year's end even the right-handed hitters were getting in on the fun. His season may have been the best advertisement yet for the wisdom of putting rookie pitchers in middle relief: even with the protection afforded his arm, Weaver was unprepared for the mental demands that came with starting every fifth day.

What does all this mean for his future? The good news is that he's physically healthy. In his final start, the Tigers finally got Weaver to try a new cut fastball as an out pitch against left-handed hitters, and they hold hope it will be the weapon he needs. But ultimately, Jeff Weaver got himself into this mess, and he has to make the effort to pull himself out.

Alan Webb　　　　**Throws L**　　　**Age 20**

YEAR	TEAM	LGE	IP	H	ER	HR	BB	K	ERA	W	L	H/9	HR/9	BB/9	K/9	KWH	PERA
1998	W Michgn	Mid	156.0	159	103	14	74	138	5.94	6	11	9.17	0.81	4.27	7.96	1.21	4.67
1999	Jacksnvl	Sou	131.0	163	98	18	68	73	6.73	5	10	11.20	1.24	4.67	5.02	0.36	6.53

Despite skipping a level and landing in Double-A while still in his teens, Webb got off to a great start. In his last 44 innings, though, he posted an 8.39 ERA and had more walks (26) than strikeouts (24). Webb is in the Billy Wagner class of small, at 5'10" and 170 pounds and for a teenager his size to be worked as hard as he has been the last two years is, to be kind, unwise. He may just be the Rangers' best long-term pitching prospect, following his inclusion in the Gonzalez deal.

Support-Neutral Records — DETROIT TIGERS — Park Effect: +2.8%

PITCHER	GS	IP	R	SNW	SNL	SNPCT	W	L	RA	APW	SNVA	SNWAR
Willie Blair	16	81.3	79	3.1	8.4	.267	3	8	8.74	-2.87	-2.59	-1.81
David Borkowski	12	66.3	56	2.8	5.8	.325	1	6	7.60	-1.56	-1.41	-0.86
Nelson Cruz	6	31.3	28	1.4	2.8	.326	2	3	8.04	-0.88	-0.70	-0.42
Bryce Florie	3	15.3	8	0.8	0.9	.466	1	0	4.70	0.09	-0.05	0.07
Beiker Graterol	1	4.0	7	0.0	0.8	.028	0	1	15.75	-0.43	-0.39	-0.33
Dave Mlicki	31	191.7	108	11.8	10.3	.535	14	12	5.07	0.45	0.63	2.42
Brian Moehler	32	196.3	116	11.2	11.7	.490	10	16	5.32	-0.04	-0.13	1.48
C.J. Nitkowski	7	37.3	19	2.7	1.4	.654	2	2	4.58	0.27	0.64	0.95
Justin Thompson	24	142.7	85	9.2	8.2	.529	9	11	5.36	-0.09	0.33	1.82
Jeff Weaver	29	162.7	104	9.7	10.7	.476	9	12	5.75	-0.76	-0.60	1.05
TOTALS	161	929.0	610	52.8	61.1	.463	51	71	5.91	-5.81	-4.27	4.37

Early in the season, Jeff Weaver was called the next David Cone. But by the end of the year, he was pitching more like the next Dave Otto. Through his first 14 starts, he had a terrific .738 Support-Neutral Winning Percentage, but in his last 15 starts, it was a horrible .266. That doesn't quite match the extreme split-personality season of John Snyder (see the White Sox SNW/L comment), but it's close.

Pitcher Abuse Points

PITCHER	AGE	GS	PAP	PAP/S	WKLD	MAX	1-90	91-100	101-110	111-120	121-130	131-140	141+
Willie Blair	33	16	0	0.0	0.0	97	10	6	0	0	0	0	0
David Borkowski	22	12	96	8.0	21.3	123	5	2	2	1	2	0	0
Nelson Cruz	26	6	28	4.7	9.3	114	1	3	1	1	0	0	0
Bryce Florie	29	3	0	0.0	0.0	83	3	0	0	0	0	0	0
Beiker Graterol	24	1	0	0.0	0.0	79	1	0	0	0	0	0	0
Dave Mlicki	31	31	156	5.0	5.9	120	7	8	12	4	0	0	0
Brian Moehler	27	32	283	8.8	16.2	130	8	7	9	6	2	0	0
C. J. Nitkowski	26	7	16	2.3	4.6	111	2	3	1	1	0	0	0
Justin Thompson	26	24	274	11.4	22.8	131	8	6	3	2	4	1	0
Jeff Weaver	22	29	63	2.2	5.8	111	13	5	10	1	0	0	0
DETROIT		161	916	5.7	10.9	131	58	40	38	16	8	1	0
Ranking (AL)				12	11								

Jeff Weaver's contribution helped keep the Tigers' overall PAP scores close to the bottom of the league, but Larry Parrish's record is not without a blemish or two: David Borkowski was not protected nearly as carefully as Weaver, and despite four and a half years of minor-league experience, Borkowski is actually six months *younger* than Weaver. Another case of a manager burdening his pitchers based on their experience, not on their age. . . . Justin Thompson, despite years of trouble with his balky elbow, had Workloads of 22.8 and 21.7 the last two years, and suffered through a disappointing season before he was shut down in mid-August. . . . The good news for Tiger fans is that new manager Phil Garner has become as protective with his starters as anyone in the game, so hopefully he'll sign onto the plan to protect the few arms the Tigers have worth protecting.

Kansas City Royals

On the field, the Royals reached the bottom of what has been an entire decade of lows. But that they finished with the worst record in franchise history obscures the fact that they may have finally turned a corner as an organization and are now firmly on the path back to contention.

The Royals can take comfort in the knowledge that all their losses last year were not in vain. The seeds of almost every great team are planted in the rubble of a 90-game loser. Much as the 1989-90 Braves featured John Smoltz, Tom Glavine, Ron Gant, David Justice and Jeff Blauser, and the 1991-92 Indians played Albert Belle, Carlos Baerga, Jim Thome, Charles Nagy and Kenny Lofton, the 1999 Royals featured the development of some of the potential stars of the new millennium. Rookie of the Year Carlos Beltran displayed speed and power at the age of 22, while Carlos Febles showed off much the same skill set, with less power but more plate discipline. But as impressive as the Class of 1999 was, almost equally important to the Royals' future was the final maturation of their previous youth movement, the Class of 1996—a class that came precariously close to flunking out before the year began.

The pride of that crop, Johnny Damon, at long last realized his considerable promise. Damon, who in 1998 was finally allowed to play without the threat of losing his job, reestablished himself as an everyday player. He built on that performance in 1999 with a distinguished all-around season. Mike Sweeney, whose defensive skills as a catcher had been so vilified that the Royals nearly traded him away in March, was granted a temporary stay when Jeremy Giambi went on the disabled list with a bad hamstring. Sweeney turned a one-week stint as the team's DH into a rebirth, posting the highest OPS by a Royal since 1991. Jermaine Dye, whose acquisition from the Braves for Michael Tucker was roundly criticized by analysts, made the organization proud with a breakout season many of us didn't think he had in him.

For all these successes, Manager Tony Muser deserves credit. Muser is a patient man and a positive thinker, exactly what players like Damon and Sweeney needed. A player like Dye needed a manager who would give him another chance after he botched his first two, while rookies like the Dos Carlos needed a manager who would not play mind games with them or bench them at the first sign of a slump.

But there is another side to this coin. Muser's patience in giving so many players the opportunity to develop works fine when the player has talent and can contribute. But when patience means waiting all season for Chad Kreuter to start hitting or for Scott Service to start getting batters out, it becomes stubbornness. Despite a significant improvement in the Royals' core talent, the contributions of players like Kreuter, Service and Jeff Montgomery were so disastrous that they sank the Royals towards their worst record ever.

And the bullpen...oh, that bullpen. While not the manager's most important job, his handling of the bullpen may be the part of his job over which he has the most control. The bullpen is baseball's proving ground, where roster turnover is at its greatest. As a result, almost every bullpen is stocked with rookies or journeymen still waiting for their first taste of success. It is up to the manager to evaluate his options in March and pick the best relief candidates, and it is up to him and his pitching coach to get the most out of the pen during the season.

On both counts, Muser and pitching coach Mark Wiley—who had been fired by the Indians the year before—failed miserably, creating a disaster of such proportions that the Royals can lay claim to the distinction of having The Worst Bullpen of All Time. Here's what went wrong:

1. Muser, somewhere in his travels, picked up the notion that the ideal reliever throws a fastball that tops out around 91 mph and has no movement whatsoever. Look at the parade of "relievers" who attracted more big flies than a picnic in August: Don Wengert, Brian Barber, Jim Pittsley, Ken Ray, Marc Pisciotta, Mac Suzuki. Wengert, whose glacier-like movement on his fastball has made him the poster boy for this class of pitcher, gave up 25

Royals Prospectus

1999 record: 64-97; Fourth place, AL Central

Pythagorean W/L: 76-86

Runs scored: 856 (7th in AL)

Runs allowed: 921 (14th in AL)

Team EQA: .258 (9th in AL)

1999 team age: 26.7 (3rd-youngest in AL)

1999 park: Kauffman Stadium; slight hitters' park, increased run scoring by 2%.

1999: A historically bad bullpen undermined the progress of their young hitters.

2000: At least a year away, but for the first time in a while, there's hope.

runs in 24 innings before the Royals pulled the plug, setting an example that his comrades did their best to live up to.

2. Pitchers who should have been successful weren't. Scott Service, who had a 3.48 ERA in 1998, lost his slider and turned into Service-with-a-smile for opposing hitters, pummeled for a .507 slugging average. Left-hander Matt Whisenant continued to display great stuff and continued to do little with it, giving up 66 baserunners in 40 innings for a 6.35 ERA. After being picked up by the Padres on waivers in August, he cut his ERA nearly in half.

3. Unrealistic expectations. The Royals re-signed Jeff Montgomery for $2.6 million, and by the end of the year there were 2.6 million reasons why this was a mistake. He had nothing.

4. Injuries. The Royals were generally healthy for most of the season, but Jose Santiago, their only good reliever in the early going, and Orber Moreno, their best closer prospect, both went down for the second half with biceps tendinitis.

How bad was it? The Royals' bullpen broke more records than White Sox fans on Disco Demolition Night. In 728 at-bats in "Close and Late" situations, Royals' opponents hit a ridiculous .328/.404/.520, turning every hitter into Gary Sheffield. Never before had a team blown more saves than they had recorded; the Royals saved just 29 of 59 opportunities. The Royals were the first team in league history to record a Rolaids relief score below zero.

According to Tom Ruane, the Royals' 11-32 record in one-run games was the worst by any team in over 60 years. Table 1 lists the four worst winning percentages in one-run games this century.

Table 1

Year	Team	W	L	Pct.
1935	Boston (NL)	7	31	.184
1937	St. Louis (AL)	10	31	.244
1999	Kansas City	11	32	.256
1916	Philadelphia (AL)	11	32	.256

The 1937 St. Louis Browns finished 46-108, and they were the best of the three other teams on this list. The 1935 Braves finished 38-115, the second-worst record this century. The worst? Those 1916 Athletics (36-117). Three teams with overall winning percentages in the .200s and last year's Royals. Wow.

As historic as their futility in close games was, it was the Royals' collapse at the end of games that damns the bullpen. The Royals, owners of the third-worst record in baseball, were better than .500 through six innings. Consider Table 2, where "Expected Wins" assumes the Royals won all the

games they were leading and half of the games in which they were tied.

Table 2

Inning	6	7	8	Final
Ahead	73	70	66	64
Tied	20	15	14	0
Behind	68	76	81	97
Expected Wins	83	77.5	73	64

Through six innings, the Royals were 73-68 with 20 ties, yet at game's end they were 64-97. They slipped 19 games in the standings after the sixth inning. Inning-by-inning data is not available prior to 1980, but with Keith Woolner's help, we found that over the last 20 years, the 1985 Pirates had held the record with an 18-game drop. The Royals' 13½-game drop after seven innings broke the record of 12 held by the 1997 Cubs.

You get the point. This isn't your standard "we would have won 10 more games with a good bullpen" sob story. This is the Real McCoy. The 1999 Royals were the worst late-inning team of at least the last 20 years, and the worst close-game team of the last 60.

After all this, Mark Wiley was retained as pitching coach. He then left voluntarily, accepting a senior position with the Colorado Rockies. While his replacement has not been named yet, the Royals can't help but hope to improve without him. No one, with the marginal exception of Jeff Suppan, pitched above expectations, and you could fill the Kauffman fountains with all the pitchers who disappointed.

Making the situation more galling is that the Royals had several young prospects who might have been reasonably effective in the bullpen and could have used the experience to prepare for more demanding roles in the future. These prospects—Chris Fussell, Dan Reichert and Jay Witasick—are all starting pitchers, and the Royals were too inflexible to break in a starting pitcher in the bullpen. We've harped on the Scott Elarton strategy numerous times, but in this case the Royals could have reaped an extra benefit: they could have shored up their bullpen in the process.

Instead, Fussell went 0-4, 7.82 in eight starts and was banished to the minors, while Reichert had a 9.08 ERA before a line drive nicked his arm and mercifully ended his season. Witasick was three different flavors of awful through July, but Muser was patient—or was it stubborn?—enough to keep him in the rotation all year, and he posted a 3.86 ERA from August 1 to the end of the season.

We've expressed enough frustration over Herk Robinson in these pages, so let's credit him for what he did right in 1999. He finally gave his full support to the youth movement, and the impact of trading Jeff Conine right before Opening Day cannot be underestimated. It gave full-time jobs to both

Dye and Sweeney. Robinson restrained himself—barely—from bringing in another mediocre veteran when Jeff King retired. His theft of Jeff Suppan from the Diamondbacks paid nice dividends. And two of his most-maligned moves, trading Tucker for Dye and former first-rounder Juan LeBron for Joe Randa, worked out perfectly.

Robinson's biggest weakness is no longer his poor evaluation of talent. His problem is that there's no guiding vision behind his moves, no firm plan for how the Royals are to get from point A to point B. Every transaction and trade is made in reaction to what's going on at that moment, and never in advance of an anticipated need, whether it's a young player approaching free agency or a veteran who needs to be replaced. He also changes his mind like a teenage girl going through her wardrobe before a big date. Last July, the Padres offered a pair of players for Whisenant; he turned them down, only to put Whisenant on waivers five days later.

Now, more than ever, the Royals need a GM with courage and foresight. They suddenly have a lot of players approaching arbitration, and they don't have the financial resources to go year-to-year and pay market price. They need a GM who will sign Carlos Beltran to an eight-year contract with a couple of option years tacked on at the end. That gives Beltran financial security while giving the Royals the power to keep him until he's 33. Instead, Robinson signed Jermaine Dye to a two-year contract. That's acceptable, but the deal had no club options or other leverage that might keep Dye under contract longer for less than his market value.

Even more than a new GM, though, what the Royals need is a new owner. Any owner. We exhausted this topic last year, and remarkably, the ownership situation moved not an inch until early November, when Major League Baseball told Miles Prentice to take a hike. Prentice is an intelligent, well-intentioned, reasonable man whose shallow pockets and fan-friendly plans made him anathema to the establishment. The powers that be were nice enough to let Prentice twist in the wind for more than a year before rejecting him.

David Glass, Wal-Mart CEO and Ewing Kauffman's hand-picked choice to be his successor, has now tossed his hat into the ring. No one questions Glass's wealth, his passion for baseball or his willingness to stand up for small-market teams when dealing with other owners. The question is why he waited more than six years to set the wheels in motion on what should have been a fait accompli. Conspiracy rumors abounded several years ago that Glass was purposely dragging his feet to let the market value of the franchise drop. Subsequent events revealed that theory to be rather far-fetched, but the negative public sentiment towards Glass was a major factor in his choosing not to make an offer the first time around. Public support has shifted from Prentice to Glass so abruptly that city hospitals are dealing with an epidemic of whiplash. More importantly, the other owners want Glass to buy the team, so if he makes an acceptable offer, the transaction will probably be completed by season's end.

So there's a happy ending, right? Maybe not. Glass is an admitted labor hawk who was one of the few owners to vote against the current bargaining agreement and is adamant that revenue sharing and a more favorable Collective Bargaining Agreement are essential for small-market teams to survive. That the other owners want him in the club is a sign that they're planning to go to war after the 2001 season, and fully expect to lose most, if not all, of 2002. And they want to keep out any new owners who would be too squeamish to see their dirty deed through.

In the meantime, predicting improvement for the Royals in 2000 is like predicting a big gross for the next *Star Wars* movie: it tells you nothing about the quality of the product. The Royals lost 97 games last year, and even a 10-game improvement, significant for most teams, would hardly be noticed. Frankly, 10 games would be a disappointing jump for this bunch. The Royals have enough talent to break .500 with ease, and if their luck in close games is as good this year as it was bad last year, they could be this year's Cincinnati Reds: the best story in baseball come late September.

HITTERS (Averages: BA: .270 / OBP: .340 / SLG: .430 / EQA: .260)

Carlos Beltran   CF   Bats B   Age 23

YEAR	TEAM	LGE	AB	H	DB	TP	HR	BB/SO	R	RBI	SB	CS	OUT	BA	OBP	SLG	EQA	EQR	DEFENSE
1997	Wilmngtn	Car	431	97	15	3	11	35/96	48	41	9	4	338	.225	.288	.350	.217	37	119-OF 97
1998	Wilmngtn	Car	201	53	9	0	7	23/38	28	32	5	3	151	.264	.343	.413	.257	25	50-OF 110
1998	Wichita	Tex	177	51	10	2	10	18/33	34	30	4	1	127	.288	.356	.537	.292	29	44-OF 96
1999	KansasCy	AL	658	189	28	7	20	38/123	102	98	27	8	477	.287	.330	.442	.261	83	154-CF 89
2000	*KansasCy*	*AL*	*576*	*166*	*23*	*4*	*23*	*52/109*	*100*	*99*	*23*	*8*	*418*	*.288*	*.347*	*.462*	*.269*	*79*	

Was he the best rookie in the AL? His case rests on two arguments: 1) even though his offense was barely league-average, he had by far the most playing time of any rookie, and 2) he's a terrific defensive center fielder. The problem with the second argument is that as good as he looked, the numbers say he was the worst regular center fielder in baseball last year.

(Carlos Beltran *continued*)

So Beltran might not have been as valuable as Freddy Garcia or Jeff Zimmerman or even Chris Singleton. But when we look back at previous winners, the ones that make us say "what were they thinking?" aren't the Beltrans of the world. They're the 25-year-olds playing the best baseball of their life—Bob Hamelin and Pat Listach and Jerome Walton. Beltran might not have been the best rookie in 1999, but he was clearly the one every team would want to build around. As talented as he is, his ability to remake himself from a total hacker in April to a more disciplined hitter in September (14 of his 46 walks came in the season's final month) is what makes us excited about his future, starting this year.

Dee Brown   OF   Bats L   Age 22

YEAR	TEAM	LGE	AB	H	DB	TP	HR	BB/SO	R	RBI	SB	CS	OUT	BA	OBP	SLG	EQA	EQR	DEFENSE
1997	Spokane	Nwn	296	71	16	3	9	23/69	36	41	4	2	227	.240	.297	.405	.235	30	66-OF 83
1998	Wilmngtn	Car	460	117	27	2	12	49/111	57	57	12	5	348	.254	.332	.400	.250	55	104-OF 78
1999	Wilmngtn	Car	231	67	9	1	14	37/54	40	40	10	5	169	.290	.394	.519	.301	42	53-OF 96
1999	Wichita	Tex	234	70	12	2	9	28/45	42	41	5	4	168	.299	.380	.483	.286	37	60-OF 92
2000	*KansasCy*	*AL*	*460*	*136*	*21*	*2*	*21*	*58/102*	*91*	*88*	*17*	*7*	*331*	*.296*	*.375*	*.487*	*.286*	*72*	

As expected, Brown—who officially changed his first name from Dermal—had a breakout season, and in fact his career path is awfully similar to Beltran's. Like Beltran, Brown got a midseason promotion to Double-A at age 21 and tore through the Texas League. Brown hit much better in Wilmington than Beltran did, and is probably the best power prospect the Royals have developed since Bo Jackson. His defense also conjures up images of Jackson . . . after the hip replacement. Regardless, the Royals have to find a way of getting his bat into the lineup this year.

Mike Curry   OF   Bats L   Age 23

YEAR	TEAM	LGE	AB	H	DB	TP	HR	BB/SO	R	RBI	SB	CS	OUT	BA	OBP	SLG	EQA	EQR	DEFENSE
1998	Spokane	Nwn	232	50	8	1	1	32/46	29	17	10	4	186	.216	.315	.272	.211	19	64-OF 109
1999	Charl-WV	SAL	333	91	10	2	1	39/60	42	21	23	7	249	.273	.358	.324	.248	38	86-OF 99
1999	Wilmngtn	Car	208	48	5	2	1	28/39	23	15	12	5	165	.231	.324	.288	.221	19	50-OF 96
2000	*KansasCy*	*AL*	*350*	*90*	*9*	*2*	*1*	*52/74*	*65*	*30*	*23*	*7*	*267*	*.257*	*.353*	*.303*	*.237*	*37*	

Rotisserie players, take note. Curry, a sixth-round pick out of college in 1998, is making Royals executives whisper "Willie Wilson" while wiping away their drool. In one respect he's even more talented than Wilson, in that he drew 82 walks last year—more than Wilson drew in his best *two* seasons combined. Of course, when Wilson was 22 he was already in the major leagues. The Royals are deeper in outfield prospects than any team needs to be and should peddle Curry to a speed-obsessed GM for some talent they can really use. "Mr. Robinson? I'm sorry, sir, but Mr. Woodward doesn't work here anymore."

Johnny Damon   LF   Bats L   Age 26

YEAR	TEAM	LGE	AB	H	DB	TP	HR	BB/SO	R	RBI	SB	CS	OUT	BA	OBP	SLG	EQA	EQR	DEFENSE
1997	KansasCy	AL	469	127	12	8	8	39/67	67	46	16	10	352	.271	.331	.382	.243	51	137-OF 99
1998	KansasCy	AL	636	172	29	10	17	56/82	95	61	22	12	476	.270	.333	.428	.256	79	153-OF 103
1999	KansasCy	AL	576	173	38	9	13	60/50	92	70	36	6	409	.300	.369	.465	.287	90	131-LF 102
2000	*KansasCy*	*AL*	*548*	*158*	*25*	*9*	*17*	*57/58*	*105*	*91*	*27*	*8*	*398*	*.288*	*.355*	*.460*	*.274*	*78*	

He's the player everyone thought he would be; it just took him four years to get there. In 1998, Damon's road to stardom still had two enormous potholes: he was a free swinger and he couldn't hit left-handed pitchers. Last year, he cut his strikeout-to-walk ratio nearly in half and hit .329 against southpaws. He's durable, a terrific baserunner and went from slap-hitter to gap-hitter with 48 combined doubles and triples, second in the league behind Jermaine Dye. His range is completely wasted in left field. Since he's approaching free agency and is represented by Scott Boras, trading him to the Yankees for D'Angelo Jimenez and Ed Yarnall makes almost too much sense to actually happen.

Jeremy Dodson   OF   Bats L   Age 23

YEAR	TEAM	LGE	AB	H	DB	TP	HR	BB/SO	R	RBI	SB	CS	OUT	BA	OBP	SLG	EQA	EQR	DEFENSE
1998	Spokane	Nwn	268	73	18	2	7	15/66	35	37	2	2	197	.272	.319	.433	.250	31	60-OF 87
1999	Wichita	Tex	452	101	16	1	17	42/103	48	44	5	3	354	.223	.292	.376	.225	42	126-OF 85
2000	*KansasCy*	*AL*	*265*	*65*	*11*	*1*	*13*	*26/75*	*36*	*43*	*2*	*1*	*201*	*.245*	*.313*	*.442*	*.248*	*31*	

Dodson, a sixth-round pick in 1998, was promoted to Double-A in his first full pro season, so his inconsistent numbers are not surprising. After hitting .226/.299/.396 through June 20, he hit .283/.361/.488 the rest of the way. He's a capable corner outfielder who was voted as having the best throwing arm in the Texas League. Grade B- prospect; if everything breaks right, he could be Rusty Greer.

Jermaine Dye — RF — Bats R — Age 26

YEAR	TEAM	LGE	AB	H	DB	TP	HR	BB/SO	R	RBI	SB	CS	OUT	BA	OBP	SLG	EQA	EQR	DEFENSE
1997	KansasCy	AL	262	61	12	0	8	15/49	25	22	2	1	202	.233	.277	.370	.216	22	67-OF 101
1997	Omaha	AA	142	38	4	0	9	8/26	18	22	0	1	105	.268	.312	.486	.259	18	25-OF 89
1998	Omaha	PCL	156	42	5	0	10	16/30	22	28	5	0	114	.269	.340	.494	.280	24	33-OF 112
1998	KansasCy	AL	213	49	4	1	5	10/45	22	22	2	2	166	.230	.268	.329	.197	14	57-OF 108
1999	KansasCy	AL	602	175	44	8	25	51/119	87	108	2	3	430	.291	.347	.515	.281	90	154-RF 115
2000	KansasCy	AL	571	166	31	1	30	52/111	93	116	4	3	408	.291	.350	.506	.278	83	

Never underestimate the power of plate discipline, and never underestimate a player who is committed to improving himself. Dye was not prepared for the major leagues when he first had success with the Braves in 1996, but after spending time in Triple-A in 1997 and 1998, he learned to use the opposite field and lay off bad pitches.

Armed with his new knowledge and healthy for the first time in three years, Dye had a breakout year and deserves credit for making himself into a solid everyday player. As a 26-year-old "proven run producer" who plays good defense, he is perceived as a valuable commodity. The Royals should explore trading him even more aggressively than Damon, but his new contract is an indication they won't.

Mark Ellis — SS — Bats R — Age 23

YEAR	TEAM	LGE	AB	H	DB	TP	HR	BB/SO	R	RBI	SB	CS	OUT	BA	OBP	SLG	EQA	EQR	DEFENSE
1999	Spokane	Nwn	283	73	6	0	7	30/45	36	30	7	3	213	.258	.332	.353	.238	29	71-SS 107
2000	KansasCy	AL	145	41	2	0	5	22/38	25	24	3	1	105	.283	.377	.400	.268	19	

Ellis played above his ninth-round selection last year, running the Northwest League ragged with a .424 OBP and 67 runs scored in just 71 games. He's still several years away from the majors, but the Royals have never had a star-caliber shortstop, so be understanding if they promote Ellis aggressively.

Sal Fasano — C — Bats R — Age 28

YEAR	TEAM	LGE	AB	H	DB	TP	HR	BB/SO	R	RBI	SB	CS	OUT	BA	OBP	SLG	EQA	EQR	DEFENSE
1997	Wichita	Tex	131	24	4	0	8	15/45	17	16	0	1	108	.183	.293	.397	.230	14	
1997	Omaha	AA	152	22	7	0	3	10/59	15	12	0	0	130	.145	.222	.250	.144	5	
1998	KansasCy	AL	215	48	8	0	8	9/55	19	29	1	0	167	.223	.306	.372	.231	21	67-C 107
1999	Omaha	PCL	279	63	10	0	15	34/75	43	34	2	1	217	.226	.351	.423	.264	39	78-C 92
1999	KansasCy	AL	60	14	1	0	5	6/17	10	15	0	1	47	.233	.370	.500	.283	10	
2000	KansasCy	AL	321	69	9	0	18	35/90	37	48	1	1	253	.215	.292	.411	.230	32	

After losing the backup job to Tim Spehr, Fasano remade himself as a hitter and forced himself back into the Royals' long-term plans. After taking just six walks in his first 113 at-bats, Fasano converted to the Church of Plate Discipline, drawing 34 walks in his next 167 at-bats. That, along with a PCL-record 26 HBPs, helped him rack up a .415 OBP. He performed ably in his September audition and figures to have the starting job this spring. Catchers frequently take longer to develop their offense than other position players; I expect him to have a good year.

Carlos Febles — 2B — Bats R — Age 24

YEAR	TEAM	LGE	AB	H	DB	TP	HR	BB/SO	R	RBI	SB	CS	OUT	BA	OBP	SLG	EQA	EQR	DEFENSE
1997	Wilmngtn	Car	451	107	28	6	3	39/95	60	27	25	7	351	.237	.310	.346	.232	45	115-2B 96
1998	Wichita	Tex	422	112	23	6	10	64/78	70	36	25	9	319	.265	.372	.419	.275	63	115-2B 97
1999	KansasCy	AL	450	113	22	9	9	41/91	65	48	20	4	341	.251	.326	.400	.252	54	121-2B 95
2000	KansasCy	AL	424	113	24	6	8	51/83	79	57	21	6	317	.267	.345	.408	.258	53	

As advertised, Febles showed no one outstanding attribute in his rookie year but contributed in every phase of the game. On defense, he showed good range along with an ability to turn the double play. Offensively, he drew walks, stole bases and drove the ball. He played with a bum shoulder for much of the year, which hurt him in the field and held him to a .205 average after the All-Star break. A torn finger ligament ended his season. Second basemen are susceptible to injuries that impede their development, so there is some concern about this. Febles adjusts from at-bat to at-bat as well as any player on the team; if healthy and rested—the Royals made him sit out winter ball—he's almost a sure bet to improve.

Jeremy Giambi   1B/OF   Bats L   Age 25

YEAR	TEAM	LGE	AB	H	DB	TP	HR	BB/SO	R	RBI	SB	CS	OUT	BA	OBP	SLG	EQA	EQR	DEFENSE
1997	Lansing	Mid	118	32	8	1	4	17/17	22	15	2	1	87	.271	.370	.458	.279	18	
1997	Wichita	Tex	265	73	11	1	10	36/53	37	39	2	2	194	.275	.372	.438	.275	38	56-OF 100
1998	Omaha	PCL	321	110	19	2	17	51/64	55	55	6	4	215	.343	.440	.573	.331	68	61-OF 90
1999	Omaha	PCL	125	38	5	1	9	27/31	24	21	1	1	88	.304	.431	.576	.328	27	16-OF 116
1999	KansasCy	AL	285	80	12	1	3	36/67	31	31	0	0	205	.281	.367	.361	.255	34	25-1B 82
2000	KansasCy	AL	361	117	16	0	16	59/78	77	81	3	1	245	.324	.419	.501	.309	65	

He can't help himself; despite doing his best to disprove the idea that minor-league performance is meaningful, Giambi still had a promising rookie season. It was easy to see how the Royals' lack of confidence in him manifested itself at the plate. At times, it appeared he had decided to swing at a pitch before it even left the pitcher's hand, which was rather astonishing for such an ordinarily patient hitter. Not coincidentally, his power completely disappeared: his slugging average was lower than that of Rey Sanchez. In 452 Triple-A at-bats, Giambi has hit .365 with 32 homers and 88 walks. It would be almost unprecedented for such a dominant Triple-A hitter to fail in the majors.

Jed Hansen   IF   Bats R   Age 27

YEAR	TEAM	LGE	AB	H	DB	TP	HR	BB/SO	R	RBI	SB	CS	OUT	BA	OBP	SLG	EQA	EQR	DEFENSE	
1997	Omaha	AA	377	89	19	2	8	27/82	36	36	6	1	289	.236	.291	.361	.222	34	85-2B 100	24-SS 99
1997	KansasCy	AL	93	28	6	1	1	12/28	10	13	3	2	67	.301	.388	.419	.277	13	25-2B 97	
1998	Omaha	PCL	416	98	17	5	11	35/137	45	41	11	6	324	.236	.299	.380	.230	41	115-2B 99	
1999	Omaha	PCL	175	39	7	5	4	26/78	25	15	5	2	138	.223	.331	.389	.248	21	32-2B 93	21-SS 97
1999	KansasCy	AL	79	16	0	0	3	9/32	14	5	0	1	64	.203	.284	.316	.200	6		
2000	San Dieg	NL	268	56	9	2	8	36/98	32	30	6	3	215	.209	.303	.347	.231	28		

The Royals have given up on him, but I'm more convinced than ever of his ability to be a fabulous bench player. His skills do not include hitting for a high average, and the Royals have yet to adjust to the idea that a player with skills like power and plate discipline can be useful off the bench. The Padres claimed him off waivers; he should get more of an opportunity to contribute for an NL team.

Ken Harvey   1B   Bats R   Age 22

YEAR	TEAM	LGE	AB	H	DB	TP	HR	BB/SO	R	RBI	SB	CS	OUT	BA	OBP	SLG	EQA	EQR	DEFENSE
1999	Spokane	Nwn	202	65	11	0	7	14/33	29	26	2	1	138	.322	.376	.480	.287	30	35-1B 98
2000	KansasCy	AL	107	39	4	0	7	9/43	21	29	1	0	68	.364	.414	.598	.328	21	

Harvey was actually considered a bit of a reach in the fifth round last year, despite leading the nation in hitting in his junior year. All tools are not created equal: if you can hit like Frank Thomas, you're going to make a lot of money in this game, even if you do everything else as well as . . . er . . . Frank Thomas. Harvey hit .397 in his debut, nearly breaking the Northwest League record for batting average, with power and walks. It's not a stretch to think he could be in Triple-A by year's end. Disregard that projection; like the Wiltons of Ben Broussard and Sean Burroughs, it can't be taken seriously.

Ray Holbert   SS   Bats R   Age 29

YEAR	TEAM	LGE	AB	H	DB	TP	HR	BB/SO	R	RBI	SB	CS	OUT	BA	OBP	SLG	EQA	EQR	DEFENSE
1997	Toledo	Int	379	86	18	5	6	24/116	35	31	10	5	298	.227	.279	.348	.212	31	104-SS 152
1998	Ottawa	Int	265	70	14	3	1	21/73	28	19	5	3	198	.264	.318	.351	.229	25	74-SS 91
1999	Omaha	PCL	127	32	3	0	3	9/38	18	9	8	3	98	.252	.301	.346	.226	12	21-SS 101
1999	KansasCy	AL	99	27	2	0	0	7/20	12	4	7	4	76	.273	.321	.293	.216	8	
2000	KansasCy	AL	271	70	13	2	4	23/74	39	30	11	5	206	.258	.316	.365	.231	26	

Holbert defines the term "replacement player." He's been bouncing from one organization to another as a competent shortstop for any Triple-A team that needs one. Given an everyday job when both Febles and Rey Sanchez were out with injuries, he played just well enough to get consideration from the Royals as Sanchez's successor. With the Royals re-signing Sanchez, he'll be back in Triple-A.

Chad Kreuter   C   Bats B   Age 35

YEAR	TEAM	LGE	AB	H	DB	TP	HR	BB/SO	R	RBI	SB	CS	OUT	BA	OBP	SLG	EQA	EQR	DEFENSE
1997	Anaheim	AL	217	51	7	1	4	20/55	18	17	0	2	168	.235	.300	.332	.212	17	
1998	ChiSox	AL	245	63	9	1	2	31/44	25	32	1	0	182	.257	.348	.327	.238	25	73-C 101
1999	KansasCy	AL	322	71	10	0	6	31/65	27	33	0	0	251	.220	.301	.307	.209	25	87-C 102
2000	*KansasCy*	*AL*	*219*	*50*	*4*	*0*	*6*	*28/44*	*24*	*26*	*0*	*0*	*169*	*.228*	*.316*	*.329*	*.218*	*19*	

It's not his fault the Royals put him in a role they should have known he couldn't handle. He's a decent backup catcher, good for 30 starts a year against tough right-handed pitchers. He has no business playing every day, and Muser's decision to make him a starter stunted the offense and forced Mike Sweeney to give up catching for the year. Kreuter hit .102 in August and September, and whether his career is over depends on just how naive managers can be.

Mendy Lopez   SS/3B   Bats R   Age 25

YEAR	TEAM	LGE	AB	H	DB	TP	HR	BB/SO	R	RBI	SB	CS	OUT	BA	OBP	SLG	EQA	EQR	DEFENSE
1997	Wichita	Tex	356	74	14	2	5	28/79	42	33	4	3	285	.208	.270	.301	.191	23	100-SS 94
1998	Omaha	PCL	195	33	4	1	3	16/44	15	12	2	2	164	.169	.235	.246	.150	7	56-SS 102
1998	KansasCy	AL	205	49	10	2	1	11/39	17	14	4	2	158	.239	.281	.322	.203	15	64-SS 110
1999	Omaha	PCL	219	60	5	0	10	15/42	31	31	1	1	160	.274	.321	.434	.251	25	52-SS 102
2000	*KansasCy*	*AL*	*336*	*82*	*9*	*1*	*10*	*29/68*	*38*	*42*	*4*	*2*	*256*	*.244*	*.304*	*.366*	*.223*	*30*	

Lopez was overmatched in his first major-league opportunity in 1998, but returned to Triple-A last year and was much improved, adding power to his game. As an adequate shortstop who is considered an outstanding third baseman, Lopez was on his way to winning at least a bench job for 2000 when an Aaron Sele pitch fractured his ulna and ended his season. He should be healthy, and is capable of making a contribution if he gets the opportunity.

Felix Martinez   SS   Bats R   Age 26

YEAR	TEAM	LGE	AB	H	DB	TP	HR	BB/SO	R	RBI	SB	CS	OUT	BA	OBP	SLG	EQA	EQR	DEFENSE
1997	Omaha	AA	407	92	17	3	2	25/88	46	31	16	8	323	.226	.283	.297	.200	29	110-SS 93
1998	KansasCy	AL	85	11	0	1	0	5/21	6	4	3	1	75	.129	.187	.153	—	0	27-SS 102
1998	Omaha	PCL	163	37	7	2	2	13/41	21	13	4	2	128	.227	.287	.331	.211	13	41-SS 101
1999	Wichita	Tex	328	70	18	1	2	26/53	37	25	8	5	263	.213	.276	.293	.192	21	76-SS 97
2000	*Philadel*	*NL*	*299*	*67*	*15*	*2*	*2*	*24/58*	*33*	*22*	*13*	*5*	*237*	*.224*	*.282*	*.308*	*.201*	*21*	

Just when you thought it was safe to go back to the ballpark. . . . The year's worst September call-up returned to the major leagues because Herk Robinson thought he had learned to control his emotions. Of course, the reason Martinez doesn't belong in the majors has nothing to do with his character; it has to do with the fact that HE SUCKS. Mercifully claimed off waivers by the Phillies, so with any luck this will be the last time I have to write about him.

Sean McNally   3B/1B   Bats R   Age 27

YEAR	TEAM	LGE	AB	H	DB	TP	HR	BB/SO	R	RBI	SB	CS	OUT	BA	OBP	SLG	EQA	EQR	DEFENSE	
1997	Wilmngtn	Car	334	73	18	1	12	27/114	37	47	1	0	261	.219	.280	.386	.222	30	85-3B 96	
1998	Wichita	Tex	316	63	18	1	3	27/108	28	27	1	2	255	.199	.264	.291	.183	18	32-3B 92	27-1B 106
1999	Wichita	Tex	445	94	17	1	22	69/162	62	66	3	1	352	.211	.323	.402	.247	53	118-3B 94	
2000	*Florida*	*NL*	*369*	*76*	*15*	*1*	*14*	*48/134*	*42*	*45*	*2*	*1*	*294*	*.206*	*.297*	*.366*	*.230*	*37*		

A solid organizational player who had absolutely no prospect status, McNally started taking pitches out of desperation, nearly doubling his career high with 93 walks, and—stop me if you've heard this before—hitting for power, more than doubling his career high with 36 home runs. He did his best in the Arizona Fall League to prove his season was no fluke. As a 27-year-old corner infielder with no previous history of success, he'll have to take the Kevin Millar/Brian Daubach path to the majors. Traded to Florida for Todd Dunwoody.

Kit Pellow   3B   Bats R   Age 26

YEAR	TEAM	LGE	AB	H	DB	TP	HR	BB/SO	R	RBI	SB	CS	OUT	BA	OBP	SLG	EQA	EQR	DEFENSE
1997	Lansing	Mid	258	60	13	1	8	16/85	26	34	1	0	198	.233	.289	.384	.226	24	49-3B 72
1997	Wichita	Tex	240	51	11	1	8	16/84	29	30	3	1	190	.213	.266	.367	.211	20	65-3B 102
1998	Wichita	Tex	368	76	18	1	18	18/130	44	44	2	1	293	.207	.251	.408	.216	32	87-3B 90
1999	Omaha	PCL	469	113	23	3	24	15/127	62	69	4	3	359	.241	.284	.456	.242	52	126-3B 90
2000	*KansasCy*	*AL*	*482*	*116*	*21*	*1*	*24*	*28/143*	*53*	*73*	*2*	*1*	*367*	*.241*	*.282*	*.438*	*.233*	*48*	

The answer to that killer SAT question: "Who comes next in the following sequence: Phil Hiatt, Craig Paquette, ???" Pellow's light-tower power occasionally obscures the fact that his swing has more holes than Jeff Bower's socks. The Royals wisely excluded him from their September call-ups, but Royals fans are kept awake at night by the knowledge that he's an injury away from the starting job.

Paul Phillips   C   Bats R   Age 23

YEAR	TEAM	LGE	AB	H	DB	TP	HR	BB/SO	R	RBI	SB	CS	OUT	BA	OBP	SLG	EQA	EQR	DEFENSE
1998	Spokane	Nwn	235	61	12	1	3	9/21	34	16	4	1	175	.260	.293	.357	.220	20	47-C 101
1999	Wichita	Tex	392	92	20	1	2	20/41	46	44	4	4	304	.235	.275	.306	.192	25	97-C 102
2000	*KansasCy*	*AL*	*248*	*65*	*13*	*1*	*2*	*13/28*	*26*	*25*	*2*	*2*	*185*	*.262*	*.299*	*.347*	*.212*	*19*	

An outfielder in college, Phillips was converted to catcher after he was drafted in 1998 and played so well that he was ranked the #1 prospect in the Northwest League. Like Dodson, he jumped a pair of levels to play in Double-A last year. Also like Dodson, he recovered slightly from a terrible start, hitting 40 points higher in the second half of the season. He needs another year at Wichita to consolidate; then we'll know if he's really a prospect.

Scott Pose   OF   Bats L   Age 33

YEAR	TEAM	LGE	AB	H	DB	TP	HR	BB/SO	R	RBI	SB	CS	OUT	BA	OBP	SLG	EQA	EQR	DEFENSE
1997	Columbus	Int	230	62	10	6	1	25/31	39	25	8	3	171	.270	.353	.378	.255	28	56-OF 98
1997	NY Yanks	AL	87	20	2	1	0	9/11	18	5	3	1	68	.230	.302	.276	.204	6	31-OF 83
1998	Columbus	Int	487	124	20	7	2	39/80	54	36	25	9	372	.255	.316	.337	.229	47	100-OF 89
1999	KansasCy	AL	135	37	3	0	0	20/22	25	11	6	2	100	.274	.368	.296	.243	15	
2000	*KansasCy*	*AL*	*228*	*56*	*8*	*2*	*1*	*31/36*	*35*	*21*	*7*	*3*	*175*	*.246*	*.336*	*.311*	*.226*	*21*	

Rarely is a player so perfectly matched to his role. There are some things Pose can't do, like hit the ball more than about 200 feet. However, he can play all three outfield positions, reach first base and steal second. Placed in exactly that role as the team's fourth outfielder, Pose excelled. The turnover in bench roles means that Pose will lose his job in the middle of his first slump, but there's always another team looking to employ John Cangelosi Jr.

Mark Quinn   LF   Bats R   Age 26

YEAR	TEAM	LGE	AB	H	DB	TP	HR	BB/SO	R	RBI	SB	CS	OUT	BA	OBP	SLG	EQA	EQR	DEFENSE
1997	Wilmngtn	Car	309	81	18	2	12	31/51	38	51	1	1	229	.262	.340	.450	.264	41	57-OF 78
1997	Wichita	Tex	94	30	6	0	3	12/22	18	15	1	1	65	.319	.409	.479	.299	16	17-OF 97
1998	Wichita	Tex	362	95	18	3	10	30/66	51	51	2	1	268	.262	.330	.412	.251	42	87-OF 89
1999	Omaha	PCL	420	125	17	0	19	21/75	47	60	5	6	300	.298	.342	.474	.268	56	101-OF 98
1999	KansasCy	AL	59	19	4	1	6	4/11	10	17	1	0	40	.322	.375	.729	.338	13	
2000	*KansasCy*	*AL*	*463*	*142*	*21*	*1*	*25*	*44/83*	*80*	*99*	*5*	*3*	*324*	*.307*	*.367*	*.518*	*.288*	*72*	

The Royals have no room for any more outfield prospects, but the Mighty Quinn refuses to make their decisions any easier. Despite a swing so awkward and violent that he nearly falls down on his follow-through, he has now won batting titles in each of the last two years, a feat doubly impressive for a right-handed hitter. Last year he was rated the best defensive outfielder in the PCL, and he was so awed by the majors that he became the first player in 35 years to hit two homers in his first game. He's supposed to be too old to have real star potential. Then again, he's torn off every other label slapped on him, so why should he stop now?

Joe Randa   3B   Bats R   Age 30

YEAR	TEAM	LGE	AB	H	DB	TP	HR	BB/SO	R	RBI	SB	CS	OUT	BA	OBP	SLG	EQA	EQR	DEFENSE
1997	Pittsbrg	NL	447	134	30	9	7	40/63	58	59	3	2	315	.300	.365	.454	.276	63	115-3B 96
1998	Detroit	AL	458	115	21	2	9	39/68	53	48	7	7	350	.251	.320	.365	.232	45	108-3B 99
1999	KansasCy	AL	622	192	36	8	15	42/80	84	77	5	4	434	.309	.355	.465	.273	85	154-3B 102
2000	KansasCy	AL	518	153	27	4	13	47/69	80	86	4	4	369	.295	.354	.438	.263	66	

Ironically, the acquisition of Randa from the Mets for former #1 draft pick Juan LeBron raised such a fury in Kansas City that it threatened to finally cost Robinson his job. LeBron injured himself in spring training and missed the entire year, while Randa had a wonderful season. I generally don't believe in fluke seasons; if a player can sustain a new level of performance for an entire year, it's improvement. His defense has improved since his first tour of duty in Kansas City and he's only 30. At less than $800,000, he's a hell of a bargain.

Rey Sanchez   SS   Bats R   Age 32

YEAR	TEAM	LGE	AB	H	DB	TP	HR	BB/SO	R	RBI	SB	CS	OUT	BA	OBP	SLG	EQA	EQR	DEFENSE	
1997	ChiCubs	NL	205	50	4	0	3	11/26	13	13	3	2	157	.244	.282	.307	.197	14	36-SS 88	24-2B 99
1997	NY Yanks	AL	139	45	9	0	2	4/20	20	16	0	4	98	.324	.348	.432	.252	16	29-2B 107	
1998	San Fran	NL	321	96	16	2	2	16/46	46	31	0	0	225	.299	.341	.380	.246	34	56-SS 104	21-2B 111
1999	KansasCy	AL	476	138	16	6	2	16/48	59	52	11	5	343	.290	.319	.361	.232	44	128-SS 113	
2000	KansasCy	AL	295	87	11	1	2	17/33	36	35	3	3	211	.295	.333	.359	.232	27		

With excellent defense and the unique ability to hit singles on pitches at his shoetops, Sanchez was better than advertised. Sanchez is always going to be overrated as long as batting average is considered a seminal statistic, and there are dozens of players with his skills available on the cheap. That didn't stop the Royals from signing him to a two-year, $4.7 million deal. It's a mistake, even though he's an excellent fielder.

Tim Spehr   C   Bats R   Age 33

YEAR	TEAM	LGE	AB	H	DB	TP	HR	BB/SO	R	RBI	SB	CS	OUT	BA	OBP	SLG	EQA	EQR	DEFENSE
1997	Richmond	Int	122	22	4	0	3	9/39	11	12	0	0	100	.180	.242	.287	.170	6	
1999	KansasCy	AL	157	32	6	0	9	20/47	24	24	1	0	125	.204	.317	.414	.248	19	52-C 93
2000	KansasCy	AL	111	22	2	0	6	15/54	13	15	0	0	89	.198	.294	.378	.223	10	

The Royals' bizarre Spehr fetish—this was his third tour of duty with the team—continues to fly directly in the face of reason. Spehr, who had a career average of .195 in parts of seven major-league seasons coming into last year, nevertheless set a career high in at-bats and hit .206 while throwing out just eight of 43 base-stealers. With that kind of performance, I doubt he'll be seen again in a Royals uniform. At least not until Opening Day, anyway.

Larry Sutton   1B   Bats L   Age 30

Year	Team	Lge	AB	H	DB	TP	HR	BB/SO	R	RBI	SB	CS	Out	BA	OBP	SLG	EQA	EQR	Defense
1997	Omaha	AA	377	92	21	1	13	50/64	46	53	0	0	285	.244	.333	.408	.252	45	101-1B 100
1998	KansasCy	AL	308	74	14	2	5	27/45	27	40	2	3	237	.240	.308	.347	.222	27	72-OF 93
1999	Omaha	PCL	148	34	6	1	2	22/26	20	9	2	1	115	.230	.332	.324	.231	15	31-1B 91
1999	KansasCy	AL	101	22	3	0	3	12/17	12	15	1	0	79	.218	.301	.337	.220	9	22-1B 92
2000	St Louis	NL	204	47	6	0	6	32/34	26	26	1	1	158	.230	.335	.348	.237	22	

Tony Muser looks at Sutton and sees himself looking back, which led to the pointless tirades about the importance of good defense at first base, and forced Giambi to stew in Omaha after Jeff King retired. Sutton passed through waivers after the season without getting claimed, which should tell Muser all he needs to know. Sutton signed a minor-league contract with the Cardinals.

Mike Sweeney   1B/C   Bats R   Age 26

YEAR	TEAM	LGE	AB	H	DB	TP	HR	BB/SO	R	RBI	SB	CS	OUT	BA	OBP	SLG	EQA	EQR	DEFENSE
1997	Omaha	AA	143	30	7	1	8	16/20	19	24	0	1	114	.210	.299	.441	.243	17	
1997	KansasCy	AL	239	57	5	0	8	15/32	28	30	3	2	184	.238	.303	.360	.225	22	
1998	KansasCy	AL	280	71	13	0	9	23/37	29	33	2	3	212	.254	.315	.396	.238	29	82-C 98
1999	KansasCy	AL	568	180	43	2	21	47/48	92	93	6	1	389	.317	.379	.511	.296	93	72-1B 89
2000	KansasCy	AL	454	132	27	1	19	44/44	75	86	3	1	323	.291	.353	.480	.275	64	

(Mike Sweeney *continued*)

After coming thisclose to being sent to the White Sox in March—even the Royals' front office won't deny he was as good as gone before Giambi went on the disabled list—he had the season we all thought he was capable of. That it came as a first baseman detracts from his value, especially since his defensive shortcomings behind the plate have been grossly exaggerated by the Royals. But catching prospects frequently don't reach their offensive potential as well as other players, and Sweeney's offense proved to be more than enough to carry first base. Even now, Muser, who played 10 major-league seasons as a good-field, no-hit first baseman, is not convinced that Sweeney can play the position. Wake up, Tony: defense at first base isn't very important.

Geoffrey Tomlinson   OF   Bats L   Age 23

YEAR	TEAM	LGE	AB	H	DB	TP	HR	BB/SO	R	RBI	SB	CS	OUT	BA	OBP	SLG	EQA	EQR	DEFENSE
1997	Spokane	Nwn	209	54	9	0	4	19/21	25	18	5	1	156	.258	.333	.359	.242	22	55-OF 105
1998	Lansing	Mid	280	70	14	4	8	32/35	40	31	8	3	213	.250	.333	.414	.255	35	61-OF 109
1998	Wilmngtn	Car	141	39	8	1	0	13/25	15	15	1	1	103	.277	.338	.348	.236	14	29-OF 105
1999	Wichita	Tex	480	114	28	2	3	59/89	75	35	13	9	375	.237	.325	.323	.226	45	128-OF 108
2000	*KansasCy*	*AL*	*452*	*122*	*25*	*2*	*9*	*56/75*	*76*	*62*	*12*	*7*	*337*	*.270*	*.350*	*.394*	*.252*	*54*	

Tomlinson, a Rice alumnus, is well thought of for his ability to hit line drives and draw walks. While both skills are certainly useful, he does neither often enough to be anything more than a marginal prospect. Think "Orlando Palmeiro," and you'll be neither disappointed nor particularly impressed.

Joe Vitiello   DH/1B   Bats R   Age 30

YEAR	TEAM	LGE	AB	H	DB	TP	HR	BB/SO	R	RBI	SB	CS	OUT	BA	OBP	SLG	EQA	EQR	DEFENSE
1997	KansasCy	AL	129	31	5	0	5	13/36	10	17	0	0	98	.240	.321	.395	.243	14	18-OF 105
1998	Omaha	PCL	374	91	17	1	13	31/74	32	52	0	0	283	.243	.309	.398	.238	39	89-1B 89
1999	Omaha	PCL	443	115	21	1	20	53/91	49	69	2	2	330	.260	.343	.447	.265	59	39-1B 84
1999	KansasCy	AL	41	6	0	0	1	2/9	3	3	0	0	35	.146	.222	.220	.126	1	
2000	*Seattle*	*AL*	*388*	*97*	*13*	*0*	*15*	*45/80*	*51*	*59*	*1*	*1*	*292*	*.250*	*.328*	*.399*	*.249*	*45*	

Like Fasano, he appeared to be washed up in this organization, but avoided the guillotine with a fine season in Triple-A. Unlike Fasano, he found himself under the blade after the season anyway, and with good reason. The Royals have several first-base options, and most of them are better than playing a 30-year-old former failed prospect who's slower than a Commodore 64.

PITCHERS (Averages: ERA: 4.50 / H/9: 9.00 / HR/9: 1.00 / BB/9: 3.50 / K/9: 6.50 / KWH: 1.00)

Jeff Austin   Throws R   Age 23

YEAR	TEAM	LGE	IP	H	ER	HR	BB	K	ERA	W	L	H/9	HR/9	BB/9	K/9	KWH	PERA
1999	Wilmngtn	Car	103.0	141	67	13	45	69	5.85	4	7	12.32	1.14	3.93	6.03	0.56	6.82
1999	Wichita	Tex	32.7	45	21	1	13	17	5.79	2	2	12.40	0.28	3.58	4.68	0.37	5.79

After protracted negotiations that were declared dead on more than one occasion, the Royals finally signed the 1998 College Player of the Year for $2.7 million in February. Austin was far from overpowering: a 3.77 ERA at Wilmington is simply not that impressive. He showed more consistency as the year went on and pitched fairly well in six starts for Wichita. He was then shut down with elbow soreness, but returned to pitch well in the Arizona Fall League. If healthy, I think he could be a poor man's Kris Benson, which sounds a lot better now than it did a year ago.

Brian Barber   Throws R   Age 27

YEAR	TEAM	LGE	IP	H	ER	HR	BB	K	ERA	W	L	H/9	HR/9	BB/9	K/9	KWH	PERA
1997	Louisvil	AmA	90.0	124	89	19	51	65	8.90	2	8	12.40	1.90	5.10	6.50	0.50	8.40
1998	Omaha	PCL	127.7	128	69	22	62	81	4.86	6	8	9.02	1.55	4.37	5.71	0.62	5.43
1998	KansasCy	AL	43.3	42	24	5	14	25	4.98	2	3	8.72	1.04	2.91	5.19	0.79	4.15
1999	Omaha	PCL	111.0	142	74	19	35	59	6.00	4	8	11.51	1.54	2.84	4.78	0.52	6.32

Great arm, no pitching instincts. It is a law of physics that when a moving object strikes a wall, its rebound velocity will be in direct proportion to its original velocity. What that means, Brian, is that the harder you throw your straight fastball, the more home runs (21 in Triple-A, six in just 19 major-league innings) you'll give up. Barber's unhealthy fear of throwing strikes to major-league hitters renders him worse than useless.

Jamie Bluma — Throws R — Age 28

YEAR	TEAM	LGE	IP	H	ER	HR	BB	K	ERA	W	L	H/9	HR/9	BB/9	K/9	KWH	PERA
1998	Wichita	Tex	58.0	75	54	9	45	29	8.38	1	5	11.64	1.40	6.98	4.50	0.19	8.07
1998	Omaha	PCL	13.0	21	14	4	8	6	9.69	0	1	14.54	2.77	5.54	4.15	0.16	11.08
1999	Wichita	Tex	34.3	50	31	9	22	15	8.13	1	3	13.11	2.36	5.77	3.93	0.15	9.70
1999	Omaha	PCL	20.7	24	11	5	5	15	4.79	1	1	10.45	2.18	2.18	6.53	1.40	6.10

The one-time closer-of-the-future disappeared completely from public view in his second year of rehab from shoulder surgery, yet quietly made impressive strides in his comeback. His velocity picked up during the season, and his command was close to his pre-injury form in the second half, with an excellent strikeout-to-walk ratio of 19-to-4. His pitches are still too straight to fool major-league hitters, but Bluma knows how to pitch well enough to compensate. It's hard to say whether he'll recover enough to pitch effectively in the majors; in all honesty, I'm impressed that he's made it back this far.

Tim Byrdak — Throws L — Age 26

YEAR	TEAM	LGE	IP	H	ER	HR	BB	K	ERA	W	L	H/9	HR/9	BB/9	K/9	KWH	PERA
1997	Wilmngtn	Car	37.7	44	22	4	15	32	5.26	2	2	10.51	0.96	3.58	7.65	1.16	5.26
1998	Wichita	Tex	49.7	62	30	3	36	29	5.44	2	4	11.23	0.54	6.52	5.26	0.28	6.52
1998	Omaha	PCL	34.7	33	14	3	23	27	3.63	2	2	8.57	0.78	5.97	7.01	0.72	4.93
1999	Omaha	PCL	46.7	41	21	0	33	40	4.05	3	2	7.91	0.00	6.36	7.71	0.88	4.05
1999	KansasCy	AL	25.0	31	22	5	19	17	7.92	1	2	11.16	1.80	6.84	6.12	0.37	8.28

As horrible as his rookie season was, I'm not entirely convinced Byrdak can't help a major-league team. The Royals had him alter his motion in spring training, turning him into a sidearm pitcher and making him deadly against left-handers, holding them to an incredible .135/.182/.154 in Triple-A. In the major leagues, while right-handers took more shots at him than at a clay pigeon, left-handed hitters still hit only .212. Success as a one-out specialist is rare for a young pitcher, and even specialists end up without the platoon advantage at least half the time, so I'm skeptical.

Lance Carter — Throws R — Age 25

YEAR	TEAM	LGE	IP	H	ER	HR	BB	K	ERA	W	L	H/9	HR/9	BB/9	K/9	KWH	PERA
1998	Lansing	Mid	36.3	50	11	1	13	24	2.72	3	1	12.39	0.25	3.22	5.94	0.66	5.45
1998	Wilmngtn	Car	46.7	68	31	7	21	41	5.98	2	3	13.11	1.35	4.05	7.91	0.88	7.71
1999	Wichita	Tex	65.7	58	12	1	35	57	1.64	6	1	7.95	0.14	4.80	7.81	1.20	3.56

In a season full of bizarre twists for the Royals, this may be the most surreal fact of all: despite having one of the worst bullpens of all time, they simply ignored a relief prospect with an ERA under 1.00 in a hitters' park. Carter is a Tommy-John-surgery survivor whose fastball tops out around 90 mph but *moves*, and he changes speeds and varies his delivery so that no two pitches are the same. He was grudgingly called up in September and impressed Muser in a half-dozen outings. The Royals finally call him a prospect, but if they had used any common sense, they might already be calling him their closer.

Jeffrey D'Amico — Throws R — Age 25

YEAR	TEAM	LGE	IP	H	ER	HR	BB	K	ERA	W	L	H/9	HR/9	BB/9	K/9	KWH	PERA
1997	Modesto	Cal	90.0	133	63	6	39	62	6.30	3	7	13.30	0.60	3.90	6.20	0.55	6.80
1997	Edmonton	PCL	29.3	42	25	6	6	16	7.67	1	2	12.89	1.84	1.84	4.91	0.76	7.06
1999	Midland	Tex	44.0	58	34	4	22	29	6.95	1	4	11.86	0.82	4.50	5.93	0.49	6.34
1999	Vancouvr	PCL	15.0	18	7	1	11	8	4.20	1	1	10.80	0.60	6.60	4.80	0.24	6.60
1999	Omaha	PCL	17.3	31	14	1	4	10	7.27	1	1	16.10	0.52	2.08	5.19	0.60	7.79

The other Jeff D'Amico is a converted infielder who supposedly throws in the mid-90s, so despite no history of actually getting hitters out, the Royals insisted on getting him in the Kevin Appier deal. Given his lack of experience, he's a better prospect than his numbers would suggest, which means nothing: his numbers suck. Check back next year. Or don't; it probably won't matter either way.

Chad Durbin   Throws R   Age 22

YEAR	TEAM	LGE	IP	H	ER	HR	BB	K	ERA	W	L	H/9	HR/9	BB/9	K/9	KWH	PERA
1997	Lansing	Mid	134.7	199	103	19	66	82	6.88	4	11	13.30	1.27	4.41	5.48	0.38	7.82
1998	Wilmngtn	Car	136.3	161	76	14	79	116	5.02	7	8	10.63	0.92	5.22	7.66	0.79	6.07
1999	Wichita	Tex	150.0	174	96	20	60	99	5.76	6	11	10.44	1.20	3.60	5.94	0.70	5.58

Durbin doesn't have flashy stats or a first-round pedigree to herald his advance through the minor leagues, and going 8-10 with a 4.64 ERA in Double-A is hardly a sign of greatness. But he's very poised on the mound, and has the guts to throw his outstanding change-up on any count to any batter—doing so to great effect in his major-league debut. A 22-year-old with a strikeout-to-walk ratio of 2.5-to-1 (in a good hitters' park), with no injury history, a record of success and a strong finish is exactly the kind of pitcher who could surprise everyone and become a star.

Chris Fussell   Throws R   Age 24

YEAR	TEAM	LGE	IP	H	ER	HR	BB	K	ERA	W	L	H/9	HR/9	BB/9	K/9	KWH	PERA
1997	Frederck	Car	47.7	52	27	6	35	40	5.10	2	3	9.82	1.13	6.61	7.55	0.66	6.42
1997	Bowie	Eas	74.7	119	79	11	62	57	9.52	1	7	14.34	1.33	7.47	6.87	0.33	10.00
1998	Bowie	Eas	90.0	99	60	14	59	69	6.00	4	6	9.90	1.40	5.90	6.90	0.61	6.50
1998	Rochestr	Int	55.7	56	33	4	30	45	5.34	2	4	9.05	0.65	4.85	7.28	0.90	4.69
1999	Omaha	PCL	77.3	70	36	10	30	66	4.19	5	4	8.15	1.16	3.49	7.68	1.55	4.19
1999	KansasCy	AL	56.7	69	45	8	35	38	7.15	2	4	10.96	1.27	5.56	6.04	0.45	6.83

Shrewdly acquired from Baltimore for Jeff Conine just before the 1999 season, Fussell pitched well in Omaha. In the major leagues he would usually keep his composure for about two innings before he remembered he was facing major-league hitters, at which point his outings would degenerate into a series of four-pitch walks and grooved fastballs. He was finally moved to the bullpen in August, but by then his season was shot. I have little doubt that with good tutelage he can be successful in the major leagues.

Chris George   Throws L   Age 20

YEAR	TEAM	LGE	IP	H	ER	HR	BB	K	ERA	W	L	H/9	HR/9	BB/9	K/9	KWH	PERA
1999	Wilmngtn	Car	135.7	177	80	11	61	104	5.31	6	9	11.74	0.73	4.05	6.90	0.75	6.04

The minor leagues were impossibly deep in left-handed teenage pitching prospects last year, and while Rick Ankiel, Matt Riley and Ryan Anderson got the headlines, Chris George quietly staked his own claim on being the next great southpaw. Most teams were surprised when George was taken as a supplemental first-rounder in 1998, because his fastball is only in the high 80s, but George impressed the Royals enough that they started him in the Carolina League in his first full year. He matched Jeff Austin start-for-start despite spotting Austin three years of experience. There's a lot of quiet excitement in the organization about George, and with good reason.

Junior Guerrero   Throws R   Age 20

YEAR	TEAM	LGE	IP	H	ER	HR	BB	K	ERA	W	L	H/9	HR/9	BB/9	K/9	KWH	PERA
1999	Charl-WV	SAL	95.3	122	55	8	63	73	5.19	5	6	11.52	0.76	5.95	6.89	0.52	6.70
1999	Wilmngtn	Car	48.7	39	12	3	29	49	2.22	4	1	7.21	0.55	5.36	9.06	1.59	3.88

Even less heralded than George, Guerrero pitched well for a bad Charleston club, then posted a 1.40 ERA in nine starts for Wilmington, with 68 strikeouts against just 30 hits. He led the organization with 181 strikeouts, and on the precept that the best pitching prospect is a power pitcher, Guerrero is the best pitching prospect the Royals have. He's just the kind of pitcher who could get called up in July and go 8-4 down the stretch, so watch him closely this year.

Mike MacDougal   Throws R   Age 23

YEAR	TEAM	LGE	IP	H	ER	HR	BB	K	ERA	W	L	H/9	HR/9	BB/9	K/9	KWH	PERA
1999	Spokane	Nwn	40.3	59	32	3	19	36	7.14	1	3	13.17	0.67	4.24	8.03	0.86	6.92

The second of the Royals' two first-round picks last year, MacDougal teamed with fellow first-rounder Kyle Snyder and second-rounder Brian Sanches to lead Spokane to an easy romp over the Northwest League. The trio combined for 133 strikeouts in 104 innings, and represent the Royals' best hope of rebuilding their pathetic pitching staff. They were all named among the top 10 prospects in the league by *Baseball America;* the one with the brightest future will be the one who, five years from now, has no idea what general anesthesia feels like.

Jeff Montgomery — Throws R — Age 38

YEAR	TEAM	LGE	IP	H	ER	HR	BB	K	ERA	W	L	H/9	HR/9	BB/9	K/9	KWH	PERA
1997	KansasCy	AL	60.0	52	22	8	18	49	3.30	5	2	7.80	1.20	2.70	7.35	1.92	3.75
1998	KansasCy	AL	58.0	54	29	7	23	55	4.50	3	3	8.38	1.09	3.57	8.53	1.82	4.19
1999	KansasCy	AL	51.3	70	36	6	20	28	6.31	2	4	12.27	1.05	3.51	4.91	0.42	6.49

He deserved to go out on better terms, but we hope people remember him as one of the game's best closers from 1989 to 1993, and as a loyal, honorable player who took less money to stay with the same team for essentially his entire career. Every great player leaves a subtle impact on the game, and Montgomery's legacy will be having shown that a four-pitch pitcher with only an average fastball can be just as effective a closer as a flamethrower. He may have been the first closer to use his change-up as his out pitch, a style that has found an outstanding disciple in Trevor Hoffman.

Orber Moreno — Throws R — Age 23

YEAR	TEAM	LGE	IP	H	ER	HR	BB	K	ERA	W	L	H/9	HR/9	BB/9	K/9	KWH	PERA
1997	Lansing	Mid	129.7	189	100	19	56	91	6.94	4	10	13.12	1.32	3.89	6.32	0.58	7.57
1998	Wilmngtn	Car	32.3	9	4	2	13	35	1.11	4	0	2.51	0.56	3.62	9.74	7.82	1.11
1998	Wichita	Tex	34.3	28	12	1	14	33	3.15	3	1	7.34	0.26	3.67	8.65	2.08	2.88
1999	Omaha	PCL	24.7	18	6	2	5	25	2.19	2	1	6.57	0.73	1.82	9.12	5.19	2.55

The Royals certainly can't blame their terrible record on injuries, because the lineup and rotation were both essentially healthy all year. Moreno, who followed up his amazing 1998 with an outstanding winter campaign, developed biceps tendinitis just as he was poised to take over the closer role in June, and was lost for the year. There is some concern that what appeared to be a three-week problem took three months to go away. Moreno's health is absolutely essential to the revival of the Royals' bullpen and, with it, any chance for respectability this season.

Robbie Morrison — Throws R — Age 23

YEAR	TEAM	LGE	IP	H	ER	HR	BB	K	ERA	W	L	H/9	HR/9	BB/9	K/9	KWH	PERA
1998	Spokane	Nwn	22.7	22	11	3	21	22	4.37	2	1	8.74	1.19	8.34	8.74	0.78	6.35
1999	Wilmngtn	Car	41.0	40	17	3	15	33	3.73	3	2	8.78	0.66	3.29	7.24	1.36	3.95
1999	Wichita	Tex	21.3	29	8	0	9	17	3.38	1	1	12.23	0.00	3.80	7.17	0.83	5.48

No doubt happy that Warren Morris had his great rookie season in the NL, Morrison figures to make his own mark on the AL before long. The Florida State closer blew through Wilmington and showed surprisingly good command in his first full year. As the Royals await Congressional approval of disaster funding for their bullpen, Morrison will be awfully tempting as a setup man if he has a good March.

Dan Murray — Throws R — Age 26

YEAR	TEAM	LGE	IP	H	ER	HR	BB	K	ERA	W	L	H/9	HR/9	BB/9	K/9	KWH	PERA
1997	St Lucie	Fla	145.7	189	100	6	78	67	6.18	6	10	11.68	0.37	4.82	4.14	0.23	5.93
1998	Binghmtn	Eas	153.3	189	84	14	67	120	4.93	8	9	11.09	0.82	3.93	7.04	0.85	5.69
1999	Norfolk	Int	141.0	155	88	20	77	82	5.62	6	10	9.89	1.28	4.91	5.23	0.42	5.87

Herk Robinson loves to trade with the Mets, and the Royals have had their eye on Murray for years. They gave up on Glendon Rusch to acquire him, which is probably best for all involved. Murray has a good breaking ball and supposedly has good command of all his pitches, though you wouldn't know it from his performance at Norfolk last year.

Ken Ray — Throws R — Age 25

YEAR	TEAM	LGE	IP	H	ER	HR	BB	K	ERA	W	L	H/9	HR/9	BB/9	K/9	KWH	PERA
1997	Omaha	AmA	118.7	132	81	19	73	89	6.14	5	8	10.01	1.44	5.54	6.75	0.61	6.45
1998	Wichita	Tex	115.0	156	78	7	56	58	6.10	5	8	12.21	0.55	4.38	4.54	0.29	6.26
1999	Wichita	Tex	19.7	27	15	3	13	14	6.86	1	1	12.36	1.37	5.95	6.41	0.42	8.24
1999	Omaha	PCL	40.3	45	29	9	14	29	6.47	1	3	10.04	2.01	3.12	6.47	1.00	6.02
1999	KansasCy	AL	11.3	22	11	2	6	0	8.74	0	1	17.47	1.59	4.76	0.00	0.00	11.12

The Wengert Company is proud to unveil its new model. Ray had been teasing the Royals with his high-velocity, no-movement fastball for years, and was marginally successful in the minors after adding a change-up and moving to relief. He pitched five scoreless innings after a midseason call-up, but then the wheels came off, along with the axles, transmission, both side doors

(Ken Ray *continued*)

and the steering column: 24 of the next 43 batters he faced reached base before Ray was shipped out. His fastball was so straight that exactly zero of the 56 major-league batters he faced struck out. Any success he has will be purely accidental.

Dan Reichert — Throws R — Age 23

YEAR	TEAM	LGE	IP	H	ER	HR	BB	K	ERA	W	L	H/9	HR/9	BB/9	K/9	KWH	PERA
1997	Spokane	Nwn	34.0	53	32	3	20	22	8.47	1	3	14.03	0.79	5.29	5.82	0.34	8.21
1998	Lansing	Mid	33.0	35	22	0	25	24	6.00	1	3	9.55	0.00	6.82	6.55	0.49	5.18
1998	Wichita	Tex	35.3	53	38	7	34	20	9.68	1	3	13.50	1.78	8.66	5.09	0.17	10.70
1999	Omaha	PCL	106.3	95	51	8	56	101	4.32	6	6	8.04	0.68	4.74	8.55	1.43	4.15
1999	KansasCy	AL	37.0	46	34	2	32	21	8.27	1	3	11.19	0.49	7.78	5.11	0.22	7.05

This is why Mark Wiley should have been fired. Reichert, who was leading the PCL in strikeouts when he was recalled, completely lost confidence in a fastball that Triple-A observers had called "filthy." With only his slider to throw for strikes, Reichert gave up 20 walks and 23 hits in 14 innings over four starts. He pitched better in August (4.76 ERA) before a line drive left him with a stress fracture in his right arm and ended his season. On one hand, it disabled Reichert just as he was regaining confidence in himself, but on the other it gave his arm some rest after he had worked deep into a lot of games in Triple-A. One thing is for sure: he only adds to the uncertainty regarding the Royals' pitching staff this year.

Brad Rigby — Throws R — Age 27

YEAR	TEAM	LGE	IP	H	ER	HR	BB	K	ERA	W	L	H/9	HR/9	BB/9	K/9	KWH	PERA
1997	Edmonton	PCL	78.3	96	46	9	27	41	5.29	4	5	11.03	1.03	3.10	4.71	0.48	5.51
1997	Oakland	AL	80.7	84	37	13	22	34	4.13	5	4	9.37	1.45	2.45	3.79	0.47	4.80
1998	Edmonton	PCL	65.0	96	56	4	20	28	7.75	2	5	13.29	0.55	2.77	3.88	0.31	6.23
1999	Oakland	AL	62.7	66	27	4	25	27	3.88	4	3	9.48	0.57	3.59	3.88	0.33	4.31
1999	KansasCy	AL	21.3	33	18	5	4	10	7.59	1	1	13.92	2.11	1.69	4.22	0.57	8.02

Your standard 10th pitcher, Rigby is able to stay in the major leagues by virtue of a sinking fastball that gets him enough double-play balls to eliminate some of the many baserunners he yields. He's everything Marc Pisciotta was supposed to be, and Pisciotta wasn't supposed to be that good.

Jose Rosado — Throws L — Age 25

YEAR	TEAM	LGE	IP	H	ER	HR	BB	K	ERA	W	L	H/9	HR/9	BB/9	K/9	KWH	PERA
1997	KansasCy	AL	206.3	202	107	24	74	131	4.67	11	12	8.81	1.05	3.23	5.71	0.86	4.32
1998	KansasCy	AL	180.7	166	89	22	60	138	4.43	10	10	8.27	1.10	2.99	6.87	1.43	3.99
1999	KansasCy	AL	209.0	189	91	21	70	145	3.92	13	10	8.14	0.90	3.01	6.24	1.19	3.75

10-14, my rear end. Rosado is one of the 10 best pitchers in the league, and his record reflects an almost comic betrayal by his teammates. He's only 25 this year, and has thrown enough pitches over the last four years that the possibility of serious injury has to be a consideration. In the past, he has responded to overwork by losing his command and getting hit hard, so even if he's healthy enough to pitch, he may not be healthy enough to pitch well.

Jose Santiago — Throws R — Age 25

YEAR	TEAM	LGE	IP	H	ER	HR	BB	K	ERA	W	L	H/9	HR/9	BB/9	K/9	KWH	PERA
1997	Wichita	Tex	25.3	34	13	1	9	10	4.62	1	2	12.08	0.36	3.20	3.55	0.24	5.33
1998	Wichita	Tex	70.3	83	34	8	32	25	4.35	4	4	10.62	1.02	4.09	3.20	0.18	5.76
1999	KansasCy	AL	47.3	44	21	7	14	15	3.99	3	2	8.37	1.33	2.66	2.85	0.27	4.18

Despite no real history of success in the minor leagues, and no out pitch with which to rack up strikeouts, Santiago has been a Royals favorite because he throws the best pitch in baseball: a live, moving fastball. He was a surprise addition to the Opening Day roster and pitched quite well before a sore shoulder cost him three months. He resembles Hipolito Pichardo, who also had a fastball that danced enough that he could get away with throwing it 90% of the time. Like Pichardo, Santiago can be a league-average reliever for many years, but unless he develops a second pitch, that's his upside.

Scott Service   Throws R   Age 33

YEAR	TEAM	LGE	IP	H	ER	HR	BB	K	ERA	W	L	H/9	HR/9	BB/9	K/9	KWH	PERA
1997	Indianap	AmA	32.3	35	18	5	14	45	5.01	2	2	9.74	1.39	3.90	12.53	3.09	5.57
1997	KansasCy	AL	17.3	16	8	1	5	19	4.15	1	1	8.31	0.52	2.60	9.87	3.37	3.12
1998	KansasCy	AL	85.3	64	29	6	36	97	3.06	6	3	6.75	0.63	3.80	10.23	3.05	3.06
1999	KansasCy	AL	76.7	82	44	11	41	70	5.17	4	5	9.63	1.29	4.81	8.22	1.09	5.75

A disastrous year. Given a dozen opportunities to seize the closer role, Service treated each one the way Kate Moss treats a dessert cart. His fastball didn't appear to lose anything, but his out pitch, the slider, was useless. With nothing to fool left-handed hitters with, Service was helpless as they hit .339/.448/.627 against him. His stuff may return as suddenly as it vanished, but the Royals would be fools if they put him on their roster to check.

Blake Stein   Throws R Age 26

YEAR	TEAM	LGE	IP	H	ER	HR	BB	K	ERA	W	L	H/9	HR/9	BB/9	K/9	KWH	PERA
1997	Arkansas	Tex	120.3	154	80	18	58	96	5.98	5	8	11.52	1.35	4.34	7.18	0.77	6.73
1997	Huntsvil	Sou	32.3	41	25	3	22	20	6.96	1	3	11.41	0.84	6.12	5.57	0.33	6.96
1998	Edmonton	PCL	22.3	24	14	1	12	26	5.64	1	1	9.67	0.40	4.84	10.48	1.75	4.84
1998	Oakland	AL	117.0	112	85	21	74	90	6.54	4	9	8.62	1.62	5.69	6.92	0.73	5.85
1999	Vancouvr	PCL	99.3	107	63	8	50	86	5.71	4	7	9.69	0.72	4.53	7.79	1.03	4.98
1999	KansasCy	AL	70.7	56	29	9	40	44	3.69	5	3	7.13	1.15	5.09	5.60	0.65	4.20

Give the Royals credit: though largely criticized for the return on Kevin Appier at the trading deadline, Robinson had the wisdom to pick up a good minor-league starter who had already received his initiation the year before. An obscene lack of run support left Stein with just one win to show for an impressive six-week run. His two-seam fastball tails away from left-handed hitters and his out pitch is a four-seam fastball. Pitchers who rely on a fastball high in the strike zone walk a tightrope each time out. Given his mediocre strikeout-to-walk ratio, I'm not convinced that Stein has major-league hitters licked yet.

Jeff Suppan   Throws R   Age 25

YEAR	TEAM	LGE	IP	H	ER	HR	BB	K	ERA	W	L	H/9	HR/9	BB/9	K/9	KWH	PERA
1997	Pawtuckt	Int	59.7	55	27	7	16	34	4.07	4	3	8.30	1.06	2.41	5.13	0.98	3.77
1997	Boston	AL	114.7	132	66	11	37	68	5.18	6	7	10.36	0.86	2.90	5.34	0.71	4.87
1998	Arizona	NL	65.7	87	57	12	23	38	7.81	2	5	11.92	1.64	3.15	5.21	0.54	6.85
1998	Tucson	PCL	69.0	69	23	4	20	54	3.00	6	2	9.00	0.52	2.61	7.04	1.58	3.65
1999	KansasCy	AL	210.0	213	100	24	60	106	4.29	12	11	9.13	1.03	2.57	4.54	0.66	4.24

His success was a surprise only to those who don't trust minor-league performance or who don't appreciate how important age is when evaluating players. He's never going to be Greg Maddux; Suppan's fastball is a bit slower, and apparently only one player per generation gets to throw four pitches with last-second movement in either direction. The one cause for concern is Suppan's low strikeout rate, but I think he's young enough and savvy enough to reverse that trend.

Mac Suzuki   Throws R   Age 25

YEAR	TEAM	LGE	IP	H	ER	HR	BB	K	ERA	W	L	H/9	HR/9	BB/9	K/9	KWH	PERA
1997	Tacoma	PCL	78.3	77	54	11	65	54	6.20	3	6	8.85	1.26	7.47	6.20	0.44	6.32
1998	Tacoma	PCL	122.3	142	75	18	77	99	5.52	6	8	10.45	1.32	5.66	7.28	0.67	6.62
1998	Seattle	AL	27.0	32	20	3	15	19	6.67	1	2	10.67	1.00	5.00	6.33	0.56	6.00
1999	Seattle	AL	43.0	44	39	6	33	33	8.16	1	4	9.21	1.26	6.91	6.91	0.56	6.28
1999	KansasCy	AL	68.3	74	40	8	29	37	5.27	3	5	9.75	1.05	3.82	4.87	0.48	5.14

By virtue of a strong September, Suzuki did just enough to tease the Royals into thinking he might be worth a rotation spot this April. This would be a mistake; Suzuki has yet to show that he can throw strikes consistently enough to succeed. Unlike Witasick, his stuff isn't good enough to get hitters out on a 2-1 count.

Derek Wallace — Throws R — Age 28

YEAR	TEAM	LGE	IP	H	ER	HR	BB	K	ERA	W	L	H/9	HR/9	BB/9	K/9	KWH	PERA
1998	Norfolk	Int	59.3	60	31	3	30	42	4.70	3	4	9.10	0.46	4.55	6.37	0.73	4.40
1999	Norfolk	Int	54.0	54	23	6	28	33	3.83	3	3	9.00	1.00	4.67	5.50	0.54	5.00

Another Met refugee who was also an ex-Royal, Wallace was John Franco's heir apparent before an aneurysm in his shoulder cost him most of 1997. In all honesty, he wasn't having a particularly good season for Norfolk when the Royals traded for him, but to give you an idea of how bad the Royals' relievers were, if they had gone with six Derek Wallaces in their bullpen all year, they would have won five to 10 more games. He pitched eight effective innings for Kansas City before his shoulder started bothering him, and I suspect that's going to be the story of his career: sometimes effective, often hurt.

Kris Wilson — Throws R — Age 23

YEAR	TEAM	LGE	IP	H	ER	HR	BB	K	ERA	W	L	H/9	HR/9	BB/9	K/9	KWH	PERA
1997	Spokane	Nwn	65.0	133	62	8	26	41	8.58	2	5	18.42	1.11	3.60	5.68	0.36	10.80
1998	Lansing	Mid	107.7	163	71	11	20	52	5.93	4	8	13.63	0.92	1.67	4.35	0.62	6.44
1998	Wilmngtn	Car	22.7	24	14	0	8	14	5.56	1	2	9.53	0.00	3.18	5.56	0.76	3.57
1999	Wilmngtn	Car	45.7	33	9	0	12	32	1.77	4	1	6.50	0.00	2.36	6.31	1.93	1.97
1999	Wichita	Tex	70.7	104	56	11	17	36	7.13	2	6	13.25	1.40	2.17	4.58	0.55	7.00

For every hitter who jumps from Wilmington to Wichita and hits better than ever, there is a Kris Wilson. He was as dominant as any pitcher in the minor leagues not named Rick Ankiel (1.13 ERA, just 36 baserunners in 48 innings) before getting an unwelcome reception by the state of Kansas. He's an extreme control pitcher who is probably several years from his prime. Wilson has a chance to become the next Bob Tewksbury.

Jay Witasick — Throws R — Age 27

YEAR	TEAM	LGE	IP	H	ER	HR	BB	K	ERA	W	L	H/9	HR/9	BB/9	K/9	KWH	PERA
1997	Edmonton	PCL	25.7	26	13	3	15	14	4.56	1	2	9.12	1.05	5.26	4.91	0.38	5.26
1998	Edmonton	PCL	141.0	141	81	17	57	126	5.17	7	9	9.00	1.09	3.64	8.04	1.48	4.66
1998	Oakland	AL	26.3	36	22	8	16	29	7.52	1	2	12.30	2.73	5.47	9.91	1.09	9.57
1999	KansasCy	AL	160.0	183	95	20	80	105	5.34	7	11	10.29	1.13	4.50	5.91	0.56	5.79

Muser refused to believe that Witasick couldn't pitch in the major leagues despite his awful start, and by year's end, Witasick was beginning to justify that faith. On raw stuff alone—a crackling fastball and a slider with bite—he's a potential 15-game winner, and he was always successful in the minor leagues. After starting 4-10 with a 6.67 ERA, he finished by going 5-2 with a 3.24 ERA in his last seven starts. It was, however, only seven starts. He's another reason why this year's Royals could be sipping champagne or drinking out of the toilet.

Support-Neutral Records							KANSAS CITY ROYALS				Park Effect: +5.5%		
PITCHER	GS	IP	R	SNW	SNL	SNPCT	W	L	RA	APW	SNVA	SNWAR
Kevin Appier	22	140.3	81	8.0	7.4	.519	9	9	5.19	0.25	0.33	1.45
Brian Barber	3	10.0	15	0.3	1.7	.147	1	2	13.50	-0.83	-0.71	-0.56
Chris Fussell	8	38.0	37	1.2	3.9	.240	0	4	8.76	-1.31	-1.27	-0.95
Terry Mathews	1	4.7	4	0.1	0.4	.180	0	0	7.71	-0.11	-0.13	-0.13
Jim Pittsley	5	23.3	22	0.6	2.5	.199	1	2	8.49	-0.74	-0.87	-0.71
Dan Reichert	8	36.7	38	1.6	4.0	.284	2	2	9.33	-1.48	-1.12	-0.78
Jose Rosado	33	208.0	103	13.8	9.1	.604	10	14	4.46	1.94	2.09	4.10
Blake Stein	11	67.3	30	4.8	3.0	.614	1	2	4.01	0.93	0.92	1.49
Jeff Suppan	32	208.7	113	12.9	10.2	.557	10	12	4.87	1.06	1.29	3.04
Mac Suzuki	9	42.3	31	2.3	3.3	.415	1	2	6.59	-0.52	-0.47	-0.06
Don Wengert	1	5.0	8	0.0	0.8	.046	0	1	14.40	-0.46	-0.38	-0.31
Jay Witasick	28	151.0	103	8.6	10.3	.454	9	11	6.14	-1.18	-0.84	0.54
TOTALS	161	935.3	585	54.2	56.6	.489	44	61	5.63	-2.45	-1.15	7.12

Kevin Appier earns the unhappy distinction of being the unluckiest starter of the decade. His Support-Neutral W/L record during the decade exceeded his actual record to a greater extent than any other starter's. We don't have the Support-Neutral numbers for other decades, but some quick number crunching with Bill James's Pythagorean formula reveals these previous titleholders: Jim Beattie for the 1980s, Bert Blyleven for the 1970s, Bob Friend for the 1960s, Bob Rush for the 1950s, Hal Newhouser for the 1940s, Milt Gaston for the 1930s, Dolf Luque for the 1920s, Walter Johnson for the 1910s, and Ned Garvin for the 1900s. The unluckiest starter of the century, by a wide margin, is the Big Train. That's right: the winner of 417 games could have won 66 more with average support. See the Red Sox Support-Neutral comment for the luckiest pitchers in history.

Pitcher Abuse Points													
PITCHER	AGE	GS	PAP	PAP/S	WKLD	MAX	1-90	91-100	101-110	111-120	121-130	131-140	141+
Kevin Appier	31	22	194	8.8	10.3	129	4	6	9	0	3	0	0
Brian Barber	26	3	0	0.0	0.0	82	3	0	0	0	0	0	0
Chris Fussell	23	8	3	0.4	0.9	103	4	3	1	0	0	0	0
Terry Mathews	34	1	0	0.0	0.0	82	1	0	0	0	0	0	0
Jim Pittsley	25	5	0	0.0	0.0	97	4	1	0	0	0	0	0
Dan Reichert	22	8	6	0.8	2.0	106	3	4	1	0	0	0	0
Jose Rosado	24	33	603	18.3	42.6	132	8	4	5	7	7	2	0
Blake Stein	25	11	285	25.9	56.1	134	2	3	0	2	2	2	0
Jeff Suppan	24	32	174	5.4	12.7	121	4	11	12	4	1	0	0
Mac Suzuki	24	9	2	0.2	0.5	102	8	0	1	0	0	0	0
Don Wengert	29	1	0	0.0	0.0	94	0	1	0	0	0	0	0
Jay Witasick	26	28	261	9.3	18.6	137	12	9	2	1	3	1	0
KANSAS CITY		161	1528	9.5	19.9	137	53	42	31	14	16	5	0
Ranking (AL)			5	2									

This is how a bad bullpen can affect an entire staff. Tony Muser, who a year ago was the rock of sensibility in handling the Royals' rotation, became increasingly terrified of entrusting late-inning leads to his bullpen, with the result that starters were kept in to pitch as long as they were effective, regardless of their age. Jose Rosado, still just 24, topped 120 pitches nine times, and for the second time in three years had a pronounced second-half slide: 3.01 ERA at the break, 4.87 after. . . . Blake Stein, who was acquired after Muser was well into ride-the-starter mode, had a Workload that would have ranked him fourth in all of baseball had he made enough starts to qualify. . . . Even Jay Witasick threw more pitches than you would expect from a rookie with a 5.57 ERA. . . . Jeff Suppan, to his credit, was much more efficient with his pitches than Rosado, finishing with less than 30% as many PAPs despite averaging more innings per start. Still, he faded in the second half (5.42 ERA vs. 3.86) nearly as much as Rosado. All of this affects our confidence in the Royals' rotation this season.

Minnesota Twins

Okay, the joke's on us. Last year, we envisioned a future in which the Twins were going to play a bunch of rookies and sneak up on people. Sure enough, they played 17 rookies, but they didn't do much sneaking—not unless you count giving the Tigers and Royals a fight for third place in the AL Central.

Our enthusiasm was especially out of line considering how difficult General Manager Terry Ryan's job is. Owner Carl Pohlad has little commitment to do anything for the team until the twin issues of the team's sale and the construction of a new stadium are resolved. Pohlad's ultimatum on cutting salary cost the team starting shortstop Pat Meares, which left observers wailing about the Twins' failure to give big bucks to a mediocre player. I guess that's what passes for a commitment to excellence in some circles.

The flip-flop over Rick Aguilera—Ryan signed him to a multi-year deal then had to trade him at Pohlad's command—won't help with free-agent shopping as long as Pohlad owns the team. We've obviously been much too enthusiastic about the Twins in the short term. Still, despite the off-field problems, Ryan and his staff have slowly been creating an organization that is hard not to be enthusiastic about, especially when looking at the team they'll be able to field in a few years.

The Twins went into the season thinking they weren't going to win, but had the benefit of knowing that nobody expected them to. While this hardly seems worth getting excited about, there was a major change: a realization that there was no difference between what they could expect in 1999 and what they had gotten in the seasons during which they'd spent more. So why bother stumbling around with mercenary stiffs like Orlando Merced or Otis Nixon? Guys like that weren't going to help build the next mediocre Twins team, let alone the next good one. They were players who needed the jobs more than the Twins needed them. Why pay Pat Meares a million dollars or more just because he was arbitration-eligible? He was never going to be much better than Denny Hocking in the first place.

Thus the Twins got back to doing what they should have been doing for years: using major-league trials to evaluate their minor-league talent. Teams like the Twins will contend through player development, controlling the first six years of a player's career and having the opportunity to get the best years of that career. They'd started the process before, back in 1995, with players like Marty Cordova, Rich Becker and Scott Stahoviak. The mistake they made was settling for those guys. What could have been a relentless improve-or-die cycle of player development only got as far as 78 wins in 1996, as good as that outfit was going to get.

Repeating the process in 1999, the results were mixed. It would be simple to say the tools goofs struggled and the baseball players earned jobs, but that is basically how things worked out. Guys like Jacque Jones and Corey Koskie, who were going to hit if they got regular playing time, did. Marginal players like Torii Hunter and Chad Allen got to show what they could do: Hunter has value in a limited role, while Allen should start campaigning for a pension plan for Pacific Coast League veterans. Cristian Guzman showed physical skill afield and very little ability at the plate. Sorting through these players to separate the wheat from the chaff is a useful way for the organization to spend its time, until it has the young talent in place to mount a major push for contention.

It isn't that these players are going to be the core of the next good Twins team, like the Gary Gaetti/Kirby Puckett/Kent Hrbek group in the early 1980s. What they will be is a solid group of experienced players to surround and support the organization's outstanding crop of prospects: Mike Cuddyer, Matt LeCroy, Mike Restovich and possibly Bobby Kielty. If the Twins allow themselves to get as attached to the current group of young players as they did to the best players in the 1995 group, they'll be undercutting their best opportunity to improve.

The more interesting problem going into 1999 was the pitching staff. Analysts and media creatures alike have been

Twins Prospectus

1999 record: 63-97; Fifth place, AL Central

Pythagorean W/L: 66-96

Runs scored: 686 (14th in AL)

Runs allowed: 845 (5th in AL)

Team EQA: .233 (14th in AL)

1999 team age: 26.3 (2nd-youngest in AL)

1999 park: Metrodome; good hitters' park, increased run scoring by 10%.

1999: Sifted through the bit players while waiting for the real prospects.

2000: By the end of the year, they'll be a very exciting team.

bashing Tom Kelly and pitching coach Dick Such for their perceived failures in developing young pitchers. For years, the Twins have been remarkable in their ability to promote and discard young arms. Consider the young pitchers who have come up with the Twins in the last 10 years or so: Pat Mahomes was starting in the majors at 21; Brad Radke, Scott Erickson, Denny Neagle, Eddie Guardado, LaTroy Hawkins, Paul Abbott and Mike Dyer were all 22. Frankie Rodriguez and Jose Parra were both 22 when they were acquired and fitted for major-league uniforms.

It isn't as though these guys were polished college pitchers with little need for minor-league experience. Most of them were drafted out of high school, as risky a breed as you can find as far as prospects go. How easy can it be to teach pitchers this young to pitch at the major-league level? It's extraordinary for any team to try so many different pitchers at such a young age, and it shouldn't surprise anyone that it burned the Twins regularly.

The strategy is also foolhardy because bringing up pitchers this young starts arbitration and free-agency clocks ticking much too soon—and for not nearly enough of a payoff to be worthwhile. Also, an affiliation with Salt Lake City makes it difficult for a pitching prospect to get useful Triple-A experience before he reaches the majors. The Twins of the 1990s might be the best example of a team that should have followed the Earl Weaver maxim about breaking in young pitchers in middle relief. If they'd been a bit more willing to let pitchers like Abbott, Mahomes or Todd Ritchie get their feet wet pitching low-leverage relief, they might have gotten the same results they got this year with Joe Mays.

So what's really wrong with the Twins? It would be easy to lay everything at Carl Pohlad's feet, as the argument over which direction Minnesota baseball needs to take swirls around him. The intertwined stadium/ownership issue is similar to the muck the Giants wallowed in with Bob Lurie in the 1980s, when he was alternately trying to sell the team, threatening to move the team and trying to bully various local governments into giving him a new stadium. Like voters were throughout the Bay Area, the people of Minnesota are sensible enough to call Pohlad's bluff. The team isn't going anywhere because there's no viable place to go, and they haven't caved in to his attempts to get an ugly neo-retro monstrosity ballpark on his, or any potential buyer's, terms.

Increasingly, it is Pohlad's existence that is the lightning rod for public and political rejection of any and every scheme. A potential buyer for the team can reap the benefits of this on two levels. First, because Pohlad can't really move the team, the longer he owns it the more his existence hurts the franchise's value. The more people have to hear about the whiny billionaire who envies the profit Dick Jacobs turned on the Tribe, the more likely it becomes that the Twins will

cost less than Kevin Brown. Second, anyone who buys the Twins stands to inherit a measure of public support just by not being Carl Pohlad—a la Kevin McClatchy when he started out in Pittsburgh.

Nobody should pity Pohlad. He waited too long to try to blackmail state and local government into giving him a new stadium. Bud Selig has gone out of his way to point out that the Expos will have Major League Baseball's support to remain in Montreal, in no small part because of the good attendance the Expos enjoyed in the late 1970s and early 1980s. By that logic, the Twin Cities can laugh off the specter of the Twins moving to North Carolina, because public support of the Twins in good times has been outstanding. The Twins were the first team in the AL to draw three million fans (1988) and attendance prior to the 1994 strike was consistently over two million per year. That the Twins haven't gotten the same support since the strike has everything to do with a mediocre team's being further undermined by an ownership/stadium controversy that keeps baseball in the background. As in every market, Twins fans will support a winner; more than most markets, they will even support a mediocre team. Once the team isn't Carl Pohlad's, that will happen again.

The central problem in assessing the Twins, or any team currently struggling, lies in being able to distinguish between what things cannot be changed and what things will change. The idea that nothing is permanent might be particle physics for a Denver doofus like Jerry McMorris, but it's the basis for why the Twins aren't going to be bad forever. Nor will they stay great forever once the LeCroy/Cuddyer/Restovich/Kielty group makes it up for good, even if the group turns out better than we expect. If the Twins were truly a problem franchise, they wouldn't be expending effort in new directions. They wouldn't be starting a scouting effort in Australia that's beginning to bear fruit, and they wouldn't be building a baseball academy in Puerto Rico.

While Pohlad's problems persist, the organization has more than endured: it has expanded and improved. This is hardly a desperate situation like Charlie Finley's last years of owning the A's, when MC Hammer was working in the front office and a major-league team was run out of a shoebox. Make no mistake about what's on life support here. It isn't Major League Baseball in Minnesota. It's Carl Pohlad's attempt to make a few bucks more than anyone is willing to pay.

The AL Central is an armed camp where good teams for the new millennium are being built. The progress as the White Sox and the Royals work on their rosters to mount challenges to an aging Indians team is as plain as day. But one of baseball's so-called problem franchises is poised to blow by both of them and the Tribe. Not this year—we've been there and blown that—but by 2002.

HITTERS (Averages: BA: .270 / OBP: .340 / SLG: .430 / EQA: .260)

Chad Allen   LF   Bats R   Age 25

YEAR	TEAM	LGE	AB	H	DB	TP	HR	BB/SO	R	RBI	SB	CS	OUT	BA	OBP	SLG	EQA	EQR	DEFENSE
1997	Ft Myers	Fla	412	114	20	3	3	33/58	51	38	11	6	304	.277	.333	.362	.239	42	103-OF 97
1997	New Brit	Eas	117	29	10	1	3	6/22	17	15	1	0	88	.248	.285	.427	.236	12	25-OF 86
1998	New Brit	Eas	515	130	31	6	8	42/79	61	76	13	6	391	.252	.315	.383	.238	54	132-OF 86
1999	Minnesot	AL	476	127	20	3	9	31/89	61	41	14	7	356	.267	.314	.378	.236	48	126-LF 96
2000	Minnesot	AL	472	131	23	4	9	47/80	76	65	13	6	347	.278	.343	.400	.252	56	

His winning the left-field job was definitely unscripted, but a club-record 35 hits in spring training couldn't be ignored. Even among Twins' rookies, Allen was especially green. If he wasn't blowing defensive assignments, he was flubbing hit-and-run chores. Because he hit out of a deep crouch, pitchers started busting him inside, and he never adjusted. Things got so bad that by the end of the year some people were accusing him of being just plain dumb. While that's probably overstated, he should never again get 500 plate appearances at the major-league level. Once upon a time there was a team that could win with Dan Gladden. That doesn't mean finding the next Dan Gladden should be an organizational goal.

Brian Buchanan   OF   Bats R   Age 26

YEAR	TEAM	LGE	AB	H	DB	TP	HR	BB/SO	R	RBI	SB	CS	OUT	BA	OBP	SLG	EQA	EQR	DEFENSE
1997	Norwich	Eas	474	132	25	2	7	21/91	58	54	7	5	347	.278	.320	.384	.238	48	111-OF 92
1998	SaltLake	PCL	488	114	23	2	13	29/93	53	61	9	2	376	.234	.286	.369	.222	44	122-OF 98
1999	SaltLake	PCL	379	88	17	1	6	22/92	44	40	6	1	292	.232	.286	.330	.210	30	97-OF 90
2000	Minnesot	AL	390	94	17	1	8	26/84	42	41	6	2	298	.241	.288	.351	.213	31	

A poor man's Chad Allen. Not phony poor, like big-market versus small-market poor. More like "Can I pay you with pencil shavings?" poor. Buchanan was part of the bounty for Knoblauch, so he's guaranteed a cup of coffee at some point.

Dan Cey   2B   Bats R   Age 24

YEAR	TEAM	LGE	AB	H	DB	TP	HR	BB/SO	R	RBI	SB	CS	OUT	BA	OBP	SLG	EQA	EQR	DEFENSE
1997	Ft Myers	Fla	532	141	35	3	9	28/93	70	54	10	4	395	.265	.306	.393	.236	54	63-SS 91
1998	New Brit	Eas	579	146	30	2	8	33/93	75	48	16	5	438	.252	.295	.352	.222	51	135-2B 96
1999	SaltLake	PCL	391	98	16	2	8	27/65	46	41	7	1	294	.251	.308	.363	.231	38	110-2B 96
2000	Minnesot	AL	446	118	19	2	8	32/73	60	52	13	3	331	.265	.314	.370	.233	43	

Cey is too impatient ever to turn into somebody you want playing every day, but Todd Walker looks like he needs a platoon-mate, and Brent Gates is gone. Cey is the son of the original Penguin, but he didn't get his old man's build. His lack of range and occasional carelessness was a problem at shortstop and persists at second base, so he'll go only as far as his bat takes him.

Ron Coomer   1B/3B   Bats R   Age 33

YEAR	TEAM	LGE	AB	H	DB	TP	HR	BB/SO	R	RBI	SB	CS	OUT	BA	OBP	SLG	EQA	EQR	DEFENSE	
1997	Minnesot	AL	522	157	32	2	13	19/87	61	83	4	3	368	.301	.325	.444	.256	61	110-3B 99	
1998	Minnesot	AL	528	146	22	1	15	16/70	52	69	2	2	384	.277	.298	.407	.234	51	72-3B 101	44-1B 108
1999	Minnesot	AL	463	118	24	1	15	24/69	47	59	2	1	346	.255	.293	.408	.233	45	61-1B 112	46-3B 119
2000	Minnesot	AL	418	114	17	0	17	25/61	50	67	1	1	305	.273	.314	.435	.247	46		

The Twins' token All-Star and a guy to root for. Not everybody has to spend nearly six years kicking around the Southern and Pacific Coast leagues. He's stretched as a regular at either corner, but he can still be a valuable pinch-hitter and platoon partner once the Twins decide which kids will win the jobs at first base and DH. While that projection looks optimistic, if Coomer plays less often against right-handed pitching, his performance will improve.

Marty Cordova   DH/LF   Bats R   Age 30

YEAR	TEAM	LGE	AB	H	DB	TP	HR	BB/SO	R	RBI	SB	CS	OUT	BA	OBP	SLG	EQA	EQR	DEFENSE
1997	Minnesot	AL	377	93	19	4	15	28/88	43	49	5	3	287	.247	.305	.438	.246	43	94-OF 100
1998	Minnesot	AL	437	111	19	2	10	48/101	49	66	2	6	332	.254	.335	.375	.241	47	111-OF 95
1999	Minnesot	AL	419	115	30	3	12	42/96	55	62	12	4	308	.274	.353	.446	.271	59	20-RF 83
2000	Minnesot	AL	387	106	21	2	12	47/88	65	62	6	3	284	.274	.353	.432	.264	51	

He seems over his battle with plantar fascitis, but he's still injury-prone, even managing to hurt himself running into an outfield wall during one of his few games in the field. He dumped his big leg-kick at the plate, which helped his batting average. Cordova spent the year alienating everyone in the organization, bitching about how he was tired of playing for a bunch of losers and how he'd come back only if the only other job was in the Northern League. His agent could probably do him a favor by pointing out that designated hitters with little power and bad attitudes shouldn't kid about working in the Northern League.

Mike Cuddyer — 3B — Bats R — Age 21

YEAR	TEAM	LGE	AB	H	DB	TP	HR	BB/SO	R	RBI	SB	CS	OUT	BA	OBP	SLG	EQA	EQR	DEFENSE
1998	Ft Wayne	Mid	513	128	34	4	14	50/110	67	68	6	3	388	.250	.323	.413	.249	60	122-SS 90
1999	Ft Myers	Fla	479	133	22	3	18	65/100	73	72	7	2	348	.278	.371	.449	.279	71	126-3B 93
2000	Minnesot	AL	402	121	21	2	17	56/86	80	81	6	2	283	.301	.386	.490	.293	66	

One of the trinity of prospects, along with Mike Restovich and Matt LeCroy, on whom the organization's future rests. He's the best of the three. Now that he's been moved from shortstop after a 61-error season in 1998, the hope is that he'll be the next Scott Rolen. The Twins would like to see him tinker with his swing to get a little more power. While still raw at third base, he has a good arm and was named the best defensive third baseman in the Florida State League. A good start this year could earn him a call-up in September.

Cleatus Davidson — 2B — Bats B — Age 23

YEAR	TEAM	LGE	AB	H	DB	TP	HR	BB/SO	R	RBI	SB	CS	OUT	BA	OBP	SLG	EQA	EQR	DEFENSE
1997	Ft Wayne	Mid	489	117	18	5	7	38/104	57	43	17	5	377	.239	.295	.339	.220	43	122-2B 100
1998	Ft Myers	Fla	534	123	14	6	2	37/110	69	38	18	8	419	.230	.283	.290	.197	36	124-2B 99
1999	New Brit	Eas	498	118	18	8	2	42/113	70	35	22	8	388	.237	.299	.317	.216	42	111-2B 96
2000	Minnesot	AL	473	114	20	4	4	42/102	61	43	18	6	365	.241	.303	.326	.216	40	

Nabbing 40 bases and taking an occasional walk makes Davidson a borderline prospect, but he needs to improve at both before he'll be able to shoot for a Mark McLemore-type career. A hamate bone broken during batting practice in September should be healed by spring. Even so, he isn't likely to force Todd Walker out of town anytime soon.

Brent Gates — IF — Bats B — Age 30

YEAR	TEAM	LGE	AB	H	DB	TP	HR	BB/SO	R	RBI	SB	CS	OUT	BA	OBP	SLG	EQA	EQR	DEFENSE	
1997	Seattle	AL	151	37	5	0	4	13/20	17	21	0	0	114	.245	.305	.358	.225	14	23-3B 104	12-2B 93
1998	Minnesot	AL	332	83	8	0	5	35/45	29	42	3	3	252	.250	.325	.319	.223	30	70-3B 101	
1999	Minnesot	AL	302	73	12	2	3	31/56	35	34	1	3	232	.242	.314	.325	.218	26	43-3B 109	30-2B 104
2000	Minnesot	AL	230	55	6	0	5	28/38	27	26	1	2	177	.239	.322	.330	.221	20		

Gates was a major beneficiary of Tom Kelly's policy of giving all of his hitters some playing time. Having repaired his resume in two seasons with the Twins, he should end up getting something better than a non-roster invite. Now that he's reached the big 3-0, he's ready for the Orioles.

Cristian Guzman — SS — Bats B — Age 22

YEAR	TEAM	LGE	AB	H	DB	TP	HR	BB/SO	R	RBI	SB	CS	OUT	BA	OBP	SLG	EQA	EQR	DEFENSE
1997	Greensbr	SAL	505	130	23	3	4	15/106	55	44	9	6	381	.257	.288	.339	.210	39	119-SS 101
1998	New Brit	Eas	575	158	32	4	1	15/108	62	38	16	9	426	.275	.294	.350	.217	47	139-SS 102
1999	Minnesot	AL	418	91	10	3	1	17/90	41	23	9	7	334	.218	.253	.263	.166	19	121-SS 95
2000	Minnesot	AL	428	110	17	2	2	21/87	44	37	11	7	325	.257	.292	.320	.203	30	

Mosquito country's answer to Rey Ordonez was almost as green as Allen. While Guzman has good range and hands, he seemed to forget where to go on plays when the ball wasn't hit at him. The Twins say he's coachable, but they can't seem to decide whether he should dump switch-hitting. He's been awful batting left-handed, with a 471 OPS last year. He has the advantage of having gotten to the majors first over Luis Rivas, but he'll have a hard time hitting enough to keep the job.

Steve Hacker DH Bats R Age 25

YEAR	TEAM	LGE	AB	H	DB	TP	HR	BB/SO	R	RBI	SB	CS	OUT	BA	OBP	SLG	EQA	EQR	DEFENSE
1997	Macon	SAL	468	127	24	1	28	29/95	63	88	0	0	341	.271	.318	.506	.269	64	49-1B 113
1998	Ft Myers	Fla	254	53	9	0	9	12/48	22	28	0	0	201	.209	.248	.350	.195	17	
1999	New Brit	Eas	466	120	25	0	22	26/116	54	73	0	1	347	.258	.301	.453	.248	53	
2000	Minnesot	AL	415	114	16	0	27	35/97	60	85	0	0	301	.275	.331	.508	.273	59	

Snagged from the Braves in exchange for Greg Myers in 1997, he missed almost three months in 1998 with a broken forearm. He bounced back to put up an All-Star season with New Britain and is now a dark-horse candidate for the DH job. The Twins haven't had anyone hit 30 taters since 1987. Hacker is their best internal candidate to break the streak, because he can hit and because he doesn't have David Ortiz's problems with people in the organization.

Denny Hocking ALL Bats B Age 30

YEAR	TEAM	LGE	AB	H	DB	TP	HR	BB/SO	R	RBI	SB	CS	OUT	BA	OBP	SLG	EQA	EQR	DEFENSE	
1997	Minnesot	AL	253	65	13	4	2	16/49	27	24	3	5	193	.257	.304	.364	.222	22	33-SS 98	21-3B 89
1998	Minnesot	AL	198	40	6	1	3	15/43	31	14	2	1	159	.202	.258	.288	.180	11	17-SS 94	
1999	Minnesot	AL	383	98	19	2	6	17/54	42	37	10	7	292	.256	.293	.363	.220	33	38-SS 89	33-2B 93
2000	Minnesot	AL	273	66	13	1	4	20/44	29	27	4	4	211	.242	.294	.341	.209	21		

Hocking has even been an emergency catcher, so when we say "all" positions, we mean it. He can run a little, he switch-hits, he can do everything but help his team score runs. He's a nifty bottom-of-the-bench guy miscast as a regular. Once the Twins come up with a few great position players, they'll have a good bench already in place to support them.

Torii Hunter CF Bats R Age 24

YEAR	TEAM	LGE	AB	H	DB	TP	HR	BB/SO	R	RBI	SB	CS	OUT	BA	OBP	SLG	EQA	EQR	DEFENSE
1997	New Brit	Eas	480	107	25	2	6	35/97	48	48	6	5	378	.223	.279	.321	.201	34	125-OF 102
1998	New Brit	Eas	313	85	24	3	6	16/63	39	30	8	6	234	.272	.314	.425	.245	35	82-OF 104
1998	SaltLake	PCL	89	25	3	0	4	1/13	11	16	2	1	65	.281	.295	.449	.245	10	21-OF 112
1999	Minnesot	AL	381	94	17	2	8	21/72	46	31	10	6	293	.247	.297	.365	.224	35	87-CF 106
2000	Minnesot	AL	364	95	19	1	8	26/69	46	45	8	6	275	.261	.310	.385	.231	35	

He could end up having a career like Gerald Williams's because he has similar strengths—great defense, good arm, hammers left-handers—and weaknesses—no plate discipline, mostly harmless against right-handers. The combination of skills makes him a good complementary player to Jacque Jones, and gives the Twins a good situation in center field until Bobby Kielty is ready. Tom Kelly took Hunter to task for missing hit-and-run signs—to the point where he was hauled onto the field in the wee hours after a game in August to practice reading them.

Jacque Jones CF Bats L Age 25

YEAR	TEAM	LGE	AB	H	DB	TP	HR	BB/SO	R	RBI	SB	CS	OUT	BA	OBP	SLG	EQA	EQR	DEFENSE
1997	Ft Myers	Fla	550	147	32	4	15	26/125	67	68	10	5	408	.267	.303	.422	.242	59	130-OF 106
1998	New Brit	Eas	528	149	37	2	20	29/135	68	76	12	7	386	.282	.324	.473	.262	68	129-OF 106
1999	SaltLake	PCL	192	47	11	1	3	7/37	23	19	6	1	146	.245	.271	.359	.214	15	52-OF 113
1999	Minnesot	AL	319	89	24	2	8	13/63	48	39	3	4	234	.279	.315	.442	.249	36	65-CF 109
2000	Minnesot	AL	511	145	32	2	16	31/111	75	80	10	5	371	.284	.325	.448	.256	61	

A fun player to watch, although not somebody I'd want on my team. He's a singles hitter who swings from his heels. While he isn't the type who draws walks, simply calling him impatient doesn't do him justice. With nobody on, he's hacking early to get the ball in play. With somebody on, he seems to foul everything off and work the pitcher until he gets the pitch he wants to put in play. Naturally, he's a great bad-ball hitter. He can make the highlight-reel catch in center field, and he throws well. Only on a Tom Kelly team can a young player get in trouble for smiling too often, as Jones did.

Bobby Kielty CF Bats R Age 23

YEAR	TEAM	LGE	AB	H	DB	TP	HR	BB/SO	R	RBI	SB	CS	OUT	BA	OBP	SLG	EQA	EQR	DEFENSE
1999	Quad Cit	Mid	252	65	10	1	11	32/60	37	31	5	2	189	.258	.346	.437	.265	34	56-OF 111
2000	Minnesot	AL	129	35	4	0	11	26/51	28	33	2	1	95	.271	.394	.558	.309	25	

His signing was a major coup for Twins' player development. After his senior season at Mississippi was marred by a skiing accident, he went undrafted in 1998. He went on to star in the Cape Cod League, then chose to sign with the Twins because he thinks his best shot at the majors is with them. Remember that the next time you hear somebody argue that only "big market" teams would be able to sign great amateur talent without the draft. Guys want to end up in the majors, not rotting in Columbus waiting for Darryl Strawberry's next indictment. Kielty will stay in center field until he proves he can't play there; so far, he gets a good jump on the ball.

Corey Koskie   3B   Bats L   Age 27

YEAR	TEAM	LGE	AB	H	DB	TP	HR	BB/SO	R	RBI	SB	CS	OUT	BA	OBP	SLG	EQA	EQR	DEFENSE
1997	New Brit	Eas	449	110	26	5	15	69/120	64	56	5	3	342	.245	.352	.425	.264	61	124-3B 81
1998	SaltLake	PCL	491	115	25	3	17	39/114	60	69	9	4	380	.234	.298	.401	.235	51	131-3B 88
1999	Minnesot	AL	336	100	15	0	12	36/72	37	53	4	4	240	.298	.374	.449	.277	48	69-3B 115
2000	*Minnesot*	*AL*	*392*	*102*	*16*	*1*	*17*	*47/89*	*60*	*66*	*4*	*2*	*292*	*.260*	*.339*	*.436*	*.260*	*50*	

Koskie was old for a rookie, and you can see he has old-players' skills in that he slugs well and draws walks, so he may not have a long career. He is a good athlete who played more hockey and volleyball than baseball in Canada before college, so he could surprise people. He was platooned and played well, but he did have to endure a punitive benching for hammering Chuck Knoblauch with a takeout slide. Having Coomer and Gates around forced Koskie to stumble around in right field for a few games. He'll spend most of 2000 at third base, but once Cuddyer is up, the Twins will make room for Koskie's bat somewhere.

Chris Latham   CF   Bats B   Age 27

YEAR	TEAM	LGE	AB	H	DB	TP	HR	BB/SO	R	RBI	SB	CS	OUT	BA	OBP	SLG	EQA	EQR	DEFENSE
1997	SaltLake	PCL	475	119	16	3	6	45/116	52	39	14	13	369	.251	.320	.335	.223	44	118-OF 102
1998	SaltLake	PCL	365	90	17	2	7	44/108	52	33	17	4	279	.247	.329	.362	.244	41	93-OF 100
1998	Minnesot	AL	94	15	0	0	1	13/35	13	5	4	2	81	.160	.262	.191	.155	4	27-OF 98
1999	SaltLake	PCL	370	90	18	5	9	42/103	59	32	10	8	288	.243	.322	.392	.241	41	94-OF 110
2000	*Colorado*	*NL*	*341*	*89*	*14*	*2*	*9*	*46/99*	*54*	*46*	*13*	*9*	*261*	*.261*	*.349*	*.393*	*.230*	*33*	

A nifty fifth outfielder in the making, but his window of opportunity was 1999, and both Jones and Hunter jumped past him. Now he can only hope he gets bumped off the 40-man roster so that he can take a chance somewhere else, before he winds up like Allen Battle. Picked up by the Rox, where he may get to back up Tom Goodwin.

Matt Lawton   OF   Bats L   Age 28

YEAR	TEAM	LGE	AB	H	DB	TP	HR	BB/SO	R	RBI	SB	CS	OUT	BA	OBP	SLG	EQA	EQR	DEFENSE
1997	Minnesot	AL	458	114	29	3	14	73/78	71	58	7	4	348	.249	.366	.417	.269	65	130-OF 95
1998	Minnesot	AL	555	154	36	6	21	83/63	86	74	14	8	409	.277	.386	.477	.290	93	147-OF 104
1999	Minnesot	AL	400	98	13	0	8	52/42	52	49	26	4	306	.245	.341	.338	.247	46	94-RF 94
2000	*Minnesot*	*AL*	*417*	*112*	*20*	*2*	*11*	*66/48*	*83*	*61*	*16*	*4*	*309*	*.269*	*.369*	*.405*	*.269*	*58*	

After a career year in 1998, 1999 was an unending horror show for Lawton. He started off in an awful slump, then had his eye socket broken by a Dennis Reyes pitch in June. He came back late and never got on track offensively. Part of the Twins' chance to improve their offense in 2000 depends on Lawton's getting back to where he was in 1998 instead of settling back to his 1997 level, as Wilton projects.

Matthew LeCroy   C   Bats R   Age 24

YEAR	TEAM	LGE	AB	H	DB	TP	HR	BB/SO	R	RBI	SB	CS	OUT	BA	OBP	SLG	EQA	EQR	DEFENSE
1998	Ft Wayne	Mid	234	57	12	1	9	27/48	27	32	0	0	177	.244	.334	.419	.255	29	46-C 95
1998	Ft Myers	Fla	203	53	7	1	10	17/40	25	38	1	0	150	.261	.327	.453	.260	26	42-C 95
1999	Ft Myers	Fla	341	80	15	1	17	33/61	42	51	0	0	261	.235	.305	.434	.246	39	64-C 92
1999	SaltLake	PCL	115	29	2	1	8	5/22	17	22	0	1	87	.252	.288	.496	.251	14	
2000	*Minnesot*	*AL*	*319*	*87*	*14*	*1*	*25*	*41/67*	*56*	*76*	*0*	*0*	*232*	*.273*	*.356*	*.558*	*.294*	*54*	

LeCroy came into 1999 needing to improve his footwork and his game calling, because his hitting is already fine. He did improve, but he'll probably never be a good catcher. He spent time with the Pan Am Games team, then suffered a broken finger in the PCL playoffs that spoiled his chance for a call-up. He's been gifted with Antone Williamson's good looks and Steve McMichael's hair. Just try to tell me that won't sell tickets in a land that loved Kent Hrbek. LeCroy is a very good candidate for 2000 AL Rookie of the Year.

Doug Mientkiewicz   1B   Bats L   Age 26

YEAR	TEAM	LGE	AB	H	DB	TP	HR	BB/SO	R	RBI	SB	CS	OUT	BA	OBP	SLG	EQA	EQR	DEFENSE
1997	New Brit	Eas	479	112	29	2	11	80/71	67	48	13	5	372	.234	.349	.372	.253	60	106-1B 87
1998	New Brit	Eas	519	148	31	0	17	79/62	79	77	6	3	374	.285	.385	.443	.283	79	136-1B 94
1999	Minnesot	AL	324	72	19	3	2	38/51	30	29	1	1	253	.222	.311	.318	.218	28	96-1B 99
2000	*Minnesot*	*AL*	*365*	*96*	*23*	*1*	*8*	*58/51*	*66*	*53*	*4*	*2*	*271*	*.263*	*.364*	*.397*	*.262*	*47*	

The new Scott Stahoviak, brought to you by the same team that brought you the old one. Like Dan Perkins, he was a high-school teammate of Alex Rodriguez. He managed to irk both Tom Kelly and hitting coach Scott Ullger with his long swing, his defensiveness at the plate and his unwillingness to listen. There are enough people in the world who can hit some and play first base, so making a bad impression can kill a career. Like Stahoviak the First, Mientkiewicz is doomed to be an Iowa Cub someday.

Chad Moeller   C   Bats R   Age 25

YEAR	TEAM	LGE	AB	H	DB	TP	HR	BB/SO	R	RBI	SB	CS	OUT	BA	OBA	SA	EQA	EQR	DEFENSE
1997	FtWayne	Mid	393	97	17	2	8	36/82	43	29	4	4	300	.247	.326	.361	.235	40	
1998	FtMyers	Fla	259	67	18	1	5	23/45	27	28	1	1	193	.259	.324	.394	.243	28	56-C88
1998	NewBrit	Eas	191	43	7	0	7	21/41	19	22	1	1	149	.225	.310	.372	.232	19	55-C98
1999	NewBrit	Eas	253	56	11	2	3	15/50	24	19	0	0	197	.221	.275	.316	.198	17	79-C92
2000	*Minnesot*	*AL*	*285*	*68*	*10*	*1*	*6*	*26/56*	*31*	*32*	*2*	*1*	*218*	*.239*	*.302*	*.344*	*.217*	*24*	

Now that Steinbach's retired, Moeller is sort of in the running for some catching duties after a nice AFL. Doesn't have a great opportunity to beat out LeCroy, and hasn't earned one.

Mike Moriarty   SS   Bats R   Age 26

YEAR	TEAM	LGE	AB	H	DB	TP	HR	BB/SO	R	RBI	SB	CS	OUT	BA	OBP	SLG	EQA	EQR	DEFENSE	
1997	New Brit	Eas	430	90	23	4	5	40/73	48	41	8	3	343	.209	.280	.316	.204	32	135-SS 116	
1998	New Brit	Eas	115	28	5	0	4	14/17	18	13	0	2	89	.243	.338	.391	.244	13	30-3B 96	
1998	SaltLake	PCL	158	29	8	1	2	19/40	15	14	1	1	130	.184	.274	.285	.189	10	29-2B 102	17-SS 107
1999	SaltLake	PCL	372	74	15	5	2	44/67	42	34	4	2	300	.199	.291	.282	.198	26	124-SS 102	
2000	*Minnesot*	*AL*	*303*	*63*	*16*	*3*	*3*	*34/56*	*32*	*26*	*2*	*1*	*241*	*.208*	*.288*	*.310*	*.200*	*22*		

Moriarty is a glove man out of Seton Hall, and a good one. His chance depends on Hocking's getting traded or Guzman's getting sent down before Rivas is considered ready. He should be nicknamed "Professor" for you Arthur Conan Doyle fans. Maybe Jon Miller will crack a joke if he ever bats against Darren "Sherlock" Holmes.

David Ortiz   1B/DH   Bats L   Age 24

YEAR	TEAM	LGE	AB	H	DB	TP	HR	BB/SO	R	RBI	SB	CS	OUT	BA	OBP	SLG	EQA	EQR	DEFENSE
1997	Ft Myers	Fla	245	73	10	0	14	19/58	39	50	1	0	172	.298	.350	.510	.283	37	58-1B 93
1997	New Brit	Eas	262	77	23	2	11	15/81	33	45	2	3	188	.294	.339	.523	.278	38	32-1B 84
1998	Minnesot	AL	277	77	14	0	11	38/70	44	46	1	0	200	.278	.375	.448	.280	42	67-1B 101
1999	SaltLake	PCL	459	121	27	2	22	68/104	61	78	1	1	339	.264	.361	.475	.279	70	110-1B 95
2000	*Minnesot*	*AL*	*455*	*133*	*25*	*1*	*25*	*68/112*	*88*	*101*	*1*	*1*	*323*	*.292*	*.384*	*.516*	*.297*	*78*	

The organization's litmus test to see if they want to get better in a hurry or just do things their way. Ortiz is accused of having an attitude, and he catches flak for bad glovework and his weight. Ullger says he's gotten into bad habits at the plate: he had been pitched outside for so long that he wasn't adjusting to anything inside in the majors, diving across the plate without keeping his head or hands still. Despite all that, he has the best power in the organization, so the question is whether Kelly will work with Ortiz or bury him.

Tommy Peterman   1B   Bats L   Age 25

YEAR	TEAM	LGE	AB	H	DB	TP	HR	BB/SO	R	RBI	SB	CS	OUT	BA	OBP	SLG	EQA	EQR	DEFENSE	
1997	Ft Wayne	Mid	424	109	12	0	9	18/74	36	46	0	2	317	.257	.289	.349	.212	33	58-OF 82	28-1B 79
1998	Ft Myers	Fla	529	133	30	1	16	47/104	53	78	1	0	396	.251	.316	.403	.243	57	123-1B 91	
1999	New Brit	Eas	546	124	19	1	17	44/95	53	66	0	1	423	.227	.287	.359	.217	46	135-1B 102	
2000	*Minnesot*	*AL*	*500*	*130*	*16*	*0*	*19*	*45/90*	*61*	*76*	*0*	*1*	*371*	*.260*	*.321*	*.406*	*.242*	*54*		

He's a lumbering left-handed slugger, drafted after leading Division I baseball in home runs at Georgia Southern. While he doesn't have the power of Hacker or Ortiz, he warrants a mention because this is the team that kept Mientkiewicz over Ortiz last year. As Chad Allen proved, one good camp can win you a job with this club.

A.J. Pierzynski — C — Bats L — Age 23

YEAR	TEAM	LGE	AB	H	DB	TP	HR	BB/SO	R	RBI	SB	CS	OUT	BA	OBP	SLG	EQA	EQR	DEFENSE
1997	Ft Myers	Fla	418	109	21	1	10	14/65	44	56	1	0	309	.261	.292	.388	.227	38	
1998	New Brit	Eas	216	63	6	0	5	7/24	28	17	0	1	154	.292	.319	.389	.237	21	56-C 103
1998	SaltLake	PCL	204	45	6	1	6	7/24	22	23	2	1	160	.221	.246	.348	.194	13	58-C 101
1999	SaltLake	PCL	223	50	4	0	2	13/29	21	20	0	0	173	.224	.267	.269	.174	11	63-C 93
2000	*Minnesot*	*AL*	*347*	*94*	*10*	*0*	*10*	*21/45*	*37*	*48*	*1*	*1*	*254*	*.271*	*.313*	*.386*	*.232*	*33*	

He's a young catcher with a reputation for good glove work. Pierzynski would make an ideal caddy for LeCroy if the Twins trade Javier Valentin. He will end up catching somewhere in the major leagues someday.

Michael Restovich — OF — Bats R — Age 21

YEAR	TEAM	LGE	AB	H	DB	TP	HR	BB/SO	R	RBI	SB	CS	OUT	BA	OBP	SLG	EQA	EQR	DEFENSE
1998	Elizbthn	App	244	66	13	1	9	38/64	40	38	1	1	179	.270	.380	.443	.280	37	60-OF 89
1999	Quad Cit	Mid	505	139	27	3	18	56/105	70	81	3	4	370	.275	.357	.448	.270	70	123-OF 93
2000	*Minnesot*	*AL*	*305*	*89*	*16*	*1*	*15*	*45/79*	*58*	*64*	*1*	*1*	*217*	*.292*	*.383*	*.498*	*.292*	*50*	

The third member of the Twins' trinity, Restovich turned down a Notre Dame scholarship to sign. He's a big kid with power to all fields who knows what to do with different pitches and knows how to drive the ball. His defense in either outfield corner needs work, but he has a good arm, so right field should be his eventual destination. The Twins are conservative about call-ups for hitters, so he probably won't come up until 2001, after Cuddyer and LeCroy.

Brian Richardson — 3B — Bats R — Age 24

YEAR	TEAM	LGE	AB	H	DB	TP	HR	BB/SO	R	RBI	SB	CS	OUT	BA	OBP	SLG	EQA	EQR	DEFENSE
1997	SanAnton	Tex	486	128	22	8	13	33/111	56	69	2	3	361	.263	.319	.422	.247	55	130-3B 95
1999	SaltLake	PCL	439	103	19	3	13	46/103	57	53	0	0	336	.235	.314	.380	.236	45	107-3B 93
2000	*Minnesot*	*AL*	*319*	*88*	*16*	*3*	*11*	*33/100*	*49*	*55*	*1*	*1*	*232*	*.276*	*.344*	*.448*	*.264*	*41*	

After missing 1998 with injuries, Richardson escaped from the Dodgers, where he had no hope with Adrian Beltre in place. After a decent year in 1999, he's stuck in the organization that has Cuddyer about to rocket past him. Like Scott McClain, he could be better than some major-league third basemen, but he's going to have to pick his next employer carefully.

Luis Rivas — SS — Bats R — Age 20

YEAR	TEAM	LGE	AB	H	DB	TP	HR	BB/SO	R	RBI	SB	CS	OUT	BA	OBP	SLG	EQA	EQR	DEFENSE
1997	Ft Wayne	Mid	427	95	21	5	1	23/94	44	25	12	9	341	.222	.269	.302	.190	27	120-SS 93
1998	Ft Myers	Fla	466	122	23	4	4	10/83	43	42	14	4	348	.262	.280	.354	.215	37	124-SS 95
1999	New Brit	Eas	533	129	32	6	6	31/95	64	42	17	8	412	.242	.285	.358	.218	46	123-SS 95
2000	*Minnesot*	*AL*	*517*	*139*	*28*	*5*	*7*	*34/94*	*71*	*61*	*15*	*8*	*386*	*.269*	*.314*	*.383*	*.234*	*51*	

What are the differences between Rivas and Guzman? Rivas also has the arm, range and hands to be a great shortstop. Unlike Guzman, the young Venezuelan was showing improving power and getting a handle on the strike zone, all before he turned 20. He's the better prospect, and ought to beat out Guzman faster than you can say "Lenny Faedo," but it won't happen for keeps until 2001.

Mike Ryan — 2B — Bats L — Age 22

YEAR	TEAM	LGE	AB	H	DB	TP	HR	BB/SO	R	RBI	SB	CS	OUT	BA	OBP	SLG	EQA	EQR	DEFENSE
1997	Elizbthn	App	223	50	4	0	3	26/42	25	18	1	1	174	.224	.309	.283	.205	17	55-3B 74
1998	Ft Wayne	Mid	425	120	22	4	11	35/95	58	60	3	1	306	.282	.339	.431	.259	52	108-3B 89
1999	Ft Myers	Fla	519	133	28	4	9	53/66	76	62	2	2	388	.256	.329	.378	.241	55	124-2B 93
2000	*Minnesot*	*AL*	*513*	*142*	*23*	*2*	*14*	*56/80*	*77*	*80*	*3*	*2*	*373*	*.277*	*.348*	*.411*	*.256*	*62*	

With Cuddyer around, Ryan was moved to second base. The Twins like his patience at the plate and were impressed with his second-half improvement in the field. He's got improving power and he's young. If he survives the jump to Double-A, he'll eventually give the Twins reason to trade Todd Walker.

Jon Schaeffer | C | Bats R Age 24

YEAR	TEAM	LGE	AB	H	DB	TP	HR	BB/SO	R	RBI	SB	CS	OUT	BA	OBP	SLG	EQA	EQR	DEFENSE	
1997	Elizbthn	App	167	40	5	0	5	23/34	20	20	0	0	127	.240	.338	.359	.242	18		
1998	Ft Wayne	Mid	429	107	29	3	10	43/124	63	50	1	2	324	.249	.337	.401	.251	51	54-C 97	48-1B 107
1999	Quad Cit	Mid	405	94	25	2	13	67/79	67	43	1	1	312	.232	.357	.400	.261	54	68-C 89	35-1B 74
2000	Minnesot	AL	338	85	18	1	12	55/76	57	55	1	1	254	.251	.356	.417	.262	45		

Picked out of Stanford in 1997, Schaeffer was old for his league and is not a great catcher. Still, he's someone to think about when you hear how you can never find enough catchers. The Twins are loaded with good catching, and Schaeffer was forced to repeat in the Midwest League because the organization had Pierzynski, LeCroy and Chad Moeller ahead of him. In another organization, he'd be moving up.

Terry Steinbach | F | Casts R Age 38

YEAR	TEAM	LGE	AB	H	DB	TP	HR	BB/SO	R	RBI	SB	CS	OUT	BA	OBP	SLG	EQA	EQR	DEFENSE
1997	Minnesot	AL	446	112	26	1	13	32/102	58	54	6	1	335	.251	.303	.401	.238	46	
1998	Minnesot	AL	421	102	25	2	14	36/87	43	52	0	1	320	.242	.308	.411	.240	45	114-C 103
1999	Minnesot	AL	333	91	14	4	4	34/54	31	38	2	2	244	.273	.344	.375	.247	37	92-C 97

The "F" is for "Fisherman," now that he's retired. Steinbach's reactions behind the plate had slowed to glacial, so his decision was well-timed. Steinbach falls into that category of players who make a Hall of Fame ballot but never garner a vote. He played for 13 years, won a World Series and made a couple of All-Star teams. That's not a bad little career.

Mario Valdez | 1B | Bats L Age 25

YEAR	TEAM	LGE	AB	H	DB	TP	HR	BB/SO	R	RBI	SB	CS	OUT	BA	OBP	SLG	EQA	EQR	DEFENSE	
1997	Nashvill	AA	284	74	19	1	13	39/79	40	55	1	1	211	.261	.369	.472	.282	44	74-1B 98	
1997	ChiSox	AL	115	29	4	0	2	16/37	10	14	1	0	86	.252	.361	.339	.249	13	30-1B 91	
1998	Calgary	PCL	436	125	20	0	18	51/102	65	64	1	1	312	.287	.373	.456	.280	65	117-1B 96	
1999	Charlott	Int	398	95	15	2	20	65/94	61	57	1	0	303	.239	.360	.437	.271	58	96-1B 95	16-OF 92
2000	Minnesot	AL	417	110	19	1	19	67/100	73	78	1	0	307	.264	.366	.451	.275	61		

Valdez has an outstanding opportunity here, having been claimed on waivers from the White Sox. He's got a good defensive reputation, solid power and he'll take a walk. The Sox had their own problems with him, thinking he had a "big league" attitude. Unlike Ortiz or Mientkiewicz, those problems were in somebody else's organization, and not with Tom Kelly or Scott Ullger. He has a chance to win the first-base job in camp.

Javier Valentin | C | Bats B Age 24

YEAR	TEAM	LGE	AB	H	DB	TP	HR	BB/SO	R	RBI	SB	CS	OUT	BA	OBP	SLG	EQA	EQR	DEFENSE
1997	New Brit	Eas	376	88	11	0	9	22/63	34	45	2	2	290	.234	.278	.335	.204	27	
1998	Minnesot	AL	162	32	8	1	3	10/29	11	18	0	0	130	.198	.244	.315	.181	9	45-C 93
1999	Minnesot	AL	216	52	13	1	4	19/39	20	25	0	0	164	.241	.305	.366	.227	20	62-C 107
2000	Minnesot	AL	242	62	11	1	6	19/43	29	32	1	0	180	.256	.310	.384	.233	23	

Valentin is caught in a bind. While he won't be the star people expected after his big year at 19 in the Midwest League, he's a solid backup catcher and could count on playing time as long as Steinbach was around. Now LeCroy should be coming to town, so Valentin will either get used to being his caddy or hope for a trade to avoid that worst of all possible things, a summer in Utah.

Todd Walker | 2B | Bats L Age 27

YEAR	TEAM	LGE	AB	H	DB	TP	HR	BB/SO	R	RBI	SB	CS	OUT	BA	OBP	SLG	EQA	EQR	DEFENSE
1997	Minnesot	AL	156	37	8	1	3	10/29	15	16	7	0	119	.237	.288	.359	.227	15	31-3B 107
1997	SaltLake	PCL	308	88	14	1	8	36/52	47	36	3	3	223	.286	.362	.416	.264	40	73-3B 97
1998	Minnesot	AL	526	166	41	3	12	45/64	80	59	17	7	367	.316	.372	.473	.284	79	133-2B 100
1999	Minnesot	AL	524	140	35	4	5	46/83	55	41	17	10	394	.267	.327	.378	.241	56	94-2B 97
2000	Minnesot	AL	479	133	27	2	10	51/71	81	67	15	6	352	.278	.347	.405	.256	59	

It was a disappointing season for Walker. The collapse of the offense around him was made worse by his getting frustrated with a lack of home runs in the first half. He got into bad habits trying to hit them the rest of the way. You could compare the situation to what George Brett endured in 1986. While lineup protection has been debunked pretty thoroughly, players don't play in a vacuum. When expectations lead to pressing, you see these sorts of breakdowns. Because he hasn't hit left-handed pitchers in his two full seasons so far, he's earned a platoon label. Walker should bounce back better than that projection.

PITCHERS (Averages: ERA: 4.50 / H/9: 9.00 / HR/9: 1.00 / BB/9: 3.50 / K/9: 6.50 / KWH: 1.00)

Grant Balfour   Throws R   Age 22

YEAR	TEAM	LGE	IP	H	ER	HR	BB	K	ERA	W	L	H/9	HR/9	BB/9	K/9	KWH	PERA
1998	Elizbthn	App	70.3	92	44	8	35	46	5.63	3	5	11.77	1.02	4.48	5.89	0.49	6.53
1999	Quad Cit	Mid	84.3	86	49	9	42	67	5.23	4	5	9.18	0.96	4.48	7.15	0.93	4.91

Balfour is probably the best prospect among the Twins' crop of Australian pitchers, although Brad Thomas tossed a no-hitter against Charlotte in the Florida State League. A great athlete who throws hard—though you don't want to get too excited about guys with only A-ball experience. Still, his peripheral numbers are very good compared to other guys who have only pitched in the Midwest League.

Jason Bell   Throws R   Age 25

YEAR	TEAM	LGE	IP	H	ER	HR	BB	K	ERA	W	L	H/9	HR/9	BB/9	K/9	KWH	PERA
1997	New Brit	Eas	148.7	200	86	18	68	114	5.21	7	10	12.11	1.09	4.12	6.90	0.71	6.72
1998	New Brit	Eas	157.3	181	113	23	70	130	6.46	6	11	10.35	1.32	4.00	7.44	1.00	5.83
1999	New Brit	Eas	44.3	55	25	4	13	26	5.08	2	3	11.17	0.81	2.64	5.28	0.71	5.28
1999	SaltLake	PCL	75.0	97	54	10	41	59	6.48	3	5	11.64	1.20	4.92	7.08	0.65	6.96

One of the ghosts of a heralded draft turned disappointing. Bell was the second-round pick in 1995, after Mark Redman was picked in the first round. Both were expected to be contributing in the majors by now. It might seem perverse to keep sending somebody the organization has invested so much in to New Britain year after year, but Bell doesn't throw hard, relying heavily on breaking stuff and a nice change-up. Without dominating stuff, sending him to Salt Lake would be like throwing him into a pit of wild dogs just to see which limbs got torn off first.

Hector Carrasco   Throws R   Age 30

YEAR	TEAM	LGE	IP	H	ER	HR	BB	K	ERA	W	L	H/9	HR/9	BB/9	K/9	KWH	PERA
1997	Cincnnti	NL	52.3	50	24	3	27	43	4.13	3	3	8.60	0.52	4.64	7.39	1.02	4.30
1997	KansasCy	AL	35.3	28	19	4	16	31	4.84	2	2	7.13	1.02	4.08	7.90	1.60	3.82
1998	Minnesot	AL	62.7	72	27	4	32	47	3.88	4	3	10.34	0.57	4.60	6.75	0.72	5.31
1999	Minnesot	AL	50.0	45	25	3	18	36	4.50	3	3	8.10	0.54	3.24	6.48	1.20	3.42

Carrasco had a nice little season after having surgery in March to remove a blood clot and correct circulatory problems in his right shoulder. He surprised everybody by returning by the All-Star break. A strikeout/groundball middle reliever, if he's sound he could give his employer 80 good innings.

Jack Cressend   Throws R   Age 25

YEAR	TEAM	LGE	IP	H	ER	HR	BB	K	ERA	W	L	H/9	HR/9	BB/9	K/9	KWH	PERA
1997	Sarasota	Fla	155.0	206	125	19	76	115	7.26	5	12	11.96	1.10	4.41	6.68	0.63	6.79
1998	Trenton	Eas	142.7	192	99	14	64	103	6.25	5	11	12.11	0.88	4.04	6.50	0.65	6.43
1999	New Brit	Eas	135.3	182	95	10	59	95	6.32	5	10	12.10	0.67	3.92	6.32	0.63	6.12

Claimed on waivers from the Red Sox in April, courtesy of Dan Duquette's inveterate roster shuffling. He's not really a prospect, because he doesn't have great heat, but he has command of four pitches he can throw for strikes. He generated twice as many groundball outs as flyball outs in 1999, so with some good infield defense he could worm his way into being a fifth starter or a very effective middle reliever.

Eddie Guardado   Throws L   Age 29

YEAR	TEAM	LGE	IP	H	ER	HR	BB	K	ERA	W	L	H/9	HR/9	BB/9	K/9	KWH	PERA
1997	Minnesot	AL	46.7	44	21	7	17	55	4.05	3	2	8.49	1.35	3.28	10.61	3.02	4.44
1998	Minnesot	AL	66.3	64	30	9	29	54	4.07	4	3	8.68	1.22	3.93	7.33	1.17	4.75
1999	Minnesot	AL	49.0	34	21	6	24	52	3.86	3	2	6.24	1.10	4.41	9.55	2.48	3.49

Another part of the Twins' unheralded but effective bullpen, and someone with considerable value in a trade market where a Ricky Rincon can fetch a Brian Giles. His rubber-arm reputation did take a hit this year, as he went on the disabled list in June for the first time in his career, but he was back in action after the All-Star break. He's waiting for his moment to outshine other great situational left-handers like Graeme Lloyd or Paul Assenmacher. As an ex-starter, he can do more than just pitch in situational relief if given the chance.

LaTroy Hawkins   Throws R   Age 27

YEAR	TEAM	LGE	IP	H	ER	HR	BB	K	ERA	W	L	H/9	HR/9	BB/9	K/9	KWH	PERA
1997	SaltLake	PCL	73.7	97	48	4	17	45	5.86	3	5	11.85	0.49	2.08	5.50	0.92	5.01
1997	Minnesot	AL	105.0	130	65	17	47	59	5.57	5	7	11.14	1.46	4.03	5.06	0.43	6.51
1998	Minnesot	AL	193.0	219	114	25	64	107	5.32	9	12	10.21	1.17	2.98	4.99	0.61	5.18
1999	Minnesot	AL	178.7	224	117	25	59	107	5.89	7	13	11.28	1.26	2.97	5.39	0.65	5.89

Hawkins's career is becoming an episode of "Unsolved Mysteries." After watching him get smacked around early and often (the Twins were outscored 33-2 while he was on the mound in his first six starts), Kelly complained that Hawkins either had mechanical problems or concentration problems. He would routinely fall behind hitters while struggling to find a consistent release point for his fastball. Then he tossed seven shutout innings against the Cardinals in mid-July, relying more on his curve and splitter. He credited Dick Such for helping him with the splitter, but opponents complained that Hawkins was scuffing the ball. If he was, he wasn't caught. I won't predict a Mike Scott-style comeback; while there are reasons to believe he's making progress, this is the make-or-break year.

Matt Kinney   Throws R   Age 23

YEAR	TEAM	LGE	IP	H	ER	HR	BB	K	ERA	W	L	H/9	HR/9	BB/9	K/9	KWH	PERA
1997	Michigan	Mid	107.7	120	74	5	93	86	6.19	4	8	10.03	0.42	7.77	7.19	0.50	6.19
1998	Sarasota	Fla	114.0	129	83	6	96	75	6.55	4	9	10.18	0.47	7.58	5.92	0.34	6.32
1998	Ft Myers	Fla	34.7	37	22	0	23	30	5.71	2	2	9.61	0.00	5.97	7.79	0.79	4.67
1999	New Brit	Eas	58.0	78	59	8	39	41	9.16	1	5	12.10	1.24	6.05	6.36	0.41	7.76

Kinney is the prospect stolen from the Red Sox in exchange for two months of Flounder Swindell's valuable time. He had surgery to remove bone chips from his elbow; before the injury he had command of a great sinking fastball and an off-the-table curve. The injury wasn't as severe as initially thought, and he was throwing in the high 90s in the Arizona Fall League. He'll move up fast if he improves his command.

Mike Lincoln   Throws R   Age 25

YEAR	TEAM	LGE	IP	H	ER	HR	BB	K	ERA	W	L	H/9	HR/9	BB/9	K/9	KWH	PERA
1997	Ft Myers	Fla	118.7	181	66	6	34	57	5.01	6	7	13.73	0.46	2.58	4.32	0.39	6.29
1998	New Brit	Eas	159.7	219	102	14	40	86	5.75	7	11	12.34	0.79	2.25	4.85	0.63	5.75
1999	SaltLake	PCL	57.7	84	49	10	25	32	7.65	2	4	13.11	1.56	3.90	4.99	0.36	7.80
1999	Minnesot	AL	78.0	97	51	9	25	28	5.88	3	6	11.19	1.04	2.88	3.23	0.24	5.54

How far can a guy go with great command of adequate stuff? After an All-Star season in 1998 he made the Twins in 1999, only to get rocked out of the gate. He made it worse by overthrowing, which flattened out his curveball. So then he didn't have the great command that was his calling card, at which point there weren't any strengths to talk about. There's no reason to suspect he's going to grow up to be Brad Radke.

Kyle Lohse   Throws R   Age 21

YEAR	TEAM	LGE	IP	H	ER	HR	BB	K	ERA	W	L	H/9	HR/9	BB/9	K/9	KWH	PERA
1998	Rockford	Mid	155.3	215	107	12	59	84	6.20	6	11	12.46	0.70	3.42	4.87	0.42	6.20
1999	Daytona	Fla	50.3	56	24	5	21	33	4.29	3	3	10.01	0.89	3.75	5.90	0.69	5.01
1999	Ft Myers	Fla	38.0	58	35	6	11	27	8.29	1	3	13.74	1.42	2.61	6.39	0.85	7.58
1999	New Brit	Eas	67.0	98	54	10	25	34	7.25	2	5	13.16	1.34	3.36	4.57	0.35	7.39

The prize of the Aguilera deal. There's hope that as he matures physically he'll pick up velocity. In the meantime, he's got good command of his slider and throws strikes with his fastball and change-up. He should end up spending 2000 in New Britain, since he's already zipped through high-A ball.

Alan Mahaffey — Throws L — Age 26

YEAR	TEAM	LGE	IP	H	ER	HR	BB	K	ERA	W	L	H/9	HR/9	BB/9	K/9	KWH	PERA
1997	Ft Myers	Fla	42.3	67	43	3	11	40	9.14	1	4	14.24	0.64	2.34	8.50	1.62	6.80
1997	New Brit	Eas	20.7	24	13	2	11	23	5.66	1	1	10.45	0.87	4.79	10.02	1.50	5.66
1998	New Brit	Eas	46.7	79	36	6	20	46	6.94	1	4	15.24	1.16	3.86	8.87	1.00	8.68
1999	New Brit	Eas	89.3	136	57	15	41	66	5.74	4	6	13.70	1.51	4.13	6.65	0.58	8.26
1999	SaltLake	PCL	21.0	28	17	1	18	9	7.29	1	1	12.00	0.43	7.71	3.86	0.12	7.29

He got knocked around in his stints as a starter. When he pitches in relief, his fastball gets up over 90 mph, but he lacks a consistent change-up. He has a cutter he can run in on right-handed hitters, but nothing to freeze lefties. Mahaffey is a longshot.

Joe Mays — Throws R — Age 24

YEAR	TEAM	LGE	IP	H	ER	HR	BB	K	ERA	W	L	H/9	HR/9	BB/9	K/9	KWH	PERA
1997	Wisconsn	Mid	75.7	82	28	4	28	55	3.33	5	3	9.75	0.48	3.33	6.54	0.98	4.28
1997	Lancastr	Cal	93.0	121	57	9	39	59	5.52	4	6	11.71	0.87	3.77	5.71	0.55	6.10
1998	Ft Myers	Fla	86.3	126	57	9	31	62	5.94	4	6	13.14	0.94	3.23	6.46	0.74	6.78
1998	New Brit	Eas	53.7	74	48	4	24	36	8.05	1	5	12.41	0.67	4.02	6.04	0.55	6.37
1999	Minnesot	AL	175.3	166	77	20	65	119	3.95	11	8	8.52	1.03	3.34	6.11	0.98	4.21

This is a great example of a good development pattern for a rookie pitcher. Unlike Lincoln and Perkins, Mays started off pitching middle relief, usually mopping up whatever mess Hawkins or Lincoln had created. He struggled initially, but Dick Such was credited with teaching him a four-seam fastball. Dropped into the rotation out of desperation, he quickly impressed by going after batters and pitching inside and mixing in his slider or change-up anywhere in the count. After a great two months, he struggled down the stretch but impressed Kelly again by going straight to the manager when his rotation spot was rumored to be in danger. While he poor-mouths himself as "Average Joe" for the local press, there are concerns that he's too hyper and prone to tantrums. Assuming they don't overreact and start shoveling Ritalin into him, I like his future.

Travis Miller — Throws L — Age 27

YEAR	TEAM	LGE	IP	H	ER	HR	BB	K	ERA	W	L	H/9	HR/9	BB/9	K/9	KWH	PERA
1997	SaltLake	PCL	121.0	134	66	10	61	73	4.91	6	7	9.97	0.74	4.54	5.43	0.49	5.21
1997	Minnesot	AL	49.0	62	44	7	24	26	8.08	1	4	11.39	1.29	4.41	4.78	0.34	6.61
1998	SaltLake	PCL	58.0	59	31	3	37	54	4.81	3	3	9.16	0.47	5.74	8.38	1.00	4.97
1998	Minnesot	AL	23.7	24	9	0	11	23	3.42	2	1	9.13	0.00	4.18	8.75	1.50	3.80
1999	Minnesot	AL	50.7	52	15	3	15	41	2.66	4	2	9.24	0.53	2.66	7.28	1.61	3.91

An old-fashioned story: failed starter turns into decent reliever. He was used mostly in garbage time as the second left-hander behind Guardado but should have been given more to do. He's first in line to do more if Guardado is traded. Miller still has the nifty slider that attracted people's attention in the first place.

Ryan Mills — Throws All Over The Place — Age 22

YEAR	TEAM	LGE	IP	H	ER	HR	BB	K	ERA	W	L	H/9	HR/9	BB/9	K/9	KWH	PERA
1999	Ft Myers	Fla	83.7	147	131	9	106	57	14.09	1	8	15.81	0.97	11.40	6.13	0.16	12.48

The highly-touted left-hander was picked out of Arizona State in the first round in 1998, amidst concerns that he was overworked in college after he came up with a weak rotator cuff. He struggled early in Florida, got demoted to the Gulf Coast League, received all sorts of specialized instruction, and by season's end was still no better. What you don't see in his DT is that he beaned 16 guys and threw 20 wild pitches. The Twins claim he's still got that mid-90s heat and a good curve and change-up, and make sunny comparisons of Mills to a golfer off his game. If he isn't hurt, he could probably lick those control problems in a league where the batters are nine feet tall and home plate is three feet wide. Probably.

Eric Milton   Throws L   Age 24

YEAR	TEAM	LGE	IP	H	ER	HR	BB	K	ERA	W	L	H/9	HR/9	BB/9	K/9	KWH	PERA
1997	Tampa	Fla	88.7	98	45	11	18	74	4.57	5	5	9.95	1.12	1.83	7.51	2.32	4.47
1997	Norwich	Eas	73.7	67	31	2	38	54	3.79	5	3	8.19	0.24	4.64	6.60	0.86	3.79
1998	Minnesot	AL	174.3	188	103	23	74	109	5.32	8	11	9.71	1.19	3.82	5.63	0.64	5.21
1999	Minnesot	AL	210.0	178	94	24	62	168	4.03	13	10	7.63	1.03	2.66	7.20	1.91	3.47

He started the year having problems putting away hitters early, racking up big pitch counts by the sixth inning. As the season wore on, he gained greater command of a slider to freeze right-handed hitters and developed a change-up to drop on the left-ies who were sitting on the slider. Add that to a fastball consistently in the low 90s and a snapping curve, and you've suddenly got one of the league's best left-handed starters. The no-hitter may have been against a no-stars Angels lineup, but the stuff is there for Milton to do it against anybody, and the Angels weren't all that special with Mo Vaughn in the lineup, anyway. By himself, Milton will end up rehabilitating the way the Knoblauch deal gets remembered. But then, he has to.

Daniel Mota   Throws R   Age 24

YEAR	TEAM	LGE	IP	H	ER	HR	BB	K	ERA	W	L	H/9	HR/9	BB/9	K/9	KWH	PERA
1997	Oneonta	NYP	24.7	31	12	0	23	25	4.38	2	1	11.31	0.00	8.39	9.12	0.65	6.93
1997	Greensbr	SAL	27.7	23	8	2	15	20	2.60	2	1	7.48	0.65	4.88	6.51	0.87	3.90
1998	Ft Wayne	Mid	29.7	32	19	3	11	26	5.76	1	2	9.71	0.91	3.34	7.89	1.43	4.85
1998	Ft Myers	Fla	43.0	56	26	4	28	37	5.44	2	3	11.72	0.84	5.86	7.74	0.65	6.91
1999	Ft Myers	Fla	16.7	24	7	0	7	16	3.78	1	1	12.96	0.00	3.78	8.64	1.14	5.94
1999	New Brit	Eas	12.0	13	5	2	6	10	3.75	1	0	9.75	1.50	4.50	7.50	0.96	6.00

A damaged elbow burned most of his 1999 season, and he wasn't able to get a roster spot in any of the winter leagues. It may take him a few months to get back up to full speed, but he will pitch in 2000, and he has the talent to be in the Twins' bullpen by year's end.

Dan Perkins   Throws R   Age 25

YEAR	TEAM	LGE	IP	H	ER	HR	BB	K	ERA	W	L	H/9	HR/9	BB/9	K/9	KWH	PERA
1997	New Brit	Eas	130.0	192	112	16	57	91	7.75	4	10	13.29	1.11	3.95	6.30	0.57	7.41
1998	New Brit	Eas	107.7	169	81	9	36	62	6.77	4	8	14.13	0.75	3.01	5.18	0.47	7.11
1998	SaltLake	PCL	47.7	46	26	7	23	29	4.91	2	3	8.69	1.32	4.34	5.48	0.59	4.91
1999	Minnesot	AL	89.3	110	59	12	42	46	5.94	4	6	11.08	1.21	4.23	4.63	0.34	6.25

The other Twin who was a high-school teammate of Alex Rodriguez. Did a Twins' scout go to their games and say, "There's no way we'll get A-Rod, so let's watch everyone else"? Perkins was a second-round pick in 1993, and despite making the majors, he's been a big disappointment. His fastball has decent movement and he's got a nice overhand curve. Like Lincoln, he started to nibble and overthrow, making his weekly beatings even worse.

Brad Radke   Throws R   Age 27

YEAR	TEAM	LGE	IP	H	ER	HR	BB	K	ERA	W	L	H/9	HR/9	BB/9	K/9	KWH	PERA
1997	Minnesot	AL	241.7	231	104	26	48	176	3.87	16	11	8.60	0.97	1.79	6.55	2.09	3.61
1998	Minnesot	AL	216.3	230	98	21	45	148	4.08	13	11	9.57	0.87	1.87	6.16	1.58	4.08
1999	Minnesot	AL	222.7	225	83	24	43	125	3.35	16	9	9.09	0.97	1.74	5.05	1.21	3.84

Radke is that rare right-hander who doesn't have a blazing fastball, but is nevertheless better off when he isn't relying on his breaking stuff. When he's on, he's just alternating his fastball and his amazing change-up to generate lots of groundballs, while mixing in the slider and curve for show. He had some problems after taking a line drive off his knee; overcompensating may have created his subsequent groin problems. The declining strikeout rate is a source for concern. He's never been overpowering, and if he stops fooling some of the people some of the time, he could end up being a lot less effective very quickly.

Rob Radlosky — Throws R — Age 26

YEAR	TEAM	LGE	IP	H	ER	HR	BB	K	ERA	W	L	H/9	HR/9	BB/9	K/9	KWH	PERA
1997	Ft Myers	Fla	113.0	130	71	13	52	79	5.65	5	8	10.35	1.04	4.14	6.29	0.69	5.58
1998	New Brit	Eas	119.0	163	83	17	46	87	6.28	4	9	12.33	1.29	3.48	6.58	0.75	6.81
1999	SaltLake	PCL	98.3	102	48	10	45	54	4.39	6	5	9.34	0.92	4.12	4.94	0.47	4.85

This is another of the Twins' good-command, adequate-stuff, cannon-fodder types. He surrendered an eye-popping seven home runs in 8⅔ innings during a brief, ugly call-up. This being the Twins, chances are he'll be back to start another souvenir shower, which might at least help attendance. "Hey kids, Radlosky's pitching! Bleacher seats for everybody!"

Fred Rath — Throws R — Age 27

YEAR	TEAM	LGE	IP	H	ER	HR	BB	K	ERA	W	L	H/9	HR/9	BB/9	K/9	KWH	PERA
1997	Ft Myers	Fla	19.0	28	8	3	5	15	3.79	1	1	13.26	1.42	2.37	7.11	1.20	7.11
1997	New Brit	Eas	44.7	56	24	1	15	24	4.84	2	3	11.28	0.20	3.02	4.84	0.51	4.84
1997	SaltLake	PCL	10.3	11	2	1	2	9	1.74	1	0	9.58	0.87	1.74	7.84	2.75	4.35
1998	SaltLake	PCL	32.0	35	15	4	10	12	4.22	2	2	9.84	1.13	2.81	3.38	0.31	4.78
1998	ColSprin	PCL	29.3	35	15	2	18	17	4.60	1	2	10.74	0.61	5.52	5.22	0.34	5.83
1999	SaltLake	PCL	80.3	91	41	8	30	29	4.59	4	5	10.20	0.90	3.36	3.25	0.23	5.04

One of a number of Twins pitchers drafted or signed out of the Florida colleges not named Florida State or Miami (those guys are expensive) and occasionally called a pitching prospect. He's a reliever with decent control and no single dominant pitch. If things break his way, he could be the 11th or 12th guy on a staff.

Gary Rath — Throws L — Age 27

YEAR	TEAM	LGE	IP	H	ER	HR	BB	K	ERA	W	L	H/9	HR/9	BB/9	K/9	KWH	PERA
1997	Albuquer	PCL	133.7	159	86	15	53	85	5.79	6	9	10.71	1.01	3.57	5.72	0.64	5.52
1998	Albuquer	PCL	156.7	184	85	15	63	98	4.88	8	9	10.57	0.86	3.62	5.63	0.62	5.29
1999	SaltLake	PCL	96.7	135	74	10	33	54	6.89	3	8	12.57	0.93	3.07	5.03	0.49	6.33

In case you're wondering, he is not Fred's twin, although they were born only five days apart. After years of getting his ears pinned back in the PCL, you'd hope somebody would pick up the tab for shell-shock treatment. He's past the point where he can help a team as a fifth starter, but if Andrew Lorraine can finally get a chance, Rath may yet as well.

Mark Redman — Throws L — Age 26

YEAR	TEAM	LGE	IP	H	ER	HR	BB	K	ERA	W	L	H/9	HR/9	BB/9	K/9	KWH	PERA
1997	SaltLake	PCL	153.7	191	106	17	82	108	6.21	6	11	11.19	1.00	4.80	6.33	0.56	6.33
1998	New Brit	Eas	42.3	53	17	4	21	38	3.61	3	2	11.27	0.85	4.46	8.08	0.97	6.17
1998	SaltLake	PCL	100.0	110	68	11	48	75	6.12	4	7	9.90	0.99	4.32	6.75	0.80	5.31
1999	SaltLake	PCL	130.3	145	85	10	62	91	5.87	5	9	10.01	0.69	4.28	6.28	0.69	5.04
1999	Minnesot	AL	13.0	16	11	3	7	11	7.62	0	1	11.08	2.08	4.85	7.62	0.81	7.62

The team's top pick in the 1995 draft, he had been a major disappointment coming into 1999. Much of that had to do with trying to hone his craft in a Utah bandbox, but in his third try, Redman seems to have exorcised his PCL demons. He had a brilliant June, going 6-0 with an ERA under 3.00, and the organization buzzed about his newfound aggressiveness, willingness to spot his fastball inside and improved command of his curve. Something is amiss, though, because Tom Kelly seems to blow a gasket every time the idea of calling him up is broached. After making one start with the Twins, Redman complained of fatigue, and that was enough to kill off his opportunity.

Juan Rincon — Throws R — Age 21

YEAR	TEAM	LGE	IP	H	ER	HR	BB	K	ERA	W	L	H/9	HR/9	BB/9	K/9	KWH	PERA
1998	Ft Wayne	Mid	88.7	107	64	9	69	51	6.50	3	7	10.86	0.91	7.00	5.18	0.26	7.00
1999	Quad Cit	Mid	148.3	187	84	11	75	108	5.10	7	9	11.35	0.67	4.55	6.55	0.62	5.95

Made big strides in his second year in the Midwest League: a 2.92 ERA and 153 strikeouts in 163 innings. He'd already been an All-Star in the league in 1998. Signed as a free agent out of Venezuela, Rincon should start appearing on prospect lists now that Pedro Martinez has given right-handed pitchers under six feet tall a good name.

J.C. Romero   Throws L   Age 24

YEAR	TEAM	LGE	IP	H	ER	HR	BB	K	ERA	W	L	H/9	HR/9	BB/9	K/9	KWH	PERA
1997	Elizbthn	App	21.0	37	19	4	10	16	8.14	0	2	15.86	1.71	4.29	6.86	0.52	10.29
1997	Ft Myers	Fla	10.7	16	10	2	5	7	8.44	0	1	13.50	1.69	4.22	5.91	0.46	8.44
1998	New Brit	Eas	73.0	59	34	3	48	63	4.19	4	4	7.27	0.37	5.92	7.77	1.05	3.82
1999	New Brit	Eas	50.0	60	27	6	37	42	4.86	3	3	10.80	1.08	6.66	7.56	0.59	7.02
1999	SaltLake	PCL	19.7	17	10	1	16	17	4.58	1	1	7.78	0.46	7.32	7.78	0.79	4.58

The wild left-hander came over from Puerto Rico to play for the University of Mobile and has shot up the ladder since being drafted in 1997. This summer, he jumped to the majors after pitching in the Pan Am Games. He generates groundball outs, flashing a good fastball, curve and slider. Romero is the guy who's going to make Eddie Guardado expendable.

Jason Ryan   Throws R   Age 24

YEAR	TEAM	LGE	IP	H	ER	HR	BB	K	ERA	W	L	H/9	HR/9	BB/9	K/9	KWH	PERA
1997	Daytona	Fla	167.3	193	116	26	73	111	6.24	7	12	10.38	1.40	3.93	5.97	0.65	5.92
1998	WestTenn	Sou	142.3	186	94	21	56	100	5.94	6	10	11.76	1.33	3.54	6.32	0.72	6.51
1999	WestTenn	Sou	41.7	36	15	1	17	43	3.24	3	2	7.78	0.22	3.67	9.29	2.26	3.24
1999	New Brit	Eas	48.0	55	32	6	27	34	6.00	2	3	10.31	1.13	5.06	6.38	0.58	6.00
1999	SaltLake	PCL	53.7	56	33	7	28	29	5.53	2	4	9.39	1.17	4.70	4.86	0.40	5.37
1999	Minnesot	AL	41.3	44	19	8	16	15	4.14	3	2	9.58	1.74	3.48	3.27	0.24	5.66

Like anybody the Twins drafted earlier in the decade, Ryan has command of four pitches but lacks velocity. Unlike the others, there's a catch. After being picked up from the Cubs in the Aguilera trade, Ryan got a crack at the rotation because he was still standing and the Twins needed a body. After one start in which he crossed up Steinbach repeatedly, the Twins figured out Ryan needed glasses because he couldn't pick up the signs. His next start out, he dominated the Blue Jays for eight innings. That brings to light the extent to which some major-league teams let things like vision tests get done sloppily, if at all. You would think that with the amount of money invested in the industry, something like this wouldn't happen, but here we have it. In addition to finally seeing his catcher for the first time in years, Ryan also added an improved slider. Don't expect greatness, but he may turn out to be a decent fourth or fifth starter.

Benj Sampson   Throws L   Age 25

YEAR	TEAM	LGE	IP	H	ER	HR	BB	K	ERA	W	L	H/9	HR/9	BB/9	K/9	KWH	PERA
1997	New Brit	Eas	106.7	137	68	11	52	74	5.74	5	7	11.56	0.93	4.39	6.24	0.57	6.33
1998	SaltLake	PCL	164.3	193	87	21	59	115	4.76	8	10	10.57	1.15	3.23	6.30	0.87	5.48
1998	Minnesot	AL	17.3	9	3	0	7	16	1.56	2	0	4.67	0.00	3.63	8.31	3.04	1.56
1999	Minnesot	AL	73.3	101	56	15	33	58	6.87	2	6	12.40	1.84	4.05	7.12	0.75	7.85
1999	SaltLake	PCL	15.7	26	15	3	1	6	8.62	0	2	14.94	1.72	0.57	3.45	1.03	8.04

Stop me if you've heard this one. There's this left-hander with a nice curve and change-up, but a spotty fastball, who gets tossed into the rotation to give it some southpaw flavor. He gets hammered and bumped to mop-up duties; he gets hammered some more and gets sent to the PCL, where he gets hammered again. Like Gary Rath, Sampson may yet become useful, and his chance is currently better than Rath's.

Brent Stentz   Throws R   Age 24

YEAR	TEAM	LGE	IP	H	ER	HR	BB	K	ERA	W	L	H/9	HR/9	BB/9	K/9	KWH	PERA
1997	Ft Myers	Fla	62.3	74	30	5	31	55	4.33	4	3	10.68	0.72	4.48	7.94	0.99	5.63
1998	New Brit	Eas	55.3	54	17	4	31	52	2.77	4	2	8.78	0.65	5.04	8.46	1.21	4.55
1999	SaltLake	PCL	25.7	42	30	5	24	19	10.52	0	3	14.73	1.75	8.42	6.66	0.27	11.22
1999	New Brit	Eas	30.0	27	15	3	14	35	4.50	2	1	8.10	0.90	4.20	10.50	2.42	4.20

After he won the Eastern League's MVP award in 1998, the PCL chased him back inside of two months. He's exactly the sort of guy who should never pitch for Salt Lake, flyball-prone with spotty control and an average fastball. There's never been any such thing as a closer prospect, and Stentz doesn't change that. He's the new-and-improved Gus Gandarillas, if you remember the last great Twins minor-league closer-to-be. He can pitch; just don't expect him to be Armando Benitez.

Mike Trombley   Throws R   Age 33

YEAR	TEAM	LGE	IP	H	ER	HR	BB	K	ERA	W	L	H/9	HR/9	BB/9	K/9	KWH	PERA
1997	Minnesot	AL	83.3	74	39	6	32	75	4.21	5	4	7.99	0.65	3.46	8.10	1.77	3.56
1998	Minnesot	AL	97.7	86	37	15	43	90	3.41	7	4	7.92	1.38	3.96	8.29	1.64	4.42
1999	Minnesot	AL	89.0	88	36	13	27	85	3.64	6	4	8.90	1.31	2.73	8.60	2.27	4.45

He's been a dramatically better pitcher since adding a forkball in 1996, courtesy of Salt Lake pitching coach Rick Anderson, so put him on the list of people who had a career because of the pitch, rather than one destroyed by it. Trombley was victimized by Carl Pohlad's whim when he and his agent made it clear he'd love to sign a multi-year deal for less than market value if it meant staying in the Twin Cities. The Twins ought to be wishing they could bottle that sort of enthusiasm for a team currently going nowhere, and send a case to the governor and the state legislature. Instead, Terry Ryan had to put Trombley off because Pohlad didn't feel like making a decision. The Orioles signed him to a three-year deal, which amounts to a youth movement for the Birds. He'll set up Mike Timlin and collect a few saves along the way.

Bob Wells   Throws R   Age 34

YEAR	TEAM	LGE	IP	H	ER	HR	BB	K	ERA	W	L	H/9	HR/9	BB/9	K/9	KWH	PERA
1997	Seattle	AL	69.3	82	42	10	18	52	5.45	3	5	10.64	1.30	2.34	6.75	1.37	5.32
1998	Seattle	AL	53.0	50	33	12	17	29	5.60	2	4	8.49	2.04	2.89	4.92	0.74	5.09
1999	Minnesot	AL	89.0	74	35	7	27	45	3.54	6	4	7.48	0.71	2.73	4.55	0.76	3.13

Here's another guy who gets away from Lou Piniella and turns into a good reliever. This time, the non-news event took place in Minnesota. After Aguilera was traded, Wells was bumped up into Mike Trombley's setup role. He was brought into any inning in which the opposition got runners aboard, and showed remarkable effectiveness pitching from the stretch. He stranded two-thirds of the runners he inherited—not a league-leading figure, but considering he inherited a lot of runners, not bad at all. Would you call that clutch pitching? Or a canny use of one journeyman's specific skill? I don't think it's a skill that you can count on, but it worked in 1999 and it bears watching in 2000.

Support-Neutral Records   MINNESOTA TWINS   Park Effect: -1.8%

PITCHER	GS	IP	R	SNW	SNL	SNPCT	W	L	RA	APW	SNVA	SNWAR
LaTroy Hawkins	33	174.3	136	8.1	14.8	.355	10	14	7.02	-3.33	-3.21	-1.61
Mike Lincoln	15	69.7	57	3.1	6.2	.330	3	9	7.36	-1.58	-1.40	-0.88
Joe Mays	20	118.7	54	8.0	5.7	.582	6	9	4.10	1.33	1.15	2.16
Eric Milton	34	206.3	111	13.0	11.1	.541	7	11	4.84	0.72	0.87	2.79
Dan Perkins	12	53.7	54	1.6	6.1	.209	1	7	9.06	-2.16	-2.10	-1.65
Brad Radke	33	218.7	97	15.2	9.1	.625	12	14	3.99	2.69	2.80	4.87
Gary Rath	1	3.0	5	0.0	0.6	.056	0	1	15.00	-0.31	-0.26	-0.24
Mark Redman	1	4.7	3	0.1	0.4	.240	0	0	5.79	-0.03	-0.09	-0.10
Jason Ryan	8	40.7	23	2.6	2.4	.511	1	4	5.09	0.04	0.07	0.43
Benj Sampson	4	9.0	21	0.2	2.6	.063	0	1	21.00	-1.48	-1.22	-1.02
TOTALS	161	898.7	561	51.9	59.1	.468	40	70	5.62	-4.10	-3.39	4.74

Isn't it about time to give up on LaTroy Hawkins? I know he had promise, and he's still relatively young, but he has 98 major league starts now and still hasn't cracked the .400 Support-Neutral Winning Percentage (SNPct) mark in five seasons. Last year was his worst year yet, and it moved him past Todd Van Poppel to rank as the second-worst starter since the Support-Neutral stats were developed, at 4.1 wins below replacement level. He's second to Scott Aldred, another pitcher to whom the Twins gave tons of starts in the hopes that he would eventually fulfill his promise. Yes, Hawkins improved over the course of the year, from a .261 SNPct in the first half to a .464 in the second half. But even that second half is not the level of pitching most teams are dying to get. At this point it seems that Hawkins's ceiling is fairly low, and the risk you take in trying to reach that ceiling is high.

Pitcher Abuse Points

PITCHER	AGE	GS	PAP	PAP/S	WKLD	MAX	1-90	91-100	101-110	111-120	121-130	131-140	141+
LaTroy Hawkins	26	33	120	3.6	7.3	123	11	12	7	1	2	0	0
Mike Lincoln	24	15	0	0.0	0.0	96	12	3	0	0	0	0	0
Joe Mays	23	20	124	6.2	15.5	126	3	11	1	4	1	0	0
Eric Milton	23	34	348	10.2	25.6	128	10	4	10	7	3	0	0
Dan Perkins	24	12	5	0.4	1.0	104	9	1	2	0	0	0	0
Brad Radke	26	33	155	4.7	9.4	118	7	10	10	6	0	0	0
Gary Rath	26	1	0	0.0	0.0	70	1	0	0	0	0	0	0
Mark Redman	25	1	0	0.0	0.0	96	0	1	0	0	0	0	0
Jason Ryan	23	8	35	4.4	10.9	120	3	3	1	1	0	0	0
Benj Sampson	24	4	0	0.0	0.0	88	4	0	0	0	0	0	0
MINNESOTA		161	787	4.9	11.4	128	60	45	31	19	6	0	0
Ranking (AL)				13	10								

Tom Kelly and Dick Such finally quieted talk about their inability to develop young pitchers, as Eric Milton and Joe Mays both had fine years. Perhaps even more relevant to the Twins' future was the return to form of Brad Radke, who had a miserable second half in 1998 after posting a Workload of 37.5. Kelly tightened the reins on Radke, never letting him throw more than 118 pitches in a start, and Radke responded with the fourth-best ERA in the league. . . . Mays, who spent two months in middle relief before joining the rotation, was handled much more carefully than Milton, who, though a sophomore, is the same age as Mays. That Mays had to be eased into the rotation by gradually stretching his pitch counts was a beneficial by-product of having a rookie pitcher earn his stripes in the bullpen for a time. . . . Milton's workload, while not unconscionable, was excessive, and I wouldn't be surprised if he failed to build on last year's success this season.

New York Yankees

It was just another year at the office for the Team of the Century. The 1990s Yankees continue to move up on the list of the best teams in franchise history, surpassing the 1976-81 teams to be the best since at least the post-Casey Stengel Yankees of the early 1960s. It's a team unique among the great ones in the franchise's history, with an offense built less on left-handed power and more on team on-base skills and balance. Like most of the great Yankees teams, it has been built from within through player development and trades. Among players with at least 100 plate appearances or 40 innings pitched, DH Chili Davis and left-handed reliever Mike Stanton were free-agent signings.

Of course, that doesn't tell the entire story. While the roster hasn't been put together by signing free agents, it certainly has been kept together by a committment to paying good players large sums of money. Tino Martinez, Chuck Knoblauch and Roger Clemens were all acquired from teams that didn't want to continue paying their salaries. Bernie Williams, Scott Brosius and David Cone have been retained at great expense when they've become eligible for free agency. The Yankees' payroll has been among the highest in the game throughout their successful run, and at no point have they declined to improve the team due to financial concerns.

They've been able to maintain this approach thanks to a confluence of factors that have given the Yankees the deepest revenue stream in baseball. First, the Yankees have sports' most lucrative local television contract, courtesy of the Madison Square Garden network. Their total local media revenues of $50 million per year are far greater than those of any other baseball team and provide the Yankees their greatest financial advantage.

It's not their only one. The economic wave that all of America has ridden in the late 1990s has been a boon for New York City. There's been a marked increase in discretionary income available for entertainment, which has increased demand for Yankee tickets. The Yankees have been able to parlay the increased demand *and* their run of success into higher ticket prices across the board, with the most dramatic rise occurring in the price of premium seats. The Yankees are getting many more people to pay a significantly higher price for their product.

Finally, the Yankees have played 51 postseason games in the past five years, 25 at home. Postseason revenue provides a big boost to a team, with higher ticket prices and fewer unsold seats. Merely making one October run can be the difference between a small profit and a large one. The Yankees have been getting at least some of that pie every year since the strike, extra money that has made it even harder for their rivals to close the gap.

Consider: the Yankees have a team in a large market. The team used its advantage in local cable revenue to finance player development and find talent outside the United States (Bernie Williams, Mariano Rivera). As the team got better due to these efforts, demand increased. The Yankees were able to broaden their talent base at the major-league level thanks to their improved player-development process, giving them the depth to make trades (John Wetteland, Cone, Knoblauch). They were also able to plow the extra revenue into international signings, adding talent to the organization (Jackson Melian, Ricardo Aramboles, Orlando Hernandez). The continuing success has increased their revenue stream, which has enabled them to keep the team together (Williams, Cone), which has in turn allowed the organization to raise prices without damaging demand.

Those of us who produce *Baseball Prospectus* believe that quality management is more important than payroll. We believe that the incessant yammering over large and small markets is at best a waste of time, and at worst a controversy based on falsehoods promoted by Major League Baseball and team owners. There is no absolute relationship between payroll and success, and there is no team whose circumstances will never allow it to be successful. Even the terms

Yankees Prospectus

1999 record: 98-64; First place, AL East; Beat Braves in World Series, 4-0

Pythagorean W/L: 96-66

Runs scored: 900 (3rd in AL)

Runs allowed: 731 (2nd in AL)

Team EQA: .281 (1st in AL)

1999 team age: 30.8 (2nd-oldest in AL)

1999 park: Yankee Stadium; excellent pitchers' park, decreased run scoring by 18%.

1999: Declined by almost 20 games and still won the World Series.

2000: A transition year, as age and farm system reshape the roster.

"small market" and "large market" are misused so badly that, until some effort is made to define and use them accurately, serious debate will be doomed.

But the Yankees—and only the Yankees—now present an interesting question. Is it possible for a team to have such an advantage, by virtue of its market, that it puts the competition at a perennial disadvantage? Remember that this all began with the Yankees' generous local television contract, which is largely due to the size of the New York cable market. There are more potential eyeballs than anywhere else in the country. That's not an advantage the Yankees are going to lose. The same goes for their attendance base: even sharing the city with the Mets, the Yankees have one of baseball's largest population pools from which to draw fans.

Of course, the large population and big cable deal were in place for a number of years without the team running rough-shod. It took an injection of quality management, focused on player development, to turn these advantages into on-field success. Gene Michael, Buck Showalter and Bill Livesey have never gotten enough credit for the jobs they did prior to the Joe Torre/Brian Cashman era, but they were the architects of this team. Quality management is a necessary ingredient, because a large payroll and poor decision-making just makes you the Orioles or Dodgers.

But so long as all of these pieces are in place—a good team run well, inordinately popular, in a big city with a good economy that provides enough money for the team to do whatever it wants—it's going to be very hard to beat the Yankees. The economics of baseball aren't anywhere near as bad as those who run the game would have you believe, but that doesn't mean there couldn't be a team in a perfect situation capable of exploiting its advantages. The Yankees are an outlier, and it's possible to recognize this—even to acknowledge that it may be a problem—without buying into the myths of baseball economics.

Of course, the rules aren't going to change for 2000, so the Yankees will have a good opportunity to make it three in a row. The 1999 team was more or less the same as the 1998 version, so the questions heading into 2000 are similar. Will they integrate their young position players, replacing the declining veterans they have at first base, third base and right field? By the end of 1999, Ricky Ledee and Jorge Posada had finally cemented starting jobs in the Yankees' lineup. Now the Yankees have two of the best dozen prospects in the game in D'Angelo Jimenez and Nick Johnson, each poised for an opportunity to win jobs from Chuck Knoblauch (or Scott Brosius) and Tino Martinez.

Last winter, it was Bernie Williams who graduated from being a relatively cheap core player to one requiring an expensive long-term contract. This winter, Derek Jeter and Mariano Rivera are going to get huge raises, possibly in the form of long-term commitments. To afford these players, the Yankees will have to work in younger, cheaper talent, in much the same way that the Atlanta Braves subsidized their pitching staff by breaking in Chipper Jones, Javy Lopez, Andruw Jones and Ryan Klesko in the mid-1990s. In addition to the two exceptional talents knocking on the door, the Yankees have B prospects like Ed Yarnall, Alfonso Soriano, Jackson Melian and Ryan Bradley who can be used to fill holes at the major-league level or to trade for established players, such as the right fielder the Yankees will need soon.

The Yankees are an old team. Their Opening Day lineup will contain just three players under 30, and their top three starting pitchers average 36 years of age. Last year's championship occurred in spite of age-related declines from their first baseman, third baseman and right fielder. All three will be back on Opening Day, and none can be counted on to arrest their decline. The rotation, a strength in both championship seasons, also slipped in 1999.

It's one thing to be relying on one or two players in their mid-to-late 30s, but six of the Yankees' top 13 players are significantly past their primes. That's a recipe for a collapse, as the Baltimore Orioles discovered last year. Not only will there be a decline in runs scored, but an aging defense can undermine even the best pitching staff. It is imperative that the Yankees find a way to integrate Jimenez and Johnson this year, and Soriano and Melian afterwards.

As the Yankees come back towards mortality, the competition is improving. Even after the Shawn Green/Raul Mondesi trade, the Blue Jays appear ready for a 90-win season. The Red Sox have some good young arms to support Pedro Martinez and Nomar Garciaparra, and by 2001 will have added a few very good hitters to the lineup. The Yankees found themselves in a race for only a week or so last September; you can bet they're going to spend a lot more time scoreboard-watching in 2000.

HITTERS (Averages: BA: .270 / OBP: .340 / SLG: .430 / EQA: .260)

Chris Ashby   1B/LF   Bats L   Age 25

YEAR	TEAM	LGE	AB	H	DB	TP	HR	BB/SO	R	RBI	SB	CS	OUT	BA	OBP	SLG	EQA	EQR	DEFENSE	
1997	Norwich	Eas	465	107	21	1	20	66/98	74	66	7	4	362	.230	.331	.409	.252	57	116-1B 93	
1998	Norwich	Eas	446	119	16	0	13	55/100	55	50	11	2	329	.267	.355	.390	.260	57	91-OF 85	21-1B 107
1999	Norwich	Eas	110	24	5	1	2	8/23	8	12	1	2	88	.218	.283	.336	.205	8		
1999	Columbus	Int	208	53	13	1	7	17/40	38	26	4	2	157	.255	.316	.428	.249	24	60-OF 90	
2000	*NY Yanks*	*AL*	*395*	*99*	*16*	*1*	*17*	*50/83*	*60*	*63*	*6*	*3*	*299*	*.251*	*.335*	*.425*	*.264*	*53*		

Ashby is a converted catcher who is nothing special as a left fielder and DH. In the Devil Rays' chapter, Jeff Bower sings the praises of Tom Wilson, a 29-year-old catcher with significant offensive skills. Ashby is four years younger and a comparable player, but unless he's asked to catch again—unlikely—he has no shot at a career. Wilson, by the way, is back in the Yankee system, and would be a great backup for Jorge Posada.

Scott Brosius   3B   Bats R   Age 33

YEAR	TEAM	LGE	AB	H	DB	TP	HR	BB/SO	R	RBI	SB	CS	OUT	BA	OBP	SLG	EQA	EQR	DEFENSE	
1997	Oakland	AL	478	97	20	1	11	31/98	57	40	9	4	385	.203	.258	.318	.193	31	96-3B 105	17-SS 84
1998	NY Yanks	AL	531	162	27	0	22	50/95	82	98	10	8	377	.305	.376	.480	.285	81	150-3B 112	
1999	NY Yanks	AL	476	122	28	1	17	34/74	61	69	9	3	357	.256	.314	.426	.249	55	129-3B 114	
2000	*NY Yanks*	*AL*	*415*	*99*	*14*	*0*	*15*	*41/70*	*50*	*55*	*5*	*3*	*319*	*.239*	*.307*	*.381*	*.239*	*44*		

While still a good defender, Brosius's decline at the plate left the Yankees with $5 million worth of average at third base. With the Yankees facing major raises for their young stars, they're looking to move Brosius, whose glove and reputation as a World Series hero could make him attractive to other teams. He'll outperform the projection, but not by much.

Bubba Carpenter   LF   Bats L   Age 31

YEAR	TEAM	LGE	AB	H	DB	TP	HR	BB/SO	R	RBI	SB	CS	OUT	BA	OBP	SLG	EQA	EQR	DEFENSE	
1997	Columbus	Int	276	67	11	4	4	38/49	38	31	3	5	214	.243	.334	.355	.236	29	79-OF 99	
1998	Columbus	Int	199	38	12	1	5	29/53	21	18	2	1	162	.191	.296	.337	.218	18	29-OF 97	25-1B 102
1999	Columbus	Int	330	82	17	3	16	63/75	60	61	4	2	250	.248	.374	.464	.283	53	103-OF 94	
2000	*NY Yanks*	*AL*	*313*	*74*	*16*	*2*	*13*	*62/72*	*57*	*53*	*2*	*2*	*241*	*.236*	*.363*	*.425*	*.276*	*48*		

Just in case you see his name bandied about as 2000's Bruce Aven or something, know that he isn't. His massive 1999 was completely out of line with the rest of his career and does not constitute evidence that he deserves a chance at a major-league job. It was a fluke.

Chad Curtis   LF   Bats R   Age 31

YEAR	TEAM	LGE	AB	H	DB	TP	HR	BB/SO	R	RBI	SB	CS	OUT	BA	OBP	SLG	EQA	EQR	DEFENSE
1997	NY Yanks	AL	322	98	21	1	13	34/47	51	51	13	6	230	.304	.381	.497	.292	53	84-OF 99
1998	NY Yanks	AL	457	114	20	1	11	73/78	76	56	19	5	348	.249	.362	.370	.260	60	129-OF 107
1999	NY Yanks	AL	196	53	6	0	5	41/35	35	23	8	4	147	.270	.404	.378	.278	30	52-LF 94
2000	*Texas*	*AL*	*239*	*63*	*8*	*0*	*7*	*43/40*	*46*	*35*	*7*	*3*	*179*	*.264*	*.376*	*.385*	*.263*	*32*	

With Bernie Williams healthy all year, Curtis was able to return to the fourth-outfielder role at which he excels, and he bounced back from his sub-par 1998. His performance may vary wildly from season to season given his limited playing time; even so, he'll be a valuable player for at least another three years. Curtis is one of only a handful of men to live the dream we all had as kids: a walk-off home run in the World Series. His role remains the same in Texas.

Chili Davis   DH   Bats B   Age 40

YEAR	TEAM	LGE	AB	H	DB	TP	HR	BB/SO	R	RBI	SB	CS	OUT	BA	OBP	SLG	EQA	EQR	DEFENSE
1997	KansasCy	AL	472	131	19	0	30	81/92	67	86	6	3	344	.278	.385	.508	.296	82	
1998	NY Yanks	AL	103	30	5	0	4	14/18	11	9	0	1	74	.291	.376	.456	.278	15	
1999	NY Yanks	AL	478	134	27	1	19	68/100	57	76	4	1	345	.280	.372	.460	.282	73	

Davis was pretty useless after a hot start and deserved the platoon role he was thrust into during September and the post-season. He's utterly one-dimensional, and what he does—crush left-handed pitchers—is available in cheaper and better players. Released and retired, so we've seen the last of the Chili Dawg.

Joe Girardi   C   Bats R   Age 35

YEAR	TEAM	LGE	AB	H	DB	TP	HR	BB/SO	R	RBI	SB	CS	OUT	BA	OBP	SLG	EQA	EQR	DEFENSE
1997	NY Yanks	AL	400	111	24	1	1	24/51	38	51	2	3	292	.278	.322	.350	.228	36	
1998	NY Yanks	AL	254	71	11	4	3	14/37	30	30	2	4	187	.280	.322	.390	.237	26	74-C 98
1999	NY Yanks	AL	211	53	17	1	2	7/26	22	27	3	1	159	.251	.275	.370	.215	17	62-C 94
2000	*ChiCubs*	*NL*	*182*	*47*	*12*	*1*	*2*	*16/24*	*22*	*21*	*1*	*1*	*136*	*.258*	*.318*	*.368*	*.228*	*17*	

His defensive reputation is growing in inverse proportion to his offensive production, a phenomenon known as Nichols' Law of Catcher Defense. He was the catcher for all three of the Yankees' English-speaking starting pitchers in the postseason, garnering a much greater percentage of the playing time than he did in the regular season. Girardi signed a three-year deal with the Cubs for oodles of cash. <Yankee fan>YES!!!!!</Yankee fan>

Drew Henson   3B   Bats R   Age 20

YEAR	TEAM	LGE	AB	H	DB	TP	HR	BB/SO	R	RBI	SB	CS	OUT	BA	OBP	SLG	EQA	EQR	DEFENSE
1999	Tampa	Fla	257	65	10	0	13	21/78	30	31	1	1	193	.253	.311	.444	.250	30	49-3B 78
2000	*NY Yanks*	*AL*	*132*	*33*	*3*	*0*	*11*	*13/64*	*19*	*28*	*1*	*0*	*99*	*.250*	*.317*	*.523*	*.281*	*21*	

Henson spent most of the year unable to win the starting job, hampered by a decision-maker unwilling to recognize his superior talent—not with Tampa but with the Michigan Wolverines, where Lloyd Carr insisted on alternating him at quarterback with Tom Brady. As a baseball player, you can't take Henson seriously on just two months a year, which is a shame. If he dropped football tomorrow, he'd be about the 15th-best prospect in the game.

Michel Hernandez   C   Bats R   Age 21

YEAR	TEAM	LGE	AB	H	DB	TP	HR	BB/SO	R	RBI	SB	CS	OUT	BA	OBP	SLG	EQA	EQR	DEFENSE
1998	Oneonta	NYP	211	49	9	1	0	15/20	22	18	1	2	164	.232	.283	.284	.188	13	52-C 97
1999	Tampa	Fla	283	66	10	1	2	15/54	22	19	1	1	218	.233	.276	.297	.190	17	83-C 97
2000	*NY Yanks*	*AL*	*189*	*46*	*4*	*0*	*2*	*12/36*	*16*	*16*	*1*	*1*	*144*	*.243*	*.289*	*.296*	*.200*	*13*	

A less-heralded Cuban defector, Hernandez is a good defensive catcher who still has a lot to learn as a hitter. He's behind Victor Valencia in the system but doesn't demonstrate Valencia's extremes. I think he's the better prospect and, with a few good months at Tampa, will jump to Double-A with a growing reputation.

Derek Jeter   SS   Bats R   Age 26

YEAR	TEAM	LGE	AB	H	DB	TP	HR	BB/SO	R	RBI	SB	CS	OUT	BA	OBP	SLG	EQA	EQR	DEFENSE
1997	NY Yanks	AL	657	199	33	8	10	71/120	117	71	24	13	471	.303	.381	.423	.275	94	155-SS 97
1998	NY Yanks	AL	627	208	25	9	19	55/116	123	82	28	6	425	.332	.390	.491	.299	104	147-SS 92
1999	NY Yanks	AL	629	229	41	10	23	84/116	130	99	20	9	409	.364	.448	.571	.336	134	157-SS 92
2000	*NY Yanks*	*AL*	*600*	*199*	*30*	*6*	*20*	*76/110*	*127*	*121*	*17*	*7*	*408*	*.332*	*.407*	*.502*	*.314*	*112*	

Analysts can argue all day about his defense, but the fact is that his reputation is very good, so he's not moving off shortstop anytime soon. It's not like he's Howard Johnson, and he may improve slightly as he continues to learn positioning. His pivot is still poor, but his arm makes up for some of that. This is all just nit-picking: Jeter is one of the best players in baseball, four years into a Hall of Fame career.

D'Angelo Jimenez   SS   Bats B   Age 22

YEAR	TEAM	LGE	AB	H	DB	TP	HR	BB/SO	R	RBI	SB	CS	OUT	BA	OBP	SLG	EQA	EQR	DEFENSE
1997	Tampa	Fla	360	88	14	4	7	43/55	44	40	4	6	278	.244	.328	.364	.235	37	93-SS 99
1998	Norwich	Eas	155	40	5	2	2	22/25	19	19	4	3	118	.258	.356	.355	.248	18	40-SS 103
1998	Columbus	Int	343	80	17	3	7	39/68	46	43	4	4	267	.233	.313	.362	.229	34	87-SS 97
1999	Columbus	Int	529	167	29	4	14	50/75	81	76	19	12	374	.316	.376	.465	.281	78	118-SS 99
1999	NY Yanks	AL	20	8	3	0	0	3/4	3	4	0	0	12	.400	.478	.550	.348	4	
2000	*NY Yanks*	*AL*	*550*	*156*	*28*	*4*	*16*	*66/86*	*95*	*89*	*12*	*8*	*402*	*.284*	*.360*	*.436*	*.276*	*81*	

Jimenez would have been playing shortstop and batting second by June for about 25 other teams. He isn't going to hit for the power that the Trinity does, but he actually does some things better than they do, including play defense. With Jeter being Jeter, and Knoblauch being expensive and difficult to move, Jimenez's first shot at a job is likely to come in another organization. He's a superior talent who deserves an opportunity.

Nick Johnson 1B Bats L Age 21

YEAR	TEAM	LGE	AB	H	DB	TP	HR	BB/SO	R	RBI	SB	CS	OUT	BA	OBP	SLG	EQA	EQR	DEFENSE
1997	Greensbr	SAL	454	114	18	1	17	67/100	63	65	6	2	342	.251	.363	.407	.266	63	124-1B 81
1998	Tampa	Fla	309	83	12	1	15	57/84	55	44	0	2	228	.269	.404	.460	.293	53	91-1B 95
1999	Norwich	Eas	430	138	33	4	13	107/91	98	75	4	3	295	.321	.481	.507	.340	99	131-1B 98
2000	*NY Yanks*	*AL*	*433*	*134*	*21*	*2*	*20*	*91/98*	*101*	*97*	*4*	*2*	*301*	*.309*	*.429*	*.506*	*.325*	*90*	

Johnson is the best prospect in baseball, a ranking very difficult for a first baseman to achieve. Like Jimenez, he could have been a major-league player last year and is on track to be a devastating hitter. One word of caution: he was hit by pitches 37 times this year and has yet to stay healthy for a complete season.

Chuck Knoblauch 2B Bats R Age 31

YEAR	TEAM	LGE	AB	H	DB	TP	HR	BB/SO	R	RBI	SB	CS	OUT	BA	OBP	SLG	EQA	EQR	DEFENSE
1997	Minnesot	AL	608	176	24	11	9	80/81	113	56	63	10	442	.289	.390	.410	.288	98	149-2B 96
1998	NY Yanks	AL	604	163	26	4	17	74/68	112	62	28	12	453	.270	.367	.411	.269	85	147-2B 98
1999	NY Yanks	AL	606	185	38	4	18	76/57	116	67	30	10	431	.305	.401	.470	.298	104	148-2B 96
2000	*NY Yanks*	*AL*	*576*	*154*	*28*	*4*	*17*	*88/60*	*114*	*86*	*26*	*8*	*430*	*.267*	*.364*	*.418*	*.279*	*88*	

Knoblauch arrested his offensive decline just in time to be the defensive story of the year. He made 14 throwing errors, most on routine plays. He is flipping the ball as opposed to throwing it hard, a problem to which second basemen are occasionally prone. For all the talk about his mental state, the problem is mechanical, and I expect it to have disappeared by the time people are paying attention again. He's a second baseman with a ton of mileage on him; if the Yankees can find someone to take him so they can make room for Jimenez, they need to jump at the chance, no matter what they get in return.

Ricky Ledee LF Bats L Age 26

YEAR	TEAM	LGE	AB	H	DB	TP	HR	BB/SO	R	RBI	SB	CS	OUT	BA	OBP	SLG	EQA	EQR	DEFENSE
1997	Columbus	Int	172	51	12	1	9	17/48	33	34	3	0	121	.297	.363	.535	.296	29	32-OF 90
1998	Columbus	Int	359	90	19	1	15	44/113	56	33	4	1	270	.251	.338	.435	.261	47	75-OF 92
1998	NY Yanks	AL	79	19	6	2	1	7/28	13	12	3	1	61	.241	.302	.405	.240	9	24-OF 98
1999	NY Yanks	AL	251	72	12	6	9	26/73	43	39	4	3	182	.287	.354	.490	.278	37	61-LF 105
1999	Columbus	Int	116	26	6	1	3	14/32	14	12	2	1	92	.224	.308	.371	.231	12	26-OF 100
2000	*NY Yanks*	*AL*	*364*	*95*	*19*	*3*	*15*	*47/109*	*62*	*62*	*7*	*3*	*272*	*.261*	*.345*	*.453*	*.276*	*54*	

It was something of a wasted year for him as Zimmer, then Torre, mismanaged the left-field situation. Ledee deserved, and still does deserve, at least a platoon role with Shane Spencer. He might hit left-handers well enough to play full-time, given the quality of his defense. For a team with expensive problems at a number of positions, Ledee is a good, cheap solution for a couple of years.

Donny Leon 3B Bats R Age 24

YEAR	TEAM	LGE	AB	H	DB	TP	HR	BB/SO	R	RBI	SB	CS	OUT	BA	OBP	SLG	EQA	EQR	DEFENSE
1997	Greensbr	SAL	525	125	27	1	13	13/107	39	64	2	2	402	.238	.261	.368	.206	39	131-3B 84
1998	Tampa	Fla	386	96	20	1	9	18/73	43	45	0	0	290	.249	.290	.376	.223	34	98-3B 81
1999	Norwich	Eas	463	128	31	2	18	24/108	59	82	0	0	335	.276	.315	.469	.258	57	113-3B 82
2000	*NY Yanks*	*AL*	*441*	*115*	*20*	*1*	*16*	*30/96*	*52*	*66*	*0*	*0*	*326*	*.261*	*.308*	*.420*	*.249*	*50*	

Yick. Leon continues to march through the system despite showing nothing more than a decent power stroke. There's just nothing here to like. Where he goes next depends on what happens to Scott Brosius, Alfonso Soriano and, to a lesser extent, D'Angelo Jimenez.

Jim Leyritz   DH/C   Bats R   Age 36

YEAR	TEAM	LGE	AB	H	DB	TP	HR	BB/SO	R	RBI	SB	CS	OUT	BA	OBP	SLG	EQA	EQR	DEFENSE
1997	Anaheim	AL	292	81	7	0	11	35/54	45	48	1	1	212	.277	.362	.414	.265	38	
1997	Texas	AL	84	24	4	0	0	22/21	11	13	1	0	60	.286	.452	.333	.295	14	
1998	Boston	AL	129	37	4	0	9	20/33	16	24	0	0	92	.287	.391	.527	.303	23	
1998	San Dieg	NL	148	43	8	0	6	21/39	18	21	0	0	105	.291	.406	.466	.298	25	
1999	San Dieg	NL	135	33	5	0	8	13/37	16	20	0	0	102	.244	.331	.459	.263	18	
1999	NY Yanks	AL	66	15	5	1	0	13/17	8	5	0	0	51	.227	.354	.333	.244	8	
2000	NY Yanks	AL	168	38	6	0	5	31/43	26	22	0	0	130	.226	.347	.351	.251	21	

Leyritz's willingness to catch makes him an asset on the bench even in an off-year. He can't play the position well enough to be a backup, though. As a third catcher, backup first baseman, occasional DH and a pinch-hitter who can be used at any point in an inning, Leyritz can still push a team towards a title.

Tino Martinez   1B   Bats L   Age 32

YEAR	TEAM	LGE	AB	H	DB	TP	HR	BB/SO	R	RBI	SB	CS	OUT	BA	OBP	SLG	EQA	EQR	DEFENSE
1997	NY Yanks	AL	597	185	34	2	46	72/72	97	143	3	1	413	.310	.387	.605	.318	117	146-1B 107
1998	NY Yanks	AL	532	153	32	1	29	59/81	90	121	2	1	380	.288	.365	.515	.290	86	139-1B 98
1999	NY Yanks	AL	592	163	31	2	28	63/86	92	103	3	4	433	.275	.348	.476	.273	84	151-1B 118
2000	NY Yanks	AL	528	143	21	1	30	68/76	86	105	2	1	386	.271	.354	.485	.286	85	

In retrospect, the trade that brought him to New York and the subsequent five-year, $20-million contract he signed weren't that bad. Martinez had a big 1997 and hasn't been a complete offensive disaster, while the $4 million a year he makes is chicken feed for a starting first baseman. His contract is up in 2000, and with Johnson coming up hard behind him, one of the safest bets in the world is that he'll be elsewhere in 2001.

Donzell McDonald   CF   Bats R   Age 25

YEAR	TEAM	LGE	AB	H	DB	TP	HR	BB/SO	R	RBI	SB	CS	OUT	BA	OBP	SLG	EQA	EQR	DEFENSE
1997	Tampa	Fla	305	77	24	6	3	40/85	48	18	15	7	235	.252	.345	.400	.257	39	78-OF 104
1998	Norwich	Eas	503	118	21	7	5	46/128	67	32	22	14	399	.235	.303	.334	.219	45	128-OF 102
1999	Norwich	Eas	546	130	19	8	3	68/124	66	26	24	11	426	.238	.327	.319	.229	53	135-OF 100
2000	NY Yanks	AL	505	122	25	6	4	66/122	81	50	21	10	393	.242	.329	.339	.240	56	

McDonald hasn't hit for any power since suffering a broken hand in 1997. Analyst Daniel Levine posits that young players may struggle more than older ones when trying to recover from their first injury, with Travis Lee being a significant recent example. Some, like McDonald, never seem to recover completely. His speed and range give him a chance to be a fifth outfielder.

Jackson Melian   RF   Bats R   Age 20

YEAR	TEAM	LGE	AB	H	DB	TP	HR	BB/SO	R	RBI	SB	CS	OUT	BA	OBP	SLG	EQA	EQR	DEFENSE
1998	Greensbr	SAL	476	108	17	1	8	33/121	51	36	6	5	373	.227	.283	.317	.202	34	130-OF 94
1999	Tampa	Fla	472	120	20	9	8	41/107	54	51	5	4	356	.254	.322	.386	.240	50	127-OF 100
2000	NY Yanks	AL	358	90	13	4	6	33/90	45	42	5	2	270	.251	.315	.360	.237	37	

Melian hasn't had the explosive development some predicted, but his game is getting better each year. The spike in power in 1999 should be the start of a trend, and his strike-zone judgment was considerably improved over 1998. In an organization thin on outfielders, Melian stands out. He still has significant upside, and his 2000 will excite people once more.

Paul O'Neill   RF   Bats L   Age 37

YEAR	TEAM	LGE	AB	H	DB	TP	HR	BB/SO	R	RBI	SB	CS	OUT	BA	OBP	SLG	EQA	EQR	DEFENSE
1997	NY Yanks	AL	556	189	34	0	26	72/88	89	123	11	8	375	.340	.416	.541	.315	104	143-OF 99
1998	NY Yanks	AL	603	196	40	2	25	55/101	93	115	14	1	408	.325	.383	.522	.302	102	147-OF 99
1999	NY Yanks	AL	600	177	42	4	19	60/89	67	107	11	10	433	.295	.361	.473	.276	87	146-RF 101
2000	NY Yanks	AL	484	133	24	1	19	61/75	80	84	5	3	354	.275	.356	.446	.278	72	

At 36, O'Neill finally began to slip, even reverting to his pre-Yankee helplessness against left-handed pitchers. He should be platooned for the rest of his career and can be productive in that role for a couple of years, especially if given some time at DH. He has the admiration of many, myself included, for playing in Game 4 of the World Series just hours after his father's death.

Jorge Posada   C   Bats B   Age 28

YEAR	TEAM	LGE	AB	H	DB	TP	HR	BB/SO	R	RBI	SB	CS	OUT	BA	OBP	SLG	EQA	EQR	DEFENSE
1997	NY Yanks	AL	189	50	11	0	7	29/32	29	26	1	2	141	.265	.373	.434	.273	27	
1998	NY Yanks	AL	359	99	18	0	19	45/90	54	63	0	1	261	.276	.356	.485	.279	53	88-C 106
1999	NY Yanks	AL	381	97	21	2	12	49/91	48	56	1	0	284	.255	.344	.415	.259	48	99-C 95
2000	*NY Yanks*	*AL*	*282*	*70*	*11*	*0*	*12*	*42/67*	*43*	*46*	*0*	*0*	*212*	*.248*	*.346*	*.415*	*.266*	*39*	

He suffered through a first half so bad that the Yankees, worried by his spiraling strikeout rate and a spate of passed balls, had his eyesight tested. Nothing unusual was detected, and Posada played much better in the second half, despite which he still was on the bench for most of the postseason. He hits much better from the right side, and will play a few weeks of winter ball to work on his swing from the left side. Still, the Yankees would be well served to find a left-handed-hitting backup. He will outperform that projection with more playing time, especially now that Personal Catcher to the Stars is gone.

Juan Rivera   OF   Bats R   Age 21

YEAR	TEAM	LGE	AB	H	DB	TP	HR	BB/SO	R	RBI	SB	CS	OUT	BA	OBP	SLG	EQA	EQR	DEFENSE
1999	Tampa	Fla	429	102	18	1	15	21/73	42	64	3	2	329	.238	.278	.389	.221	38	93-OF 97
2000	*NY Yanks*	*AL*	*221*	*57*	*8*	*0*	*11*	*14/53*	*25*	*36*	*1*	*1*	*165*	*.258*	*.302*	*.443*	*.252*	*26*	

He's a tools player signed out of Venezuela for first-round money. At this point, Rivera isn't the player Melian is, but keep in mind that he has less than half of Melian's professional experience. He's young and inexperienced enough to make me regret this statement, but I think he looks more like Gerald Williams to Melian's Bernie.

Luis Sojo   IF   Bats R   Age 34

YEAR	TEAM	LGE	AB	H	DB	TP	HR	BB/SO	R	RBI	SB	CS	OUT	BA	OBP	SLG	EQA	EQR	DEFENSE
1997	NY Yanks	AL	216	69	7	1	2	15/13	27	25	3	1	148	.319	.367	.389	.261	26	58-2B 91
1998	NY Yanks	AL	147	34	4	1	0	4/15	16	14	1	0	113	.231	.252	.272	.167	6	
1999	NY Yanks	AL	128	33	4	0	3	3/17	19	17	1	0	95	.258	.275	.359	.211	10	
2000	*NY Yanks*	*AL*	*100*	*26*	*2*	*0*	*1*	*6/11*	*9*	*10*	*1*	*0*	*74*	*.260*	*.302*	*.310*	*.215*	*8*	

Like O'Neill, Sojo lost his father in October and came back to be with the team for two of the four World Series games. Sojo isn't much of a player at this point, really not worth the roster spot, but give him credit for his fortitude during a tough time. He's a free agent, and will probably end up as an NRI. No value.

Alfonso Soriano   SS   Bats R   Age 22

YEAR	TEAM	LGE	AB	H	DB	TP	HR	BB/SO	R	RBI	SB	CS	OUT	BA	OBP	SLG	EQA	EQR	DEFENSE
1999	Norwich	Eas	366	103	19	2	14	24/69	46	57	13	9	272	.281	.330	.459	.260	47	87-SS 102
1999	Columbus	Int	83	15	4	1	2	4/18	7	10	1	1	69	.181	.218	.325	.171	4	
2000	*NY Yanks*	*AL*	*241*	*63*	*13*	*0*	*13*	*17/76*	*36*	*40*	*9*	*6*	*183*	*.261*	*.310*	*.477*	*.264*	*33*	

Soriano primed a hype machine that had already been set in motion by his two-homer performance in the Futures Game. While he's a good athlete with power and speed, he's not nearly the prospect Jimenez is. Soriano has some plate discipline issues, was a disaster at Triple-A and may end up somewhere other than shortstop, so you could say I'm not terribly excited about him.

Shane Spencer   LF   Bats R   Age 28

YEAR	TEAM	LGE	AB	H	DB	TP	HR	BB/SO	R	RBI	SB	CS	OUT	BA	OBP	SLG	EQA	EQR	DEFENSE
1997	Columbus	Int	460	99	32	3	23	56/112	63	67	0	1	362	.215	.305	.448	.249	56	109-OF 89
1998	Columbus	Int	340	91	22	1	13	30/66	49	49	0	2	251	.268	.331	.453	.260	43	63-OF 95
1998	NY Yanks	AL	67	25	7	0	10	5/12	18	26	0	1	43	.373	.417	.925	.381	19	
1999	Columbus	Int	50	16	0	0	2	8/9	13	8	0	0	34	.320	.414	.440	.295	8	
1999	NY Yanks	AL	206	50	8	0	8	16/51	24	19	0	4	160	.243	.304	.398	.229	20	40-LF 107
2000	*NY Yanks*	*AL*	*297*	*71*	*10*	*0*	*15*	*35/67*	*38*	*48*	*0*	*2*	*228*	*.239*	*.319*	*.424*	*.254*	*37*	

A year removed from his magical September, Spencer suffered through a difficult season. The inability of Zimmer and Torre to commit to either him or Ledee, or even to a strict platoon, made it difficult for either player to establish himself. Then, in the middle of a minor hot streak, Spencer had to sit down when we was diagnosed with an irregular heartbeat. He was healthy at the end of the year, and his outlook is the same: he can be a useful platoon left fielder and DH.

Darryl Strawberry   DH   Bats L   Age 38

YEAR	TEAM	LGE	AB	H	DB	TP	HR	BB/SO	R	RBI	SB	CS	OUT	BA	OBP	SLG	EQA	EQR	DEFENSE
1998	NY Yanks	AL	296	75	12	2	24	44/88	42	55	7	7	228	.253	.356	.551	.289	51	
1999	Columbus	Int	74	18	4	1	3	9/14	9	11	1	1	57	.243	.325	.446	.256	9	
1999	NY Yanks	AL	49	17	5	0	3	16/16	9	6	2	0	32	.347	.508	.633	.379	14	
2000	NY Yanks	AL	104	25	3	0	8	26/38	22	24	1	1	80	.240	.392	.500	.305	21	

Strawberry is still a productive hitter. At some point, though, his endless absences due to injury and personal problems have to outweigh his value. The Yankees stuck with him through 1999's peccadillo, an arrest for drug possession that led to a suspension. They've even picked up his option for 2000, so you can expect him to give the team 100 to 300 good at-bats as a platoon DH.

Victor Valencia   C   Bats R   Age 23

YEAR	TEAM	LGE	AB	H	DB	TP	HR	BB/SO	R	RBI	SB	CS	OUT	BA	OBP	SLG	EQA	EQR	DEFENSE
1997	Greensbr	SAL	365	76	11	1	13	37/117	38	37	1	0	289	.208	.290	.351	.218	32	
1998	Tampa	Fla	414	84	14	1	15	20/154	44	34	0	0	330	.203	.243	.350	.193	27	115-C 97
1999	Norwich	Eas	403	86	16	0	21	36/146	51	63	0	0	317	.213	.284	.409	.230	40	113-C 97
2000	NY Yanks	AL	356	77	11	0	17	35/129	38	48	0	0	279	.216	.286	.390	.232	36	

The Yankees' most advanced catching prospect, Valencia is a package similar to Donny Leon. He has moderate power, serious problems controlling the strike zone and plays a position at which the team has better prospects. He'll be the starting catcher at Columbus, and should make at least one trip to the Bronx this summer. Hernandez will push him out of the way in about 16 months.

Bernie Williams   CF   Bats B   Age 31

YEAR	TEAM	LGE	AB	H	DB	TP	HR	BB/SO	R	RBI	SB	CS	OUT	BA	OBP	SLG	EQA	EQR	DEFENSE
1997	NY Yanks	AL	511	175	36	7	22	71/77	108	101	16	9	344	.342	.424	.569	.324	103	126-OF 101
1998	NY Yanks	AL	500	172	30	6	26	72/79	97	95	13	9	337	.344	.428	.584	.327	103	120-OF 110
1999	NY Yanks	AL	593	210	32	7	24	93/95	111	111	9	11	394	.354	.443	.553	.327	120	152-CF 101
2000	NY Yanks	AL	484	154	25	4	21	84/76	107	106	8	7	337	.318	.419	.517	.319	97	

Williams stayed healthy in 1999, adding to his game the missing piece that made him the best center fielder in baseball. It's interesting to note that NBC jumped all over his moderate platoon split in 1999 as "evidence" that Williams is a better hitter from the left side. This was actually the first season since 1991 in which Williams hadn't hit left-handed pitchers better than right-handed ones. Sample size, guys.

PITCHERS (Averages: ERA: 4.50 / H/9: 9.00 / HR/9: 1.00 / BB/9: 3.50 / K/9: 6.50 / KWH: 1.00)

Ryan Bradley   Throws R   Age 24

YEAR	TEAM	LGE	IP	H	ER	HR	BB	K	ERA	W	L	H/9	HR/9	BB/9	K/9	KWH	PERA
1997	Oneonta	NYP	24.0	32	8	2	8	14	3.00	2	1	12.00	0.75	3.00	5.25	0.57	5.62
1998	Tampa	Fla	90.3	70	34	6	39	83	3.39	6	4	6.97	0.60	3.89	8.27	1.89	3.19
1998	Norwich	Eas	24.7	9	4	1	9	20	1.46	3	0	3.28	0.36	3.28	7.30	3.69	1.09
1998	Columbus	Int	15.7	16	12	4	13	11	6.89	1	1	9.19	2.30	7.47	6.32	0.43	8.04
1998	NY Yanks	AL	12.7	12	8	2	9	13	5.68	0	1	8.53	1.42	6.39	9.24	1.17	5.68
1999	Columbus	Int	140.3	168	106	26	76	105	6.80	5	11	10.77	1.67	4.87	6.73	0.65	6.93

In 1998, Bradley shot from the Florida State League to Yankee Stadium in a span of six weeks. In 1999, he never sniffed the Bronx; his mechanics got fouled up early and led to an abysmal season at Triple-A. He's still a solid pitching prospect with a decent health and workload record. The Yankees can afford to be patient with him.

Mike Buddie — Throws R — Age 29

YEAR	TEAM	LGE	IP	H	ER	HR	BB	K	ERA	W	L	H/9	HR/9	BB/9	K/9	KWH	PERA
1997	Columbus	Int	71.0	98	28	4	27	54	3.55	5	3	12.42	0.51	3.42	6.85	0.82	5.96
1998	Columbus	Int	42.3	36	15	0	17	25	3.19	3	2	7.65	0.00	3.61	5.31	0.76	2.98
1998	NY Yanks	AL	41.0	47	28	5	14	20	6.15	2	3	10.32	1.10	3.07	4.39	0.45	5.27
1999	Columbus	Int	75.7	85	30	2	24	58	3.57	5	3	10.11	0.24	2.85	6.90	1.23	4.04

The additions of Jason Grimsley and Dan Naulty forced Buddie back to Triple-A, where he had a second good season. Buddie is good enough to be a middle reliever in the majors, and if he winds up in Kansas City or Seattle, he might be the best pitcher in the bullpen. The same could be said for about 35 other Triple-A relievers, a half-dozen NFL quarterbacks, three *Prospectus* authors, two of our wives and Eric Cartman.

Roger Clemens — Throws R — Age 37

YEAR	TEAM	LGE	IP	H	ER	HR	BB	K	ERA	W	L	H/9	HR/9	BB/9	K/9	KWH	PERA
1997	Toronto	AL	264.3	198	59	8	68	294	2.01	24	5	6.74	0.27	2.32	10.01	4.80	2.28
1998	Toronto	AL	236.7	161	70	10	92	274	2.66	19	7	6.12	0.38	3.50	10.42	3.79	2.47
1999	NY Yanks	AL	184.0	182	94	18	87	165	4.60	10	10	8.90	0.88	4.26	8.07	1.28	4.60

Clemens never got into a groove in New York, missing time with a pulled groin that never seemed to get completely healthy. His velocity wasn't affected, but his command was. He pitched behind in the count more, which took away the splitter he throws for swinging strikes. Clemens pitched better on long rest; five months should be long enough for him to have a more typical season in 2000.

David Cone — Throws R — Age 37

YEAR	TEAM	LGE	IP	H	ER	HR	BB	K	ERA	W	L	H/9	HR/9	BB/9	K/9	KWH	PERA
1997	NY Yanks	AL	195.3	149	60	16	86	223	2.76	16	6	6.87	0.74	3.96	10.27	2.90	3.27
1998	NY Yanks	AL	205.7	188	86	19	61	211	3.76	14	9	8.23	0.83	2.67	9.23	2.90	3.59
1999	NY Yanks	AL	189.3	163	79	19	86	180	3.76	12	9	7.75	0.90	4.09	8.56	1.73	3.95

The beginning of the end. Cone is really struggling with the transition as his fastball continues to lose steam. He still delivers an assortment of hard breaking stuff from a few arm angles, but without a heater that can get him out of trouble, he is forced to nibble. The deterioration in his numbers is comparable to that of Clemens, but Cone wasn't injured: he's simply losing his best pitch. Cone still has a couple of years left; he's just a #3 starter now instead of a #1.

Todd Erdos — Throws R — Age 26

YEAR	TEAM	LGE	IP	H	ER	HR	BB	K	ERA	W	L	H/9	HR/9	BB/9	K/9	KWH	PERA
1997	Mobile	Sou	56.3	50	23	4	25	39	3.67	4	2	7.99	0.64	3.99	6.23	0.91	3.83
1997	San Dieg	NL	13.7	17	9	1	4	12	5.93	1	1	11.20	0.66	2.63	7.90	1.58	5.27
1998	Columbus	Int	48.3	54	27	4	22	43	5.03	2	3	10.06	0.74	4.10	8.01	1.16	5.03
1999	Columbus	Int	56.0	75	47	9	28	45	7.55	2	4	12.05	1.45	4.50	7.23	0.72	7.23

As good as his stuff is, it's possible that Erdos has missed his window of opportunity to be a star. The innings that should have been his last year went to Dan Naulty while Erdos got his head handed to him in Ohio. He's added a change-up to his fastball/slider mix and is still capable of being a cheap solution in the sixth through eighth innings. Waived by the Yankees, he's a sleeper wherever he surfaces next.

Randy Flores — Throws L — Age 24

YEAR	TEAM	LGE	IP	H	ER	HR	BB	K	ERA	W	L	H/9	HR/9	BB/9	K/9	KWH	PERA
1997	Oneonta	NYP	66.0	93	49	5	35	44	6.68	2	5	12.68	0.68	4.77	6.00	0.44	6.82
1998	Greensbr	SAL	119.3	158	64	7	46	87	4.83	6	7	11.92	0.53	3.47	6.56	0.78	5.66
1998	Tampa	Fla	22.3	32	27	3	21	11	10.88	0	2	12.90	1.21	8.46	4.43	0.13	9.27
1999	Tampa	Fla	125.3	145	71	6	51	74	5.10	6	8	10.41	0.43	3.66	5.31	0.55	4.74
1999	Norwich	Eas	23.7	36	23	0	13	15	8.75	1	2	13.69	0.00	4.94	5.70	0.36	6.85

Flores chewed up the Florida State League, thanks to his command. Flores is short and doesn't throw hard, so he's fighting a couple of biases as he works his way towards New York. He'll need an adjustment period at both Double-A and Triple-A, so it could be 2002 before he arrives. He will eventually be a good major-league pitcher.

Ben Ford   Throws R   Age 24

YEAR	TEAM	LGE	IP	H	ER	HR	BB	K	ERA	W	L	H/9	HR/9	BB/9	K/9	KWH	PERA
1997	Tampa	Fla	35.3	33	10	2	18	29	2.55	3	1	8.41	0.51	4.58	7.39	1.06	4.08
1997	Norwich	Eas	40.3	40	31	1	20	30	6.92	1	3	8.93	0.22	4.46	6.69	0.84	4.02
1998	Tucson	PCL	70.3	61	34	6	37	55	4.35	4	4	7.81	0.77	4.73	7.04	1.00	4.09
1999	Columbus	Int	68.3	70	40	4	41	36	5.27	3	5	9.22	0.53	5.40	4.74	0.34	4.87

It's funny the way things develop. The Diamondbacks traded Ford back to the Yankees at the end of 1999 spring training in exchange for Darren Holmes. To no one's surprise, Holmes got hurt, and the general disaster in the D'Back bullpen eventually inspired them to trade Tony Batista, Brad Penny and Vladimir Nunez to fix it. If they'd simply kept Ford—who had more upside, a lower salary and less injury risk than Holmes—perhaps the bullpen would have been deeper and more effective, and the D'Backs would still have some excellent players.

Jason Grimsley   Throws R   Age 32

YEAR	TEAM	LGE	IP	H	ER	HR	BB	K	ERA	W	L	H/9	HR/9	BB/9	K/9	KWH	PERA
1997	Tucson	PCL	79.3	96	68	5	46	53	7.71	2	7	10.89	0.57	5.22	6.01	0.48	5.79
1997	Omaha	AmA	32.3	37	27	3	35	20	7.52	1	3	10.30	0.84	9.74	5.57	0.23	7.79
1998	Buffalo	Int	84.3	84	43	9	63	57	4.59	4	5	8.96	0.96	6.72	6.08	0.46	5.76
1999	NY Yanks	AL	73.0	66	36	6	39	50	4.44	4	4	8.14	0.74	4.81	6.16	0.73	4.32

A running theme in these player comments is that there are any number of Triple-A pitchers with two good pitches who could be effective as a middle reliever. Now, while Grimsley moved from Triple-A to the Yankee bullpen and pitched reasonably well in 1999, I wouldn't use him as an illustration of the point. He wasn't especially effective outside of May, had mediocre peripherals and this *was* his upside.

Orlando Hernandez   Throws R   Age 34

YEAR	TEAM	LGE	IP	H	ER	HR	BB	K	ERA	W	L	H/9	HR/9	BB/9	K/9	KWH	PERA
1998	Columbus	Int	42.0	43	19	2	19	50	4.07	3	2	9.21	0.43	4.07	10.71	2.29	4.29
1998	NY Yanks	AL	139.3	114	51	10	54	132	3.29	10	5	7.36	0.65	3.49	8.53	2.11	3.29
1999	NY Yanks	AL	210.0	185	101	22	83	160	4.33	12	11	7.93	0.94	3.56	6.86	1.25	3.86

The fiction of his 1970 birthdate was finally exposed in October, so he'll go to arbitration at the end of the season as a 35-year-old with an unknown amount of wear on his arm. El Duque is a lot of fun to watch, and his postseason performance has been otherworldly. He's still a poor risk if you're thinking about giving him Chuck Finley money. He showed some decline in 1999, a trend I expect to continue in 2000.

Hideki Irabu   Throws R   Age 31

YEAR	TEAM	LGE	IP	H	ER	HR	BB	K	ERA	W	L	H/9	HR/9	BB/9	K/9	KWH	PERA
1997	Columbus	Int	26.0	22	8	1	6	23	2.77	2	1	7.62	0.35	2.08	7.96	2.99	2.77
1997	NY Yanks	AL	53.0	68	43	14	20	56	7.30	2	4	11.55	2.38	3.40	9.51	1.72	7.64
1998	NY Yanks	AL	171.0	149	76	25	79	127	4.00	11	8	7.84	1.32	4.16	6.68	1.02	4.42
1999	NY Yanks	AL	166.0	177	92	24	44	135	4.99	8	10	9.60	1.30	2.39	7.32	1.75	4.72

Irabu is a #4 starter and not a terrible one. He improved his command significantly and is in line for his best year now that he has escaped to Montreal. Olympic Stadium should be a better place for Irabu and his flyball tendencies, particularly if Peter Bergeron can win the center-field job.

Mark Johnson   Throws R   Age 25

YEAR	TEAM	LGE	IP	H	ER	HR	BB	K	ERA	W	L	H/9	HR/9	BB/9	K/9	KWH	PERA
1997	Kissimme	Fla	141.7	197	93	11	52	97	5.91	6	10	12.52	0.70	3.30	6.16	0.69	6.16
1998	Portland	Eas	140.3	158	95	13	70	96	6.09	6	10	10.13	0.83	4.49	6.16	0.62	5.39
1999	Norwich	Eas	81.7	105	62	7	45	39	6.83	3	6	11.57	0.77	4.96	4.30	0.24	6.39

Johnson was part of the Ed Yarnall heist, one of the two #1 picks the Marlins threw in with Yarnall to get Mike Lowell. Unfortunately, Johnson stalled at Norwich, pitching ineffectively at Double-A for the second straight year. The Tigers took him in the Rule 5 draft, so Johnson should get a chance with them in middle relief.

Oswaldo Mairena		Throws L					Age 24										
YEAR	TEAM	LGE	IP	H	ER	HR	BB	K	ERA	W	L	H/9	HR/9	BB/9	K/9	KWH	PERA
1997	Greensbr	SAL	57.0	56	32	3	22	51	5.05	3	3	8.84	0.47	3.47	8.05	1.58	3.95
1998	Tampa	Fla	50.7	63	28	6	30	38	4.97	3	3	11.19	1.07	5.33	6.75	0.57	6.57
1999	Norwich	Eas	54.3	55	27	3	30	37	4.47	3	3	9.11	0.50	4.97	6.13	0.62	4.64

Mairena could end up in the Bronx this year when Allen Watson returns to earth, freeing up the #2 left-hander spot in the bullpen. He throws a big curveball that makes him tough on left-handed hitters, and complements it with a fastball that can reach 90 mph. He'll be effective in a restricted role initially and will eventually move up to be one of the better relievers in the league.

Ramiro Mendoza		Throws R					Age 28										
YEAR	TEAM	LGE	IP	H	ER	HR	BB	K	ERA	W	L	H/9	HR/9	BB/9	K/9	KWH	PERA
1997	NY Yanks	AL	134.0	151	61	14	28	82	4.10	8	7	10.14	0.94	1.88	5.51	1.19	4.43
1998	NY Yanks	AL	128.7	133	50	8	31	56	3.50	9	5	9.30	0.56	2.17	3.92	0.57	3.71
1999	NY Yanks	AL	120.7	140	64	11	26	81	4.77	6	7	10.44	0.82	1.94	6.04	1.35	4.55

Mendoza continues to be more effective as a reliever despite having the repertoire of a starter. He's such an extreme ground-ball pitcher that he should be successful in any role. In this organization, he is unlikely to get the chance to start regularly, but will be quite valuable in the swingman role until he's traded or leaves on his own. He does have a fairly big platoon split, about 100 points of OPS worse against left-handed hitters over his career.

Dan Naulty		Throws R					Age 30										
YEAR	TEAM	LGE	IP	H	ER	HR	BB	K	ERA	W	L	H/9	HR/9	BB/9	K/9	KWH	PERA
1997	Minnesot	AL	30.7	29	18	7	10	23	5.28	1	2	8.51	2.05	2.93	6.75	1.36	4.99
1998	Minnesot	AL	24.0	24	14	3	11	15	5.25	1	2	9.00	1.13	4.13	5.63	0.64	4.87
1999	NY Yanks	AL	48.0	41	23	7	21	25	4.31	3	2	7.69	1.31	3.94	4.69	0.54	4.31

Naulty won a roster spot when the Yankees found a taker for Darren Holmes, and was the team's 11th pitcher until August. He didn't hurt or help the Yankees much, but may have reestablished himself so that he can begin bouncing around the league with the "veteran" tag. He's not going to be even this effective again. He's been traded to the Dodgers, and has almost no chance of making the team.

Jeff Nelson		Throws R					Age 33										
YEAR	TEAM	LGE	IP	H	ER	HR	BB	K	ERA	W	L	H/9	HR/9	BB/9	K/9	KWH	PERA
1997	NY Yanks	AL	78.7	51	29	7	37	81	3.32	6	3	5.83	0.80	4.23	9.27	2.60	2.86
1998	NY Yanks	AL	40.0	44	18	1	23	35	4.05	2	2	9.90	0.22	5.18	7.88	0.90	4.95
1999	NY Yanks	AL	29.7	27	13	2	21	35	3.94	2	1	8.19	0.61	6.37	10.62	1.61	4.85

One of the deleterious effects of the expanded playoffs has been that the best teams in the league can treat the regular season as a six-month warm-up. The Indians are the obvious example, the Yankees a less obvious one. The past two years, they have spent most of the season letting Nelson nurse various back and elbow injuries, all with an eye towards having him available in October. He didn't throw more than 10 innings in any month but was his usual nasty self in the postseason.

Todd Noel		Throws R					Age 21										
YEAR	TEAM	LGE	IP	H	ER	HR	BB	K	ERA	W	L	H/9	HR/9	BB/9	K/9	KWH	PERA
1998	KaneCnty	Mid	34.3	58	33	2	22	18	8.65	1	3	15.20	0.52	5.77	4.72	0.19	8.65
1998	Rockford	Mid	82.0	110	60	2	48	49	6.59	3	6	12.07	0.22	5.27	5.38	0.34	6.15
1999	Tampa	Fla	88.0	117	64	4	42	65	6.55	3	7	11.97	0.41	4.30	6.65	0.64	5.93

Noel is a hard-throwing suspect who, like Johnson, is a former #1 pick acquired in the Mike Lowell trade with the Marlins. He's at least two years out, as he's primarily a fastball pitcher with considerable control issues. A project, but one that bears watching. The Yankees have added him to the 40-man roster.

Andy Pettitte — Throws L — Age 28

YEAR	TEAM	LGE	IP	H	ER	HR	BB	K	ERA	W	L	H/9	HR/9	BB/9	K/9	KWH	PERA
1997	NY Yanks	AL	241.3	222	77	7	65	167	2.87	19	8	8.28	0.26	2.42	6.23	1.44	3.02
1998	NY Yanks	AL	214.0	227	107	18	91	147	4.50	12	12	9.55	0.76	3.83	6.18	0.78	4.67
1999	NY Yanks	AL	187.3	212	98	18	86	123	4.71	10	11	10.19	0.86	4.13	5.91	0.62	5.28

His loss of effectiveness calls to mind the collapse of Steve Avery, another left-hander who had a lot of success and threw a lot of pitches before turning 26. Pettitte's strikeout rate has been stable amidst his problems with location and off-speed pitches. I think he's going to arrest the decline and pitch well in 2000—and for many years to follow.

Mariano Rivera — Throws R — Age 30

YEAR	TEAM	LGE	IP	H	ER	HR	BB	K	ERA	W	L	H/9	HR/9	BB/9	K/9	KWH	PERA
1997	NY Yanks	AL	72.0	62	15	5	20	68	1.88	7	1	7.75	0.63	2.50	8.50	2.79	3.12
1998	NY Yanks	AL	60.3	50	13	3	17	36	1.94	6	1	7.46	0.45	2.54	5.37	1.14	2.83
1999	NY Yanks	AL	67.7	43	14	2	18	53	1.86	7	1	5.72	0.27	2.39	7.05	2.71	1.86

Rivera's best year since 1996 came about because he developed a completely unhittable pitch, a cut fastball that just destroys left-handed hitters. He presents a philosophical question: can a pitcher survive on one pitch if that one pitch is perhaps the best in baseball? I am still skeptical, but it's increasingly difficult to remain so in light of his performance. Does anyone realize he's already 30?

Mike Stanton — Throws L — Age 33

YEAR	TEAM	LGE	IP	H	ER	HR	BB	K	ERA	W	L	H/9	HR/9	BB/9	K/9	KWH	PERA
1997	NY Yanks	AL	67.0	48	17	3	34	70	2.28	6	1	6.45	0.40	4.57	9.40	2.24	2.96
1998	NY Yanks	AL	78.0	72	49	12	27	70	5.65	3	6	8.31	1.38	3.12	8.08	1.88	4.38
1999	NY Yanks	AL	61.0	70	28	4	17	60	4.13	4	3	10.33	0.59	2.51	8.85	2.26	4.43

Stanton is a good left-handed reliever who doesn't dominate left-handed batters enough to be a great specialist. Like many relievers thrust into this role, Stanton would be more effective pitching an inning or two at a time. Because the Yankees get so many innings from their starters, they don't really need him that way. Giving him a three-year deal was overkill.

Jay Tessmer — Throws R — Age 28

YEAR	TEAM	LGE	IP	H	ER	HR	BB	K	ERA	W	L	H/9	HR/9	BB/9	K/9	KWH	PERA
1997	Norwich	Eas	55.7	96	51	6	29	37	8.25	1	5	15.52	0.97	4.69	5.98	0.37	9.05
1998	Norwich	Eas	47.0	60	9	0	16	42	1.72	4	1	11.49	0.00	3.06	8.04	1.37	4.79
1998	Columbus	Int	18.3	8	2	1	1	12	0.98	2	0	3.93	0.49	0.49	5.89	13.45	0.98
1999	Columbus	Int	54.3	56	22	4	13	36	3.64	4	2	9.28	0.66	2.15	5.96	1.33	3.81
1999	NY Yanks	AL	6.3	16	10	1	4	3	14.21	0	1	22.74	1.42	5.68	4.26	0.11	15.63

Now that the hype surrounding him has died, it will be interesting to see if he can carve out a career in the middle innings. Tessmer is a submariner with decent stuff who throws strikes and gets ground balls. He doesn't have the upside of Ford and will possibly have to go elsewhere to get a real chance. He's a sleeper once that happens.

Allen Watson — Throws L — Age 29

YEAR	TEAM	LGE	IP	H	ER	HR	BB	K	ERA	W	L	H/9	HR/9	BB/9	K/9	KWH	PERA
1997	Anaheim	AL	202.7	211	109	34	74	143	4.84	11	12	9.37	1.51	3.29	6.35	0.98	5.15
1998	Anaheim	AL	91.7	122	64	11	35	65	6.28	3	7	11.98	1.08	3.44	6.38	0.74	6.28
1999	NY Mets	NL	39.0	37	18	5	21	31	4.15	2	2	8.54	1.15	4.85	7.15	0.92	4.85
1999	Seattle	AL	3.0	6	7	4	2	2	21.00	0	0	18.00	12.00	6.00	6.00	0.25	33.00
1999	NY Yanks	AL	33.7	30	7	3	10	31	1.87	3	1	8.02	0.80	2.67	8.29	2.39	3.48

Watson was part of a bizarre sequence in which the Mariners acquired him from the Mets, with whom he'd been pitching fairly well, then released him a week later after three ineffective outings. The Yankees signed him to a minor-league deal, and a month later he resumed his good season. Watson might have more years like this one, contributing as both a spot left-hander and swingman, but they're going to be interspersed with years like his 1998.

Ed Yarnall — Throws L — Age 24

YEAR	TEAM	LGE	IP	H	ER	HR	BB	K	ERA	W	L	H/9	HR/9	BB/9	K/9	KWH	PERA
1997	St Lucie	Fla	101.3	111	39	7	40	90	3.46	7	4	9.86	0.62	3.55	7.99	1.36	4.62
1997	Binghmtn	Eas	32.0	21	11	2	12	26	3.09	3	1	5.91	0.56	3.38	7.31	2.00	2.53
1998	Binghmtn	Eas	45.0	24	7	0	19	42	1.40	5	0	4.80	0.00	3.80	8.40	2.89	1.80
1998	Charlott	Int	69.3	80	58	10	42	42	7.53	2	6	10.38	1.30	5.45	5.45	0.39	6.49
1999	Columbus	Int	142.3	138	57	5	60	130	3.60	10	6	8.73	0.32	3.79	8.22	1.53	3.79
1999	NY Yanks	AL	16.7	16	7	1	10	13	3.78	1	1	8.64	0.54	5.40	7.02	0.79	4.32

He's going to be special. Yarnall throws four pitches for strikes, hides the ball well and has a major-league fastball. Like many young left-handers, his control can be a problem, but that's the only negative here. He even has a good health record and hasn't been worked that hard. Yarnall could be the best left-hander in the league by 2002.

Support-Neutral Records — NEW YORK YANKEES — Park Effect: -8.1%

PITCHER	GS	IP	R	SNW	SNL	SNPCT	W	L	RA	APW	SNVA	SNWAR
Roger Clemens	30	187.7	101	11.0	10.4	.513	14	10	4.84	0.33	0.27	1.88
David Cone	31	193.3	84	12.6	8.7	.591	12	9	3.91	2.24	1.84	3.53
Orlando Hernandez	33	214.3	108	13.5	10.4	.566	17	9	4.53	1.07	1.43	3.36
Hideki Irabu	27	158.0	92	8.7	9.9	.467	11	7	5.24	-0.39	-0.57	0.78
Jeff Juden	1	3.7	6	0.0	0.7	.042	0	1	14.73	-0.38	-0.32	-0.28
Ramiro Mendoza	6	39.7	24	2.3	2.3	.502	2	3	5.45	-0.18	-0.05	0.36
Andy Pettitte	31	191.7	105	11.1	11.2	.499	14	11	4.93	0.16	-0.07	1.64
Mike Stanton	1	4.0	0	0.4	0.0	1.000	0	0	0.00	0.21	0.21	0.26
Ed Yarnall	2	10.3	8	0.4	0.9	.327	1	0	6.97	-0.21	-0.25	-0.13
TOTALS	162	1002.7	528	60.1	54.5	.524	71	50	4.74	2.85	2.49	11.40

It may seem surprising given the good performance by their rotation, but the Yankees suffered the majors' third-biggest drop in starting pitching performance from 1998 to 1999. The Yankees fell by more than seven wins, according to Support-Neutral Value Added, from around 9½ games above average in 1998 to just 2½ wins above average in 1999. The only two teams that slipped by more were the Braves—another surprise—and the Cubs. Every regular member of the rotation declined, with the biggest drops coming from the spot taken by Wells in '98 and Clemens in '99 (2½ wins) and Hideki Irabu (2 wins). As a result, the Yankees had to settle for having the third-best rotation in the league, behind Boston and Seattle. . . . David Cone had another fine season in 1999, but it looked a little better than it actually was, thanks to the league-best support he got from the bullpen. Cone turned 21 runners over to his relievers in 1999; given where they were and the number of outs in the inning when Cone left, those runners would have been expected to score 6.6 runs. Only two of them actually scored, saving Cone 4.6 runs and knocking .22 runs off his per-game average (RA). New York relievers bailed Cone out of an amazing five bases-loaded jams (three with one out, two with two out), without a run scoring.

Pitcher Abuse Points

PITCHER	AGE	GS	PAP	PAP/S	WKLD	MAX	1-90	91-100	101-110	111-120	121-130	131-140	141+
Roger Clemens	36	30	763	25.4	25.4	138	4	1	8	7	7	3	0
David Cone	36	31	394	12.7	12.7	131	5	5	10	8	2	1	0
Orlando Hernandez	33	33	791	24.0	24.0	137	7	3	4	10	5	4	0
Hideki Irabu	30	27	197	7.3	9.7	127	9	6	6	4	2	0	0
Jeff Juden	28	1	0	0.0	0.0	85	1	0	0	0	0	0	0
Ramiro Mendoza	27	6	36	6.0	11.0	117	0	1	4	1	0	0	0
Andy Pettitte	27	31	404	13.0	23.9	134	5	7	9	6	3	1	0
Mike Stanton	32	1	0	0.0	0.0	57	1	0	0	0	0	0	0
Ed Yarnall	23	2	9	4.5	11.3	109	1	0	1	0	0	0	0
NEW YORK (AL)		162	2594	16.0	18.8	138	33	23	42	36	19	9	0
Ranking (AL)				1	3								

It's hard to criticize Joe Torre for what he's done the last four years, but it seems strange that with five dependable starters, an outstanding closer and an experienced corps of middle relievers, he couldn't spread the work around a little more. These are the Yankees: are you telling me they didn't have a five-run lead in the seventh inning once or twice a week? . . . The addition of Roger Clemens vaulted the Yankees into the AL lead in PAPs per start, and while under normal circumstances I wouldn't care—Clemens is as accomplished a workhorse as any pitcher in baseball—don't you think his high Workload contributed to his persistent groin injury? . . . Andy Pettitte continued to throw too many pitches, although his Workload dropped from 40.1 to 23.9 because he wasn't pitching well enough to go deep into games. . . . We can stop worrying about Orlando Hernandez now that we know his real age.

Oakland Athletics

The A's didn't win anything, but as we warned you last year, they managed to contend. That, along with their continued success in player development, earned them *Baseball America*'s Organization of the Year award.

And because this is baseball, Jerry McMorris wants to break up the team before it really puts an exclamation point on that old saying about a fool and his money.

Going into 1999, what General Manager Billy Beane and his staff wanted to accomplish was pretty straightforward. At the major-league level, they wanted to be competitive with a potent lineup and a pitching staff built around Kenny Rogers and a group of retreads. The lineup had been assembled as a reflection of an organizational offensive philosophy: work the pitcher, take a walk, hit the ball hard. It's still the easiest way to score runs, and has been since the days of John McGraw.

The danger zone was the pitching staff, which featured a lot of senior citizens: Tom Candiotti, Doug Jones, Billy Taylor. But while it was old, it was also designed to be re-built on the fly, depending on how things played out. If the A's were really competitive a few months into the season, they could upgrade their pitching with trades, thanks to a deep farm system. If they weren't competitive, they could turn to that same farm system and rebuild the staff from within, getting an early start on 2000.

Pitching is a commodity synonymous with unpredictability. If you're a major-league team with financial limitations that keep you from chasing Kevin Brown, why go shopping for Tim Belcher or Doc Gooden? That commits your limited resources to pitchers no more likely to give you a big year than Mike Oquist. Instead, the A's would wait and see where they stood relative to the rest of the league, then start cherry-picking useful starters from the hopeless teams. Of course, while the A's managed to land Omar Olivares and Kevin Appier while giving up very little in return, in retrospect it looks like they waited a bit too long. The best you can say in their defense is that the July deadline encourages more procrastination among the teams

looking to trade players away than among the teams looking to add them.

In some ways, the organization's plan of action was similar to that of the Cincinnati Reds, another team built to win on a budget. Both teams demonstrated that you can win without spending $40 million. But the significant difference between the A's and the Reds reflects the difference between Jim Bowden and Billy Beane. Whereas Bowden built a high-risk team that was going to be disassembled during or after the year, win or lose, Beane's goal is to build a consistent winner. Bowden's roster moves and free-wheeling ways with the Reds are grounded in the present, in present opportunities and present payoffs. For the Reds, it has to be that way because their player development has been spotty at best, and their commitment to building a good development program seems dubious. Beane built a team that could win this year—armed with the expectation that tomorrow is filled with promise, thanks to the A's investment in player development.

So while Bowden and Beane pursued similar goals in 1999, they're in the process of building different futures. And by winning 183 games between them, they demonstrated how easy it can be for a smart management team to assemble winning talent without spending Huizenga cash.

And the lineup? Is a lineup that features old players like John Jaha, Tony Phillips, Randy Velarde and Matt Stairs really supposed to last? We'll tell you yes, because those aren't the signature players who will help the A's score 800 or more runs year after year. They're the supporting players, the guys the organization identified as ones who would give the team a good, cost-effective offense. None of them got a Devon White contract—not that the A's would commit their limited financial resources to such a marginally useful player like Devon White in the first place. To a certain extent, the A's are the only team that plays the market for available players this way, whether it's getting Olmedo Saenz for nothing or nabbing an underused Rich Becker.

Athletics Prospectus

1999 record: 87-75; Second place, AL West

Pythagorean W/L: 85-77

Runs scored: 893 (4th in AL)

Runs allowed: 846 (6th in AL)

Team EQA: .265 (5th in AL)

1999 team age: 29.8 (5th-oldest in AL)

1999 park: Network Associates Coliseum; slight pitchers' park, decreased run scoring by 3%.

1999: Not as young as people think, but still a great story.

2000: A consolidation year; they should win the division, anyway.

It would be easy to associate the offensive future of the A's with the futures of Eric Chavez and Ben Grieve. While they're the best bets to be the lineup's core for a number of years, consider that they're just advanced representatives of an organizational offensive plan of action. The players in the A's lineup are all there to achieve one goal: scoring runs. Amusing as it is to have Randy Hundley, in his best Hank Hill drawl, enlighten us with, "I tellyoowut, th'team with the most runs wins," not every organization has that part of the game figured out.

On the A's, whoever contributes more to scoring runs is going to play. Sometimes that commitment to scoring runs carries defensive risks, such as when Phillips played center field between Stairs and Grieve. (Mmmm. . . triples.) But the goal of outscoring the opposition will depend more on the young players than on the current fun bunch of beer leaguers like Stairs and Jaha. The expectation right now is that the key players will be Chavez and Grieve. Three years from now, Mario Encarnacion, Esteban German or Ryan Ludwick could be the key players.

That the A's have such a bevy of talented prospects reflects more than just the survival strategy of a team that can't afford to flush $60 million as easily as the Cubs can. Beyond good scouting and a peerless academy in the Dominican Republic, the A's do a better job than any other organization in working with hitters. In addition to the prospects you'll find here, the A's have at least a half-dozen young hitters, maybe more, who deserve to be in this book but who didn't make it because there's not enough room.

While a thoughtful program for developing hitters makes building a good lineup look easy, it can't do everything for an organization. It doesn't eliminate the risk of over-committing to veteran hitters, or help turn around what has been one of the game's worst records of pitcher development.

Offseason commitments to veterans with health records as bad as John Jaha's or Randy Velarde's may make for a political win in the clubhouse, in the local media and even with season-ticket holders, but they also limit Oakland's freedom of action. If Stairs or Grieve needs to move to DH because Mario Encarnacion is ready, now Jaha is in the way. If you don't want Jose Ortiz to turn into the next Tony Batista, starring for somebody else, you have to ensure that if he earns the chance to play, he'll get to. A cynic could point out that these problems solve themselves when fragile players like Jaha or Velarde hurt themselves. And because neither player is signed to a contract of notable length or size, the A's can survive even if either or both flop, as long as their presence isn't a sign that Billy Beane is getting satisfied with a team that hasn't actually won anything.

Whether or not the A's start developing pitching is the question on which the organization's future rests. The alternative is signing free-agent pitchers, but Pedro Martinez and Kevin Brown and Randy Johnson are rare—as well as prohibitively expensive—while Tim Belcher and Jeff Fassero are not the answer when you want to run with the Yankees and Braves. If the A's are going to win the World Series, or even be in a position to get there, it will have to be on the strength of the pitching they develop.

Understanding how lineups score runs, what players put runs on the board and which ones will grow into good hitters is facilitated by the availability of reams of data. But determining what works on the mound, who's going to turn into a good pitcher and which pitchers get the most out of what they have is still more art than science. The A's have been burdened with a good 15 to 20 years of poor pitcher development. The boneyard is full of pitchers with "limitless" potential: the Four Aces, Mike Morgan, Tim Conroy, Ariel Prieto, John Wasdin...even Mike Rossiter and Benji Grigsby.

That track record has led to innumerable trades for other teams' pitching prospects. The prospect pickups used to work (Rick Langford, Mike Norris, Jose Rijo), but lately they've been disastrous. Of the seven pitchers Sandy Alderson got from the Cardinals in exchange for Mark McGwire, Todd Stottlemyre and Dennis Eckersley between January 1996 and July 1997, exactly one, T.J. Mathews, is left. At that rate of exchange, the A's would do better to let players leave as free agents and take the draft picks, because the track record of their own picks is better than whatever Carl Dale had to offer.

The hope for improvement depends greatly on the work of men like major-league pitching coach Rick Peterson and minor-league pitching coordinator Ron Romanick. While Tim Hudson's spectacular arrival overstates the possibilities, there are many talented pitchers in the farm system. Among Mark Mulder, Barry Zito and Brett Laxton, rookie pitchers should be able to win the last two spots in the rotation. These three should be the point men for what looks like the most pitching talent the organization has had in years.

That core is a reflection of a pitcher-development philosophy as coherent as the one the organization uses with hitters. At the A-ball level, the A's use eight-man rotations. They pair off pitchers (for example, Mark Seaver and Jon Adkins were a pair at Modesto) and flip them back and forth between starting and relieving when their turn comes up. Everyone is kept around 75 pitches starting and 50 pitches relieving per outing every four days, and everyone gets pulled at those points, no matter what the game situation. The objective is to make sure nobody gets overworked for the greater glory of the Visalia Oaks, while guaranteeing that everyone on the roster gets to pitch for the purpose of evaluation.

How well the A's convert their pitching prospects into major leaguers will define the range of success they can enjoy with this team. Without good young pitching, the best they can hope for is to duplicate the recent regular-season success of teams like the Rangers and Indians. The worst case without generating their own pitching would be ending up like the 1990-93 Tigers or the 1995-97 Mariners, scoring lots of runs and amusing folks, but never adding up to much.

So the A's are in a precarious spot, positioned to become the dominant team in the AL West for the next decade, or to lapse into a Mariner-like state of entertaining irrelevance. Even with the Giants' new Pac Bell Park likely to generate a big attendance boost for the orange and black, the A's ought to be able to count on improved attendance in support of newly competitive team. Attendance increases are year-after phenomena: witness the 1988 Twins or the 1999 Cubs.

Unfortunately, fan sentiment has been undermined by two persistent problems. First, there's the annoying ownership dance and the derision it earns. Whether or not Steve Schott and Ken Hofman intend to sell to someone who will keep the team in Oakland, intend to maneuver their way to San Jose or intend to get a stadium somewhere between Fresno and Redding is all up in the air. It's also kept deliberately vague so that every scenario is potentially feasible if the right events occur. That's great for Schott and Hofman for creating competing financial opportunities, but it's bad for public confidence in a public institution. Second, Al Davis's

mausoleum has had a terribly adverse effect on public support for professional sports in the East Bay.

Those problems handicap the franchise right now, but the talent is in place for a chance at greatness, a chance just as tangible as the chance the Braves and Indians had 10 years ago. The A's have built a first-class organization and the best player-development program in baseball, and they have started to contend without spending oodles of cash on marginal players like Dante Bichette. You can understand why somebody like Jerry McMorris would be frightened of seeing it happen. If the A's demonstrate that phony labels like "small market" aren't synonymous with an inability to contend, people might start reevaluating all sorts of modern assumptions, from the necessity of public financing of stadiums, to whether anyone really needs to spend $60 or $70 million to win.

If an organization proves it can win with intelligence, good scouting and some calculated risks, it could hasten the death of the owners' already-doomed drive for a salary cap. The Lords can't have that, so it's better to argue that smarter organizations than McMorris' Rockies should be disbanded before they start winning. Here's hoping the A's succeed beyond their wildest dreams, because nothing will put the lie to the current ownership bleating faster than a World Series winner with a $40 million payroll.

HITTERS (Averages: BA: .270 / OBP: .340 / SLG: .430 / EQA: .260)

Danny Ardoin — C — Bats R — Age 25

YEAR	TEAM	LGE	AB	H	DB	TP	HR	BB/SO	R	RBI	SB	CS	OUT	BA	OBP	SLG	EQA	EQR	DEFENSE
1997	Visalia	Cal	146	29	7	1	2	16/39	12	14	0	0	117	.199	.290	.301	.202	11	
1997	Huntsvil	Sou	208	43	10	1	3	13/41	20	18	1	2	167	.207	.261	.308	.186	12	
1998	Huntsvil	Sou	369	84	14	0	16	46/93	52	50	5	2	287	.228	.322	.396	.245	43	84-C 101
1999	Vancouvr	PCL	339	79	11	2	7	43/79	43	39	2	2	262	.233	.332	.339	.233	34	81-C 105
2000	Oakland	AL	316	72	10	1	9	38/75	39	38	3	1	245	.228	.311	.351	.229	31	

Ardoin is a nifty receiver from bayou country. Even if communicating in English was a problem, could he make less sense than Jean-Claude Van Damme? His immediate future depends on Ramon Hernandez's winning the catching job, and the A's deciding to go with a rookie as a defensive replacement instead of signing another graybeard. He's a backup catcher in the Tom Prince or Mark Parent mold, not quite up to Todd Pratt standards, but a better defensive catcher.

Rich Becker — OF — Bats L — Age 28

YEAR	TEAM	LGE	AB	H	DB	TP	HR	BB/SO	R	RBI	SB	CS	OUT	BA	OBP	SLG	EQA	EQR	DEFENSE
1997	Minnesot	AL	441	117	23	3	10	59/125	59	44	17	5	329	.265	.354	.399	.262	58	128-OF 102
1998	NY Mets	NL	102	21	6	2	3	21/41	16	11	3	1	82	.206	.341	.392	.255	13	24-OF 110
1998	Baltimor	AL	113	24	1	0	3	22/33	22	11	2	0	89	.212	.351	.301	.238	12	33-OF 96
1999	Milwauke	NL	139	35	4	2	5	31/38	14	15	5	0	104	.252	.388	.417	.285	23	
1999	Oakland	AL	124	33	2	0	1	23/43	19	9	3	2	93	.266	.389	.306	.253	15	24-CF 93
2000	Oakland	AL	230	60	9	1	6	44/71	46	34	7	2	172	.261	.380	.387	.273	34	

(Rich Becker *continued*)

Here's a great example of a fourth outfielder and an organization made for each other. Becker's primary skill is his ability to get on base, and Billy Beane has said he wants to build a team that can put up a .400 OBP. Becker's problem is that he may no longer have the range for center field; he did not impress Art Howe or his teammates with his tendency to position himself too deep and give up extra bases on hits. The A's haven't had a great center fielder since Dwayne Murphy and Mike Davis ran into each other; Becker will be another temporary solution.

Mark Bellhorn — IF — Bats B — Age 25

YEAR	TEAM	LGE	AB	H	DB	TP	HR	BB/SO	R	RBI	SB	CS	OUT	BA	OBP	SLG	EQA	EQR	DEFENSE	
1997	Edmonton	PCL	228	62	14	2	8	53/60	37	31	4	4	170	.272	.413	.456	.295	40	40-2B 103	22-SS 94
1997	Oakland	AL	223	51	10	1	6	30/67	32	19	7	1	173	.229	.320	.363	.240	24	28-3B 108	
1998	Edmonton	PCL	307	69	17	3	9	55/90	46	36	5	2	240	.225	.351	.388	.257	40	44-3B 87	33-2B 106
1999	Midland	Tex	57	13	1	0	2	8/16	8	6	0	0	44	.228	.323	.351	.233	6		
2000	Oakland	AL	166	41	10	1	5	28/47	30	25	2	1	126	.247	.356	.410	.265	23		

He spent most of the year recuperating from nagging wrist and hand injuries after missing a good chunk of 1998 to injury. The A's admit they rushed him, so he may yet resurface somewhere with a team that needs a second baseman or third baseman with some pop and the ability to get on base. There can't be more than 15 or 20 of those.

Eric Byrnes — OF — Bats R — Age 24

YEAR	TEAM	LGE	AB	H	DB	TP	HR	BB/SO	R	RBI	SB	CS	OUT	BA	OBP	SLG	EQA	EQR	DEFENSE
1998	So Oregn	Nwn	169	42	9	1	5	8/19	22	19	2	1	128	.249	.287	.402	.229	16	38-OF 92
1998	Visalia	Cal	107	37	9	1	3	14/16	17	14	4	1	71	.346	.425	.533	.321	21	23-OF 117
1999	Modesto	Cal	361	96	20	1	5	42/39	52	44	10	3	268	.266	.351	.368	.252	43	90-OF 87
1999	Midland	Tex	163	32	8	0	2	14/36	18	18	3	2	133	.196	.269	.282	.186	10	38-OF 81
2000	Oakland	AL	345	93	19	1	9	40/54	55	51	6	2	254	.270	.345	.409	.261	44	

Byrnes is a speedy hustler drafted out of UCLA in 1998, and an interesting variant on the A's OBP obsession. Instead of being a slugger with patience, Byrnes hits for a good average, takes his share of walks (75 last year) and can run. Sort of like Roberto Vaz, but better. As you can see, he's already old for A ball, so he's going to have jump up to Sacramento to really earn a shot.

Eric Chavez — 3B — Bats L — Age 22

YEAR	TEAM	LGE	AB	H	DB	TP	HR	BB/SO	R	RBI	SB	CS	OUT	BA	OBP	SLG	EQA	EQR	DEFENSE
1997	Visalia	Cal	519	123	24	2	15	26/89	49	75	6	3	399	.237	.275	.378	.217	44	119-3B 99
1998	Huntsvil	Sou	338	104	21	1	21	29/63	51	68	7	3	236	.308	.364	.562	.300	58	77-3B 93
1998	Edmonton	PCL	191	56	13	0	10	10/32	30	33	2	2	137	.293	.331	.518	.275	27	46-3B 75
1999	Oakland	AL	355	88	23	2	12	41/56	44	46	1	1	268	.248	.326	.425	.252	43	95-3B 89
2000	Oakland	AL	483	142	27	1	25	45/81	81	98	5	2	343	.294	.354	.509	.287	76	

Expectations were high, so in some quarters Chavez was perceived as a disappointment. He had to be platooned, and his defense needs work, but the A's believe he's coachable. His hitting got better as the season went on; before a torn plantar fascia sidelined him from mid-August to mid-September, he was on the verge of becoming the big stick in the lineup. Among 1999 AL rookies, Chavez is still the guy who should have the best offensive career.

Ryan Christenson — CF — Bats R — Age 26

YEAR	TEAM	LGE	AB	H	DB	TP	HR	BB/SO	R	RBI	SB	CS	OUT	BA	OBP	SLG	EQA	EQR	DEFENSE
1997	Visalia	Cal	310	69	14	4	9	52/77	43	34	8	4	245	.223	.337	.381	.248	38	82-OF 101
1997	Huntsvil	Sou	119	37	9	2	1	18/25	27	12	3	2	84	.311	.401	.445	.289	19	29-OF 114
1998	Edmonton	PCL	88	20	5	1	1	12/25	13	6	3	1	69	.227	.320	.341	.232	9	21-OF 119
1998	Oakland	AL	372	99	23	2	5	35/104	55	40	4	6	279	.266	.331	.379	.240	39	102-OF 109
1999	Oakland	AL	267	55	11	1	4	35/58	37	22	7	5	217	.206	.300	.300	.208	21	78-CF 104
1999	Vancouvr	PCL	129	38	4	1	1	18/23	22	12	5	1	92	.295	.381	.364	.267	17	32-OF 111
2000	Oakland	AL	433	110	19	3	9	58/101	69	56	11	6	329	.254	.342	.374	.250	51	

American League ▬▬▬▬▬▬▬▬▬▬▬▬▬▬▬▬▬▬▬ **163**

If Becker is the regular center fielder, there are worse platoon mates than Christenson. The disappointment is that more was expected of him: he wasn't supposed to be so pathetic against right-handed pitching. The ultimatum has been issued: the A's want Christenson to hit the weight room or get really familiar with the Sacramento area as long as he's under contract with the organization. A word of advice: cruising Fair Oaks Boulevard is probably still cool in Sacto.

Mario Encarnacion   CF   Bats R   Age 22

YEAR	TEAM	LGE	AB	H	DB	TP	HR	BB/SO	R	RBI	SB	CS	OUT	BA	OBP	SLG	EQA	EQR	DEFENSE	
1997	Modesto	Cal	368	97	15	5	16	32/118	52	60	7	5	276	.264	.329	.462	.262	48	80-OF 95	
1998	Huntsvil	Sou	362	92	14	2	14	45/127	55	49	6	5	275	.254	.342	.420	.257	46	93-OF 96	
1999	Midland	Tex	349	89	16	2	14	38/94	50	51	5	4	264	.255	.329	.433	.255	43	72-OF 88	
1999	Vancouvr	PCL	145	33	4	0	3	5/43	15	15	4	3	115	.228	.261	.317	.191	9	36-OF 110	
2000	*Oakland*	*AL*	*459*	*121*	*15*	*2*	*21*	*59/136*	*73*	*80*	*7*	*5*	*343*	*.264*	*.347*	*.442*	*.268*	*64*		

Because the A's know what they're doing, Encarnacion is more than just a young Dominican with great power and a great arm. He'll take a walk, and while he hasn't mastered breaking stuff, he's smart enough to foul it off or take it. The major question is whether or not he can play center field; he only moved to right field this year after Terrence Long was acquired. The A's think he can handle it, but may just put him in right field anyway for his arm.

Josue Espada   SS/2B   Bats R   Age 24

YEAR	TEAM	LGE	AB	H	DB	TP	HR	BB/SO	R	RBI	SB	CS	OUT	BA	OBP	SLG	EQA	EQR	DEFENSE	
1997	Visalia	Cal	445	108	8	2	2	57/67	60	30	22	8	345	.243	.337	.283	.226	42	115-SS 93	
1998	Huntsvil	Sou	163	39	7	1	1	21/15	23	18	4	2	126	.239	.338	.313	.231	16	42-SS 90	
1999	Midland	Tex	429	116	12	2	4	49/57	59	36	10	7	320	.270	.347	.336	.238	44	83-SS 85	23-2B 94
2000	*Oakland*	*AL*	*351*	*93*	*12*	*1*	*3*	*46/46*	*57*	*37*	*13*	*6*	*264*	*.265*	*.350*	*.330*	*.243*	*38*		

After nabbing 46 bags at Visalia in 1997, Espada had knee problems that ate up most of 1998. He had a brief shot at beating out Cristian Guzman for the starting shortstop job in Minnesota via the Rule 5 draft, but the Twins had to offer him back. While he has a good arm, he's in the midst of having some problems throwing accurately. Promoted for Vancouver's playoff drive, Espada was moved over to second base while Jose Ortiz manned shortstop, and he was more comfortable there. Playing behind fragile Randy Velarde, that's good for him.

Esteban German   2B   Bats R   Age 21

YEAR	TEAM	LGE	AB	H	DB	TP	HR	BB/SO	R	RBI	SB	CS	OUT	BA	OBP	SLG	EQA	EQR	DEFENSE
1999	Modesto	Cal	496	135	16	8	5	83/124	73	39	18	7	368	.272	.380	.367	.265	67	110-2B 95
2000	*Oakland*	*AL*	*236*	*66*	*9*	*3*	*2*	*52/93*	*55*	*32*	*8*	*3*	*173*	*.280*	*.410*	*.369*	*.283*	*37*	

He's another gem from the A's expansive Dominican program, and proof that you can walk off the islands if you try. German is one of the fastest players in the game today. A's fans who remember Lance Blankenship: imagine if Blankenship could have hit for a better average, was faster and happened to be a good defensive second baseman. Plans for moving German to center field are only at the talking stages and may or may not be implemented.

Jason Giambi   1B   Bats L   Age 29

YEAR	TEAM	LGE	AB	H	DB	TP	HR	BB/SO	R	RBI	SB	CS	OUT	BA	OBP	SLG	EQA	EQR	DEFENSE	
1997	Oakland	AL	516	152	41	2	20	51/86	63	78	0	1	365	.295	.366	.498	.286	80	55-OF 90	42-1B 114
1998	Oakland	AL	565	173	24	0	30	80/100	91	112	2	2	394	.306	.397	.508	.301	98	142-1B 86	
1999	Oakland	AL	569	179	32	3	32	97/106	105	115	1	1	391	.315	.420	.550	.321	114	136-1B 79	
2000	*Oakland*	*AL*	*576*	*175*	*26*	*1*	*32*	*98/103*	*118*	*133*	*1*	*1*	*402*	*.304*	*.405*	*.519*	*.311*	*109*		

Right now, he's the franchise's best left-handed hitter since Reggie Jackson, a title he won't hold for long with Chavez and Ben Grieve in the fold. Perhaps taking a cue from Mr. October, Giambi has talked his way into an interesting niche within the organization. Billy Beane seems to go out of his way to get Giambi's opinions on roster moves. He's obviously the team's most vocal player, so it could just be good politics on Beane's part. It's time to come to terms with the fact that Giambi's glovework is bad. Frank Thomas bad. He's a Garveyesque pillar of immobility, and having Jaha around keeps him on the field. It's a problem.

Oakland Athletics

Ben Grieve   OF   Bats L   Age 24

YEAR	TEAM	LGE	AB	H	DB	TP	HR	BB/SO	R	RBI	SB	CS	OUT	BA	OBP	SLG	EQA	EQR	DEFENSE
1997	Huntsvil	Sou	370	106	24	1	20	65/80	73	80	3	1	265	.286	.402	.519	.307	69	97-OF 94
1997	Edmonton	PCL	101	37	9	1	5	9/16	19	19	0	1	65	.366	.422	.624	.333	21	25-OF 99
1997	Oakland	AL	92	29	5	0	3	13/24	11	23	0	0	63	.315	.407	.467	.298	15	16-OF 103
1998	Oakland	AL	587	176	40	3	19	83/120	93	90	2	2	413	.300	.395	.475	.294	97	147-OF 89
1999	Oakland	AL	484	129	18	0	28	57/108	73	81	4	0	355	.267	.353	.477	.278	72	111-LF 99
2000	*Oakland*	*AL*	*500*	*147*	*24*	*1*	*28*	*77/107*	*97*	*111*	*2*	*1*	*354*	*.294*	*.388*	*.514*	*.303*	*89*	

Grieve hit 28 home runs, and it was considered a bad year. Talk about a tough audience. His improvement as a power hitter is frightening for what it could mean for the next four or five years. Jackson hit more than 40 home runs only once, and no other left-handed hitter in A's history has done it. Grieve's chances aren't as good as Chavez's over the course of a career, yet even Grieve could do it more than once if the current offensive environment prevails. The problem for the A's is that, as with Giambi and Stairs, Grieve's best position might be DH.

Jason Hart   1B   Bats R   Age 22

YEAR	TEAM	LGE	AB	H	DB	TP	HR	BB/SO	R	RBI	SB	CS	OUT	BA	OBP	SLG	EQA	EQR	DEFENSE
1998	So Oregn	Nwn	297	61	12	1	15	23/75	37	42	0	0	236	.205	.266	.404	.221	27	67-1B 108
1999	Modesto	Cal	545	146	36	2	18	42/102	72	92	1	2	401	.268	.323	.440	.254	65	127-1B 99
2000	*Oakland*	*AL*	*330*	*81*	*15*	*1*	*15*	*29/71*	*41*	*52*	*0*	*1*	*250*	*.245*	*.306*	*.433*	*.247*	*38*	

Hart is a big kid out of Southwest Missouri State who led both the Missouri Valley Conference and the Northwest League in home runs in 1998. He hits with power to all fields already, and the A's expect him to hit for even more power and improve as a hitter as he finishes filling out. Be patient: he's a good year and a half away from being close to ready.

Ramon Hernandez   C   Bats R   Age 24

YEAR	TEAM	LGE	AB	H	DB	TP	HR	BB/SO	R	RBI	SB	CS	OUT	BA	OBP	SLG	EQA	EQR	DEFENSE	
1997	Visalia	Cal	328	102	16	1	13	26/46	43	64	1	2	228	.311	.372	.485	.285	49		
1997	Huntsvil	Sou	162	29	4	0	3	14/25	21	19	0	0	133	.179	.254	.259	.167	8		
1998	Huntsvil	Sou	484	135	20	1	15	40/63	67	80	2	3	352	.279	.353	.417	.261	61	50-C 96	19-1B 76
1999	Vancouvr	PCL	292	73	10	3	11	20/37	32	46	1	1	220	.250	.311	.418	.243	32	43-C 103	
1999	Oakland	AL	135	37	4	0	4	17/11	12	21	1	0	98	.274	.359	.393	.261	17	38-C 93	
2000	*Oakland*	*AL*	*433*	*121*	*15*	*1*	*15*	*37/53*	*58*	*70*	*1*	*1*	*313*	*.279*	*.336*	*.423*	*.258*	*53*		

Everything came together in 1999 for Hernandez. He came to camp in shape for the first time, impressing the organization. Although he wasn't having his best year at the plate, he'd worked hard while Hinch had flopped. After his call-up, he gave the A's some desperately needed right-handed power. His defense still needs work; he has problems sitting still and making a good target for his pitchers. He's always been injury-prone, so while he should win the job outright, the A's will need to carry a good caddy.

A.J. Hinch   C   Bats R   Age 26

YEAR	TEAM	LGE	AB	H	DB	TP	HR	BB/SO	R	RBI	SB	CS	OUT	BA	OBP	SLG	EQA	EQR	DEFENSE
1997	Modesto	Cal	336	85	21	1	14	30/73	47	49	3	1	252	.253	.327	.446	.259	43	
1997	Edmonton	PCL	118	37	3	0	4	16/13	16	18	1	0	81	.314	.406	.441	.293	19	
1998	Oakland	AL	339	82	8	0	10	29/87	33	35	3	0	257	.242	.309	.354	.228	32	107-C 102
1999	Oakland	AL	205	44	3	1	7	9/41	24	22	6	2	163	.215	.255	.341	.200	15	64-C 94
1999	Vancouvr	PCL	61	20	1	0	2	2/13	7	6	1	1	42	.328	.357	.443	.266	8	
2000	*Oakland*	*AL*	*303*	*74*	*5*	*0*	*11*	*24/66*	*35*	*38*	*6*	*1*	*230*	*.244*	*.300*	*.370*	*.230*	*29*	

He was close to having it made, so close he could taste it, but then he started to press. Hinch is a better player than he showed in 1999, but he couldn't afford this kind of season in an organization with Hernandez ready and several more catching prospects on the way. If he settles down and plays his game, he can be somebody worth 250 at-bats. If he continues to struggle, he'll get the blistering pleasures of a Sacramento summer.

John Jaha · DH · Bats R · Age 34

YEAR	TEAM	LGE	AB	H	DB	TP	HR	BB/SO	R	RBI	SB	CS	OUT	BA	OBP	SLG	EQA	EQR	DEFENSE
1997	Milwauke	AL	162	41	5	0	12	24/38	24	26	1	0	121	.253	.361	.506	.287	27	22-1B 91
1998	Milwauke	NL	218	46	6	2	7	49/64	30	39	1	3	175	.211	.371	.353	.255	29	50-1B 84
1999	Oakland	AL	453	125	21	0	35	94/129	86	104	2	0	328	.276	.410	.554	.317	93	
2000	Oakland	AL	308	74	9	0	20	75/87	63	65	1	1	235	.240	.389	.464	.293	54	

The feel-good story on the AL's feel-good-story team, topped off with an All-Star game appearance. It was enough to win Jaha his first multi-year contract. He's your classic DH: the guy who can't do everything a baseball player does and stay healthy. Like Harold Baines or Edgar Martinez, he shouldn't do anything other than hit. The DH rule generally doesn't take off the field people who can still play a position; it extends the careers of guys who'd be dead without it, or allows a player like Rafael Palmeiro to help his team without increasing the risk that he'll suffer a career-altering injury. Is that so bad? Jaha's health record is bad enough that he'll probably never pass another physical in his life.

Rusty Keith · OF · Bats R · Age 22

YEAR	TEAM	LGE	AB	H	DB	TP	HR	BB/SO	R	RBI	SB	CS	OUT	BA	OBP	SLG	EQA	EQR	DEFENSE
1999	Visalia	Cal	446	122	27	2	9	66/57	66	47	5	4	327	.274	.372	.404	.268	61	112-OF 99
2000	Oakland	AL	198	58	11	1	6	39/40	43	37	1	1	141	.293	.409	.449	.298	34	

After starring at Portland State, Keith looks the like the best of a group of good young outfielders the A's had in the California League. The problem is that jobs will be tight in the fight to get to Midland. Gary Thomas is a center fielder who can fly, Juan Camilo and Hipolito Martinez both look like prospects, and even Modesto's utility infielder, Oscar Salazar, spent his time at DH when he wasn't on the field. This was before they stole Ryan Ludwick in the 1999 draft. There are whole organizations that don't have half as many prospects as the A's have at A ball.

Terrence Long · OF · Bats L · Age 24

YEAR	TEAM	LGE	AB	H	DB	TP	HR	BB/SO	R	RBI	SB	CS	OUT	BA	OBP	SLG	EQA	EQR	DEFENSE
1997	St Lucie	Fla	475	108	29	5	9	34/112	41	52	10	4	371	.227	.281	.366	.219	41	120-OF 97
1998	Binghmtn	Eas	460	127	19	8	16	54/103	59	52	15	7	340	.276	.354	.457	.273	66	128-OF 95
1999	Norfolk	Int	303	94	19	3	6	19/41	33	39	10	5	214	.310	.353	.452	.270	41	78-OF 107
1999	Vancouvr	PCL	154	35	4	2	2	9/29	13	18	6	4	123	.227	.274	.318	.199	11	37-OF 109
2000	Oakland	AL	458	124	19	5	13	44/85	70	68	13	7	341	.271	.335	.419	.257	57	

If there's something to be said about a guy, it's been said about Long. Some people say he'll be a five-tool, 30/30 guy who can play center field. Some people think he'll need to move to first base and won't hit enough to stick. Given such extremes, it's safe to say the truth is somewhere in between. He can play center field, he has a strong arm and he can hit to all fields, but he won't be the offensive superstar the Mets projected. Long was named MVP of the Triple-A World Series after also starring in the PCL playoffs. If Becker's defense becomes too much of an issue, Long will get a chance to flash the leather and win the job.

Mike MacFarlane · C · Bats R · Age 36

YEAR	TEAM	LGE	AB	H	DB	TP	HR	BB/SO	R	RBI	SB	CS	OUT	BA	OBP	SLG	EQA	EQR	DEFENSE
1997	KansasCy	AL	256	60	14	2	8	22/45	33	33	0	2	198	.234	.312	.398	.238	27	
1998	Oakland	AL	208	54	8	0	9	11/33	27	36	1	0	154	.260	.310	.428	.247	23	55-C 99
1999	Oakland	AL	226	55	14	0	5	10/52	22	30	0	0	171	.243	.278	.372	.216	18	60-C 106
2000	Oakland	AL	181	40	7	0	6	14/37	17	20	0	0	141	.221	.277	.359	.213	15	

There are some things a Bay Area sports team shouldn't do: the 49ers should never hire Mike Ditka, the Raiders should never employ Franco Harris in any capacity, and the green and gold shouldn't give jobs to ex-Royals. They're evil. MacFarlane claimed he was retiring and got a nice hand from the fans, then filed for free agency. He should just go back to writing those neat *Spawn* comics; they're a hoot.

T.R. Marcinczyk · 1B · Bats R · Age 26

YEAR	TEAM	LGE	AB	H	DB	TP	HR	BB/SO	R	RBI	SB	CS	OUT	BA	OBP	SLG	EQA	EQR	DEFENSE	
1997	Modesto	Cal	471	107	29	1	17	51/114	61	63	2	2	366	.227	.312	.401	.240	52	94-1B 106	17-3B 96
1998	Huntsvil	Sou	508	119	21	1	21	30/144	66	63	1	3	392	.234	.286	.404	.228	49	109-1B 85	
1999	Midland	Tex	475	100	23	1	15	44/134	56	70	1	0	375	.211	.289	.358	.219	42	124-1B 105	
2000	Oakland	AL	488	105	22	1	17	49/135	52	59	1	1	384	.215	.287	.369	.221	44		

(T.R. Marcinczyk *continued*)

First basemen who can hit are about as rare as Furbies, and only the very few aren't pre-programmed to hit with some power. Despite being a Texas League All-Star, Marcinczyk isn't a prospect. Midland made it appear that he survived the jump to Double-A, but take out the park and league effects, and he looks like a non-prospect who would struggle anywhere else.

Jason McDonald OF Bats B Age 28

YEAR	TEAM	LGE	AB	H	DB	TP	HR	BB/SO	R	RBI	SB	CS	OUT	BA	OBP	SLG	EQA	EQR	DEFENSE
1997	Edmonton	PCL	268	52	10	4	2	57/65	45	18	18	6	222	.194	.346	.284	.236	30	77-OF 107
1997	Oakland	AL	234	60	11	4	4	35/47	45	13	13	8	182	.256	.356	.389	.256	30	67-OF 95
1998	Oakland	AL	176	46	6	0	2	27/32	24	17	10	4	134	.261	.369	.330	.253	22	48-OF 105
1999	Vancouvr	PCL	130	36	6	1	3	15/36	19	14	5	3	97	.277	.358	.408	.262	17	31-OF 108
1999	Oakland	AL	187	39	1	1	3	22/48	23	8	6	3	151	.209	.302	.273	.203	14	39-CF 110
2000	Texas	AL	290	71	10	2	6	45/69	49	35	11	6	225	.245	.346	.355	.241	32	

He could help a team looking for somebody who can get on base, pinch-run and do some defensive subbing. He could do more than that for a team totally lacking a viable center fielder, like the Expos in 1999 or the Cubs the last year or two. If he takes up playing the infield again, he'd be extremely valuable as a utilityman.

Frank Menechino UT Bats R Age 29

YEAR	TEAM	LGE	AB	H	DB	TP	HR	BB/SO	R	RBI	SB	CS	OUT	BA	OBP	SLG	EQA	EQR	DEFENSE	
1997	Nashvill	AA	115	22	3	0	3	22/35	16	9	2	1	94	.191	.351	.296	.236	13	28-2B 94	
1997	Birmnghm	Sou	323	76	23	2	8	58/93	51	39	4	2	249	.235	.364	.393	.264	44	77-2B 99	
1998	Edmonton	PCL	377	85	8	5	7	57/82	51	28	6	6	298	.225	.338	.329	.233	39	73-2B 91	
1999	Vancouvr	PCL	505	135	26	8	10	59/105	78	66	3	3	373	.267	.352	.410	.260	64	55-3B 93	38-SS 109
2000	Oakland	AL	392	99	18	4	9	64/88	65	57	3	3	296	.253	.357	.388	.259	51		

After years of his being just another nice little minor-league second baseman, the A's decided to turn Menechino into a utility player. This is the only way he has a shot at a big-league career, and it worked better than expected. Between his versatility and his hitting, he was Vancouver's key player. In addition to shortstop and third base, he played second base and the outfield. Given the choice between carrying a sad sack like Jorge Velandia or a baseball player like Menechino, Frankie is the more useful choice.

Mike Neill OF Bats L Age 30

YEAR	TEAM	LGE	AB	H	DB	TP	HR	BB/SO	R	RBI	SB	CS	OUT	BA	OBP	SLG	EQA	EQR	DEFENSE
1997	Huntsvil	Sou	483	126	23	1	9	50/137	80	51	8	4	361	.261	.334	.369	.242	52	117-OF 90
1998	Edmonton	PCL	369	91	15	3	7	52/99	52	35	4	3	281	.247	.342	.360	.244	41	94-OF 92
1999	Vancouvr	PCL	368	94	19	3	6	47/105	45	46	6	3	277	.255	.342	.372	.247	42	78-OF 90
2000	Seattle	AL	324	80	12	1	9	48/91	49	45	4	3	247	.247	.344	.373	.250	38	

Shoulder injuries derailed what could have been a very good career, because Neill knows how to hit. He had a moment worth remembering: after Lance Berkman was called up by the Astros, Neill made the Pan Am Games team and delivered the game-winning hit against Mexico that put Team USA in the Olympics. Neill is a minor-league free agent and a good bet to be on the Olympic squad.

Miguel Olivo C Bats R Age 21

YEAR	TEAM	LGE	AB	H	DB	TP	HR	BB/SO	R	RBI	SB	CS	OUT	BA	OBP	SLG	EQA	EQR	DEFENSE
1999	Modesto	Cal	241	64	14	3	8	15/58	34	30	2	2	179	.266	.312	.448	.251	28	67-C 98
2000	Oakland	AL	124	33	8	1	6	10/66	19	22	1	1	92	.266	.321	.492	.268	17	

Another product of the A's peerless Dominican program, this was his first year in a full-season league after starring in both the Dominican and Arizona rookie leagues. Behind the plate, he's shown a good arm and great receiving and plate-blocking skills. He still needs to pick up English to improve his work with pitchers, and he needs to work on his command of the strike zone, but he already has good power. It will be a couple of years before he's ready.

Jose Ortiz   SS   Bats R   Age 23

YEAR	TEAM	LGE	AB	H	DB	TP	HR	BB/SO	R	RBI	SB	CS	OUT	BA	OBP	SLG	EQA	EQR	DEFENSE	
1997	Modesto	Cal	503	111	22	4	15	47/104	69	46	11	6	398	.221	.293	.370	.225	48	114-SS 98	
1998	Huntsvil	Sou	358	94	25	1	6	35/65	54	45	13	5	269	.263	.335	.388	.250	42	58-2B 98	31-SS 93
1999	Vancouvr	PCL	378	102	29	2	7	25/49	55	38	10	3	279	.270	.327	.413	.252	44	99-SS 96	
2000	*Oakland*	*AL*	*381*	*104*	*23*	*2*	*9*	*36/60*	*63*	*53*	*13*	*4*	*281*	*.273*	*.336*	*.415*	*.259*	*48*		

Nagging injuries keep holding him back; in 1998, he missed time with a broken hand. While he has the great arm at shortstop that can turn a single through the hole into an out, some feel he's going to have to move to second base. Similar things were said about Tony Batista coming up, and like Batista, Ortiz has good power. The question is whether the A's have room for him.

Tony Phillips   UT   Bats B   Age 41

YEAR	TEAM	LGE	AB	H	DB	TP	HR	BB/SO	R	RBI	SB	CS	OUT	BA	OBP	SLG	EQA	EQR	DEFENSE	
1997	ChiSox	AL	129	42	3	0	3	28/28	22	9	4	1	88	.326	.450	.419	.310	24	19-OF 118	
1997	Anaheim	AL	402	105	28	2	6	70/86	70	46	9	9	306	.261	.374	.386	.262	54	37-2B 99	26-OF 96
1998	NY Mets	NL	191	45	10	0	4	39/43	26	15	1	1	147	.236	.365	.351	.253	24	48-OF 95	
1999	Oakland	AL	404	98	25	4	14	66/94	70	45	11	3	309	.243	.356	.428	.269	58	54-2B 106	20-CF 104
2000	*Oakland*	*AL*	*266*	*60*	*13*	*1*	*6*	*56/60*	*48*	*34*	*3*	*2*	*208*	*.226*	*.360*	*.350*	*.253*	*34*		

Love him or hate him, Tony Phillips is the salt on your margarita. For some guys, it's easy to mistake a style of playing for a way of life. During the LaRussa mini-dynasty, Phillips was in the background, but he was always playing in the shadow of Jose Canseco or Rickey Henderson or Dave Henderson or Dave Stewart. Years later, he's the one still hanging around as a crazed veteran, playing every day as if it were his last. He's constantly mixing things up, talking trash, threatening to retire and homering on the same day, making the impossible game-saving diving catch or barreling into second base to break up the double play. The highs come with lows, as that last tactic earned him a broken leg in mid-August. Whether he comes back, and if so, where, are open questions.

Adam Piatt   3B   Bats R   Age 24

YEAR	TEAM	LGE	AB	H	DB	TP	HR	BB/SO	R	RBI	SB	CS	OUT	BA	OBP	SLG	EQA	EQR	DEFENSE
1997	So Oregn	Nwn	217	47	5	0	10	22/62	33	21	5	2	172	.217	.290	.378	.227	21	50-3B 87
1998	Modesto	Cal	511	125	29	2	18	61/104	64	80	9	3	389	.245	.325	.415	.251	62	121-3B 76
1999	Midland	Tex	470	130	32	2	28	74/113	88	91	3	2	342	.277	.381	.532	.299	84	114-3B 93
2000	*Oakland*	*AL*	*492*	*131*	*29*	*1*	*23*	*82/112*	*95*	*93*	*7*	*2*	*363*	*.266*	*.371*	*.470*	*.287*	*80*	

In seasonal notation, you can't pick out where Piatt suddenly figured out how to hit: in the second half at Modesto, he smacked 17 home runs, and went through the Texas League as if it were a step down from the California League. He's gotten away from trying to pull everything, and now he's hitting to all fields. While he was athletic enough to play shortstop in college, he won't be following the path Scott Spiezio blazed over to second base. His play at third base isn't great, and there's a Chavez-sized roadblock in that direction. The A's are talking about moving him to first base or the outfield.

Tim Raines   HOF   Bats B   Age 40

YEAR	TEAM	LGE	AB	H	DB	TP	HR	BB/SO	R	RBI	SB	CS	OUT	BA	OBP	SLG	EQA	EQR	DEFENSE
1997	NY Yanks	AL	272	91	22	2	4	40/33	56	38	8	5	186	.335	.420	.474	.303	47	44-OF 92
1998	NY Yanks	AL	321	95	14	1	5	54/48	51	46	7	3	229	.296	.402	.393	.280	48	39-OF 87
1999	Oakland	AL	134	28	5	0	4	25/17	19	16	4	1	107	.209	.333	.336	.239	15	29-LF 102
2000	*Oakland*	*AL*	*134*	*33*	*3*	*0*	*4*	*26/18*	*23*	*19*	*3*	*2*	*103*	*.246*	*.369*	*.358*	*.258*	*17*	

Beating lupus isn't going to be easy. There's no cure, and people who have it endure severe fatigue problems and a tough regimen of medications. That's going to make it hard for Raines to continue any kind of playing career. If you're interested in learning what you can do to help people with lupus, you can contact the Lupus Foundation of America at (800) 558-0121, or check out its website at www.lupus.org.

With his battle in mind, let's review a great player's career. He's managed a career .306 EqA (tied for 97th), 1,628 EqR (43rd, just behind Lou Brock) and 833 runs above replacement (also 43rd). There have been just six left fielders who were more valuable offensively: Ted Williams, Stan Musial, Rickey Henderson, Barry Bonds, Carl Yastrzemski and Harry Heilmann. In his glory years, from 1983 to 1987, Raines was the best player in the NL:

(Tim Raines *continued*)

1983: 124 EqR, second to Dale Murphy's 125, and tied for fifth with a .315 EqA

1984: .330 EqA, 137 EqR, league leader in both

1985: .338 EqA, second to Pedro Guerrero's .357; his 133 EqR led the league

1986: .334 EqA, 127 EqR, led league in both

1987: .333 EqA, tied for fourth; 115 EqR, tied for fifth

While not the greatest left fielder in the history of the game, he's the best leadoff hitter the NL has ever seen. When the time comes, hopefully the voters will remember his peak, and not just the recent years when he stuck around as a solid part-time player because he has fun playing the game.

Olmedo Saenz 3B/1B Bats R Age 29

YEAR	TEAM	LGE	AB	H	DB	TP	HR	BB/SO	R	RBI	SB	CS	OUT	BA	OBP	SLG	EQA	EQR	DEFENSE
1998	Calgary	PCL	455	113	18	0	21	35/54	60	70	2	2	344	.248	.323	.426	.251	54	114-3B 98
1999	Oakland	AL	254	70	14	1	11	19/47	37	39	1	1	185	.276	.361	.469	.277	37	43-3B 93
2000	Oakland	AL	210	56	9	0	12	20/45	30	40	1	0	154	.267	.330	.481	.271	29	

He was an outstanding free talent pickup. After he tore his Achilles tendon in 1997, the White Sox doubted he'd recover his defensive skills at third base and took him off their 40-man roster. The A's signed him as a free agent, giving them the right-handed bat they needed to back up Giambi and Chavez at the corner infield positions. He suffered nagging leg injuries all season, including a bum knee and a pulled hamstring. Guys like Saenz and Jeff Manto and Scott McClain are floating around, waiting for people to stop handing jobs to Gary Gaetti and Dave Hollins just because they're famous.

Scott Spiezio 2B/3B Bats B Age 27

YEAR	TEAM	LGE	AB	H	DB	TP	HR	BB/SO	R	RBI	SB	CS	OUT	BA	OBP	SLG	EQA	EQR	DEFENSE	
1997	Oakland	AL	536	131	28	4	14	41/72	56	63	9	3	408	.244	.300	.390	.233	54	143-2B 98	
1998	Oakland	AL	408	110	21	1	9	43/55	54	50	1	3	301	.270	.342	.392	.249	47	110-2B 105	
1999	Oakland	AL	246	60	20	0	9	26/36	28	32	0	0	186	.244	.321	.435	.253	30	32-2B 123	23-3B 84
1999	Vancouvr	PCL	105	35	7	1	4	12/17	20	20	0	0	70	.333	.409	.533	.313	19	20-2B 113	
2000	Anaheim	AL	346	91	21	1	11	40/49	53	54	2	1	256	.263	.339	.425	.260	44		

Spiezio tops some people's shopping lists as a guy who could be a cheap power source. Either they're really hard up, or they haven't noticed that we're in the middle of a high-offense era. If the choice is between Spiezio and Luis Castillo, then yes, Spiezio has more power. His 1998 knee injury has limited his range at second base severely, so much so that nobody thinks he can play it regularly. Keep in mind that those good 1999 fielding numbers are small samples.

Matt Stairs OF Bats L Age 31

YEAR	TEAM	LGE	AB	H	DB	TP	HR	BB/SO	R	RBI	SB	CS	OUT	BA	OBP	SLG	EQA	EQR	DEFENSE
1997	Oakland	AL	349	104	17	1	27	48/58	59	70	3	2	247	.298	.388	.585	.313	68	77-OF 83
1998	Oakland	AL	526	160	30	2	28	58/91	87	107	7	3	369	.304	.380	.529	.299	90	
1999	Oakland	AL	528	135	26	3	37	82/124	86	95	2	7	400	.256	.358	.527	.285	87	136-RF 93
2000	Oakland	AL	519	139	20	1	35	81/108	93	114	3	3	383	.268	.367	.513	.292	88	

Before the 1999 season, Stairs decided to change his beer-league body. He dumped 25 pounds of fat, put on 12 of muscle and quit smoking. I guess this isn't the same game Babe Ruth played after all. Given how cavalier the A's are about who plays where, they could probably swap Jason Giambi and Matt Stairs between right field and first base and improve themselves defensively, except Stairs might kill himself hustling to run down pop-ups. One of the more entertaining moments of the season was when he crushed a Keith Foulke palmball into the Coliseum seats, followed by plenty of White Sox whining that the A's must be stealing signs. Foulke's out pitch is the palmball, so how hard would it have been for Stairs to know what was coming?

Miguel Tejada SS Bats R Age 24

YEAR	TEAM	LGE	AB	H	DB	TP	HR	BB/SO	R	RBI	SB	CS	OUT	BA	OBP	SLG	EQA	EQR	DEFENSE
1997	Huntsvil	Sou	501	121	19	2	18	37/106	62	73	10	6	386	.242	.301	.395	.234	51	128-SS 97
1997	Oakland	AL	99	20	3	2	2	1/21	10	10	2	0	79	.202	.237	.333	.189	6	23-SS 95
1998	Oakland	AL	367	88	20	1	12	27/84	52	45	4	6	285	.240	.305	.398	.233	37	105-SS 100
1999	Oakland	AL	591	147	36	4	19	51/94	86	77	8	7	451	.249	.319	.420	.247	68	155-SS 105
2000	Oakland	AL	506	127	25	2	18	50/91	70	74	8	6	385	.251	.318	.415	.248	59	

He improved across the board but is still short of the stardom people hoped for. He'll uncork a Steve Sax special when instead of eating the ball he tries to make the impossible play. Tejada wore down late in the season after Jorge Velandia got hurt, because Art Howe decided he wouldn't need any rest. Assuming he doesn't get burned out, it looks like he'll have a better career than the people he could be compared to—Shawon Dunston or Mariano Duncan—but remain well short of the Trinity.

Roberto Vaz   OF   Bats L   Age 25

YEAR	TEAM	LGE	AB	H	DB	TP	HR	BB/SO	R	RBI	SB	CS	OUT	BA	OBP	SLG	EQA	EQR	DEFENSE
1997	So Oregn	Nwn	77	18	4	0	2	4/4	6	8	1	1	60	.234	.276	.364	.212	6	
1998	Huntsvil	Sou	462	124	17	3	8	38/67	40	48	13	9	347	.268	.327	.370	.238	48	121-OF 91
1999	Vancouvr	PCL	369	90	16	4	5	45/73	43	31	5	4	283	.244	.329	.350	.234	37	64-OF 88
2000	Oakland	AL	464	122	19	3	7	53/81	68	57	8	5	347	.263	.338	.362	.244	51	

Because he's chunky and African-American, Vaz gets compared to Tony Gwynn. At 24, Gwynn had played more than 300 major-league games and won his first batting title. Vaz was a two-way star for Alabama the same year that Tim Hudson was a two-way star for Auburn. He broke his foot in the regional playoffs and missed the Crimson Tide's shot at LSU for the title in 1996. He doesn't have good instincts afield, although he'll flash a pitcher's velocity when he gets to throw the ball. Vaz is not a prospect, just a guy with an interesting career.

Randy Velarde   2B   Bats R   Age 37

YEAR	TEAM	LGE	AB	H	DB	TP	HR	BB/SO	R	RBI	SB	CS	OUT	BA	OBP	SLG	EQA	EQR	DEFENSE	
1996	Calfrnia	AL	525	148	27	3	13	62/118	73	49	7	8	385	.282	.364	.419	.265	70	108-2B 85	19-3B 106
1998	Anaheim	AL	188	50	14	1	4	34/41	28	26	6	2	140	.266	.381	.415	.277	28	49-2B 100	
1999	Anaheim	AL	372	112	16	4	8	39/56	52	44	13	4	264	.301	.373	.430	.277	53	93-2B 107	
1999	Oakland	AL	253	84	11	3	6	24/42	44	25	11	4	173	.332	.394	.470	.294	40	59-2B 108	
2000	Oakland	AL	328	93	12	2	8	47/61	62	50	11	3	238	.284	.373	.405	.274	47		

While he was a nice stretch-drive pickup and exceeded expectations once he came over, is this really somebody you give a lot of guaranteed money if your payroll is limited? Maybe his elbow will be fine, but Velarde has a knack for hurting himself. His noisy campaigning to stay, combined with Giambi's public statements in favor of the idea, should have you wondering if the A's are a bit too eager to avoid anything that might create a Duquette-versus-the-clubhouse situation.

PITCHERS (Averages: ERA: 4.50 / H/9: 9.00 / HR/9: 1.00 / BB/9: 3.50 / K/9: 6.50 / KWH: 1.00)

Kevin Appier   Throws R   Age 32

YEAR	TEAM	LGE	IP	H	ER	HR	BB	K	ERA	W	L	H/9	HR/9	BB/9	K/9	KWH	PERA
1997	KansasCy	AL	238.7	209	88	22	75	199	3.32	17	10	7.88	0.83	2.83	7.50	1.89	3.47
1998	Omaha	PCL	29.7	45	27	7	14	18	8.19	1	2	13.65	2.12	4.25	5.46	0.38	9.10
1998	KansasCy	AL	15.3	20	11	3	5	9	6.46	1	1	11.74	1.76	2.93	5.28	0.61	7.04
1999	KansasCy	AL	141.3	147	72	16	49	80	4.58	8	8	9.36	1.02	3.12	5.09	0.66	4.58
1999	Oakland	AL	69.0	73	43	7	32	54	5.61	3	5	9.52	0.91	4.17	7.04	0.93	4.96

After a year lost to an unfortunate collection of injuries (shoulder reconstruction, moving, motorcycles, and a bum colon), his most significant victory was making 34 starts and throwing 209 innings despite a hamstring injury that plagued him down the stretch. The velocity isn't there anymore, and it's not coming back, but he came to the right team at the right time. The A's offense should dress up his coming free agency with a number of run-support-generated wins. He's still got that amazing, funky delivery, bringing his left leg straight up and tight, then sweeping his arm forward.

Jesus Colome   Throws R   Age 21

YEAR	TEAM	LGE	IP	H	ER	HR	BB	K	ERA	W	L	H/9	HR/9	BB/9	K/9	KWH	PERA
1999	Modesto	Cal	123.3	134	62	7	65	94	4.52	7	7	9.78	0.51	4.74	6.86	0.76	4.89

Colome is another product of the A's Dominican development program. Is it any surprise teams like the Twins and White Sox are playing catch-up there? Colome has a blazing fastball that got him named the best prospect in the 1998 Arizona Rookie League and the #6 prospect in the 1999 California League by Baseball America. He can occasionally get it up to 100 mph, has a slider he can get up to 90 mph and has a good sense of how and when to use his change-up. It's dicey to say too many nice things about pitchers with only A-ball experience, since even among the good ones, so many wash out. Colome is one of those rare A-ball pitchers we'd almost call a prospect.

Eric DuBose   Throws L   Age 24

YEAR	TEAM	LGE	IP	H	ER	HR	BB	K	ERA	W	L	H/9	HR/9	BB/9	K/9	KWH	PERA
1997	Visalia	Cal	36.7	48	38	4	32	28	9.33	1	3	11.78	0.98	7.85	6.87	0.38	8.10
1998	Visalia	Cal	68.3	67	40	6	44	57	5.27	3	5	8.82	0.79	5.80	7.51	0.82	5.14
1998	Huntsvil	Sou	78.3	95	38	3	33	54	4.37	5	4	10.91	0.34	3.79	6.20	0.70	5.06
1999	Midland	Tex	75.3	94	58	10	55	54	6.93	2	6	11.23	1.19	6.57	6.45	0.42	7.41

DuBose was supposed to come into the year with a new delivery designed to help him avoid injury, but he and Chris Enochs both came in hurt and tried to hide it. Both finished with dead arms and time off, but according to Dr. Lewis Yocum, no damage. When healthy, DuBose has low-90s heat and a nice curve. He's behind both Mark Mulder and Barry Zito and will have to prove he can stay healthy.

Kevin Gregg   Throws R   Age 22

YEAR	TEAM	LGE	IP	H	ER	HR	BB	K	ERA	W	L	H/9	HR/9	BB/9	K/9	KWH	PERA
1997	Visalia	Cal	112.3	126	83	9	84	98	6.65	4	8	10.09	0.72	6.73	7.85	0.68	6.17
1998	Modesto	Cal	132.3	169	86	9	94	96	5.85	6	9	11.49	0.61	6.39	6.53	0.43	6.73
1999	Visalia	Cal	60.7	66	36	4	25	35	5.34	3	4	9.79	0.59	3.71	5.19	0.55	4.60
1999	Midland	Tex	91.3	76	44	7	37	53	4.34	5	5	7.49	0.69	3.65	5.22	0.75	3.45

He's another big kid out of the Pacific Northwest, one of the few high-school pitchers the A's have picked, drafted with the expectation that his velocity will improve as he fills out. The velocity hasn't come, but he has started to polish a good slider. Why are there so many big kids from the Northwest? Isn't there an "X-Files" episode about something like this? You know, the one where Bigfoot decides he simply cannot resist the charms of the local housewives in some small town in the Cascades?

Buddy Groom   Throws L   Age 34

YEAR	TEAM	LGE	IP	H	ER	HR	BB	K	ERA	W	L	H/9	HR/9	BB/9	K/9	KWH	PERA
1997	Oakland	AL	67.0	69	31	8	24	46	4.16	4	3	9.27	1.07	3.22	6.18	0.95	4.57
1998	Oakland	AL	57.3	60	28	4	20	36	4.40	3	3	9.42	0.63	3.14	5.65	0.81	4.24
1999	Oakland	AL	46.3	45	25	1	18	33	4.86	2	3	8.74	0.19	3.50	6.41	1.00	3.50

If you look through Michael Wolverton's Reliever Evaluation Tools, you'll see that Groom was the reliever most let down by the relievers who came in after him. For a situational guy who gets brought in for a batter or two, and who usually leaves before the inning is over, that produced a season in which his actual ERA was significantly higher than what you would have expected from his baserunners allowed. It also explains the big discrepancy between his PERA and his ERA. Groom is leaving the team after giving them four good seasons, and he's still a serviceable left-handed reliever. He's just not going to get as many job offers as he would like, thanks to his buddies in the pen.

Chad Harville   Throws R   Age 23

YEAR	TEAM	LGE	IP	H	ER	HR	BB	K	ERA	W	L	H/9	HR/9	BB/9	K/9	KWH	PERA
1997	Visalia	Cal	17.7	28	14	2	15	17	7.13	1	1	14.26	1.02	7.64	8.66	0.51	9.68
1998	Visalia	Cal	66.7	67	28	1	39	52	3.78	4	3	9.05	0.14	5.27	7.02	0.77	4.32
1998	Huntsvil	Sou	14.0	7	4	0	13	20	2.57	2	0	4.50	0.00	8.36	12.86	3.28	3.21
1999	Midland	Tex	22.3	13	6	1	11	28	2.42	2	0	5.24	0.40	4.43	11.28	4.10	2.42
1999	Vancouvr	PCL	24.0	25	6	0	13	29	2.25	2	1	9.38	0.00	4.88	10.88	1.93	4.12
1999	Oakland	AL	14.7	17	10	2	9	15	6.14	1	1	10.43	1.23	5.52	9.20	1.10	6.14

Stop short of nominating him as the right-handed answer to Billy Wagner. While he's also short and gets his fastball up into the high 90s, his change of pace is a slider, not a curve. He could have been a big part of the A's stretch drive, but Art Howe was reluctant to trust him, and then a hamstring injury ended his year prematurely. If he's left alone for a couple of months, the A's will have a great reliever on their hands. Should Jason Isringhausen falter, Harville could end up closing.

Jimmy Haynes Throws R Age 27

YEAR	TEAM	LGE	IP	H	ER	HR	BB	K	ERA	W	L	H/9	HR/9	BB/9	K/9	KWH	PERA
1997	Rochestr	Int	99.7	98	51	9	59	94	4.61	5	6	8.85	0.81	5.33	8.49	1.14	4.97
1997	Edmonton	PCL	28.3	36	20	4	11	20	6.35	1	2	11.44	1.27	3.49	6.35	0.75	6.35
1997	Oakland	AL	76.0	67	32	6	41	66	3.79	5	3	7.93	0.71	4.86	7.82	1.18	4.14
1998	Oakland	AL	194.0	222	114	23	91	135	5.29	9	13	10.30	1.07	4.22	6.26	0.67	5.61
1999	Oakland	AL	143.0	150	99	19	77	95	6.23	5	11	9.44	1.20	4.85	5.98	0.58	5.54

Haynes entered the year as a pitcher with promise and left it a source of tremendous confusion. After scuffling at the start, pitching coach Rick Peterson had him junk his big-bending curve for a slider and dump his change-up to resurrect the splitter the Orioles had taken away from him after he was drafted. The results were mixed. At the All-Star break, he had a 4.61 ERA and looked like he'd finally settled in. He was a disaster after that, putting up an 11.68 ERA after the break.

Changing a pitcher's entire repertoire midseason was a risk, and it blew up in the team's face. Because Haynes doesn't talk much or go through the clubhouse ritual of beating himself up after a loss, guys like Phillips, MacFarlane and Giambi grew to loathe him. Everyone in the organization appears to have had enough, but there's still enough talent there to tantalize people. He logged 14 quality starts in 25 attempts (three would be blown by Howe leaving him in or by the pen), and in a world where Mike Oquist gets a shot, somebody should be able to use a guy who does that. Haynes was traded to Milwaukee in an effort to clear payroll

Gil Heredia Throws R Age 34

YEAR	TEAM	LGE	IP	H	ER	HR	BB	K	ERA	W	L	H/9	HR/9	BB/9	K/9	KWH	PERA
1997	Ottawa	Int	42.0	56	32	5	10	33	6.86	2	3	12.00	1.07	2.14	7.07	1.45	5.79
1997	Iowa	AmA	43.3	66	29	6	10	25	6.02	2	3	13.71	1.25	2.08	5.19	0.71	7.06
1998	Edmonton	PCL	136.3	174	77	12	21	81	5.08	7	8	11.49	0.79	1.39	5.35	1.34	4.89
1998	Oakland	AL	42.7	42	13	4	3	27	2.74	4	1	8.86	0.84	0.63	5.70	4.32	3.16
1999	Oakland	AL	201.7	215	103	19	33	120	4.60	11	11	9.60	0.85	1.47	5.36	1.52	3.88

What is it some people say about expansion pitching? Without expansion, Heredia wouldn't be pitching in major television markets. All he does is throw strikes, work fast and keep his infielders busy. Early in the season, he had problems getting past the sixth inning, but he got stronger down the stretch. Some teams got frustrated watching him beat them; Mike Hargrove accused him of throwing a spitball. If he was, he didn't get caught. Heredia logged 12 quality starts in 15 that came on five or more days' rest (three were blown by managerial decision or the pen), so it looks like he's more effective with long rest. Bob Tewksbury managed to be good into his late 30s, which is reason to think Heredia will give the A's a couple of good years.

Tim Hudson Throws R Age 24

YEAR	TEAM	LGE	IP	H	ER	HR	BB	K	ERA	W	L	H/9	HR/9	BB/9	K/9	KWH	PERA
1997	So Oregn	Nwn	27.3	16	10	0	18	21	3.29	2	1	5.27	0.00	5.93	6.91	1.14	2.63
1998	Modesto	Cal	35.7	23	12	0	23	32	3.03	3	1	5.80	0.00	5.80	8.07	1.45	2.78
1998	Huntsvil	Sou	126.0	153	88	15	68	85	6.29	5	9	10.93	1.07	4.86	6.07	0.52	6.29
1999	Midland	Tex	18.0	9	0	0	4	14	0.00	2	0	4.50	0.00	2.00	7.00	4.07	1.00
1999	Vancouvr	PCL	45.3	42	18	2	23	50	3.57	3	2	8.34	0.40	4.57	9.93	1.93	3.97
1999	Oakland	AL	137.0	114	48	7	60	135	3.15	10	5	7.49	0.46	3.94	8.87	1.99	3.35

We told you to watch out for him last year, but nobody could have expected him to be this good this fast. His assortment is dynamite, from the darting, moving sinker to a good forkball, a nice change-up and a slider he mixes in for show. For a strike-out pitcher, he's economical with his pitches, and Howe deserves credit for not overworking him. Perhaps the most basic thing he gave the A's was the ability to go beat Randy Johnson or Pedro Martinez behind a good pitching performance.

Jason Isringhausen Throws R Age 27

YEAR	TEAM	LGE	IP	H	ER	HR	BB	K	ERA	W	L	H/9	HR/9	BB/9	K/9	KWH	PERA
1997	Norfolk	Int	19.3	22	10	4	9	14	4.66	1	1	10.24	1.86	4.19	6.52	0.74	6.52
1997	NY Mets	NL	29.0	43	28	3	23	23	8.69	1	2	13.34	0.93	7.14	7.14	0.40	8.69
1999	Norfolk	Int	50.0	34	17	4	22	44	3.06	4	2	6.12	0.72	3.96	7.92	1.93	2.88
1999	NY Mets	NL	38.7	44	28	7	21	30	6.52	1	3	10.24	1.63	4.89	6.98	0.73	6.52
1999	Oakland	AL	25.7	19	5	2	12	20	1.75	3	0	6.66	0.70	4.21	7.01	1.31	3.16

(Jason Isringhausen *continued*)

I don't invest much faith in closers or closing, but it would be foolish to ignore that the clubhouse leadership, Giambi foremost among them, came out and said they wanted Isringhausen in that role. After seeing his stuff, they had confidence he would do the job. But what about a closer's "makeup" or the need for experience? It's an interesting thing when players ditch the untrue truisms that many journalists hold sacred. Restricted to relief, Izzy should be able to succeed with his mid-90s heat and his still-good curve, reclaiming the career Dallas Green almost stole from him.

Doug Jones   Throws R   Age 43

YEAR	TEAM	LGE	IP	H	ER	HR	BB	K	ERA	W	L	H/9	HR/9	BB/9	K/9	KWH	PERA
1997	Milwauke	AL	81.0	59	18	4	9	83	2.00	8	1	6.56	0.44	1.00	9.22	9.69	1.89
1998	Milwauke	NL	55.0	65	30	15	12	41	4.91	3	3	10.64	2.45	1.96	6.71	1.61	6.55
1998	Clevelnd	AL	32.7	32	10	2	6	29	2.76	3	1	8.82	0.55	1.65	7.99	3.27	3.31
1999	Oakland	AL	105.0	99	37	9	24	65	3.17	8	4	8.49	0.77	2.06	5.57	1.33	3.43

Doug Jones tossing more than 100 innings? The last time it happened was 1992, and Art Howe was his manager then, too. The usage patterns were different this time around. Jones was a middle-relief godsend for the A's early on, giving them three-inning outings nobody would have guessed he had in him. He hasn't had back-to-back good seasons since 1989 and 1990, and the last time he tossed 100 innings, he followed it with a terrible year in 1993, the year that got Art Howe fired. As much fun as it was to see Jones have a good year, he's a risk. The A's have re-signed him for 2000.

Tim Kubinski   Throws L   Age 28

YEAR	TEAM	LGE	IP	H	ER	HR	BB	K	ERA	W	L	H/9	HR/9	BB/9	K/9	KWH	PERA
1997	Edmonton	PCL	71.7	66	38	7	37	44	4.77	4	4	8.29	0.88	4.65	5.53	0.59	4.40
1998	Edmonton	PCL	70.7	86	44	7	26	44	5.60	3	5	10.95	0.89	3.31	5.60	0.65	5.48
1999	Vancouvr	PCL	66.0	79	36	2	31	43	4.91	3	4	10.77	0.27	4.23	5.86	0.56	5.05
1999	Oakland	AL	12.3	13	7	3	5	7	5.11	0	1	9.49	2.19	3.65	5.11	0.56	5.84

Now that Buddy Groom is leaving town, Kubinski can take heart that the A's aren't likely to spend money to drag in some veteran left-handed carcass. He'll have to fight for a job with Ron Mahay and possibly Leo Vasquez, but there's also the chance that Mahay may get to start a few games. Kubinski is like a late-night 900-number commercial: he occupies time until something better comes along.

Brett Laxton   Throws R   Age 26

YEAR	TEAM	LGE	IP	H	ER	HR	BB	K	ERA	W	L	H/9	HR/9	BB/9	K/9	KWH	PERA
1997	Visalia	Cal	131.0	165	69	7	61	81	4.74	7	8	11.34	0.48	4.19	5.56	0.49	5.56
1998	Huntsvil	Sou	118.0	132	75	5	82	62	5.72	5	8	10.07	0.38	6.25	4.73	0.27	5.57
1998	Edmonton	PCL	43.3	49	36	5	27	18	7.48	1	4	10.18	1.04	5.61	3.74	0.18	6.02
1999	Vancouvr	PCL	145.0	180	82	7	58	87	5.09	7	9	11.17	0.43	3.60	5.40	0.54	5.21

Until now, the high point of his career was his freshman year at LSU in 1993, when he was 12-1 with a 1.98 ERA. Since then, he's battled a variety of minor injuries and muscle pulls, never getting seriously hurt. The various aches and pains led to small changes in his delivery, to the point where he didn't have a good idea of what he was doing. You have to wonder how many guys blow careers by slowly losing command of their strengths. Work on his mechanics in the past year led to a dramatic improvement in control, while his assortment has remained the same: good fastball, sharp slider and a change-up every once in a while. He's a slow starter and needs a couple of batters to warm up and get command, so a move to the pen is unlikely. He'll be in the race for one of the last two spots in the rotation behind Hudson, Appier and Heredia.

Julian Leyva   Throws R   Age 22

YEAR	TEAM	LGE	IP	H	ER	HR	BB	K	ERA	W	L	H/9	HR/9	BB/9	K/9	KWH	PERA
1997	Modesto	Cal	130.0	170	107	22	43	64	7.41	4	10	11.77	1.52	2.98	4.43	0.42	6.51
1998	Modesto	Cal	127.3	190	84	12	31	62	5.94	5	9	13.43	0.85	2.19	4.38	0.49	6.43
1999	Visalia	Cal	78.3	95	50	10	27	49	5.74	3	6	10.91	1.15	3.10	5.63	0.70	5.63
1999	Midland	Tex	62.3	91	45	10	15	32	6.50	2	5	13.14	1.44	2.17	4.62	0.56	6.93

Another of the A's infrequent high-school-pitcher draftees, Leyva was throwing in the low 90s when he was drafted, heat that didn't come back until this year. He has a good feel for his change and breaking stuff, and loves to pitch. Conditioning has been an issue.

Ron Mahay   **Throws L**   **Age 29**

YEAR	TEAM	LGE	IP	H	ER	HR	BB	K	ERA	W	L	H/9	HR/9	BB/9	K/9	KWH	PERA
1997	Trenton	Eas	37.3	37	21	0	15	34	5.06	2	2	8.92	0.00	3.62	8.20	1.56	3.62
1997	Boston	AL	25.3	18	6	3	11	22	2.13	2	1	6.39	1.07	3.91	7.82	1.83	3.20
1998	Pawtuckt	Int	40.0	40	20	8	21	35	4.50	2	2	9.00	1.80	4.73	7.88	1.09	5.85
1998	Boston	AL	26.0	25	15	2	16	14	5.19	1	2	8.65	0.69	5.54	4.85	0.37	4.85
1999	Vancouvr	PCL	94.3	132	67	11	53	56	6.39	3	7	12.59	1.05	5.06	5.34	0.33	7.35
1999	Oakland	AL	19.3	8	3	2	2	15	1.40	2	0	3.72	0.93	0.93	6.98	10.51	0.93

The A's claimed the ex-outfielder on waivers from the Red Sox at the end of spring training, and he's now probably the best bet to fill the situational left-hander role in the bullpen. The A's are intrigued by what he could do as a starter. Since it's unlikely that the A's will sign a starter of note, he could break through in camp.

Tim Manwiller   **Throws R**   **Age 25**

YEAR	TEAM	LGE	IP	H	ER	HR	BB	K	ERA	W	L	H/9	HR/9	BB/9	K/9	KWH	PERA
1997	So Oregn	Nwn	27.0	25	10	0	13	16	3.33	2	1	8.33	0.00	4.33	5.33	0.59	3.33
1997	Modesto	Cal	19.3	24	8	1	8	12	3.72	1	1	11.17	0.47	3.72	5.59	0.56	5.12
1998	Modesto	Cal	140.7	195	93	11	61	81	5.95	6	10	12.48	0.70	3.90	5.18	0.41	6.40
1998	Edmonton	PCL	10.3	9	1	0	2	9	0.87	1	0	7.84	0.00	1.74	7.84	3.36	2.61
1999	Midland	Tex	82.3	104	45	6	32	44	4.92	4	5	11.37	0.66	3.50	4.81	0.43	5.47
1999	Vancouvr	PCL	48.3	80	47	8	16	24	8.75	1	4	14.90	1.49	2.98	4.47	0.34	8.57

Since he was drafted in the 30th round, it's been a nice surprise to see him come this far. As you'd expect from someone drafted low, he doesn't throw hard, but he's got a deceptive delivery in which he hides the ball well with his lead arm, and he mixes in a good slider and change-up off of that. While he got flattened at Vancouver, pitching well in Midland's bandbox was surprising: untranslated, he had a 3.51 ERA. He's an overachiever with no star potential and a longshot for the rotation in 2000.

T.J. Mathews   **Throws R**   **Age 30**

YEAR	TEAM	LGE	IP	H	ER	HR	BB	K	ERA	W	L	H/9	HR/9	BB/9	K/9	KWH	PERA
1997	St Louis	NL	45.7	42	14	5	18	43	2.76	4	1	8.28	0.99	3.55	8.47	1.83	4.14
1997	Oakland	AL	29.3	32	15	5	12	24	4.60	1	2	9.82	1.53	3.68	7.36	1.12	5.52
1998	Oakland	AL	72.7	68	40	6	30	53	4.95	4	4	8.42	0.74	3.72	6.56	1.03	3.96
1999	Oakland	AL	59.3	43	24	8	20	43	3.64	4	3	6.52	1.21	3.03	6.52	1.61	3.19

Since he's basically all that's left from the multiple deals with the Cardinals that turned St. Louis half-red, half-green and thinking every day was Christmas, you can forgive A's fans if they're disappointed that Mathews didn't turn out to be the next John Wetteland. He has become a solid reliever but not a particularly consistent one: he had two great months, followed by two months in which he tried to pitch with a sore shoulder, followed by two months split between the disabled list and trying to pitch with a sore elbow. The A's gave him a three-year contract, too much job security for a pitcher with his resume.

Greg McMichael   **Throws R**   **Age 33**

YEAR	TEAM	LGE	IP	H	ER	HR	BB	K	ERA	W	L	H/9	HR/9	BB/9	K/9	KWH	PERA
1997	NY Mets	NL	86.3	77	35	8	28	75	3.65	6	4	8.03	0.83	2.92	7.82	1.95	3.54
1998	NY Mets	NL	53.0	67	32	8	31	42	5.43	2	4	11.38	1.36	5.26	7.13	0.63	7.13
1998	LosAngls	NL	14.0	18	8	1	6	10	5.14	1	1	11.57	0.64	3.86	6.43	0.69	5.79
1999	NY Mets	NL	18.0	21	10	3	8	17	5.00	1	1	10.50	1.50	4.00	8.50	1.29	6.00
1999	Oakland	AL	15.3	14	8	3	11	3	4.70	1	1	8.22	1.76	6.46	1.76	0.04	5.87

He's already outward bound. If his agent lands him more than a non-roster invitation to camp for any guaranteed money at all, the man deserves a medal.

Mark Mulder   **Throws L**   **Age 22**

YEAR	TEAM	LGE	IP	H	ER	HR	BB	K	ERA	W	L	H/9	HR/9	BB/9	K/9	KWH	PERA
1999	Vancouvr	PCL	117.0	166	76	12	34	66	5.85	5	8	12.77	0.92	2.62	5.08	0.58	6.31

Does Mulder actually have a great fastball or not? As much as it's been rumored to exist, no one seems to have seen it. He does throw hard—wait for it—for a left-hander, getting up into the high 80s. He's got a nice change-up, improving curve and

(Mark Mulder *continued*)

good mechanics. He isn't afraid to pitch inside. Although he suffered through a dead-arm period, after it he was Team USA's ace in the Pan Am Games, then tossed 17 consecutive scoreless innings in the PCL playoffs on the way to being named the Triple-A postseason MVP. He'll get every opportunity to win a rotation spot in camp. While he's a good prospect, he isn't a great one yet.

Omar Olivares   Throws R   Age 32

YEAR	TEAM	LGE	IP	H	ER	HR	BB	K	ERA	W	L	H/9	HR/9	BB/9	K/9	KWH	PERA
1997	Detroit	AL	115.0	110	65	7	53	75	5.09	6	7	8.61	0.55	4.15	5.87	0.72	4.07
1997	Seattle	AL	64.3	75	36	9	29	29	5.04	3	4	10.49	1.26	4.06	4.06	0.29	5.88
1998	Anaheim	AL	181.3	188	88	17	95	113	4.37	10	10	9.33	0.84	4.72	5.61	0.53	5.01
1999	Anaheim	AL	129.0	136	60	10	47	50	4.19	8	6	9.49	0.70	3.28	3.49	0.29	4.40
1999	Oakland	AL	75.7	77	38	7	31	37	4.52	4	4	9.16	0.83	3.69	4.40	0.43	4.52

Picked up pretty cheaply from the Angels, Olivares surprised me by pitching even better in 1999 than he did in 1998. That's great for his free agency, courtesy of two months with A's run support. He throws harder than Heredia, but fools fewer people with his stuff. I'm still not optimistic about his chances to pitch this well over the life of his next contract, but he is an extreme groundball pitcher. If he goes to a team that has a great offense and a tight infield defense, like the Indians, he could surprise.

Mike Oquist   Throws R   Age 32

YEAR	TEAM	LGE	IP	H	ER	HR	BB	K	ERA	W	L	H/9	HR/9	BB/9	K/9	KWH	PERA
1997	Edmonton	PCL	50.0	58	23	3	18	31	4.14	3	3	10.44	0.54	3.24	5.58	0.69	4.68
1997	Oakland	AL	111.3	101	52	14	43	73	4.20	6	6	8.16	1.13	3.48	5.90	0.92	4.12
1998	Oakland	AL	174.7	204	116	26	59	113	5.98	7	12	10.51	1.34	3.04	5.82	0.79	5.56
1999	Oakland	AL	141.7	150	75	16	61	91	4.76	8	8	9.53	1.02	3.88	5.78	0.68	4.96

Most game shows have a rule against letting the same contestant win twice, but Oquist managed to beg, bribe and bully his way into another year as the fifth starter. Strictly in terms of results, he's not anyone's first choice, but if you look around the AL and compare him to the other fifth starters out there, he's better than most. He'll never get any better than that. The Tigers have signed him to a minor-league deal.

Bert Snow   Throws R   Age 23

YEAR	TEAM	LGE	IP	H	ER	HR	BB	K	ERA	W	L	H/9	HR/9	BB/9	K/9	KWH	PERA
1998	So Oregn	Nwn	41.3	65	44	3	21	23	9.58	1	4	14.15	0.65	4.57	5.01	0.29	7.62
1999	Visalia	Cal	61.0	61	45	5	45	65	6.64	2	5	9.00	0.74	6.64	9.59	1.15	5.46
1999	Midland	Tex	20.7	15	3	3	10	26	1.31	2	0	6.53	1.31	4.35	11.32	3.37	3.92

Another one of the SEC guys the A's seem to favor in the draft, picked out of Vanderbilt in 1998. During his first season, his arm turned black and blue, and he had to have surgery to remove both a blood clot and a rib that was affecting his delivery. Early in 1999, the A's moved him to the pen and he shot all the way up to Vancouver. Moving, low-90s heat and the organization's best slider could get him to the majors in 2000.

Leo Vasquez   Throws L   Age 26

YEAR	TEAM	LGE	IP	H	ER	HR	BB	K	ERA	W	L	H/9	HR/9	BB/9	K/9	KWH	PERA
1997	Columbia	SAL	49.3	90	56	5	34	32	10.22	1	4	16.42	0.91	6.20	5.84	0.25	10.40
1998	St Lucie	Fla	61.0	64	33	3	36	30	4.87	3	4	9.44	0.44	5.31	4.43	0.29	4.87
1998	Binghmtn	Eas	27.0	34	20	1	31	21	6.67	1	2	11.33	0.33	10.33	7.00	0.31	8.00
1999	Binghmtn	Eas	40.0	47	21	4	34	33	4.72	2	2	10.58	0.90	7.65	7.43	0.51	6.97
1999	Midland	Tex	22.3	19	12	2	18	18	4.84	1	1	7.66	0.81	7.25	7.25	0.71	4.84

Where does relief talent come from? In this case, from the now-empty fields of the defunct Pioneer League, where Vasquez pitched for Aberdeen before hooking up with the Mets in 1996. While he's supposed to have good velocity, he was also older than most of the people he was playing against. Vasquez has a good shot at making the A's in camp.

Luis Vizcaino   Throws R   Age 23

YEAR	TEAM	LGE	IP	H	ER	HR	BB	K	ERA	W	L	H/9	HR/9	BB/9	K/9	KWH	PERA
1997	So Oregn	Nwn	42.3	80	60	6	33	24	12.76	1	4	17.01	1.28	7.02	5.10	0.16	11.69
1997	Modesto	Cal	13.3	26	24	4	15	11	16.20	0	1	17.55	2.70	10.13	7.43	0.23	15.52
1998	Modesto	Cal	95.7	88	47	7	52	73	4.42	6	5	8.28	0.66	4.89	6.87	0.87	4.33
1998	Huntsvil	Sou	35.3	50	28	8	21	21	7.13	1	3	12.74	2.04	5.35	5.35	0.31	8.92
1999	Midland	Tex	103.3	127	72	17	59	72	6.27	4	7	11.06	1.48	5.14	6.27	0.52	6.97
1999	Vancouvr	PCL	11.7	14	5	0	7	6	3.86	1	0	10.80	0.00	5.40	4.63	0.27	5.40

He's another one of the A's Dominicans. Stuff like this leaves me wondering about the superiority of Latin civilization. Take the difference in children's television: Americans give their kids saccharine visions of horror, like Barney, Bananas in Pajamas or, heaven help us, the Teletubbies. Latins have Madonna wannabes like Xuxa running variety shows populated by showgirls. What competent adult wouldn't make the right choice here?

Vizcaino has a mid-90s fastball and a sharp slider, but he hasn't picked up a change-up. There are concerns that his delivery and the slider put stress on his elbow, and because of the struggle to pick up an off-speed pitch, he has a good chance of becoming of reliever. He didn't fare too well in Midland, but few do. Merle Haggard, I guess.

Denny Wagner   Throws R   Age 23

YEAR	TEAM	LGE	IP	H	ER	HR	BB	K	ERA	W	L	H/9	HR/9	BB/9	K/9	KWH	PERA
1997	So Oregn	Nwn	11.3	38	32	3	17	6	25.41	0	1	30.18	2.38	13.50	4.76	0.04	27.00
1999	Modesto	Cal	108.3	126	57	8	47	71	4.74	6	6	10.47	0.66	3.90	5.90	0.64	5.15
1999	Midland	Tex	27.7	28	22	1	17	10	7.16	1	2	9.11	0.33	5.53	3.25	0.16	4.55

Wagner missed 1998 with a slight impingement or tendinitis; nobody could figure out which. In 1999, he was finally healthy enough to pitch, and had regained the great moving fastball he had when the A's picked him out of Virginia Tech. That first-round pick came courtesy of Mike Bordick's signing with the Orioles, one of three picks the A's got as compensation. The other two were spent on Nathan Haynes, who was part of the package sent to the Angels for Olivares, and Eric DuBose. Not a bad haul for a mediocre shortstop; in fact, it was better than what the A's got for Todd Stottlemyre and Mark McGwire combined.

Tim Worrell   Throws R   Age 32

YEAR	TEAM	LGE	IP	H	ER	HR	BB	K	ERA	W	L	H/9	HR/9	BB/9	K/9	KWH	PERA
1997	San Dieg	NL	104.3	120	69	15	52	75	5.95	4	8	10.35	1.29	4.49	6.47	0.67	6.04
1998	Detroit	AL	62.0	65	38	10	20	48	5.52	3	4	9.44	1.45	2.90	6.97	1.32	4.94
1998	Oakland	AL	36.0	33	15	5	8	33	3.75	2	2	8.25	1.25	2.00	8.25	3.08	3.75
1999	Oakland	AL	70.0	65	32	5	33	64	4.11	4	4	8.36	0.64	4.24	8.23	1.43	4.11

In a superficially good-looking season, Worrell was toxic when it came to letting other people's runs score, allowing more than half of the runners he inherited to cross home plate. That's the sort of situational performance no team can live with. Guys who can get right-handed batters out aren't rare. Sometimes a nice strikeout rate means zip in terms of being a useful reliever, and Worrell's year is an example of that.

Barry Zito   Throws L   Age 22

YEAR	TEAM	LGE	IP	H	ER	HR	BB	K	ERA	W	L	H/9	HR/9	BB/9	K/9	KWH	PERA
1999	Visalia	Cal	39.0	23	14	4	24	46	3.23	3	1	5.31	0.92	5.54	10.62	2.86	3.23
1999	Midland	Tex	22.0	23	15	1	13	24	6.14	1	1	9.41	0.41	5.32	9.82	1.44	4.91
1999	Vancouvr	PCL	5.7	5	1	0	3	5	1.59	1	0	7.94	0.00	4.76	7.94	1.25	3.18

The A's 1999 first-rounder was named the top pitching prospect in the California League after only eight starts. Zito racked up three 16-strikeout games for USC in the Pac-10, then rocketed through the California and Texas leagues before pitching for Vancouver in the PCL playoffs and Triple-A World Series. He has outstanding command of a great curve and change-up. He can get predictable with his curve, but he's as advanced as a college pitcher gets and has a shot to win a spot in the rotation this spring.

Support-Neutral Records — OAKLAND ATHLETICS — Park Effect: +3.0%

PITCHER	GS	IP	R	SNW	SNL	SNPCT	W	L	RA	APW	SNVA	SNWAR
Kevin Appier	12	68.7	50	3.8	4.9	.440	7	5	6.55	-0.88	-0.48	0.13
Tom Candiotti	11	56.7	46	2.4	5.2	.314	3	5	7.31	-1.16	-1.26	-0.84
Jimmy Haynes	25	135.0	98	8.1	9.7	.454	7	12	6.53	-1.70	-0.76	0.52
Gil Heredia	33	200.3	119	11.9	11.4	.512	13	8	5.35	-0.08	0.24	2.03
Tim Hudson	21	136.3	56	10.0	5.0	.665	11	2	3.70	2.24	2.26	3.60
Kevin Jarvis	1	4.3	6	0.1	0.6	.092	0	1	12.46	-0.32	-0.28	-0.23
Brett Laxton	2	8.0	11	0.1	1.2	.085	0	1	12.38	-0.58	-0.49	-0.44
Ron Mahay	1	5.0	1	0.4	0.1	.863	1	0	1.80	0.18	0.18	0.22
Omar Olivares	12	74.7	43	3.8	4.6	.452	7	2	5.18	0.09	-0.37	0.22
Mike Oquist	24	125.0	80	7.2	8.1	.468	9	10	5.76	-0.58	-0.36	0.66
Kenny Rogers	19	119.3	66	7.0	6.2	.530	5	3	4.98	0.40	0.39	1.39
Blake Stein	1	2.7	5	0.0	0.7	.035	0	0	16.88	-0.32	-0.31	-0.26
TOTALS	162	936.0	581	54.8	57.7	.487	63	49	5.59	-2.69	-1.24	7.00

It's still not clear to me why the A's traded Kenny Rogers in the middle of the pennant race, rather than taking the draft picks if he left as a free agent. There's no doubt he would have helped them down the stretch. Looking at the A's pitching assignments after the Rogers trade, it seems reasonable to guess that Rogers would have gotten all of Jimmy Haynes's starts from late July, all of Mike Oquist's starts from mid-August, and Kevin Jarvis's important start against the Rangers in late September. Those pitchers combined to be an abysmal two games below average in those 11 starts, according to SNVA, while Rogers was about a half-game above average in his 12 starts with the Mets. The resulting 2½ game swing wouldn't have made up the difference between the A's and Red Sox for the AL wild card, but it does demonstrate the difference a good starter can make, even over a few months. . . . Tim Hudson couldn't sustain his blistering pace. In his first 11 starts, Hudson's Support-Neutral Winning Percentage was .783, an amazing rate for any pitcher, much less a rookie. In his last 10 starts, it was a less-amazing .537. Even if his performance is closer to that second number over the next few years, I don't think the A's are going to complain.

Pitcher Abuse Points

PITCHER	AGE	GS	PAP	PAP/S	WKLD	MAX	1-90	91-100	101-110	111-120	121-130	131-140	141+
Kevin Appier	31	12	53	4.4	5.2	117	4	2	5	1	0	0	0
Tom Candiotti	41	11	40	3.6	3.6	119	3	4	3	1	0	0	0
Jimmy Haynes	26	25	198	7.9	15.8	126	6	7	3	8	1	0	0
Gil Heredia	33	33	41	1.2	1.2	112	20	5	7	1	0	0	0
Tim Hudson	23	21	189	9.0	22.5	136	2	7	9	1	1	1	0
Kevin Jarvis	29	1	0	0.0	0.0	90	1	0	0	0	0	0	0
Brett Laxton	25	2	0	0.0	0.0	82	2	0	0	0	0	0	0
Ron Mahay	28	1	0	0.0	0.0	74	1	0	0	0	0	0	0
Omar Olivares	31	12	28	2.3	2.7	111	1	4	6	1	0	0	0
Mike Oquist	31	24	48	2.0	2.3	115	9	8	5	2	0	0	0
Kenny Rogers	34	19	172	9.1	9.1	121	3	3	6	5	2	0	0
Blake Stein	25	1	0	0.0	0.0	83	1	0	0	0	0	0	0
OAKLAND		162	769	4.7	7.9	136	53	40	44	20	4	1	0
Ranking (AL)				14	14								

Art Howe did a much better job running his rotation last year, as the A's Workload dropped from 14.5 to 7.9. Jimmy Haynes (24.4 to 15.8) was lousy for fewer pitches than in 1998, and Blake Stein, who had 218 PAPs in 1998, made only one start for the A's before he was traded to Kansas City. . . . In the best news for the beleaguered A's rotation in some time, they not only developed their first quality starter in 15 years, but Tim Hudson was handled with admirable restraint by Howe, when you consider just how magnificent he was and how crucial he was to their pennant hopes. Hudson's 136-pitch outing came in a one-run, must-win game in September. If ever there was a reason to throw caution to the wind, that was it.

Seattle Mariners

The roof opened and the window of opportunity closed. The midseason debut of Safeco Field, which was to usher in a new era of Seattle baseball, instead dropped the final curtain on a team whose performance never matched its talent.

Ken Griffey Jr.'s request to be traded and Alex Rodriguez's looming (after the 2000 season) free agency make it likely that neither will be with the team come Opening Day. With Randy Johnson already redefining the term "desert heat" in Arizona, it's possible that only Edgar Martinez, Jay Buhner and Dan Wilson will remain from the 1995 team that played for the league championship. That team had a remarkable core of talent, and it seemed their magical season would be a springboard to even bigger things. But the front office never surrounded that talent with an adequate supporting cast, so while the All-Star nucleus remained intact for the rest of the decade, the Mariners made the playoffs just one other time, bowing out in the 1997 Division Series.

While baseball fans in the Pacific Northwest view the late 1990s as a period of great success— after 18 years of misery, that's understandable—eventually, it will be remembered for what might have been. Indeed, what should have been. That will be the ultimate legacy of former General Manager Woody Woodward and Manager Lou Piniella. Their influences on the failure of the franchise are inexorably linked. While Piniella was responsible for creating many of the crises, Woodward never identified him as part of the problem, instead deferring to his advice on how to solve them. The solutions in almost every case can be described by the adjectives "old," "short-term" and "ineffective."

Most damaging were trades made under duress in the middle of the season. Veterans acquired at the trade deadline from 1995 to 1997 in an attempt to nudge the Mariners to the AL West title included Andy Benes, Salomon Torres, Terry Mulholland, Jamie Moyer, Roberto Kelly, Dave Hollins, Mike Timlin, Paul Spoljaric and Heathcliff Slocumb. Most of these players played in Seattle for just a few months; only Moyer

was with the ballclub for more than a season and a half. Prospects were always used as the bait, a strategy that caused little public outcry and advanced the notion that the team was serious about winning. Marc Newfield, Shawn Estes, Desi Relaford, Darren Bragg, David Ortiz, Joe Mays, Jose Cruz Jr., Jason Varitek and Derek Lowe were sent packing in the deals. While not all of these guys developed into good players, many offered long-term solutions to the team's problems and would have been cheap for a few years. The effect of the string of trades was the complete stripping of the upper levels of the minors, with nothing to show for the damage.

Having exhausted all of their chips in previous campaigns, Seattle opened the 1998 season with an aging team and a combustible back end of the rotation and bullpen that seemed to date back to when Danny Kaye owned the team. Fortunately, the Randy Johnson debacle provided a welcome diversion from the team's on-field problems. After all, how could they possibly be expected to win with the Big Unit making waves in the clubhouse? The ruse was perpetuated as long as possible, to within minutes of the trade deadline. By the time Johnson was dealt to the Astros for three prospects, the Mariners were deep in the background of the playoff picture, and the blame for the failed season was packed in the Big Unit's luggage as he boarded the plane for Houston.

The trade with the Astros should have been used as the catalyst for a complete team makeover before the 1999 season. Moyer, Jeff Fassero, David Segui and Russ Davis were all entering the last year of their contracts, while the club had options on Buhner and Wilson for 2000. Any or all of these players should have been moved for whatever prospects could be had. Instead, Woodward and Piniella stayed the course that had landed the organization on the rocks, collecting still more relics via trades and free agency. The elderly (Mark Leiter), infirm (Butch Henry) and ineffective (Jose Mesa) were labeled solutions to the perennial pitching problems, while light-hitting John Mabry and backup catcher

---

Mariners Prospectus

1999 record: 79-83; Third place, AL West

Pythagorean W/L: 77-85

Runs scored: 859 (6th in AL)

Runs allowed: 905 (12th in AL)

Team EQA: .259 (7th in AL)

1999 team age: 28.7 (6th-youngest in AL)

1999 parks: Kingdome (until All-Star break); extreme hitters' park, increased run scoring by 23%. Safeco Field (after All-Star break); moderate pitchers' park, decreased run scoring by 9%.

1999: A very disappointing era ends with just one postseason series win.

2000: They'll be within five games of .500 either way, and could luck into October.

Tom Lampkin were brought in to provide still more veteran leadership. Despite promises not to trade any young pitchers, Woodward dipped into the low levels of the nearly-dry minor-league well, trading hard-throwing reliever Lesli Brea for Butch Huskey.

Having traded, released and lost through free agency and injury seven pitchers from the 1998 team, the Mariners had little choice but to open the '99 season with five rookies on the staff. Given Piniella's track record for impatience with young pitchers, it seemed a recipe for disaster. A month into the season, it clearly was. Seattle's team ERA was at the bottom of the league, and Piniella began shuffling pitchers on and off the team randomly, more for effect than results. By the end of June, the Mariners had used 22 pitchers, 10 of whom hadn't received even a 15-inning audition.

More appalling than Piniella's roster management was the team's "solution" to its offensive woes, brought on in part when Alex Rodriguez tore knee cartilage in early April. Brian L. Hunter's one-man offensive wrecking machine, which had been shackled to the bench in Motown, was hauled in and inserted at the top of the order. It remained there for three months despite a .277 OBP. Hunter was a prime reason for Seattle's lackluster second-half attack, although the trades of Segui and Huskey for more arms boosted the number of line-up holes to four. The offense, which ranked second in the league in scoring before the All-Star break, was 12th afterwards, averaging just 4.4 runs per game.

Certainly, moving to Safeco Field had an impact on run scoring. Before the stadium opened, it was hailed as the cure-all for the team's ailments ("Just look at what happened in Baltimore and Cleveland!"). Within a few weeks of moving in, the outlook changed; now it was blamed for the team's continued malaise. Although the pitching staff flourished in the new digs, the offense stalled because, according to management, many of the players weren't a good fit for the ballpark. Of course, no details were given about what type of player is, other than "fast." The organization acted as though it couldn't have anticipated how Safeco's larger dimensions and cooler temperatures would play compared to the Kingdome. It was as if the ballpark had appeared on the Seattle skyline overnight.

While Griffey and Rodriguez have completely different personalities, they share a common trait: neither has ever made excuses for not playing well. That's a stark contrast to the organization that has employed them. After four years of listening to management defend its failures by pointing fingers, and seeing no heads roll, is it any wonder they want to move to a winning environment?

It's a scenario that most definitely troubles Mariner ownership. They have a new stadium to fill and probably will have to pick up a sizable chunk of the $100 million tab for cost overruns during its construction. Having Griffey and Rodriguez on the team is money in their pockets. After major public-relations gaffes the last two years, involving running Randy Johnson out of town and attempting to back out on the construction overruns, they're being very careful about saying and appearing to do the right things.

When Howard Lincoln was named Mariners CEO, he promised to be a more visible link to ownership and met with the all the players to assure them of his commitment to winning. Soon thereafter he announced that the team payroll for 2000 would be increased to nearly $70 million, and made very public contract offers to Griffey and Rodriguez, emphasizing that the deals would make them the two highest-paid players in the game. While these announcements were meant to send signals that it's all about winning, make no mistake: it's all about re-signing the team's two most marketable players. In the worst-case scenario, the team figures to gain some public sympathy when the duo leaves.

How unusual is it for a club to have such a wonderful collection of players—in this case, four potential Hall of Famers—yet never reach the World Series? Table 1 lists the teams that had the same four Hall of Fame teammates for at least four consecutive years and didn't reach the World Series during those seasons.

Two of the teams, the 1929 Philadelphia Athletics and 1925 Pittsburgh Pirates, played in the World Series the following year, while the 1962 San Francisco Giants had played in October the year before their run started. The Cleveland Indians (1948 and 1954) and John McGraw's New York Giants (1926 and 1933) appeared in the Fall Classic both the year before and the year after their drought.

Martinez may be a stretch to list as a future Hall of Famer, but he was arguably one of the top ten players of the decade and is the greatest DH ever. A few more seasons at his current level will give him a reasonable case for enshrinement. He certainly is as worthy as four or five of the players in the table who are cast in bronze. However, the point isn't Martinez's Cooperstown credentials, but the level of the Mariners' ineptitude at filling in the pieces around a great quartet of players.

The team's public-relations focus continued when Pat Gillick was named to succeed Woodward as general manager. As should be the case with a new hire, he was the best person for the job—the job being to keep the two superstars in the fold. Gillick was brought in because he is perceived as a winner, while Piniella, who has never created a mess that he couldn't distance himself from, was retained for 2000 for the same reason. In a move that smacked of treating the symptoms but not the disease, coaches Jesse Barfield, Steve Smith and Stan Williams were fired, while discussions were underway to extend the virus' stay with the host.

Despite ownership's elaborate maneuvering, their efforts apparently are going to fail, as Griffey Jr. has requested a trade

Table 1

Years	Team	Win Pct.	Hall of Famers
1949-53	Cleveland	.596	Doby, Feller, Lemon, Wynn
1925-28	Philadelphia (AL)	.591	Cochrane, Foxx, Grove, Simmons
1921-24	Pittsburgh	.573	Carey, Cuyler, Maranville, Traynor
1927-32	New York (NL)	.563	Hubbell**, Jackson, Lindstrom, Ott, Terry
1963-71	San Francisco	.557	Cepeda*, Marichal, Mays, McCovey, Perry
1937-41	Boston (AL)	.557	Cronin, Doerr, Foxx, Grove
1932-37	Pittsburgh	.547	Traynor, Vaughan, L. Waner, P. Wane
1995-98	Seattle	.525	Griffey, Johnson, Martinez, Rodriguez
1921-26	Chicago (AL)	.471	Collins, Faber, Hooper**, Lyons*, Schalk

* Was on the team for four years of the streak
** Was on the team for five years of the streak

and Rodriguez has said that regardless of what happens, he plans on testing the market. So where do the Mariners go from here? Gillick and Piniella will supply the answers, and their pasts provide glimpses into the team's future.

Gillick has two dissimilar experiences on his resume with the Blue Jays and Orioles, and at age 62 seems unlikely to embark on a rebuilding program. His stint in Baltimore was marked by overspending on past-prime talent, and he was responsible for assembling one of the oldest teams in major-league history. That approach meshes perfectly with Piniella, who prefers players with as much hair in their ears as on their head. Piniella has never been involved in rebuilding a team, and his history of mishandling young talent indicates that the situation would get very ugly, very quickly. It certainly appears that the Mariners are destined for an Oriole redux. Crabcakes with that latte, sir?

HITTERS (Averages: BA: .270 / OBP: .340 / SLG: .430 / EQA: .260)

David Bell   2B/3B   Bats R   Age 27

YEAR	TEAM	LGE	AB	H	DB	TP	HR	BB/SO	R	RBI	SB	CS	OUT	BA	OBP	SLG	EQA	EQR	DEFENSE	
1997	St Louis	NL	143	31	8	2	1	10/28	9	12	1	0	112	.217	.268	.322	.197	10	18-3B 92	14-2B 93
1998	Clevelnd	AL	337	85	22	2	9	20/53	35	37	0	3	255	.252	.298	.409	.233	33	93-2B 102	
1998	Seattle	AL	80	26	8	0	0	5/8	11	8	0	0	54	.325	.365	.425	.268	10		
1999	Seattle	AL	591	154	31	2	19	51/90	82	70	7	4	441	.261	.321	.416	.248	68	147-2B 96	
2000	Seattle	AL	439	113	20	1	14	43/67	58	64	2	2	328	.257	.324	.403	.247	50		

Pressed into full-time service in the first week of the season, he was one of the few pleasant surprises among Mariner position players and laid claim to the second-base job. He showed surprising power and a nifty double-play pivot, phenomena unseen during the Joey Cora era. Unfortunately, he didn't contribute much after May. He's expected to play third base in the wake of Russ Davis's departure.

Mike Blowers   1B/3B   Bats R   Age 35

YEAR	TEAM	LGE	AB	H	DB	TP	HR	BB/SO	R	RBI	SB	CS	OUT	BA	OBP	SLG	EQA	EQR	DEFENSE
1997	Seattle	AL	149	44	6	0	5	20/32	22	20	0	0	105	.295	.379	.436	.278	21	30-1B 124
1998	Oakland	AL	411	101	27	2	11	38/113	56	71	1	0	310	.246	.311	.401	.240	44	103-3B 93
1999	HAN	JpC	261	59	7	2	8	28/83	28	37	0	0	202	.226	.306	.360	.227	25	
1999	Seattle	AL	46	11	1	0	2	3/12	2	7	0	0	35	.239	.286	.391	.225	4	
2000	Seattle	AL	143	34	4	0	5	16/38	17	19	0	0	109	.238	.314	.371	.235	15	

I can accept most baseball superstitions. Not changing socks or underwear? Repulsive, but OK. Brushing teeth between innings? It's out there, but I'll buy it. Signing detritus like Blowers as a lucky charm because he was on your two playoff teams? Now you've crossed the line. His September playing time should have been used to see if Ozzie Timmons could handle first base or if team mascots are an untapped source of major-league talent.

Rafael Bournigal   IF   Bats R   Age 34

YEAR	TEAM	LGE	AB	H	DB	TP	HR	BB/SO	R	RBI	SB	CS	OUT	BA	OBP	SLG	EQA	EQR	DEFENSE	
1997	Oakland	AL	221	61	4	0	3	15/18	27	21	2	1	161	.276	.335	.335	.232	21	61-SS 100	
1998	Oakland	AL	210	49	6	0	3	9/11	22	21	6	1	162	.233	.272	.305	.197	14	30-SS 102	30-2B 104
1999	Oklahoma	PCL	55	17	4	0	2	10/5	11	10	1	1	39	.309	.415	.491	.303	10		
1999	Seattle	AL	94	25	4	0	2	6/6	14	13	0	0	69	.266	.310	.372	.230	9		
2000	*Seattle*	*AL*	*145*	*37*	*2*	*0*	*4*	*14/10*	*18*	*18*	*3*	*1*	*109*	*.255*	*.321*	*.352*	*.234*	*14*		

The last of six players tried at shortstop while Rodriguez was on the disabled list, he put up a 971 OPS prior to A-Rod's return. After that he was, well, Rafael Bournigal. He has absolutely no value except as a late-inning defensive replacement; the Mariners aren't good enough to afford that luxury.

Jay Buhner   RF   Bats R   Age 35

YEAR	TEAM	LGE	AB	H	DB	TP	HR	BB/SO	R	RBI	SB	CS	OUT	BA	OBP	SLG	EQA	EQR	DEFENSE
1997	Seattle	AL	537	132	20	2	40	116/168	101	106	0	0	405	.246	.385	.514	.298	98	150-OF 96
1998	Seattle	AL	244	60	7	1	15	37/69	32	43	0	0	184	.246	.348	.467	.272	36	66-OF 94
1999	Seattle	AL	262	56	10	0	13	65/100	33	34	0	0	206	.214	.379	.401	.273	40	78-RF 89
2000	*Seattle*	*AL*	*244*	*53*	*7*	*0*	*16*	*59/83*	*46*	*48*	*0*	*0*	*191*	*.217*	*.370*	*.443*	*.280*	*40*	

Some careers burn slowly towards the end while others are extinguished quickly. Buhner's looks to be the latter. A decade of all-out play on the Kingdome Astroturf ravaged his body, rendering him worthless in right field and robbing him of much of his power. Bone's keen eye at the plate and 1109 OPS against southpaws would make him a valuable platoon player. After declining his option, the Mariners signed him to a one-year deal.

Raul Chavez   C   Bats R   Age 27

YEAR	TEAM	LGE	AB	H	DB	TP	HR	BB/SO	R	RBI	SB	CS	OUT	BA	OBP	SLG	EQA	EQR	DEFENSE
1997	Ottawa	Int	313	74	11	0	5	13/42	27	42	1	2	241	.236	.275	.319	.196	21	
1998	Tacoma	PCL	234	47	2	0	4	18/45	21	28	1	1	188	.201	.266	.261	.173	12	74-C 114
1999	Tacoma	PCL	354	83	16	1	2	23/68	30	31	1	2	273	.234	.290	.302	.199	24	92-C 103
2000	*Seattle*	*AL*	*257*	*58*	*6*	*0*	*4*	*19/47*	*21*	*21*	*1*	*1*	*200*	*.226*	*.279*	*.296*	*.192*	*16*	

A good defensive backstop, he got contact lenses last winter and had his best offensive season in years. If he ponies up a few more bucks and undergoes laser surgery, maybe he'll hook on somewhere as a backup.

Ryan Christianson   C   Bats R   Age 19

YEAR	TEAM	LGE	AB	H	DB	TP	HR	BB/SO	R	RBI	SB	CS	OUT	BA	OBP	SLG	EQA	EQR	DEFENSE
1999	Everett	Nwn	108	25	5	0	6	8/34	11	10	1	0	83	.231	.293	.444	.245	12	
2000	*Seattle*	*AL*	*53*	*13*	*3*	*0*	*5*	*6/40*	*8*	*13*	*0*	*0*	*40*	*.245*	*.322*	*.585*	*.290*	*9*	

The 11th overall pick in the June draft, he signed late and proceeded to strain his shoulder after the layoff, curtailing his time behind the plate. There are no questions about his defense and now there are fewer about his offense, as he hit for a good average, was patient at the plate and showed excellent power to all fields. There's absolutely nobody in the organization blocking his path, so Christianson will advance as quickly as his performance dictates.

Jermaine Clark   2B   Bats L   Age 23

YEAR	TEAM	LGE	AB	H	DB	TP	HR	BB/SO	R	RBI	SB	CS	OUT	BA	OBP	SLG	EQA	EQR	DEFENSE
1998	Wisconsn	Mid	461	132	24	9	8	46/66	59	45	15	7	336	.286	.353	.430	.266	61	114-2B 99
1999	Lancastr	Cal	488	122	24	4	5	43/80	69	40	13	6	372	.250	.312	.346	.227	46	121-2B 102
2000	*Seattle*	*AL*	*337*	*92*	*16*	*4*	*4*	*37/58*	*56*	*42*	*11*	*4*	*249*	*.273*	*.345*	*.380*	*.254*	*40*	

Talent runs in cycles, and this seems to be a good one for second basemen, with a number of talented ones breaking into the majors. Even the Mariners' thin farm system has a pair of keystone prospects nearly ready to make the jump. Clark is the better of the two, with superior plate discipline, more power and more speed. Defense has always been the soft spot in his game, but hard work seems to have shored that up.

Russe Davis 3B Bats R Age 30

YEAR	TEAM	LGE	AB	H	DB	TP	HR	BB/SO	R	RBI	SB	CS	OUT	BA	OBP	SLG	EQA	EQR	DEFENSE
1997	Seattle	AL	419	115	28	1	21	25/96	55	62	6	2	306	.274	.319	.496	.267	57	115-3B 97
1998	Seattle	AL	501	131	27	1	21	33/131	65	80	4	3	373	.261	.311	.445	.250	58	132-3B 101
1999	Seattle	AL	429	102	16	1	20	27/111	49	53	3	3	330	.238	.291	.420	.235	44	119-3B 93
2000	*Seattle*	*AL*	*394*	*99*	*16*	*1*	*19*	*34/100*	*51*	*64*	*3*	*2*	*297*	*.251*	*.311*	*.442*	*.252*	*47*	

In 1998, Davis made 34 errors and was mercilessly ripped in the Seattle media for how his defense cost the team games. Last year, he was lauded for his defensive improvement when his error total dropped to 12, though he still had the range of a lamp-post. Barely a word was said about how he had become the second-worst everyday third baseman in the league offensively. Is there much difference between the two vintages of Davis, in terms of helping a team win? Not really, which again demonstrates that errors are overrated as an indicator of defensive performance. At this point in his career, Davis is sub-par in every phase of the game. He was non-tendered by the Mariners, becoming a free agent.

Alex Fernandez OF Bats L Age 19

YEAR	TEAM	LGE	AB	H	DB	TP	HR	BB/SO	R	RBI	SB	CS	OUT	BA	OBP	SLG	EQA	EQR	DEFENSE
1999	Lancastr	Cal	417	98	22	1	13	13/81	42	44	9	5	324	.235	.262	.386	.214	34	112-OF 85
2000	*Seattle*	*AL*	*215*	*55*	*10*	*0*	*10*	*8/65*	*24*	*32*	*3*	*2*	*162*	*.256*	*.283*	*.442*	*.239*	*23*	

Fernandez demonstrated 30/30 potential while posting totals of .282/.320/.458 with 21 steals as the youngest player in the California League. I'd have him begin the season back at Lancaster, focusing on plate discipline until he learns to take a free pass. Given his youth, there is no reason to advance him to the Double-A proving grounds until he dominates at high-A ball.

Jose Flores IF Bats R Age 27

YEAR	TEAM	LGE	AB	H	DB	TP	HR	BB/SO	R	RBI	SB	CS	OUT	BA	OBP	SLG	EQA	EQR	DEFENSE	
1997	Scran-WB	Int	207	50	13	1	1	24/51	28	16	2	1	158	.242	.326	.329	.228	20	32-2B 97	29-3B 72
1998	Scran-WB	Int	350	94	18	1	4	38/50	41	27	6	4	260	.269	.343	.360	.243	38	82-SS 92	
1999	Scran-WB	Int	230	50	4	2	0	30/47	26	15	8	2	182	.217	.323	.252	.210	18	61-SS 86	
1999	Tacoma	PCL	145	37	5	1	2	31/25	25	11	3	2	110	.255	.399	.345	.268	20	41-SS 97	
2000	*Seattle*	*AL*	*335*	*79*	*13*	*2*	*2*	*54/61*	*55*	*31*	*11*	*4*	*260*	*.236*	*.342*	*.304*	*.234*	*34*		

The Mariners pulled off a nice little heist when they acquired him at midseason from the Phillies for Domingo Cedeno. Flores has developed into an on-base machine and is fundamentally sound on defense. He is certainly qualified for a utility role, and there are much worse players starting at shortstop in the majors right now.

Charles Gipson UT Bats R Age 27

YEAR	TEAM	LGE	AB	H	DB	TP	HR	BB/SO	R	RBI	SB	CS	OUT	BA	OBP	SLG	EQA	EQR	DEFENSE	
1997	Memphis	Sou	321	69	9	2	1	23/83	35	21	16	4	256	.215	.286	.265	.197	22	30-3B 91	29-SS 101
1998	Tacoma	PCL	279	59	12	2	0	21/55	29	10	9	7	227	.211	.277	.269	.184	17	38-OF 100	
1999	Tacoma	PCL	174	46	5	2	0	11/26	18	17	11	3	131	.264	.317	.316	.226	16	22-SS 81	
1999	Seattle	AL	80	17	4	2	0	5/13	14	8	3	4	67	.213	.267	.313	.188	5		
2000	*Seattle*	*AL*	*278*	*60*	*12*	*3*	*0*	*24/50*	*30*	*17*	*11*	*5*	*223*	*.216*	*.278*	*.281*	*.192*	*18*		

It may require a fistful of hallucinogens, but visualize Rich Amaral Lite. Gipson might be the fastest player on the team and can play six positions—half of them passably, half exceptionally. He also can't hit a lick. He has value as a defensive chess piece and pinch-runner. Anything beyond that, and the Mariners will be sabotaging their offense.

Ken Griffey Jr. CF Bats L Age 30

YEAR	TEAM	LGE	AB	H	DB	TP	HR	BB/SO	R	RBI	SB	CS	OUT	BA	OBP	SLG	EQA	EQR	DEFENSE
1997	Seattle	AL	605	186	36	3	56	72/116	122	142	15	4	423	.307	.389	.655	.328	131	155-OF 108
1998	Seattle	AL	632	182	33	3	56	73/118	115	141	18	5	455	.288	.368	.616	.312	124	150-OF 111
1999	Seattle	AL	597	165	27	3	44	83/108	111	119	24	7	439	.276	.371	.553	.302	110	148-CF 96
2000	*Seattle*	*AL*	*568*	*156*	*28*	*2*	*40*	*78/104*	*109*	*127*	*11*	*4*	*416*	*.275*	*.362*	*.542*	*.298*	*101*	

Not bad for an off-year. His second-half OPS was down 140 points compared to his first half, a performance attributable more to playing on a tender knee than to the move to Safeco Field. The ailment also affected his range in center field. Griffey has decided to leave Seattle to pursue a championship; the fans should be thankful he hung around as long as he did and wish him the best.

Carlos Guillen   2B/SS   Bats B   Age 24

YEAR	TEAM	LGE	AB	H	DB	TP	HR	BB/SO	R	RBI	SB	CS	OUT	BA	OBP	SLG	EQA	EQR	DEFENSE
1997	Jackson	Tex	390	89	15	1	9	31/88	37	31	4	3	304	.228	.288	.341	.212	31	109-SS 93
1998	New Orln	PCL	378	107	19	3	11	27/61	59	45	3	3	274	.283	.337	.437	.259	47	98-SS 95
1998	Tacoma	PCL	92	20	0	1	1	8/17	7	4	1	2	74	.217	.280	.272	.181	5	23-2B 96
1999	Seattle	AL	19	3	0	0	1	1/6	2	3	0	0	16	.158	.200	.316	.157	1	
2000	Seattle	AL	201	51	7	1	7	19/38	26	29	2	1	151	.254	.318	.403	.245	23	

A torn ACL, courtesy of a leg-whip from Tony Phillips that would have made Conrad Dobler proud, ended his season after one week. Injuries have kept him from playing a full season in any of his five years as a pro, so despite his considerable talent, it's difficult to count on him in any long-range plans. To minimize further collisions, the Mariners are talking about moving him to third base, but he may be forced to return to his original position of shortstop if Rodriguez is traded.

Adonis Harrison   2B   Bats L   Age 23

YEAR	TEAM	LGE	AB	H	DB	TP	HR	BB/SO	R	RBI	SB	CS	OUT	BA	OBP	SLG	EQA	EQR	DEFENSE
1997	Wisconsn	Mid	419	113	25	3	7	42/77	43	47	10	8	314	.270	.343	.394	.250	49	114-2B 87
1998	Lancastr	Cal	258	70	18	2	2	38/49	41	25	10	6	194	.271	.368	.380	.260	33	66-2B 92
1998	Orlando	Sou	192	40	7	1	3	22/31	26	16	3	2	154	.208	.298	.302	.207	15	56-2B 95
1999	New Havn	Eas	453	115	6	0	5	28/77	43	41	13	10	348	.254	.303	.300	.206	33	116-2B 89
2000	Seattle	AL	481	128	17	2	8	50/84	75	55	22	11	364	.266	.335	.360	.243	53	

This is the organization's other second-base prospect. Harrison lost all semblance of his previous plate discipline, and his line-drive stroke, which wasn't all that great to begin with, suffered. He should have fallen behind Clark on the Mariners' depth chart, but he's speedy, flashy on defense and has a cool name, so maybe not.

Brian Hunter   LF/CF   Bats R   Age 29

YEAR	TEAM	LGE	AB	H	DB	TP	HR	BB/SO	R	RBI	SB	CS	OUT	BA	OBP	SLG	EQA	EQR	DEFENSE
1997	Detroit	AL	656	175	27	8	4	62/116	107	43	74	18	499	.267	.331	.351	.248	77	162-OF 107
1998	Detroit	AL	593	150	29	3	4	34/92	62	34	37	12	455	.253	.296	.332	.220	52	132-OF 116
1999	Detroit	AL	55	13	1	1	0	4/11	7	2	0	3	45	.236	.300	.291	.185	3	
1999	Seattle	AL	481	107	9	5	4	27/80	64	31	44	5	379	.222	.265	.287	.203	35	105-LF 110
2000	Seattle	AL	497	120	16	4	3	40/83	68	39	31	8	385	.241	.298	.308	.217	42	

We once had a heifer on our family farm that repeatedly broke through fences and would lead us on merry chases for hours at a time. We tried reinforcing the fence, adding barbed wire, installing electric fencing and even subtle attention-getting with a two-by-four, all to no avail. The only solution was to get rid of the beast. Like Bossie gone bad, Hunter tends to be everywhere but where you want a leadoff hitter to be: on base. Although I don't know if a two-by-four would help as a tool of instruction, Hunter would undoubtedly be tastier on the grill than in the lineup.

Raul Ibanez   OF/1B   Bats L   Age 28

YEAR	TEAM	LGE	AB	H	DB	TP	HR	BB/SO	R	RBI	SB	CS	OUT	BA	OBP	SLG	EQA	EQR	DEFENSE
1997	Tacoma	PCL	427	105	23	3	10	22/84	55	55	4	3	325	.246	.284	.384	.222	38	111-OF 95
1998	Tacoma	PCL	191	36	9	1	4	20/51	19	19	1	1	156	.188	.265	.309	.192	13	39-OF 97
1998	Seattle	AL	98	25	7	1	2	5/22	12	12	0	0	73	.255	.291	.408	.232	9	
1999	Seattle	AL	207	52	5	0	9	15/32	20	25	5	1	156	.251	.302	.406	.240	22	24-RF 106
2000	Seattle	AL	257	61	12	1	8	21/51	31	32	3	1	197	.237	.295	.385	.231	25	

Lou Piniella likes reserves who can play multiple positions for the purpose of in-game maneuvering. Unfortunately, last year's bench—Ibanez, Bournigal, Gipson, John Mabry—had plenty of versatility but not much talent. A lack of outfield prospects in the upper minors will probably enable Ibanez to again make the squad, but unless he becomes more selective at the plate and hits for more power, he won't be in the majors long enough to draw a full pension.

Craig Kuzmic — UT — Bats B — Age 23

YEAR	TEAM	LGE	AB	H	DB	TP	HR	BB/SO	R	RBI	SB	CS	OUT	BA	OBP	SLG	EQA	EQR	DEFENSE	
1998	Everett	Nwn	187	41	10	1	7	23/62	22	29	1	1	147	.219	.313	.396	.240	21	25-3B 89	
1999	Lancastr	Cal	107	18	2	0	4	16/43	12	10	1	0	89	.168	.280	.299	.201	8		
1999	Wisconsn	Mid	330	67	13	1	9	46/91	35	40	3	2	265	.203	.303	.330	.218	30	50-3B 96	23-OF 78
2000	Seattle	AL	264	54	9	0	11	35/87	31	33	1	1	211	.205	.298	.364	.226	26		

It's not often we predict a major-league career for a utility player in low-A ball, but Kuzmic will have one. He's a switch-hitter, will take a walk and has some sock in his bat. He can also play any position on the diamond and proved it on the last day of the season, using a knuckleball to earn a save.

Tom Lampkin — C — Bats L — Age 36

YEAR	TEAM	LGE	AB	H	DB	TP	HR	BB/SO	R	RBI	SB	CS	OUT	BA	OBP	SLG	EQA	EQR	DEFENSE
1997	St Louis	NL	232	58	7	1	8	28/30	28	23	2	1	175	.250	.341	.392	.252	28	
1998	St Louis	NL	218	52	13	1	6	23/31	25	28	3	2	168	.239	.332	.390	.247	25	53-C 99
1999	Seattle	AL	204	58	11	2	8	10/32	26	30	1	3	149	.284	.333	.475	.263	27	49-C 108
2000	Seattle	AL	189	46	9	1	6	20/28	25	26	1	2	145	.243	.316	.397	.240	21	

He had a career year offensively after coming home to Seattle as a free agent. Lampkin has always been solid behind the dish and last year nailed 46% of base-stealers, thanks to nimble footwork and a quick release. He smacked right-handed pitching for an 877 OPS and as a result could see his playing time boosted this season.

John Mabry — OF/3B/1B — Bats L — Age 29

YEAR	TEAM	LGE	AB	H	DB	TP	HR	BB/SO	R	RBI	SB	CS	OUT	BA	OBP	SLG	EQA	EQR	DEFENSE	
1997	St Louis	NL	394	115	12	0	8	38/76	40	38	0	1	280	.292	.359	.383	.255	46	60-OF 96	35-1B 95
1998	St Louis	NL	380	97	16	0	12	29/74	41	49	0	2	285	.255	.310	.392	.235	38	29-3B 79	48-OF 96
1999	Seattle	AL	260	62	11	0	9	17/60	30	30	2	1	199	.238	.285	.385	.224	24	28-RF 101	
2000	Seattle	AL	325	83	10	0	13	30/69	40	49	1	1	243	.255	.318	.406	.246	36		

Used sparingly, Mabry is a handy guy to have in reserve at the infield and outfield corners. Of course, he was on pace for 400 plate appearances before fracturing his kneecap, helping to fuel the Mariners' descent to offensive mediocrity. Seattle gave him to a two-year, $3-million deal after the 1998 season, so while there are cheaper facsimiles readily available, he'll be back for a return engagement.

Edgar Martinez — DH — Bats R — Age 37

YEAR	TEAM	LGE	AB	H	DB	TP	HR	BB/SO	R	RBI	SB	CS	OUT	BA	OBP	SLG	EQA	EQR	DEFENSE
1997	Seattle	AL	538	179	32	2	29	114/83	100	106	2	4	363	.333	.460	.561	.339	121	
1998	Seattle	AL	554	181	40	2	31	103/94	83	100	1	1	374	.327	.435	.574	.332	118	
1999	Seattle	AL	490	161	32	1	23	90/99	77	77	7	2	331	.329	.438	.539	.327	101	
2000	Seattle	AL	457	132	20	1	25	103/84	104	104	2	1	326	.289	.420	.501	.314	90	

While his teammates were kvetching about how tough it is to hit at Safeco Field, he did what he always does, quietly going about his business to the tune of .394/.479/.535 at the new digs. So why isn't Edgar used as the prototype when assembling the offense for the "new Mariners"? He re-signed with Seattle for two more years of line-drive doubles.

Shane Monahan — OF — Bats L — Age 25

YEAR	TEAM	LGE	AB	H	DB	TP	HR	BB/SO	R	RBI	SB	CS	OUT	BA	OBP	SLG	EQA	EQR	DEFENSE
1997	Memphis	Sou	399	107	22	4	10	21/107	38	57	9	4	296	.268	.307	.419	.243	43	91-OF 94
1997	Tacoma	PCL	83	21	3	0	2	4/22	11	9	4	1	63	.253	.294	.361	.227	8	20-OF 113
1998	Tacoma	PCL	277	65	8	5	3	16/47	27	28	5	3	215	.235	.276	.332	.204	20	64-OF 105
1998	Seattle	AL	211	51	9	1	4	7/52	17	27	1	2	162	.242	.266	.351	.201	15	57-OF 95
1999	Tacoma	PCL	399	95	19	3	5	15/82	41	27	6	2	306	.238	.270	.338	.203	29	89-OF 103
2000	Seattle	AL	418	102	16	2	9	26/91	43	46	6	3	319	.244	.288	.356	.218	35	

The essence of Monahan was on display in his first meeting with Mike Mussina two years ago: Moose threw him nothing but knuckle-curves in the dirt, and Monahan swung at every one until his third at-bat, when he managed to check his swing on the second pitch. He didn't progress at all last year with Tacoma and apparently sees the writing on the wall—he asked the Mariners to send him to the instructional league to become a catcher and "better focus his intensity." Brown-noser.

Adrian Myers　OF　Bats R　Age 25

YEAR	TEAM	LGE	AB	H	DB	TP	HR	BB/SO	R	RBI	SB	CS	OUT	BA	OBP	SLG	EQA	EQR	DEFENSE
1997	Charlott	Fla	296	68	10	3	0	29/83	31	18	7	6	234	.230	.303	.284	.202	21	72-OF 108
1998	Charlott	Fla	463	105	19	5	5	41/119	52	47	17	10	368	.227	.292	.322	.211	38	98-OF 103
1999	Tulsa	Tex	361	73	11	2	1	33/75	39	22	15	4	292	.202	.273	.252	.184	21	94-OF 97
2000	Seattle	AL	390	86	14	3	2	40/91	46	28	15	6	310	.221	.293	.287	.204	29	

He was picked up from Texas in the Jeff Fassero deal, so Mariner fans shouldn't have been expecting much. He seems to fit the organizational concept of the perfect Safeco player, a speedy singles hitter who can go fetch 'em in the outfield, OBP be damned.

Ryan Radmanovich　OF　Bats L　Age 28

YEAR	TEAM	LGE	AB	H	DB	TP	HR	BB/SO	R	RBI	SB	CS	OUT	BA	OBP	SLG	EQA	EQR	DEFENSE
1997	SaltLake	PCL	473	98	18	3	18	50/155	59	49	7	3	378	.207	.287	.372	.223	45	129-OF 90
1998	Tacoma	PCL	397	102	27	2	11	37/91	55	49	1	3	298	.257	.321	.418	.247	45	95-OF 91
1999	Tacoma	PCL	422	105	21	2	12	43/90	51	60	6	3	320	.249	.323	.393	.244	47	93-OF 95
2000	San Dieg	NL	417	90	17	1	13	47/101	46	47	5	2	329	.216	.295	.355	.229	41	

Just another usable part that the Mariners didn't try in left field. It appears that he's been branded like Hester Prynne, except with three scarlet As instead of one. The Padres have signed him as a minor-league free agent.

Bo Robinson　3B　Bats R　Age 24

YEAR	TEAM	LGE	AB	H	DB	TP	HR	BB/SO	R	RBI	SB	CS	OUT	BA	OBP	SLG	EQA	EQR	DEFENSE
1998	Everett	Nwn	205	44	11	1	3	14/39	21	17	0	0	161	.215	.268	.322	.196	14	33-3B 82
1999	Wisconsn	Mid	509	130	36	2	10	77/86	68	66	1	0	379	.255	.356	.393	.259	65	82-3B 94
2000	Seattle	AL	275	70	16	1	7	41/56	44	41	0	0	205	.255	.351	.396	.259	35	

He had a monster year for the Timber Rattlers while showing exceptional plate discipline. Normally, we'd be raving about his Midwest-League-record 50 doubles and how that will translate into future homers with age, but there's the rub—Robinson turned 24 last August. The Mariners need to push him to Double-A immediately and see if he floats.

Alex Rodriguez　SS　Bats R　Age 24

YEAR	TEAM	LGE	AB	H	DB	TP	HR	BB/SO	R	RBI	SB	CS	OUT	BA	OBP	SLG	EQA	EQR	DEFENSE
1997	Seattle	AL	586	177	42	3	23	37/95	97	82	29	6	415	.302	.350	.502	.285	90	139-SS 98
1998	Seattle	AL	685	214	35	6	41	42/118	116	119	41	13	484	.312	.361	.561	.300	119	159-SS 98
1999	Seattle	AL	496	137	24	0	39	49/109	98	99	21	7	366	.276	.347	.560	.293	85	125-SS 102
2000	Seattle	AL	573	173	28	2	42	56/111	115	133	23	7	407	.302	.364	.578	.308	107	

He probably would have been the first shortstop to hit 50 home runs had he not missed 32 games with torn cartilage in his left knee. Still only 24 years old, Rodriguez has a tremendous work ethic; when he learns to lay off breaking pitches away, he will put up absolutely mind-boggling numbers. Given his age, ability and defensive position, re-signing Rodriguez is more critical to the future of the Mariners than keeping Griffey Jr.

Chris Snelling　CF　Bats L　Age 18

YEAR	TEAM	LGE	AB	H	DB	TP	HR	BB/SO	R	RBI	SB	CS	OUT	BA	OBP	SLG	EQA	EQR	DEFENSE
1999	Everett	Nwn	265	64	13	2	7	21/26	28	30	3	3	204	.242	.304	.385	.231	26	70-OF 109
2000	Seattle	AL	143	39	7	1	5	12/30	20	23	1	1	105	.273	.329	.441	.259	18	

Seattle is one of the few clubs with a strong presence in Australia. In Snelling and Everett ace Craig Anderson, scout Jim Colborn picked a couple of plums off the Sydney Storm roster. The youngest player in the Northwest League, Snelling showed good plate discipline and credits Yoda and the Force for his surprising power. Seriously. Also a fine defensive center fielder, he should only get better as his thin frame fills out.

Ichiro Suzuki　OF　Bats L　Age 25

YEAR	TEAM	LGE	AB	H	DB	TP	HR	BB/SO	R	RBI	SB	CS	OUT	BA	OBP	SLG	EQA	EQR	DEFENSE
1998	ORX	JpP	507	158	35	2	10	30/43	68	60	8	4	353	.312	.358	.448	.271	68	
1999	ORX	JpP	418	131	29	2	17	36/51	73	58	10	6	293	.313	.377	.514	.293	68	
2000	Seattle	AL	423	132	26	1	16	37/45	74	81	7	4	295	.312	.367	.492	.288	66	

Already a six-time Pacific League batting champ, he spent part of spring training in Peoria in an exchange between Seattle and its sister city, Kobe. Suzuki is listed only as a tease—he is tethered to the Japanese League through 2001, after which he would be free to sign with any team.

Ozzie Timmons OF Bats R Age 29

YEAR	TEAM	LGE	AB	H	DB	TP	HR	BB/SO	R	RBI	SB	CS	OUT	BA	OBP	SLG	EQA	EQR	DEFENSE
1997	Indianap	AA	417	96	14	1	11	50/112	40	48	1	2	323	.230	.316	.348	.227	40	92-OF 92
1998	Indianap	Int	329	76	19	2	9	21/72	36	28	1	1	254	.231	.284	.383	.222	30	93-OF 85
1999	Tacoma	PCL	300	70	16	0	16	43/88	41	49	0	1	231	.233	.332	.447	.260	40	52-OF 94
1999	Seattle	AL	44	5	1	0	1	4/12	3	3	0	1	40	.114	.188	.205	.067	0	
2000	TampaBay	AL	328	76	14	1	14	46/87	46	51	0	1	253	.232	.326	.409	.248	39	

He made the short trip up from Tacoma at the All-Star break and didn't even get 50 plate appearances for a team in desperate need of runs. He has a long swing, like Juan Gonzalez, that requires regular work to maintain and makes him susceptible to breaking stuff. Timmons crushes left-handed pitchers, but with the dearth of southpaws in the league, a modified platoon is needed to keep him sharp—maybe left-handers and hard-throwing right-handers. He was released and has signed with the Devil Rays as a minor-league free agent.

Peanut Williams 1B Bats R Age 22

YEAR	TEAM	LGE	AB	H	DB	TP	HR	BB/SO	R	RBI	SB	CS	OUT	BA	OBP	SLG	EQA	EQR	DEFENSE
1997	Everett	Nwn	255	54	4	0	9	9/99	23	29	0	0	201	.212	.243	.333	.186	15	
1998	Wisconsn	Mid	233	52	5	0	11	13/80	28	30	2	1	182	.223	.271	.386	.218	20	
1999	Lancastr	Cal	264	70	7	0	21	27/86	42	40	0	0	194	.265	.339	.530	.282	41	49-1B 94
2000	Seattle	AL	295	84	6	0	22	40/98	51	69	0	0	211	.285	.370	.529	.298	51	

The nickname "Peanut" doesn't conjure up images of strapping, free-swinging first base/DH types, but that's exactly what Williams is. He is also the best power-hitting prospect in the Mariners' organization, returning from a broken hand to belt 26 round-trippers in a little over two months with the JetHawks. His production was partially a phenomenon of The Hanger, as he hit 19 of his homers there and slugged .879 at home versus .412 on the road. Williams also struck out once every 3.5 plate appearances and needs to learn more patience at the plate, or he will be exposed as he moves up the ladder.

Dan Wilson C Bats R Age 31

YEAR	TEAM	LGE	AB	H	DB	TP	HR	BB/SO	R	RBI	SB	CS	OUT	BA	OBP	SLG	EQA	EQR	DEFENSE
1997	Seattle	AL	507	139	29	1	16	36/69	64	73	7	2	370	.274	.329	.430	.256	61	
1998	Seattle	AL	325	83	17	1	9	23/55	38	42	2	1	243	.255	.315	.397	.240	34	92-C 99
1999	Seattle	AL	411	106	24	2	6	24/83	42	34	5	0	305	.258	.302	.370	.229	38	112-C 97
2000	Seattle	AL	332	85	16	1	8	24/60	40	42	3	1	248	.256	.306	.383	.234	33	

His health returned this year but his offense didn't; it's on permanent sabbatical. Wilson's ability to handle pitchers is largely a myth, and the team has a better option against right-handers, so it's time for Piniella to stop penciling him in for 120 starts a season. He's been given a three-year extension, so that's not likely to happen.

PITCHERS (Averages: ERA: 4.50 / H/9: 9.00 / HR/9: 1.00 / BB/9: 3.50 / K/9: 6.50 / KWH: 1.00)

Paul Abbott Throws R Age 32

YEAR	TEAM	LGE	IP	H	ER	HR	BB	K	ERA	W	L	H/9	HR/9	BB/9	K/9	KWH	PERA
1997	Tacoma	PCL	88.3	84	47	10	31	96	4.79	5	5	8.56	1.02	3.16	9.78	2.64	4.18
1998	Tacoma	PCL	14.3	10	2	2	6	16	1.26	2	0	6.28	1.26	3.77	10.05	3.19	3.14
1998	Seattle	AL	25.3	22	9	2	11	22	3.20	2	1	7.82	0.71	3.91	7.82	1.49	3.55
1999	Seattle	AL	73.7	47	26	8	31	70	3.18	5	3	5.74	0.98	3.79	8.55	2.51	2.81

Abbott is a scrap-heap find who throws 93 mph, is effective against both left-handed and right-handed hitters, strikes batters out and has decent control. He was a top prospect in the Twins' organization before his career was derailed by a string of bizarre, unrelated injuries. He would be better utilized as a starter, but Piniella plans to use him as the setup man for Mesa. Regardless of the role, he'll be effective if he can stay healthy.

Pat Ahearne Throws R Age 30

YEAR	TEAM	LGE	IP	H	ER	HR	BB	K	ERA	W	L	H/9	HR/9	BB/9	K/9	KWH	PERA
1997	SanAnton	Tex	72.7	135	63	1	17	35	7.80	2	6	16.72	0.12	2.11	4.33	0.40	7.56
1997	Albuquer	PCL	60.7	76	36	8	22	37	5.34	3	4	11.27	1.19	3.26	5.49	0.61	5.93
1999	New Havn	Eas	115.3	141	52	6	33	59	4.06	7	6	11.00	0.47	2.58	4.60	0.56	4.68

He was signed out of the independent Atlantic League in early June and went on to win the Eastern League ERA title. In a best-case scenario, he's the next Dave Eiland. Is that really something to get excited about?

Ryan Anderson Throws L Age 20

YEAR	TEAM	LGE	IP	H	ER	HR	BB	K	ERA	W	L	H/9	HR/9	BB/9	K/9	KWH	PERA
1998	Wisconsn	Mid	105.3	107	56	6	85	106	4.78	6	6	9.14	0.51	7.26	9.06	0.92	5.55
1999	New Havn	Eas	129.7	148	84	10	94	134	5.83	5	9	10.27	0.69	6.52	9.30	0.96	6.18

Very green at age 19, he made the two-level jump up to Double-A and scuffled most of the season, but posted a 3.19 ERA in seven starts after returning from the Pan Am Games. Meche's success has made Anderson seem a bit of a disappointment in the Mariners' eyes, even though he led the Eastern League in strikeouts and is more advanced than Randy Johnson was at the same age. Because he's one of the few coveted commodities in the farm system, there are rumblings that he'll be dealt to acquire major-league help. His strong Arizona Fall League performance boosted his trade value while making it less likely that he will be dealt.

Mel Bunch Throws R Age 28

YEAR	TEAM	LGE	IP	H	ER	HR	BB	K	ERA	W	L	H/9	HR/9	BB/9	K/9	KWH	PERA
1997	Harrisbg	Eas	45.7	55	32	7	26	37	6.31	2	3	10.84	1.38	5.12	7.29	0.72	6.70
1997	Ottawa	Int	74.0	115	69	13	49	47	8.39	2	6	13.99	1.58	5.96	5.72	0.29	9.36
1998	Ottawa	Int	100.0	112	62	16	54	84	5.58	4	7	10.08	1.44	4.86	7.56	0.87	6.21
1999	Tacoma	PCL	114.0	127	62	10	47	91	4.89	6	7	10.03	0.79	3.71	7.18	1.04	4.97

He took one for the team in relief against Texas on June 26, finishing the game and giving up eight runs in 3 1/3 innings. Rewarded with a bus ticket to Tacoma as he left the mound, he didn't don the teal and blue again. Rainiers' pitching coach Jim Slaton put Humpty back together again, and Bunch ended up winning the Pacific Coast League's ERA title. Bunch has a plus arm, improved command and could help a number of teams as a fifth starter, were he given a clean shot at the job. Don't expect it to happen with the Mariners.

Ken Cloude Throws R Age 25

YEAR	TEAM	LGE	IP	H	ER	HR	BB	K	ERA	W	L	H/9	HR/9	BB/9	K/9	KWH	PERA
1997	Memphis	Sou	124.0	151	68	15	52	102	4.94	6	8	10.96	1.09	3.77	7.40	0.99	5.88
1997	Seattle	AL	52.3	37	27	8	26	47	4.64	3	3	6.36	1.38	4.47	8.08	1.72	3.78
1998	Seattle	AL	158.7	176	103	27	84	116	5.84	7	11	9.98	1.53	4.76	6.58	0.68	6.18
1999	Tacoma	PCL	36.0	21	13	3	18	26	3.25	3	1	5.25	0.75	4.50	6.50	1.34	2.75
1999	Seattle	AL	74.3	100	58	9	44	36	7.02	2	6	12.11	1.09	5.33	4.36	0.22	7.26

He has been ravaged in the type of tag-team attack usually seen in the WWF. Piniella handled the mental side, destroying his confidence, while Stan Williams altered his delivery and screwed up his mechanics. Within two weeks of being demoted to Tacoma and put in Slaton's care, he was completely dominating the Pacific Coast League. If Cloude is given the ball on a consistent basis and allowed to work through his struggles, he'll return to the form that made him one of the top pitching prospects in baseball a couple of years ago. In what would be a wonderful move for his career, Cloude will probably be dealt over the winter.

Tom Davey Throws R Age 26

YEAR	TEAM	LGE	IP	H	ER	HR	BB	K	ERA	W	L	H/9	HR/9	BB/9	K/9	KWH	PERA
1997	Dunedin	Fla	37.0	56	27	5	21	27	6.57	1	3	13.62	1.22	5.11	6.57	0.46	8.27
1997	Knoxvill	Sou	91.3	113	63	5	57	59	6.21	3	7	11.14	0.49	5.62	5.81	0.40	6.01
1998	Knoxvill	Sou	73.3	81	37	2	54	60	4.54	4	4	9.94	0.25	6.63	7.36	0.61	5.52
1999	Toronto	AL	44.3	38	24	4	26	43	4.87	2	3	7.71	0.81	5.28	8.73	1.40	4.26
1999	Syracuse	Int	32.3	33	16	1	21	17	4.45	2	2	9.19	0.28	5.85	4.73	0.31	4.73
1999	Seattle	AL	21.7	20	11	0	14	18	4.57	1	1	8.31	0.00	5.82	7.48	0.86	4.15

A tall, flame-throwing right-hander, he fits the closer stereotype and is being groomed for that role. However, like most of his Seattle pen pals, Davey has little idea where the ball is going after it leaves his hand. The Mariner bullpen ranked last in the league, averaging 5.6 walks per nine innings. Yet inexplicably, the team keeps bringing in relievers with a history of control problems. Piniella believes that he can help them simply by screaming "Throw strikes!" but it seems likely that the notion has already crossed their minds.

Freddy Garcia   Throws R   Age 23

YEAR	TEAM	LGE	IP	H	ER	HR	BB	K	ERA	W	L	H/9	HR/9	BB/9	K/9	KWH	PERA
1997	Kissimme	Fla	165.3	211	85	9	64	102	4.63	9	9	11.49	0.49	3.48	5.55	0.58	5.39
1998	Jackson	Tex	112.0	105	52	8	66	94	4.18	6	6	8.44	0.64	5.30	7.55	0.95	4.50
1998	Tacoma	PCL	30.3	33	15	6	15	25	4.45	2	1	9.79	1.78	4.45	7.42	0.94	6.23
1999	Seattle	AL	205.7	191	81	15	87	175	3.54	14	9	8.36	0.66	3.81	7.66	1.38	3.94

"Chief" put a stranglehold on a rotation spot with a sparkling spring training and didn't let go despite an unhealthy helping of Piniella-dispensed abuse. In recent years, young pitchers haven't fared well with the Mariners, but Garcia has a couple things working in his favor: he was schooled in the Astros' organization, and his tenuous grasp of the English language may enable him to ignore much of Piniella's bluster. He has the stuff and makeup to be a number one starter. With Piniella returning, all bets are off concerning Garcia's future.

John Halama   Throws L   Age 28

YEAR	TEAM	LGE	IP	H	ER	HR	BB	K	ERA	W	L	H/9	HR/9	BB/9	K/9	KWH	PERA
1997	New Orln	AmA	160.7	178	73	9	38	106	4.09	10	8	9.97	0.50	2.13	5.94	1.24	4.03
1998	New Orln	PCL	111.3	135	57	11	18	69	4.61	6	6	10.91	0.89	1.46	5.58	1.46	4.69
1998	Houston	NL	32.3	38	21	0	14	20	5.85	1	3	10.58	0.00	3.90	5.57	0.56	4.45
1999	Seattle	AL	182.7	180	74	17	54	108	3.65	12	8	8.87	0.84	2.66	5.32	0.90	3.94

A few excerpts from the Piniella Primer: no high-fives with the Mariner Moose, never take anything from the post-game buffet that can't be ingested with a straw and don't put three soft-tossing left-handers in your starting rotation. The last dictum caused Halama to be miscast as a situational reliever to open the season. Not long after Butch Henry tore his labrum, Halama was dropped into the rotation and reeled off eight consecutive quality starts. His repertoire is uncannily similar to Jamie Moyer's, so if anything trickles down from the off-speed master, he should have a nice little career.

Jeff Heaverlo   Throws R   Age 22

YEAR	TEAM	LGE	IP	H	ER	HR	BB	K	ERA	W	L	H/9	HR/9	BB/9	K/9	KWH	PERA
1999	Everett	Nwn	8.0	7	6	1	2	6	6.75	0	1	7.88	1.13	2.25	6.75	1.92	3.37
1999	Wisconsn	Mid	16.7	18	7	2	8	17	3.78	1	1	9.72	1.08	4.32	9.18	1.50	5.40

Part of the bountiful Northwest harvest in last June's draft, he was a sandwich pick out of the University of Washington. Heaverlo signed late, breezed through a short stint with Everett and was promoted to Wisconsin for the playoffs. He really turned it on there, allowing only one earned run in 17 innings. The son of former Mariner Dave "Kojak" Heaverlo is polished, throws four pitches for strikes and will be pushed hard through the system.

Brett Hinchliffe   Throws R   Age 25

YEAR	TEAM	LGE	IP	H	ER	HR	BB	K	ERA	W	L	H/9	HR/9	BB/9	K/9	KWH	PERA
1997	Memphis	Sou	135.3	183	88	20	49	88	5.85	6	9	12.17	1.33	3.26	5.85	0.65	6.65
1998	Tacoma	PCL	149.0	144	85	20	97	85	5.13	7	10	8.70	1.21	5.86	5.13	0.39	5.50
1999	Tacoma	PCL	119.0	155	86	16	51	85	6.50	4	9	11.72	1.21	3.86	6.43	0.68	6.50
1999	Seattle	AL	31.7	38	26	9	20	14	7.39	1	3	10.80	2.56	5.68	3.98	0.19	8.53

He peaked in March, which helped him make the Mariners' Opening Day roster. There's nothing about his game to get excited about. If he keeps the ball down, he can be effective; if he doesn't, dash out to the bleachers and do battle for souvenirs.

Mark Leiter   Throws R   Age 37

YEAR	TEAM	LGE	IP	H	ER	HR	BB	K	ERA	W	L	H/9	HR/9	BB/9	K/9	KWH	PERA
1997	Philadel	NL	181.3	222	133	26	68	138	6.60	6	14	11.02	1.29	3.38	6.85	0.94	5.96
1998	Philadel	NL	89.7	67	35	8	50	81	3.51	6	4	6.72	0.80	5.02	8.13	1.46	3.61

(Mark Leiter *continued*)

Another marcher in Seattle's parade of overpaid veteran mediocrities dubbed "relief solutions," he was as much a solution in the bullpen as Butch Henry—four starts, five months on the disabled list—was in the rotation. Are there any three words more terrifying to a 37-year-old pitcher than "rotator cuff rehabilitation"? How about "Demoted to Altoona"? Or "Mom's moving in"?

Chris Mears · Throws R · Age 22

YEAR	TEAM	LGE	IP	H	ER	HR	BB	K	ERA	W	L	H/9	HR/9	BB/9	K/9	KWH	PERA
1997	Everett	Nwn	57.0	103	54	6	25	27	8.53	1	5	16.26	0.95	3.95	4.26	0.21	9.16
1998	Everett	Nwn	91.3	113	49	8	38	45	4.83	5	5	11.14	0.79	3.74	4.43	0.35	5.62
1999	Wisconsn	Mid	84.7	91	38	2	19	56	4.04	5	4	9.67	0.21	2.02	5.95	1.36	3.51
1999	Lancastr	Cal	53.7	75	40	12	20	34	6.71	2	4	12.58	2.01	3.35	5.70	0.58	7.88

Mears was named the best pitching prospect in the Midwest League by league managers, despite being old for the league and having only average stuff. He relies on pinpoint control, and the margin for error gets smaller as you move up the chain, which he discovered upon promotion to Lancaster.

Gil Meche · Throws R · Age 21

YEAR	TEAM	LGE	IP	H	ER	HR	BB	K	ERA	W	L	H/9	HR/9	BB/9	K/9	KWH	PERA
1997	Everett	Nwn	69.0	95	45	8	30	35	5.87	3	5	12.39	1.04	3.91	4.57	0.32	6.78
1998	Wisconsn	Mid	140.7	169	93	13	81	117	5.95	6	10	10.81	0.83	5.18	7.49	0.75	6.08
1999	New Havn	Eas	57.0	58	26	3	28	46	4.11	3	3	9.16	0.47	4.42	7.26	0.97	4.42
1999	Tacoma	PCL	28.3	33	13	3	15	20	4.13	2	1	10.48	0.95	4.76	6.35	0.60	5.72
1999	Seattle	AL	87.3	68	41	8	55	48	4.23	5	5	7.01	0.82	5.67	4.95	0.46	4.02

Go to the head of the class if you saw this coming. Meche was the youngest hurler to advance four levels in less than a year and throw at least 75 league-average innings in the majors since Dwight Gooden lit up the Big Apple as a teenager in 1984. Overworked, Gooden tore his rotator cuff at age 24 and was never the same. There is a lesson to be learned from Gooden's demise. While Piniella deserves credit for using Meche judiciously last year, there is a misguided tendency to increase a young pitcher's workload based on major-league experience instead of age, which is the relevant variable.

With the Mariners, Meche often had difficulty controlling his breaking pitches, so he would abandon them and survive by spotting his fastball. That's not a recipe for continued success.

Jose Mesa · Throws R · Age 34

YEAR	TEAM	LGE	IP	H	ER	HR	BB	K	ERA	W	L	H/9	HR/9	BB/9	K/9	KWH	PERA
1997	Clevelnd	AL	82.7	80	25	7	28	69	2.72	7	2	8.71	0.76	3.05	7.51	1.59	3.92
1998	Clevelnd	AL	56.0	58	31	6	21	36	4.98	3	3	9.32	0.96	3.38	5.79	0.80	4.66
1998	San Fran	NL	30.0	32	15	1	19	27	4.50	2	1	9.60	0.30	5.70	8.10	0.90	5.10
1999	Seattle	AL	70.3	79	36	9	39	43	4.61	4	4	10.11	1.15	4.99	5.50	0.45	5.89

So that's all it takes to be a closer? Insiders claim his statistics are grotesque because he was battered in non-save situations and focuses better when the game hangs in the balance. Malarkey. He has lost five mph off his fastball since his heyday, and his command keeps deteriorating. Mesa is as good a bet to completely collapse as any reliever in the game.

Ivan Montane · Throws R · Age 27

YEAR	TEAM	LGE	IP	H	ER	HR	BB	K	ERA	W	L	H/9	HR/9	BB/9	K/9	KWH	PERA
1997	Lancastr	Cal	29.0	50	32	2	18	21	9.93	1	2	15.52	0.62	5.59	6.52	0.37	9.00
1997	Memphis	Sou	62.7	102	80	15	60	48	11.49	1	6	14.65	2.15	8.62	6.89	0.28	11.92
1999	New Havn	Eas	51.7	47	20	2	26	52	3.48	4	2	8.19	0.35	4.53	9.06	1.65	3.83

Given Seattle's ongoing bullpen miseries, any reliever who strikes out 11.5 batters per nine innings in Double-A should get some attention. Montane was moved to relief after missing nearly all of 1998 with a torn ACL. He has always had a live arm, but this was the first time in his professional career that his walk rate dipped below four per nine innings. If the command is for real, he could be a sleeper.

Jamie Moyer — Throws L — Age 37

YEAR	TEAM	LGE	IP	H	ER	HR	BB	K	ERA	W	L	H/9	HR/9	BB/9	K/9	KWH	PERA
1997	Seattle	AL	193.3	172	69	19	44	114	3.21	14	7	8.01	0.88	2.05	5.31	1.28	3.31
1998	Seattle	AL	238.7	220	85	21	44	160	3.21	18	9	8.30	0.79	1.66	6.03	1.98	3.24
1999	Seattle	AL	232.3	219	91	20	47	141	3.53	16	10	8.48	0.77	1.82	5.46	1.44	3.37

He had an ERA of 7.96 on April 23, when the Mariners boldly extended his contract through 2001 with a club option for 2002. From that point on, he was the second-best starter in the league. Moyer is a master in the art of pitching, befuddling batters with off-speed pitches that never cross the heart of the plate. He lives and dies with his control, and I expect him to be on life support by the end of his contract.

Jose Paniagua — Throws R — Age 26

YEAR	TEAM	LGE	IP	H	ER	HR	BB	K	ERA	W	L	H/9	HR/9	BB/9	K/9	KWH	PERA
1997	Ottawa	Int	134.7	174	80	13	46	74	5.35	6	9	11.63	0.87	3.07	4.95	0.51	5.75
1998	Tacoma	PCL	64.0	72	28	2	25	50	3.94	4	3	10.13	0.28	3.52	7.03	1.04	4.36
1998	Seattle	AL	22.3	13	4	3	6	16	1.61	2	0	5.24	1.21	2.42	6.45	2.45	2.42
1999	Seattle	AL	80.0	68	30	4	51	76	3.38	6	3	7.65	0.45	5.74	8.55	1.24	4.05

He was so effective in April and May that he was overused and posted a 4.85 ERA over the last four months of the season. Paniagua racks up strikeouts and ground balls with his 95 mph heater and a sharp breaking slider, and can be nearly untouchable when his control is on. He still seems to have Piniella's confidence and should be first in line for the closer job when Mesa implodes.

Brandon Parker — Throws R — Age 24

YEAR	TEAM	LGE	IP	H	ER	HR	BB	K	ERA	W	L	H/9	HR/9	BB/9	K/9	KWH	PERA
1998	Wisconsn	Mid	118.3	154	104	12	104	104	7.91	3	10	11.71	0.91	7.91	7.91	0.50	7.91
1999	Lancastr	Cal	134.0	182	98	13	81	103	6.58	5	10	12.22	0.87	5.44	6.92	0.54	7.12

Unlike most of the 1998 Timber Rattler rotation, he headed west to the unfriendly environs of the California League, where he improved his command and earned an All-Star selection. Parker will probably be in the rotation at New Haven, but unless he can develop a third pitch to go with his low-90s fastball and vicious slider, he'll begin the young pitcher's death march to the Mariners' bullpen.

Joel Pineiro — Throws R — Age 21

YEAR	TEAM	LGE	IP	H	ER	HR	BB	K	ERA	W	L	H/9	HR/9	BB/9	K/9	KWH	PERA
1997	Everett	Nwn	45.3	68	39	3	22	33	7.74	1	4	13.50	0.60	4.37	6.55	0.54	7.15
1998	Wisconsn	Mid	90.7	114	48	11	37	58	4.76	5	5	11.32	1.09	3.67	5.76	0.60	6.06
1998	Lancastr	Cal	42.3	70	45	7	28	34	9.57	1	4	14.88	1.49	5.95	7.23	0.44	9.99
1999	New Havn	Eas	159.3	215	115	19	57	96	6.50	6	12	12.14	1.07	3.22	5.42	0.56	6.33

He was pushed up to New Haven after logging only 45 unsuccessful innings at Lancaster in 1998. Meche and Anderson skipped Lancaster altogether, which makes me wonder if the Mariners are merely fast-tracking certain players or if the organization doesn't want to subject their best pitching prospects to the California League. One of the younger pitchers in Double-A, Pineiro struggled with the promotion; however, he maintained a good strikeout-to-walk ratio and remains a player to watch.

Robert Ramsay — Throws L — Age 26

YEAR	TEAM	LGE	IP	H	ER	HR	BB	K	ERA	W	L	H/9	HR/9	BB/9	K/9	KWH	PERA
1997	Sarasota	Fla	123.3	176	121	19	89	85	8.83	3	11	12.84	1.39	6.49	6.20	0.34	8.61
1998	Trenton	Eas	153.0	166	85	11	61	125	5.00	8	9	9.76	0.65	3.59	7.35	1.15	4.59
1999	Pawtuckt	Int	112.0	121	79	19	40	68	6.35	4	8	9.72	1.53	3.21	5.46	0.71	5.38
1999	Tacoma	PCL	30.7	23	7	2	16	29	2.05	2	1	6.75	0.59	4.70	8.51	1.71	3.23
1999	Seattle	AL	19.0	21	11	3	9	11	5.21	1	1	9.95	1.42	4.26	5.21	0.48	5.68

(Robert Ramsay *continued*)

The huge southpaw was acquired from Boston for Butch Huskey in the annual Great Northwest Pitching Hunt. He was the Red Sox minor-league pitcher of the year at Trenton in 1998, but was wild in the strike zone at Pawtucket. Under the tutelage of Jim Slaton, he found his command at Tacoma, striking out 37 in 33 innings with a 1.08 ERA. He'll be given a long look in spring training, but will likely open the season in Triple-A. His talents would be wasted in a relief role.

Frankie Rodriguez   Throws R   Age 27

YEAR	TEAM	LGE	IP	H	ER	HR	BB	K	ERA	W	L	H/9	HR/9	BB/9	K/9	KWH	PERA
1997	Minnesot	AL	143.7	142	76	11	61	66	4.76	8	8	8.90	0.69	3.82	4.13	0.38	4.26
1998	Minnesot	AL	71.3	84	52	6	32	63	6.56	3	5	10.60	0.76	4.04	7.95	1.10	5.43
1998	SaltLake	PCL	96.3	97	50	8	42	65	4.67	5	6	9.06	0.75	3.92	6.07	0.77	4.48
1999	SaltLake	PCL	41.0	43	33	7	17	26	7.24	1	4	9.44	1.54	3.73	5.71	0.69	5.49
1999	Seattle	AL	75.3	88	40	10	29	49	4.78	4	4	10.51	1.19	3.46	5.85	0.70	5.62

He signed on with Lou Piniella after being released from his long-term lease in Tom Kelly's doghouse. Talk about out of the frying pan and into the fire. Actually, Piniella seemed to take a shine to him, making him the Mariners' designated retaliator. When not earning suspensions defending the team's honor, Rodriguez pitched pretty well as the long reliever. An ex-shortstop, he's fun to watch play defense.

Aaron Scheffer   Throws R   Age 24

YEAR	TEAM	LGE	IP	H	ER	HR	BB	K	ERA	W	L	H/9	HR/9	BB/9	K/9	KWH	PERA
1997	Lancastr	Cal	89.0	107	60	17	47	75	6.07	4	6	10.82	1.72	4.75	7.58	0.84	6.98
1998	Lancastr	Cal	40.7	57	23	1	15	44	5.09	2	3	12.61	0.22	3.32	9.74	1.69	5.75
1998	Orlando	Sou	31.3	26	8	3	13	27	2.30	2	1	7.47	0.86	3.73	7.76	1.61	3.73
1999	Tacoma	PCL	55.7	51	28	6	26	51	4.53	3	3	8.25	0.97	4.20	8.25	1.47	4.37

Recalled at the peak of Seattle's self-inflicted bullpen massacre, he was allotted all of five innings to prove himself. He really didn't pitch poorly, but at that point Piniella had a ridiculously quick trigger finger, even by his standards. Scheffer has aspirations of being the next Doug Jones, who didn't establish himself in the majors until age 30, so he's way ahead of schedule.

Steve Sinclair   Throws L   Age 28

YEAR	TEAM	LGE	IP	H	ER	HR	BB	K	ERA	W	L	H/9	HR/9	BB/9	K/9	KWH	PERA
1997	Dunedin	Fla	61.3	85	52	5	40	45	7.63	2	5	12.47	0.73	5.87	6.60	0.45	7.34
1998	Syracuse	Int	47.0	44	19	2	25	38	3.64	3	2	8.43	0.38	4.79	7.28	0.98	4.02
1998	Toronto	AL	15.0	12	6	0	6	8	3.60	1	1	7.20	0.00	3.60	4.80	0.66	2.40
1999	Syracuse	Int	38.0	27	12	3	13	26	2.84	3	1	6.39	0.71	3.08	6.16	1.44	2.61
1999	Seattle	AL	14.0	14	7	1	10	15	4.50	1	1	9.00	0.64	6.43	9.64	1.20	5.14

Sinclair is a specialist obtained from the Blue Jays for David Segui. He had quit professional baseball and was playing in a beer league a couple of years ago, so both his travels and talent are half as remarkable as Jeff Zimmerman's. He is going to have to refine his control if he expects to survive a full season of camping near Mt. Piniella.

Sean Spencer   Throws L   Age 25

YEAR	TEAM	LGE	IP	H	ER	HR	BB	K	ERA	W	L	H/9	HR/9	BB/9	K/9	KWH	PERA
1997	Lancastr	Cal	58.3	47	13	4	18	50	2.01	5	1	7.25	0.62	2.78	7.71	2.21	2.93
1998	Orlando	Sou	41.0	38	19	4	18	35	4.17	3	2	8.34	0.88	3.95	7.68	1.34	4.17
1999	Tacoma	PCL	45.0	46	24	6	26	42	4.80	2	3	9.20	1.20	5.20	8.40	1.10	5.60

Piniella's keen pitching acumen enabled him to judge Spencer in a two-game trial in early May, after which he was returned to Tacoma. The team's chaotic search for a situational left-hander continued into the offseason, even though they had some worthy candidates on the roster. Of course, Spencer doesn't come with a multi-million-dollar contract, an artificial hip or a rap sheet for bar fighting, so he can't possibly be the solution.

Denny Stark — Throws R — Age 25

YEAR	TEAM	LGE	IP	H	ER	HR	BB	K	ERA	W	L	H/9	HR/9	BB/9	K/9	KWH	PERA
1997	Wisconsn	Mid	85.0	71	38	4	41	71	4.02	5	4	7.52	0.42	4.34	7.52	1.29	3.49
1998	Lancastr	Cal	19.7	21	15	2	23	14	6.86	1	1	9.61	0.92	10.53	6.41	0.30	7.78
1999	New Havn	Eas	137.0	183	100	15	73	79	6.57	5	10	12.02	0.99	4.80	5.19	0.35	6.83

After missing almost all of 1998 due to reconstructive ankle surgery, it took him more than half the season to harness his slider and change-up. He finished strongly at New Haven, posting a 3.06 ERA in his last eight starts, and was rewarded with a spot in the Mariners' bullpen when the rosters expanded. Piniella believes in baptism by fire, so with Seattle out of the playoff hunt, he ad-libbed and had Stark make his debut when he was sick with the flu. It's the kind of experience you just can't get in other organizations. Stark needs to consolidate last year's gains if he wants to have a career.

Matt Thornton — Throws L — Age 23

YEAR	TEAM	LGE	IP	H	ER	HR	BB	K	ERA	W	L	H/9	HR/9	BB/9	K/9	KWH	PERA
1999	Wisconsn	Mid	26.3	49	22	1	29	24	7.52	1	2	16.75	0.34	9.91	8.20	0.30	11.62

Despite the ongoing chaos at the major-league level, Seattle has done an outstanding job of scouting amateur talent, evidenced by the fact that every #1 draft pick from 1979 through 1996 has reached the majors. 1997 selection Ryan Anderson looks to be a lock, but the streak may end with Thornton, a reliever who is very raw for a college product and plagued by arm woes.

Enmanuel Ulloa — Throws R — Age 21

YEAR	TEAM	LGE	IP	H	ER	HR	BB	K	ERA	W	L	H/9	HR/9	BB/9	K/9	KWH	PERA
1999	Wisconsn	Mid	82.0	110	57	11	42	70	6.26	3	6	12.07	1.21	4.61	7.68	0.79	7.02

He's probably ill-suited to be a Mariner due to his outstanding control, though he didn't come close to matching 1998's obscene strikeout-to-walk ratio of 61-to-1. His fastball doesn't light up the radar guns, but he carves up batters by mixing it with an outstanding curve and change-up. Ulloa moved from the bullpen into the rotation at midseason, an indication that the organization is starting to take him seriously as a prospect.

Todd Williams — Throws R — Age 29

YEAR	TEAM	LGE	IP	H	ER	HR	BB	K	ERA	W	L	H/9	HR/9	BB/9	K/9	KWH	PERA
1997	Chattang	Sou	52.3	44	19	1	31	34	3.27	4	2	7.57	0.17	5.33	5.85	0.63	3.61
1998	Indianap	Int	55.7	60	21	0	26	29	3.40	4	2	9.70	0.00	4.20	4.69	0.40	4.20
1999	Indianap	Int	40.0	43	26	3	14	30	5.85	1	3	9.68	0.68	3.15	6.75	1.12	4.50
1999	Seattle	AL	9.7	11	4	1	6	7	3.72	1	0	10.24	0.93	5.59	6.52	0.55	5.59

Lou Piniella: "That damn bunch in the pen isn't responding to my leadership. I need you to go get me a proven guy."

Woody Woodward: "Come on, Lou . . . I've been dealing for bullpen help since you got here in '93. Of course, it's not your fault none of them pan out. Lately, I've had my eye on a sidearmer at Indianapolis. He has 24 saves already this year, and he had 26 last season. Of course, he's younger than you like: only 28."

Piniella (drooling): "Mmmm . . . saves."

Woodward: "Okay, I'll call Jim Bowden. By the way, did you know that I'm a legend in the Queen City? Yup . . . hit my only home run with the Reds. That was a long time ago, years before Bowie got into that whole androgyny scene."

Piniella: "Mmmm . . . androgyny."

Jordan Zimmerman — Throws L — Age 25

YEAR	TEAM	LGE	IP	H	ER	HR	BB	K	ERA	W	L	H/9	HR/9	BB/9	K/9	KWH	PERA
1997	Everett	Nwn	35.7	47	33	3	29	30	8.33	1	3	11.86	0.76	7.32	7.57	0.49	7.57
1998	Lancastr	Cal	15.0	27	12	3	11	5	7.20	1	1	16.20	1.80	6.60	3.00	0.06	11.40
1999	New Havn	Eas	31.7	31	10	0	22	25	2.84	3	1	8.81	0.00	6.25	7.11	0.68	4.55
1999	Seattle	AL	8.0	14	7	0	3	3	7.88	0	1	15.75	0.00	3.38	3.38	0.16	7.87
1999	Tacoma	PCL	6.0	14	4	1	5	3	6.00	0	1	21.00	1.50	7.50	4.50	0.10	15.00

It's said that bad things happen in threes; with Zimmerman, the Mariners hoped good things might come packaged that way as well. His older brother's success with the Rangers has been well-chronicled, and his father survived being one yank on a power cord away from death. This Zimmerman was promoted from New Haven and couldn't complete the hat trick, but since he is relatively young, throws hard and is left-handed, I think he eventually will.

Support-Neutral Records				SEATTLE MARINERS							Park Effect: +8.2%		
PITCHER	GS	IP	R	SNW	SNL	SNPCT	W	L	RA	APW	SNVA	SNWAR
Paul Abbott	7	43.7	22	2.6	2.1	.557	3	2	4.53	0.40	0.27	0.62
Ken Cloude	6	23.0	29	0.6	3.4	.146	1	2	11.35	-1.37	-1.36	-1.12
Jeff Fassero	24	131.0	113	6.0	12.0	.332	4	13	7.76	-3.07	-2.94	-1.66
Freddy Garcia	33	201.3	96	14.0	8.7	.618	17	8	4.29	2.34	2.58	4.37
John Halama	24	152.0	75	10.0	6.8	.597	9	8	4.44	1.54	1.53	2.88
Butch Henry	4	23.3	13	1.6	1.1	.584	2	0	5.01	0.10	0.27	0.43
Brett Hinchliffe	4	14.3	20	0.4	2.2	.160	0	3	12.56	-1.03	-0.89	-0.70
Gil Meche	15	84.0	45	5.3	4.2	.558	8	4	4.82	0.53	0.55	1.27
Jamie Moyer	32	228.0	108	15.7	8.8	.642	14	8	4.26	2.72	3.35	5.31
Robert Ramsay	3	14.7	10	0.6	1.0	.380	0	1	6.14	-0.10	-0.16	-0.07
Frankie Rodriguez	5	26.0	15	1.9	1.2	.610	2	1	5.19	0.07	0.22	0.58
Mac Suzuki	4	18.7	19	0.6	2.0	.228	0	2	9.16	-0.70	-0.65	-0.50
TOTALS	162	962.7	568	59.5	53.7	.526	60	52	5.31	1.30	2.73	11.41

It's rare for one team to have a pair of rookie starters as good as Freddy Garcia and John Halama. How rare? A non-exhaustive search turned up only one rookie duo better than Garcia/Halama in the post-war era: Hideo Nomo and Ismael Valdes for the Dodgers in 1995. Nomo's total of 4.9 Support-Neutral Wins Above Replacement (SNWAR) bested Garcia's total from last year, while Valdes's 3.7 SNWAR likewise edged out Halama. Before the Dodger pair, though, I had to go back to the terrific debuts of Milkman Jim Turner and Lou Fette for the 1937 Boston Braves to find any competition for last year's Mariner pair. Add in Gil Meche's fine 15 starts, and the Mariners may well have had the best collective performance from rookie starters of any team in history. Lou Piniella has a deserved reputation for mishandling young pitchers, but give him credit for the way his rookies pitched in 1999. . . . If you'd told a Mariner fan the day after Randy Johnson was traded that the team's 1999 rotation would be one of the best in the history of the club, you might have been beaten with a blunt object. This group was probably the third-best in the Mariner's short history. In years for which the Support-Neutral stats are available (1980-85, 1992-present), only the 1993 Johnson/Erik Hanson/Chris Bosio/Dave Fleming staff had better numbers than the 1999 edition: a .549 Support-Neutral Winning Percentage for 1993 vs. .526 last year. In years for which there is no Support-Neutral data, only the 1990 Hanson/Matt Young/Johnson/Brian Holman staff looks better than 1999's.

Pitcher Abuse Points													
PITCHER	AGE	GS	PAP	PAP/S	WKLD	MAX	1-90	91-100	101-110	111-120	121-130	131-140	141+
Paul Abbott	31	7	62	8.9	10.3	128	3	2	1	0	1	0	0
Ken Cloude	24	6	0	0.0	0.0	99	5	1	0	0	0	0	0
Jeff Fassero	36	24	354	14.8	14.8	134	9	3	2	6	3	1	0
Freddy Garcia	22	33	656	19.9	53.0	139	6	4	7	7	6	3	0
John Halama	27	24	172	7.2	13.1	126	7	5	8	2	2	0	0
Butch Henry	30	4	31	7.8	10.3	120	2	0	1	1	0	0	0
Brett Hinchliffe	24	4	0	0.0	0.0	93	3	1	0	0	0	0	0
Gil Meche	20	15	63	4.2	12.6	112	4	1	9	1	0	0	0
Jamie Moyer	36	32	564	17.6	17.6	143	5	3	8	11	4	0	1
Robert Ramsay	25	3	1	0.3	0.7	101	2	0	1	0	0	0	0
Frankie Rodriguez	26	5	8	1.6	3.2	108	2	2	1	0	0	0	0
Mac Suzuki	24	4	12	3.0	7.0	107	1	1	2	0	0	0	0
SEATTLE		162	1923	11.9	20.6	143	50	23	40	28	16	4	1
Ranking (AL)			2	1									

Death. Taxes. Lou Piniella mishandling young pitchers. Actually, Piniella even mishandles his old pitchers: just look at Jeff Fassero, who ranked seventh in the majors with 787 PAPs in 1998 and then pitched hurt in 1999. At least Freddy Garcia, was handled better than Livan Hernandez. . . . Jamie Moyer, who had a much lighter workload in 1998 and relies on the strength-saving technique of changing speeds, had another fine year. . . . It seems like a sick joke that Gil Meche, the youngest pitcher in baseball to make more than five starts last year, should be under Piniella's loving care. Either Meche will get off to a bad start this year, and Piniella will turn him into Ken Cloude, or he'll pitch well, and Piniella will turn him into mincemeat.

Tampa Bay Devil Rays

For nearly a decade, Tampa and St. Petersburg tried to lure a major-league baseball team to vacant Tropicana Field. Since being awarded an expansion franchise, the ownership group, led by Vince Naimoli, has been trying to lure paying customers using time-honored methods such as task forces, pleas to city government and fan ridicule. Last offseason, the Devil Rays hired Mike Veeck as Vice President of Marketing. He masterminded the "Off the Wall" campaign, which featured promotions including Lawyer Appreciation Night and Duct Tape Night. The most innovative plan, however, has been torn out of the pages of the Veeck family scrapbook and carried out by General Manager Chuck LaMar. In the spirit of Eddie Gaedel and Ila Borders, LaMar has acquired uniformed curiosities for the Tampa Bay roster, at the expense of player development at the major-league level.

The players brought in to sell tickets fall into four basic categories: 1) free agent signings, 2) local heroes, 3) record chasers and 4) human-interest stories. In some cases, the categories overlap, all the better from a promotional standpoint.

The strategy was hatched before the fledgling Devil Rays even played their first game. The first wave was costly, as it involved signing free agents to show the locals that management was serious about fielding a competitive team. To stabilize the mound corps, Rolando Arrojo, Wilson Alvarez and Roberto Hernandez were signed, while Wade Boggs, Dave Martinez and Paul Sorrento were added to the offense—giving it a mild, aged flavor. Boggs and Martinez are local products, and they were soon joined by Tampa's own Fred McGriff, generously donated by the Braves.

Altogether, the plan worked about as well as could have been expected, with the pitching better and the offense worse than projected. It was during 1998's season-long offensive malaise that the first signs of an unwillingness to play youngsters for fear of decreasing the gate became apparent. Bubba Trammell and Scott McClain were nifty in-house options to improve production at DH and third base,

but while Trammell forced his way into a couple hundred plate appearances, McClain barely got a sniff. The Devil Rays finished '98 at an expansion-like 63-99, but drew more than 2.5 million fans to their suburban circus tent, enabling them to rank seventh in the AL in attendance despite having the league's worst record. Nevertheless, the turnout didn't meet ownership's expectations.

Naimoli wasn't going to throw good money after bad, and since dipping into the free-agent trough hadn't produced the desired results, he didn't repeat the exercise in 1999. Jose Canseco was signed to an incentive-laden contract, but with Sorrento and Trammell already on the roster, Canseco's presence purely for the seductive value of potential home-run milestones. With no prospects introduced into the '99 lineup, patrons were essentially asked to buy tickets to a horror show they had already seen.

The Devil Rays recognized the problem and focused on selling sizzle instead of steak. The centerpieces were Veeck's offbeat promotions, Canseco swinging from his heels and Boggs' protracted limp towards 3,000 hits. However, the locals didn't bite, and in spite of a surprising 21-19 record at the quarter pole, attendance at The Trop plummeted.

Desperate times call for desperate measures, so LaMar sprang into action when Boggs went on the disabled list with a strained hamstring. Needing to replace his top gate attraction, he again passed over McClain, instead recalling Florida native and three-year rehabilitation project Herb Perry. A study in perseverance, Perry was the first obvious human-interest story to be added to the roster, though certainly not the most blatant.

That honor falls to former high-school biology teacher Jim Morris, who hadn't pitched professionally in a decade and who had thrown only 28 minor-league innings prior to donning the Devil Ray knits in September. Hauling Julio Franco's carcass in from Mexico for the Triple-A playoffs and a late-season cameo would be considered equally overt, except that the only engaging thing about Franco is that nobody seems to

Devil Rays Prospectus

1999 record: 69-93; Fifth place, AL East

Pythagorean W/L: 69-93

Runs scored: 772 (11th in AL)

Runs allowed: 913 (13th in AL)

Team EQA: .249 (11th in AL)

1999 team age: 29.7 (6th-oldest in AL)

1999 park: Tropicana Field; neutral park, increased run scoring by less than 1%.

1999: Their core of Boggs, McGriff and Canseco was dominant. In 1988.

2000: Offseason moves indicate a lack of recognition; they need to start over.

know his real age. None of these human-interest stories earned their way onto the Tampa Bay roster by being good baseball players, and while only Perry saw significant playing time, each was an opportunity wasted by a last-place team going nowhere. Young prospects who deserved a chance to show what they could do and gain valuable experience at the big-league level were kept at bay.

As big a mistake as it was to add these sideshows to the squad, the decision not to trade some of them away was equally as bad. By the time the trading deadline arrived on July 31, the Devil Rays had reverted to form and were anchored in the basement of the AL East with a 43-61 record. While some of the highly-paid players on the wrong side of 30 were enjoying seasons they'll never see again, Tampa Bay failed to make a single deal that could have helped set the team up for the future while getting rid of some unnecessary salary.

The most glaring example was the 35-year-old McGriff, having his best season since 1994. Steve Cox was doing a fine John Olerud imitation at Durham, showing that he was fully ready to take the final step on his climb, but not only was the Crime Dog retained, in September he was given a no-trade contract extension, putting Cox's promising career on hold. Other clubs certainly had an interest in John Flaherty, Dave Martinez and Roberto Hernandez. Dealing Flaherty would have finally given Tom Wilson the chance he so richly deserves, while moving Martinez would have guaranteed full-time duty for Trammell, one of the team's few offensive weapons. As for Hernandez, well, a closer on a last-place team is as valuable as stock in Braniff Air. The prospect he might have fetched would have had much more long-term value.

Why did an organization that had so adamantly voiced its plans to build through its farm system not give prospects who were ready an opportunity to play? After all, none of the veteran roadblocks will even be around when the first good Devil Ray team takes the field. Apparently, the powers that be didn't want to send their fans any signals that could be misinterpreted as not wanting to be competitive—especially with their handsome siblings, the Arizona Diamondbacks, on their way to a division title.

The organization's decisions were uniformly terrible in terms of putting the best team on the field. But how effective were they at gaining and retaining fans? Not very. 1999 attendance at Tropicana Field dropped more than 30% from 1998. Is that a steep decline compared to other recent second-year expansion teams? The answer is in Table 1.

Of the five other clubs, only the 1978 Seattle Mariners suffered a bigger tumble at the turnstiles. The obvious common thread between those Mariners and last year's Rays is that both played in high-capacity tombs. But ballpark ambiance aside, a sizable drop in attendance should be expected in a team's second year, as the euphoria of a new entertainment source is soon replaced by the realization that you're paying to watch crummy baseball. As Seattle went on to demonstrate, until ownership assembles a winning team, no amount of promotion can produce fundamental change in the interest level of the public.

So the question becomes how to go about fielding a winning team that will enable the Devil Rays to make a profit—or, depending on who is doing the bookkeeping, minimize their losses.

The answer is to actually follow their own five-year plan of building from within, which must include giving youngsters a genuine opportunity to play when ready. Though the winning part of the equation may take a few years, the financial benefits can be felt immediately. For a prime example of this, Naimoli and LaMar need look no further than the Kansas City Royals. The Royals committed to a youth movement that played fresh, exciting baseball, and increased their attendance while slashing the payroll by almost 20%. Although they finished with the league's worst record, their future looks brighter and they actually made a profit.

Where around the diamond can Tampa Bay plug in prospects to get the process underway? The best two options were at first base and catcher. Unfortunately, the ill-considered contracts given to McGriff and Flaherty at the end of last season means that Cox and Wilson won't inherit those spots. While Wilson has escaped to the Yankee organization, Manager Larry Rothschild has said that Cox will be tried in

Table 1

Team	Year	Attendance	W/L	Year	Attendance	Attn Diff	W/L	W/L Diff
Sea.	1977	1,338,511	64-98	1978	877,440	-34.4%	56-104	-7
Tor.	1977	1,701,052	54-107	1978	1,562,585	-8.1%	59-102	+5
Col.	1993	4,483,350	67-95	1994	4,663,200*	+4.0%	73-89*	+6
Fla.	1993	3,064,847	64-98	1994	2,659,912*	-13.2%	72-90*	+8
Ari.	1998	3,602,856	65-97	1999	3,015,948	-16.3%	100-62	+35
T.B.	1998	2,506,023	63-99	1999	1,749,657	-30.2%	69-93	+6

* Strike year. Figures projected
to a 162-game season.

left field. Given the same chance that Sorrento got, Cox could very well lay claim to the job. In a best-case scenario, Trammell slides over to right field, a move that will require Rothschild to overcome his obsession with speed in the outfield. That scenario would also have McClain getting regular playing time at third base until Aubrey Huff is ready in 2001.

That scenario is dead. Pauly Shore dead. "Mambo No. 5" dead. At December's winter meetings, the Rays picked up about $50 million worth of slow right-handed hitters with fair to medium power and on-base issues. Greg Vaughn will be the new left fielder, at $34 million over four years. Tampa also traded nominal ace Rolando Arrojo to the Rockies for nominal power-hitter Vinny Castilla. Naimoli has all but double-dared the Tampa/St. Petersburg area to support the team, claiming that he's fulfilled his end of the bargain by spending money on the roster while holding ticket prices steady.

The problem is that the team isn't any better. It's more expensive, and more famous. It will even hit more home runs. But the lineup isn't appreciably improved over the 1999 team, and the rotation is one arm shorter. Like the best-case scenario, the Devil Rays' chances in 2000 are dead.

In contrast to that silliness, the team has been eager to promote young hurlers, almost to the point of rushing them. Obviously, as an ex-pitching coach, Rothschild feels comfortable developing pitching prospects. After just 18 minor-league starts, Ryan Rupe joined the staff last year and has had some success, while Dan Wheeler will head to spring training penciled into the rotation despite only a year of experience above low-A ball. A notch or two below Rupe and Wheeler is a cadre of hard throwers, any of whom could find themselves up with the parent club if everything comes together for a few months. This fact is both a credit to and an indictment of the organization.

Consistent with the organizational plan, Tampa Bay has invested heavily in scouting and player development. LaMar employs the philosophy used by the Braves during his time in Atlanta, focusing the team's efforts on drafting and signing high-school players who have high upsides but who take longer to develop than collegians. It's a risky strategy and has yet to yield any major-league products. Outfielders Paul Wilder and Josh Pressley, the club's top picks in '96 and '98, have been stiffs. Second-rounders Kenny Kelly and Doug Johnson show tremendous athleticism, but have slowed their development by playing college football. Josh Hamilton, the #1 pick in the '99 draft, won't be ready for about three years but looks like a future stud.

Up until December 13, the Devil Rays' biggest capital venture had been in the young-arms market, including loophole free-agents Matt White and Bobby Seay, and '97 first-round selection Jason Standridge. Only Standridge has made consistent progress; White and Seay have to be considered disappointments. All three could still develop into mainstays of the Tampa Bay pitching staff in the new millennium, but as of yet none has conquered even Orlando. It's premature to issue a final verdict about LaMar's developmental approach, but there are certainly no stone-cold locks among the prep selections.

If the raw talent in Tampa Bay's farm system develops, the team's long-term outlook is encouraging. That's a big "if." Right now, the lengthy contracts given to fading mediocrities are strangling the franchise, and Naimoli's raised expectations are going to lead to fireworks when the team struggles in 2000. Only after the commitments to old people end, and some of the youngsters arrive on the scene, will the Devil Rays have a chance to build a real contender.

HITTERS (Averages: BA: .270 / OBP: .340 / SLG: .430 / EQA: .260)

Wade Boggs   3B   Bats L   Age 42

YEAR	TEAM	LGE	AB	H	DB	TP	HR	BB/SO	R	RBI	SB	CS	OUT	BA	OBP	SLG	EQA	EQR	DEFENSE	
1997	NY Yanks	AL	355	108	26	1	4	46/37	56	28	0	1	248	.304	.384	.417	.275	49	64-3B 110	
1998	TampaBay	AL	431	119	21	4	7	45/53	48	49	3	2	314	.276	.345	.392	.252	50	72-3B 97	
1999	TampaBay	AL	289	86	14	1	2	34/23	37	27	1	0	203	.298	.372	.374	.260	35	65-3B 88	

With a kiss of home plate, the self-indulgent chase ended, taking with it a potential attendance windfall. No doubt Naimoli was hoping for a well-timed 0-for-24, but darned if Boggs didn't get the three hits needed for 3,000 in the second game of the home-stand. He retired in November, a certain Hall of Famer and the rare high-average hitter who managed to be underrated.

Miguel Cairo   2B   Bats R   Age 26

YEAR	TEAM	LGE	AB	H	DB	TP	HR	BB/SO	R	RBI	SB	CS	OUT	BA	OBP	SLG	EQA	EQR	DEFENSE	
1997	Iowa	AA	576	158	35	4	4	20/55	75	44	33	12	429	.274	.306	.370	.233	56	106-2B 104	28-SS 98
1998	TampaBay	AL	512	135	25	5	5	22/43	45	43	16	8	385	.264	.302	.361	.226	46	141-2B 99	
1999	TampaBay	AL	463	134	14	5	3	18/46	56	33	22	7	336	.289	.326	.361	.239	47	112-2B 105	
2000	TampaBay	AL	478	138	24	4	3	26/46	72	53	22	7	347	.289	.325	.374	.242	50		

(Miguel Cairo *continued*)

An undisciplined slap-hitter, Cairo is a novelty because he uses a split grip at the plate. His greatest assets are his speed and range, both of which were limited last year by hamstring injuries in both legs. Deceived by his batting average, the Devil Rays consider him a solution, not a problem. Rumors persist that he will be traded to the Angels.

Jose Canseco — DH — Bats R — Age 35

YEAR	TEAM	LGE	AB	H	DB	TP	HR	BB/SO	R	RBI	SB	CS	OUT	BA	OBP	SLG	EQA	EQR	DEFENSE
1997	Oakland	AL	386	90	17	0	24	49/117	54	72	8	2	298	.233	.325	.464	.264	53	31-OF 98
1998	Toronto	AL	582	137	24	0	46	62/155	91	102	25	17	462	.235	.316	.514	.267	85	63-OF 92
1999	TampaBay	AL	426	118	17	1	33	53/136	68	88	3	0	308	.277	.366	.554	.299	75	
2000	TampaBay	AL	465	111	14	0	34	65/137	74	92	7	4	358	.239	.332	.488	.270	68	

He was leading the league in home runs and outrageous quotes when he had surgery for a herniated disc in his back at the All-Star break. When he returned, his power didn't: he hit only three bombs in 138 plate appearances the rest of the way. Canseco has never found a weight room he didn't like, so I expect him to be back at full strength this season. He plans on playing until he reaches 500 home runs, and the Rays are more than happy to oblige. He's a nice diversion from the on-field drudgery and has agreed to have the manta immortalized in bronze if the BBWAA overlooks his inadequacies and rubber-stamps him a Hall of Famer.

Dustin Carr — 2B — Bats R — Age 25

YEAR	TEAM	LGE	AB	H	DB	TP	HR	BB/SO	R	RBI	SB	CS	OUT	BA	OBP	SLG	EQA	EQR	DEFENSE
1997	HudsnVal	NYP	293	68	11	1	5	31/49	33	34	1	1	226	.232	.308	.328	.218	25	71-2B 77
1998	St Pete	Fla	526	112	22	3	5	52/104	62	38	4	2	416	.213	.293	.295	.202	38	135-2B 85
1999	Orlando	Sou	466	119	19	3	4	52/70	57	47	3	1	348	.255	.334	.335	.233	46	125-2B 103
2000	TampaBay	AL	477	116	17	1	7	60/80	62	52	3	1	362	.243	.328	.327	.227	45	

A 22nd-round find by legendary scout "Gas Pipe" Gassaway, he is forcing the organization to take notice by steadily improving as he moves through the system. Carr won't wow anybody with pure athleticism, but he's steady with the glove and finds a way to get on base. He turns 25 in June, so the development trend needs to continue at Durham this year. He played well in the Arizona Fall League.

Danny Clyburn — OF — Bats R — Age 26

YEAR	TEAM	LGE	AB	H	DB	TP	HR	BB/SO	R	RBI	SB	CS	OUT	BA	OBP	SLG	EQA	EQR	DEFENSE
1997	Rochestr	Int	523	150	32	4	19	43/104	79	67	10	3	376	.287	.350	.472	.275	75	133-OF 92
1998	Rochestr	Int	325	87	18	1	12	27/75	48	46	7	4	242	.268	.331	.440	.258	41	71-OF 94
1999	Durham	Int	303	64	11	1	6	14/81	29	25	1	0	239	.211	.258	.314	.188	18	68-OF 90
1999	TampaBay	AL	81	16	3	0	3	6/21	7	5	0	0	65	.198	.261	.346	.201	6	
2000	TampaBay	AL	350	86	16	1	12	29/85	44	47	5	2	266	.246	.303	.400	.236	36	

Results like this won't encourage LaMar to make more trades. While Jason Johnson was in Camden Yards showing signs of becoming a fair starting pitcher, Clyburn spent the year in Durham looking like the next Wes Chamberlain. He threw away the offensive gains he had made at the plate the two previous years by constantly burying himself in the count, and his defense in left field regressed from barely adequate to frightful. At this point his career could head in any direction, only one of which is up.

Steve Cox — 1B — Bats L — Age 25

YEAR	TEAM	LGE	AB	H	DB	TP	HR	BB/SO	R	RBI	SB	CS	OUT	BA	OBP	SLG	EQA	EQR	DEFENSE
1997	Edmonton	PCL	450	102	23	1	12	73/92	59	65	1	2	350	.227	.337	.362	.242	50	126-1B 87
1998	Durham	Int	433	105	23	2	11	47/102	56	58	2	3	331	.242	.319	.381	.237	45	114-1B 92
1999	Durham	Int	531	166	43	3	21	56/77	87	102	2	2	367	.313	.383	.524	.298	89	123-1B 94
2000	TampaBay	AL	551	156	38	2	22	71/95	97	105	1	2	397	.283	.365	.479	.282	84	

He hit the weights and improved his agility to try and steer clear of the injuries that have nagged him his entire career. Call it an unqualified success. He was healthy all year, and the added strength sent his power numbers skyrocketing, leading to his being named International League Player of the Year. Despite the honors, LaMar seems more enamored of prospects the organization has drafted and didn't feel Cox could outperform an aging Crime Dog, inking McGriff to a two-year extension. He has a history of struggling when first exposed to a new level, and given the Rays' track record of impatience with players such as Bubba Trammell and Terrell Lowery, I don't like his chances. Cox could be trade bait, as he is out of minor-league options.

Mike DiFelice   C   Bats R   Age 31

YEAR	TEAM	LGE	AB	H	DB	TP	HR	BB/SO	R	RBI	SB	CS	OUT	BA	OBP	SLG	EQA	EQR	DEFENSE
1997	St Louis	NL	263	64	12	1	4	19/60	17	30	1	1	200	.243	.302	.342	.218	22	
1998	TampaBay	AL	247	56	11	3	3	14/55	16	22	0	0	191	.227	.271	.332	.200	17	76-C 104
1999	TampaBay	AL	178	54	8	0	7	6/23	19	26	0	0	124	.303	.337	.466	.267	23	50-C 103
2000	TampaBay	AL	194	52	11	1	5	14/34	25	28	0	0	142	.268	.317	.412	.244	21	

Behold the miraculous powers of a small sample size. His statistical illusion and Flaherty's hollow numbers had the local media beating its chest about how the Devil Rays had the second-most productive catching situation in the league. It was an ugly public spectacle that won't be repeated this year.

John Flaherty   C   Bats R   Age 32

YEAR	TEAM	LGE	AB	H	DB	TP	HR	BB/SO	R	RBI	SB	CS	OUT	BA	OBP	SLG	EQA	EQR	DEFENSE
1997	San Dieg	NL	447	127	24	1	10	33/61	40	48	3	4	324	.284	.333	.409	.249	50	
1998	TampaBay	AL	303	61	8	0	4	21/45	19	23	0	5	247	.201	.255	.267	.164	13	86-C 105
1999	TampaBay	AL	444	122	15	0	15	14/64	48	67	0	2	324	.275	.306	.410	.237	44	112-C 107
2000	TampaBay	AL	346	93	7	0	10	23/50	36	47	0	2	255	.269	.314	.376	.231	33	

Pretzel logic, Devil Ray style. They were so disillusioned with Flaherty after 1998 that they cut his salary by the maximum 20%. His increased production last year was above his established norms, yet his EqA was still in the bottom third of catchers. Thanks to the hypnotic power of batting average and an overemphasis on defense, Tampa Bay gave him a new three-year, $9-million contract. That would be asinine even if he wasn't already 32 years old.

Julio Franco   1B/DH   Bats R   Age 41

YEAR	TEAM	LGE	AB	H	DB	TP	HR	BB/SO	R	RBI	SB	CS	OUT	BA	OBP	SLG	EQA	EQR	DEFENSE
1997	Clevelnd	AL	290	86	14	1	3	36/72	46	25	8	5	209	.297	.374	.383	.263	37	28-2B 114
1997	Milwauke	AL	141	35	3	0	4	30/39	21	19	7	1	107	.248	.384	.355	.270	20	
1998	CHB	JpP	492	126	28	2	14	53/130	69	66	5	3	369	.256	.333	.407	.251	58	
2000	TampaBay	AL	134	32	3	0	3	19/35	18	16	1	0	102	.239	.333	.328	.232	13	

I don't give a whit if he led the Mexican League with a .423 average and .656 slugging percentage playing for the Devil Rays' affiliate in Mexico City last year. Who was holding the crack pipe when they decided to sign him in the first place? Franco plans to play as long as he is better than at least one other player, so his retirement should coincide with Brian L. Hunter's.

Tony Graffanino   2B/SS   Bats R   Age 28

YEAR	TEAM	LGE	AB	H	DB	TP	HR	BB/SO	R	RBI	SB	CS	OUT	BA	OBP	SLG	EQA	EQR	DEFENSE
1997	Atlanta	NL	189	49	9	1	9	25/46	33	21	5	4	144	.259	.349	.460	.268	27	50-2B 116
1998	Atlanta	NL	292	64	17	1	5	23/66	33	23	1	4	232	.219	.281	.336	.204	22	72-2B 110
1999	Durham	Int	344	92	21	5	6	29/51	48	43	9	6	258	.267	.329	.410	.249	40	84-2B 97
1999	TampaBay	AL	129	40	9	4	2	7/22	18	18	3	2	91	.310	.350	.488	.276	18	
2000	TampaBay	AL	338	89	17	4	9	34/59	51	49	8	7	256	.263	.331	.417	.250	40	

He hooked on with Tampa Bay after being released by the Braves. Graffanino is a solid defender, has a decent eye at the plate and good gap power for a middle infielder. Recalled from Triple-A at the end of July, he finished with the fourth-highest EqA on the team. Rothschild took notice and is talking about Graffanino as being more than a backup middle infielder, possibly giving him extensive playing time at shortstop. The trade of Aaron Ledesma helps him considerably.

Jose Guillen   RF   Bats R   Age 24

YEAR	TEAM	LGE	AB	H	DB	TP	HR	BB/SO	R	RBI	SB	CS	OUT	BA	OBP	SLG	EQA	EQR	DEFENSE
1997	Pittsbrg	NL	501	133	20	5	15	16/87	58	70	1	2	370	.265	.299	.415	.237	50	135-OF 94
1998	Pittsbrg	NL	578	157	38	2	16	20/97	61	86	3	6	427	.272	.304	.427	.240	60	144-OF 99
1999	Pittsbrg	NL	121	32	4	0	2	8/21	17	19	1	0	89	.264	.310	.347	.225	11	30-RF 106
1999	Nashvill	PCL	130	40	6	0	5	7/21	22	19	0	1	91	.308	.351	.469	.271	17	26-OF 105
1999	TampaBay	AL	168	41	6	0	3	8/36	21	13	0	0	127	.244	.306	.333	.218	14	46-RF 95
2000	TampaBay	AL	509	148	22	1	20	31/91	68	88	1	2	363	.291	.331	.456	.261	63	

(Jose Guillen *continued*)

Tampa Bay fans cackled with glee over how LaMar "fleeced" Cam Bonifay and picked up a gifted outfielder for Joe Oliver. However, the Pirates will probably laugh last, as the key component of the deal was not Oliver, but low-A backstop Humberto Cota, who projects as a dynamite player.

Guillen's reputation as a future star is based on two things. The first is his cannon arm, which is indeed impressive (however, even the best outfield arm is worth less than 10 runs over the course of a season). The second is the rare four-level jump to the majors he made for the 1997 season. While he survived the promotion, it appears to have stunted his development. Guillen's biggest problem is that he will swing at anything chucked in the general direction of home plate. He has also put on excess weight, costing him speed and prompting the Pirates to question his work ethic. Right now, it doesn't look like he'll develop into a better player than Rich Butler.

Josh Hamilton — OF — Bats L — Age 19

YEAR	TEAM	LGE	AB	H	DB	TP	HR	BB/SO	R	RBI	SB	CS	OUT	BA	OBP	SLG	EQA	EQR	DEFENSE
1999	Princetn	App	233	59	16	2	6	6/46	25	26	4	1	175	.253	.272	.416	.228	22	55-OF 92
1999	HudsnVal	NYP	73	15	3	0	0	0/14	6	6	0	0	58	.205	.211	.247	.120	1	
2000	TampaBay	AL	146	37	9	1	4	4/69	16	18	1	0	109	.253	.273	.411	.225	13	

The #1 pick in the nation last year, he signed quickly and laid waste to the Appalachian League. Promoted to Hudson Valley, Hamilton struggled, but righted himself in the playoffs and helped lead the Renegades to the New York-Penn League title. He has a full tool belt but needs to tighten his strike zone to continue his rapid ascent up the ladder. Exactly the type of impact player the Devil Rays must have if they are to be taken seriously.

Paul Hoover — C — Bats R — Age 24

YEAR	TEAM	LGE	AB	H	DB	TP	HR	BB/SO	R	RBI	SB	CS	OUT	BA	OBP	SLG	EQA	EQR	DEFENSE
1997	Princetn	App	251	58	15	2	2	12/40	31	21	2	1	194	.231	.274	.331	.202	18	64-SS 97
1998	HudsnVal	NYP	280	68	18	1	4	30/47	33	28	9	2	214	.243	.329	.357	.241	30	52-C 96
1998	Charl-SC	SAL	128	30	10	1	2	18/30	18	14	1	0	98	.234	.343	.375	.250	15	23-C 84
1999	St Pete	Fla	413	93	13	3	8	42/97	45	40	9	3	323	.225	.310	.329	.223	38	88-C 91
2000	TampaBay	AL	438	111	18	2	10	48/94	66	54	13	4	331	.253	.327	.372	.242	48	

Leave it to the Devil Rays to find a catcher who can run. Actually, Hoover has emerged as a good prospect, and his rapid progress made LaMar feel comfortable enough to trade Cota. Previously a shortstop, he is already adequate defensively and getting better. If he hits Double-A pitching in his first attempt this year, his future looks promising.

Aubrey Huff — 3B — Bats L — Age 23

YEAR	TEAM	LGE	AB	H	DB	TP	HR	BB/SO	R	RBI	SB	CS	OUT	BA	OBP	SLG	EQA	EQR	DEFENSE
1998	Charl-SC	SAL	270	73	16	1	11	19/40	29	41	1	0	197	.270	.318	.459	.258	33	69-3B 100
1999	Orlando	Sou	494	137	36	2	20	51/79	71	63	1	2	359	.277	.348	.480	.274	71	134-3B 111
2000	TampaBay	AL	317	90	21	1	16	34/57	54	64	1	1	228	.284	.353	.508	.283	49	

Last year, after his outstanding half-season debut with Charleston, we said to check back to see if it was for real. It was. Aggressively pushed up two levels to Double-A, Huff improved his walk rate while maintaining his 900 OPS against much tougher competition. According to Clay Davenport's rating system, which combines hitting, fielding and age, Huff was the best player in the Southern League. His defense at the hot corner is said to be inconsistent, but you wouldn't guess it from his numbers. His poor Arizona Fall League stint and the Castilla pickup will mean Huff will spend 2000 at Triple-A.

Kenny Kelly — OF — Bats R — Age 21

YEAR	TEAM	LGE	AB	H	DB	TP	HR	BB/SO	R	RBI	SB	CS	OUT	BA	OBP	SLG	EQA	EQR	DEFENSE
1998	Charl-SC	SAL	222	56	6	4	3	15/52	31	14	7	2	168	.252	.307	.356	.229	21	54-OF 110
1999	St Pete	Fla	207	52	12	3	3	15/50	30	17	7	3	157	.251	.309	.382	.236	21	51-OF 106
2000	TampaBay	AL	165	42	7	3	3	13/44	24	20	6	2	125	.255	.309	.388	.238	17	

Tampa Bay spent a second-round pick on Kelly in 1997 and since then has been sharing him with the University of Miami, where he is the starting quarterback. Even though his baseball seasons have been abbreviated due to football commitments, he has successfully advanced a level in each of his three years, while displaying tremendous speed and power. Kelly has better baseball skills than most similar athletes do; all he lacks is plate discipline and polish. While I suspect that he will eventually opt for baseball, by then it may be too late for him to reach his full potential. He's missed a lot of development time.

David Lamb — SS/2B — Bats B — Age 25

YEAR	TEAM	LGE	AB	H	DB	TP	HR	BB/SO	R	RBI	SB	CS	OUT	BA	OBP	SLG	EQA	EQR	DEFENSE	
1997	Frederck	Car	254	61	18	1	2	18/33	24	32	1	1	194	.240	.301	.343	.218	22	59-2B 94	
1997	Bowie	Eas	273	84	20	2	3	26/36	38	32	0	0	189	.308	.374	.429	.274	37	45-SS 97	19-3B 79
1998	Bowie	Eas	242	66	8	1	2	23/33	25	22	1	2	178	.273	.338	.339	.233	23	64-SS 98	
1998	Rochestr	Int	179	51	5	1	1	14/25	21	14	1	4	132	.285	.346	.341	.232	17	38-SS 92	
1999	TampaBay	AL	124	28	5	1	1	8/18	16	12	0	1	97	.226	.273	.306	.189	8	25-SS 91	
2000	TampaBay	AL	254	68	14	1	2	23/35	33	29	1	2	188	.268	.329	.354	.232	24		

Lamb was added to the LaMar collection of lightweight Hummel diamond figurines via the Rule 5 draft. Like the others, it's best if he doesn't see much playing time. He'll probably be shipped to Durham and used every day, but don't fret if he gets broken: his model is not all that valuable and very replaceable.

Aaron Ledesma — IF — Bats R — Age 29

YEAR	TEAM	LGE	AB	H	DB	TP	HR	BB/SO	R	RBI	SB	CS	OUT	BA	OBP	SLG	EQA	EQR	DEFENSE
1997	Rochestr	Int	327	93	21	1	2	27/51	30	34	7	2	236	.284	.344	.373	.249	36	81-SS 94
1997	Baltimor	AL	88	32	5	1	2	12/9	23	11	1	0	56	.364	.446	.511	.327	17	14-2B 95
1998	TampaBay	AL	297	94	13	3	1	8/50	27	28	8	7	210	.316	.337	.391	.244	31	51-SS 100
1999	TampaBay	AL	293	77	11	0	1	11/35	28	29	1	1	217	.263	.296	.311	.204	20	48-SS 91
2000	Colorado	NL	306	96	15	1	1	20/41	43	38	5	3	213	.314	.356	.379	.229	27	

Ledesma dislocated his thumb at the end of spring training, and the effects of the injury seemed to linger, dragging down his batting average. Having won the Coors Lottery, he'll battle Terry Shumpert for the fifth infielder job while hoping Mike Lansing's back continues to hurt. His versatility makes him a very handy player to have on the roster.

Terrell Lowery — CF — Bats R — Age 29

YEAR	TEAM	LGE	AB	H	DB	TP	HR	BB/SO	R	RBI	SB	CS	OUT	BA	OBP	SLG	EQA	EQR	DEFENSE
1997	Iowa	AA	396	105	26	3	12	55/109	57	58	6	5	296	.265	.356	.437	.267	55	105-OF 105
1998	Iowa	PCL	245	61	13	1	8	21/69	30	35	3	1	185	.249	.312	.408	.243	27	62-OF 113
1999	Durham	Int	274	78	16	4	11	35/68	50	41	6	4	200	.285	.367	.493	.284	43	70-OF 94
1999	TampaBay	AL	184	47	14	1	2	17/53	23	16	0	2	139	.255	.322	.375	.234	18	31-CF 89
2000	TampaBay	AL	368	95	21	2	13	50/98	60	60	4	4	277	.258	.347	.432	.262	49	

Called up at the All-Star break when Rothschild finally had his fill of Winn's weak waves, Lowery put up a couple of solid months before fading in September. He won't satisfy the Rays' lust for stolen bases, but he's every bit the player Dave Martinez is. Unbelievably, it seems that Rothschild was dissatisfied with Lowery's defense on carpet, and he was released. A smarter team will snag him.

Dave Martinez — OF — Bats L — Age 35

YEAR	TEAM	LGE	AB	H	DB	TP	HR	BB/SO	R	RBI	SB	CS	OUT	BA	OBP	SLG	EQA	EQR	DEFENSE	
1997	ChiSox	AL	505	149	16	7	12	52/66	77	55	12	6	362	.295	.365	.426	.270	68	93-OF 97	38-1B 95
1998	TampaBay	AL	307	77	7	0	4	33/51	28	19	7	7	237	.251	.328	.313	.221	27	81-OF 101	
1999	TampaBay	AL	510	143	25	5	5	54/76	72	60	13	6	373	.280	.355	.378	.255	61	87-RF 97	43-CF 92
2000	TampaBay	AL	415	104	15	3	5	49/65	57	45	8	6	317	.251	.330	.337	.230	40		

After an injury-plagued 1998, he returned to his old self: a patient line-drive hitter who isn't quite good enough to play every day. Other clubs have expressed interest in Martinez for his versatility and experience, and the Rays would be wise to move him before it becomes obvious that Father Time is starting to inhabit his uniform.

Scott McClain — 3B — Bats R — Age 28

YEAR	TEAM	LGE	AB	H	DB	TP	HR	BB/SO	R	RBI	SB	CS	OUT	BA	OBP	SLG	EQA	EQR	DEFENSE	
1997	Norfolk	Int	434	106	25	2	16	50/99	56	50	1	2	330	.244	.325	.422	.250	52	92-3B 96	20-SS 100
1998	Durham	Int	474	121	26	0	26	52/126	69	82	3	1	354	.255	.331	.475	.267	65	123-3B 103	
1999	Durham	Int	535	117	27	1	21	58/171	80	77	2	1	419	.219	.298	.391	.232	54	82-3B 91	
2000	Colorado	NL	466	125	21	0	26	63/135	75	91	3	1	342	.268	.355	.481	.255	56		

(Scott McClain *continued*)

He should have broken camp with the Devil Rays, but Wade Boggs sells more tickets. Worse yet, even after the tedious 3K crawl was over, McClain wasn't called up, and it seems that his inability to hit for average has reduced him to a Triple-A lifer. While he compensates by drawing lots of walks, a respectable OBP just doesn't have the sexy allure of a high batting average. In a sign of desperation, he is trying his hand at catching. The Castilla pickup buries him.

Quinton McCracken   OF   Bats B   Age 30

YEAR	TEAM	LGE	AB	H	DB	TP	HR	BB/SO	R	RBI	SB	CS	OUT	BA	OBP	SLG	EQA	EQR	DEFENSE
1997	Colorado	NL	322	89	10	1	3	41/61	61	33	22	11	243	.276	.360	.342	.249	38	109-OF 92
1998	TampaBay	AL	609	175	35	7	7	39/105	71	55	17	10	444	.287	.333	.402	.249	69	147-OF 109
1999	TampaBay	AL	147	35	6	1	1	13/23	18	16	6	5	117	.238	.304	.313	.211	12	
2000	*TampaBay*	*AL*	*283*	*76*	*15*	*3*	*3*	*29/48*	*44*	*34*	*9*	*6*	*213*	*.269*	*.337*	*.375*	*.243*	*31*	

He missed the last four months of the campaign with a torn right ACL after getting tangled up with an outfield wall. Some people in the baseball media said his loss devastated the Devil Rays' offense. They're the ones who still can't fathom the Orioles' "collapse." McCracken is expected to be healthy in 2000, but with Greg Vaughn and Gerald Williams on the team, there's no job waiting for him.

Fred McGriff   1B   Bats L   Age 36

YEAR	TEAM	LGE	AB	H	DB	TP	HR	BB/SO	R	RBI	SB	CS	OUT	BA	OBP	SLG	EQA	EQR	DEFENSE
1997	Atlanta	NL	572	161	25	1	24	67/111	78	99	4	0	411	.281	.361	.455	.276	82	137-1B 90
1998	TampaBay	AL	559	157	25	0	21	76/115	68	78	6	2	404	.281	.369	.438	.275	80	135-1B 90
1999	TampaBay	AL	523	161	26	1	32	79/107	68	97	1	0	362	.308	.400	.545	.311	98	120-1B 103
2000	*TampaBay*	*AL*	*437*	*118*	*17*	*0*	*21*	*74/88*	*79*	*84*	*1*	*0*	*319*	*.270*	*.376*	*.453*	*.282*	*67*	

The rumble felt in Tampa in early September was Branch Rickey turning in his grave after McGriff's contract was extended through 2001. Most great players have a season in the twilight of their career when the stars are in alignment and the old magic returns. McGriff's was last year. A Tampa native, he was re-signed partly because the Rays think he attracts fans. Unless he hails from a family of practicing polygamists, I don't think that's accurate.

Herb Perry   3B/1B   Bats R   Age 30

YEAR	TEAM	LGE	AB	H	DB	TP	HR	BB/SO	R	RBI	SB	CS	OUT	BA	OBP	SLG	EQA	EQR	DEFENSE
1996	Buffalo	Int	153	46	8	1	3	7/22	18	24	3	0	107	.301	.339	.425	.261	19	23-1B 108
1999	Durham	Int	102	27	6	0	4	5/23	16	15	0	0	75	.265	.310	.441	.249	12	
1999	TampaBay	AL	208	52	9	1	6	14/42	26	30	0	0	156	.250	.328	.389	.244	23	
2000	*TampaBay*	*AL*	*143*	*38*	*5*	*0*	*7*	*9/49*	*17*	*24*	*0*	*0*	*105*	*.266*	*.309*	*.448*	*.250*	*16*	

Is Luis Mandoki on the Rays' payroll, or what? In this tearjerker, a small-town hero overcomes five knee operations and returns to his home state to play in the majors after being given up for dead. Cut to reality. Perry doesn't hit enough to be of much value at the infield corners or DH. He's also a health risk, and The Trop is one of three artificial turf fields in the league. Rothschild has many better options, if only he would recognize them.

Alex Sanchez   CF   Bats L   Age 23

YEAR	TEAM	LGE	AB	H	DB	TP	HR	BB/SO	R	RBI	SB	CS	OUT	BA	OBP	SLG	EQA	EQR	DEFENSE
1997	Charl-SC	SAL	551	151	16	4	1	32/73	47	29	36	20	419	.274	.316	.323	.222	49	130-OF 104
1998	St Pete	Fla	547	160	19	7	1	25/77	51	39	26	16	403	.293	.324	.358	.233	53	130-OF 105
1999	Orlando	Sou	503	122	12	3	2	17/91	51	25	28	16	397	.243	.267	.290	.188	31	124-OF 105
2000	*TampaBay*	*AL*	*489*	*134*	*15*	*4*	*1*	*27/78*	*63*	*44*	*25*	*13*	*368*	*.274*	*.312*	*.327*	*.220*	*42*	

In keeping with their blossoming tradition of fast, hacking center fielders, Tampa Bay views him as their leadoff man of the future. Sanchez lost nearly 80 points off his batting average in the move to Double-A and has no plate discpline, leading to an abysmal .290 on-base percentage. Nevertheless, he was promoted to Durham for the playoffs, indicating the Rays still think highly of him. He'll start the season in Triple-A, and any hint of success could land him in the majors.

Jared Sandberg   3B   Bats R   Age 22

YEAR	TEAM	LGE	AB	H	DB	TP	HR	BB/SO	R	RBI	SB	CS	OUT	BA	OBP	SLG	EQA	EQR	DEFENSE
1997	Princetn	App	271	61	11	3	10	28/101	32	37	3	1	211	.225	.300	.399	.236	28	40-2B 98
1998	Charl-SC	SAL	196	34	7	0	4	22/77	24	22	2	0	162	.173	.263	.270	.181	11	56-3B 84
1998	HudsnVal	NYP	283	71	11	1	12	33/78	35	41	5	2	214	.251	.335	.424	.257	36	69-3B 111
1999	St Pete	Fla	508	126	19	1	22	42/146	59	79	4	1	383	.248	.312	.419	.246	57	134-3B 108
2000	TampaBay	AL	517	131	19	1	24	63/156	76	87	3	1	387	.253	.334	.433	.259	66	

After washing out of the Sally League a year earlier, he more than held his own in the Florida State League, finishing second in the loop in homers. He also tied for the league lead in strikeouts, courtesy of a long swing riddled with holes. Sandberg will be severely tested in Double-A, but even if he falters, his tools and surname will get him plenty of chances.

Bobby Smith   3B/SS   Bats R   Age 26

YEAR	TEAM	LGE	AB	H	DB	TP	HR	BB/SO	R	RBI	SB	CS	OUT	BA	OBP	SLG	EQA	EQR	DEFENSE
1997	Richmond	Int	361	86	9	3	11	37/106	42	42	5	4	279	.238	.320	.371	.236	38	98-SS 105
1998	TampaBay	AL	367	100	13	3	11	33/108	41	52	4	3	270	.272	.343	.414	.256	45	85-3B 100
1999	TampaBay	AL	199	35	4	1	3	14/64	16	18	4	4	168	.176	.234	.251	.151	7	46-3B 103
1999	Durham	Int	224	65	14	2	10	21/67	38	34	8	3	162	.290	.360	.504	.286	35	53-3B 101
2000	TampaBay	AL	293	67	10	1	9	31/89	35	35	5	4	230	.229	.302	.362	.224	27	

The Devil Rays had high expectations, but a dreadful start earned him a demotion to Durham in mid-May. He pasted International League pitching for a 1018 OPS, then fell apart upon being recalled. He looked lost at the plate, striking out nearly once every three at-bats, including a streak of six consecutive times looking. Smith has lost Rothschild's confidence, and I wouldn't be surprised to see him wearing a different uniform in 2000.

Ramon Soler   SS   Bats B   Age 18

YEAR	TEAM	LGE	AB	H	DB	TP	HR	BB/SO	R	RBI	SB	CS	OUT	BA	OBP	SLG	EQA	EQR	DEFENSE
1999	Charl-SC	SAL	403	91	18	1	1	47/94	51	25	18	7	319	.226	.310	.283	.212	33	89-SS 95
2000	TampaBay	AL	202	50	5	0	2	28/68	33	18	11	3	155	.248	.339	.302	.233	20	

The extended forecast in the Tampa area is for hailstorms of bad headline puns. Soler was the youngest position player in a full-season minor league yet already has one unusual skill for a hitter his age: he draws walks. His whippet-like build doesn't generate much power, but that should come in time. He's very raw now but could become something really special.

Paul Sorrento   1B/DH/LF   Bats L   Age 34

YEAR	TEAM	LGE	AB	H	DB	TP	HR	BB/SO	R	RBI	SB	CS	OUT	BA	OBP	SLG	EQA	EQR	DEFENSE	
1997	Seattle	AL	456	124	19	0	32	48/108	66	79	0	2	334	.272	.346	.524	.282	71	118-1B 122	
1998	TampaBay	AL	432	96	21	0	18	52/130	37	54	2	3	339	.222	.310	.396	.238	47	25-1B 104	
1999	TampaBay	AL	292	68	15	1	10	45/101	37	38	1	1	225	.233	.343	.394	.253	36	50-LF 98	22-1B 89
2000	TampaBay	AL	213	47	5	0	9	34/66	28	31	0	1	167	.221	.328	.371	.239	23		

There was no position for him after Canseco was signed, so to keep his bat in the lineup he was again tried in left field. Again, it didn't work. Sorrento was mediocre with the glove and confirmed that his 1998 hitting collapse was no fluke. He is a free agent and may be useful to another team as a pinch-hitter, but he still considers himself an everyday player. As of late December, he was still unemployed, with the Royals apparently interested in him.

Kevin Stocker   SS   Bats B   Age 30

YEAR	TEAM	LGE	AB	H	DB	TP	HR	BB/SO	R	RBI	SB	CS	OUT	BA	OBP	SLG	EQA	EQR	DEFENSE
1997	Philadel	NL	511	139	26	5	4	50/90	51	40	9	6	378	.272	.339	.366	.243	55	145-SS 95
1998	TampaBay	AL	334	68	10	3	6	26/78	34	23	4	3	269	.204	.278	.305	.197	23	107-SS 99
1999	TampaBay	AL	252	73	11	2	1	21/41	35	25	9	7	186	.290	.354	.361	.246	28	72-SS 92
2000	TampaBay	AL	264	68	11	2	4	27/50	37	31	6	4	200	.258	.326	.360	.235	27	

It may not be Lou Brock for Ernie Broglio, but even the sleepy fans of Tampa are beginning to wish they still had Bobby Abreu instead of a reliable shortstop. Well, kind of reliable. For the second straight season Stocker couldn't stay healthy, missing the latter part of the campaign with what was called tendinitis in his left knee. It could turn out to be much more serious than that, and since the Trop has plastic grass, he may hobble right to the end of his contract, which runs through 2002.

Bubba Trammell   OF/DH   Bats R   Age 28

YEAR	TEAM	LGE	AB	H	DB	TP	HR	BB/SO	R	RBI	SB	CS	OUT	BA	OBP	SLG	EQA	EQR	DEFENSE
1997	Toledo	Int	326	75	13	1	23	30/97	46	60	1	1	252	.230	.304	.488	.258	43	75-OF 49
1997	Detroit	AL	123	28	3	0	5	14/34	13	13	3	1	96	.228	.307	.374	.234	13	18-OF 112
1998	Durham	Int	219	55	9	0	12	30/47	34	36	3	1	165	.251	.341	.457	.268	31	55-OF 96
1998	TampaBay	AL	197	55	17	1	12	16/44	26	33	0	2	144	.279	.333	.558	.283	31	33-OF 90
1999	Durham	Int	186	44	8	0	6	11/40	19	24	0	0	142	.237	.279	.376	.218	16	42-OF 87
1999	TampaBay	AL	280	80	15	1	14	40/37	44	36	0	2	202	.286	.377	.496	.288	45	53-LF 106
2000	TampaBay	AL	464	122	19	1	24	57/91	71	86	1	2	344	.263	.344	.463	.269	64	

He was healthy all year and still received just 328 plate appearances for one of the worst offensive teams in the league. Rothschild's fetish for banjo-hitting, jackrabbit outfielders was most conspicuously on display while Trammell rotted in Durham until mid-June. Trammell is an awkward but adequate outfielder who also happens to be the best hitter the Devil Rays have. There is no doubt that he is an effective major-league player. What isn't clear is whether Rothschild yet knows that, which casts doubt on whether *he* can be an effective major-league manager.

Tom Wilson   C   Bats R   Age 29

YEAR	TEAM	LGE	AB	H	DB	TP	HR	BB/SO	R	RBI	SB	CS	OUT	BA	OBP	SLG	EQA	EQR	DEFENSE
1997	Norwich	Eas	429	103	20	4	13	63/147	63	55	1	2	328	.240	.341	.396	.252	52	
1998	Tucson	PCL	361	87	13	2	8	32/89	41	37	2	1	275	.241	.311	.355	.228	34	92-C 86
1999	Orlando	Sou	105	24	2	0	5	14/40	9	15	0	0	81	.229	.330	.390	.247	12	17-C 88
1999	Durham	Int	216	51	14	0	12	41/65	30	32	0	1	166	.236	.358	.468	.275	33	60-C 101
2000	NY Yanks	AL	280	64	10	1	11	47/86	42	42	1	1	217	.229	.339	.389	.257	36	

Having failed to catch the eye of either expansion team, what does he do now? Head back to the Yankees system. Given an opportunity, Wilson could be Chris Hoiles for a few years, drawing walks, hitting for power and taking unnecessary criticism about his defense. There's really nothing not to like about his game, although with his mom lurking in the Devil Rays' Usenet newsgroup, I admit that I tread lightly. Did I do OK, Mrs. Wilson?

Randy Winn   CF   Bats B   Age 26

YEAR	TEAM	LGE	AB	H	DB	TP	HR	BB/SO	R	RBI	SB	CS	OUT	BA	OBP	SLG	EQA	EQR	DEFENSE
1997	Brevard	Fla	147	39	9	1	0	12/34	17	12	5	3	111	.265	.336	.340	.235	15	36-OF 110
1997	Portland	Eas	381	91	14	5	5	31/98	44	25	20	11	301	.239	.304	.341	.223	35	91-OF 100
1998	Durham	Int	123	32	5	1	1	13/25	19	13	6	3	94	.260	.331	.341	.235	13	26-OF 97
1998	TampaBay	AL	335	91	8	9	1	28/67	46	16	22	12	256	.272	.330	.358	.238	35	81-OF 108
1999	TampaBay	AL	302	79	15	4	2	13/63	40	22	9	9	232	.262	.294	.358	.216	25	70-CF 101
1999	Durham	Int	205	62	16	2	2	12/30	27	22	5	4	147	.302	.343	.429	.258	25	47-OF 108
2000	TampaBay	AL	495	131	25	6	5	39/98	73	54	22	13	377	.265	.318	.370	.234	50	

Rothschild views players with Winn's skill set through rose-colored glasses, but even that wasn't enough to make Winn's first-half performance look good. At bat, he is undisciplined and overmatched, while on the basepaths he hurts the team with his poor base-stealing percentage. Undoubtedly, his outfield speed and two-month out-of-body experience at Durham will get him another opportunity this year.

PITCHERS (Averages: ERA: 4.50 / H/9: 9.00 / HR/9: 1.00 / BB/9: 3.50 / K/9: 6.50 / KWH: 1.00)

Wilson Alvarez   Throws L   Age 30

YEAR	TEAM	LGE	IP	H	ER	HR	BB	K	ERA	W	L	H/9	HR/9	BB/9	K/9	KWH	PERA
1997	ChiSox	AL	147.3	119	54	8	55	111	3.30	10	6	7.27	0.49	3.36	6.78	1.41	3.05
1997	San Fran	NL	66.0	55	36	10	37	64	4.91	3	4	7.50	1.36	5.05	8.73	1.50	4.64
1998	TampaBay	AL	143.3	129	73	16	72	109	4.58	8	8	8.10	1.00	4.52	6.84	0.96	4.40
1999	TampaBay	AL	162.0	149	79	19	77	131	4.39	9	9	8.28	1.06	4.28	7.28	1.12	4.44

He pitched in pain most of the season, twice landing on the disabled list with arm problems. In contrast to 1998, Rothschild didn't baby Alvarez in the least, letting him run up high pitch counts within a week after returning from the DL each time. The portly left-hander will never meet the expectations that came with his immense contract, but he will toss 180 very good innings if handled with care. Rothschild seems to want him to do more than that, which makes Alvarez a very high risk.

Rolando Arrojo Throws R Age 31

YEAR	TEAM	LGE	IP	H	ER	HR	BB	K	ERA	W	L	H/9	HR/9	BB/9	K/9	KWH	PERA
1997	St Pete	Fla	77.7	112	70	8	20	49	8.11	2	7	12.98	0.93	2.32	5.68	0.80	6.26
1998	TampaBay	AL	203.0	195	80	19	68	155	3.55	14	9	8.65	0.84	3.01	6.87	1.35	3.95
1999	TampaBay	AL	143.0	151	71	20	58	110	4.47	8	8	9.50	1.26	3.65	6.92	1.03	5.10

If human ages could be determined like trees' ages are, he would be undergoing microsurgery to reattach a limb. There's no way he is only 31 years old. Arrojo's desire to pitch was questioned when he went on the disabled list at the end of May with shoulder inflammation and a 7.31 ERA. He was vindicated upon returning, posting a 4.08 ERA the remainder of the season. The increases in his walk and home-run rates, even after his return, and his continuing problems (969 OPS) with left-handed batters make me think he still isn't completely healthy. Arrojo was traded to Colorado in the Vinny Castilla deal; he puts the ball in play, which doesn't bode well for his chances on Planet Coors.

Cedrick Bowers Throws L Age 22

YEAR	TEAM	LGE	IP	H	ER	HR	BB	K	ERA	W	L	H/9	HR/9	BB/9	K/9	KWH	PERA
1997	Charl-SC	SAL	144.0	161	103	15	109	112	6.44	5	11	10.06	0.94	6.81	7.00	0.53	6.44
1998	St Pete	Fla	139.3	171	104	17	102	120	6.72	5	10	11.05	1.10	6.59	7.75	0.62	7.11
1999	Orlando	Sou	119.7	140	98	19	82	115	7.37	4	9	10.53	1.43	6.17	8.65	0.86	6.99

In mid-July, his ERA was a grisly 8.10, and there was talk of demoting him to A ball. He made some mechanical changes that improved both his command and velocity, and pared his ERA to 3.27 over his final ten starts. Bowers has a live arm but is as wild as Belushi on acid and needs to develop consistency with his breaking pitches. One indirect benefit of the dreadful start to his campaign was that it kept his overall workload low, after he had been ridden hard the previous two seasons.

Mickey Callaway Throws R Age 25

YEAR	TEAM	LGE	IP	H	ER	HR	BB	K	ERA	W	L	H/9	HR/9	BB/9	K/9	KWH	PERA
1997	St Pete	Fla	154.3	218	107	12	53	83	6.24	6	11	12.71	0.70	3.09	4.84	0.45	6.18
1998	Orlando	Sou	84.3	118	59	8	44	46	6.30	3	6	12.59	0.85	4.70	4.91	0.30	7.04
1998	Durham	Int	45.7	54	29	6	17	17	5.72	2	3	10.64	1.18	3.35	3.35	0.24	5.52
1999	Durham	Int	79.7	89	43	4	30	49	4.86	4	5	10.05	0.45	3.39	5.54	0.67	4.52
1999	TampaBay	AL	20.0	27	17	2	14	11	7.65	1	1	12.15	0.90	6.30	4.95	0.24	7.65

Apparently the fact that Callaway was healthy was enough to earn him a look in late June. The Devil Rays were so impressed that they didn't mail him a return ticket when the rosters expanded in September. He could be the next Bob Milacki if his innards can endure another ten years of truck-stop coffee. Outrighted to Durham.

Norm Charlton Throws L Age 37

YEAR	TEAM	LGE	IP	H	ER	HR	BB	K	ERA	W	L	H/9	HR/9	BB/9	K/9	KWH	PERA
1997	Seattle	AL	71.7	83	52	6	48	56	6.53	3	5	10.42	0.75	6.03	7.03	0.59	6.15
1998	Baltimor	AL	34.7	45	25	5	26	41	6.49	1	3	11.68	1.30	6.75	10.64	1.07	7.79
1998	Atlanta	NL	12.7	8	2	0	8	6	1.42	1	0	5.68	0.00	5.68	4.26	0.42	2.84
1999	Durham	Int	30.3	30	13	7	11	25	3.86	2	1	8.90	2.08	3.26	7.42	1.42	5.64
1999	TampaBay	AL	51.7	45	25	4	35	46	4.35	3	3	7.84	0.70	6.10	8.01	1.00	4.53

Like a B-movie psychopath who is flattened by a semi, mauled by a pack of rabid Rottweilers and run through a hay baler—only to keep returning to terrorize the village—Charlton won't go away. He still has pretty good velocity but lost all command of his pitches years ago. Hide the children and bar the doors.

Mike Duvall Throws L Age 25

YEAR	TEAM	LGE	IP	H	ER	HR	BB	K	ERA	W	L	H/9	HR/9	BB/9	K/9	KWH	PERA
1997	Portland	Eas	67.7	67	20	4	22	40	2.66	6	2	8.91	0.53	2.93	5.32	0.81	3.72
1998	Durham	Int	70.3	80	33	3	33	49	4.22	4	4	10.24	0.38	4.22	6.27	0.68	4.86
1999	Durham	Int	29.3	33	19	4	13	24	5.83	1	2	10.13	1.23	3.99	7.36	1.00	5.52
1999	TampaBay	AL	40.3	44	18	4	26	18	4.02	2	2	9.82	0.89	5.80	4.02	0.21	5.80

Pigeonholed as a situational southpaw, Duvall received an extended trial after the All-Star break and blew it. His control completely abandoned him, enabling left-handed pitchers to whack him for a .324 average. He'll be participating in the Rays' Spring Training Sweepstakes, where ten effective innings can win lots of great prizes, including another chance in the majors.

Dave Eiland   Throws R   Age 33

YEAR	TEAM	LGE	IP	H	ER	HR	BB	K	ERA	W	L	H/9	HR/9	BB/9	K/9	KWH	PERA
1997	Columbus	Int	58.3	92	53	8	16	35	8.18	1	5	14.19	1.23	2.47	5.40	0.62	7.56
1998	Durham	Int	163.0	200	80	12	30	94	4.42	9	9	11.04	0.66	1.66	5.19	1.10	4.58
1999	Durham	Int	57.7	63	25	7	10	39	3.90	3	3	9.83	1.09	1.56	6.09	1.80	4.37
1999	TampaBay	AL	81.7	92	51	7	26	54	5.62	4	5	10.14	0.77	2.87	5.95	0.91	4.63

It's nice to see somebody who has persevered be rewarded. He won his first game in the majors since 1995 and was Kevin Costner's body double in *For Love of the Game*. Costner claims he did all the pitching scenes, which is possible since Eiland's stuff may not have appeared "major league." The quintessential junkballer, Eiland is nothing more than cheap staff filler until the Rays' pitching prospects are ready.

Eddie Gaillard   Throws R   Age 29

YEAR	TEAM	LGE	IP	H	ER	HR	BB	K	ERA	W	L	H/9	HR/9	BB/9	K/9	KWH	PERA
1997	Toledo	Int	49.3	61	31	7	26	43	5.66	2	3	11.13	1.28	4.74	7.84	0.87	6.57
1997	Detroit	AL	20.3	16	11	2	10	12	4.87	1	1	7.08	0.89	4.43	5.31	0.67	3.54
1998	Durham	Int	18.3	31	19	5	12	18	9.33	0	2	15.22	2.45	5.89	8.84	0.65	11.29
1999	Durham	Int	60.7	70	29	5	26	57	4.30	4	3	10.38	0.74	3.86	8.46	1.33	5.19

Gaillard was handed the closer job in Durham, stayed healthy and collected 26 saves. Given his age and middling stuff, if he ever finds permanent employment in the majors, he should send a personal thank-you note to Jerome Holtzman for popularizing that overblown statistic. Designated for assignment after the season, he signed with the Reds.

Travis Harper   Throws R   Age 24

YEAR	TEAM	LGE	IP	H	ER	HR	BB	K	ERA	W	L	H/9	HR/9	BB/9	K/9	KWH	PERA
1998	HudsnVal	NYP	50.7	57	22	3	28	48	3.91	3	3	10.13	0.53	4.97	8.53	1.08	5.15
1999	St Pete	Fla	73.0	109	51	5	31	60	6.29	3	5	13.44	0.62	3.82	7.40	0.80	6.90
1999	Orlando	Sou	68.7	83	49	10	28	55	6.42	3	5	10.88	1.31	3.67	7.21	0.97	6.03

Originally drafted by Boston, he was released before he threw a pitch when they claimed he'd hidden his elbow tendinitis from them. Since signing with the Devil Rays, Harper has been a strike-throwing machine with a bit of a wild streak (10 hit batters in 72 innings with Orlando). He's a very similar pitcher to Dan Wheeler; like Wheeler, Harper will probably perform under the big top at some point this season.

Roberto Hernandez   Throws R   Age 35

YEAR	TEAM	LGE	IP	H	ER	HR	BB	K	ERA	W	L	H/9	HR/9	BB/9	K/9	KWH	PERA
1997	ChiSox	AL	48.0	37	13	5	24	47	2.44	4	1	6.94	0.94	4.50	8.81	1.86	3.75
1997	San Fran	NL	32.0	31	9	2	14	32	2.53	3	1	8.72	0.56	3.94	9.00	1.76	3.94
1998	TampaBay	AL	71.7	55	31	4	43	56	3.89	5	3	6.91	0.50	5.40	7.03	0.99	3.64
1999	TampaBay	AL	74.3	63	23	1	32	71	2.78	6	2	7.63	0.12	3.87	8.60	1.87	3.03

He avoided the extreme wildness that plagued him in 1998 and fashioned an effective season. All the more reason that LaMar should be spanked for not moving him. The demand for veteran relievers always swells near the trading deadline, so if the erratic Hernandez can keep it together for four months, LaMar will have another chance to do the right thing.

Cory Lidle   Throws R   Age 28

YEAR	TEAM	LGE	IP	H	ER	HR	BB	K	ERA	W	L	H/9	HR/9	BB/9	K/9	KWH	PERA
1997	Norfolk	Int	40.7	51	21	1	10	28	4.65	2	3	11.29	0.22	2.21	6.20	1.15	4.43
1997	NY Mets	NL	80.3	91	40	7	21	50	4.48	5	4	10.20	0.78	2.35	5.60	0.98	4.48
1999	TampaBay	AL	5.3	7	3	0	2	4	5.06	0	1	11.81	0.00	3.38	6.75	0.85	5.06

Like the Red Sox, the Devil Rays have a habit of collecting rehabilitation projects, except that theirs don't have much upside. Lidle is coming off Tommy John surgery and will be part of the group grope for long-relief work this spring.

Albie Lopez   Throws R   Age 28

YEAR	TEAM	LGE	IP	H	ER	HR	BB	K	ERA	W	L	H/9	HR/9	BB/9	K/9	KWH	PERA
1997	Clevelnd	AL	77.0	98	56	10	40	63	6.55	3	6	11.45	1.17	4.68	7.36	0.76	6.66
1998	TampaBay	AL	80.3	72	30	6	34	63	3.36	6	3	8.07	0.67	3.81	7.06	1.21	3.81
1999	TampaBay	AL	64.7	62	34	7	23	38	4.73	3	4	8.63	0.97	3.20	5.29	0.76	4.18

The portly right-hander's totals were scarred by a horrific April when he was tagged for six home runs before revealing that he had been pitching with a strained oblique muscle. After being shut down for seven weeks, Lopez returned and posted a 2.04 ERA after the All-Star break. His performance prompted whispers about making him the closer. If that means shedding Hernandez's salary for a couple of hot prospects, it's a good thing.

Ben McDonald — Throws R — Age 32

YEAR	TEAM	LGE	IP	H	ER	HR	BB	K	ERA	W	L	H/9	HR/9	BB/9	K/9	KWH	PERA
1995	Baltimor	AL	80.0	67	36	9	36	66	4.05	5	4	7.54	1.01	4.05	7.43	1.35	3.94
1996	Milwauke	AL	221.7	217	90	21	63	151	3.65	15	10	8.81	0.85	2.56	6.13	1.25	3.90
1997	Milwauke	AL	134.0	115	62	12	37	111	4.16	8	7	7.72	0.81	2.49	7.46	2.16	3.22

If the third operation on his right shoulder last summer was successful, Big Ben might someday be able to rassle alligators again. It's pretty much guaranteed that he won't be throwing a baseball. Still, the minor-league contract Tampa Bay gave him achieved what they wanted: they're now in Scott Boras's good graces. McDonald is a free agent at this writing.

Jim Mecir — Throws R — Age 30

YEAR	TEAM	LGE	IP	H	ER	HR	BB	K	ERA	W	L	H/9	HR/9	BB/9	K/9	KWH	PERA
1997	Columbus	Int	26.0	16	5	0	7	27	1.73	3	0	5.54	0.00	2.42	9.35	4.86	1.73
1997	NY Yanks	AL	33.7	35	21	5	10	25	5.61	2	2	9.36	1.34	2.67	6.68	1.33	4.81
1998	TampaBay	AL	84.3	68	29	5	35	78	3.09	6	3	7.26	0.53	3.74	8.32	1.91	3.20
1999	TampaBay	AL	21.0	14	6	0	13	15	2.57	2	0	6.00	0.00	5.57	6.43	0.92	2.57

He missed the last four and a half months of the season after tripping over a bat and fracturing his elbow. Mecir throws a screwball that is very effective against left-handers, and by some measures he was one of the top relievers in the game in 1998. Expected to be fully recovered by spring training and should pick up right where he left off.

Jim Morris — Throws L — Age 36

YEAR	TEAM	LGE	IP	H	ER	HR	BB	K	ERA	W	L	H/9	HR/9	BB/9	K/9	KWH	PERA
1999	Orlando	Sou	4.7	7	1	0	2	5	1.93	1	0	13.50	0.00	3.86	9.64	1.33	5.79
1999	Durham	Int	22.0	22	14	3	21	14	5.73	1	1	9.00	1.23	8.59	5.73	0.32	6.95
1999	TampaBay	AL	4.7	3	3	1	2	3	5.79	0	1	5.79	1.93	3.86	5.79	1.12	3.86

By now, all of you know Morris's incredible story. If somehow you missed it, be sure to watch it on "Oprah Winfrey Presents" this fall. What's next for the oldest rookie in the majors in 29 years? There isn't much data to go on, but we do know this: he is left-handed, he legitimately throws in the mid-90s, and for goodness sakes—it's the Devil Rays! The fairy tale will continue.

Alan Newman — Throws L — Age 30

YEAR	TEAM	LGE	IP	H	ER	HR	BB	K	ERA	W	L	H/9	HR/9	BB/9	K/9	KWH	PERA
1997	Birmnghm	Sou	66.0	66	42	0	47	47	5.73	3	4	9.00	0.00	6.41	6.41	0.53	4.64
1998	LasVegas	PCL	75.3	54	27	2	59	62	3.23	5	3	6.45	0.24	7.05	7.41	0.90	3.70
1999	Durham	Int	79.0	61	23	2	22	65	2.62	7	2	6.95	0.23	2.51	7.41	2.35	2.39
1999	TampaBay	AL	16.0	21	10	2	9	21	5.63	1	1	11.81	1.13	5.06	11.81	1.74	6.75

A few years ago, he resembled Newman from "Seinfeld," almost eating his way out of professional baseball. The long trip back included a stint in the independent leagues and was aided by his ability to strike people out. However, it wasn't until last year with Durham that he finally reigned in his wildness. As long as that continues, he'll have chances in the major leagues.

Bryan Rekar — Throws R — Age 28

YEAR	TEAM	LGE	IP	H	ER	HR	BB	K	ERA	W	L	H/9	HR/9	BB/9	K/9	KWH	PERA
1997	ColSprin	PCL	140.7	167	86	18	43	96	5.50	6	10	10.68	1.15	2.75	6.14	0.96	5.31
1998	TampaBay	AL	87.3	95	52	15	22	56	5.36	4	6	9.79	1.55	2.27	5.77	1.12	5.05
1999	Durham	Int	34.0	31	15	3	9	22	3.97	2	2	8.21	0.79	2.38	5.82	1.30	3.44
1999	TampaBay	AL	95.7	115	59	12	39	56	5.55	4	7	10.82	1.13	3.67	5.27	0.52	5.74

Rekar appears to be one of the first identified casualties of an assignment to Planet Coors. First he lost his confidence, then his control. He can still get Triple-A batters out, but when promoted, he's taterrific.

Ryan Rupe — Throws R — Age 25

YEAR	TEAM	LGE	IP	H	ER	HR	BB	K	ERA	W	L	H/9	HR/9	BB/9	K/9	KWH	PERA
1998	Charl-SC	SAL	52.0	47	27	4	14	37	4.67	3	3	8.13	0.69	2.42	6.40	1.55	3.29
1999	Orlando	Sou	25.3	21	15	1	7	17	5.33	1	2	7.46	0.36	2.49	6.04	1.47	2.84
1999	TampaBay	AL	144.0	127	70	15	55	100	4.38	8	8	7.94	0.94	3.44	6.25	1.07	3.81

The early leader for steal of the 1998 draft. A sixth-round pick, Jeff Weaver nosed him out by three weeks to be the first starting pitcher from that draft to make the majors. But while Weaver took his licks the second time through the league, Rupe was Tampa Bay's most consistent starter, logging a team-high 14 quality starts. Rothschild handled him sensibly and shut him down in late September when Rupe complained of a tired shoulder. Rupe is the future ace of the Devil Ray staff, if he hasn't claimed that title already.

Tony Saunders — Throws L — Age 26

YEAR	TEAM	LGE	IP	H	ER	HR	BB	K	ERA	W	L	H/9	HR/9	BB/9	K/9	KWH	PERA
1997	Florida	NL	110.3	101	62	13	67	95	5.06	5	7	8.24	1.06	5.47	7.75	1.00	4.89
1998	TampaBay	AL	194.3	188	90	13	117	176	4.17	12	10	8.71	0.60	5.42	8.15	1.05	4.68
1999	TampaBay	AL	42.3	50	34	5	29	31	7.23	1	4	10.63	1.06	6.17	6.59	0.50	6.59

Last seen writhing in pain after breaking the humerus bone in his left arm while throwing a pitch. The three major-league pitchers who suffered a similar injury—Dave Dravecky, Tom Browning and John Smiley—also were left-handed. I'm no Vegas odds-maker, but since only about a third of the pitchers in the majors are southpaws, the probability of that happening randomly is about 80 to 1. None of the other three returned to pitch successfully, but they were in their thirties, while Saunders is only 26. He's not expected to play in 2000.

Bobby Seay — Throws L — Age 22

YEAR	TEAM	LGE	IP	H	ER	HR	BB	K	ERA	W	L	H/9	HR/9	BB/9	K/9	KWH	PERA
1997	Charl-SC	SAL	55.7	75	48	3	52	44	7.76	2	4	12.13	0.49	8.41	7.11	0.37	7.92
1998	Charl-SC	SAL	63.0	77	50	11	40	48	7.14	2	5	11.00	1.57	5.71	6.86	0.56	7.29
1999	St Pete	Fla	53.0	68	31	1	29	37	5.26	3	3	11.55	0.17	4.92	6.28	0.52	5.60
1999	Orlando	Sou	16.0	25	15	2	16	13	8.44	0	2	14.06	1.13	9.00	7.31	0.32	10.12

He started harnessing both his command and volatile personality and was named to Team USA for the Pan Am Games. Promoted to Double-A after the event, but it all came crashing down. Seay is blessed with great stuff and is the type of pitcher for whom everything could suddenly click, but right now, he's just another example of the risk involved in developing high-school pitchers. His inability to stay healthy has some scouts projecting him as a setup man, which isn't exactly what the Devil Rays envisioned when they signed him as the first loophole free agent. Seay suffered an injury in the Arizona Fall League, a tear of his labrum that the D-Rays are hoping will heal without surgery.

Jason Standridge — Throws R — Age 21

YEAR	TEAM	LGE	IP	H	ER	HR	BB	K	ERA	W	L	H/9	HR/9	BB/9	K/9	KWH	PERA
1998	Princetn	App	53.7	111	77	5	37	29	12.91	1	5	18.61	0.84	6.20	4.86	0.15	11.74
1999	Charl-SC	SAL	107.3	112	53	6	44	54	4.44	6	6	9.39	0.50	3.69	4.53	0.44	4.28
1999	St Pete	Fla	44.3	60	27	1	26	21	5.48	2	3	12.18	0.20	5.28	4.26	0.21	6.29

The Devil Rays' top pick in the 1997 draft dominated at Charleston, allowing fewer baserunners than innings pitched, and was named the #2 prospect in the Sally League by *Baseball America*. He didn't fare as well after his promotion to St. Petersburg, primarily because he hasn't developed a true strikeout pitch. That should come with experience, as Standridge offers a full buffet: 94-mph fastball, big overhand curve and improving change-up. In addition to the requisite caveats that come with any A-ball hurler, the organization needs to more closely watch his workload, which was too high for a 20-year-old.

Dan Wheeler — Throws R — Age 22

YEAR	TEAM	LGE	IP	H	ER	HR	BB	K	ERA	W	L	H/9	HR/9	BB/9	K/9	KWH	PERA
1997	HudsnVal	NYP	75.3	107	57	4	26	50	6.81	2	6	12.78	0.48	3.11	5.97	0.67	5.97
1998	Charl-SC	SAL	164.3	273	127	19	41	88	6.96	5	13	14.95	1.04	2.25	4.82	0.52	7.67
1999	Orlando	Sou	55.7	63	29	8	9	44	4.69	3	3	10.19	1.29	1.46	7.11	2.55	4.69
1999	Durham	Int	81.7	104	53	15	26	52	5.84	3	6	11.46	1.65	2.87	5.73	0.75	6.39
1999	TampaBay	AL	30.7	34	17	6	13	33	4.99	1	2	9.98	1.76	3.82	9.68	1.84	6.16

A former 34th-round pick, he made more progress in 1999 than any other prospect in the Rays' system. Wheeler cemented his status with an exceptional performance in the Pan Am Games, earning a six-start audition with the parent club in September. He throws strikes and has decent breaking pitches that he mixes with a low-90s fastball, but gives up a lot of hits due to wildness within the strike zone. Rothchild was impressed and intends to give him a clean shot at the rotation in spring training. I expect him to struggle and would rather see him begin the season working out of the bullpen, as he did for Team USA.

Matt White   Throws R   Age 21

YEAR	TEAM	LGE	IP	H	ER	HR	BB	K	ERA	W	L	H/9	HR/9	BB/9	K/9	KWH	PERA
1997	HudsnVal	NYP	74.0	111	65	5	44	51	7.91	2	6	13.50	0.61	5.35	6.20	0.40	7.54
1998	St Pete	Fla	88.7	127	82	12	52	49	8.32	2	8	12.89	1.22	5.28	4.97	0.27	7.92
1999	St Pete	Fla	104.7	154	93	9	42	75	8.00	3	9	13.24	0.77	3.61	6.45	0.65	6.88

Publicly the Devil Rays are staying positive, but privately they're worried. They expected White to dominate at high-A St. Petersburg after he spent the last half of 1998 there. Instead, his 5.18 ERA was well above the league average, he gave up more than a hit an inning and his strikeout rate was nothing special. The problem is that while White has great mechanics and very good control, his 95-mph fastball is as straight as Al Gore. The Rays are far from giving up on such a big investment—a simple mechanical tweak might add some movement to his heater—but it's reaching the point where they need to see results.

Rick White   Throws R   Age 31

YEAR	TEAM	LGE	IP	H	ER	HR	BB	K	ERA	W	L	H/9	HR/9	BB/9	K/9	KWH	PERA
1997	Orlando	Sou	76.3	116	69	7	26	48	8.14	2	6	13.68	0.83	3.07	5.66	0.57	6.96
1998	Durham	Int	50.3	71	33	3	12	26	5.90	2	4	12.70	0.54	2.15	4.65	0.59	5.54
1998	TampaBay	AL	68.7	67	31	7	24	40	4.06	4	4	8.78	0.92	3.15	5.24	0.74	4.19
1999	TampaBay	AL	109.3	124	48	7	37	83	3.95	7	5	10.21	0.58	3.05	6.83	1.12	4.53

Exhibit #453 in how easy it is to find cheap, effective relievers. White serves up more slop than an Army mess hall, but knows how to set up a hitter and consumed a lot of innings for the wounded Rays' bullpen. Chuck LaMar should sign him to a bloated, multi-year contract, then call Seattle.

Bobby Witt   Throws R   Age 36

YEAR	TEAM	LGE	IP	H	ER	HR	BB	K	ERA	W	L	H/9	HR/9	BB/9	K/9	KWH	PERA
1997	Texas	AL	214.0	231	104	30	75	123	4.37	12	12	9.71	1.26	3.15	5.17	0.65	5.05
1998	Texas	AL	73.0	88	53	13	34	31	6.53	3	5	10.85	1.60	4.19	3.82	0.24	6.53
1998	St Louis	NL	48.0	56	31	7	21	27	5.81	2	3	10.50	1.31	3.94	5.06	0.46	5.81
1999	TampaBay	AL	183.0	200	112	20	93	126	5.51	8	12	9.84	0.98	4.57	6.20	0.64	5.41

Witt stayed in the Tampa Bay rotation the entire season because of what has always been his greatest asset: the ability to take the ball every fifth day. As they head out of spring training this year, the Rays should have enough healthy bodies and lofty delusions for their young hurlers that they don't resort to this again.

Esteban Yan   Throws R   Age 26

YEAR	TEAM	LGE	IP	H	ER	HR	BB	K	ERA	W	L	H/9	HR/9	BB/9	K/9	KWH	PERA
1997	Rochestr	Int	117.0	116	55	13	38	112	4.23	7	6	8.92	1.00	2.92	8.62	2.13	4.23
1998	TampaBay	AL	89.3	77	39	10	43	78	3.93	6	4	7.76	1.01	4.33	7.86	1.37	4.13
1999	TampaBay	AL	62.0	72	35	7	31	47	5.08	3	4	10.45	1.02	4.50	6.82	0.74	5.81

He didn't do himself any favors in the eyes of the organization when he played winter ball against its wishes. Season-long shoulder problems followed, which made his usually nasty stuff very hittable. Still, Yan gave more than he got, ranking among the league leaders by allowing a mere seven of 31 inherited runners to score. Rothschild is making noise about having him start, which would increase his value, but I don't think his arm troubles are behind him.

Support-Neutral Records — TAMPA BAY DEVIL RAYS — Park Effect: +4.1%

PITCHER	GS	IP	R	SNW	SNL	SNPCT	W	L	RA	APW	SNVA	SNWAR
Wilson Alvarez	28	160.0	92	10.3	8.8	.540	9	9	5.18	0.26	0.66	2.19
Rolando Arrojo	24	140.7	84	8.1	8.4	.493	7	12	5.37	-0.06	-0.01	1.13
Mickey Callaway	4	15.3	14	0.8	1.4	.369	1	2	8.22	-0.45	-0.33	-0.13
Dave Eiland	15	68.0	45	4.0	4.8	.458	4	7	5.96	-0.43	-0.37	0.29
Cory Lidle	1	2.0	2	0.1	0.3	.183	0	0	9.00	-0.07	-0.08	-0.09
Bryan Rekar	12	63.0	48	3.0	4.7	.394	5	5	6.86	-0.98	-0.80	-0.24
Ryan Rupe	24	142.3	81	8.9	8.1	.523	8	9	5.12	0.31	0.43	1.68
Julio Santana	5	26.0	29	0.9	2.8	.235	1	3	10.04	-1.25	-0.90	-0.70
Tony Saunders	9	42.0	39	2.3	4.3	.350	3	3	8.36	-1.30	-0.96	-0.50
Dan Wheeler	6	30.7	20	1.6	2.0	.454	0	4	5.87	-0.17	-0.18	0.10
Rick White	1	2.3	2	0.1	0.3	.263	0	0	7.71	-0.06	-0.10	-0.07
Bobby Witt	32	180.3	130	9.3	13.3	.412	7	15	6.49	-2.13	-1.97	-0.29
Esteban Yan	1	4.0	2	0.3	0.1	.678	0	0	4.50	0.03	0.04	0.12
TOTALS	162	876.7	588	49.9	59.3	.457	45	69	6.04	-6.30	-4.57	3.49

In 1998, Tampa Bay had the best starting staff ever for a first-year expansion team. The fans had to know it couldn't last. Last year, three of the Rays' top '98 performers—Rolando Arrojo, Julio Santana and Tony Saunders—fell off significantly, and Ryan Rupe's impressive debut wasn't enough to compensate. Tampa Bay's rotation was 4½ wins below average, according to SNVA—24th in the league. . . . Whenever a noteworthy rookie makes a significant number of starts, it's a good idea to examine his first-half and second-half performance. If he was worse the second time through the league, it may indicate that his initial success was due to the league's unfamiliarity with him, and that hitters went on to figure out his quirks, such as a deceptive motion. On the other hand, if he was better the second time through, it may indicate that he learned something about getting major-league hitters out. The results for Rupe are encouraging on that front: in his first 12 starts, his Support Neutral Winning Percentage was .497; in his last 12, it was .551.

Pitcher Abuse Points

PITCHER	AGE	GS	PAP	PAP/S	WKLD	MAX	1-90	91-100	101-110	111-120	121-130	131-140	141+
Wilson Alvarez	29	28	568	20.3	30.4	144	9	3	4	5	3	3	1
Rolando Arrojo	30	24	306	12.8	17.0	138	9	4	5	1	4	1	0
Mickey Callaway	24	4	0	0.0	0.0	97	2	2	0	0	0	0	0
Dave Eiland	32	15	40	2.7	2.7	122	12	1	1	0	1	0	0
Cory Lidle	27	1	0	0.0	0.0	39	1	0	0	0	0	0	0
Bryan Rekar	27	12	44	3.7	6.7	120	6	2	3	1	0	0	0
Ryan Rupe	24	24	138	5.8	13.4	120	7	7	5	5	0	0	0
Julio Santana	26	5	0	0.0	0.0	95	2	3	0	0	0	0	0
Tony Saunders	25	9	53	5.9	12.8	127	4	3	1	0	1	0	0
Dan Wheeler	21	6	22	3.7	10.4	111	2	1	2	1	0	0	0
Rick White	30	1	0	0.0	0.0	34	1	0	0	0	0	0	0
Bobby Witt	35	32	413	12.9	12.9	130	8	5	10	3	6	0	0
Esteban Yan	25	1	0	0.0	0.0	96	0	1	0	0	0	0	0
TAMPA BAY		162	1584	9.8	14.2	144	63	32	31	16	15	4	1
Ranking (AL)				4	7								

Larry Rothschild continued to work his starters a little harder than you'd like the manager of an expansion team to do. Wilson Alvarez showed a glimmer of his form from his White Sox days and was immediately put back on the White Sox workload that caused him to lose that form in the first place. . . . Even if Rolando Arrojo is only 30, his workload can't be blamed for the health problems he suffered last season. . . . Tony Saunders paid a rather ugly (and painful) price for a Workload of 37.3 in 1998, but at least Ryan Rupe, who battled back from severe elbow problems to have a very nice rookie season, was handled carefully.

Texas Rangers

As the 1990 season ended, the three-time defending AL champion Oakland A's were getting old. Players such as Carney Lansford, Rickey and Dave Henderson, Harold Baines and Mike Gallego were in their 30s, while those who weren't were still on the wrong side of 27: Terry Steinbach, Mark McGwire, Walt Weiss. Rather than infusing youth into the team gradually, the A's adopted an organizational philosophy of retaining their aging lineup and attempting to plug holes with other older players, like Willie Wilson and Ernest Riles. Though they did manage to squeeze one more playoff appearance out of the team in 1992, the eventual result was a miserable six-year rebuilding period that is just now ending.

The tale of the Baltimore Orioles of the late 1990s is similar. After winning the AL East championship in 1997, the Orioles decided to stick with their over-30 offense—Baines, Cal Ripken, Eric Davis, Brady Anderson, B.J. Surhoff, Rafael Palmeiro, Geronimo Berroa, Chris Hoiles, Mike Bordick and Roberto Alomar—and bring in even older players, such as Joe Carter, to keep the success going. The result so far has been a two-year malaise with no end in sight.

The Texas Rangers just won their third AL West title in the past four years with an aging offense similar to those of the A's and Orioles. Almost all the key hitters of the 1999 team—Palmeiro, Juan Gonzalez, Rusty Greer, Todd Zeile, Lee Stevens, Royce Clayton, Mark McLemore, Roberto Kelly, Tom Goodwin and Luis Alicea—would be older than 30 by Opening Day 2000. Palmeiro, Zeile, McLemore, Alicea and Kelly would all be over 34. The only important offensive player who would still be under 30 was 28-year-old Ivan Rodriguez. Remember, that's 28 in Catcher Years—well past 30 to other players. How the Rangers deal with this situation will determine whether or not they repeat the quick decline pattern of the other aging teams.

Why should we care how old players are, as long as they can still play? Because having a lineup filled with players on the wrong side of 30 makes offensive decline almost inevitable. While it's not at all unusual for a player in his 30s

Rangers Prospectus

1999 record: 95-67; First place, AL West; Lost to Yankees in Division Series, 3-0

Pythagorean W/L: 88-74

Runs scored: 945 (2nd in AL)

Runs allowed: 859 (7th in AL)

Team EQA: .271 (3rd in AL)

1999 team age: 30.4 (3rd-oldest in AL)

1999 park: The Ballpark in Arlington; moderate hitters' park, increased run scoring by 8%.

1999: Another October flop mars an otherwise successful season.

2000: Gonzalez trade makes them younger, cheaper and better.

to see his performance improve in a given year—Rafael Palmeiro, for example, just had a career year at age 34—it's more probable that he will decline. When you have a number of players all facing that probability, the odds that they're going to improve as a group are microscopic. It may be possible to keep an old team's head temporarily above water by bringing in more older, high-priced talent to fill holes—Palmeiro is again an example—but this short-sighted strategy can only delay the collapse, not prevent it.

Another price you pay for having older players on the roster is an increased risk of injury. While the 1998 Rangers were lucky to avoid the disabled list almost completely, last year's edition, with players who were a year older, saw the odds catch up to them. Mike Simms, 32, spent the entire year on the DL. Clayton spent almost a month there. Goodwin spent almost two months out of action (hey, we never claimed all injuries hurt the team). Palmeiro, Kelly and McLemore, while never on the DL, all battled through injuries that cost them playing time or, in Palmeiro's case, restricted what he could do. The result was loss of platoon opportunities and some significant playing time for subpar replacements.

So how do the Rangers avoid becoming Orioles West? Here are a few strategies, many of which General Manager Doug Melvin is already implementing:

1. Look for opportunities to get younger through trades. Melvin has done this in a big way this offseason by trading one year of Juan Gonzalez to the Tigers for a package that includes quality younger players Gabe Kapler, Frank Catalanotto and Francisco Cordero. This trade is a big step in the right direction for the Rangers' future, and could help the Rangers in the short term as well.

2. Avoid rent-a-veteran trades. In baseball's new and improved postseason format ("Just Like the NHL! Without the Ice!"), it makes less sense than ever to mortgage your team's future for a couple of months of a veteran who merely improves your shot at entering the 1-in-8

World Series crapshoot. Melvin may have learned this lesson after watching two young players he traded away in 1998, Fernando Tatis and Warren Morris, emerge as stars for other teams in 1999. To his credit, Melvin resisted making any trades of this nature in 1999, though the end result—AL West crown, first-round playoff loss—was exactly the same as the result of the short-sighted trades of 1998.

3. Don't sign or re-sign mediocre veterans. When a GM has as large a budget as Melvin does, it's tempting to fill a hole in the lineup by giving a two- or three-year contract to a 35-year-old "proven major leaguer." Tempting, but unwise. By the time that contract is up, that middling veteran is likely to have declined to near replacement level. A younger player, even one who isn't thought of as a top-flight prospect, should at least improve over time. Using him frees up the team's money for premier free agents who will make a real difference. Melvin's handling of free agents Mark McLemore and Todd Zeile has been encouraging in this regard.

The Rangers' roster on Opening Day 2000 will have several key position players under 27, a big improvement over the roster just six months earlier. Still, the 2000 Rangers will be top-heavy with older players; it's a situation that needs to be addressed constantly over the next few seasons for the Rangers to avoid the fate of the A's and Orioles. Melvin has already taken some positive steps, and those, along with an increasing willingness to use the club's improving farm system, should help keep this team young. Or at least middle-aged.

With the Rangers suffering their second straight October embarrassment, everyone is searching for reasons that might explain why the usually potent Ranger offense goes limp against Yankee pitchers. Actually, that may be overstating the inquisitiveness of most baseball fans. It's more the case that everyone seems to *know why* Texas has scored a grand total of two runs in six playoff games against New York in 1998 and 1999.

The most popular theory, which I've heard advocated confidently by respected baseball analysts and talk-show callers alike, goes something like this: during the regular season, facing pitchers of varying quality, the Rangers' talented free swingers can succeed because they beat up on the mediocre and poor pitchers of the league. But in the playoffs the past two years, the Rangers didn't have the luxury of facing second- and third-tier pitching. The elite Yankee staff was able to exploit the vulnerable Rangers—especially their poor command of the strike zone—and turn them into out machines.

When I first heard this theory, I wasn't too impressed. For one thing, despite a few prominent free swingers on the club, the Rangers are simply not that undisciplined. They ranked third in the league in on-base percentage last year, second in 1998. They ranked fifth in the AL in walks last year, fourth in 1998. Even taking their offense-friendly ballpark into account, it's hard to see anything that would make them look like the 1962 Mets against good pitching.

The theory can easily be tested. If the idea is that the Rangers are vulnerable to good pitching in October, then it serves to reason that they would underperform against good pitching in April through September as well. So are the Rangers especially vulnerable to the league's best pitchers?

We looked at every Ranger game of the past two years, dividing the games according to quality of starter the Rangers faced. We looked only at starters because we wanted a large sample of innings to determine the pitcher's quality. As another sample size consideration, we threw out all pitcher-seasons with fewer than 10 starts. The Support-Neutral measures were used to partition the pitchers: Good pitchers were those with a final season Support-Neutral Winning Percentage (SNPct) above .550; Average pitchers were those with SNPcts between .450 and .550; and Bad pitchers were those with SNPcts below .450.

Obviously the Rangers are going to perform worse against good pitchers—every team does. The question is how they perform relative to an average team. Does their offense suffer more against a good pitcher than does the league as a whole? To estimate how the league would score against the same lineup of pitchers the Rangers faced, we summed up the pitchers' runs-per-inning rates, weighted by the number of innings each pitched against the Rangers. Here is the Rangers' performance compared to league average for Good, Average and Bad pitching:

	Games	R/G Avg	R/G Tex	Texas compared to Average
Good pitching	87	4.29	5.15	+20%
Average pitching	128	5.46	6.13	+12%
Bad pitching	70	7.16	7.16	0%

The results do not support the theory that the Rangers are especially vulnerable to good pitching. In fact, they indicate exactly the opposite. The better the pitching, the better the Rangers, relative to the league. They score 20% more runs than you'd expect an average team to score against good pitching, and 12% more against mediocre pitching. It's actually against the worst pitching that the Rangers do not exceed expectations: against the league's cannon fodder, they play exactly like an average team.

There are still other theories to explain the Rangers' poor October performance: good Yankee scouting, the Rangers being worn down by a season in the Texas heat, the Rangers collectively being intimidated by the Yankee mystique. But until anyone can provide at least a little evidence to go along with the barstool speculation, I think the most plausible explanation is the most obvious one: plain old bad luck. The Rangers faced an elite team, largely in a poor run-scoring environment (Yankee Stadium in cold weather) and were just unlucky to have a couple of team slumps at the wrong times.

HITTERS (Averages: BA: .270 / OBP: .340 / SLG: .430 / EQA: .260)

Luis Alicea — 2B/3B — Bats B — Age 34

YEAR	TEAM	LGE	AB	H	DB	TP	HR	BB/SO	R	RBI	SB	CS	OUT	BA	OBP	SLG	EQA	EQR	DEFENSE
1997	Anaheim	AL	386	97	15	7	5	66/62	56	35	22	8	297	.251	.373	.365	.264	53	103-2B 98
1998	Texas	AL	255	68	12	3	6	36/39	46	30	3	3	190	.267	.368	.408	.266	35	39-2B 99
1999	Texas	AL	162	31	6	0	4	26/32	29	16	2	1	132	.191	.303	.302	.212	14	31-2B 96
2000	Texas	AL	189	46	8	1	4	37/32	35	25	4	3	146	.243	.367	.360	.251	23	

Much of the blame for that terrible 1999 line belongs to a wrist injury that hampered him through most of the first half. In the second half, he hit as well as could be expected: .254/.329/.463. If healthy, he should outperform the projection by a little. At his age, the "if" is a big one.

Andy Barkett — 1B — Bats L — Age 25

YEAR	TEAM	LGE	AB	H	DB	TP	HR	BB/SO	R	RBI	SB	CS	OUT	BA	OBP	SLG	EQA	EQR	DEFENSE
1997	Tulsa	Tex	468	122	31	6	7	51/97	63	49	1	2	348	.261	.339	.397	.250	55	129-1B 89
1998	Tulsa	Tex	158	36	10	1	1	22/25	18	23	0	0	122	.228	.325	.323	.226	15	42-1B 91
1998	Oklahoma	PCL	255	75	17	4	3	30/43	32	30	2	3	183	.294	.368	.427	.269	34	69-1B 84
1999	Oklahoma	PCL	480	129	28	4	7	37/72	54	58	5	5	356	.269	.327	.387	.242	51	119-1B 97
2000	Texas	AL	495	140	28	4	9	55/79	79	74	3	4	359	.283	.355	.410	.255	59	

Barkett has never developed the power that could have changed his title from Professional Minor League Hitter to The Next Paul Sorrento. He's likely to be squeezed out of the Ranger organization soon by the line of solid first-base prospects coming up behind him. He could help some big league teams over the next few years as a backup first baseman and left-handed pinch-hitter.

Cliff Brumbaugh — OF/1B — Bats R — Age 26

YEAR	TEAM	LGE	AB	H	DB	TP	HR	BB/SO	R	RBI	SB	CS	OUT	BA	OBP	SLG	EQA	EQR	DEFENSE	
1997	Charlott	Fla	535	120	26	2	13	36/119	61	54	5	4	419	.224	.279	.353	.211	43	126-3B 110	
1998	Tulsa	Tex	486	104	23	1	11	38/94	46	53	1	1	383	.214	.275	.333	.204	36	97-1B 92	23-3B 86
1999	Tulsa	Tex	518	114	27	2	16	52/108	62	58	7	2	406	.220	.293	.373	.226	49	113-OF 88	21-1B 85
2000	Texas	AL	490	112	21	1	17	50/101	58	63	4	2	380	.229	.300	.380	.225	46		

On the surface, Brumbaugh's untranslated 1999 numbers look promising: .281/.368/.507. Ignore them. He was repeating Double A, was too old to be there and the converted first baseman showed little ability in the outfield. He's not a prospect.

Royce Clayton — SS — Bats R — Age 30

YEAR	TEAM	LGE	AB	H	DB	TP	HR	BB/SO	R	RBI	SB	CS	OUT	BA	OBP	SLG	EQA	EQR	DEFENSE
1997	St Louis	NL	583	158	42	5	10	32/108	73	62	24	10	435	.271	.312	.412	.245	65	145-SS 102
1998	St Louis	NL	358	86	20	1	4	39/50	60	29	20	7	279	.240	.319	.335	.231	36	88-SS 108
1998	Texas	AL	184	51	10	1	5	12/31	27	22	4	5	138	.277	.325	.424	.246	21	51-SS 97
1999	Texas	AL	460	129	19	5	13	33/100	61	47	8	6	337	.280	.334	.428	.255	55	129-SS 98
2000	Texas	AL	488	133	29	3	11	43/93	76	67	14	7	362	.273	.331	.412	.248	55	

A shoulder injury hampered both his fielding and hitting in the first half (639 pre-break OPS). After the break, he joined the growing list of players converting to the new Sam Bat, and he suddenly started hitting like he wanted to join the Jeter/Rodriguez/Garciaparra club (912 post-break OPS). With the shoulder problem behind him, I think there's a good chance we'll see a career year from Clayton in 2000.

Kelly Dransfeldt — SS — Bats R — Age 25

YEAR	TEAM	LGE	AB	H	DB	TP	HR	BB/SO	R	RBI	SB	CS	OUT	BA	OBP	SLG	EQA	EQR	DEFENSE
1997	Charlott	Fla	477	102	21	5	7	34/130	51	51	10	7	382	.214	.269	.323	.198	33	130-SS 88
1998	Charlott	Fla	249	64	11	0	14	22/81	31	52	2	1	186	.257	.321	.470	.261	32	65-SS 99
1998	Tulsa	Tex	226	50	14	2	7	14/90	31	26	4	1	177	.221	.271	.394	.222	21	57-SS 102
1999	Oklahoma	PCL	356	75	18	3	7	20/110	42	34	4	2	283	.211	.257	.337	.197	24	94-SS 89
1999	Texas	AL	53	10	1	0	1	2/12	3	5	0	0	43	.189	.218	.264	.141	2	
2000	Texas	AL	398	88	20	2	12	33/124	45	45	6	2	312	.221	.281	.372	.215	33	

Last year we urged caution amidst the Dransfeldt hype, but we can't claim to have foreseen the magnitude of the disaster to come. He was actually hitting fairly well in late April when he was promoted to the majors to fill in for Clayton, but he was brutally overmatched by major-league pitching. He then seemed to take his problems back to Oklahoma with him. The Rangers were undeterred, moving him to second base over the winter because there's no full-time spot for him at shortstop. I hate to break the news to them, but there should be no full-time spot anywhere for someone who's consistently shown so little hitting ability.

Tom Evans — 3B — Bats R — Age 25

YEAR	TEAM	LGE	AB	H	DB	TP	HR	BB/SO	R	RBI	SB	CS	OUT	BA	OBP	SLG	EQA	EQR	DEFENSE
1997	Syracuse	Int	381	98	17	1	14	45/101	54	59	1	1	284	.257	.349	.417	.261	49	104-3B 106
1998	Syracuse	Int	400	111	26	1	14	42/75	48	47	7	5	294	.278	.356	.452	.271	56	110-3B 84
1999	Oklahoma	PCL	436	107	31	2	9	56/102	65	52	4	3	332	.245	.341	.388	.250	52	123-3B 108
2000	Texas	AL	393	106	22	1	14	51/88	66	66	4	2	289	.270	.354	.438	.264	52	

Once the Blue Jays' third baseman of the future, Evans was stolen off waivers from Toronto in the spring. He rewarded the Rangers by being the third-best hitter on their PCL American Conference champion. Evans was removed from the 40-man roster after the season, then signed to a minor-league contract with an invitation to spring training. He is still the perfect guy to have around while Mike Lamb makes the transition to the majors—as a stopgap, an insurance policy or even a platoon partner.

Shawn Gallagher — 1B — Bats R — Age 23

YEAR	TEAM	LGE	AB	H	DB	TP	HR	BB/SO	R	RBI	SB	CS	OUT	BA	OBP	SLG	EQA	EQR	DEFENSE
1997	Pulaski	App	198	48	10	2	9	5/53	23	28	1	0	150	.242	.268	.449	.235	20	49-1B 65
1997	Charlott	Fla	100	16	5	0	0	4/38	7	8	0	0	84	.160	.198	.210	.087	1	26-1B 81
1998	Charlott	Fla	530	143	32	3	24	54/128	86	95	7	3	390	.270	.343	.477	.272	76	128-1B 65
1999	Tulsa	Tex	452	114	25	2	15	20/91	49	61	1	0	338	.252	.289	.416	.234	45	107-1B 77
2000	Texas	AL	488	134	25	1	22	45/109	72	88	2	1	355	.275	.336	.465	.262	63	

He took a step backwards from his great 1998, but not too big a step. He's always had the reputation of a great hitter prior to 1999, including a dominating high-school career, and his subpar 1999 can be partially blamed on a paintball accident in April that separated his shoulder. 2000 will be his age-23 season, when a lot of hitters make big strides in their development. If he gets a chance to play every day, look for him to rebound with a big season at the plate and to work his way back into the Rangers' crowded 1B/DH picture. Space limitations, along with the obscenity laws of some states, prevent me from discussing his defense.

Juan Gonzalez — RF — Bats R — Age 30

YEAR	TEAM	LGE	AB	H	DB	TP	HR	BB/SO	R	RBI	SB	CS	OUT	BA	OBP	SLG	EQA	EQR	DEFENSE
1997	Texas	AL	531	159	25	3	42	30/103	84	127	0	0	372	.299	.341	.595	.298	90	56-OF 97
1998	Texas	AL	598	186	44	3	44	43/123	102	146	2	1	413	.311	.363	.615	.310	111	114-OF 88
1999	Texas	AL	554	176	32	1	38	44/105	102	117	3	3	381	.318	.372	.585	.307	99	125-RF 95
2000	Detroit	AL	535	164	23	1	39	46/104	90	130	1	1	372	.307	.361	.572	.303	94	

Mr. Consistency. Gonzalez's 1999 was about as valuable as any of his previous four years, including his "MVP" seasons. Last year even featured a career-high walk rate. Unfortunately for Gonzalez, last year also featured Tom Goodwin's return to earth—say goodbye to 20 RBIs, say goodbye to postseason trophies. Traded to the Tigers, Gonzalez will be missed in Arlington. He is far and away the best hitter in Rangers history.

Tom Goodwin   CF   Bats L   Age 31

YEAR	TEAM	LGE	AB	H	DB	TP	HR	BB/SO	R	RBI	SB	CS	OUT	BA	OBP	SLG	EQA	EQR	DEFENSE
1997	KansasCy	AL	365	98	12	4	2	17/49	48	21	34	10	277	.268	.305	.340	.230	35	94-OF 102
1997	Texas	AL	206	48	13	2	0	24/36	37	16	16	6	164	.233	.316	.316	.227	20	47-OF 110
1998	Texas	AL	512	142	12	3	2	70/88	90	30	32	19	389	.277	.366	.324	.246	58	129-OF 109
1999	Texas	AL	401	100	11	5	3	35/61	57	29	39	12	313	.249	.310	.324	.229	39	103-CF 98
2000	*Colorado*	*NL*	*467*	*139*	*18*	*5*	*2*	*51/75*	*89*	*51*	*37*	*17*	*344*	*.298*	*.367*	*.370*	*.236*	*46*	

We all knew 1998 was a mirage, right? Goodwin's return to earth was an especially hard one, featuring a hip flexor injury that robbed him of his one valuable skill, defense. Ruben Mateo made him obsolete in Arlington, so the baseball fans of Denver will get to watch him hit .300, steal 40 bases and still be below-average.

Jason Grabowski   3B   Bats L   Age 24

YEAR	TEAM	LGE	AB	H	DB	TP	HR	BB/SO	R	RBI	SB	CS	OUT	BA	OBP	SLG	EQA	EQR	DEFENSE
1997	Pulaski	App	178	39	8	0	3	28/34	20	14	2	1	140	.219	.325	.315	.225	17	
1998	Savannah	SAL	365	84	12	5	11	45/97	45	39	6	4	285	.230	.316	.381	.237	39	60-C 93
1999	Charlott	Fla	442	112	28	4	10	50/79	50	63	5	4	334	.253	.333	.403	.249	52	115-3B 89
2000	*Texas*	*AL*	*359*	*92*	*16*	*2*	*9*	*49/73*	*56*	*51*	*5*	*3*	*270*	*.256*	*.346*	*.387*	*.248*	*41*	

Grabowski has gotten some people excited with his 1999, but I'm not quite as high on him. He has hit pretty well at low-A and high-A the past two years, but he was really old to be playing at those levels. It's not clear that his defense at third base—he just converted from catcher—will be good enough to keep him at that position. He's likely to wear a major-league uniform someday, but has a low ceiling.

Scarborough Green   OF   Bats B   Age 26

YEAR	TEAM	LGE	AB	H	DB	TP	HR	BB/SO	R	RBI	SB	CS	OUT	BA	OBP	SLG	EQA	EQR	DEFENSE
1997	Arkansas	Tex	249	65	13	2	2	29/56	32	21	6	3	187	.261	.342	.353	.242	27	75-OF 113
1997	Louisvil	AA	211	51	9	2	3	20/56	24	12	9	5	165	.242	.307	.346	.225	20	52-OF 119
1998	Memphis	PCL	81	15	4	0	0	7/23	9	2	1	3	69	.185	.250	.235	.145	3	20-OF 116
1999	Oklahoma	PCL	357	74	14	4	2	27/93	47	21	16	8	291	.207	.267	.286	.189	23	102-OF 99
1999	*Texas*	*AL*	*13*	*4*	*0*	*0*	*0*	*1/2*	*2*	*0*	*0*	*1*	*10*	*.308*	*.357*	*.308*	*.209*	*1*	

It's not clear why Johnny Oates suddenly decided he needed to carry a player whose only asset is . . . what is it, again? Green spent 35 days with the team before the September roster expansion, and another four on the playoff roster, and in that time got into 10 games and had four plate appearances. That's certainly better than playing him a lot, but why not use the roster spot on someone who might occasionally do something useful?

Rusty Greer   LF   Bats L   Age 31

YEAR	TEAM	LGE	AB	H	DB	TP	HR	BB/SO	R	RBI	SB	CS	OUT	BA	OBP	SLG	EQA	EQR	DEFENSE
1997	Texas	AL	597	193	42	3	26	78/84	108	84	9	5	409	.323	.405	.534	.310	109	152-OF 92
1998	Texas	AL	589	175	31	5	15	76/91	99	99	1	4	418	.297	.381	.443	.279	86	150-OF 91
1999	Texas	AL	546	160	41	3	18	88/67	96	90	2	2	388	.293	.396	.478	.295	91	143-LF 101
2000	*Texas*	*AL*	*520*	*154*	*34*	*2*	*18*	*85/69*	*106*	*102*	*2*	*2*	*368*	*.296*	*.395*	*.473*	*.290*	*83*	

As we predicted, he bounced back from his subpar 1998. While he's often mentioned in talk-show trade proposals, Greer is exactly the kind of player the Rangers should keep. He has underappreciated skills—drawing walks and hitting doubles—so you're not likely to get equal value in a trade. Plus, he's relatively cheap.

Travis Hafner   1B   Bats L   Age 23

YEAR	TEAM	LGE	AB	H	DB	TP	HR	BB/SO	R	RBI	SB	CS	OUT	BA	OBP	SLG	EQA	EQR	DEFENSE	
1998	Savannah	SAL	419	88	15	3	14	56/140	49	66	3	1	332	.210	.309	.360	.230	42	65-1B 85	21-3B 85
1999	Savannah	SAL	502	126	28	2	23	55/157	75	86	2	2	378	.251	.332	.452	.261	66	108-1B 93	
2000	*Texas*	*AL*	*369*	*89*	*16*	*1*	*18*	*47/129*	*53*	*62*	*1*	*1*	*281*	*.241*	*.327*	*.436*	*.251*	*45*		

Those 1999 numbers look pretty good, and they won Hafner all sorts of accolades. Unfortunately, they are the result of repeating a low level, and that makes them suspicious. He has a great batting eye, but I don't know whether he can maintain the power numbers he put up last year.

Roberto Kelly   OF   Bats R   Age 35

YEAR	TEAM	LGE	AB	H	DB	TP	HR	BB/SO	R	RBI	SB	CS	OUT	BA	OBP	SLG	EQA	EQR	DEFENSE	
1997	Minnesot	AL	246	71	19	2	5	16/48	38	36	7	4	179	.289	.338	.443	.261	31	47-OF 98	
1997	Seattle	AL	121	36	5	0	8	4/16	18	22	2	1	86	.298	.326	.537	.279	18	19-OF 111	
1998	Texas	AL	254	80	7	3	15	7/45	44	42	0	2	176	.315	.341	.543	.284	38	57-OF 106	
1999	Texas	AL	287	84	18	1	7	17/57	37	33	6	1	204	.293	.343	.436	.265	37	30-RF 104	28-CF 93
2000	*Texas*	*AL*	*269*	*77*	*13*	*1*	*12*	*19/50*	*39*	*49*	*2*	*2*	*194*	*.286*	*.333*	*.476*	*.262*	*34*		

The key for Kelly is how he's used. He's a very consistent hitter with a large platoon split. If his team is healthy enough and his manager diligent enough that Kelly can bat mostly against left-handed pitchers, as he did in 1998, his overall numbers will look excellent. If not, as was the case in 1999, they won't. He's a free agent.

Cesar King   C   Bats R   Age 22

YEAR	TEAM	LGE	AB	H	DB	TP	HR	BB/SO	R	RBI	SB	CS	OUT	BA	OBP	SLG	EQA	EQR	DEFENSE
1997	Charlott	Fla	316	86	14	3	7	30/64	44	33	3	3	233	.272	.337	.402	.250	36	
1998	Tulsa	Tex	318	65	16	1	2	23/75	32	31	1	1	254	.204	.261	.280	.177	17	86-C 102
1999	Tulsa	Tex	323	66	16	1	10	26/76	33	36	1	1	258	.204	.267	.353	.206	25	92-C 99
2000	*Texas*	*AL*	*294*	*69*	*16*	*1*	*7*	*30/68*	*36*	*35*	*2*	*1*	*226*	*.235*	*.306*	*.367*	*.224*	*27*	

Two years ago he looked like the next Pudge Rodriguez. After flopping for the second consecutive year at Double-A, he now looks like he won't even get the chance to be the next John Orton. The two things he still has going for him: a great arm and his youth.

Mike Lamb   3B   Bats L   Age 24

YEAR	TEAM	LGE	AB	H	DB	TP	HR	BB/SO	R	RBI	SB	CS	OUT	BA	OBP	SLG	EQA	EQR	DEFENSE
1997	Pulaski	App	234	58	15	2	5	20/19	32	26	2	1	177	.248	.312	.393	.238	25	58-3B 101
1998	Charlott	Fla	543	143	32	2	9	35/72	64	73	7	3	403	.263	.311	.379	.234	53	133-3B 105
1999	Tulsa	Tex	544	149	42	3	16	41/73	74	73	2	1	396	.274	.331	.450	.261	69	136-3B 103
2000	*Texas*	*AL*	*470*	*134*	*29*	*1*	*13*	*44/60*	*72*	*76*	*2*	*2*	*338*	*.285*	*.346*	*.434*	*.259*	*57*	

1999 was a breakthrough year for Lamb. He had a big jump in power with 21 homers and a Tulsa-record 51 doubles, and was named Rangers' minor-league player of the year. He was a little old to be in Double-A, and he's never done anything like this before, so we should wait until he repeats those numbers at a higher level before cranking the hype meter too high. If he approaches that performance again this year, the Rangers have found their third baseman of the future, a future that may arrive sometime in 2000.

Ruben Mateo   OF   Bats R   Age 22

YEAR	TEAM	LGE	AB	H	DB	TP	HR	BB/SO	R	RBI	SB	CS	OUT	BA	OBP	SLG	EQA	EQR	DEFENSE
1997	Charlott	Fla	393	114	23	5	14	18/60	51	59	8	2	281	.290	.329	.481	.269	53	89-OF 100
1998	Tulsa	Tex	432	118	29	2	14	22/62	58	57	9	4	319	.273	.324	.447	.257	54	107-OF 106
1999	Oklahoma	PCL	249	76	10	0	15	12/36	41	50	4	2	175	.305	.353	.526	.287	39	55-OF 103
1999	Texas	AL	122	28	9	1	5	2/28	15	17	3	0	94	.230	.248	.443	.229	12	30-CF 91
2000	*Texas*	*AL*	*405*	*123*	*21*	*2*	*23*	*26/64*	*67*	*86*	*7*	*3*	*285*	*.304*	*.346*	*.536*	*.283*	*61*	

The two big concerns about Mateo are his lack of plate discipline and his fragility. The former is just part of the package; he should be an excellent hitter—if overrated—even with a poor walk rate. I don't know what to make of the latter. I know some bodies are just more brittle than others, but with Mateo I'm inclined to blame some of his fragility on bad luck; it's not as if he's injuring the same body part over and over. If healthy in 2000, he's the frontrunner for AL Rookie of the Year.

Mark McLemore   2B   Bats B   Age 35

YEAR	TEAM	LGE	AB	H	DB	TP	HR	BB/SO	R	RBI	SB	CS	OUT	BA	OBP	SLG	EQA	EQR	DEFENSE
1997	Texas	AL	348	91	18	2	1	37/52	45	24	7	5	262	.261	.336	.333	.233	34	84-2B 104
1998	Texas	AL	455	109	13	1	5	86/63	72	49	10	4	350	.240	.363	.305	.243	51	121-2B 97
1999	Texas	AL	558	147	19	7	5	76/79	94	40	16	8	419	.263	.352	.349	.246	63	130-2B 105
2000	*Seattle*	*AL*	*428*	*106*	*14*	*3*	*3*	*69/60*	*68*	*45*	*8*	*5*	*327*	*.248*	*.352*	*.315*	*.239*	*46*	

McLemore is 35 years old, has established himself as below average at his position and is playing with knees that can explode at any time. In other words, he's not the kind of player you should sign to a two-year, seven-figure contract. McLemore has signed with the Mariners; as a utility player who gets 350 at-bats and plays some second base and right field, he can help them.

Rafael Palmeiro — 1B/DH — Bats L — Age 35

YEAR	TEAM	LGE	AB	H	DB	TP	HR	BB/SO	R	RBI	SB	CS	OUT	BA	OBP	SLG	EQA	EQR	DEFENSE
1997	Baltimor	AL	614	160	26	2	39	63/105	94	109	5	2	456	.261	.335	.500	.274	90	152-1B 105
1998	Baltimor	AL	622	191	34	2	45	77/89	97	121	10	7	438	.307	.390	.585	.313	120	158-1B 106
1999	Texas	AL	554	175	27	1	45	89/69	86	134	2	4	383	.316	.413	.612	.327	117	28-1B 89
2000	Texas	AL	534	155	21	1	40	90/72	109	135	3	3	382	.290	.393	.558	.306	99	

This was a spectacular year at the plate for Palmeiro. If he'd been the run-saving first baseman he was in 1998, you could have made a case for him as MVP. He wasn't, because his knees limited him to 28 games at the position, and that's cause for concern. He had the right one operated on twice in the spring, and it's still causing serious problems. Take a look at Kirk Gibson's career to see how quickly bad knees can bring down a great player. That's not something the Rangers want to hear about a guy who's still owed about $40 million.

There's not much to say about his Gold Glove award, other than to hope it has shed some light on how meaningless the honor is. Here's hoping fans, the media and people within the game take them less seriously in the future, and use this opportunity to take a long, hard look at how defense is evaluated.

Carlos Pena — 1B — Bats L — Age 22

YEAR	TEAM	LGE	AB	H	DB	TP	HR	BB/SO	R	RBI	SB	CS	OUT	BA	OBP	SLG	EQA	EQR	DEFENSE
1998	Savannah	SAL	115	32	8	0	6	7/25	15	16	1	1	84	.278	.334	.504	.273	16	26-1B 97
1999	Charlott	Fla	509	118	28	5	19	63/148	71	85	1	2	393	.232	.327	.418	.251	62	133-1B 100
2000	Texas	AL	279	73	14	1	16	39/88	48	56	1	1	207	.262	.352	.491	.275	41	

Last year he was considered a disappointment as the Rangers' top pick in 1998, but there was actually a lot to like. His batting average was lower than anyone would have hoped, but he showed good isolated power and a much higher walk rate than he had shown previously. Pena is a good bet to reestablish himself as a top prospect this year.

Juan Piniella — OF — Bats R — Age 22

YEAR	TEAM	LGE	AB	H	DB	TP	HR	BB/SO	R	RBI	SB	CS	OUT	BA	OBP	SLG	EQA	EQR	DEFENSE
1997	Pulaski	App	126	27	2	2	1	5/24	10	11	3	2	101	.214	.244	.286	.170	6	32-OF 100
1998	Savannah	SAL	262	78	13	4	3	25/48	35	31	11	5	189	.298	.365	.412	.267	35	70-OF 98
1998	Charlott	Fla	226	64	9	2	2	20/42	26	19	9	3	165	.283	.343	.367	.248	25	50-OF 97
1999	Tulsa	Tex	461	108	20	1	8	50/131	53	37	8	3	356	.234	.317	.334	.226	43	124-OF 106
2000	Texas	AL	437	115	18	2	8	46/107	63	55	9	4	326	.263	.333	.368	.238	45	

After Mateo, the Rangers' outfield-prospect situation is bleak. Piniella stumbled in his first season in Double-A, yet he still has the highest ceiling of any outfielder in the farm system. As with Pena, it's encouraging that only Piniella's batting average dropped; his walk rate stayed high and power was unchanged from 1998. Look for him to improve in 2000.

Ivan Rodriguez — C — Bats R — Age 28

YEAR	TEAM	LGE	AB	H	DB	TP	HR	BB/SO	R	RBI	SB	CS	OUT	BA	OBP	SLG	EQA	EQR	DEFENSE
1997	Texas	AL	594	187	34	4	20	34/86	94	74	7	3	410	.315	.361	.487	.282	87	
1998	Texas	AL	571	179	38	4	20	30/86	81	84	8	0	392	.313	.351	.499	.283	83	136-C 111
1999	Texas	AL	593	191	27	1	33	17/64	103	102	24	13	414	.322	.342	.538	.285	89	136-C 110
2000	Texas	AL	610	198	32	2	28	38/75	109	125	17	5	417	.325	.364	.521	.289	94	

It's tempting to look at Rodriguez's consistent improvement at the plate and attribute it to the normal progression of a young player. But there's more than that here. 1999 marked the fourth consecutive year that Rodriguez improved his OPS by 20 points or more over the previous year. He's only the 15th player in major-league history to accomplish that feat with a minimum 400 at-bats in each year. Nevertheless, a player can't improve forever, especially one who endures the abuse of catching at least 130 games every year. Rodriguez is now on the wrong side of 27, so the safe money is on his dropping off a bit from his outstanding 1999.

(Ivan Rodriguez *continued*)

He wasn't the most valuable player in the AL in 1999. That said, this wasn't like the Juan Gonzalez awards in 1996 and 1998, when Gonzalez had no business in the discussion. Rodriguez had an excellent offensive season, excels at the one part of catching we can measure well and would have been a great candidate in a lot of years. Just not this one.

Jason Romano   2B   Bats R   Age 21

YEAR	TEAM	LGE	AB	H	DB	TP	HR	BB/SO	R	RBI	SB	CS	OUT	BA	OBP	SLG	EQA	EQR	DEFENSE	
1998	Savannah	SAL	535	131	19	4	6	38/95	50	42	15	8	412	.245	.301	.329	.216	45	132-2B 98	
1999	Charlott	Fla	463	129	28	10	14	32/79	64	58	16	8	342	.279	.335	.473	.268	64	109-2B 93	
2000	Texas	AL	371	110	17	4	14	29/74	64	66	13	5	266	.296	.347	.477	.271	51		

Romano, the Rangers' top draft choice in 1997, established himself as their #2 position-player prospect with his big season. He showed line-drive power, speed (34 steals and 14 triples) and decent plate discipline. His defense at second base is still a little raw, but that's to be expected from a converted third baseman. Romano reminds some people of a young Chuck Knoblauch.

Tom Sergio   2B   Bats L   Age 25

YEAR	TEAM	LGE	AB	H	DB	TP	HR	BB/SO	R	RBI	SB	CS	OUT	BA	OBP	SLG	EQA	EQR	DEFENSE	
1997	Pulaski	App	228	53	11	2	5	25/47	26	21	6	2	177	.232	.313	.364	.234	23	55-2B 99	
1998	Charlott	Fla	460	111	29	4	4	34/72	59	28	11	4	353	.241	.303	.348	.224	42	108-2B 92	
1999	Tulsa	Tex	514	122	32	3	7	43/70	60	51	8	3	395	.237	.301	.352	.223	46	123-2B 99	
2000	Texas	AL	480	124	27	2	8	49/70	70	58	9	4	360	.258	.327	.373	.236	49		

Sergio basically repeated at Double-A what he'd done the year before at high-A. He's old for his level, but he could potentially make a decent major-league utility infielder through his peak years.

Jon Shave   IF   Bats R   Age 32

YEAR	TEAM	LGE	AB	H	DB	TP	HR	BB/SO	R	RBI	SB	CS	OUT	BA	OBP	SLG	EQA	EQR	DEFENSE	
1997	SaltLake	PCL	380	98	21	2	4	28/70	49	38	4	4	286	.258	.317	.355	.228	36	22-3B 104	22-SS 99
1998	SaltLake	PCL	306	80	14	1	2	26/50	42	27	5	5	231	.261	.337	.333	.232	30	55-2B 90	
1999	Texas	AL	72	20	4	0	0	4/17	9	8	1	0	52	.278	.333	.333	.233	7		
2000	Texas	AL	154	40	4	0	2	14/28	18	16	2	2	116	.260	.321	.325	.216	13		

I don't know exactly how it happened, but Jon Shave is now a Proven Major Leaguer. When the *Dallas Morning News* gave end-of-season grades to all Ranger players, it gave Shave a higher grade than Gonzalez, Greer or Rick Helling, along with this bit of "praise": "He is willing to do anything. With the Rangers, that mostly means sitting on the bench." Presumably, it also means detailing Doug Melvin's car. Shave does hit left-handed pitchers a bit. He's been released.

Scott Sheldon   UT   Bats R   Age 31

YEAR	TEAM	LGE	AB	H	DB	TP	HR	BB/SO	R	RBI	SB	CS	OUT	BA	OBP	SLG	EQA	EQR	DEFENSE	
1997	Edmonton	PCL	406	98	28	3	12	43/117	55	47	3	1	309	.241	.321	.414	.248	48	79-SS 98	28-2B 105
1998	Oklahoma	PCL	495	109	28	3	21	50/156	56	71	1	1	387	.220	.295	.416	.237	53	122-SS 95	
1999	Oklahoma	PCL	448	115	29	2	19	45/121	65	68	7	2	335	.257	.328	.458	.262	59	57-2B 107	29-SS 99
2000	Texas	AL	449	109	21	1	20	55/127	65	72	3	1	341	.243	.325	.428	.249	53		

1999 was probably Sheldon's career season—.311/.385/.587 unadjusted—and he spent it punishing minor-league pitching while the likes of Shave and Dransfeldt got valuable major-league plate appearances. I could fill pages on all the times the Rangers have blown opportunities to use Sheldon. Here's just one example. Coming into 1999, Mark McLemore had gone the previous three years with a 675 OPS against left-handed pitchers—55 points worse than his performance against right-handers. At the same time, Sheldon was coming off a 1998 season in which he murdered Triple-A left-handers to the tune of a 950 OPS. Can you say "platoon opportunity"? The Rangers couldn't: last year Sheldon had a Ruthian 1190 OPS against left-handers, again against Triple-A pitching, while McLemore had an Ordonezian 473.

Mike Simms   DH   Bats R   Age 33

YEAR	TEAM	LGE	AB	H	DB	TP	HR	BB/SO	R	RBI	SB	CS	OUT	BA	OBP	SLG	EQA	EQR	DEFENSE
1997	Texas	AL	111	28	6	0	6	7/26	12	22	0	1	84	.252	.297	.468	.248	13	
1998	Texas	AL	183	52	9	0	16	23/46	33	43	0	1	132	.284	.373	.596	.307	35	27-OF 85
1999	Oklahoma	PCL	73	16	0	0	2	13/27	5	13	0	0	57	.219	.337	.301	.227	7	
2000	Texas	AL	116	29	2	0	7	18/30	18	22	0	0	87	.250	.351	.448	.265	16	

Injuries to his Achilles tendon and his heel limited Simms to 115 at-bats in the minors and two with Texas. It would have been extremely tough for Simms to approach his career-best numbers of 1998 while entering 1999 at age 32. Now, a year older, coming off two serious injuries and a year of relative inactivity, it will be that much tougher.

Danny Solano   SS   Bats R   Age 21

YEAR	TEAM	LGE	AB	H	DB	TP	HR	BB/SO	R	RBI	SB	CS	OUT	BA	OBP	SLG	EQA	EQR	DEFENSE
1998	Charlott	Fla	268	63	9	0	3	35/60	36	27	4	3	208	.235	.327	.302	.221	24	68-SS 102
1999	Charlott	Fla	429	105	17	3	8	63/81	51	37	11	7	330	.245	.346	.354	.245	49	114-SS 102
2000	Texas	AL	271	71	8	1	7	43/56	46	39	6	3	203	.262	.363	.376	.254	33	

Solano is a rare breed: a Dominican shortstop who walks like crazy. He also hits for average and is a slick fielder. He hasn't drawn much attention from other minor-league analysts, which will change if he makes the important transition to Double-A smoothly.

Lee Stevens   1B/DH   Bats L   Age 33

YEAR	TEAM	LGE	AB	H	DB	TP	HR	BB/SO	R	RBI	SB	CS	OUT	BA	OBP	SLG	EQA	EQR	DEFENSE	
1997	Texas	AL	424	128	24	2	21	21/80	56	71	1	3	299	.302	.337	.517	.276	60	51-1B 99	13-OF 97
1998	Texas	AL	340	87	16	4	19	30/91	48	54	0	2	255	.256	.316	.494	.263	45	22-1B 98	
1999	Texas	AL	511	140	29	1	23	46/132	68	73	2	3	374	.274	.334	.470	.265	68	130-1B 87	
2000	Texas	AL	366	96	17	1	18	35/91	51	65	0	1	271	.262	.327	.462	.257	45		

Injuries to Simms and Palmeiro forced Stevens to make the transition from the left-handed half of a DH platoon to full-time first baseman. In one respect, the full-time job suited him surprisingly well, as he hit left-handers even better than he hit right-handers. In another respect, it didn't: the increased playing time in the Texas heat really wore Stevens down. His OPS before the All-Star break: 885; after: 766.

Pedro Valdes   OF/DH   Bats L   Age 27

YEAR	TEAM	LGE	AB	H	DB	TP	HR	BB/SO	R	RBI	SB	CS	OUT	BA	OBP	SLG	EQA	EQR	DEFENSE
1997	Iowa	AA	472	129	27	1	13	42/71	59	56	7	2	345	.273	.335	.417	.256	57	117-OF 104
1998	Iowa	PCL	227	60	7	0	13	22/42	35	29	1	1	168	.264	.329	.467	.263	30	54-OF 97
1999	Tulsa	Tex	34	9	2	0	1	6/7	2	3	0	0	25	.265	.375	.412	.272	5	
1999	Oklahoma	PCL	389	104	19	1	15	42/65	51	51	1	1	286	.267	.346	.437	.264	51	21-OF 107
2000	Texas	AL	359	101	12	0	18	46/60	59	70	2	1	259	.281	.363	.465	.274	51	

Valdes, like his Oklahoma teammates Scott Sheldon and Tom Evans, is a strong candidate for the Ken Phelps All-Stars: major-league-caliber players who somehow get that last promotion and get caught up in front-office circular reasoning: "Why won't you call him up?" "Because he's a career minor leaguer." "Why is he a career minor leaguer?" "Because we won't call him up." Most teams, including the Rangers, could use a left-handed-hitting fifth outfielder who'll hit .280 with some pop and patience.

Corey Wright   OF   Bats L   Age 20

YEAR	TEAM	LGE	AB	H	DB	TP	HR	BB/SO	R	RBI	SB	CS	OUT	BA	OBP	SLG	EQA	EQR	DEFENSE
1998	Pulaski	App	137	29	4	1	3	33/25	23	17	4	2	110	.212	.367	.321	.250	17	40-OF 104
1999	Savannah	SAL	334	78	17	3	1	54/74	49	19	5	6	262	.234	.345	.311	.231	34	94-OF 97
2000	Texas	AL	193	45	10	2	1	40/51	36	20	3	2	150	.233	.365	.321	.242	22	

Nobody's talking about Wright, but his walk rate blows me away. In the Appalachian League in 1998, 25% of his plate appearances resulted in walks. Last year, it was 17%. He looks like the second coming of Max Bishop. One of two things will happen to Wright at this point. Either he'll bomb as he gets to higher levels with pitchers who can actually throw strikes, or he'll learn to complement his batting eye by hitting the ball hard once in a while. Given his age, there's at least some hope for the latter.

Gregg Zaun   C   Bats B   Age 29

YEAR	TEAM	LGE	AB	H	DB	TP	HR	BB/SO	R	RBI	SB	CS	OUT	BA	OBP	SLG	EQA	EQR	DEFENSE
1997	Florida	NL	146	45	11	2	2	26/18	22	20	1	0	101	.308	.420	.452	.302	25	
1998	Florida	NL	302	61	13	2	6	34/51	20	31	5	2	243	.202	.285	.318	.207	24	83-C 100
1999	Texas	AL	92	22	2	1	1	9/7	11	11	1	0	70	.239	.307	.315	.216	8	26-C 108
2000	*Detroit*	*AL*	*150*	*35*	*7*	*1*	*3*	*19/20*	*21*	*17*	*2*	*0*	*115*	*.233*	*.320*	*.353*	*.235*	*15*	

Some of the world's least demanding jobs: Bruce Willis's hair stylist, O.J. Simpson Fan Club chairman, Scott Baio's casting agent, ESPN movie critic, backup catcher to Pudge Rodriguez. Gregg Zaun has exactly the right skill set for one of those. He'll back up Brad Ausmus in Detroit, having traded jobs with Bill Haselman.

Todd Zeile   3B   Bats R   Age 34

YEAR	TEAM	LGE	AB	H	DB	TP	HR	BB/SO	R	RBI	SB	CS	OUT	BA	OBP	SLG	EQA	EQR	DEFENSE
1997	LosAngls	NL	589	166	17	0	35	85/111	93	96	6	7	430	.282	.378	.489	.287	95	157-3B 91
1998	LosAngls	NL	161	43	7	1	8	10/23	24	29	1	1	119	.267	.314	.472	.258	20	39-3B 75
1998	Florida	NL	238	73	12	1	7	31/33	38	41	2	4	169	.307	.392	.454	.284	36	64-3B 99
1998	Texas	AL	178	45	12	1	6	27/31	24	26	1	0	133	.253	.354	.433	.268	25	51-3B 96
1999	Texas	AL	581	166	36	2	23	49/94	71	89	1	2	417	.286	.345	.473	.271	80	152-3B 94
2000	*NY Mets*	*NL*	*535*	*145*	*21*	*1*	*21*	*67/88*	*77*	*89*	*3*	*3*	*393*	*.271*	*.352*	*.432*	*.268*	*73*	

Zeile aged gracefully in 1999, but Mets' GM Steve Phillips keep this in mind: the list of Zeile-caliber third baseman who stayed effective into their late 30s is awfully short. Much longer is the list of third basemen at least as good as Zeile who crashed and burned in their mid-30s. Tim Wallach, Buddy Bell, Kevin Seitzer and Bobby Bonilla are just a few of the names on that second list. The Mets have signed Zeile to a three-year, $18-million deal to play first base; he will be one of the worst first basemen in the NL.

Mike Zywica   OF   Bats R   Age 25

YEAR	TEAM	LGE	AB	H	DB	TP	HR	BB/SO	R	RBI	SB	CS	OUT	BA	OBP	SLG	EQA	EQR	DEFENSE
1997	Charlott	Fla	474	108	25	3	12	42/131	61	53	8	8	374	.228	.303	.369	.226	46	110-OF 97
1998	Charlott	Fla	256	76	19	2	8	26/48	45	33	5	2	182	.297	.370	.480	.285	39	61-OF 89
1998	Tulsa	Tex	214	52	14	2	4	14/64	28	33	3	2	164	.243	.300	.383	.230	21	50-OF 100
1999	Oklahoma	PCL	490	115	27	2	7	28/121	62	62	3	1	376	.235	.284	.341	.210	38	130-OF 94
2000	*Texas*	*AL*	*431*	*105*	*22*	*2*	*10*	*36/106*	*52*	*51*	*5*	*3*	*329*	*.244*	*.302*	*.374*	*.223*	*39*	

Reason number 1,492 not to pay attention to a good performance by an older player repeating a low-level league—in this case, Zywica's 1998 Charlotte line. Kelly Dransfeldt's 1998 was reason number 1,491.

PITCHERS (Averages: ERA: 4.50 / H/9: 9.00 / HR/9: 1.00 / BB/9: 3.50 / K/9: 6.50 / KWH: 1.00)

John Burkett   Throws R   Age 35

YEAR	TEAM	LGE	IP	H	ER	HR	BB	K	ERA	W	L	H/9	HR/9	BB/9	K/9	KWH	PERA
1997	Texas	AL	194.0	227	93	18	31	141	4.31	11	11	10.53	0.84	1.44	6.54	2.11	4.41
1998	Texas	AL	204.3	211	109	17	48	134	4.80	11	12	9.29	0.75	2.11	5.90	1.32	3.88
1999	Tulsa	Tex	6.0	9	7	0	4	2	10.50	0	1	13.50	0.00	6.00	3.00	0.08	7.50
1999	Texas	AL	152.3	168	78	15	45	99	4.61	8	9	9.93	0.89	2.66	5.85	0.97	4.55

Last year we predicted that Burkett would bounce back to his usual league-average self, and he did . . . eventually. Specifically, he was an above-average pitcher June through September, but that was only after a disastrous April and May in which he allowed more than a run per inning. Maybe I'm refusing to learn from past mistakes, but I'm once again going to predict improvement for Burkett. All signs are that his early-season velocity problems, which were making his off-speed pitches ineffective, have been fixed. His fastball was in the high 80s by August. The prediction goes double since Burkett won't be back with the Rangers. His ERA in Arlington, 1997-99: 6.12; outside Arlington: 4.41.

Mark Clark Throws R Age 32

YEAR	TEAM	LGE	IP	H	ER	HR	BB	K	ERA	W	L	H/9	HR/9	BB/9	K/9	KWH	PERA
1997	NY Mets	NL	139.3	166	77	18	50	67	4.97	7	8	10.72	1.16	3.23	4.33	0.40	5.56
1997	ChiCubs	NL	64.0	54	20	6	13	48	2.81	5	2	7.59	0.84	1.83	6.75	2.45	2.95
1998	ChiCubs	NL	214.3	242	115	23	51	154	4.83	11	13	10.16	0.97	2.14	6.47	1.44	4.58
1999	Texas	AL	76.3	96	62	15	33	45	7.31	2	6	11.32	1.77	3.89	5.31	0.48	6.96

The last consistently average pitcher to come crashing down was John Burkett in 1998. So what was the cause for Clark? The league switch? Dick Bosman tinkering too much? A Ranger curse? Ranger fans hope it was the elbow injury that eventually ended his season, and that eight months of prescribed rest will get him back to his old self.

Tim Crabtree Throws R Age 30

YEAR	TEAM	LGE	IP	H	ER	HR	BB	K	ERA	W	L	H/9	HR/9	BB/9	K/9	KWH	PERA
1997	Toronto	AL	40.7	64	30	7	17	26	6.64	2	3	14.16	1.55	3.76	5.75	0.46	8.41
1998	Texas	AL	89.3	77	33	3	37	61	3.32	6	4	7.76	0.30	3.73	6.15	0.98	3.22
1999	Texas	AL	67.0	65	21	3	17	56	2.82	5	2	8.73	0.40	2.28	7.52	2.12	3.36

If there's a down side to having the deepest bullpen in baseball, it's that excellent pitchers like Crabtree are wasted by not pitching or by pitching in low-leverage situations. Crabtree threw just 65 innings, low for a good middle reliever, and 34% of his appearances occurred with the Rangers' lead or deficit at four runs or greater. By comparison, those figures were 20% for Zimmerman and 15% for Wetteland. To make better use of their pitching resources, the Rangers might convert a reliever into a starter. Zimmerman's name has been floated, but I think Crabtree might be a better candidate. He's the hardest thrower on the team, a big sturdy guy who has never had stamina problems, and he doesn't have a key role in the current bullpen. He also doesn't have a good third pitch, something that can be taught.

Douglas Davis Throws L Age 24

YEAR	TEAM	LGE	IP	H	ER	HR	BB	K	ERA	W	L	H/9	HR/9	BB/9	K/9	KWH	PERA
1997	Charlott	Fla	45.0	38	26	3	42	41	5.20	2	3	7.60	0.60	8.40	8.20	0.79	5.20
1998	Charlott	Fla	138.7	170	95	10	96	129	6.17	5	10	11.03	0.65	6.23	8.37	0.76	6.43
1999	Tulsa	Tex	69.0	79	32	9	31	62	4.17	4	4	10.30	1.17	4.04	8.09	1.17	5.61
1999	Oklahoma	PCL	73.3	82	30	4	35	61	3.68	5	3	10.06	0.49	4.30	7.49	0.97	4.91

The most promising Rangers pitching prospect. I wish that Oates had found a way to get him out of his major-league debut before he gave up 10 runs. Then again, Davis has had too much success in the minors to let one drubbing shatter his confidence. The Rangers would love to have left-handed pitchers in their rotation, so Davis has a good chance of starting for them sometime during 2000.

David Elder Throws R Age 24

YEAR	TEAM	LGE	IP	H	ER	HR	BB	K	ERA	W	L	H/9	HR/9	BB/9	K/9	KWH	PERA
1997	Pulaski	App	30.0	25	10	2	16	31	3.00	2	1	7.50	0.60	4.80	9.30	1.80	3.90
1999	Charlott	Fla	40.0	42	21	3	34	32	4.72	2	2	9.45	0.68	7.65	7.20	0.54	6.07

The Rangers' 1997 fourth-round pick missed 1998 after reconstructive elbow surgery. He came back to be effective in relief last year, holding high-A hitters to a .213 average and striking out nearly a batter an inning. Some think he has the best arm in the system.

Jeff Fassero Throws L Age 37

YEAR	TEAM	LGE	IP	H	ER	HR	BB	K	ERA	W	L	H/9	HR/9	BB/9	K/9	KWH	PERA
1997	Seattle	AL	240.3	208	91	19	84	191	3.41	17	10	7.79	0.71	3.15	7.15	1.56	3.45
1998	Seattle	AL	228.7	210	99	30	69	178	3.90	14	11	8.27	1.18	2.72	7.01	1.63	3.98
1999	Seattle	AL	142.3	177	105	30	71	104	6.64	5	11	11.19	1.90	4.49	6.58	0.64	7.27
1999	Texas	AL	18.0	18	10	1	10	13	5.00	1	1	9.00	0.50	5.00	6.50	0.70	4.50

Historically, the odds of an aging pitcher's bouncing back from a season like Fassero's 1999 are pretty low. His park-adjusted ERA was a whopping 42% higher than the AL average. Seventeen pitchers in major-league history have had full seasons at age 36 or older with a park-adjusted ERA at least 30% higher than the league average. Of those 17, none managed an above-average park-adjusted ERA over the remainder of his career, and only three—Bert Blyleven, Frank Tanana and Jim Kaat—managed to keep their figures within 10% of the league average.

Ryan Glynn — Throws R — Age 25

YEAR	TEAM	LGE	IP	H	ER	HR	BB	K	ERA	W	L	H/9	HR/9	BB/9	K/9	KWH	PERA
1997	Charlott	Fla	119.0	196	112	17	59	73	8.47	3	10	14.82	1.29	4.46	5.52	0.34	8.92
1998	Tulsa	Tex	139.7	175	86	12	75	89	5.54	6	10	11.28	0.77	4.83	5.74	0.45	6.12
1999	Oklahoma	PCL	83.7	89	51	6	42	44	5.49	4	5	9.57	0.65	4.52	4.73	0.39	4.84
1999	Texas	AL	56.7	66	39	9	34	40	6.19	2	4	10.48	1.43	5.40	6.35	0.53	6.67

Glynn earned a promotion to the Rangers with six excellent starts in Oklahoma (1.85 ERA) before his season fell apart. His control deserted him with the Rangers, and he wasn't able to regain it after being sent back to Triple-A. I expect him to find the strike zone again and to have limited success in the majors.

Rick Helling — Throws R — Age 29

YEAR	TEAM	LGE	IP	H	ER	HR	BB	K	ERA	W	L	H/9	HR/9	BB/9	K/9	KWH	PERA
1997	Florida	NL	75.3	62	38	13	50	49	4.54	4	4	7.41	1.55	5.97	5.85	0.58	5.14
1997	Texas	AL	56.0	44	25	5	21	47	4.02	3	3	7.07	0.80	3.38	7.55	1.79	3.21
1998	Texas	AL	225.3	189	89	24	82	167	3.55	15	10	7.55	0.96	3.28	6.67	1.34	3.59
1999	Texas	AL	224.3	211	107	36	83	135	4.29	13	12	8.47	1.44	3.33	5.42	0.78	4.57

The ERA dropped off a bit from 1998, but the peripheral numbers took a bigger tumble. Helling recorded fewer strikeouts and more walks than in 1998, and his opponents' OPS went up by almost 100 points, thanks mostly to a league-leading 41 home runs allowed. I wouldn't read too much into that, though. Pitchers are flaky, and their peripheral numbers are flaky, too. My best guess is that we'll get more of the same from Helling in 2000; he'll be a league-average workhorse.

Brandon Knight — Throws R — Age 24

YEAR	TEAM	LGE	IP	H	ER	HR	BB	K	ERA	W	L	H/9	HR/9	BB/9	K/9	KWH	PERA
1997	Charlott	Fla	84.7	108	46	12	29	71	4.89	4	5	11.48	1.28	3.08	7.55	1.20	6.06
1997	Tulsa	Tex	83.3	94	57	13	40	72	6.16	3	6	10.15	1.40	4.32	7.78	1.03	5.94
1998	Tulsa	Tex	77.0	113	64	11	43	71	7.48	2	7	13.21	1.29	5.03	8.30	0.78	8.06
1998	Oklahoma	PCL	59.7	107	76	15	32	44	11.46	1	6	16.14	2.26	4.83	6.64	0.42	11.31
1999	Oklahoma	PCL	151.3	189	102	21	53	80	6.07	6	11	11.24	1.25	3.15	4.76	0.48	5.95

A former top prospect in the Texas system, Knight bounced back a bit from his disastrous 1998, but not enough to catch up with some of his peers (Davis, Lee, Glynn, and Kolb). He'll probably get one more chance in Oklahoma to show major-league readiness. The improved control he exhibited last year should help his chances.

Danny Kolb — Throws R — Age 25

YEAR	TEAM	LGE	IP	H	ER	HR	BB	K	ERA	W	L	H/9	HR/9	BB/9	K/9	KWH	PERA
1997	Charlott	Fla	117.0	193	127	14	83	64	9.77	2	11	14.85	1.08	6.38	4.92	0.19	9.54
1997	Tulsa	Tex	10.3	8	7	1	13	5	6.10	0	1	6.97	0.87	11.32	4.35	0.18	6.10
1998	Tulsa	Tex	141.7	228	129	11	90	66	8.20	4	12	14.48	0.70	5.72	4.19	0.16	8.51
1999	Oklahoma	PCL	55.0	80	39	4	31	17	6.38	2	4	13.09	0.65	5.07	2.78	0.09	7.20
1999	Texas	AL	31.7	30	15	2	15	15	4.26	2	2	8.53	0.57	4.26	4.26	0.37	3.98

Despite showing very little in the minors, Kolb surprisingly found himself on the "Oklahoma shuttle" of minor leaguers rotating through Arlington. Even more surprisingly, he pitched pretty well for the big club. He impressed the Ranger coaches enough to earn a shot at fifth starter or long reliever in spring training, but I don't expect much. Those three years of mediocrity in the minors are more telling than 31 good innings in the majors.

Corey Lee — Throws L — Age 25

YEAR	TEAM	LGE	IP	H	ER	HR	BB	K	ERA	W	L	H/9	HR/9	BB/9	K/9	KWH	PERA
1997	Charlott	Fla	145.0	177	94	12	79	112	5.83	6	10	10.99	0.74	4.90	6.95	0.67	5.96
1998	Tulsa	Tex	127.3	132	100	16	119	105	7.07	4	10	9.33	1.13	8.41	7.42	0.52	6.86
1999	Tulsa	Tex	115.0	166	100	11	58	91	7.83	3	10	12.99	0.86	4.54	7.12	0.64	7.20
1999	Oklahoma	PCL	25.0	24	7	2	9	20	2.52	2	1	8.64	0.72	3.24	7.20	1.38	3.96

Lee rediscovered the control that had deserted him in 1998, and saw his stock rise from its already-high pre-1999 level, especially because of those four Oklahoma starts. He will probably compete with Perisho and Davis for a left-handed-starter or long reliever role in spring training, with the most likely scenario bring at least another half season at Triple-A.

Esteban Loaiza   Throws R   Age 28

YEAR	TEAM	LGE	IP	H	ER	HR	BB	K	ERA	W	L	H/9	HR/9	BB/9	K/9	KWH	PERA
1997	Pittsbrg	NL	202.3	201	85	17	59	114	3.78	13	9	8.94	0.76	2.62	5.07	0.82	3.87
1998	Pittsbrg	NL	92.3	97	49	13	32	51	4.78	5	5	9.45	1.27	3.12	4.97	0.63	4.87
1998	Texas	AL	83.3	95	48	14	24	56	5.18	4	5	10.26	1.51	2.59	6.05	1.03	5.40
1999	Texas	AL	123.3	117	54	9	39	79	3.94	8	6	8.54	0.66	2.85	5.76	1.02	3.65

After a first half spent relegated to the bullpen, the disabled list and Johnny Oates's doghouse, Loaiza was the Rangers' best pitcher during the second half. So now will he finally do what the Pirates had long hoped he would—consistently produce results that match his stuff? You never know with pitchers, but I'm a little skeptical. His second half featured a strikeout rate below his career average, and a walk rate well above—not what you'd expect from a pitcher who had suddenly learned how to use his great stuff.

Juan Moreno   Throws L   Age 25

YEAR	TEAM	LGE	IP	H	ER	HR	BB	K	ERA	W	L	H/9	HR/9	BB/9	K/9	KWH	PERA
1999	Tulsa	Tex	57.7	42	26	5	41	62	4.06	3	3	6.55	0.78	6.40	9.68	1.67	4.06

Sidelined by injuries in 1997 and 1998, Moreno returned to pro ball with a vengeance last year. He struck out 83 batters in 62⅔ innings and had the Drillers' best ERA. Better control would be nice, but when the league hits .153 off of you, and left-handed hitters hit .104, that's nitpicking.

Mike Morgan   Throws R   Age 40

YEAR	TEAM	LGE	IP	H	ER	HR	BB	K	ERA	W	L	H/9	HR/9	BB/9	K/9	KWH	PERA
1997	Cincnnti	NL	164.0	163	86	13	52	96	4.72	9	9	8.95	0.71	2.85	5.27	0.81	3.95
1998	Minnesot	AL	99.0	105	37	12	25	51	3.36	7	4	9.55	1.09	2.27	4.64	0.74	4.45
1998	ChiCubs	NL	23.0	31	22	9	16	10	8.61	1	2	12.13	3.52	6.26	3.91	0.15	10.96
1999	Texas	AL	143.7	171	92	22	47	63	5.76	6	10	10.71	1.38	2.94	3.95	0.37	5.70

During spring training Johnny Oates was quoted as saying, "[Morgan is] resilient. He can throw every day. He has a rubber arm." He was talking about a guy who had made 11 trips to the disabled list in the previous six years. It makes you wonder exactly how much research goes into club personnel decisions. Another thing Oates called Morgan is "a survivor," and he was certainly right about that. It's tempting to write Morgan off now, but he's come back from the grave so many times that it's hard to pronounce him dead.

Mike Munoz   Throws L   Age 34

YEAR	TEAM	LGE	IP	H	ER	HR	BB	K	ERA	W	L	H/9	HR/9	BB/9	K/9	KWH	PERA
1997	Colorado	NL	48.3	48	21	4	14	25	3.91	3	2	8.94	0.74	2.61	4.66	0.69	3.91
1998	Colorado	NL	45.3	50	28	2	18	24	5.56	2	3	9.93	0.40	3.57	4.76	0.48	4.37
1999	Texas	AL	54.0	48	20	5	17	28	3.33	4	2	8.00	0.83	2.83	4.67	0.72	3.50

Everyone wants left-handed pitchers in their bullpens, but Mike Munoz defeats the purpose. For the third year in a row, he was far more effective against right-handed hitters than against left-handed ones. He was quite effective overall, though. In addition to the solid ERA, he was very good at preventing inherited runners from scoring. 1999 was about at the level of his previous peak seasons, so don't expect him to be as good this year.

Danny Patterson   Throws R   Age 29

YEAR	TEAM	LGE	IP	H	ER	HR	BB	K	ERA	W	L	H/9	HR/9	BB/9	K/9	KWH	PERA
1997	Texas	AL	72.7	66	25	3	23	70	3.10	5	3	8.17	0.37	2.85	8.67	2.41	3.22
1998	Texas	AL	63.0	59	25	10	20	34	3.57	4	3	8.43	1.43	2.86	4.86	0.73	4.43
1999	Texas	AL	61.7	72	32	4	18	44	4.67	3	4	10.51	0.58	2.63	6.42	1.12	4.52

His 1999 numbers look terrible next to those of his bullpen cohorts, but he wasn't bad, only average. Patterson is tough to use in critical situations because of his vulnerability to left-handed hitters. Over the past two years, lefties have hit like Mo Vaughn against him: .340/.405/.519. He was part of the Gonzalez trade, and should have a prominent role in the Tiger bullpen.

Matt Perisho — Throws L — Age 25

YEAR	TEAM	LGE	IP	H	ER	HR	BB	K	ERA	W	L	H/9	HR/9	BB/9	K/9	KWH	PERA
1997	Midland	Tex	72.0	61	24	5	30	54	3.00	6	2	7.63	0.63	3.75	6.75	1.19	3.50
1997	Vancouvr	PCL	46.7	70	42	3	29	39	8.10	1	4	13.50	0.58	5.59	7.52	0.56	7.71
1997	Anaheim	AL	46.3	56	31	6	29	36	6.02	2	3	10.88	1.17	5.63	6.99	0.60	6.60
1998	Oklahoma	PCL	84.7	97	44	6	46	51	4.68	4	5	10.31	0.64	4.89	5.42	0.44	5.42
1999	Oklahoma	PCL	144.7	173	93	12	90	121	5.79	6	10	10.76	0.75	5.60	7.53	0.70	6.10

Perisho had a very encouraging 1999. He struggled through the first half after rotator-cuff surgery the previous August: on July 4 he had a 6.13 ERA and was coughing up about 11 hits per nine innings. Then he finished the season with a flourish, posting a 2.82 ERA and allowing just 6.8 hits per nine innings in his last 60⅔ innings with Oklahoma, followed by a terrific start—12 strikeouts in six shutout innings—for the Rangers. He's out of options, so he'll be given every chance to make the big-league club in spring training, probably as a fifth starter.

Aaron Sele — Throws R — Age 30

YEAR	TEAM	LGE	IP	H	ER	HR	BB	K	ERA	W	L	H/9	HR/9	BB/9	K/9	KWH	PERA
1997	Boston	AL	181.3	184	102	23	81	123	5.06	9	11	9.13	1.14	4.02	6.10	0.76	4.91
1998	Texas	AL	223.0	217	95	12	89	171	3.83	14	11	8.76	0.48	3.59	6.90	1.13	3.87
1999	Texas	AL	210.7	225	95	18	69	192	4.06	13	10	9.61	0.77	2.95	8.20	1.77	4.40

It was another solid year from Sele, rescued by his second half (a 4.08 ERA, vs. 5.51 in the first half). I still don't see how he's going to keep it up for many more years. The league hit .293 off him, .305 outside of Arlington. And it's not as if he has pin-point control to compensate for all those hits. He won't earn the huge contract he got this winter.

Chuck Smith — Throws R — Age 30

YEAR	TEAM	LGE	IP	H	ER	HR	BB	K	ERA	W	L	H/9	HR/9	BB/9	K/9	KWH	PERA
1997	Birmnghm	Sou	56.3	76	42	4	32	42	6.71	2	4	12.14	0.64	5.11	6.71	0.54	6.71
1997	Nashvill	AmA	30.7	44	37	8	28	25	10.86	0	3	12.91	2.35	8.22	7.34	0.38	10.86
1999	Oklahoma	PCL	78.7	83	36	6	33	60	4.12	5	4	9.50	0.69	3.78	6.86	0.98	4.58

The Rangers had such good luck with Jeff Zimmerman, they're spending more time mining the Northern League for talent. Their latest two success stories are Matt Miller, who was overpowering in Double-A, and Chuck Smith, a nine-year pro who spent 1998 with the Sioux Falls Canaries. Smith struggled early then dominated late, ending up with the Redhawks' best ERA. He has a good chance of seeing action with the Rangers in 2000.

Mike Venafro — Throws L — Age 26

YEAR	TEAM	LGE	IP	H	ER	HR	BB	K	ERA	W	L	H/9	HR/9	BB/9	K/9	KWH	PERA
1997	Charlott	Fla	38.7	69	25	3	29	26	5.82	1	3	16.06	0.70	6.75	6.05	0.25	10.01
1998	Tulsa	Tex	45.7	55	29	5	32	34	5.72	2	3	10.84	0.99	6.31	6.70	0.49	6.70
1999	Texas	AL	69.7	58	24	3	21	38	3.10	5	3	7.49	0.39	2.71	4.91	0.89	2.84

Venafro is a sidewinder who came out of Double-A to be the most effective left-handed reliever in the league. Any time a pitcher has a quirky motion, you wonder whether he'll lose effectiveness as hitters get a chance to study him. The results for Venafro: in the first half, the league had a 573 OPS against him; in the second half, 748. Even if that second number comes closer to his true ability, he's still a valuable one-out left-hander.

John Wetteland — Throws R — Age 33

YEAR	TEAM	LGE	IP	H	ER	HR	BB	K	ERA	W	L	H/9	HR/9	BB/9	K/9	KWH	PERA
1997	Texas	AL	66.3	39	15	5	21	64	2.04	6	1	5.29	0.68	2.85	8.68	3.74	2.17
1998	Texas	AL	63.7	43	13	5	15	73	1.84	6	1	6.08	0.71	2.12	10.32	6.17	2.26
1999	Texas	AL	67.3	62	25	8	19	62	3.34	5	2	8.29	1.07	2.54	8.29	2.44	3.74

There's a lot to be concerned about here. Wetteland is now at an age where the injuries he fought through in 1999 are the rule rather than the exception, and 1999 was easily his worst year in almost a decade. Given how quickly relievers—even great ones—can drop off the face of the earth, and the exaggerated value attached to "proven closers," the Rangers would be wise to look for an opportunity to get some return for Wetteland before his contract expires.

Jeff Zimmerman Throws R Age 27

YEAR	TEAM	LGE	IP	H	ER	HR	BB	K	ERA	W	L	H/9	HR/9	BB/9	K/9	KWH	PERA
1998	Tulsa	Tex	56.3	52	25	5	26	50	3.99	3	3	8.31	0.80	4.15	7.99	1.38	4.15
1999	Texas	AL	88.7	46	19	8	22	69	1.93	8	2	4.67	0.81	2.23	7.00	3.52	1.73

Through the end of July, Zimmerman was having perhaps the most dominating relief season ever: 59⅔ innings, 0.75 ERA, 3.2 hits per nine innings and 5.4 baserunners per nine innings. If his season had ended right then, those last two numbers would have been records, and the ERA would have been the third-best all-time (minimum 50 IP). Unfortunately, his season did not end right then, and in August and September the league seemed to figure out his unusually quick rock-and-fire motion: 28 innings, 5.79 ERA, 9.3 hits per nine innings, 11.9 baserunners per nine innings. Which is the real Jeff Zimmerman? He's somewhere in between, and that's pretty good. He's got a wicked slider that he throws for strikes, and he's dominated at every professional level he's pitched, so I like his chances for success in the long run.

Support-Neutral Records				**TEXAS RANGERS**							Park Effect: +13.7%	
PITCHER	GS	IP	R	SNW	SNL	SNPCT	W	L	RA	APW	SNVA	SNWAR
John Burkett	25	129.3	89	7.8	9.1	.461	9	8	6.19	-0.78	-0.54	0.61
Mark Clark	15	74.3	73	3.0	7.3	.293	3	7	8.84	-2.41	-2.01	-1.37
Jeff Fassero	3	14.0	5	1.2	0.4	.741	1	0	3.21	0.33	0.36	0.50
Ryan Glynn	10	50.3	42	2.0	4.4	.314	2	4	7.51	-0.96	-1.24	-0.70
Rick Helling	35	219.3	127	12.9	11.8	.522	13	11	5.21	0.83	0.55	2.41
Esteban Loaiza	15	91.7	41	6.4	3.6	.638	8	4	4.03	1.43	1.35	2.15
Mike Morgan	25	123.0	100	5.9	10.7	.357	11	8	7.32	-2.12	-2.28	-1.14
Matt Perisho	1	6.0	0	0.7	0.0	1.000	0	0	0.00	0.33	0.33	0.42
Aaron Sele	33	205.0	115	12.1	10.9	.525	18	9	5.05	1.11	0.64	2.31
TOTALS	162	913.0	592	52.1	58.3	.472	65	51	5.84	-2.24	-2.84	5.20

Texas once again demonstrated that a good rotation is not necessary for regular-season success. For the third year in a row, the Ranger rotation was worth at least 2½ wins below average, according to SNVA, and two of those years ended in division championships. 1999 did represent improvement over the previous two years, as the starters ranked 19th in the majors, compared to 23rd in 1997 and 26th in 1998. That improvement was entirely due to the rotation's strong second-half showing. Before the All-Star break, the Rangers Support-Neutral Winning Percentage was .420, but after it was .532. . . . Texas' starting pitching problems the past three years are especially frustrating to Ranger fans because of all the good starters Texas let get away. You could build a quality rotation with pitchers who came up through the Ranger organization only to have their best years with another club. The combined 1999 Support-Neutral W/L record of Kevin Brown, Darren Oliver, Kenny Rogers and Wilson Alvarez was 51.9-37.7 (.579). Add in Brian Bohanon or Bobby Witt as a replacement-level fifth starter, and the collection of starters developed by but no longer with Texas is better and deeper than the corresponding collection for any other team, and far better than Texas' current rotation.

Pitcher Abuse Points

PITCHER	AGE	GS	PAP	PAP/S	WKLD	MAX	1-90	91-100	101-110	111-120	121-130	131-140	141+
John Burkett	34	25	92	3.7	3.7	118	14	3	6	2	0	0	0
Mark Clark	31	15	41	2.7	3.2	120	8	4	2	1	0	0	0
Jeff Fassero	36	3	0	0.0	0.0	73	3	0	0	0	0	0	0
Ryan Glynn	24	10	10	1.0	2.3	107	3	5	2	0	0	0	0
Rick Helling	28	35	646	18.5	30.8	131	4	5	9	8	8	1	0
Esteban Loaiza	27	15	92	6.1	11.2	126	5	5	3	1	1	0	0
Mike Morgan	39	25	46	1.8	1.8	120	20	3	0	2	0	0	0
Matt Perisho	24	1	0	0.0	0.0	78	1	0	0	0	0	0	0
Aaron Sele	29	33	474	14.4	21.5	126	8	5	4	10	6	0	0
TEXAS		162	1401	8.6	13.4	131	66	30	26	24	15	1	0
Ranking (AL)				7	8								

You can't exactly blame the Rangers' postseason woes on their pitching staff, but it doesn't help that Rick Helling, after Workloads of 32.5 and 30.8 the last two seasons, had nothing in September (7.68 ERA, 15 homers in 35 IP) while setting a new Ranger record with 41 gopher balls. . . . Aaron Sele has had identical Workloads of 21.5 in each of the last two years, and not coincidentally, he was still pitching well at year's end. . . . One piece of encouraging news for the Rangers was that Esteban Loaiza, who is younger than either Helling or Sele, was given a nice, slow reintroduction to the rotation, and thrived the last two months of the season. . . . Overall, Oates isn't particularly good or bad when it comes to handling young pitchers, but it hardly matters, since the Rangers have few young pitchers to worry about anyway.

Toronto Blue Jays

To be blunt, the Blue Jays screwed themselves out of a playoff spot in 1999. They did it by switching managers at a very inopportune time. They did it by trading their best pitcher without improving the team and by aping the Seattle Mariners' strategy of surrounding a superior talent core with complete stiffs. The organization has no place to look for answers but at itself.

The Jays' problems began in the spring, when it became clear that Manager Tim Johnson wasn't going to be able to overcome the derision he'd earned. Johnson had invented a persona built around what he claimed was his service in the Vietnam Conflict as a United States Marine. When the truth about his service—he never left the States, and the closest he came to conflict was heated conversation with the recruits he was responsible for training—came to light after the 1998 season, there was considerable speculation that his players would no longer respect him.

General Manager Gord Ash probably deserves some credit for trying to stand behind Johnson, who hadn't shown himself to be anything out of the ordinary as a manager. But the decision to backtrack from that commitment in mid-March, after the team had already suffered the loss of Roger Clemens, contributed to the chaos surrounding the team and may have damaged its chances to get off to a good start. Ash brought in veteran manager Jim Fregosi as a replacement during spring training. Fregosi lacked Johnson's best quality—his willingness to play talent over experience—but had his worst quality—a tendency to push starting pitchers too hard—in spades.

Fregosi inherited a team that had just traded the two-time reigning Cy Young Award winner for a package that wouldn't have passed the giggle test in a good Strat-O-Matic league. The Jays sent Clemens to the Yankees, upgrading their chief divisional competitor's #1 starter slot, in exchange for David Wells, Homer Bush and Graeme Lloyd. The Jays maintained that they'd helped themselves significantly, filling their second-base hole with a budding young star and getting a pitcher comparable to Clemens. People might even

---

Blue Jays Prospectus

1999 record: 84-78; Third place, AL East

Pythagorean W/L: 83-79

Runs scored: 883 (5th in AL)

Runs allowed: 862 (9th in AL)

Team EQA: .263 (6th in AL)

1999 team age: 28.1 (5th-youngest in AL)

1999 park: Skydome; slight hitters' park, increased run scoring by 3%.

1999: A good talent core is sabotaged by a poor supporting cast.

2000: They will be better than anyone expects and play in October.

---

have bought this line of reasoning...if Yankee GM Brian Cashman had stopped grinning from ear to ear at any point before Memorial Day.

Yet even with the disaster that was March in Dunedin, the Jays entered the season as one of the favorites for the AL wild card. They had young hitters with upside in Carlos Delgado, Shawn Green, Shannon Stewart, Jose Cruz and Alex Gonzalez. The only significant hole in the lineup was at second base; Bush injured a finger in the first week of the season, and the Jays patched together a Pat Kelly/Craig Grebeck solution in the interim. This was bullet two in the year-long "Shoot Ourselves in the Foot" festival.

Bullet one was the "Dave Hollins Extravaganza." Hollins, unwanted by the Angels even as insurance for sophomore third baseman Troy Glaus, was picked up on March 30 in exchange for Triple-A defensive replacment Tomas Perez. Fregosi, no doubt happy to see a familiar face—Hollins had been his third baseman in Philadelphia—quickly made Hollins his everyday designated hitter and inserted him into the cleanup spot between Shawn Green and Carlos Delgado.

The concept wasn't bad: put a switch-hitter with some pop from the right side between the two left-handed hitters. The execution, however, was brutal: Hollins hasn't hit right-handed pitchers worth a damn since the 1993 season, in which he played for Fregosi and hit .273/.372/.442 for the pennant-winning Phillies. His 1998 performance—.242/.334/.388—gave every indication of an average player who had hit the wall in his early 30s and was done. Hollins batted .233/.283/.279, lost the cleanup spot and was on the verge of losing his DH job when he broke his right wrist April 17, knocking him out for six weeks.

Two and a half weeks into the season, the Jays had made a handful of poor decisions, were going with four rookies in the bullpen, were missing their #3 starter, Joey Hamilton... and were in first place. They had a DH platoon, at this point, of Willie Greene and Geronimo Berroa, which didn't look that bad. The aliens had settled into Tony Fernandez's body, Alex

Gonzalez was shoehorning four years of lost development into one great month and even Darrin Fletcher was hitting. Roy Halladay and Chris Carpenter were setting the league on fire, and the unheralded rookies in the pen, Peter Munro and Tom Davey, were pitching wonderfully.

Then they went 16-31. The pitching collapsed, led by the implosion of Kelvim Escobar. Alex Gonzalez's career year was interrupted by a season-ending shoulder injury. Willie Greene went 5-for-44 on his way to Syracuse. The team began what would be a three-month tryout camp in the DH slot, beginning with moving Tony Fernandez there and playing waiver pickup Willis Otanez at third base. With a healthy Bush now at shortstop and Pat Kelly playing most of the innings at second base, the infield defense had gone from respectable to abysmal. Jose Cruz broke his finger. Chris Carpenter's effectiveness waned until he had to rest a sore elbow. It was one of the ugliest stretches you would ever wish on a team, and it cost them a postseason berth.

On June 12, the Jays caught a break that helped them regain respectability in 1999 and should give them a big leg up in 2000 and beyond. The Arizona Diamondbacks, getting their first taste of a pennant race and having bullpen problems, traded shortstop Tony Batista and right-handed reliever John Frascatore to Toronto in exchange for left-handed reliever Dan Plesac. The trade looked bad for Arizona at the time, and even worse in retrospect. Batista became the starting shortstop, moving Bush back to second base and Kelly to Australia, which upgraded the offense and was a huge boon to the defense. Frascatore gave the Jays a serviceable setup man in front of Billy Koch, who had taken over the closer role during the May slump.

The Jays were 28-36 at the time of the trade. With Batista hitting .271/.338/.571, the Jays went 26-9 in the next six weeks, passing the Boston Red Sox on July 23 to move into first place in the wild-card race. At *Baseball Prospectus Online*, we ran what amounted to a coronation of the Jays as the AL wild card, doing everything but speculating on their playoff rotation:

"... it looks like the Blue Jays are simply too good to be held back by poor roster and player usage decisions." — Transaction Analysis, July 27, 1999

We were wrong. "The Internet is just a fad" kind of wrong. We simply underestimated the ability of Gord Ash to make terrible decisions under pressure.

On August 6, the Jays picked up Curtis Goodwin on waivers. To make room for him, the team sent Jose Cruz to Syracuse, planning to split the center field job between Goodwin and Jacob Brumfield. Here's what the three players had done to that point:

Jose Cruz:	.228/.343/.407	11 HR in 307 AB	54 walks	11 SB	3 CS
Jacob Brumfield:	.235/.310/.373	1 HR in 102 AB	12 walks	1 SB	1 CS
Curtis Goodwin:	.242/.298/.293	0 HR in 157 AB	13 walks	2 SB	4 CS

Even conceding that there might have been a defensive gain, there is just no way that this decision made any sense. The Jays didn't compare Cruz to their intended replacements and make a reasoned decision. They merely compared Cruz to their expectations for him, declared him a disappointment and gave his job to two clearly inferior players.

Three days later, the Blue Jays acquired Brian McRae from the Colorado Rockies. McRae was more expensive than the Goodwin/Brumfield solution, but it would be hard to argue that he was much of an improvement. His performance to that point:

Brian McRae:	.224/.323/.358	9 HR in 321 AB	41 walks	2 SB	6 CS

Cruz's last game for the Jays prior to the demotion was on August 3. At the end of the game, Toronto was 60-49 and held a 1½-game lead over the Red Sox in the wild-card race. Four weeks later they were 68-61, 4½ games behind the Sox, and effectively done.

Sometimes, a team misses an opportunity due to circumstances it can't control. In this case, the Jays did everything they could to sabotage their own season, but their fate came down to three key elements:

1. Trading Roger Clemens for some shiny rocks
2. Not filling the designated hitter slot with an actual hitter
3. Giving up on Jose Cruz and replacing him with terrible players

The good news for Toronto fans is that the talent core that inspired optimism last year is still there. In fact, it's even better: the Jays' top prospect, Vernon Wells, is a true center fielder and should be up to stay by August. He's ready defensively, but he isn't the hitter Cruz is right now. Tony Batista is in town for a full season; he will move to third base if Alex Gonzalez is healthy and a Blue Jay, or play shortstop if he isn't. Billy Koch has come back from Tommy John surgery to be a nasty right-handed reliever at the end of games, and the rotation is almost certain to improve on its 1999 performance. Trading Shawn Green for Raul Mondesi is a step backward, unfortunately, as Green is a better player at the same position. It is unlikely that the gap between the two players will be as wide as it was in 1999, and isn't a move that torpedoes the Jays' chances in 2000.

The best Blue Jays team in 2000 would have Jose Cruz in center field. The Jays will be tempted to give Vernon Wells the job, but it's an open question whether Wells can hit enough to stay in the majors; he is just 20, so it's a fair question. The Jays need only pick the right third baseman and DH to complete a 95-win team. Yes, Homer Bush has serious flaws, but the Jays aren't going to recognize that; in all fairness, if Bush is their worst player, that's not a disaster.

The Jays may trade Cruz for a third baseman. They could have filled the DH slot with an internal solution like a Kevin Witt/Kevin Thompson platoon, or one of the myriad hitters available for the minimum salary. 2000's Brian Daubach is out there just waiting to be discovered. Steve Cox, Roberto Petagine and Jon Nunnally are just three candidates. Unfortunately, their decision to offer David Segui arbitration backfired, as he accepted, and will split first base and DH with Carlos Delagdo.

This is a critical time for the franchise, and illustrates just how diverse a range of talents it takes to build a winning team. The Blue Jays have assembled excellent front-line talent through the draft, international signings and their player-development process. They have surrounded that core with a few good pieces acquired in astute trades. But now, on the brink of a run, they need to fill the last couple of holes with the right players. The ability to do so will be the difference between 87 wins and 93, an early winter or a trip to the playoffs.

The Jays have the highest upside of any team in the division, possibly of any team in the league. It would be a shame if that upside were wasted because management couldn't handle the short strokes for a second straight year.

HITTERS (Averages: BA: .270 / OBP: .340 / SLG: .430 / EQA: .260)

Brent Abernathy — 2B — Bats R — Age 22

YEAR	TEAM	LGE	AB	H	DB	TP	HR	BB/SO	R	RBI	SB	CS	OUT	BA	OBP	SLG	EQA	EQR	DEFENSE
1997	Hagerstn	SAL	387	106	28	1	1	26/32	53	21	8	6	287	.274	.326	.359	.234	38	100-2B 99
1998	Dunedin	Fla	484	137	32	1	3	35/42	59	50	13	6	353	.283	.332	.372	.242	51	121-2B 91
1999	Knoxvill	Sou	579	155	31	1	14	42/48	83	52	19	9	433	.268	.322	.397	.245	64	132-2B 99
2000	Toronto	AL	492	138	30	1	8	43/41	77	64	14	6	360	.280	.338	.394	.252	57	

Abernathy is still developing, although the excitement surrounding him has died down. Walk fetishists that we are, we'd like to see him show the kind of development in his plate discipline this year that he showed in his power in 1999. That's really the only thing keeping him from being a top-tier second-base prospect. By August, he'll be a better player than Homer Bush.

Tony Batista — SS — Bats R — Age 26

YEAR	TEAM	LGE	AB	H	DB	TP	HR	BB/SO	R	RBI	SB	CS	OUT	BA	OBP	SLG	EQA	EQR	DEFENSE	
1997	Oakland	AL	188	38	10	1	4	13/30	21	17	2	2	152	.202	.262	.330	.196	13	49-SS 103	
1997	Edmonton	PCL	119	31	8	1	2	14/18	17	14	1	1	89	.261	.342	.395	.251	14	30-SS 94	
1998	Arizona	NL	296	83	17	1	19	17/51	47	42	1	1	214	.280	.327	.537	.278	44	32-2B 94	28-SS 105
1999	Arizona	NL	145	38	4	0	5	14/17	15	20	2	0	107	.262	.336	.393	.252	17	38-SS 118	
1999	Toronto	AL	372	105	24	1	25	18/79	55	72	2	0	267	.282	.322	.554	.282	56	97-SS 111	
2000	Toronto	AL	436	115	20	1	25	36/78	62	81	2	1	322	.264	.320	.486	.266	59		

In a way, Batista was the best thing to come out of the Clemens trade. The Jays picked up Graeme Lloyd in that deal, which made Dan Plesac expendable when the Diamondbacks decided to do something dumb. Batista is a much better defensive shortstop than his reputation would have it; a fair fight between him and Alex Gonzalez would be too close to call. The more likely scenario is that a healthy Gonzalez is traded in the spring. That projection is low; he'll have a .280 EqA this year.

Josephang Bernhardt — 3B — Bats R — Age 19

YEAR	TEAM	LGE	AB	H	DB	TP	HR	BB/SO	R	RBI	SB	CS	OUT	BA	OBP	SLG	EQA	EQR	DEFENSE	
1997	Med Hat	Pio	198	34	2	0	1	4/66	13	10	1	1	165	.172	.190	.197	.047	0	57-SS 76	
1998	St Cath	NYP	187	34	11	1	2	12/63	15	16	0	0	153	.182	.231	.283	.161	8	29-SS 79	24-3B 93
1999	St Cath	NYP	271	60	9	1	5	5/68	17	28	1	0	211	.221	.237	.317	.177	14	61-3B 73	
2000	Toronto	AL	227	49	5	0	4	10/64	13	16	1	0	178	.216	.249	.291	.171	11		

Bernhardt is just one example of the silliness involved in signing 16-year-old baseball players from countries without real development systems. The Jays gave Bernhardt, originally from the Dominican Republic, $700,000 in 1996, amidst great fanfare. It's hard enough to project the career path of 18-to-21-year-olds coming through the United States' amateur system; signing younger players at prices like this is mostly a waste of money. See also Williams, Glenn. Bernhardt still has a lot of physical development left; realistically, he's a non-prospect.

Casey Blake   3B   Bats R   Age 26

YEAR	TEAM	LGE	AB	H	DB	TP	HR	BB/SO	R	RBI	SB	CS	OUT	BA	OBP	SLG	EQA	EQR	DEFENSE
1997	Dunedin	Fla	456	93	14	0	8	37/109	40	32	7	4	367	.204	.270	.287	.188	28	119-3B 87
1998	Dunedin	Fla	338	85	21	2	7	20/104	38	39	2	2	255	.251	.304	.388	.232	33	86-3B 96
1998	Knoxvill	Sou	168	50	13	2	5	14/28	26	24	4	0	118	.298	.357	.488	.284	25	44-3B 88
1999	Syracuse	Int	388	81	13	2	16	49/90	50	54	5	4	311	.209	.307	.376	.232	40	109-3B 89
1999	Toronto	AL	39	10	2	0	1	1/7	5	2	0	0	29	.256	.275	.385	.217	3	
2000	Toronto	AL	408	93	17	2	12	44/97	50	50	5	2	317	.228	.303	.368	.229	40	

He may be the Jays' answer to the third-base question in 2000, but Blake is more problem than solution. His defensive reputation is good, in contrast to his numbers, and that's the best part of his game. If Toronto is going to contend, they'll have to do better than this at the hot corner.

Kevin Brown   C   Bats R   Age 27

YEAR	TEAM	LGE	AB	H	DB	TP	HR	BB/SO	R	RBI	SB	CS	OUT	BA	OBP	SLG	EQA	EQR	DEFENSE
1997	Oklahoma	AA	405	89	17	2	16	32/117	49	44	2	1	317	.220	.286	.390	.226	39	
1998	Toronto	AL	110	29	8	1	2	8/30	17	15	0	0	81	.264	.325	.409	.248	12	35-C 98
1999	Syracuse	Int	294	66	16	2	9	15/87	29	37	0	1	229	.224	.266	.384	.213	24	83-C 88
2000	Toronto	AL	231	54	12	1	9	18/67	26	32	0	0	177	.234	.289	.411	.233	23	

Another of the ways the Jays beat themselves in 1999 was by choosing Mike Matheny over Brown as their right-handed-hitting catcher. Brown has been ready for at least a slice of a major-league job for three years, a rare backup catcher with some secondary skills. He's been released and is still young enough to catch on somewhere and push a team towards the postseason. He would make an excellent backup for Dave Nilsson, wherever Nilsson lands.

Jacob Brumfield   OF   Bats R   Age 35

YEAR	TEAM	LGE	AB	H	DB	TP	HR	BB/SO	R	RBI	SB	CS	OUT	BA	OBP	SLG	EQA	EQR	DEFENSE
1997	Toronto	AL	175	37	6	1	2	13/30	22	20	4	4	142	.211	.271	.291	.186	11	42-OF 101
1998	Charlott	Int	230	36	7	0	4	26/46	18	23	4	1	195	.157	.252	.239	.165	11	74-OF 85
1999	Toronto	AL	169	39	7	3	2	17/39	22	17	1	2	132	.231	.301	.343	.217	14	32-CF 102
2000	Toronto	AL	165	29	5	1	3	19/36	13	11	2	1	137	.176	.261	.273	.184	10	

Because Brumfield can play center field and hit left-handed pitchers a little, he has some value as a fifth outfielder. There are better players in the category, though, and the roster spot a team might use on Brumfield would be better used on a younger player with similar skills and more upside.

Homer Bush   2B   Bats B   Age 27

YEAR	TEAM	LGE	AB	H	DB	TP	HR	BB/SO	R	RBI	SB	CS	OUT	BA	OBP	SLG	EQA	EQR	DEFENSE
1997	LasVegas	PCL	151	35	9	1	2	4/42	17	10	3	1	117	.232	.260	.344	.201	11	34-2B 95
1997	Columbus	Int	278	66	11	2	2	20/56	31	23	9	5	217	.237	.291	.313	.207	21	74-2B 104
1998	NY Yanks	AL	71	27	2	0	1	5/19	16	5	6	3	47	.380	.421	.451	.297	11	
1999	Toronto	AL	481	151	23	4	5	15/82	62	50	32	9	338	.314	.343	.410	.261	59	106-2B 103
2000	Toronto	AL	405	121	23	3	6	26/74	74	52	26	7	291	.299	.341	.415	.263	51	

The case against Bush, as made by performance analysts, is that he doesn't have the plate discipline or power to put runs on the board. Implicit in this is that he is not a .320 hitter. Bush has almost 600 major-league at-bats with a career batting average of .328. Now, even if Bush hits .320, he's not a great player—the walks and power still aren't there—but he would be a good one. That Homer Bush may be good is a possibility we have to entertain. I still think the average is a fluke and expect he'll hit .280 this year and really hurt the Jays.

Jose Cruz   CF   Bats B   Age 26

YEAR	TEAM	LGE	AB	H	DB	TP	HR	BB/SO	R	RBI	SB	CS	OUT	BA	OBP	SLG	EQA	EQR	DEFENSE
1997	Tacoma	PCL	186	44	14	1	5	28/45	24	22	2	0	142	.237	.339	.403	.256	23	45-OF 93
1997	Seattle	AL	183	50	13	1	12	12/43	28	33	1	0	133	.273	.318	.552	.280	28	36-OF 102
1997	Toronto	AL	213	52	6	0	15	26/69	31	35	6	2	163	.244	.326	.484	.268	30	49-OF 96
1998	Toronto	AL	351	89	14	3	11	55/97	52	40	10	4	266	.254	.355	.405	.262	47	96-OF 110
1998	Syracuse	Int	141	37	14	1	5	28/34	23	18	5	3	107	.262	.385	.482	.289	24	41-OF 117
1999	Toronto	AL	345	80	19	3	13	60/91	57	40	14	4	269	.232	.346	.417	.263	48	88-CF 102
1999	Syracuse	Int	104	16	3	1	2	24/22	13	10	3	0	88	.154	.313	.260	.213	9	29-OF 108
2000	*Toronto*	*AL*	*462*	*112*	*24*	*2*	*19*	*78/119*	*88*	*73*	*16*	*4*	*354*	*.242*	*.352*	*.426*	*.269*	*66*	

A good player in a bad organization. Cruz hasn't been a superstar so far and has been prone to long slumps that have made him an easy target for management dissatisfaction. His stat line—heavy on walks, light on batting average and RBIs—provides a convenient excuse to mishandle him when the team struggles. The decision to use anybody but him in center field in August was inexcusable. The Jays would be better off in 2000 with him in center field, rather than Vernon Wells.

Carlos Delgado   1B   Bats L   Age 28

YEAR	TEAM	LGE	AB	H	DB	TP	HR	BB/SO	R	RBI	SB	CS	OUT	BA	OBP	SLG	EQA	EQR	DEFENSE
1997	Toronto	AL	520	142	45	3	31	61/128	79	91	0	3	381	.273	.360	.550	.293	88	117-1B 88
1998	Toronto	AL	528	156	37	2	39	70/136	90	111	3	0	372	.295	.390	.595	.317	105	141-1B 94
1999	Toronto	AL	567	152	35	0	43	78/142	102	123	1	1	416	.268	.371	.557	.301	103	147-1B 91
2000	*Toronto*	*AL*	*561*	*158*	*33*	*1*	*40*	*82/139*	*108*	*134*	*1*	*1*	*404*	*.282*	*.373*	*.558*	*.304*	*103*	

About as consistent a power threat as you can ask for, Delgado continues to improve his game each season. His defense, once a disaster, has become passable, and he's gotten better at hitting left-handers every year that he's been a regular. He's a younger, more lithe Mo Vaughn. In something of a surprise, the Jays re-signed Delgado to a three-year deal worth about $36 million.

Tony Fernandez   3B   Bats B   Age 38

YEAR	TEAM	LGE	AB	H	DB	TP	HR	BB/SO	R	RBI	SB	CS	OUT	BA	OBP	SLG	EQA	EQR	DEFENSE	
1997	Clevelnd	AL	411	122	21	1	12	19/45	55	45	6	6	295	.297	.332	.440	.256	49	106-2B 96	
1998	Toronto	AL	484	155	35	2	9	43/52	67	69	11	8	337	.320	.389	.457	.285	73	77-2B 107	49-3B 94
1999	Toronto	AL	477	153	26	0	10	70/62	64	72	6	8	332	.321	.418	.438	.293	77	125-3B 92	
2000	*Toronto*	*AL*	*341*	*93*	*10*	*0*	*10*	*43/41*	*52*	*51*	*4*	*3*	*251*	*.273*	*.354*	*.390*	*.256*	*42*		

Fernandez's inability to play either middle-infield position makes him a risky signing this winter. While this late-career surge has been impressive, it's mostly in his batting average, and that's not likely to stay in the .320 range. If he drops into the .280s, which is probable, you have an aging third baseman who is average defensively and not putting runs on the board. Fernandez is a poor risk.

Darrin Fletcher   C   Bats L   Age 33

YEAR	TEAM	LGE	AB	H	DB	TP	HR	BB/SO	R	RBI	SB	CS	OUT	BA	OBP	SLG	EQA	EQR	DEFENSE
1997	Montreal	NL	312	86	18	1	18	17/35	39	54	1	1	227	.276	.323	.513	.272	44	
1998	Toronto	AL	406	115	21	1	10	23/38	36	51	0	0	291	.283	.331	.414	.251	46	112-C 96
1999	Toronto	AL	409	117	21	0	19	21/47	43	75	0	0	292	.286	.330	.477	.267	54	105-C 97
2000	*Toronto*	*AL*	*368*	*98*	*14*	*0*	*15*	*27/39*	*45*	*58*	*0*	*0*	*270*	*.266*	*.316*	*.427*	*.249*	*42*	

In the shallow pool that is "American League Catchers," Darrin Fletcher stands tall. He doesn't throw particularly well, but the rest of his defense is good. A left-handed-hitting catcher who can contribute with the bat is valuable. The projection is low; I expect him to produce in the .260 EqA area for a few more years.

Ryan Freel   OF   Bats R   Age 24

YEAR	TEAM	LGE	AB	H	DB	TP	HR	BB/SO	R	RBI	SB	CS	OUT	BA	OBP	SLG	EQA	EQR	DEFENSE
1997	Dunedin	Fla	186	47	10	1	3	40/31	30	14	10	2	141	.253	.403	.366	.281	29	23-SS 101
1997	Knoxvill	Sou	93	16	0	1	0	16/14	12	3	3	2	79	.172	.303	.194	.179	5	29-SS 96
1998	Knoxvill	Sou	250	63	15	2	4	23/33	33	27	10	5	192	.252	.317	.376	.237	26	53-OF 98
1998	Syracuse	Int	119	26	3	0	2	22/16	15	11	6	3	96	.218	.357	.294	.238	13	26-OF 93
1999	Knoxvill	Sou	46	11	3	1	1	7/4	6	7	2	1	36	.239	.340	.413	.257	6	
1999	Syracuse	Int	77	22	1	2	1	6/13	12	9	8	3	57	.286	.364	.390	.268	11	
2000	Toronto	AL	253	62	10	3	4	37/35	45	28	14	6	196	.245	.341	.356	.247	30	

Freel was on his way to a September call-up when he injured his rotator cuff in May. He doesn't do any one thing very well; what he does is play both the infield and the outfield, get on base and run a little. Assuming he's healthy in March, he's the player with whom the Jays should fill Jacob Brumfield's roster spot.

Tim Giles   1B   Bats L   Age 24

YEAR	TEAM	LGE	AB	H	DB	TP	HR	BB/SO	R	RBI	SB	CS	OUT	BA	OBP	SLG	EQA	EQR	DEFENSE
1997	Hagerstn	SAL	392	113	20	0	14	40/96	45	46	1	1	280	.288	.356	.446	.270	53	50-1B 96
1998	Dunedin	Fla	363	90	17	1	15	24/95	40	47	1	1	274	.248	.295	.424	.238	38	70-1B 116
1999	Knoxvill	Sou	507	140	20	1	16	42/99	61	89	0	1	368	.276	.337	.414	.253	59	102-1B 107
2000	Toronto	AL	464	131	17	0	20	49/100	68	84	0	1	334	.282	.351	.448	.269	63	

Giles isn't anything special but since he racked up a lot of RBIs at Knoxville this year the Jays took notice. Now that the Jays have re-signed Delgado, Giles's chances for a career lie elsewhere. The projection is pretty accurate and is not good enough for a starting first baseman.

Alex Gonzalez   SS   Bats R   Age 27

YEAR	TEAM	LGE	AB	H	DB	TP	HR	BB/SO	R	RBI	SB	CS	OUT	BA	OBP	SLG	EQA	EQR	DEFENSE
1997	Toronto	AL	427	105	26	2	12	32/90	46	35	15	6	328	.246	.307	.400	.240	46	124-SS 105
1998	Toronto	AL	567	136	25	1	14	26/118	66	50	19	6	437	.240	.281	.362	.219	49	157-SS 102
1999	Toronto	AL	152	43	9	0	3	15/23	19	11	4	2	111	.283	.359	.401	.261	19	36-SS 118
2000	Toronto	AL	311	78	11	0	10	24/60	40	39	10	3	236	.251	.304	.383	.235	32	

Gonzalez gave the True Believers a month of excitement, hitting well in April with his usual great defense and a big uptick in walk rate. Pain in his right shoulder shut him down May 14, and the surgery he underwent a month later ended his season. He should be healthy and back at shortstop this spring. There's considerable speculation that he'll be with another team, possibly the Braves. That projection is very pessimistic.

Curtis Goodwin   OF   Bats L   Age   27

YEAR	TEAM	LGE	AB	H	DB	TP	HR	BB/SO	R	RBI	SB	CS	OUT	BA	OBP	SLG	EQA	EQR	DEFENSE
1997	Cincnnti	NL	266	66	6	0	3	24/52	24	12	18	13	214	.248	.313	.305	.213	22	67-OF 106
1997	Indianap	AA	118	30	2	1	1	14/21	12	6	9	6	94	.254	.333	.314	.227	12	25-OF 105
1998	Colorado	NL	156	34	4	0	2	16/39	24	6	5	1	123	.218	.291	.282	.201	11	42-OF 112
1999	ChiCubs	NL	157	37	5	1	0	11/38	13	8	1	4	124	.236	.286	.280	.183	9	35-CF 101
2000	ChiCubs	NL	201	48	6	1	2	20/47	25	16	11	7	160	.239	.308	.308	.208	16	

We can dismiss a player's intangibles all we like, but in real life, being a jackass can be an expensive proposition. The other Goodwin, Tom, signed a three-year deal with the Rockies for more than $10 million. This Goodwin, more or less the same player but better known for his temper and some highly-publicized run-ins, was dumped twice in two weeks during 1999. He can still help a team in a specialized role, but who wants a part-time player who complains all the time?

Craig Grebeck   IF   Bats R   Age 35

YEAR	TEAM	LGE	AB	H	DB	TP	HR	BB SO	R	RBI	SB	CS	OUT	BA	OBP	SLG	EQA	EQR	DEFENSE	
1997	Anaheim	AL	125	34	6	0	2	17 11	11	6	0	1	92	.272	.359	.368	.251	14	21-2B 102	11-SS 101
1998	Toronto	AL	300	77	16	2	2	28 41	31	26	2	2	225	.257	.329	.343	.231	29	82-2B 110	
1999	Toronto	AL	111	40	6	0	0	13 13	16	9	0	0	71	.360	.436	.414	.300	17		
2000	Toronto	AL	139	38	5	0	2	18 17	21	18	1	1	102	.273	.357	.353	.248	16		

Grebeck is one of the better utility infielders in baseball, thanks to his good secondary skills. He really can't play shortstop, which keeps him from being one of the best, and it's doubtful that he could even be an effective platoon second baseman. He's a good example of a player who is successful if used within his limits.

Shawn Green			**RF**				**Bats L**		**Age 27**									
YEAR	TEAM	LGE	AB	H	DB	TP	HR	BB	SO	R	RBI	SB	CS	OUT	BA	OBP	SLG	EQA	EQR	DEFENSE
1997	Toronto	AL	430	128	24	5	16	34	95	57	53	14	3	305	.298	.351	.488	.281	64	86-OF 96
1998	Toronto	AL	628	174	33	4	35	48	139	100	96	31	12	466	.277	.333	.510	.277	94	150-OF 98
1999	Toronto	AL	607	184	38	0	42	58	117	120	113	20	8	431	.303	.374	.573	.306	111	150-RF 108
2000	LosAngls	NL	573	156	27	2	34	59/119		98	105	25	7	424	.272	.340	.504	.287	93	

Like Delgado, Green has improved steadily over the past four years, especially when it comes to hitting left-handed pitchers (pre-1999: .243/.293/.373 in 378 at-bats; 1999: .280/.376/.506 in 164 at-bats) and playing defense, even winning a Gold Glove in 1999. I think last year was about the top of his range and expect him to settle into the .290-.300 EqA level for the next few years. He will help the Dodgers, who will have to avoid appearing disappointed when he slips back to a .290 EqA with traditional statistics that look worse thanks to the park switch.

Willie Greene			**DH/3B**				**Bats L**		**Age 28**									
YEAR	TEAM	LGE	AB	H	DB	TP	HR	BB/SO	R	RBI	SB	CS	OUT	BA	OBP	SLG	EQA	EQR	DEFENSE
1997	Cincnnti	NL	498	124	21	1	27	77/110	61	89	5	0	374	.249	.351	.458	.273	73	102-3B 92 / 29-OF 110
1998	Cincnnti	NL	360	100	19	1	15	56/78	58	50	6	3	263	.278	.380	.461	.284	57	70-3B 105 / 21-OF 96
1999	Toronto	AL	225	45	5	0	12	18/56	20	38	0	0	180	.200	.259	.382	.212	19	
1999	Syracuse	Int	52	15	0	0	4	4/15	9	8	0	0	37	.288	.339	.519	.280	8	
2000	Toronto	AL	291	73	10	0	15	46/68	47	53	1	1	219	.251	.353	.440	.269	41	

Greene picked a really bad time to go into the worst slump of his life. In April, Dave Hollins's broken hand left the DH job to him, but from April 26 until his demotion to Syracuse May 21, he hit .068/.163/.091. That slump was a significant contributor to the Jays' horrid stretch and may have sealed the perception of Greene as unfit for a regular job. He'll always be a classic example of a good young player whose career was badly damaged by his organization. He can still give a team 400 good plate appearances as a platoon third baseman.

Cesar Izturis			**SS/2B**				**Bats B**		**Age 20**									
YEAR	TEAM	LGE	AB	H	DB	TP	HR	BB	SO	R	RBI	SB	CS	OUT	BA	OBP	SLG	EQA	EQR	DEFENSE
1997	St Cath	NYP	236	46	1	0	2	11	31	24	10	2	2	192	.195	.232	.225	.132	6	40-2B 90 / 30-SS 98
1998	Hagerstn	SAL	415	97	12	1	1	16	43	40	30	8	4	322	.234	.264	.275	.177	21	125-SS 94
1999	Dunedin	Fla	538	150	33	10	3	17	64	60	63	15	8	396	.279	.305	.394	.235	53	84-SS 93 / 44-2B 103
2000	Toronto	AL	422	115	19	4	2	20	49	47	44	8	6	313	.273	.305	.351	.221	36	

Like some very young players, Izturis is making big leaps with the bat as he matures physically. He has a significant defensive reputation and was named the best defensive second baseman in the Florida State League. While he has been sharing time at both middle-infield positions with Mike Young, he projects as a shortstop. He's young enough to improve the plate discipline; as with Abernathy, it's the biggest thing keeping him from being a top-tier prospect.

Joe Lawrence			**3B**				**Bats R**		**Age 23**									
YEAR	TEAM	LGE	AB	H	DB	TP	HR	BB/SO	R	RBI	SB	CS	OUT	BA	OBP	SLG	EQA	EQR	DEFENSE
1997	Hagerstn	SAL	457	95	19	1	9	42/108	52	32	3	5	367	.208	.280	.313	.198	32	116-SS 87
1998	Dunedin	Fla	459	117	27	4	10	87/97	77	33	6	5	347	.255	.377	.397	.268	65	119-SS 88
1999	Knoxvill	Sou	252	59	16	1	6	48/49	42	19	4	3	196	.234	.361	.377	.257	33	66-3B 94
2000	Toronto	AL	363	94	20	1	10	59/75	63	55	4	4	273	.259	.363	.402	.263	49	

A torn ankle ligament ended his season in June, costing him a trip to Fenway Park for the Futures Game. He should get to see the Fens soon enough, as he's a much better prospect than Casey Blake. Lawrence should be up with the Jays no later than this September, with a good chance at a starting job in 2001. The idea of moving him to catcher is dead.

Felipe Lopez SS Bats B Age 20

YEAR	TEAM	LGE	AB	H	DB	TP	HR	BB/SO	R	RBI	SB	CS	OUT	BA	OBP	SLG	EQA	EQR	DEFENSE
1998	St Cath	NYP	85	27	6	1	1	2/14	10	8	1	1	59	.318	.333	.447	.258	10	
1999	Hagerstn	SAL	551	131	28	2	12	50/159	67	63	8	6	426	.238	.303	.361	.225	51	129-SS 83
2000	*Toronto*	*AL*	*265*	*67*	*12*	*1*	*7*	*27/83*	*36*	*35*	*3*	*2*	*200*	*.253*	*.322*	*.385*	*.241*	*28*	

The Jays' 1998 #1 was named the #4 prospect in the Sally League, mostly due to his physical tools and power bat. He's not the fielder Izturis is; combined with his power, that will probably move him to third base or the outfield in the next couple of years. Lopez has significant offensive potential; a year from now, he'll be all over lists of top prospects.

Luis Lopez 1B/3B Bats R Age 26

YEAR	TEAM	LGE	AB	H	DB	TP	HR	BB/SO	R	RBI	SB	CS	OUT	BA	OBP	SLG	EQA	EQR	DEFENSE	
1997	Hagerstn	SAL	519	145	38	2	9	47/50	72	69	1	3	377	.279	.345	.412	.256	62	88-1B 106	
1998	Knoxvill	Sou	445	113	20	1	11	37/62	48	56	0	1	333	.254	.314	.378	.234	44	60-1B 102	28-3B 89
1999	Syracuse	Int	526	146	26	2	3	29/64	57	52	1	0	380	.278	.316	.352	.227	47	79-1B 103	28-3B 91
2000	*Toronto*	*AL*	*457*	*121*	*23*	*1*	*8*	*37/56*	*56*	*57*	*1*	*1*	*337*	*.265*	*.320*	*.372*	*.235*	*45*		

Lopez is a first baseman who hits for average and not much else. If he could really play third base, he might be a C prospect. He can't, and he's not. The Delgado signing cuts off any future he might have had here.

Mike Matheny C Bats R Age 29

YEAR	TEAM	LGE	AB	H	DB	TP	HR	BB/SO	R	RBI	SB	CS	OUT	BA	OBP	SLG	EQA	EQR	DEFENSE
1997	Milwauke	AL	320	79	17	1	4	15/65	28	31	0	1	242	.247	.298	.344	.216	26	
1998	Milwauke	NL	322	78	9	0	8	10/61	24	28	1	0	244	.242	.282	.345	.210	25	91-C 95
1999	Toronto	AL	163	34	3	0	4	10/37	14	17	0	0	129	.209	.259	.301	.183	9	50-C 102
2000	*St Louis*	*NL*	*185*	*42*	*3*	*0*	*5*	*12/39*	*13*	*18*	*0*	*0*	*143*	*.227*	*.274*	*.324*	*.198*	*12*	

Matheny is not a major-league-quality baseball player. You don't need us to tell you that. Unless you're Gord Ash, in which case this may well be worth repeating: Mike Matheny is not a major-league-quality baseball player. At 29, he's likely to be around for many more years. The Cardinals have signed him.

Brian McRae CF Bats B Age 32

YEAR	TEAM	LGE	AB	H	DB	TP	HR	BB/SO	R	RBI	SB	CS	OUT	BA	OBP	SLG	EQA	EQR	DEFENSE
1997	ChiCubs	NL	418	98	27	5	6	51/61	60	27	11	6	326	.234	.324	.366	.238	45	106-OF 103
1997	NY Mets	NL	147	37	6	2	5	12/22	23	15	2	4	114	.252	.317	.422	.242	16	25-OF 108
1998	NY Mets	NL	562	156	41	5	23	80/88	83	83	21	13	419	.278	.373	.491	.286	92	144-OF 104
1999	NY Mets	NL	300	67	11	1	8	36/56	33	34	1	6	239	.223	.318	.347	.224	28	77-CF 87
1999	Colorado	NL	22	5	0	0	1	2/7	1	1	0	0	17	.227	.350	.364	.250	3	
1999	Toronto	AL	81	15	2	1	3	15/22	10	10	0	1	67	.185	.326	.346	.232	9	
2000	*Toronto*	*AL*	*384*	*105*	*21*	*2*	*15*	*61/69*	*69*	*68*	*8*	*8*	*286*	*.273*	*.373*	*.456*	*.254*	*46*	

How's that for a tease? McRae, in the last year of his contract and having an abysmal year, gets traded to Colorado on July 31. He had to be thinking, "OK, two good months here, and I set myself up for a new deal." A week later, he was shipped off Planet Coors. If you're Brian McRae, you must feel just a little gypped. He's worth an NRI, or a cheap one-year deal, as a fourth outfielder.

Adam Melhuse OF/1B Bats B Age 28

YEAR	TEAM	LGE	AB	H	DB	TP	HR	BB/SO	R	RBI	SB	CS	OUT	BA	OBP	SLG	EQA	EQR	DEFENSE	
1997	Knoxvill	Sou	87	15	2	0	2	14/23	9	6	0	0	72	.172	.287	.264	.191	6		
1997	Syracuse	Int	120	26	4	1	2	9 /19	6	8	1	1	95	.217	.276	.317	.198	8		
1998	Knoxvill	Sou	239	54	11	0	11	50/46	35	26	2	2	187	.226	.360	.410	.264	34	51-C 95	
1999	Knoxvill	Sou	381	87	15	1	14	83/88	55	47	2	3	297	.228	.370	.383	.262	52	42-OF 86	24-1B 99
1999	Syracuse	Int	71	17	2	0	2	8/22	11	12	1	1	55	.239	.316	.352	.228	7		
2000	*Toronto*	*AL*	*390*	*90*	*11*	*0*	*17*	*78/90*	*66*	*62*	*2*	*2*	*302*	*.231*	*.359*	*.390*	*.260*	*52*		

Melhuse moved out from behind the plate in 1999, playing part-time in the outfield. He's lost his prospect tag, but as a switch-hitter who can catch and get on base, he could help a lot of teams, the Jays included. He deserves a break, if for no other reason than as compensation for parts of three summers in Knoxville, Tennessee.

Jorge Nunez 　　　　2B 　　　Bats R 　Age 22

YEAR	TEAM	LGE	AB	H	DB	TP	HR	BB/SO	R	RBI	SB	CS	OUT	BA	OBP	SLG	EQA	EQR	DEFENSE
1998	Med Hat	Pio	311	77	8	6	5	11/52	35	29	10	2	236	.248	.274	.360	.216	25	65-SS 93
1999	Hagerstn	SAL	574	136	27	7	13	33/104	81	49	20	4	442	.237	.280	.376	.224	52	119-2B 91
2000	*LosAngls*	*NL*	*371*	*94*	*15*	*5*	*10*	*23/78*	*48*	*46*	*14*	*2*	*279*	*.253*	*.297*	*.402*	*.245*	*41*	

Nunez was the throw-in with Shawn Green in the trade with the Dodgers. He's a toolsy player with significant power and speed. Moving from the Blue Jay organization to the Dodgers helps him significantly, as the Jays are flush with middle-infield prospects, while the Dodgers have Alex Cora.

Willis Otanez 　　　　3B 　　　Bats R 　Age 27

YEAR	TEAM	LGE	AB	H	DB	TP	HR	BB/SO	R	RBI	SB	CS	OUT	BA	OBP	SLG	EQA	EQR	DEFENSE
1997	Bowie	Eas	79	22	5	0	3	6/22	9	10	0	1	58	.278	.329	.456	.257	10	
1997	Rochestr	Int	170	34	5	0	6	11/35	17	24	0	0	136	.200	.249	.335	.191	11	40-3B 91
1998	Rochestr	Int	484	122	24	1	20	30/116	70	77	1	0	362	.252	.303	.430	.244	53	116-3B 111
1999	Baltimor	AL	80	17	3	0	2	5/16	6	10	0	0	63	.213	.267	.325	.197	5	
1999	Toronto	AL	126	31	7	0	5	8/30	19	12	0	0	95	.246	.296	.421	.238	13	
2000	*Toronto*	*AL*	*277*	*69*	*11*	*0*	*12*	*20/64*	*32*	*41*	*0*	*0*	*208*	*.249*	*.300*	*.419*	*.242*	*30*	

In May, the Jays claimed Otanez off waivers, where he'd ended up after the Orioles realized he wasn't 35. It wasn't a bad gamble; Otanez was a potential solution for the DH/third base problem, with upside and some defensive ability. He didn't hit and played only sporadically after the All-Star break. He's a free agent.

Josh Phelps 　　　　C 　　　Bats R 　Age 22

YEAR	TEAM	LGE	AB	H	DB	TP	HR	BB/SO	R	RBI	SB	CS	OUT	BA	OBP	SLG	EQA	EQR	DEFENSE
1997	Hagerstn	SAL	237	47	7	1	7	13/73	22	20	1	1	191	.198	.256	.325	.191	15	
1998	Hagerstn	SAL	390	89	21	1	7	32/81	37	34	1	0	301	.228	.295	.341	.216	33	82-C 96
1999	Dunedin	Fla	408	119	23	2	21	23/114	59	72	3	2	291	.292	.337	.512	.277	59	19-C 99
2000	*Toronto*	*AL*	*389*	*105*	*15*	*1*	*16*	*32/101*	*51*	*64*	*1*	*1*	*285*	*.270*	*.325*	*.437*	*.255*	*47*	

Moved out from behind the plate, his bat sparked to life. With Guillermo Quiroz, he'll need to hit enough to carve out a job elsewhere, most likely as a DH. I'm not optimistic.

Guillermo Quiroz 　　　　C 　　　Bats R 　Age 18

YEAR	TEAM	LGE	AB	H	DB	TP	HR	BB/SO	R	RBI	SB	CS	OUT	BA	OBP	SLG	EQA	EQR	DEFENSE
1999	Med Hat	Pio	208	37	6	0	6	10/63	15	16	0	1	172	.178	.222	.293	.159	9	59-C 95
2000	*Toronto*	*AL*	*99*	*18*	*4*	*0*	*5*	*6/55*	*7*	*10*	*0*	*0*	*81*	*.182*	*.229*	*.374*	*.193*	*7*	

Quiroz is another expensive international signing, a tall Venezuelan catcher with a lot of physical development left. His defense is ahead of his bat at this point. Merely playing professionally at 17 in a foreign country is impressive; doing so well enough to be the sixth-best prospect in your league is more so. Look for Quiroz to jump to full-season ball in 2000 and make a nice offensive gain as he gets stronger.

David Segui 　　　　1B 　　　Bats B 　Age 33

YEAR	TEAM	LGE	AB	H	DB	TP	HR	BB/SO	R	RBI	SB	CS	OUT	BA	OBP	SLG	EQA	EQR	DEFENSE
1997	Montreal	NL	463	141	22	3	22	56/65	75	67	1	0	322	.305	.381	.508	.295	76	122-1B 100
1998	Seattle	AL	521	161	31	2	20	47/78	76	82	3	1	361	.309	.366	.491	.285	79	133-1B 137
1999	Seattle	AL	341	97	22	3	8	28/43	39	35	1	2	246	.284	.341	.437	.260	42	85-1B 115
1999	Toronto	AL	94	29	4	0	5	7/17	12	12	0	0	65	.309	.356	.511	.285	14	
2000	*Toronto*	*AL*	*413*	*116*	*19*	*1*	*18*	*47/58*	*65*	*77*	*1*	*1*	*298*	*.281*	*.354*	*.462*	*.275*	*59*	

Picking up Segui in August was irrelevant. He didn't improve the team's offense significantly, and the Jays couldn't play him at first base without ticking off Carlos Delgado. The pitchers the Jays gave up, Tom Davey and Steve Sinclair, are middle relievers at best. One of the more insignificant moves of the season. Segui will be back with the Jays in 2000, having accepted an offer of arbitration.

　　We often criticize teams for not offering arbitration to departing free agents, as they forego draft picks by not doing so. In this case, the Jays did make the offer—solely for the compensation—and were tripped up by it, as Segui didn't find many takers. Jim Fregosi will have to find a way to convince Carlos Delgado to DH, so Segui can play first base. He has some value there.

Shannon Stewart — LF — Bats R — Age 26

YEAR	TEAM	LGE	AB	H	DB	TP	HR	BB/SO	R	RBI	SB	CS	OUT	BA	OBP	SLG	EQA	EQR	DEFENSE
1997	Syracuse	Int	210	69	10	1	5	32/25	35	21	7	4	145	.329	.426	.457	.303	37	55-OF 103
1997	Toronto	AL	168	49	12	8	0	18/23	24	22	10	3	122	.292	.376	.458	.285	26	40-OF 105
1998	Toronto	AL	514	142	28	3	12	65/75	83	52	45	18	390	.276	.374	.412	.274	77	129-OF 102
1999	Toronto	AL	602	178	28	2	10	51/83	92	61	36	15	439	.296	.359	.399	.262	77	136-LF 88
2000	Toronto	AL	548	158	26	4	13	64/76	109	79	34	12	402	.288	.363	.422	.272	78	

It was a disappointing year for a player who looked ready to explode. Stewart regressed in almost every area of his game despite being healthy most of the year. I don't think it's a trend; I think he'll be one of the best left fielders in the league in 2000.

Andy Thompson — RF — Bats R — Age 24

YEAR	TEAM	LGE	AB	H	DB	TP	HR	BB/SO	R	RBI	SB	CS	OUT	BA	OBP	SLG	EQA	EQR	DEFENSE
1997	Knoxvill	Sou	440	104	20	2	12	49/81	53	50	0	3	339	.236	.319	.373	.234	45	104-3B 88
1999	Knoxvill	Sou	256	56	13	2	13	27/58	43	41	4	2	202	.219	.307	.438	.248	31	65-OF 88
1999	Syracuse	Int	228	63	14	2	14	17/45	34	35	4	0	165	.276	.331	.539	.284	35	44-OF 98
2000	Toronto	AL	334	83	16	2	19	39/107	52	62	3	1	252	.249	.327	.479	.268	47	

Thompson is one of the many victims of Prospect's Disease. If he could hit like he did in 1999 while playing third base, he'd make a lot of money in this game. He can't, and he won't. As a right fielder, he's nothing special and certainly isn't going to keep Raul Mondesi up at night. Thompson could be mildly interesting as part of a DH platoon with Kevin Witt. That's a $500,000 solution that would be much better than, say, $2 million worth of Gregg Jefferies.

Vernon Wells — CF — Bats R — Age 21

YEAR	TEAM	LGE	AB	H	DB	TP	HR	BB/SO	R	RBI	SB	CS	OUT	BA	OBP	SLG	EQA	EQR	DEFENSE
1997	St Cath	NYP	274	69	15	1	9	23/50	37	22	3	3	208	.252	.311	.412	.241	30	61-OF 102
1998	Hagerstn	SAL	515	124	29	3	9	39/85	64	49	5	3	394	.241	.295	.361	.221	45	131-OF 102
1999	Dunedin	Fla	267	81	14	1	12	22/37	34	36	6	1	187	.303	.358	.498	.285	41	69-OF 103
1999	Knoxvill	Sou	106	33	4	2	3	9/15	14	14	3	1	74	.311	.365	.472	.281	16	26-OF 106
1999	Syracuse	Int	128	37	8	1	3	8/22	16	17	4	1	92	.289	.335	.438	.262	16	33-OF 104
1999	Toronto	AL	88	23	4	0	1	3/18	7	7	1	1	66	.261	.286	.341	.208	6	23-CF 93
2000	Toronto	AL	537	159	26	2	17	44/86	86	89	11	4	382	.296	.349	.447	.270	72	

The A-ball-to-the-major-leagues storyline is nice, but was more a product of the Jays' desperation than Wells's talent. He's an excellent prospect who didn't do anything at Syracuse that demanded he be called up. I think he's being rushed and would be better off playing at least three months in Triple-A before being given the starting job in Toronto. A great prospect for 2001 and beyond.

Kevin Witt — 1B/LF — Bats L — Age 24

YEAR	TEAM	LGE	AB	H	DB	TP	HR	BB/SO	R	RBI	SB	CS	OUT	BA	OBP	SLG	EQA	EQR	DEFENSE	
1997	Knoxvill	Sou	492	120	21	3	23	32/117	53	64	1	0	372	.244	.293	.439	.242	54	65-1B 109	32-3B 84
1998	Syracuse	Int	456	116	19	3	20	44/126	62	57	2	2	342	.254	.328	.441	.257	57	102-1B 98	
1999	Syracuse	Int	419	109	23	3	20	56/109	60	58	0	0	310	.260	.351	.473	.275	61	63-1B 110	49-OF 88
1999	Toronto	AL	34	7	0	0	1	2/9	2	4	0	0	27	.206	.250	.294	.175	2		
2000	Toronto	AL	473	125	22	2	25	63/123	78	92	1	0	348	.264	.351	.478	.278	71		

At 24, Witt has nowhere left to go on the defensive spectrum, having moved from shortstop to first base in just three years, with stops at third base and left field. Witt can hit, and as mentioned above, could be part of a cheap DH solution for the Jays. Even more fun: live with the mediocre gloves and make them the third-base platoon. Witt should have some type of job in Toronto this year, and will meet that projection in less playing time.

Chris Woodward   SS   Bats R   Age 24

YEAR	TEAM	LGE	AB	H	DB	TP	HR	BB/SO	R	RBI	SB	CS	OUT	BA	OBP	SLG	EQA	EQR	DEFENSE
1997	Dunedin	Fla	320	82	14	3	1	44/57	32	31	2	3	241	.256	.353	.328	.239	34	88-SS 102
1998	Knoxvill	Sou	253	56	7	0	4	17/49	27	22	2	3	200	.221	.277	.296	.190	16	71-SS 105
1998	Syracuse	Int	85	16	5	0	2	6/20	8	5	1	1	70	.188	.242	.318	.181	5	24-SS 101
1999	Syracuse	Int	279	76	18	2	1	33/49	38	17	3	1	204	.272	.351	.362	.249	31	58-SS 101
1999	Toronto	AL	26	6	0	0	0	2/6	1	2	0	0	20	.231	.286	.231	.170	1	
2000	*Toronto*	*AL*	*311*	*77*	*13*	*1*	*2*	*34/58*	*38*	*30*	*2*	*2*	*236*	*.248*	*.322*	*.315*	*.220*	*27*	

He can thank Alex Gonzalez for his lines in *Total Baseball*. Woodward is a defensive replacement who would be among the league's worst shortstops if he tripped into a job. He also doesn't do enough with his bat or legs to be a contributor off the bench.

Mike Young   2B/SS   Bats R   Age 23

YEAR	TEAM	LGE	AB	H	DB	TP	HR	BB/SO	R	RBI	SB	CS	OUT	BA	OBP	SLG	EQA	EQR	DEFENSE	
1997	St Cath	NYP	287	73	13	2	9	25/67	34	35	3	2	216	.254	.322	.408	.246	32	44-SS 89	28-2B 98
1998	Hagerstn	SAL	529	126	31	3	13	44/97	63	64	6	4	406	.238	.302	.382	.231	52	121-2B 92	13-SS 95
1999	Dunedin	Fla	501	137	36	2	5	50/88	64	66	13	3	367	.273	.342	.383	.252	58	73-2B 96	52-SS 85
2000	*Toronto*	*AL*	*470*	*129*	*26*	*2*	*11*	*52/86*	*77*	*68*	*10*	*3*	*344*	*.274*	*.347*	*.409*	*.260*	*59*		

He's moved through the organization with Cesar Izturis, but this may be the end of their pairing. Young isn't the shortstop Izturis is, and he's a year younger than Brent Abernathy while being about the same player. Young is a B or B- prospect in his own right; he's just stuck behind a B+ one. He could move to the major leagues quickly in a different organization.

PITCHERS (Averages: ERA: 4.50 / H/9: 9.00 / HR/9: 1.00 / BB/9: 3.50 / K/9: 6.50 / KWH: 1.00)

Clayton Andrews   Throws L   Age 22

YEAR	TEAM	LGE	IP	H	ER	HR	BB	K	ERA	W	L	H/9	HR/9	BB/9	K/9	KWH	PERA
1997	Hagerstn	SAL	109.7	148	85	11	67	78	6.98	4	8	12.15	0.90	5.50	6.40	0.46	7.14
1998	Hagerstn	SAL	150.7	152	81	8	64	125	4.84	8	9	9.08	0.48	3.82	7.47	1.20	4.12
1999	Knoxvill	Sou	127.7	158	89	14	74	77	6.27	5	9	11.14	0.99	5.22	5.43	0.38	6.49
1999	Syracuse	Int	14.3	11	13	5	14	8	8.16	0	2	6.91	3.14	8.79	5.02	0.31	8.16

After a good second season at Hagerstown, Andrews struggled early at Double-A before putting it together in the second half. Like many pitchers without a dominant fastball, Andrews appears to need an adjustment period at every level. His arm hasn't been abused and he has three above-average pitches, so I think he'll eventually have a career, starting in 2002 or so.

Chris Carpenter   Throws R   Age 25

YEAR	TEAM	LGE	IP	H	ER	HR	BB	K	ERA	W	L	H/9	HR/9	BB/9	K/9	KWH	PERA
1997	Syracuse	Int	116.7	123	66	16	55	83	5.09	6	7	9.49	1.23	4.24	6.40	0.76	5.32
1997	Toronto	AL	81.7	105	52	7	38	55	5.73	3	6	11.57	0.77	4.19	6.06	0.57	6.06
1998	Toronto	AL	177.0	171	88	17	63	138	4.47	10	10	8.69	0.86	3.20	7.02	1.32	4.07
1999	Toronto	AL	151.7	169	71	14	46	109	4.21	9	8	10.03	0.83	2.73	6.47	1.14	4.63

His mistreatment at the hands of Tim Johnson haunted the Jays well after Johnson's dismissal, as Carpenter missed most of last June with a sore elbow. Fregosi wasn't particularly gentle with him, either, as he averaged 110 pitches per start before the DL stint. Carpenter has the build, the arm and the repertoire to be one of the best starters in the league.

Kelvim Escobar   Throws R   Age 24

YEAR	TEAM	LGE	IP	H	ER	HR	BB	K	ERA	W	L	H/9	HR/9	BB/9	K/9	KWH	PERA
1997	Dunedin	Fla	11.3	19	10	0	4	13	7.94	0	1	15.09	0.00	3.18	10.32	1.66	7.15
1997	Knoxvill	Sou	24.3	20	12	1	18	26	4.44	2	1	7.40	0.37	6.66	9.62	1.40	4.07
1997	Toronto	AL	31.0	28	11	1	19	36	3.19	2	1	8.13	0.29	5.52	10.45	1.82	4.06
1998	Syracuse	Int	57.3	58	29	7	25	57	4.55	3	3	9.10	1.10	3.92	8.95	1.67	4.87
1998	Toronto	AL	80.3	69	33	5	37	73	3.70	5	4	7.73	0.56	4.15	8.18	1.56	3.59
1999	Toronto	AL	176.0	193	103	16	79	133	5.27	8	12	9.87	0.82	4.04	6.80	0.87	5.01

(Kelvim Escobar *continued*)

Another pitcher Tim Johnson damaged. In 1998, Escobar ranked second in the major leagues in Workload in just ten starts. In 1999, he was a completely different pitcher, without the dominant fastball he had displayed in his first two seasons. His ineffectiveness kept his workload down in 1999, a small blessing. Like Carpenter, he has the tools to be a top starting pitcher, and I think he's going to be above average in 2000.

John Frascatore — Throws R — Age 30

YEAR	TEAM	LGE	IP	H	ER	HR	BB	K	ERA	W	L	H/9	HR/9	BB/9	K/9	KWH	PERA
1997	St Louis	NL	79.3	75	24	5	35	54	2.72	7	2	8.51	0.57	3.97	6.13	0.83	3.97
1998	St Louis	NL	96.7	95	47	11	39	47	4.38	6	5	8.84	1.02	3.63	4.38	0.45	4.47
1999	Arizona	NL	32.0	32	16	6	12	14	4.50	2	2	9.00	1.69	3.38	3.94	0.38	5.06
1999	Toronto	AL	37.0	41	14	4	9	23	3.41	3	1	9.97	0.97	2.19	5.59	1.07	4.62

He's just some middle-relief fodder picked up in the Batista heist. Frascatore is arbitration-eligible and eminiently replaceable, so look for him to have a comparable season in a different uniform in 2000.

Gary Glover — Throws R — Age 23

YEAR	TEAM	LGE	IP	H	ER	HR	BB	K	ERA	W	L	H/9	HR/9	BB/9	K/9	KWH	PERA
1997	Hagerstn	SAL	166.7	203	114	12	83	107	6.16	7	12	10.96	0.65	4.48	5.78	0.51	5.67
1998	Dunedin	Fla	102.7	142	79	10	47	68	6.93	3	8	12.45	0.88	4.12	5.96	0.52	6.66
1998	Knoxvill	Sou	36.0	45	36	3	27	12	9.00	1	3	11.25	0.75	6.75	3.00	0.09	7.00
1999	Knoxvill	Sou	83.7	77	41	5	29	64	4.41	5	4	8.28	0.54	3.12	6.88	1.37	3.55
1999	Syracuse	Int	74.3	98	48	9	37	52	5.81	3	5	11.87	1.09	4.48	6.30	0.56	6.78

Glover is a big, hard-throwing right-hander who finally experienced some success in 1999. His best pitch is a slider, and his improvement in 1999 is in part due to the improvement of his off-speed stuff. Glover moved to the bullpen in the Arizona Fall League. He's a year away, but a good bet to show up in Toronto as a middle reliever this season.

Roy Halladay — Throws R — Age 23

YEAR	TEAM	LGE	IP	H	ER	HR	BB	K	ERA	W	L	H/9	HR/9	BB/9	K/9	KWH	PERA
1997	Knoxvill	Sou	36.3	49	25	4	12	25	6.19	1	3	12.14	0.99	2.97	6.19	0.79	6.19
1997	Syracuse	Int	122.0	143	77	13	55	55	5.68	5	9	10.55	0.96	4.06	4.06	0.29	5.61
1998	Syracuse	Int	110.7	122	58	10	55	63	4.72	6	6	9.92	0.81	4.47	5.12	0.44	5.20
1998	Toronto	AL	14.0	9	4	2	2	13	2.57	2	0	5.79	1.29	1.29	8.36	7.02	2.57
1999	Toronto	AL	150.7	149	67	16	76	84	4.00	9	8	8.90	0.96	4.54	5.02	0.47	4.78

Halladay had only sporadic command of his four pitches in 1999, despite which he was an above-average starter. His pitches, particularly his cutter and knuckle-curve, have great movement. His control should improve with innings. No team in the league has three young starters that can compare to the Jays' trio.

Joey Hamilton — Throws R — Age 29

YEAR	TEAM	LGE	IP	H	ER	HR	BB	K	ERA	W	L	H/9	HR/9	BB/9	K/9	KWH	PERA
1997	San Dieg	NL	190.0	202	100	23	72	115	4.74	10	11	9.57	1.09	3.41	5.45	0.68	4.88
1998	San Dieg	NL	208.3	236	123	16	111	138	5.31	10	13	10.20	0.69	4.80	5.96	0.54	5.40
1999	Toronto	AL	99.0	113	64	11	38	58	5.82	4	7	10.27	1.00	3.45	5.27	0.59	5.18

Dave Stewart was given credit for Hamilton's good second half in 1998, but whatever Stewart was able to do as a pitching coach didn't work as well from the front office. Hamilton doesn't resemble, in any way, shape or form, the pitcher who looked so good through 1994. An optimist would point to his sore shoulder and say it caused the bad year; a realist points to the loss of velocity and lack of movement and thinks, "He's done."

Pat Hentgen — Throws R — Age 31

YEAR	TEAM	LGE	IP	H	ER	HR	BB	K	ERA	W	L	H/9	HR/9	BB/9	K/9	KWH	PERA
1997	Toronto	AL	264.0	247	108	29	71	161	3.68	17	12	8.42	0.99	2.42	5.49	1.10	3.75
1998	Toronto	AL	179.7	202	99	26	72	95	4.96	9	11	10.12	1.30	3.61	4.76	0.46	5.51
1999	Toronto	AL	201.0	214	101	28	64	121	4.52	11	11	9.58	1.25	2.87	5.42	0.80	4.84

He's a league-average innings-muncher at this point, which has value. Traded to the Cardinals, a team that has desperately needed starters to give them innings. Rotoheads: Hentgen's a great bet for big wins in 2000 if you can live with the ERA and ratio.

Billy Koch — Throws R — Age 25

YEAR	TEAM	LGE	IP	H	ER	HR	BB	K	ERA	W	L	H/9	HR/9	BB/9	K/9	KWH	PERA
1997	Dunedin	Fla	20.0	35	13	2	4	15	5.85	1	1	15.75	0.90	1.80	6.75	1.20	7.65
1998	Dunedin	Fla	113.7	155	86	9	58	78	6.81	4	9	12.27	0.71	4.59	6.18	0.51	6.57
1999	Syracuse	Int	25.0	29	11	3	11	19	3.96	2	1	10.44	1.08	3.96	6.84	0.85	5.76
1999	Toronto	AL	64.3	52	22	4	29	59	3.08	5	2	7.27	0.56	4.06	8.25	1.72	3.36

Koch throws very hard for someone two years removed from Tommy John surgery. Converted to the bullpen in the spring, he was the Toronto closer by June. That blazing fastball isn't his only pitch, but it's the only good one right now. He'll get even better as his breaking stuff improves and is going to be nasty for the next four years or so.

Graeme Lloyd — Throws L — Age 33

YEAR	TEAM	LGE	IP	H	ER	HR	BB	K	ERA	W	L	H/9	HR/9	BB/9	K/9	KWH	PERA
1997	NY Yanks	AL	49.0	53	22	6	20	26	4.04	3	2	9.73	1.10	3.67	4.78	0.48	5.14
1998	NY Yanks	AL	37.0	27	10	3	6	20	2.43	3	1	6.57	0.73	1.46	4.86	1.84	2.19
1999	Toronto	AL	72.3	65	31	10	23	48	3.86	5	3	8.09	1.24	2.86	5.97	1.15	3.98

Lloyd is the player lost in the Clemens deal whom the Yankees missed most. Without him, they used fodder like Tony Fossas and Greg McCarthy as spot lefties, finally getting lucky when Allen Watson put together 30 innings that didn't suck. Lloyd signed a three-year deal with the Expos, a strange signing in that the Expos aren't at a place where they need to throw money at a spot left-hander.

Peter Munro — Throws R — Age 25

YEAR	TEAM	LGE	IP	H	ER	HR	BB	K	ERA	W	L	H/9	HR/9	BB/9	K/9	KWH	PERA
1997	Trenton	Eas	107.7	133	86	11	51	87	7.19	3	9	11.12	0.92	4.26	7.27	0.83	5.93
1998	Pawtuckt	Int	105.0	116	48	9	37	67	4.11	7	5	9.94	0.77	3.17	5.74	0.78	4.63
1998	Syracuse	Int	42.0	66	46	7	24	37	9.86	1	4	14.14	1.50	5.14	7.93	0.65	9.00
1999	Syracuse	Int	68.0	75	30	6	35	60	3.97	4	4	9.93	0.79	4.63	7.94	1.02	5.29
1999	Toronto	AL	56.0	67	33	5	23	39	5.30	3	3	10.77	0.80	3.70	6.27	0.74	5.46

Munro has the repertoire of a starter, with a good fastball that can break 90, an effective change-up and an improving breaking ball. The Jays seem to want him to be a reliever, which isn't the best use of his talents. With Hentgen gone, Munro has a line on his job. Postseason surgery to clear out some bone chips in his elbow won't hinder him in the spring.

Paul Quantrill — Throws R — Age 31

YEAR	TEAM	LGE	IP	H	ER	HR	BB	K	ERA	W	L	H/9	HR/9	BB/9	K/9	KWH	PERA
1997	Toronto	AL	88.3	100	23	5	17	56	2.34	8	2	10.19	0.51	1.73	5.71	1.38	3.97
1998	Toronto	AL	81.0	85	24	5	23	60	2.67	7	2	9.44	0.56	2.56	6.67	1.38	3.89
1999	Toronto	AL	49.3	50	16	4	17	29	2.92	4	1	9.12	0.73	3.10	5.29	0.74	4.20

After an offseason snowmobile accident sparked speculation that his career was over, Quantrill returned in May and had the same year he'd had the previous two, just 40% shorter. Since becoming a full-time reliever in 1997, his ERA has been much better than his peripherals; in 1997 and 1998, that was due to a phenomenal performance with runners on base. Last year, it was just random: he was hit harder with runners on.

John Sneed — Throws R — Age 24

YEAR	TEAM	LGE	IP	H	ER	HR	BB	K	ERA	W	L	H/9	HR/9	BB/9	K/9	KWH	PERA
1997	Med Hat	Pio	64.7	54	23	5	28	47	3.20	5	2	7.52	0.70	3.90	6.54	1.09	3.48
1998	Hagerstn	SAL	148.7	168	83	10	82	133	5.02	8	9	10.17	0.61	4.96	8.05	0.96	5.33
1999	Dunedin	Fla	114.3	139	72	13	49	108	5.67	5	8	10.94	1.02	3.86	8.50	1.28	5.83
1999	Knoxvill	Sou	27.0	37	18	2	23	23	6.00	1	2	12.33	0.67	7.67	7.67	0.46	8.00

The Jays' best pitching prospect is a big right-hander out of Texas A&M. Sneed throws hard, mixes in a slider and change-up and has been handled well by the Jays so far. Sneed is a year away, one of the better early-line candidates for 2001 Rookie of the Year.

Paul Spoljaric   Throws L   Age 29

YEAR	TEAM	LGE	IP	H	ER	HR	BB	K	ERA	W	L	H/9	HR/9	BB/9	K/9	KWH	PERA
1997	Toronto	AL	48.0	36	16	3	21	43	3.00	3	2	6.75	0.56	3.94	8.06	1.83	3.00
1997	Seattle	AL	23.3	22	11	1	16	27	4.24	2	1	8.49	0.39	6.17	10.41	1.55	4.63
1998	Seattle	AL	85.0	79	59	13	58	90	6.25	3	6	8.36	1.38	6.14	9.53	1.32	5.61
1999	Philadel	NL	11.7	23	22	1	6	10	16.97	0	1	17.74	0.77	4.63	7.71	0.54	10.03
1999	Toronto	AL	62.7	59	36	8	31	65	5.17	3	4	8.47	1.15	4.45	9.34	1.73	4.74

In his 12 career starts, he has an ERA of 11.07. The rest of the time? 4.31. So after four excellent months in the Toronto bullpen, Jim Fregosi couldn't help himself and gave Spoljaric two starts down the stretch, in which he was bludgeoned. Spoljaric can be one of the best left-handed relievers in the league, and not just in the spot role: he gets righties out and can handle 90 innings. He's been traded to St. Louis, so he may end up pigeonholed in the specialist role by LaRussa.

David Wells   Throws L   Age 37

YEAR	TEAM	LGE	IP	H	ER	HR	BB	K	ERA	W	L	H/9	HR/9	BB/9	K/9	KWH	PERA
1997	NY Yanks	AL	218.7	230	99	23	45	157	4.07	13	11	9.47	0.95	1.85	6.46	1.78	4.07
1998	NY Yanks	AL	211.7	199	84	27	30	164	3.57	15	9	8.46	1.15	1.28	6.97	3.37	3.49
1999	Toronto	AL	233.7	235	115	28	60	174	4.43	13	13	9.05	1.08	2.31	6.70	1.60	4.16

Wells declined from his career-year 1998 back to his normal level of performance. He's a tough call: his age and weight would seem to make him a risk, but his pitch counts are reasonable thanks to his control. His strikeout rates have been constant and he doesn't miss starts. I expect one more year at around his 1997 level of performance with about 50 fewer innings, then a sharp decline that's going to look very bad.

Support-Neutral Records — TORONTO BLUE JAYS — Park Effect: +4.5%

PITCHER	GS	IP	R	SNW	SNL	SNPCT	W	L	RA	APW	SNVA	SNWAR
Chris Carpenter	24	150.0	81	8.9	8.2	.522	9	8	4.86	0.74	0.38	1.65
Kelvim Escobar	30	168.0	116	9.0	11.6	.438	14	11	6.21	-1.49	-1.28	0.27
Roy Halladay	18	104.3	54	7.4	5.4	.577	5	6	4.66	0.73	1.06	1.95
Joey Hamilton	18	94.7	69	5.7	7.0	.451	7	8	6.56	-1.17	-0.66	0.33
Pat Hentgen	34	199.0	115	11.4	11.8	.492	11	12	5.20	0.29	-0.18	1.56
Peter Munro	2	8.0	13	0.1	1.3	.075	0	1	14.63	-0.76	-0.57	-0.49
Paul Spoljaric	2	10.0	15	0.1	1.5	.053	0	2	13.50	-0.83	-0.69	-0.58
David Wells	34	231.7	132	13.9	12.1	.534	17	10	5.13	0.51	0.76	2.83
TOTALS	162	965.7	595	56.6	58.9	.490	63	58	5.55	-1.96	-1.19	7.51

In two years, the Blue Jays have gone from having one of the elite starting rotations in baseball to being below average. Last year alone their starters dropped by more than five wins, according to Support-Neutral Value Added (SNVA). All of that drop can be accounted for by the replacement of Roger Clemens's 1998 with David Wells's 1999, and the replacement of Woody Williams's 1998 with Joey Hamilton's 1999. Not that the Clemens/Wells trade played a part in the drop. Confounding the expectations of most people, Wells pitched better than Clemens in 1999 by about half a win, according to SNVA.... Going into the 1999 season, Roy Halladay was touted as one of the leading candidates for the AL Rookie of the Year award. He pitched about as well as anyone could have expected, but his season went largely unnoticed because of two things: he was jerked in and out of the Blue Jays' starting rotation for no apparent reason, and an unusually strong crop of rookie starters in the AL—Freddy Garcia, Tim Hudson and John Halama—overshadowed his fine season.

Pitcher Abuse Points

PITCHER	AGE	GS	PAP	PAP/S	WKLD	MAX	1-90	91-100	101-110	111-120	121-130	131-140	141+
Chris Carpenter	24	24	268	11.2	26.1	130	5	3	8	6	2	0	0
Kelvim Escobar	23	30	246	8.2	20.5	132	12	4	6	7	0	1	0
Roy Halladay	22	18	107	5.9	15.9	115	3	6	5	4	0	0	0
Joey Hamilton	28	18	83	4.6	7.7	118	9	3	3	3	0	0	0
Pat Hentgen	30	34	251	7.4	9.8	123	14	5	7	7	1	0	0
Peter Munro	24	2	0	0.0	0.0	94	1	1	0	0	0	0	0
Paul Spoljaric	28	2	28	14.0	23.3	119	1	0	0	1	0	0	0
David Wells	36	34	344	10.1	10.1	129	5	7	11	8	3	0	0
TORONTO		162	1327	8.2	14.7	132	50	29	40	36	6	1	0
Ranking (AL)				8	6								

The Blue Jays' inability to make the playoffs last year, when they had an enormous talent advantage over the Red Sox, was somehow missed by the national media as a major story. A big part of their collapse was due to the pitching, and while Jim Fregosi deserves to be fried for his part in the collapse of the post-1993 Phillies rotation, he is largely faultless here. The blame lies squarely on the shoulders of Tim Johnson, who certainly ran his rotation as if it were a platoon on the Ho Chi Minh Trail. Chris Carpenter (37.2 Workload in 1998) had a 6.95 ERA from August on and was shut down in September, while Kelvim Escobar, who amassed more PAPs (274) in 10 starts in 1998 than he did all last season, was a disappointment. Fregosi certainly could have treated the pair more kindly, but he had already inherited damaged goods.... Fregosi did a fairly good job with the enigmatic Roy Halladay and did his best to counteract the years of damage done to Pat Hentgen's right arm. The only starter on the staff who came into the season healthy was David Wells, and he was the only starter on the Blue Jays who finished the season strong.

Arizona Diamondbacks

The Diamondbacks' 1999 season was remarkable. Whatever the near future holds for the D'backs, they deserved every bit of the satisfaction that comes from winning 100 games, no matter how old or young the franchise. Of course, a key to understanding Arizona lies in that issue of old versus young: it is a young franchise, but an old team.

The historic nature of a second-year franchise's winning its division forces us to ask how it was done, and the importance of money in creating success seems to offer an easy explanation. While it has always been better to be smart than to be rich when it came to baseball, it is more clear than ever that the best way to win is to be both smart *and* rich. Arizona won a divisional title in their second season, and their rich owner spent a lot of money. For many, this is enough evidence to prove that the Diamondbacks were also smart. But a closer look suggests they had a funny way of showing their intelligence.

Take Tony Womack. (Please.) Womack is the Omar Moreno of his day. Moreno was the center fielder on the 1979 "We Are Family" Pirates. He hit .282/.334/.381 with 77 stolen bases and 110 runs scored, and played good defense. You can use a player like Moreno at his peak, as long as you appreciate that the .334 OBP is more indicative of his contributions than the 110 runs scored.

Last year, Tony Womack hit .277/.332/.370 with 72 steals and 111 runs scored—a good season for Omar Moreno. Of course, Womack's defense wasn't as good; he looked like a converted infielder playing right field. And Womack's offense compared to other NL right fielders wasn't as impressive as Moreno's compared to center fielders. Finally, Womack plays in an extreme offensive era, so his hitting isn't as impressive relative to his league as was Moreno's. That's Tony Womack: not as impressive as Omar Moreno. Yet the Diamondbacks made him their regular right fielder.

Womack wasn't the only example of Arizona's curious talent evaluation. You can understand, somewhat, the Matt Mantei acquisition, given the state of their bullpen at the

time. But how to explain Dan Plesac? The team wanted another left-hander in the bullpen, so they sent John Frascatore to Toronto for the 37-year-old Plesac. That's not a bad deal, right? Oh . . . they also included Tony Batista in the deal. Batista, a 25-year-old shortstop with power and a good glove, slugged .565 for the Jays, with 26 home runs in fewer than 100 games. Batista's replacements, mostly Andy Fox, Hanley Frias and Womack, didn't slug .565 or hit 26 homers.

But a hundred wins is a hundred wins, and certainly Arizona did a lot of things right, beginning with Randy Johnson. The team's starting pitching was excellent, and the bullpen post-Mantei was effective. The most amazing aspect of the D'backs' season, though, was the performance of the offense. You can expect Randy Johnson to pitch well, but no one could have predicted that this lineup would outscore every other team in the National League. The miracle was accomplished thanks to four veterans: Jay Bell, Matt Williams, Luis Gonzalez and Steve Finley. It is important to examine what these four players did in 1999, because it speaks volumes about the upcoming season for Arizona, and for any team that might try to emulate the Diamondbacks' success.

Jay Bell's 38 homers were 17 more than he had ever hit in a season. His OBP was his highest since 1993. His slugging percentage was 150 points higher than his career average. Matt Williams hit his most home runs since 1994, and after watching his slugging percentage drop from .510 to .439 in two years, he raised it back to .536. Luis Gonzalez set personal highs in runs, hits, doubles, home runs, OBP, slugging percentage and batting average. Steve Finley also set a personal high in home runs while lifting his slugging percentage by 124 points over his 1998 performance. If these four players had performed closer to expectations, the Diamondbacks would not have won 100 games.

It's important to note that all of these players had had fine seasons in the past; it isn't as if four non-entities somehow turned themselves into Murderers Row. But their past

---

Diamondbacks Prospectus

1999 record: 100-62; First place, NL West; Lost to Mets in Division Series, 3-1

Pythagorean W/L: 103-59

Runs scored: 908 (1st in NL)

Runs allowed: 676 (3rd in NL)

Team EQA: .273 (3rd in NL)

1999 team age: 30.4 (2nd-oldest in NL)

1999 park: Bank One Ballpark; slight pitchers' park, decreased run scoring by 6%.

1999: Surprising seasons by thirtysomething hitters led to a division title.

2000: It won't last; look for Arizona to slip by at least 12 games.

successes may have blinded people to the stunning unpredictability of what they did in 1999. If you heard that Bell, Williams, Gonzalez and Finley had fine years, you wouldn't be surprised, because they are fine players. But the unpredictable nature of their seasons is central to appreciating just how unusual 1999 was for Arizona. Four hitters at an age (Gonzalez, 31; Bell and Williams, 33; Finley 34) when they should have been in decline, and all having declined in the past year, all raised their performance significantly and led their team to a division title.

It behooves the Arizona front office, and the front office of any team thinking the Arizona plan warrants emulation, to keep this particular aspect of 1999 in mind. Despite the 100 wins, the division title and the acclaim, it remains a bad idea to build your offense around players in their 30s. The Diamondbacks might think 1999 proves the wisdom of signing aging hitters, but they would be wrong. Performance analysis tells us that the probability of a team's leading the league in runs scored with a lineup full of aging hitters is not very high. The current version of the Diamondbacks is reminiscent of the Philadelphia Phillies of the early 1980s, and the comparison doesn't leave much room for optimism.

The Phillies won their first-ever World Series in 1980. They had a Hall-of-Famer, Steve Carlton, anchoring a solid rotation. And they had one of the oldest lineups in the league: Pete Rose, at first base, was 39; the shortstop, Larry Bowa, was 34; the catcher, Bob Boone, was 32; two of the regular outfielders were in their 30s and Mike Schmidt, at third base, was 30. They won the division by one game on the next-to-last day of the season, barely squeaked by Houston in one of the most memorable playoff series of all times, and finally won the World Series in six games over Kansas City.

By 1983, the Phillies had gotten older. Rose and Schmidt and Garry Maddox were still around; Rose was now 42. The team's new second baseman was Joe Morgan, a sprightly 39. Nonetheless, they won the NL pennant before losing to the Orioles in five games in the Series.

The next year, the Phillies fell to fourth place, and they didn't make the postseason again until 1993.

The 1980-83 Phillies are one of the better "old" teams of recent times; they represent the best the D'backs can hope for with their old-hitters strategy. It must be noted that as good as the Arizona players are, Jay Bell isn't Joe Morgan, and Matt Williams isn't Mike Schmidt. No one is Pete Rose, for better or worse.

The Arizona Diamondbacks are ripe for a fall if they misinterpret those 100 wins and continue to pursue aging hitters as answers to offensive problems. In fact, despite their magnificent 1999 season, the team needs to start rebuilding immediately. They cannot afford to wait until the hitters decline; they need to act as if their hitters are already declining.

How does Arizona look for the near future? You want to say the team is in good hands, but then you realize this is a front office that thought Batista and Frascatore for Plesac was a good idea, a front office that thought Womack would be a good regular right fielder, and yes, a front office that thought it was a good idea to build an offense around guys in their 30s. Sure, they went out and got Randy Johnson, but that took money, not smarts. A lot needs to be done, but the first step is simply to *recognize* that a lot needs to be done, to avoid the complacency that might set in after a 100-win season.

The starting rotation seems like a strength, but once you get past Johnson and Omar Daal, what you really have are question marks. The team is counting on Brian Anderson's finally having a big year, hoping his 2.56 ERA after the All-Star break is indicative of an emergence. But Anderson's strikeout rate is unimpressive: even during his late-season spurt, he struck out only 36 batters in 70 innings. It is not clear if he's capable of becoming a solid #3 starter. It would be nice to have Brad Penny coming out of the minors, but of course he was traded, along with Vladimir Nunez, for Mantei.

It's also unclear whether or not the D'Backs know they have other problems. Tony Womack is not good enough to be a regular right fielder and is being moved to shortstop, having signed a four-year, $17 million deal. If Gonzalez and Finley decline, as we would expect, this could be a very ugly outfield in 2000. Bell and Williams are now 34 years old. If Erubiel Durazo declines and Travis Lee continues to scuffle as he learns right field, Arizona could go from scoring the most runs in the league to the fewest. If that happens, even Randy Johnson won't be able to keep the team over .500.

If the team had a new generation of regulars waiting in the farm system, they could have smooth sailing. But that doesn't appear to be the case. Outside of Durazo, the team's best prospect might be pitcher John Patterson, who looks good but who struggled in his first exposure to Triple-A. Jack Cust looks like a wonderful hitter, but he's a first baseman, the one position on the diamond where the D'backs have youth and depth. Cust switched to left field this season with uncertain results; his ability to adapt to the position is crucial to the D'backs' future. The team's best hitting prospects are a few years away from the majors. It would appear that Arizona fans should treasure the 1999 season, because another like it might be a long time coming.

HITTERS (Averages: BA: .270 / OBP: .340 / SLG: .430 / EQA: .260)

Rod Barajas   C   Bats R   Age 24

YEAR	TEAM	LGE	AB	H	DB	TP	HR	BB/SO	R	RBI	SB	CS	OUT	BA	OBP	SLG	EQA	EQR	DEFENSE
1997	High Des	Cal	197	45	5	0	7	4/40	17	23	0	1	153	.228	.246	.360	.195	13	
1998	High Des	Cal	436	105	14	0	19	17/85	45	55	0	0	331	.241	.277	.404	.225	40	96-C 99
1999	El Paso	Tex	500	130	29	1	11	17/82	55	67	1	0	370	.260	.292	.388	.227	46	111-C 99
2000	Arizona	NL	394	105	16	0	16	26/69	45	60	0	0	289	.266	.312	.429	.245	43	

Barajas was named the best defensive catcher in the Texas League in 1999 by *Baseball America*. He has some pop, which is always useful behind the plate. He could stick around for a few years as a backup, but he's just too impatient a hitter to have much impact in the major leagues.

Jay Bell   2B   Bats L   Age 34

YEAR	TEAM	LGE	AB	H	DB	TP	HR	BB/SO	R	RBI	SB	CS	OUT	BA	OBP	SLG	EQA	EQR	DEFENSE
1997	KansasCy	AL	568	164	30	3	20	67/97	85	87	10	6	410	.289	.368	.458	.278	83	146-SS 105
1998	Arizona	NL	555	143	29	5	22	80/126	80	69	3	6	418	.258	.359	.447	.270	79	134-SS 99
1999	Arizona	NL	592	171	34	6	37	74/131	126	106	6	4	425	.289	.372	.554	.300	105	143-2B 85
2000	Arizona	NL	434	118	21	2	21	68/95	74	83	3	3	319	.272	.371	.475	.281	67	

Charles Atlas-cized. Bell used to be a skinny wimp, one who led the league in sacrifice bunts for two years straight—when he wasn't getting sand kicked in his face by the bullies on the beach. Last year, he topped the league in home runs by a middle infielder. Bell has had one of those bizarre developmental curves that keep analysts on their toes. He should be more than passable in 2000, though he'll have to get out of Jackie Rexrode's way sooner or later.

Jeffrey Brooks   3B   Bats R   Age 20

YEAR	TEAM	LGE	AB	H	DB	TP	HR	BB/SO	R	RBI	SB	CS	OUT	BA	OBP	SLG	EQA	EQR	DEFENSE
1998	Lethbrid	Pio	241	50	8	1	1	12/61	19	22	0	0	191	.207	.252	.261	.163	10	66-3B 85
1999	Missoula	Pio	290	75	15	2	8	8/89	26	33	1	1	216	.259	.284	.407	.228	27	69-3B 82
2000	Arizona	NL	170	42	8	1	4	7/63	15	19	0	0	128	.247	.277	.376	.214	14	

Brooks led Missoula with a .349 average while hitting 18 doubles and 11 home runs. He is a reasonable hitting prospect, but his defense is terrible, and it isn't just the 38 errors: his range is almost nonexistent and his arm is scattershot. He probably doesn't have the bat to move to the outfield in this organization, and reportedly worked hard this offseason on making his D a bit more tenacious.

J.D. Closser   C   Bats B   Age 20

YEAR	TEAM	LGE	AB	H	DB	TP	HR	BB/SO	R	RBI	SB	CS	OUT	BA	OBP	SLG	EQA	EQR	DEFENSE
1999	Missoula	Pio	276	65	10	0	8	49/66	39	30	2	1	212	.236	.353	.359	.250	33	64-C 97
1999	Sth Bend	Mid	179	39	4	0	4	27/39	23	22	0	0	140	.218	.322	.307	.221	16	30-C 88
2000	Arizona	NL	224	53	7	0	8	49/81	39	34	1	0	171	.237	.374	.375	.263	30	

Closser cemented his standing as one of the most exciting young catching prospects in baseball with an awesome year split between Missoula and South Bend. His .462 on-base percentage at Missoula was due in large part to a great batting eye, especially great for a player this young. Damian Miller and Kelly Stinnett need to watch their backs, because Closser could be a habitual All-Star in a few years.

Greg Colbrunn   1B   Bats R   Age 30

YEAR	TEAM	LGE	AB	H	DB	TP	HR	BB/SO	R	RBI	SB	CS	OUT	BA	OBP	SLG	EQA	EQR	DEFENSE
1997	Minnesot	AL	217	62	11	0	6	6/37	23	26	1	2	157	.286	.309	.419	.240	22	51-1B 101
1998	Colorado	NL	120	34	7	2	2	7/22	11	12	3	3	89	.283	.328	.425	.249	14	22-1B 114
1999	Arizona	NL	136	44	5	3	5	10/23	19	23	1	1	93	.324	.389	.515	.298	23	27-1B 106
2000	Arizona	NL	131	41	7	1	5	10/23	20	25	1	1	91	.313	.362	.496	.282	19	

Enjoyed a solid season as the Snakes' second bat off the bench. Colbrunn has always swung enough to make Hugh Hefner blush, but his walk rate this year was about league average. He's not really qualified to play anywhere but first base, despite his willingness to be an emergency catcher and third baseman. With Durazo and Lee likely to be on the Opening Day 2000 roster, he may have to look elsewhere for continued employment.

Jason Conti CF Bats L Age 25

YEAR	TEAM	LGE	AB	H	DB	TP	HR	BB/SO	R	RBI	SB	CS	OUT	BA	OBP	SLG	EQA	EQR	DEFENSE
1997	Sth Bend	Mid	467	124	23	7	3	32/107	55	33	12	8	351	.266	.324	.364	.235	47	117-OF 105
1998	Tulsa	Tex	530	142	26	7	12	48/110	88	49	10	7	395	.268	.336	.411	.253	63	116-OF 95
1999	Tucson	PCL	504	119	18	6	6	46/91	70	40	14	5	390	.236	.305	.331	.221	45	126-OF 104
2000	Arizona	NL	442	113	18	4	11	48/88	61	58	11	7	336	.256	.329	.389	.242	49	

Conti was named the system's 1998 player of the year while helping Tulsa to the Texas League title. He regressed in almost every facet of the game in 1999. Conti has a broad skill set, but he doesn't do anything notably except play defense. He'd be a better choice than someone like Darren Lewis for a major-league center-field job right now.

Darryl Conyer CF Bats L Age 20

YEAR	TEAM	LGE	AB	H	DB	TP	HR	BB/SO	R	RBI	SB	CS	OUT	BA	OBP	SLG	EQA	EQR	DEFENSE
1999	Missoula	Pio	192	39	8	1	2	30/65	27	13	5	3	156	.203	.318	.286	.215	17	45-OF 90
2000	Arizona	NL	89	18	1	0	2	18/70	13	8	2	1	72	.202	.336	.281	.222	8	

Arizona drafted Conyer in the third round in 1998, then signed him away from a football scholarship at the University of Arizona. As you might expect, Conyer covers a ton of ground in center field and is one of the fastest men in baseball. Better still, unlike lots of tools players, he's got a good idea of the strike zone.

Jack Cust LF/1B Bats L Age 21

YEAR	TEAM	LGE	AB	H	DB	TP	HR	BB/SO	R	RBI	SB	CS	OUT	BA	OBP	SLG	EQA	EQR	DEFENSE
1998	Lethbrid	Pio	216	49	13	1	6	57/83	35	25	4	3	170	.227	.392	.380	.273	33	59-OF 85
1999	High Des	Cal	435	114	28	2	24	75/141	71	70	1	2	323	.262	.372	.501	.289	72	108-OF 78
2000	Arizona	NL	250	68	15	1	14	56/93	53	54	1	1	183	.272	.405	.508	.304	47	

He had a brilliant season at High Desert, threatening for the Triple Crown. Cust was the organization's minor-league player of the year, and it isn't hard to see why: he couples great power with great patience and is one of the most dangerous hitting prospects in baseball. Just like Brooks, though, he's defensively challenged. With the logjam at first base in Arizona, he needs to get used to the idea of playing left field every day.

David Dellucci OF Bats L Age 26

YEAR	TEAM	LGE	AB	H	DB	TP	HR	BB/SO	R	RBI	SB	CS	OUT	BA	OBP	SLG	EQA	EQR	DEFENSE
1997	Bowie	Eas	391	115	29	3	15	45/74	55	43	7	2	278	.294	.372	.499	.290	63	89-OF 97
1998	Arizona	NL	420	111	21	13	5	32/100	44	52	3	6	315	.264	.321	.412	.244	46	105-OF 98
1999	Arizona	NL	109	43	6	1	1	10/24	25	14	2	0	66	.394	.461	.495	.331	21	
2000	Arizona	NL	226	68	15	3	5	27/50	41	38	4	2	160	.301	.375	.460	.281	33	

Dellucci was having a nice season as a fill-in when he was sidelined by a degenerative bone condition, called Kienbock's disease, in his left wrist. Nobody has ever had this kind of disorder and returned to play baseball. It would be a shame if Dellucci's career came to an end so soon, as he was coming into his own as a hitter and would have had a good chance to take part of the right-field job.

Edwin Diaz 2B Bats R Age 25

YEAR	TEAM	LGE	AB	H	DB	TP	HR	BB/SO	R	RBI	SB	CS	OUT	BA	OBP	SLG	EQA	EQR	DEFENSE	
1997	Tulsa	Tex	437	105	23	1	14	25/115	49	35	4	5	337	.240	.291	.394	.227	41	105-2B 102	
1998	Tucson	PCL	500	115	25	9	2	22/105	47	38	7	4	389	.230	.267	.328	.198	34	107-2B 103	
1999	Tucson	PCL	401	102	18	1	8	13/78	51	36	4	4	303	.254	.287	.364	.216	33	56-2B 104	43-SS 93
2000	Texas	AL	469	121	23	3	9	31/99	54	57	5	4	352	.258	.304	.377	.224	42		

Again, he didn't hit. At his peak, Diaz will be a reliable defensive second baseman who does nothing right with a bat in his hands, so he might as well be there already. A team with a huge offense and a hole at second base could deal with a guy like this, but the Diamondbacks really don't need someone with Diaz's skill set.

Erubiel Durazo 1B Bats L Age 26

YEAR	TEAM	LGE	AB	H	DB	TP	HR	BB/SO	R	RBI	SB	CS	OUT	BA	OBP	SLG	EQA	EQR	DEFENSE
1999	El Paso	Tex	220	63	14	1	8	31/46	33	32	1	0	157	.286	.378	.468	.286	34	61-1B 96
1999	Tucson	PCL	112	35	3	0	7	10/19	17	18	1	0	77	.313	.373	.527	.297	18	27-1B 98
1999	Arizona	NL	155	51	3	2	11	24/43	29	28	1	1	105	.329	.423	.587	.327	32	39-1B 99
2000	Arizona	NL	258	88	10	1	26	50/111	61	84	1	0	170	.341	.448	.690	.358	65	

Every once in a while, you find a Mexican League All-Star who amounts to something north of the border. Durazo is a terror with the bat, and he's got a stranglehold on first base for the Snakes for about as long as he wants it. He's pushed prodigal son Travis Lee to either right field or another organization. Durazo is a devastating and patient hitter and a nice story as well. He's for real.

Steve Finley CF Bats L Age 35

YEAR	TEAM	LGE	AB	H	DB	TP	HR	BB/SO	R	RBI	SB	CS	OUT	BA	OBP	SLG	EQA	EQR	DEFENSE
1997	San Dieg	NL	570	156	28	5	31	42/91	104	97	13	3	417	.274	.327	.504	.273	82	141-OF 105
1998	San Dieg	NL	635	173	48	7	16	44/100	102	74	13	4	466	.272	.323	.446	.258	78	147-OF 112
1999	Arizona	NL	594	158	34	10	33	55/93	96	98	7	4	440	.266	.332	.524	.277	89	148-CF 101
2000	Arizona	NL	596	152	31	6	27	67/95	88	101	7	3	447	.255	.330	.463	.262	79	

He got his stroke back in a big way. Finley is notoriously streaky, and when he's on he can hit anything out of the park. The defense is still good. He was another seemingly past-prime signing who turned in a good year for the 1999 Diamondbacks.

Andy Fox UT Bats L Age 29

YEAR	TEAM	LGE	AB	H	DB	TP	HR	BB/SO	R	RBI	SB	CS	OUT	BA	OBP	SLG	EQA	EQR	DEFENSE	
1997	Columbus	Int	324	79	10	4	4	43/68	50	26	18	7	252	.244	.334	.336	.238	35	48-3B 94	22-2B 97
1998	Arizona	NL	507	143	21	6	10	42/94	68	45	15	8	372	.282	.360	.406	.263	66	50-2B 88	22-3B 107
1999	Arizona	NL	276	71	11	2	6	29/60	32	31	4	1	206	.257	.349	.377	.253	33	69-SS 99	
2000	Arizona	NL	344	92	11	3	9	41/71	52	48	11	5	257	.267	.345	.395	.253	41		

Still a valuable ballplayer, Fox had a good season overall but didn't get the job done defensively at shortstop after the Diamondbacks ran Batista out of town. He seems like he has a lot of trouble going to his right, not a task with which you want your shortstop to struggle. After Hanley Frias took over the everyday job, Fox resumed his utility-player role and probably will do more of the same in 2000.

Hanley Frias SS Bats R Age 26

YEAR	TEAM	LGE	AB	H	DB	TP	HR	BB/SO	R	RBI	SB	CS	OUT	BA	OBP	SLG	EQA	EQR	DEFENSE
1997	Oklahoma	AA	486	120	16	4	4	49/74	56	42	28	11	377	.247	.317	.321	.226	46	129-SS 96
1998	Tucson	PCL	247	60	7	3	1	20/42	23	16	11	5	192	.243	.300	.308	.211	20	55-SS 96
1999	Arizona	NL	151	41	3	2	1	27/18	25	15	3	3	113	.272	.382	.338	.255	19	38-SS 98
2000	Arizona	NL	278	74	10	2	2	36/43	45	29	13	5	209	.266	.350	.338	.243	30	

Frias lucked into a starting spot after the front office freaked about a left-handed specialist in the pen. He's a reliable bottom-of-the-league shortstop who isn't making much and isn't declining yet, but don't expect him to do in 2000 what he did in 1999 with the bat; that kind of jump in walk rate screams "small sample size." The move of Womack makes Frias the D'backs' fifth infielder in 2000.

Bernard Gilkey OF Bats R Age 33

YEAR	TEAM	LGE	AB	H	DB	TP	HR	BB/SO	R	RBI	SB	CS	OUT	BA	OBP	SLG	EQA	EQR	DEFENSE
1997	NY Mets	NL	525	131	30	1	20	69/110	84	79	5	11	405	.250	.343	.425	.256	67	125-OF 99
1998	NY Mets	NL	268	64	12	0	6	32/64	35	31	6	1	205	.239	.330	.351	.239	29	69-OF 98
1998	Arizona	NL	102	26	0	0	1	11/14	8	5	4	2	78	.255	.334	.284	.221	9	27-OF 93
1999	Arizona	NL	205	60	16	1	8	26/42	27	37	2	2	147	.293	.378	.498	.290	33	31-RF 108
2000	Arizona	NL	222	55	8	0	9	32/46	32	34	3	2	169	.248	.343	.405	.253	27	

He was less popular than former governor Evan Mecham after deep-sixing a trade to the Pirates that would have landed Womack and Al Martin, then went on to his first solid season since his monster 1996 in New York. He gets paid far too much for a bench player, but he's a legitimate threat as a pinch-hitter and spot starter for the Snakes. With Womack moving back to the infield, Gilkey could end up platooning in right field, a role in which he'd be valuable.

Luis Gonzalez   LF   Bats L   Age 32

YEAR	TEAM	LGE	AB	H	DB	TP	HR	BB/SO	R	RBI	SB	CS	OUT	BA	OBP	SLG	EQA	EQR	DEFENSE
1997	Houston	NL	560	150	34	2	11	70/66	80	71	8	7	417	.268	.354	.395	.256	69	146-OF 97
1998	Detroit	AL	545	145	37	5	22	54/61	79	67	10	7	407	.266	.341	.473	.269	77	129-OF 91
1999	Arizona	NL	617	207	47	4	25	58/62	107	105	8	5	415	.335	.400	.546	.310	111	145-LF 94
2000	Arizona	NL	590	162	36	2	17	68/73	90	91	6	4	432	.275	.350	.429	.262	76	

Gonzalez is a prototypical "unspectacular" player who had an All-Star season after signing with the Diamondbacks. Maybe it's something in the water? Gonzalez is visibly slowing down in left field and on the basepaths, which makes his big season all the more unpredictable. I wouldn't want to rely on him to hit .320 with power again.

Lenny Harris   UT   Bats L   Age 35

YEAR	TEAM	LGE	AB	H	DB	TP	HR	BB/SO	R	RBI	SB	CS	OUT	BA	OBP	SLG	EQA	EQR	DEFENSE	
1997	Cincnnti	NL	239	64	14	1	3	18/18	31	27	3	3	178	.268	.324	.372	.236	24	25-OF 89	13-2B 98
1998	Cincnnti	NL	123	37	8	0	0	8/9	12	10	1	3	89	.301	.349	.366	.240	13		
1998	NY Mets	NL	170	41	7	0	7	9/12	19	18	5	2	131	.241	.284	.406	.231	17	36-OF 107	
1999	Colorado	NL	154	40	11	0	0	4/6	13	11	1	1	115	.260	.278	.331	.201	10		
1999	Arizona	NL	29	11	1	0	1	0/1	2	7	1	0	18	.379	.379	.517	.302	5		
2000	Arizona	NL	152	38	5	0	3	10/9	15	16	3	2	116	.250	.296	.342	.213	12		

For some reason, Harris just won't go away. He's a super-sub in that he can almost play any position except catcher. It's a mystery why teams don't realize that there are lots of guys in the minors like that: guys who hit well and take a lot less space on your payroll. He was a silly midseason acquisition, especially for a team that had Andy Fox on its roster already.

Danny Klassen   SS/2B   Bats R   Age 24

YEAR	TEAM	LGE	AB	H	DB	TP	HR	BB/SO	R	RBI	SB	CS	OUT	BA	OBP	SLG	EQA	EQR	DEFENSE	
1997	El Paso	Tex	499	133	23	3	12	37/117	75	55	9	5	371	.267	.327	.397	.246	56	130-SS 86	
1998	Tucson	PCL	275	70	21	1	8	15/54	35	36	4	1	206	.255	.304	.425	.244	30	51-SS 95	18-2B 123
1998	Arizona	NL	109	22	2	1	3	9/32	12	8	1	1	88	.202	.270	.321	.197	8	27-2B 93	
1999	Tucson	PCL	238	54	14	2	4	17/50	27	24	3	2	186	.227	.281	.353	.212	19	58-SS 108	
2000	Arizona	NL	286	74	18	1	6	24/64	38	35	6	2	214	.259	.316	.392	.239	30		

A former hot property after his El Paso campaign in 1997, Klassen was soundly thrashed by Tony Batista last year. His defense and impatience at the plate keep him from being a real prospect. The ridiculous contract given to Womack, in addition to Jay Bell's deal, means Klassen's future is in another organization. The International Brotherhood of Electrical Workers comes to mind.

Travis Lee   1B   Bats L   Age 25

YEAR	TEAM	LGE	AB	H	DB	TP	HR	BB/SO	R	RBI	SB	CS	OUT	BA	OBP	SLG	EQA	EQR	DEFENSE
1997	High Des	Cal	221	63	11	1	13	36/36	42	41	2	0	158	.285	.390	.520	.303	40	54-1B 128
1997	Tucson	PCL	221	58	15	1	11	25/47	31	33	1	0	163	.262	.342	.489	.275	32	38-1B 106
1998	Arizona	NL	568	156	21	1	24	66/120	73	74	9	1	413	.275	.350	.442	.269	78	144-1B 101
1999	Arizona	NL	377	90	16	2	9	53/49	53	48	15	3	290	.239	.333	.363	.246	43	95-1B 102
2000	Arizona	NL	435	126	20	1	17	62/74	83	76	14	2	311	.290	.378	.457	.285	68	

Lee had an inexplicably bad season last year and ended up on the disabled list with torn ankle ligaments. He was left off the D'backs' postseason roster. With Durazo coming out of nowhere, Lee's future is uncertain. The organization plans to move him to right field, which will give them a dandy player once Lee figures out whatever is troubling him; he's always been too good defensively to be stuck at first base, anyway.

Damian Miller   C   Bats R   Age 30

YEAR	TEAM	LGE	AB	H	DB	TP	HR	BB/SO	R	RBI	SB	CS	OUT	BA	OBP	SLG	EQA	EQR	DEFENSE
1997	SaltLake	PCL	302	80	14	2	7	20/70	31	52	4	1	223	.265	.316	.394	.241	32	
1998	Arizona	NL	170	50	16	2	3	10/42	18	14	1	0	120	.294	.341	.465	.269	23	44-C 100
1999	Arizona	NL	298	81	16	0	12	15/77	33	46	0	0	217	.272	.312	.446	.251	34	79-C 103
2000	Arizona	NL	177	48	9	0	7	13/45	22	28	1	0	129	.271	.321	.441	.253	21	

Miller is a reliable backstop who won't win any awards. His stick isn't terrible, and other teams certainly sport catchers with less offensive potential. The Diamondbacks would be making a mistake giving Miller the first crack at the job in 2000, but he'll keep a roster spot warm until Barajas is finished with Tucson.

Corey Myers — SS — Bats R — Age 20

YEAR	TEAM	LGE	AB	H	DB	TP	HR	BB/SO	R	RBI	SB	CS	OUT	BA	OBP	SLG	EQA	EQR	DEFENSE
1999	Missoula	Pio	271	59	11	2	3	12/75	24	26	1	1	213	.218	.253	.306	.181	15	55-SS 99
2000	Arizona	NL	120	27	2	0	3	7/71	8	11	0	0	93	.225	.268	.317	.190	7	

He's a solid power-hitting prospect who had a reasonable campaign in Missoula. Myers considers himself a natural third baseman, and made 29 errors in 1999 at shortstop. With Jeff Brooks at third base, hitting ground balls to the left side was a good strategy against the Osprey. Myers is another hot prospect who has baseball in his blood: his father is Clint Myers, a former minor leaguer in the St. Louis chain.

Abraham Nunez — OF — Bats B — Age 20

YEAR	TEAM	LGE	AB	H	DB	TP	HR	BB/SO	R	RBI	SB	CS	OUT	BA	OBP	SLG	EQA	EQR	DEFENSE
1998	Sth Bend	Mid	379	86	13	1	10	56/84	36	40	5	6	299	.227	.329	.346	.233	39	109-OF 102
1999	High Des	Cal	474	103	22	3	18	67/119	66	61	17	6	377	.217	.316	.390	.243	55	129-OF 99
2000	Florida	NL	315	71	12	1	13	53/88	49	45	8	3	247	.225	.337	.394	.257	41	

Nunez may be the best of Diamondbacks' Latin American Coordinator Junior Noboa's prospect parade. He was rated the #2 prospect in the California League last year by *Baseball America*, ahead of teammate Jack Cust. Unlike Cust, he's good defensively. Just when you thought the Mantei trade couldn't get any worse, the Diamondbacks made Nunez the last player in the deal in December. He has a better opportunity for rapid advancement with the Fish.

Dante Powell — CF — Bats R — Age 26

YEAR	TEAM	LGE	AB	H	DB	TP	HR	BB/SO	R	RBI	SB	CS	OUT	BA	OBP	SLG	EQA	EQR	DEFENSE
1997	Phoenix	PCL	443	91	21	2	9	41/108	64	30	24	8	360	.205	.277	.323	.210	36	107-OF 109
1998	Fresno	PCL	446	90	14	2	12	61/142	62	42	29	7	363	.202	.312	.323	.230	46	133-OF 100
1999	Tucson	PCL	180	46	12	1	4	11/41	18	19	12	4	138	.256	.301	.400	.241	20	44-OF 99
2000	St Louis	NL	303	65	16	1	7	35/83	47	27	25	7	245	.215	.296	.343	.228	30	

Powell has been a prospect forever, and time is rapidly running out for him to have a career. He didn't do much for himself this year, and with many better players between him and playing time in the Arizona outfield, his future is less promising than a Martha Stewart IPO.

Jackie Rexrode — 2B — Bats L — Age 21

YEAR	TEAM	LGE	AB	H	DB	TP	HR	BB/SO	R	RBI	SB	CS	OUT	BA	OBP	SLG	EQA	EQR	DEFENSE
1997	Sth Bend	Mid	340	87	11	4	2	43/49	45	22	7	3	256	.256	.342	.329	.237	35	92-2B 89
1998	Sth Bend	Mid	184	49	8	2	0	39/32	24	8	9	2	137	.266	.396	.332	.269	26	49-2B 90
1998	High Des	Cal	206	57	6	2	1	36/43	32	16	8	1	150	.277	.384	.340	.264	27	42-2B 88
1999	Birmnghm	Sou	215	54	8	4	0	23/31	27	21	8	2	163	.251	.324	.326	.230	21	65-2B 94
1999	El Paso	Tex	142	37	7	1	1	23/17	21	7	3	1	106	.261	.364	.345	.252	17	37-2B 89
2000	Arizona	NL	458	128	23	5	2	72/72	87	55	16	3	333	.279	.377	.365	.264	60	

Remember the season Lance Blankenship had in 1992, when he walked about as often as he got a hit? Rexrode is a threat to do that every season. He flashes Luis Castillo-quality power, but he's never failed to produce a .400 OBP in the leadoff spot. If Arizona is willing to give him a chance in 2001, they won't be sorry. He's still learning on defense, although his pivot move is excellent.

Rob Ryan — OF — Bats L — Age 27

YEAR	TEAM	LGE	AB	H	DB	TP	HR	BB/SO	R	RBI	SB	CS	OUT	BA	OBP	SLG	EQA	EQR	DEFENSE
1997	Sth Bend	Mid	438	103	28	2	6	61/71	46	47	4	1	336	.235	.331	.349	.237	46	111-OF 92
1998	Tucson	PCL	384	95	14	1	11	50/67	47	44	5	2	291	.247	.345	.375	.250	45	112-OF 93
1999	Tucson	PCL	402	88	21	3	12	44/76	46	56	2	2	316	.219	.310	.376	.233	41	102-OF 91
2000	Arizona	NL	381	92	18	2	12	58/72	58	54	4	1	290	.241	.342	.394	.252	46	

(Rob Ryan *continued*)

Ryan's window of opportunity is closing rapidly; last year, we mentioned that he'd probably make a good platoon mate for Bernard Gilkey, but that's not going to happen now. He's got the bat a good fifth outfielder should have, without the defensive ability.

Jhensy Sandoval   OF   Bats R   Age 21

YEAR	TEAM	LGE	AB	H	DB	TP	HR	BB/SO	R	RBI	SB	CS	OUT	BA	OBP	SLG	EQA	EQR	DEFENSE
1997	Lethbrid	Pio	154	41	10	0	5	5/43	16	19	2	1	114	.266	.296	.429	.240	16	38-OF 100
1998	High Des	Cal	394	92	18	1	4	9/131	35	38	4	4	306	.234	.256	.315	.185	22	106-OF 96
1999	El Paso	Tex	125	24	5	1	1	5/46	8	19	1	0	101	.192	.228	.272	.155	5	33-OF 101
2000	*Arizona*	*NL*	*240*	*62*	*13*	*1*	*5*	*10/83*	*25*	*27*	*3*	*1*	*179*	*.258*	*.288*	*.383*	*.222*	*21*	

An injured hamstring ended Sandoval's season after an inauspicious start at El Paso. With Cust and Nunez breathing down his neck, Sandoval needs to start off strong next year or he's going to be a statistic. The chances of that happening certainly aren't any worse than Magic Johnson's chances of starring in an entertaining talk show.

Kelly Stinnett   C   Bats R   Age 30

YEAR	TEAM	LGE	AB	H	DB	TP	HR	BB/SO	R	RBI	SB	CS	OUT	BA	OBP	SLG	EQA	EQR	DEFENSE
1997	Tucson	PCL	203	51	13	2	6	32/52	33	27	1	1	153	.251	.366	.424	.270	29	
1998	Arizona	NL	277	73	15	1	12	34/72	36	35	0	1	205	.264	.358	.455	.272	40	81-C 104
1999	Arizona	NL	286	67	12	0	14	21/82	34	36	2	1	220	.234	.299	.423	.241	31	78-C 101
2000	*Arizona*	*NL*	*284*	*70*	*12*	*0*	*14*	*35/79*	*38*	*47*	*1*	*1*	*215*	*.246*	*.329*	*.437*	*.255*	*35*	

Stinnett has always been a favorite of ours, and we were pulling for him to take the catching job in Arizona and run with it. He had a disappointing season, largely sabotaged by injuries, and it doesn't look like he'll be able to shake Miller anytime soon. He's still got time for a couple of All-Star games if he hits the way he's capable of hitting.

Carlos Urquiola   2B   Bats L   Age 20

YEAR	TEAM	LGE	AB	H	DB	TP	HR	BB/SO	R	RBI	SB	CS	OUT	BA	OBP	SLG	EQA	EQR	DEFENSE	
1998	Sth Bend	Mid	170	49	10	3	0	7/15	22	13	4	3	124	.288	.319	.382	.236	17	37-2B 78	
1999	Sth Bend	Mid	388	125	11	2	1	12/34	47	27	9	7	270	.322	.348	.369	.244	40	37-2B 90	28-OF 89
2000	*Arizona*	*NL*	*231*	*77*	*5*	*2*	*0*	*9/29*	*30*	*29*	*6*	*4*	*158*	*.333*	*.358*	*.372*	*.249*	*24*		

Urquiola is a second-base prospect with a nice swing who has had two good seasons with the bat in South Bend. Expect the Diamondbacks to push him harder from now on, and for Urquiola to start the season at High Desert. The team is trying to figure out where to put him, which seems to indicate they're taking Rexrode seriously; Urquiola may end up in center field.

Turner Ward   OF   Bats B   Age 35

YEAR	TEAM	LGE	AB	H	DB	TP	HR	BB/SO	R	RBI	SB	CS	OUT	BA	OBP	SLG	EQA	EQR	DEFENSE
1997	Calgary	PCL	198	50	14	2	5	17/29	27	26	4	1	149	.253	.324	.419	.252	24	52-OF 88
1997	Pittsbrg	NL	169	59	18	1	7	17/17	33	33	3	1	111	.349	.415	.592	.327	34	41-OF 97
1998	Pittsbrg	NL	285	76	13	3	10	26/39	34	47	5	4	214	.267	.337	.439	.259	36	66-OF 111
1999	Nashvill	PCL	89	22	3	1	1	13/15	11	12	2	1	68	.247	.348	.337	.242	10	
1999	Pittsbrg	NL	91	19	1	0	0	12/9	4	7	2	2	74	.209	.308	.220	.185	5	
2000	*Arizona*	*NL*	*202*	*52*	*11*	*1*	*5*	*25/28*	*31*	*27*	*5*	*2*	*152*	*.257*	*.339*	*.396*	*.251*	*24*	

Pittsburgh made its problem Arizona's problem by foisting Ward off on the Diamondbacks for the stretch run in 1999. At his peak, Ward was a reasonable center fielder who wouldn't hurt you with his glove, but there's no compelling reason—except his contract—that he's still in baseball. He lucked out in 1997 with a strong 150 at-bats; it won't be so easy for him to find someone to sign on the dotted line again.

Matt Williams   3B   Bats R   Age 34

YEAR	TEAM	LGE	AB	H	DB	TP	HR	BB/SO	R	RBI	SB	CS	OUT	BA	OBP	SLG	EQA	EQR	DEFENSE
1997	Clevelnd	AL	599	165	37	3	33	30/104	87	106	12	4	438	.275	.315	.513	.270	83	148-3B 105
1998	Arizona	NL	515	140	25	1	22	42/99	73	73	5	1	376	.272	.331	.452	.262	66	128-3B 106
1999	Arizona	NL	631	192	37	2	35	33/92	94	136	2	0	439	.304	.341	.536	.285	95	150-3B 112
2000	*Arizona*	*NL*	*526*	*149*	*24*	*1*	*27*	*44/86*	*75*	*98*	*5*	*1*	*378*	*.283*	*.339*	*.487*	*.272*	*73*	

Williams looked finished in 1998, when he was way behind any serious heat. In 1999, he showed up with quicker wrists and had a vintage Matt Williams season. He's still an awesome defensive third baseman, and I can't help but wonder what the result of leaving him at shortstop out of college would have been.

Tony Womack — RF/SS — Bats L — Age 30

YEAR	TEAM	LGE	AB	H	DB	TP	HR	BB/SO	R	RBI	SB	CS	OUT	BA	OBP	SLG	EQA	EQR	DEFENSE
1997	Pittsbrg	NL	646	181	30	9	6	42/108	81	50	50	7	472	.280	.327	.382	.253	76	145-2B 95
1998	Pittsbrg	NL	661	191	30	7	3	37/91	88	46	62	9	479	.289	.327	.369	.251	76	149-2B 107
1999	Arizona	NL	618	173	25	10	4	44/67	102	39	64	13	458	.280	.330	.372	.253	74	105-RF 111
2000	*Arizona*	*NL*	*578*	*163*	*24*	*7*	*4*	*50/74*	*103*	*60*	*47*	*9*	*424*	*.282*	*.339*	*.369*	*.252*	*68*	

Don't let the stolen bases or runs scored fool you: Womack was the worst right fielder in the league. Those defensive numbers look very forgiving to me; Womack is a track star, but his arm isn't good enough for right field, and he didn't get good jumps on the ball. At the plate . . . well, if you've got no power, no on-base skills and you're being compared to Bob Abreu and Larry Walker, you're bound to look bad. He'll be the everyday shortstop this year.

Ernie Young — CF — Bats R — Age 30

YEAR	TEAM	LGE	AB	H	DB	TP	HR	BB/SO	R	RBI	SB	CS	OUT	BA	OBP	SLG	EQA	EQR	DEFENSE
1997	Edmonton	PCL	187	45	5	0	6	28/52	24	27	3	1	143	.241	.354	.364	.252	23	43-OF 106
1997	Oakland	AL	174	39	6	0	5	18/55	21	14	1	3	138	.224	.305	.345	.218	15	59-OF 100
1998	Omaha	PCL	294	81	10	1	16	23/74	42	40	4	3	216	.276	.336	.480	.268	40	75-OF 102
1999	Tucson	PCL	440	99	18	1	19	44/140	50	61	2	1	342	.225	.301	.400	.236	46	105-OF 83
2000	*Arizona*	*NL*	*395*	*97*	*12*	*1*	*19*	*54/119*	*54*	*65*	*2*	*1*	*299*	*.246*	*.336*	*.425*	*.256*	*50*	

Young bashed 30 home runs while playing full-time at Tucson in 1999. A refugee from the Oakland system, he was a Quadruple-A player at his peak: enough defense to play center field, enough pop to poke balls out of the park. Now, age is rearing its head; his wheels aren't what they once were, and he didn't do much with the bat besides those home runs. Young's still a reasonable reserve outfielder for a team that could use the power off the bench.

PITCHERS (Averages: ERA: 4.50 / H/9: 9.00 / HR/9: 1.00 / BB/9: 3.50 / K/9: 6.50 / KWH: 1.00)

Brian Anderson — Throws L — Age 28

YEAR	TEAM	LGE	IP	H	ER	HR	BB	K	ERA	W	L	H/9	HR/9	BB/9	K/9	KWH	PERA
1997	Buffalo	AmA	78.7	98	45	13	17	50	5.15	4	5	11.21	1.49	1.94	5.72	1.12	5.72
1997	Clevelnd	AL	48.0	53	26	7	11	22	4.88	2	3	9.94	1.31	2.06	4.13	0.62	4.87
1998	Arizona	NL	205.7	235	114	39	25	91	4.99	10	13	10.28	1.71	1.09	3.98	1.05	5.03
1999	Arizona	NL	127.7	147	68	17	27	72	4.79	7	7	10.36	1.20	1.90	5.08	0.98	4.86

He pitched like a man possessed in spring training; the Diamondbacks probably should have traded him then, because he started getting roughed up as soon as the games counted, and needed a good second half to make his numbers look passable. Anderson is a useful pitcher and a reliable spot starter, but this team certainly doesn't need the pitching depth. Anderson is good at helping his outfielders work off the clubhouse buffet.

Jeff Andrews — Throws R — Age 25

YEAR	TEAM	LGE	IP	H	ER	HR	BB	K	ERA	W	L	H/9	HR/9	BB/9	K/9	KWH	PERA
1997	Lethbrid	Pio	43.3	74	35	3	15	29	7.27	1	4	15.37	0.62	3.12	6.02	0.57	7.89
1997	Sth Bend	Mid	49.3	68	48	5	34	22	8.76	1	4	12.41	0.91	6.20	4.01	0.16	7.66
1998	Sth Bend	Mid	112.7	168	81	6	39	43	6.47	4	9	13.42	0.48	3.12	3.43	0.21	6.39
1999	El Paso	Tex	70.7	98	52	6	32	30	6.62	3	5	12.48	0.76	4.08	3.82	0.21	6.50

Converted to relief after a so-so season at South Bend in 1998, Andrews has moved up the chain steadily and had a solid season in El Paso's pen in 1999. He makes use of the defense, so Arizona isn't a bad team for him to play with, but he needs better control to make it in the majors. He showed some improvement in the Arizona Fall League.

Andy Benes — Throws R — Age 32

YEAR	TEAM	LGE	IP	H	ER	HR	BB	K	ERA	W	L	H/9	HR/9	BB/9	K/9	KWH	PERA
1997	St Louis	NL	175.7	152	63	10	63	162	3.23	13	7	7.79	0.51	3.23	8.30	2.05	3.28
1998	Arizona	NL	229.3	234	116	25	79	157	4.55	12	13	9.18	0.98	3.10	6.16	1.00	4.43
1999	Arizona	NL	195.0	221	114	31	79	136	5.26	9	13	10.20	1.43	3.65	6.28	0.79	5.72

He's had a rough ride since coming to Arizona. Benes has been easier to hit in the last two years than at any other time in his career, and word is that he's lost a few feet on his heater. He seems healthy, so this may be the beginning of the end for him. He had terminated his contract with Arizona and was a free agent at this writing.

Nick Bierbrodt — Throws L — Age 22

YEAR	TEAM	LGE	IP	H	ER	HR	BB	K	ERA	W	L	H/9	HR/9	BB/9	K/9	KWH	PERA
1997	Sth Bend	Mid	68.3	100	55	5	45	45	7.24	2	6	13.17	0.66	5.93	5.93	0.34	7.64
1998	High Des	Cal	126.0	141	73	9	80	61	5.21	6	8	10.07	0.64	5.71	4.36	0.25	5.64
1999	El Paso	Tex	76.0	80	45	3	46	45	5.33	3	5	9.47	0.36	5.45	5.33	0.41	4.86
1999	Tucson	PCL	44.0	53	36	8	34	36	7.36	1	4	10.84	1.64	6.95	7.36	0.54	7.77

He's been pushed hard since being the organization's first #1 pick, and in large part he's responded. Bierbrodt had a rough end to the season after pitching for Team USA in the Pan Am Games last year. He has to get those ratios under control to be truly dominant; there's plenty of time for him to work out the kinks in Tucson next season.

Bobby Chouinard — Throws R — Age 28

YEAR	TEAM	LGE	IP	H	ER	HR	BB	K	ERA	W	L	H/9	HR/9	BB/9	K/9	KWH	PERA
1997	Edmonton	PCL	93.0	135	77	16	29	48	7.45	3	7	13.06	1.55	2.81	4.65	0.44	7.35
1998	Louisvil	Int	39.7	58	34	5	16	28	7.71	1	3	13.16	1.13	3.63	6.35	0.63	7.26
1998	Arizona	NL	38.0	44	25	6	11	25	5.92	1	3	10.42	1.42	2.61	5.92	0.96	5.45
1999	Tucson	PCL	62.0	70	30	7	16	50	4.35	4	3	10.16	1.02	2.32	7.26	1.67	4.65
1999	Arizona	NL	39.3	32	16	3	12	22	3.66	2	2	7.32	0.69	2.75	5.03	0.94	2.97

I didn't think he'd keep it up, but Chouinard had the best year of his career in 1999. Unfortunately, his postseason wasn't anything to write home about. He'll have a spot in Arizona's bullpen, rather than Tucson's, in 2000; whether he can hold it depends in large part on his ability to keep balls out of the cheap seats—something he's had a problem with over the course of his career.

Omar Daal — Throws L — Age 28

YEAR	TEAM	LGE	IP	H	ER	HR	BB	K	ERA	W	L	H/9	HR/9	BB/9	K/9	KWH	PERA
1997	Montreal	NL	30.7	49	35	4	16	15	10.27	0	3	14.38	1.17	4.70	4.40	0.21	8.51
1997	Syracuse	Int	32.7	20	2	0	11	23	0.55	4	0	5.51	0.00	3.03	6.34	1.80	1.65
1997	Toronto	AL	26.7	34	12	3	6	28	4.05	2	1	11.48	1.01	2.03	9.45	2.87	5.40
1998	Arizona	NL	161.3	155	64	12	54	126	3.57	11	7	8.65	0.67	3.01	7.03	1.42	3.79
1999	Arizona	NL	210.7	194	90	19	75	143	3.84	13	10	8.29	0.81	3.20	6.11	1.05	3.80

He's been one of the best left-handed pitchers in the league. Daal is kind of a cool story, and as an added bonus for the Diamondbacks, his arm has been cared for throughout his career, so he could be effective for the next ten seasons. Why someone didn't give him a reasonable chance earlier in his career is a very good question.

Nelson Figueroa — Throws R — Age 26

YEAR	TEAM	LGE	IP	H	ER	HR	BB	K	ERA	W	L	H/9	HR/9	BB/9	K/9	KWH	PERA
1997	Binghmtn	Eas	138.0	152	79	13	75	92	5.15	6	9	9.91	0.85	4.89	6.00	0.55	5.41
1998	Binghmtn	Eas	115.0	163	90	20	54	88	7.04	4	9	12.76	1.57	4.23	6.89	0.66	7.75
1998	Tucson	PCL	42.0	44	19	7	18	24	4.07	3	2	9.43	1.50	3.86	5.14	0.54	5.36
1999	Tucson	PCL	127.3	126	53	13	50	85	3.75	8	6	8.91	0.92	3.53	6.01	0.86	4.38

Figueroa was a throw-in in the Willie Blair/Bernard Gilkey trade with the Mets in 1998, and nobody expected much out of him in 1999. So naturally, he ended up with the finest season of his career. He's obviously old for prospect status, and a good split-finger fastball is his only real out pitch. More work on his curveball could turn him into a bottom-of-the-rotation starter for a major-league team.

Andrew Good Throws R Age 20

YEAR	TEAM	LGE	IP	H	ER	HR	BB	K	ERA	W	L	H/9	HR/9	BB/9	K/9	KWH	PERA
1999	Sth Bend	Mid	140.0	202	99	12	48	104	6.36	5	11	12.99	0.77	3.09	6.69	0.83	6.43

Good is a developing pitcher who has reasonable control of four pitches. He was tough on opposing hitters in his first full season in South Bend, ending up with a 4.10 ERA. His control is pretty good for a power pitcher, he keeps the ball in the park and he's got quite a bit of time for his arm to develop. Keep an eye on him this year. It would be fun to see him make it: he's a headline writer's dream.

Darren Holmes Throws R Age 34

YEAR	TEAM	LGE	IP	H	ER	HR	BB	K	ERA	W	L	H/9	HR/9	BB/9	K/9	KWH	PERA
1997	Colorado	NL	95.7	106	50	12	39	67	4.70	5	6	9.97	1.13	3.67	6.30	0.81	5.27
1998	NY Yanks	AL	50.7	54	19	4	14	31	3.38	4	2	9.59	0.71	2.49	5.51	0.95	4.09
1999	Arizona	NL	48.0	51	21	3	24	34	3.94	3	2	9.56	0.56	4.50	6.38	0.71	4.69

Acquired from the Yankees for Ben Ford and Izzy Molina before last season began—which means Holmes missed out on another piece of gaudy jewelry. In his prime, Holmes was one of the premier relievers in the league; now, he can be counted on for 50 league-average innings and two DL trips a year.

Randy Johnson Throws L Age 36

YEAR	TEAM	LGE	IP	H	ER	HR	BB	K	ERA	W	L	H/9	HR/9	BB/9	K/9	KWH	PERA
1997	Seattle	AL	217.3	134	49	18	78	294	2.03	20	4	5.55	0.75	3.23	12.17	6.18	2.40
1998	Seattle	AL	162.7	137	78	17	63	216	4.32	9	9	7.58	0.94	3.49	11.95	4.04	3.65
1998	Houston	NL	84.0	59	12	4	27	110	1.29	8	1	6.32	0.43	2.89	11.79	5.68	2.36
1999	Arizona	NL	268.7	211	83	28	67	351	2.78	22	8	7.07	0.94	2.24	11.76	6.51	2.95

The Big Unit had another Cy Young season, showing no ill effects from carrying the Mariners on his back all those years. That back appears to be cranky but basically sound. As we predicted last year, he ended up with more than 350 strikeouts. His well-publicized postseason woes still appear to be more bad luck than anything else, but he didn't do much for the Diamondbacks in the Division Series.

Byung-Hyun Kim Throws R Age 21

YEAR	TEAM	LGE	IP	H	ER	HR	BB	K	ERA	W	L	H/9	HR/9	BB/9	K/9	KWH	PERA
1999	El Paso	Tex	21.7	5	5	0	11	26	2.08	2	0	2.08	0.00	4.57	10.80	9.18	0.83
1999	Tucson	PCL	30.3	19	7	2	17	34	2.08	2	1	5.64	0.59	5.04	10.09	2.67	2.97
1999	Arizona	NL	26.7	21	14	2	20	30	4.72	1	2	7.09	0.68	6.75	10.13	1.60	4.39

He started his career with a bang, making the majors within months of joining the Diamondback organization. He wasn't ready, as evidenced by all those free passes he gave up. It's critical that he gets control of those; nobody wants to see Buck Showalter doing Mylanta shots in the dugout. Kim is as close to an unhittable pitcher as the Diamondbacks have—perhaps even more so than Randy Johnson.

Jeff Kubenka Throws L Age 25

YEAR	TEAM	LGE	IP	H	ER	HR	BB	K	ERA	W	L	H/9	HR/9	BB/9	K/9	KWH	PERA
1997	San Bern	Cal	37.7	29	5	1	12	43	1.19	4	0	6.93	0.24	2.87	10.27	3.97	2.63
1997	SanAnton	Tex	24.3	13	3	1	7	33	1.11	3	0	4.81	0.37	2.59	12.21	8.94	1.48
1998	Albuquer	PCL	40.7	30	9	1	14	34	1.99	4	1	6.64	0.22	3.10	7.52	2.06	2.43
1999	Albuquer	PCL	65.7	61	31	5	27	51	4.25	4	3	8.36	0.69	3.70	6.99	1.18	3.97

The Diamondbacks have made some canny waiver-wire acquisitions over the last couple of seasons, and Kubenka is their latest. He's a former Dodger who has made a habit of being unkind to opposing hitters, and will make a great setup man for Matt Mantei. Of course, that's if the Diamondbacks don't fritter him away like they did Amaury Telemaco.

Matt Mantei Throws R Age 26

YEAR	TEAM	LGE	IP	H	ER	HR	BB	K	ERA	W	L	H/9	HR/9	BB/9	K/9	KWH	PERA
1998	Florida	NL	54.3	39	19	1	24	60	3.15	4	2	6.46	0.17	3.98	9.94	2.87	2.65
1999	Florida	NL	35.3	26	11	4	24	48	2.80	3	1	6.62	1.02	6.11	12.23	2.76	4.33
1999	Arizona	NL	29.0	20	10	1	19	47	3.10	2	1	6.21	0.31	5.90	14.59	4.34	3.10

(Matt Mantei *continued*)

Yes, he's one of the better closers in the league, but was he really worth Brad Penny and Vlad Nunez? Nevertheless, for the dear price they paid, the Diamondbacks picked up a fine pitcher who is young, has no health issues or platoon split to speak of, and isn't making a lot of money. I can't blame the front office for wanting a closer like this, rather than Gregg Olson.

Ben Norris   **Throws L**   **Age 22**

YEAR	TEAM	LGE	IP	H	ER	HR	BB	K	ERA	W	L	H/9	HR/9	BB/9	K/9	KWH	PERA
1997	Lethbrid	Pio	73.3	120	76	7	32	33	9.33	2	6	14.73	0.86	3.93	4.05	0.21	8.10
1997	Sth Bend	Mid	54.0	89	55	9	38	28	9.17	1	5	14.83	1.50	6.33	4.67	0.17	10.00
1998	Sth Bend	Mid	83.7	120	52	9	35	37	5.59	4	5	12.91	0.97	3.76	3.98	0.24	6.88
1998	High Des	Cal	39.0	57	30	8	23	12	6.92	1	3	13.15	1.85	5.31	2.77	0.08	9.00
1999	High Des	Cal	41.7	38	23	4	27	34	4.97	2	3	8.21	0.86	5.83	7.34	0.84	4.75
1999	El Paso	Tex	118.0	140	60	13	65	71	4.58	6	7	10.68	0.99	4.96	5.42	0.41	6.10

Norris was a 13th-round pick in 1996. After making his way through the chain as a reliever, he was converted to starter in El Paso following a strong couple of outings at High Desert. Since he moved up one level in the process, it's tough to say whether the change in roles was successful.

Gregg Olson   **Throws R**   **Age 33**

YEAR	TEAM	LGE	IP	H	ER	HR	BB	K	ERA	W	L	H/9	HR/9	BB/9	K/9	KWH	PERA
1997	Omaha	AmA	36.0	31	12	4	12	17	3.00	3	1	7.75	1.00	3.00	4.25	0.58	3.75
1997	KansasCy	AL	42.3	38	17	3	17	28	3.61	3	2	8.08	0.64	3.61	5.95	0.91	3.61
1998	Arizona	NL	68.0	60	27	4	26	53	3.57	5	3	7.94	0.53	3.44	7.01	1.35	3.44
1999	Arizona	NL	59.7	56	27	8	24	43	4.07	4	3	8.45	1.21	3.62	6.49	1.03	4.37

His Cinderella story hit a snag with a rough start in 1999. By the time the Diamondbacks acquired Mantei, Olson had already blown twice as many saves as he had in 1998. Chances are, it was bad luck more than anything else, since he ended up with only slightly inferior peripherals than he had in his 30-save season. Now that he's out of the closer's role, the pressure is off and he should be a fine reliever as long as his elbow holds up. Tick...tick...tick....

John Patterson   **Throws R**   **Age 22**

YEAR	TEAM	LGE	IP	H	ER	HR	BB	K	ERA	W	L	H/9	HR/9	BB/9	K/9	KWH	PERA
1997	Sth Bend	Mid	72.3	81	41	4	41	66	5.10	4	4	10.08	0.50	5.10	8.21	0.98	5.23
1998	High Des	Cal	123.7	120	59	14	53	102	4.29	7	7	8.73	1.02	3.86	7.42	1.22	4.51
1999	El Paso	Tex	99.0	105	60	15	51	96	5.45	4	7	9.55	1.36	4.64	8.73	1.29	5.64
1999	Tucson	PCL	31.7	40	23	3	21	25	6.54	1	3	11.37	0.85	5.97	7.11	0.56	6.82

He's probably the best pitching prospect the Diamondbacks have, which is saying something in an organization not wanting for pitching prospects. He has overpowering stuff, and his curve is already legendary. Patterson has been worked fairly hard and, like fellow pitching prospect Bierbrodt, he was ineffective after pitching for Team USA last season. He'll spend a full season at Tucson this year.

Dan Plesac   **Throws L**   **Age 38**

YEAR	TEAM	LGE	IP	H	ER	HR	BB	K	ERA	W	L	H/9	HR/9	BB/9	K/9	KWH	PERA
1997	Toronto	AL	50.3	46	20	8	19	61	3.58	4	2	8.23	1.43	3.40	10.91	3.18	4.47
1998	Toronto	AL	50.3	39	20	4	17	56	3.58	4	2	6.97	0.72	3.04	10.01	3.53	3.04
1999	Toronto	AL	23.3	26	18	4	9	27	6.94	1	2	10.03	1.54	3.47	10.41	2.33	5.79
1999	Arizona	NL	21.7	22	9	3	8	26	3.74	1	1	9.14	1.25	3.32	10.80	2.87	4.57

Come on, did the Diamondbacks really need this guy more than a 26-year-old shortstop with power, a good glove and a low salary? I wasn't a fan of the Mantei trade, but that one looks like genius compared to this move. That's not really Plesac's fault—he's a reliable left-hander out of the pen—but the Diamondbacks would have done better if they'd coaxed Jerry Don Gleaton out of retirement or something. An indefensible move by the Arizona front office.

Armando Reynoso — Throws R — Age 34

YEAR	TEAM	LGE	IP	H	ER	HR	BB	K	ERA	W	L	H/9	HR/9	BB/9	K/9	KWH	PERA
1997	NY Mets	NL	89.7	100	49	7	31	44	4.92	5	5	10.04	0.70	3.11	4.42	0.47	4.62
1998	NY Mets	NL	67.7	66	32	4	34	38	4.26	4	4	8.78	0.53	4.52	5.05	0.48	4.26
1999	Arizona	NL	163.3	183	88	18	64	76	4.85	8	10	10.08	0.99	3.53	4.19	0.37	5.12

Reynoso had a terrible September, which isn't all that surprising; he has trouble pitching an entire season without running into some kind of problem. When he's healthy and strong, he's good, but it's frustrating to watch his season disintegrate because of fatigue or injury. He's slated to remain in the rotation in 2000.

Todd Stottlemyre — Throws R Age 35

YEAR	TEAM	LGE	IP	H	ER	HR	BB	K	ERA	W	L	H/9	HR/9	BB/9	K/9	KWH	PERA
1997	St Louis	NL	180.0	156	85	17	69	149	4.25	11	9	7.80	0.85	3.45	7.45	1.54	3.70
1998	St Louis	NL	163.0	146	71	20	55	141	3.92	10	8	8.06	1.10	3.04	7.79	1.85	3.92
1998	Texas	AL	63.7	61	26	4	32	59	3.68	4	3	8.62	0.57	4.52	8.34	1.33	4.24
1999	Arizona	NL	99.3	109	50	11	38	71	4.53	5	6	9.88	1.00	3.44	6.43	0.91	4.98

He came back from surgery on his ACL quicker than anyone expected and pitched well during the stretch run. His war of words with Giants third baseman Charlie Hayes was one of the more amusing sound-bite generators of 1999. Stottlemyre was consistently overrated while he was with Toronto, but since then he has been one of the most consistent pitchers in the league. Look for a return to 180 innings in 2000.

Greg Swindell — Throws L — Age 35

YEAR	TEAM	LGE	IP	H	ER	HR	BB	K	ERA	W	L	H/9	HR/9	BB/9	K/9	KWH	PERA
1997	Minnesot	AL	116.3	99	42	11	25	76	3.25	9	4	7.66	0.85	1.93	5.88	1.74	3.09
1998	Minnesot	AL	66.7	65	24	9	19	46	3.24	5	2	8.78	1.22	2.57	6.21	1.28	4.18
1998	Boston	AL	24.3	24	12	3	14	18	4.44	2	1	8.88	1.11	5.18	6.66	0.72	5.18
1999	Arizona	NL	63.3	56	19	7	20	49	2.70	5	2	7.96	0.99	2.84	6.96	1.60	3.69

The Flounder has completely reinvented himself since signing with Minnesota in 1997; he began his stint there as a broken-down left-handed starter with an attitude problem and ended it as a sought-after long reliever. He's one of the most productive relievers in the majors and has no problem pitching two or three innings in an outing, though he's usually held to less than that. He's the front end of a potent 1-2 punch with closer Mantei.

Ed Vosberg — Throws L — Age 38

YEAR	TEAM	LGE	IP	H	ER	HR	BB	K	ERA	W	L	H/9	HR/9	BB/9	K/9	KWH	PERA
1997	Texas	AL	41.7	42	20	3	15	29	4.32	3	2	9.07	0.65	3.24	6.26	1.00	4.10
1999	Tucson	PCL	34.7	25	4	0	9	24	1.04	4	0	6.49	0.00	2.34	6.23	1.91	2.08

Vosberg completely missed 1998 due to an injured shoulder. What you see is what you get; Vosberg has relied on location and accuracy for years and is a good bet to succeed as a strict left-handed specialist. He didn't help himself in his return to the majors, but we're talking about 10 innings here. If Arizona had given him more than a two-inning tryout, they might still have Tony Batista on the roster.

Jeremy Ward — Throws R — Age 22

YEAR	TEAM	LGE	IP	H	ER	HR	BB	K	ERA	W	L	H/9	HR/9	BB/9	K/9	KWH	PERA
1999	El Paso	Tex	25.7	19	7	1	11	21	2.45	2	1	6.66	0.35	3.86	7.36	1.58	2.81

A very advanced pitching prospect drafted out of Long Beach State, Ward started the season in High Desert and ended it in Tucson after pitching well at three stops in 1999. Ward says all the right things about trying to strike people out ("I'm happier when I see a ground ball to the shortstop.") but he's got the stuff to be a strikeout pitcher. Ward is excellent at moving the ball within the strike zone. The organization likes him, even more so after his excellent Arizona Fall League stint.

| Support-Neutral Records | | | ARIZONA DIAMONDBACKS | | | | | | | Park Effect: +3.9% | |
PITCHER	GS	IP	R	SNW	SNL	SNPCT	W	L	RA	APW	SNVA	SNWAR
Brian Anderson	19	111.7	56	7.7	5.3	.590	7	1	4.51	0.75	1.23	2.15
Andy Benes	32	196.3	116	10.8	11.7	.480	13	12	5.32	-0.31	-0.48	1.23
Omar Daal	32	214.7	92	14.4	8.3	.633	16	9	3.86	2.91	2.95	4.74
Randy Johnson	35	271.7	86	21.0	7.2	.745	17	9	2.85	6.52	6.65	9.03
Armando Reynoso	27	161.0	86	10.0	8.3	.546	10	6	4.81	0.59	0.85	2.22
Todd Stottlemyre	17	101.3	51	5.9	5.4	.523	6	3	4.53	0.67	0.24	1.10
TOTALS	162	1056.7	487	69.8	46.3	.601	69	40	4.15	11.13	11.42	20.47

Who says you can't buy happiness? Certainly not Diamondback fans. Arizona's rent-a-rotation strategy paid off in a big way last year, as their starting staff was easily the majors' best. In 1998, their rotation was worth about three wins below average, certainly respectable for a first-year expansion team. But with the additions of Johnson, Reynoso and Stottlemyre, the '99 rotation was good for about 11½ games above average. That 14½-game improvement by the starting rotation doesn't account for all of the Diamondbacks' 35-game swing in the standings, but it was a big part of it.... In July, at *Baseball Prospectus Online*, Rany Jazayerli wrote that Pedro Martinez was having "one of those historic Lefty Grove seasons." If that's true, then Randy Johnson, who was about as good as Martinez compared to league average (SNVA), and better compared to replacement level (SNWAR), had one, too. I don't want to take away from the fabulous seasons Johnson and Martinez had, but doesn't it strike anyone as odd that these "historic Lefty Grove seasons" seems to occur about once per season lately? Maddux 1994 and '95, Johnson '95, Brown '96, Clemens '97 and now Johnson and Martinez. Consider two six-year periods, 1980–85 and 1994–99. The latter six years produced three seasons with SNPcts greater than .800; the former produced none. 1994–99 produced twenty seasons with SNPcts greater than .700; 1980-85 produced four. The results are similar for any statistic normalized to league-scoring levels (e.g., ERA+). Maybe the best pitchers today are just better than they were 20 years ago. On the other hand, maybe it's somehow easier for the top pitchers to put up fabulous numbers relative to the league when league scoring is through the roof. I don't have a solution here, just the observation.

Pitcher Abuse Points

PITCHER	AGE	GS	PAP	PAP/S	WKLD	MAX	1-90	91-100	101-110	111-120	121-130	131-140	141+
Brian Anderson	27	19	84	4.4	8.1	123	13	2	1	2	1	0	0
Andy Benes	31	32	446	13.9	16.3	127	5	2	7	15	3	0	0
Omar Daal	27	32	316	9.9	18.1	125	4	6	14	6	2	0	0
Randy Johnson	35	35	1358	38.8	38.8	143	0	1	9	7	10	6	2
Armando Reynoso	33	27	120	4.4	4.4	121	9	3	11	3	1	0	0
Todd Stottlemyre	34	17	73	4.3	4.3	120	2	6	6	3	0	0	0
ARIZONA		162	2397	14.8	17.3	143	33	20	48	36	17	6	2
Ranking (NL)				2	5								

It's funny how adding Randy Johnson to your rotation can raise your team's rank from 11th to 5th in the league in Workload. Showalter has shown himself to be a rather shrewd handler of pitchers, at least during the regular season. Brian Anderson was babied for the second straight year, and continues to show signs of putting it all together. The only real concern is for Omar Daal, who bounced around forever before finding success in the desert, but was still only 27, and who wore down a little in September (5.20 ERA).... And Johnson, who led baseball in PAPs for the second straight year and ranked ahead of all but 11 *teams?* We've speculated before that his physique may give him extra protection from the rigors of pitching, but there is another reason for his apparent indestructibility. Johnson, who was to the 1990s what Nolan Ryan was to the 1970s and 1980s, has, like Ryan, shown no signs of slowing down in his late 30s. And you know what else he has in common with Ryan? Neither entered a major-league rotation for good until he turned 25.

Atlanta Braves

The Braves have now played in eight consecutive postseasons, a feat unmatched in baseball history. They have never lost a Division Series; in the five years of the opening round, their record is 15-2. They appeared in five World Series in the 1990s, turning over their roster completely in that time. Since the 1994 strike, the Braves have been challenged for a postseason berth just once—last year—when everything broke right for the New York Mets and enabled them to reach September 20 with a chance to catch and pass Atlanta. They didn't, of course.

Elsewhere in this book, you'll read about the AL Central. Since 1995, the Cleveland Indians have enjoyed a run of success similar to the Braves', with five consecutive division crowns. But as you read about the Tribe, and the Twins and the Royals and the White Sox, you realize that the Indians' period of dominance is over. The nominal "small market" organizations of the AL Central are building strong teams for the '00s, breaking in excellent young hitters and talented pitchers. For the most part, they're following the example set by Cleveland at the start of the decade, establishing a young, improving talent core that they'll eventually support with judicious trades and signings. The "inevitable" playoff berth for the Indians could be in question as early as this fall.

The New York Yankees, thanks to their three World Championships in four years, may better fit some fans' definition of dominance, but the Yankees have won their division in just three of the past five seasons, and only one of those seasons was a runaway win. The Yankees face a challenge in 2000, as the Red Sox have upgraded their offense and the Blue Jays have a young team with the potential for dramatic improvement. It's hard to see the Yankees owning the AL East for any extended period of time.

In the NL East, though, there is no reason to believe the Braves won't be the favorites for at least a few more years. While the Mets challenged in 1999, they are a very old team and don't have any contributors coming up through the system. Exchanging John Olerud for Todd Zeile will accelerate

the decline of their offense, while the only thing in Queens older than the Met rotation is that globe left over from the World's Fair. The trade of Roger Cedeno and Octavio Dotel for Mike Hampton and Derek Bell makes them older and worse. The Phillies appear to be emerging from their funk, and have one of the game's better prospects in Pat Burrell. Still, there's nothing about them that screams juggernaut: their best players, Scott Rolen and Curt Schilling, have health questions, and there's nothing much in the system other than Burrell. The Expos and Marlins are in the middle of rebuilding projects and probably won't be ready to contend until 2002 or '03.

So the Braves find themselves roughly where the Indians were in 1997, able to treat the regular season as a six-month exhibition in preparation for the only 11 wins that matter. The perception of the Braves is that they're "chokers," a team that wins 100 games with regularity but doesn't have the heart, guts, thyroid, hemoglobin... whatever the body part is that would help a team win more than one World Series in eight postseasons. In reality, though, the Braves' decade has more to do with poor fortune (Eric Gregg) and some questionable decisions (Charlie Leibrandt) than with any collective shortcomings in character.

Poor fortune isn't something the team can change. Poor decision-making, on the other hand, can be addressed by taking advantage of weak competition. Although winning 100 games and another NL East title would be nice, the Braves really need to spend the regular season focused on building a roster that can win three short series. While the basics are the same—score and prevent runs—the nature of a playoff series is such that the best 25 men for getting you there aren't necessarily the best 25 for keeping you there. Short series are won primarily by front-line talent: the eight or nine regulars, top three starting pitchers and two best relievers. That doesn't mean that a good bench is unimportant; on the contrary, short series highlight a bench's tactical importance, because rather than starting the occasional day

---

Braves Prospectus

1999 record: 103-59; First place, NL East; Lost to Yankees in World Series, 4-0

Pythagorean W/L: 99-63

Runs scored: 840 (7th in NL)

Runs allowed: 661 (1st in NL)

Team EQA: .267 (5th in NL)

1999 team age: 29.3 (5th-oldest in NL)

1999 park: Turner Field; good pitchers' park, decreased run scoring by 12%.

1999: Injuries and age hurt them, yet they still played deep into October.

2000: Offense gets a needed OBP infusion to help it pick up an aging rotation.

game after a night game on artificial turf, or filling in for injuries, bench players are used in the postseason solely in game-critical situations.

The Yankees and Indians have pioneered one approach, leaving key players on extended rehabilitation, only to have them return when the weather gets cold. They run open tryouts for the last two or three roster spots, all in an effort to have the best short-series team. The results aren't always optimal—the Indians had about four healthy pitchers against the Red Sox, while the Yankees repeatedly carry Luis Sojo like so much ship's ballast—but it's the approach that sets these teams apart.

The Braves will have about two more chances to learn. Bobby Cox has taken a lot of heat for his postseason foibles—from the 1985 ALCS, when Dick Howser played chess to Cox's tiddlywinks, to last year when Cox ignored his two right-handed relief pitchers in all but the most dire straits. Cox's postseason roster choices have ranged from the bizarre—Joe Ayrault?—to the detrimental—Ozzie Guillen comes to mind. In a great career that should eventually land him in the Hall of Fame, Cox's strange October moves stand out like a discussion of the flat tax on "Sex in the City."

In 2000 and '01, Cox and GM John Schuerholz have to find players who can contribute in important situations. If Cox insists on carrying three catchers, Schuerholz has to make sure that the third one has value—a Jim Leyritz who can provide some offense in a key spot. If Cox wants to carry just nine pitchers, Schuerholz needs to make sure he'll use all nine, and not treat perfectly good relievers such as Kevin McGlinchy and Russ Springer like a father treats his daughter's first boyfriend. When a quality pinch-hitter spends most of the season on the roster and puts up a .278 EqA, as Randall Simon did, he—not a third shortstop—needs to be on that bench in October.

Cox isn't a bad postseason manager. His willingness to be unconventional and use his starting pitchers out of the bullpen is a nice touch and a sign he does realize that things are different in October. He needs to sift through what he likes to do, keep what works and discard what doesn't. He did this once before, after Howser ran Cox's Blue Jay platoons through the shredder on his way to the 1985 World Championship. Cox needs to go through the process again to give the Braves their best chance at a second World Series title.

Amidst their success, there has been something of a disturbing trend in Atlanta. The 1991 team was an amalgam of

innocuous free agents surrounding a few good products of the farm system. From that point through 1996, the Braves filled most of their holes internally, either by trading talent for established players (Fred McGriff, Kenny Lofton) or letting the products of a strong farm system win jobs (Javy Lopez, Ryan Klesko, Chipper Jones, Andruw Jones). Greg Maddux was the only significant free agent signed during this period.

Since then, however, the Braves have signed a number of free agents to fill holes, including Walt Weiss, Andres Galarraga and Brian Jordan. Along with the acquisition of Bret Boone, these moves have transformed the Braves into an old, expensive team with OBP issues. While they have gotten some good years out of these players—Weiss and Galarraga were both very good in 1998—for the most part these moves have not improved the team. The moves that have helped the Braves have been the ones akin to those from the 1992–96 period: making first Kerry Ligtenberg, then John Rocker, the closer; allowing Kevin Millwood to win the fifth starter spot in 1998.

The Braves need to get back to that. They have to let George Lombard win at least a piece of the left-field job. Rather than jerk Bruce Chen around based on a poor spring, they need to work him in as a middle reliever and let him win the #5 starter job. When Rafael Furcal and Marcus Giles are ready in 2001 or '02, the Braves have to give them an opportunity to play, as opposed to chasing people like Jeff Kent or Mark Grudzielanek.

Most importantly, as the contracts of the big three starters end over the next few years, the Braves have to have the courage to let them leave. All three are in decline, to one degree or another, yet will command large salaries based on their track records. The Braves have enough pitching depth to watch Hall of Fame starters leave, and they should do so to give people like Jason Marquis and Jimmy Osting a chance to be the John Smoltz and Tom Glavine of the '00s.

The Braves already have set a record for consecutive postseason appearances, a mark they should run to at least ten over the next two years. If they can make the right choices in the next few winters, they have a real chance to extend their run and begin to approach some of the longest playoff streaks in sports history. All the elements are in place: management simply needs to make the right decisions.

HITTERS (Averages: BA: .270 / OBP: .340 / SLG: .430 / EQA: .260)

Wilson Betemit   SS   Bats B   Age 19

YEAR	TEAM	LGE	AB	H	DB	TP	HR	BB/SO	R	RBI	SB	CS	OUT	BA	OBP	SLG	EQA	EQR	DEFENSE
1999	Danville	App	260	63	14	1	3	15/68	22	30	1	1	198	.242	.285	.338	.208	20	68-SS 89
2000	Atlanta	NL	122	29	3	0	3	9/52	10	13	0	0	93	.238	.290	.336	.212	10	

He was just 18, yet this was Betemit's third year as a pro—and the first one in which he hit after two unimpressive Gulf Coast League campaigns. There's potential here for explosive growth, as he's shown some extra-base power at a young age and impressed the organization with how easily he adapted to switch-hitting. He's already 6'2″ and has a much better shortstop in front of him in Rafael Furcal, so look for a position switch soon. Betemit has one of the highest upsides in baseball and will be garnering a lot of attention in 2000. There are rumors he was signed at 15, which could impact his status or bring discipline down on the Braves.

Bret Boone   2B   Bats R   Age 31

YEAR	TEAM	LGE	AB	H	DB	TP	HR	BB/SO	R	RBI	SB	CS	OUT	BA	OBP	SLG	EQA	EQR	DEFENSE
1997	Cincnnti	NL	445	99	23	1	8	44/100	39	46	4	5	351	.222	.298	.333	.214	37	133-2B 98
1998	Cincnnti	NL	589	161	36	1	27	47/101	77	98	6	5	433	.273	.332	.475	.266	79	154-2B 103
1999	Atlanta	NL	615	158	36	1	21	39/111	97	62	12	9	466	.257	.307	.421	.242	67	142-2B 108
2000	San Dieg	NL	440	106	24	1	14	46/83	57	57	7	3	337	.241	.313	.395	.248	52	

Part of the problem. Boone is exactly the type of hitter bad teams build their offense around: a right-handed batter with middling power and lousy plate discipline. His defensive performance is catching up with his reputation. The Braves have traded him to San Diego, where it looks like he'll again bat high in the lineup.

Troy Cameron   3B   Bats B   Age 21

YEAR	TEAM	LGE	AB	H	DB	TP	HR	BB/SO	R	RBI	SB	CS	OUT	BA	OBP	SLG	EQA	EQR	DEFENSE	
1997	Danville	App	211	37	5	1	4	17/86	17	15	0	1	175	.175	.242	.265	.160	9	35-SS 95	
1998	Macon	SAL	480	91	18	2	17	54/163	53	48	1	1	390	.190	.276	.342	.208	39	69-SS 75	59-3B 81
1999	Macon	SAL	479	100	25	1	19	57/163	58	61	3	4	383	.209	.297	.384	.229	48	119-3B 84	
2000	Atlanta	NL	440	93	16	1	19	59/155	50	59	1	2	349	.211	.305	.382	.234	46		

The Braves' 1997 #1 pick is a non-prospect, a Russ Branyan-type player without the lumberjack power. Despite making a second run through the Sally League, he didn't stand out offensively, which is a bad sign. His defense at third base is . . . er . . . better than it was at shortstop.

Jorge Fabregas   C   Bats L   Age 30

YEAR	TEAM	LGE	AB	H	DB	TP	HR	BB/SO	R	RBI	SB	CS	OUT	BA	OBP	SLG	EQA	EQR	DEFENSE
1997	ChiSox	AL	323	93	11	1	7	9/41	31	48	1	1	231	.288	.310	.393	.235	31	
1998	Arizona	NL	152	31	2	0	2	13/25	8	16	0	0	121	.204	.271	.257	.175	8	38-C 118
1999	Florida	NL	226	48	11	2	3	23/27	20	21	0	0	178	.212	.292	.319	.208	18	67-C 110
2000	Atlanta	NL	221	50	8	1	4	20/28	20	22	0	0	171	.226	.290	.326	.210	17	

Fabregas is miscast badly as a starting catcher, and his presence on the Braves' playoff roster is an indictment of Bobby Cox as a postseason manager. I can see a scenario in which Fabregas could contribute to a team, backing up a right-handed-hitting catcher with poor defensive skills who plays 90% of the time. Preferably in the International League.

Rafael Furcal   SS   Bats B   Age 19

YEAR	TEAM	LGE	AB	H	DB	TP	HR	BB/SO	R	RBI	SB	CS	OUT	BA	OBP	SLG	EQA	EQR	DEFENSE
1998	Danville	App	269	70	14	2	0	24/32	25	15	17	7	206	.260	.325	.327	.231	26	64-2B 93
1999	Macon	SAL	348	107	13	1	1	34/36	45	25	29	11	251	.307	.374	.359	.262	44	75-SS 95
1999	Myrtle B	Car	188	53	12	2	0	11/41	24	10	11	5	140	.282	.322	.367	.238	19	42-SS 102
2000	Atlanta	NL	329	97	10	2	1	32/57	61	32	29	8	240	.295	.357	.347	.257	40	

He's one of the top two prospects in the game, along with Yankee first baseman Nick Johnson. Furcal is a very good defensive shortstop who might also be the best base-stealer in organized baseball. On top of that, he showed excellent plate discipline for an 18-year-old. With the Braves having little more than a scar at shortstop, look for Furcal to make an appearance in Atlanta when rosters expand, and have the major-league job all to himself by April 2001. He is exactly what the Braves need: a middle infielder who can get on base.

Andres Galarraga   1B   Bats R   Age 39

YEAR	TEAM	LGE	AB	H	DB	TP	HR	BB/SO	R	RBI	SB	CS	OUT	BA	OBP	SLG	EQA	EQR	DEFENSE
1996	Colorado	NL	610	160	36	2	40	38/156	100	123	13	7	457	.262	.325	.525	.275	91	158-1B 95
1997	Colorado	NL	595	177	29	3	39	52/139	110	128	11	8	425	.297	.370	.553	.298	103	152-1B 94
1998	Atlanta	NL	562	174	24	1	48	63/142	105	124	7	7	395	.310	.405	.612	.323	117	145-1B 83
2000	*Atlanta*	*NL*	*279*	*73*	*10*	*0*	*18*	*37/72*	*43*	*54*	*4*	*3*	*209*	*.262*	*.348*	*.491*	*.279*	*43*	

The Braves missed him desperately, as his at-bats went to Otis Nixon and Gerald Williams. Optimists and Braves fans can point to Dave Winfield for hope. Winfield had the third-best season of his career in 1988 before missing the entire '89 season with a back injury. He returned to play five more years and helped the Blue Jays win the World Series in 1992. Of course, he was 35 when he missed his season, while the Big Cat was 38. Galarraga should be right around league average. That's a great accomplishment after cancer.

Freddy Garcia   3B/RF   Bats R   Age 27

YEAR	TEAM	LGE	AB	H	DB	TP	HR	BB/SO	R	RBI	SB	CS	OUT	BA	OBP	SLG	EQA	EQR	DEFENSE	
1997	Carolina	Sou	280	66	15	2	13	11/66	31	37	0	0	214	.236	.275	.443	.235	29	68-3B 102	
1997	Calgary	PCL	118	23	4	0	4	6/21	14	12	0	0	95	.195	.239	.331	.184	7	29-3B 76	
1998	Nashvill	PCL	326	77	20	3	16	19/97	39	41	0	1	250	.236	.284	.463	.243	36	66-3B 99	18-1B 103
1998	Pittsbrg	NL	174	46	10	1	10	17/44	27	27	0	2	130	.264	.337	.506	.272	25	45-3B 102	
1999	Pittsbrg	NL	131	30	6	0	6	2/41	16	22	0	0	101	.229	.241	.412	.211	10		
2000	*Atlanta*	*NL*	*255*	*57*	*13*	*1*	*13*	*17/73*	*26*	*36*	*0*	*0*	*198*	*.224*	*.272*	*.435*	*.234*	*26*		

Garcia is a useful bench player, a cheap source of power who can play all four corners and pinch-hit. He is more valuable to an NL team for the in-game flexibility and the lack of temptation to use him as a DH. His career from this point forward depends on getting lucky.

Marcus Giles   2B   Bats R   Age 22

YEAR	TEAM	LGE	AB	H	DB	TP	HR	BB/SO	R	RBI	SB	CS	OUT	BA	OBP	SLG	EQA	EQR	DEFENSE
1997	Danville	App	208	53	10	1	5	22/51	29	25	1	1	156	.255	.330	.385	.244	23	42-2B 94
1998	Macon	SAL	513	137	33	2	28	69/104	79	75	4	2	378	.267	.361	.503	.285	82	126-2B 105
1999	Myrtle B	Car	510	154	39	6	14	43/86	70	62	4	3	359	.302	.359	.484	.280	74	119-2B 99
2000	*Atlanta*	*NL*	*521*	*154*	*29*	*2*	*25*	*65/98*	*89*	*104*	*4*	*2*	*369*	*.296*	*.374*	*.503*	*.294*	*86*	

Giles, the darling of the system in 1998, had another good year in '99. No one noticed, thanks to the performance of Furcal and the fact that Giles's numbers were superficially worse. As you can see above, though, the seasons were nearly identical in value. There's still some talk of moving him to left field; he doesn't look like a second baseman, although he clearly can play the position. The Braves could have a top-tier middle infield from 2001 through 2003 for what they're paying Bret Boone this year.

Ozzie Guillen   SS   Bats L   Age 36

YEAR	TEAM	LGE	AB	H	DB	TP	HR	BB/SO	R	RBI	SB	CS	OUT	BA	OBP	SLG	EQA	EQR	DEFENSE
1997	ChiSox	AL	491	124	21	7	4	19/23	58	52	5	3	370	.253	.280	.348	.209	37	137-SS 101
1998	Atlanta	NL	267	76	16	1	1	24/24	36	22	1	5	195	.285	.346	.363	.240	28	63-SS 94
1999	Atlanta	NL	235	58	11	0	3	12/17	20	21	4	2	179	.247	.283	.332	.207	17	46-SS 108
2000	*Atlanta*	*NL*	*181*	*42*	*8*	*1*	*1*	*14/13*	*17*	*14*	*2*	*2*	*141*	*.232*	*.287*	*.304*	*.200*	*13*	

Ugh. At least Jorge Fabregas can catch. Guillen's calling card at this point is his reputation as a good guy, and that's just not enough. The Braves must replace players like Guillen, Fabregas and Nixon if they're going to keep the dynasty going into the '00s. Their bench is really an embarrassment.

Wes Helms   1B/3B   Bats R   Age 24

YEAR	TEAM	LGE	AB	H	DB	TP	HR	BB/SO	R	RBI	SB	CS	OUT	BA	OBP	SLG	EQA	EQR	DEFENSE
1997	Richmond	Int	111	21	4	0	3	8/33	10	14	1	1	91	.189	.273	.306	.195	8	31-3B 92
1997	Greenvil	Sou	307	75	12	1	8	25/53	35	30	2	2	234	.244	.310	.368	.230	30	83-3B 94
1998	Richmond	Int	448	113	21	1	12	27/105	46	64	4	1	336	.252	.311	.384	.236	46	122-3B 93
1999	Greenvil	Sou	111	28	5	0	6	4/36	11	18	0	0	83	.252	.283	.459	.242	12	24-1B 102
2000	*Atlanta*	*NL*	*243*	*62*	*8*	*0*	*11*	*19/62*	*27*	*37*	*1*	*1*	*182*	*.255*	*.309*	*.424*	*.246*	*27*	

Helms was never as good a prospect as the organization thought he was, and now injuries have really knocked him off the track. He returned from surgery on a torn right rotator cuff just in time to separate his left shoulder. The positive is that he adapted reasonably well to first base. Helms has no real upside, and will bounce up and down between Triple-A and the majors for a few years as Mike Blowers Lite.

Jose Hernandez   SS   Bats R   Age 30

YEAR	TEAM	LGE	AB	H	DB	TP	HR	BB/SO	R	RBI	SB	CS	OUT	BA	OBP	SLG	EQA	EQR	DEFENSE	
1997	ChiCubs	NL	183	48	8	5	7	14/42	31	25	1	5	140	.262	.315	.475	.252	22	25-3B 82	13-2B 89
1998	ChiCubs	NL	493	128	24	6	25	39/136	77	76	4	7	372	.260	.315	.485	.259	64	57-3B 109	35-SS 98
1999	ChiCubs	NL	340	89	11	2	14	36/100	52	39	6	2	253	.262	.342	.429	.262	44	79-SS 112	
1999	Atlanta	NL	168	44	5	0	5	10/44	21	19	4	1	125	.262	.303	.381	.233	16	39-SS 108	
2000	*Milwauke*	*NL*	*489*	*126*	*16*	*3*	*22*	*50/137*	*64*	*79*	*6*	*5*	*368*	*.258*	*.327*	*.438*	*.253*	*59*		

In addition to the strange decisions by Bobby Cox in putting his postseason bench together, his treatment of Hernandez was just bizarre. After Hernandez struggled in the Division Series, Cox limited him to just seven at-bats in the NLCS and World Series, and no starts at shortstop. Benching your best shortstop in favor of the 1999 version of Walt Weiss isn't too bright. Hernandez has signed with the Brewers and is expected to be their everyday third baseman, a role for which he's ill-suited.

Brian Hunter   1B   Bats R   Age 32

YEAR	TEAM	LGE	AB	H	DB	TP	HR	BB/SO	R	RBI	SB	CS	OUT	BA	OBP	SLG	EQA	EQR	DEFENSE	
1997	Indianap	AA	514	130	35	3	16	34/85	62	72	6	4	388	.253	.305	.426	.243	56	76-1B 93	52-OF 95
1998	St Louis	NL	113	24	9	1	4	7/22	11	13	1	1	90	.212	.265	.416	.223	11		
1999	Atlanta	NL	183	47	12	1	6	29/40	27	29	0	1	137	.257	.372	.432	.273	27	49-1B 94	
2000	*Atlanta*	*NL*	*168*	*38*	*12*	*1*	*5*	*20/33*	*22*	*22*	*1*	*1*	*131*	*.226*	*.309*	*.399*	*.240*	*18*		

Hunter is a useful player who stood out on this bench like Chris Kahrl at a "Thin is In!" rally. He is the perfect dance partner for a maladroit, left-handed-hitting first baseman. With the return of Andres Galarraga and the acquisition of Wally Joyner, Hunter doesn't fit as well. He'll be a contributor on someone's bench.

Andruw Jones   CF   Bats R   Age 23

YEAR	TEAM	LGE	AB	H	DB	TP	HR	BB/SO	R	RBI	SB	CS	OUT	BA	OBP	SLG	EQA	EQR	DEFENSE
1997	Atlanta	NL	404	94	19	1	19	56/106	59	71	16	11	321	.233	.332	.426	.254	52	129-OF 102
1998	Atlanta	NL	588	164	36	8	33	39/126	92	92	29	4	428	.279	.328	.536	.285	93	153-OF 120
1999	Atlanta	NL	598	167	38	5	25	69/102	93	80	21	12	443	.279	.364	.485	.281	93	159-CF 119
2000	*Atlanta*	*NL*	*549*	*154*	*32*	*5*	*32*	*76/108*	*111*	*109*	*29*	*11*	*406*	*.281*	*.368*	*.532*	*.298*	*99*	

To many observers, his year didn't look as impressive as his breakthrough 1998. However, the dramatic improvement in his strikeout-to-walk ratio signifies a player developing rapidly. Look for a big power spike this year, as Jones outperforms that projection. His defense is fast becoming legendary and makes him a legitimate MVP candidate even at the .280 EqA level.

Chipper Jones   3B   Bats B   Age 28

YEAR	TEAM	LGE	AB	H	DB	TP	HR	BB/SO	R	RBI	SB	CS	OUT	BA	OBP	SLG	EQA	EQR	DEFENSE
1997	Atlanta	NL	606	180	46	3	22	76/87	100	112	16	5	431	.297	.375	.492	.290	98	141-3B 98
1998	Atlanta	NL	610	196	30	5	37	96/91	127	111	17	7	421	.321	.415	.569	.321	123	159-3B 101
1999	Atlanta	NL	572	188	36	2	47	119/93	112	108	23	3	387	.329	.446	.645	.352	142	152-3B 88
2000	*Atlanta*	*NL*	*553*	*175*	*32*	*2*	*37*	*117/87*	*139*	*137*	*19*	*4*	*382*	*.316*	*.436*	*.582*	*.339*	*128*	

For the first time since his rookie year, that "B" is for real. Jones hit .352/.450/.739 from the right side, a far sight from his .281/.363/.399 career mark coming into the season. That took a key weapon—turning Jones around late in games—away from the opposition. Clutch players are a myth, but clutch performances aren't; what Jones did to the Mets in the next-to-last week of the season—really, what he did all of September—called to mind Ken Caminiti's 1996 stretch drive. He's a great player in the prime of his career.

Brian Jordan   RF   Bats R   Age 33

YEAR	TEAM	LGE	AB	H	DB	TP	HR	BB/SO	R	RBI	SB	CS	OUT	BA	OBP	SLG	EQA	EQR	DEFENSE
1997	St Louis	NL	147	36	6	0	0	9/21	17	10	5	1	112	.245	.315	.286	.214	12	31-OF 113
1998	St Louis	NL	569	181	34	7	27	39/64	101	92	18	6	394	.318	.372	.545	.300	97	129-OF 99
1999	Atlanta	NL	582	167	30	4	23	44/80	96	111	11	8	423	.287	.348	.471	.271	81	141-RF 95
2000	*Atlanta*	*NL*	*507*	*147*	*24*	*3*	*22*	*43/67*	*77*	*90*	*9*	*4*	*364*	*.290*	*.345*	*.479*	*.277*	*73*	

Players who don't walk much toe a fine line with regard to their value. In his best year, 1998, Jordan hit .300 with significant power and was an excellent player. Last year, hindered by a bad hand, his average and power slipped, making him an average right fielder. He's unlikely to see the heights of '98 again; that projection looks accurate.

Ryan Klesko   1B/LF   Bats L   Age 29

YEAR	TEAM	LGE	AB	H	DB	TP	HR	BB/SO	R	RBI	SB	CS	OUT	BA	OBP	SLG	EQA	EQR	DEFENSE	
1997	Atlanta	NL	473	125	26	6	25	47/129	68	85	3	4	352	.264	.336	.503	.273	69	105-OF 90	10-1B 80
1998	Atlanta	NL	432	122	28	1	20	56/64	70	72	5	3	313	.282	.369	.491	.286	68	105-OF 88	
1999	Atlanta	NL	408	124	31	2	21	48/68	54	78	4	2	286	.304	.380	.544	.302	72	58-1B 85	43-LF 80
2000	*San Dieg*	*NL*	*391*	*102*	*21*	*1*	*19*	*52/71*	*60*	*69*	*3*	*2*	*291*	*.261*	*.348*	*.465*	*.280*	*60*		

Klesko's best year since 1996 occurred in the year his status as a platoon player was sealed. He had just 49 at-bats against left-handed pitchers and couldn't muster even a 400 OPS against them. Klesko has old players' skills; I think he'll be an excellent hitter from 2000 through 2002, then suffer a steep decline. The Padres will probably use him at first base, given their outfield prospects.

Ryan Langerhans   RF   Bats L   Age 20

YEAR	TEAM	LGE	AB	H	DB	TP	HR	BB/SO	R	RBI	SB	CS	OUT	BA	OBP	SLG	EQA	EQR	DEFENSE
1999	Macon	SAL	462	110	24	1	9	44/100	51	41	7	5	357	.238	.310	.353	.226	43	110-OF 95
2000	*Atlanta*	*NL*	*226*	*58*	*9*	*0*	*7*	*27/81*	*31*	*31*	*4*	*2*	*170*	*.257*	*.336*	*.389*	*.251*	*27*	

He's a toolsy 1998 draftee whom the organization is excited about. Langerhans showed a broad range of skills at Macon, with better plate discipline than a typical tools prospect. His arm in right field is excellent. The Braves have a dearth of outfield prospects; Langerhans is second only to George Lombard and will progress rapidly. The Braves' tendency to draft high-school athletes and try to make them baseball players is a problem.

Keith Lockhart   2B/PH   Bats L   Age 35

YEAR	TEAM	LGE	AB	H	DB	TP	HR	BB/SO	R	RBI	SB	CS	OUT	BA	OBP	SLG	EQA	EQR	DEFENSE
1997	Atlanta	NL	149	42	7	3	6	14/17	26	32	0	0	107	.282	.348	.490	.277	22	12-2B 107
1998	Atlanta	NL	370	99	15	0	12	28/36	50	40	2	2	273	.268	.321	.405	.244	40	83-2B 109
1999	Atlanta	NL	163	44	3	1	1	17/21	19	21	3	1	120	.270	.343	.319	.234	16	
2000	*Atlanta*	*NL*	*151*	*37*	*6*	*1*	*3*	*16/17*	*17*	*18*	*0*	*0*	*114*	*.245*	*.317*	*.358*	*.233*	*15*	

Lockhart is a good enough left-handed pinch-hitter to be worth the roster spot, even though he can't play shortstop well enough to be a fifth infielder. His 1999 performance—just five extra-base hits—aside, Lockhart can be used either to start or finish an inning. He was one of the good players on the Braves' bench; that's not unlike being one of the well-read people in NASCAR.

George Lombard   LF   Bats L   Age 24

YEAR	TEAM	LGE	AB	H	DB	TP	HR	BB/SO	R	RBI	SB	CS	OUT	BA	OBP	SLG	EQA	EQR	DEFENSE
1997	Durham	Car	473	117	25	5	13	52/144	50	60	17	4	360	.247	.330	.404	.253	58	126-OF 100
1998	Greenvil	Sou	418	114	22	3	19	53/145	59	48	19	3	307	.273	.360	.476	.284	66	114-OF 82
1999	Richmond	Int	234	47	10	3	6	31/98	20	25	16	5	192	.201	.301	.346	.230	24	62-OF 87
2000	*Atlanta*	*NL*	*265*	*66*	*11*	*2*	*12*	*34/99*	*45*	*41*	*14*	*4*	*203*	*.249*	*.334*	*.442*	*.267*	*37*	

His lost year got a whole lot better when he hit 11 homers in the Arizona Fall League. Prior to that, he'd watched the Braves give his potential job to Brian Jordan, then missed more than two months with a pulled groin. The Braves could use Lombard's left-handed bat and low price tag, but his opportunity was again limited by Atlanta's decision to pick up an outfielder over the winter; this time it was Reggie Sanders.

Javy Lopez   C   Bats R   Age 29

YEAR	TEAM	LGE	AB	H	DB	TP	HR	BB/SO	R	RBI	SB	CS	OUT	BA	OBP	SLG	EQA	EQR	DEFENSE
1997	Atlanta	NL	420	125	27	1	25	39/81	53	69	1	1	296	.298	.364	.545	.296	70	
1998	Atlanta	NL	494	144	22	1	36	30/83	75	108	5	3	353	.291	.340	.559	.289	79	126-C 102
1999	Atlanta	NL	249	80	19	1	11	17/41	33	44	0	3	172	.321	.373	.538	.294	40	54-C 96
2000	*Atlanta*	*NL*	*300*	*87*	*16*	*1*	*17*	*25/53*	*44*	*60*	*1*	*2*	*215*	*.290*	*.345*	*.520*	*.284*	*46*	

The torn right ACL that ended his season was the single biggest reason there was a race in the NL East last year. The gap between Lopez and the Greg Myers/Eddie Perez platoon that replaced him was worth at least two games, possibly more. Lopez was the Braves' best player at the time of the injury, and is about as good as a player who walks 30 times a year can be. He's expected to be healthy and ready to go in March.

Pat Manning   SS/2B   Bats R   Age 20

YEAR	TEAM	LGE	AB	H	DB	TP	HR	BB/SO	R	RBI	SB	CS	OUT	BA	OBP	SLG	EQA	EQR	DEFENSE
1999	Macon	SAL	174	40	11	2	3	12/42	20	15	1	0	134	.230	.286	.368	.220	15	38-SS 105
2000	*Atlanta*	*NL*	*84*	*20*	*5*	*1*	*2*	*6/63*	*9*	*10*	*0*	*0*	*64*	*.238*	*.289*	*.393*	*.229*	*8*	

The Braves' third-round pick in the 1999 draft outplayed the Gulf Coast League for a month, forcing a promotion to Macon. Manning, a shortstop in high school, will be moved to second base. At either position, he'll have to be impressive to beat out the players in front of him. He's going to move up quickly.

Greg Myers   C   Bats L   Age 34

YEAR	TEAM	LGE	AB	H	DB	TP	HR	BB/SO	R	RBI	SB	CS	OUT	BA	OBP	SLG	EQA	EQR	DEFENSE
1997	Minnesot	AL	165	45	12	1	5	14 28	23	28	0	0	120	.273	.330	.448	.260	21	
1998	San Dieg	NL	176	48	7	0	6	17 35	20	23	0	1	129	.273	.337	.415	.253	21	38-C 103
1999	San Dieg	NL	129	38	4	0	3	11 14	9	15	0	0	91	.295	.350	.395	.255	15	32-C 96
1999	Atlanta	NL	73	17	2	0	2	12 16	10	9	0	0	56	.233	.341	.342	.240	8	20-C 111
2000	*Baltimor*	*AL*	*176*	*46*	*4*	*0*	*5*	*23/29*	*24*	*25*	*0*	*0*	*130*	*.261*	*.347*	*.369*	*.251*	*20*	

Myers is very consistent for a player who doesn't get a lot of playing time. Look at Eddie Perez for an example of what the performance record of a guy like this usually is. Myers is an underrated player who is well-suited for the role of #2 catcher and pinch-hitter. He's perfectly capable of being the good half of a platoon if he finds a manager who likes him. Myers doesn't have a good defensive reputation, despite evidence that he's fine behind the plate. He'll back up Charles Johnson in Baltimore.

Otis Nixon   LF/PR   Bats B   Age 41

YEAR	TEAM	LGE	AB	H	DB	TP	HR	BB/SO	R	RBI	SB	CS	OUT	BA	OBP	SLG	EQA	EQR	DEFENSE
1997	Toronto	AL	402	109	12	1	1	50 52	53	26	49	11	303	.271	.352	.313	.251	48	103-OF 106
1997	LosAngls	NL	178	52	7	2	1	13 24	30	19	11	2	128	.292	.340	.371	.252	20	31-OF 120
1998	Minnesot	AL	446	133	5	6	1	43 55	66	20	34	7	320	.298	.363	.343	.257	53	102-OF 103
1999	Atlanta	NL	152	32	2	1	0	22 15	28	8	23	7	127	.211	.310	.237	.215	14	32-LF 81
2000	*Atlanta*	*NL*	*264*	*62*	*5*	*2*	*0*	*38/31*	*40*	*18*	*17*	*6*	*208*	*.235*	*.331*	*.269*	*.223*	*24*	

Nixon is an unusual player in that, while he probably doesn't deserve a roster spot during the regular season, he's a pretty good guy to have around in the playoffs. His one skill, stealing bases, can be highlighted, while all the things he doesn't do aren't as important. In the postseason, you can afford to carry bench players who play specific roles in winning a baseball game. During the regular season, it's more important that your bench have players who can start for you if needed. The regular season requires a strategic bench, while a postseason bench should be tactical. Nixon fits the second type.

Asdrubal Oropeza   3B   Bats R   Age 19

YEAR	TEAM	LGE	AB	H	DB	TP	HR	BB/SO	R	RBI	SB	CS	OUT	BA	OBP	SLG	EQA	EQR	DEFENSE
1998	Eugene	Nwn	109	25	4	0	5	7/35	13	15	0	0	84	.229	.276	.404	.225	10	28-3B 112
1999	Jamestwn	NYP	273	68	8	1	12	24/61	41	34	3	1	206	.249	.317	.418	.247	31	73-3B 115
2000	*Atlanta*	*NL*	*161*	*41*	*5*	*0*	*9*	*15/46*	*21*	*27*	*1*	*0*	*120*	*.255*	*.318*	*.453*	*.260*	*21*	

Like Betemit, Oropeza was in his third professional season at 18. He was by far the best defensive third baseman in the New York-Penn League, and made considerable progress as a hitter this year. Despite his youth and the low level of competition, he is one of the best third-base prospects in baseball. Look for him to have a big year at Macon.

Eddie Perez   **C**   **Bats R**   **Age 32**

YEAR	TEAM	LGE	AB	H	DB	TP	HR	BB/SO	R	RBI	SB	CS	OUT	BA	OBP	SLG	EQA	EQR	DEFENSE
1997	Atlanta	NL	193	43	4	0	7	9/35	20	19	0	1	151	.223	.265	.352	.202	14	
1998	Atlanta	NL	151	52	8	0	8	15/27	18	34	1	1	100	.344	.411	.556	.317	28	37-C 99
1999	Atlanta	NL	312	79	14	0	8	14/40	29	30	0	1	234	.253	.300	.375	.226	28	83-C 102
2000	Atlanta	NL	242	62	7	0	8	18/35	25	32	0	1	181	.256	.308	.384	.234	24	

Perez returned to earth at the wrong time for the Braves, just in time for Lopez to miss half the season. He's a serviceable back-up catcher at around 150 at-bats. Any more playing time and his problems with the bat become an issue. He's still Greg Maddux's personal catcher, which is pretty good job security.

Randall Simon   **1B**   **Bats L**   **Age 25**

YEAR	TEAM	LGE	AB	H	DB	TP	HR	BB/SO	R	RBI	SB	CS	OUT	BA	OBP	SLG	EQA	EQR	DEFENSE
1997	Richmond	Int	523	155	37	1	15	9/74	55	93	1	4	372	.296	.313	.457	.252	59	125-1B 90
1998	Richmond	Int	482	114	19	1	11	17/63	44	59	2	3	371	.237	.265	.349	.201	34	116-1B 83
1999	Richmond	Int	59	15	3	0	1	2/10	6	7	0	1	45	.254	.279	.356	.205	4	
1999	Atlanta	NL	220	71	11	1	6	15/25	25	25	2	2	151	.323	.369	.464	.278	31	53-1B 87
2000	Atlanta	NL	378	105	20	1	10	21/50	44	53	2	2	275	.278	.316	.415	.246	41	

Simon had a year at the top of his range while standing in for Andres Galarraga. His absence from the postseason roster was criminal, as the Braves really needed an extra bat. Simon is stretched as a starter; he does have the profile of "classic" pinch-hitter, and should stick around for a number of years in that role.

Walt Weiss   **SS**   **Bats B**   **Age 36**

YEAR	TEAM	LGE	AB	H	DB	TP	HR	BB/SO	R	RBI	SB	CS	OUT	BA	OBP	SLG	EQA	EQR	DEFENSE
1997	Colorado	NL	390	99	23	4	4	64/55	49	35	4	2	293	.254	.362	.364	.255	48	114-SS 99
1998	Atlanta	NL	352	102	16	2	1	59/52	66	28	8	1	251	.290	.397	.355	.271	48	90-SS 99
1999	Atlanta	NL	282	65	13	4	2	32/48	36	28	6	3	220	.230	.316	.326	.224	26	76-SS 103
2000	Atlanta	NL	244	59	10	2	1	39/39	36	24	3	1	186	.242	.346	.311	.237	25	

Walt Weiss, April 1998: .435/.506/.580. Walt Weiss since: .233/.335/.303. Like Michael Tucker before him, Weiss has been terrible after his initial month with the Braves. He isn't a championship-caliber shortstop anymore, despite Bobby Cox's insistence on playing him over Jose Hernandez in October. Signed through 2000, he's a problem for this team.

Gerald Williams   **OF**   **Bats R**   **Age 33**

YEAR	TEAM	LGE	AB	H	DB	TP	HR	BB/SO	R	RBI	SB	CS	OUT	BA	OBP	SLG	EQA	EQR	DEFENSE	
1997	Milwauke	AL	567	145	34	2	10	15/86	71	40	23	9	431	.256	.284	.376	.223	51	157-OF 106	
1998	Atlanta	NL	269	83	19	2	11	17/47	47	45	12	6	192	.309	.357	.517	.286	42	66-OF 108	
1999	Atlanta	NL	427	119	24	1	17	27/66	71	65	16	11	319	.279	.332	.459	.261	55	81-LF 90	20-RF 97
2000	TampaBay	AL	393	102	19	1	15	30/62	53	58	10	7	298	.260	.312	.427	.245	44		

Like Simon and Perez, Williams is a good backup who got too much playing time due to the Braves' injuries. Hitting him lead-off just exacerbated the Braves' OBP problems at the top of the lineup, particularly against right-handed pitching. He's one of the better fourth outfielders in the game. The Devil Rays signed him as a free agent. Whether he'll be the everyday center fielder or platoon with Randy Winn or Quinton McCracken is unclear.

Glenn Williams   **2B**   **Bats R**   **Age 22**

YEAR	TEAM	LGE	AB	H	DB	TP	HR	BB/SO	R	RBI	SB	CS	OUT	BA	OBP	SLG	EQA	EQR	DEFENSE
1997	Macon	SAL	302	71	14	1	13	21/106	41	41	3	3	234	.235	.292	.417	.235	31	73-SS 91
1998	DanvillC	Car	480	101	23	1	11	35/127	40	43	1	1	380	.210	.269	.331	.200	34	125-2B 91
1999	Greenvil	Sou	202	40	7	0	4	4/60	15	12	1	2	164	.198	.224	.292	.157	8	51-2B 98
2000	Atlanta	NL	300	68	8	0	10	22/89	26	33	1	1	233	.227	.280	.353	.213	24	

This is another case of getting far too excited about a very young player from a foreign country. The money it took to sign Williams out of Australia in 1996 ($700,000) could have signed and developed dozens of Rafael Furcals and Asdrubal Oropezas. It's hard enough to project 16-year-olds coming through the relatively established United States development process. To throw hundreds of thousands of dollars at a Williams, a Josephang Bernhardt or a Jose Pett is a waste. That money is better spent on international scouting and infrastructure.

PITCHERS (Averages: ERA: 4.50 / H/9: 9.00 / HR/9: 1.00 / BB/9: 3.50 / K/9: 6.50 / KWH: 1.00)

Sean Bergman   Throws R   Age 30

YEAR	TEAM	LGE	IP	H	ER	HR	BB	K	ERA	W	L	H/9	HR/9	BB/9	K/9	KWH	PERA
1997	San Dieg	NL	97.7	129	73	12	39	69	6.73	3	8	11.89	1.11	3.59	6.36	0.71	6.36
1998	Houston	NL	171.3	189	82	20	45	95	4.31	10	9	9.93	1.05	2.36	4.99	0.79	4.62
1999	Houston	NL	98.3	127	55	8	24	36	5.03	5	6	11.62	0.73	2.20	3.29	0.32	5.22

After a surprising 1998, even the magic touch of Larry Dierker couldn't make Bergman effective, and the Astros released him in August. If his missing fastball returns, he can have some value as an 11th man on a staff, mopping up and spot starting. He's latched on with the Twins, where he'll have first crack at the #5 starter spot.

Bruce Chen   Throws L   Age 23

YEAR	TEAM	LGE	IP	H	ER	HR	BB	K	ERA	W	L	H/9	HR/9	BB/9	K/9	KWH	PERA
1997	Macon	SAL	139.3	155	83	23	62	125	5.36	6	9	10.01	1.49	4.00	8.07	1.21	5.81
1998	Greenvil	Sou	136.0	116	55	13	46	136	3.64	9	6	7.68	0.86	3.04	9.00	2.59	3.44
1998	Richmond	Int	24.0	17	5	1	20	26	1.88	3	0	6.38	0.38	7.50	9.75	1.49	4.12
1998	Atlanta	NL	20.0	25	9	3	9	16	4.05	1	1	11.25	1.35	4.05	7.20	0.85	6.30
1999	Richmond	Int	76.3	76	34	9	27	81	4.01	4	4	8.96	1.06	3.18	9.55	2.39	4.36
1999	Atlanta	NL	49.7	40	31	11	26	43	5.62	2	4	7.25	1.99	4.71	7.79	1.33	5.07

Not that Odalis Perez isn't a good pitcher, but it's silly the way teams let a handful of innings in the spring derail the careers of their top prospects. Chen's lousy March cost him the Braves' #5 starter job, although he returned in May. He needs only to work on keeping the ball—particularly his curve—in the park to be another great Braves' starter.

David Cortes   Throws R   Age 26

YEAR	TEAM	LGE	IP	H	ER	HR	BB	K	ERA	W	L	H/9	HR/9	BB/9	K/9	KWH	PERA
1997	Macon	SAL	30.3	21	4	0	6	20	1.19	3	0	6.23	0.00	1.78	5.93	2.37	1.78
1997	Durham	Car	18.3	19	6	1	6	11	2.95	1	1	9.33	0.49	2.95	5.40	0.79	3.93
1998	Richmond	Int	44.3	39	15	2	15	40	3.05	3	2	7.92	0.41	3.05	8.12	2.04	3.25
1999	Richmond	Int	44.0	53	19	2	16	36	3.89	3	2	10.84	0.41	3.27	7.36	1.14	4.91

The closer at Richmond last year has absolutely no profile. Still he's given up just six home runs in four professional seasons and gets ground balls. Should Kerry Ligtenberg struggle in his return, Cortes would be a front-runner to get setup innings in front of John Rocker. Sleeper, one I'm very high on.

Derrin Ebert   Throws L   Age 23

YEAR	TEAM	LGE	IP	H	ER	HR	BB	K	ERA	W	L	H/9	HR/9	BB/9	K/9	KWH	PERA
1997	Greenvil	Sou	171.7	209	94	23	53	84	4.93	9	10	10.96	1.21	2.78	4.40	0.48	5.56
1998	Richmond	Int	162.7	203	92	13	52	79	5.09	8	10	11.23	0.72	2.88	4.37	0.44	5.26
1999	Richmond	Int	147.3	178	75	12	46	74	4.58	8	8	10.87	0.73	2.81	4.52	0.50	5.01

Ebert would be the #3 starter for about a dozen other teams. Here, he's insurance against a massive Y2K problem in the Braves' rotation. Ebert doesn't have a major-league fastball; he'll eventually find his way into a bullpen and be a successful middle reliever. Check back in 2002.

Tom Glavine   Throws L   Age 34

YEAR	TEAM	LGE	IP	H	ER	HR	BB	K	ERA	W	L	H/9	HR/9	BB/9	K/9	KWH	PERA
1997	Atlanta	NL	234.3	210	93	20	83	141	3.57	16	10	8.07	0.77	3.19	5.42	0.85	3.65
1998	Atlanta	NL	226.0	216	74	13	79	150	2.95	17	8	8.60	0.52	3.15	5.97	0.99	3.66
1999	Atlanta	NL	227.0	268	117	17	79	132	4.64	12	13	10.63	0.67	3.13	5.23	0.61	4.96

Glavine's decline was popularly attributed to the change in the strike zone, with umpires purportedly calling the sides of the plate tighter while giving the pitcher the high strike. Glavine's strikeout and walk rates were mostly unchanged, however; he was just getting his head handed to him by NL batters. A sudden decline for a pitcher in his thirties who lacks an overpowering fastball isn't surprising. Glavine should bounce back somewhat, but his days as a Cy Young candidate are over.

Kerry Ligtenberg — Throws R — Age 29

YEAR	TEAM	LGE	IP	H	ER	HR	BB	K	ERA	W	L	H/9	HR/9	BB/9	K/9	KWH	PERA
1996	Durham	Car	54.0	79	30	4	23	51	5.00	3	3	13.17	0.67	3.83	8.50	1.07	6.83
1997	Greenvil	Sou	34.0	24	9	3	17	32	2.38	3	1	6.35	0.79	4.50	8.47	1.88	3.18
1997	Richmond	Int	24.0	25	15	3	2	28	5.63	1	2	9.38	1.13	0.75	10.50	11.72	3.75
1997	Atlanta	NL	14.7	13	5	4	4	18	3.07	1	1	7.98	2.45	2.45	11.05	4.66	4.91
1998	Atlanta	NL	72.0	55	25	6	25	75	3.13	5	3	6.88	0.75	3.13	9.38	3.06	3.00

Let's get something straight: even if Ligtenberg returns healthy and effective, John Rocker has established himself as the Braves' closer and should keep the job. Ligtenberg is expected to be back for spring training and would team with Rudy Seanez or Kevin McGlinchy to make an exceptional setup tandem. The Braves have plenty of live arms with which to assemble a bullpen in 2000.

Greg Maddux — Throws R — Age 34

YEAR	TEAM	LGE	IP	H	ER	HR	BB	K	ERA	W	L	H/9	HR/9	BB/9	K/9	KWH	PERA
1997	Atlanta	NL	227.0	215	64	9	21	164	2.54	19	6	8.52	0.36	0.83	6.50	4.45	2.70
1998	Atlanta	NL	248.3	213	81	13	48	194	2.94	20	8	7.72	0.47	1.74	7.03	2.75	2.68
1999	Atlanta	NL	212.7	266	105	15	35	130	4.44	12	12	11.26	0.63	1.48	5.50	1.36	4.61

See above. Maddux's walk rate actually dropped in 1999, which is pretty good evidence he wasn't throwing a lot more balls because of the strike zone. He was missing up in the zone a lot, leading to more balls hit in the air and more extra-base hits. Expect him to return to his 1998 level in 2000. This was the first year since 1991 in which Maddux posted an ERA above 2.72. Think about that.

Jason Marquis — Throws R — Age 21

YEAR	TEAM	LGE	IP	H	ER	HR	BB	K	ERA	W	L	H/9	HR/9	BB/9	K/9	KWH	PERA
1997	Macon	SAL	134.7	198	97	13	79	85	6.48	5	10	13.23	0.87	5.28	5.68	0.35	7.69
1998	DanvillC	Car	107.7	151	85	4	56	98	7.11	3	9	12.62	0.33	4.68	8.19	0.85	6.35
1999	Myrtle B	Car	30.0	30	4	0	19	30	1.20	3	0	9.00	0.00	5.70	9.00	1.18	4.20
1999	Greenvil	Sou	56.0	54	31	7	32	30	4.98	3	3	8.68	1.13	5.14	4.82	0.39	5.14

Continuous improvement is a factor I weigh heavily in judging a prospect. Marquis added a curve in 1998 and a change-up in 1999, giving him three plus pitches. He has good command and gets points for his intelligence, so there's not much here to not like. With the usual health caveats, Marquis is an excellent pitching prospect.

Kevin McGlinchy — Throws R — Age 23

YEAR	TEAM	LGE	IP	H	ER	HR	BB	K	ERA	W	L	H/9	HR/9	BB/9	K/9	KWH	PERA
1997	Durham	Car	134.0	172	88	16	45	84	5.91	6	9	11.55	1.07	3.02	5.64	0.68	5.91
1998	DanvillC	Car	134.7	153	72	10	40	93	4.81	7	8	10.23	0.67	2.67	6.22	1.06	4.54
1998	Greenvil	Sou	31.7	38	18	5	15	17	5.12	2	2	10.80	1.42	4.26	4.83	0.38	6.25
1999	Atlanta	NL	68.7	68	25	6	29	64	3.28	5	3	8.91	0.79	3.80	8.39	1.55	4.33

Despite having only a month of experience above A-ball, McGlinchy moved to the bullpen last winter and put together a good year throwing low-leverage relief for the Braves. As you might expect, he struggled when used on consecutive days, with an ERA over 8.00. If he's traded, he will probably move back to the rotation; otherwise, he'll be a quality cog in the Braves' pen.

Kevin Millwood — Throws R — Age 25

YEAR	TEAM	LGE	IP	H	ER	HR	BB	K	ERA	W	L	H/9	HR/9	BB/9	K/9	KWH	PERA
1997	Greenvil	Sou	60.3	64	36	8	26	51	5.37	3	4	9.55	1.19	3.88	7.61	1.17	5.22
1997	Richmond	Int	58.7	43	14	2	17	39	2.15	6	1	6.60	0.31	2.61	5.98	1.55	2.30
1997	Atlanta	NL	50.0	59	28	1	22	39	5.04	3	3	10.62	0.18	3.96	7.02	0.88	4.68
1998	Atlanta	NL	173.0	185	90	18	59	156	4.68	9	10	9.62	0.94	3.07	8.12	1.67	4.63
1999	Atlanta	NL	222.0	177	81	22	56	197	3.28	16	9	7.18	0.89	2.27	7.99	2.93	2.96

Millwood took his first turn as the best pitcher in the best rotation in baseball, displaying better command of all his pitches. Of some concern is his workload; Cox and Leo Mazzone haven't been as careful with Millwood as they have with their other starters, and his Workload score has topped 20 in each of the past two seasons. Millwood's 2000 will be somewhere between his 1998 and 1999. He's not *this* good.

Terry Mulholland **Throws L** **Age 37**

YEAR	TEAM	LGE	IP	H	ER	HR	BB	K	ERA	W	L	H/9	HR/9	BB/9	K/9	KWH	PERA
1997	ChiCubs	NL	159.3	161	75	20	48	70	4.24	10	8	9.09	1.13	2.71	3.95	0.47	4.35
1997	San Fran	NL	29.3	29	20	4	6	23	6.14	1	2	8.90	1.23	1.84	7.06	2.27	3.99
1998	ChiCubs	NL	112.3	102	49	7	41	69	3.93	7	5	8.17	0.56	3.28	5.53	0.85	3.53
1999	ChiCubs	NL	112.7	131	62	14	31	43	4.95	6	7	10.46	1.12	2.48	3.43	0.34	5.03
1999	Atlanta	NL	58.3	67	25	5	12	37	3.86	3	3	10.34	0.77	1.85	5.71	1.27	4.32

Mulholland has allowed five stolen bases since the strike ended, or as many as Todd Hundley allowed while you were reading this. That, and his ability to be effective in a variety of roles, makes him an asset despite being quite hittable. His value tends to go up with the temperature: he's been traded at midseason in three of the past four years.

Jimmy Osting **Throws L** **Age 23**

YEAR	TEAM	LGE	IP	H	ER	HR	BB	K	ERA	W	L	H/9	HR/9	BB/9	K/9	KWH	PERA
1997	Macon	SAL	55.0	68	35	4	41	43	5.73	2	4	11.13	0.65	6.71	7.04	0.50	6.71
1999	Macon	SAL	134.7	181	74	16	43	82	4.95	7	8	12.10	1.07	2.87	5.48	0.65	6.15

Osting recovered from elbow surgery in 1997 to reestablish himself as a solid prospect. His best pitch is a change-up, and enough of his fastball survived the surgery to make it effective. He returned a better pitcher than he was before the injury, so I expect him to make rapid progress through the system. The Braves made a point of babying him this year.

Odalis Perez **Throws L** **Age 22**

YEAR	TEAM	LGE	IP	H	ER	HR	BB	K	ERA	W	L	H/9	HR/9	BB/9	K/9	KWH	PERA
1997	Macon	SAL	84.0	84	39	5	38	68	4.18	5	4	9.00	0.54	4.07	7.29	1.08	4.29
1998	Greenvil	Sou	128.3	139	66	16	51	119	4.63	7	7	9.75	1.12	3.58	8.35	1.49	5.12
1998	Richmond	Int	24.0	27	10	4	8	20	3.75	2	1	10.13	1.50	3.00	7.50	1.38	5.62
1999	Atlanta	NL	90.3	105	65	11	50	79	6.48	3	7	10.46	1.10	4.98	7.87	0.89	6.08

Perez beat out Bruce Chen in spring training for the #5 starter spot, then watched his career implode. He had problems with his control and was handled badly by Cox and Mazzone, surpassing 120 pitches on April 27 and June 14 despite showing obvious fatigue around the 100-pitch mark. In August, he had Tommy John surgery and will be out until at least 2001. Maybe those two starts didn't cause the injury, but they certainly didn't help.

Mike Remlinger **Throws L** **Age 34**

YEAR	TEAM	LGE	IP	H	ER	HR	BB	K	ERA	W	L	H/9	HR/9	BB/9	K/9	KWH	PERA
1997	Cincnnti	NL	125.7	98	57	11	64	136	4.08	8	6	7.02	0.79	4.58	9.74	2.20	3.65
1998	Cincnnti	NL	165.7	166	94	23	93	138	5.11	8	10	9.02	1.25	5.05	7.50	0.92	5.38
1999	Atlanta	NL	81.3	70	25	8	34	78	2.77	7	2	7.75	0.89	3.76	8.63	1.91	3.76

Remlinger had the best year of any player in the Boone/Neagle trade, putting up the eighth-best relief performance in baseball. He was somewhat miscast as a starting pitcher; returned to the pen full-time, he was able to rely on his fastball more. There's no good reason he can't do this again.

Luis Rivera **Throws R** **Age 22**

YEAR	TEAM	LGE	IP	H	ER	HR	BB	K	ERA	W	L	H/9	HR/9	BB/9	K/9	KWH	PERA
1997	Danville	App	39.0	34	16	2	23	31	3.69	2	2	7.85	0.46	5.31	7.15	0.92	3.92
1997	Macon	SAL	20.0	17	5	1	10	18	2.25	2	0	7.65	0.45	4.50	8.10	1.42	3.60
1998	Macon	SAL	89.0	93	61	9	56	77	6.17	3	7	9.40	0.91	5.66	7.79	0.85	5.46
1999	Myrtle B	Car	63.0	60	33	4	26	59	4.71	3	4	8.57	0.57	3.71	8.43	1.67	3.86

Blister problems helped limit Rivera to just 67 innings this year. He's got a great fastball and a good change-up, and the blister problems and an earlier back injury have kept his workload down in his early 20s. Rivera may be headed for the bullpen, where his two-pitch arsenal and the blisters won't be detriments.

John Rocker — Throws L — Age 25

YEAR	TEAM	LGE	IP	H	ER	HR	BB	K	ERA	W	L	H/9	HR/9	BB/9	K/9	KWH	PERA
1997	Durham	Car	34.0	39	24	4	26	28	6.35	1	3	10.32	1.06	6.88	7.41	0.58	6.88
1997	Greenvil	Sou	111.0	128	67	11	68	80	5.43	5	7	10.38	0.89	5.51	6.49	0.55	6.00
1998	Richmond	Int	18.7	14	4	1	10	19	1.93	2	0	6.75	0.48	4.82	9.16	1.93	3.37
1998	Atlanta	NL	37.7	24	11	4	23	40	2.63	3	1	5.73	0.96	5.50	9.56	2.17	3.35
1999	Atlanta	NL	70.7	50	24	5	35	100	3.06	5	3	6.37	0.64	4.46	12.74	4.27	3.06

What's not to like? Rocker throws in the high 90s out of a funky motion and mixes in a good slider. That motion works both ways: he's hard to pick up, but he also occasionally gets out of whack and loses the strike zone completely, particularly against right-handed hitters. That's a small concern; Rocker is a top-tier closer. It is unknown what impact the *Sports Illustrated* interview, in which he came off as a xenophobic jackass, will have on his career.

Rudy Seanez — Throws R — Age 31

YEAR	TEAM	LGE	IP	H	ER	HR	BB	K	ERA	W	L	H/9	HR/9	BB/9	K/9	KWH	PERA
1997	Omaha	AmA	48.0	57	43	12	30	40	8.06	1	4	10.69	2.25	5.63	7.50	0.70	7.87
1998	Richmond	Int	20.7	14	9	1	8	28	3.92	1	1	6.10	0.44	3.48	12.19	5.23	2.61
1998	Atlanta	NL	35.7	27	13	2	17	48	3.28	3	1	6.81	0.50	4.29	12.11	3.75	3.28
1999	Atlanta	NL	52.3	49	21	3	20	39	3.61	4	2	8.43	0.52	3.44	6.71	1.16	3.61

This is one of the great triumphs of the Cox/Mazzone Braves, taking the oft-maligned Seanez and getting 90 good innings from him over two seasons. Losing him to a broken elbow in September was what led to Cox's interesting pitcher usage in October, using three starters out of the pen and essentially ignoring McGlinchy and Russ Springer in meaningful situations. Seanez is expected to be healthy in the spring.

John Smoltz — Throws R — Age 33

YEAR	TEAM	LGE	IP	H	ER	HR	BB	K	ERA	W	L	H/9	HR/9	BB/9	K/9	KWH	PERA
1997	Atlanta	NL	250.3	251	105	22	66	224	3.77	16	12	9.02	0.79	2.37	8.05	2.26	3.88
1998	Atlanta	NL	166.0	154	62	10	47	165	3.36	12	6	8.35	0.54	2.55	8.95	2.81	3.36
1999	Atlanta	NL	181.3	175	71	13	38	150	3.52	12	8	8.69	0.65	1.89	7.44	2.53	3.37

His performance is essentially unchanged, despite a cranky elbow that has cost him his slider and limited his availability. Smoltz had to rework his delivery at midseason to diminish the stress on his elbow and was just as effective with the new mechanics. It doesn't look like this problem is going to go away, but Smoltz should continue to be effective, albeit with a reduced workload.

Russ Springer — Throws R — Age 31

YEAR	TEAM	LGE	IP	H	ER	HR	BB	K	ERA	W	L	H/9	HR/9	BB/9	K/9	KWH	PERA
1997	Houston	NL	54.7	49	28	4	29	69	4.61	3	3	8.07	0.66	4.77	11.36	2.50	4.12
1998	Arizona	NL	32.3	31	16	4	15	35	4.45	2	2	8.63	1.11	4.18	9.74	1.97	4.73
1998	Atlanta	NL	20.0	23	11	0	17	18	4.95	1	1	10.35	0.00	7.65	8.10	0.62	5.85
1999	Atlanta	NL	46.0	33	20	5	21	47	3.91	3	2	6.46	0.98	4.11	9.20	2.38	3.33

With very little fanfare, Springer has developed into a decent middle reliever. On a staff with as many live arms as the Braves have, his chance to move into any kind of glamour role was nil. He's signed a two-year, $4 million contract with the Diamondbacks, where he should be the setup man for Matt Mantei. I think 2000 will be an exceptional year for him.

Support-Neutral Records | ATLANTA BRAVES | Park Effect: -10.0%

PITCHER	GS	IP	R	SNW	SNL	SNPCT	W	L	RA	APW	SNVA	SNWAR
Bruce Chen	7	40.0	23	2.3	2.5	.477	1	2	5.18	-0.15	-0.11	0.26
Tom Glavine	35	234.0	115	13.3	12.0	.526	14	11	4.42	0.99	0.54	2.55
Greg Maddux	33	219.3	103	14.0	10.9	.563	19	9	4.23	1.39	1.42	3.42
Kevin Millwood	33	228.0	80	16.0	7.9	.670	18	7	3.16	4.06	3.74	5.85
Terry Mulholland	8	52.0	21	3.7	1.8	.672	3	2	3.63	0.66	0.80	1.34
Odalis Perez	17	92.0	65	4.2	7.4	.363	4	6	6.36	-1.52	-1.38	-0.72
John Smoltz	29	186.3	70	13.4	7.1	.653	11	8	3.38	2.87	2.79	4.69
TOTALS	162	1051.7	477	66.9	49.6	.574	70	45	4.08	8.29	7.80	17.40

The Braves' reign as best starting rotation in the majors has finally come to an end. For the first time in eight years, another team's starters finished with better numbers than Atlanta's. The new reigning champion is Arizona, as the Braves plummeted all the way to second. It says a lot about the Braves' depth that it took the worst year of the past eight by both Maddux and Glavine to dethrone them. If you replace the 1999 line of either of those guys with what they did in 1998, the Braves would have had better Support-Neutral stats than the Diamondbacks.... Another thing that contributed to the "collapse" of the Braves' rotation was their inability to find a good fifth starter until August. For most teams, it's a given that the fifth starter will be below average, usually significantly so. But not for the Braves. Odalis Perez's season was easily the worst by a Braves starter with more than 15 starts since 1990. It's tempting to think that the Braves wouldn't have had fifth-starter problems if they hadn't traded Denny Neagle, but it's not true. Neagle didn't start pitching effectively until August, by which time the Braves were getting good starts from Terry Mulholland.... 1999 marked the first year since 1992 that no Brave was among the top three starters in the majors.

Pitcher Abuse Points

PITCHER	AGE	GS	PAP	PAP/S	WKLD	MAX	1-90	91-100	101-110	111-120	121-130	131-140	141+
Bruce Chen	22	7	19	2.7	7.2	107	3	1	3	0	0	0	0
Tom Glavine	33	35	599	17.1	17.1	133	6	4	9	9	5	2	0
Greg Maddux	33	33	93	2.8	2.8	118	13	10	7	3	0	0	0
Kevin Millwood	24	33	296	9.0	20.9	128	5	12	9	4	3	0	0
Terry Mulholland	36	8	7	0.9	0.9	107	4	3	1	0	0	0	0
Odalis Perez	21	17	130	7.6	21.7	124	3	5	5	2	2	0	0
John Smoltz	32	29	145	5.0	5.0	122	10	7	8	3	1	0	0
ATLANTA		162	1289	8.0	12.1	133	44	42	42	21	11	2	0
Ranking (NL)				7	8								

That the best rotation in baseball, year in and year out, continues to score right around the league average in PAPs is a testimony of the ability of Bobby Cox and Leo Mazzone to pull their starters before they get tired. But their one mistake in 1999 may have cost Odalis Perez a promising career. Their error highlights the importance of pitch counts: the first time Perez threw more than 120 pitches—and in the process blew an eighth-inning lead—Cox became more than a little irritated at the press for asking whether he left Perez out there too long. And given the success the Braves have had keeping their pitchers healthy over the years, shouldn't we have trusted that he knew what he was doing? But Perez's lame elbow reminds us that Cox and Mazzone don't have some sort of magic touch; they've kept their pitchers healthy because they've kept them from throwing too much. And when they got away from that plan with Perez, they suffered the consequences.... You'll also notice that Kevin Millwood had nearly as high a Workload as Perez, and this is the second straight year that his Workload has been over 20. I hate to invoke the name "Steve Avery," given that Millwood is a different type of pitcher, but it would be foolish to ignore history.

Chicago Cubs

I know what you're thinking. Another essay in which we all enjoy a few more laughs at the Cubs' expense for some dopey moves, ill-considered big contracts, spotty player development and general Cubbiness, right? To heck with all of that. I'm tired of beating the dead horse's bones into dust. Besides, the 1999 Cubs offer some valuable lessons and a few interesting opportunities.

If negative reinforcement is the most potent learning tool, then the Cubs' 1999 season should be about as educational as sticking your tongue in a power outlet. The experience provided a number of concrete do's and don'ts that team President Andy MacPhail and General Manager Ed Lynch must take to heart. First, they should have learned to not get too sentimental about success. Whatever the inadequacies of the 1998 wild-card team, there's no doubt that it was a potential stepping stone to further success. But instead of building on that, Mac-Phail and Lynch were comfortable with merely bringing back most of the aging regulars from that team. The Cubs neither promoted new talent nor bought better talent. They stood still, hoping the applause wouldn't end and basking in the glory of getting blown out by the Braves.

Only one real move was made. The Cubs pulled off a coup in exchanging a borderline player like Brant Brown for a quality starting pitcher in Jon Lieber. For the most part, though, the Cubs were satisfied with rewarding the people associated with the team's first meaningful season in ten years.

Elective stagnation is no way to run a baseball club. The genius of George Weiss, GM of the Yankees' dynasty after World War II, was that he never got close to his players and never made a roster move on any basis other than talent and the ability to contribute in the future. What people remember about the Yankees' dynasties is their predatory relationship with sad-sack organizations like the Red Sox in the 1920s or the Kansas City A's in the 1950s. A more important element was that Weiss was smart enough—as well as ruthless enough—to dump valued Yankees' contributors simply because he was always looking to improve.

Because it's a part of their own history, it's a lesson the Cubs should have been familiar with. Both 1985 and 1990 saw the organization cling to almost every marginal contributor from the previous season's success. It's interesting that most observers think MacPhail and Lynch spend more time in the clubhouse than is considered normal for front-office people, hobnobbing with the players on a daily basis. In their own ways, both Lynch and MacPhail grew up with the game and in professional clubhouses, and they seem to have forgotten that management's responsibilities do not include "hanging out."

While 1999 was a predictable disaster, the fact that Mac-Phail and Lynch got to experience it firsthand should mean they'll learn something from it, as opposed to someone like Bill Bavasi who completely blew it and doesn't even recognize that he did. The lessons of 1999 are clear. First, you don't overpay for old offensive talent. Despite playing in the best hitters' park in baseball outside of Colorado, a lineup featuring old men like Mickey Morandini, Lance Johnson, Glenallen Hill and Gary Gaetti having decent years wasn't even close to being the league's best offense in 1998. As the Lieber pickup highlighted, improving the pitching staff had been the offseason priority; the offense was ignored and subsequently collapsed, finishing 13th in the league in runs scored.

Second, the Cubs made the mistake of believing a veteran team is automatically a good defensive team. While the injury to Lance Johnson and the daily atrocity of Tyler Houston at third base made things worse, the Cubs as a team had poor range and bad hands. Third, they did one of the worst jobs of any major-league team in filling their last five to seven roster spots. When you're carrying only 14 position players, a bench that features guys like Manny Alexander or Sandy Martinez or Curtis Goodwin leaves you with lousy pinch-hitters, not to mention few better options to start instead of people like Gaetti, Johnson and Houston.

The back end of the pitching staff included last-minute pickups like Dan Serafini and Brad Woodall and Triple-A

Cubs Prospectus

1999 record: 67-95; Sixth place, NL Central

Pythagorean W/L: 66-96

Runs scored: 747 (13th in NL)

Runs allowed: 920 (15th in NL)

Team EQA: .246 (14th in NL)

1999 team age: 30.3 (3rd-oldest in NL)

1999 park: Wrigley Field; good hitters' park, increased run scoring by 13%.

1999: Basking in the glow of 1998, the Cubs didn't even try to improve, and it showed.

2000: The rotation should be better, but they'll struggle to reach 750 runs.

careerists like Rodney Myers and Kurt Miller. Injuries to Kerry Wood, Rod Beck and Terry Adams made the Opening Day pitching staff look weak, but using guys like Woodall, Serafini and Scott Sanders didn't keep the Cubs from playing well: they rushed out to a 32-23 start. Time brought injuries, which meant more innings for the spare guys, which made a weak pitching staff and weaker lineup look even worse.

But the lesson that was probably the hardest to accept was that they had to name a fall guy. Jim Riggleman was the manager they'd brought in when MacPhail took over from Larry Himes after 1994. While they were comfortable with him, and while he's generally regarded as a sound tactician, somebody had to take the blame. The lesson should be that everybody, no matter how popular or how snuggly, is expendable, but whether Lynch and MacPhail take this lesson to heart remains to be seen.

Riggleman isn't destined for a permanent place in the history of managing, but his tenure in Chicago can teach the Cubs—and the rest of us—a thing or two about progress. Fifteen years ago, Riggleman would have been hailed as one of the better managers in baseball. He's good at observing and securing platoon advantages with his relievers during a game, he's not particularly irresponsible about working his starting pitchers and he's willing to build platoons at positions where he doesn't have a good everyday player. You could call him a mild-mannered Tony LaRussa. He's open-minded enough to have read Bill James back in the '80s. Riggleman represents a good blend of baseball experience and sabermetric knowledge . . . circa 1987.

Riggleman's record as a manager proves that there are larger managerial responsibilities than being smart enough to look up players' platoon splits. Riggleman's bullpen management may play righty/lefty percentages well enough, but is that necessarily a good thing in every situation? Situational usage patterns are great if you want to win individual matchups in individual games, but running a bullpen isn't simply about securing matchups. Constantly warming guys up for potential situations, and then re-warming them up two innings later if you missed those opportunities, is no way to keep relievers ready and useful over the course of a six-month season.

As Jack McKeon and Jerry Manuel demonstrated in 1999, running a bullpen well can just as easily be about giving relievers enough time on the mound that they're sharp, even if it means not having them handy as often because you're letting them pitch multiple innings in their appearances. It can mean punting the occasional situational advantage because you know batters make outs 65% of the time. It can mean learning to exercise discretion about which situational advantages are game-critical, and which ones aren't worth it if it means using four relievers every night.

A larger issue is whether you let a focus on situational matchups start to dictate who's on your roster and how you use them. Take Terry Adams. For the second straight year, Adams had serious problems against right-handed hitters. Riggleman was a platoon-oriented manager, so Adams would get brought in to face right-handed hitters, and time and again the Cubs were hurt by it. By contrast, Rick Aguilera was great against right-handed hitters in 1999. But why let those factors alone dictate who to use and when? Aguilera works high with good control, getting plenty of flyball outs, while Adams keeps the ball down and gets ground balls. Between the two of them, the Cubs had an opportunity to mix and match closers not based on platoon matchups, but on whether they needed grounders or fly balls.

The lesson of Tony LaRussa's managerial career—particularly his success with Oakland in the late 1980s—isn't that every bullpen should be made up of pitchers in specialized roles tailored to their physical limitations. It's that you should manage in a way that takes advantage of the talent you have available. Felix Heredia isn't Rick Honeycutt, an old guy who is good for 50 innings spread out over 70 games. Heredia is a 24-year-old who needs to get experience to sort out how his pitches work; trotting him out to face Barry Bonds and Larry Walker is a lousy way to do that.

Riggleman's predilection for specialized roles carried over to the back end of his bench: a third catcher, a light-hitting utility infielder and a pinch-runner. This is similar to Bobby Cox's approach to postseason rosters, and just like the Braves, Riggleman's teams use marginal players like Curtis Goodwin or Manny Alexander more than they should because they don't carry bench players who could hit.

Hmmm . . . I've spent a lot of time talking about what the Cubs screwed up after all. Other than the hope that MacPhail and Lynch learned anything from all this, what is there to look forward to? Plenty. First off, the organization may not have much depth, but the guys with talent are among the best prospects in the game today. Corey Patterson looks like he's going to be ready much sooner than expected. He could easily make a Vernon Wells-style three- or four-level jump and be in the majors by Labor Day. Mike Meyers is one of the best pitching prospects in the game and represents a brilliant scouting coup for farm director Jim Hendry's player-development program.

Jeff Goldbach and Eric Hinske are good prospects at the perennial sore spots of catcher and third base, and Roosevelt Brown looks like he'll hit enough to be an above-average player in either outfield corner. While Hee Seop Choi is only one high-profile signing out of Korea, as opposed to the product of a major Asian scouting effort, he's a legitimate prospect. Everybody else in the Lansing Lugnuts' lineup was hailed as a prospect in his own right, but they're all several steps behind Patterson, Choi and Goldbach. With this kind of talent on the way, it's hard not to be optimistic about the team the Cubs could put on the field in 2001 and 2002.

Second, in replacing Riggleman, they've brought in a

pretty good manager. Don Baylor may not be Earl Weaver or Billy Martin, but his record with the Rockies was notable for his ability to build a good bullpen and use it well. The league's best bullpen is what propelled the Rockies to their lone postseason appearance in 1995. It can't hurt that he's already used to managing in a high-offense environment. Wrigley isn't Coors, but it's still a bandbox. Baylor is coming in talking about getting the Cubs to be more aggressive, but I doubt he'll engage in Trebelhorn-style kamikaze baserunning. The talent for it simply isn't there, and while tough talk about fundamentals is a normal "new sheriff in town" gesture, too much of the running game carries an increased risk for injuries. If Sammy Sosa starts coming up with hamstring pulls and jammed fingers, that sort of nonsense will quickly be discouraged.

The Cubs are saying they're looking to be competitive in 2000, and while there's nowhere to go but up, their offseason acquisitions didn't address the team's real needs. Getting Ismael Valdes from the Dodgers for Terry Adams improves the rotation, but having to take Eric Young in the deal blocks Chad Meyers at second base. The Cubs believe they've solved their problem in center field by trading Manny Alexander to the Red Sox for Damon Buford, a good idea in that trading Alexander for anything that isn't disease-ridden helps, but bad if they expect Buford to be the everyday center fielder. He isn't going to hit enough for the job. Adding to the lineup's woes, the Cubs brought Joe Girardi home for three years. With the few good hitters in the lineup likely to decline, there's a real chance that this team could slip from even 1999's poor showing and challenge the Expos and Padres as the worst offense in the league.

The Cubs needed to use this year to start building a good team by breaking in some of their good young starting pitchers in middle relief and playing Chad Meyers and Rosie Brown. Most importantly, they needed to get away from chasing a temporary goal like the wild card. It's clear that the focus is still on the immediate future, at scraping to the 88-win level in the hopes of extending the season by one week. It's a sign that no matter how clear the lessons, perhaps some people just don't want to learn.

HITTERS (Averages: BA: .270 / OBP: .340 / SLG: .430 / EQA: .260)

Manny Alexander — SLB — Bats R — Age 29

YEAR	TEAM	LGE	AB	H	DB	TP	HR	BB/SO	R	RBI	SB	CS	OUT	BA	OBP	SLG	EQA	EQR	DEFENSE	
1997	NY Mets	NL	150	38	11	3	2	9/38	25	15	9	0	112	.253	.300	.407	.248	17	17-SS 109	17-2B 104
1997	ChiCubs	NL	99	28	3	1	1	8/16	11	7	2	1	72	.283	.349	.364	.247	11	22-SS 109	
1998	ChiCubs	NL	266	62	12	1	5	18/64	35	25	4	1	205	.233	.284	.342	.213	21	28-SS 91	
1999	ChiCubs	NL	177	47	11	2	0	7/38	15	14	3	0	130	.266	.293	.350	.219	15		
2000	Boston	AL	188	49	11	1	2	14/42	25	21	4	0	139	.261	.312	.362	.231	18		

SLB? "Sammy's Little Buddy." If the Cubs were a Western, Manny would be the sidekick with the hyena laugh. "Want me to bunt him over, Sammito?" Because he'll hack at anything, he can be a useful "get it in play no matter what" pinch-hitter. With the Red Sox, he'll join a fight to the death with Jeff Frye and Donnie Sadler for a utility infielder job. Watch for pay-per-view details.

Shane Andrews — 3B — Bats R — Age 28

YEAR	TEAM	LGE	AB	H	DB	TP	HR	BB/SO	R	RBI	SB	CS	OUT	BA	OBP	SLG	EQA	EQR	DEFENSE
1996	Montreal	NL	376	83	15	2	19	35/118	41	61	2	1	294	.221	.291	.423	.237	40	115-3B 108
1998	Montreal	NL	504	132	30	1	30	58/133	52	77	1	7	379	.262	.338	.504	.272	73	139-3B 114
1999	Montreal	NL	281	49	7	0	11	40/87	26	34	1	0	232	.174	.277	.317	.203	22	65-3B 101
1999	ChiCubs	NL	67	16	4	0	5	6/21	12	13	0	1	52	.239	.312	.522	.265	9	
2000	ChiCubs	NL	266	63	10	0	18	36/87	37	50	0	1	204	.237	.328	.477	.260	35	

Andrews is a good example of the kind of player the Expos had no idea how to use, but who has value to certain teams in certain ballparks. The Expos kept focusing on what he couldn't do, such as situational hitting and poking the ball to right field. The Cubs were smart enough to identify his strengths. Hitting coach Jeff Pentland opened Andrews's stance back up and he went back to hitting like he can. He's a good defensive player at third base, especially at starting the double play. That playing time projection is low because of the injuries that cost him 1997. If he plays regularly in Wrigley, his rate stats might come up a peg, and he could easily smack 30 home runs.

Jeff Blauser IF Bats R Age 34

YEAR	TEAM	LGE	AB	H	DB	TP	HR	BB/SO	R	RBI	SB	CS	OUT	BA	OBP	SLG	EQA	EQR	DEFENSE
1997	Atlanta	NL	528	165	35	4	18	69/100	92	71	4	1	364	.313	.412	.496	.307	95	133-SS 99
1998	ChiCubs	NL	365	83	14	3	4	59/91	51	27	2	2	284	.227	.348	.315	.236	38	100-SS 92
1999	ChiCubs	NL	199	45	5	2	8	24/51	38	23	2	2	156	.226	.336	.392	.249	24	
2000	ChiCubs	NL	205	51	7	1	7	36/48	32	32	1	1	155	.249	.361	.395	.256	26	

Blauser is flogged routinely in Chicago, but at the time signing him was a reasonable risk for a team that needed someone to play up the middle. His ability to get on base in the first half of 1998 has been forgotten, but he's a good player to sign and keep as an offense-oriented part-timer at second base and shortstop. The arm injuries make it unlikely he can handle third base or play regularly, but I like his chances of having a 1985 Toby Harrah-style last hurrah in one of the next few years.

Roosevelt Brown OF Bats L Age 24

YEAR	TEAM	LGE	AB	H	DB	TP	HR	BB/SO	R	RBI	SB	CS	OUT	BA	OBP	SLG	EQA	EQR	DEFENSE
1997	KaneCnty	Mid	215	46	7	1	4	16/54	23	25	2	2	171	.214	.271	.312	.194	14	55-OF 87
1997	Brevard	Fla	116	26	8	1	1	6/34	8	10	0	1	91	.224	.262	.336	.194	8	28-OF 89
1998	Daytona	Fla	243	68	14	3	7	18/52	36	30	1	1	176	.280	.333	.449	.260	30	58-OF 93
1998	WestTenn	Sou	160	38	6	0	7	8/31	15	20	2	1	123	.237	.281	.406	.228	15	33-OF 96
1999	WestTenn	Sou	127	35	7	0	4	11/31	9	11	3	1	93	.276	.340	.425	.260	16	25-OF 107
1999	Iowa	PCL	264	87	21	2	18	16/53	39	63	2	2	179	.330	.373	.629	.315	50	64-OF 96
1999	ChiCubs	NL	64	14	5	1	1	1/14	5	9	1	0	50	.219	.231	.375	.198	4	
2000	ChiCubs	NL	480	143	26	2	24	42/106	76	95	6	2	339	.298	.354	.510	.280	71	

Brown can flat-out hit any kind of pitching, but the Cubs need a center fielder, which is something he can't be between Sammy Sosa and Henry Rodriguez. If they decide to stick him out there just to get him playing time until Patterson comes up, Cub pitchers would have to live with plenty of triples to the gaps. The Cubs can definitely help themselves by trading Rodriguez for the best package they can get and putting Brown in left field for the next five years.

Hee Seop Choi 1B Bats L Age 21

YEAR	TEAM	LGE	AB	H	DB	TP	HR	BB/SO	R	RBI	SB	CS	OUT	BA	OBP	SLG	EQA	EQR	DEFENSE
1999	Lansing	Mid	290	76	14	3	15	37/71	50	47	1	0	214	.262	.348	.486	.277	43	78-1B 81
2000	ChiCubs	NL	154	45	9	1	14	23/84	31	42	0	0	109	.292	.384	.636	.317	31	

Signed out of college on Asia scout Leon Lee's recommendation, Choi is already one of the Cubs' best prospects. He's obviously a hitter and credited with having a great learning curve, but there are some issues. He's sort of flabby and needs to start working out, having taken to fast food. He OD'd on Mountain Dew, drinking so much that he had to be hospitalized for dehydration. He's still on the hook for a three-year military stint that has to start sometime in the next five years. Choi was bumped off of Korea's Asian Games team because Chan Ho Park wanted a veteran team, as the players would be exempted from their service if they made it to the Olympics, which they did.

Pat Cline C Bats R Age 25

YEAR	TEAM	LGE	AB	H	DB	TP	HR	BB/SO	R	RBI	SB	CS	OUT	BA	OBP	SLG	EQA	EQR	DEFENSE
1997	Orlando	Sou	273	64	12	0	8	20/83	29	31	1	1	210	.234	.296	.366	.223	25	
1997	Iowa	AA	97	22	2	0	3	8/25	6	10	0	1	76	.227	.286	.340	.207	7	
1998	Iowa	PCL	421	109	20	2	11	31/59	43	50	2	2	314	.259	.320	.394	.241	45	108-C 87
1999	Iowa	PCL	289	59	15	1	5	22/74	21	33	1	1	231	.204	.268	.315	.194	19	26-C 69
2000	ChiCubs	NL	377	92	20	1	10	34/84	43	47	1	1	286	.244	.307	.382	.227	35	

The man who ran Terry Kennedy out of Iowa. In addition to managing there for the last two years, Kennedy was supposed to turn Cline into a major-league catcher. Although Cline is a good athlete, his footwork and release inspire despair and, after the year, Kennedy said he'd had enough.

Nate Frese   SS   Bats R   Age 22

YEAR	TEAM	LGE	AB	H	DB	TP	HR	BB/SO	R	RBI	SB	CS	OUT	BA	OBP	SLG	EQA	EQR	DEFENSE	
1998	Willmspt	NYP	179	37	5	0	3	11/39	21	15	2	1	143	.207	.257	.285	.178	10	53-SS 103	
1999	Lansing	Mid	375	84	24	2	4	43/70	48	35	4	2	293	.224	.309	.331	.221	34	103-SS 120	
2000	ChiCubs	NL	216	51	13	1	4	27/62	28	25	2	1	166	.236	.321	.361	.229	21		

The 1999 Lansing crop has been touted as the Cubs' saving wave of future prospects. Frese doesn't get as much consideration as the others, but he's a good fielder with college experience (University of Iowa). Unless Jason Smith heals enough to play regularly, there's no one in the organization between Frese and Nieves.

Gary Gaetti   3B   Bats R   Age 41

YEAR	TEAM	LGE	AB	H	DB	TP	HR	BB/SO	R	RBI	SB	CS	OUT	BA	OBP	SLG	EQA	EQR	DEFENSE	
1997	St Louis	NL	508	130	24	1	19	36/87	64	71	6	3	381	.256	.313	.419	.245	57	120-3B 102	11-1B 93
1998	St Louis	NL	309	83	23	1	12	30/38	39	44	1	1	227	.269	.344	.466	.270	43	76-3B 93	
1998	ChiCubs	NL	130	42	11	0	9	11/22	22	28	0	0	88	.323	.399	.615	.324	26	32-3B 112	
1999	ChiCubs	NL	280	55	10	1	8	18/50	20	41	0	1	226	.196	.251	.325	.188	17	65-3B 102	
2000	ChiCubs	NL	292	66	9	0	11	27/47	28	36	1	1	227	.226	.292	.370	.217	25		

Gaetti is the poster boy for last winter's stand-pat philosophy. He really should call it a career, but keeps saying he still wants to play. He's even threatened to go back to the Twins, where he can't do anything that Ron Coomer doesn't do better. It's like Bill Clinton saying he wants to move to your block. You let him down gently to avoid an airstrike, then breathe a sigh of relief once he's out the door.

Jeff Goldbach   C   Bats R   Age 20

YEAR	TEAM	LGE	AB	H	DB	TP	HR	BB/SO	R	RBI	SB	CS	OUT	BA	OBP	SLG	EQA	EQR	DEFENSE
1999	Lansing	Mid	401	90	21	2	15	48/69	59	50	0	2	313	.224	.314	.399	.240	44	82-C 94
2000	ChiCubs	NL	200	52	10	1	12	31/54	33	41	0	1	149	.260	.359	.500	.278	30	

Not that there's much competition, but he's the best catching prospect in the organization. Goldbach is a Midwest League All-Star and the second-best prospect on the Lugnuts behind Patterson. He's still considered raw behind the plate, so you have to hope the organization has learned from Cline's failures to come up with a better way to work on catching instruction.

Mark Grace   1B   Bats L   Age 36

YEAR	TEAM	LGE	AB	H	DB	TP	HR	BB/SO	R	RBI	SB	CS	OUT	BA	OBP	SLG	EQA	EQR	DEFENSE
1997	ChiCubs	NL	557	173	33	5	13	86/45	85	75	1	4	388	.311	.405	.458	.293	90	148-1B 110
1998	ChiCubs	NL	603	191	42	3	18	92/55	94	91	4	8	420	.317	.410	.486	.300	103	156-1B 104
1999	ChiCubs	NL	588	175	42	5	15	75/44	98	82	2	4	417	.298	.379	.463	.283	89	156-1B 98
2000	ChiCubs	NL	498	146	28	2	12	77/40	90	83	3	3	355	.293	.388	.430	.276	71	

So much was made over the fact that last winter was the first time Grace had worked out, which led to lots of wasted speculation that he'd finally pop 20 home runs. He didn't. What's important if you're the Cubs? Chip Caray's blubbering over Grace's 2000th career hit with two outs in the ninth inning of a 5-1 loss? The public debate over what could be done to insure that Grace wound up as the decade's hits leader over Rafael Palmeiro, the man the Cubs should have kept instead of Grace? He's the fifth-best first baseman in a six-team division, and that's only if Kevin Barker doesn't develop. Grace is currently threatening to leave the Cubs after 2000, and because it's the Cubs, they're worried.

Glenallen Hill   DH   Bats R   Age 35

YEAR	TEAM	LGE	AB	H	DB	TP	HR	BB/SO	R	RBI	SB	CS	OUT	BA	OBP	SLG	EQA	EQR	DEFENSE	
1997	San Fran	NL	403	108	29	4	12	18/86	48	65	6	4	299	.268	.306	.449	.249	46	79-OF 93	
1998	Seattle	AL	259	76	20	2	12	13/44	36	32	1	1	184	.293	.335	.525	.279	38	60-OF 88	
1998	ChiCubs	NL	133	47	4	0	9	14/33	26	24	0	0	86	.353	.415	.586	.326	26	27-OF 101	
1999	ChiCubs	NL	252	74	8	1	19	18/60	39	50	4	1	179	.294	.341	.560	.291	41	27-LF 88	22-RF 81
2000	ChiCubs	NL	344	96	17	1	17	29/76	50	62	4	1	249	.279	.335	.483	.266	46		

There's plenty of talk about what he would do if only he was allowed to play full-time or DH every day, but that's wasted breath. Every time he got a regular opportunity to play, he didn't hit well enough to let teams turn a blind eye to his awful glove-work. What he's done with the Cubs over the last year and a half is what you get when he's used in the spots that best suit him: to mash left-handers or pinch-hit or take advantage of warm days in Wrigley. Play him more often, and he'll only struggle against the better right-handers in the league. He re-signed with the Cubs, saying he liked the direction the club was heading. Seventh?

Eric Hinske   3B/1B   Bats L   Age 22

YEAR	TEAM	LGE	AB	H	DB	TP	HR	BB/SO	R	RBI	SB	CS	OUT	BA	OBP	SLG	EQA	EQR	DEFENSE	
1998	Willmspt	NYP	257	66	11	0	10	27/63	30	44	7	2	193	.257	.330	.416	.255	32	69-1B 117	
1999	Daytona	Fla	450	117	24	4	19	52/99	60	63	8	5	338	.260	.340	.458	.266	62	58-3B 96	56-1B 115
2000	*ChiCubs*	*NL*	*340*	*103*	*18*	*2*	*20*	*45/90*	*67*	*75*	*8*	*2*	*239*	*.303*	*.384*	*.544*	*.301*	*59*		

After starring at Arkansas in 1998, Hinske was a good example of a college player who didn't need to start off at Lansing. While the initial expectation was that he wouldn't stick at third base, the Cubs are willing to see if he can cut it there while also having him play both outfield corners. Showing power in the Florida State League is extremely difficult, yet Hinske showed enough to be an All-Star in his first full pro season. If he survives the jump to Double-A, he could be in Chicago by September.

Robin Jennings   OF   Bats L   Age 28

YEAR	TEAM	LGE	AB	H	DB	TP	HR	BB/SO	R	RBI	SB	CS	OUT	BA	OBP	SLG	EQA	EQR	DEFENSE
1997	Iowa	AA	473	117	25	4	15	47/82	57	59	4	2	358	.247	.322	.412	.248	55	118-OF 90
1998	Iowa	PCL	298	63	21	1	11	26/54	42	45	3	3	238	.211	.284	.399	.227	29	71-OF 92
1999	Iowa	PCL	256	66	14	4	6	20/37	33	30	4	3	193	.258	.313	.414	.243	28	61-OF 101
2000	*Minnesot*	*AL*	*292*	*74*	*16*	*1*	*11*	*28/47*	*42*	*44*	*4*	*1*	*219*	*.253*	*.319*	*.428*	*.249*	*34*	

A jammed thumb cost him his shot at winning the fifth outfielder's job in camp. Because of that, Curtis Goodwin was picked up on waivers, and once Lance Johnson went on the disabled list in June, the Cubs made the mistake of playing Goodwin and forgetting that Jennings was the better player. Signed with the Twins in a rare reverse commute from the Cubs, he has no shot at a career.

Lance Johnson   CF   Bats L   Age 36

YEAR	TEAM	LGE	AB	H	DB	TP	HR	BB/SO	R	RBI	SB	CS	OUT	BA	OBP	SLG	EQA	EQR	DEFENSE
1997	NY Mets	NL	269	83	11	6	1	33/21	41	24	12	10	196	.309	.384	.405	.268	37	55-OF 116
1997	ChiCubs	NL	145	43	6	2	4	9/10	16	14	4	2	104	.297	.338	.448	.263	18	29-OF 108
1998	ChiCubs	NL	307	87	10	4	2	26/21	52	21	10	7	227	.283	.339	.362	.240	32	69-OF 99
1999	ChiCubs	NL	334	84	10	6	1	32/20	41	19	11	3	253	.251	.317	.326	.226	31	81-CF 107
2000	*ChiCubs*	*NL*	*296*	*81*	*9*	*3*	*1*	*36/19*	*45*	*31*	*9*	*4*	*219*	*.274*	*.352*	*.334*	*.238*	*30*	

Johnson spent the summer fighting Riggleman, Lynch and rumors floated by the team that his strained abdomen wasn't really hurting. In the last few years, the Cubs have dumped anyone who is both black and outspoken about the team's problems (Brian McRae, Shawon Dunston, Curtis Goodwin). Whether it's coincidence or a real problem, it should be over now that Baylor is aboard. That's still too late for Johnson, who was released in November and looks done.

Dave Kelton   3B   Bats R   Age 20

YEAR	TEAM	LGE	AB	H	DB	TP	HR	BB/SO	R	RBI	SB	CS	OUT	BA	OBP	SLG	EQA	EQR	DEFENSE
1999	Lansing	Mid	509	118	16	2	12	25/127	52	50	9	4	395	.232	.269	.342	.205	37	113-3B 73
2000	*ChiCubs*	*NL*	*251*	*62*	*6*	*0*	*8*	*14/82*	*24*	*29*	*4*	*1*	*190*	*.247*	*.287*	*.367*	*.215*	*20*	

He's already touted as the organization's top third-base prospect after slipping to the second round of the 1998 draft because of a dislocated shoulder. His hitting numbers suffered after he wore down in the second half. Kelton will have to improve his command of the strike zone, and he needs to work on his defense after moving over from his high-school position of shortstop. He is at least two years away from being ready.

Cole Liniak   3B   Bats R   Age 23

YEAR	TEAM	LGE	AB	H	DB	TP	HR	BB/SO	R	RBI	SB	CS	OUT	BA	OBP	SLG	EQA	EQR	DEFENSE
1997	Sarasota	Fla	220	65	12	0	7	18/34	27	36	0	1	156	.295	.355	.445	.268	29	58-3B 100
1997	Trenton	Eas	203	54	7	0	3	12/30	16	16	0	1	150	.266	.309	.345	.220	17	45-3B 100
1998	Pawtuckt	Int	429	104	25	1	16	31/72	55	51	3	3	328	.242	.300	.417	.238	45	107-3B 90
1999	Pawtuckt	Int	346	84	17	0	12	34/57	45	35	0	4	266	.243	.312	.396	.235	36	92-3B 98
1999	ChiCubs	NL	29	7	1	0	0	1/4	2	2	0	1	23	.241	.267	.276	.163	1	
2000	*ChiCubs*	*NL*	*428*	*122*	*17*	*0*	*19*	*38/71*	*58*	*75*	*2*	*3*	*309*	*.285*	*.343*	*.458*	*.261*	*54*	

(Cole Liniak *continued*)

By season's end, the Cubs were casting about for anybody who could play third base. They picked up Liniak from the Red Sox in the Rod Beck deal, not knowing that a week later the Expos would be fed up with Andrews. He's now hosed but is still useful, a steady defender who hasn't hit for the power some expected. He has a lot of Triple-A experience for his age and is young enough to improve.

Sandy Martinez — C — Bats L — Age 27

YEAR	TEAM	LGE	AB	H	DB	TP	HR	BB/SO	R	RBI	SB	CS	OUT	BA	OBP	SLG	EQA	EQR	DEFENSE
1997	Syracuse	Int	326	72	10	1	4	21/76	24	27	5	2	256	.221	.278	.294	.194	21	
1998	ChiCubs	NL	88	24	10	1	0	13/20	7	7	1	0	64	.273	.373	.409	.272	12	20-C 95
1999	ChiCubs	NL	30	5	0	0	1	0/11	1	1	0	0	25	.167	.167	.267	.097	0	
1999	Iowa	PCL	124	25	4	0	2	4/31	6	15	1	0	99	.202	.227	.282	.158	5	31-C 97
2000	Florida	NL	157	34	3	0	4	12/40	14	14	4	0	123	.217	.272	.312	.205	12	

Useless. The Cubs were convinced he'd be claimed if waived and kept him as a third catcher because they were messing around with Tyler Houston at third base. When they finally did send him down after picking up Reed, they were shocked to discover that everyone else knows he can't play.

Tydus Meadows — OF — Bats R — Age 22

YEAR	TEAM	LGE	AB	H	DB	TP	HR	BB/SO	R	RBI	SB	CS	OUT	BA	OBP	SLG	EQA	EQR	DEFENSE
1998	Rockford	Mid	138	37	3	0	7	12/33	27	20	2	1	102	.268	.337	.442	.262	18	29-OF 100
1999	Lansing	Mid	449	112	25	3	15	49/89	54	51	7	5	342	.249	.332	.419	.253	55	120-OF 84
2000	ChiCubs	NL	279	80	15	1	16	39/69	52	58	5	2	201	.287	.374	.520	.290	46	

He was named the Midwest League's best hitting prospect over Patterson, which is silly. He didn't really have any business spending a full year at the level. He'd already hit well in the Southeastern Conference and the Midwest League in 1998, and Daytona didn't have a single outfield prospect. But Daytona was a bad team not going anywhere while Lansing had a shot at the playoffs, and the organization needed something to brag about.

Chad Meyers — 2B/OF — Bats R — Age 24

YEAR	TEAM	LGE	AB	H	DB	TP	HR	BB/SO	R	RBI	SB	CS	OUT	BA	OBP	SLG	EQA	EQR	DEFENSE	
1997	Rockford	Mid	449	120	27	3	4	58/75	60	46	23	8	337	.267	.361	.367	.258	57	97-2B 90	18-OF 90
1998	Daytona	Fla	187	48	8	3	2	26/33	24	18	8	3	142	.257	.358	.364	.255	23	45-2B 86	
1998	WestTenn	Sou	292	73	9	0	1	45/44	43	21	22	6	225	.250	.356	.291	.242	32	72-2B 87	
1999	WestTenn	Sou	241	65	16	2	3	20/42	34	24	12	5	181	.270	.343	.390	.254	29	60-2B 97	
1999	Iowa	PCL	173	55	11	2	0	25/20	30	13	12	5	123	.318	.411	.405	.287	27	38-2B 89	
1999	ChiCubs	NL	142	32	9	0	0	7/27	15	5	3	2	112	.225	.278	.289	.191	9	28-2B 93	
2000	ChiCubs	NL	537	149	31	3	4	72/87	104	59	35	11	399	.277	.363	.369	.255	66		

He was a college outfielder at Creighton who hasn't turned into a good second baseman. I'd leave him at second base for another year. If he can adjust, he's what this lineup needs; if he can't, the Cubs still have Eric Young lying around. Meyers is sort of a faster version of Jody Reed at the plate in that he won't hit home runs, but he'll still give you 40 or 50 extra-base hits. In addition to his willingness to take a free pass, he was plunked by 16 pitches last year, so Baylor should love him.

Mickey Morandini — 2B — Bats L — Age 34

YEAR	TEAM	LGE	AB	H	DB	TP	HR	BB/SO	R	RBI	SB	CS	OUT	BA	OBP	SLG	EQA	EQR	DEFENSE
1997	Philadel	NL	561	167	42	2	1	62/90	81	39	12	13	407	.298	.376	.385	.261	71	139-2B 95
1998	ChiCubs	NL	589	179	20	4	9	71/82	95	54	14	1	411	.304	.388	.397	.277	83	144-2B 103
1999	ChiCubs	NL	455	105	16	5	4	42/60	54	34	5	6	356	.231	.305	.314	.211	37	112-2B 101
2000	ChiCubs	NL	419	112	19	2	4	56/59	63	49	6	4	311	.267	.354	.351	.241	44	

He was a victim of the front office's tin ears almost as much as his own lousy year. He fired on Lynch after Ben Christensen was drafted; shortly thereafter, Meyers was called up and handed Morandini's job. He kvetched about how he deserved to play, but after watching him duke it out with Marlon Anderson for "league's worst second baseman" for four months, you can forgive the Cubs for not wanting to wait and see who'd win. His problem is his salary expectation: he's never been much better than a half-dozen guys you can dig up and pay the minimum for in any given year. He's the most recent winner of the Jody Reed Negotiation Boner award, for rejecting a multi-year deal last spring. He'll never be offered one again.

Jose Nieves   SS   Bats R   Age 25

YEAR	TEAM	LGE	AB	H	DB	TP	HR	BB/SO	R	RBI	SB	CS	OUT	BA	OBP	SLG	EQA	EQR	DEFENSE
1997	Daytona	Fla	331	79	18	1	4	13/62	38	34	6	2	255	.239	.274	.335	.204	24	64-SS 93
1998	WestTenn	Sou	314	80	24	3	7	8/59	30	28	9	5	239	.255	.275	.417	.228	30	79-SS 89
1998	Iowa	PCL	75	18	4	0	0	1/11	6	4	1	1	58	.240	.250	.293	.172	4	
1999	Iowa	PCL	389	92	22	3	8	19/66	42	46	8	5	303	.237	.278	.370	.216	33	100-SS 90
1999	ChiCubs	NL	181	43	8	1	2	6/25	15	16	0	2	140	.238	.279	.326	.198	12	51-SS 109
2000	*ChiCubs*	*NL*	*478*	*124*	*28*	*2*	*11*	*28/81*	*56*	*58*	*10*	*5*	*359*	*.259*	*.300*	*.395*	*.229*	*45*	

He's probably not one of the 20 best shortstop prospects who were in the minor leagues in 1999, but he's the guy the Cubs have, so he'll get a shot. He has good range to his left, the strong arm to make the play in the hole and can spray pitches all over the park. If it's my choice, I go shopping for somebody else. The Cubs concurred, picking up Ricky Gutierrez for two years.

Corey Patterson   CF   Bats L   Age 20

YEAR	TEAM	LGE	AB	H	DB	TP	HR	BB/SO	R	RBI	SB	CS	OUT	BA	OBP	SLG	EQA	EQR	DEFENSE
1999	Lansing	Mid	472	126	30	9	18	13/89	61	54	13	4	350	.267	.291	.483	.254	57	102-OF 103
2000	*ChiCubs*	*NL*	*269*	*90*	*19*	*4*	*21*	*10/76*	*55*	*68*	*15*	*3*	*182*	*.335*	*.358*	*.669*	*.319*	*52*	

In the deeply incisive words of Tom Paciorek, "He's good." Already an excellent center fielder, in his first year with a wooden bat he led the Midwest League in extra-base hits, triples and slugging average, easily winning the league's top prospect awards. The organization loves his attitude, and he busted up the Arizona Fall League. Even a good camp probably won't win him the job in center field, but my guess is that he'll be ready by June. Patterson has been called Kenny Lofton with power, but he isn't as patient as Lofton was. A better comparison might be a faster Griffey, but there's a chance that there really is nobody to compare him to.

Bo Porter   OF   Bats R   Age 27

YEAR	TEAM	LGE	AB	H	DB	TP	HR	BB/SO	R	RBI	SB	CS	OUT	BA	OBP	SLG	EQA	EQR	DEFENSE
1997	Daytona	Fla	445	99	16	3	12	44/147	55	41	7	4	350	.222	.295	.353	.221	40	118-OF 96
1998	WestTenn	Sou	464	107	21	7	7	56/137	54	44	22	9	366	.231	.319	.351	.235	49	126-OF 98
1999	Iowa	PCL	412	97	19	1	18	53/131	59	43	10	10	325	.235	.331	.417	.250	51	107-OF 102
2000	*Oakland*	*AL*	*381*	*84*	*16*	*2*	*9*	*55/122*	*55*	*42*	*11*	*8*	*305*	*.220*	*.319*	*.344*	*.230*	*39*	

How can you not like a 40th-round pick who played defensive back for Iowa? He can get on base and hit for a little power. Porter is too old to need any more seasoning, so it's now or never. The A's snagged him in the Rule 5 draft, and he should be their fifth outfielder.

Jaisen Randolph   OF   Bats R   Age 21

YEAR	TEAM	LGE	AB	H	DB	TP	HR	BB/SO	R	RBI	SB	CS	OUT	BA	OBP	SLG	EQA	EQR	DEFENSE
1998	Rockford	Mid	502	132	21	7	1	31/116	58	27	12	10	379	.263	.310	.339	.220	43	122-OF 98
1999	Daytona	Fla	514	125	18	4	2	36/94	55	30	13	12	401	.243	.299	.305	.205	38	131-OF 101
2000	*ChiCubs*	*NL*	*370*	*98*	*14*	*3*	*1*	*28/82*	*45*	*34*	*11*	*6*	*278*	*.265*	*.317*	*.327*	*.217*	*30*	

Called a leadoff prospect by some, but he doesn't get on base that well, and if he was a good base thief he'd do better than get caught 24 times in 49 attempts. Although young enough to improve, he'll need a Korean press gang to accidentally kidnap Patterson to fulfill Choi's military service to even deserve consideration for Double-A this year.

Jeff Reed   C   Bats L   Age 37

YEAR	TEAM	LGE	AB	H	DB	TP	HR	BB/SO	R	RBI	SB	CS	OUT	BA	OBP	SLG	EQA	EQR	DEFENSE
1997	Colorado	NL	254	71	10	0	16	34/54	40	43	1	1	184	.280	.369	.508	.289	41	
1998	Colorado	NL	253	66	16	1	8	36/55	39	34	0	0	187	.261	.355	.427	.266	34	71-C 102
1999	Colorado	NL	103	22	3	0	2	15/24	9	9	0	1	82	.214	.320	.301	.215	9	26-C 91
1999	ChiCubs	NL	149	37	10	2	1	26/34	17	15	1	1	113	.248	.368	.362	.257	19	42-C 96
2000	*ChiCubs*	*NL*	*165*	*40*	*5*	*0*	*5*	*28/37*	*24*	*23*	*0*	*0*	*125*	*.242*	*.352*	*.364*	*.245*	*19*	

Reed is another ex-Twin who got to be a graying MacPhail Cubbie, and he's the inspiration for Jim Riggleman's pathetic July 8 statement that the Cubs hadn't given up on the year because they'd just gotten this good-hittin' catcher off waivers. The man has 57 career home runs in almost 3,300 plate appearances, with 22 of those hit in a little more than 500 PAs with the Rockies from 1996-98. While he's a nice caddy, he's not going to turn an offense around.

Henry Rodriguez   LF   Bats L   Age 32

YEAR	TEAM	LGE	AB	H	DB	TP	HR	BB/SO	R	RBI	SB	CS	OUT	BA	OBP	SLG	EQA	EQR	DEFENSE
1997	Montreal	NL	479	116	29	2	27	41/147	54	82	2	3	366	.242	.305	.480	.256	60	109-OF 94
1998	ChiCubs	NL	419	107	22	1	33	54/110	57	87	1	3	315	.255	.340	.549	.285	68	96-OF 101
1999	ChiCubs	NL	444	130	24	0	26	50/112	65	80	1	4	318	.293	.364	.523	.288	71	111-LF 94
2000	ChiCubs	NL	398	106	15	0	27	58/105	65	84	1	1	293	.266	.360	.508	.281	61	

A conveniently timed back injury in September ended his year two weeks early, protecting his first-ever .300 batting average. The Cubs already have Henry and Shane Andrews, and they're looking to add Chris Widger. I wouldn't have thought rebuilding the 1997 Expos was high on anyone's list of priorities, but it's a better plan than collecting ex-Twins.

Benito Santiago   C   Bats R   Age 35

YEAR	TEAM	LGE	AB	H	DB	TP	HR	BB/SO	R	RBI	SB	CS	OUT	BA	OBP	SLG	EQA	EQR	DEFENSE
1996	Philadel	NL	489	132	24	2	31	48/103	73	85	2	0	357	.270	.337	.517	.279	74	
1997	Toronto	AL	342	86	9	0	14	15/77	31	42	1	0	256	.251	.288	.401	.229	32	
1999	ChiCubs	NL	349	84	18	3	6	28/70	26	32	1	1	266	.241	.301	.361	.224	32	95-C 104
2000	ChiCubs	NL	202	47	10	1	4	19/59	21	22	0	0	155	.233	.299	.351	.215	17	

While you might think he's milked a great 1996 for about all it's worth, keep in mind how long Rick Cerone hung around after his good 1980: twelve years. Hell, Mike Matheny hasn't had a good year since Little League, and he's still employed. Santiago still has good catching skills, but his days as a useful everyday player are long gone.

Tony Schrager   2B   Bats R   Age 23

YEAR	TEAM	LGE	AB	H	DB	TP	HR	BB/SO	R	RBI	SB	CS	OUT	BA	OBP	SLG	EQA	EQR	DEFENSE
1998	Rockford	Mid	175	39	10	1	6	36/33	31	16	1	1	137	.223	.361	.394	.262	24	48-2B 81
1999	Lansing	Mid	396	84	22	2	13	79/109	56	48	3	1	313	.212	.347	.376	.253	50	119-2B 99
2000	ChiCubs	NL	197	45	9	1	9	47/57	38	34	1	0	152	.228	.377	.421	.272	29	

Even more than Meadows, Schrager had little business spending the whole year at Lansing. He played second base for perennial college powerhouse Stanford, and after being drafted in 1998 had already demonstrated his core skills—patience and power—in the Midwest League. Daytona's second baseman, Dennis Abreu, looks like a washout. While I wouldn't exactly call Schrager a prospect, there's nobody of value between him and Meyers, and he's the kind of guy who could help for a year or two, making Young expendable.

Sammy Sosa   RF/CF   Bats R   Age 31

YEAR	TEAM	LGE	AB	H	DB	TP	HR	BB/SO	R	RBI	SB	CS	OUT	BA	OBP	SLG	EQA	EQR	DEFENSE	
1997	ChiCubs	NL	643	156	31	4	36	44/172	85	114	17	12	499	.243	.293	.471	.249	77	159-OF 98	
1998	ChiCubs	NL	651	203	24	0	68	72/166	137	159	19	10	458	.312	.381	.662	.324	137	156-OF 98	
1999	ChiCubs	NL	621	172	23	2	59	70/169	103	127	5	8	457	.277	.353	.605	.300	113	138-RF 101	22-CF 120
2000	ChiCubs	NL	552	162	17	1	54	72/147	102	148	8	5	395	.293	.375	.621	.310	106		

No Sammy issue is too small for Sammyvision. Sick wife? A city wails, wondering if their hero has a heart of stone for not rushing to her bedside. See Sammy talk. See Sammy breathe. Hear that Sammy will meet Bubba, build a new home or buy Robin Leach to do voice-overs on all Sammy advertising. Up next, the burgeoning controversy over whether Sammy will get to play his music in the clubhouse! The local media is desperately short of Michael Jordan footage these days, so all things Sammy get to be stories.

Scott Vieira   OF/1B   Bats R   Age 26

YEAR	TEAM	LGE	AB	H	DB	TP	HR	BB/SO	R	RBI	SB	CS	OUT	BA	OBP	SLG	EQA	EQR	DEFENSE	
1996	Rockford	Mid	454	123	24	2	8	64/101	59	59	4	3	334	.271	.380	.385	.267	62	118-1B 96	
1997	Daytona	Fla	482	104	20	2	14	54/150	60	56	3	2	380	.216	.310	.353	.228	47	125-1B 89	
1999	WestTenn	Sou	462	114	37	3	7	37/147	46	42	4	3	351	.247	.313	.385	.236	48	97-OF 86	24-1B 92
2000	ChiCubs	NL	244	56	14	1	5	30/91	30	28	2	1	189	.230	.314	.357	.225	23		

Borderline prospect drafted off of the Tennessee team that got wiped out by the Mark Kotsay steamroller (aka Cal State Fullerton) back in 1995. He lost 1998 to a dislocated thumb and now has a marginal opportunity to show up as a pinch-hitter and spare part, if only to give the Cubs a chance to say they've got somebody in the bushes.

Ron Walker   3B   Bats R   Age 24

YEAR	TEAM	LGE	AB	H	DB	TP	HR	BB/SO	R	RBI	SB	CS	OUT	BA	OBP	SLG	EQA	EQR	DEFENSE
1997	Willmspt	NYP	193	53	9	0	8	13/55	22	27	0	0	140	.275	.329	.446	.259	24	42-3B 87
1998	Daytona	Fla	359	84	14	1	19	36/91	41	54	2	1	276	.234	.312	.437	.250	43	71-3B 80
1999	WestTenn	Sou	308	64	17	1	9	30/91	35	36	1	0	244	.208	.289	.357	.219	27	50-3B 91
2000	ChiCubs	NL	322	80	14	0	16	41/91	45	54	1	0	242	.248	.333	.441	.256	40	

Is extra instruction always a good thing, or does it end up being a distraction? A decent power prospect, Walker needed work on his defense and on his command of the strike zone. So the Cubs sent Richie Zisk to work on his hitting and Sandy Alomar Sr. to work on his defense, and he didn't do anything right. With Liniak now at Iowa, Walker will repeat Triple-A.

Julio Zuleta   1B   Bats R   Age 25

YEAR	TEAM	LGE	AB	H	DB	TP	HR	BB/SO	R	RBI	SB	CS	OUT	BA	OBP	SLG	EQA	EQR	DEFENSE
1997	Rockford	Mid	436	107	28	4	5	24/95	45	57	2	2	331	.245	.299	.362	.223	39	103-1B 101
1998	Daytona	Fla	364	95	17	1	12	26/72	46	56	2	1	270	.261	.327	.412	.250	42	76-1B 105
1998	WestTenn	Sou	139	37	4	0	3	5/32	13	16	0	1	103	.266	.303	.360	.221	12	26-1B 103
1999	WestTenn	Sou	487	125	33	3	16	23/138	58	72	2	1	363	.257	.308	.435	.247	55	115-1B 92
2000	ChiCubs	NL	482	127	30	2	15	33/123	59	69	2	1	356	.263	.311	.427	.241	51	

He's currently being mistaken for a good prospect. Zuleta played for Panama in the Pan Am Games, was a Southern League All-Star and has a good defensive reputation. While he doesn't have nearly good enough command of the strike zone, he did let himself get hit by 20 pitches. Don Baylor likes that sort of thing.

PITCHERS (Averages: ERA: 4.50 / H/9: 9.00 / HR/9: 1.00 / BB/9: 3.50 / K/9: 6.50 / KWH: 1.00)

Terry Adams   Throws R   Age 27

YEAR	TEAM	LGE	IP	H	ER	HR	BB	K	ERA	W	L	H/9	HR/9	BB/9	K/9	KWH	PERA
1997	ChiCubs	NL	76.0	91	41	3	43	61	4.86	4	4	10.78	0.36	5.09	7.22	0.71	5.45
1998	ChiCubs	NL	73.3	73	39	7	44	70	4.79	4	4	8.96	0.86	5.40	8.59	1.14	5.03
1999	ChiCubs	NL	66.3	58	29	8	27	55	3.93	4	3	7.87	1.09	3.66	7.46	1.44	4.07

This year's health problems? He started off on the disabled list with a strained elbow, went back on it a few months later with a strained groin and finished up scuffling down the stretch. Throwing more than 100 innings in his rookie season and making 143 appearances in his first two years probably didn't help him stay healthy. We're still researching usage patterns for relievers and hope to have some findings in the next year or two. Adams was traded to the Dodgers in the Ismael Valdes deal and will help Alan Mills set up Jeff Shaw.

Rick Aguilera   Throws R   Age 38

YEAR	TEAM	LGE	IP	H	ER	HR	BB	K	ERA	W	L	H/9	HR/9	BB/9	K/9	KWH	PERA
1997	Minnesot	AL	69.0	63	26	8	22	69	3.39	5	3	8.22	1.04	2.87	9.00	2.57	3.91
1998	Minnesot	AL	75.0	73	31	7	15	58	3.72	5	3	8.76	0.84	1.80	6.96	2.30	3.60
1999	Minnesot	AL	21.3	9	3	2	2	13	1.27	2	0	3.80	0.84	0.84	5.48	7.02	1.27
1999	ChiCubs	NL	47.0	42	19	6	9	31	3.64	3	2	8.04	1.15	1.72	5.94	1.90	3.45

Aguilera struggled after coming over to the Cubs, which they claimed was because he was sad about being traded. Others said his forkball looked like it was being served on a plate. He settled down as the season went on, although he missed August with a strained calf.

Bobby Ayala   Throws R   Age 30

YEAR	TEAM	LGE	IP	H	ER	HR	BB	K	ERA	W	L	H/9	HR/9	BB/9	K/9	KWH	PERA
1997	Seattle	AL	99.3	84	38	13	41	93	3.44	7	4	7.61	1.18	3.71	8.43	1.88	3.99
1998	Seattle	AL	77.0	95	58	8	27	69	6.78	3	6	11.10	0.94	3.16	8.06	1.39	5.49
1999	Montreal	NL	67.3	57	30	5	33	62	4.01	4	3	7.62	0.67	4.41	8.29	1.53	3.74
1999	ChiCubs	NL	16.0	11	6	4	5	15	3.38	1	1	6.19	2.25	2.81	8.44	3.06	3.94

(Bobby Ayala *continued*)

It will be interesting to see who picks up Ayala. Freed from bullpen hell pitching for Lou Piniella, he had a superficially successful season, as if he were another of Felipe Alou's famed rehab jobs. Unfortunately, he was one of the league's worst pitchers when it came to allowing inherited runners to score. He obviously has value in middle relief, but his next manager will have to pick his spots.

Micah Bowie   Throws L   Age 25

YEAR	TEAM	LGE	IP	H	ER	HR	BB	K	ERA	W	L	H/9	HR/9	BB/9	K/9	KWH	PERA
1997	Durham	Car	37.3	36	18	2	31	32	4.34	2	2	8.68	0.48	7.47	7.71	0.69	5.30
1997	Greenvil	Sou	43.0	36	19	3	29	34	3.98	3	2	7.53	0.63	6.07	7.12	0.83	4.40
1998	Greenvil	Sou	157.7	147	74	13	64	129	4.22	10	8	8.39	0.74	3.65	7.36	1.32	3.94
1999	Richmond	Int	71.3	68	23	4	15	72	2.90	6	2	8.58	0.50	1.89	9.08	3.80	3.15
1999	ChiCubs	NL	48.7	71	48	7	29	38	8.88	1	4	13.13	1.29	5.36	7.03	0.52	8.14

The Cubs oversold what he could do because they expected too much, but he was not the key player in the Hernandez trade with the Braves. Bowie rattled off four quality starts in his first six at Richmond before suffering a strained elbow that hampered him for the rest of the year. He's had problems with the elbow before, so it's an issue. There are plenty of left-handed pitchers who throw in the high 80s with a nice change-up. Bowie's key pitch is his curve: if he's healthy, it's supposed to cut instead of tumble. He'll have to fight to win the fifth spot in the rotation.

Scott Downs   Throws L   Age 24

YEAR	TEAM	LGE	IP	H	ER	HR	BB	K	ERA	W	L	H/9	HR/9	BB/9	K/9	KWH	PERA
1997	Willmspt	NYP	21.0	21	16	0	11	17	6.86	1	1	9.00	0.00	4.71	7.29	0.93	3.86
1997	Rockford	Mid	35.0	21	5	2	9	30	1.29	4	0	5.40	0.51	2.31	7.71	3.56	1.80
1998	Daytona	Fla	156.0	203	89	14	73	89	5.13	7	10	11.71	0.81	4.21	5.13	0.40	6.17
1999	New Brit	Eas	18.3	38	22	5	11	18	10.80	0	2	18.65	2.45	5.40	8.84	0.58	13.75
1999	Daytona	Fla	44.7	51	15	3	15	31	3.02	3	2	10.28	0.60	3.02	6.25	0.94	4.63
1999	WestTenn	Sou	75.7	67	16	3	31	81	1.90	7	1	7.97	0.36	3.69	9.63	2.36	3.45

The Cubs obviously regretted giving him up in the 1998 deal for Mike Morgan and got him back in the Aguilera trade. He's mastered his sinker and mixes in a good curve and a nice change-up. He isn't really a power pitcher as much as a groundball artist. His chances of turning into a good major-league starter are better than Bowie's or McNichol's.

Kyle Farnsworth   Throws R   Age 24

YEAR	TEAM	LGE	IP	H	ER	HR	BB	K	ERA	W	L	H/9	HR/9	BB/9	K/9	KWH	PERA
1997	Daytona	Fla	154.3	203	99	17	63	84	5.77	6	11	11.84	0.99	3.67	4.90	0.41	6.24
1998	WestTenn	Sou	79.0	76	32	7	20	60	3.65	5	4	8.66	0.80	2.28	6.84	1.77	3.65
1998	Iowa	PCL	98.0	135	88	17	40	67	8.08	3	8	12.40	1.56	3.67	6.15	0.62	7.26
1999	Iowa	PCL	37.0	41	17	5	10	24	4.14	2	2	9.97	1.22	2.43	5.84	1.05	4.86
1999	ChiCubs	NL	132.3	136	71	25	50	68	4.83	7	8	9.25	1.70	3.40	4.62	0.51	5.37

A big guy who can get his fastball up into the mid-90s, Farnsworth was called up after Jon Lieber got hurt in a freak batting-practice accident. He struggled with his breaking stuff, putting up only three quality starts in his first 15, but a stint in the pen and a couple of demotions were enough to inspire improved command of a sharp slider and a good splitter. He was rushed and will have to continue to improve to hold a rotation spot, but he's a prospect.

Jeremi Gonzalez   Throws R   Age 25

YEAR	TEAM	LGE	IP	H	ER	HR	BB	K	ERA	W	L	H/9	HR/9	BB/9	K/9	KWH	PERA
1997	Iowa	AmA	59.3	55	32	8	23	52	4.85	3	4	8.34	1.21	3.49	7.89	1.60	4.40
1997	ChiCubs	NL	146.3	124	69	16	73	87	4.24	8	8	7.63	0.98	4.49	5.35	0.62	4.12
1998	ChiCubs	NL	110.7	127	72	13	44	67	5.86	4	8	10.33	1.06	3.58	5.45	0.60	5.37

Here as a cautionary tale for people wondering about Kerry Wood, because the same men making decisions on Gonzalez's fitness to pitch will be making those decisions about Wood in the spring. Like Wood, Gonzalez was a talented young pitcher who had an elbow problem that shut him down in 1998. Although some doctors recommended that Gonzalez have a full Tommy John ligament transplant, the Cubs opted for just realigning the ulnar nerve so that he could pitch in 1999. After 25 rehab innings, Gonzalez complained that his elbow hurt. The Cubs responded by publicly accusing him of being a whiner before finally letting him have reconstructive surgery. He might pitch an inning or two in September, but he's more likely gone until 2001.

Mark Guthrie   Throws L   Age 34

YEAR	TEAM	LGE	IP	H	ER	HR	BB	K	ERA	W	L	H/9	HR/9	BB/9	K/9	KWH	PERA
1997	LosAngls	NL	66.7	77	47	12	31	39	6.35	2	5	10.40	1.62	4.19	5.27	0.48	6.34
1998	LosAngls	NL	53.0	58	27	3	26	43	4.58	3	3	9.85	0.51	4.42	7.30	0.92	4.75
1999	Boston	AL	47.7	46	26	8	19	37	4.91	2	3	8.69	1.51	3.59	6.99	1.17	4.91
1999	ChiCubs	NL	12.3	7	5	1	4	9	3.65	1	0	5.11	0.73	2.92	6.57	2.16	2.19

Andy MacPhail collects ex-Twins like they were Pokémon cards, except there won't be a rush on ex-Twins at Christmas. Guthrie isn't your typical left-handed reliever, because he doesn't own left-handed hitters. He's a useful second left-hander and middle man on a team that has someone else to bust Sean Casey or Jeromy Burnitz inside.

Felix Heredia   Throws L   Age 24

YEAR	TEAM	LGE	IP	H	ER	HR	BB	K	ERA	W	L	H/9	HR/9	BB/9	K/9	KWH	PERA
1997	Florida	NL	56.3	54	30	3	31	50	4.79	3	3	8.63	0.48	4.95	7.99	1.12	4.31
1998	Florida	NL	41.0	39	30	1	34	36	6.59	2	3	8.56	0.22	7.46	7.90	0.73	5.05
1998	ChiCubs	NL	18.0	19	9	1	7	15	4.50	1	1	9.50	0.50	3.50	7.50	1.26	4.50
1999	ChiCubs	NL	53.0	54	31	6	25	49	5.26	3	3	9.17	1.02	4.25	8.32	1.33	4.92

Heredia has a great fastball, but it's extremely difficult for a young pitcher to stay sharp throwing fewer than 60 innings a year, especially when they're spread over 70 appearances. Riggleman was so busy trying to turn Heredia into Rick Honeycutt that he blew the opportunity to find out if Heredia could be more than that.

Matt Karchner   Throws R   Age 33

YEAR	TEAM	LGE	IP	H	ER	HR	BB	K	ERA	W	L	H/9	HR/9	BB/9	K/9	KWH	PERA
1997	Nashvill	AmA	18.3	13	5	1	7	9	2.45	2	0	6.38	0.49	3.44	4.42	0.67	2.45
1997	ChiSox	AL	53.3	47	16	4	27	30	2.70	4	2	7.93	0.68	4.56	5.06	0.53	4.05
1998	ChiSox	AL	36.7	32	19	2	20	30	4.66	2	2	7.85	0.49	4.91	7.36	1.05	3.93
1998	ChiCubs	NL	28.0	31	18	6	15	21	5.79	1	2	9.96	1.93	4.82	6.75	0.71	6.75
1999	ChiCubs	NL	18.3	15	4	3	9	9	1.96	2	0	7.36	1.47	4.42	4.42	0.45	4.42

That whiny sound you hear is Andy MacPhail telling people—over their laughter—that he got a major-league pitcher for Jon Garland. That's proof positive of good player development, if not enough sense to avoid drowning in the tub. Karchner's persistent groin problems aren't going away, and it isn't like the Cubs are the Yankees and can afford to wait around for him as the Yankees do with Jeff Nelson. It's time to cut bait and admit they screwed up.

Ray King   Throws L   Age 26

YEAR	TEAM	LGE	IP	H	ER	HR	BB	K	ERA	W	L	H/9	HR/9	BB/9	K/9	KWH	PERA
1997	Durham	Car	66.3	112	67	7	32	42	9.09	1	6	15.20	0.95	4.34	5.70	0.37	8.68
1997	Greenvil	Sou	63.3	94	53	8	28	34	7.53	2	5	13.36	1.14	3.98	4.83	0.33	7.53
1998	WestTenn	Sou	28.3	26	9	1	11	20	2.86	2	1	8.26	0.32	3.49	6.35	1.05	3.49
1998	Iowa	PCL	30.7	38	21	4	17	22	6.16	1	2	11.15	1.17	4.99	6.46	0.56	6.46
1999	Iowa	PCL	40.3	33	13	1	26	32	2.90	3	1	7.36	0.22	5.80	7.14	0.89	3.79
1999	ChiCubs	NL	11.0	11	7	2	10	5	5.73	0	1	9.00	1.64	8.18	4.09	0.17	7.36

Ray King was acquired from the Braves for Jon Ratliff, who was the guy drafted with one of the picks the Cubs got for Greg Maddux. So there's your payoff for Larry Himes's sunny personality: a spot left-hander with a nice over-the-top delivery. King is good enough to help a major-league pen if given the chance.

Jon Lieber   Throws R   Age 30

YEAR	TEAM	LGE	IP	H	ER	HR	BB	K	ERA	W	L	H/9	HR/9	BB/9	K/9	KWH	PERA
1997	Pittsbrg	NL	193.7	182	90	23	53	149	4.18	12	10	8.46	1.07	2.46	6.92	1.72	3.86
1998	Pittsbrg	NL	172.7	184	91	23	43	132	4.74	9	10	9.59	1.20	2.24	6.88	1.65	4.53
1999	ChiCubs	NL	207.0	218	93	25	44	181	4.04	13	10	9.48	1.09	1.91	7.87	2.55	4.22

(Jon Lieber *continued*)

Is he on the verge of being an ace? He's extremely close, despite his continuing problems with left-handed hitters. Marty DeMerritt tried to get Lieber to add a change-up to complement a good fastball and a slider with so much movement that hitters have problems spotting the seams. Some guys with extreme platoon splits turn the corner, like Alex Fernandez or David Cone or Kevin Appier, but every once in a while you get Danny Darwin. That's nice, but the Cubs are guessing that he'll go towards the high end, inking him to a three-year, $15 million contract.

Andrew Lorraine　Throws L　Age 27

YEAR	TEAM	LGE	IP	H	ER	HR	BB	K	ERA	W	L	H/9	HR/9	BB/9	K/9	KWH	PERA
1997	Edmonton	PCL	111.7	145	69	11	36	64	5.56	5	7	11.69	0.89	2.90	5.16	0.59	5.72
1997	Oakland	AL	31.0	42	19	2	15	18	5.52	1	2	12.19	0.58	4.35	5.23	0.38	6.39
1998	Tacoma	PCL	73.0	105	50	9	42	56	6.16	3	5	12.95	1.11	5.18	6.90	0.53	7.77
1999	Iowa	PCL	132.3	165	74	14	40	75	5.03	7	8	11.22	0.95	2.72	5.10	0.64	5.44
1999	ChiCubs	NL	63.0	68	37	8	22	39	5.29	3	4	9.71	1.14	3.14	5.57	0.76	4.86

He tossed a three-hit shutout in his season debut against the Astros, followed by 42 runs in the remaining 52⅔ innings he pitched for the Cubs. It was the first shutout by a Cubs' left-hander since Jamie Moyer tossed one in 1988. You know the drill: left-handed, no heat, nice changeup, good command, lots of buses in his past and his future, one hell of a game to remember.

David Manning　Throws R　Age 27

YEAR	TEAM	LGE	IP	H	ER	HR	BB	K	ERA	W	L	H/9	HR/9	BB/9	K/9	KWH	PERA
1997	Tulsa	Tex	68.3	91	54	8	33	44	7.11	2	6	11.99	1.05	4.35	5.80	0.48	6.72
1997	Oklahoma	AmA	28.3	37	18	6	10	13	5.72	1	2	11.75	1.91	3.18	4.13	0.34	6.99
1999	WestTenn	Sou	110.0	145	79	8	60	58	6.46	4	8	11.86	0.65	4.91	4.75	0.29	6.38

He's not a prospect, having scuffled through the Rangers' chain before a circulatory problem shut him down in 1998. He does have a bulldog reputation, and he tossed a no-hitter against Jacksonville after losing one with a strike to go in his previous start. If you remember Tom Drees, the last guy to throw consecutive no-hitters in the minors, you spend too much time reading or writing books like this.

Brian McNichol　Throws L　Age 26

YEAR	TEAM	LGE	IP	H	ER	HR	BB	K	ERA	W	L	H/9	HR/9	BB/9	K/9	KWH	PERA
1997	Daytona	Fla	37.0	40	18	2	14	29	4.38	2	2	9.73	0.49	3.41	7.05	1.12	4.38
1997	Orlando	Sou	107.7	177	99	18	47	77	8.28	3	9	14.80	1.50	3.93	6.44	0.53	8.94
1998	WestTenn	Sou	169.0	196	95	15	65	129	5.06	8	11	10.44	0.80	3.46	6.87	0.98	5.11
1999	Iowa	PCL	147.0	215	119	18	65	94	7.29	4	12	13.16	1.10	3.98	5.76	0.47	7.35
1999	ChiCubs	NL	11.0	14	7	4	7	12	5.73	0	1	11.45	3.27	5.73	9.82	1.10	9.82

He doesn't throw hard, his best pitch is a change-up, he has spotty command of a curveball and he has no star potential. McNichol tossed just nine quality starts for Iowa in 28 starts. He's a poor man's Micah Bowie, without the obvious Knife Night promotional tie-in.

Mike Meyers　Throws R　Age 22

YEAR	TEAM	LGE	IP	H	ER	HR	BB	K	ERA	W	L	H/9	HR/9	BB/9	K/9	KWH	PERA
1998	Rockford	Mid	78.3	102	52	5	41	60	5.97	3	6	11.72	0.57	4.71	6.89	0.64	6.09
1999	Daytona	Fla	102.3	81	34	11	49	99	2.99	8	3	7.12	0.97	4.31	8.71	1.85	3.78
1999	WestTenn	Sou	31.3	25	6	1	11	42	1.72	3	0	7.18	0.29	3.16	12.06	4.79	2.87

Here's a nice piece of scouting. The Cubs snagged Meyers out of Blackhawk College in nearby Moline in the 26th round of the 1997 draft, and now he's one of the best pitching prospects in the country. He already had a good fastball and change-up, but he added a biting curve. The man gave up only 89 hits and 50 walks in 140⅔ innings while missing some time pitching for Canada in the Pan Am Games. Don't be surprised if he's pitching on Austin Powers Night, '60s Night, Strange Brew Night . . . he might as well start wearing crushed velvet now.

Rodney Myers Throws R Age 31

YEAR	TEAM	LGE	IP	H	ER	HR	BB	K	ERA	W	L	H/9	HR/9	BB/9	K/9	KWH	PERA
1997	Iowa	AmA	130.7	171	98	17	46	67	6.75	5	10	11.78	1.17	3.17	4.61	0.43	6.20
1998	Iowa	PCL	95.7	91	50	9	52	70	4.70	5	6	8.56	0.85	4.89	6.59	0.77	4.61
1998	ChiCubs	NL	18.3	27	14	3	6	14	6.87	1	1	13.25	1.47	2.95	6.87	0.90	7.36
1999	Iowa	PCL	28.7	32	20	3	13	19	6.28	1	2	10.05	0.94	4.08	5.97	0.65	5.34
1999	ChiCubs	NL	64.7	69	30	9	24	40	4.18	4	3	9.60	1.25	3.34	5.57	0.72	5.01

A fastball/slider mop-up guy who credits departed pitching coach Marty DeMerritt with helping him with his off-speed stuff over the last two years. It's made him moderately more effective, but not enough for him to be more than an 11th pitcher. Myers is one of the few Rule 5 picks the Cubs made and kept. On that level, he's not a good example of positive reinforcement.

Joe Nation Throws L Age 21

YEAR	TEAM	LGE	IP	H	ER	HR	BB	K	ERA	W	L	H/9	HR/9	BB/9	K/9	KWH	PERA
1997	Danville	App	24.0	32	14	2	7	22	5.25	1	2	12.00	0.75	2.63	8.25	1.61	5.62
1998	Macon	SAL	137.0	216	116	18	54	92	7.62	4	11	14.19	1.18	3.55	6.04	0.54	7.95
1999	Macon	SAL	25.3	36	14	2	13	20	4.97	1	2	12.79	0.71	4.62	7.11	0.64	6.75
1999	Myrtle B	Car	90.0	114	65	9	43	64	6.50	3	7	11.40	0.90	4.30	6.40	0.62	6.10
1999	Daytona	Fla	12.7	9	2	0	3	9	1.42	1	0	6.39	0.00	2.13	6.39	2.24	2.13

Nation is a highly touted left-hander out of the Braves system, and as with Ruben Quevedo, a much more important part of the Jose Hernandez deal than Bowie. He's still filling out, but he's got good command and he throws harder than your average left-hander. Nation is a long way from being a prospect, but he's someone to keep an eye on and may make Lynch look good two or three years from now.

Phillip Norton Throws L Age 24

YEAR	TEAM	LGE	IP	H	ER	HR	BB	K	ERA	W	L	H/9	HR/9	BB/9	K/9	KWH	PERA
1997	Rockford	Mid	104.0	109	59	6	54	80	5.11	5	7	9.43	0.52	4.67	6.92	0.81	4.67
1997	Daytona	Fla	41.7	46	11	6	16	35	2.38	4	1	9.94	1.30	3.46	7.56	1.24	5.40
1998	Daytona	Fla	64.3	62	32	5	35	41	4.48	4	3	8.67	0.70	4.90	5.74	0.58	4.62
1998	WestTenn	Sou	117.0	127	58	12	49	99	4.46	7	6	9.77	0.92	3.77	7.62	1.18	5.00
1999	WestTenn	Sou	80.7	86	38	6	46	65	4.24	5	4	9.60	0.67	5.13	7.25	0.80	5.13
1999	Iowa	PCL	73.7	104	63	18	37	50	7.70	2	6	12.71	2.20	4.52	6.11	0.49	8.67

Variations on a theme: Norton's another one of the Cubs' left-handers who doesn't throw that hard, but his curve is one of the best breaking pitches in the organization. He was named the Southern League's top pitching prospect after mastering the change-up. That got him promoted, and the PCL ate him alive. Of the various left-handed pitchers the Cubs have to sort through, Norton is probably the best after Downs and should turn up for a few major-league starts this year.

Ruben Quevedo Throws R Age 21

YEAR	TEAM	LGE	IP	H	ER	HR	BB	K	ERA	W	L	H/9	HR/9	BB/9	K/9	KWH	PERA
1997	Danville	App	64.3	57	43	6	38	42	6.02	3	4	7.97	0.84	5.32	5.88	0.61	4.48
1998	Macon	SAL	107.3	137	55	15	43	76	4.61	6	6	11.49	1.26	3.61	6.37	0.73	6.29
1998	DanvillC	Car	30.7	35	29	3	18	25	8.51	1	2	10.27	0.88	5.28	7.34	0.74	5.87
1999	Richmond	Int	103.0	117	62	24	36	88	5.42	4	7	10.22	2.10	3.15	7.69	1.37	6.29
1999	Iowa	PCL	42.3	35	19	1	24	41	4.04	3	2	7.44	0.21	5.10	8.72	1.50	3.40

Quevedo is a rapidly improving Venezuelan picked up from the Braves in the Hernandez/Mulholland deal. His velocity is increasing as he matures, he has excellent movement, a good knuckle-curve and he can trot out a slider for show. If the Cubs bring him up, they would be wise to put him in long relief and give him 70 or 80 innings there. There are plenty of other starting pitchers to choose from, and Quevedo's future isn't worth risking just to make the Braves deal look good sooner.

Steve Rain   **Throws R**   **Age 25**

YEAR	TEAM	LGE	IP	H	ER	HR	BB	K	ERA	W	L	H/9	HR/9	BB/9	K/9	KWH	PERA
1997	Orlando	Sou	13.3	19	8	2	8	9	5.40	0	1	12.83	1.35	5.40	6.08	0.40	8.10
1997	Iowa	AmA	41.7	59	35	8	38	45	7.56	1	4	12.74	1.73	8.21	9.72	0.67	9.72
1998	Iowa	PCL	99.0	121	82	13	71	71	7.45	3	8	11.00	1.18	6.45	6.45	0.44	7.18
1999	WestTenn	Sou	41.3	42	12	3	18	42	2.61	4	1	9.15	0.65	3.92	9.15	1.74	4.35
1999	ChiCubs	NL	15.3	27	15	1	7	12	8.80	0	2	15.85	0.59	4.11	7.04	0.57	8.80

Rain has been terribly inconsistent since pitching his way into prospect status in 1996. There are whispers that he'd been enjoying himself too much at one point but is a model citizen nowadays. He's a huge man, which has made him a nightmare mechanically. Rain isn't really a sleeper, but he can help a team.

Chad Ricketts   **Throws R**   **Age 25**

YEAR	TEAM	LGE	IP	H	ER	HR	BB	K	ERA	W	L	H/9	HR/9	BB/9	K/9	KWH	PERA
1997	Rockford	Mid	27.3	24	10	1	14	22	3.29	2	1	7.90	0.33	4.61	7.24	1.08	3.62
1997	Daytona	Fla	20.0	15	4	0	8	14	1.80	2	0	6.75	0.00	3.60	6.30	1.22	2.70
1998	Daytona	Fla	47.3	48	17	0	16	42	3.23	3	2	9.13	0.00	3.04	7.99	1.72	3.42
1998	WestTenn	Sou	14.7	20	7	0	4	10	4.30	1	1	12.27	0.00	2.45	6.14	0.93	4.91
1999	WestTenn	Sou	61.3	70	32	9	24	61	4.70	3	4	10.27	1.32	3.52	8.95	1.65	5.58

Like Rain, Ricketts is a good minor-league reliever and someone who might earn a shot in the major-league pen. He can throw low-90s heat with good location but has severe problems with left-handed hitters. He's another potentially useful guy for the Cubs pen, but he'll have to impress them in camp. Ricketts pitched for Canada in the Pan Am Games, and shared WestTenn's closing duties down the stretch with Eric Newman after Rain was called up. Tossed into the Young/Valdes deal, he's another potentially useful guy for the Dodgers' pen, but he'll have to be impressive in camp.

Scott Sanders   **Throws R**   **Age 31**

YEAR	TEAM	LGE	IP	H	ER	HR	BB	K	ERA	W	L	H/9	HR/9	BB/9	K/9	KWH	PERA
1997	Seattle	AL	67.0	68	42	15	39	63	5.64	3	4	9.13	2.01	5.24	8.46	1.12	6.45
1997	Detroit	AL	74.3	79	42	13	24	59	5.09	4	4	9.57	1.57	2.91	7.14	1.37	5.21
1998	LasVegas	PCL	36.3	34	13	2	14	35	3.22	3	1	8.42	0.50	3.47	8.67	1.92	3.72
1998	San Dieg	NL	29.7	35	21	6	5	24	6.37	1	2	10.62	1.82	1.52	7.28	2.46	5.46
1999	ChiCubs	NL	106.3	109	61	17	51	87	5.16	5	7	9.23	1.44	4.32	7.36	1.02	5.42

Initially, Sanders was signed to be an 11th pitcher and insurance policy. But all hell broke loose in camp, and after Kerry Wood and Rod Beck went down, Sanders was promoted to fourth starter. He was more useful to the Cubs than his final stats show; in May and June, he was a workhorse in the bullpen before completely falling apart in July and August amidst the team-wide collapse. He still has value as an 11th man, but insurance policies always seem better the less you have to use them.

Dan Serafini   **Throws L**   **Age 26**

YEAR	TEAM	LGE	IP	H	ER	HR	BB	K	ERA	W	L	H/9	HR/9	BB/9	K/9	KWH	PERA
1997	SaltLake	PCL	148.0	158	75	16	56	102	4.56	8	8	9.61	0.97	3.41	6.20	0.88	4.80
1997	Minnesot	AL	26.3	27	10	1	11	15	3.42	2	1	9.23	0.34	3.76	5.13	0.57	4.10
1998	SaltLake	PCL	54.0	55	27	4	24	33	4.50	3	3	9.17	0.67	4.00	5.50	0.62	4.50
1998	Minnesot	AL	76.0	92	53	9	31	47	6.28	3	5	10.89	1.07	3.67	5.57	0.58	5.80
1999	ChiCubs	NL	64.0	83	46	8	31	17	6.47	2	5	11.67	1.13	4.36	2.39	0.08	6.61
1999	Iowa	PCL	12.0	13	7	1	6	9	5.25	0	1	9.75	0.75	4.50	6.75	0.78	5.25

Purchased from the Twins before Opening Day, Serafini is further proof that Andy MacPhail needs a Twins fix or he gets the shakes so bad it wrecks his golf game. He was spectacularly awful mopping up but was almost adequate in a few spot starts against teams with problems against left-handed pitchers, like the Twins and Pirates. He pitched his way off the roster in August when he offended Riggleman by allowing a home run to Matt Williams after being instructed to not give Baldy anything to hit.

Kevin Tapani · Throws R · Age 36

YEAR	TEAM	LGE	IP	H	ER	HR	BB	K	ERA	W	L	H/9	HR/9	BB/9	K/9	KWH	PERA
1997	ChiCubs	NL	86.3	76	31	7	24	52	3.23	7	3	7.92	0.73	2.50	5.42	1.11	3.34
1998	ChiCubs	NL	219.7	251	119	30	66	130	4.88	11	13	10.28	1.23	2.70	5.33	0.76	5.16
1999	ChiCubs	NL	138.3	145	72	11	32	71	4.68	7	8	9.43	0.72	2.08	4.62	0.81	3.90

Last year, we fretted that he was on the verge of blowing out his arm. Instead, his season died a slow death as he did everything in his power to stay on the mound. A strained shoulder cost him half of April, but he came back to rattle off seven quality starts in eight games despite a broken bone in his left wrist. He started having hip problems and chronic lower back pain. He started tinkering with his delivery to pitch through it, but after two months of lousy starts, the Cubs finally pulled the plug. While it might impress some people that he kept trying to pitch, he'd signed a multi-year extension and should have been shut down sooner to protect that investment.

Steve Trachsel · Throws R · Age 29

YEAR	TEAM	LGE	IP	H	ER	HR	BB	K	ERA	W	L	H/9	HR/9	BB/9	K/9	KWH	PERA
1997	ChiCubs	NL	205.3	225	105	32	73	151	4.60	11	12	9.86	1.40	3.20	6.62	1.04	5.30
1998	ChiCubs	NL	209.0	208	106	27	89	143	4.56	11	12	8.96	1.16	3.83	6.16	0.83	4.78
1999	ChiCubs	NL	209.7	218	117	29	61	145	5.02	10	13	9.36	1.24	2.62	6.22	1.18	4.59

He's certain to sign anywhere other than Chicago, but I'll miss him. He had the right attitude about flirting with 20 losses, taking the Roger Craig, "You gotta be pretty good to keep getting the ball" approach. He might irk some with his willingness to blame his fielders for a bad day, and he's good for a laugh when he shrugs off a 10-run outing by pointing out that good hitters can hit good pitches, and he made good pitches. If he gets into a bigger ballpark with a decent lineup to score him some runs, he'll look like one of this winter's best free-agent signings.

Kerry Wood · Throws R · Age 23

YEAR	TEAM	LGE	IP	H	ER	HR	BB	K	ERA	W	L	H/9	HR/9	BB/9	K/9	KWH	PERA
1996	Daytona	Fla	112.3	83	59	9	88	113	4.73	6	6	6.65	0.72	7.05	9.05	1.31	4.33
1997	Orlando	Sou	88.0	67	53	2	84	86	5.42	4	6	6.85	0.20	8.59	8.80	0.98	4.50
1997	Iowa	AmA	55.3	40	40	2	58	71	6.51	2	4	6.51	0.33	9.43	11.55	1.62	4.72
1998	ChiCubs	NL	168.0	118	67	14	90	222	3.59	12	7	6.32	0.75	4.82	11.89	3.47	3.32

While everyone else feared for what might happen to their pitching prospects after Wood's elbow blew up, it isn't clear the Cubs have learned their lesson. They blamed his high-school pitching coach as much as possible. They seem determined to keep his rehabilitation at around a year, which means he could be pitching in the majors by May 1 if he makes a full complement of rehab starts, sooner if they push harder. They dismissed his having surgery to correct a heart condition; it would have set back his rehab by a couple of weeks. The payoff may be an extra month of starts at the risk of further damage during a season in which the Cubs' chances of contending are marginal at best.

Jeff Yoder · Throws R · Age 24

YEAR	TEAM	LGE	IP	H	ER	HR	BB	K	ERA	W	L	H/9	HR/9	BB/9	K/9	KWH	PERA
1996	Rockford	Mid	144.3	177	87	15	56	89	5.42	7	9	11.04	0.94	3.49	5.55	0.60	5.61
1998	Daytona	Fla	137.3	182	108	18	62	97	7.08	4	11	11.93	1.18	4.06	6.36	0.62	6.68
1999	WestTenn	Sou	124.0	139	65	11	77	88	4.72	7	7	10.09	0.80	5.59	6.39	0.54	5.73

He left a good fastball on the surgeon's table after blowing out his shoulder in 1997. Using a sharp curve and a change-up, he won the Southern League ERA title in 1999. Yoder isn't really a prospect as much as he's a survivor, so he'll go as far as guile can take him.

Support-Neutral Records — CHICAGO CUBS — Park Effect: -1.8%

PITCHER	GS	IP	R	SNW	SNL	SNPCT	W	L	RA	APW	SNVA	SNWAR
Micah Bowie	11	47.0	54	1.2	6.4	.158	2	6	10.34	-2.63	-2.43	-2.04
Kyle Farnsworth	21	116.7	75	6.1	8.2	.424	5	8	5.79	-0.94	-1.00	-0.02
Jon Lieber	31	203.3	107	11.9	10.7	.527	10	11	4.74	0.61	0.60	2.30
Andrew Lorraine	11	61.7	42	3.0	4.5	.394	2	5	6.13	-0.72	-0.71	-0.23
Brian McNichol	2	9.0	8	0.4	0.9	.329	0	2	8.00	-0.28	-0.24	-0.12
Terry Mulholland	16	94.3	63	5.0	6.5	.437	6	6	6.01	-0.98	-0.72	0.13
Scott Sanders	6	30.7	19	1.7	2.3	.421	0	3	5.58	-0.18	-0.31	-0.02
Dan Serafini	4	19.0	14	0.7	1.7	.304	1	1	6.63	-0.32	-0.46	-0.30
Kevin Tapani	23	136.0	81	7.5	8.3	.477	6	12	5.36	-0.48	-0.47	0.82
Steve Trachsel	34	205.7	133	11.6	13.1	.470	8	18	5.82	-1.73	-0.80	1.10
Brad Woodall	3	12.0	10	0.4	1.1	.271	0	1	7.50	-0.31	-0.31	-0.24
TOTALS	162	935.3	606	49.6	63.8	.437	40	73	5.83	-7.97	-6.84	1.40

It took an across-the-board collapse for the Cubs to drop 22 games in the standings from 1998 to 1999, and the starting pitchers certainly did their share. The 1998 staff was worth two wins above average according to SNVA, making them the ninth-best rotation in the majors. But the 1999 staff fell to seven games below average, next to last in the majors and just barely ahead of the Marlins. . . . Having the worst starter in the league in Micah Bowie certainly didn't help matters, but I think a more important factor in the Cubs' problems is that they simply didn't have anybody who was very good. Just look at all those minus signs in the SNVA column. Even their one above-average starter, Jon Lieber, didn't exactly set the world on fire. That makes the problem of rebuilding this rotation a difficult one. Other teams with struggling rotations often have a couple of good starters to build on and can expect to see a big improvement in overall staff performance by plugging a few gaping holes. The Cubs' holes are smaller but more numerous; plugging just one or two of them won't help that much.

Pitcher Abuse Points

PITCHER	AGE	GS	PAP	PAP/S	WKLD	MAX	1-90	91-100	101-110	111-120	121-130	131-140	141+
Micah Bowie	24	11	32	2.9	6.8	111	5	2	3	1	0	0	0
Kyle Farnsworth	23	21	83	4.0	9.9	121	7	4	8	1	1	0	0
Jon Lieber	29	31	263	8.5	12.7	133	6	9	12	2	0	2	0
Andrew Lorraine	26	11	31	2.8	5.6	114	6	1	3	1	0	0	0
Brian McNichol	25	2	0	0.0	0.0	98	1	1	0	0	0	0	0
Terry Mulholland	36	16	95	5.9	5.9	125	7	4	2	2	1	0	0
Scott Sanders	30	6	12	2.0	2.7	109	2	2	2	0	0	0	0
Dan Serafini	25	4	0	0.0	0.0	85	4	0	0	0	0	0	0
Kevin Tapani	35	23	208	9.0	9.0	132	8	7	1	5	1	1	0
Steve Trachsel	28	34	255	7.5	12.5	123	9	6	10	7	2	0	0
Brad Woodall	30	3	0	0.0	0.0	75	3	0	0	0	0	0	0
CHICAGO		162	979	6.0	9.2	133	58	36	41	19	5	3	0
Ranking (NL)				12	12								

Jim Riggleman deserved the axe, but it wasn't because he was playing fast and loose with his starters. In 1999, at least, not one of his starting pitchers took on a burden he couldn't bear. As for 1998, well, Riggleman didn't treat Kerry Wood any worse than most managers in the game would have. As for Wood's future . . . this may sound crazy, but I am now more optimistic about Wood's long-term future than I was before he tore up his elbow. Tearing the medial collateral ligament is no longer a career-threatening injury; surgeons have 25 years' experience with transplanting a fresh, healthy ligament from the hand, an extra ligament that no one needs. With the proper rehabilitation time, almost all pitchers who undergo the surgery come back throwing as hard, if not harder, than before. Wood only needs to look at Blue Jays rookie Billy Koch for encouragement. Also, the rest that Wood got last year, along with the extra care he figures to get when he comes back, should do wonders for his rotator cuff. It's a torn rotator cuff—where surgery doesn't involve bringing in fresh tissue, but rather restoring the old to new—that causes a career to wither and die. If Dwight Gooden had torn an elbow ligament after his 1985 season, he might not have torn his rotator cuff in 1989, and he might still be more than a shadow of his former self.

Cincinnati Reds

When Herman Franks, the manager of the 1979 Chicago Cubs, decided to protect Bruce Sutter from injury by letting Sutter pitch only when the Cubs had a lead, he could not have foreseen the impact his decision would have on baseball. Franks was fired in 1980, but 20 years later baseball teams—every last one of them—still hold to the mantra that your best reliever should be your "closer," and that the closer should pitch only in save situations.

Never mind that there isn't a single compelling piece of evidence justifying the closer role as we've come to know it. Should your best reliever sit in the bullpen while a setup man tries to escape an eighth-inning jam in a tie game in the hopes that the reliever can come in to protect a ninth-inning lead that may never materialize? Does a manager really need to use his best reliever to protect a three-run lead in the ninth, creating another save that will then be used against the team in arbitration?

The term "evolution" evokes deep-seated reactions from people, ranging from complete acceptance to cries of heresy. But the concept behind evolution, that every environment selects for certain traits that improve chances for survival, has been used to explain everything from why all politicians are spineless and dishonest, to why the .400 hitter has disappeared. Evolution is why some teams are now building their offense around players with high on-base percentages: it is a successful strategy, and successful strategies are replicated while unsuccessful ones are discarded.

What's troubling about the modern usage of relievers is that it *doesn't* fit into evolutionary theory. The philosophy that your best reliever should pitch only when he can earn a save, almost always for just one inning, is not more successful than the philosophy of the 1970s. At that time, closers pitched two or three innings at a time, frequently in tie games or even when their team was behind by a run. While they had only half as many saves, they frequently won 10 or more games.

Evolution usually begins with a change to the existing system. In baseball, it's typically the newer, younger managers who are more willing to deviate from conventional wisdom, going to the bullpen more, using non-standard lineups, issuing intentional walks with the bases loaded. . . . Last year, what we saw in Cincinnati was a case of evolutionary forces bringing the Reds' bullpen back to an older, but more successful, strategy. It's hardly surprising that the man behind this move was Jack McKeon, who started his managerial career in 1973 and, at 69, is one of the oldest managers in baseball history.

What did McKeon do that was so different? To begin with, he allowed his relievers to have longer outings: the Reds threw the most relief innings (530) of any NL team, but only the Astros, who had the fewest relief innings in baseball, made fewer relief changes. The usage patterns for the Reds' bullpen look like something straight out of 1974: 62 games, 93 innings for Scott Williamson; 75 games, 111 innings for Danny Graves; 79 games, 114 innings for Scott Sullivan. The Reds' bullpen was only the third this decade to have three relievers pitch 90 innings apiece, and they did so largely in chunks of two or three innings at a time.

But it wasn't just that the Reds relievers had longer outings; what was so unique was that it was the closers who were being stretched out. Williamson and Graves combined for 45 of the Reds' league-leading 55 saves, yet they weren't restricted to one-inning outings any more than the Reds' setup men were. Actually, McKeon was more likely to let Williamson or Graves pitch two innings than, say, Dennis Reyes. In more than half of the Reds' saves (28), the closer went more than an inning to sew up the win. No other NL team had more than 14 saves of the inning-plus variety. The only other team to convert even 20 of these long saves in the last four years was . . . the 1998 Reds.

So McKeon had a pair of excellent closers who occasionally notched two-inning saves. If that was all—if Williamson and Graves were coming into games with a two-run lead in the eighth, instead of a two-run lead in the ninth—we'd call

Reds Prospectus

1999 record: 96-67; Second place, NL Central; Lost one-game wild-card playoff to Mets, 5-0

Pythagorean W/L: 96-66

Runs scored: 865 (4th in NL)

Runs allowed: 711 (4th in NL)

Team EQA: .267 (6th in NL)

1999 team age: 28.4 (6th-youngest in NL)

1999 park: Cinergy Field; slight pitchers' park, decreased run scoring by 3%.

1999: A great run, fueled by a dominant bullpen and some career years.

2000: They will probably be disappointing; getting Griffey would keep them in the race.

it interesting and leave it at that. But there's more to it than that. Table 1 breaks down Williamson's and Graves's appearances, along with those of Mike Jackson and Paul Shuey, the Indians' closer and set-up man.

Table 1

Name	Inning		Score			
	1-7	9+	-1/0	+1/+2	+3	+4 or more
Scott Williamson	23	21	22	19	9	0
Danny Graves	16	28	19	22	14	6
Mike Jackson	0	71	7	26	15	19
Paul Shuey	17	21	17	23	7	14

Jackson was the ultimate one-inning closer. Only once all season did he come into a game before the ninth inning. Even Shuey, his setup man, was more likely to come into a game in the ninth inning than in the seventh or earlier. By contrast, Williamson and Graves came in to pitch before the eighth inning 39 times combined, more than twice as often as Jackson and Shuey.

But it's the breakdown by score that really makes you scratch your head. Only seven times all year was Mike Jackson brought into a game with the Indians tied or losing by one, key situations in which a single run can swing the game toward victory or defeat. Williamson pitched in 22 such games, and while pitching in so many tight games might have cost him some saves, it also meant that he picked up 12 wins. Not once was Williamson wasted on preserving a lead of four or more runs; McKeon rightly presumed that any reliever in his bullpen was capable of such a mundane task. In contrast, Jackson was brought in to protect leads of four or more runs 19 times.

This is the inevitable result of using your closer only in "save situations." When Jerome Holtzman invented the save, he did so in an attempt to credit an underappreciated segment of baseball players, not to define the way that pitchers should be used. By keeping Jackson in the bullpen until a save situation emerged, Mike Hargrove left crucial situations in the hands of lesser relievers. Meanwhile, because there weren't enough save situations for Jackson to pitch in, Hargrove "kept him sharp" by wasting him in the ninth inning of decided contests 19 times, instead of bringing him in when games were in doubt before the ninth inning.

McKeon did none of that. He didn't use his best relievers according to a statistic. He brought them in to put out fires, regardless of whether the fire blazed in the ninth inning or the sixth. And those relievers put out enough fires to bring the Reds within a game of the postseason.

This was just the first salvo in the war against the 1990s-style bullpen, and it may be years before another battle is won. But eventually the tide will turn. It has to. Baseball is ruled by the modern concept of the bullpen, the way the earth was once ruled by dinosaurs. The dinosaurs died out, and one day, so too must the 45-save, 60-inning closer. It's fitting that it took McKeon, one of baseball's own dinosaurs, to help to push the evolutionary forces along.

The Reds' bullpen was the team's MVP last year, when they surprised everyone by reaching 96 wins and forcing a one-game playoff for the NL wild card. The Reds also benefited from the best years some of their players will ever have, from Sean Casey's breakout to the peak efforts of Pokey Reese, Aaron Boone and Eddie Taubensee. And General Manager Jim Bowden's big move, the acquisition of $5 million left fielder Greg Vaughn, paid off as Vaughn provided much-needed power. All together, the Reds got good years from just about everyone in 1999, while no major contributor had a bad year.

So it's inevitable that the 2000 Reds are going to struggle to reach 96 wins again. The 1999 team was fairly cheap, with a payroll around $35 million, but it wasn't notably young. The Reds' AL counterparts, the Oakland A's, were structured similiarly—and neither team was filled with 23- and 24-year-olds. The A's have a few such players, but their best players in 1999 were veterans like Jason Giambi, Matt Stairs, Randy Velarde and Omar Olivares. The Reds, in turn, were led by veterans Vaughn, Taubensee and Barry Larkin. The team's best younger players, like Reese, Mike Cameron and Dmitri Young, are already at their peak, and there are very few blue-chip prospects in the organization ready to step in.

With a not-so-young team and some payroll restrictions still in place, Bowden attempted to recreate his Vaughn pickup by trading Jeffrey Hammonds and Stan Belinda for another left fielder in his 30s with a year to go on his contract. Unfortunately, Dante Bichette is the poster boy for altitude effects on a player's statistics, having put up so-called monster seasons that are really nothing special after his environment is factored in. The outfielder Bowden traded, Hammonds, is a better player than Bichette; Bichette's sole advantage over him has been durability. But when Bichette puts up a .270/.320/.410 season this year, that "advantage" is going to hurt the Reds dearly.

The Bichette acquisition was a poor one for the Reds, one that will cost them considerable ground in 2000, and one that has nothing at all to do with the Reds' revenues or their desire to keep a low payroll. It was a bad baseball decision. It also wasn't their only one.

At this writing, the Reds are in negotiations to acquire Ken Griffey Jr. from the Seattle Mariners. Griffey has asked to be traded and, as a player with "10-and-5" rights, must approve any deal, and has more or less restricted the Mariners to working with Cincinnati. The Reds, perhaps sensing the Mariners' distress, have held to an offer of a starting pitcher (either Brett Tomko or Denny Neagle), Rookie of the Year reliever Scott Williamson and center fielder Mike Cameron. The sticking point appears to be the Reds' refusal to add Pokey Reese to the deal.

Reese had his best season in 1999, playing a fantastic second base, poking 52 extra-base hits and stealing 38 bases while being caught just seven times. All that added up to an unimpressive EqA of just .255, thanks mainly to a mere 32 unintentional walks and a .330 OBP. Reese, at his best, is an above-average second baseman thanks to his glove and legs. This was as good as he gets, though, and Bowden's refusal to include him in a trade for Griffey is stubborn to the point of inexcusable. Griffey would add four or five wins to the Reds'

2000 total and bring, conservatively, an extra half-million people to Cinergy Field. There's no reason to pass him up for a second baseman whose value is more perceived than real.

When the Reds decline this year, their performance will be used to support the notion that "small market" teams cannot compete consistently in an age of rising salaries. The rhetoric will flow, and the owners will sit back and smile in anticipation of an NBA-style war in 2002. Just remember that the Reds' fall from grace in 2000 will be due to their decisions, not the economic conditions of the industry. 1999 proved that the Reds are perfectly capable of making good personnel decisions and assuming some risk to build a contender. That they aren't doing so is their own fault.

HITTERS (Averages: BA: .270 / OBP: .340 / SLG: .430 / EQA: .260)

Aaron Boone — 3B — Bats R — Age 27

YEAR	TEAM	LGE	AB	H	DB	TP	HR	BB/SO	R	RBI	SB	CS	OUT	BA	OBP	SLG	EQA	EQR	DEFENSE
1997	Indianap	AA	484	135	32	4	18	34/85	71	68	9	3	352	.279	.328	.473	.266	64	118-3B 110
1998	Indianap	Int	334	72	16	1	5	23/79	42	30	9	3	265	.216	.280	.314	.204	25	76-3B 108
1998	Cincnnti	NL	183	53	15	2	2	15/35	25	29	6	1	131	.290	.361	.426	.272	25	48-3B 112
1999	Cincnnti	NL	475	132	29	5	13	23/78	52	68	14	6	349	.278	.323	.442	.256	58	123-3B 113
2000	Cincnnti	NL	516	134	31	3	12	40/94	71	64	17	6	388	.260	.313	.401	.241	56	

The defense pushes him up to average as a player; he's not that different from his older brother. Bret's defensive reputation at second base is comparable to Aaron's performance at third. Boone isn't a star in the making; he's Steve Buechele or Vance Law. He wore down badly in September.

Ben Broussard — 1B/LF — Bats L — Age 23

YEAR	TEAM	LGE	AB	H	DB	TP	HR	BB/SO	R	RBI	SB	CS	OUT	BA	OBP	SLG	EQA	EQR	DEFENSE
1999	Billings	Pio	142	41	7	1	8	22/36	20	23	0	0	101	.289	.391	.521	.302	25	30-OF 88
1999	Clinton	Mid	19	9	1	1	2	2/4	5	4	0	0	10	.474	.524	.947	.440	6	
1999	Chattang	Sou	128	26	4	0	7	8/42	21	17	1	0	102	.203	.262	.398	.219	11	
2000	Cincnnti	NL	145	41	8	1	12	21/79	27	37	0	0	104	.283	.373	.600	.310	28	

Generating a .302 EqA in the Pioneer League is an otherworldly feat. Broussard is just a hitter with great bat speed; the Reds are messing with him in left field, but his future is at first base or DH, hitting line drives and trying not to get hurt when on the field. That Wilton is just silly, of course, based solely on the hottest two months of Broussard's life, but he is a B prospect.

Mike Cameron — CF — Bats R — Age 27

YEAR	TEAM	LGE	AB	H	DB	TP	HR	BB/SO	R	RBI	SB	CS	OUT	BA	OBP	SLG	EQA	EQR	DEFENSE
1997	Nashvill	AA	121	30	6	2	5	16/33	18	14	3	1	92	.248	.351	.455	.272	18	26-OF 106
1997	ChiSox	AL	379	101	19	3	15	53/101	63	56	24	2	280	.266	.365	.451	.284	60	111-OF 106
1998	ChiSox	AL	396	84	16	5	8	35/99	49	42	24	11	323	.212	.286	.338	.217	35	108-OF 112
1999	Cincnnti	NL	544	138	35	9	20	73/144	86	62	32	12	418	.254	.349	.461	.274	82	139-CF 97
2000	Cincnnti	NL	467	118	23	5	17	65/123	89	67	32	9	358	.253	.344	.433	.267	66	

This was a good gamble by the Reds: picking up a part they needed—a center fielder—for Paul Konerko, a talented hitter whom they weren't sure what to do with. Cameron has power, speed, plate discipline and is a good defensive center fielder, so even in a year in which he hits .250, he's a considerable asset. If he hits .280, he's a star. I expect him to approach that level and be one of the best center fielders in the league this year.

Sean Casey   1B   Bats L   Age 25

YEAR	TEAM	LGE	AB	H	DB	TP	HR	BB/SO	R	RBI	SB	CS	OUT	BA	OBP	SLG	EQA	EQR	DEFENSE
1997	Akron	Eas	241	84	18	1	8	17/35	30	52	0	1	158	.349	.400	.531	.307	41	49-1B 94
1997	Buffalo	AA	74	26	7	0	5	9/11	12	18	0	0	48	.351	.429	.649	.344	17	
1998	Indianap	Int	95	29	7	1	1	12/10	12	12	0	0	66	.305	.388	.432	.282	14	20-1B 92
1998	Cincnnti	NL	306	86	22	1	8	42/44	45	54	1	1	221	.281	.374	.438	.276	44	78-1B 91
1999	Cincnnti	NL	595	196	43	3	24	54/87	98	93	0	2	401	.329	.395	.533	.305	103	144-1B 76
2000	*Cincnnti*	*NL*	*511*	*175*	*36*	*2*	*25*	*64/74*	*101*	*123*	*0*	*1*	*337*	*.342*	*.416*	*.568*	*.322*	*99*	

Casey showed the expected ability to hit for average and draw some walks; his power was a bit of a surprise. While I think the doubles are real, I'm just as convinced that the 24 bombs are his high end. That would make him Jeff Bagwell Lite, which will suffice. His second-half slump could have been anticipated: due to injuries, Casey hadn't played in more than 96 games in a season as a professional.

Brady Clark   OF   Bats R   Age 27

YEAR	TEAM	LGE	AB	H	DB	TP	HR	BB/SO	R	RBI	SB	CS	OUT	BA	OBP	SLG	EQA	EQR	DEFENSE
1997	Burlingt	Mid	466	109	21	3	8	50/86	61	38	9	7	363	.234	.312	.343	.225	43	114-OF 106
1998	Chattang	Sou	223	50	11	1	1	20/40	26	11	5	2	175	.224	.297	.296	.206	17	58-OF 105
1999	Chattang	Sou	508	129	29	2	12	65/68	69	50	11	8	387	.254	.340	.390	.249	60	133-OF 93
2000	*Cincnnti*	*NL*	*447*	*115*	*20*	*1*	*11*	*60/68*	*68*	*59*	*11*	*6*	*338*	*.257*	*.345*	*.380*	*.249*	*52*	

Clark is a non-prospect still living off his Midwest League MVP in 1997. You can't overemphasize the importance of age in evaluating a player as a prospect. Every performance has to be placed in the context of age and level, which is why a 24-year-old who tears up a low-A circuit really isn't a prospect, while an 18-year-old who just holds his own at high-A is. The principle is the same at the major-league level: a 26-year-old Rookie of the Year is peaking as he accepts the award, while a 21-year-old with a job has time to become something special.

Travis Dawkins   SS   Bats R   Age 21

YEAR	TEAM	LGE	AB	H	DB	TP	HR	BB/SO	R	RBI	SB	CS	OUT	BA	OBP	SLG	EQA	EQR	DEFENSE
1997	Billings	Pio	252	48	4	0	3	20/45	24	23	5	2	206	.190	.250	.242	.160	11	69-SS 99
1998	Burlingt	Mid	373	92	9	5	1	30/62	36	25	15	5	286	.247	.304	.306	.214	30	101-SS 95
1999	Rockford	Mid	309	75	9	4	8	25/40	36	24	16	7	241	.243	.299	.375	.231	31	74-SS 90
1999	Chattang	Sou	128	42	3	0	3	11/18	18	11	9	3	89	.328	.381	.422	.279	18	30-SS 93
2000	*Cincnnti*	*NL*	*413*	*113*	*12*	*3*	*10*	*42/63*	*67*	*53*	*24*	*7*	*307*	*.274*	*.341*	*.390*	*.254*	*50*	

Dawkins took a big step forward as a hitter last year, driving the ball more and making contact more frequently. He is extremely fast and a good defensive shortstop, the heir apparent to Barry Larkin. Continuous improvement is something to look for in a top prospect, a trait Dawkins has shown. While he had a cup of coffee with the Reds this year, he should start 2000 at Chattanooga. He has a big upside.

Alejandro Diaz   OF   Bats R   Age 21

YEAR	TEAM	LGE	AB	H	DB	TP	HR	BB/SO	R	RBI	SB	CS	OUT	BA	OBP	SLG	EQA	EQR	DEFENSE
1999	Clinton	Mid	221	54	14	2	5	7/37	24	29	11	5	172	.244	.271	.394	.223	20	56-OF 108
1999	Chattang	Sou	220	53	9	7	6	5/32	22	28	3	1	168	.241	.265	.427	.227	21	55-OF 114
2000	*Cincnnti*	*NL*	*237*	*65*	*14*	*4*	*8*	*9/81*	*35*	*35*	*13*	*3*	*175*	*.274*	*.301*	*.468*	*.257*	*29*	

a/k/a Alejandro Quezada. The Reds signed Diaz, a Dominican who played in Japan in 1998, after winning his rights in a sealed-bid auction last winter. The system is designed to cut Japanese League teams in on the money generated when players wish to leave for the States. Diaz is tools-positive and one of the best defensive outfielders in the minor leagues, but needs to be introduced to the strike zone. He's young enough to show explosive growth.

Adam Dunn   OF   Bats L   Age 20

YEAR	TEAM	LGE	AB	H	DB	TP	HR	BB/SO	R	RBI	SB	CS	OUT	BA	OBP	SLG	EQA	EQR	DEFENSE
1998	Billings	Pio	124	27	1	1	3	12/27	13	7	1	1	98	.218	.294	.315	.207	10	32-OF 74
1999	Rockford	Mid	317	84	15	1	10	35/67	43	33	9	5	238	.265	.349	.413	.260	41	67-OF 79
2000	*Cincnnti*	*NL*	*162*	*46*	*5*	*0*	*8*	*23/42*	*28*	*30*	*4*	*2*	*118*	*.284*	*.373*	*.463*	*.281*	*25*	

The Reds caught a break when Dunn elected to play baseball full-time rather than return to the University of Texas, where he was the backup quarterback. Given the play of Major Applewhite last fall, it looks like a good decision. Dunn is 6'6", weighs 230 pounds and is fast, a tremendous physical talent who can hit and run. His outfield play so far has been shaky, but is expected to improve as he gains experience. With Casey and Broussard ahead of him at first base, he doesn't have much choice but to improve.

Mike Frank — OF — Bats L — Age 25

YEAR	TEAM	LGE	AB	H	DB	TP	HR	BB/SO	R	RBI	SB	CS	OUT	BA	OBP	SLG	EQA	EQR	DEFENSE
1997	Billings	Pio	259	66	16	3	5	22/30	28	30	5	3	196	.255	.316	.398	.241	28	67-OF 98
1998	Chattang	Sou	230	66	11	3	10	11/30	32	31	3	1	165	.287	.322	.491	.267	30	52-OF 104
1998	Indianap	Int	88	29	3	0	0	5/9	7	12	1	0	59	.330	.366	.364	.255	10	18-OF 115
1998	Cincnnti	NL	90	21	6	0	0	7/12	14	7	0	0	69	.233	.289	.300	.198	6	24-OF 112
1999	Indianap	Int	435	121	33	7	7	29/57	60	52	7	5	319	.278	.333	.434	.257	53	111-OF 97
2000	*Cincnnti*	*NL*	*405*	*111*	*24*	*4*	*9*	*32/53*	*56*	*57*	*7*	*3*	*297*	*.274*	*.327*	*.420*	*.251*	*47*	

Frank showed few ill effects from being rushed to the majors in 1998, returning to Indianapolis and having a good season. He's not a threat to Mike Cameron, nor will he hit enough to start on an outfield corner. With Jeffrey Hammonds gone, Frank is the only real option at the upper levels to back up center field, so he has a good chance to make the team as the fifth outfielder.

Jeffrey Hammonds — OF — Bats R — Age 29

YEAR	TEAM	LGE	AB	H	DB	TP	HR	BB/SO	R	RBI	SB	CS	OUT	BA	OBP	SLG	EQA	EQR	DEFENSE
1997	Baltimor	AL	397	107	20	4	21	30/70	70	54	15	1	291	.270	.326	.499	.275	58	107-OF 102
1998	Baltimor	AL	172	48	14	1	6	25/37	35	28	6	2	126	.279	.380	.477	.289	28	45-OF 102
1998	Cincnnti	NL	87	27	5	1	0	13/18	15	11	1	1	61	.310	.400	.391	.276	12	24-OF 116
1999	Cincnnti	NL	263	72	12	0	17	24/63	40	39	2	6	197	.274	.337	.513	.271	38	37-RF 108
2000	*Colorado*	*NL*	*261*	*82*	*15*	*1*	*16*	*35/57*	*53*	*62*	*5*	*3*	*182*	*.314*	*.395*	*.563*	*.287*	*40*	

You wonder just how many old ladies you have to help across the street, or how many cats you have to rescue from trees, to have this kind of luck. Hammonds is an average right fielder who, without his game changing much at all, is about to be considered a star, having been dealt to Colorado for 1992 lottery winner Dante Bichette. He's not a bad player, and will help the Rockies more than Bichette did. As ever, his health is the biggest question; Tom Goodwin's presence will keep him out of center field, which should help.

Darron Ingram — "OF" — Bats R — Age 24

YEAR	TEAM	LGE	AB	H	DB	TP	HR	BB/SO	R	RBI	SB	CS	OUT	BA	OBP	SLG	EQA	EQR	DEFENSE	
1997	Burlingt	Mid	515	118	20	2	25	33/204	55	71	3	2	399	.229	.276	.421	.230	50	83-OF 88	21-1B 94
1998	Chattang	Sou	469	100	19	6	17	27/175	48	51	2	2	371	.213	.256	.388	.211	38	115-OF 89	
1999	Chattang	Sou	269	53	9	3	9	21/101	33	31	3	4	220	.197	.255	.353	.199	19	53-OF 88	
1999	Clinton	Mid	76	20	4	0	3	10/23	9	10	0	0	56	.263	.349	.434	.265	10		
2000	*Cincnnti*	*NL*	*412*	*93*	*15*	*2*	*17*	*38/156*	*44*	*54*	*3*	*2*	*321*	*.226*	*.291*	*.396*	*.228*	*40*		

The organization has long been in love with his power, but it's time to give up the ghost. Ingram struck out in more than a third of his at-bats over a year and a half at Chattanooga, he can't really play the outfield and there are better first-base prospects everywhere you look in this organization. His success at Clinton may buy him some time, but don't be fooled: Ingram is done.

Brian Johnson — C — Bats R — Age 32

YEAR	TEAM	LGE	AB	H	DB	TP	HR	BB/SO	R	RBI	SB	CS	OUT	BA	OBP	SLG	EQA	EQR	DEFENSE
1997	Detroit	AL	139	33	7	1	2	4/18	13	18	1	0	106	.237	.259	.345	.199	9	
1997	San Fran	NL	182	52	7	2	12	13/26	20	28	0	1	131	.286	.340	.544	.284	28	
1998	San Fran	NL	313	78	10	1	14	27/65	36	36	0	2	237	.249	.320	.422	.247	36	85-C 101
1999	Cincnnti	NL	118	27	8	0	5	7/31	12	17	0	0	91	.229	.272	.424	.228	11	27-C 102
2000	*KansasCy*	*AL*	*197*	*49*	*6*	*0*	*10*	*17/41*	*24*	*32*	*0*	*0*	*148*	*.249*	*.308*	*.431*	*.243*	*21*	

A knee injury in June more or less ended his season. Johnson has enough power to be the right-handed half of a platoon and could repeat his 1998 performance given the playing time. The Royals have signed him, striking fear into the hearts of the Kansas Sabermetric Mafia, starting with Rob Neyer and Rany Jazayerli.

Austin Kearns   OF   Bats R   Age 20

YEAR	TEAM	LGE	AB	H	DB	TP	HR	BB/SO	R	RBI	SB	CS	OUT	BA	OBP	SLG	EQA	EQR	DEFENSE
1998	Billings	Pio	106	24	3	0	2	14/26	9	8	0	0	82	.226	.319	.311	.220	9	27-OF 83
1999	Rockford	Mid	433	99	33	3	12	36/126	52	36	9	4	338	.229	.296	.402	.235	45	120-OF 89
2000	Cincnnti	NL	224	51	15	1	7	26/79	29	29	2	1	174	.228	.308	.397	.237	24	

Kearns is another young tools outfielder who doesn't control the strike zone as well as you'd like. There was a sale, apparently. He was the Reds' 1998 #1 pick, and he showed good power and speed at Rockford. In Kearns, Diaz and Dunn, the Reds have three guys with significant upside, one of whom should turn out to be a player. Kearns is the middle talent of the three, without the power of Dunn or the arm and glove of Diaz, but with fewer large holes in his game than either.

Barry Larkin   SS   Bats R   Age 36

YEAR	TEAM	LGE	AB	H	DB	TP	HR	BB/SO	R	RBI	SB	CS	OUT	BA	OBP	SLG	EQA	EQR	DEFENSE
1997	Cincnnti	NL	226	71	18	3	4	46/24	32	20	11	3	158	.314	.436	.473	.315	44	54-SS 108
1998	Cincnnti	NL	545	173	36	10	19	79/67	97	75	28	3	375	.317	.406	.525	.315	104	140-SS 94
1999	Cincnnti	NL	584	170	32	4	11	86/56	101	70	26	8	422	.291	.384	.416	.279	87	152-SS 99
2000	Cincnnti	NL	436	120	20	3	12	74/46	85	67	16	5	321	.275	.380	.417	.276	64	

It looks like the decline is finally here, after a delayed peak from 1995-98 during which he was a remarkable player. Larkin is now an average defensive shortstop; in another year, the Reds will have to decide whether to move him to third base to create room for Dawkins. It will be interesting to see if his hitting spikes upward when he makes the move to an easier position, a la Paul Molitor and, more recently, Tony Fernandez.

Jason LaRue   C   Bats R   Age 26

YEAR	TEAM	LGE	AB	H	DB	TP	HR	BB/SO	R	RBI	SB	CS	OUT	BA	OBP	SLG	EQA	EQR	DEFENSE
1997	Charl-WV	SAL	490	127	42	2	7	38/100	58	60	4	2	365	.259	.317	.396	.241	52	
1998	Chattang	Sou	381	113	32	5	10	23/68	48	53	2	1	269	.297	.349	.486	.276	54	92-C 95
1999	Indianap	Int	264	60	10	2	9	11/57	33	28	0	2	206	.227	.267	.383	.212	21	67-C 102
1999	Cincnnti	NL	90	19	6	0	3	10/32	11	9	4	1	72	.211	.306	.378	.238	10	27-C 108
2000	Cincnnti	NL	374	94	21	2	11	32/84	47	50	5	2	282	.251	.310	.406	.240	40	

The injury to Brian Johnson brought him to the majors as Eddie Taubensee's caddy, a role that fits him. He won't hit enough to be a regular, so backing up a left-handed-hitting catcher who is below average defensively makes the most of what he does well. LaRue has no star value.

Mark Lewis   3B   Bats R   Age 30

YEAR	TEAM	LGE	AB	H	DB	TP	HR	BB/SO	R	RBI	SB	CS	OUT	BA	OBP	SLG	EQA	EQR	DEFENSE	
1997	San Fran	NL	345	94	15	6	11	23/61	51	43	2	2	253	.272	.325	.446	.256	42	50-3B 97	17-2B 98
1998	Philadel	NL	521	131	20	2	10	47/108	52	54	3	3	393	.251	.317	.355	.229	50	139-2B 98	
1999	Cincnnti	NL	174	44	13	0	7	5/24	17	27	0	0	130	.253	.274	.448	.236	17	35-3B 96	
2000	Cincnnti	NL	265	70	16	1	7	23/48	34	37	1	1	196	.264	.323	.411	.245	29		

I'm not sure what was worse: Lewis's performance in 1999, or Cincinnati's November decision to sign him to a one-year deal. Lewis is a slow backup infielder who can't play shortstop anymore and is a borderline pinch-hitter. He's a waste of a roster spot.

Hal Morris   PH/1B   Bats L   Age 35

YEAR	TEAM	LGE	AB	H	DB	TP	HR	BB/SO	R	RBI	SB	CS	OUT	BA	OBP	SLG	EQA	EQR	DEFENSE	
1997	Cincnnti	NL	335	92	22	1	1	22/43	42	33	2	1	244	.275	.325	.355	.233	32	88-1B 92	
1998	KansasCy	AL	467	142	26	2	1	31/51	47	37	1	0	325	.304	.349	.375	.249	50	40-1B 110	33-OF 81
1999	Cincnnti	NL	102	29	8	0	0	9/21	9	15	0	0	73	.284	.342	.363	.243	11		
2000	Cincnnti	NL	166	44	10	0	0	15/23	20	16	0	0	122	.265	.326	.325	.223	14		

Morris will be around for another half-dozen years as a pinch-hitter, the role he was born to play. Mercifully, he's past the point where someone will try to make him a regular, or pay him like one, so he could be an asset well into the next recession.

Roberto Petagine   1B   Bats L   Age 29

YEAR	TEAM	LGE	AB	H	DB	TP	HR	BB/SO	R	RBI	SB	CS	OUT	BA	OBP	SLG	EQA	EQR	DEFENSE	
1996	Norfolk	Int	319	88	21	2	9	43/85	38	50	2	1	232	.276	.373	.439	.277	47	93-1B 92	
1996	NY Mets	NL	101	25	4	0	4	9/27	11	17	0	2	78	.248	.330	.406	.244	11	28-1B 101	
1997	Norfolk	Int	446	122	23	1	25	68/98	70	77	0	1	325	.274	.378	.498	.291	74	114-1B_89	
1998	Indianap	Int	365	102	23	1	18	56/79	61	82	2	1	264	.279	.379	.496	.292	61	67-1B 102	14-OF 105
1998	Cincnnti	NL	63	17	3	1	3	16/11	15	7	1	0	46	.270	.418	.492	.310	12		
1999	Yakult	JpC	442	126	26	2	33	99/97	84	91	9	5	321	.285	.424	.577	.325	97		

Petagine, long deserving of a major-league job, spent 1999 in Japan and hit .325/.469/.677. The only thing he needs to be Geronimo Berroa is a chance. John Olerud signed for about $6 million a year more than Petagine would; the difference between them on the field is negligible. Petagine will be in Japan again in 2000; he's listed here because we're stubborn.

Pokey Reese   2B   Bats R   Age 27

YEAR	TEAM	LGE	AB	H	DB	TP	HR	BB/SO	R	RBI	SB	CS	OUT	BA	OBP	SLG	EQA	EQR	DEFENSE
1997	Indianap	AA	73	17	1	0	4	8/13	10	11	3	0	56	.233	.309	.411	.249	9	
1997	Cincnnti	NL	399	88	10	0	6	30/81	45	27	21	7	318	.221	.283	.291	.202	29	102-SS 96
1998	Cincnnti	NL	134	35	3	2	1	14/27	21	16	3	2	101	.261	.331	.336	.231	13	24-3B 111
1999	Cincnnti	NL	588	167	40	5	9	28/80	79	49	33	7	428	.284	.324	.415	.255	70	135-2B 112
2000	*Cincnnti*	*NL*	*417*	*112*	*22*	*2*	*6*	*31/64*	*64*	*45*	*26*	*6*	*311*	*.269*	*.319*	*.374*	*.242*	*45*	

The power and glove Reese displayed in 1999 made him a good second baseman. While the defense is for real, there's no way I expect him to slug .400 again, which is something he needs to do to keep from hurting the team. Despite his adequate season, his inability to get on base more will keep him from being a star. Getting him out of the top of the lineup is mandatory if the Reds are going to stay in contention.

Chris Stynes   2B   Bats R   Age 27

YEAR	TEAM	LGE	AB	H	DB	TP	HR	BB/SO	R	RBI	SB	CS	OUT	BA	OBP	SLG	EQA	EQR	DEFENSE	
1997	Omaha	AA	329	78	17	1	6	15/26	44	37	2	1	252	.237	.270	.350	.206	24	22-OF 106	20-2B 88
1997	Indianap	AA	87	30	4	0	2	1/5	12	17	3	1	58	.345	.360	.460	.277	12	19-2B 114	
1997	Cincnnti	NL	199	69	7	1	6	11/13	29	27	9	2	132	.347	.393	.482	.298	32	28-OF 114	
1998	Cincnnti	NL	351	92	9	1	7	31/35	53	28	16	1	260	.262	.330	.353	.244	38	60-OF 98	
1999	Cincnnti	NL	114	27	2	0	2	10/13	17	14	4	2	89	.237	.298	.307	.209	9	26-2B 96	
2000	*Cincnnti*	*NL*	*249*	*68*	*9*	*1*	*7*	*21/23*	*35*	*34*	*9*	*2*	*183*	*.273*	*.330*	*.402*	*.251*	*29*		

He's a marginally useful bench player who can play second base and the outfield and run a little. He's worth the roster spot as opposed to, say, Mark Lewis, which isn't a ringing endorsement. Stynes will play less than that projection indicates.

Mark Sweeney   PH/LF   Bats L   Age 30

YEAR	TEAM	LGE	AB	H	DB	TP	HR	BB/SO	R	RBI	SB	CS	OUT	BA	OBP	SLG	EQA	EQR	DEFENSE
1997	San Dieg	NL	105	35	2	0	3	11/18	11	21	2	2	72	.333	.397	.438	.283	15	10-OF 90
1998	San Dieg	NL	197	51	11	3	2	27/36	19	16	1	2	148	.259	.351	.376	.250	23	21-OF 97
1999	Cincnnti	NL	31	11	2	0	2	4/9	5	6	0	0	20	.355	.429	.613	.337	7	
1999	Indianap	Int	314	88	14	1	9	49/44	51	39	2	1	227	.280	.383	.417	.276	46	49-OF 98
2000	*Cincnnti*	*NL*	*236*	*68*	*10*	*1*	*7*	*40/38*	*42*	*41*	*1*	*1*	*169*	*.288*	*.391*	*.428*	*.281*	*35*	

He's an infinitely better player than Hal Morris, despite which he spent most of the summer in Indianapolis. Sweeney is comparable to the Dodgers' Dave Hansen in that both players, who are similar hitters, garnered reputations as "pinch-hitters" early in their career and were never given much chance to play regularly. He deserves a job, even if it is just a pinch-hitting role.

Eddie Taubensee   C   Bats L   Age 31

YEAR	TEAM	LGE	AB	H	DB	TP	HR	BB/SO	R	RBI	SB	CS	OUT	BA	OBP	SLG	EQA	EQR	DEFENSE
1997	Cincnnti	NL	255	67	14	1	11	22/65	25	34	0	1	189	.263	.324	.455	.257	32	
1998	Cincnnti	NL	436	125	20	1	14	52/91	62	76	1	0	311	.287	.363	.433	.271	59	114-C 94
1999	Cincnnti	NL	426	133	23	2	20	24/66	55	82	0	2	295	.312	.351	.516	.283	63	108-C 91
2000	*Cincnnti*	*NL*	*345*	*102*	*17*	*1*	*13*	*35/63*	*52*	*62*	*0*	*1*	*244*	*.296*	*.361*	*.464*	*.274*	*48*	

(Eddie Taubensee *continued*)

Taubensee is one of the most underrated players in baseball, known more for being traded for Kenny Lofton than for his productive left-handed bat. His tremendous stretch drive (1129 OPS after August 31) was an unheralded factor in the Reds' getting to game 163. The bad part: Taubensee is probably the worst-throwing catcher in baseball.

Michael Tucker   RF   Bats L   Age 29

YEAR	TEAM	LGE	AB	H	DB	TP	HR	BB/SO	R	RBI	SB	CS	OUT	BA	OBP	SLG	EQA	EQR	DEFENSE
1997	Atlanta	NL	506	144	28	7	15	43/115	80	57	9	7	369	.285	.348	.457	.268	68	108-OF 100
1998	Atlanta	NL	419	106	29	3	14	48/109	56	47	8	3	316	.253	.334	.437	.260	55	108-OF 97
1999	Cincnnti	NL	297	75	9	5	10	34/80	51	41	9	4	226	.253	.336	.418	.256	38	
2000	*Cincnnti*	*NL*	*345*	*94*	*15*	*3*	*14*	*46/90*	*58*	*59*	*9*	*5*	*256*	*.272*	*.358*	*.455*	*.272*	*49*	

In a parallel universe, the Royals leave Tucker at second base and he makes a lot of money playing baseball. I'm taller there, too. In this universe, Tucker is a corner outfielder who doesn't hit enough to keep a job. Like many Reds, he has skills that could make him an asset off the bench.

Greg Vaughn   LF   Bats R   Age 34

YEAR	TEAM	LGE	AB	H	DB	TP	HR	BB/SO	R	RBI	SB	CS	OUT	BA	OBP	SLG	EQA	EQR	DEFENSE
1997	San Dieg	NL	368	84	10	0	20	56/109	62	60	6	4	288	.228	.333	.418	.254	47	79-OF 96
1998	San Dieg	NL	592	176	33	4	58	80/118	124	133	12	5	421	.297	.386	.660	.327	128	147-OF 98
1999	Cincnnti	NL	552	135	22	2	44	78/136	99	111	13	2	419	.245	.342	.531	.286	91	132-LF 102
2000	*TampaBay*	*AL*	*493*	*124*	*18*	*1*	*38*	*81/116*	*91*	*110*	*7*	*2*	*371*	*.252*	*.357*	*.523*	*.290*	*84*	

He wasn't the fourth most valuable player in the NL; that was just sportswriters being silly. He was important to the Reds' season, both for what his acquisition represented and what he contributed to a team shy on power. Power hitters in their mid-30s are dangerous free agents, but Vaughn has been a very good player in three of the past four seasons. I think he can contribute for two more; that Wilton looks about right. Signed by Tampa Bay, where he will hit and no one will care.

DeWayne Wise   OF   Bats L   Age 22

YEAR	TEAM	LGE	AB	H	DB	TP	HR	BB/SO	R	RBI	SB	CS	OUT	BA	OBP	SLG	EQA	EQR	DEFENSE
1997	Billings	Pio	261	61	11	4	5	5/56	26	22	6	3	203	.234	.251	.364	.202	19	61-OF 98
1998	Burlingt	Mid	504	105	18	8	2	31/114	47	37	10	8	407	.208	.255	.288	.178	27	124-OF 105
1999	Rockford	Mid	508	116	19	8	12	28/85	48	62	15	7	399	.228	.275	.368	.216	43	132-OF 108
2000	*Cincnnti*	*NL*	*485*	*117*	*20*	*7*	*9*	*37/93*	*59*	*52*	*17*	*7*	*375*	*.241*	*.295*	*.367*	*.224*	*45*	

Yadda, yadda, tools...yadda, yadda, outfielder...yadda, yadda, control of the strike zone...yadda, yadda, the Reds love these guys. Wise has no future in an organization with better players of his ilk both next to him and ahead of him.

Dmitri Young   Bats B   OF   Age 26

YEAR	TEAM	LGE	AB	H	DB	TP	HR	BB/SO	R	RBI	SB	CS	OUT	BA	OBP	SLG	EQA	EQR	DEFENSE	
1997	Louisvil	AA	85	22	6	0	4	12/15	9	13	1	1	64	.259	.351	.471	.272	12		
1997	St Louis	NL	338	90	16	3	5	37/62	38	34	5	5	253	.266	.342	.376	.245	38	70-1B 92	
1998	Cincnnti	NL	543	173	43	2	17	46/91	82	87	2	5	375	.319	.374	.499	.288	83	37-1B 96	93-OF 87
1999	Cincnnti	NL	375	113	32	2	13	25/70	60	53	3	1	263	.301	.349	.501	.280	55	58-RF 107	
2000	*Cincnnti*	*NL*	*426*	*129*	*26*	*1*	*17*	*46/77*	*71*	*81*	*4*	*3*	*300*	*.303*	*.371*	*.488*	*.285*	*65*		

It's no secret that Young can hit, since he's been a doubling machine as long as he's been a professional. In 1999, however, it was his defense that raised eyebrows. It's not just his DFT above that looks good: his range factor and zone rating were also well above average. He should be the full-time starter in 2000; I think he'll outperform that projection and post a .300 EqA.

PITCHERS (Averages: ERA: 4.50 / H/9: 9.00 / HR/9: 1.00 / BB/9: 3.50 / K/9: 6.50 / KWH: 1.00)

Steve Avery   Throws L   Age 30

YEAR	TEAM	LGE	IP	H	ER	HR	BB	K	ERA	W	L	H/9	HR/9	BB/9	K/9	KWH	PERA
1997	Boston	AL	99.0	120	68	14	49	52	6.18	4	7	10.91	1.27	4.45	4.73	0.34	6.36
1998	Boston	AL	123.7	127	69	12	67	58	5.02	6	8	9.24	0.87	4.88	4.22	0.30	5.02
1999	Cincnnti	NL	93.7	81	62	10	75	49	5.96	4	6	7.78	0.96	7.21	4.71	0.30	5.19

He was inexpensive and gave the Reds a couple of good months before shoulder surgery ended his season, so you could say the gamble worked. He's become a very painful pitcher to watch, though, constantly scuffling. The memory of those two months will get him many more opportunities, but I have to believe he has little chance to be even this effective again. I'd rather have William Avery. Or Avery Brundage.

Manny Barrios   Throws R   Age 25

YEAR	TEAM	LGE	IP	H	ER	HR	BB	K	ERA	W	L	H/9	HR/9	BB/9	K/9	KWH	PERA
1997	New Orln	AmA	78.7	80	38	5	37	68	4.35	5	4	9.15	0.57	4.23	7.78	1.17	4.46
1998	Charlott	Int	24.0	19	9	3	10	20	3.38	2	1	7.13	1.13	3.75	7.50	1.57	3.75
1998	Albuquer	PCL	36.7	45	22	7	17	29	5.40	2	2	11.05	1.72	4.17	7.12	0.82	6.87
1999	Indianap	Int	85.7	103	63	8	37	64	6.62	3	7	10.82	0.84	3.89	6.72	0.80	5.57

Barrios is a skinny guy with a good fastball who can't find an organization that likes him. He's pitched at Triple-A for four teams in three years, with just 6⅔ major-league innings to show for it. The Phillies claimed him off waivers in October; they're neither deep nor talented in the bullpen, so this is Barrios's best chance at a career. I expect him to make their pen and be one of the league's better rookie relievers.

Stan Belinda   Throws R   Age 33

YEAR	TEAM	LGE	IP	H	ER	HR	BB	K	ERA	W	L	H/9	HR/9	BB/9	K/9	KWH	PERA
1997	Cincnnti	NL	100.7	83	39	11	34	106	3.49	7	4	7.42	0.98	3.04	9.48	2.98	3.49
1998	Cincnnti	NL	61.7	46	23	8	30	54	3.36	4	3	6.71	1.17	4.38	7.88	1.58	3.79
1999	Cincnnti	NL	42.0	44	26	11	17	39	5.57	2	3	9.43	2.36	3.64	8.36	1.52	6.43

DTs can adjust for offensive levels, caliber of competition and ballpark, but there's no translation that can do justice to what Belinda did in 1999, returning to the major leagues while battling the onset of multiple sclerosis. The MS didn't shorten his season; a sore elbow did. Belinda was traded to Colorado in the Dante Bichette deal. At his best, Belinda gets strikeouts and allows walks, keeping the ball out of play. That's a style I feel may be effective at altitude, so he has some chance for success.

Rob Bell   Throws R   Age 23

YEAR	TEAM	LGE	IP	H	ER	HR	BB	K	ERA	W	L	H/9	HR/9	BB/9	K/9	KWH	PERA
1997	Macon	SAL	139.7	184	89	19	59	97	5.74	6	10	11.86	1.22	3.80	6.25	0.65	6.57
1998	DanvillC	Car	167.3	215	104	11	63	142	5.59	7	12	11.56	0.59	3.39	7.64	1.11	5.49
1999	Chattang	Sou	69.7	83	31	7	19	57	4.00	4	4	10.72	0.90	2.45	7.36	1.54	4.91

Solely on ability, Bell is one of the best pitching prospects in baseball. That said, he spent about three months on the disabled list with a sore elbow, two words you do not want to hear in connection with a pitcher whose best pitch is a curveball. When Bell pitched, he was as effective as ever, but that elbow is a huge red flag. Look for him to have surgery before he reaches 200 major-league innings.

Jim Crowell   Throws L   Age 26

YEAR	TEAM	LGE	IP	H	ER	HR	BB	K	ERA	W	L	H/9	HR/9	BB/9	K/9	KWH	PERA
1997	Kinston	Car	101.7	135	63	5	32	64	5.58	4	7	11.95	0.44	2.83	5.67	0.71	5.31
1998	Chattang	Sou	22.0	44	30	2	18	8	12.27	0	2	18.00	0.82	7.36	3.27	0.06	11.86
1998	Charl-WV	SAL	11.7	39	33	1	15	5	25.46	0	1	30.09	0.77	11.57	3.86	0.03	23.14
1999	Chattang	Sou	136.0	208	118	13	102	61	7.81	4	11	13.76	0.86	6.75	4.04	0.13	8.67

The first year after surgery is a difficult one, as a pitcher sorts through what he still has and what was left on the table. Crowell had rotator-cuff surgery in the summer of 1998, and may have come back a bit too soon. His velocity is gone, and as you can see, he's learning to command what he has left. Now, Crowell is primarily an example of the transitory nature of the label "pitching prospect."

Bo Donaldson — Throws R — Age 25

YEAR	TEAM	LGE	IP	H	ER	HR	BB	K	ERA	W	L	H/9	HR/9	BB/9	K/9	KWH	PERA
1997	Boise	Nwn	48.3	42	13	0	25	48	2.42	4	1	7.82	0.00	4.66	8.94	1.64	3.35
1998	Lk Elsin	Cal	67.3	88	51	8	52	62	6.82	2	5	11.76	1.07	6.95	8.29	0.63	7.75
1999	Rockford	Mid	27.3	24	10	0	16	31	3.29	2	1	7.90	0.00	5.27	10.21	1.87	3.62
1999	Chattang	Sou	49.3	35	21	3	19	51	3.83	3	2	6.39	0.55	3.47	9.30	2.92	2.74

Despite two pretty good years, the Angels gave up on Donaldson, and he migrated to the Reds' system, where he was the same pitcher he'd been in 1997. He is a serviceable reliever who throws strikes and keeps the ball in the park. The Reds showed that a bullpen doesn't have to be famous to be effective, so Donaldson is in the right place to get the chance I believe he deserves. If Williamson is traded, his opportunity increases.

Keith Glauber — Throws R — Age 28

YEAR	TEAM	LGE	IP	H	ER	HR	BB	K	ERA	W	L	H/9	HR/9	BB/9	K/9	KWH	PERA
1997	Arkansas	Tex	52.0	61	30	3	32	41	5.19	3	3	10.56	0.52	5.54	7.10	0.64	5.71
1998	Burlingt	Mid	12.3	19	13	1	9	8	9.49	0	1	13.86	0.73	6.57	5.84	0.28	8.76
1998	Indianap	Int	15.0	22	18	1	16	13	10.80	0	2	13.20	0.60	9.60	7.80	0.36	9.00
1999	Chattang	Sou	46.7	52	16	0	10	20	3.09	3	2	10.03	0.00	1.93	3.86	0.57	3.47
1999	Indianap	Int	63.3	94	52	7	22	43	7.39	2	5	13.36	0.99	3.13	6.11	0.67	6.96

Glauber's comeback from rotator-cuff surgery continued, as he had his first success in two years, a good start in Double-A. Moved up to Indianapolis, he scuffled, still fighting a loss of velocity. He will be in the major-league camp in the spring, trying to take Stan Belinda's job as the sixth reliever.

Danny Graves — Throws R — Age 26

YEAR	TEAM	LGE	IP	H	ER	HR	BB	K	ERA	W	L	H/9	HR/9	BB/9	K/9	KWH	PERA
1997	Buffalo	AmA	40.3	53	26	3	12	19	5.80	2	2	11.83	0.67	2.68	4.24	0.42	5.36
1998	Cincnnti	NL	81.3	77	31	6	30	42	3.43	6	3	8.52	0.66	3.32	4.65	0.57	3.87
1999	Cincnnti	NL	108.3	95	43	9	48	67	3.57	7	5	7.89	0.75	3.99	5.57	0.74	3.82

Graves was the best reliever in the NL, as measured by Michael Wolverton's Reliever Evaluation Tools. Graves was particularly effective at stranding inherited runners, allowing just nine of 44 to score and leading the majors in Inherited Runs Prevented. An extreme groundball pitcher, Graves benefited from the improved infield defense of the Reds. His strikeout rate is unimpressive, and he's thrown a lot of innings the past two years, so I believe there will be some decline in 2000.

Juan Guzman — Throws R — Age 33

YEAR	TEAM	LGE	IP	H	ER	HR	BB	K	ERA	W	L	H/9	HR/9	BB/9	K/9	KWH	PERA
1997	Toronto	AL	60.3	46	39	14	31	52	5.82	3	4	6.86	2.09	4.62	7.76	1.42	4.92
1998	Toronto	AL	146.3	129	75	17	67	114	4.61	8	8	7.93	1.05	4.12	7.01	1.12	4.18
1998	Baltimor	AL	65.3	59	32	4	34	55	4.41	4	3	8.13	0.55	4.68	7.58	1.13	3.99
1999	Baltimor	AL	121.7	123	59	16	63	97	4.36	7	7	9.10	1.18	4.66	7.18	0.91	5.18
1999	Cincnnti	NL	75.3	74	34	9	20	58	4.06	4	4	8.84	1.08	2.39	6.93	1.70	4.06

Traded at midseason for the second straight year, effective in a doomed effort for a second straight year. He's a free agent again; while he's coming off the first back-to-back 200-inning seasons of his career, his PAP data indicate he hasn't been overworked, so I think he's a good signing for a team looking for a #3 starter. Given the thin supply of pitching this winter, he's likely to be paid like a #1. Signed by the Devil Rays.

Pete Harnisch — Throws R — Age 33

YEAR	TEAM	LGE	IP	H	ER	HR	BB	K	ERA	W	L	H/9	HR/9	BB/9	K/9	KWH	PERA
1997	NY Mets	NL	25.3	36	24	6	12	11	8.53	1	2	12.79	2.13	4.26	3.91	0.21	8.53
1997	Milwauke	AL	14.3	12	8	1	12	10	5.02	1	1	7.53	0.63	7.53	6.28	0.52	5.02
1998	Cincnnti	NL	209.7	178	77	24	68	150	3.31	15	8	7.64	1.03	2.92	6.44	1.39	3.56
1999	Cincnnti	NL	193.0	201	89	23	54	116	4.15	11	10	9.37	1.07	2.52	5.41	0.93	4.38

The star of the best game I attended all year, a 3-0 Reds win over the Padres in San Diego. Harnisch threw a 110-pitch, three-hit shutout and hit a two-run homer that put the game away in the seventh inning. It's cool to feel like you may have seen the best game of a player's career. For the second straight season, Harnisch was more effective when given an extra day of rest. As much as Harnisch slipped this year, McKeon would be well served to handle him with kid gloves in 2000.

Marty Janzen   Throws R   Age 27

YEAR	TEAM	LGE	IP	H	ER	HR	BB	K	ERA	W	L	H/9	HR/9	BB/9	K/9	KWH	PERA
1997	Syracuse	Int	62.0	85	62	12	38	47	9.00	1	6	12.34	1.74	5.52	6.82	0.51	8.27
1997	Toronto	AL	25.3	22	10	4	13	17	3.55	2	1	7.82	1.42	4.62	6.04	0.76	4.62
1998	Norwich	Eas	31.7	51	35	4	23	28	9.95	1	3	14.49	1.14	6.54	7.96	0.50	9.38
1998	Columbus	Int	67.3	82	49	7	43	46	6.55	2	5	10.96	0.94	5.75	6.15	0.45	6.55
1999	Chattang	Sou	50.3	66	39	6	35	31	6.97	2	4	11.80	1.07	6.26	5.54	0.31	7.51
1999	Indianap	Int	15.7	18	10	0	9	7	5.74	1	1	10.34	0.00	5.17	4.02	0.23	4.60

Janzen is Exhibit A in the case for trading pitching prospects for established players, particularly during a pennant race. On occasion, one will become John Smoltz. More often, they end up like Janzen: mishandled, injured and ineffective. Janzen was one of three pitchers traded by the Yankees to Toronto for David Cone in 1995. He's had the best career of any of them. I'm no fan of trading Brad Penny or Jason Grilli for mid-level talents, but the evidence is very strong that the team trading away the minor leaguers usually wins the deal.

Phil Merrell   Throws R   Age 22

YEAR	TEAM	LGE	IP	H	ER	HR	BB	K	ERA	W	L	H/9	HR/9	BB/9	K/9	KWH	PERA
1997	Billings	Pio	64.3	92	63	7	38	37	8.81	1	6	12.87	0.98	5.32	5.18	0.29	7.55
1998	Charl-WV	SAL	137.7	211	111	13	59	76	7.26	4	11	13.79	0.85	3.86	4.97	0.35	7.39
1999	Clinton	Mid	98.3	90	36	4	36	62	3.29	7	4	8.24	0.37	3.29	5.67	0.89	3.39
1999	Indianap	Int	10.3	22	21	4	5	5	18.29	0	1	19.16	3.48	4.35	4.35	0.17	15.68
1999	Chattang	Sou	33.3	54	35	3	15	13	9.45	1	3	14.58	0.81	4.05	3.51	0.16	7.83

Merrell is a slow developer who parlayed an improved change-up into prospect status. The Reds do not have a lot of pitching in the system; behind Rob Bell, Merrell may actually be their best pitching prospect. His fastball is average at best, so his progress will continue to be slow. Long-term, I like him, so check back in 2002.

Denny Neagle   Throws L   Age 31

YEAR	TEAM	LGE	IP	H	ER	HR	BB	K	ERA	W	L	H/9	HR/9	BB/9	K/9	KWH	PERA
1997	Atlanta	NL	228.0	218	93	18	51	160	3.67	15	10	8.61	0.71	2.01	6.32	1.72	3.43
1998	Atlanta	NL	208.0	208	96	25	64	158	4.15	12	11	9.00	1.08	2.77	6.84	1.40	4.28
1999	Cincnnti	NL	108.7	102	55	21	38	73	4.56	6	6	8.45	1.74	3.15	6.05	1.03	4.80

Don't be fooled: Neagle's overall numbers were dragged down by six starts in the spring (8.17 ERA) when he was suffering from shoulder tendinitis. He simply wasn't able to pitch and had no business trying. Allowed to rest until after the All-Star break, he was his old self (13 starts, 3.13 ERA). He should pitch at his 1998 level for a few more years.

Steve Parris   Throws R   Age 32

YEAR	TEAM	LGE	IP	H	ER	HR	BB	K	ERA	W	L	H/9	HR/9	BB/9	K/9	KWH	PERA
1997	Chattang	Sou	75.0	93	50	8	35	51	6.00	3	5	11.16	0.96	4.20	6.12	0.60	6.00
1997	Indianap	AmA	33.3	31	18	4	13	23	4.86	2	2	8.37	1.08	3.51	6.21	0.98	4.32
1998	Indianap	Int	80.7	83	42	8	29	86	4.69	4	5	9.26	0.89	3.24	9.60	2.30	4.46
1998	Cincnnti	NL	99.3	90	43	9	34	73	3.90	6	5	8.15	0.82	3.08	6.61	1.30	3.71
1999	Indianap	Int	33.3	44	17	5	10	26	4.59	2	2	11.88	1.35	2.70	7.02	1.15	6.21
1999	Cincnnti	NL	125.0	132	60	14	50	83	4.32	7	7	9.50	1.01	3.60	5.98	0.78	4.82

Parris's 1999 gives us a chance to illustrate the importance of plate discipline to an offense. Parris made 21 starts and one relief appearance, split evenly against teams in the top and bottom half of their leagues in walks. Against the teams who walked less, Parris was 8-0 with a 3.23 ERA, averaging just over seven innings per start with a 52/18 strikeout-to-walk ratio. In 11 starts against the teams that walked more, he was 3-4 with a 3.86 ERA, averaging just over five innings per start with a dead-even 34 walks and 34 strikeouts. Same pitcher, but the teams that didn't walk allowed him to throw two extra innings per start with greater effectiveness. That's the advantage being patient gives an offense.

Parris was worked hard by McKeon last year, and has never been able to stay healthy. He'll be moderately effective as a swingman and make at least one trip to the disabled list.

Brandon Puffer   Throws R   Age 24

YEAR	TEAM	LGE	IP	H	ER	HR	BB	K	ERA	W	L	H/9	HR/9	BB/9	K/9	KWH	PERA
1997	Boise	Nwn	14.3	13	7	0	3	8	4.40	1	1	8.16	0.00	1.88	5.02	1.23	2.51
1997	CedarRpd	Mid	16.3	11	8	0	12	8	4.41	1	1	6.06	0.00	6.61	4.41	0.36	3.31
1998	Charl-WV	SAL	44.7	88	58	5	32	23	11.69	1	4	17.73	1.01	6.45	4.63	0.14	11.49
1999	Clinton	Mid	59.3	67	25	3	30	40	3.79	4	3	10.16	0.46	4.55	6.07	0.59	5.01

Puffer is a closer suspect thanks to 34 saves with Clinton. Here's a free hint to fantasy players, Strat geeks and player-development people: there's no such thing as a pitching prospect. Even if there were, there would *certainly* be no such thing as a relief-pitching prospect. There's nothing about Puffer that makes me think he'll survive Double-A.

Dennis Reyes   Throws L   Age 23

YEAR	TEAM	LGE	IP	H	ER	HR	BB	K	ERA	W	L	H/9	HR/9	BB/9	K/9	KWH	PERA
1997	SanAnton	Tex	73.3	91	38	7	32	57	4.66	4	4	11.17	0.86	3.93	7.00	0.83	5.77
1997	Albuquer	PCL	58.7	60	31	4	34	39	4.76	3	4	9.20	0.61	5.22	5.98	0.56	4.91
1997	LosAngls	NL	45.3	55	23	4	19	33	4.57	2	3	10.92	0.79	3.77	6.55	0.78	5.56
1998	Albuquer	PCL	44.0	29	11	5	20	50	2.25	4	1	5.93	1.02	4.09	10.23	3.22	3.07
1998	LosAngls	NL	28.3	28	18	1	21	31	5.72	1	2	8.89	0.32	6.67	9.85	1.22	5.08
1998	Cincnnti	NL	39.0	36	18	2	28	42	4.15	2	2	8.31	0.46	6.46	9.69	1.31	4.62
1999	Cincnnti	NL	60.3	56	30	5	38	69	4.48	4	3	8.35	0.75	5.67	10.29	1.67	4.77

Reyes has been ready for a rotation job for more than a year. That he hasn't been given one is a good thing in the long term, saving him hundreds of innings at the ages of 21 and 22, while his arm is still vulnerable. The Reds are deep in starters at the major-league level, so Reyes could spend another year in the pen. Once he gets a rotation slot, he's going to keep it for a while.

Scott Sullivan   Throws R   Age 29

YEAR	TEAM	LGE	IP	H	ER	HR	BB	K	ERA	W	L	H/9	HR/9	BB/9	K/9	KWH	PERA
1997	Indianap	AmA	26.7	19	5	0	5	19	1.69	3	0	6.41	0.00	1.69	6.41	2.84	1.69
1997	Cincnnti	NL	98.7	77	33	12	32	90	3.01	8	3	7.02	1.09	2.92	8.21	2.46	3.28
1998	Cincnnti	NL	102.3	100	62	14	38	82	5.45	4	7	8.79	1.23	3.34	7.21	1.32	4.57
1999	Cincnnti	NL	111.0	94	43	9	45	75	3.49	7	5	7.62	0.73	3.65	6.08	0.99	3.57

Despite the ineffectiveness and fatigue that rendered him unavailable in September of 1998, Sullivan was once again worked like a dray horse in 1999, throwing 113 innings. He managed to stay healthy, but there was another drop in his effectiveness after July. Even sidearmers can get tired. With his peripherals in a slow retreat, I think he's in for a difficult 2000.

David Therneau   Throws R   Age 24

YEAR	TEAM	LGE	IP	H	ER	HR	BB	K	ERA	W	L	H/9	HR/9	BB/9	K/9	KWH	PERA
1998	Billings	Pio	40.3	64	30	2	18	37	6.69	1	3	14.28	0.45	4.02	8.26	0.89	7.36
1998	Burlingt	Mid	37.7	45	21	4	23	29	5.02	2	2	10.75	0.96	5.50	6.93	0.61	6.21
1999	Rockford	Mid	90.7	124	53	8	41	70	5.26	4	6	12.31	0.79	4.07	6.95	0.72	6.45
1999	Chattang	Sou	20.0	25	8	3	9	9	3.60	1	1	11.25	1.35	4.05	4.05	0.27	6.30
1999	Indianap	Int	34.0	56	36	9	14	20	9.53	1	3	14.82	2.38	3.71	5.29	0.38	10.06

The Reds' 1998 #9 pick jumped all the way to Triple-A in his first full season. While he pitched well, the rapid ascent was primarily due to a glossy record (14-3) and the aforementioned dearth of pitching prospects in the system. Therneau throws four pitches, including a plus slider, and has a future. It's just not going to arrive as quickly as it looks here.

Brett Tomko   Throws R   Age 27

YEAR	TEAM	LGE	IP	H	ER	HR	BB	K	ERA	W	L	H/9	HR/9	BB/9	K/9	KWH	PERA
1997	Indianap	AmA	58.7	61	24	7	10	52	3.68	4	3	9.36	1.07	1.53	7.98	3.31	3.99
1997	Cincnnti	NL	127.3	104	47	15	49	89	3.32	9	5	7.35	1.06	3.46	6.29	1.16	3.68
1998	Cincnnti	NL	211.7	201	109	22	68	155	4.63	12	12	8.55	0.94	2.89	6.59	1.31	3.95
1999	Cincnnti	NL	167.7	184	103	29	58	127	5.53	8	11	9.88	1.56	3.11	6.82	1.13	5.48
1999	Indianap	Int	12.0	17	8	1	1	8	6.00	0	1	12.75	0.75	0.75	6.00	2.81	5.25

Chemistry is a vastly overrated concept, primarily used—in lieu of serious analysis—as an ex post facto justification for why a team over- or underperformed. Occasionally, though, there are clear examples of interpersonal problems affecting the performance of individuals. The war between Tomko and the McKeon/Don Gullett team has had a detrimental effect on the pitcher's development, and it would be best for everyone involved if he was traded. He has the talent to succeed; I fully expect him to get back to his 1997 level.

Ron Villone　　　　**Throws L**　　　**Age 30**

YEAR	TEAM	LGE	IP	H	ER	HR	BB	K	ERA	W	L	H/9	HR/9	BB/9	K/9	KWH	PERA
1997	Milwauke	AL	53.3	52	21	4	36	40	3.54	4	2	8.78	0.68	6.08	6.75	0.64	5.06
1998	Buffalo	Int	21.3	22	12	2	13	24	5.06	1	1	9.28	0.84	5.48	10.13	1.50	5.48
1998	Clevelnd	AL	28.3	28	16	3	23	15	5.08	1	2	8.89	0.95	7.31	4.76	0.26	6.04
1999	Indianap	Int	18.0	10	3	1	14	19	1.50	2	0	5.00	0.50	7.00	9.50	1.93	3.00
1999	Cincnnti	NL	139.0	122	71	7	70	94	4.60	7	8	7.90	0.45	4.53	6.09	0.77	3.76

On one hand, you have to credit McKeon for getting Villone out of the specialist role. On the other, keeping Villone in the rotation when he was clearly less effective as a starter than in the long-relief role was a bit stubborn. Dennis Reyes and Gabe White are both better suited for the rotation. At this point, it's not clear what Villone's role will be in 2000.

Gabe White　　　　**Throws L**　　　**Age 28**

YEAR	TEAM	LGE	IP	H	ER	HR	BB	K	ERA	W	L	H/9	HR/9	BB/9	K/9	KWH	PERA
1997	Indianap	AmA	111.7	140	57	9	21	52	4.59	6	6	11.28	0.73	1.69	4.19	0.69	4.84
1997	Cincnnti	NL	41.3	39	19	6	8	23	4.14	3	2	8.49	1.31	1.74	5.01	1.27	3.92
1998	Cincnnti	NL	98.7	88	46	17	28	79	4.20	6	5	8.03	1.55	2.55	7.21	1.89	4.10
1999	Cincnnti	NL	59.7	71	31	12	13	59	4.68	3	4	10.71	1.81	1.96	8.90	2.82	5.73

The opposite of Villone, in that his flyball tendencies and lack of a platoon split or dominant pitch would make him a more effective starter than reliever. White is comparable to Denny Neagle and capable of having the same kind of success.

Scott Williamson　　　**Throws R**　　　**Age 24**

YEAR	TEAM	LGE	IP	H	ER	HR	BB	K	ERA	W	L	H/9	HR/9	BB/9	K/9	KWH	PERA
1997	Billings	Pio	77.7	88	32	5	32	61	3.71	5	4	10.20	0.58	3.71	7.07	0.99	4.87
1998	Chattang	Sou	96.3	95	49	4	44	87	4.58	5	6	8.88	0.37	4.11	8.13	1.35	4.02
1998	Indianap	Int	20.0	22	9	2	9	15	4.05	1	1	9.90	0.90	4.05	6.75	0.85	4.95
1999	Cincnnti	NL	91.3	59	29	7	41	103	2.86	7	3	5.81	0.69	4.04	10.15	3.28	2.76

Williamson's dominant year was a key to the Reds' surprising success, giving McKeon a third reliever to use with Sullivan and Graves and guaranteeing that he'd have at least one effective right-handed reliever available every night. Like Sullivan in 1998, Williamson scuffled late in the year. It will be interesting to see if McKeon continues to use his relievers the same way in 2000, or elects to make Williamson his closer and use Graves and Sullivan as setup men. If the rumored trade to the Mariners does happen, I think a most intriguing subplot will be how Williamson handles the transition from McKeon to Lou Piniella.

Mark Wohlers　　　　**Throws R**　　　**Age 30**

YEAR	TEAM	LGE	IP	H	ER	HR	BB	K	ERA	W	L	H/9	HR/9	BB/9	K/9	KWH	PERA
1997	Atlanta	NL	68.3	60	30	4	40	86	3.95	5	3	7.90	0.53	5.27	11.33	2.30	4.08
1998	Atlanta	NL	20.7	19	23	2	35	21	10.02	0	2	8.27	0.87	15.24	9.15	0.50	8.71
1998	Richmond	Int	11.7	24	30	5	41	14	23.14	0	1	18.51	3.86	31.63	10.80	0.15	30.09

We'll spare you the DTs on this one. In 4⅔ innings over seven appearances at four levels, Wohlers gave up 10 runs and 16 walks. It may have been the first time in baseball history that Tommy John surgery was the highlight of a player's season. Wohlers is out until at least September, more likely 2001, at which time he'll get a few more chances.

Support-Neutral Records — CINCINNATI REDS — Park Effect: +0.7%

PITCHER	GS	IP	R	SNW	SNL	SNPCT	W	L	RA	APW	SNVA	SNWAR
Steve Avery	19	96.0	62	6.0	6.7	.472	6	7	5.81	-0.73	-0.33	0.59
Jason Bere	10	40.3	31	2.2	3.9	.361	3	0	6.92	-0.77	-0.78	-0.39
Juan Guzman	12	77.3	33	5.2	3.3	.615	6	3	3.84	1.01	0.91	1.62
Pete Harnisch	33	198.3	86	13.9	8.8	.612	16	10	3.90	2.45	2.32	4.25
Denny Neagle	19	109.3	53	7.2	5.4	.570	9	5	4.36	0.82	0.90	1.82
Steve Parris	21	125.3	56	8.1	5.7	.586	10	4	4.02	1.39	1.25	2.23
Dennis Reyes	1	2.7	6	0.0	0.8	.011	0	1	20.25	-0.42	-0.39	-0.34
Brett Tomko	26	157.3	99	8.3	10.7	.438	5	7	5.66	-0.95	-1.14	0.24
Ron Villone	22	125.0	69	7.5	7.3	.509	8	7	4.97	0.15	0.16	1.24
TOTALS	163	931.7	495	58.3	52.5	.527	63	44	4.78	2.94	2.90	11.25

The title of Most Underrated Starter in baseball might belong to Pete Harnisch. Over the past two seasons, Harnisch has the eighth-best Support-Neutral W/L record in the majors, better than Mike Hampton, John Smoltz, Roger Clemens, Mike Mussina and a host of other starters who get more ink than he does. Jamie Moyer, who ranks fifth on the list, would give Harnisch a run for his money in the balloting.

Pitcher Abuse Points

PITCHER	AGE	GS	PAP	PAP/S	WKLD	MAX	1-90	91-100	101-110	111-120	121-130	131-140	141+
Steve Avery	29	19	57	3.0	4.5	118	9	6	2	2	0	0	0
Jason Bere	28	10	4	0.4	0.7	104	6	3	1	0	0	0	0
Juan Guzman	32	12	130	10.8	10.8	123	2	4	2	3	1	0	0
Pete Harnisch	32	33	98	3.0	3.0	117	17	5	8	3	0	0	0
Denny Neagle	30	19	51	2.7	3.6	118	7	8	3	1	0	0	0
Steve Parris	31	21	220	10.5	12.2	135	4	8	4	3	1	1	0
Dennis Reyes	22	1	0	0.0	0.0	71	1	0	0	0	0	0	0
Brett Tomko	26	26	314	12.1	24.2	131	8	3	7	3	4	1	0
Ron Villone	29	22	60	2.7	4.1	121	7	9	5	0	1	0	0
CINCINNATI		163	934	5.7	8.4	135	61	46	32	15	7	2	0
Ranking (NL)				13	14								

You know, it's difficult to work your starting pitchers too hard when you have half a dozen relievers capable of throwing three innings at a time. Jack McKeon, once again, kept the kid gloves on with his starters, and the results were impressive. Pete Harnisch had another fine season, Denny Neagle returned from early-season arm troubles (you think the Braves knew something we didn't?) to pitch well in the second half and Juan Guzman was effective after being picked up at the trade deadline. . . . Brett Tomko led the team in workload for the second straight season, and once again drove the Reds batty with his inconsistency. . . . I would be remiss not to mention that Steve Parris, whose career has been marred by one injury after another, was used as if McKeon wasn't aware of his macabre health record.

Colorado Rockies

Four years ago, in the first edition of *Baseball Prospectus*, we spent a large portion of the chapter on the Colorado Rockies talking about park effects, Coors Field and the apparent lack of understanding Rockies' management had of the effect of their environment on the game.

Three years ago, in *Baseball Prospectus 1997*, we spent a large portion of the chapter on the Colorado Rockies talking about park effects, Coors Field and management's continuing difficulties understanding what effect playing at high altitude has on the game of baseball.

Two years ago, we talked about Coors and management. We thought perhaps the team had turned a corner and didn't know what to make of Don Baylor.

Last year, we talked about the team's most important new signing, manager Jim Leyland. The word "Coors" didn't appear until more than halfway through the chapter. The Rockies lost 90 games, finishing in last place for the first time in their history. General Manager Bob Gebhard resigned in August, and Leyland announced in early September that he would retire at the end of the season.

So this year, we're going back to talking about Coors Field and management.

We'll begin with a bit of honesty: no one knows what makes a good "Coors Field" team. For starters, it isn't Coors Field that distorts the game, but the altitude of the city of Denver. The term "park effect," which is normally on point, is too specific when discussing the Rockies. It leads to the erroneous conclusion that the park is responsible for the conditions, as is the case in the Astrodome or Wrigley Field. It's not; short of a pressurized dome, no ballpark will counter the effects of thinner air at altitude. So from here on out, we won't be discussing Coors Field or park effects; we'll be discussing altitude or environmental effects.

As we suggested a few years ago, the altitude has such an extreme effect on the game that it may be many years before we can get a handle on the best way to build a winner in Denver. That doesn't mean we give up trying to understand the effects; it means that we can't approach the issue with our usual air of certainty.

To date, the Rockies have done a poor job of identifying good players. The distorting effects of altitude on player statistics have blinded the team to the relative mediocrity of its hitting and the decent quality of its pitching. The result has been the retention of too many overrated hitters and a lack of respect for pitchers who have been fairly effective. Of course, even in 1999, the Rockies' pitching was disappointing.

So with the primary problem still a front office one, the most important new signing for the Colorado Rockies will again be someone who won't play a single game: new General Manager Dan O'Dowd. O'Dowd, who has spent 16 years in the front offices of Baltimore and Cleveland, gets the next opportunity to build a winner in Denver.

O'Dowd's job isn't an easy one; even here at the *Prospectus* there is disagreement about what kind of player is best under the extreme conditions. Joe Sheehan theorizes that balls in play are worse for the defense in Coors than anywhere else, since those balls are more likely to become hits and extra-base hits in the thinner Denver air. This would suggest that the best pitchers would be guys who keep the ball out of play, even if they walked lots of hitters in the process. Similarly, free-swinging hitters who put the ball in play, even those who don't walk much, might be more valuable in Colorado than anywhere else.

On the other hand, given the increase in home runs in this environment, perhaps the best pitcher is one who doesn't walk guys who are then on base when their teammate homers. Ground balls would be nice, except that the breaking balls that normally lead to grounders break less at high elevation, making them easier to hit in the air and over the fence. We know the conditions are extreme, but we are a long way from knowing the proper way to build a winning team under these conditions.

In the meantime, the Rockies need a general manager who can filter out the altitude effects when evaluating talent. There are some concepts that all GMs should follow: get good players, avoid bad ones. Younger, cheaper and underrated players are more valuable than older, expensive and overrated ones.

Rockies Prospectus

1999 record: 72-90; Fifth place, NL West

Pythagorean W/L: 72-90

Runs scored: 906 (2nd in NL)

Runs allowed: 1,028 (16th in NL)

Team EQA: .245 (15th in NL)

1999 team age: 29.2 (7th-oldest in NL)

1999 park: Coors Field; ridiculous hitters' park, increased run scoring by 63%.

1999: A disappointment as the team fought age and injuries.

2000: The new management team provides hope; early returns are mixed.

In addition to these basics, a Rockies' GM needs an additional level of insight, because the environment muddies the waters. It's harder to separate the good players from the bad ones, to recognize the mediocre hitters and the effective pitchers in this context.

That's why O'Dowd's first player-personnel move was encouraging for Colorado fans. O'Dowd dumped Dante Bichette on the Cincinnati Reds. If the key to Colorado's future is to recognize and acquire good baseball players while jettisoning their overrated and overpaid "stars," then O'Dowd is on the right track. Bichette, average to slightly above in his prime, is the poster child for the effects the environment has on hitting statistics. Until 1999, Bichette was never a terrible player. He was merely a mediocre one whose raw statistics were inflated by his environment and, to some extent, a learned ability to take advantage of that environment. He was never a slugging stud who belonged in the middle of the lineup regularly. And if O'Dowd knows this, he is already the best general manager in club history.

What O'Dowd got for Bichette is not as important as the recognition that he needed to be traded. In Jeffrey Hammonds and Stan Belinda, however, he got back two players who are not stars but who have a reasonable chance at being better in 2000 than they were in 1999.

O'Dowd's subsequent moves at the winter meetings were a mixed bag. He traded Vinny Castilla—who like Bichette has been vastly overrated—and Jamey Wright in a four-team deal that netted Jeff Cirillo. Cirillo is a tremendous player and part of the solution to the Colorado OBP problems. O'Dowd's next move, though, was a real disappointment, as he signed Tom Goodwin to a three-year deal to play center field. Goodwin's lack of on-base skills makes him a real problem, especially in the leadoff spot. O'Dowd also signed both halves of the San Francisco Giants' catching platoon, Brent Mayne and Scott Servais, which doesn't bode well for the team's top prospect, catcher Ben Petrick.

We've seen that the Rockies' GM faces difficulties not found elsewhere. But what makes a good manager under these conditions? There are certain managerial qualities that seem important no matter what, leadership being the foremost. But the in-game and day-to-day strategies involved in running a team at altitude would seem to be different. Again, we aren't yet sure what those differences might be.

Since Don Baylor hadn't managed anywhere but Colorado, it was hard to tell what, if anything, he was doing differently than he would have done elsewhere. He didn't appear to be the best tactician, and his handling of the pitching staff wasn't anything special, but how much of that was Don Baylor and how much of it was thin air? After six years and just one successful season, the Rockies decided it was Baylor, firing him after the 1998 campaign.

To replace him, they got Super Genius Jim Leyland. Leyland, of course, was also a super pain for pitchers. Given the number of extra pitches a Rockies' starter is likely to throw, this seemed to guarantee trouble. Leyland was predictably awful in this regard, although a bit better than with the 1998 Marlins. Pedro Astacio took the brunt of the abuse, throwing 130 or more pitches five times, including the major-league high of 153 on June 6.

Will Buddy Bell be any better? He admitted when he signed on that the whole "Coors Effect" thing was hard for him to believe; he said defense and keeping opposing hitters off base were priorities, which is the kind of thing a new manager is supposed to say. His Detroit stint is inconclusive, with the team's failures late in his stay being attributed more to a lack of ownership funds than to anything Bell did wrong. He didn't show any great understanding of how an offense works.

There is no quick fix for a team as bad as this. There is some excellent talent in the farm system, if the team can wait a bit. Ben Petrick is the best catching prospect in baseball: he throws well, and his .323 average in 19 games at the end of the 1999 season is a positive sign. Left-hander Josh Kalinowski is their top pitching prospect, a 23-year-old who has looked good against younger competition. Jody Gerut tore up A ball and could be a Rockie as soon as September.

Ultimately, the Rockies' future depends on solving the mystery of baseball at 5,280 feet, while making good decisions in the talent market. It's good to trade Dante Bichette and Vinny Castilla, but if those moves just clear space for Tom Goodwin, there's no progress being made. There have been signs that O'Dowd understands he's playing a different game now; Colorado fans have to hope he plays it well.

HITTERS (Averages: BA: .270 / OBP: .340 / SLG: .430 / EQA: .260)

Kurt Abbott   IF   Bats R   Age 31

YEAR	TEAM	LGE	AB	H	DB	TP	HR	BB/SO	R	RBI	SB	CS	OUT	BA	OBP	SLG	EQA	EQR	DEFENSE
1997	Florida	NL	255	71	21	2	6	14/67	36	30	2	1	185	.278	.319	.447	.254	30	45-2B 93
1998	Oakland	AL	124	35	8	1	2	9/33	17	9	2	1	90	.282	.336	.411	.253	15	25-SS 91
1999	Colorado	NL	280	67	13	2	7	12/68	33	34	2	2	215	.239	.271	.375	.213	22	55-2B 93
2000	*Colorado*	*NL*	*171*	*49*	*13*	*1*	*5*	*10/42*	*24*	*27*	*3*	*1*	*123*	*.287*	*.326*	*.462*	*.239*	*17*	

He had serious problems all year making contact. Was it his eyes acting up again? If not, Abbott may be through. There was a period of time when he was one of the best middle infielders in the league, but he sure didn't play like it last year. The best thing you can say about his defense is that it didn't get any more porous. He's a free agent, and this town's not big enough for both Abbott and Terry Shumpert.

Jeff Barry   CF   Bats B   Age 31

YEAR	TEAM	LGE	AB	H	DB	TP	HR	BB/SO	R	RBI	SB	CS	OUT	BA	OBP	SLG	EQA	EQR	DEFENSE
1997	ColSprin	PCL	263	60	10	2	8	21/51	29	42	3	0	203	.228	.293	.373	.226	25	71-OF 100
1998	ColSprin	PCL	341	69	15	4	5	36/57	37	37	3	1	273	.202	.288	.314	.206	26	93-OF 94
1999	ColSprin	PCL	179	47	9	0	7	14/34	23	18	4	2	134	.263	.316	.430	.250	21	43-OF 97
1999	Colorado	NL	163	37	10	0	5	17/29	15	21	0	3	129	.227	.308	.380	.228	16	27-CF 102
2000	*Colorado*	*NL*	*274*	*70*	*15*	*1*	*9*	*27/50*	*36*	*39*	*4*	*2*	*206*	*.255*	*.322*	*.416*	*.225*	*25*	

If you're a minor-league veteran who can't hack a full-time job in the majors, setting a course for Colorado's system ought to be the first thing on your agent's mind. If you're lucky, you'll pull a Mike Kingery and luck into a couple years of seven-figure income. Barry is in the right place; unfortunately, there are better players in front of him.

Dante Bichette   LF   Bats R   Age 36

YEAR	TEAM	LGE	AB	H	DB	TP	HR	BB/SO	R	RBI	SB	CS	OUT	BA	OBP	SLG	EQA	EQR	DEFENSE
1997	Colorado	NL	557	162	30	2	25	28/89	75	109	4	5	400	.291	.328	.487	.266	73	119-OF 95
1998	Colorado	NL	649	198	43	2	21	26/74	88	109	13	4	455	.305	.333	.475	.268	85	150-OF 94
1999	Colorado	NL	575	150	32	2	28	45/83	84	106	4	5	430	.261	.317	.470	.258	73	140-LF 93
2000	*Cincnnti*	*NL*	*605*	*158*	*26*	*1*	*24*	*50/84*	*75*	*91*	*5*	*3*	*450*	*.261*	*.318*	*.426*	*.247*	*69*	

I remember liking this girl in high school; one day we were talking and I got up my courage to ask her out. She hit me with the "let's just be friends" line, which I wasn't very happy about. A couple of days later, she called to ask for my buddy's phone number.

    Now, that whole experience sucked, but given the choice I'd take that every day over Fonzie Bichette soaking up 600 at-bats a year for a team that I care about. He's moved on to Cincinnati, where his chance of imploding is very high.

Henry Blanco   C   Bats R   Age 28

YEAR	TEAM	LGE	AB	H	DB	TP	HR	BB/SO	R	RBI	SB	CS	OUT	BA	OBP	SLG	EQA	EQR	DEFENSE
1997	Albuquer	PCL	281	66	12	1	4	27/71	23	29	4	3	218	.235	.304	.327	.216	24	
1998	Albuquer	PCL	132	28	4	0	4	18/30	13	17	1	0	104	.212	.307	.333	.222	12	27-C 107
1999	Colorado	NL	257	51	11	2	5	29/38	25	22	1	1	207	.198	.282	.315	.203	19	78-C 108
2000	*Milwauke*	*NL*	*237*	*52*	*10*	*1*	*5*	*27/44*	*25*	*24*	*1*	*1*	*186*	*.219*	*.299*	*.333*	*.213*	*20*	

Blanco is your basic defensive substitute. He doesn't do anything with the bat, but he's a reliable backstop without any defensive weaknesses. Of course, if you have this guy and Manwaring as your catchers, you have a situation that's easy to improve. He's been traded to Milwaukee, where he'll fight Bobby Hughes for playing time.

Vinny Castilla   3B   Bats R   Age 32

YEAR	TEAM	LGE	AB	H	DB	TP	HR	BB/SO	R	RBI	SB	CS	OUT	BA	OBP	SLG	EQA	EQR	DEFENSE
1997	Colorado	NL	607	173	24	2	38	43/107	87	103	1	4	438	.285	.340	.519	.279	90	156-3B 94
1998	Colorado	NL	632	184	25	4	42	38/87	96	127	4	9	457	.291	.338	.543	.281	95	162-3B 95
1999	Colorado	NL	599	144	18	1	28	44/74	67	82	1	3	458	.240	.294	.414	.234	61	153-3B 95
2000	*TampaBay*	*AL*	*529*	*139*	*18*	*1*	*31*	*43/71*	*69*	*98*	*1*	*3*	*393*	*.263*	*.318*	*.476*	*.260*	*68*	

(Vinny Castilla *continued*)

Few worse things could have happened to the Rockies than Castilla's bat going AWOL last year. Once the Rockies finally admitted they were out of the race, trade rumors fluttered around Castilla like rose petals in *American Beauty*, but by then nobody wanted to take a chance on him. Traded to Tampa Bay after the season, his power numbers should stay high enough to give the illusion that he's contributing. Don't be fooled.

Edgard Clemente		**CF**			**Bats R**	**Age 24**												
YEAR	TEAM	LGE	AB	H	DB	TP	HR	BB/SO	R	RBI	SB	CS	OUT	BA	OBP	SLG	EQA	EQR	DEFENSE
1997	ColSprin	PCL	423	99	20	6	13	26/122	48	50	4	2	326	.234	.286	.402	.229	41	116-OF 99
1998	ColSprin	PCL	482	103	17	5	17	33/116	59	61	4	3	382	.214	.268	.376	.214	40	128-OF 98
1999	ColSprin	PCL	265	68	19	1	12	17/54	33	43	4	3	201	.257	.305	.472	.254	33	62-OF 96
1999	Colorado	NL	159	35	8	2	7	5/46	20	21	0	0	124	.220	.244	.428	.217	14	38-CF 103
2000	*Colorado*	*NL*	*491*	*140*	*32*	*5*	*24*	*41/119*	*79*	*95*	*7*	*3*	*354*	*.285*	*.340*	*.517*	*.257*	*59*	

After his big 1996, he was one of the best prospects in baseball, but other than changing his name from Velazquez, Clemente has done little since then. His defense isn't good enough for center field at the major-league level. Of course, this is the team that put up with Ellis Burks out there. He's with the right team to turn it around, but I don't like his chances, especially now that the Rockies have signed Tom Goodwin.

Angel Echevarria		**OF**			**Bats R**	**Age 29**													
YEAR	TEAM	LGE	AB	H	DB	TP	HR	BB/SO	R	RBI	SB	CS	OUT	BA	OBP	SLG	EQA	EQR	DEFENSE	
1997	ColSprin	PCL	282	69	13	0	9	20/53	36	49	4	1	214	.245	.305	.387	.235	29	61-OF 96	
1998	ColSprin	PCL	290	74	16	1	10	10/51	33	40	0	1	217	.255	.285	.421	.232	28	45-1B 93	26-OF 89
1999	Colorado	NL	185	47	6	0	9	15/34	23	28	1	3	141	.254	.321	.432	.248	22	21-RF 107	
2000	*Colorado*	*NL*	*241*	*70*	*10*	*0*	*12*	*23/43*	*36*	*46*	*2*	*2*	*173*	*.290*	*.352*	*.481*	*.252*	*28*		

Echevarria hung around Coors Field for much of 1999, but didn't grab his chance to impress. He's your average lumbering, power-hitting corner outfielder, a guy that seems made for Colorado. Unfortunately, the Rockies have better outfield options. Echevarria needs a few Benny Agbayani weeks to cash in and will probably have another chance in 2000.

Chone Figgins		**SS**			**Bats B**	**Age 22**												
YEAR	TEAM	LGE	AB	H	DB	TP	HR	BB/SO	R	RBI	SB	CS	OUT	BA	OBP	SLG	EQA	EQR	DEFENSE
1998	Portland	Nwn	272	67	9	2	1	14/63	23	18	8	2	207	.246	.286	.305	.203	19	66-SS 103
1999	Salem VA	Car	453	107	11	3	1	31/83	52	20	14	8	353	.236	.288	.280	.195	29	122-SS 99
2000	*Colorado*	*NL*	*281*	*77*	*10*	*1*	*1*	*19/68*	*35*	*25*	*11*	*3*	*207*	*.274*	*.320*	*.327*	*.203*	*19*	

He's here for one of two reasons: because the Rockies' farm system is not as well-stocked as Chris Kahrl's refrigerator, or because he's got the coolest name in baseball since Razor Shines hung 'em up. You be the judge.

Choo Freeman		**CF**			**Bats R**	**Age 20**												
YEAR	TEAM	LGE	AB	H	DB	TP	HR	BB/SO	R	RBI	SB	CS	OUT	BA	OBP	SLG	EQA	EQR	DEFENSE
1999	Ashevlle	SAL	492	116	21	2	12	32/133	62	51	6	2	378	.236	.288	.360	.219	42	130-OF 100
2000	*Colorado*	*NL*	*242*	*66*	*10*	*1*	*10*	*19/83*	*32*	*39*	*3*	*1*	*177*	*.273*	*.326*	*.446*	*.235*	*24*	

Freeman was Colorado's second supplemental pick in the bonanza draft of 1998, and they signed him away from a football scholarship at Texas A&M. He's a wonderful athlete whose defense and baserunning should only improve as he moves up the ladder. Like many tools prospects, he has serious problems with good breaking stuff.

Jody Gerut		**OF**			**Bats L**	**Age 22**												
YEAR	TEAM	LGE	AB	H	DB	TP	HR	BB/SO	R	RBI	SB	CS	OUT	BA	OBP	SLG	EQA	EQR	DEFENSE
1999	Salem VA	Car	510	136	33	8	12	48/63	65	53	12	7	380	.267	.332	.433	.257	64	127-OF 96
2000	*Colorado*	*NL*	*284*	*101*	*24*	*4*	*11*	*32/74*	*69*	*66*	*11*	*3*	*186*	*.356*	*.421*	*.585*	*.305*	*48*	

If you play some type of fantasy-baseball keeper league, make it your top priority to get this guy. Gerut hit well at Salem in his first season out of Stanford, and is on the fast track to play in the Rockies' outfield. He'll start next season at Carolina and should end it in Denver. Gerut has good patience, didn't have much trouble adjusting to a wooden bat and should be good for 40 home runs a couple of times in his career.

Derrick Gibson   RF   Bats R   Age 25

YEAR	TEAM	LGE	AB	H	DB	TP	HR	BB/SO	R	RBI	SB	CS	OUT	BA	OBP	SLG	EQA	EQR	DEFENSE
1997	New Havn	Eas	465	134	23	2	19	25/104	70	60	13	8	339	.288	.334	.469	.265	61	114-OF 92
1998	ColSprin	PCL	483	119	17	2	11	29/110	62	61	10	4	368	.246	.292	.358	.221	42	119-OF 90
1999	ColSprin	PCL	376	86	17	4	12	24/83	48	48	8	4	294	.229	.283	.391	.226	36	100-OF 88
2000	Colorado	NL	475	138	21	2	23	38/105	76	86	15	6	342	.291	.343	.488	.253	55	

Gibson's recent history has been eerily similar to Clemente's; perhaps there's something going on at Colorado Springs? He has serious problems with making contact, plate discipline and defense, and he doesn't have much time to get them ironed out with Gerut right behind him. He underwent Achilles' surgery; his status for 2000 is uncertain.

Chris Hatcher   OF   Bats R   Age 31

YEAR	TEAM	LGE	AB	H	DB	TP	HR	BB/SO	R	RBI	SB	CS	OUT	BA	OBP	SLG	EQA	EQR	DEFENSE
1997	Omaha	AA	221	43	8	0	8	13/76	27	19	0	1	179	.195	.259	.339	.197	15	36-OF 82
1998	Omaha	PCL	480	126	20	1	33	19/137	60	76	5	4	358	.262	.294	.515	.260	62	74-OF 92
1999	ColSprin	PCL	322	86	19	1	13	17/96	40	44	7	2	238	.267	.319	.453	.258	40	55-OF 82
2000	Colorado	NL	380	107	14	0	25	26/112	53	76	6	2	275	.282	.328	.516	.252	44	

Hatcher had a big power year at Omaha in 1998 and was looking for a better chance to break camp with the big club than he got last year. He's a late bloomer who has already had his best season, and he plays defense like Shakes the Clown coming off a three-day bender. Still, you could do worse—and Colorado routinely does—for an end-of-the-bench bat. A minor-league free agent, he's probably bound for another PCL team in 2000.

Todd Helton   1B   Bats L   Age 26

YEAR	TEAM	LGE	AB	H	DB	TP	HR	BB/SO	R	RBI	SB	CS	OUT	BA	OBP	SLG	EQA	EQR	DEFENSE	
1997	ColSprin	PCL	370	108	23	1	12	49/70	60	60	2	1	263	.292	.375	.457	.281	55	79-1B 98	18-OF 108
1998	Colorado	NL	518	149	31	1	24	51/53	70	87	3	3	372	.288	.359	.490	.281	78	137-1B 119	
1999	Colorado	NL	557	156	36	4	28	58/76	93	89	5	5	406	.280	.355	.510	.283	86	148-1B 103	
2000	Colorado	NL	552	187	38	2	35	71/71	117	147	4	3	368	.339	.414	.605	.304	94		

I'm pretty disappointed; Helton didn't put up sky-high raw numbers in 1999 after a solid debut. He was very streaky last year, and didn't hit well on the road. The minute he gets that worked out, he'll become one of the richest men in baseball. If he hits like he can while playing half his games in Coors, he'll be the guy to challenge Larry Walker for the batting title next year. That projection looks right.

Matt Holliday   3B   Bats R   Age 20

YEAR	TEAM	LGE	AB	H	DB	TP	HR	BB/SO	R	RBI	SB	CS	OUT	BA	OBP	SLG	EQA	EQR	DEFENSE
1999	Ashevlle	SAL	453	102	19	0	15	44/117	58	51	4	1	352	.225	.301	.366	.227	43	107-3B 79
2000	Colorado	NL	241	70	9	0	15	29/80	41	52	3	0	171	.290	.367	.515	.269	32	

The Rockies are big on high-school two-sport stars, a policy I don't think much of. So far their investment in Holliday, another player the team signed away from a football scholarship, looks pretty good. He's got some power, hitting 16 home runs and 28 doubles at Asheville last year, but his defense at third base has to improve if he wants a career there. Take that projection, based on just one year, with a fistful of salt.

Mike Lansing   2B   Bats R   Age 32

YEAR	TEAM	LGE	AB	H	DB	TP	HR	BB/SO	R	RBI	SB	CS	OUT	BA	OBP	SLG	EQA	EQR	DEFENSE
1997	Montreal	NL	576	160	43	2	22	44/91	84	70	9	5	421	.278	.334	.474	.267	78	137-2B 99
1998	Colorado	NL	574	144	35	3	11	37/86	66	59	9	3	433	.251	.302	.380	.231	56	145-2B 93
1999	Colorado	NL	141	38	6	0	4	5/22	20	12	2	0	103	.270	.300	.397	.235	14	34-2B 98
2000	Colorado	NL	270	78	21	1	10	22/41	43	47	4	1	193	.289	.342	.485	.252	31	

Message for Dan O'Dowd: don't sign players like Lansing to contracts like his. The Rockies bought high when they brought Lansing in after his career year in Montreal, and his creaky back has been haunting all parties ever since. He hasn't been healthy for two years now, and the back problem is starting to look like a career-killer. The organization says he'll be back at second base in 2000.

Kirt Manwaring   C   Bats R   Age 34

YEAR	TEAM	LGE	AB	H	DB	TP	HR	BB/SO	R	RBI	SB	CS	OUT	BA	OBP	SLG	EQA	EQR	DEFENSE	
1997	Colorado	NL	335	72	5	4	1	29/77	20	25	0	5	268	.215	.281	.263	.178	18		
1998	Colorado	NL	286	64	10	3	2	36/48	27	23	1	5	227	.224	.317	.301	.211	23	90-C 100	
1999	Colorado	NL	133	34	5	1	2	10/23	14	11	0	0	99	.256	.333	.353	.237	14	39-C 91	
2000	Colorado	NL	185	44	4	1	4	23/33	19	21	0	2	143	.238	.322	.335	.200	13		

Teflon would be a possible explanation. Either that, or he can get front-office people dates with Anna Nicole Smith. A completely inoffensive player whose defense isn't what it once was, Manwaring has more lives than Morris the Cat. The Rockies bought out his contract, so that's certainly a step in the sane direction.

Elvis Pena   2B   Bats B   Age 23

YEAR	TEAM	LGE	AB	H	DB	TP	HR	BB/SO	R	RBI	SB	CS	OUT	BA	OBP	SLG	EQA	EQR	DEFENSE	
1997	Salem VA	Car	286	63	8	2	1	29/53	32	27	8	3	226	.220	.295	.273	.199	20	37-2B 97	27-SS 92
1998	Ashevlle	SAL	434	103	21	3	5	56/86	59	35	14	5	336	.237	.337	.334	.238	46	110-2B 88	
1999	Carolina	Sou	360	102	24	5	2	39/66	46	26	12	4	262	.283	.360	.394	.262	46	78-2B 89	24-SS 105
2000	Colorado	NL	436	130	24	4	4	53/81	86	56	24	7	312	.298	.374	.399	.249	48		

How old is he? If he's 23, he's a prospect; if he's 25, he's filler. Questions abound with Pena, who hit well at Carolina in 1999. He's got a solid all-around game with the doubles that can develop into home runs as a player gets older. He should be with Colorado Springs full-time in 2000.

Neifi Perez   SS   Bats B   Age 25

YEAR	TEAM	LGE	AB	H	DB	TP	HR	BB/SO	R	RBI	SB	CS	OUT	BA	OBP	SLG	EQA	EQR	DEFENSE	
1997	ColSprin	PCL	288	88	19	2	6	11/28	46	32	5	1	202	.306	.331	.448	.261	35	68-SS 95	
1997	Colorado	NL	311	85	14	9	5	20/43	43	29	3	3	229	.273	.319	.424	.248	35	39-SS 109	35-2B 106
1998	Colorado	NL	637	160	22	8	9	36/68	72	53	5	6	483	.251	.292	.353	.216	52	158-SS 105	
1999	Colorado	NL	675	166	25	9	10	19/53	88	57	10	4	513	.246	.268	.354	.207	50	155-SS 106	
2000	Colorado	NL	646	203	27	11	16	41/59	97	111	11	6	448	.314	.355	.464	.251	70		

Rey Ordonez, NL West Edition. Perez has atrophied terribly in Colorado, getting worse every year. Batting a guy like this at the top of the order is borderline insanity. Nice things are said about Perez's offense by people who should know better, and his defense is good, so O'Dowd should have no problem foisting Perez off on another team for more than fair value, should he choose to do so.

Ben Petrick   C   Bats R   Age 23

YEAR	TEAM	LGE	AB	H	DB	TP	HR	BB/SO	R	RBI	SB	CS	OUT	BA	OBP	SLG	EQA	EQR	DEFENSE	
1997	Salem VA	Car	423	98	21	2	14	49/99	53	47	15	6	331	.232	.314	.390	.241	47		
1998	New Havn	Eas	357	82	19	3	18	49/87	48	47	5	5	280	.230	.327	.451	.258	47	81-C 90	
1999	Carolina	Sou	69	20	3	1	4	7/15	14	18	2	1	50	.290	.361	.536	.292	12		
1999	ColSprin	PCL	273	72	13	4	14	38/57	41	46	6	4	205	.264	.359	.495	.281	43	65-C 89	
1999	Colorado	NL	59	16	1	0	4	9/13	11	10	1	0	43	.271	.368	.492	.288	10		
2000	Colorado	NL	446	135	25	4	26	70/98	98	102	16	7	317	.303	.397	.552	.287	70		

Petrick improved across the board in 1999. The only question was whether he'd hit for average, and he did that at three levels. He's got no real weaknesses in his offensive game, with power that is still developing. He'll be an excellent source of offense for the team over the next five years. That is, if they let him: the Rockies have signed both Brent Mayne and Scott Servais.

J.R. Phillips   1B/OF   Bats R   Age 30

YEAR	TEAM	LGE	AB	H	DB	TP	HR	BB/SO	R	RBI	SB	CS	OUT	BA	OBP	SLG	EQA	EQR	DEFENSE	
1997	New Orln	AA	422	113	22	0	19	31/125	51	64	0	1	310	.268	.318	.455	.255	51	55-OF 85	37-1B 111
1998	New Orln	PCL	227	61	13	0	17	17/71	39	47	1	1	167	.269	.322	.551	.279	34	37-1B 101	
1999	ColSprin	PCL	465	113	14	0	27	42/155	56	65	2	2	354	.243	.307	.447	.249	55	124-1B 114	
2000	Colorado	NL	427	121	17	0	30	41/137	64	94	0	1	307	.283	.346	.534	.262	54		

Unlike some recent Rockies' properties, Phillips had no problem with Colorado Springs, doing his usual damage to PCL pitching. He got a short trial with the big club, although any shot at a major-league career disappeared when he signed with the team that has Todd Helton at first base. He'd be a kick to watch in beer-league softball.

Terry Shumpert   2B   Bats R   Age 33

YEAR	TEAM	LGE	AB	H	DB	TP	HR	BB/SO	R	RBI	SB	CS	OUT	BA	OBP	SLG	EQA	EQR	DEFENSE	
1997	LasVegas	PCL	106	24	4	1	1	6/22	11	11	2	0	82	.226	.283	.311	.205	8		
1998	ColSprin	PCL	364	85	22	5	7	27/64	43	32	7	7	285	.234	.291	.379	.223	34	41-2B 96	27-OF 82
1999	ColSprin	PCL	76	23	5	1	4	3/10	10	11	2	1	54	.303	.329	.553	.283	12		
1999	Colorado	NL	251	77	23	2	8	26/41	47	29	11	0	174	.307	.377	.510	.300	43	46-2B 105	
2000	Colorado	NL	297	90	23	2	9	28/48	54	52	9	3	210	.303	.363	.485	.260	36		

Shumpert took the second-base job after Lansing's injury and ran with it in a big way. He also hit well at Colorado Springs after a mediocre campaign in 1998. He probably changed his choice in breakfast cereal or something. Shumpert is a slick defensive second baseman, reasonable utility infielder material for the last three or four years, who seems to have suddenly found his bat.

Juan Sosa   SS/2B   Bats R   Age 24

YEAR	TEAM	LGE	AB	H	DB	TP	HR	BB/SO	R	RBI	SB	CS	OUT	BA	OBP	SLG	EQA	EQR	DEFENSE	
1997	Vero Bch	Fla	252	53	5	1	6	11/43	24	26	9	4	203	.210	.248	.310	.186	15	43-SS 89	28-2B 96
1998	Salem VA	Car	541	140	20	10	9	39/83	66	42	27	8	409	.259	.312	.383	.240	58	121-SS 93	
1999	Carolina	Sou	494	126	20	4	7	21/69	52	35	20	9	377	.255	.287	.354	.218	42	113-SS 103	
2000	Colorado	NL	556	166	22	8	12	43/79	94	80	30	10	400	.299	.349	.432	.244	59		

If it isn't an axiom yet, it should be: once you're named to the Utility Infielder spot of your league's All-Star team, the die is cast. Sosa regressed in 1999 after a promising season with Salem, where he won the aforementioned honor. Wilton likes him; if that projection turns out to be accurate, he'll be a long-on-offense, short-on-defense utility player for a few years. Heck, he might even out-hit Neifi Perez over that period.

Juan Uribe   SS   Bats B   Age 20

YEAR	TEAM	LGE	AB	H	DB	TP	HR	BB/SO	R	RBI	SB	CS	OUT	BA	OBP	SLG	EQA	EQR	DEFENSE
1999	Asheville	SAL	433	100	25	3	7	17/80	44	36	4	3	336	.231	.265	.351	.203	31	124-SS 102
2000	Colorado	NL	221	61	13	1	5	10/58	24	29	1	1	161	.276	.307	.412	.216	17	

He's a defensive wizard who handled the jump to Asheville with little difficulty. Uribe has the arm, the range and the consistency you look for in a major-league shortstop. His offense has a long way to go, and it would be really nice if he had a stronger knowledge of the strike zone, but he's ready to move up to high-A.

Larry Walker   RF   Bats L   Age 33

YEAR	TEAM	LGE	AB	H	DB	TP	HR	BB/SO	R	RBI	SB	CS	OUT	BA	OBP	SLG	EQA	EQR	DEFENSE
1997	Colorado	NL	561	194	45	3	47	76/89	131	119	26	8	375	.346	.436	.688	.353	139	129-OF 94
1998	Colorado	NL	441	148	40	3	22	61/59	103	60	14	4	297	.336	.421	.590	.330	93	114-OF 97
1999	Colorado	NL	416	138	22	3	30	49/51	87	90	8	4	282	.332	.418	.615	.331	89	107-RF 99
2000	Colorado	NL	418	155	29	1	35	66/54	112	132	13	5	267	.371	.457	.696	.339	89	

Mister Consistent. Chalk up another great year for the right fielder, who hit .379 with 37 home runs in only 127 games. Walker again had injury problems and also missed some time after his best friend was killed in a motorcycle accident. He had surgery after the season to smooth out the cartilage in his troublesome left knee and is expected to be ready for spring training.

Jeff Winchester   C   Bats R   Age 20

YEAR	TEAM	LGE	AB	H	DB	TP	HR	BB/SO	R	RBI	SB	CS	OUT	BA	OBP	SLG	EQA	EQR	DEFENSE
1999	Asheville	SAL	315	64	14	0	15	22/93	35	36	0	0	251	.203	.266	.390	.217	28	70-C 85
2000	Colorado	NL	158	38	6	0	15	14/67	21	35	0	0	120	.241	.302	.563	.252	19	

Winchester was a sandwich pick in the Rockies' big 1998 draft and had a very impressive first season in the Sally League. There's little question that he has the bat to be a major-league player, but his defense is very much in question; scouts hate it, and so do our ratings. He has time to learn, although he may be moved to the outfield before he does.

PITCHERS (Averages: ERA: 4.50 / H/9: 9.00 / HR/9: 1.00 / BB/9: 3.50 / K/9: 6.50 / KWH: 1.00)

Pedro Astacio — Throws R — Age 30

YEAR	TEAM	LGE	IP	H	ER	HR	BB	K	ERA	W	L	H/9	HR/9	BB/9	K/9	KWH	PERA
1997	LosAngls	NL	148.0	163	81	15	49	106	4.93	7	9	9.91	0.91	2.98	6.45	1.05	4.74
1997	Colorado	NL	51.3	45	19	9	15	48	3.33	4	2	7.89	1.58	2.63	8.42	2.55	4.21
1998	Colorado	NL	227.7	233	137	36	82	169	5.42	10	15	9.21	1.42	3.24	6.68	1.12	4.98
1999	Colorado	NL	253.7	226	103	32	74	210	3.65	17	11	8.02	1.14	2.63	7.45	1.97	3.76

Dan O'Dowd is calling Astacio his ace and saying that Cleveland didn't have anyone outside of Bartolo Colon who pitched like Astacio did last year. He's right, and it's a sign that he may understand park effects. Astacio was worked very hard by Jim Leyland, so hopefully Buddy Bell will go easier on him in 2000.

Rigo Beltran — Throws L — Age 30

YEAR	TEAM	LGE	IP	H	ER	HR	BB	K	ERA	W	L	H/9	HR/9	BB/9	K/9	KWH	PERA
1997	Louisvil	AmA	52.7	51	20	7	25	39	3.42	4	2	8.72	1.20	4.27	6.66	0.89	4.78
1997	St Louis	NL	54.3	47	24	3	18	46	3.98	3	3	7.79	0.50	2.98	7.62	1.87	3.15
1998	Norfolk	Int	92.0	112	51	15	44	83	4.99	4	6	10.96	1.47	4.30	8.12	1.04	6.55
1999	Norfolk	Int	22.0	16	4	1	13	23	1.64	2	0	6.55	0.41	5.32	9.41	1.90	3.27
1999	NY Mets	NL	30.3	31	14	5	12	34	4.15	2	1	9.20	1.48	3.56	10.09	2.32	5.04
1999	Colorado	NL	13.0	18	7	2	7	15	4.85	0	1	12.46	1.38	4.85	10.38	1.33	7.62

Acquired from the Mets in the Darryl Hamilton trade, Beltran may be the best of the Rockies' left-handed relievers. He has picked up a wrinkle or two since 1997 and his strikeouts have gone through the roof since then. I like his chances to be Colorado's top left-hander out of the pen in 2000, especially if he keeps striking out one batter an inning.

Brian Bohanon — Throws L — Age 31

YEAR	TEAM	LGE	IP	H	ER	HR	BB	K	ERA	W	L	H/9	HR/9	BB/9	K/9	KWH	PERA
1997	Norfolk	Int	92.7	99	40	9	35	68	3.88	6	4	9.62	0.87	3.40	6.60	1.00	4.66
1997	NY Mets	NL	92.7	100	51	9	36	62	4.95	5	5	9.71	0.87	3.50	6.02	0.80	4.76
1998	NY Mets	NL	53.3	50	22	4	22	37	3.71	4	2	8.44	0.68	3.71	6.24	0.93	3.88
1998	LosAngls	NL	95.3	77	36	9	38	68	3.40	7	4	7.27	0.85	3.59	6.42	1.18	3.49
1999	Colorado	NL	218.0	207	110	25	92	121	4.54	12	12	8.55	1.03	3.80	5.00	0.57	4.38

He resembled kindling-in-waiting after signing with Colorado following a career year. Smokey the Bear put out an advisory not to leave Bohanon unattended. Nevertheless, he got the job done for the Rockies in 1999. Bohanon underwent surgery to remove bone chips in his elbow during the offseason; he's expected to be at full strength by spring training.

Heath Bost — Throws R — Age 25

YEAR	TEAM	LGE	IP	H	ER	HR	BB	K	ERA	W	L	H/9	HR/9	BB/9	K/9	KWH	PERA
1997	New Havn	Eas	40.3	51	21	3	11	36	4.69	2	2	11.38	0.67	2.45	8.03	1.73	5.13
1998	New Havn	Eas	44.3	49	22	2	12	38	4.47	3	2	9.95	0.41	2.44	7.71	1.83	4.06
1999	ColSprin	PCL	87.0	118	52	9	14	55	5.38	4	6	12.21	0.93	1.45	5.69	1.37	5.48

Bost didn't get a call-up in 1999 and wasn't particularly happy about it. His control has improved from good to great, but at the same time he was fairly hittable in Colorado Springs, not a trait you want in your relievers, especially at altitude. Bost's slider/fastball combination is intact, and I expect an improvement in his peripherals and a call-up in 2000. If he turns the corner, Bost could be useful for 90 high-leverage innings a year. That kind of relief work is essential for the Rockies to be successful.

Mark Brownson — Throws R — Age 25

YEAR	TEAM	LGE	IP	H	ER	HR	BB	K	ERA	W	L	H/9	HR/9	BB/9	K/9	KWH	PERA
1997	New Havn	Eas	172.0	203	114	23	59	137	5.97	7	12	10.62	1.20	3.09	7.17	1.17	5.49
1998	ColSprin	PCL	128.7	122	70	19	42	71	4.90	6	8	8.53	1.33	2.94	4.97	0.74	4.34
1999	ColSprin	PCL	102.7	118	66	21	28	66	5.79	4	7	10.34	1.84	2.45	5.79	0.99	5.79
1999	Colorado	NL	32.7	38	20	7	8	21	5.51	2	2	10.47	1.93	2.20	5.79	1.08	5.79

Brownson looked like a real prospect a couple of years ago. The New Haven pitch-o-rama in 1997 couldn't have been fun for him; since then, his performance hasn't been the same. It could be the higher levels of play or it could be some problem with his arm; either way, Brownson wouldn't be the first pitcher to be felled by the high-altitude blues.

Shawn Chacon — Throws R — Age 22

YEAR	TEAM	LGE	IP	H	ER	HR	BB	K	ERA	W	L	H/9	HR/9	BB/9	K/9	KWH	PERA
1997	Ashevlle	SAL	155.0	197	100	17	90	104	5.81	6	11	11.44	0.99	5.23	6.04	0.46	6.68
1998	Salem VA	Car	53.3	64	44	7	42	40	7.43	2	4	10.80	1.18	7.09	6.75	0.44	7.26
1999	Salem VA	Car	69.7	83	51	4	39	49	6.59	3	5	10.72	0.52	5.04	6.33	0.55	5.56

A sprained elbow ligament sidelined Chacon in 1998, and he was back with the Avalanche in 1999. His sweeping change and a fastball with plus speed but minus movement make him a prospect. He has trouble staying in shape, and he's never going to be a starter in the majors if he doesn't take care of that. Of course, there's always room for an out-of-shape analyst on the *Baseball Prospectus* team. Right, Rany?

Tsao Chin-Hui — Throws R — Age 19

Pacific Rim scout Tim Ireland's first move was a lulu. Chin-Hui, already a legend in his native Taiwan, signed for a massive $2.2 million bonus in October. He's supposedly got a fastball in the low 90s, as well as a deceptive change and a serviceable curve and slider. Scouts have been calling him "first-round talent." While that isn't necessarily indicative of much, keep an eye on him this year. He'll be tested early and often.

Mike DeJean — Throws R — Age 29

YEAR	TEAM	LGE	IP	H	ER	HR	BB	K	ERA	W	L	H/9	HR/9	BB/9	K/9	KWH	PERA
1997	Colorado	NL	71.7	68	28	4	26	36	3.52	5	3	8.54	0.50	3.27	4.52	0.55	3.64
1998	Colorado	NL	80.0	73	25	4	27	27	2.81	6	3	8.21	0.45	3.04	3.04	0.28	3.37
1999	Colorado	NL	68.3	74	47	11	32	31	6.19	3	5	9.75	1.45	4.21	4.08	0.30	5.66

Mike DeJean missed the end of the 1998 season after breaking his hand hitting his locker in frustration. I hate it when good players do silly things and get themselves injured, but since DeJean isn't all that good, I guess I don't have an issue with him. In 1999, he gave up the home run, the walk and the stolen base much more readily than before. He's still young, he's still got the great forkball and he should be back to normal in 2000. With Dave Veres gone to St. Louis and Curtis Leskanic in Milwaukee, he could pick up some saves.

Jerry DiPoto — Throws R — Age 32

YEAR	TEAM	LGE	IP	H	ER	HR	BB	K	ERA	W	L	H/9	HR/9	BB/9	K/9	KWH	PERA
1997	Colorado	NL	101.7	100	48	6	36	70	4.25	6	5	8.85	0.53	3.19	6.20	1.02	3.81
1998	Colorado	NL	76.0	57	26	7	27	48	3.08	5	3	6.75	0.83	3.20	5.68	1.12	3.08
1999	Colorado	NL	95.0	79	32	8	44	69	3.03	8	3	7.48	0.76	4.17	6.54	1.02	3.69

DiPoto was the Rockies' closer for most of 1998, but didn't get much in the way of save opportunities in 1999. He had a good season as their top setup man, stranding 28 of 32 inherited runners. He re-signed with Colorado for two years, with a team option for 2002. DiPoto is ahead of DeJean for the closer job.

Lariel Gonzalez — Throws R — Age 24

YEAR	TEAM	LGE	IP	H	ER	HR	BB	K	ERA	W	L	H/9	HR/9	BB/9	K/9	KWH	PERA
1997	Salem VA	Car	54.0	54	23	3	26	58	3.83	3	3	9.00	0.50	4.33	9.67	1.79	4.33
1998	New Havn	Eas	55.3	53	35	6	44	51	5.69	2	4	8.62	0.98	7.16	8.30	0.83	5.69
1999	Carolina	Sou	32.0	44	29	5	24	33	8.16	1	3	12.38	1.41	6.75	9.28	0.77	8.44

The Rockies envision Gonzalez as their future closer due to his excellent splitter and fastball. He's got the stuff to throw balls right past hitters, but he doesn't yet have the control to be effective. Gonzalez doesn't have a lot of experience playing baseball, despite which his ceiling is pretty high if he can develop control. Guys like this can always find someone who will take a chance on their arm, even if their previous performance doesn't merit it. To be fair, that's how pitchers like Rudy Seanez find jobs, so sometimes the process works.

Luther Hackman   Throws R   Age 25

YEAR	TEAM	LGE	IP	H	ER	HR	BB	K	ERA	W	L	H/9	HR/9	BB/9	K/9	KWH	PERA
1997	Salem VA	Car	73.3	128	74	15	43	43	9.08	2	6	15.71	1.84	5.28	5.28	0.25	10.68
1997	New Havn	Eas	46.0	69	54	11	36	27	10.57	1	4	13.50	2.15	7.04	5.28	0.22	10.37
1998	New Havn	Eas	131.3	191	117	20	63	71	8.02	4	11	13.09	1.37	4.32	4.87	0.31	7.81
1999	Carolina	Sou	58.3	62	38	4	32	38	5.86	2	4	9.57	0.62	4.94	5.86	0.54	4.94
1999	ColSprin	PCL	101.3	99	42	6	52	72	3.73	7	4	8.79	0.53	4.62	6.39	0.75	4.35

He turned the corner in 1999. Hackman's game has improved by leaps and bounds, and he got his first cup of coffee as a what-the-heck call-up in September. He jumped two levels this year due to an improved mix of pitches and better control over his fastball. Traded to St. Louis in the Darryl Kile deal, he'll have trouble making the Cardinals and should spend the year at Memphis.

Jason Jennings   Throws R   Age 21

YEAR	TEAM	LGE	IP	H	ER	HR	BB	K	ERA	W	L	H/9	HR/9	BB/9	K/9	KWH	PERA
1999	Ashevlle	SAL	56.7	70	33	4	11	45	5.24	3	3	11.12	0.64	1.75	7.15	1.97	4.61

Jennings was the 16th overall pick in 1999 after being named *Baseball America*'s College Player of the Year. He was the best pitcher—and most fearsome hitter—on a very good Baylor squad. At Asheville in the Sally League, Jennings put up some great peripherals including an impressive strikeout-to-walk ratio. His mechanics on the mound are very smooth and consistent. He'll make Carolina next season and pitch in Coors by 2001.

Bobby M. Jones   Throws L   Age 28

YEAR	TEAM	LGE	IP	H	ER	HR	BB	K	ERA	W	L	H/9	HR/9	BB/9	K/9	KWH	PERA
1997	ColSprin	PCL	129.0	130	80	14	77	86	5.58	6	8	9.07	0.98	5.37	6.00	0.55	5.23
1998	Colorado	NL	153.7	143	74	11	73	108	4.33	9	8	8.38	0.64	4.28	6.33	0.83	4.10
1999	Colorado	NL	125.3	116	69	20	77	75	4.95	6	8	8.33	1.44	5.53	5.39	0.47	5.39

Business as usual for Jones; pitchers like this are useful because they'll give you tons of work soaking up garbage time so you can save your good pitchers for a day when the game is close. As you know, in Colorado the game is often not close.

Josh Kalinowski   Throws L   Age 23

YEAR	TEAM	LGE	IP	H	ER	HR	BB	K	ERA	W	L	H/9	HR/9	BB/9	K/9	KWH	PERA
1998	Ashevlle	SAL	164.3	196	110	17	91	141	6.02	6	12	10.73	0.93	4.98	7.72	0.83	6.02
1999	Salem VA	Car	156.7	146	55	4	84	126	3.16	11	6	8.39	0.23	4.83	7.24	0.97	3.91

Kalinowski is the best pitching prospect the Rockies have, and one of the best in baseball. Coming off a successful campaign at Asheville in which he fanned 215 batters, he led the Carolina League in ERA with a 2.11 mark at Salem. Kalinowski has a power curveball that he uses to set up his impressive fastball; his lack of a third pitch hasn't hurt him yet. He's going to start next season with Carolina. The Rockies are taking care not to rush him, and since they won't be contending for anything anytime soon, will continue to be patient.

Darryl Kile   Throws R   Age 31

YEAR	TEAM	LGE	IP	H	ER	HR	BB	K	ERA	W	L	H/9	HR/9	BB/9	K/9	KWH	PERA
1997	Houston	NL	251.7	215	88	19	98	190	3.15	19	9	7.69	0.68	3.50	6.79	1.28	3.47
1998	Colorado	NL	250.7	242	120	26	106	157	4.31	15	13	8.69	0.93	3.81	5.64	0.72	4.38
1999	Colorado	NL	211.7	197	113	28	109	117	4.80	11	13	8.38	1.19	4.63	4.97	0.48	4.80

By now, it should be apparent to the Rockies that 1997 was the outlier; were their expectations reasonable, the team would have little reason to be disappointed with Kile's performance as a Rockie. He reportedly has a lot of problems getting his curve to break at home, but he wasn't much better on the road (5.89 ERA) than he was at Coors (7.44) in 1999. He's been traded to St. Louis, where he'll be the 230-inning rotation anchor the Cardinals have needed. His 1998 performance is the one he's most likely to repeat.

David Lee · Throws R · Age 27

YEAR	TEAM	LGE	IP	H	ER	HR	BB	K	ERA	W	L	H/9	HR/9	BB/9	K/9	KWH	PERA
1997	Ashevlle	SAL	46.7	88	45	6	39	36	8.68	1	4	16.97	1.16	7.52	6.94	0.28	11.76
1998	Salem VA	Car	51.7	78	39	3	24	34	6.79	2	4	13.59	0.52	4.18	5.92	0.46	6.97
1999	Colorado	NL	54.0	35	15	4	29	38	2.50	5	1	5.83	0.67	4.83	6.33	1.06	3.00

Lee was the best of the Colorado relief corps in 1999, which was an unlikely occurrence, to say the least. He had been a closer during his climb through the Colorado chain, but nothing in his background indicated he was capable of this kind of performance, which makes me very suspicious. Lee is great at keeping the ball in the park and is very tough on right-handed hitters, so he'll be a useful pitcher even if he can't repeat last season's heroics.

Curt Leskanic · Throws R · Age 32

YEAR	TEAM	LGE	IP	H	ER	HR	BB	K	ERA	W	L	H/9	HR/9	BB/9	K/9	KWH	PERA
1997	Colorado	NL	61.7	54	31	8	26	50	4.52	3	4	7.88	1.17	3.79	7.30	1.33	4.23
1998	Colorado	NL	82.3	69	32	8	45	55	3.50	6	3	7.54	0.87	4.92	6.01	0.73	4.15
1999	Colorado	NL	94.0	75	40	6	48	77	3.83	6	4	7.18	0.57	4.60	7.37	1.23	3.54

Leskanic is the last remaining connection to the great Rockies' bullpens of 1995-97. He's still going strong and has apparently recovered from the tired arm he had. Leyland increased Leskanic's innings without putting him in more games in 1999, and Leskanic seems to have had no problem with the workload. He's a groundball pitcher, which may help him in this environment.

Mike Porzio · Throws L · Age 27

YEAR	TEAM	LGE	IP	H	ER	HR	BB	K	ERA	W	L	H/9	HR/9	BB/9	K/9	KWH	PERA
1998	DanvillC	Car	85.7	107	56	9	48	59	5.88	4	6	11.24	0.95	5.04	6.20	0.51	6.41
1998	Salem VA	Car	37.7	57	31	7	19	29	7.41	1	3	13.62	1.67	4.54	6.93	0.58	8.60
1999	ColSprin	PCL	42.3	41	14	5	36	26	2.98	3	2	8.72	1.06	7.65	5.53	0.34	6.17
1999	Colorado	NL	16.3	20	11	4	10	10	6.06	1	1	11.02	2.20	5.51	5.51	0.37	8.27

Porzio was picked up in the Greg Colbrunn trade with Atlanta in 1998. He's another player who kicked around the independent leagues for years before a major-league team took notice. There may be a reason for that, as he was overmatched in limited duty in Colorado, allowing five home runs in only 14⅔ innings. Porzio doesn't figure prominently in the Rockies' plans for 2000; then again, neither would Greg Colbrunn had the team not traded him.

Roberto Ramirez · Throws L · Age 27

YEAR	TEAM	LGE	IP	H	ER	HR	BB	K	ERA	W	L	H/9	HR/9	BB/9	K/9	KWH	PERA
1998	LasVegas	PCL	29.3	23	13	2	12	27	3.99	2	1	7.06	0.61	3.68	8.28	1.97	3.07
1999	ColSprin	PCL	61.0	64	23	5	20	44	3.39	4	3	9.44	0.74	2.95	6.49	1.13	4.28
1999	Colorado	NL	46.0	62	33	7	22	33	6.46	2	3	12.13	1.37	4.30	6.46	0.60	7.24

Ramirez can be tough on left-handed hitters, but he shouldn't be counted on for high-leverage innings yet. He's another Rockies' pitcher who had problems keeping the ball in play last season, allowing a home run about once every five innings. He's a Mexican League import who has good stuff for a left-hander and strikes batters out, so the Rockies might have something on their hands if they're patient with him.

Scott Randall · Throws R · Age 24

YEAR	TEAM	LGE	IP	H	ER	HR	BB	K	ERA	W	L	H/9	HR/9	BB/9	K/9	KWH	PERA
1997	Salem VA	Car	165.3	209	114	9	74	95	6.21	6	12	11.38	0.49	4.03	5.17	0.44	5.55
1998	New Havn	Eas	195.0	231	112	16	69	109	5.17	9	13	10.66	0.74	3.18	5.03	0.56	5.03
1999	Carolina	Sou	94.7	114	56	7	37	82	5.32	5	6	10.84	0.67	3.52	7.80	1.19	5.23
1999	ColSprin	PCL	42.3	59	35	4	25	21	7.44	1	4	12.54	0.85	5.31	4.46	0.22	7.23

Randall is a well regarded prospect who has thrown a lot of innings over the last three years. I'd be fairly worried about his arm by now; other than the two no-hitters he's been involved in, it isn't like he pitches a lot of 1-2-3 innings. Randall has a fastball and a curve and needs another quality pitch to have any success in the majors.

Kevin Ritz   Throws R   Age 35

YEAR	TEAM	LGE	IP	H	ER	HR	BB	K	ERA	W	L	H/9	HR/9	BB/9	K/9	KWH	PERA
1996	Colorado	NL	237.7	211	107	21	121	104	4.05	14	12	7.99	0.80	4.58	3.94	0.32	4.17
1997	Colorado	NL	114.7	134	62	16	49	54	4.87	6	7	10.52	1.26	3.85	4.24	0.33	5.81
1998	New Havn	Eas	16.3	20	9	4	3	10	4.96	1	1	11.02	2.20	1.65	5.51	1.25	6.06
1998	ColSprin	PCL	17.7	24	21	2	11	6	10.70	0	2	12.23	1.02	5.60	3.06	0.10	7.13
1998	Colorado	NL	10.3	17	10	1	2	3	8.71	0	1	14.81	0.87	1.74	2.61	0.20	6.97

He missed most of 1998 and all of 1999 with multiple shoulder surgeries. The Rockies won't be re-signing Ritz, but he's supposedly going to be healthy by spring training, so some team is bound to take a chance on him. There are certainly riskier gambles; flying ValuJet, for instance.

Matt Roney   Throws R   Age 20

Roney missed the entire season after having a torn labrum in his shoulder repaired. He was the Rockies' first pick in their big 1998 draft, and the team is eager to appraise his recovery. Keep an eye out for him in 2000. He had the fastball to make things happen quickly, so if it comes back, he'll make noise.

Mike Saipe   Throws R   Age 26

YEAR	TEAM	LGE	IP	H	ER	HR	BB	K	ERA	W	L	H/9	HR/9	BB/9	K/9	KWH	PERA
1997	New Havn	Eas	126.3	154	68	17	32	96	4.84	6	8	10.97	1.21	2.28	6.84	1.40	5.41
1997	ColSprin	PCL	60.0	68	34	9	25	35	5.10	3	4	10.20	1.35	3.75	5.25	0.54	5.70
1998	ColSprin	PCL	144.0	159	82	16	60	106	5.13	7	9	9.94	1.00	3.75	6.63	0.88	5.12
1999	ColSprin	PCL	53.3	62	33	10	24	31	5.57	2	4	10.46	1.69	4.05	5.23	0.48	6.41

Nobody bothered picking him up when the Rockies dropped him from the 40-man roster last year, so he's still with the organization. In three stints at Colorado Springs, he hasn't been able to recapture the success he had earlier in his career, and that's due in large part to his repertoire. His curve is his money pitch, so he'd probably be better off somewhere else. I'd like to see what he would do in a full season at sea level.

John Thomson   Throws R   Age 26

YEAR	TEAM	LGE	IP	H	ER	HR	BB	K	ERA	W	L	H/9	HR/9	BB/9	K/9	KWH	PERA
1997	ColSprin	PCL	41.7	33	15	4	15	43	3.24	3	2	7.13	0.86	3.24	9.29	2.79	3.24
1997	Colorado	NL	176.7	178	79	15	55	101	4.02	11	9	9.07	0.76	2.80	5.15	0.78	4.02
1998	Colorado	NL	174.0	164	73	19	54	105	3.78	11	8	8.48	0.98	2.79	5.43	0.93	3.93
1999	Colorado	NL	70.3	76	48	9	36	34	6.14	3	5	9.73	1.15	4.61	4.35	0.32	5.50

Thomson pitched through pain most of the season and underwent postseason surgery for a torn right labrum. A healthy Thomson's value to the Rockies is almost incalculable; he's shown he can pitch successfully at altitude, and he allows the team to save the money they'd have to spend to replace him with quality innings. The recovery period for his surgery isn't long; if he doesn't have any collateral damage, he'll be back in the rotation in 2000.

Jermaine Van Buren   Throws R   Age 19

YEAR	TEAM	LGE	IP	H	ER	HR	BB	K	ERA	W	L	H/9	HR/9	BB/9	K/9	KWH	PERA
1999	Ashevlle	SAL	136.7	180	107	18	100	88	7.05	4	11	11.85	1.19	6.59	5.80	0.32	7.77

A second-round pick in the 1998 draft, Van Buren led the Arizona Fall League in ERA and strikeouts. In his first full season of action at Asheville, what really stands out is the walks. He gives up a load of them. He's got a plus fastball and a good curve and change-up, and if the team's treatment of Kalinowski is any indication, they'll be very patient with Van Buren.

Dave Veres   Throws R   Age 33

YEAR	TEAM	LGE	IP	H	ER	HR	BB	K	ERA	W	L	H/9	HR/9	BB/9	K/9	KWH	PERA
1997	Montreal	NL	62.7	69	27	5	28	44	3.88	4	3	9.91	0.72	4.02	6.32	0.75	4.88
1998	Colorado	NL	81.3	62	22	5	30	73	2.43	7	2	6.86	0.55	3.32	8.08	2.14	2.88
1999	Colorado	NL	85.0	77	34	12	37	71	3.60	5	4	8.15	1.27	3.92	7.52	1.32	4.45

He's consistently one of the better relievers in the league. Veres got the chance to close games regularly for the first time in his career in 1999, and he ended up setting the club record for saves with 31. When looking at the performance, it becomes apparent that last year wasn't really one of his better seasons. He'll be the Cardinal closer in 2000.

David Wainhouse　　　Throws R　　　Age 32

YEAR	TEAM	LGE	IP	H	ER	HR	BB	K	ERA	W	L	H/9	HR/9	BB/9	K/9	KWH	PERA
1997	Calgary	PCL	38.3	41	19	4	14	20	4.46	2	2	9.63	0.94	3.29	4.70	0.52	4.70
1997	Pittsbrg	NL	28.7	33	26	2	18	20	8.16	1	2	10.36	0.63	5.65	6.28	0.50	5.65
1998	ColSprin	PCL	51.0	44	22	3	28	37	3.88	3	3	7.76	0.53	4.94	6.53	0.83	3.88
1999	ColSprin	PCL	42.0	42	17	6	8	33	3.64	3	2	9.00	1.29	1.71	7.07	2.42	4.07
1999	Colorado	NL	32.0	33	16	5	16	18	4.50	2	2	9.28	1.41	4.50	5.06	0.46	5.62

Wainhouse is another one of a number of Colorado pitchers who have seen a sharp upward spike in effectiveness since joining the organization. In Wainhouse's case, he went from a marginal reliever in Pittsburgh to one of the better pitchers in the PCL. He wasn't terrible in a short stint in Colorado at the end of the season; obviously, he's too old to have much ahead of him, but he'll probably get some time in the Rockies' pen this year.

Jamey Wright　　　Throws R　　　Age 25

YEAR	TEAM	LGE	IP	H	ER	HR	BB	K	ERA	W	L	H/9	HR/9	BB/9	K/9	KWH	PERA
1997	Colorado	NL	160.7	185	98	19	77	57	5.49	7	11	10.36	1.06	4.31	3.19	0.17	5.71
1998	Colorado	NL	225.0	222	124	22	105	86	4.96	11	14	8.88	0.88	4.20	3.44	0.24	4.60
1999	Colorado	NL	104.7	96	39	8	55	49	3.35	8	4	8.25	0.69	4.73	4.21	0.34	4.21
1999	ColSprin	PCL	100.7	128	78	11	45	61	6.97	3	8	11.44	0.98	4.02	5.45	0.48	6.17

He's still learning to pitch. Wright was actually impressive in the limited duty he saw with the Rockies in 1999, despite which he received a punitive demotion. He's got a "heavy ball" that induces loads of grounders and double plays, a style that served him well with players like Neifi Perez and Todd Helton behind him. Wright doesn't strike a lot of guys out, but he's about two walks per nine innings from millions of dollars in cash and prizes. We still can't believe he pitched as much as he did in 1998. He's been traded to the Brewers, who also have a fairly good infield defense. He's a decent candidate for what will look like a breakout season in 2000.

Support-Neutral Records				COLORADO ROCKIES							Park Effect: +52.5%	
PITCHER	GS	IP	R	SNW	SNL	SNPCT	W	L	RA	APW	SNVA	SNWAR
Pedro Astacio	34	232.0	140	14.8	11.7	.558	17	11	5.43	2.05	1.39	3.52
Brian Bohanon	33	197.3	146	10.6	13.1	.449	12	12	6.66	-0.52	-1.07	0.56
Mark Brownson	7	29.7	26	2.1	2.4	.459	0	2	7.89	-0.42	-0.11	0.15
Luther Hackman	3	14.0	17	0.4	1.5	.216	0	2	10.93	-0.59	-0.48	-0.39
Bobby M. Jones	20	100.0	78	4.9	7.0	.411	6	9	7.02	-0.60	-0.85	-0.17
Darryl Kile	32	190.7	150	10.3	13.0	.442	8	13	7.08	-1.25	-1.23	0.40
Roberto Ramirez	4	16.7	20	0.6	1.8	.253	1	3	10.80	-0.69	-0.51	-0.42
John Thomson	13	60.7	62	2.4	6.2	.283	1	10	9.20	-1.60	-1.70	-1.22
Jamey Wright	16	94.3	52	6.4	4.3	.598	4	3	4.96	1.25	1.00	1.87
TOTALS	162	935.3	691	52.6	61.0	.463	49	65	6.65	-2.36	-3.55	4.30

The Rockies' rotation is regular as clockwork. For the past four years, Colorado starters have been worth between three and four wins below average each season according to SNVA, ranking no better than 20th and no worse than 24th in the majors during that time. Consistency is nice, but I bet Rockies' management could do without this particular kind.... Once again, Colorado's starters had some trouble pitching in Denver, although the home/road split wasn't as large as it has been in previous years. At home, the Rockies' Support-Neutral Winning Percentage (SNPct) was .452, while on the road it was .473. Remember that the Support-Neutral stats are park-adjusted, so the extra trouble they're having at home is genuine and not a park illusion.... Tony LaRussa, take note: Darryl Kile was one of the few Rockies who pitched better at home: .460 at Coors and .427 away.... Pedro Astacio's season was the best by a Rockies starter in the short history of the franchise, as measured by Support-Neutral Wins Above Replacement (SNWAR). Marvin Freeman's 1994 is Astacio's toughest competition, and while Freeman produced at a better rate than Astacio (beating him in SNPct .709 to .558), he didn't have enough innings in the strike-shortened season to compete with Astacio's cumulative production last year.

Pitcher Abuse Points													
PITCHER	AGE	GS	PAP	PAP/S	WKLD	MAX	1-90	91-100	101-110	111-120	121-130	131-140	141+
Pedro Astacio	29	34	816	24.0	36.0	153	6	3	7	9	5	3	1
Brian Bohanon	30	33	455	13.8	18.4	137	10	4	8	6	4	1	0
Mark Brownson	24	7	0	0.0	0.0	99	5	2	0	0	0	0	0
Luther Hackman	24	3	10	3.3	7.8	110	1	1	1	0	0	0	0
Bobby M. Jones	27	20	118	5.9	10.8	120	8	4	4	4	0	0	0
Darryl Kile	30	32	320	10.0	13.3	123	7	4	11	6	4	0	0
Roberto Ramirez	26	4	0	0.0	0.0	94	2	2	0	0	0	0	0
John Thomson	25	13	0	0.0	0.0	100	8	5	0	0	0	0	0
Jamey Wright	24	16	228	14.3	33.3	141	4	3	4	4	0	0	1
COLORADO		162	1947	12.0	18.7	153	51	28	35	29	13	4	2
Ranking (NL)				3	2								

Take the most abusive manager in the game in 1998, add 5,000 feet, sprinkle in some frustration and you have a recipe for disaster. It could have tasted worse, but Leyland lost the services of John Thomson before he could really abuse him, leaving the Rockies "only" second in the league in Workload.... It seems that the only thing that held Leyland back was his starters' ineffectiveness; Darryl Kile had another awful season and finished with a reasonable workload, while Brian Bohanon paid a slightly higher price for his fast start.... Pedro Astacio had a remarkable season (he went 12-6 with a 3.60 ERA on the road) and ranked fourth in baseball in PAPs, while throwing the longest outing of the season.... Jamey Wright, who after missing half the season came back and somehow finished with a 4.87 ERA, didn't escape Leyland's wrath. Thankfully for the Rockies, new manager Buddy Bell did a fine job protecting his starters in Detroit.

Florida Marlins

It's time to start moving forward again. The Florida Marlins are 30 months removed from a celebratory dogpile on the field at Pro Player Stadium, and ten times further in spirit from that shining moment. The team has lost 206 games since that night in October, 1997. The franchise has been stripped, ridiculed and sold, and at one late-season game last year had fewer people in the stands than we had buyers of *Baseball Prospectus 1996*.

All that should be behind them now, because while the major-league Marlins were being battered from pillar to post, the organization was adding loads of talent at the lower levels. Some of the trades the team made were stellar (Matt Mantei for Brad Penny, et al) and some were startlingly bad (Ed Yarnall, et al for the redundant Mike Lowell), but nearly all of them sacrificed major-league players for prospects with more upside and lower prices, and few were received well by baseball fans in South Florida or the baseball media at large.

Starting in 2000, however, Marlins GM Dave Dombrowski will begin to see the return on his efforts. The Marlins aren't going to contend this year—they won't score enough runs to be a significant threat—but they are going to improve to around the .500 level, enough to generate some excitement among the riddled Marlins' fan base and encourage new owner John Henry to write some checks to help the 2001 team make a wild-card push.

Why such an optimistic outlook? After all, this is a team that finished last in the National League in runs scored and 12th in runs allowed. Their best prospects from two years ago have been terrible disappointments; center fielder Todd Dunwoody and first baseman Derrek Lee spent significant parts of 1999 back at Triple-A Calgary, while right fielder Mark Kotsay was one of the league's worst regulars at his position for the second year in a row. Their best pitchers in 1998, Brian Meadows and Jesus Sanchez, were terrible in 1999. Their best pitchers in 1999, Alex Fernandez and Dennis Springer, are well past 30.

Still, a number of Very Good Things happened last season. Longtime prospect Luis Castillo finally established himself, hitting the ball past the infielders often enough to make his combination of plate discipline, speed and defense valuable. Suspect Preston Wilson snagged a job in the wake of Dunwoody's struggles and slugged .502 while posting a surprising .350 OBP. Fernandez returned from shoulder surgery to be one of the most effective pitchers in the league, and the team handled him superbly, even shutting him down over some minor soreness with three weeks to go.

This season, the Marlins will really start seeing the benefits of the trades they've been making. Already in the second half of 1999, the team was getting contributions from Wilson, Armando Almanza, Braden Looper and Vladimir Nunez, all acquired in so-called "dump" deals. The 2000 rotation should include A.J. Burnett, picked up from the Mets for Al Leiter. As the year progresses, Pablo Ozuna and Brad Penny could be called up to play second base and take a rotation spot, respectively.

So if 2000 is going to be the start of the Marlins' recovery, what has to be done to help it along? Talent acquisition is just one aspect of a rebuilding effort, and the most important. Dombrowski has done an exceptional job of turning major-league veterans into minor leaguers with upside. Now that the talent base is in place, it's critical that the organization begin to make moves that craft the talent into the shape of a baseball team. As teams like the late 1990s Angels have shown, a poor distribution of talent can doom a team that has a good base on which to build.

Right now, the Marlins have an excess of middle infielders, tools outfielders and young pitchers with upside. They lack players with on-base skills, have no top-tier prospects at catcher or third base, and need a big left-handed hitter. Taking from that first list and adding players who fill their needs has to be Dombrowski's highest priority. The Marlins have to decide which of Wilson, Kotsay, Julio Ramirez, Abraham Nunez and Chip Ambres they want to build

Marlins Prospectus

1999 record: 64-98; Fifth place, NL East

Pythagorean W/L: 66-96

Runs scored: 691 (16th in NL)

Runs allowed: 852 (12th in NL)

Team EQA: .250 (13th in NL)

1999 team age: 25.6 (2nd-youngest in NL)

1999 park: Pro Player Stadium; excellent pitchers' park, decreased run scoring by 13%.

1999: Year two of the rebuilding saw little progress, but lots of talent arriving in the system.

2000: The talent base is there for a .500 season, with much more to come.

around, and shop the others. They have to decide whether Ozuna or Castillo is going to be their second baseman and which of their collection of great arms can be invested in the trade market.

There's an organizational precedent for this. In 1993, the Marlins put the first piece of a championship team in place by trading Trevor Hoffman, Andres Berumen and Pedro Martinez to the San Diego Padres for Gary Sheffield. (No, the other Pedro Martinez.) Sheffield was coming off a near-MVP season with the Padres and had established himself as a devastating right-handed hitter, a package of average, power and plate discipline. The Marlins got the prime of Sheffield's career before sending him to Los Angeles in their own fire sale in 1998.

That move, in the middle of Florida's inaugural season, gave the Marlins a legitimate star, a player a cut above the expansion fodder that littered their roster. It set the stage for the decisions that followed, such as the signings of Devon White, Kevin Brown, Bobby Bonilla and Moises Alou. It converted the strength of the young Marlins—depth in live young arms—into something that would make them a better baseball team.

Entering 2000, the Marlins need to contemplate a similar move. Dombrowski has to identify and obtain a player or two that the Marlins can construct a lineup around. It would be unrealistic to point to the Seattle Mariners' imminent free agents, both with Florida ties, because it's unlikely that Henry will write a check that big. But that's the type of player Dombrowski has the talent base to acquire. If he aims high, he can provide the Marlins with a lineup anchor for the 2000-03 seasons, in the same way that Sheffield anchored the 1993-97 teams.

If he can't get Ken Griffey Jr. or Alex Rodriguez, he should probably focus on a high-upside hitter in the Sheffield mold, as that is the type of player the Marlins don't have many of in the system. Oakland's Ben Grieve, the Yankees' Nick Johnson, the Cardinals' J.D. Drew and the Diamondbacks' Travis Lee are just a few names that come to mind. Of course, none of these players may be available, but they serve as an illustration of the guys Dombrowski should try to bring in, so that he can build a great baseball *team* out of his current collection of baseball *talent*.

Two years from now, the Marlins are going be contenders. At that point, Dombrowski's job will change again, and he will have to focus on getting the missing pieces. Some may be large, like a #2 starter or a first baseman who can hit in the middle of the lineup. Others may be smaller, the chess pieces a competing team needs to give itself advantages on a daily basis: a left-handed relief specialist or a platoon right fielder.

It was at this phase that Blue Jays' GM Gord Ash failed so terribly in 1999. He had the front-line talent in place for a 95-win season but was unable to patch the holes at third base, DH and on the bench. The Mariners' Woody Woodward was also guilty of this, getting only one postseason series win in the last half of the decade out of a team that featured four all-time greats.

Every team, be it the two-time champion Yankees or the cellar-dwelling Marlins, is at a specific point in its development cycle. The best general managers, people like Gerry Hunsicker and Billy Beane, are adept at recognizing where they are and adjusting their actions accordingly: getting younger and dumping payroll, or adding and developing core players, or acquiring the supporting and spare parts to complete a contender.

Other GMs get caught up in doing what they do best, be it developing and giving jobs to young players, like Bill Bavasi, or constantly making small moves to patch leaks, like Dan Duquette. The ability to recognize and adjust to changing circumstances is what separates, and will continue to separate, the best GMs from the next group down. Not reacting to, or worse, not anticipating your team's changing needs is the fastest way to be labeled a disappointment. Ask Bavasi, who never recognized that the Angels' OBP problem needed to be solved by dumping favorites like Gary DiSarcina and Garret Anderson. The 1990s Angels fared even worse than the aforementioned Mariners: they haven't been to the postseason since 1986, and Bavasi was finally pushed into a resignation in October.

Some teams show no recognition of where they are in the cycle, or even that there is one. Organizations like the Cubs and Tigers seem lost in an endless loop, flitting from poor to average, never able to commit to the first phase of the cycle—the talent-acquisition phase—long enough to establish a base. Without the core of good young players, the subsequent acquisitions of supporting parts don't push the team towards a championship, and when there isn't any tangible success, the team changes management personnel and starts over.

Dombrowski has completed a near-perfect first phase. His ability to implement the second and third phases will determine how quickly the Marlins get back and how successful they will be when they get there. Given his track record, the future looks very bright in Miami.

HITTERS (Averages: BA: .270 / OBP: .340 / SLG: .430 / EQA: .260)

Chip Ambres — OF — Bats R — Age 20

YEAR	TEAM	LGE	AB	H	DB	TP	HR	BB/SO	R	RBI	SB	CS	OUT	BA	OBP	SLG	EQA	EQR	DEFENSE
1999	Utica	NYP	110	25	4	3	5	17/25	16	11	3	2	87	.227	.333	.455	.262	15	25-OF 93
2000	Florida	NL	53	13	1	1	4	10/21	10	11	2	1	41	.245	.365	.528	.297	10	

Ambres, the Marlins' 1998 #1 draft pick, started the year in rookie ball after passing up a drooling Texas A&M football program. After his promotion, he quickly proved that he was too good for the New York-Penn League. Ambres is a great athlete who has control of the strike zone, which is exactly the kind of player the Marlins need to develop. He could move through the system quickly.

Bruce Aven — LF — Bats R — Age 28

YEAR	TEAM	LGE	AB	H	DB	TP	HR	BB/SO	R	RBI	SB	CS	OUT	BA	OBP	SLG	EQA	EQR	DEFENSE
1997	Buffalo	AA	444	117	26	3	13	41/111	59	67	7	2	329	.264	.341	.423	.260	57	105-OF 97
1999	Florida	NL	386	115	20	2	12	39/81	56	69	3	0	271	.298	.377	.453	.283	58	62-LF 105
2000	Pittsbrg	NL	250	74	11	1	9	29/88	41	44	3	0	176	.296	.369	.456	.280	36	

Because of their desire to keep payroll down, the Marlins gave opportunities to some good hitters who had been stuck in the upper minors for a few years. Aven, who missed almost all of 1998 after Tommy John surgery, won a piece of the left-field job in June. His second trip around the league wasn't as successful (about 150 points of OPS worse). The Marlins traded him to the Pirates for Brant Brown; his path is crowded in Pittsburgh, but he should end up with a reserve outfielder job.

Danny Bautista — OF — Bats R — Age 28

YEAR	TEAM	LGE	AB	H	DB	TP	HR	BB/SO	R	RBI	SB	CS	OUT	BA	OBP	SLG	EQA	EQR	DEFENSE
1997	Richmond	Int	172	43	12	2	1	14/32	23	22	1	0	129	.250	.310	.360	.229	16	38-OF 113
1997	Atlanta	NL	104	26	4	2	3	5/24	15	9	2	0	78	.250	.291	.413	.238	11	29-OF 98
1998	Atlanta	NL	145	37	7	0	5	7/20	17	19	1	0	108	.255	.289	.407	.232	14	33-OF 84
1999	Calgary	PCL	130	32	5	1	5	9/19	16	18	2	2	100	.246	.299	.415	.236	14	35-OF 108
1999	Florida	NL	208	62	10	1	5	1/30	31	24	3	0	146	.298	.305	.428	.246	22	23-RF 98
2000	Florida	NL	219	56	10	1	5	14/34	24	26	2	1	164	.256	.300	.379	.233	21	

Bautista is a useful spare part on a good team, thanks to his defense and above-average speed. On a team going nowhere, like the 1999 Marlins, all he does is take up space. He was in a good situation in Atlanta as Ryan Klesko's caddy; I'm sure he'll eventually stumble into another opportunity.

David Berg — IF — Bats R — Age 29

YEAR	TEAM	LGE	AB	H	DB	TP	HR	BB/SO	R	RBI	SB	CS	OUT	BA	OBP	SLG	EQA	EQR	DEFENSE
1997	Charlott	Int	425	107	23	4	7	42/76	58	36	10	4	322	.252	.323	.374	.240	45	108-SS 92
1998	Florida	NL	186	61	6	0	4	26/45	18	23	4	0	125	.328	.410	.425	.293	29	19-2B 93
1999	Florida	NL	308	91	19	1	3	23/58	41	25	2	2	219	.295	.349	.393	.253	35	
2000	Florida	NL	302	86	15	1	5	35/61	47	41	5	2	218	.285	.359	.391	.264	39	

One of the Aven class, Berg actually won his job in the second half of 1998. He should be one of the best fifth infielders in baseball for the next few years; he can play three positions, is patient, has doubles power and can start for a week and not hurt the team.

Luis Castillo — 2B — Bats B — Age 24

YEAR	TEAM	LGE	AB	H	DB	TP	HR	BB/SO	R	RBI	SB	CS	OUT	BA	OBP	SLG	EQA	EQR	DEFENSE
1997	Charlott	Int	129	41	5	0	0	14/21	21	6	6	4	92	.318	.385	.357	.259	16	35-2B 92
1997	Florida	NL	267	67	5	0	1	26/52	25	10	13	11	211	.251	.317	.281	.207	21	63-2B 97
1998	Florida	NL	155	34	4	2	1	22/32	22	11	3	0	121	.219	.321	.290	.219	14	42-2B 93
1998	Charlott	Int	380	100	7	2	1	65/69	57	15	26	11	291	.263	.371	.300	.246	44	100-2B 92
1999	Florida	NL	493	152	18	5	1	61/84	70	28	45	18	359	.308	.384	.371	.269	67	120-2B 102
2000	Florida	NL	501	133	15	4	1	74/91	95	44	40	14	382	.265	.360	.317	.252	61	

Castillo finally got the ball out of the infield enough to keep a job. He was a much improved player last year, particularly on the bases and with the glove. He got better as the year went on before missing most of September with a dislocated left shoulder. He has to hit .270 or so with some doubles to keep his job; I expect he'll do that and more.

Ramon Castro — C — Bats R — Age 24

YEAR	TEAM	LGE	AB	H	DB	TP	HR	BB/SO	R	RBI	SB	CS	OUT	BA	OBP	SLG	EQA	EQR	DEFENSE
1997	Kissimme	Fla	421	109	20	1	9	46/80	47	57	0	0	312	.259	.334	.375	.243	46	
1998	Jackson	Tex	168	38	4	0	7	10/34	21	20	0	1	131	.226	.281	.375	.217	14	46-C 104
1998	Portland	Eas	89	22	2	0	3	6/21	8	10	0	0	67	.247	.295	.371	.223	8	
1999	Calgary	PCL	341	75	13	0	13	20/63	31	47	0	0	266	.220	.266	.372	.211	27	91-C 100
1999	Florida	NL	68	13	4	0	2	9/14	4	4	0	0	55	.191	.286	.338	.212	6	20-C 109
2000	*Florida*	*NL*	*399*	*97*	*12*	*0*	*17*	*40/79*	*45*	*58*	*0*	*0*	*302*	*.243*	*.312*	*.401*	*.245*	*45*	

The nominal catcher of the future hasn't shown as much offensive development as you'd like to see, but reached the majors last August anyway. Castro is a good defensive catcher who will hit enough to be a starter right now and is young enough to improve. He should be up to stay.

Chris Clapinski — UT — Bats B — Age 28

YEAR	TEAM	LGE	AB	H	DB	TP	HR	BB/SO	R	RBI	SB	CS	OUT	BA	OBP	SLG	EQA	EQR	DEFENSE	
1997	Charlott	Int	342	78	22	1	9	37/68	47	40	8	2	266	.228	.318	.377	.240	38	39-2B 84	32-SS 93
1998	Charlott	Int	312	72	16	1	6	30/59	40	26	6	2	242	.231	.307	.346	.225	29	25-OF 98	24-3B 109
1999	Calgary	PCL	258	64	16	5	4	23/57	33	22	3	1	195	.248	.313	.395	.240	28	33-3B 106	14-SS 94
1999	Florida	NL	57	14	1	2	0	8/12	6	3	1	0	43	.246	.350	.333	.244	6		
2000	*Florida*	*NL*	*285*	*66*	*14*	*3*	*6*	*36/61*	*39*	*33*	*5*	*2*	*221*	*.232*	*.318*	*.365*	*.239*	*31*		

Perhaps the reason the Braves couldn't find a decent utility infielder for their postseason roster was because the Marlins had all of them. In Berg, Clapinski and Amaury Garcia, Florida has a glut of extra infielders who can contribute with the bat and play multiple positions. Clapinski made the team in August thanks to injuries; there's no room here for him when everyone is healthy.

Todd Dunwoody — CF — Bats L — Age 25

YEAR	TEAM	LGE	AB	H	DB	TP	HR	BB/SO	R	RBI	SB	CS	OUT	BA	OBP	SLG	EQA	EQR	DEFENSE
1997	Charlott	Int	402	100	15	6	21	31/126	62	54	18	2	304	.249	.307	.473	.262	54	107-OF 106
1998	Charlott	Int	102	29	7	2	5	9/28	16	18	2	1	74	.284	.363	.539	.293	17	25-OF 129
1998	Florida	NL	440	116	29	7	6	20/110	55	29	5	1	325	.264	.302	.402	.237	44	96-OF 112
1999	Florida	NL	188	43	6	3	2	10/41	19	20	2	4	149	.229	.272	.324	.194	12	38-CF 89
1999	Calgary	PCL	240	54	13	5	6	7/57	24	25	5	5	191	.225	.252	.396	.210	19	65-OF 106
2000	*KansasCy*	*AL*	*370*	*92*	*16*	*6*	*11*	*26/92*	*48*	*50*	*9*	*4*	*282*	*.249*	*.298*	*.414*	*.235*	*38*	

He had a better year than Moises Alou. Seriously, Dunwoody hasn't done anything at the major-league level in two chances and even struggled after his return to Calgary last year. He's not going to be Andy Van Slyke, and if he doesn't start controlling the strike zone, he's not going to be playing baseball for a living much longer. At this point, he's a potential fourth outfielder, nothing more. He'll try to revive his career with the Royals, a team with even more outfielders than the Marlins.

Matt Erickson — 2B — Bats L — Age 24

YEAR	TEAM	LGE	AB	H	DB	TP	HR	BB/SO	R	RBI	SB	CS	OUT	BA	OBP	SLG	EQA	EQR	DEFENSE
1997	Utica	NYP	246	63	6	0	5	37/41	29	31	3	1	184	.256	.366	.341	.252	29	62-3B 114
1998	KaneCnty	Mid	457	127	29	1	5	57/66	63	51	6	3	333	.278	.371	.379	.262	58	102-3B 94
1999	Portland	Eas	362	86	14	2	1	40/69	31	29	1	2	278	.238	.317	.296	.212	29	104-2B 94
2000	*Florida*	*NL*	*396*	*102*	*17*	*1*	*4*	*56/70*	*58*	*44*	*5*	*2*	*296*	*.258*	*.350*	*.336*	*.246*	*44*	

Erickson looked like a heck of a prospect two years ago, a great defensive third baseman with plate discipline. Moved to second base, he played passable defense and stopped hitting. In this organization, he has a better chance to make the majors at the hot corner and should be returned there posthaste.

Cliff Floyd   LF   Bats L   Age 27

YEAR	TEAM	LGE	AB	H	DB	TP	HR	BB/SO	R	RBI	SB	CS	OUT	BA	OBP	SLG	EQA	EQR	DEFENSE
1997	Florida	NL	139	33	11	1	6	24/33	23	19	5	2	108	.237	.358	.460	.276	22	25-OF 112
1997	Charlott	Int	130	43	7	0	8	8/29	21	27	5	2	89	.331	.374	.569	.305	23	28-OF 94
1998	Florida	NL	598	176	48	3	24	46/109	89	94	29	16	438	.294	.348	.505	.279	90	144-OF 88
1999	Florida	NL	254	78	20	1	11	27/47	36	47	4	6	182	.307	.379	.524	.291	42	58-LF 99
2000	*Florida*	*NL*	*361*	*101*	*22*	*1*	*19*	*43/72*	*63*	*67*	*12*	*7*	*267*	*.280*	*.356*	*.504*	*.288*	*59*	

A strained MCL in his left knee and a torn right Achilles' tendon were the latest additions to Floyd's long list of owies. He's cracked 400 plate appearances exactly once in his six-year career, so you have to expect him to miss time every year. When he's healthy, he's an above-average hitter in left field and can contribute to a winning team. The Marlins really need his power.

Amaury Garcia   2B   Bats R   Age 25

YEAR	TEAM	LGE	AB	H	DB	TP	HR	BB/SO	R	RBI	SB	CS	OUT	BA	OBP	SLG	EQA	EQR	DEFENSE
1997	Brevard	Fla	490	127	28	1	8	41/110	56	37	18	5	368	.259	.321	.369	.240	52	123-2B 94
1998	Portland	Eas	548	135	19	5	12	36/127	66	54	14	9	422	.246	.295	.365	.222	49	135-2B 91
1999	Calgary	PCL	463	120	28	6	12	36/80	65	37	11	7	350	.259	.319	.423	.248	54	119-2B 94
1999	Florida	NL	24	6	0	1	2	3/11	6	3	0	0	18	.250	.333	.583	.291	4	
2000	*Florida*	*NL*	*538*	*137*	*27*	*5*	*14*	*51/113*	*75*	*70*	*17*	*8*	*409*	*.255*	*.319*	*.401*	*.249*	*63*	

Garcia is a pretty good offensive second baseman caught behind a better one in Castillo. He is attempting to learn other positions in an effort to make the Marlins as a utility player. He'll go into camp with a chance to make the roster, albeit behind Berg as the backup second baseman. Garcia deserves a job.

Alex Gonzalez   SS   Bats R   Age 23

YEAR	TEAM	LGE	AB	H	DB	TP	HR	BB/SO	R	RBI	SB	CS	OUT	BA	OBP	SLG	EQA	EQR	DEFENSE
1997	Portland	Eas	447	100	15	3	15	18/86	53	49	3	4	351	.224	.262	.371	.207	34	130-SS 93
1998	Charlott	Int	421	108	20	9	8	21/81	60	43	2	5	318	.257	.300	.404	.232	41	106-SS 93
1998	Florida	NL	87	14	3	0	3	9/29	12	7	0	0	73	.161	.248	.299	.180	5	22-SS 94
1999	Florida	NL	567	161	30	8	14	8/112	79	58	2	5	411	.284	.310	.439	.246	62	129-SS 90
2000	*Florida*	*NL*	*508*	*135*	*24*	*5*	*15*	*26/105*	*56*	*70*	*4*	*5*	*378*	*.266*	*.301*	*.421*	*.243*	*55*	

He wasn't expected to walk much, but this is ridiculous. It's nearly impossible to be a good player with this kind of walk rate, and Gonzalez isn't going to hit the .330 or so he's going to need to carry that kind of plate discipline. Because he can hit for average and has some power, he's going to be overrated. The Marlins are moving Pablo Ozuna to second base; they'd be better off trading Gonzalez after this season.

Jaime Jones   OF   Bats L   Age 23

YEAR	TEAM	LGE	AB	H	DB	TP	HR	BB/SO	R	RBI	SB	CS	OUT	BA	OBP	SLG	EQA	EQR	DEFENSE
1997	Brevard	Fla	383	96	25	3	11	37/94	55	52	3	1	288	.251	.318	.418	.248	44	58-OF 86
1998	Portland	Eas	442	117	20	0	12	47/115	52	59	3	1	326	.265	.339	.391	.250	51	106-OF 85
1999	Calgary	PCL	135	28	5	0	0	8/30	9	5	1	2	109	.207	.252	.244	.153	5	34-OF 96
1999	Portland	Eas	245	56	12	0	7	39/83	32	26	1	0	189	.229	.338	.363	.244	28	71-OF 83
2000	*Florida*	*NL*	*372*	*93*	*13*	*0*	*10*	*43/105*	*47*	*47*	*3*	*1*	*280*	*.250*	*.328*	*.366*	*.243*	*41*	

Jones is a tools outfielder who doesn't play like one, hitting better than the rest of the species without showing the speed or glove. He's been passed by Julio Ramirez and won't be able to hold off Abraham Nunez, so his shot in this organization is minimal. He was outrighted to Calgary after the season, a very bad sign.

Mark Kotsay   RF   Bats L   Age 24

YEAR	TEAM	LGE	AB	H	DB	TP	HR	BB/SO	R	RBI	SB	CS	OUT	BA	OBP	SLG	EQA	EQR	DEFENSE
1997	Portland	Eas	434	115	24	2	15	59/67	76	57	11	3	322	.265	.353	.433	.268	60	113-OF 102
1998	Florida	NL	587	172	30	7	12	33/59	77	72	11	6	421	.293	.332	.429	.255	69	138-OF 106
1999	Florida	NL	501	140	24	9	8	23/49	55	49	6	6	367	.279	.311	.411	.240	52	111-RF 99
2000	*Florida*	*NL*	*519*	*146*	*27*	*6*	*13*	*41/56*	*75*	*76*	*13*	*6*	*379*	*.281*	*.334*	*.432*	*.263*	*67*	

(Mark Kotsay *continued*)

Kotsay regressed in his second full season and has yet to show any of the plate discipline or power that made him a top prospect in 1997. Unlike Dunwoody, he's hit for a respectable average; that has helped him keep his job but is not helping the Marlins much. With Ramirez coming up behind him, he's got about two months to get it together. I think he'll show a big power jump this year, possibly at the expense of some average, and post a .280 EqA.

Derrek Lee   **1B**   **Bats R**   **Age 24**

YEAR	TEAM	LGE	AB	H	DB	TP	HR	BB/SO	R	RBI	SB	CS	OUT	BA	OBP	SLG	EQA	EQR	DEFENSE
1997	LasVegas	PCL	453	124	20	1	11	47/119	60	46	12	2	331	.274	.342	.395	.255	55	124-1B 110
1998	Florida	NL	461	113	28	1	20	46/117	65	79	5	2	350	.245	.328	.440	.258	59	119-1B 111
1999	Florida	NL	221	47	11	1	5	14/69	21	20	2	1	175	.213	.260	.339	.198	15	56-1B 106
1999	Calgary	PCL	330	79	16	1	14	25/89	44	53	2	3	254	.239	.299	.421	.238	35	90-1B 105
2000	*Florida*	*NL*	*537*	*136*	*26*	*1*	*23*	*61/150*	*75*	*84*	*6*	*2*	*403*	*.253*	*.329*	*.434*	*.262*	*71*	

Like Kotsay, Lee hasn't at all resembled the hitter who generated such excitement in 1997. Striking out a third of the time hasn't helped the perception of his play, either. Lee is a big guy who can be a devastating power source, something the Marlins need. He goes into camp trying to win a piece of the first-base job. As with Kotsay, I think he'll establish himself this year, at least job-sharing with Kevin Millar.

Mike Lowell   **3B**   **Bats R**   **Age 26**

YEAR	TEAM	LGE	AB	H	DB	TP	HR	BB/SO	R	RBI	SB	CS	OUT	BA	OBP	SLG	EQA	EQR	DEFENSE
1997	Norwich	Eas	289	89	13	1	12	38/32	46	37	1	1	201	.308	.394	.484	.295	47	64-3B 97
1997	Columbus	Int	212	56	11	1	14	19/33	32	39	2	3	159	.264	.333	.524	.275	32	42-3B 88
1998	Columbus	Int	507	138	31	2	21	27/89	64	79	2	0	369	.272	.316	.465	.258	63	117-3B 103
1999	Calgary	PCL	80	19	1	0	2	7/21	8	7	0	0	61	.237	.299	.325	.212	6	18-3B 124
1999	Florida	NL	312	81	14	0	13	22/68	31	47	0	0	231	.260	.320	.429	.251	36	81-3B 97
2000	*Florida*	*NL*	*433*	*120*	*20*	*1*	*21*	*43/86*	*60*	*79*	*1*	*1*	*314*	*.277*	*.342*	*.473*	*.276*	*63*	

While Lowell has some power and can play third base, he's not special enough to be worth Ed Yarnall. That move was Dave Dombrowski's one misstep during this rebuilding process; given the pitchers he's picked up since then, it shouldn't be fatal. Lowell goes into camp as the starting third baseman after the Kevin Orie trade, and that Wilton looks accurate.

Kevin Millar   **1B**   **Bats R**   **Age 28**

YEAR	TEAM	LGE	AB	H	DB	TP	HR	BB/SO	R	RBI	SB	CS	OUT	BA	OBP	SLG	EQA	EQR	DEFENSE
1997	Portland	Eas	504	131	27	1	19	45/62	60	80	1	1	374	.260	.328	.431	.255	61	122-1B 100
1999	Calgary	PCL	139	33	9	1	4	8/21	16	17	1	0	106	.237	.279	.403	.227	13	19-OF 94
1999	Florida	NL	355	104	18	4	9	36/63	47	65	1	0	251	.293	.371	.442	.277	51	87-1B 98
2000	*Florida*	*NL*	*278*	*70*	*14*	*1*	*8*	*30/55*	*36*	*38*	*1*	*0*	*208*	*.252*	*.325*	*.396*	*.250*	*32*	

Millar is a good hitter who, like Aven, wasn't quite as impressive the second time through the league. Unless Lee hits like Jimmie Foxx on uppers in March, Millar should have at least half of the first base job when the season starts. That projection is low; I think he'll match his 1999 performance.

Kevin Orie   **3B**   **Bats R**   **Age 27**

YEAR	TEAM	LGE	AB	H	DB	TP	HR	BB/SO	R	RBI	SB	CS	OUT	BA	OBP	SLG	EQA	EQR	DEFENSE
1997	ChiCubs	NL	365	98	24	5	8	38/56	39	42	1	2	269	.268	.346	.427	.260	47	99-3B 114
1998	ChiCubs	NL	206	39	10	0	4	17/34	24	24	1	1	168	.189	.262	.296	.185	12	54-3B 106
1998	Iowa	PCL	91	28	5	0	7	9/16	19	18	1	0	63	.308	.379	.593	.313	17	19-3B 101
1998	Florida	NL	178	49	8	1	7	13/23	24	18	1	0	129	.275	.344	.449	.267	24	47-3B 105
1999	Florida	NL	243	64	13	0	7	19/43	25	29	1	0	179	.263	.326	.403	.247	27	59-3B 103
1999	Calgary	PCL	70	17	6	0	2	10/8	7	5	0	0	53	.243	.344	.414	.258	9	16-3B 93
2000	*LosAngls*	*NL*	*388*	*98*	*20*	*1*	*14*	*44/63*	*51*	*58*	*1*	*1*	*291*	*.253*	*.329*	*.418*	*.258*	*49*	

Orie had taken advantage of Mike Lowell's absence to grab the third base job with a good May, but injured his groin and quadriceps in rapid succession, reopening the door for Lowell. He's been dealt to the Dodgers, primarily as insurance in case they lose Adrian Beltre. If Beltre is a Dodger, Orie will be an Albuquerque Duke. Or a Backstreet Boy.

Pablo Ozuna   SS/2B   Bats R   Age 21

YEAR	TEAM	LGE	AB	H	DB	TP	HR	BB/SO	R	RBI	SB	CS	OUT	BA	OBP	SLG	EQA	EQR	DEFENSE
1997	JohnsnCy	App	230	58	9	1	3	5/26	19	14	7	2	174	.252	.270	.339	.205	17	55-SS 88
1998	Peoria	Mid	547	172	25	7	11	22/58	85	50	23	12	337	.314	.348	.446	.266	71	123-SS 92
1999	Portland	Eas	501	129	24	6	6	5/51	48	38	16	9	381	.257	.278	.365	.215	41	115-SS 90
2000	*Florida*	*NL*	*482*	*139*	*20*	*5*	*9*	*18/52*	*62*	*61*	*19*	*8*	*351*	*.288*	*.314*	*.407*	*.248*	*54*	

Concerns about his throwing arm had the Marlins moving Ozuna to second base last winter. He was one of the youngest players in Double-A in 1999, so his regression as a hitter isn't too worrisome. The move to second base is, as it puts him behind a better player in Castillo. The potential for a Gonzalez/Ozuna middle infield in 2002, walking a total of 50 times, should send shudders down the spines of Marlin fans. Ozuna will have to show some offensive development in 2000 to maintain his status as a top prospect.

Julio Ramirez   CF   Bats R   Age 22

YEAR	TEAM	LGE	AB	H	DB	TP	HR	BB/SO	R	RBI	SB	CS	OUT	BA	OBP	SLG	EQA	EQR	DEFENSE
1997	KaneCnty	Mid	383	88	17	4	14	27/127	47	42	18	4	299	.230	.287	.405	.237	41	98-OF 103
1998	Brevard	Fla	564	140	19	9	14	36/163	60	47	28	13	437	.248	.297	.388	.233	57	136-OF 110
1999	Portland	Eas	569	138	31	7	12	27/154	64	53	33	9	440	.243	.279	.385	.228	54	138-OF 109
1999	Florida	NL	21	3	1	0	0	1/6	2	2	0	1	19	.143	.182	.190	—	0	
2000	*Florida*	*NL*	*610*	*157*	*26*	*8*	*17*	*48/176*	*97*	*75*	*45*	*13*	*466*	*.257*	*.312*	*.410*	*.254*	*75*	

Ramirez is a scout's wet dream, and an illustration of how performance analysis and talent analysis can come together to provide a complete picture of a player. Ramirez is the proverbial five-tool prospect; he looks great in a uniform and impresses talent evaluators with his great speed, strong arm and power. However, because he doesn't control the strike zone, he's not making a significant offensive contribution. He's not being selective enough, so he's not getting into hitters' counts—which would boost his average and power—or garnering walks, which would help his OBP. Plate discipline can be taught, and it's up to the Marlins' development staff to both recognize the weakness in Ramirez's game and develop that missing skill. Frankly, it's about the only thing missing: Ramirez is a star in the making.

Mike Redmond   C   Bats R   Age 29

YEAR	TEAM	LGE	AB	H	DB	TP	HR	BB/SO	R	RBI	SB	CS	OUT	BA	OBP	SLG	EQA	EQR	DEFENSE
1998	Florida	NL	120	41	7	0	3	5/16	10	13	0	0	79	.342	.379	.475	.287	17	35-C 108
1999	Florida	NL	245	76	3	0	3	23/34	21	28	0	0	169	.310	.382	.359	.261	29	73-C 106
2000	*Florida*	*NL*	*117*	*34*	*2*	*0*	*2*	*11/24*	*14*	*16*	*0*	*0*	*83*	*.291*	*.352*	*.359*	*.251*	*13*	

This is a quality backup/platoon catcher. Redmond is fair defensively and can pinch-hit, so he should be around for a long time; his immediate future will involve sharing time with Ramon Castro. He'll play more than that projection indicates.

John Roskos   LF/1B/C   Bats R   Age 25

YEAR	TEAM	LGE	AB	H	DB	TP	HR	BB/SO	R	RBI	SB	CS	OUT	BA	OBP	SLG	EQA	EQR	DEFENSE	
1997	Portland	Eas	447	119	24	1	19	37/84	49	62	3	3	331	.266	.322	.452	.256	55		
1998	Charlott	Int	415	109	19	1	9	35/85	46	53	0	3	309	.263	.324	.378	.237	42	72-1B 97	
1999	Calgary	PCL	489	129	26	0	19	43/114	59	64	1	1	361	.264	.326	.434	.254	59	85-OF 75	27-1B 100
2000	*SanDieg*	*NL*	*450*	*116*	*18*	*0*	*19*	*43/104*	*56*	*69*	*1*	*1*	*335*	*.258*	*.323*	*.424*	*.258*	*57*		

That "C" is just a reminder that Roskos is capable of catching. He's not going to be more than a third/emergency catcher in the majors, though. Still, a player who can pinch-hit, play some first base or left field and strap on the tools 10 times a year has a lot of value. The Marlins' logjam of better players at left field and first base creates a problem for Roskos, who may need to go elsewhere to get a chance.

Preston Wilson   CF   Bats R   Age 25

YEAR	TEAM	LGE	AB	H	DB	TP	HR	BB/SO	R	RBI	SB	CS	OUT	BA	OBP	SLG	EQA	EQR	DEFENSE
1997	St Lucie	Fla	246	53	10	1	10	6/75	26	38	1	2	195	.215	.236	.386	.199	17	59-OF 92
1997	Binghmtn	Eas	259	67	12	1	15	14/73	28	36	4	1	193	.259	.300	.486	.258	33	64-OF 97
1998	Charlott	Int	355	91	24	2	21	28/123	58	63	9	4	268	.256	.314	.513	.269	50	92-OF 102
1999	Florida	NL	488	141	24	4	26	40/154	66	69	10	4	351	.289	.355	.514	.286	77	101-CF 94
2000	*Florida*	*NL*	*453*	*119*	*23*	*2*	*25*	*39/147*	*65*	*80*	*10*	*3*	*337*	*.263*	*.321*	*.488*	*.272*	*65*	

(Preston Wilson *continued*)

To his credit, he got a chance and took advantage, putting together his best season as a professional. Realistically, this is the top of his range; he didn't fundamentally change as a player, he just did the things he does pretty well. He hit .414 when not striking out, which won't last. Even when he returns to Earth, Wilson would make a good platoon right fielder, as he hits left-handers and is a good glove man on the outfield corners. The Marlins need to not get discouraged with him this year when he slips and focus on what he can do to contribute.

PITCHERS (Averages: ERA: 4.50 / H/9: 9.00 / HR/9: 1.00 / BB/9: 3.50 / K/9: 6.50 / KWH: 1.00)

Antonio Alfonseca   Throws R   Age 28

YEAR	TEAM	LGE	IP	H	ER	HR	BB	K	ERA	W	L	H/9	HR/9	BB/9	K/9	KWH	PERA
1997	Charlott	Int	57.0	64	35	8	22	37	5.53	2	4	10.11	1.26	3.47	5.84	0.73	5.37
1997	Florida	NL	25.3	38	16	3	10	18	5.68	1	2	13.50	1.07	3.55	6.39	0.64	7.46
1998	Florida	NL	70.3	77	36	10	35	44	4.61	4	4	9.85	1.28	4.48	5.63	0.54	5.76
1999	Florida	NL	75.7	81	28	4	27	44	3.33	5	3	9.63	0.48	3.21	5.23	0.66	4.16

Alfonseca has consistently posted a DT-ERA better than his peripherals would predict, thanks in part to his effectiveness with runners on: he allowed just a .568 OPS in those situations in 1999 and is 99 points of OPS better with runners on for his career. He's not an overpowering pitcher, but does the things that keep runs off the board, controlling the running game and getting ground balls. There's not much upside—except for roto-heads and their save category—but Alfonseca should contribute on this level for a while.

Armando Almanza   Throws L   Age 27

YEAR	TEAM	LGE	IP	H	ER	HR	BB	K	ERA	W	L	H/9	HR/9	BB/9	K/9	KWH	PERA
1997	Pr Willm	Car	58.3	55	27	4	41	52	4.17	3	3	8.49	0.62	6.33	8.02	0.90	4.94
1998	Arkansas	Tex	29.3	34	17	2	23	34	5.22	1	2	10.43	0.61	7.06	10.43	1.10	6.44
1998	Memphis	PCL	33.0	39	20	1	22	36	5.45	2	2	10.64	0.27	6.00	9.82	1.13	5.73
1999	Portland	Eas	11.0	6	6	1	5	15	4.91	0	1	4.91	0.82	4.09	12.27	5.60	2.45
1999	Calgary	PCL	17.0	28	25	3	22	16	13.24	0	2	14.82	1.59	11.65	8.47	0.31	12.71
1999	Florida	NL	15.7	8	4	1	9	19	2.30	2	0	4.60	0.57	5.17	10.91	3.75	2.30

He's a hard thrower who should be ready to contribute right about the time the Marlins are good enough to make use of this type of player. In the meantime, they should focus less on using him tactically and more on getting him enough work to develop.

Josh Beckett   Throws R   Age 19

The #2 overall pick in the 1999 draft, Beckett demanded and received a major-league contract from the Marlins. This puts a tremendous amount of pressure on him and the organization, and almost guarantees that he'll be asked to do too much before he's physically ready. Drafting high-school pitchers is risky enough without mandating that they take up valuable space on your 40-man roster. Beckett is a fastball/curveball pitcher, just like Kerry Wood.

Brent Billingsley   Throws L   Age 25

YEAR	TEAM	LGE	IP	H	ER	HR	BB	K	ERA	W	L	H/9	HR/9	BB/9	K/9	KWH	PERA
1997	KaneCnty	Mid	157.0	193	89	12	62	119	5.10	7	10	11.06	0.69	3.55	6.82	0.88	5.39
1998	Portland	Eas	168.3	186	93	25	82	146	4.97	9	10	9.94	1.34	4.38	7.81	1.04	5.77
1999	Calgary	PCL	117.0	127	71	12	57	65	5.46	5	8	9.77	0.92	4.38	5.00	0.44	5.23
1999	Florida	NL	7.3	11	13	3	10	3	15.95	0	1	13.50	3.68	12.27	3.68	0.06	14.73

Billingsley could be an intermediate solution while Brad Penny, A.J. Burnett, Jason Grilli and Nate Bump get innings in Triple-A. Billingsley doesn't throw particularly hard, with his best pitch a change-up. He's the type of left-hander who pitches much better after the age of 28 or so. Picked up by the Expos on waivers over the winter.

Nate Bump — Throws R — Age 23

YEAR	TEAM	LGE	IP	H	ER	HR	BB	K	ERA	W	L	H/9	HR/9	BB/9	K/9	KWH	PERA
1998	San Jose	Cal	55.3	53	20	3	29	41	3.25	4	2	8.62	0.49	4.72	6.67	0.82	4.23
1999	Portland	Eas	42.7	62	39	3	13	27	8.23	1	4	13.08	0.63	2.74	5.70	0.68	6.12
1999	Shrevprt	Tex	84.3	105	51	9	39	47	5.44	4	5	11.21	0.96	4.16	5.02	0.40	5.98

Bump was picked up in the Livan Hernandez swindle, one of two Giants' #1 picks the Marlins nabbed in that deal. He's behind the Marlins' big three, needing to develop his off-speed pitches and have some success in Double-A. I like his future, in part because he doesn't rely on the more-damaging slider or curve, instead throwing a cut fastball and knuckle-curve. Check back in a year.

A.J. Burnett — Throws R — Age 23

YEAR	TEAM	LGE	IP	H	ER	HR	BB	K	ERA	W	L	H/9	HR/9	BB/9	K/9	KWH	PERA
1997	Pittsfld	NYP	37.3	42	40	5	51	30	9.64	1	3	10.13	1.21	12.29	7.23	0.31	9.16
1998	KaneCnty	Mid	112.7	97	35	5	57	128	2.80	9	4	7.75	0.40	4.55	10.22	2.21	3.59
1999	Portland	Eas	119.7	144	93	15	78	101	6.99	4	9	10.83	1.13	5.87	7.60	0.68	6.69
1999	Florida	NL	40.0	39	23	3	24	32	5.18	2	2	8.78	0.68	5.40	7.20	0.82	4.72

There was considerable talk in the spring that Burnett would open the season in the major leagues, jumping from the Midwest League. He ended up at Portland, where he struggled and was eventually removed from the rotation. Burnett throws hard with a knee-buckling curveball and improving change-up and should be up for good by midseason. They're nipple rings, people: get over it.

Scott Comer — Throws L — Age 23

YEAR	TEAM	LGE	IP	H	ER	HR	BB	K	ERA	W	L	H/9	HR/9	BB/9	K/9	KWH	PERA
1997	Pittsfld	NYP	84.7	104	39	7	18	60	4.15	5	4	11.06	0.74	1.91	6.38	1.44	4.78
1998	KaneCnty	Mid	90.0	122	55	17	11	58	5.50	4	6	12.20	1.70	1.10	5.80	1.87	6.20
1999	Brevard	Fla	121.3	148	47	5	6	66	3.49	8	5	10.98	0.37	0.45	4.90	3.67	3.78

At one point this season, Comer went 65 innings without walking a batter. You know our position on A-ball pitching prospects; still, Comer has displayed amazing control at the lower levels. He won't rocket through the system; he should move up a level a year and make a cameo in September, 2001. Don't worry too much about his poor Arizona Fall League stint.

Vic Darensbourg — Throws L — Age 29

YEAR	TEAM	LGE	IP	H	ER	HR	BB	K	ERA	W	L	H/9	HR/9	BB/9	K/9	KWH	PERA
1997	Charlott	Int	24.3	24	12	4	17	17	4.44	2	1	8.88	1.48	6.29	6.29	0.53	5.92
1998	Florida	NL	70.7	53	29	5	31	70	3.69	5	3	6.75	0.64	3.95	8.92	2.23	3.18
1999	Florida	NL	33.7	51	36	3	20	15	9.62	1	3	13.63	0.80	5.35	4.01	0.16	8.02

Woof. Michael Wolverton's Reliever Evaluation Tools peg Darensbourg as the worst reliever in baseball in 1999, a neat trick given he threw just 34⅔ innings. Even with the bad year, his outlook is the same: interchangeable left-handed reliever capable of giving a team 70 good innings. Almanza should reduce his importance.

Ryan Dempster — Throws R — Age 23

YEAR	TEAM	LGE	IP	H	ER	HR	BB	K	ERA	W	L	H/9	HR/9	BB/9	K/9	KWH	PERA
1997	Brevard	Fla	152.0	238	127	25	60	103	7.52	4	13	14.09	1.48	3.55	6.10	0.56	8.23
1998	Portland	Eas	43.7	37	21	9	17	27	4.33	3	2	7.63	1.85	3.50	5.56	0.87	4.53
1998	Charlott	Int	33.0	33	13	4	13	21	3.55	2	2	9.00	1.09	3.55	5.73	0.77	4.64
1998	Florida	NL	54.7	74	47	6	40	33	7.74	2	4	12.18	0.99	6.59	5.43	0.27	7.74
1999	Calgary	PCL	31.0	29	14	5	11	24	4.06	2	1	8.42	1.45	3.19	6.97	1.35	4.65
1999	Florida	NL	143.0	151	75	20	89	121	4.72	8	8	9.50	1.26	5.60	7.62	0.81	5.92

To his credit, he bounced back from a 1998 in which he was rushed to the majors as part of the Marlins' Pitcher-Eating Program. Dempster doesn't have exceptional stuff, but he can be a placeholder while the real pitchers develop, hopefully picking up some trade value along the way. See Meadows, Brian.

Mike Drumright   Throws R   Age 26

YEAR	TEAM	LGE	IP	H	ER	HR	BB	K	ERA	W	L	H/9	HR/9	BB/9	K/9	KWH	PERA
1997	Jacksnvl	Sou	26.7	20	9	0	14	19	3.04	2	1	6.75	0.00	4.73	6.41	0.96	2.70
1997	Toledo	Int	125.0	153	85	23	93	97	6.12	5	9	11.02	1.66	6.70	6.98	0.49	7.85
1998	Toledo	Int	146.7	204	137	20	101	78	8.41	4	12	12.52	1.23	6.20	4.79	0.22	8.10
1999	Toledo	Int	113.7	130	92	15	65	65	7.28	4	9	10.29	1.19	5.15	5.15	0.37	6.18
1999	Calgary	PCL	20.7	39	31	5	16	12	13.50	0	2	16.98	2.18	6.97	5.23	0.17	13.06

Drumright is another piece of evidence in the case against pitching prospects. Three years ago, he was a #1 pick out of Wichita State, one of the top young arms in baseball. He simply wasn't good enough to get Triple-A hitters out, and after 400 innings, it looks like he's not going to solve them. It isn't an injury: Drumright just doesn't have it.

Brian Edmondson   Throws R   Age 27

YEAR	TEAM	LGE	IP	H	ER	HR	BB	K	ERA	W	L	H/9	HR/9	BB/9	K/9	KWH	PERA
1997	Binghmtn	Eas	21.0	19	4	0	9	14	1.71	2	0	8.14	0.00	3.86	6.00	0.86	3.43
1997	Norfolk	Int	66.0	70	29	5	39	54	3.95	4	3	9.55	0.68	5.32	7.36	0.80	5.18
1998	Atlanta	NL	16.7	15	10	2	8	8	5.40	1	1	8.10	1.08	4.32	4.32	0.40	4.32
1998	Florida	NL	59.0	64	28	8	30	30	4.27	4	3	9.76	1.22	4.58	4.58	0.35	5.64
1999	Florida	NL	91.0	109	64	10	42	55	6.33	3	7	10.78	0.99	4.15	5.44	0.49	5.84

In 1998, the Marlins' rotation was a disaster while the bullpen was quietly effective. The roles reversed in 1999, with Edmondson a large part of the decline. Wolverton's RET pegs Edmondson as the third-worst reliever in baseball. Unlike his teammate Darensbourg, who was brutal in fewer than 40 innings, Edmondson was merely bad, with more than twice as much work. The Marlins have a lot of live arms they need to make room for, so Edmondson is going to have a hard time making the team.

Alex Fernandez   Throws R   Age 30

YEAR	TEAM	LGE	IP	H	ER	HR	BB	K	ERA	W	L	H/9	HR/9	BB/9	K/9	KWH	PERA
1997	Florida	NL	219.0	195	92	26	73	170	3.78	14	10	8.01	1.07	3.00	6.99	1.52	3.82
1999	Florida	NL	137.3	139	60	9	39	87	3.93	9	6	9.11	0.59	2.56	5.70	1.04	3.80

He returned as pretty much the same pitcher he was before the injury. He's lost a little off his fastball, but his command is better. The Marlins handled him wonderfully: he threw more than 100 pitches exactly once all season, and he was shut down in September when he experienced some shoulder soreness. His value to the Marlins is what they can get for him in a trade. With two years left at about $6 million per year, he's a bargain in the current pitching market.

Jason Grilli   Throws R   Age 23

YEAR	TEAM	LGE	IP	H	ER	HR	BB	K	ERA	W	L	H/9	HR/9	BB/9	K/9	KWH	PERA
1998	Shrevprt	Tex	113.0	132	69	11	43	82	5.50	5	8	10.51	0.88	3.42	6.53	0.89	5.18
1998	Fresno	PCL	40.7	51	29	7	20	32	6.42	2	3	11.29	1.55	4.43	7.08	0.75	6.86
1999	Fresno	PCL	100.0	121	61	19	44	64	5.49	4	7	10.89	1.71	3.96	5.76	0.57	6.66
1999	Calgary	PCL	41.7	53	42	6	26	23	9.07	1	4	11.45	1.30	5.62	4.97	0.29	7.13

Grilli has the makings of a good pitcher, with a top-notch fastball, changeup and curve. Scouts give him high marks for his mechanics and makeup, as befits the son of a major leaguer. Grilli's performance hasn't been that impressive to date, even taking into account the environments in which he's pitched. With barely 300 professional innings under his belt, Grilli needs to experience some success at Triple-A before the Marlins can even think about promoting him. He will be very good, eventually.

Braden Looper   Throws R   Age 25

YEAR	TEAM	LGE	IP	H	ER	HR	BB	K	ERA	W	L	H/9	HR/9	BB/9	K/9	KWH	PERA
1997	Pr Willm	Car	59.3	89	47	7	29	42	7.13	2	5	13.50	1.06	4.40	6.37	0.51	7.74
1997	Arkansas	Tex	19.3	28	16	3	8	17	7.45	1	1	13.03	1.40	3.72	7.91	0.96	7.45
1998	Memphis	PCL	38.3	46	17	3	15	37	3.99	2	2	10.80	0.70	3.52	8.69	1.48	5.17
1999	Florida	NL	80.7	98	43	7	30	48	4.80	4	5	10.93	0.78	3.35	5.36	0.59	5.36

Looper may have been rushed to the majors following his acquisition in the Renteria trade. He stayed healthy in 1999, something he'd yet to do as a professional, and got a lot of ground balls. Looper needs an out pitch against left-handed hitters—who posted an .875 OPS against him—to move into a bigger role.

Brian Meadows — Throws R — Age 24

YEAR	TEAM	LGE	IP	H	ER	HR	BB	K	ERA	W	L	H/9	HR/9	BB/9	K/9	KWH	PERA
1997	Portland	Eas	171.7	224	100	21	53	94	5.24	8	11	11.74	1.10	2.78	4.93	0.56	5.92
1998	Florida	NL	173.7	227	106	20	49	84	5.49	8	11	11.76	1.04	2.54	4.35	0.47	5.75
1999	Florida	NL	173.0	219	116	29	54	69	6.03	7	12	11.39	1.51	2.81	3.59	0.30	6.19

For the past two years, he's stayed healthy, taken his turn and been the spitting image of a replacement-level starting pitcher. For a team like the Marlins in 1998 and 1999, soaking up innings has value. As the young pitchers behind Meadows mature, his usefulness disappears. He's been traded to San Diego for Dan Miceli, which opens up a rotation slot and upgrades the Marlins' bullpen, both signs that Dombrowski recognizes how the team's goals are changing. Meadows should be the #4 starter in San Diego and his numbers should improve thanks to the ballpark.

Rafael Medina — Throws R — Age 25

YEAR	TEAM	LGE	IP	H	ER	HR	BB	K	ERA	W	L	H/9	HR/9	BB/9	K/9	KWH	PERA
1997	LasVegas	PCL	65.7	82	50	11	40	43	6.85	2	5	11.24	1.51	5.48	5.89	0.42	7.26
1998	Charlott	Int	57.3	54	24	7	27	36	3.77	4	2	8.48	1.10	4.24	5.65	0.66	4.55
1998	Florida	NL	67.0	78	50	8	55	47	6.72	2	5	10.48	1.07	7.39	6.31	0.38	7.12
1999	Calgary	PCL	35.3	25	13	1	25	28	3.31	3	1	6.37	0.25	6.37	7.13	0.94	3.57
1999	Florida	NL	22.3	21	15	3	20	15	6.04	1	1	8.46	1.21	8.06	6.04	0.40	6.45

Medina managed to place fifth on the Pitcher Abuse Points list in 1998 despite making just 12 starts. He was essentially useless in 1999, moving to the bullpen and scuffling in a brief stint in Florida. The Marlins no longer have room for him, so he'll be back at Triple-A, hoping to be a trade throw-in.

Vladimir Nunez — Throws R — Age 25

YEAR	TEAM	LGE	IP	H	ER	HR	BB	K	ERA	W	L	H/9	HR/9	BB/9	K/9	KWH	PERA
1997	High Des	Cal	152.0	199	106	35	47	101	6.28	6	11	11.78	2.07	2.78	5.98	0.81	7.11
1998	Tucson	PCL	97.7	95	48	11	42	68	4.42	6	5	8.75	1.01	3.87	6.27	0.87	4.52
1999	Arizona	NL	33.7	30	14	2	19	27	3.74	2	2	8.02	0.53	5.08	7.22	0.96	4.01
1999	Florida	NL	73.0	68	47	9	32	55	5.79	3	5	8.38	1.11	3.95	6.78	1.04	4.44

The split by teams you see above is also a reflection of how he pitched as a reliever (effectively, with Arizona) and a starter (poorly, with Florida). He stranded 17 of 18 inherited runners, an amazing rate. Nunez's future is as a reliever; it's a role that suits him and fits the Marlins' needs better as well. Like Looper, he scuffles against left-handed hitters.

Brad Penny — Throws R — Age 22

YEAR	TEAM	LGE	IP	H	ER	HR	BB	K	ERA	W	L	H/9	HR/9	BB/9	K/9	KWH	PERA
1997	Sth Bend	Mid	110.0	119	57	5	51	80	4.66	6	6	9.74	0.41	4.17	6.55	0.79	4.58
1998	High Des	Cal	159.7	164	71	17	44	142	4.00	10	8	9.24	0.96	2.48	8.00	2.09	4.17
1999	El Paso	Tex	90.7	115	55	9	31	82	5.46	4	6	11.42	0.89	3.08	8.14	1.41	5.66
1999	Portland	Eas	32.0	30	15	4	15	29	4.22	2	2	8.44	1.13	4.22	8.16	1.40	4.50

The best pitching prospect in baseball, once you factor the likelihood of injury into the equation. Penny battled tendinitis early this season, which kept his workload down yet didn't impact his development. The movement on his fastball gets him a lot of ground balls and helps him keep the ball in the park. Still a year away, he'll be a significant contributor to a good Marlins team in 2002.

Jesus Sanchez — Throws L — Age 25

YEAR	TEAM	LGE	IP	H	ER	HR	BB	K	ERA	W	L	H/9	HR/9	BB/9	K/9	KWH	PERA
1997	Binghmtn	Eas	161.3	160	86	23	66	143	4.80	8	10	8.93	1.28	3.68	7.98	1.45	4.80
1998	Florida	NL	172.7	182	98	18	96	131	5.11	8	11	9.49	0.94	5.00	6.83	0.73	5.32
1999	Florida	NL	74.3	87	52	15	57	59	6.30	3	5	10.53	1.82	6.90	7.14	0.52	7.87

Sanchez may have felt the strain of the workload he carried in 1998 under Jim Leyland. He pitched poorly in the spring and declined from there, losing his rotation spot in May. Already operating on a thin margin, Sanchez fell apart when he started getting the ball up in the zone. He's still young enough to reestablish himself as a swingman or one-batter left-hander.

Dennis Springer Throws R Age 35

YEAR	TEAM	LGE	IP	H	ER	HR	BB	K	ERA	W	L	H/9	HR/9	BB/9	K/9	KWH	PERA
1997	Anaheim	AL	198.0	189	106	29	74	76	4.82	10	12	8.59	1.32	3.36	3.45	0.31	4.55
1998	TampaBay	AL	116.3	120	73	19	63	47	5.65	5	8	9.28	1.47	4.87	3.64	0.22	5.72
1998	Durham	Int	35.7	39	15	1	16	19	3.79	2	2	9.84	0.25	4.04	4.79	0.43	4.54
1999	Florida	NL	190.3	237	121	21	61	79	5.72	8	13	11.21	0.99	2.88	3.74	0.32	5.53

Like Meadows, Springer was valuable for his ability to take the ball and throw six innings once a week. He doesn't have any useful second pitch, so if the knuckleball isn't working, he gets obliterated. He'll be at the back of a rotation somewhere.

Mike Tejera Throws L Age 23

YEAR	TEAM	LGE	IP	H	ER	HR	BB	K	ERA	W	L	H/9	HR/9	BB/9	K/9	KWH	PERA
1997	Utica	NYP	63.7	91	49	11	17	42	6.93	2	5	12.86	1.55	2.40	5.94	0.85	7.07
1998	KaneCnty	Mid	50.7	61	29	5	16	32	5.15	3	3	10.84	0.89	2.84	5.68	0.78	5.15
1998	Portland	Eas	106.3	120	55	15	41	79	4.66	6	6	10.16	1.27	3.47	6.69	0.95	5.42
1999	Portland	Eas	153.7	147	54	13	50	126	3.16	11	6	8.61	0.76	2.93	7.38	1.61	3.81

The influx of pitching talent acquired through trades has pushed Tejera into the background. He's a short left-hander who defected from Cuba in 1995 at the age of 17 and may be the least-publicized Cuban defector in recent memory. He's ahead of the Penny/Grilli class, without their upside, and is a real sleeper this spring.

Support-Neutral Records — FLORIDA MARLINS — Park Effect: -19.0%

PITCHER	GS	IP	R	SNW	SNL	SNPCT	W	L	RA	APW	SNVA	SNWAR
A.J. Burnett	7	41.3	23	2.4	2.2	.525	4	2	5.01	-0.19	0.05	0.47
Reid Cornelius	2	13.7	3	1.3	0.1	.902	1	0	1.98	0.39	0.53	0.66
Ryan Dempster	25	147.0	77	8.9	8.4	.514	7	8	4.71	-0.20	0.21	1.54
Alex Fernandez	24	141.0	60	8.6	6.8	.556	7	8	3.83	1.18	0.90	2.02
Livan Hernandez	20	136.0	78	6.9	8.1	.458	5	9	5.16	-0.85	-0.62	0.50
Brian Meadows	31	178.3	117	7.4	13.6	.353	11	15	5.90	-2.58	-3.00	-1.52
Vladimir Nunez	12	68.0	45	3.4	5.1	.401	3	7	5.96	-1.02	-0.85	-0.21
Jesus Sanchez	10	42.7	34	1.7	4.7	.267	1	4	7.17	-1.21	-1.39	-1.00
Dennis Springer	29	174.3	105	8.3	12.8	.393	6	14	5.42	-1.59	-2.22	-0.68
TOTALS	162	945.0	550	48.9	63.1	.437	45	68	5.24	-6.72	-6.92	1.31

For the second year in the row, the Marlins had the worst starting rotation in the majors according to SNVA. This is the first time since we started tracking the Support-Neutral numbers in 1992 that any team has finished at the very bottom for two consecutive years. The Marlins' closest competition for back-to-back futility in recent years is the Minnesota Twins, who had the third-worst rotation in 1994 and by far the worst in 1995.... That's not to say that all the news was bad for the Marlins. The 1999 staff actually was quite a bit better than the disastrous rotation of 1998. The '98 starting staff was worth 14 wins below average, while last year's rotation "only" cost the Marlins seven wins and narrowly missed being beat out by the Cubs for last place.... Alex Fernandez returned from a career-threatening injury and picked up right where he had left off. Ryan Dempster had 25 starts that must have made the Rangers regret trading him for Bobby Witt, and the highly touted A.J. Burnett debuted with seven above-average outings. With prospects Brad Penny, Jason Grilli, Nate Bump and others on their way up, the future looks bright for this rotation.... Has there ever been a less effective brother duo than Dennis and Russ Springer? Between them they have nine seasons in which they were used as starters. All of those seasons were below average, and only two of them were above replacement level (a .425 Support-Neutral Winning Percentage). Knuckleballer Dennis is the better of the pair, his career having resulted in a merely bad .406 SNPct and -1.2 SNWAR over 93 starts. Meanwhile, brother Russ has been among the decade's very worst starters, putting together a .275 SNPct and -2.8 SNWAR in 27 starts. I know that each has had variable success as a reliever, but please, major-league managers, no more penciling them into the rotation, OK?

Pitcher Abuse Points

PITCHER	AGE	GS	PAP	PAP/S	WKLD	MAX	1-90	91-100	101-110	111-120	121-130	131-140	141+
A.J. Burnett	22	7	48	6.9	18.3	121	1	3	2	0	1	0	0
Reid Cornelius	29	2	0	0.0	0.0	89	2	0	0	0	0	0	0
Ryan Dempster	22	25	258	10.3	27.5	122	8	4	2	10	1	0	0
Alex Fernandez	29	24	2	0.1	0.1	102	9	14	1	0	0	0	0
Livan Hernandez	24	20	644	32.2	75.1	141	1	3	1	5	9	0	1
Brian Meadows	23	31	48	1.5	3.9	114	16	8	6	1	0	0	0
Vladimir Nunez	24	12	26	2.2	5.1	111	6	2	3	1	0	0	0
Jesus Sanchez	24	10	12	1.2	2.8	106	6	1	3	0	0	0	0
Dennis Springer	34	29	278	9.6	9.6	134	13	6	4	2	3	1	0
FLORIDA		162	1316	8.1	17.3	141	64	41	22	19	14	1	1
Ranking (NL)			5	4									

He didn't vacillate as much as Lou Piniella, but John Boles engaged in a bit of doublespeak last year. First, he admitted that Livan Hernandez had thrown too many pitches in 1998 and vowed to protect him. Then he let him throw more than 120 pitches in 10 of his 20 starts for the Marlins. That Dave Dombrowski could turn a sore-armed pitcher who hadn't pitched well in two years into a pair of fine prospects shows us just how much smarter Dombrowski is than Brian Sabean. Then again, we already knew that.... On the other hand, few decisions were more admirable last season than the Marlins' resolve to protect Alex Fernandez at all costs. Fernandez had a remarkable return from rotator cuff surgery, one that might not have been possible had the Marlins not gone to such lengths to keep his pitch counts in double digits.... Brian Meadows, for the second straight year, was also well protected, but Boles didn't do Ryan Dempster any favors. It is a sad irony of baseball that the arms most worth protecting—the ones belonging to power pitchers—are the ones that work deep into counts and, if not carefully watched, throw the most pitches.

Houston Astros

Bad teams make excuses. They blame injuries, they blame luck, they say they would be in first place if they could only drive home the runner from third with one out. They lose their direction so often, they can't even remember who today's scapegoat is. When the manager is on the hot seat, the front office extends his contract to remind the players who's in charge, then pulls the other lever and fires him two months later. Management rips into the team, complaining about a lack of "character" and "chemistry" in the clubhouse, while holding up their shortstop—who's cleared a .300 OBP twice in nine years—as a role model for team behavior.

Good teams create opportunity out of adversity. Good teams have the depth to overcome injuries and the talent to overcome luck, and they know that the best way to bring home more runners from third base is to get more runners to third base. They remain calm under pressure, and they stay loyal to their personnel because they brought in the right personnel in the first place. They let other teams worry about how to improve their clubhouse; they spend their time improving the team on the field.

The Astros are a good team.

That may seem obvious, given that the Astros have won three straight division titles. Unfortunately, their 2-9 postseason record over that time has left them with a reputation as one of the NL's second-tier teams, the best in a weak division—and little more than an ugly stepsister to the real powerhouses in baseball, the Braves, Yankees and Indians. This is an injustice. How many other teams could lose their left fielder before spring training, their starting catcher by the end of April and their center fielder in August, play half the season without their starting third baseman, withstand a charge by a 96-win team and still win the division?

The Astros' ascension to a spot among the elite teams in baseball was something few had foreseen. We could hardly have predicted it when Drayton McLane bought the team in 1992 and started throwing money at free agents. It would

have been even more difficult to envision after two of those free agents, Doug Drabek and Greg Swindell, were nearly released six months after signing, before someone explained to McLane that their contracts were guaranteed. The roller-coaster atmosphere surrounding the Astros' front office had fans longing for the relative sanity of a Peter Angelos operation.

McLane fooled us. We all thought he was another owner with more money than common sense and more ego than money. In fact, all he had was a learning curve. He just needed time to learn not to sign pitchers in their thirties to long-term deals, time to understand the importance of building an elite farm system, time to accept the wisdom of hiring good baseball men and letting them do their jobs without interference. He learned, and as a result, the Astros have been one of the best-run organizations in baseball over the last five years.

The Cleveland Indians get all the credit for signing their best young players to long-term deals at bargain salaries, but the Astros, with Bagwell and Biggio under contract for a little more than $6 million each, had the lowest Opening Day payroll of any playoff team last year. The Oakland Athletics and New York Yankees get all the publicity for giving plate discipline the importance it deserves, but the Astros led the NL in walks last year, after finishing third in both 1997 and 1998. Actually, the Astros may have the best understanding of the importance of walks, both on offense and on defense, of any team in baseball. Not only did they lead the NL in most walks drawn, but with control freaks like Jose Lima and Shane Reynolds, they also lapped the field in walks allowed.

If ever there was a team that used the power of the base on balls to its advantage, it was these Astros. Look at their hitters' totals compared to the totals for their opponents in Table 1.

The Astros attempted many more stolen bases than their opponents, but they weren't successful any more often. Their running game didn't add more than an extra couple of

Astros Prospectus

1999 record: 97-65; First place, NL Central; Lost to Braves in Division Series, 3-1

Pythagorean W/L: 96-66

Runs scored: 823 (8th in NL)

Runs allowed: 675 (2nd in NL)

Team EQA: .267 (6th in NL)

1999 team age: 28.8 (8th-youngest in NL)

1999 park: Astrodome; good pitchers' park, decreased run scoring by 11%. Moving to Enron Field for 2000 season.

1999: Survived a slew of injuries to win the division, yet were quickly bounced again.

2000: Team is aging a bit and needs to work in good young hitters; great offseason.

Table 1

Team	1B	2B	3B	HR	TB	SB	CS	GIDP	Runs
Astros	979	293	23	168	2306	166	75	128	823
Opponents	1051	271	35	128	2210	94	43	136	675
Difference	-72	+22	-12	+40	+96	+72	+32	-8	+148

runs over their opponents. The Astros did have a 40-home-run advantage, which is not trivial, but their opponents had more hits, so Astro hitters had only 96 more total bases than their pitchers gave up.

And yet the Astros outscored their opponents by nearly a run a game, because of the one piece of information not listed above: the Astros drew 728 walks, and their pitchers gave up only 478. A 250-walk difference—more than 1.5 walks per game—isn't just impressive, it's historic. Take a look at Table 2, which shows the teams with the greatest walk advantages over their opponents in major-league history.

Table 2

Team	Year	BB (Hit)	BB (Pit)	Difference
Houston	1999	728	478	250
San Francisco	1969	711	461	250
New York (AL)	1927	643	409	234
New York (AL)	1931	750	543	207
New York (NL)	1908	494	288	206
New York (AL)	1937	712	506	206
New York (AL)	1932	765	561	204
Oakland	1999	770	569	201

When Dierker was hired to run the Astros straight out of the broadcast booth, his education in sabermetric principles was on trial as much as he was. His loyalty to those principles was an open question when he was hired, but is there any doubt now? The power of the walk as an offensive weapon has been one of the key tenets of sabermetrics. That Dierker has placed it front and center in the Astros' plan for winning speaks volumes about his beliefs, while the success of the Astros since he was hired speaks volumes about the validity of those beliefs.

In a way, the Astros are even more ahead of their time than they appear. As more organizations sign on to the idea that a patient hitter is better than an aggressive one, it places an evolutionary pressure on pitchers. Those with control problems are giving up more walks, falling behind more hitters and letting them tee off on hitters' counts more than they would have 20 or even 10 years ago. The game is changing, as pitchers who once made their living on the impatience of hitters are going broke. And as the modern hitter becomes more patient, the model for success as a pitcher is going to change—from one who fools hitters with breaking balls out of the strike zone to one who changes speeds, uses a variety of deliveries and, above all, throws strikes.

The Astros' rotation is evidence that the transformation has begun. Shane Reynolds was 26 before he finally stuck in the major leagues, and has held hitters to fewer hits than innings exactly once in his career. He's won 60 games over the last four years because of control that only Greg Maddux can match in the NL. Jose Lima's fastball was so straight that he had a career ERA of 5.92 after his first three seasons in the majors. Now, with a change-up that is among the best in baseball and control so good that he can spot that fastball on the corners of the plate, he's one of the 10 best starters in the league.

Still, even with their rotation evolving and their manager embracing the power of the walk, the Astros lost in the Division Series for the third straight season. That they put up their best fight yet only served to make the experience that much more painful. The Astros had gone the entire season without an injury to any of their significant pitchers, but in the end it was an injury to their one indispensable pitcher, Billy Wagner, that sealed their fate. Wagner's inability to pitch probably cost the Astros Game 3, and ultimately, the series.

Well, that and the continuing saga of Jeff Bagwell and Craig Biggio in the playoffs. There are many reasons why neither star has hit a lick in the playoffs, and heaven knows all those reasons have already been discussed. But no combination of opposition aces, bad lighting or just plain awful luck is enough to excuse their performances. Table 3 compares the postseason stats of Bagwell and Biggio with the career playoff numbers of another pair of noted hitters, "X" and "Y."

The identities of X and Y? Tom Glavine and John Smoltz, who—against playoff pitching staffs, remember—have out-hit two of the best players in Astro history.

It's not enough that they realize the problem. They have to solve it, and solve it this year, because the Astros don't have a permanent lease on a playoff spot, and the last three Octobers have shown us that they can't win without their big guns.

No team stays together forever, and no dynasty can be built on the efforts of just one group of players. If the Astros want to sustain a run of success for five or more years, they're going to have to replenish their talent pool quickly. In trading Mike Hampton to the Mets for Roger Cedeno and Octavio Dotel, and gulling the Mets into taking Derek Bell too, the Astros cleared payroll space while improving the lineup. They extended the contract of Craig Biggio and signed Jose Lima through 2002, and now have just one open issue—the contract of Jeff Bagwell, which will be up after 2001. This kind of proactive management is a credit to GM Gerry Hunsicker and assistant GM Tim Purpura, and a model for other organizations to follow.

The Astros' outfield is probably going to be 50 runs better than it was last year now that they've disposed of Bell.

Table 3

Player	AB	H	DB	TP	HR	R	RBI	BB	SO	AVG	OBP	SLG
Jeff Bagwell	39	5	0	0	0	3	4	7	15	.128	.261	.128
Craig Biggio	42	5	1	0	0	4	1	6	9	.119	.229	.143
X	54	12	1	0	0	3	2	4	21	.222	.286	.241
Y	46	8	1	1	0	4	3	5	13	.174	.255	.239

And with four legitimate starting outfielders even before the Cedeno trade (Alou, Lance Berkman, Richard Hidalgo and Daryle Ward), they were able to trade Carl Everett to the Red Sox for what they needed, a high-ceiling shortstop prospect in Adam Everett. Bringing Everett in made it easier to let Ricky Gutierrez leave as free agent. Gutierrez is exactly the sort of average player who can command way too much money from a team desperate to fill a key position, money the Astros were better off investing in their better players. It's a decision that took some courage: there are no quality shortstops on the trade market, and shortstop-in-waiting Julio Lugo may not be ready, forcing some combination of Tim Bogar, Bill Spiers and Russ Johnson into the role.

The management clinic put on by Hunsicker and Purpura will keep the Astros in among baseball's elite for the next five years. Enjoy watching them, and remember that the Astros are a good team. A very good team.

HITTERS (Averages: BA: .270 / OBP: .340 / SLG: .430 / EQA: .260)

Moises Alou · LF · Bats R · Age 33

YEAR	TEAM	LGE	AB	H	DB	TP	HR	BB/SO	R	RBI	SB	CS	OUT	BA	OBP	SLG	EQA	EQR	DEFENSE
1996	Montreal	NL	542	149	29	2	21	48/83	84	92	7	4	397	.275	.336	.452	.263	71	132-OF 101
1997	Florida	NL	547	162	31	5	25	70/84	89	118	7	5	390	.296	.380	.508	.294	91	145-OF 94
1998	Houston	NL	594	190	36	5	41	83/85	108	128	12	3	407	.320	.408	.604	.327	124	153-OF 88
2000	Houston	NL	337	97	15	2	19	55/50	65	71	6	2	242	.288	.388	.513	.302	61	

The team missed his contributions on the field, especially since he became a distraction off of it. Beyond the mystery surrounding how he injured himself in the first place, his original return date of August was delayed more times than a takeoff from O'Hare in January. Alou's commitment to his rehabilitation was questioned, and he didn't help himself by re-injuring the knee horsing around with his son. Finally, he didn't even bother to show up to root for the Astros in the playoffs. If he's healthy and productive this year, all may be forgiven. Neither is a safe assumption.

Jeff Bagwell · 1B · Bats R · Age 32

YEAR	TEAM	LGE	AB	H	DB	TP	HR	BB/SO	R	RBI	SB	CS	OUT	BA	OBP	SLG	EQA	EQR	DEFENSE
1997	Houston	NL	580	170	40	2	47	127/121	109	140	26	10	420	.293	.433	.612	.336	138	155-1B 103
1998	Houston	NL	550	173	32	1	38	109/88	128	117	20	8	385	.315	.435	.584	.332	123	149-1B 109
1999	Houston	NL	566	173	31	0	43	143/126	136	121	27	12	405	.306	.455	.588	.341	137	155-1B 106
2000	Houston	NL	505	146	21	0	38	123/104	123	123	16	6	365	.289	.428	.556	.328	112	

His playoff struggles aside, he is one amazing ballplayer. In some ways, last season was his best, because the never-friendly Astrodome became downright hostile: Bagwell hit 30 of his 42 homers on the road, where he put up a Ruthian .337/.477/.709. If Enron Field is half as hospitable to right-handed hitters as it is supposed to be, you're looking at 45 to 50 homers a year. This is all the more reason for the Astros to extend his contract now. Does anyone think of Bagwell as a 40/40 player? He led all of baseball with a power/speed number of 35.0, garnishing his homers with 30 steals, two more than Biggio.

Paul Bako · C · Bats L · Age 28

YEAR	TEAM	LGE	AB	H	DB	TP	HR	BB/SO	R	RBI	SB	CS	OUT	BA	OBP	SLG	EQA	EQR	DEFENSE
1997	Indianap	AA	327	73	14	1	6	28/91	30	37	0	3	257	.223	.289	.327	.206	25	
1998	Detroit	AL	304	83	11	1	3	22/80	22	29	1	1	222	.273	.322	.345	.228	28	86-C 101
1999	Houston	NL	217	57	14	1	2	24/56	16	17	1	1	161	.263	.336	.364	.241	23	61-C 103
2000	Houston	NL	235	59	13	1	3	28/63	31	27	1	1	177	.251	.331	.353	.237	24	

A curious addition to the Brad Ausmus trade, Bako's value was no mystery after Mitch Meluskey went out for the season in late April. A .260 hitter who can work the count a little and throw out 35% of attempted base-stealers can make a useful player: just look at Tony Eusebio. When you can do that and bat left-handed like Bako, you can stay in the majors for 10 years. Now that Eusebio has been re-signed, Bako may be the odd man out in Houston.

Glen Barker   OF   Bats B Age 29

YEAR	TEAM	LGE	AB	H	DB	TP	HR	BB/SO	R	RBI	SB	CS	OUT	BA	OBP	SLG	EQA	EQR	DEFENSE
1997	Jacksnvl	Sou	258	59	8	2	4	19/87	30	19	9	4	203	.229	.290	.322	.211	21	64-OF 106
1998	Jacksnvl	Sou	459	109	26	5	4	36/140	62	38	14	4	354	.237	.297	.342	.221	41	109-OF 114
1999	Houston	NL	74	21	0	0	2	10/19	21	12	15	6	59	.284	.377	.365	.268	11	
2000	Houston	NL	206	52	9	1	3	21/63	30	21	11	5	159	.252	.322	.350	.235	21	

Ever since the Pirates nabbed Roberto Clemente from an unsuspecting Dodger team, conventional wisdom has stated that the Rule 5 draft is a chance for teams to discover another organization's unwanted player and turn him into a star. But for every George Bell or Dave Hollins, there are dozens of William Canates and Jamie Walkers. So who's to say it's not a better use of the draft to select a player like Barker, who has absolutely no star potential but has the skills (patience, speed and defense) to be a fine fourth outfielder for the league minimum? If anything, he may play better knowing that he can't be sent down without being offered back to his original team. Barker may be out of a job because of the Astros' amazing outfield depth.

Derek Bell   RF   Bats R Age 31

YEAR	TEAM	LGE	AB	H	DB	TP	HR	BB/SO	R	RBI	SB	CS	OUT	BA	OBP	SLG	EQA	EQR	DEFENSE	
1997	Houston	NL	501	142	32	3	16	39/93	67	73	12	7	366	.283	.350	.455	.269	69	84-OF 98	26-OF 112
1998	Houston	NL	639	206	43	2	24	50/123	115	111	14	3	436	.322	.376	.509	.295	103	150-OF 96	
1999	Houston	NL	514	124	16	0	14	44/128	57	66	16	6	396	.241	.307	.354	.228	49	123-RF 88	
2000	NY Mets	NL	409	109	15	1	14	41/92	58	59	11	3	303	.267	.333	.411	.257	51		

He gave back all the gains he made in 1998 with enough interest to satisfy a loan shark. Bell has never been the model of consistency, but this wasn't just an off year: it was a disaster. He was as much a liability in the field as at the plate. Dumping him off on the Mets and getting Roger Cedeno in return was an absolute steal. The other half of that trade—Mike Hampton for Octavio Dotel—doesn't begin to make up for it, once you factor in Hampton's cost and impending free agency. Right now, Gerry Hunsicker has as good a case as anyone for the title of Baseball's Best Executive.

Lance Berkman   OF   Bats B Age 24

YEAR	TEAM	LGE	AB	H	DB	TP	HR	BB/SO	R	RBI	SB	CS	OUT	BA	OBP	SLG	EQA	EQR	DEFENSE
1997	Kissimme	Fla	191	50	8	0	12	32/42	27	30	1	0	141	.262	.372	.492	.289	32	43-OF 92
1998	Jackson	Tex	426	112	23	0	20	69/91	60	66	3	2	316	.263	.369	.458	.279	65	115-OF 95
1999	New Orln	PCL	225	68	14	0	8	34/46	33	42	5	1	158	.302	.394	.471	.295	37	51-OF 97
1999	Houston	NL	94	23	2	0	4	11/21	10	15	5	1	72	.245	.324	.394	.250	11	
2000	Houston	NL	319	92	13	0	17	55/69	62	65	6	1	228	.288	.393	.489	.301	57	

Alou's absence opened the door wide open for Berkman, but arthroscopic surgery on his knee for a torn meniscus allowed Daryle Ward to walk through instead. It wasn't a completely lost season for Berkman. Coming back early on a knee that still wasn't 100%, some of his homers turned into loud doubles. Still, he showed he had as little to learn from Triple-A pitchers as from the ones in Double-A the year before. Berkman has developed to the point where another season in the minors could hurt him more than help.

Craig Biggio   2B   Bats R Age 34

YEAR	TEAM	LGE	AB	H	DB	TP	HR	BB/SO	R	RBI	SB	CS	OUT	BA	OBP	SLG	EQA	EQR	DEFENSE
1997	Houston	NL	632	199	41	8	24	84/106	145	84	40	10	443	.315	.423	.519	.319	127	153-2B 100
1998	Houston	NL	656	220	48	3	23	64/110	128	92	55	9	445	.335	.415	.523	.320	128	154-2B 91
1999	Houston	NL	645	191	41	0	21	80/106	114	73	25	15	469	.296	.384	.457	.284	101	150-2B 98
2000	Houston	NL	606	176	32	2	22	81/102	113	102	23	10	440	.290	.374	.459	.284	95	

Excuse me, but was that supposed to be an off year? Biggio reached base nearly 300 times, scored 123 runs and hit 56 doubles, the most in baseball since George Kell hit the same number in 1950. He's missed four games in the last four years. After spending 500 words on the subject last year, I'll limit myself to five: he's a Hall of Famer. He holds Astro records for career runs, doubles and total bases, and is second in games, at-bats, hits and stolen bases. Even at 34, he's one of the three best second basemen in baseball.

Tim Bogar — SS — Bats R — Age 33

YEAR	TEAM	LGE	AB	H	DB	TP	HR	BB/SO	R	RBI	SB	CS	OUT	BA	OBP	SLG	EQA	EQR	DEFENSE
1997	Houston	NL	245	63	18	4	4	23/42	31	31	3	1	183	.257	.329	.412	.251	29	70-SS 96
1998	Houston	NL	157	26	4	1	1	9/35	12	8	2	1	132	.166	.221	.223	.129	4	33-SS 115
1999	Houston	NL	312	76	16	2	4	34/51	42	30	2	5	241	.244	.327	.346	.229	30	75-SS 102
2000	Houston	NL	220	52	10	2	4	26/39	27	25	2	2	170	.236	.317	.355	.231	22	

When a hitter gets rewarded with a two-year contract for hitting .154, as Bogar did in 1998, you know that this long-term-contract craze has gone a little too far. For a utility player, he fields a mean shortstop, making him adequate insurance for Julio Lugo and Adam Everett.

Ken Caminiti — 3B — Bats B — Age 37

YEAR	TEAM	LGE	AB	H	DB	TP	HR	BB/SO	R	RBI	SB	CS	OUT	BA	OBP	SLG	EQA	EQR	DEFENSE
1997	San Dieg	NL	498	150	25	0	30	80/117	95	95	10	2	350	.301	.401	.532	.310	94	127-3B 109
1998	San Dieg	NL	466	129	29	0	35	73/105	96	93	7	2	339	.277	.380	.564	.306	88	119-3B 88
1999	Houston	NL	275	80	12	1	13	43/57	43	54	5	2	197	.291	.393	.484	.295	47	69-3B 93
2000	Houston	NL	342	91	12	0	19	62/74	62	66	5	1	252	.266	.379	.468	.289	57	

Tony Gwynn is fond of saying that, far from being a martyr for staying with the Padres through some lean years, he was loyal for selfish reasons. A stable home was a higher priority than a few extra million or the opportunity to be part of more winning teams. I'm sure that Caminiti has just as few regrets that he turned down twice as much guaranteed money from Detroit to return home to Houston. He's still a fine hitter when healthy, but his all-out style of play has taken a toll on his defense. At 37, it's simply unwise for the Astros to expect him to play every day.

Tony Eusebio — C — Bats R — Age 33

YEAR	TEAM	LGE	AB	H	DB	TP	HR	BB/SO	R	RBI	SB	CS	OUT	BA	OBP	SLG	EQA	EQR	DEFENSE
1997	Houston	NL	167	48	2	0	1	19/27	12	18	0	1	120	.287	.374	.317	.245	18	
1998	Houston	NL	184	48	7	1	1	18/30	13	32	1	0	136	.261	.330	.326	.229	17	44-C 102
1999	Houston	NL	326	91	9	0	6	36/66	29	34	0	0	235	.279	.351	.362	.247	36	85-C 104
2000	Houston	NL	202	49	2	0	3	25/39	21	21	0	0	153	.243	.326	.297	.219	17	

An underrated catcher for most of his career, Eusebio reached free agency not a moment too soon. At 33, the end is near, making this his one and only chance to sign a multi-year contract and ensure that any post-baseball career he has won't be for the money. The Astros kept him around for two years and $2.4 million; he'll split the job with Mitch Meluskey.

Carl Everett — CF — Bats B — Age 30

YEAR	TEAM	LGE	AB	H	DB	TP	HR	BB/SO	R	RBI	SB	CS	OUT	BA	OBP	SLG	EQA	EQR	DEFENSE
1997	NY Mets	NL	447	112	28	3	15	32/101	57	57	14	9	344	.251	.311	.427	.246	52	115-OF 97
1998	Houston	NL	474	143	37	4	16	43/99	74	78	14	13	344	.302	.364	.498	.281	72	114-OF 116
1999	Houston	NL	468	153	37	3	24	45/93	83	103	24	7	322	.327	.400	.573	.318	92	109-CF 98
2000	Boston	AL	460	133	28	2	19	51/93	85	84	14	8	335	.289	.360	.483	.279	69	

We harp on the importance of not confusing tools with performance. When a player learns how to use the former to produce the latter, though, it's a beautiful thing to see. Everett got better as the season progressed, slugging above .700 after the break. He even hit well from the right side of the plate for the first time in his career, although he still has a marked platoon split. He's been traded to the Red Sox; while he'll be an improvement over the detritus the Sox have been playing in center field, keep in mind that Everett is 30: he's not a young star on the rise.

Ricky Gutierrez — SS — Bats R — Age 30

YEAR	TEAM	LGE	AB	H	DB	TP	HR	BB/SO	R	RBI	SB	CS	OUT	BA	OBP	SLG	EQA	EQR	DEFENSE	
1997	Houston	NL	307	83	16	4	3	21/49	34	35	4	2	226	.270	.323	.378	.239	32	49-SS 95	15-3B 112
1998	Houston	NL	497	135	26	3	2	54/82	57	47	14	8	370	.272	.351	.348	.244	55	129-SS 103	
1999	Houston	NL	271	72	8	5	1	33/45	32	25	1	5	204	.266	.350	.343	.238	28	75-SS 90	
2000	ChiCubs	NL	273	72	15	3	2	33/46	39	32	4	4	205	.264	.343	.363	.237	28		

His absence from the lineup due to assorted injuries throughout all of May and most of July might have been to his advantage, reminding the Astros of how ill-prepared they are for his departure as he enters free agency. He didn't help his cause with a grand total of three extra-base hits after the All-Star break. While the Astros would like to have him back, I wouldn't expect them to shed any tears now that he's a Cub. Julio Lugo is just as good, and in any industry, you don't stay in business by paying 10 times more for labor than you have to.

Carlos Hernandez — SS/2B — Bats R — Age 24

YEAR	TEAM	LGE	AB	H	DB	TP	HR	BB/SO	R	RBI	SB	CS	OUT	BA	OBP	SLG	EQA	EQR	DEFENSE
1997	Jackson	Tex	362	96	10	1	4	26/66	46	26	10	5	271	.265	.320	.331	.226	33	91-2B 101
1998	New Orln	PCL	497	144	21	2	1	18/81	54	49	24	9	362	.290	.327	.346	.235	48	122-2B 97
1999	New Orln	PCL	353	94	9	0	1	23/64	44	37	17	9	268	.266	.326	.300	.220	31	82-SS 91
2000	Houston	NL	364	98	13	1	2	26/65	48	33	17	6	272	.269	.318	.327	.227	34	

I'm sure there are many people who think that he would make a fine replacement for Gutierrez, but they're all members of Hernandez's extended family. The reality is that Hernandez has yet to put to rest the doubts that he can handle shortstop, and his bat was no livelier in 1999 than it was in 1998. He may be a candidate for Bogar's job next year, which lacks sex appeal but will put food on the table for all those supportive relatives.

Richard Hidalgo — OF — Bats R — Age 24

YEAR	TEAM	LGE	AB	H	DB	TP	HR	BB/SO	R	RBI	SB	CS	OUT	BA	OBP	SLG	EQA	EQR	DEFENSE	
1997	New Orln	AA	538	152	39	5	10	30/58	73	77	6	8	393	.283	.331	.429	.253	63	127-OF 101	
1998	Houston	NL	214	67	11	0	9	17/36	31	37	3	4	151	.313	.370	.491	.282	32	54-OF 110	
1999	Houston	NL	387	90	26	2	15	51/72	47	54	7	5	302	.233	.329	.426	.254	49	78-LF 117	22-CF 102
2000	Houston	NL	342	92	21	1	13	42/58	56	55	9	5	255	.269	.349	.450	.270	48		

He needs to learn to take care of himself, because injuries are the only obstructions on his road to superstardom. He was well down that path last year before his take-no-prisoners style of defense wore out his knee. His month-by-month slugging averages: .500, .505, .449, .264, .304. He hit .154 after the All-Star break before finally shutting it down in August. Before his season ended, he showed dramatic improvement in his strike zone judgment—he had never drawn even 40 walks in a season before—and a terrific arm that killed 15 baserunners in barely two-thirds of a season. Given a job and his health, he's as good a candidate for a breakout season as anyone in the game.

Stan Javier — OF — Bats B — Age 36

YEAR	TEAM	LGE	AB	H	DB	TP	HR	BB/SO	R	RBI	SB	CS	OUT	BA	OBP	SLG	EQA	EQR	DEFENSE	
1997	San Fran	NL	448	132	17	4	9	55/69	69	52	22	3	319	.295	.378	.411	.278	65	119-OF 98	
1998	San Fran	NL	426	133	14	5	5	65/61	67	53	23	6	299	.312	.405	.404	.287	66	105-OF 99	
1999	San Fran	NL	338	97	16	1	3	25/54	47	30	11	6	247	.287	.338	.367	.243	36	47-LF 101	30-RF 101
1999	Houston	NL	65	22	4	1	0	8/8	12	4	3	1	44	.338	.411	.431	.293	10		
2000	Seattle	AL	371	101	14	2	4	52/56	63	45	10	5	275	.272	.362	.353	.254	45		

He was acquired at the trading deadline for Joe Messman, your standard A-ball-pitcher-with-a-live-arm. Javier played so well down the stretch that the Astros were able to keep Derek Bell on the bench when Bell returned from the disabled list, an unexpected bonus. For years, Javier has been among the best fourth outfielders in baseball. With everyone healthy, he wouldn't even be the Astros' sixth outfielder, so he signed with the Mariners. He shoud get a lot of playing time in left field.

Russ Johnson — 3B/SS — Bats R — Age 27

YEAR	TEAM	LGE	AB	H	DB	TP	HR	BB/SO	R	RBI	SB	CS	OUT	BA	OBP	SLG	EQA	EQR	DEFENSE
1997	New Orln	AA	459	125	18	6	3	59/82	69	48	6	3	337	.272	.357	.357	.250	53	104-3B 95
1998	New Orln	PCL	463	125	26	1	5	75/70	75	41	8	7	345	.270	.376	.363	.259	59	109-3B 101
1999	Houston	NL	157	45	9	0	5	19/31	23	22	2	3	115	.287	.364	.439	.268	21	24-3B 96
1999	New Orln	PCL	77	22	3	0	1	13/14	12	9	1	2	57	.286	.394	.364	.263	10	
2000	Houston	NL	361	103	18	1	7	55/64	62	53	5	5	263	.285	.380	.399	.270	50	

Speaking of good bench players, Johnson would be the best fifth infielder in baseball if the Astros would stop optioning him to Triple-A (three times last year) and notice how much he can contribute. He can play shortstop in a pinch and the rest of the infield in style, and has a better stick than a dozen of the starting first basemen in baseball. He was used as a pinch-hitter 39 times last year and hit .343/.410/.514. As long as Johnson is around, Astro fans can rest easy knowing their playoff hopes don't hinge on Ken Caminiti's health.

Randy Knorr   C   Bats R   Age 31

YEAR	TEAM	LGE	AB	H	DB	TP	HR	BB/SO	R	RBI	SB	CS	OUT	BA	OBP	SLG	EQA	EQR	DEFENSE
1997	New Orln	AA	250	57	8	0	5	18/43	20	26	0	0	193	.228	.280	.320	.201	17	
1998	Charlott	Int	200	54	8	0	6	27/46	22	29	1	1	147	.270	.359	.400	.261	25	58-C 91
1999	New Orln	PCL	266	79	15	1	8	16/44	24	30	0	1	188	.297	.339	.451	.262	33	69-C 93
2000	*Pittsbrg*	*NL*	*240*	*63*	*7*	*0*	*8*	*24/45*	*28*	*35*	*0*	*0*	*177*	*.262*	*.330*	*.392*	*.244*	*26*	

Before you write him off as just another backup catcher biding his time in Triple-A until he can get a coaching job, consider that over the last two years he has hit .342 with 37 doubles, 18 home runs and 54 walks at Triple-A. He may be 31, but I have enough faith in minor-league performance to say that any team courageous enough to give him their backup job won't be disappointed.

Julio Lugo   SS   Bats R   Age 24

YEAR	TEAM	LGE	AB	H	DB	TP	HR	BB/SO	R	RBI	SB	CS	OUT	BA	OBP	SLG	EQA	EQR	DEFENSE
1997	Kissimme	Fla	516	130	24	11	9	39/109	71	54	15	4	390	.252	.306	.393	.239	54	115-SS 104
1998	Kissimme	Fla	516	136	21	11	7	38/82	55	49	19	9	388	.264	.317	.388	.241	55	100-SS 92
1999	Jackson	Tex	445	121	20	3	8	35/59	55	31	12	6	330	.272	.328	.384	.243	48	113-SS 90
2000	*Houston*	*NL*	*497*	*139*	*21*	*8*	*11*	*49/77*	*79*	*71*	*19*	*7*	*365*	*.280*	*.344*	*.421*	*.263*	*65*	

While it's fairly common to see top prospects skip Triple-A on their way to the majors, Lugo is a less-publicized prospect who may still be ready for the major leagues this season. His numbers have improved steadily as he has climbed the ladder, and his ability to add power while making the jump to Double-A was impressive, especially since he suffered a series of annoying injuries during the season. He has great defensive range even though he still makes too many errors; it's generally easier to teach a prospect to make the routine play than to make the difficult one. I'm in the minority, but I think if the Astros give him a chance to win the shortstop job, he'll do so and be a contributor in 2000.

Aaron McNeal   1B   Bats R   Age 22

YEAR	TEAM	LGE	AB	H	DB	TP	HR	BB/SO	R	RBI	SB	CS	OUT	BA	OBP	SLG	EQA	EQR	DEFENSE
1998	Quad Cit	Mid	379	96	11	1	15	25/115	46	51	1	1	284	.253	.305	.406	.238	39	102-1B 95
1999	Michigan	Mid	534	139	20	2	31	25/127	67	90	3	1	396	.260	.295	.479	.253	64	130-1B 121
2000	*Houston*	*NL*	*344*	*94*	*13*	*1*	*23*	*25/94*	*46*	*68*	*1*	*0*	*250*	*.273*	*.322*	*.517*	*.276*	*50*	

The Astros' minor-league player of the year is still very much a work in progress. The Astros readily admit he needs better plate discipline and more work on defense. Still, you hit 38 home runs and slug .588 as a 21-year-old—in any league—and you're a prospect. Bagwell has already driven Daryle Ward off of first base, and McNeal played 17 games in the outfield last year, not that there's any room for him there, either. He's still two years away, but they don't have to wait that long to trade him.

Mitch Meluskey   C   Bats B   Age 26

YEAR	TEAM	LGE	AB	H	DB	TP	HR	BB/SO	R	RBI	SB	CS	OUT	BA	OBP	SLG	EQA	EQR	DEFENSE
1997	Jackson	Tex	240	70	11	0	13	24/45	36	34	1	2	172	.292	.362	.500	.283	37	
1997	New Orln	AA	177	46	4	0	4	23/39	21	23	0	0	131	.260	.349	.350	.244	19	
1998	New Orln	PCL	404	134	28	0	18	76/61	63	63	2	0	270	.332	.440	.535	.327	83	104-C 95
1999	Houston	NL	33	7	1	0	1	5/6	4	3	1	0	26	.212	.316	.333	.232	3	
2000	*Houston*	*NL*	*180*	*56*	*8*	*0*	*9*	*30/31*	*35*	*39*	*1*	*0*	*124*	*.311*	*.410*	*.506*	*.311*	*33*	

His much-anticipated rookie season ended after 33 at-bats, and while the Astros soldiered on, his absence was a big reason why they ranked just eighth in runs scored, after leading the league in 1998. Well, that and Derek Bell. The Astros are confident that he'll be ready to start the season, but he didn't exactly throw like Charles Johnson before surgery on his right shoulder. I think he'll be an above-average hitter, and the Astros really have no choice but to put up with his defense. What are they going to do, move him to first base?

Matt Mieske OF Bats R Age 32

YEAR	TEAM	LGE	AB	H	DB	TP	HR	BB/SO	R	RBI	SB	CS	OUT	BA	OBP	SLG	EQA	EQR	DEFENSE
1997	Milwauke	AL	253	64	17	3	5	17/48	39	21	1	0	189	.253	.300	.403	.236	25	67-OF 94
1998	ChiCubs	NL	98	30	5	0	2	11/17	16	13	0	0	68	.306	.382	.418	.276	14	24-OF 85
1999	Seattle	AL	40	14	2	0	3	2/9	10	6	0	0	26	.350	.381	.625	.320	8	
1999	Houston	NL	110	32	5	0	5	5/22	13	21	0	0	78	.291	.322	.473	.262	14	
2000	Houston	NL	158	44	4	0	7	15/34	20	27	0	0	114	.278	.341	.437	.264	20	

After being stuck in Milwaukee for five years, Mieske has picked up a deserved reputation as the kind of player a playoff team can use, making it into October with the Cubs in 1998 and the Astros last year. It's deserved because Mieske does one thing and does it very well. His batting averages against left-handed pitchers, working back from 1999: .354, .389, .255, .352, .306, .299. His slugging averages: .622, .481, .462, .641, .587, .657. For his career he's hit .319/.380/.579 against southpaws, .231/.310/.347 against northpaws. The Astros, who are waist-deep in both outfielders and right-handed hitters, are actually about the last team that needs him, so expect him to turn up on another contender—maybe Boston?—this September.

Aaron Miles 2B Bats B Age 23

YEAR	TEAM	LGE	AB	H	DB	TP	HR	BB/SO	R	RBI	SB	CS	OUT	BA	OBP	SLG	EQA	EQR	DEFENSE
1997	Quad Cit	Mid	377	92	14	1	1	21/47	41	28	8	5	290	.244	.287	.294	.196	25	82-2B 91
1998	Quad Cit	Mid	377	87	25	5	2	19/54	32	31	11	6	296	.231	.269	.340	.204	28	99-2B 93
1999	Michigan	Mid	467	120	25	4	9	16/36	48	48	6	5	352	.257	.283	.385	.221	41	72-2B 84
2000	Houston	NL	414	106	24	3	5	25/42	46	44	8	5	313	.256	.298	.365	.225	37	

Miles is a 1960s-edition speedy second baseman stuck in the era of Jeff Kent and Edgardo Alfonzo. He's trying to pick up the big man's game despite standing all of 5'8": he hit 10 homers in 1999 after poking just three in his first 307 career games. The tarot cards show that he'll make it to the major leagues in September 2004, go 4-for-20 and disappear after that. But what do they know?

Mike Rose C Bats B Age 23

YEAR	TEAM	LGE	AB	H	DB	TP	HR	BB/SO	R	RBI	SB	CS	OUT	BA	OBP	SLG	EQA	EQR	DEFENSE
1997	Quad Cit	Mid	239	57	5	1	3	21/65	17	22	1	1	183	.238	.308	.305	.211	19	
1998	Quad Cit	Mid	278	73	12	1	8	44/58	39	33	4	4	209	.263	.365	.399	.262	37	75-C 97
1999	Kissimme	Fla	310	75	14	1	11	49/72	48	26	6	3	238	.242	.349	.400	.258	40	87-C 96
2000	Houston	NL	365	92	12	1	13	62/86	60	55	8	4	277	.252	.361	.397	.264	50	

On a Kissimmee team loaded with Grade B and C prospects, Rose had the fewest thorns. He's a switch-hitting catcher with an impressive amount of power for the Florida State League, and impressive plate discipline for any league. He was promoted to Double-A for the last two weeks of the season, and had more walks (13) and extra bases (12) than hits (11). It may be from my gut and not my head, but I have a really good feeling about him.

Bill Spiers UT Bats L Age 34

YEAR	TEAM	LGE	AB	H	DB	TP	HR	BB/SO	R	RBI	SB	CS	OUT	BA	OBP	SLG	EQA	EQR	DEFENSE	
1997	Houston	NL	299	98	32	4	4	61/42	52	50	8	5	206	.328	.443	.502	.319	59	63-3B 100	19-SS 93
1998	Houston	NL	389	110	30	4	4	45/60	69	44	12	2	281	.283	.365	.411	.270	53	83-3B 95	
1999	Houston	NL	397	116	19	5	4	42/45	54	38	9	5	286	.292	.360	.395	.260	49	57-3B 107	
2000	Houston	NL	374	106	24	3	4	57/48	69	51	9	5	273	.283	.378	.396	.271	52		

There's more to building a championship team than having two superstars. Spiers hit .288 while starting at six positions. On a largely veteran team that's going to have its share of injuries, you can't overstate the importance of a super-utility player like Spiers. It's not as crazy as it sounds for Spiers to take over as a semi-regular shortstop, freeing up the utility job for Russ Johnson; he made it to the major leagues at the position, and gave the Astros nine starts there last year.

Chris Truby 3B Bats R Age 26

YEAR	TEAM	LGE	AB	H	DB	TP	HR	BB/SO	R	RBI	SB	CS	OUT	BA	OBP	SLG	EQA	EQR	DEFENSE	
1997	Quad Cit	Mid	272	64	13	1	5	15/37	23	33	5	2	210	.235	.277	.346	.210	21	68-3B 101	
1997	Kissimme	Fla	201	45	7	0	3	6/48	17	25	3	1	157	.224	.251	.303	.182	11	54-3B 85	
1998	Kissimme	Fla	214	51	12	1	9	13/39	23	30	2	1	164	.238	.288	.430	.237	23	51-3B 114	
1998	Jackson	Tex	307	72	18	3	10	13/61	30	41	4	2	237	.235	.272	.410	.225	29	70-3B 99	
1999	Jackson	Tex	465	105	17	2	18	25/108	50	57	8	4	364	.226	.268	.387	.218	40	120-3B 106	
2000	*Houston*	*NL*	*496*	*111*	*19*	*0*	*19*	*35/107*	*51*	*57*	*11*	*3*	*388*	*.224*	*.275*	*.377*	*.221*	*45*		

After finally elevating himself to prospect status at the age of 25, Truby lost out to Carlos Villalobos in spring training and had to repeat Double-A. He showed that his power surge in 1998 was no fluke, but he's now 26 and no higher than fourth on the Astros' depth chart at third base.

Carlos Villalobos 3B Bats R Age 26

YEAR	TEAM	LGE	AB	H	DB	TP	HR	BB/SO	R	RBI	SB	CS	OUT	BA	OBP	SLG	EQA	EQR	DEFENSE	
1997	Lakeland	Fla	149	33	4	0	1	8/30	16	12	0	0	116	.221	.268	.268	.175	7	27-3B 90	
1997	Lancastr	Cal	294	75	15	1	7	44/45	46	33	2	2	221	.255	.360	.384	.258	37	71-3B 92	
1998	Jacksnvl	Sou	501	138	28	1	15	34/96	69	58	4	0	363	.275	.324	.425	.253	58	125-3B 103	
1999	New Orln	PCL	497	120	23	1	7	43/108	59	38	7	2	379	.241	.304	.334	.219	43	99-3B 113	20-2B 80
2000	*Detroit*	*AL*	*392*	*99*	*15*	*1*	*9*	*43/80*	*52*	*50*	*4*	*1*	*294*	*.253*	*.326*	*.365*	*.239*	*41*		

Brad Ausmus is no superstar, but it's a little puzzling that the Astros would trade him and C.J. Nitkowski away for what boiled down to organizational depth. Villalobos was probably the best of the five players acquired, but regressed badly. Reclaimed by the Tigers over the winter.

Daryle Ward LF/1B Bats L Age 25

YEAR	TEAM	LGE	AB	H	DB	TP	HR	BB/SO	R	RBI	SB	CS	OUT	BA	OBP	SLG	EQA	EQR	DEFENSE	
1997	Jackson	Tex	420	124	16	0	19	37/77	55	71	3	1	297	.295	.356	.469	.276	59	109-1B 98	
1998	New Orln	PCL	468	139	27	1	22	36/78	68	86	2	0	329	.297	.349	.500	.281	69	58-OF 92	48-1B 112
1999	New Orln	PCL	238	76	13	1	22	20/44	43	50	1	1	163	.319	.378	.660	.323	49	59-1B 95	
1999	Houston	NL	152	42	7	0	8	7/31	11	29	0	0	110	.276	.308	.480	.258	19	23-LF 96	
2000	*Houston*	*NL*	*440*	*133*	*17*	*0*	*32*	*44/82*	*71*	*102*	*1*	*0*	*307*	*.302*	*.366*	*.559*	*.303*	*77*		

His impersonations of an outfielder are no more convincing now than they were a year ago, but Ward is one spectacular hitter. Alou's return may throw the Astros' outfield into as much disarray as his absence did last year, because Ward is absolutely deserving of an everyday job. With a lot less ground to cover in left field at Enron, his defensive inadequacies become less of an issue. If Dan O'Dowd grabs one of the Astros' extra outfielders, they'll hit more homers by July than Dante Bichette will hit all year with the Reds.

George Williams C Bats B Age 31

YEAR	TEAM	LGE	AB	H	DB	TP	HR	BB/SO	R	RBI	SB	CS	OUT	BA	OBP	SLG	EQA	EQR	DEFENSE
1997	Oakland	AL	199	57	9	1	3	34/44	29	21	0	1	143	.286	.397	.387	.274	28	
1999	New Orln	PCL	100	20	2	0	3	11/21	13	11	1	1	81	.200	.289	.310	.204	8	
1999	SaltLake	PCL	222	51	12	1	3	33/55	25	20	0	2	173	.230	.341	.333	.234	23	53-C 90
2000	*SanDieg*	*NL*	*173*	*39*	*5*	*0*	*4*	*30/59*	*22*	*20*	*0*	*2*	*136*	*.225*	*.340*	*.324*	*.238*	*19*	

After finally establishing himself as a quality backup catcher in 1997, injuries cost him all of 1998, and he spent last year trying to rebuild his career in Triple-A. He can't turn on a pitch quite as well as he used to, but he still draws walks and he still bats from both sides of the plate. All he needs is a break to get his butt back on a major-league bench where it belongs.

PITCHERS (Averages: ERA: 4.50 / H/9: 9.00 / HR/9: 1.00 / BB/9: 3.50 / K/9: 6.50 / KWH: 1.00)

Jose Cabrera — Throws R — Age 28

YEAR	TEAM	LGE	IP	H	ER	HR	BB	K	ERA	W	L	H/9	HR/9	BB/9	K/9	KWH	PERA
1997	New Orln	AmA	43.7	37	16	2	15	40	3.30	3	2	7.63	0.41	3.09	8.24	2.15	3.09
1997	Houston	NL	15.0	7	2	1	6	17	1.20	2	0	4.20	0.60	3.60	10.20	5.14	1.80
1999	New Orln	PCL	48.0	37	20	3	15	32	3.75	3	2	6.94	0.56	2.81	6.00	1.38	2.81
1999	Houston	NL	29.0	21	6	3	9	27	1.86	3	0	6.52	0.93	2.79	8.38	2.88	2.79

There's an awful lot to like here. Cabrera was acquired from the Indians in 1997 for Alvin Morman, but he lost almost all of 1998 to injury just as he made a place for himself in the Astros' bullpen. He came back as good as ever, and his dominance down the stretch did wonders for a bullpen that was hurting after Scott Elarton moved into the rotation. Cabrera is a very good bet to pitch well. There's something about him that whispers "Mariano Rivera" to me, but maybe that's just a reminder to refill my prescription.

Scott Elarton — Throws R — Age 24

YEAR	TEAM	LGE	IP	H	ER	HR	BB	K	ERA	W	L	H/9	HR/9	BB/9	K/9	KWH	PERA
1997	Jackson	Tex	125.7	112	60	7	54	121	4.30	7	7	8.02	0.50	3.87	8.67	1.81	3.65
1997	New Orln	AmA	51.3	58	42	5	19	44	7.36	2	4	10.17	0.88	3.33	7.71	1.31	4.91
1998	New Orln	PCL	86.3	76	45	6	45	84	4.69	5	5	7.92	0.63	4.69	8.76	1.54	3.96
1998	Houston	NL	56.7	42	21	5	21	53	3.34	4	2	6.67	0.79	3.34	8.42	2.38	3.02
1999	Houston	NL	123.3	109	50	7	41	116	3.65	8	6	7.95	0.51	2.99	8.46	2.25	3.28

The October news that he had a partially torn rotator cuff was more than a little disturbing, given that the way the Astros broke him in is a model for all organizations. It's just another reminder that pitching is an inordinately stressful task. The tear was small, and while there is no such thing as "routine" surgery on the rotator cuff, you have to ask: if he can put up a 3.64 ERA pitching hurt, what might he do when he's healthy? Dierker is smart enough to not push him when he comes back, and the Astros don't need him to be anything more than a #4 starter. This is reminiscent of the arm injury Roger Clemens suffered in 1985, and we all know what happened in 1986.

Wayne Franklin — Throws L — Age 26

YEAR	TEAM	LGE	IP	H	ER	HR	BB	K	ERA	W	L	H/9	HR/9	BB/9	K/9	KWH	PERA
1997	Savannah	SAL	70.7	114	62	13	53	37	7.90	2	6	14.52	1.66	6.75	4.71	0.17	10.32
1998	Vero Bch	Fla	78.0	107	59	8	39	52	6.81	3	6	12.35	0.92	4.50	6.00	0.48	6.81
1999	Kissimme	Fla	16.0	15	6	0	9	15	3.38	1	1	8.44	0.00	5.06	8.44	1.25	3.94
1999	Jackson	Tex	46.0	40	16	3	22	29	3.13	3	2	7.83	0.59	4.30	5.67	0.71	3.72

No eyebrows were raised when Franklin, a 25-year-old who had never pitched above high-A ball, was taken in the minor-league Rule 5 draft from the Dodgers. I hope the scout who recommended the move got a raise, because Franklin was six kinds of unhittable in the Texas League last year. Trever Miller didn't cut it as the Astros' left-handed setup man, so expect Franklin to get every opportunity to make the major-league roster in April.

Mike Hampton — Throws L — Age 27

YEAR	TEAM	LGE	IP	H	ER	HR	BB	K	ERA	W	L	H/9	HR/9	BB/9	K/9	KWH	PERA
1997	Houston	NL	219.3	224	107	16	81	129	4.39	12	12	9.19	0.66	3.32	5.29	0.69	4.19
1998	Houston	NL	210.7	235	94	18	86	131	4.02	13	10	10.04	0.77	3.67	5.60	0.63	4.91
1999	Houston	NL	237.7	202	78	11	96	170	2.95	18	8	7.65	0.42	3.64	6.44	1.11	3.26

I don't think the cozier dimensions of Enron Field will affect him, because he keeps the ball down better than anyone in baseball. In 1999, he gave up just 12 home runs and induced a league-leading 38 double plays. The question is, can he get even better? He still walked 101 batters, and when you consider the Astros' recent record of improving their pitchers' control, as well as the histories of many left-handed power pitchers, it wouldn't have been unreasonable to think he could become a left-handed Kevin Brown. Now that he's been traded to the Mets, his outlook dims a bit. He's a groundball pitcher in front of a good infield defense, though, so he should still be successful. Hampton is probably the best-hitting pitcher in the game, having set Astros' records for hits (23) and total bases (32) by a pitcher.

Doug Henry — Throws R — Age 36

YEAR	TEAM	LGE	IP	H	ER	HR	BB	K	ERA	W	L	H/9	HR/9	BB/9	K/9	KWH	PERA
1997	San Fran	NL	70.3	71	45	5	43	64	5.76	3	5	9.09	0.64	5.50	8.19	1.00	4.99
1998	Houston	NL	70.3	57	26	9	37	56	3.33	5	3	7.29	1.15	4.73	7.17	1.11	4.22
1999	Houston	NL	40.3	45	22	8	23	35	4.91	2	2	10.04	1.79	5.13	7.81	0.88	6.69

He had a miserable year that was at least partially explained by surgery to clean up bone chips in his elbow. I don't think he's done, but as a 36-year-old homer-prone pitcher, there are some questions about his future. The Astros signed him to a one-year deal, so he'll be back under Dierker's care.

Chris Holt — Throws R — Age 28

YEAR	TEAM	LGE	IP	H	ER	HR	BB	K	ERA	W	L	H/9	HR/9	BB/9	K/9	KWH	PERA
1997	Houston	NL	205.3	220	102	18	64	88	4.47	12	11	9.64	0.79	2.81	3.86	0.41	4.38
1999	Houston	NL	163.0	189	85	11	54	110	4.69	9	9	10.44	0.61	2.98	6.07	0.89	4.69

Hey, it's great that he was able to come back after completely blowing out his arm in 1997. That still doesn't excuse the Astros' keeping him in the rotation almost all season, which almost single-handedly kept them from clinching a playoff spot until the last day. Holt pitched much better (2.65 ERA) on six or more days' rest, and got stronger as the season progressed. If they move him to the bullpen as a long reliever, giving him at least two days off between appearances with a spot start thrown in once a month, I think he could be effective.

Rick Huisman — Throws R — Age 31

YEAR	TEAM	LGE	IP	H	ER	HR	BB	K	ERA	W	L	H/9	HR/9	BB/9	K/9	KWH	PERA
1997	Omaha	AmA	61.3	61	29	6	43	50	4.26	4	3	8.95	0.88	6.31	7.34	0.71	5.43
1998	Fresno	PCL	68.0	71	44	16	40	65	5.82	3	5	9.40	2.12	5.29	8.60	1.11	6.75
1999	New Orln	PCL	49.0	46	25	6	19	52	4.59	2	3	8.45	1.10	3.49	9.55	2.31	4.22

In a fair world, Huisman would get another chance. He was one of the 10 best pitching prospects in the game in 1991, only to see his career ruined because the Giants thought it would be cool to have Clinton lead the Midwest League in complete games. After having his elbow rebuilt, Huisman adapted well to relief and got a few innings with the Royals in 1995 and 1996. He reminds me of Scott Service, as he racks up lots of strikeouts but gets hurt by too many hanging breaking balls.

Eric Ireland — Throws R — Age 23

YEAR	TEAM	LGE	IP	H	ER	HR	BB	K	ERA	W	L	H/9	HR/9	BB/9	K/9	KWH	PERA
1997	Auburn	NYP	98.3	151	75	7	33	49	6.86	3	8	13.82	0.64	3.02	4.48	0.36	6.77
1998	Quad Cit	Mid	184.0	246	120	22	92	132	5.87	7	13	12.03	1.08	4.50	6.46	0.58	6.80
1999	Kissimme	Fla	158.3	182	77	16	39	105	4.38	9	9	10.35	0.91	2.22	5.97	1.16	4.66

We got all over the Astros for letting Ireland throw a minor-league high 206 innings in 1998, but they defended themselves by saying that Ireland is extremely efficient with his pitches. Unfortunately, minor-league pitch counts are charted only by organizations, and trying to pry the data out of them is like trying to pull Bobby Bonilla away from a card game. We do know that Ireland averaged 14.7 pitches per inning in 1998, which comes out to 106 pitches per start. By comparison, six major-league pitchers were between 105 and 107 pitches per start last year, including Randy Wolf, Freddy Garcia and Blake Stein. Ireland, at 21 in 1998, was younger than any of them.

In the Astros' defense, Ireland was outstanding last year, with a 145/32 strikeout-to-walk ratio and a perfect game. He also threw 185 innings. The Astros are unyielding in their philosophy of giving minor-league pitchers a full year at each level, a rigidity that may bite them in the butt in a few years.

Jose Lima — Throws R — Age 27

Year	Team	Lge	IP	H	ER	HR	BB	K	ERA	W	L	H/9	HR/9	BB/9	K/9	KWH	PERA
1997	Houston	NL	73.7	83	47	10	16	58	5.74	3	5	10.14	1.22	1.95	7.09	1.89	4.76
1998	Houston	NL	232.3	237	101	34	34	161	3.91	15	11	9.18	1.32	1.32	6.24	2.40	4.07
1999	Houston	NL	244.7	251	98	28	41	180	3.60	16	11	9.23	1.03	1.51	6.62	2.35	3.90

For someone who gave up 256 hits and 30 home runs, it was one hell of a year. Lima is one of the most flamboyant players in the game, cocky and a little bit of a hothead. In other words, he's only a degree or two more stable than Joaquin Andujar was, and the low-pressure atmosphere of the Astros clubhouse is an essential element of his success. More than any other player on the team, I think that Lima's success is tied to Dierker's presence as the manager. Which means I think he'll have another fine year.

Tony McKnight   Throws R   Age 23

YEAR	TEAM	LGE	IP	H	ER	HR	BB	K	ERA	W	L	H/9	HR/9	BB/9	K/9	KWH	PERA
1997	Quad Cit	Mid	106.3	145	86	9	67	64	7.28	3	9	12.27	0.76	5.67	5.42	0.32	7.11
1998	Kissimme	Fla	141.0	232	123	15	64	80	7.85	4	12	14.81	0.96	4.09	5.11	0.32	8.30
1999	Jackson	Tex	151.0	158	71	16	53	95	4.23	9	8	9.42	0.95	3.16	5.66	0.81	4.53

McKnight is a former #1 draft pick with a terrific curveball, and he showed the mark of a great pitching prospect last year: he jumped to Double-A while improving his performance. McKnight missed some time at midseason with shoulder tendinitis and still threw 160 innings. The Astros can either put him in their bullpen as a middle reliever this year, or take the chance that he's going to ruin his arm as a starter and end up pitching junk relief in a few years anyway.

Trever Miller   Throws L   Age 27

YEAR	TEAM	LGE	IP	H	ER	HR	BB	K	ERA	W	L	H/9	HR/9	BB/9	K/9	KWH	PERA
1997	New Orln	AmA	153.0	205	87	15	62	85	5.12	7	10	12.06	0.88	3.65	5.00	0.42	6.24
1998	Houston	NL	53.3	59	21	4	21	29	3.54	4	2	9.96	0.68	3.54	4.89	0.51	4.72
1999	Houston	NL	49.3	57	27	6	28	36	4.93	2	3	10.40	1.09	5.11	6.57	0.61	6.02

One of the myths of left-handed relief specialists is that they face left-handed hitters the majority of the time. Miller was mildly effective against left-handed hitters (.237/.363/.408), but right-handed hitters lit him up for a .339 average with power, and he faced them 61% of the time. This is about as good as he's going to get, and it's not good enough.

Wade Miller   Throws R   Age 23

YEAR	TEAM	LGE	IP	H	ER	HR	BB	K	ERA	W	L	H/9	HR/9	BB/9	K/9	KWH	PERA
1997	Quad Cit	Mid	55.7	57	33	8	12	35	5.34	2	4	9.22	1.29	1.94	5.66	1.34	4.37
1997	Kissimme	Fla	94.0	101	38	4	19	59	3.64	6	4	9.67	0.38	1.82	5.65	1.36	3.64
1998	Jackson	Tex	58.0	55	25	7	31	39	3.88	3	3	8.53	1.09	4.81	6.05	0.67	4.81
1999	New Orln	PCL	152.3	164	88	14	72	111	5.20	7	10	9.69	0.83	4.25	6.56	0.78	5.02

The Astros love this guy, and it's hard not to love a 95-mph fastball, power slider and consistent track record of success. He missed half of 1998 because of tendinitis in his right middle finger that required surgery, which may have served to keep his arm fresh. Last year marked the first time in his career that he didn't dominate his league, and he still needs another year before he's ready to join the rotation. These are the Astros, so expect him to spend the year throwing two or three innings at a time in the major-league bullpen, and expect him to throw well.

Tony Mounce   Throws L   Age 25

YEAR	TEAM	LGE	IP	H	ER	HR	BB	K	ERA	W	L	H/9	HR/9	BB/9	K/9	KWH	PERA
1997	Jackson	Tex	133.7	179	94	19	75	99	6.33	5	10	12.05	1.28	5.05	6.67	0.55	7.34
1998	Kissimme	Fla	22.3	45	29	2	18	11	11.69	0	2	18.13	0.81	7.25	4.43	0.11	11.69
1998	Jackson	Tex	99.7	146	81	14	57	66	7.31	3	8	13.18	1.26	5.15	5.96	0.39	8.13
1999	Jackson	Tex	62.3	78	41	6	39	60	5.92	3	4	11.26	0.87	5.63	8.66	0.88	6.64
1999	New Orln	PCL	10.0	10	3	0	14	8	2.70	1	0	9.00	0.00	12.60	7.20	0.34	7.20

Mounce never had an ERA above 2.72 before he hit Double-A, and until last year he hadn't had an ERA below 5.00 since then. The Astros still thought highly of him, and last year's move to the bullpen took. I don't think his repertoire is ever going to be major-league quality, and I think the best he can hope for is a Mike Magnante career, pitching just well enough to say in the major leagues for five or six years. That's better than a dot-com IPO, folks.

Mike Nannini   Throws R   Age 19

YEAR	TEAM	LGE	IP	H	ER	HR	BB	K	ERA	W	L	H/9	HR/9	BB/9	K/9	KWH	PERA
1999	Michigan	Mid	82.3	130	63	10	36	49	6.89	3	6	14.21	1.09	3.94	5.36	0.38	7.98
1999	Auburn	NYP	73.0	70	22	3	22	53	2.71	6	2	8.63	0.37	2.71	6.53	1.36	3.45

(Mike Nannini *continued*)

Nannini's been described as a short (5'11") Scott Elarton and a right-handed Billy Wagner, which is weighty praise for a teenager. The Astros think he can handle it: they started him in the Midwest League in his first full season, a very unusual move for an organization as conservative as the Astros. He was impressive if not particularly dominant there; after moving down to the New York-Penn League when their season started, he may have been the best pitcher in the circuit. The Astros have shown an admirable disregard for height when acquiring pitchers: Nannini, Hampton and Wagner all stand well under six feet tall. He's several years away, but worth keeping tabs on anyway.

Scott Navarro   Throws L   Age 25

YEAR	TEAM	LGE	IP	H	ER	HR	BB	K	ERA	W	L	H/9	HR/9	BB/9	K/9	KWH	PERA
1999	Kissimme	Fla	99.3	150	61	6	26	60	5.53	4	7	13.59	0.54	2.36	5.44	0.69	6.25

Navarro, an independent-league find who was pitching for Chico in the Western League in 1998, was astonishingly effective in his first year of National Association baseball. A left-hander with an 86/17 strikeout-to-walk ratio is not someone to be trifled with, and we've seen enough independent-league successes to know better than to write him off.

Roy Oswalt   Throws R   Age 22

YEAR	TEAM	LGE	IP	H	ER	HR	BB	K	ERA	W	L	H/9	HR/9	BB/9	K/9	KWH	PERA
1997	Auburn	NYP	47.3	68	41	2	24	28	7.80	1	4	12.93	0.38	4.56	5.32	0.36	6.65
1998	Auburn	NYP	65.3	68	32	5	42	42	4.41	4	3	9.37	0.69	5.79	5.79	0.46	5.23
1999	Michigan	Mid	144.3	175	88	10	63	103	5.49	6	10	10.91	0.62	3.93	6.42	0.72	5.36

From modest beginnings—he was a 23rd-round draft pick in 1996—Oswalt has become a highly-regarded prospect. He missed half of 1998 while rehabbing from a sprained elbow but was healthy last year and very impressive in the Midwest League. His curveball may be the best in the organization, and his fastball tops out in the mid-90s. Along with Nannini, Oswalt gives Houston a second wave of pitching prospects as a fallback if their more polished prospects flop.

Jay Powell   Throws R   Age 28

YEAR	TEAM	LGE	IP	H	ER	HR	BB	K	ERA	W	L	H/9	HR/9	BB/9	K/9	KWH	PERA
1997	Florida	NL	79.3	72	34	3	31	60	3.86	5	4	8.17	0.34	3.52	6.81	1.21	3.40
1998	Florida	NL	36.0	38	19	5	23	23	4.75	2	2	9.50	1.25	5.75	5.75	0.45	6.00
1998	Houston	NL	34.0	22	9	1	16	36	2.38	3	1	5.82	0.26	4.24	9.53	2.75	2.38
1999	Houston	NL	74.7	81	35	3	38	74	4.22	4	4	9.76	0.36	4.58	8.92	1.33	4.70

Powell was not nearly as dominant as the Astros expected him to be, forcing Elarton to be used more as Wagner's setup man than in the long-relief role the Astros would have preferred. My suspicion is that Powell was pitching through a nagging injury all year. He had trouble throwing strikes and was way too hittable for someone with his stuff. He's a better pitcher than he showed, and I expect him to bounce back some this year.

Shane Reynolds   Throws R   Age 32

YEAR	TEAM	LGE	IP	H	ER	HR	BB	K	ERA	W	L	H/9	HR/9	BB/9	K/9	KWH	PERA
1997	Houston	NL	178.3	195	94	20	49	141	4.74	9	11	9.84	1.01	2.47	7.12	1.55	4.59
1998	Houston	NL	232.7	266	100	25	56	199	3.87	15	11	10.29	0.97	2.17	7.70	1.99	4.68
1999	Houston	NL	230.0	245	99	21	35	189	3.87	15	11	9.59	0.82	1.37	7.40	3.11	3.83

Reynolds and Lima look vastly different on the mound, but their performances were eerily similar. Both gave up more than a hit per inning. Reynolds led the league in strikeout-to-walk ratio and walks per nine innings, while Lima finished third in both categories. That Lima went 21-10 while Reynolds went 16-14 with almost identical performances and similar run support is a fluke. If I had to bet on one of the Astro starters to win 20 games this year, my money would be on Reynolds. He's arguably the most underrated pitcher in the game today.

Jeromie Robertson   Throws L   Age 23

YEAR	TEAM	LGE	IP	H	ER	HR	BB	K	ERA	W	L	H/9	HR/9	BB/9	K/9	KWH	PERA
1997	Quad Cit	Mid	135.0	189	105	16	68	94	7.00	4	11	12.60	1.07	4.53	6.27	0.51	7.20
1998	Kissimme	Fla	161.0	226	101	16	68	101	5.65	7	11	12.63	0.89	3.80	5.65	0.50	6.71
1999	Jackson	Tex	178.7	217	95	23	55	107	4.79	9	11	10.93	1.16	2.77	5.39	0.72	5.49

He's another polished pitching prospect with too much mileage on his arm. Robertson led the Florida State League with 175 innings in 1998, then led the Texas League with 191 innings last year. Even if he stays healthy, I don't think he has the stuff to be a successful starter in the major leagues. Far lesser left-handers have crafted long careers out of the bullpen.

Wilfredo Rodriguez — Throws L — Age 21

YEAR	TEAM	LGE	IP	H	ER	HR	BB	K	ERA	W	L	H/9	HR/9	BB/9	K/9	KWH	PERA
1998	Quad Cit	Mid	149.0	174	104	11	80	117	6.28	6	11	10.51	0.66	4.83	7.07	0.73	5.56
1999	Kissimme	Fla	143.7	132	68	11	77	120	4.26	8	8	8.27	0.69	4.82	7.52	1.06	4.32

Of the Astros' many fine pitching prospects, Rodriguez may have the best combination of performance and projectability. He has been unstoppable in the low minors, and his stuff is wicked, particularly a curveball that moves so much that one opposing manager thought it was a slider. Last year we said he was about three years away, which means he's now two years away. When he arrives, it's not going to be quietly.

Doug Sessions — Throws R — Age 23

YEAR	TEAM	LGE	IP	H	ER	HR	BB	K	ERA	W	L	H/9	HR/9	BB/9	K/9	KWH	PERA
1998	Auburn	NYP	29.3	30	13	3	14	25	3.99	2	1	9.20	0.92	4.30	7.67	1.11	4.91
1999	Michigan	Mid	12.7	8	1	1	1	12	0.71	1	0	5.68	0.71	0.71	8.53	13.45	1.42
1999	Kissimme	Fla	42.7	44	14	1	18	43	2.95	3	2	9.28	0.21	3.80	9.07	1.74	4.01

Relievers in the low minors are hardly worth mentioning most of the time, but since Sessions was drafted in 1998, he has made life hell for hitters in three different leagues. His career numbers: 90 innings, 63 hits, 25 walks, 114 strikeouts. The minor-league closers who are still racking up strikeouts when they get to Double-A have a chance to be something, so this season should tell us all we need to know about Sessions's future.

Billy Wagner — Throws L — Age 28

YEAR	TEAM	LGE	IP	H	ER	HR	BB	K	ERA	W	L	H/9	HR/9	BB/9	K/9	KWH	PERA
1997	Houston	NL	65.7	51	23	5	32	98	3.15	5	2	6.99	0.69	4.39	13.43	4.40	3.43
1998	Houston	NL	60.0	48	19	6	26	92	2.85	5	2	7.20	0.90	3.90	13.80	5.07	3.60
1999	Houston	NL	74.3	35	12	5	22	119	1.45	7	1	4.24	0.61	2.66	14.41	13.74	1.57

Why isn't Wagner one of the most well-known and popular players in the game? He should be a national folk hero, the little guy from the Appalachian wilderness who by some measures is the most unhittable closer of all time. Before last year, the highest strikeout-to-hit ratio for a pitcher (a good measure of dominance) was 2.63, by Troy Percival in 1996. Wagner's ratio last year was a ridiculous 3.54. He's well on his way to becoming the best left-handed closer in history.

One of the problems with the trend towards inflating pitchers' radar-gun readings is, now that so many pitchers can claim to hit 95 mph with their fastball, we don't appreciate how unique Wagner is to throw 97-98 mph as a left-hander, something only he and Randy Johnson can claim. His fastball has so much life to it that he became a great closer throwing nothing else. His improvement last year stems from learning a slider from Vern Ruhle, and he's still tinkering with a change-up on the sidelines. Right now, hitters go to the plate with their bats dialed up to hit something in the 90s. If he can add a change-up, even if it's just for show, he could improve on one of the 20 best relief seasons in history.

Brian Williams — Throws R — Age 31

YEAR	TEAM	LGE	IP	H	ER	HR	BB	K	ERA	W	L	H/9	HR/9	BB/9	K/9	KWH	PERA
1997	Rochestr	Int	67.0	76	36	8	26	64	4.84	3	4	10.21	1.07	3.49	8.60	1.55	5.24
1997	Baltimor	AL	24.0	20	8	0	18	14	3.00	2	1	7.50	0.00	6.75	5.25	0.41	3.75
1999	Houston	NL	67.0	68	32	4	33	51	4.30	4	3	9.13	0.54	4.43	6.85	0.87	4.43

Williams was one of the biggest surprises on an Opening Day roster, given that he hadn't pitched on American soil in 1998 and hadn't been effective since, what, his rookie year? His performance was more than adequate for the 11th pitcher on the staff, but if Dierker and Ruhle can get *Brian Williams* to pitch this well, don't you think they can do better this year by letting him leave as a free agent and giving the spot to Wade Miller or Tony McKnight?

PITCHER	GS	IP	R	SNW	SNL	SNPCT	W	L	RA	APW	SNVA	SNWAR
Sean Bergman	16	93.0	55	4.8	6.5	.426	4	6	5.32	-0.57	-0.84	0.01
Scott Elarton	15	84.7	43	5.1	4.4	.538	4	3	4.57	0.17	0.24	1.08
Mike Hampton	34	239.0	86	17.1	8.2	.676	22	4	3.24	3.93	4.20	6.34
Chris Holt	26	158.0	86	8.1	9.6	.457	5	13	4.90	-0.24	-0.66	0.56
Jose Lima	35	246.3	108	15.5	11.2	.582	21	10	3.95	2.17	2.00	4.18
Wade Miller	1	3.0	7	0.0	0.8	.018	0	1	21.00	-0.53	-0.39	-0.33
Shane Reynolds	35	231.7	108	14.8	11.6	.561	16	14	4.20	1.41	1.45	3.58
TOTALS	162	1055.7	493	65.4	52.2	.556	72	51	4.20	6.35	6.00	15.42

In the three years prior to Larry Dierker's arrival, the Astros' best Support-Neutral Winning Percentage (SNPct) was .471, and their best rank in the majors was 21st. In the three years since Dierker took the helm, their worst SNPct is .538 and their worst rank in the majors is sixth.... Everything Larry Dierker Touches Turns to Gold, Part 12: in 1997, the Astros had a left-handed starter named Mike Hampton who was a disaster. Through his first 14 starts of the season, Hampton was the worst starter in the league with a 2.6-7.4 SNWL record (.262 SNPct). Many managers would have given up at that point and relegated Hampton to the bullpen or the minors. Dierker, though, was patient, and was rewarded for that patience with a fantastic 11.0-4.7 (.698) SNWL record from Hampton the rest of the season.... Jump ahead to 1999. The Astros faced a similar situation with Chris Holt, who was near the bottom of the league with a 3.3-6.1 (.350) SNWL record through his first 14 starts. Once again, Dierker showed patience with his struggling starter and kept him in the rotation. And once again the patience paid off, this time with a 4.8-3.5 (.579) second half from Holt. Holt may not turn into a Mike Hampton in the long run, but his story shows how you can afford to be patient if you have the talent-evaluation skills of Larry Dierker.

Pitcher Abuse Points

PITCHER	AGE	GS	PAP	PAP/S	WKLD	MAX	1-90	91-100	101-110	111-120	121-130	131-140	141+
Sean Bergman	29	16	0	0.0	0.0	99	13	3	0	0	0	0	0
Scott Elarton	23	15	95	6.3	15.8	131	4	6	3	1	0	1	0
Mike Hampton	26	34	467	13.7	27.5	129	3	9	6	12	4	0	0
Chris Holt	27	26	136	5.2	9.6	135	9	9	5	2	0	1	0
Jose Lima	26	35	378	10.8	21.6	132	5	8	11	9	1	1	0
Wade Miller	22	1	0	0.0	0.0	64	1	0	0	0	0	0	0
Shane Reynolds	31	35	185	5.3	6.2	123	10	9	11	3	2	0	0
HOUSTON		162	1261	7.8	14.8	135	45	44	36	27	7	3	0
Ranking (NL)				8	7								

The Astros dropped from sixth to eighth in PAPs per start and from fourth to seventh in Workload, which is entirely due to not having Randy Johnson make 11 starts in 1999. When you consider that Astro starters threw the second-most innings of any rotation in baseball, their ranking becomes even more impressive.... With the exception of one start, Scott Elarton was handled extremely well as he eased into the Astros' rotation, while control freak Shane Reynolds threw 232 innings without breaking a sweat. Jose Lima was worked a little more than I would like (his Workload increased slightly from 20.3 to 21.6), but it's still remarkably low when you consider he averaged more than seven innings per start. The Astros' other 26-year-old ace, Mike Hampton, walked more batters than Lima and Reynolds combined, and his workload is cause for some concern. As the most prolific groundball pitcher in the game, though, he's less susceptible to injury than the numbers suggest.

Los Angeles Dodgers

A year ago, in the wake of the disastrous 1998 season, the Dodgers hired a new general manager, Kevin Malone, and a new manager, Davey Johnson. The new Fox ownership group had turned its first season into a nightmare. Their trading of Mike Piazza was a bad idea poorly executed; the subsequent decision to make Dodger icon Tommy Lasorda the GM, and the havoc he wrought, was much, much worse. The new management team also fired Bill Russell at midseason and replaced him with the over-matched Glenn Hoffman, contributing to the sense of chaos surrounding the team and doing nothing to push it towards a post-season berth.

These moves all failed while antagonizing the fan base. So bringing in two people with histories of success and no prior connection to Fox was well-received. The results, unfortunately, were even worse. Malone embarked on a series of signings—Alan Mills, Carlos Perez, Devon White, Kevin Brown—that exacerbated the existing Dodgers' problems of age and payroll inflexibility. He also made the high-risk trade of outfielder Roger Cedeno for injured catcher Todd Hundley, a move that imploded when it became obvious that Hundley's elbow was not fully healed, leaving him a shadow of the player he'd been in 1997.

Meanwhile, Johnson had to make do with a roster that had many holes, notably a lack of left-handed hitters, the usual Dodgers' problems with getting on base and a thin bullpen. He inherited a team that had highly-paid full-time starters at most positions, which didn't work well for a manager who liked to use the entire roster. He spent much of the 1999 season with his hands tied, unable to run the team in his preferred manner. For the first time in his managerial career, his team finished the season in a place other than first or second.

With 1999 even worse than 1998, Fox decided to declare victory and get out. On October 27, the team introduced Bob Daly, former Warner Brothers executive and self-proclaimed lifelong Dodger fan, as the team's president and chief executive officer. The myriad Fox suits that had been involved since the spring of 1998 would be fading into the background, and the team would now be run by Daly. The new man said all the right things at his introduction, earning praise from a media happy to see anyone not affiliated with the Evil Empire in charge.

In reality, not much has changed. Daly has no more baseball experience than any of the Fox representatives, and while his status as a Dodgers' fan is nice, it doesn't necessarily make him qualified to run the team. He's also not a particularly formidable barrier to continued changes at Chavez Ravine: Dodger Stadium is still going to be renovated, the atmosphere at the park is still going to be "enhanced" by loud music and non-baseball distractions, and if Fox decides it can generate revenue by serving Dodger Dogs smothered in salsa, well, grab a few extra napkins at the concession stand.

The biggest gain for Fox is the removal of their people, or the corporation itself, as the primary target for fan and media dissatisfaction. Daly can drape himself in Dodger Blue and be the front man for what is still corporate ownership, while regaling beat writers with stories of a childhood spent rooting for Duke Snider. This isn't an entirely bad thing, as a good relationship with the media goes a long way, but it really doesn't signal a sea change in how the Dodgers will be run.

On the field, the Dodgers are in a world of hurt. The payroll problems Malone inherited have only been made worse on his watch, and the farm system is in no danger of burping up a contributor anytime before mid-2001. The team's expensive players have very little trade value, due in varying degrees to their performance (Raul Mondesi, Devon White, Todd Hundley), age (White), perceived attitude problems (Mondesi, Gary Sheffield) or injury history (Hundley, Eric Young).

So you have to give Malone a considerable amount of credit for his first big move this winter, trading Mondesi to the Blue Jays for Shawn Green. While the difference between the two players isn't as large as their 1999 performances

Dodgers Prospectus

1999 record: 77-85; Third place, NL West

Pythagorean W/L: 82-80

Runs scored: 793 (11th in NL)

Runs allowed: 787 (8th in NL)

Team EQA: .260 (9th in NL)

1999 team age: 28.9 (8th-oldest in NL)

1999 park: Dodger Stadium; moderate pitchers' park, decreased run scoring by 7%.

1999: A massive disappointment to most, given manager, payroll and reputation.

2000: In a weak division, they could win 87 games and march into the playoffs.

would indicate, Green fits the Dodgers' desperate need for a left-handed hitter who can get on base and he comes with much less off-field baggage than Mondesi. He does add to the Dodgers' payroll problems, having signed a six-year, $84-million contract, but there's no question that this deal makes the Dodgers a better team in 2000.

Malone's other major move was a blatant salary dump, as the Dodgers sent Eric Young and Ismael Valdes to the Cubs for middle reliever Terry Adams and some minor-league arms. The Dodgers desperately wanted to be rid of Young and basically shopped Valdes with the second baseman attached. To get the right-hander, you had to take the expensive, fragile infielder. That Malone couldn't get more back was criminal, and the inevitable result of the previous winter's mistakes.

The loss of Valdes will hurt the Dodgers, but Green over Mondesi helps, and not having Young around will give the team some flexibility. So with the roster improved, we're left with a key question: in Davey we trust?

He's still one of the best managers in the game. As mentioned, the roster he inherited lacked flexibility, and he didn't have his typical bench. Johnson did the best he could, carving out roles for Todd Hollandsworth and Dave Hansen in an effort to give his lineup balance and increase the number of runners on base. He sorted through his bullpen options in the spring and got pretty good years out of Onan Masaoka and Pedro Borbon, performances that helped him use his bullpen in the aggressive manner he prefers. The loss of Antonio Osuna was a significant blow.

Johnson has to take some of the blame for last year, though. His war with Eric Young alienated his only real lead-off hitter and contributed to the perception that Johnson had lost control of the team. He endured sniping from every one of his starting outfielders at one time or another, and frequently complained to Malone about the lack of useful left-handed hitters at his disposal. If the Dodgers are going to contend in 2000, Johnson is going to have to work with Malone in the offseason to bring in the elements he feels he needs to make the Dodgers successful. And once the season starts, he's going to have to accept what he has and not complain publicly about the roster.

The team has re-signed Hansen, a Johnson favorite, but traded Pedro Borbon in the Green deal, which will force Johnson to find a left-handed reliever to go with Masaoka. The team's pursuit of Arthur Rhodes was in vain. Young's departure opens up second base for Jose Vizcaino. While that helps the team's lefty/righty balance, it's really not much of an upgrade. Johnson can also be expected to expand Todd Hollandsworth's role; Hollandsworth could become the best fourth outfielder in the league.

The signings of Devon White and Kevin Brown saddled the Dodgers with large obligations for a number of years to players who are declining or will be soon. That's going to be a roster and payroll-management issue. But more significantly, these signings meant the Dodgers had no picks in the first two rounds of the 1999 draft. Added to the export of prospects by Lasorda in 1998 and the age of the roster, the damage to the Dodger player-development process was significant.

The Dodgers have used non-draft methods to acquire talent for years, and they are continuing their efforts in the international talent market. Taiwan export Chin-Feng Chen is one of the top prospects in baseball, and pitcher Jesus Cordero has significant upside. High-profile international signings can be an expensive route, though. Drafting well is the best path to success, and giving away high draft picks for the last few years of Devon White's career torpedoes an organization in the long term. Very few free agents are worth the draft-pick investment.

As this is written in mid-December, it appears that the Dodgers are going to get away with signing Adrian Beltre at 15. The third baseman claims that the team altered his birth certificate so they could sign him in July of 1994, nine months before his 16th birthday. The details are murky, but Beltre apparently related this information to his agent, Scott Boras, in the spring of 1999, and Boras informed the Dodgers of the problem. Major League Baseball has allowed the Dodgers to keep Beltre, while assessing them a fine and suspending their activities in the Dominican Republic for one year.

The issue is a complicated one, made more so by the lack of an official MLB policy on the issue. Recent precedents, such as the signings of Richard Aramboles and Juan Diaz, indicate that Beltre would be declared a free agent. In this case, this potential remedy has caused a lot of consternation, primarily from people who believe that Beltre should not receive a financial windfall for his role, whatever it was, in the deception.

Whether Adrian Beltre actively sought to deceive the Dodgers, or his altered birth certificate was an idea hatched in the mind of a scout, is difficult to determine. By the time this book is released, there will probably be better evidence available, so the issue of the degree of Beltre's involvement won't be addressed here.

Regardless of Beltre's actions, the only appropriate solution is to declare him a free agent. The Dodgers must relinquish his rights, because the initial contract between the organization and the player violated baseball's rules. That contract also denied the other 27 teams the chance to sign Beltre legally, and they must be allowed the opportunity that was denied them by the Dodgers' illegal actions. Additionally, losing Beltre is the only penalty strong enough to discourage this kind of behavior in the future.

Beltre may make a lot of money as a result of this remedy, but that is not, and should not, be the issue here. The violation and its handling are between MLB and the Dodgers, and

MLB and the rest of its entities. The rule on underage signing applies to clubs, not players. MLB's rules, and the rights of the other clubs to Beltre, were violated here. Any solution that doesn't have that at its center is at best ill-founded, and at worst motivated by a desire to keep money out of Beltre's pocket.

What should come of this is a firm statement by Major League Baseball that the practice of underage signing stops now. A policy to handle all future cases needs to be established, one with both a punitive element, to deter teams from the practice, and a preventative element, to keep players from actively deceiving teams. It needs to be implemented immediately, before MLB is faced with a rash of claims.

Letting a player become a free agent because he was signed before the age of 16 is not a perfect solution. It is the one that comes closest, the one that follows precedents set by MLB, punishes the entity that violated the rule and re-establishes the competitive condition that was in place before the violation.

HITTERS (Averages: BA: .270 / OBP: .340 / SLG: .430 / EQA: .260)

Adrian Beltre · 3B · Bats R · Age 21

YEAR	TEAM	LGE	AB	H	DB	TP	HR	BB/SO	R	RBI	SB	CS	OUT	BA	OBP	SLG	EQA	EQR	DEFENSE	
1997	Vero Bch	Fla	443	123	19	1	25	57/72	73	84	10	4	324	.278	.366	.494	.286	71	119-3B 98	
1998	SanAnton	Tex	248	72	18	1	11	32/41	36	44	11	3	179	.290	.375	.504	.294	42	59-3B 95	
1998	LosAngls	NL	198	46	9	0	8	14/36	19	24	3	1	153	.232	.294	.399	.233	20	59-3B 97	
1999	LosAngls	NL	541	149	29	5	14	54/104	79	63	15	7	399	.275	.349	.425	.263	71	147-3B 96	
2000	LosAngls	NL	485	136	23	1	23	60/91	84	86	16	5	354	.280	.360	.474	.287	78		

What isn't in dispute in the Beltre case is his real birth date of April 7, 1979. This means that last year he was a 20-year-old putting up a .263 EqA with fair defense. That separates him from Scott Rolen and puts him on par with Andruw Jones and Alex Rodriguez as one of the most valuable properties in baseball. As with the draft free agents from 1996 (Travis Lee, et al), if Beltre is allowed to become a free agent, it will serve as an illustration of just how much the current system restricts the earnings of players in their early 20s. Regardless of his age or contract status, he's on the brink of stardom.

Hiram Bocachica · 2B · Bats R · Age 24

YEAR	TEAM	LGE	AB	H	DB	TP	HR	BB/SO	R	RBI	SB	CS	OUT	BA	OBP	SLG	EQA	EQR	DEFENSE	
1997	Harrisbg	Eas	444	111	19	2	9	30/101	61	28	18	7	340	.250	.311	.363	.233	44	54-SS 78	27-2B 96
1998	Harrisbg	Eas	300	77	20	3	4	18/60	34	25	13	5	228	.257	.318	.383	.241	33	73-OF 106	
1998	Albuquer	PCL	99	20	5	1	3	12/24	12	12	4	2	81	.202	.316	.364	.236	11	25-OF 132	
1999	SanAnton	Tex	486	125	20	7	10	48/80	63	48	15	8	369	.257	.336	.389	.249	57	121-2B 94	
2000	LosAngls	NL	495	128	22	4	12	51/94	74	62	22	9	376	.259	.328	.392	.254	61		

Bocachica has a decent mix of offensive skills and adapted fairly well to second base last year, being voted the best defensive second baseman in the Texas League in a *Baseball America* poll. The big improvement in his plate discipline was a welcome surprise. He's not going to be a star, but I think Johnson could get a lot out of him as a utility player if given a chance.

Chin-Feng Chen · OF · Bats R · Age 22

YEAR	TEAM	LGE	AB	H	DB	TP	HR	BB/SO	R	RBI	SB	CS	OUT	BA	OBP	SLG	EQA	EQR	DEFENSE
1999	San Bern	Cal	508	143	20	5	29	59/125	69	92	14	4	368	.281	.360	.512	.289	82	116-OF 89
2000	LosAngls	NL	254	77	11	2	18	39/80	54	59	10	2	179	.303	.396	.575	.325	54	

Chen had a fantastic year in what is, admittedly, an excellent environment for a hitter. While his ability to hit was known, he really surprised people with his speed. Chen is one of the best offensive prospects in baseball and could be in a Dodger uniform as early as this September.

Alex Cora · SS · Bats L · Age 24

YEAR	TEAM	LGE	AB	H	DB	TP	HR	BB/SO	R	RBI	SB	CS	OUT	BA	OBP	SLG	EQA	EQR	DEFENSE
1997	SanAnton	Tex	447	96	19	3	3	19/68	40	38	8	5	356	.215	.251	.291	.177	23	127-SS 105
1998	Albuquer	PCL	294	68	15	4	4	12/38	32	35	7	5	231	.231	.267	.350	.205	22	80-SS 104
1999	Albuquer	PCL	296	80	10	6	3	9/37	39	29	6	3	219	.270	.306	.375	.230	28	76-SS 98
1999	LosAngls	NL	30	5	1	0	0	0/4	2	3	0	0	25	.167	.197	.200	.066	0	
2000	LosAngls	NL	272	66	11	4	5	14/36	27	29	6	3	209	.243	.280	.368	.222	24	

(Alex Cora *continued*)

Joey's little brother is a much better defensive player than he was, but he can't hit and isn't likely to learn anytime soon. If you had to have a guy like this on the roster, you'd be better off with Juan Castro, who is a fantastic defender and an even worse hitter. Even if something were to happen to Mark Grudzielanek, the Dodgers would be better off moving Jose Vizcaino to shortstop and playing Bocachica or Adam Riggs. In other words, forget Cora.

Craig Counsell · 2B · Bats L · Age 29

YEAR	TEAM	LGE	AB	H	DB	TP	HR	BB/SO	R	RBI	SB	CS	OUT	BA	OBP	SLG	EQA	EQR	DEFENSE
1997	ColSprin	PCL	358	91	22	3	3	32/43	47	38	7	2	269	.254	.323	.358	.236	36	91-2B 89
1997	Florida	NL	167	51	10	2	1	18/17	21	16	1	1	117	.305	.383	.407	.272	23	47-2B 103
1998	Florida	NL	341	90	23	5	4	51/46	45	42	3	0	251	.264	.367	.396	.266	46	101-2B 100
1999	Florida	NL	67	11	1	0	0	4/10	4	2	0	0	56	.164	.211	.179	.069	0	
1999	LosAngls	NL	109	29	6	0	0	7/14	19	9	1	0	80	.266	.310	.321	.217	9	25-2B 111
2000	*LosAngls*	*NL*	*246*	*62*	*16*	*2*	*2*	*30/32*	*34*	*28*	*2*	*1*	*185*	*.252*	*.333*	*.358*	*.243*	*27*	

The Dodgers' desperate need for left-handed-hitting bench help led them to pick up Counsell at midseason after he lost the Marlins' second base job to Luis Castillo. He's a very limited contributor, as he can't play anywhere but second base, doesn't hit left-handers, run or hit for any power. Unless you're trying to make the Braves' World Series roster, those things count against you. He's been removed from the Dodgers' 40-man roster.

Bubba Crosby · LF · Bats L · Age 23

YEAR	TEAM	LGE	AB	H	DB	TP	HR	BB/SO	R	RBI	SB	CS	OUT	BA	OBP	SLG	EQA	EQR	DEFENSE
1998	San Bern	Cal	201	40	9	1	0	13/39	20	11	2	2	163	.199	.248	.254	.158	8	50-OF 101
1999	San Bern	Cal	370	97	20	2	1	31/71	37	28	8	4	277	.262	.325	.335	.229	35	89-OF 99
2000	*LosAngls*	*NL*	*204*	*49*	*7*	*2*	*0*	*18/46*	*21*	*16*	*3*	*1*	*156*	*.240*	*.302*	*.294*	*.211*	*16*	

Crosby, the Dodgers' 1998 #1 pick out of Rice, hasn't adjusted to professional baseball. He illustrates the problems with drafting college players in the middle or at the left end of the defensive spectrum: if they don't hit, they're completely useless. It's better to draft collegians from the right end of the spectrum. It's better still to eschew college hitters entirely and draft college pitchers and high school position players. Crosby has about six weeks to save his career.

Glenn Davis · 1B · Bats B · Age 24

YEAR	TEAM	LGE	AB	H	DB	TP	HR	BB/SO	R	RBI	SB	CS	OUT	BA	OBP	SLG	EQA	EQR	DEFENSE	
1997	San Bern	Cal	230	49	9	0	9	37/75	32	29	3	1	182	.213	.326	.370	.241	26	57-1B 99	
1998	Vero Bch	Fla	382	76	11	1	17	56/121	46	46	5	2	308	.199	.304	.366	.230	39	50-OF 96	30-1B 116
1998	SanAnton	Tex	70	18	2	0	5	8/24	11	12	1	0	52	.257	.333	.500	.276	10		
1999	SanAnton	Tex	503	117	29	4	8	55/146	58	51	3	3	389	.233	.308	.354	.226	47	70-OF 88	62-1B 106
2000	*LosAngls*	*NL*	*492*	*106*	*22*	*1*	*14*	*68/151*	*59*	*57*	*4*	*2*	*388*	*.215*	*.311*	*.350*	*.233*	*51*		

See Crosby, Bubba. Davis hasn't struggled quite as badly, but this isn't what the team expected when they made him their #1 pick in 1997. An excellent defensive first baseman, he's learning left field with some difficulty. It would be better to leave him at first base and see if he can make it easy for the team to let Eric Karros go after the 2000 season. Davis is likely to have good statistics this year, thanks to Albuquerque, so look for him to get some positive press.

Juan Diaz · 1B · Bats R · Age 24

YEAR	TEAM	LGE	AB	H	DB	TP	HR	BB/SO	R	RBI	SB	CS	OUT	BA	OBP	SLG	EQA	EQR	DEFENSE
1997	Savannah	SAL	477	104	22	1	24	42/157	56	70	1	1	374	.218	.285	.419	.233	49	69-1B 72
1998	Vero Bch	Fla	250	60	10	1	13	17/59	25	35	0	1	191	.240	.295	.444	.243	28	53-1B 93
1998	SanAnton	Tex	189	45	10	0	11	12/50	20	23	0	0	144	.238	.289	.466	.247	22	43-1B 79
1999	SanAnton	Tex	258	69	16	1	8	21/86	34	42	0	0	189	.267	.328	.430	.254	31	58-1B 90
2000	*LosAngls*	*NL*	*403*	*102*	*19*	*1*	*20*	*40/124*	*52*	*67*	*0*	*0*	*301*	*.253*	*.321*	*.454*	*.264*	*54*	

Diaz isn't a prospect, despite superficially good numbers at San Antonio and some supporters within the organization. He's a big guy who doesn't hit like one, and while some of last year's improvement is real, Diaz doesn't have the upside of Davis or Crosby. He could sneak in if those two continue to struggle, which wouldn't be the best thing for the Dodgers in the long term.

Kevin Gibbs   DL   Bats B   Age 26

YEAR	TEAM	LGE	AB	H	DB	TP	HR	BB/SO	R	RBI	SB	CS	OUT	BA	OBP	SLG	EQA	EQR	DEFENSE
1997	SanAnton	Tex	357	102	19	4	2	58/56	59	25	27	11	266	.286	.393	.378	.274	52	99-OF 106
1999	Albuquer	PCL	21	5	1	0	0	3/6	2	1	1	1	17	.238	.354	.286	.226	2	
2000	LosAngls	NL	64	18	4	0	0	11/21	12	7	3	2	48	.281	.387	.344	.265	9	

In case you were wondering, we've confirmed the rumor: life isn't fair. Two years ago, Kevin Gibbs looked like he could be a minor star, packaging plate discipline and speed with good outfield defense. Since then, he's had 29 at-bats. In April, 1998, Gibbs's knee exploded. This year, he suffered a slap lesion in his shoulder and missed the season. His chance at any kind of career is shot, and what he's left with is trying to get healthy, knock the rust off and hope for a 25th-man spot somewhere. Good luck, Kevin: you deserve a break.

Geronimo Gil   C   Bats R   Age 24

YEAR	TEAM	LGE	AB	H	DB	TP	HR	BB/SO	R	RBI	SB	CS	OUT	BA	OBP	SLG	EQA	EQR	DEFENSE	
1997	Vero Bch	Fla	215	49	12	1	6	12/45	25	20	1	0	166	.228	.278	.377	.219	19		
1998	SanAnton	Tex	242	64	15	2	5	11/48	21	23	1	1	179	.264	.296	.405	.233	23	23-C 91	19-OF 92
1999	SanAnton	Tex	350	88	20	1	13	40/65	37	47	1	0	262	.251	.331	.426	.256	43	72-C 96	19-OF 98
2000	LosAngls	NL	237	59	13	1	8	25/46	31	34	1	0	178	.249	.321	.414	.254	29		

There's some rumbling that Gil is a prospect, helped by Angel Pena's weight problem and a growing perception that Pena is a head case. While Gil played well in 1999, the performance was out of line with his career and occurred as a Double-A repeater in a good offensive environment. Pena is still a better player, but Gil has created an opportunity for himself.

Mark Grudzielanek   SS   Bats R   Age 30

YEAR	TEAM	LGE	AB	H	DB	TP	HR	BB/SO	R	RBI	SB	CS	OUT	BA	OBP	SLG	EQA	EQR	DEFENSE
1997	Montreal	NL	653	178	57	3	4	22/75	74	50	20	9	484	.273	.307	.387	.235	65	152-SS 96
1998	Montreal	NL	405	121	19	1	9	21/49	56	45	12	6	290	.299	.349	.417	.260	50	101-SS 94
1998	LosAngls	NL	197	56	4	0	3	4/22	12	23	8	0	141	.284	.306	.350	.230	18	50-SS 111
1999	LosAngls	NL	491	159	23	5	7	25/64	68	44	5	6	338	.324	.370	.434	.271	64	115-SS 96
2000	LosAngls	NL	528	150	27	2	8	31/67	64	66	8	6	384	.284	.324	.388	.246	58	

This is the top of his range, and it isn't all that impressive. Grudzielanek is overrated thanks to a couple of high batting averages and the 50-double season. He's in the Garret Anderson class, a player who helps you if he hits .320, but doesn't if he hits his more typical .280. He'll take 1999's .326 batting average to arbitration, so he's a lock to be overpaid for his 2000 performance. Grudzielanek's defense has advanced to "passable."

Dave Hansen   PH/1B/3B   Bats L   Age 31

YEAR	TEAM	LGE	AB	H	DB	TP	HR	BB/SO	R	RBI	SB	CS	OUT	BA	OBP	SLG	EQA	EQR	DEFENSE
1997	ChiCubs	NL	152	46	8	2	3	30/32	18	20	1	2	108	.303	.421	.441	.295	26	29-3B 94
1999	LosAngls	NL	107	27	8	1	2	25/20	14	16	0	0	80	.252	.404	.402	.284	17	
2000	LosAngls	NL	82	21	5	1	2	19/26	17	13	0	0	61	.256	.396	.415	.290	14	

Hansen is an excellent bench player who was cheated out of millions of dollars by Tommy Lasorda. This on-base machine wasted away on The Pastaman's bench from 1993 to 1995 after the team signed Tim Wallach to play third base. Hansen is a tremendous early-inning pinch-hitter who can still platoon at the hot corner if needed.

Todd Hollandsworth   OF   Bats L   Age 27

YEAR	TEAM	LGE	AB	H	DB	TP	HR	BB/SO	R	RBI	SB	CS	OUT	BA	OBP	SLG	EQA	EQR	DEFENSE
1997	LosAngls	NL	301	78	23	2	4	17/59	40	32	4	5	228	.259	.299	.389	.228	28	87-OF 98
1998	LosAngls	NL	179	52	9	4	3	8/41	25	21	4	3	130	.291	.325	.436	.252	21	42-OF 101
1999	LosAngls	NL	263	75	12	2	9	20/60	37	31	4	2	190	.285	.338	.449	.263	34	29-CF 103
2000	LosAngls	NL	257	68	13	2	8	19/60	33	36	5	3	192	.265	.315	.424	.253	31	

Now that the expectations created by his ill-gotten Rookie of the Year award have been tempered, Hollandsworth can settle into a nice career as a fourth outfielder. The acquisition of Shawn Green means he won't have to play much right field, but with Devon White and Gary Sheffield still around, there will be a lot of opportunity for Hollandsworth to flash his left-handed bat and good range. He might even end up in a platoon situation with White before the year is over. Hollandsworth can be a contributor to a championship team.

Trenidad Hubbard OF Bats R Age 34

YEAR	TEAM	LGE	AB	H	DB	TP	HR	BB/SO	R	RBI	SB	CS	OUT	BA	OBP	SLG	EQA	EQR	DEFENSE
1997	Buffalo	AA	388	109	21	1	13	48/58	59	52	18	7	286	.281	.365	.441	.275	57	89-OF 108
1998	LosAngls	NL	213	68	10	1	8	18/45	31	19	10	6	151	.319	.381	.488	.288	34	54-OF 105
1999	Albuquer	PCL	120	32	8	1	3	13/29	15	16	9	3	91	.267	.338	.425	.263	16	28-OF 113
1999	LosAngls	NL	105	33	4	0	1	12/24	20	12	3	3	75	.314	.385	.381	.263	13	
2000	LosAngls	NL	242	64	10	1	7	32/53	39	34	9	5	183	.264	.350	.401	.264	33	

Hubbard started 1999 at Albuquerque because Davey Johnson picked Jacob Brumfield over him for the last roster spot. It was an inexplicable decision, as there is nothing Brumfield does that Hubbard doesn't do better. By Memorial Day, Johnson concurred, bringing Hubbard back and releasing Brumfield. Hubbard is a good bench player and should have a job somewhere in 2000.

Todd Hundley C Bats L Age 31

YEAR	TEAM	LGE	AB	H	DB	TP	HR	BB/SO	R	RBI	SB	CS	OUT	BA	OBP	SLG	EQA	EQR	DEFENSE
1997	NY Mets	NL	424	117	24	2	31	82/115	79	87	1	3	310	.276	.397	.561	.310	83	
1998	NY Mets	NL	126	22	3	0	4	15/54	8	14	1	1	105	.175	.268	.294	.189	8	24-OF 91
1999	LosAngls	NL	379	79	15	0	24	39/112	47	53	3	0	300	.208	.290	.438	.242	43	98-C 92
2000	LosAngls	NL	283	61	8	0	16	42/89	36	44	1	1	223	.216	.317	.413	.252	36	

That was truly an ugly year, seemingly made worse by the great season Roger Cedeno, for whom Hundley was acquired, had with the Mets. While Hundley is never going to be the player he was from 1995 to 1997, before the surgery, there's enough ability here to make him a contributor. He's already given up batting right-handed. Hundley slugged .492 against right-handed pitchers last year, so he can help the Dodgers as a platoon player. While his throwing was terrible, it wasn't the worst in the league (Eddie Taubensee and Dave Nilsson were both worse) and it did improve in the second half. A Hundley/Pena platoon, with Pena being used against all left-handed pitchers, would be a strong catching situation. Hundley will jump back to the .270 EqA level this season.

Eric Karros 1B Bats R Age 32

YEAR	TEAM	LGE	AB	H	DB	TP	HR	BB/SO	R	RBI	SB	CS	OUT	BA	OBP	SLG	EQA	EQR	DEFENSE
1997	LosAngls	NL	641	179	26	0	36	60/115	89	112	13	7	469	.279	.343	.488	.274	92	160-1B 105
1998	LosAngls	NL	520	164	20	1	27	46/91	64	95	8	2	358	.315	.375	.513	.295	84	133-1B 106
1999	LosAngls	NL	581	177	35	0	35	46/118	70	107	7	5	409	.305	.358	.546	.292	95	145-1B 111
2000	LosAngls	NL	598	168	19	0	35	61/117	86	115	6	3	433	.281	.347	.488	.283	92	

All this for $5 million? I'll take two, thanks. Karros has had a delayed peak, with every aspect of his game better in his early thirties than in his twenties. His contract is up at the end of 2000, and while he wants an extension, the team is taking a hard line. He should be elsewhere in 2001, a bad free-agent signing for a team like the Orioles.

Nick Leach 1B Bats L Age 22

YEAR	TEAM	LGE	AB	H	DB	TP	HR	BB/SO	R	RBI	SB	CS	OUT	BA	OBP	SLG	EQA	EQR	DEFENSE
1997	Yakima	Nwn	194	46	13	1	5	20/39	19	28	1	0	148	.237	.319	.392	.242	21	43-1B 95
1997	Savannah	SAL	136	34	7	0	0	13/23	13	11	0	1	103	.250	.328	.301	.218	11	25-1B 100
1998	San Bern	Cal	474	98	24	1	7	32/97	38	38	3	5	381	.207	.262	.306	.186	29	117-1B 99
1999	Vero Bch	Fla	450	110	14	0	20	52/80	45	59	5	3	342	.244	.327	.409	.250	53	126-1B 92
2000	NY Yanks	AL	397	96	13	0	12	46/75	51	51	4	3	304	.242	.321	.365	.241	43	

The Dodgers made some happy noises about his performance in the Florida State League. Realistically, Leach is a nonprospect, kept alive only by the organization's decision to demote him to easier competition and the disappointing performance of Glenn Davis ahead of him. Leach was traded to the Yankees for Dan Naulty; behind Nick Johnson, he's doomed.

Paul LoDuca   C   Bats R   Age 28

YEAR	TEAM	LGE	AB	H	DB	TP	HR	BB/SO	R	RBI	SB	CS	OUT	BA	OBP	SLG	EQA	EQR	DEFENSE	
1997	SanAnton	Tex	383	99	22	1	5	33/34	40	46	7	4	288	.258	.321	.360	.233	38		
1998	Albuquer	PCL	440	112	23	2	5	47/44	47	39	12	5	333	.255	.331	.350	.237	46	90-C 99	17-1B 112
1999	LosAngls	NL	96	22	2	0	3	8/9	11	11	1	2	76	.229	.304	.344	.217	8	28-C 104	
1999	Albuquer	PCL	74	22	5	0	1	8/1	12	6	1	1	53	.297	.398	.405	.278	11		
2000	LosAngls	NL	264	67	12	1	4	31/22	36	30	5	3	200	.254	.332	.352	.243	29		

The current organizational frown directed at Angel Pena could earn LoDuca some more time towards his pension. He may actually be a better fit than Pena for the platoon/defensive replacement role. LoDuca deserves a major-league job, certainly ahead of the Kirt Manwaring and Joe Girardi types.

Raul Mondesi   RF   Bats R   Age 29

YEAR	TEAM	LGE	AB	H	DB	TP	HR	BB/SO	R	RBI	SB	CS	OUT	BA	OBP	SLG	EQA	EQR	DEFENSE
1997	LosAngls	NL	630	202	45	5	33	43/104	96	91	26	15	443	.321	.370	.565	.300	109	159-OF 98
1998	LosAngls	NL	592	177	30	5	34	29/109	92	97	17	12	427	.299	.335	.539	.280	89	141-OF 103
1999	LosAngls	NL	605	154	31	5	32	63/133	92	94	31	9	460	.255	.328	.481	.270	87	154-RF 101
2000	Toronto	AL	587	159	31	3	31	55/118	98	107	18	9	437	.271	.333	.492	.273	85	

I expect Mondesi to have his best year in 2000. While he continued to decline from his 1997 peak season, the loss was primarily in his batting average: his walk rate was way up, his power about the same as it's always been and he improved as a base-stealer. Give him the missing 20 singles, and there would be no difference between 1998 and 1999. Shawn Green is a better player than Mondesi, but the gap is considerably less than it appeared in 1999; they'll be within a game of each other this year.

Tony Mota   OF   Bats B   Age 22

YEAR	TEAM	LGE	AB	H	DB	TP	HR	BB/SO	R	RBI	SB	CS	OUT	BA	OBP	SLG	EQA	EQR	DEFENSE
1997	San Bern	Cal	422	92	15	7	5	20/95	40	39	5	4	334	.218	.258	.322	.191	27	108-OF 109
1998	Vero Bch	Fla	254	68	17	4	6	14/30	33	26	5	4	190	.268	.310	.437	.247	29	53-OF 105
1998	SanAnton	Tex	223	50	9	4	2	9/40	14	18	9	5	178	.224	.254	.327	.194	15	55-OF 91
1999	SanAnton	Tex	351	104	28	1	13	34/61	52	61	7	3	250	.296	.358	.493	.282	53	57-OF 98
2000	LosAngls	NL	411	106	20	3	15	37/73	56	60	9	5	310	.258	.319	.431	.257	52	

Manny's son, which counts for something, even with the Fox Dodgers. He became a prospect in 1999 with a good year in the hitters' haven of San Antonio. While I'd normally be skeptical, the development of his secondary skills can't be ignored. Mota missed the last month of the season after tearing a ligament in his left thumb. He's still on track for a September call-up this year and in the mix for a fourth outfielder spot in 2001.

Angel Pena   C   Bats R   Age 25

YEAR	TEAM	LGE	AB	H	DB	TP	HR	BB/SO	R	RBI	SB	CS	OUT	BA	OBP	SLG	EQA	EQR	DEFENSE
1997	San Bern	Cal	323	76	19	2	12	23/84	39	45	2	2	249	.235	.289	.418	.234	33	
1998	SanAnton	Tex	485	142	27	1	17	36/91	60	78	5	3	346	.293	.347	.458	.269	65	112-C 98
1999	Albuquer	PCL	125	31	7	1	1	8/24	11	19	2	1	95	.248	.293	.344	.216	10	28-C 100
1999	LosAngls	NL	121	25	4	0	5	10/24	13	21	0	1	97	.207	.267	.364	.207	9	36-C 100
2000	LosAngls	NL	339	83	18	1	10	30/70	39	44	2	2	258	.245	.306	.392	.240	37	

It was a tough year for the Dodgers' most advanced prospect. Pena didn't hit or field when given the starting job in the wake of Todd Hundley's problems. Sent to Albuquerque, he was suspended for a week before suffering a strained right forearm that ended his season. Pena's weight problems appear to be here to stay, so developing a reputation as a head case isn't going to help him. He will be a part-time player, at best, in 2000.

Jason Repko   SS   Bats R   Age 19

YEAR	TEAM	LGE	AB	H	DB	TP	HR	BB/SO	R	RBI	SB	CS	OUT	BA	OBP	SLG	EQA	EQR	DEFENSE
1999	GreatFls	Pio	203	45	7	4	6	13/50	25	17	3	2	160	.222	.273	.384	.218	18	47-SS 76
2000	LosAngls	NL	100	23	3	2	4	8/58	11	14	2	1	78	.230	.287	.420	.241	11	

Los Angeles Dodgers

(Jason Repko *continued*)

The Dodgers' first selection in the 1999 draft, as compensation for Scott Radinsky. Hmmm...a dispensable left-handed reliever for one of the top amateur players in the country, with a 5-10% chance of being very good, and a 100% chance of being very cheap until 2005 or so. For a significant number of Type-A free agents, and all Type-B free agents—such as Radinsky—this kind of trade is terribly unbalanced against the signing team. Repko is a very fast infielder who may eventually move to center field.

Adam Riggs 2B Bats R Age 27

YEAR	TEAM	LGE	AB	H	DB	TP	HR	BB/SO	R	RBI	SB	CS	OUT	BA	OBP	SLG	EQA	EQR	DEFENSE
1997	Albuquer	PCL	217	52	6	2	9	22/41	38	18	8	2	167	.240	.317	.410	.249	26	56-2B 96
1998	Albuquer	PCL	164	47	10	3	2	17/32	20	17	7	4	121	.287	.361	.421	.266	22	43-2B 90
1999	Albuquer	PCL	504	118	22	5	8	42/123	58	55	15	10	396	.234	.303	.345	.221	46	113-2B 90
2000	*LosAngls*	*NL*	*333*	*74*	*12*	*3*	*7*	*37/80*	*41*	*33*	*12*	*8*	*267*	*.222*	*.300*	*.339*	*.224*	*32*	

Riggs' window is just about closed, with Bocachica coming up hard behind him. His performance slipped a bit last year as well, although as with Mondesi, it was mostly in his batting average. Riggs isn't cut out to be a utility infielder, so he needs to get to an organization with a muddled second-base situation and hope to get lucky.

Gary Sheffield LF Bats R Age 31

YEAR	TEAM	LGE	AB	H	DB	TP	HR	BB/SO	R	RBI	SB	CS	OUT	BA	OBP	SLG	EQA	EQR	DEFENSE
1997	Florida	NL	454	116	23	1	23	121/78	87	74	9	7	345	.256	.428	.463	.305	88	127-OF 98
1998	Florida	NL	139	40	11	1	7	26/16	22	30	4	2	101	.288	.408	.532	.310	27	36-OF 91
1998	LosAngls	NL	312	108	19	1	19	70/29	57	64	20	6	210	.346	.475	.596	.354	78	87-OF 96
1999	LosAngls	NL	551	166	18	0	34	94/63	97	96	9	5	390	.301	.407	.519	.308	103	136-LF 99
2000	*LosAngls*	*NL*	*510*	*148*	*18*	*0*	*31*	*107/62*	*107*	*111*	*11*	*6*	*368*	*.290*	*.413*	*.508*	*.316*	*103*	

Sheffield may be the most underappreciated hitter in the game. It's either him or Edgar Martinez, a similar batsman. There's no one reason why he's never gotten the proper credit: some ill-timed comments, some incomplete reporting, his early-career fragility and playing in bad hitters' parks on losing teams have all contributed. He's got a lot of quality years ahead of him, and I expect he'll outperform that 2000 projection.

Jose Vizcaino SS Bats B Age 32

YEAR	TEAM	LGE	AB	H	DB	TP	HR	BB/SO	R	RBI	SB	CS	OUT	BA	OBP	SLG	EQA	EQR	DEFENSE
1997	San Fran	NL	576	157	23	7	5	47/86	78	51	6	8	427	.273	.327	.363	.234	56	138-SS 105
1998	LosAngls	NL	242	69	5	0	5	17/34	32	33	8	4	177	.285	.335	.368	.242	25	63-SS 100
1999	LosAngls	NL	268	68	6	0	2	17/23	25	29	2	1	201	.254	.301	.299	.204	19	38-SS 97
2000	*LosAngls*	*NL*	*242*	*60*	*6*	*1*	*3*	*20/28*	*23*	*24*	*2*	*2*	*184*	*.248*	*.305*	*.318*	*.217*	*20*	

A free-agent signing that worked about as well as was expected. Vizcaino's association with the 1997 NL West champion San Francisco Giants gave him perceived value far beyond his actual value and led to a three-year, $9 million commitment from the Dodgers. He's spent two years fighting injuries and hitting like the fifth infielder he is. He's an asset in that role; with the Young trade, though, he's the second baseman. I've got May 4 in the disabled list pool.

Devon White CF Bats B Age 37

YEAR	TEAM	LGE	AB	H	DB	TP	HR	BB/SO	R	RBI	SB	CS	OUT	BA	OBP	SLG	EQA	EQR	DEFENSE
1997	Florida	NL	269	68	12	1	7	32/64	36	35	11	5	206	.253	.348	.383	.254	33	65-OF 109
1998	Arizona	NL	568	160	29	1	25	41/99	85	87	23	9	417	.282	.341	.468	.270	79	138-OF 109
1999	LosAngls	NL	477	128	23	2	13	33/87	57	64	16	5	354	.268	.332	.407	.253	57	119-CF 96
2000	*LosAngls*	*NL*	*333*	*80*	*13*	*1*	*12*	*35/63*	*42*	*44*	*7*	*4*	*257*	*.240*	*.313*	*.393*	*.245*	*38*	

Another of the moves that made the Dodgers older and more expensive without really improving the team. Both his Fielding Translation and Zone Rating indicate that White may have lost a step defensively. If it doesn't come back, he's a real liability for the Dodgers, because there's no place in their outfield to move him. As a switch-hitter with some speed and power, he would be a useful bench player.

Eric Young   2B   Bats R   Age 33

YEAR	TEAM	LGE	AB	H	DB	TP	HR	BB/SO	R	RBI	SB	CS	OUT	BA	OBP	SLG	EQA	EQR	DEFENSE
1997	Colorado	NL	464	122	29	5	6	56/37	70	41	24	11	353	.263	.349	.386	.255	58	115-2B 103
1997	LosAngls	NL	157	45	6	2	2	14/17	28	17	11	2	114	.287	.360	.389	.267	21	32-2B 96
1998	LosAngls	NL	463	143	27	1	9	45/31	84	47	47	16	335	.309	.377	.430	.281	70	110-2B 94
1999	LosAngls	NL	458	127	23	2	2	58/26	66	39	44	22	353	.277	.365	.349	.254	57	108-2B 103
2000	*ChiCubs*	*NL*	*432*	*122*	*25*	*2*	*4*	*61/29*	*89*	*48*	*34*	*15*	*325*	*.282*	*.371*	*.377*	*.259*	*55*	

Ankle and hamstring injuries dogged Eric Young throughout the season, a situation made worse by Johnson's reluctance to put Young on the disabled list. After he relented and gave Young a few weeks off at the end of July, Young came back to have his best month in August. He's an above-average second baseman who needs to be rested a little more than usual. He'll be the Cubs' leadoff hitter, arguably their best since Ivan DeJesus.

PITCHERS (Averages: ERA: 4.50 / H/9: 9.00 / HR/9: 1.00 / BB/9: 3.50 / K/9: 6.50 / KWH: 1.00)

Jamie Arnold   Throws R   Age 26

YEAR	TEAM	LGE	IP	H	ER	HR	BB	K	ERA	W	L	H/9	HR/9	BB/9	K/9	KWH	PERA
1997	Durham	Car	22.3	32	26	2	16	15	10.48	0	2	12.90	0.81	6.45	6.04	0.33	8.06
1998	Greenvil	Sou	78.0	107	54	12	48	37	6.23	3	6	12.35	1.38	5.54	4.27	0.20	7.85
1998	Richmond	Int	20.3	32	22	1	18	9	9.74	0	2	14.16	0.44	7.97	3.98	0.11	8.85
1999	Albuquer	PCL	18.7	28	13	1	9	10	6.27	1	1	13.50	0.48	4.34	4.82	0.30	6.75
1999	LosAngls	NL	68.3	81	47	5	33	25	6.19	3	5	10.67	0.66	4.35	3.29	0.17	5.40

Arnold is decidedly a non-prospect, a six-year free agent who landed with the Albuquerque Dukes in April. When the Dodger bullpen imploded they had no choice but to turn to him. At best, he's an 11th man who gets ground balls and can spot start and throw mop-up innings. He has a good change-up; unfortunately, it's his fastball. That change-up, and the rest of his pitches, were pounded in the Arizona Fall League.

Pedro Borbon   Throws L   Age 32

YEAR	TEAM	LGE	IP	H	ER	HR	BB	K	ERA	W	L	H/9	HR/9	BB/9	K/9	KWH	PERA
1998	Greenvil	Sou	17.3	25	16	2	15	8	8.31	0	2	12.98	1.04	7.79	4.15	0.13	8.83
1998	Richmond	Int	23.3	31	18	1	9	13	6.94	1	2	11.96	0.39	3.47	5.01	0.45	5.40
1999	LosAngls	NL	50.3	39	22	5	28	32	3.93	3	3	6.97	0.89	5.01	5.72	0.70	3.93

Borbon completed his long and arduous comeback by being a stellar left-handed reliever for about three months. He tired in July, which is understandable: his 39 appearances in the first half matched his total for 1997 and 1998 combined. Another year removed from surgery, he'll be among the better left-handed relievers in baseball. Borbon was dealt to Toronto in the Green trade.

Kevin Brown   Throws R   Age 35

YEAR	TEAM	LGE	IP	H	ER	HR	BB	K	ERA	W	L	H/9	HR/9	BB/9	K/9	KWH	PERA
1997	Florida	NL	235.3	218	75	10	69	190	2.87	18	8	8.34	0.38	2.64	7.27	1.79	3.21
1998	San Dieg	NL	249.3	240	83	9	51	241	3.00	19	9	8.66	0.32	1.84	8.70	3.55	3.07
1999	LosAngls	NL	251.0	207	92	17	57	213	3.30	18	10	7.42	0.61	2.04	7.64	2.87	2.76

The perception among Los Angeles fans and media that Brown was a disappointment stemmed from the confluence of his worst stretch of the season with that of the team in June. He was exactly the pitcher the Dodgers paid $573 billion for, and he wasn't at all culpable in the team's sorry season. Brown threw 120 pitches just three times, a good sign for a team committed to him for six more years. Nevertheless, it's just a matter of time before he gets hurt: he's 35 and has thrown a ton of innings since the strike.

Robinson Checo — Throws R — Age 28

YEAR	TEAM	LGE	IP	H	ER	HR	BB	K	ERA	W	L	H/9	HR/9	BB/9	K/9	KWH	PERA
1997	Sarasota	Fla	48.7	76	54	10	42	43	9.99	1	4	14.05	1.85	7.77	7.95	0.43	10.73
1997	Pawtuckt	Int	53.3	48	24	8	17	45	4.05	3	3	8.10	1.35	2.87	7.59	1.85	4.05
1997	Boston	AL	13.7	11	4	0	3	14	2.63	1	1	7.24	0.00	1.98	9.22	4.44	1.98
1998	Pawtuckt	Int	51.7	52	31	8	29	39	5.40	2	4	9.06	1.39	5.05	6.79	0.75	5.57
1999	LosAngls	NL	15.3	24	18	5	13	11	10.57	0	2	14.09	2.93	7.63	6.46	0.29	12.33
1999	Albuquer	PCL	76.0	69	38	13	47	78	4.50	4	4	8.17	1.54	5.57	9.24	1.40	5.45

Checo has seen more American cities than Charles Kuralt, all in the past three seasons. And while he may have a library of human-interest tales to show for his travels, what he doesn't have is a baseball career. The small right-hander is a bit miscast as a starter, but would be a huge asset to the Dodger bullpen if given a chance there. He has considerable upside, and I think Johnson can make him a contributor this year. If he's still around, that is: Checo was designated for assignment in December.

Randey Dorame — Throws L — Age 21

YEAR	TEAM	LGE	IP	H	ER	HR	BB	K	ERA	W	L	H/9	HR/9	BB/9	K/9	KWH	PERA
1999	San Bern	Cal	143.7	153	60	11	41	117	3.76	9	7	9.58	0.69	2.57	7.33	1.63	4.13
1999	Vero Bch	Fla	10.0	19	11	2	2	4	9.90	0	1	17.10	1.80	1.80	3.60	0.31	9.90

Another Mike Brito Production, Dorame is a very polished young pitcher who spent 1998 in the Mexican League. A-ball pitching prospects come with more disclaimers than the words "$39 each way to anywhere in the country," and Dorame's lack of a plus fastball will become an issue at Double-A. That said, he's a good long-term prospect.

Darren Dreifort — Throws R — Age 28

YEAR	TEAM	LGE	IP	H	ER	HR	BB	K	ERA	W	L	H/9	HR/9	BB/9	K/9	KWH	PERA
1997	LosAngls	NL	61.0	49	23	3	35	58	3.39	4	3	7.23	0.44	5.16	8.56	1.47	3.69
1998	LosAngls	NL	177.3	177	87	13	60	159	4.42	10	10	8.98	0.66	3.05	8.07	1.78	3.96
1999	LosAngls	NL	177.7	176	98	18	73	135	4.96	9	11	8.92	0.91	3.70	6.84	1.06	4.46

His self-perception is keeping him from being a great pitcher. Dreifort wants to start, over the wishes of Johnson, who wants to use him as a reliever. Regular readers know how we feel about this: Dreifort can be a dominant reliever, and since he consistently breaks down at around the 180-inning mark, there's every reason to move him to the bullpen. He is slated to be the Dodgers' #3 starter.

Eric Gagne — Throws R — Age 24

YEAR	TEAM	LGE	IP	H	ER	HR	BB	K	ERA	W	L	H/9	HR/9	BB/9	K/9	KWH	PERA
1998	Vero Bch	Fla	132.7	140	79	18	63	108	5.36	6	9	9.50	1.22	4.27	7.33	0.99	5.36
1999	SanAnton	Tex	154.0	149	68	18	78	143	3.97	10	7	8.71	1.05	4.56	8.36	1.31	4.79
1999	LosAngls	NL	30.0	18	7	3	14	29	2.10	2	1	5.40	0.90	4.20	8.70	2.49	2.70

Gagne is sporting a halo after his excellent September call-up capped a remarkable comeback from elbow surgery in 1997. He was dominant at San Antonio and goes into the spring fighting Carlos Perez for the #4 starter slot. He throws four pitches and will eventually be a middle-of-the-rotation starter. For 2000, he would be well served by a year in middle relief.

Mike Judd — Throws R — Age 25

YEAR	TEAM	LGE	IP	H	ER	HR	BB	K	ERA	W	L	H/9	HR/9	BB/9	K/9	KWH	PERA
1997	Vero Bch	Fla	82.3	82	46	5	52	80	5.03	4	5	8.96	0.55	5.68	8.74	1.12	4.92
1997	SanAnton	Tex	72.3	79	32	1	38	56	3.98	4	4	9.83	0.12	4.73	6.97	0.78	4.60
1998	Albuquer	PCL	95.7	93	54	15	50	67	5.08	5	6	8.75	1.41	4.70	6.30	0.72	5.27
1999	Albuquer	PCL	107.7	132	84	19	55	99	7.02	3	9	11.03	1.59	4.60	8.28	1.01	6.85
1999	LosAngls	NL	27.7	30	16	4	12	21	5.20	1	2	9.76	1.30	3.90	6.83	0.92	5.53

Judd's flyball tendencies work in Albuquerque the way Rany Jazayerli's pickup lines worked with the women of Johns Hopkins. Only one, however, led to lots of home runs. Judd is a good pitcher in a bad environment; he needs to have a good enough spring to win a job with the Dodgers and avoid another summer in New Mexico.

Mike Maddux				**Throws R**				**Age 38**									
YEAR	TEAM	LGE	IP	H	ER	HR	BB	K	ERA	W	L	H/9	HR/9	BB/9	K/9	KWH	PERA
1997	LasVegas	PCL	15.3	22	10	0	9	11	5.87	1	1	12.91	0.00	5.28	6.46	0.46	6.46
1997	Seattle	AL	11.3	19	11	1	8	7	8.74	0	1	15.09	0.79	6.35	5.56	0.24	9.53
1998	Montreal	NL	54.0	54	27	3	16	31	4.50	3	3	9.00	0.50	2.67	5.17	0.83	3.67
1999	Montreal	NL	5.3	8	4	1	3	4	6.75	0	1	13.50	1.69	5.06	6.75	0.50	8.44
1999	LosAngls	NL	54.3	53	19	5	19	40	3.15	4	2	8.78	0.83	3.15	6.63	1.19	4.14

The world tour continues, as Maddux needs only to pitch in Florida this year to hit all four corners of the MLB map in four years. He's a useful middle reliever who gets ground balls and can pitch often: he's more effective on no or short rest than on long rest. I can see him doing this for another year or two.

Onan Masaoka				**Throws L**				**Age 22**									
YEAR	TEAM	LGE	IP	H	ER	HR	BB	K	ERA	W	L	H/9	HR/9	BB/9	K/9	KWH	PERA
1997	Vero Bch	Fla	142.0	137	86	19	72	104	5.45	6	10	8.68	1.20	4.56	6.59	0.82	4.94
1998	SanAnton	Tex	99.0	131	90	11	72	77	8.18	3	8	11.91	1.00	6.55	7.00	0.47	7.55
1999	LosAngls	NL	66.0	56	31	7	45	59	4.23	4	3	7.64	0.95	6.14	8.05	1.03	4.77

Masaoka combined with Borbon to give Johnson two excellent left-handed relievers in the first half. Neither held up past midseason, an unheralded factor in the Dodgers' fade. Masaoka throws hard and is very effective against left-handers. His curveball can get him in trouble and led to a good chunk of the eight home runs he allowed. As a converted starter, he should be better with a year of relief experience under his belt.

Alan Mills				**Throws R**				**Age 33**									
YEAR	TEAM	LGE	IP	H	ER	HR	BB	K	ERA	W	L	H/9	HR/9	BB/9	K/9	KWH	PERA
1997	Baltimor	AL	38.7	41	22	5	33	32	5.12	2	2	9.54	1.16	7.68	7.45	0.57	6.75
1998	Baltimor	AL	76.0	54	30	7	52	57	3.55	5	3	6.39	0.83	6.16	6.75	0.86	3.91
1999	LosAngls	NL	72.0	69	31	9	42	47	3.88	5	3	8.63	1.13	5.25	5.88	0.57	5.12

There's no way Mills is $2 million better than a random hard-throwing Triple-A right-hander who can't find home plate without a Sherpa. He was the first silly Dodger signing in the winter of 1998-99, the first notes of a symphony of questionable decision-making. With two years and $4.3 million left on the deal, he's got job security. Mills pitches up in the zone way too much to have Gary Sheffield and Devon White chasing his mistakes.

Antonio Osuna				**Throws R**				**Age 27**									
YEAR	TEAM	LGE	IP	H	ER	HR	BB	K	ERA	W	L	H/9	HR/9	BB/9	K/9	KWH	PERA
1997	Albuquer	PCL	14.0	8	2	0	4	22	1.29	2	0	5.14	0.00	2.57	14.14	11.30	1.29
1997	LosAngls	NL	60.0	50	17	7	19	63	2.55	5	2	7.50	1.05	2.85	9.45	3.12	3.45
1998	LosAngls	NL	63.3	53	27	9	33	68	3.84	4	3	7.53	1.28	4.69	9.66	1.98	4.41
1999	LosAngls	NL	4.7	4	4	0	3	5	7.71	0	1	7.71	0.00	5.79	9.64	1.56	3.86
1999	San Bern	Cal	17.0	24	8	0	8	17	4.24	1	1	12.71	0.00	4.24	9.00	1.12	5.82

To his credit, he tried like hell to pitch through an elbow injury, enduring a couple of disabled-list stints and, as you can see, a lot of California League time before undergoing Tommy John surgery in July. He probably came back too quickly from the minor surgery he had in the fall of 1998. Now, he'll miss 2000 and hope his fastball returns in 2001.

Chan Ho Park				**Throws R**				**Age 27**									
YEAR	TEAM	LGE	IP	H	ER	HR	BB	K	ERA	W	L	H/9	HR/9	BB/9	K/9	KWH	PERA
1997	LosAngls	NL	186.0	161	87	25	73	153	4.21	11	10	7.79	1.21	3.53	7.40	1.49	4.06
1998	LosAngls	NL	216.0	208	104	16	101	181	4.33	12	12	8.67	0.67	4.21	7.54	1.17	4.25
1999	LosAngls	NL	193.0	208	111	28	96	168	5.18	9	12	9.70	1.31	4.48	7.83	1.06	5.64

It's not every day a pitcher gets the chance to give up 11 runs in an inning. The performance better known as "Fernando Tatis' two-grand-slam-inning" was more notable, to me, for the fact that Park was still pitching after giving up seven runs and loading the bases. In Davey we . . . oh, never mind. . . . Park eventually regained control of his curve and pitched much better in the second half. He should revert to his 1997-98 form in 2000.

Carlos Perez — Throws Tantrums — Age 29

YEAR	TEAM	LGE	IP	H	ER	HR	BB	K	ERA	W	L	H/9	HR/9	BB/9	K/9	KWH	PERA
1997	Montreal	NL	206.7	209	107	21	50	103	4.66	11	12	9.10	0.91	2.18	4.49	0.76	3.96
1998	Montreal	NL	156.7	192	88	13	35	77	5.06	8	9	11.03	0.75	2.01	4.42	0.66	4.83
1998	LosAngls	NL	75.7	71	31	9	31	43	3.69	5	3	8.44	1.07	3.69	5.11	0.63	4.28
1999	LosAngls	NL	89.0	115	72	21	38	39	7.28	3	7	11.63	2.12	3.84	3.94	0.26	7.58
1999	Albuquer	PCL	36.7	47	27	5	12	11	6.63	1	3	11.54	1.23	2.95	2.70	0.16	6.14

Perez hit much better than he pitched, with an .826 OPS and a one-round knockout of a water cooler before he was demoted. He's probably better than his 1999 performance, just not by much. He's always pitched well against left-handed hitters: given the Dodger rotation depth, it might not be a bad idea to make him the second left-hander behind Masaoka, at least at the start of the year.

Luke Prokopec — Throws R — Age 22

YEAR	TEAM	LGE	IP	H	ER	HR	BB	K	ERA	W	L	H/9	HR/9	BB/9	K/9	KWH	PERA
1997	Savannah	SAL	37.3	52	30	10	17	30	7.23	1	3	12.54	2.41	4.10	7.23	0.76	8.68
1998	San Bern	Cal	103.3	122	52	13	41	101	4.53	5	6	10.63	1.13	3.57	8.80	1.52	5.66
1998	SanAnton	Tex	24.0	18	6	0	15	20	2.25	2	1	6.75	0.00	5.63	7.50	1.11	3.00
1999	SanAnton	Tex	144.0	203	135	19	55	102	8.44	4	12	12.69	1.19	3.44	6.38	0.70	6.94

Prokopec is a converted catcher who cooks with gas. At Double-A, however, it helps to have skills with electric stoves and barbecue grills as well. Tortured metaphors aside, Prokopec struggled for the first time since his conversion. Long-term, he's going to fight the prejudice against short right-handers and may be best-suited to a short reliever role. The Dodgers exposed him to the Rule 5 draft but didn't lose him.

Johnny Ruffin — Throws R — Age 28

YEAR	TEAM	LGE	IP	H	ER	HR	BB	K	ERA	W	L	H/9	HR/9	BB/9	K/9	KWH	PERA
1997	Pawtuckt	Int	13.7	6	8	0	17	13	5.27	1	1	3.95	0.00	11.20	8.56	1.24	3.95
1998	Louisvil	Int	57.3	44	29	4	53	48	4.55	3	3	6.91	0.63	8.32	7.53	0.74	4.87
1998	Norfolk	Int	38.3	32	15	2	22	34	3.52	2	2	7.51	0.47	5.17	7.98	1.23	3.76
1999	Albuquer	PCL	52.3	41	20	6	31	52	3.44	4	2	7.05	1.03	5.33	8.94	1.59	4.13

I think I speak for everyone when I say, "He's just 28!?" It seems like forever since he had a dominant year setting up for the post-Nasty Boys Reds. Since then, he's been to the Far East and back and is much the same pitcher he was during his great 1994. Ruffin just needs an opportunity and he'll have another year just like that one.

Jeff Shaw — Throws R — Age 33

YEAR	TEAM	LGE	IP	H	ER	HR	BB	K	ERA	W	L	H/9	HR/9	BB/9	K/9	KWH	PERA
1997	Cincnnti	NL	95.3	78	23	7	12	69	2.17	9	2	7.36	0.66	1.13	6.51	3.80	2.45
1998	Cincnnti	NL	49.3	42	11	2	12	28	2.01	4	1	7.66	0.36	2.19	5.11	1.16	2.74
1998	LosAngls	NL	34.7	36	11	7	7	24	2.86	3	1	9.35	1.82	1.82	6.23	1.71	4.93
1999	LosAngls	NL	67.3	64	23	5	14	41	3.07	5	2	8.55	0.67	1.87	5.48	1.40	3.34

His decline leveled off as Johnson—and the Dodgers ineffectual play—limited his workload. He was used like a 1990s closer for the first time, with the fewest innings per appearance of his career. He's not going to fall off a cliff, so he's going to be the Dodger closer and pick up a bunch of saves. Make no mistake, though: he's fading.

Ismael Valdes — Throws R — Age 26

YEAR	TEAM	LGE	IP	H	ER	HR	BB	K	ERA	W	L	H/9	HR/9	BB/9	K/9	KWH	PERA
1997	LosAngls	NL	190.0	184	75	17	49	129	3.55	13	8	8.72	0.81	2.32	6.11	1.38	3.69
1998	LosAngls	NL	170.7	178	85	18	69	115	4.48	10	9	9.39	0.95	3.64	6.06	0.80	4.75
1999	LosAngls	NL	201.7	212	90	29	55	138	4.02	12	10	9.46	1.29	2.45	6.16	1.22	4.64

The Dodgers have no idea how good he is, eternally focused on his unspectacular won/lost record and a reputation as a head case. Admittedly, he hasn't been the pitcher many analysts—OK, we—thought he would be. He was given to the Cubs as a reward for the Snugglies taking Eric Young off the Dodgers' hands. Wrigley isn't the best place for Valdes; despite that, he's still capable of being a #1 starter.

Jeff Williams   Throws L   Age 28

YEAR	TEAM	LGE	IP	H	ER	HR	BB	K	ERA	W	L	H/9	HR/9	BB/9	K/9	KWH	PERA
1997	San Bern	Cal	102.0	138	74	8	45	44	6.53	4	7	12.18	0.71	3.97	3.88	0.23	6.26
1997	SanAnton	Tex	24.7	37	22	3	9	11	8.03	1	2	13.50	1.09	3.28	4.01	0.27	7.30
1998	SanAnton	Tex	36.7	54	25	3	16	26	6.14	1	3	13.25	0.74	3.93	6.38	0.58	6.87
1998	Albuquer	PCL	120.7	160	82	13	59	77	6.12	5	8	11.93	0.97	4.40	5.74	0.47	6.56
1999	Albuquer	PCL	121.3	153	75	12	56	68	5.56	5	8	11.35	0.89	4.15	5.04	0.40	6.01

Williams is an Australian left-hander who has only been a professional for three seasons. The organization likes him, and he pitched well enough in a cup of coffee in September and in the AFL to stay in the Dodgers' plans. Johnson needs a second left-hander in the pen, and the team also has two rotation spots up for grabs, so I think Williams will be on the team in 2000.

Support-Neutral Records				LOS ANGELES DODGERS						Park Effect: -12.9%		
PITCHER	GS	IP	R	SNW	SNL	SNPCT	W	L	RA	APW	SNVA	SNWAR
Jamie Arnold	3	15.3	12	1.0	1.3	.422	1	0	7.04	-0.38	-0.18	-0.01
Kevin Brown	35	252.3	99	17.7	9.5	.651	18	9	3.53	3.31	3.84	6.14
Robinson Checo	2	5.3	5	0.4	0.8	.325	1	1	8.44	-0.21	-0.19	-0.12
Darren Dreifort	29	177.0	105	9.0	11.1	.446	13	13	5.34	-1.14	-1.01	0.43
Eric Gagne	5	30.0	8	2.4	0.9	.716	1	1	2.40	0.76	0.67	0.96
Mike Judd	4	23.7	13	1.1	1.5	.414	3	1	4.94	-0.05	-0.22	-0.03
Chan Ho Park	33	194.3	120	10.4	12.3	.458	13	11	5.56	-1.71	-1.09	0.76
Carlos Perez	16	85.3	76	3.2	8.3	.282	2	10	8.02	-3.02	-2.44	-1.64
Ismael Valdes	32	203.3	97	12.2	10.3	.542	9	14	4.29	0.99	0.78	2.63
Jeff Williams	3	15.7	9	0.7	1.1	.369	2	0	5.17	-0.07	-0.20	-0.10
TOTALS	162	1002.3	544	58.0	57.2	.503	63	60	4.88	-1.53	-0.05	9.04

You really can't fault the Dodgers for expecting their rotation to be better than this in 1999. They spent gazillions to get Kevin Brown and figured that he, Ismael Valdes, Chan Ho Park and Carlos Perez would perform at their established levels. Then no matter what wild-card Darren Dreifort gave them, they'd have a nice year from their starters. It sounded good, but only Brown came through. If Valdes, Park and Perez had performed at the levels they had established in 1997–98, the Dodgers' rotation would have been worth about five games above average according to SNVA, good enough to be the fifth-best rotation in the majors. Instead it ended up with a 0 SNVA, 11th in the majors.

Pitcher Abuse Points

PITCHER	AGE	GS	PAP	PAP/S	WKLD	MAX	1-90	91-100	101-110	111-120	121-130	131-140	141+
Jamie Arnold	25	3	1	0.3	0.7	101	2	0	1	0	0	0	0
Kevin Brown	34	35	444	12.7	12.7	126	1	4	12	15	3	0	0
Robinson Checo	27	2	0	0.0	0.0	82	2	0	0	0	0	0	0
Darren Dreifort	27	29	57	2.0	3.6	117	7	13	8	1	0	0	0
Eric Gagne	23	5	18	3.6	9.0	109	0	2	3	0	0	0	0
Mike Judd	24	4	0	0.0	0.0	96	3	1	0	0	0	0	0
Chan Ho Park	26	33	163	4.9	9.9	120	9	6	11	7	0	0	0
Carlos Perez	28	16	52	3.3	5.4	122	9	3	3	0	1	0	0
Ismael Valdes	25	32	336	10.5	22.8	125	8	6	6	8	4	0	0
Jeff Williams	27	3	0	0.0	0.0	85	3	0	0	0	0	0	0
LOS ANGELES		162	1071	6.6	10.7	126	44	35	44	31	8	0	0
Ranking (NL)				11	10								

Davey Johnson tasted failure for the first time last year, but he deserves credit for doing his best to counteract years of damage to Dodgers' starters done by Tommy Lasorda and his disciples. After finishing second in the NL in Workload in 1998, the Dodgers plunged to 10th. Every starter benefited from Johnson's mercy: Chan Ho Park (31.9 Workload in 1998, 9.9 in 1999), Darren Dreifort (16.7 to 3.6), Ismael Valdes (26.4 to 22.8) and even Carlos Perez (25.0 to 5.4). Of course, except for Valdes all of these guys were lousy last year, but that's just the point: the Dodgers had been overworking their starters for years, and the piper finally came to collect in 1999. . . . Kevin Brown, who was as good as advertised, still had his Workload cut from 14.6 to 12.7, throwing more than 120 pitches just three times. With six more years and $90 million left on Brown's contract, Johnson did the sensible thing. It may be too late to restore their established starters to complete health, but Dodgers' fans can feel good knowing that Eric Gagne's surgically-repaired arm is in good hands.

Milwaukee Brewers

It was one of the worst years in the history of Milwaukee baseball—much worse than the Paul Householder years, and almost as bad as when the Braves left town. But while the team sucked for the seventh year in a row, and the crane collapse at Miller Park was tragic and avoidable, the most important thing about what happened to the Brewers in 1999 is that for the first time since 1992, *something happened.*

Actually, a lot of things happened, a chain of events that may have finally put the Brewers on the road to relevance. Now, instead of continuing to live out life as baseball's happy herd-animal franchise, the Brewers may finally be in a situation so desperate that they have no choice but to help themselves. It's been a long time coming.

To discuss the Brewers' immediate future, we'll have to talk about how it very nearly never happened. The season began with the usual suspects doing the usual things. With a sense of solemn tedium honed by years of practice, General Manager Sal Bando and Manager Phil Garner talked about the futility of it all. They railed about competing with franchises that had more money, the difficulty of keeping players in Milwaukee or drafting talented players because of their financial expectations and evil agents. You've heard the whine before; for the last decade, it's been served up at every press conference and in every public statement like a four-buck bottle of Chardonnay.

So the Brewers sat still, complaining about the world that had grown up around them. We all have family like that, and we probably all indulge in it one way or another ourselves. It's human nature to invent the "good old days," a time period when we thought everything was going our way. For the Brewers, 1982 looms large. But in a competitive baseball world, this attitude reflected poorly on an organization that had run out of ideas right around the time everyone noticed that Harry Dalton's highly-touted farm system wasn't cranking out as much talent as people had expected.

Dalton's removal had led to the hiring of Bando and Garner in 1992, but things basically remained the same.

Brewers Prospectus

1999 record: 74-87; Fifth place, NL Central

Pythagorean W/L: 75-87

Runs scored: 815 (9th in NL)

Runs allowed: 886 (14th in NL)

Team EQA: .263 (7th in NL)

1999 team age: 28.0 (4th-youngest in NL)

1999 park: County Stadium; neutral park, increased run scoring by less than 1%.

1999: A difficult year made worse by an off-field tragedy.

2000: Another swan song for County Stadium should see another under-.500 team.

Bando had been a special assistant to Dalton from the moment he retired as a player after 1981, and once upon a time was thought of as the team's next manager. His loyalty to the organization, to the people in it and to the Selig family in particular, is unquestioned. Unfortunately, handing the team over to a trusted family retainer put the organization in an unenviable position. The only way the Brewers would appreciate the need for real change would be to experience an extended, multi-year train wreck.

If you look back at the Brewers of 1991, there's a lot of talent on the roster: Gary Sheffield, Greg Vaughn, Darryl Hamilton, Bill Spiers, B.J. Surhoff. With Chris Bosio, Bill Wegman and Jaime Navarro, they had three-fifths of a good major-league rotation. Paul Molitor was still going strong, and the farm system had guys like Cal Eldred, John Jaha, Dave Nilsson and Troy O'Leary. But after 1992's flirtation with competitiveness, Bando's Brewers started their slow, steady collapse.

The first jump off the tracks was the decision to trade Gary Sheffield. Rather than start over with the organization's most talented prospect, Bando decided to cut bait before the Brewers had played a game in 1992. It might have made sense if the deal had given the Brew Crew a clean shot at winning that year, but it didn't bring them the ace starter they needed, or even a power hitter to replace Sheffield. It brought them a fifth starter (Ricky Bones) and two borderline prospects who were two years away (Matt Mieske and Jose Valentin). The Brewers went down to the season's last weekend and fell four games short, then treated the season as a success despite not winning and no longer having their best prospect.

The second poor decision was Phil Garner's sacrifice of Cal Eldred. Six straight losing seasons have taken the spring out of his step, but it seems quaint to remember Garner in his early days, brash and arrogant, aggressive, riding into town on attitude. He offered pre-packaged wisdom on the subjects of intensity, sacrifice, hard work and getting back to the good old days when pitchers finished what they started.

It's hard to remember how good Eldred was, but when he came up he was a better pitcher than Alex Fernandez. There was every reason to expect Eldred would grow into a staff ace, the kind of guy who makes the job of building a solid rotation seem almost easy. But Garner couldn't wait for it to happen. Everyone rushed to call him a genius in 1992, so he had to keep putting up a good front. Eldred's career was sacrificed in the seventh and eighth innings of his starts during meaningless 1993 and 1994 seasons, where the only goal was satisfying Phil Garner's sense of self-worth.

It isn't every day that an organization throws away the careers of its best hitting and pitching prospects, but the coup de grace came from player development. Whereas Dalton's prospects had been touted, fallen short of expectations and still ended up as useful major-league players, Bando's drafts have been appalling. First-round picks were blown on Kenny Felder or Chad Green or Antone Williamson, and Brewer scouting became the butt of jokes in the industry. While their last three drafts have been slightly better, they've hardly given the organization the kind of talent base it needs. Recent decisions to resume scouting internationally and to build an academy in the Dominican Republic were years overdue.

A fourth problem was Bando's failure to understand the relationship between value and cost. Bando made many mistakes in deciding who should get long-term contracts and who shouldn't, while operating under the fear that nobody would sign with the Brewers of his own free will. Cal Eldred's multi-year deal after elbow and shoulder injuries was irresponsible, but saying so implies that Bando did it thoughtlessly. On the contrary. With the injuries and the already wasted potential staring him in the face, with all of the information at his disposal, he gave the contract to Eldred anyway.

The worry that no premier free agent would choose to come to Milwaukee led to the trade for Marquis Grissom, which did nothing for the Brewers on the field. It did give the Indians' John Hart salary and roster space to pick up Kenny Lofton, while getting Cleveland out from under a multi-year contract it shouldn't have given a past-peak Grissom in the first place. Nobody should say Sal Bando isn't a good sport.

Bando had contributed to a disaster, but not even the repeated wipeouts were enough to create a push for change. The canned bleating about small-market victimhood and mediocrity as the natural by-product of an old stadium were enough to keep anyone from appearing responsible. As long as the Brewers mucked around .500 for a bit, and nothing went terribly wrong, everyone was probably safe. It wouldn't be progress, but it would be profitable. After 1998's league-jumping act and County Stadium's farewell season, everyone could look forward to a 2000 that would have another novelty,

Miller Park. A good 1999 going into Miller Park would preserve the management team into the foreseeable future, and create the sort of warm fuzzies that make money and put fannies in the seats for a little while.

The Brewers nearly accomplished these limited goals. Going into the All-Star break, the offense was clicking thanks to a healthy Dave Nilsson and the breakthroughs of Ron Belliard and Geoff Jenkins. Despite a bad rotation reflecting Bando's lousy taste in retreads, the team was 42-44, and both Nilsson and Jeromy Burnitz were going to the All-Star game. There was reason to hope things were looking up, especially with the rest of July's schedule looking pretty soft. Burnitz even finished second in the home-run derby at the All-Star Game. Bando was only a couple of months away from sailing into the promised land of Miller Park, where everyone would be safe to make money and mark time.

The day after the All-Star break changed everything. A huge crane, operating in high winds on soft ground, collapsed on top of Miller Park, killing three men. Everyone recognized that the 2000 opening for the new park was in danger. With the future falling apart, the present started going to pieces as well. Two days after the crane collapse, Jose Rosado broke Burnitz's hand with a pitch, leaving the team without its cleanup hitter. Even so, it managed to look lively for another week, pushing up to 47-47 before hitting the road. The Brewers might still have salvaged a decent season.

Perhaps hoping to compensate for a weakened lineup, they decided to patch the rotation by calling up Kyle Peterson and giving Jim Abbott his release. Their first road series was against the pathetic Marlins, but not only were the Brewers swept, their best starter, Steve Woodard, suffered a fractured left wrist on a play at the plate in the last game. Yet Bando and Garner were so desperate to keep the present alive—and so desperate for pitching—that they asked Woodard to make three more starts. He could barely hold a bat, couldn't rub up the ball and had to take short walks around the mound between pitches while waiting for the pain to subside. The payoff was 13 runs in 16 innings over his next three starts.

Unlucky? Sure, the crane accident was a misfortune, but it shouldn't have impacted the team on the field. Having already lost their best hitter, it looked like they couldn't accept losing their best pitcher, and with him any meaning their season had. After seven straight losing seasons, they couldn't let go, even if the long-term interest of the team was to let Woodard heal. But asking him to pitch couldn't fend off a 5-13 run, and that was enough for Wendy Selig-Prieb to pull the plug on August 12. Bando and Garner were gone, and the mirage of a brilliant future disappeared. It was the end of the road for Bando and the tyranny of ex-Brewer cronyism that stretches all the way back to 1978 and the beginnings of

Harry Dalton's reign. Almost as an afterthought, the Brewers finally put Steve Woodard on the disabled list two days after firing Garner and Bando.

Was losing Burnitz and effectively losing Woodard on the heels of the accident enough to get Bando and Garner fired? Six straight years of losing hadn't been, so why should a seventh have been the last straw? The difference was that expectations were higher in 1999 than before. So much had gone right, and it was supposed to culminate in Miller Park in 2000. The fight for a new stadium stretched back more than a decade, and the Seligs and the Brewers had won. To have that victory marred by an accident, and to see that accident followed by the collapse of the team on the field, was too bitter to accept.

The good news is that for the first time since they brought in Harry Dalton and George Bamberger more than 20 years ago, the Brewers will rebuild. Whatever their misfor-

tunes, replacing Bando was long overdue, and if it took a strange combination of events to finally force him out, then better to move on and take progress in whatever shape it comes. New GM Dean Taylor, assistant GM Dave Wilder and Player Development Director Greg Riddoch may not be Branch Rickey and Whitey Herzog riding to the rescue, but they did hold the Brewers' first organizational meetings in almost a decade. Taylor hasn't been shy about firing or reassigning almost all of the old front-office crew or minor-league coaches and managers.

Of course, while I'm glad to see Davey Lopes finally get a shot as a manager, he does have some unfortunate similarities to Garner, in that both men had no managing experience coming in, and both started off by talking about fundamentals and pride. The second last bittersweet year in County Stadium won't be significantly better than the first, but there's almost nowhere to go but up.

HITTERS (Averages: BA: .270 / OBP: .340 / SLG: .430 / EQA: .260)

Jeff Alfano   C   Bats R Age 23

YEAR	TEAM	LGE	AB	H	DB	TP	HR	BB/SO	R	RBI	SB	CS	OUT	BA	OBP	SLG	EQA	EQR	DEFENSE	
1997	Ogden	Pio	170	43	9	2	4	11/37	19	15	3	1	128	.253	.306	.400	.239	18		
1997	Beloit	Mid	123	26	5	1	2	6/33	11	13	1	0	97	.211	.279	.317	.202	9		
1998	Stockton	Cal	397	89	17	1	5	28/94	31	34	3	2	310	.224	.283	.310	.200	28	107-C 96	
1999	Huntsvil	Sou	249	58	9	0	6	28/67	16	27	2	1	192	.233	.321	.341	.229	24	72-C 96	
2000	*Milwauke*	*NL*	*255*	*61*	*11*	*1*	*5*	*23/66*	*29*	*27*	*4*	*1*	*195*	*.239*	*.302*	*.349*	*.221*	*22*		

Alfano is your basic jackass. He's been suspended for the first 30 days of the 2000 season after tipping pitches against Orlando in a game with playoff implications—a loss would have kept Orlando out of the playoffs and from winning the Southern League. While he's supposed to be a good athlete and a strong-armed catcher, he's driven his managers ape for his lack of hustle, and it isn't as if he's hitting. He's not a prospect, just a legacy of a bad player-development program.

Alex Andreopoulos   C   Bats L Age 27

YEAR	TEAM	LGE	AB	H	DB	TP	HR	BB/SO	R	RBI	SB	CS	OUT	BA	OBP	SLG	EQA	EQR	DEFENSE
1998	El Paso	Tex	367	83	20	1	6	37/39	43	54	1	1	285	.226	.307	.335	.220	32	86-C 91
1999	Louisvil	Int	201	46	3	0	5	19/23	14	25	1	0	155	.229	.301	.318	.213	16	59-C 98
2000	*Milwauke*	*NL*	*176*	*42*	*3*	*0*	*4*	*23/29*	*20*	*20*	*0*	*0*	*134*	*.239*	*.327*	*.324*	*.224*	*16*	

He bats left-handed, he catches and Dave Nilsson is leaving town. Using the logic that let the dwarf in *High Plains Drifter* wear a badge after the sheriff was gone, I suppose Andreopoulos could win a share of the catcher's job. He was jerked around by the Brewers last year: they grudgingly gave him permission to play for Canada in the Pan Am Games, then promoted Robinson Cancel to the big club over him when he chose to stay.

Brian Banks   UT   Bats B Age 29

YEAR	TEAM	LGE	AB	H	DB	TP	HR	BB/SO	R	RBI	SB	CS	OUT	BA	OBP	SLG	EQA	EQR	DEFENSE	
1997	Tucson	PCL	369	89	21	2	6	25/93	35	41	4	2	282	.241	.291	.358	.219	32	74-OF 95	
1998	Louisvil	Int	302	75	15	2	15	41/80	44	50	8	2	229	.248	.341	.460	.270	43	24-OF 95	
1999	Milwauke	NL	220	53	6	1	5	22/58	31	21	5	1	168	.241	.310	.345	.228	21	26-1B 105	25-C 79
2000	*Milwauke*	*NL*	*269*	*67*	*10*	*2*	*9*	*33/71*	*39*	*38*	*6*	*1*	*203*	*.249*	*.331*	*.401*	*.250*	*32*		

With 11-man pitching staffs, if you're a good offensive team or space is tight because you're carrying three platoons, having a multi-talented spare part can be a good thing. The danger is in letting Banks play regularly if everyone else gets hurt, because he doesn't hit enough to play first base or the outfield, and he can't really catch.

Kevin Barker   1B   Bats L   Age 24

YEAR	TEAM	LGE	AB	H	DB	TP	HR	BB/SO	R	RBI	SB	CS	OUT	BA	OBP	SLG	EQA	EQR	DEFENSE
1997	Stockton	Cal	271	75	20	3	11	18/59	37	35	2	1	197	.277	.322	.494	.267	36	59-1B 86
1997	El Paso	Tex	231	51	12	3	8	22/45	25	41	2	2	182	.221	.293	.403	.232	24	46-1B 94
1998	El Paso	Tex	83	21	3	0	4	2/23	9	10	1	1	63	.253	.282	.434	.234	8	17-1B 119
1998	Louisvil	Int	465	122	27	3	20	28/99	52	83	1	3	347	.262	.308	.462	.252	55	110-1B 98
1999	Louisvil	Int	440	115	24	4	20	51/94	73	71	1	2	327	.261	.343	.470	.270	62	119-1B 107
1999	Milwauke	NL	117	33	2	0	3	8/19	12	21	1	0	84	.282	.328	.376	.241	12	27-1B 104
2000	Milwauke	NL	536	147	28	3	27	55/114	80	100	3	2	391	.274	.342	.489	.273	76	

Not the next Billy Joe Robidoux, Barker will be the first baseman the Brewers haven't had since John Jaha started falling apart after 1996. He should be the team's best first baseman since Cecil Cooper's heyday. Playing every day in the minors made it clear he needs to be platooned, but against right-handed pitching he'll eventually slug in the high .500s. He's not an outlandish Rookie of the Year candidate if he's batting behind Belliard and Burnitz.

Ron Belliard   2B   Bats R   Age 25

YEAR	TEAM	LGE	AB	H	DB	TP	HR	BB/SO	R	RBI	SB	CS	OUT	BA	OBP	SLG	EQA	EQR	DEFENSE
1997	Tucson	PCL	433	107	31	2	3	49/71	59	40	7	5	331	.247	.337	.349	.238	46	113-2B 94
1998	Louisvil	Int	508	154	35	5	13	59/78	96	64	21	9	363	.303	.383	.469	.288	81	128-2B 103
1999	Louisvil	Int	108	24	3	0	1	12/13	10	7	8	3	87	.222	.305	.278	.211	9	26-2B 91
1999	Milwauke	NL	457	133	30	4	7	58/58	56	53	3	5	329	.291	.371	.420	.269	61	113-2B 107
2000	Milwauke	NL	517	145	31	4	10	65/72	88	74	12	6	378	.280	.361	.414	.264	68	

Belliard is a significantly better player than Fernando Vina; what you can expect even if he doesn't develop isn't much worse than Vina's All-Star season, and it's a lot more likely that he's going to improve over the next three or four years. He's a smart player, in that he follows pitches and pitchers and positions himself accordingly. While he could improve his play on the deuce or covering for steals, he's an acrobatic and talented fielder. His reputation as a clutch hitter keeps him out of the lead-off slot, but he'd do the most good there. The trade of Fernando Vina cements Belliard's status as the Brewer second baseman.

Sean Berry   1B/3B   Bats R   Age 34

YEAR	TEAM	LGE	AB	H	DB	TP	HR	BB/SO	R	RBI	SB	CS	OUT	BA	OBP	SLG	EQA	EQR	DEFENSE
1997	Houston	NL	305	80	24	1	9	25/52	37	44	0	5	230	.262	.329	.436	.251	36	66-3B 99
1998	Houston	NL	304	98	19	1	14	30/49	50	54	3	1	207	.322	.397	.530	.307	54	73-3B 95
1999	Milwauke	NL	260	59	10	1	2	14/49	24	22	0	0	201	.227	.275	.296	.190	16	53-1B 94
2000	Milwauke	NL	218	57	5	0	7	21/39	25	30	0	1	162	.261	.326	.381	.238	22	

Berry should have retired after popping a ninth-inning three-run home run on Opening Day, because it was six months of misery after that. He's under contract for 2000, so they need to find a use for him. While he was awful against left-handed pitchers in 1999, he's killed them in the past and might be a good platoon mate for Barker.

Jeromy Burnitz   RF   Bats L   Age 31

YEAR	TEAM	LGE	AB	H	DB	TP	HR	BB/SO	R	RBI	SB	CS	OUT	BA	OBP	SLG	EQA	EQR	DEFENSE
1997	Milwauke	AL	493	139	38	9	26	72/107	82	82	20	13	367	.282	.380	.554	.300	91	150-OF 92
1998	Milwauke	NL	614	164	25	1	41	69/154	92	127	7	5	455	.267	.345	.511	.280	94	159-OF 97
1999	Milwauke	NL	466	123	34	2	31	85/123	82	94	6	3	346	.264	.397	.545	.309	92	124-RF 97
2000	Milwauke	NL	483	126	29	1	30	80/123	90	98	9	5	362	.261	.366	.511	.288	80	

The team's MVP, but was it for hitting well or for knocking out Vina for two months? Burnitz is either the best bad glove in right field, or the worst good one. He throws well and can do the basic things, but he's one of the worst you'll see going back on balls hit over his head. With the Brewers' pitching, that's a problem that comes up a lot. There was a lot of whining that he wasn't being protected and was being pitched around, even though he had his best season despite missing a month to a hand broken by a Jose Rosado pitch.

Robinson Cancel   C   Bats R   Age 24

YEAR	TEAM	LGE	AB	H	DB	TP	HR	BB/SO	R	RBI	SB	CS	OUT	BA	OBP	SLG	EQA	EQR	DEFENSE
1997	Stockton	Cal	214	57	4	0	3	8/39	18	15	5	2	159	.266	.297	.327	.213	17	
1998	El Paso	Tex	153	39	4	0	2	17/35	11	22	1	1	115	.255	.329	.320	.225	14	43-C 102
1999	Huntsvil	Sou	224	51	9	1	4	18/40	27	25	4	3	176	.228	.291	.330	.211	18	48-C 106
1999	Louisvil	Int	116	40	6	0	5	11/28	17	24	4	2	78	.345	.406	.526	.308	21	30-C 113
1999	Milwauke	NL	44	8	1	0	0	2/12	4	4	0	0	36	.182	.236	.205	.123	1	
2000	*Milwauke*	*NL*	*316*	*81*	*7*	*0*	*8*	*30/67*	*39*	*37*	*8*	*2*	*237*	*.256*	*.321*	*.354*	*.233*	*31*	

One hot month at Louisville got some people calling him a prospect, but his career has never had anything in it to indicate he's more than an improvement on Mike Matheny. Of course, playing Mike Matheny is sort of like eating cockroaches as an appetizer just so everything after that will taste better by comparison.

Jeff Cirillo   3B   Bats R   Age 30

YEAR	TEAM	LGE	AB	H	DB	TP	HR	BB/SO	R	RBI	SB	CS	OUT	BA	OBP	SLG	EQA	EQR	DEFENSE
1997	Milwauke	AL	579	169	47	3	10	56/71	73	81	4	3	413	.292	.370	.435	.274	81	147-3B 109
1998	Milwauke	NL	610	199	27	2	16	79/86	98	70	11	5	416	.326	.407	.456	.295	99	148-3B 108
1999	Milwauke	NL	606	195	30	2	15	67/82	91	82	6	4	415	.322	.394	.452	.288	92	150-3B 108
2000	*Colorado*	*NL*	*571*	*205*	*31*	*2*	*18*	*73/76*	*121*	*127*	*7*	*2*	*368*	*.359*	*.432*	*.515*	*.296*	*88*	

There are concerns that he's losing lateral mobility and doesn't guard the line as well as he used to, but he's still outstanding at charging bunts and starting the double play. We've compared him in the past to George Kell, but Buddy Bell works, too. The Brewers traded him to Colorado in an effort to rebuild their rotation, but it's hard to argue they got enough for him. Cirillo is about to become very famous; he can hit for more power than that Wilton indicates.

Lou Collier   IF   Bats R   Age 26

YEAR	TEAM	LGE	AB	H	DB	TP	HR	BB/SO	R	RBI	SB	CS	OUT	BA	OBP	SLG	EQA	EQR	DEFENSE	
1997	Calgary	PCL	378	103	23	3	1	28/48	44	33	8	5	280	.272	.331	.357	.236	38	85-SS 97	26-2B 85
1998	Pittsbrg	NL	337	85	15	6	2	30/68	31	34	2	2	254	.252	.325	.350	.232	33	97-SS 100	
1999	Louisvil	Int	90	29	4	0	4	12/15	17	8	4	2	63	.322	.407	.500	.303	16	17-3B 122	
1999	Milwauke	NL	135	34	5	0	3	13/32	16	20	3	2	103	.252	.318	.356	.230	13	20-SS 91	
2000	*Milwauke*	*NL*	*264*	*71*	*13*	*2*	*3*	*26/50*	*36*	*31*	*6*	*4*	*197*	*.269*	*.334*	*.367*	*.239*	*27*		

He's not a bad platoon-mate for Jose Valentin at shortstop, because he's pasted left-handed pitching for the last two years. He doesn't have the range to play shortstop every day, and there might be something wrong visually, because he seems to have a terribly slow first step.

Brandon Cromer   UT   Bats L   Age 26

YEAR	TEAM	LGE	AB	H	DB	TP	HR	BB/SO	R	RBI	SB	CS	OUT	BA	OBP	SLG	EQA	EQR	DEFENSE	
1997	Carolina	Sou	194	38	10	3	3	22/55	17	10	1	3	159	.196	.278	.325	.200	14	45-SS 89	
1997	Calgary	PCL	222	43	12	1	6	14/47	21	25	2	1	180	.194	.242	.338	.189	14	33-SS 103	27-2B 101
1998	Portland	Eas	396	78	12	5	12	34/95	42	38	2	1	319	.197	.260	.343	.201	29	64-OF 92	38-3B 95
1999	Louisvil	Int	331	62	10	1	18	32/113	34	44	4	0	269	.187	.262	.387	.218	30	44-2B 89	32-3B 105
2000	*Milwauke*	*NL*	*426*	*85*	*15*	*2*	*21*	*44/127*	*44*	*54*	*5*	*1*	*342*	*.200*	*.274*	*.392*	*.221*	*39*		

He's enjoying a bizarre career, in that he went from being a prospect in the Jays' organization to a utilityman (read: he can field all positions poorly) with power. If you had a lineup that did a good job of getting on base and you wanted a pinch-hitter who could give you more than the usual utilityman's single, Cromer could be a fun guy to have around.

Jeff Deardorff   3B   Bats R   Age 21

YEAR	TEAM	LGE	AB	H	DB	TP	HR	BB/SO	R	RBI	SB	CS	OUT	BA	OBP	SLG	EQA	EQR	DEFENSE
1997	Ogden	Pio	220	45	16	1	1	15/88	19	15	1	1	176	.205	.264	.300	.186	13	62-3B 86
1998	Beloit	Mid	333	77	12	1	12	21/129	34	38	1	0	256	.231	.282	.381	.222	30	87-3B 90
1999	Stockton	Cal	435	103	19	1	10	29/146	46	36	1	3	335	.237	.290	.354	.215	36	119-3B 86
2000	*Milwauke*	*NL*	*375*	*99*	*16*	*1*	*11*	*31/135*	*44*	*52*	*1*	*2*	*278*	*.264*	*.320*	*.400*	*.240*	*39*	

(Jeff Deardorff *continued*)

The Brewers have been pushing him up the chain in the hope that he'll start developing, and it hasn't worked. He's working on improving his visual acuity with an outfit called the Visual Fitness Institute. The idea is to produce better hand-eye coordination and pitch recognition, which means he recognizes the need to improve. He's still young enough to have a career.

Chad Green CF Bats B Age 25

YEAR	TEAM	LGE	AB	H	DB	TP	HR	BB/SO	R	RBI	SB	CS	OUT	BA	OBP	SLG	EQA	EQR	DEFENSE
1997	Stockton	Cal	520	120	28	9	2	25/139	56	35	17	7	407	.231	.268	.331	.202	37	127-OF 110
1998	Stockton	Cal	153	43	12	1	0	8/24	17	12	8	3	113	.281	.320	.373	.239	16	31-OF 108
1999	Huntsvil	Sou	425	90	19	2	8	33/123	39	34	13	7	342	.212	.271	.322	.201	31	112-OF 98
2000	Milwauke	NL	360	84	21	4	5	27/98	45	34	17	6	282	.233	.287	.356	.219	32	

Now that Antone Williamson's career has just about petered out, somebody has to be the punch line for Brewers' player development under Sal Bando. Green spent the season suffering through a variety of leg injuries, but unlike 1998's hamstring injury, he could play through them. He's got good range and a strong arm in center field, but hasn't hit left-handed pitchers, so he might grow up to be Jumpy Fox.

Marquis Grissom CF Bats R Age 33

YEAR	TEAM	LGE	AB	H	DB	TP	HR	BB/SO	R	RBI	SB	CS	OUT	BA	OBP	SLG	EQA	EQR	DEFENSE
1997	Clevelnd	AL	560	151	28	7	12	40/86	73	66	22	14	423	.270	.326	.409	.248	64	146-OF 108
1998	Milwauke	NL	546	150	28	1	11	23/76	58	61	14	9	405	.275	.307	.390	.234	53	129-OF 110
1999	Milwauke	NL	605	160	25	1	20	41/108	85	78	21	6	451	.264	.311	.408	.245	67	144-CF 98
2000	Milwauke	NL	504	129	20	1	16	39/84	61	65	15	10	385	.256	.309	.395	.235	51	

All the nice things get said about him: classy, quiet, hard-working, productive. But the 20 home runs and the 83 RBIs aren't production, they're by-products of a mediocre player's getting more than 660 plate appearances. What really hurt the Brewers was that he's losing his range, and, worse yet, managed to gun down only one baserunner in almost 1300 innings. It isn't as though the Brewer pitchers weren't putting lots of people on base or that nobody will challenge him. What hurts the most is that he's signed through 2002.

Bobby Hughes C Bats R Age 29

YEAR	TEAM	LGE	AB	H	DB	TP	HR	BB/SO	R	RBI	SB	CS	OUT	BA	OBP	SLG	EQA	EQR	DEFENSE
1997	Tucson	PCL	283	71	22	1	5	16/52	29	34	0	0	212	.251	.307	.389	.235	28	
1998	Milwauke	NL	220	51	7	2	10	15/53	29	30	1	2	171	.232	.284	.418	.231	22	59-C 93
1999	Milwauke	NL	101	26	1	0	3	4/28	9	7	0	0	75	.257	.286	.356	.214	8	25-C 99
2000	Milwauke	NL	151	36	4	0	6	12/37	14	20	0	0	115	.238	.294	.384	.225	14	

He has frustrated the Brewers with his on-again, off-again approach to conditioning and catching, with his game-calling coming under fire before he had to have surgery to remove bone chips in his elbow. Hughes is technically the leading candidate for the catcher's job, although Henry Blanco and perhaps Cancel will push him.

Buck Jacobsen OF Bats R Age 24

YEAR	TEAM	LGE	AB	H	DB	TP	HR	BB/SO	R	RBI	SB	CS	OUT	BA	OBP	SLG	EQA	EQR	DEFENSE
1997	Ogden	Pio	235	54	14	1	4	27/53	30	26	2	2	183	.230	.313	.349	.227	22	55-OF 88
1998	Beloit	Mid	517	129	20	1	26	66/141	76	78	2	1	389	.250	.340	.443	.263	69	133-OF 92
1999	Huntsvil	Sou	152	28	5	1	3	15/34	16	16	2	1	125	.184	.267	.289	.188	10	20-OF 86
1999	Stockton	Cal	156	32	3	0	5	15/43	14	16	1	1	125	.205	.284	.321	.205	12	
2000	Milwauke	NL	329	74	12	1	13	41/86	41	44	3	1	256	.225	.311	.386	.235	34	

After a good 1998, it wasn't a terrible risk to push Jacobsen up to Double-A to see if he could advance quickly. He's not really a prospect, so if he's going to have a career it's going to be because he moves up rapidly. He fell on his face—and didn't do much better once he was sent down to the California League. The Buckybackers will have to find someone else to rally to.

Geoff Jenkins   LF   Bats L   Age 25

YEAR	TEAM	LGE	AB	H	DB	TP	HR	BB/SO	R	RBI	SB	CS	OUT	BA	OBP	SLG	EQA	EQR	DEFENSE
1997	Tucson	PCL	342	71	21	2	8	26/89	33	42	0	1	272	.208	.269	.351	.205	26	66-OF 94
1998	Louisvil	Int	215	67	11	3	6	11/40	34	45	1	1	149	.312	.358	.474	.277	30	46-OF 99
1998	Milwauke	NL	264	62	11	1	10	19/59	33	29	1	3	205	.235	.292	.398	.227	25	66-OF 92
1999	Milwauke	NL	447	138	43	3	20	30/86	66	76	4	1	310	.309	.363	.553	.298	75	113-LF 111
2000	*Milwauke*	*NL*	*482*	*136*	*33*	*2*	*20*	*43/100*	*73*	*85*	*4*	*2*	*348*	*.282*	*.341*	*.483*	*.271*	*67*	

Jenkins started off low in the order and platooning, and worked his way up and out of the platoon role as he continued to produce. He's one of ex-hitting coach Jim Lefebvre's more outspoken disciples. Lefebvre is willing to try almost anything as far as gadgets and techniques, on the theory that whatever works for somebody is worthwhile. While I can't help but think that a guy who slugged .602 against right-handed pitching in 1999 is going to outperform that projection, keep in mind he isn't that young.

Scott Kirby   1B/3B   Bats R   Age 22

YEAR	TEAM	LGE	AB	H	DB	TP	HR	BB/SO	R	RBI	SB	CS	OUT	BA	OBP	SLG	EQA	EQR	DEFENSE	
1997	Helena	Pio	249	46	8	0	7	36/78	34	25	3	2	205	.185	.297	.301	.208	20	66-3B 79	
1998	Beloit	Mid	369	71	17	1	9	38/112	43	34	2	2	300	.192	.274	.317	.199	27	50-3B 96	19-2B 87
1999	Beloit	Mid	250	65	11	1	14	36/62	39	33	1	1	186	.260	.357	.480	.278	38	67-3B 96	
1999	Stockton	Cal	201	51	13	2	9	19/57	26	27	1	1	151	.254	.331	.473	.265	27	38-1B 79	
2000	*Milwauke*	*NL*	*448*	*115*	*18*	*1*	*21*	*61/126*	*66*	*77*	*3*	*2*	*335*	*.257*	*.346*	*.442*	*.264*	*60*		

He's probably the best hitting prospect in the organization now that Barker and Belliard are up. Kirby was signed as an undrafted free agent in 1996. He addressed concerns that his extreme moodiness would send him spiraling into terrible hitting and fielding funks. Between the two levels, he had a combined season in which he hit .296/.400/.559 with 27 home runs and 72 walks. With Cirillo gone, Kirby could inherit the third-base job in a year or two.

Josh Klimek   3B   Bats L   Age 26

YEAR	TEAM	LGE	AB	H	DB	TP	HR	BB/SO	R	RBI	SB	CS	OUT	BA	OBP	SLG	EQA	EQR	DEFENSE	
1997	Beloit	Mid	450	98	25	3	9	25/64	44	46	1	3	355	.218	.265	.347	.201	32	111-3B 96	
1998	Stockton	Cal	447	101	21	3	7	23/71	41	38	1	1	347	.226	.268	.333	.199	31	80-3B 87	17-SS 91
1999	Huntsvil	Sou	434	89	18	0	12	21/91	33	53	1	1	346	.205	.246	.329	.187	26	98-3B 92	
2000	*Milwauke*	*NL*	*378*	*84*	*15*	*1*	*10*	*27/71*	*33*	*38*	*1*	*1*	*295*	*.222*	*.274*	*.347*	*.204*	*28*		

Klimek shows up on the midseason Double-A All-Star squads as a token Brewer, not a prospect. His limited opportunity is that he could luck into major-league playing time now that Cirillo has been traded—if a mummy's curse kills off anyone else who applies for the job. Including Don Money.

Scott Krause   OF   Bats R   Age 26

YEAR	TEAM	LGE	AB	H	DB	TP	HR	BB/SO	R	RBI	SB	CS	OUT	BA	OBP	SLG	EQA	EQR	DEFENSE
1997	El Paso	Tex	453	128	26	7	12	13/125	62	57	6	2	327	.283	.311	.450	.253	52	115-OF 91
1998	Louisvil	Int	392	106	25	2	21	37/109	59	68	7	3	289	.270	.353	.505	.283	61	90-OF 90
1999	Louisvil	Int	497	119	22	5	11	23/114	42	66	6	4	382	.239	.288	.370	.220	44	119-OF 86
2000	*Milwauke*	*NL*	*404*	*107*	*19*	*3*	*14*	*31/101*	*52*	*60*	*7*	*4*	*301*	*.265*	*.317*	*.431*	*.248*	*46*	

Krause's skills are handy: he's a right fielder with a strong arm, some pro experience at third base and some good pop against left-handers. He's basically a latter-day Mieske—minus the Sheffield trade to propel him to the majors to prove to season-ticket holders that they got something. The problem is that he's got a funky batting stance that some people wish he would ditch.

Mickey Lopez   2B   Bats B   Age 26

YEAR	TEAM	LGE	AB	H	DB	TP	HR	BB/SO	R	RBI	SB	CS	OUT	BA	OBP	SLG	EQA	EQR	DEFENSE
1997	El Paso	Tex	468	111	20	6	2	36/70	51	38	10	5	362	.237	.297	.318	.211	37	130-2B 97
1998	El Paso	Tex	450	94	20	4	1	32/74	51	41	5	4	360	.209	.263	.278	.179	24	115-2B 94
1999	Huntsvil	Sou	317	77	14	4	3	33/54	37	28	13	2	243	.243	.321	.341	.234	32	80-2B 92
1999	Louisvil	Int	180	48	15	1	3	30/27	30	21	6	5	137	.267	.376	.411	.269	26	47-2B 97
2000	*Milwauke*	*NL*	*454*	*110*	*25*	*4*	*4*	*55/75*	*66*	*45*	*17*	*7*	*351*	*.242*	*.324*	*.341*	*.231*	*45*	

(Mickey Lopez *continued*)

He's a nice bunter, runs well, switch-hits, has a good defensive reputation and has that refreshing, minty "new second base-man" smell that always reminds you of Manny Trillo. Lopez is about as good as Vina and another reminder that second base is a loaded position, and you should never pay too much for the ones who aren't named Craig Biggio or Roberto Alomar.

Mark Loretta   IF   Bats R   Age 28

YEAR	TEAM	LGE	AB	H	DB	TP	HR	BB/SO	R	RBI	SB	CS	OUT	BA	OBP	SLG	EQA	EQR	DEFENSE	
1997	Milwauke	AL	417	121	16	6	5	45/58	54	46	5	5	301	.290	.363	.393	.259	51	56-2B 104	32-SS 88
1998	Milwauke	NL	438	139	20	0	10	42/46	55	57	10	7	306	.317	.387	.432	.279	63	43-SS 106	40-1B 87
1999	Milwauke	NL	588	168	33	5	5	44/58	87	63	3	1	421	.286	.347	.384	.251	67	66-SS 96	55-1B 98
2000	Milwauke	NL	505	154	24	3	7	54/54	81	74	7	4	355	.305	.372	.406	.266	65		

Shortstop and first base? Who does he think he is, Ernie Banks? Roy Smalley Jr.? Loretta's range is limited for everyday play at shortstop, but he's a good offensive player for a middle infielder. While this winter's rumor is that it's Jose Valentin who will be traded, thus finally settling the organization's choice between them, Loretta would fetch more because of his versatility. The organization should be scrabbling for whatever prospects they can get who play center field, shortstop or catcher.

Greg Martinez   OF   Bats B   Age 28

YEAR	TEAM	LGE	AB	H	DB	TP	HR	BB/SO	R	RBI	SB	CS	OUT	BA	OBP	SLG	EQA	EQR	DEFENSE
1997	El Paso	Tex	370	81	7	6	1	21/70	40	18	17	4	293	.219	.265	.278	.188	23	95-OF 100
1998	Louisvil	Int	379	88	5	8	3	40/89	46	20	24	5	296	.232	.305	.311	.222	35	104-OF 100
1999	Huntsvil	Sou	99	23	4	1	0	8/15	12	4	3	1	77	.232	.290	.293	.202	7	18-OF 110
1999	Louisvil	Int	419	97	10	3	3	41/55	54	22	29	6	328	.232	.305	.291	.218	36	102-OF 102
2000	Oakland	AL	424	100	12	5	2	43/70	58	34	21	5	329	.236	.306	.302	.218	37	

The first major test for the Taylor regime is going to be how quickly it rids the organization of guys like Martinez or Green or Anthony Iapoce—not to mention the scouts who recommend drafting and developing players like them. In this case, the answer is "pretty quickly," since Martinez signed a minor-league deal with the A's. He might be a defensive replacement with them.

Lyle Mouton   OF   Bats R   Age 31

YEAR	TEAM	LGE	AB	H	DB	TP	HR	BB/SO	R	RBI	SB	CS	OUT	BA	OBP	SLG	EQA	EQR	DEFENSE
1997	ChiSox	AL	243	67	5	0	7	12/63	25	24	4	4	180	.276	.313	.383	.233	23	51-OF 95
1998	Rochestr	Int	138	39	9	1	5	9/34	18	24	1	1	100	.283	.334	.471	.266	18	27-OF 101
1999	Rochestr	Int	163	33	8	1	3	9/34	19	13	2	1	131	.202	.248	.319	.186	10	32-OF 92
1999	Louisvil	Int	301	92	28	2	13	20/74	46	55	12	0	209	.306	.357	.542	.298	51	73-OF 104
2000	Milwauke	NL	245	63	16	1	8	22/59	35	35	6	1	183	.257	.318	.429	.252	29	

The next guy looking to reclaim his career by traipsing through Beertown for a year or so, so that he might eventually get to a team that needs a little bit of right-handed sock. Mouton was picked up for big washout Todd Dunn, and he can still be a solid fifth outfielder.

Dave Nilsson   C/DH   Bats L   Age 30

YEAR	TEAM	LGE	AB	H	DB	TP	HR	BB/SO	R	RBI	SB	CS	OUT	BA	OBP	SLG	EQA	EQR	DEFENSE	
1997	Milwauke	AL	553	157	26	0	23	62/85	68	82	2	3	399	.284	.359	.456	.273	77	67-1B 87	14-OF 104
1998	Milwauke	NL	312	85	15	1	13	32/47	40	57	2	2	229	.272	.342	.452	.265	41	38-1B 84	30-OF 90
1999	Milwauke	NL	342	104	19	1	20	49/63	53	57	1	2	240	.304	.395	.541	.306	62	86-C 92	
2000	Milwauke	NL	360	104	14	0	18	53/62	60	72	1	2	258	.289	.380	.478	.286	56		

He's not the world's worst catcher; he just can't throw. The Brewers deserve a lot of credit for returning him to the position at which he has the most value. A broken thumb ended his year early but should have no impact on his future. He's currently trying to choose between playing in the Olympics for Australia and signing somewhere as a free agent, and it's more likely he'll sign somewhere. The Brewers gave him an out clause in his contract at his request, restructuring his salary to pay him $2 million in each of the next two years, so they lose either way. Nilsson is better off on an AL team with a good defensive right-handed-hitting catcher, so that he can DH once in awhile.

Alex Ochoa   OF   Bats R   Age 28

YEAR	TEAM	LGE	AB	H	DB	TP	HR	BB/SO	R	RBI	SB	CS	OUT	BA	OBP	SLG	EQA	EQR	DEFENSE	
1997	NY Mets	NL	240	59	16	1	3	18/32	31	22	2	4	185	.246	.304	.358	.221	21	66-OF 89	
1998	Minnesot	AL	249	64	14	2	2	9/34	33	24	5	3	188	.257	.286	.353	.214	20	63-OF 88	
1999	Milwauke	NL	277	81	18	3	7	41/43	44	37	5	4	200	.292	.394	.455	.288	44	38-LF 103	25-RF 93
2000	Milwauke	NL	215	58	15	1	4	28/32	35	30	4	3	160	.270	.354	.405	.257	27		

Milwaukee is becoming for fourth outfielders what Montreal used to be for washed-up pitchers: a place where you get a chance to save a career. Some don't make it—Marc Newfield and Chuck Carr, for example—but others, like Ochoa or Rich Becker or Darrin Jackson or Gerald Williams, recover their livelihoods. Ochoa still has the strong arm that helped propel him to monster prospect status with the Orioles and Mets, but he's hit his ceiling.

Santiago Perez   SS   Bats B   Age 24

YEAR	TEAM	LGE	AB	H	DB	TP	HR	BB/SO	R	RBI	SB	CS	OUT	BA	OBP	SLG	EQA	EQR	DEFENSE
1997	Lakeland	Fla	448	112	22	9	5	16/108	53	39	9	4	340	.250	.278	.373	.218	38	108-SS 93
1998	El Paso	Tex	442	110	16	7	9	20/78	48	44	11	6	338	.249	.286	.378	.222	39	106-SS 92
1998	Louisvil	Int	134	35	4	2	3	4/31	15	12	4	2	101	.261	.283	.388	.224	12	31-SS 99
1999	Louisvil	Int	406	101	21	7	6	25/94	46	32	15	3	308	.249	.295	.379	.232	40	99-SS 89
2000	Milwauke	NL	509	131	22	8	12	36/112	68	64	18	5	383	.257	.306	.403	.240	54	

A thin reed at shortstop, Perez surprised a few analysts by hitting for a little bit of power even after leaving El Paso. While he has a good defensive reputation, he's error-prone. Lopez is basically wondering what cruel twist of fate has Jose Nieves and Cristian Guzman getting shots at major-league jobs while he waits behind Loretta and Valentin.

Chris Rowan   SS   Bats R   Age 21

YEAR	TEAM	LGE	AB	H	DB	TP	HR	BB/SO	R	RBI	SB	CS	OUT	BA	OBP	SLG	EQA	EQR	DEFENSE
1997	Ogden	Pio	210	39	10	1	5	18/78	26	18	1	2	173	.186	.257	.314	.188	13	35-2B 77
1998	Ogden	Pio	196	34	6	3	8	12/87	20	25	1	0	162	.173	.231	.357	.192	13	52-SS 88
1999	Stockton	Cal	431	93	23	2	11	20/138	40	43	4	2	340	.216	.260	.355	.203	32	120-SS 96
2000	Milwauke	NL	305	63	15	1	7	25/107	27	27	4	2	244	.207	.267	.331	.198	21	

If Gary Matthews has any effect working with the team's minor-league hitters in his first year or two, it will have to be with younger players like Rowan or Billy Hall or Derry Hammond, all recent high-school picks with poor command of the strike zone and good power.

Scott Sollmann   OF   Bats L   Age 25

YEAR	TEAM	LGE	AB	H	DB	TP	HR	BB/SO	R	RBI	SB	CS	OUT	BA	OBP	SLG	EQA	EQR	DEFENSE
1997	W Michgn	Mid	476	132	11	3	1	61/87	61	27	17	7	351	.277	.370	.319	.248	54	124-OF 108
1998	Lakeland	Fla	407	88	9	3	2	47/63	46	27	20	8	327	.216	.300	.268	.203	30	97-OF 109
1999	Stockton	Cal	247	62	10	2	0	37/43	32	20	10	5	190	.251	.350	.308	.236	26	49-OF 100
1999	Huntsvil	Sou	192	50	4	3	1	26/35	23	9	8	4	146	.260	.355	.328	.243	21	48-OF 99
2000	Detroit	AL	484	123	14	3	1	65/83	77	43	20	8	369	.254	.342	.302	.232	48	

The embarrassing thing about the Brewers' collection of minor-league speed guys is that they nabbed Sollmann from the Tigers in the minor-league portion of the Rule 5 draft, and he was better than the homegrown guys. Nabbed back by the Tigers.

Jose Valentin   SS   Bats B   Age 30

YEAR	TEAM	LGE	AB	H	DB	TP	HR	BB/SO	R	RBI	SB	CS	OUT	BA	OBP	SLG	EQA	EQR	DEFENSE
1997	Milwauke	AL	494	127	24	1	17	36/105	56	57	19	8	375	.257	.314	.413	.246	56	130-SS 95
1998	Milwauke	NL	431	98	20	0	18	63/102	65	50	11	8	341	.227	.327	.399	.246	51	119-SS 99
1999	Milwauke	NL	256	57	9	6	9	45/51	42	35	2	2	201	.223	.344	.410	.257	34	74-SS 96
2000	Milwauke	NL	350	82	14	2	15	51/76	51	52	7	6	274	.234	.332	.414	.250	43	

Some focus on what he can't do, like hit for average or hit left-handers, but he defines underrated: a good defensive player who hits for power and draws walks. He lost two months to a torn ulnar collateral ligament, and the Brewers missed his aggressive brand of shortstop play. Taylor's crew is evaluating what they want to do with him: they renegotiated his contract to make it more incentive-laden, and are considering whether they want to trade him or move him to center field. If he's traded and ends up in the right place, like Coors or Wrigley, he'd be star for a year or two.

Fernando Vina   2B   Bats L   Age 31

YEAR	TEAM	LGE	AB	H	DB	TP	HR	BB/SO	R	RBI	SB	CS	OUT	BA	OBP	SLG	EQA	EQR	DEFENSE
1997	Milwauke	AL	324	89	13	2	4	10/22	36	27	8	7	242	.275	.313	.364	.228	30	74-2B 104
1998	Milwauke	NL	643	199	42	7	7	53/45	102	44	23	18	462	.309	.386	.429	.276	93	157-2B 104
1999	Milwauke	NL	154	40	4	0	2	12/6	15	16	4	2	116	.260	.331	.325	.229	15	36-2B 107
2000	*St Louis*	*NL*	*288*	*79*	*13*	*1*	*4*	*25/18*	*38*	*34*	*7*	*6*	*215*	*.274*	*.332*	*.368*	*.238*	*30*	

He spent most of spring training hurt, and was knocked out for good in May by running into Burnitz while going for a pop-up in short right field. He's the new face for the Jim Gantner Test: adequacy is nice when Ron Belliard isn't around, but once he is, you don't need Vina. Bando's failure to trade him for anything of value before the season was a missed opportunity. Lucky for him there's Walt Jocketty, who took Vina off his hands in exchange for Juan Acevedo. Vina will be the starting second baseman for the Cards.

PITCHERS (Averages: ERA: 4.50 / H/9: 9.00 / HR/9: 1.00 / BB/9: 3.50 / K/9: 6.50 / KWH: 1.00)

Jim Abbott   Throws L   Age 32

YEAR	TEAM	LGE	IP	H	ER	HR	BB	K	ERA	W	L	H/9	HR/9	BB/9	K/9	KWH	PERA
1996	Calfrnia	AL	143.7	157	108	20	73	60	6.77	5	11	9.84	1.25	4.57	3.76	0.23	5.70
1998	Birmnghm	Sou	38.0	62	37	2	23	26	8.76	1	3	14.68	0.47	5.45	6.16	0.35	8.29
1998	Calgary	PCL	30.3	32	9	1	11	16	2.67	2	1	9.49	0.30	3.26	4.75	0.54	3.86
1998	ChiSox	AL	31.7	34	15	2	13	14	4.26	2	2	9.66	0.57	3.69	3.98	0.33	4.55
1999	Milwauke	NL	83.7	105	63	13	40	36	6.78	3	6	11.29	1.40	4.30	3.87	0.23	6.67

Abbott was never back, he was just pitching. The question is whether or not you think Scott Boras did the right thing. The White Sox let Abbott pitch in 1998, and he wasn't too good despite being spotted against weak teams, but they wanted him back. You could argue that Boras was smart to get his client some more money (considering he was living on borrowed time), or rotten for hosing the Sox. But since Sal Bando was dumb enough to offer the contract in the first place, why should anyone feel guilty?

Jason Bere   Throws R   Age 29

YEAR	TEAM	LGE	IP	H	ER	HR	BB	K	ERA	W	L	H/9	HR/9	BB/9	K/9	KWH	PERA
1997	ChiSox	AL	28.7	19	13	4	17	21	4.08	2	1	5.97	1.26	5.34	6.59	1.02	3.77
1998	ChiSox	AL	84.0	96	66	13	60	54	7.07	3	6	10.29	1.39	6.43	5.79	0.38	6.96
1998	Cincnnti	NL	43.7	40	20	3	22	30	4.12	3	2	8.24	0.62	4.53	6.18	0.76	4.12
1999	Cincnnti	NL	42.3	59	37	6	39	27	7.87	1	4	12.54	1.28	8.29	5.74	0.24	9.14
1999	Indianap	Int	16.0	28	21	3	21	7	11.81	0	2	15.75	1.69	11.81	3.94	0.06	13.50
1999	Louisvil	Int	25.7	22	8	0	9	23	2.81	2	1	7.71	0.00	3.16	8.06	2.00	2.81
1999	Milwauke	NL	23.3	22	13	3	10	18	5.01	1	2	8.49	1.16	3.86	6.94	1.10	4.63

It isn't time to just smell the coffee—it's time to pack the grounds into your sinuses. Bere had a nice run against lousy teams at the tail end of 1997. His lone quality start for the Brewers was in the second game of a doubleheader against a Pirates line-up that featured the three Browns, Tim Laker, John Wehner, Abraham Nunez and Dale Sveum batting cleanup. Ted Higuera could start a comeback against that bunch. He's signed to guaranteed money significantly above the minimum, so he'll hold down a rotation spot until he hands it back in May.

Rocky Coppinger   Throws R   Age 26

YEAR	TEAM	LGE	IP	H	ER	HR	BB	K	ERA	W	L	H/9	HR/9	BB/9	K/9	KWH	PERA
1997	Baltimor	AL	19.7	21	13	2	16	22	5.95	1	1	9.61	0.92	7.32	10.07	1.08	6.41
1998	Bowie	Eas	29.0	32	22	4	14	23	6.83	1	2	9.93	1.24	4.34	7.14	0.88	5.59
1998	Rochestr	Int	80.7	94	45	11	47	55	5.02	4	5	10.49	1.23	5.24	6.14	0.51	6.36
1998	Baltimor	AL	15.3	16	8	3	8	13	4.70	1	1	9.39	1.76	4.70	7.63	0.99	5.87
1999	Rochestr	Int	31.0	30	13	3	13	32	3.77	2	1	8.71	0.87	3.77	9.29	1.96	4.35
1999	Baltimor	AL	21.3	25	19	7	19	17	8.02	0	2	10.55	2.95	8.02	7.17	0.45	9.70
1999	Milwauke	NL	37.3	34	14	5	22	38	3.38	3	1	8.20	1.21	5.30	9.16	1.44	5.06

The state of Wisconsin has the highest percentage of inhabitants who fit the criteria for obesity, and that was before the Brewers added Coppinger. No word on whether Governor Thompson wants to put him on the state flag. Swiped from the Orioles in exchange for Al Reyes, he still throws hard. Coppinger will probably have a good half-season, then burn out if he isn't down to his listed 240 pounds (he's been over 270 for a couple of years now).

Jeff D'Amico   Throws R   Age 24

YEAR	TEAM	LGE	IP	H	ER	HR	BB	K	ERA	W	L	H/9	HR/9	BB/9	K/9	KWH	PERA
1996	El Paso	Tex	96.7	90	38	10	16	70	3.54	7	4	8.38	0.93	1.49	6.52	2.54	3.35
1996	Milwauke	AL	86.0	84	45	18	29	55	4.71	5	5	8.79	1.88	3.03	5.76	0.93	5.13
1997	Milwauke	AL	137.3	133	73	23	43	95	4.78	7	8	8.72	1.51	2.82	6.23	1.18	4.59

Shoulder surgery has held him back for the last two years. During his rehab outings at Beloit in 1999, his fastball was around 89 mph, which is reportedly as good as it's going to get. An enormous human being, his conditioning and mechanics have always been major issues, and most of his 1999 rehab efforts were cut short by shoulder tightness. He's not a great bet to come back.

Valerio de los Santos   Throws L   Age 24

YEAR	TEAM	LGE	IP	H	ER	HR	BB	K	ERA	W	L	H/9	HR/9	BB/9	K/9	KWH	PERA
1997	El Paso	Tex	116.7	141	72	7	45	54	5.55	5	8	10.88	0.54	3.47	4.17	0.34	5.09
1998	El Paso	Tex	67.7	80	30	2	30	52	3.99	4	4	10.64	0.27	3.99	6.92	0.84	4.92
1998	Milwauke	NL	11.0	7	7	2	20	3	5.73	0	1	5.73	1.64	16.36	2.45	0.05	9.00
1999	Milwauke	NL	8.3	12	5	1	6	5	5.40	0	1	12.96	1.08	6.48	5.40	0.26	8.64

He opened the year in the major-league bullpen but missed most of the season after surgery to repair a bulging disc in his back. He still doesn't have an off-speed pitch or change speeds well with his good fastball/forkball combination, but he could be a very effective reliever. He gave up #60 to Sosa in 1998, while Bere gave up Sammy's 60th in 1999. I guess they can't get enough history in Milwaukee.

Cal Eldred   Throws R   Age 32

YEAR	TEAM	LGE	IP	H	ER	HR	BB	K	ERA	W	L	H/9	HR/9	BB/9	K/9	KWH	PERA
1997	Milwauke	AL	204.0	199	108	29	90	123	4.76	11	12	8.78	1.28	3.97	5.43	0.63	4.85
1998	Milwauke	NL	136.3	155	77	14	65	83	5.08	7	8	10.23	0.92	4.29	5.48	0.51	5.48
1999	Milwauke	NL	83.3	98	67	17	44	58	7.24	3	6	10.58	1.84	4.75	6.26	0.58	6.91

He's now entering the last year of a four-year contract that should have gotten Sal Bando fired on the spot, since Eldred had already blown out his arm in 1995. He frustrated the Brewers all year with his unwillingness to abandon his power-pitcher mentality and start using his good curve and change-up, preferring to try to aim slow heat and get lit up. With a change of approach, he might get back to being an adequate fifth starter. Don't bet on it.

Horacio Estrada   Throws L   Age 24

YEAR	TEAM	LGE	IP	H	ER	HR	BB	K	ERA	W	L	H/9	HR/9	BB/9	K/9	KWH	PERA
1997	El Paso	Tex	156.3	167	79	11	82	112	4.55	8	9	9.61	0.63	4.72	6.45	0.68	4.95
1998	El Paso	Tex	50.3	48	24	3	25	31	4.29	3	3	8.58	0.54	4.47	5.54	0.60	4.11
1998	Louisvil	Int	11.7	10	4	1	6	4	3.09	1	0	7.71	0.77	4.63	3.09	0.20	3.86
1999	Louisvil	Int	130.3	131	80	19	68	101	5.52	6	8	9.05	1.31	4.70	6.97	0.86	5.32

This young Venezuelan lost 1998 to a hand injury and shoulder surgery, but fortunately he didn't need major reconstruction. He doesn't have one dominating pitch, just a broad assortment that he's willing to use. Estrada isn't really a top prospect, but he deserves a shot at pushing aside Bill Pulsipher and Rafael Roque.

Chad Fox   Throws R   Age 29

YEAR	TEAM	LGE	IP	H	ER	HR	BB	K	ERA	W	L	H/9	HR/9	BB/9	K/9	KWH	PERA
1997	Richmond	Int	23.0	28	12	1	15	20	4.70	1	2	10.96	0.39	5.87	7.83	0.71	5.87
1997	Atlanta	NL	26.7	26	13	4	17	26	4.39	2	1	8.78	1.35	5.74	8.78	1.14	5.74
1998	Milwauke	NL	58.3	55	25	4	21	61	3.86	3	3	8.49	0.62	3.24	9.41	2.41	3.70
1999	Milwauke	NL	7.0	11	7	1	4	12	9.00	0	1	14.14	1.29	5.14	15.43	2.45	9.00

Fox was working on a forkball to supplement his wicked slider before the slider blew out his elbow again. Without the slider, it's likely that he won't ever return to the kind of effectiveness he had in 1998.

Jose Garcia   Throws R   Age 22

YEAR	TEAM	LGE	IP	H	ER	HR	BB	K	ERA	W	L	H/9	HR/9	BB/9	K/9	KWH	PERA
1997	Beloit	Mid	143.7	184	110	12	85	88	6.89	5	11	11.53	0.75	5.32	5.51	0.37	6.45
1998	Stockton	Cal	154.0	183	110	16	110	113	6.43	6	11	10.69	0.94	6.43	6.60	0.47	6.66

Garcia missed the season after bumping elbows with another player in camp. No damage showed up in any of the numerous examinations conducted during the year, so he's expected to be fine in 2000. Previously, and probably still, one of their better young pitchers, thanks to good low-90s heat and a sharp curveball.

J.M. Gold   Throws R   Age 20

YEAR	TEAM	LGE	IP	H	ER	HR	BB	K	ERA	W	L	H/9	HR/9	BB/9	K/9	KWH	PERA
1998	Ogden	Pio	15.0	27	15	2	8	10	9.00	0	2	16.20	1.20	4.80	6.00	0.35	9.60
1999	Beloit	Mid	103.0	149	94	19	62	67	8.21	3	8	13.02	1.66	5.42	5.85	0.36	8.65

Along with Nick Neugebauer, one of a hard-throwing tandem of top high-school picks from 1998 who represented a break from previous drafts in which the Brewers focused on toolsy position players. Gold spent most of the season battling weight problems, but the larger concern is a cross-body throwing motion that is bound to cause shoulder problems. He has a mid-90s fastball and a good curve, but little command. As with all A-ball pitchers, the key is staying healthy long enough to find out if he's really a prospect.

Doug Johnston   Throws R   Age 22

YEAR	TEAM	LGE	IP	H	ER	HR	BB	K	ERA	W	L	H/9	HR/9	BB/9	K/9	KWH	PERA
1997	Helena	Pio	65.7	83	49	5	47	40	6.72	2	5	11.38	0.69	6.44	5.48	0.31	6.72
1998	Beloit	Mid	85.0	99	38	9	37	49	4.02	5	4	10.48	0.95	3.92	5.19	0.49	5.51
1998	Stockton	Cal	55.3	59	25	4	32	36	4.07	3	3	9.60	0.65	5.20	5.86	0.51	5.20
1999	Huntsvil	Sou	112.7	147	79	18	46	66	6.31	4	9	11.74	1.44	3.67	5.27	0.48	6.71

He's been pushed up the chain quickly because the Brewers say he has good pitching instincts. His curve and change are both good pitches, but because he's tall (6'5"), the expectation is that he'll add velocity as he fills out. He's the kind of project pitcher lots of organizations take a wait-and-see approach with, because not every tall guy gets his fastball over 90 mph as he matures physically.

Scott Karl   Throws L   Age 28

YEAR	TEAM	LGE	IP	H	ER	HR	BB	K	ERA	W	L	H/9	HR/9	BB/9	K/9	KWH	PERA
1997	Milwauke	AL	195.7	203	93	21	68	120	4.28	12	10	9.34	0.97	3.13	5.52	0.78	4.51
1998	Milwauke	NL	196.7	216	98	21	70	98	4.48	11	11	9.88	0.96	3.20	4.48	0.47	4.85
1999	Milwauke	NL	201.3	233	105	19	66	72	4.69	11	11	10.42	0.85	2.95	3.22	0.25	4.92

Karl is a really rare type, a junkballer without a good breaking pitch. He lives mostly with a cut fastball and a nice palmball. He's been losing ground for four straight seasons, which is why he's working on resurrecting a curveball he scrapped after college. The only thing that makes him an acceptable fourth starter has been his ability to take the ball every fifth day. Traded to Colorado; if there's a positive, it's that he doesn't have a curveball to lose, so he might not fall all the way off the cliff.

Allen Levrault   Throws R   Age 22

YEAR	TEAM	LGE	IP	H	ER	HR	BB	K	ERA	W	L	H/9	HR/9	BB/9	K/9	KWH	PERA
1997	Beloit	Mid	120.3	181	110	22	49	78	8.23	3	10	13.54	1.65	3.66	5.83	0.51	8.15
1998	Stockton	Cal	89.7	96	41	10	33	58	4.12	5	5	9.64	1.00	3.31	5.82	0.79	4.82
1998	El Paso	Tex	63.0	78	47	7	20	39	6.71	2	5	11.14	1.00	2.86	5.57	0.73	5.43
1999	Huntsvil	Sou	95.3	89	48	11	36	68	4.53	5	6	8.40	1.04	3.40	6.42	1.08	4.15
1999	Louisvil	Int	33.7	50	34	8	17	30	9.09	1	3	13.37	2.14	4.54	8.02	0.79	9.09

He's the organization's minor-league pitcher of the year, a big guy who has moved up quickly. He's gotten by so far on a low-90s fastball and a plus change-up, but his curve remains inconsistent. While it looks like he struggled after a midseason promotion for the second year in a row, note that he missed two weeks just before being promoted, when a batting-practice accident left him with a broken nose. He wasn't the same after the accident. The pattern seems clear: a midseason promotion after someone like Bere or Bill Pulsipher gets bumped.

Mike Myers — Throws L — Age 31

YEAR	TEAM	LGE	IP	H	ER	HR	BB	K	ERA	W	L	H/9	HR/9	BB/9	K/9	KWH	PERA
1997	Detroit	AL	53.7	58	34	11	25	51	5.70	2	4	9.73	1.84	4.19	8.55	1.34	6.20
1998	Milwauke	NL	50.7	44	18	5	23	38	3.20	4	2	7.82	0.89	4.09	6.75	1.07	3.91
1999	Milwauke	NL	42.0	44	21	7	12	34	4.50	3	2	9.43	1.50	2.57	7.29	1.64	4.93

He struggled with a slow start, but unlike 1998, he wasn't overused in the first half and finished strong. In November, he was traded to the Rockies for Curtis Leskanic. As a sidearming left-hander, he's an extreme specialist, and pitching in Coors won't help him. The Brewers traded him at the right time, since he's arbitration-eligible: Myers is useful, but not worth paying through the nose to keep.

Nick Neugebauer — Throws R — Age 19

YEAR	TEAM	LGE	IP	H	ER	HR	BB	K	ERA	W	L	H/9	HR/9	BB/9	K/9	KWH	PERA
1999	Beloit	Mid	76.0	63	46	5	91	90	5.45	3	5	7.46	0.59	10.78	10.66	1.06	6.16

The second-round pick from the 1998 draft led all minor leaguers in strikeout rate with nearly 14 per nine innings. He consistently throws in the mid-90s, but, like Gold, he has mechanical flaws, tending to fly open too early in his delivery. It's too early to say whether either will survive to become prospects, but both have shown the talent that got them drafted high.

Hideo Nomo — Throws R — Age 31

YEAR	TEAM	LGE	IP	H	ER	HR	BB	K	ERA	W	L	H/9	HR/9	BB/9	K/9	KWH	PERA
1997	LosAngls	NL	201.0	207	112	24	96	215	5.01	10	12	9.27	1.07	4.30	9.63	1.74	5.06
1998	LosAngls	NL	66.3	60	40	8	40	69	5.43	3	4	8.14	1.09	5.43	9.36	1.48	4.88
1998	NY Mets	NL	89.3	75	49	11	59	90	4.94	5	5	7.56	1.11	5.94	9.07	1.37	4.74
1999	Milwauke	NL	179.3	164	83	25	75	156	4.17	11	9	8.23	1.25	3.76	7.83	1.48	4.42

It was a nice comeback, but this Nomo is more of a finesse pitcher. His forkball doesn't move as much, and some people think he tips his curve. The Cubs and Indians weren't sold on him because his velocity was down at the beginning of the year. By midsummer, he was back in the low 90s. The lesson is that when a third starter drops into your lap, you don't start making excuses for Dwight Gooden or Scott Sanders. Not all of the Brewers' problems controlling the running game were Dave Nilsson's fault: Nomo allowed 41 steals while he was on the mound, and no catcher can make that sort of thing go away.

Brian Passini — Throws L — Age 25

YEAR	TEAM	LGE	IP	H	ER	HR	BB	K	ERA	W	L	H/9	HR/9	BB/9	K/9	KWH	PERA
1997	Beloit	Mid	113.7	147	60	17	44	79	4.75	6	7	11.64	1.35	3.48	6.26	0.72	6.49
1997	Stockton	Cal	39.7	53	36	8	24	24	8.17	1	3	12.03	1.82	5.45	5.45	0.34	8.17
1998	Stockton	Cal	79.3	111	54	9	41	57	6.13	3	6	12.59	1.02	4.65	6.47	0.53	7.15
1998	El Paso	Tex	80.3	68	31	5	34	42	3.47	6	3	7.62	0.56	3.81	4.71	0.57	3.47
1999	Huntsvil	Sou	34.0	42	25	3	22	17	6.62	1	3	11.12	0.79	5.82	4.50	0.23	6.35
1999	Louisvil	Int	27.0	36	23	4	18	12	7.67	1	2	12.00	1.33	6.00	4.00	0.17	7.67

Passini is your basic college left-hander. He has a big-bending curve and a nice change-up, paints the corners but can't throw the ball through the canvas. He missed most of the season with a strained lateral muscle and a bad back, but this spring's open call for starters gives him a shot at the fifth spot.

Kyle Peterson — Throws R — Age 24

YEAR	TEAM	LGE	IP	H	ER	HR	BB	K	ERA	W	L	H/9	HR/9	BB/9	K/9	KWH	PERA
1998	Stockton	Cal	86.3	126	70	6	42	72	7.30	3	7	13.14	0.63	4.38	7.51	0.73	6.88
1998	El Paso	Tex	43.7	39	21	2	19	28	4.33	3	2	8.04	0.41	3.92	5.77	0.79	3.50
1999	Louisvil	Int	108.0	92	48	12	44	86	4.00	7	5	7.67	1.00	3.67	7.17	1.37	3.83
1999	Milwauke	NL	78.3	82	40	3	24	33	4.60	4	5	9.42	0.34	2.76	3.79	0.41	3.79

He looks good for the short term as the team's third starter. Peterson isn't overpowering; he throws four pitches for strikes, fooling enough of the people enough of the time. There are reasons to doubt he'll have a long career. His mechanics are a nightmare: he throws across his body and keeps his front leg so stiff he's the anti-Seaver. It helps make his delivery more deceptive, but chances are he'll blow out his shoulder within the next three years.

Eric Plunk　　　　Throws R　　　Age 36

YEAR	TEAM	LGE	IP	H	ER	HR	BB	K	ERA	W	L	H/9	HR/9	BB/9	K/9	KWH	PERA
1997	Clevelnd	AL	65.7	61	34	11	36	66	4.66	3	4	8.36	1.51	4.93	9.05	1.48	5.21
1998	Clevelnd	AL	42.3	42	20	5	16	39	4.25	3	2	8.93	1.06	3.40	8.29	1.69	4.46
1998	Milwauke	NL	32.3	33	13	3	16	35	3.62	2	2	9.19	0.84	4.45	9.74	1.73	4.73
1999	Milwauke	NL	76.3	68	38	14	42	61	4.48	4	4	8.02	1.65	4.95	7.19	0.97	5.19

He completely collapsed in August and September, but why? Plunk's season wasn't the same after a couple of 40-pitch outings in July. Up until then, he'd kept his ERA around 3.00. Garner had been relatively careful, using him only five times on consecutive days. In the last 19 games, Lefebvre used him 11 times, six times consecutively and twice on three straight days. After that kind of flogging, it's not surprising that the Brewers elected not to pick up his option. If used carefully, Plunk can still be a valuable middle man.

Ryan Poe　　　　Throws R　　　Age 22

YEAR	TEAM	LGE	IP	H	ER	HR	BB	K	ERA	W	L	H/9	HR/9	BB/9	K/9	KWH	PERA
1998	Helena	Pio	36.0	62	32	4	16	27	8.00	1	3	15.50	1.00	4.00	6.75	0.55	8.75
1999	Beloit	Mid	90.3	116	54	11	18	77	5.38	4	6	11.56	1.10	1.79	7.67	2.12	5.38

Poe is a 1998 21st-rounder out of Saddleback Community College. He flashed extraordinary control—108 strikeouts and 13 unintentional walks—so you can put him in a category similar to the Orioles' Josh Towers. They're guys with outstanding control at a young age who aren't necessarily prospects.

Bill Pulsipher　　　Throws L　　　Age 26

YEAR	TEAM	LGE	IP	H	ER	HR	BB	K	ERA	W	L	H/9	HR/9	BB/9	K/9	KWH	PERA
1997	St Lucie	Fla	33.7	36	36	2	48	26	9.62	1	3	9.62	0.53	12.83	6.95	0.29	8.29
1997	Norfolk	Int	26.7	26	30	1	40	16	10.13	0	3	8.78	0.34	13.50	5.40	0.18	7.76
1998	Norfolk	Int	85.3	94	49	11	44	50	5.17	4	5	9.91	1.16	4.64	5.27	0.45	5.70
1998	Milwauke	NL	59.3	62	28	6	27	36	4.25	4	3	9.40	0.91	4.10	5.46	0.58	4.85
1999	Milwauke	NL	88.7	95	57	17	35	41	5.79	4	6	9.64	1.73	3.55	4.16	0.38	5.68
1999	Louisvil	Int	26.7	23	14	1	21	18	4.72	1	2	7.76	0.34	7.09	6.08	0.50	4.39

Pitching coach Bill Campbell tried to alter Pulsipher's mechanics so that his delivery was slower and he landed softly on his front foot, to avoid the back injuries that his contortions seemed likely to produce. He hurt his back all the same. Pulsipher doesn't have as strong a case as Paul Wilson for suing Dallas Green for professional irresponsibility, but he would be a good witness for the plaintiff.

Rafael Roque　　　Throws L　　　Age 28

YEAR	TEAM	LGE	IP	H	ER	HR	BB	K	ERA	W	L	H/9	HR/9	BB/9	K/9	KWH	PERA
1997	St Lucie	Fla	69.0	111	60	10	38	37	7.83	2	6	14.48	1.30	4.96	4.83	0.24	8.87
1997	Binghmtn	Eas	23.7	43	30	6	21	17	11.41	0	3	16.35	2.28	7.99	6.46	0.24	12.93
1998	El Paso	Tex	91.3	122	57	8	46	53	5.62	4	6	12.02	0.79	4.53	5.22	0.37	6.50
1998	Louisvil	Int	47.3	47	24	2	21	36	4.56	2	3	8.94	0.38	3.99	6.85	0.98	3.99
1998	Milwauke	NL	48.3	42	26	9	26	33	4.84	2	3	7.82	1.68	4.84	6.14	0.75	5.03
1999	Milwauke	NL	86.0	91	45	15	41	64	4.71	5	5	9.52	1.57	4.29	6.70	0.82	5.76

He was handed the Opening Day start by default. Roque throws a little harder than your average left-hander, getting up over 90 mph once in a while, but his curve and change are both hittable. After losing his spot in the rotation to Jim Abbott in mid-May, he was an adequate long reliever. Roque is a good 11th man, if there is such a thing.

Ben Sheets　　　　Throws R　　　Age 21

YEAR	TEAM	LGE	IP	H	ER	HR	BB	K	ERA	W	L	H/9	HR/9	BB/9	K/9	KWH	PERA
1999	Stockton	Cal	26.3	25	11	1	16	21	3.76	2	1	8.54	0.34	5.47	7.18	0.82	4.44

The Brewers' first-rounder in the 1999 draft is likely to move up fast. He flashed a good fastball, sharp curve and slider at Northeast Louisiana State and in the California League. The Brewers have to sort through stiffs like Pulsipher and Bere to open the year, so Sheets won't be up until September.

Paul Stewart   Throws R   Age 21

YEAR	TEAM	LGE	IP	H	ER	HR	BB	K	ERA	W	L	H/9	HR/9	BB/9	K/9	KWH	PERA
1997	Ogden	Pio	71.0	114	70	13	42	49	8.87	2	6	14.45	1.65	5.32	6.21	0.37	9.51
1998	Beloit	Mid	130.7	215	127	29	59	80	8.75	3	12	14.81	2.00	4.06	5.51	0.38	9.71
1999	Stockton	Cal	161.0	187	91	20	67	86	5.09	8	10	10.45	1.12	3.75	4.81	0.44	5.59

The horse at Stockton, he was saddled with a heavy workload for a 20-year-old. He's big but raw, and working this hard before your 21st birthday isn't a good way to put together a career.

Dave Weathers   Throws R   Age 30

YEAR	TEAM	LGE	IP	H	ER	HR	BB	K	ERA	W	L	H/9	HR/9	BB/9	K/9	KWH	PERA
1997	Columbus	Int	34.7	41	21	3	8	28	5.45	2	2	10.64	0.78	2.08	7.27	1.79	4.67
1997	Buffalo	AmA	63.0	88	49	7	20	43	7.00	2	5	12.57	1.00	2.86	6.14	0.78	6.43
1998	Cincnnti	NL	63.0	88	47	3	29	49	6.71	2	5	12.57	0.43	4.14	7.00	0.70	6.29
1998	Milwauke	NL	48.3	44	21	3	15	41	3.91	3	2	8.19	0.56	2.79	7.63	1.90	3.35
1999	Milwauke	NL	94.7	97	42	13	36	72	3.99	6	5	9.22	1.24	3.42	6.85	1.11	4.85

Sometimes cumulative information means something, and sometimes it doesn't. Weathers was used on consecutive days only a dozen times, allowing 12 runs in 16½ innings on the second days. Sounds bad, right? Well, he allowed five of the runs while getting nobody out the last time he turned the trick, while giving up just seven runs in 16⅓ innings the other 11 times, which looks pretty good. Stormy is your basic middle reliever: lots of gut, no glory.

Bob Wickman   Throws R   Age 31

YEAR	TEAM	LGE	IP	H	ER	HR	BB	K	ERA	W	L	H/9	HR/9	BB/9	K/9	KWH	PERA
1997	Milwauke	AL	96.7	85	29	7	42	79	2.70	8	3	7.91	0.65	3.91	7.36	1.31	3.72
1998	Milwauke	NL	84.0	77	36	5	42	68	3.86	5	4	8.25	0.54	4.50	7.29	1.07	3.96
1999	Milwauke	NL	75.7	71	26	5	37	58	3.09	5	3	8.44	0.59	4.40	6.90	0.96	4.16

Wickman has a hard slider, good sinker, and is a patriotic Green Bay, University of Wisconsin-Whitewater cheesehead through and through. He gets a ton of groundball outs, but he's also hittable. While he's now being hailed as an "established closer," he's just a solid pitcher stuck in the role. Jack McKeon or Jerry Manuel could do so much more with him.

Steve Woodard   Throws R   Age 25

YEAR	TEAM	LGE	IP	H	ER	HR	BB	K	ERA	W	L	H/9	HR/9	BB/9	K/9	KWH	PERA
1997	El Paso	Tex	138.3	131	46	8	30	85	2.99	10	5	8.52	0.52	1.95	5.53	1.37	3.19
1997	Milwauke	AL	37.0	38	23	5	6	32	5.59	2	2	9.24	1.22	1.46	7.78	3.36	4.14
1998	Milwauke	NL	168.7	168	78	19	35	129	4.16	10	9	8.96	1.01	1.87	6.88	2.11	3.84
1999	Milwauke	NL	188.0	208	88	21	34	115	4.21	11	10	9.96	1.01	1.63	5.51	1.40	4.31

While he was a solid starter, he was the victim of all sorts of bad luck. Knee surgery the previous winter led to a staph infection that left him 30 pounds lighter. As mentioned in the essay, he was having a great season up until breaking his left wrist in a collision at home plate against the Marlins. He changes speeds on his slider well and has a killer change-up, but nobody's going to coin the term "crafty right-hander" anytime soon. He'll have a better season in 2000.

Kelly Wunsch   Throws L   Age 27

YEAR	TEAM	LGE	IP	H	ER	HR	BB	K	ERA	W	L	H/9	HR/9	BB/9	K/9	KWH	PERA
1997	Stockton	Cal	117.0	203	102	12	80	60	7.85	3	10	15.62	0.92	6.15	4.62	0.17	9.77
1998	El Paso	Tex	98.0	140	85	10	40	53	7.81	3	8	12.86	0.92	3.67	4.87	0.37	6.80
1998	Louisvil	Int	49.3	59	25	6	16	30	4.56	2	3	10.76	1.09	2.92	5.47	0.71	5.47
1999	Huntsvil	Sou	47.0	50	17	1	27	26	3.26	3	2	9.57	0.19	5.17	4.98	0.37	4.60
1999	Louisvil	Int	40.3	56	23	4	15	17	5.13	2	2	12.50	0.89	3.35	3.79	0.26	6.47

Since he started throwing sidearm at the tail end of 1998, he's become a better pitcher. It's cost him velocity but given him better control, and he now keeps almost everything in the infield. He started the year recuperating from a broken foot, and he finished it a minor-league free agent. If you were looking for an adequate left-handed specialist, he would be a good choice. Signed by the White Sox, where he might make it into the Show.

Support-Neutral Records — MILWAUKEE BREWERS — Park Effect: +1.2%

PITCHER	GS	IP	R	SNW	SNL	SNPCT	W	L	RA	APW	SNVA	SNWAR
Jim Abbott	15	75.0	65	3.1	7.0	.305	2	8	7.80	-2.12	-1.89	-1.21
Jason Bere	4	22.3	15	1.1	1.2	.481	2	0	6.04	-0.22	-0.04	0.13
Cal Eldred	15	74.7	68	3.2	7.3	.303	2	8	8.20	-2.42	-2.08	-1.28
Scott Karl	33	197.7	121	10.5	11.8	.471	11	11	5.51	-0.85	-0.66	1.02
Hideo Nomo	28	176.3	96	10.3	9.1	.532	12	8	4.90	0.36	0.54	2.08
Kyle Peterson	12	70.0	39	4.2	4.2	.494	3	5	5.01	0.06	0.02	0.58
Bill Pulsipher	16	82.3	63	3.9	6.5	.376	5	6	6.89	-1.54	-1.28	-0.51
Rafael Roque	9	39.0	27	1.9	3.3	.372	0	5	6.23	-0.46	-0.63	-0.28
Steve Woodard	29	182.3	100	10.8	10.0	.519	11	8	4.94	0.31	0.34	1.97
TOTALS	161	919.7	594	49.1	60.6	.448	48	59	5.81	-6.88	-5.70	2.50

It's one thing to have bad starting pitching for two consecutive years. It's another to be bad and not do anything about it. The table above just isn't very different from the Brewers' table in *Baseball Prospectus 1999*. The 1998 rotation was worth 5.7 games below average, according to SNVA—fourth-worst in the league. The 1999 rotation was worth 5.7 games below average, fifth-worst in the league. In '98, Scott Karl and Steve Woodard were the top two Brewers in games started, with Karl performing just below average and Woodard just above. Ditto '99. The only major differences between '98 and '99 were the particular pitchers the Brewers tried as reclamation projects; in '99, their success with Hideo Nomo more or less balanced out their failure with Jim Abbott. It's hard to see how they're going to get much better following the same formula. . . . You have to wonder if it isn't time for Cal Eldred to hang 'em up. Injuries have caused this once top-flight young pitcher to plummet so fast it's been painful to watch. His Support-Neutral Winning Percentages since 1996: .602, .497, .410, .303.

Pitcher Abuse Points

PITCHER	AGE	GS	PAP	PAP/S	WKLD	MAX	1-90	91-100	101-110	111-120	121-130	131-140	141+
Jim Abbott	31	15	4	0.3	0.3	104	8	6	1	0	0	0	0
Jason Bere	28	4	1	0.3	0.4	101	0	3	1	0	0	0	0
Cal Eldred	31	15	127	8.5	9.9	131	7	3	2	2	0	1	0
Scott Karl	27	33	143	4.3	7.9	122	9	9	10	4	1	0	0
Hideo Nomo	30	28	261	9.3	12.4	129	3	8	10	4	3	0	0
Kyle Peterson	23	12	11	0.9	2.3	109	5	5	2	0	0	0	0
Bill Pulsipher	25	16	6	0.4	0.8	103	11	3	2	0	0	0	0
Rafael Roque	27	9	0	0.0	0.0	95	8	1	0	0	0	0	0
Steve Woodard	24	29	21	0.7	1.7	110	16	9	4	0	0	0	0
MILWAUKEE		161	574	3.6	5.3	131	67	47	32	10	4	1	0
Ranking (NL)				16	16								

Phil Garner has his flaws, but he has shown an ability to learn from his mistakes that other managers would do well to emulate. After ruining Cal Eldred, Garner admitted he had overworked him, and has become as protective of his pitchers as anyone in baseball. In 1998, the Brewers were 15th in the NL in PAP and Workload, ahead of only Felipe Alou's Expos, and last year they ranked dead last in all of baseball. Sixteen pitchers had more PAPs by themselves than the entire Brewer team. . . . Mind you, the Brewers have few arms worth protecting, but Hideo Nomo had the lightest workload of his career and pitched better than he had in years. . . . Steve Woodard, the Brewers' one shining light on the mound, has had fewer PAPs in his career (116) than Pedro Astacio had in one start last season. Garner is gone, but if Woodard develops into Greg Maddux Lite, his legacy will remain.

Montreal Expos

They saved baseball in Montreal. You might have missed it, because as this is written in early December, the news is being treated as a footnote to a year of idle, racy speculation that the Expos were heading to Washington, D.C. or Northern Virginia or North Carolina or just about anywhere south of Canada. Managing Partner Claude Brochu was convinced the Expos were gone when it became clear he couldn't put together a deal for a ballpark. Montreal was so dead in some writers' imaginations they speculated about what a great city it would be for a Triple-A team on the move.

There were a couple of fatal flaws with the Dead Expo Theory. First, those of us south of the border—really most of us outside the province of Quebec—don't have a good understanding about how well-connected the Expos are within the local political system. When local government swore that there wouldn't be any public financing of a stadium, Claude Brochu might have been ready to throw up his hands and give up, but his minority partners were not. It was an election year, and there wasn't any reason to worry about public statements from stumping politicians. Once the 1998 election passed, the provincial government expressed a willingness to help finance a downtown stadium.

Part of the problem was Brochu himself. Once he was moved aside, negotiations made more progress in a few months than they had in several years with him as the front man.

Second, the guy that the city of Baltimore still wishes had outbid Peter Angelos for the Orioles was willing to drop a good chunk of change to buy out Brochu and assume a controlling interest in the team. Jeff Loria is usually referred to as "a New York art dealer," but he has also owned a minor-league team, happens to speak French, is willing to keep the team in Montreal and seems to value his local partners for the political capital they represent.

Coming into the fold as a minority partner is Charles Bronfman's son Stephen, allowing the Loria group to be identified with the original owner of the Expos, and thus with a commitment to keeping the team in Montreal. And because Loria was the man who lost out in the auction of the Orioles, there's no way he'll try to relocate the team anywhere near Baltimore because of the legal fire that would draw from Clan Angelos.

The hero throughout all of this has been minority partner Jacques Menard, who slowly maneuvered Brochu out of the way. Menard patiently met every demand by Loria's group and negotiated with the city and provincial governments and the holding company that controls the Labatt Park site. While Tom Boswell was crabbing about how long the process was taking—in his hunger to see somebody take the Senators' place in D.C.—there was very little chance that the Expos were going to move. The entire deal would have sounded like a house of cards a year ago, but it had to take this long for Menard and Loria to build a partnership for a Montreal future that everyone involved would take seriously.

Now that the ownership issue is resolved, the Expos can proceed with plans for their downtown stadium. Labatt Park should be ready by 2002, at a cost of C$175 to C$200 million, and will seat around 35,000 fans, although the Expos have to meet Loria's demands for 3,000-5,000 swing seats that can be added for the playoffs. While that price sounds low, keep in mind that there isn't as much demand for construction in Canada as there is in many cities in the States.

It's also low because it doesn't include infrastructure costs and because the Expos plan on using a local firm that will handle both design and construction. That should lower the extra losses we all associate with building contractors, even the contractors not responsible for the nine-figure cost overruns on Safeco Field. Knowing how far they've come already, there's a sense of cautious optimism that the city and provincial governments will cooperate. Depending on how quickly arrangements are made with the holding company that will be selling or leasing the downtown real estate, ground may be broken in February or March.

The big question is "why?" The Expos haven't drawn well in years, although last year's especially poor attendance can be blamed in part on the uncertainty about the team's future.

Expos Prospectus

1999 record: 68-94; Fourth place, NL East

Pythagorean W/L: 68-94

Runs scored: 718 (14th in NL)

Runs allowed: 853 (13th in NL)

Team EQA: .245 (16th in NL)

1999 team age: 25.6 (youngest in NL)

1999 park: Olympic Stadium; moderate hitters' park, increased run scoring by 8%.

1999: Team continued to go nowhere, on the field or on the highway.

2000: They're staying in Quebec, so now the focus shifts to the baseball. Hopefully.

Sure, we all know Bud Selig says he wants to avoid moving franchises, but if the Expos aren't moving, who should? Basically, the Expos aren't moving because local government was willing to accede to MLB's new unwritten rule that having a major-league baseball team is dependent upon your city's willingness to fund construction of a new stadium. So despite bad attendance, the Expos will stay in Montreal and Bud Selig will talk about how good attendance was in the late 1970s and early 1980s.

He has a point: you don't have to speak English or Spanish to want to see a good baseball team, and if the Expos improve, so will attendance. Of course, this same guy is saying that baseball in Minnesota is in trouble, and the Twins have had much better attendance than the Expos. The difference is that when push came to shove, Montreal committed to building a stadium, while the voters in Minnesota aren't willing to. That, and not attendance, is driving the decisions on whether teams stay or move. Another factor is that while no major league team would go to Montreal if the Expos moved, you know one of the existing franchises would be interested in the Twin Cities if they become available.

Aside from the financial aspects of Menard's Montreal miracle, there are reasons to believe that there's a lot the Expos can do to help themselves within their market. While some people can't run out of nice things to say about Claude Brochu, the Expos have been the victim of incompetent marketing for years. From a failure to promote their own players because of a sordid fascination with team mascot Youppi, to a miserable job of getting the team's games broadcast or televised both locally and nationally, Brochu's Expos didn't do themselves any favors in encouraging people to care about the team. In a bilingual market, it seems strange that the Expos focused more on French speakers, while giving English broadcasts and advertising short shrift.

Some gossip-mongers have said Brochu is destined for better things, like working for the commissioner, but on his watch the Expos went from being broadcast throughout Canada to near invisibility. Even before Loria took over in December, Menard was firing the Brochu cronies who contributed to this disaster. It will take years to recover their previous status on television and radio, but a secure future featuring a new stadium and a better team will help after the Expos clean up their internal promotional problems.

The improvement on the field that will drive attendance back up isn't very far off. The Expos are already in position to improve a lot in a very short period of time, simply by employing the talent at hand. But they're also on the cusp of being even better than that, and they know it. While talk about contending in time for Labatt Park's opening is the kind of sunny optimism any team projects when it's about to get a new park, there are several reasons to believe the team on the field can at least dream about it.

One reason they're bound to get better is that the Expos were pretty unlucky in 1999, losing 12 more one-run games than they won, and 11 of 14 extra-inning games. Evening those numbers out would make up a lot of the difference between being one of the league's worst teams and finishing ahead of the Phillies. These sorts of things usually do even out between seasons, even if the team doesn't do much to improve its personnel. Those one-run losses were a reflection of the team's larger problems, which plagued the Expos all year: a wildly inconsistent rotation and a lousy lineup.

The problem with the pitching is that while you expect a young rotation to be a little flaky, the Expos' young starters looked like Keith Law's shoulders. Dustin Hermanson wasn't right physically for most of the year, but he finished strong. Carl Pavano hasn't given anyone reason to forget that Martinez person yet, but the promise is still there and he hasn't suffered a major injury. Javier Vazquez doesn't look like a pitcher only two years removed from A ball; he looks poised for a breakout season. Mike Thurman can pitch. Coming up, the Expos have some of the best young pitchers in the game: both Ted Lilly and Antonio Armas will do wonders for General Manager Jim Beattie's reputation after coming over in the Carlos Perez and Martinez trades, and the Expos' focus on drafting pitching over the last few years is starting to pay dividends. Right now, nobody is saying the Expos have the best young rotation in baseball. By August, you'll hear that a lot.

If the pitching was inconsistent but promising, the offense was just bad. The major-league team finished last in the league in on-base percentage, reflecting a deeper organizational problem. The Expos love to talk about situational hitting and try to teach it in the minors. While I won't say situational hitting is useless, this sort of fixation can end up blinding a team to other offensive weapons, like getting on base. It can lead to being so stubborn that you run off Shane Andrews because despite his strengths, he's never going to be a good situational hitter. Expos player development has started to get away from the fascination with situational hitting, and Beattie and Fred Ferreira have been doing a better job of finding young hitters with some command of the strike zone, from Brad Wilkerson to Albenis Machado to Valentino Pascucci. It isn't the same sort of thing you find in the A's organization, but it's a start.

Another problem is that the Expos had poor hitters at two critical offense-oriented positions: left field and first base. While it would be easy to excuse this by saying that that prime offensive players at those positions are expensive, that simply isn't true. People like Matt Stairs or Roberto Petagine or Brian Daubach work pretty cheap and are readily available if you appreciate their talent. Instead, Beattie gave guys like Orlando Merced jobs. Paying ones, even.

Again, there are reasons to believe things are getting better: Vladimir Guerrero is going to be the best player in the league during the four years he's still under contract to the

Expos. That's a great place to start. When Felipe Alou bumped Rondell White into the leadoff spot for the last 50 games of the season, the Expos' scoring increased by almost half a run per game over what they did while Alou was goofing around with Manny Martinez, Orlando Cabrera and Wilton Guerrero leading off. With Peter Bergeron expected to lead off in 2000, the Expos' lineup will simultaneously be getting a leadoff man who can get on base, and—by bumping White back into the heart of the order—someone better than Brad Fullmer batting fifth.

Putting together a good rotation is a lot more difficult than putting together a good lineup, especially in today's offensive environment, but the Expos already have the advantage of a potentially great rotation. The hope here is that Loria's desire to throw some money around early on will encourage Beattie to play for larger stakes than finding a bigger and better version of Orlando Merced or re-signing David Segui. The Expos have a great young rotation and a solid bullpen, and it looks like they have their leadoff hitter. What they need is to blow every dime Loria wants to spend for upgrades on a left-handed thumper to bat third and play first.

Unfortunately, it looks like the Expos are getting caught up in the same mistakes that the Pirates made last winter, spending too much money on bit contributors because the money is there and someone will take it. A team like the Expos has no need to worry about depth in situational left-handers. And yet, they have given Graeme Lloyd a three-year,

$9 million contract to be Steve Kline. When they already have Steve Kline.

The Expos also traded three prospects for #4 starter Hideki Irabu, who will make about $4 million in 2000. In two days in December, the Expos added $7 million to their 2000 payroll, made an extended commitment to an interchangeable part and added one win. Maybe. The Expos don't need bit parts and they don't need to spend the money just because it's there. Put the $7 million into Broadcom, take the $8.5 million you'll have in a year's time and see if you can't get a real impact player.

Better yet, take $3 million and build a couple of baseball academies in the Caribbean. Or Taiwan. Or Venezuela. International development—development, not random signings—is the gift that keeps on giving. An investment like that would pay off for a lot longer—and have more to do with an Expo championship—than anything two pitchers from the 1998 Yankees ever will.

If the Expos improve their offense and Alou continues to run his pitching staff well, the team can celebrate Loria's arrival by flirting with .500. If they trade some of the minor-league pitching the organization has been cultivating over the last three years for a young offensive star to pair with Guerrero, they'll be in a great position to do more. Giving up any pipe dreams about a glorious run at 85 wins in 2000—and spending money with an eye towards winning in 2001 and beyond—would help.

HITTERS (Averages: BA: .270 / OBP: .340 / SLG: .430 / EQA: .260)

Carlos Adolfo OF Bats R Age 24

YEAR	TEAM	LGE	AB	H	DB	TP	HR	BB/SO	R	RBI	SB	CS	OUT	BA	OBP	SLG	EQA	EQR	DEFENSE
1997	W Palm B	Fla	456	95	14	1	12	32/100	54	44	4	8	369	.208	.263	.322	.191	29	121-OF 93
1998	Jupiter	Fla	338	77	15	1	11	29/91	38	33	4	4	265	.228	.294	.376	.224	32	80-OF 92
1998	Harrisbg	Eas	132	26	3	0	3	7/32	9	17	2	0	106	.197	.242	.288	.174	7	30-OF 103
1999	Ottawa	Int	53	9	1	1	2	2/11	4	8	0	0	44	.170	.213	.340	.174	3	
1999	Harrisbg	Eas	222	53	12	0	9	18/54	29	33	1	1	170	.239	.304	.414	.240	24	46-OF 95
2000	Montreal	NL	328	78	13	0	14	28/81	36	45	4	3	253	.238	.298	.405	.231	32	

While the Expos get credit for drafting and developing tools guys, not all of them turn out well. Adolfo was pushed up to Ottawa having never played well anywhere. He was entering his sixth year in the organization and they needed to see whether or not he belonged on the 40-man roster. The answer is no.

Michael Barrett C/3B Bats R Age 23

YEAR	TEAM	LGE	AB	H	DB	TP	HR	BB/SO	R	RBI	SB	CS	OUT	BA	OBP	SLG	EQA	EQR	DEFENSE	
1997	W Palm B	Fla	431	112	20	1	11	30/54	44	55	3	2	321	.260	.314	.387	.237	44		
1998	Harrisbg	Eas	460	141	29	2	19	21/42	71	80	5	4	323	.307	.339	.502	.275	64	80-C 102	32-3B 98
1999	Montreal	NL	432	123	33	3	7	27/39	50	47	0	2	311	.285	.332	.424	.252	50	57-3B 98	50-C 92
2000	Montreal	NL	454	137	27	1	15	31/43	64	78	3	2	319	.302	.346	.465	.267	59		

Barrett is an interesting player because his talents are basically all quickness-oriented. Not speed, but quickness: quick wrists as a hitter and quick reactions and nimble footwork at third base or behind the plate. His opportunity came a few months

(Michael Barrett *continued*)

sooner than expected when both Chris Widger and Bob Henley were hurt in spring training, but it helped that he was an already an Alou favorite. Whether they'll let him become a regular at catcher or third base is up in the air, but he'll do them the most good behind the plate.

Peter Bergeron — CF — Bats L — Age 22

YEAR	TEAM	LGE	AB	H	DB	TP	HR	BB/SO	R	RBI	SB	CS	OUT	BA	OBP	SLG	EQA	EQR	DEFENSE
1997	Savannah	SAL	516	135	20	4	5	59/111	71	31	12	10	391	.262	.339	.345	.236	53	132-OF 100
1998	SanAnton	Tex	419	120	17	5	7	50/76	59	43	18	6	304	.286	.364	.401	.267	56	108-OF 107
1998	Harrisbg	Eas	137	34	10	3	0	14/25	19	9	5	2	105	.248	.318	.365	.236	14	29-OF 112
1999	Harrisbg	Eas	162	46	15	1	3	19/30	23	14	5	4	120	.284	.359	.444	.268	22	35-OF 98
1999	Ottawa	Int	191	54	13	2	2	19/40	28	16	9	6	143	.283	.350	.403	.256	24	36-OF 94
1999	Montreal	NL	45	11	2	0	0	8/5	9	2	0	0	34	.244	.358	.289	.234	4	
2000	Montreal	NL	523	157	27	4	9	64/101	101	74	29	12	378	.300	.376	.419	.272	73	

The comparisons seesaw back and forth between Steve Finley and Brett Butler. A Mark Grace who can run and play the outfield works a little better because Bergeron has better power than Butler and better on-base skills than Finley. He started the year with shoulder problems, managing to irritate the organization over them. They said he couldn't go to the Pan Am Games if his shoulder was hurting. He said it was fine and played, then came back and said that it hurt. It turned out to be a slight rotator cuff tear that required surgery. He's expected to be fully healthy before Opening Day, and he's penciled in to lead off and play center field if the arm is healed, left field if it isn't.

Geoff Blum — IF — Bats B — Age 27

YEAR	TEAM	LGE	AB	H	DB	TP	HR	BB/SO	R	RBI	SB	CS	OUT	BA	OBP	SLG	EQA	EQR	DEFENSE	
1997	Ottawa	Int	412	97	19	2	3	43/73	50	31	10	4	319	.235	.312	.313	.218	36	71-2B 88	34-SS 91
1998	Harrisbg	Eas	142	37	11	3	4	13/26	20	16	1	1	106	.261	.336	.465	.265	19		
1999	Ottawa	Int	266	59	11	1	7	29/43	31	26	4	1	208	.222	.302	.350	.224	25	56-SS 92	
1999	Montreal	NL	133	31	7	3	7	15/25	20	16	1	0	102	.233	.311	.489	.263	18	36-SS 91	
2000	Montreal	NL	316	77	16	2	11	41/56	46	46	6	2	241	.244	.331	.411	.250	38		

Stop me if you've seen the pilot episode on UPN already: surfer dude plays baseball, goes to Quebec, takes up snowboarding and finds out that Claude Brochu is the missing Wayans brother with a nefarious plot to eliminate all babes. Blum is a solid utility infielder with decent power. He's not someone who should play shortstop regularly.

Milton Bradley Jr. — CF — Bats B — Age 22

YEAR	TEAM	LGE	AB	H	DB	TP	HR	BB/SO	R	RBI	SB	CS	OUT	BA	OBP	SLG	EQA	EQR	DEFENSE
1997	Vermont	NYP	204	49	7	4	3	13/39	20	21	2	3	158	.240	.286	.358	.213	17	49-OF 101
1998	CapeFear	SAL	285	74	19	3	5	19/58	39	38	5	4	214	.260	.312	.400	.239	30	49-OF 96
1998	Jupiter	Fla	264	66	13	1	5	24/46	40	27	6	4	202	.250	.321	.364	.234	27	61-OF 109
1999	Harrisbg	Eas	345	100	22	3	10	25/63	49	39	7	6	251	.290	.342	.458	.264	45	76-OF 101
2000	Montreal	NL	396	112	20	3	12	38/75	60	62	10	7	291	.283	.346	.439	.260	50	

The Expos have been promoting him ambitiously since drafting him in 1996, and he has yet to disappoint. He had the ultimate clutch hit last year, a two-out grand slam off of the Eastern League's best closer (Joe Lisio) in the bottom of the ninth for a 12-11 win that propelled Harrisburg to a four-peat. The long-term dilemma between Bradley and Bergeron in center field has an easy solution: trade Rondell White. After two run-ins with umpires within six months, both resulting in suspensions, Milton is the ideal spokesman for the new parlor game for impolite society, "Fight the Power."

Orlando Cabrera — SS — Bats R — Age 25

YEAR	TEAM	LGE	AB	H	DB	TP	HR	BB/SO	R	RBI	SB	CS	OUT	BA	OBP	SLG	EQA	EQR	DEFENSE	
1997	W Palm B	Fla	285	71	19	1	5	22/37	40	22	13	5	219	.249	.303	.375	.233	29	62-SS 85	
1997	Harrisbg	Eas	133	37	10	2	4	11/19	25	16	5	1	97	.278	.333	.474	.271	19	33-SS 92	
1997	Ottawa	Int	123	32	5	2	2	5/16	15	13	6	1	92	.260	.299	.382	.236	12	19-SS 104	
1998	Ottawa	Int	272	59	10	3	0	23/27	25	23	12	6	219	.217	.278	.276	.191	17	44-SS 99	20-2B 100
1998	Montreal	NL	267	80	19	6	3	18/26	48	24	7	2	189	.300	.344	.449	.268	35	47-SS 94	23-2B 105
1999	Montreal	NL	383	95	24	5	7	13/38	45	36	2	2	290	.248	.279	.392	.221	33	98-SS 108	
2000	Montreal	NL	456	121	27	5	9	33/48	63	58	14	4	339	.265	.315	.406	.242	49		

Cabrera scuffled most of the year before getting hot just in time to sprain his ankle and miss the last two months. He frustrates Alou with some hotdogging in the field, leading to kvetching that he's trying too hard to make *SportsCenter*. Cabrera has worked hard to become a good shortstop, and he's a better guy to have around than Rey Ordonez. Any middle infielder with a little bit of sock and good speed is a useful player; just don't expect Cabrera to turn into a great one.

Jamey Carroll — 2B — Bats R — Age 25

YEAR	TEAM	LGE	AB	H	DB	TP	HR	BB/SO	R	RBI	SB	CS	OUT	BA	OBP	SLG	EQA	EQR	DEFENSE	
1997	W Palm B	Fla	416	95	14	2	1	35/54	44	34	7	5	326	.228	.293	.279	.195	27	60-SS 94	36-2B 97
1998	Jupiter	Fla	225	51	5	0	0	17/32	27	11	4	2	176	.227	.291	.249	.184	13	45-2B 92	
1998	Harrisbg	Eas	267	65	10	3	0	35/29	37	18	7	3	205	.243	.340	.303	.230	26	53-2B 95	21-SS 89
1999	Harrisbg	Eas	560	137	32	3	3	33/65	57	46	9	5	428	.245	.291	.329	.210	43	118-2B 105	
2000	Montreal	NL	579	145	29	3	2	56/70	72	52	13	6	440	.250	.317	.321	.218	49		

Carroll and Andy Tracy were the two holdover regulars from the Harrisburg team that won in 1998, and they won again this year. It's safe to say that anyone wearing two "Eastern League Champs" belt buckles isn't a prospect, but Carroll is good on the deuce.

Trace Coquillette — IF — Bats R — Age 26

YEAR	TEAM	LGE	AB	H	DB	TP	HR	BB/SO	R	RBI	SB	CS	OUT	BA	OBP	SLG	EQA	EQR	DEFENSE	
1997	W Palm B	Fla	193	49	15	1	6	22/32	24	23	3	3	147	.254	.343	.435	.261	25	44-2B 86	
1997	Harrisbg	Eas	294	68	18	2	7	17/43	34	38	5	2	228	.231	.295	.378	.228	28	55-2B 95	
1998	Harrisbg	Eas	190	56	7	0	8	11/44	31	19	6	2	136	.295	.349	.458	.272	26	44-2B 92	
1998	Ottawa	Int	252	58	9	0	7	12/40	24	34	2	2	196	.230	.282	.349	.211	20	45-2B 85	19-3B 96
1999	Ottawa	Int	329	88	25	2	9	34/75	39	37	6	3	244	.267	.370	.438	.275	48	84-2B 88	
1999	Montreal	NL	49	13	2	0	0	3/7	2	4	1	0	36	.265	.322	.306	.222	4		
2000	Montreal	NL	415	111	22	1	14	41/83	63	61	13	3	307	.267	.333	.427	.256	51		

Coquillette's problem is that he's an offense-oriented utility infielder in an organization already stuck with Jose Vidro's glove at second, making it more interested in the defensive skills of their utility infielders, and not whether they can hit a little. He should own Mike Mordecai's job, but the Expos gave Mordecai a multi-year contract for more than the minimum because he picks up Alou's dry cleaning.

Tomas de la Rosa — SS — Bats R — Age 22

YEAR	TEAM	LGE	AB	H	DB	TP	HR	BB/SO	R	RBI	SB	CS	OUT	BA	OBP	SLG	EQA	EQR	DEFENSE
1997	Vermont	NYP	279	63	16	4	2	24/53	30	30	6	3	219	.226	.290	.333	.212	23	68-SS 98
1998	Jupiter	Fla	394	92	21	1	3	29/67	41	36	11	4	306	.234	.293	.315	.210	31	117-SS 101
1999	Harrisbg	Eas	468	111	23	2	5	32/66	55	35	15	8	365	.237	.287	.327	.209	37	127-SS 102
2000	Montreal	NL	421	105	22	2	5	38/66	57	41	18	7	323	.249	.312	.347	.225	39	

De la Rosa gives lots of little hints that he might improve significantly in the next year or two. He's got more power than you expect from a young speed guy. As a shortstop, he has soft hands and a strong arm. If he's going to have a career, he has to improve against breaking stuff. He won't push Cabrera, but if Cabrera doesn't improve, he could get a look.

Jose Fernandez — 3B — Bats R — Age 25

YEAR	TEAM	LGE	AB	H	DB	TP	HR	BB/SO	R	RBI	SB	CS	OUT	BA	OBP	SLG	EQA	EQR	DEFENSE
1997	W Palm B	Fla	358	95	20	2	9	30/86	37	47	9	6	269	.265	.331	.408	.250	42	95-3B 107
1997	Harrisbg	Eas	97	21	3	1	3	8/29	8	9	1	0	76	.216	.281	.361	.217	8	18-3B 89
1998	Harrisbg	Eas	375	103	25	1	16	30/74	51	52	10	4	276	.275	.340	.475	.271	53	85-3B 95
1999	Ottawa	Int	461	111	26	2	11	23/141	56	53	9	5	355	.241	.283	.377	.221	41	112-3B 97
1999	Montreal	NL	24	5	1	0	0	1/7	1	1	0	0	19	.208	.240	.250	.148	1	
2000	Montreal	NL	373	95	18	1	11	32/103	47	49	8	3	281	.255	.314	.397	.238	39	

Fernandez is another one of the Expos' athletic non-prospects. He has Dunston's Syndrome: he can't accept that nobody hits breaking stuff in the dirt. Fernandez runs well, can get the ball out the infield once in a while and has good range at third, but he also managed 24 boots by July. Everyone gets tired of Nancy Sinatra after the first couple of times.

Brad Fullmer   1B   Bats L   Age 25

YEAR	TEAM	LGE	AB	H	DB	TP	HR	BB/SO	R	RBI	SB	CS	OUT	BA	OBP	SLG	EQA	EQR	DEFENSE
1997	Harrisbg	Eas	357	99	25	2	14	21/26	46	47	4	2	260	.277	.326	.476	.265	47	67-1B 107
1997	Ottawa	Int	92	27	3	0	4	1/10	11	16	1	1	66	.293	.315	.457	.253	11	
1998	Montreal	NL	517	154	46	3	16	39/68	64	81	7	7	370	.298	.350	.491	.276	74	123-1B 92
1999	Ottawa	Int	140	40	6	0	9	9/17	23	24	1	2	102	.286	.340	.521	.277	21	23-1B 96
1999	Montreal	NL	347	94	34	2	8	17/35	35	43	1	3	256	.271	.309	.450	.249	39	87-1B 96
2000	Montreal	NL	507	154	40	2	21	41/57	83	97	5	3	356	.304	.356	.515	.283	76	

Some people get along with Felipe Alou just fine, and some people don't. Fullmer was given the "Die Shane Andrews! Die! Die! DIE!" treatment for really unpopular guys, to the point that, like Andrews in 1997, he refused a punitive assignment to Ottawa. While the organization says nice things about how they think he's a better hitter now that he's working with Jeff Leonard and laying off the weights, Fullmer will lose the job at first base if Fernando Seguignol does anything in camp. If it happens, Fullmer is a solid bet for a Lee Stevens-style resurrection a few years later.

Vladimir Guerrero   RF   Bats R   Age 24

YEAR	TEAM	LGE	AB	H	DB	TP	HR	BB/SO	R	RBI	SB	CS	OUT	BA	OBP	SLG	EQA	EQR	DEFENSE
1997	Montreal	NL	327	97	24	2	11	19/39	44	39	2	4	234	.297	.349	.483	.273	45	68-OF 100
1998	Montreal	NL	641	226	42	7	44	42/92	119	120	12	11	425	.353	.399	.646	.328	131	156-OF 95
1999	Montreal	NL	608	187	37	6	39	47/61	94	119	11	7	428	.308	.365	.581	.302	107	156-RF 97
2000	Montreal	NL	558	193	36	4	42	53/65	117	150	15	6	371	.346	.403	.651	.330	116	

Rats, he only set eight new club records in his third season. Sure, 19 errors is a lot, but you're talking about the best young hitter in the league, and he has the advantage of playing in a bilingual city where he doesn't speak either language. In a lot of cities, that would mean plenty of unfair characterizations from a local media frustrated in its attempts to get interviews. In Montreal, he gets treated as an amiably mute great player. He's the perfect player to build the Expos' renaissance around.

Wilton Guerrero   Brother   Bats B   Age 25

YEAR	TEAM	LGE	AB	H	DB	TP	HR	BB/SO	R	RBI	SB	CS	OUT	BA	OBP	SLG	EQA	EQR	DEFENSE
1997	LosAngls	NL	363	110	12	10	4	8/51	41	33	5	5	258	.303	.318	.424	.245	39	89-2B 97
1998	LosAngls	NL	184	57	5	3	0	3/32	23	9	6	2	129	.310	.325	.370	.238	18	26-2B 89
1998	Albuquer	PCL	118	30	3	1	1	8/12	11	8	8	2	90	.254	.306	.322	.224	11	19-2B 90
1998	Montreal	NL	227	69	12	7	2	10/29	32	22	3	0	158	.304	.333	.445	.262	28	51-2B 96
1999	Montreal	NL	315	90	13	7	2	9/38	38	29	6	6	231	.286	.310	.390	.233	30	38-2B 94
2000	Montreal	NL	357	110	14	8	2	18/47	50	48	10	5	252	.308	.341	.409	.251	40	

What is the price of greatness? Apparently, a sidekick. While Alou talks about getting him playing time in the outfield, big bro isn't worth the trouble. Now that Vidro has broken through, there's no position for Wilton and he doesn't hit enough to play anywhere regularly, anyway. He has value as a latter-day Rodney Scott, playing the middle infield once in awhile, pinch-hitting and pinch-running. Like Chris Gwynn before him, he shows that the Dodgers have an uncanny knack of picking the right bloodline, while missing by a sibling or two.

Bob Henley   C   Bats R   Age 27

YEAR	TEAM	LGE	AB	H	DB	TP	HR	BB/SO	R	RBI	SB	CS	OUT	BA	OBP	SLG	EQA	EQR	DEFENSE
1996	Harrisbg	Eas	296	61	13	1	2	59/84	28	23	1	1	236	.206	.342	.277	.224	28	
1997	Harrisbg	Eas	280	70	14	0	9	22/45	28	35	3	1	211	.250	.312	.396	.240	30	
1998	Ottawa	Int	126	27	4	1	3	9/38	10	15	1	1	100	.214	.271	.333	.201	9	28-C 101
1998	Montreal	NL	118	39	10	1	3	11/25	17	19	3	0	79	.331	.403	.508	.308	21	30-C 101
2000	Montreal	NL	110	30	4	0	5	11/73	15	19	1	0	80	.273	.339	.445	.261	14	

Injury-prone, even for a catcher, and currently recovering from two torn muscles in his shoulder. He should be ready to take over as the backup catcher in 2000. If and when he's healthy, the Widger trade rumors will heat up. Henley has a good defensive reputation, and it helps that the Expos rave about his situational hitting skills.

Terry Jones PR/CF   Bats B   Age 29

YEAR	TEAM	LGE	AB	H	DB	TP	HR	BB/SO	R	RBI	SB	CS	OUT	BA	OBP	SLG	EQA	EQR	DEFENSE
1997	ColSprin	PCL	352	75	10	2	1	16/55	42	17	21	5	282	.213	.247	.261	.175	18	85-OF 94
1998	Ottawa	Int	279	59	3	3	0	24/53	24	17	19	4	224	.211	.274	.244	.187	17	81-OF 104
1998	Montreal	NL	216	52	10	2	1	21/45	33	17	18	5	169	.241	.308	.319	.227	21	57-OF 115
1999	Ottawa	Int	329	74	13	2	0	18/73	34	18	18	7	262	.225	.267	.277	.188	20	81-OF 98
1999	Montreal	NL	63	17	0	1	0	2/14	3	3	1	2	48	.270	.292	.302	.192	4	
2000	NYYanks	AL	316	69	8	2	0	26/65	34	17	17	6	253	.218	.278	.256	.192	20	

Jones is a jackrabbit who can beat anyone in a race from the batter's box to the dugout, and not just because he skips running the bases. If there was going to be a year in which he was useful, it would be in the one that had rag-armed catchers like Todd Hundley, Mike Piazza, Eddie Taubensee and Dave Nilsson playing regularly. As you can see, Jones didn't play.

Albenis Machado SS   Bats B   Age 21

YEAR	TEAM	LGE	AB	H	DB	TP	HR	BB/SO	R	RBI	SB	CS	OUT	BA	OBP	SLG	EQA	EQR	DEFENSE
1998	Vermont	NYP	205	48	6	1	1	25/34	22	17	4	5	162	.234	.322	.288	.211	17	55-SS 104
1999	CapeFear	SAL	457	96	16	3	2	87/78	66	27	7	12	373	.210	.341	.271	.217	41	108-SS 103
2000	Montreal	NL	276	65	9	1	1	57/53	45	25	5	6	217	.236	.366	.286	.232	28	

The new Steve Jeltz? He has a strong arm, good hands, great range and extraordinary patience. Unfortunately, he runs the bases in ways you wish he wouldn't, with 19 steals and 27 times caught in 1999. Fortunately, the minors are supposed to be a learning experience, where a guy sorts out what he can and can't do. He can get on base; the first-base coach just needs to wrestle him to the ground once he gets there.

Manny Martinez OF   Bats B   Age 29

YEAR	TEAM	LGE	AB	H	DB	TP	HR	BB/SO	R	RBI	SB	CS	OUT	BA	OBP	SLG	EQA	EQR	DEFENSE
1997	Calgary	PCL	400	101	19	1	11	22/90	46	41	10	6	305	.252	.291	.387	.227	38	106-OF 94
1998	Nashvill	PCL	75	15	4	0	1	6/22	9	5	3	2	62	.200	.259	.293	.185	5	14-OF 102
1998	Pittsbrg	NL	182	47	12	2	6	8/43	21	24	0	3	138	.258	.298	.445	.240	19	45-OF 99
1999	Montreal	NL	332	80	11	7	2	12/50	43	24	16	6	258	.241	.267	.334	.205	25	86-CF 102
2000	Montreal	NL	310	77	15	4	6	20/59	37	34	10	6	239	.248	.294	.381	.223	28	

He's a nice fifth outfielder who was forced into regular playing time during White's aches and pains. Martinez is probably going to end up coaching baserunning someday, because he does a great job of reading outfielders, anticipating throws and knowing when he can swipe an extra base on a ball hit into the gaps.

Ryan McGuire 1B/OF   Bats L   Age 28

YEAR	TEAM	LGE	AB	H	DB	TP	HR	BB/SO	R	RBI	SB	CS	OUT	BA	OBP	SLG	EQA	EQR	DEFENSE	
1997	Ottawa	Int	187	49	11	1	2	29/31	30	12	3	1	139	.262	.361	.364	.255	23	50-1B 126	
1997	Montreal	NL	200	51	15	2	3	19/34	21	16	0	4	153	.255	.320	.395	.236	21	27-OF 110	19-1B 107
1998	Montreal	NL	214	44	8	0	2	33/54	18	12	0	0	170	.206	.312	.271	.205	16	33-1B 96	27-OF 91
1999	Ottawa	Int	182	38	4	1	3	28/41	17	20	1	2	146	.209	.314	.291	.210	15	33-1B 90	
1999	Montreal	NL	140	30	6	2	2	25/33	16	17	1	1	111	.214	.333	.329	.232	14	31-1B 134	
2000	NYMets	NL	293	67	13	2	5	48/67	40	34	1	2	228	.229	.337	.338	.238	31		

A defensive first baseman on a team that doesn't have room for him because of pesky roster limits. The Expos have a couple of great pinch-runners, need defensive replacements at three infield positions, and, of course, have to carry a couple of catchers. If they could carry 30 guys, they might just have room for everyone.

Josh McKinley SS   Bats B   Age 20

YEAR	TEAM	LGE	AB	H	DB	TP	HR	BB/SO	R	RBI	SB	CS	OUT	BA	OBP	SLG	EQA	EQR	DEFENSE
1999	CapeFear	SAL	173	41	11	0	0	13/38	14	14	4	3	135	.237	.290	.301	.200	12	20-SS 83
1999	Vermont	NYP	288	61	12	1	4	25/53	35	24	3	2	229	.212	.276	.302	.194	19	44-SS 85
2000	Montreal	NL	232	55	5	0	4	22/83	24	22	5	2	179	.237	.303	.310	.208	18	

The Expos did something interesting with their 1998 first-rounder: he spent most of the first half at a higher level at DH to work on his hitting, then went down to play shortstop once the New York-Penn League began. Because Wilson Valdez is a better glove at shortstop, McKinley also played some second base; his future as a shortstop is doubtful.

Orlando Merced — OF/1B — Bats L — Age 33

YEAR	TEAM	LGE	AB	H	DB	TP	HR	BB/SO	R	RBI	SB	CS	OUT	BA	OBP	SLG	EQA	EQR	DEFENSE
1997	Toronto	AL	369	102	26	2	9	45/60	45	40	7	3	270	.276	.360	.431	.270	51	93-OF 98
1998	Minnesot	AL	203	58	8	0	6	17/28	20	32	1	4	149	.286	.344	.414	.252	24	33-1B 94
1999	Montreal	NL	193	50	13	1	7	24/27	23	23	2	1	144	.259	.341	.446	.264	26	33-LF 106
2000	Montreal	NL	178	47	7	0	6	23/26	26	27	2	1	132	.264	.348	.404	.254	22	

For the second straight year, Merced tried to maneuver his way off of a losing team's roster to sneak onto some team bound for the playoffs, this time by refusing a rehabilitation assignment. While he can be a handy bench player, who needs to put up with that kind of crap?

Mike Mordecai — IF — Bats R — Age 32

YEAR	TEAM	LGE	AB	H	DB	TP	HR	BB/SO	R	RBI	SB	CS	OUT	BA	OBP	SLG	EQA	EQR	DEFENSE	
1997	Richmond	Int	123	34	7	0	3	6/18	18	13	0	1	90	.276	.315	.407	.239	13		
1997	Atlanta	NL	82	15	2	1	0	6/16	8	3	0	1	68	.183	.239	.232	.137	2		
1998	Montreal	NL	121	27	6	2	3	9/19	13	11	1	0	94	.223	.277	.380	.220	11		
1999	Montreal	NL	226	52	8	2	5	17/31	26	23	1	5	179	.230	.287	.350	.208	18	27-SS 103	25-3B 105
2000	Montreal	NL	143	34	5	1	4	13/21	15	17	0	1	110	.238	.301	.371	.221	13		

Mordecai re-signed for 2000 with a one-year club option in an extremely ill-timed decision. Roster spots matter, and the Expos are a bad offensive team that needs every run it can get. What's the point of carrying defensive replacements if you don't have leads to protect? With better hitters like Blum and Coquillette ready, there was no reason to give Mordecai any guarantees.

James Mouton — OF — Bats R — Age 31

YEAR	TEAM	LGE	AB	H	DB	TP	HR	BB/SO	R	RBI	SB	CS	OUT	BA	OBP	SLG	EQA	EQR	DEFENSE
1997	Houston	NL	182	40	10	1	3	18/30	23	23	7	7	149	.220	.297	.335	.213	16	50-OF 95
1998	LasVegas	PCL	187	54	15	2	2	14/34	26	21	9	1	134	.289	.341	.422	.265	24	40-OF 88
1999	Montreal	NL	122	31	5	1	2	16/31	16	12	5	2	93	.254	.351	.361	.251	15	
2000	Milwauke	NL	122	31	8	1	2	13/26	20	14	6	2	93	.254	.326	.385	.245	14	

He's a good example of why older guys who get touted as prospects are more likely to disappoint: by the time he was up with the Astros, he was already 25, so it wasn't as if he was going to get considerably better from that point on. Signed by the Brewers to corner the market on Moutons.

Tootie Myers — 2B — Bats R — Age 21

YEAR	TEAM	LGE	AB	H	DB	TP	HR	BB/SO	R	RBI	SB	CS	OUT	BA	OBP	SLG	EQA	EQR	DEFENSE
1998	Vermont	NYP	279	61	17	2	0	22/89	24	19	5	3	221	.219	.283	.294	.196	19	69-2B 87
1999	CapeFear	SAL	526	110	19	5	11	29/148	46	44	12	7	423	.209	.258	.327	.195	35	136-2B 87
2000	Montreal	NL	360	79	15	3	6	24/114	32	31	8	4	285	.219	.268	.328	.196	24	

Not to be confused with Dustin Hoffman in a dress, although he started off as an outfielder before the Expos decided he should transform to a second baseman. He's one of the best athletes in the organization but has to improve in every phase of the game before he'll be a prospect.

Talmadge Nunnari — 1B — Bats L — Age 25

YEAR	TEAM	LGE	AB	H	DB	TP	HR	BB/SO	R	RBI	SB	CS	OUT	BA	OBP	SLG	EQA	EQR	DEFENSE	
1997	Vermont	NYP	244	61	10	1	4	23/43	20	29	2	1	184	.250	.319	.348	.229	23	60-1B 89	
1998	CapeFear	SAL	297	72	7	0	4	31/49	35	39	1	2	227	.242	.315	.306	.214	24	74-1B 103	
1998	Jupiter	Fla	204	48	7	0	3	23/47	13	26	0	1	157	.235	.313	.314	.215	17	53-1B 102	
1999	Jupiter	Fla	263	73	12	1	4	20/46	27	30	4	0	190	.278	.332	.376	.245	28	40-1B 91	
1999	Harrisbg	Eas	239	64	13	1	4	29/52	32	20	3	1	176	.268	.349	.381	.253	28	34-1B 86	17-OF 99
2000	Montreal	NL	410	109	15	1	8	51/80	58	53	4	1	302	.266	.347	.366	.245	45		

He's an old-fashioned ballplayer, in that his batting average reflects his value. He's been trying to help his career by hitting the weights, but it hasn't given him more power. The Expos have given him some time in left field to make him a little more useful as a bench player, and he'll have some value there. He's a better hitter than Ryan McGuire.

Thomas Pittman 1B Bats R Age 20

YEAR	TEAM	LGE	AB	H	DB	TP	HR	BB/SO	R	RBI	SB	CS	OUT	BA	OBP	SLG	EQA	EQR	DEFENSE
1998	Vermont	NYP	227	44	7	0	6	11/69	21	26	1	2	185	.194	.236	.304	.171	11	57-1B 82
1999	CapeFear	SAL	515	127	25	2	18	21/147	59	75	5	7	395	.247	.284	.408	.227	48	119-1B 96
2000	Montreal	NL	304	74	11	1	12	16/99	30	39	3	2	232	.243	.281	.405	.223	27	

Jim Beattie calls him his "Frank Thomas" because Pittman is a big kid who was heavily recruited to play college football. This sort of comparison is symbolic of bigger evaluation problems in the organization: Pittman may field like the Big Hurt, but doesn't look like he'll out-hit William Hurt. Or Mary Beth, for that matter. He's young enough to improve, but he needs to be taught to work a pitcher and take a pitch. This isn't the organization for that.

Brian Schneider C Bats L Age 23

YEAR	TEAM	LGE	AB	H	DB	TP	HR	BB/SO	R	RBI	SB	CS	OUT	BA	OBP	SLG	EQA	EQR	DEFENSE
1997	CapeFear	SAL	395	91	20	1	4	46/46	41	42	1	3	307	.230	.315	.316	.217	34	
1998	CapeFear	SAL	137	35	6	1	6	13/9	23	22	2	1	103	.255	.329	.445	.259	18	35-C 103
1998	Jupiter	Fla	304	74	11	1	3	17/42	26	24	2	2	232	.243	.285	.316	.201	21	76-C 105
1999	Harrisbg	Eas	422	101	17	1	15	23/58	40	54	1	1	322	.239	.281	.391	.223	38	109-C 104
2000	Montreal	NL	421	107	14	1	14	39/55	48	58	1	2	316	.254	.317	.392	.235	42	

The new Darrin Fletcher? He's a good receiver and game-caller, with an accurate arm that isn't very strong. Catchers who hit left-handed have better job guarantees than mailmen, and they're less likely to go postal. If Henley scuffles, Schneider could be up before September, adding another wrinkle to the choice of where to put Barrett.

Fernando Seguignol 1B/OF Bats B Age 25

YEAR	TEAM	LGE	AB	H	DB	TP	HR	BB/SO	R	RBI	SB	CS	OUT	BA	OBP	SLG	EQA	EQR	DEFENSE
1997	W Palm B	Fla	463	105	23	3	18	24/146	58	68	2	2	360	.227	.270	.406	.223	42	117-1B 113
1998	Harrisbg	Eas	286	77	11	0	23	24/78	47	61	4	1	210	.269	.336	.549	.286	46	58-1B 98
1998	Ottawa	Int	109	26	5	0	6	10/44	14	14	0	0	83	.239	.308	.450	.251	13	21-OF 87
1999	Ottawa	Int	308	76	14	2	18	34/99	41	55	2	6	238	.247	.340	.481	.266	44	49-1B 101
1999	Montreal	NL	105	26	8	0	5	4/33	13	9	0	0	79	.248	.324	.467	.262	14	
2000	Montreal	NL	463	125	22	1	29	46/147	69	91	5	3	341	.270	.336	.510	.273	66	

Despite early wrist problems, he continued to improve his command of the strike zone. With Bergeron ready and Bradley almost ready, the experiment with moving Seguignol to left field is over. Fullmer and Seguignol are only two days apart in age, and the future is now for both of them. Seguignol has more power and a better glove and carries the heavy burden of being the guy the Expos got from the Yankees for John Wetteland. Unlike Fullmer, he hasn't ticked off Alou yet.

Andrew Tracy 3B/1B Bats L Age 26

YEAR	TEAM	LGE	AB	H	DB	TP	HR	BB/SO	R	RBI	SB	CS	OUT	BA	OBP	SLG	EQA	EQR	DEFENSE
1997	CapeFear	SAL	217	53	8	1	7	17/52	23	32	2	0	164	.244	.305	.387	.235	22	52-1B 102
1998	Jupiter	Fla	256	51	12	1	7	28/89	24	33	2	1	206	.199	.283	.336	.210	21	67-1B 93
1998	Harrisbg	Eas	215	44	12	2	8	19/66	28	27	1	1	172	.205	.279	.391	.223	20	51-1B 91
1999	Harrisbg	Eas	496	108	22	1	25	50/162	67	85	2	1	389	.218	.294	.417	.237	53	109-3B 84
2000	Montreal	NL	458	104	19	1	23	52/149	56	69	2	1	355	.227	.306	.424	.240	50	

The Eastern League MVP who the Expos have been smart enough to leave off of their 40-man roster so far. While I hope the good folks in Harrisburg name a playground or a diamond after him someday, he isn't a prospect. He was repeating the league and was old for the level. While his defense has improved, he lacks the range to really stick at third base.

Jon Tucker 1B Bats L Age 23

YEAR	TEAM	LGE	AB	H	DB	TP	HR	BB/SO	R	RBI	SB	CS	OUT	BA	OBP	SLG	EQA	EQR	DEFENSE
1997	Vero Bch	Fla	426	110	18	0	15	29/93	49	66	2	1	317	.258	.309	.406	.240	45	110-1B 106
1998	SanAnton	Tex	362	96	30	1	8	33/82	36	49	2	3	269	.265	.330	.420	.251	43	73-1B 108
1998	Harrisbg	Eas	81	22	6	0	3	16/18	12	15	0	0	59	.272	.392	.457	.289	13	
1999	Harrisbg	Eas	363	83	19	1	12	40/88	44	45	2	2	282	.229	.309	.386	.235	38	88-1B 86
2000	Montreal	NL	351	94	15	1	15	45/82	52	61	1	1	258	.268	.351	.444	.265	46	

(Jon Tucker *continued*)

Jim Beattie gets credit for some things, but he needs to stop getting other people's minor-league first basemen as throw-ins. Tucker and Ryan McGuire have both turned out badly, unless Brad Fullmer's job security is high on your list of organizational priorities. Tucker's a big guy, and the hope is that he's going to add power with age, but it's going to have to be a lot more power to make him relevant.

Jose Vidro 2B/3B Bats B Age 25

YEAR	TEAM	LGE	AB	H	DB	TP	HR	BB/SO	R	RBI	SB	CS	OUT	BA	OBP	SLG	EQA	EQR	DEFENSE	
1997	Ottawa	Int	281	88	14	0	13	17/39	36	43	2	0	193	.313	.354	.502	.284	41	44-3B 110	19-2B 85
1997	Montreal	NL	170	42	13	1	2	11/20	19	17	1	0	128	.247	.301	.371	.227	16	25-3B 102	
1998	Ottawa	Int	234	63	13	1	2	19/25	29	27	3	1	172	.269	.333	.359	.239	24	29-2B 94	22-3B 104
1998	Montreal	NL	210	51	13	0	0	27/32	26	20	2	2	161	.243	.341	.305	.228	20	46-2B 97	
1999	Montreal	NL	493	145	42	2	12	23/50	62	54	0	3	351	.294	.331	.460	.261	61	107-2B 102	
2000	Montreal	NL	506	156	35	2	14	38/58	78	87	4	2	352	.308	.357	.468	.273	68		

Normally we don't do much trivia, but Vidro's 1999 was fun in that his 45 doubles were the seventh-most all-time for a player who stole no bases. Who were the top six? John Olerud holds the record with 54 (1993), followed by Don Mattingly's 53 (1986), followed by a four-way tie at 47 (Cal Ripken's 1983, Wade Boggs' 1986, Joe Medwick's 1938 and Pete Rose's 1975). As a hitter, Vidro has extremely quick wrists. One of the game's big myths is that turf hitters are supposed to be guys with great foot speed, but it's great bat speed that generates those grounders that zip through infields. He's not somebody to bank on for a long time, but a good guy to have around for the next two or three years.

Rondell White OF Bats R Age 28

YEAR	TEAM	LGE	AB	H	DB	TP	HR	BB/SO	R	RBI	SB	CS	OUT	BA	OBP	SLG	EQA	EQR	DEFENSE	
1997	Montreal	NL	596	160	31	4	29	30/110	82	81	12	8	444	.268	.315	.480	.260	76	152-OF 109	
1998	Montreal	NL	367	119	24	2	20	30/55	60	64	18	8	256	.324	.387	.564	.308	68	96-OF 112	
1999	Montreal	NL	538	163	27	6	20	25/84	76	58	8	6	381	.303	.348	.487	.275	76	71-LF 102	57-CF 96
2000	Montreal	NL	492	147	28	4	24	37/80	81	94	14	6	351	.299	.348	.518	.281	73		

He was dangled over the winter, not just because of his fragility but because he's really sick of being an Expo. He was outspoken about Shane Andrews's release and went ballistic when asked to ride pine so that Wil Guerrero could get playing time in the outfield. It doesn't help matters that he was right on both counts. He's sort of a poor man's Eric Davis for now: he'll be outstanding if he's put in an outfield corner and allowed some extra rest once in awhile, but the Expos have been unwilling to rest him in the past, and they're a turf team. He needs out.

Chris Widger C Bats R Age 29

YEAR	TEAM	LGE	AB	H	DB	TP	HR	BB/SO	R	RBI	SB	CS	OUT	BA	OBP	SLG	EQA	EQR	DEFENSE
1997	Montreal	NL	280	66	21	3	7	21/58	30	36	2	0	214	.236	.291	.407	.234	28	
1998	Montreal	NL	425	107	20	1	17	29/83	39	58	7	1	319	.252	.300	.424	.243	46	118-C 101
1999	Montreal	NL	383	98	24	1	13	23/85	38	51	0	4	289	.256	.311	.426	.243	42	100-C 94
2000	Montreal	NL	404	103	22	1	16	34/87	50	61	3	2	303	.255	.313	.433	.245	45	

Mistaken for a young star player once in a while, Widger is actually the new Scott Servais. He's a decent catcher who can hurt junk from left-handers. He's a decent guy to play regularly and bat in the seventh or eighth slots on a team with five or six good regulars. The Expos had to use him in the fifth or sixth slots a total of 60 times, which is brutal. He's under contract for two more years, plus a team option for 2002, so there are several teams interested in him.

Brad Wilkerson OF Bats L Age 23

YEAR	TEAM	LGE	AB	H	DB	TP	HR	BB/SO	R	RBI	SB	CS	OUT	BA	OBP	SLG	EQA	EQR	DEFENSE
1999	Harrisbg	Eas	425	89	20	2	7	74/103	56	40	2	3	339	.209	.333	.315	.228	42	120-OF 96
2000	Montreal	NL	190	41	9	1	4	43/81	32	23	1	1	150	.216	.361	.337	.245	22	

Considering he was a supplemental first rounder from the 1998 draft batting with wood for the first time, the Expos were daring in sending him directly to Double-A. He's got that exaggerated upright uppercut swing that Will Clark likes to show off, but the organization's fussing that he's either trying to hit home runs or he's too passive at the plate. A solid prospect, but already behind Bergeron and Bradley in the fight for the two open outfield spots, and that's only if White is elsewhere.

PITCHERS (Averages: ERA: 4.50 / H/9: 9.00 / HR/9: 1.00 / BB/9: 3.50 / K/9: 6.50 / KWH: 1.00)

Brandon Agamennone Throws R Age 24

YEAR	TEAM	LGE	IP	H	ER	HR	BB	K	ERA	W	L	H/9	HR/9	BB/9	K/9	KWH	PERA
1998	Vermont	NYP	29.7	26	8	2	16	18	2.43	2	1	7.89	0.61	4.85	5.46	0.58	3.94
1998	CapeFear	SAL	31.0	38	26	3	8	18	7.55	1	2	11.03	0.87	2.32	5.23	0.80	4.94
1999	Jupiter	Fla	58.3	72	47	5	21	31	7.25	2	4	11.11	0.77	3.24	4.78	0.47	5.40
1999	Harrisbg	Eas	50.0	53	23	5	16	33	4.14	3	3	9.54	0.90	2.88	5.94	0.96	4.50

A 1998 draft choice out of the University of Maryland, Agamennone is quickly being groomed for a bullpen job. The pen is already a bit crowded with Ugueth Urbina, Anthony Telford, Guillermo Mota, Steve Kline and Graeme Lloyd all guaranteed jobs, plus Scott Strickland and Miguel Batista, but the King of the Achaeans isn't far off from getting a shot.

Antonio Armas Throws R Age 22

YEAR	TEAM	LGE	IP	H	ER	HR	BB	K	ERA	W	L	H/9	HR/9	BB/9	K/9	KWH	PERA
1997	Greensbr	SAL	48.7	48	17	4	18	43	3.14	3	2	8.88	0.74	3.33	7.95	1.60	4.07
1997	Tampa	Fla	42.3	55	31	2	21	20	6.59	2	3	11.69	0.43	4.46	4.25	0.26	5.74
1997	Sarasota	Fla	16.3	23	17	3	16	7	9.37	0	2	12.67	1.65	8.82	3.86	0.10	9.92
1998	Jupiter	Fla	138.3	185	86	13	76	105	5.60	6	9	12.04	0.85	4.94	6.83	0.59	6.77
1999	Harrisbg	Eas	144.0	146	72	10	60	88	4.50	8	8	9.13	0.63	3.75	5.50	0.66	4.31
1999	Montreal	NL	6.3	7	3	0	2	2	4.26	1	0	9.95	0.00	2.84	2.84	0.21	4.26

Or Tony Armas Jr., if you prefer, but it seems he's leaning towards Antonio. He should be the best rookie starter in the National League, and the Expos should be credited right now for some of the things they've done right in the two years they've had him. First off, in 1998 they basically had him avoid using breaking pitches in game situations as much as possible. His curve and slider are both good, but they don't want him to rely on them until he's fully grown. In the meantime, he's perfected a change, his fastball reaches the low 90s, and he's toying with a splitter. Armas was named the best pitching prospect in the Eastern League, where he won the Double-A All-Star game. He isn't guaranteed a spot in camp, but he'll be in the rotation by June.

Miguel Batista Throws R Age 29

YEAR	TEAM	LGE	IP	H	ER	HR	BB	K	ERA	W	L	H/9	HR/9	BB/9	K/9	KWH	PERA
1997	Iowa	AmA	113.7	142	75	18	45	80	5.94	5	8	11.24	1.43	3.56	6.33	0.75	6.33
1997	ChiCubs	NL	37.0	36	23	4	26	26	5.59	2	2	8.76	0.97	6.32	6.32	0.54	5.35
1998	Montreal	NL	130.0	152	72	13	68	87	4.98	6	8	10.52	0.90	4.71	6.02	0.55	5.75
1999	Montreal	NL	139.0	136	75	9	56	92	4.86	7	8	8.81	0.58	3.63	5.96	0.83	4.01

The self-described "utility pitcher," and proud of it. He throws into the mid-90s with a rubber arm, so he's already useful. He's working on a forkball to help himself against left-handed hitters, and if he gets a handle on the pitch, he could surprise people. Otherwise, he's an adequate fifth starter and long reliever.

Shayne Bennett Throws R Age 28

YEAR	TEAM	LGE	IP	H	ER	HR	BB	K	ERA	W	L	H/9	HR/9	BB/9	K/9	KWH	PERA
1997	Harrisbg	Eas	43.3	57	34	6	24	28	7.06	1	4	11.84	1.25	4.98	5.82	0.43	7.06
1997	Ottawa	Int	33.3	25	8	0	23	24	2.16	3	1	6.75	0.00	6.21	6.48	0.75	3.24
1997	Montreal	NL	22.7	21	9	2	10	8	3.57	2	1	8.34	0.79	3.97	3.18	0.23	3.97
1998	Montreal	NL	88.0	105	67	8	48	56	6.85	3	7	10.74	0.82	4.91	5.73	0.46	5.93
1999	Ottawa	Int	88.0	101	51	11	41	61	5.22	4	6	10.33	1.13	4.19	6.24	0.67	5.73
1999	Montreal	NL	11.7	23	16	4	3	4	12.34	0	1	17.74	3.09	2.31	3.09	0.17	12.34

Bennett is a forkballing Aussie who tends to get pounded into the consistency of Vegemite. Taken off of the 40-man roster, he's not too likely to surface anywhere else for any length of time.

Matt Blank   Throws L   Age 24

YEAR	TEAM	LGE	IP	H	ER	HR	BB	K	ERA	W	L	H/9	HR/9	BB/9	K/9	KWH	PERA
1997	Vermont	NYP	87.3	108	41	4	21	52	4.23	5	5	11.13	0.41	2.16	5.36	0.89	4.53
1998	CapeFear	SAL	119.3	175	71	7	35	72	5.35	5	8	13.20	0.53	2.64	5.43	0.63	6.11
1998	Jupiter	Fla	38.3	45	21	3	13	19	4.93	2	2	10.57	0.70	3.05	4.46	0.46	4.93
1999	Jupiter	Fla	80.0	93	43	7	25	49	4.84	4	5	10.46	0.79	2.81	5.51	0.77	4.84
1999	Harrisbg	Eas	80.0	114	49	14	30	34	5.51	4	5	12.83	1.58	3.38	3.83	0.25	7.42

The organization loves him because he's competitive, knows how to use his slider and curve and keeps his fastball low. While he has been outstanding so far, he's your basic college left-hander who doesn't throw hard. Out of every five guys like this, one becomes Jamie Moyer; one gets to be Scott Karl and fade out after a good start; one gets to be Doug Johns and eke out a living on the fringe; one gets injured; and one gets to be Blaise Ilsley. As if the Expos weren't bad enough at stopping the running game, Blank's delivery is extremely slow.

Donnie Bridges   Throws R   Age 21

YEAR	TEAM	LGE	IP	H	ER	HR	BB	K	ERA	W	L	H/9	HR/9	BB/9	K/9	KWH	PERA
1998	Vermont	NYP	61.0	97	56	4	51	27	8.26	2	5	14.31	0.59	7.52	3.98	0.11	9.00
1999	CapeFear	SAL	41.7	56	21	3	24	29	4.54	2	3	12.10	0.65	5.18	6.26	0.47	6.70
1999	Jupiter	Fla	87.0	152	73	7	46	52	7.55	3	7	15.72	0.72	4.76	5.38	0.29	8.90

The Expos' 1997 first-rounder, and a good example of how Beattie isn't afraid of taking risks with high-school talent. The Expos have an odd habit of bumping up almost any pitcher if he starts the year with a good month, and doing that with Bridges in his first full season didn't help. He also suffered a slightly strained elbow. Bridges can bring it into the mid-90s, but doesn't have command of his breaking stuff yet. He's a good two years away from really wondering about, and that's if he keeps his health.

Jayson Durocher   Throws R   Age 25

YEAR	TEAM	LGE	IP	H	ER	HR	BB	K	ERA	W	L	H/9	HR/9	BB/9	K/9	KWH	PERA
1997	W Palm B	Fla	80.7	103	73	8	52	54	8.14	2	7	11.49	0.89	5.80	6.02	0.41	6.81
1998	Jupiter	Fla	31.0	65	31	4	12	20	9.00	1	2	18.87	1.16	3.48	5.81	0.38	11.03
1998	Harrisbg	Eas	10.3	12	10	0	7	9	8.71	0	1	10.45	0.00	6.10	7.84	0.72	5.23
1999	Harrisbg	Eas	48.7	55	36	5	29	28	6.66	2	3	10.17	0.92	5.36	5.18	0.37	5.92
1999	Ottawa	Int	35.7	17	11	2	21	19	2.78	3	1	4.29	0.50	5.30	4.79	0.76	2.27

People keep hoping that this great name will stay healthy long enough to snap off a few of his nasty sliders in the major leagues. He isn't going to grow up to be Jeff Nelson, just a perfectly solid middle reliever.

Keith Evans   Throws R   Age 24

YEAR	TEAM	LGE	IP	H	ER	HR	BB	K	ERA	W	L	H/9	HR/9	BB/9	K/9	KWH	PERA
1997	CapeFear	SAL	128.3	155	79	8	26	69	5.54	6	8	10.87	0.56	1.82	4.84	0.88	4.42
1997	W Palm B	Fla	41.0	52	29	5	14	16	6.37	2	3	11.41	1.10	3.07	3.51	0.26	5.93
1998	Jupiter	Fla	45.7	61	28	2	7	19	5.52	2	3	12.02	0.39	1.38	3.74	0.63	4.73
1998	Harrisbg	Eas	114.7	161	75	14	34	61	5.89	5	8	12.64	1.10	2.67	4.79	0.51	6.44
1999	Harrisbg	Eas	25.7	35	16	5	5	17	5.61	1	2	12.27	1.75	1.75	5.96	1.23	6.66
1999	Ottawa	Int	123.0	143	70	15	24	67	5.12	6	8	10.46	1.10	1.76	4.90	0.98	4.76

Beattie can't resist big pitchers, even if they don't throw hard. Evans is a control pitcher who gets a bunch of ground balls. There's some speculation that if he'd just start pushing off of his back leg in his delivery, his velocity would improve, but he hasn't done it yet. He's just Triple-A filler. Potentially interesting filler.

Bryan Hebson   Throws R   Age 24

YEAR	TEAM	LGE	IP	H	ER	HR	BB	K	ERA	W	L	H/9	HR/9	BB/9	K/9	KWH	PERA
1998	CapeFear	SAL	64.0	99	58	9	41	36	8.16	2	5	13.92	1.27	5.77	5.06	0.24	8.86
1999	CapeFear	SAL	30.0	33	21	3	25	20	6.30	1	2	9.90	0.90	7.50	6.00	0.36	6.60
1999	Jupiter	Fla	90.7	121	54	7	35	59	5.36	4	6	12.01	0.69	3.47	5.86	0.61	5.96

This is another of Beattie's big gangly pitchers. The Expos drafted Hebson as a supplemental first-rounder in 1997 out of Auburn, where he'd been the #2 starter behind the much shorter—and thus less interesting to scouts—Tim Hudson. Hebson's velocity improved in 1999 after he ditched an over-the-top delivery and dropped down to three-quarters. It got him into the low 90s, and he has a solid slider and a nice change-up as well. The interesting comparison is to Donnie Bridges, also picked in 1997, but out of high school instead of college. Hebson pitched better at the high-A Florida State League after they were promoted from the Sally League only a couple of weeks apart, but he's older and has pitched against more advanced competition. How they each do when bumped up to Harrisburg by mid-May should be interesting.

Dustin Hermanson — Throws R — Age 27

YEAR	TEAM	LGE	IP	H	ER	HR	BB	K	ERA	W	L	H/9	HR/9	BB/9	K/9	KWH	PERA
1997	Montreal	NL	158.7	135	66	15	70	127	3.74	11	7	7.66	0.85	3.97	7.20	1.28	3.80
1998	Montreal	NL	180.3	178	89	22	58	145	4.44	10	10	8.88	1.10	2.89	7.24	1.52	4.29
1999	Montreal	NL	222.0	210	92	18	66	141	3.73	15	10	8.51	0.73	2.68	5.72	1.07	3.65

A lot of hot air was vented all summer long over whether Hermanson wasn't trusting his natural ability enough, or was trusting it too much and needed to study his craft, or wasn't locating his pitches well. Everyone finally agreed that he'd spent most of the year pitching through tendinitis. A stretch of 11 second-half starts allowing three runs or less helped silence the debate, as did a 2.37 ERA after July 31. If the Expos improve at all offensively, he's poised for a great record.

Mike Johnson — Throws R — Age 24

YEAR	TEAM	LGE	IP	H	ER	HR	BB	K	ERA	W	L	H/9	HR/9	BB/9	K/9	KWH	PERA
1996	Hagerstn	SAL	149.0	228	110	9	52	99	6.64	5	12	13.77	0.54	3.14	5.98	0.62	6.70
1997	Baltimor	AL	40.0	51	34	12	16	29	7.65	1	3	11.48	2.70	3.60	6.53	0.77	8.10
1997	Montreal	NL	50.0	55	33	8	22	26	5.94	2	4	9.90	1.44	3.96	4.68	0.42	5.76
1998	Harrisbg	Eas	31.3	42	32	10	12	31	9.19	1	2	12.06	2.87	3.45	8.90	1.42	8.62
1998	Ottawa	Int	107.0	111	62	19	41	78	5.21	5	7	9.34	1.60	3.45	6.56	1.00	5.30
1999	Ottawa	Int	149.0	173	92	21	67	109	5.56	7	10	10.45	1.27	4.05	6.58	0.77	5.86

Johnson spins a nice curve, but his slider routinely winds up in the cheap seats, and his fastball isn't. He's still trying to put a career together after being snagged by the Orioles out of the Blue Jays' organization for 1997 without any high A-ball experience. He's still learning, and a long way from fulfilling the promise he had in Hagerstown.

Steve Kline — Throws L — Age 27

YEAR	TEAM	LGE	IP	H	ER	HR	BB	K	ERA	W	L	H/9	HR/9	BB/9	K/9	KWH	PERA
1997	Buffalo	AmA	47.3	64	33	4	15	35	6.27	2	3	12.17	0.76	2.85	6.65	0.95	5.89
1997	Clevelnd	AL	26.3	41	17	6	13	17	5.81	1	2	14.01	2.05	4.44	5.81	0.41	9.23
1997	Montreal	NL	26.3	32	17	4	10	19	5.81	1	2	10.94	1.37	3.42	6.49	0.84	6.15
1998	Montreal	NL	69.3	67	27	4	43	72	3.50	5	3	8.70	0.52	5.58	9.35	1.34	4.67
1999	Montreal	NL	71.3	52	27	7	32	67	3.41	5	3	6.56	0.88	4.04	8.45	2.02	3.28

Welcome to 1990s-style hyper-specialization: Kline led the NL in appearances with 82 despite missing 11 games in April during a stint on the disabled list. It's sort of a shame Alou keeps him in the situational role, because he's an all-around good pitcher. But then, I'm the kind of guy who wants Alou to put Kline in the outfield and pull the old Whitey Herzog move of alternating a right-hander and a left-hander batter by batter. Between Merced and Martinez, the Expos always had a crappy outfielder they could afford to bump for the tactical advantage. Bah, maybe next year.

Ted Lilly — Throws L — Age 24

YEAR	TEAM	LGE	IP	H	ER	HR	BB	K	ERA	W	L	H/9	HR/9	BB/9	K/9	KWH	PERA
1997	San Bern	Cal	127.7	138	59	10	36	113	4.16	8	6	9.73	0.70	2.54	7.97	1.92	4.23
1998	SanAnton	Tex	101.7	132	58	8	42	78	5.13	5	6	11.69	0.71	3.72	6.90	0.82	5.84
1998	Albuquer	PCL	31.3	38	17	3	10	22	4.88	1	2	10.91	0.86	2.87	6.32	0.95	5.17
1998	Ottawa	Int	38.3	48	27	7	20	44	6.34	1	3	11.27	1.64	4.70	10.33	1.51	7.04
1999	Ottawa	Int	89.7	80	35	11	25	71	3.51	6	4	8.03	1.10	2.51	7.13	1.88	3.71
1999	Montreal	NL	24.0	30	17	6	8	27	6.38	1	2	11.25	2.25	3.00	10.13	2.27	7.12

Lilly would have been up sooner if not for shoulder problems that knocked him out for a few weeks in June and July. He had offseason surgery to repair a slight tear in his shoulder, but they're saying he'll be 100% by spring training. While his curveball was named the International League's best breaking pitch in *Baseball America*'s tools poll, he's not just a soft-tosser; he regularly gets his heat up to 93 mph, complementing it with a good change-up. He's ahead of Armas in the line for the last two rotation spots and should hold one of them for the year.

Guillermo Mota   Throws R   Age 26

YEAR	TEAM	LGE	IP	H	ER	HR	BB	K	ERA	W	L	H/9	HR/9	BB/9	K/9	KWH	PERA
1997	CapeFear	SAL	111.0	194	99	11	51	72	8.03	3	9	15.73	0.89	4.14	5.84	0.39	8.84
1998	Jupiter	Fla	37.0	29	13	0	9	18	3.16	3	1	7.05	0.00	2.19	4.38	0.93	2.19
1998	Harrisbg	Eas	15.7	14	4	0	2	14	2.30	2	0	8.04	0.00	1.15	8.04	5.23	2.30
1999	Ottawa	Int	19.0	16	6	0	6	15	2.84	1	1	7.58	0.00	2.84	7.11	1.75	2.84
1999	Montreal	NL	57.0	50	20	5	24	26	3.16	4	2	7.89	0.79	3.79	4.11	0.42	3.79

Mota is the latest example of the trend of turning position players into pitchers, and potentially the best of them. Alou reserved him for mop-up duty, and he still has a lot to learn about setting hitters up, but doing this well on talent and very little experience is impressive. While he does have a good fastball, it remains to be seen whether it just isn't the 98 mph heater that was advertised, or whether the elbow problems he struggled with all summer kept him from throwing it. Offseason surgery to remove a bone chip shouldn't keep him out of camp, and he should be poised for a big year as a setup man.

John Nicholson   Throws R   Age 22

YEAR	TEAM	LGE	IP	H	ER	HR	BB	K	ERA	W	L	H/9	HR/9	BB/9	K/9	KWH	PERA
1997	Ashevlle	SAL	130.0	165	87	16	51	80	6.02	5	9	11.42	1.11	3.53	5.54	0.57	6.09
1998	Jupiter	Fla	137.7	198	109	6	76	94	7.13	4	11	12.94	0.39	4.97	6.15	0.44	6.80
1999	Jupiter	Fla	6.7	13	28	2	23	3	37.80	0	1	17.55	2.70	31.05	4.05	0.02	27.00

He was one of the prizes in the Lansing deal and is now a source of concern after coming down with a sore arm and a major case of Blassitis Nowherenosis. While everyone loves his hard sinker and curve, his future is in danger. Though getting Nicholson, Jacob Westbrook and Mark Mangum for Lansing still makes as much sense now as it did then, never forget that bad things happen to talented pitchers long before they're in a position to fight for a major-league job.

Carl Pavano   Throws R   Age 24

YEAR	TEAM	LGE	IP	H	ER	HR	BB	K	ERA	W	L	H/9	HR/9	BB/9	K/9	KWH	PERA
1997	Pawtuckt	Int	158.7	161	64	13	35	126	3.63	11	7	9.13	0.74	1.99	7.15	2.11	3.74
1998	Ottawa	Int	18.3	13	5	1	7	12	2.45	2	0	6.38	0.49	3.44	5.89	1.18	2.45
1998	Montreal	NL	130.0	141	77	19	45	78	5.33	6	8	9.76	1.32	3.12	5.40	0.72	5.12
1999	Montreal	NL	107.0	109	56	7	34	68	4.71	6	6	9.17	0.59	2.86	5.72	0.93	3.95

He had a wildly inconsistent year, alternating very good and very bad starts, leading to Bill Lee's observation that no real prospect can fire heat with such a small butt. Fox-quality color commentary aside, a persistent elbow problem put Pavano on the shelf. The Expos have been very careful, getting second and third opinions to make sure that the elbow only requires rest and not surgery. If that's really all there is to it, he's a great bet to finally fulfill his promise in 2000, allowing the Spaceman to tackle more important subjects.

Jeremy Powell   Throws R   Age 24

YEAR	TEAM	LGE	IP	H	ER	HR	BB	K	ERA	W	L	H/9	HR/9	BB/9	K/9	KWH	PERA
1997	W Palm B	Fla	145.0	198	93	5	81	95	5.77	6	10	12.29	0.31	5.03	5.90	0.42	6.33
1998	Harrisbg	Eas	122.3	141	69	14	42	62	5.08	6	8	10.37	1.03	3.09	4.56	0.49	5.15
1998	Montreal	NL	24.0	29	27	5	12	13	10.13	0	3	10.88	1.88	4.50	4.88	0.36	7.12
1999	Ottawa	Int	92.3	83	32	5	39	65	3.12	7	3	8.09	0.49	3.80	6.34	0.98	3.61
1999	Montreal	NL	100.0	105	51	13	43	43	4.59	5	6	9.45	1.17	3.87	3.87	0.31	5.13

Another one of Beattie's big kids who doesn't throw especially hard, Powell was called up to take Batista's place in the rotation in July. He's willing to try all sorts of things: a forkball, a curve, a nice change-up. While normally you think big kids might pick up velocity as they fill out, Powell is already full-sized. He's an adequate fifth starter; if he sticks around, it's because Lilly or Armas isn't ready.

James Serrano   Throws R   Age 24

YEAR	TEAM	LGE	IP	H	ER	HR	BB	K	ERA	W	L	H/9	HR/9	BB/9	K/9	KWH	PERA
1998	CapeFear	SAL	22.0	30	15	3	21	19	6.14	1	1	12.27	1.23	8.59	7.77	0.43	9.00
1999	Jupiter	Fla	83.3	85	40	5	37	88	4.32	5	4	9.18	0.54	4.00	9.50	1.84	4.32

At 5'8", he's one of the organization's two short short relievers out of the University of New Mexico, along with Strickland. He is not the next Chad Harville, but more of a finesse type mixing a good change-up and curve. Like Strickland before him, he could move up fast, especially after a good performance in the Arizona Fall League.

J.D. Smart   Throws R   Age 26

YEAR	TEAM	LGE	IP	H	ER	HR	BB	K	ERA	W	L	H/9	HR/9	BB/9	K/9	KWH	PERA
1997	W Palm B	Fla	92.3	139	62	13	30	47	6.04	4	6	13.55	1.27	2.92	4.58	0.40	7.31
1997	Harrisbg	Eas	66.3	88	39	7	26	34	5.29	3	4	11.94	0.95	3.53	4.61	0.38	6.24
1998	Harrisbg	Eas	70.0	87	34	2	22	35	4.37	4	4	11.19	0.26	2.83	4.50	0.48	4.76
1998	Ottawa	Int	34.0	37	23	3	12	14	6.09	1	3	9.79	0.79	3.18	3.71	0.33	4.50
1999	Montreal	NL	53.3	52	25	4	16	20	4.22	3	3	8.78	0.68	2.70	3.38	0.36	3.71
1999	Ottawa	Int	20.7	23	7	2	7	8	3.05	1	1	10.02	0.87	3.05	3.48	0.30	4.79

He's nothing more than your basic 11th pitcher, who earned the last spot in the bullpen with a great camp in 1999. Smart was used mostly in long relief: 22 of his 29 outings were two innings or longer. Other than Felipe Alou, how many managers would use a rookie reliever this well? Jack McKeon, and that's about it. Elbow tendinitis killed his shot at a September recall.

Dan Smith   Throws R   Age 24

YEAR	TEAM	LGE	IP	H	ER	HR	BB	K	ERA	W	L	H/9	HR/9	BB/9	K/9	KWH	PERA
1997	Charlott	Fla	144.3	220	125	22	85	89	7.79	4	12	13.72	1.37	5.30	5.55	0.32	8.67
1998	Tulsa	Tex	135.3	199	120	26	67	86	7.98	4	11	13.23	1.73	4.46	5.72	0.41	8.38
1999	Ottawa	Int	71.7	60	27	6	29	54	3.39	5	3	7.53	0.75	3.64	6.78	1.25	3.52
1999	Montreal	NL	92.3	98	55	11	38	70	5.36	4	6	9.55	1.07	3.70	6.82	0.98	4.97

Inserted into the rotation in June when Alou got frustrated with Vazquez, Smith quickly impressed by retiring 20 straight Red Sox in his debut. Alou likes him because he's a fast worker and throws strikes, and the Rangers' organization has been a tough place for a pitcher to learn his craft. I don't think he's much of a prospect, but Alou turned Batista into somebody useful, so Smith could turn into another handy utility pitcher. Remember the name for trivia purposes: he allowed Tony Gwynn's 3000th hit.

Scott Strickland   Throws R   Age 24

YEAR	TEAM	LGE	IP	H	ER	HR	BB	K	ERA	W	L	H/9	HR/9	BB/9	K/9	KWH	PERA
1997	Vermont	NYP	53.7	83	41	7	30	43	6.88	2	4	13.92	1.17	5.03	7.21	0.55	8.39
1998	CapeFear	SAL	32.0	51	27	4	17	34	7.59	1	3	14.34	1.13	4.78	9.56	1.00	8.44
1998	Jupiter	Fla	61.7	87	41	6	26	38	5.98	3	4	12.70	0.88	3.79	5.55	0.48	6.71
1999	Jupiter	Fla	22.7	31	17	1	5	25	6.75	1	2	12.31	0.40	1.99	9.93	3.01	5.16
1999	Harrisbg	Eas	28.0	30	10	1	11	29	3.21	2	1	9.64	0.32	3.54	9.32	1.90	4.18
1999	Ottawa	Int	28.3	22	4	0	12	31	1.27	3	0	6.99	0.00	3.81	9.85	2.72	2.54
1999	Montreal	NL	18.3	14	8	3	11	22	3.93	1	1	6.87	1.47	5.40	10.80	2.35	4.42

He came out of nowhere, one of the Expos' rare short right-handers, and is looking like a solid reliever. Strickland is already being called a flamethrower because he combined for 126 strikeouts in 100⅓ innings at four levels last year, but it isn't that he throws especially hard. His fastball tops out at 94 mph, and is usually around 90 with good movement and he mixes in a tight slider. He's been vulnerable to left-handed hitters at every level, so he'll have to be used carefully, but he's a better guy to have around than Mike Maddux.

Anthony Telford Throws R Age 34

YEAR	TEAM	LGE	IP	H	ER	HR	BB	K	ERA	W	L	H/9	HR/9	BB/9	K/9	KWH	PERA
1997	Montreal	NL	89.0	78	33	11	35	57	3.34	6	4	7.89	1.11	3.54	5.76	0.89	4.04
1998	Montreal	NL	87.3	93	51	10	38	56	5.26	4	6	9.58	1.03	3.92	5.77	0.66	5.05
1999	Montreal	NL	99.0	104	44	3	37	67	4.00	6	5	9.45	0.27	3.36	6.09	0.87	4.00

Exhibit A in Alou's case for how you can create a major-league reliever by putting a piece of meat in a covered jar and waiting two weeks. Presto! Jerky and journeyman! Telford was worn out by September, which means that sometimes even Alou makes a mistake with his bullpen. He's a thoroughly acceptable middle reliever when used correctly, not being jerked in and out of situational roles.

Mike Thurman Throws R Age 26

YEAR	TEAM	LGE	IP	H	ER	HR	BB	K	ERA	W	L	H/9	HR/9	BB/9	K/9	KWH	PERA
1997	Harrisbg	Eas	110.7	117	58	15	33	67	4.72	6	6	9.52	1.22	2.68	5.45	0.87	4.72
1997	Ottawa	Int	19.3	18	13	1	9	13	6.05	1	1	8.38	0.47	4.19	6.05	0.78	3.72
1997	Montreal	NL	11.7	8	9	3	4	7	6.94	0	1	6.17	2.31	3.09	5.40	1.14	3.86
1998	Ottawa	Int	103.0	115	51	12	53	66	4.46	6	5	10.05	1.05	4.63	5.77	0.53	5.59
1998	Montreal	NL	64.3	66	42	7	27	30	5.88	3	4	9.23	0.98	3.78	4.20	0.38	4.76
1999	Montreal	NL	150.0	130	71	15	51	83	4.26	9	8	7.80	0.90	3.06	4.98	0.78	3.60

Another one of Beattie's big college right-handers without great heat. Thurman knows how to pitch and has good command of mediocre stuff. He was also smart enough to realize that his opportunity to make it was in 1999, so he hustled back from knee surgery the previous September to claim a rotation spot in camp. He has no star potential, and he'll be hard-pressed to hold onto his rotation spot once Lilly and Armas come up, but he just set himself up for about five years of spring training invitations and guaranteed money.

T.J. Tucker Throws R Age 21

YEAR	TEAM	LGE	IP	H	ER	HR	BB	K	ERA	W	L	H/9	HR/9	BB/9	K/9	KWH	PERA
1998	Vermont	NYP	30.7	33	12	0	20	21	3.52	2	1	9.68	0.00	5.87	6.16	0.50	4.70
1999	Jupiter	Fla	40.3	33	12	3	20	28	2.68	3	1	7.36	0.67	4.46	6.25	0.89	3.57
1999	Harrisbg	Eas	112.0	129	63	12	42	71	5.06	5	7	10.37	0.96	3.38	5.71	0.70	5.22

He's a hard-throwing high-school pitcher drafted the same year as Bridges, which is where the similarities end. In an organization filled with big lanky pitchers, Tucker is a hefty kid. In part of the organizational shakeup in early May, Tucker was bumped up to Harrisburg at the same time Hebson and Bridges moved up to Jupiter. He wore out and was shut down early, not even appearing in the playoffs. Considering his age and lack of experience, it looks like a good call. Moving up faster than expected, he might get a cup of coffee by September.

Ugueth Urbina Throws R Age 26

YEAR	TEAM	LGE	IP	H	ER	HR	BB	K	ERA	W	L	H/9	HR/9	BB/9	K/9	KWH	PERA
1997	Montreal	NL	64.7	53	28	9	30	78	3.90	4	3	7.38	1.25	4.18	10.86	2.86	4.18
1998	Montreal	NL	67.0	41	12	2	35	89	1.61	6	1	5.51	0.27	4.70	11.96	4.12	2.42
1999	Montreal	NL	77.3	56	29	5	34	97	3.38	6	3	6.52	0.58	3.96	11.29	3.69	2.91

In what seems like a consistent voting pattern for sportswriters, Urbina was named the league's best closer in postseason polling in the year after his best year. If there's a guy with a great shot to rub Bobby Thigpen's name out of the record books for the single-season saves record in the next two years, it's Urbina. Like Thigpen did, Urbina has several critical factors in his favor: a good rotation, an offense that doesn't score a lot of runs, a manager who isn't afraid to bring him into a game in the eighth inning and a team that should improve.

Javier Vazquez · Throws R · Age 24

YEAR	TEAM	LGE	IP	H	ER	HR	BB	K	ERA	W	L	H/9	HR/9	BB/9	K/9	KWH	PERA
1997	W Palm B	Fla	106.3	121	50	11	37	78	4.23	6	6	10.24	0.93	3.13	6.60	1.02	4.99
1997	Harrisbg	Eas	41.3	17	5	2	12	38	1.09	5	0	3.70	0.44	2.61	8.27	5.29	1.31
1998	Montreal	NL	165.3	213	132	32	71	131	7.19	5	13	11.59	1.74	3.86	7.13	0.85	7.08
1999	Ottawa	Int	43.3	45	21	7	16	42	4.36	3	2	9.35	1.45	3.32	8.72	1.83	5.19
1999	Montreal	NL	158.3	144	83	18	50	110	4.72	9	9	8.19	1.02	2.84	6.25	1.26	3.81

Slowly but surely, he's turning into a horse. He irritated Alou a couple of times by getting too cute with his change-up, for which he was demoted. Once he started relying more on a fastball with good movement and a solid curve, he started tossing complete games. Vazquez is poised for a great third year. His development despite so little upper-level experience isn't unprecedented; it also isn't a manual for how other organizations should handle talented A-ball starters.

Jake Westbrook · Throws R · Age 22

YEAR	TEAM	LGE	IP	H	ER	HR	BB	K	ERA	W	L	H/9	HR/9	BB/9	K/9	KWH	PERA
1997	Ashevlle	SAL	162.0	225	116	20	80	64	6.44	6	12	12.50	1.11	4.44	3.56	0.17	7.11
1998	Jupiter	Fla	152.3	225	100	14	77	61	5.91	6	11	13.29	0.83	4.55	3.60	0.16	7.33
1999	Harrisbg	Eas	167.3	211	102	15	70	75	5.49	8	11	11.35	0.81	3.76	4.03	0.28	5.75

So far, Westbrook is the most famous of the three pitchers acquired in the Lansing deal. He's got a good sinker that generates a ton of groundball outs, but despite having a good infield defense behind him, he didn't pitch that well. There's debate on what to think: scouts say he can pitch, he's young and projectable, and not overly reliant on breaking stuff. The Expos are talking about having him learn to throw a splitter. If there's a guy the scouts could be right about while all of the numbers fly in the face of their spiral notebooks, it might be Westbrook. The Yankees hope so, having picked him in the Irabu deal.

Support-Neutral Records — MONTREAL EXPOS — Park Effect: -0.8%

PITCHER	GS	IP	R	SNW	SNL	SNPCT	W	L	RA	APW	SNVA	SNWAR
Antonio Armas	1	6.0	4	0.2	0.5	.296	0	1	6.00	-0.06	-0.16	-0.09
Miguel Batista	17	98.7	62	5.7	6.5	.469	7	5	5.66	-0.63	-0.32	0.54
Shayne Bennett	1	4.0	10	0.0	0.8	.015	0	1	22.50	-0.73	-0.42	-0.35
Dustin Hermanson	34	216.3	110	13.0	11.0	.542	9	14	4.58	1.07	0.86	2.81
Mike Johnson	1	4.3	6	0.1	0.5	.192	0	0	12.46	-0.34	-0.19	-0.13
Ted Lilly	3	17.7	9	0.9	1.0	.476	0	1	4.58	0.09	-0.01	0.09
Carl Pavano	18	103.0	65	6.0	6.5	.479	6	8	5.68	-0.68	-0.18	0.67
Jeremy Powell	17	97.0	60	5.5	6.1	.475	4	8	5.57	-0.53	-0.44	0.57
Dan Smith	17	83.7	61	4.1	7.0	.368	3	9	6.56	-1.33	-1.32	-0.63
Mike Thurman	27	144.7	84	9.2	8.2	.528	7	11	5.23	-0.27	0.34	1.79
Javier Vazquez	26	154.7	98	8.3	10.0	.454	9	8	5.70	-1.06	-0.82	0.53
TOTALS	162	930.0	569	52.9	57.9	.477	45	66	5.51	-4.48	-2.66	5.81

The Expos' starters were better than their runs allowed indicate. If you use their runs allowed to figure out how many wins they were worth compared to average pitchers, you get about 4½ wins below average (the Adjusted Pitching Wins column). But if you use the Support-Neutral approach (the SNVA column), they turn out to be around 2½ wins below average, almost two games better than APW indicated. . . . One of the reasons APW underestimates the Expos' starters is that they received some of the worst bullpen support in the majors last year. Montreal starters turned 93 runners over to their relievers in 1999. Given the bases the runners occupied and how many outs there were, 35.4 would have been expected to score, given average pitching. Expo relievers actually allowed 47 of them to score, costing the starters almost 12 runs above what they could have expected. Those extra 12 runs raised the rotation's collective RA by .12. Mike Thurman was the worst victim—his relievers cost him alone more than six runs.

Pitcher Abuse Points

PITCHER	AGE	GS	PAP	PAP/S	WKLD	MAX	1-90	91-100	101-110	111-120	121-130	131-140	141+
Antonio Armas	21	1	0	0.0	0.0	97	0	1	0	0	0	0	0
Miguel Batista	28	17	128	7.5	12.5	124	5	4	4	3	1	0	0
Shayne Bennett	27	1	0	0.0	0.0	83	1	0	0	0	0	0	0
Dustin Hermanson	26	34	200	5.9	11.8	126	10	11	7	5	1	0	0
Mike Johnson	23	1	0	0.0	0.0	79	1	0	0	0	0	0	0
Ted Lilly	23	3	0	0.0	0.0	100	1	2	0	0	0	0	0
Carl Pavano	23	18	88	4.9	12.2	123	6	6	3	2	1	0	0
Jeremy Powell	23	17	50	2.9	7.4	124	9	4	3	0	1	0	0
Dan Smith	23	17	23	1.4	3.4	108	9	3	5	0	0	0	0
Mike Thurman	25	27	32	1.2	2.6	114	13	10	3	1	0	0	0
Javier Vazquez	22	26	172	6.6	17.6	124	9	7	3	6	1	0	0
MONTREAL		162	693	4.3	9.5	126	64	48	28	17	5	0	0
Ranking (NL)				15	11								

The halo around Felipe Alou was tarnished a bit last year, in large part because his hitters seem to take even a three-ball count as a personal insult. He did his usual fine job of keeping his starting pitchers under a watchful eye and spread out the burden so that no single pitcher had a Workload above 18. This didn't prevent Carl Pavano from missing half the season, or Dustin Hermanson from pitching through an injury almost all year. PAP is a means to an end, not an end in itself. . . . I'll take my chances that Pavano can regain his health and become the pitcher everyone thought he could be. Injuries that occur because of acute, one-time trauma tend to heal without scarring, but chronic overuse injuries, which occur as micro-injuries get repeated over and over again, tend to result in the formation of scar tissue that may be permanent. A well-protected pitcher like Pavano may still miss time with a strained tendon or a pulled ligament throwing one awkward pitch, but with time it will heal. A pitcher like Livan Hernandez, without suffering a specific injury, may slowly weaken the muscles in his rotator cuff, lose the flexibility he once had, and the damage may never be undone.

After being stopped just short of the postseason in 1998, the Mets made a series of offseason moves that improved their talent base. Often, teams that fall just short of glory whip themselves into a frenzy, turning over the roster and writing checks in an attempt to find the missing piece. The process usually fails, because the moves get made regardless of whether they address the reason the team missed its goal.

The Mets, however, addressed their need for more offense by adding three good hitters to the lineup while retaining their best player. It was enough to help them through a harrowing race for the wild card and eventually deep into the National League Championship Series against the battered, but still superior, Atlanta Braves. The thrilling, exhausting roller-coaster ride was the first postseason appearance for the Mets since 1988, capping a season that their fans can cherish despite the team's failure to reach the World Series.

Their success was due in large part to the trade that pawned Todd Hundley off on the Dodgers, a three-team deal that brought the Mets Roger Cedeno from the Dodgers and Armando Benitez from the Orioles. Cedeno became available when the Dodgers convinced themselves that Hundley's recovery from elbow surgery would be quicker than anyone else thought. As for Benitez, the Mets had blown an opportunity to get him in 1995 when they traded Bobby Bonilla to the Orioles. They picked up tools goof Alex Ochoa instead. This time they were ready to take advantage of the Orioles' dissatisfaction with the hard-throwing reliever.

Cedeno and Benitez ended up playing far larger roles in the Mets' 1999 season than anyone expected. The team's original plan had the recently-returned Bobby Bonilla playing right field, a plan that went awry as Bonilla was both injured and incompetent. Cedeno ended up as the starter in right field against right-handed pitching after he showed terrific on-base ability and speed. Meanwhile, Benitez grabbed the closer role after John Franco went down in June and

never let it go, dominating opposing batters despite occasional lapses in control.

The other major offseason acquisition was third baseman Robin Ventura. While Ventura was clearly an upgrade—he was effectively replacing Carlos Baerga—the Mets weren't quite sure what to expect from the veteran. He looked like a player who might be on the decline. His 1998 had been his worst offensive season in years. There were whispers from Chicago that he had never recovered completely from the terrible ankle injury he suffered in 1997. Ventura dispelled the doubts quickly, playing brilliantly until a late-season knee injury limited his strength and mobility. Meanwhile, Edgardo Alfonzo, who was moved to second base to accommodate Ventura, had no trouble handling the move and may have been the team's MVP.

A cheaper but no less effective move was the signing of Rickey Henderson. Henderson had his best season since 1995, hitting .315 with more power than anyone thought he had left. With him, of course, came the occasional injuries, the quirky behavior and the antipathy towards the media, as well as a late-season demand for a new contract commensurate with his rediscovered production. How the Mets will deal with Henderson's demands is unclear, since he will be 41 in 2000, but it's safe to say that there will be some accommodation, because the Mets saw firsthand what Henderson can do for a team when he's healthy and content.

All of these transactions were set up by the big one, the signing of Mike Piazza to a seven-year, $91 million contract. The Mets were certainly justified in paying big money to Piazza, who is the best offensive catcher of all time. But the signing carried risk, given that Piazza is probably past his peak and plays a position that is physically punishing. Despite the team's success, 1999 did not go all that well for Piazza; he had the worst offensive season of his career, missed much of April with a sprained knee and was so beaten up by October that he was a shadow of himself in the playoffs. Both the organization and Piazza know that a lot of his

Mets Prospectus

1999 record: 97-66; Second place, NL East; NL wild card; Lost to Braves in NLCS, 4-2

Pythagorean W/L: 95-67

Runs scored: 853 (5th in NL)

Runs allowed: 711 (4th in NL)

Team EQA: .275 (2nd in NL)

1999 team age: 31.1 (oldest in NL)

1999 park: Shea Stadium; moderate pitchers' park, decreased run scoring by 9%.

1999: Another old lineup that outperformed expectations on its way to the playoffs.

2000: A decline or collapse is coming. The only question is: which will it be?

value is in his status as a catcher, so there is no plan to move him from behind the plate. However, Piazza could and should be given more rest than he had in 1998, especially since the Mets have a competent backup in Todd Pratt and their new first baseman, Todd Zeile, is no John Olerud.

During the season, the Mets completed the team with two major moves. One was acquiring Kenny Rogers from the Athletics for B prospect Terrence Long. Rogers' various ailments fit right in with the rest of the rotation's aches and pains, but he did pitch fairly well. His presence allowed Bobby Valentine to use a six-man rotation late in the year, giving all the starters some extra rest. The Mets also added center fielder Darryl Hamilton, who posted a .293 EqA with the team and, more importantly, was not Brian McRae.

Mets' GM Steve Phillips deserves a lot of credit for his aggressiveness in tackling the Mets' shortcomings on the heels of their devastating finish in 1998. While there was some luck involved—the free agents he signed were all 30 or older, and not even Cedeno's most ardent boosters would have predicted the season he had—the players he signed or acquired all had on-base skills. Armed with improved plate discipline, the Mets jumped from 11th to fifth in the National League in runs, and from the odd team out to a game away from a subway series.

While the improved offense was the biggest reason for the Mets' successful season, it wasn't the most-publicized. Late in 1999, at least two national publications sent their photographers to Shea Stadium. Once there, they assembled the quartet of Robin Ventura, Rey Ordonez, Edgardo Alfonzo and John Olerud for a group photograph, a photo that appeared on the cover of each magazine, both of which posed the question of whether the Mets boasted the best infield of all time.

Were they?

The question applies primarily to defense. While Ventura, Alfonzo and Olerud all had good hitting seasons, with EqAs right around .300, none of them were really great with the stick, and while Ordonez wasn't a black hole offensively, he was still a dark navy blue hole. The totals for the quartet, 369 Equivalent Runs and a .289 Equivalent Average, don't come close to units like the 1976 Reds (427, .309), the 1934 Tigers (429, .310) or the "$100,000 Infield" of the 1912-13 Philadelphia Athletics (411, .311 in 1912; 418, .319 in 1913). Each of those teams had sure-fire Hall of Famers at two positions (Joe Morgan and Pete Rose, Hank Greenberg and Charlie Gehringer, Eddie Collins and Frank Baker); the Mets don't have even one.

Defensively, the story changes. The 1999 Mets were the best team ever at not making errors, setting major-league records for fewest errors (67), best fielding percentage (.989) and fewest unearned runs allowed (20). Those records still

look good when you delve into details: unlike past record-setters such as the Orioles and Twins, the Mets did not receive an advantage from either their home scorer or their home park. In fact, the Mets made more errors in games at Shea Stadium (34 to 33) than did their opponents (54 to 51).

To look at how their fielding percentage stacks up against teams from the past, we need to normalize the statistic, which isn't as easy as it first appears. The 1876 St. Louis Brown Stockings, for instance, led the nascent National League with a .902 fielding percentage, 4.2% better than the league mark of .866. To be that much better than the league, the Mets would have needed an impossible 1.021 fielding percentage. To compensate, we can rank teams by their degree of perfection above the league, calculated as (team fielding percentage - league fielding percentage) divided by (1.000 - league fielding percentage). The best teams ever by this perfection index are listed in Table 1.

Table 1

	Team	Perfection Index
1.	1999 Mets	.450
2.	1944 Cardinals	.357
3.	1975 Reds	.333
4.	1932 Athletics	.323
5.	1932 Senators	.323
6.	1940 Reds	.321
7.	1975 Orioles	.320
8.	1980 Orioles	.318
9.	1998 Orioles	.316
10.	1945 Cubs	.310

Again, the Mets not only beat the old mark, they shattered it. In a typical year, the best-fielding team is about three or four points better than the league; the Mets were nine points better than last year's National League, the first time since 1945 that a team beat the league by that much.

The skill in avoiding errors also leads to avoiding unearned runs. The Mets saved themselves 49 runs compared to an average team; that's worth five games in the standings. Of course, even one game would have cost them their playoff spot. No team has beaten the league by that many unearned runs since 1936; only one team since then has broken 40.

That team was the 1975 Reds, with an outstanding offensive infield that outpaced the current Mets with 398 EqR and a .306 EqA. Their presence here means that the Mets were not the best infield of all time, at least when using this limited definition of defense.

Use a more expansive definition, one that considers range as well as error avoidance, and the current Mets hardly rate a mention. Rey Ordonez, for all his sparkle, consistently rates as an average fielder statistically, even with all of the adjustments (pitching staff handedness and flyball/ground-ball tendencies, overall team defense) working in his favor. It can't be a team-wide thing, because Ventura ranks at his customary Gold Glove level, Olerud rates as average and Alfonzo ranks as poor. (Caveats about fielding metrics being the dullest tools at our performance-analysis workbench apply.)

It was fortunate that the Mets slipped into the playoffs last year, even if they didn't force a subway series, because they have two factors working very much against them in 2000. The Mets were the oldest team in baseball last year, weighting the roster according to who amassed the team's plate appearances and innings. This isn't as bad as it sounds at first, since it's mostly the fault of the pitchers; the hitters only ranked 11th in age. It's better to have that combination than the reverse.

This is especially true since the Met offense didn't rely on any one person. Seven full-season Mets posted EqAs between .292 and .312 last year, and Henderson was the only player among them older than 31, giving the team plenty of room for a couple of players to have off years. The lineup can probably be relied upon to keep the offense at or near the top of the league for a couple of years. The substitutions of Todd Zeile and Derek Bell for Olerud and Roger Cedeno will hurt, though.

The pitching staff is a different story. All but one of the Mets' starting pitchers will be in their mid-30s this year. The Mets' rotation lost a lot of time to injuries last year, and was robbed of some effectiveness when pitching. There's no reason to believe that this will be any less common in the future.

The other problem is that the Mets mortgaged their future to get the players who made last year's playoff appearance possible. Prospect-for-veteran trades in the last two years have cost the team Ed Yarnall, Terrence Long, Preston Wilson, Dan Murray, Cesar Crespo, Jason Isringhausen, Jesus Sanchez, A.J. Burnett and Lindsay Gulin, as well as several lesser prospects. These moves have gutted the upper levels of the farm system, which is why so many of the players covered on the following pages are from the low minors.

The only significant near-term help already showed up in Flushing last year, in the form of Benny Agbayani and Octavio Dotel. Any use the Mets were going to get out of Jorge Toca was lost when they elected to sign Zeile instead. If the pitchers can stay healthy, that should be enough to keep the Mets in the playoff hunt this year, and maybe next. After that, the aging offense will catch up to them.

This team is going to get old pretty fast, and there's no way the organization is going to be able to fill all the holes when that happens. Mets fans better enjoy this team while it lasts, because it's not going to last for all that long.

HITTERS (Averages: BA: .270 / OBP: .340 / SLG: .430 / EQA: .260)

Benny Agbayani   OF   Bats R   Age 28

YEAR	TEAM	LGE	AB	H	DB	TP	HR	BB/SO	R	RBI	SB	CS	OUT	BA	OBP	SLG	EQA	EQR	DEFENSE	
1997	Norfolk	Int	473	127	21	1	9	52/113	68	40	18	9	355	.268	.348	.374	.250	56	121-OF 92	
1998	Norfolk	Int	322	77	18	3	8	39/65	31	40	8	4	249	.239	.326	.388	.245	37	78-OF 86	
1999	Norfolk	Int	101	31	8	1	5	13/21	15	22	3	2	72	.307	.395	.554	.307	19		
1999	NY Mets	NL	278	80	20	3	13	29/59	40	39	5	4	202	.288	.362	.522	.288	45	34-RF 110	29-LF 94
2000	NY Mets	NL	369	99	24	2	15	54/80	66	63	9	5	275	.268	.362	.466	.281	57		

Agbayani got off to a ridiculously fast start when called up in May, hitting over .400 with power. Predictably, he cooled off, but the power increase is real, not just the product of a hot streak. Agbayani should continue to platoon in right field with Roger Cedeno. He's another Hawaiian player for the Mets' all-time roster. Remember Ron Darling and Sid Fernandez?

Edgardo Alfonzo   2B   Bats R   Age 26

YEAR	TEAM	LGE	AB	H	DB	TP	HR	BB/SO	R	RBI	SB	CS	OUT	BA	OBP	SLG	EQA	EQR	DEFENSE
1997	NY Mets	NL	526	167	28	2	11	62/55	84	73	9	6	365	.317	.395	.441	.285	79	123-3B 102
1998	NY Mets	NL	567	165	30	2	19	65/75	99	82	9	3	405	.291	.367	.451	.278	82	140-3B 97
1999	NY Mets	NL	632	195	36	2	28	77/84	117	105	8	2	439	.309	.387	.505	.298	106	153-2B 93
2000	NY Mets	NL	590	174	26	1	26	83/78	105	112	8	2	418	.295	.382	.475	.293	97	

"Where do I play this year, Coach?" Even while moving from shortstop to third base and over to second base, he's made progress as a hitter and is finally turning into the player we envisioned five years ago. Alfonzo didn't make an error in picking up a ground ball the entire season. As the only one of the Mets' big guns under 30, he's a very important part of the team.

Jermaine Allensworth CF   Bats R   Age 28

YEAR	TEAM	LGE	AB	H	DB	TP	HR	BB/SO	R	RBI	SB	CS	OUT	BA	OBP	SLG	EQA	EQR	DEFENSE
1997	Pittsbrg	NL	372	95	19	2	3	43/78	53	42	11	7	284	.255	.344	.341	.239	40	102-OF 98
1998	Pittsbrg	NL	235	73	15	3	3	17/42	31	24	8	4	167	.311	.376	.438	.276	34	63-OF 106
1998	KansasCy	AL	73	15	5	0	0	8/17	14	3	6	0	58	.205	.319	.274	.228	7	18-OF 109
1999	Norfolk	Int	274	63	18	4	3	29/43	33	15	6	4	215	.230	.317	.358	.232	28	77-OF 92
1999	NY Mets	NL	74	16	3	0	3	8/23	14	9	2	1	59	.216	.302	.378	.232	8	
2000	Boston	AL	306	77	18	2	4	38/59	48	35	8	5	234	.252	.334	.363	.239	33	

He started the year figuring to be the team's fourth outfielder, but when he didn't hit like he did in Pittsburgh, Agbayani and Roger Cedeno zipped right past him. He spent the year in the Virginia Tidewater, still not hitting. After the season, Allensworth was dealt to Boston, where non-hitting outfielders fit right in.

Bobby Bonilla   PH   Bats B   Age 37

YEAR	TEAM	LGE	AB	H	DB	TP	HR	BB/SO	R	RBI	SB	CS	OUT	BA	OBP	SLG	EQA	EQR	DEFENSE
1997	Florida	NL	572	173	44	3	18	72/93	79	98	4	6	405	.302	.385	.484	.289	91	137-3B 90
1998	Florida	NL	99	29	4	0	5	12/21	12	16	0	1	71	.293	.369	.485	.282	15	24-3B 92
1998	LosAngls	NL	241	62	6	1	8	29/36	30	32	1	1	180	.257	.337	.390	.248	28	53-3B 79
1999	NY Mets	NL	120	19	3	0	5	18/16	12	19	0	1	102	.158	.274	.308	.196	9	
2000	NY Mets	NL	184	42	7	0	6	28/28	24	24	0	1	143	.228	.330	.364	.241	20	

The first time through with the Mets, Bonilla was a disappointment, putting up .290 EqAs when .310s were expected. This time he was a disaster. While he has a legitimate gripe that he's been injured almost constantly for the last two years, he's contributed to that by carrying too much weight and demanding roles he can't handle. Even his guaranteed $5.9 million wasn't enough to keep him around: the Mets released him in January.

Roger Cedeno   RF   Bats B   Age 25

YEAR	TEAM	LGE	AB	H	DB	TP	HR	BB/SO	R	RBI	SB	CS	OUT	BA	OBP	SLG	EQA	EQR	DEFENSE
1997	Albuquer	PCL	106	30	5	2	1	18/16	14	6	3	3	79	.283	.391	.396	.271	15	25-OF 100
1997	LosAngls	NL	198	57	12	2	3	25/44	32	18	8	1	142	.288	.376	.414	.277	29	59-OF 106
1998	LosAngls	NL	245	64	13	1	2	27/55	36	18	9	2	183	.261	.335	.347	.241	26	54-OF 93
1999	NY Mets	NL	456	143	23	4	4	54/99	82	34	58	17	330	.314	.390	.408	.284	71	94-RF 120
2000	Houston	NL	346	97	19	3	3	46/76	75	36	35	10	259	.280	.365	.379	.269	48	

In most reports of the three-way trade, his was the fourth name mentioned, after Todd Hundley, Charles Johnson and Armando Benitez. For the first time in his career, he was given a job and left alone, not yanked out the first time he erred. Not that he erred much: a decent center fielder, he dominated NL right fielders defensively and was a base-stealing dynamo.

Brian Cole   OF   Bats R   Age 21

YEAR	TEAM	LGE	AB	H	DB	TP	HR	BB/SO	R	RBI	SB	CS	OUT	BA	OBP	SLG	EQA	EQR	DEFENSE
1998	Kingsprt	App	228	55	12	4	4	3/25	20	22	4	3	176	.241	.251	.382	.206	17	54-OF 94
1999	Columbia	SAL	512	141	37	2	16	30/78	68	56	19	8	378	.275	.317	.449	.256	63	117-OF 104
2000	NY Mets	NL	326	89	21	2	12	21/54	49	49	14	4	241	.273	.317	.460	.264	43	

An 18th-round draft pick in 1998, Cole was asked to fill Alex Escobar's role at Columbia and did a nice job. He actually had a better batting average and more extra-base hits than Escobar did in his great 1998 season. The pint-sized (5'9", 165) center fielder finished in the league's top five in batting average, runs, hits, total bases, doubles and stolen bases. The organization is pushing him to work on his selectivity.

Shawon Dunston   UT   Bats R   Age 37

YEAR	TEAM	LGE	AB	H	DB	TP	HR	BB/SO	R	RBI	SB	CS	OUT	BA	OBP	SLG	EQA	EQR	DEFENSE
1997	ChiCubs	NL	419	117	18	4	9	8/63	53	39	24	7	309	.279	.298	.406	.240	44	88-SS 92
1998	Clevelnd	AL	155	36	10	3	3	5/18	24	11	8	2	121	.232	.261	.394	.222	14	
1999	St Louis	NL	151	46	5	2	5	0/23	21	24	5	3	108	.305	.320	.464	.258	18	
1999	NY Mets	NL	93	32	5	1	0	0/16	11	15	4	1	62	.344	.359	.419	.268	12	
2000	NY Mets	NL	209	53	9	2	4	6/32	21	22	7	3	159	.254	.274	.373	.219	18	

In 1997, he was traded from the Cubs to the Pirates and got 71 at-bats; in '98, he got 51 at-bats with the Giants after a mid-season trade; with the Mets this year, he got 93 at-bats. In those 215 at-bats following a trade, Dunston drew no walks. Nada-zero-zip-zilch-Alan Keyes's chances of winning the Republican nomination. He's a useful bench player; just don't have him play important innings in the outfield.

Alex Escobar		**OF**				**Bats R**		**Age 21**										
YEAR	TEAM	LGE	AB	H	DB	TP	HR	BB/SO	R	RBI	SB	CS	OUT	BA	OBP	SLG	EQA	EQR	DEFENSE
1998	Columbia	SAL	424	112	21	3	22	44/134	58	67	18	4	316	.264	.338	.483	.275	63	100-OF 101
2000	NY Mets	NL	82	23	4	0	7	11/31	17	19	5	1	60	.280	.366	.585	.312	16	

Escobar, who had two injury-plagued seasons in the Gulf Coast League prior to 1998, shot to the top of many prospect charts with a dazzling five-tool display that earned him the Sally League's 1998 MVP award. Unfortunately, the injuries came back this year; a stress fracture in his back kept him out until June. After two GCL games, he ruined his non-throwing shoulder while hitting a home run and was lost for the duration. He's much too talented to disappear on that note.

Matt Franco		**PH/UT**				**Bats L**		**Age 30**										
YEAR	TEAM	LGE	AB	H	DB	TP	HR	BB/SO	R	RBI	SB	CS	OUT	BA	OBP	SLG	EQA	EQR	DEFENSE
1997	NY Mets	NL	165	46	3	0	6	13/23	21	22	1	0	119	.279	.331	.406	.251	19	20-3B 106
1998	NY Mets	NL	164	47	9	2	1	23/25	21	14	0	1	118	.287	.378	.384	.264	21	
1999	NY Mets	NL	133	32	5	0	4	26/21	17	20	0	0	101	.241	.365	.368	.258	17	
2000	NY Mets	NL	105	25	4	0	3	19/16	16	14	0	0	80	.238	.355	.362	.254	13	

In nature, everything from a hawk to a crow to an elephant to an amoeba has its niche to fill in the environment, even if human eyes can't always tell what it is. Franco, who can't hit or field well enough to be a regular, has taken to the pinch-hitter role and fills it well. He set a new record by drawing 20 pinch-walks and he played five positions in emergencies, including pitching twice. It pays better than Wal-Mart.

Darryl Hamilton		**CF**				**Bats L**		**Age 35**										
YEAR	TEAM	LGE	AB	H	DB	TP	HR	BB/SO	R	RBI	SB	CS	OUT	BA	OBP	SLG	EQA	EQR	DEFENSE
1997	San Fran	NL	468	129	26	3	5	60/60	77	44	12	10	349	.276	.358	.376	.252	56	109-OF 99
1998	Colorado	NL	189	58	7	1	5	22/19	27	22	4	1	132	.307	.382	.434	.281	28	45-OF 101
1999	Colorado	NL	326	86	10	2	3	32/21	51	19	3	4	244	.264	.332	.334	.229	31	78-CF 106
1999	NY Mets	NL	169	57	8	1	5	17/18	18	20	1	3	115	.337	.401	.485	.293	27	44-CF 94
2000	NY Mets	NL	332	86	12	1	6	46/30	47	41	4	5	251	.259	.349	.355	.246	38	

When the Rockies gave up on their season and decided to dump salary, Hamilton, signed through 2000, was on their "to-go" list. The Mets had had enough of Brian McRae, whose hitting and fielding had deteriorated to the point of being unacceptable, and the deal was made. Hamilton was an upgrade in all respects, and the Mets got a bonus when he hit far better for them than he had with Colorado.

Rickey Henderson		**LF**				**Bats R**		**Age 41**										
YEAR	TEAM	LGE	AB	H	DB	TP	HR	BB/SO	R	RBI	SB	CS	OUT	BA	OBP	SLG	EQA	EQR	DEFENSE
1997	San Dieg	NL	296	86	9	0	8	72/61	63	30	26	4	214	.291	.436	.402	.306	56	68-OF 102
1997	Anaheim	AL	114	20	2	0	2	26/22	20	6	16	4	98	.175	.339	.246	.234	13	
1998	Oakland	AL	545	134	19	1	14	117/111	97	57	61	13	424	.246	.384	.361	.276	85	141-OF 99
1999	NY Mets	NL	440	138	20	0	15	77/81	81	41	33	15	317	.314	.418	.461	.301	79	99-LF 94
2000	NY Mets	NL	385	91	9	0	12	92/76	83	48	25	9	303	.236	.384	.353	.270	58	

A September fade that knocked 25 points off his EqA took some of the luster off of what was becoming a historic season for a 40-year-old. Still, the 10th-best EqR and fifth-best EqA ever for that age isn't too shabby. Don't expect him to hit .315 again, but he's still got the eye and the legs, and wants to set records for walks (41 to catch Ruth) and runs (62 behind Rose, 143 behind Cobb).

Mike Kinkade   3B/UT   Bats R   Age 27

YEAR	TEAM	LGE	AB	H	DB	TP	HR	BB/SO	R	RBI	SB	CS	OUT	BA	OBP	SLG	EQA	EQR	DEFENSE	
1997	El Paso	Tex	444	124	27	6	8	37/81	66	63	7	2	322	.279	.348	.421	.262	57	106-3B 89	
1998	Louisvil	Int	292	78	22	4	5	28/58	44	35	5	1	215	.267	.342	.421	.260	37	52-3B 88	
1998	Norfolk	Int	124	31	3	0	1	1/27	8	15	3	1	94	.250	.280	.298	.195	8	27-3B 95	
1999	Norfolk	Int	311	84	18	1	5	15/34	39	37	4	1	228	.270	.312	.383	.236	31	40-3B 89	
1999	NY Mets	NL	46	9	1	1	2	3/9	3	5	1	0	37	.196	.278	.391	.228	5		
2000	NY Mets	NL	359	91	17	2	5	30/58	43	39	7	1	269	.253	.311	.354	.232	35		

He plays third base only in the sense that he stands where the other third basemen do. The Tides also tried him at first base, in the outfield and behind the plate. Face it: he has no real position. One-dimensional players have to really, extraordinarily excel at that one dimension to be useful, and Kinkade is an average hitter at best.

Luis Lopez   IF   Bats B   Age 29

YEAR	TEAM	LGE	AB	H	DB	TP	HR	BB/SO	R	RBI	SB	CS	OUT	BA	OBP	SLG	EQA	EQR	DEFENSE	
1997	Norfolk	Int	203	59	9	1	3	5/31	25	15	1	4	148	.291	.311	.389	.229	19	37-SS 85	
1997	NY Mets	NL	180	49	12	1	1	12/42	18	19	1	4	135	.272	.332	.367	.233	18	27-SS 106	13-2B 94
1998	NY Mets	NL	270	71	16	2	2	20/58	39	23	2	2	201	.263	.324	.359	.233	26	31-2B 98	
1999	NY Mets	NL	105	22	1	0	3	11/33	10	13	1	1	84	.210	.305	.305	.210	9		
2000	NY Mets	NL	172	42	4	0	4	14/41	18	18	3	2	132	.244	.301	.337	.219	15		

Rey Ordonez was healthy almost all year and hit well enough that Lopez's role—taking over at shortstop when Ordonez was injured or lifted for a pinch-hitter—was eliminated. He wasn't on the postseason roster, which gives us a good idea of his standing with Mets' officials. Whether that was about his play, or a gesture to mollify Ordonez, with whom Lopez had a fight, isn't clear.

Melvin Mora   UT   Bats R   Age 28

YEAR	TEAM	LGE	AB	H	DB	TP	HR	BB/SO	R	RBI	SB	CS	OUT	BA	OBP	SLG	EQA	EQR	DEFENSE	
1997	New Orln	AA	381	91	14	3	1	39/58	48	34	5	5	295	.239	.328	.299	.219	33	73-OF 91	25-3B 90
1999	Norfolk	Int	305	80	16	1	6	32/59	40	27	11	6	231	.262	.344	.380	.250	36	48-SS 94	30-OF 96
1999	NY Mets	NL	31	5	0	0	0	4/7	6	1	2	1	27	.161	.280	.161	.159	1		
2000	NY Mets	NL	211	52	8	1	3	25/67	28	22	6	5	164	.246	.326	.336	.231	21		

Once an Astros' prospect, Mora spent most of 1998 playing for the Mercury Tigers in Taiwan. He came back to the States when the Mets needed warm bodies on the farm and did a surprising job as the Tides' shortstop, a performance that earned him Lopez's spot on the postseason roster. He's fast and can play seven positions without embarrassment, so he'll probably take Lopez's spot on the 2000 roster as well.

John Olerud   1B   Bats L   Age 31

YEAR	TEAM	LGE	AB	H	DB	TP	HR	BB/SO	R	RBI	SB	CS	OUT	BA	OBP	SLG	EQA	EQR	DEFENSE
1997	NY Mets	NL	532	157	34	1	24	85/66	91	104	0	0	375	.295	.405	.498	.304	95	139-1B 102
1998	NY Mets	NL	572	212	38	4	25	97/71	96	99	2	2	362	.371	.465	.582	.347	129	152-1B 107
1999	NY Mets	NL	584	175	30	0	22	118/65	102	94	3	0	409	.300	.427	.464	.308	108	154-1B 100
2000	Seattle	AL	529	160	23	1	23	108/61	116	114	1	0	369	.302	.421	.480	.311	100	

Olerud was again unable to sustain an MVP level of performance for consecutive years. 1999's level, basically his career average, is fine. He might want to check out some contact lenses: he's hit much better in day games than at night for the last few years. He's the Mariners' first baseman now; if they keep Griffey, Olerud might be enough to get them back to the postseason.

Rey Ordonez   SS   Bats R   Age 27

YEAR	TEAM	LGE	AB	H	DB	TP	HR	BB/SO	R	RBI	SB	CS	OUT	BA	OBP	SLG	EQA	EQR	DEFENSE
1997	NY Mets	NL	359	80	7	3	1	17/36	35	34	9	5	284	.223	.260	.267	.174	18	108-SS 100
1998	NY Mets	NL	512	134	22	2	1	22/58	48	44	3	7	385	.262	.294	.318	.203	36	144-SS 99
1999	NY Mets	NL	524	136	25	2	1	43/58	47	58	7	4	392	.260	.317	.321	.220	44	146-SS 101
2000	NY Mets	NL	520	133	26	2	1	38/59	55	46	6	5	392	.256	.306	.319	.215	42	

Despite much ballyhoo over his improved offense—a hot streak pushed his batting average to .300 for a day in June—there really wasn't much improvement over previous years. He did manage to post a .300 OBP for the first time, and for once didn't treat walks like stars treat paparazzi. As for the defense, well . . .

> Assists per nine innings, 1996-99, Ordonez: 3.02
>
> Assists per nine innings, 1996-99, other Mets shortstops: 3.08

However spectacular he looks, those numbers are not consistent with other great fielders. Great fielders blow their back-ups away while Ordonez, for whatever reason, doesn't. I'll admit, though: I can't tell you where the balls he misses are going.

Jay Payton   DL   Bats R   Age 27

YEAR	TEAM	LGE	AB	H	DB	TP	HR	BB/SO	R	RBI	SB	CS	OUT	BA	OBP	SLG	EQA	EQR	DEFENSE	
1998	Norfolk	Int	322	73	13	4	5	18/56	34	23	6	4	253	.227	.269	.339	.202	23	50-OF 95	23-1B 92
1999	St Lucie	Fla	27	7	2	0	0	3/6	2	2	0	0	20	.259	.333	.333	.231	3		
1999	Norfolk	Int	143	48	10	1	6	9/14	20	25	1	1	96	.336	.378	.545	.301	24	32-OF 90	
2000	*NY Mets*	*NL*	*192*	*52*	*11*	*1*	*7*	*14/33*	*25*	*30*	*2*	*2*	*142*	*.271*	*.320*	*.448*	*.257*	*24*		

His brief time in Norfolk indicated that he can still hit, but the injuries have pushed him out of the Mets' plans. If he can stay healthy, the team will be happy to give him a chance as their fifth outfielder. At this point, Payton's arms are barely held together and don't seem capable of enduring a season. He must find a way, by trade or free agency, to get to the AL and the relative safety of the DH.

Jason Phillips   C   Bats R   Age 23

YEAR	TEAM	LGE	AB	H	DB	TP	HR	BB/SO	R	RBI	SB	CS	OUT	BA	OBP	SLG	EQA	EQR	DEFENSE
1997	Pittsfld	NYP	159	31	6	0	3	10/27	11	15	2	0	128	.195	.252	.289	.180	9	
1998	Columbia	SAL	255	60	15	1	4	18/35	28	29	2	1	196	.235	.294	.349	.218	22	68-C 99
1999	St Lucie	Fla	287	67	12	1	9	18/32	31	40	0	0	220	.233	.289	.376	.223	26	68-C 99
1999	Binghmtn	Eas	142	30	5	0	6	9/21	11	19	0	0	112	.211	.268	.373	.213	12	35-C 102
2000	*NY Mets*	*NL*	*344*	*82*	*15*	*1*	*11*	*28/45*	*37*	*43*	*1*	*0*	*262*	*.238*	*.296*	*.384*	*.231*	*34*	

Phillips reached Binghamton on the strength of his arm and has reasonable power. If he can't or won't hit for a higher average, neither of those things will matter.

Mike Piazza   C   Bats R   Age 31

YEAR	TEAM	LGE	AB	H	DB	TP	HR	BB/SO	R	RBI	SB	CS	OUT	BA	OBP	SLG	EQA	EQR	DEFENSE
1997	LosAngls	NL	573	213	32	1	45	70/76	109	131	4	1	361	.372	.443	.667	.354	135	
1998	LosAngls	NL	152	46	5	0	10	11/26	21	32	0	0	106	.303	.350	.533	.288	23	35-C 94
1998	NY Mets	NL	403	146	28	1	27	47/52	70	81	1	0	257	.362	.432	.638	.344	89	99-C 97
1999	NY Mets	NL	538	166	22	0	41	44/69	96	120	2	2	374	.309	.362	.578	.301	93	129-C 96
2000	*NY Mets*	*NL*	*502*	*156*	*17*	*0*	*36*	*62/68*	*86*	*121*	*2*	*1*	*347*	*.311*	*.387*	*.560*	*.312*	*94*	

Piazza posted the worst fall-season EqA of his career. Part of that was due to wearing down, as he was unwilling to take a day off during the pennant race. He played in 136 of the Mets' 145 games after his April trip to the disabled list. He was still the anchor of the Mets' offense, holding down the cleanup spot and leading the team in home runs and slugging percentage while scoring more runs than Henderson or Cedeno. He insists he'll continue catching for at least three more years.

Todd Pratt   C   Bats R   Age 33

YEAR	TEAM	LGE	AB	H	DB	TP	HR	BB/SO	R	RBI	SB	CS	OUT	BA	OBP	SLG	EQA	EQR	DEFENSE
1997	Norfolk	Int	208	54	8	2	7	20/51	34	26	1	1	155	.260	.330	.418	.252	25	
1997	NY Mets	NL	107	31	3	0	3	13/32	12	20	0	1	77	.290	.377	.402	.267	14	
1998	Norfolk	Int	117	35	5	0	5	11/21	12	22	1	0	82	.299	.375	.470	.286	18	
1999	NY Mets	NL	141	42	4	0	3	13/32	17	20	2	0	99	.298	.371	.390	.266	18	33-C 100
2000	*NY Mets*	*NL*	*127*	*34*	*3*	*0*	*4*	*17/29*	*18*	*19*	*1*	*0*	*93*	*.268*	*.354*	*.386*	*.260*	*16*	

Pratt has gone from being out of organized baseball to playoff hero, so you could say he's having fun these days. His playing time is severely limited, as Piazza rarely comes out of the lineup and Valentine doesn't like to use his reserve catcher as a pinch-hitter. As a result, a catcher who could start for half the teams in the majors spends a lot of time watching.

Robert Stratton — RF — Bats R — Age 22

YEAR	TEAM	LGE	AB	H	DB	TP	HR	BB/SO	R	RBI	SB	CS	OUT	BA	OBP	SLG	EQA	EQR	DEFENSE
1997	Kingsprt	App	246	48	9	3	9	12/101	27	28	3	2	200	.195	.241	.366	.198	17	63-OF 90
1998	Pittsfld	NYP	128	26	5	2	6	8/57	13	13	1	1	103	.203	.250	.414	.216	11	
1999	Columbia	SAL	330	79	16	1	18	40/113	46	47	3	1	252	.239	.327	.458	.262	44	46-OF 83
2000	NY Mets	NL	220	48	8	1	11	24/82	24	32	1	1	173	.218	.295	.414	.239	24	

Stratton, a first-round pick in 1996, was traded to the Florida Marlins for Al Leiter. The Fish considered him damaged goods—he had a back problem that needed surgery—and threw him back. He's got tremendous power; he also strikes out often enough to embarrass Jim Thome and he's error-prone in the outfield. Think "Gorman Thomas," without the legendary facial hair.

Jorge Toca — 1B/OF — Bats R — Age 25/29

YEAR	TEAM	LGE	AB	H	DB	TP	HR	BB/SO	R	RBI	SB	CS	OUT	BA	OBP	SLG	EQA	EQR	DEFENSE	
1999	Binghmtn	Eas	278	68	11	1	14	23/49	42	45	2	2	212	.245	.310	.442	.249	33	47-OF 95	17-1B 99
1999	Norfolk	Int	175	54	10	1	4	4/24	20	23	0	2	123	.309	.327	.446	.253	20	44-1B 122	
2000	NY Mets	NL	285	82	20	1	5	15/90	35	39	1	1	204	.288	.323	.418	.251	32		

The media guide says he was born in 1975, but 1971 has been acknowledged as the real truth, and is the basis for his projection. He's a former member of the Cuban national team, one of the ones who made it to Costa Rica and is seeking fame; he already has the fortune, as the Mets paid one to get him. He's a sweet-fielding first baseman, and the Mets tried him in the outfield with acceptable results. The DT shows him as a .250 EqA hitter due to the age adjustment, which I'm not sure is fair in his case, since he's had plenty of other adjustments to make. Without that tweak, his EqAs would be .272 at Binghamton and .264 at Norfolk, still on the low side for a first baseman. Toca can be a solid player, not a star.

Jason Tyner — CF — Bats L — Age 23

YEAR	TEAM	LGE	AB	H	DB	TP	HR	BB/SO	R	RBI	SB	CS	OUT	BA	OBP	SLG	EQA	EQR	DEFENSE
1998	St Lucie	Fla	202	53	4	2	0	14/22	21	12	6	5	154	.262	.312	.302	.210	16	47-OF 90
1999	Binghmtn	Eas	516	146	16	4	1	49/47	67	28	26	9	379	.283	.346	.335	.242	55	127-OF 99
2000	NY Mets	NL	322	89	6	2	1	32/40	51	29	21	5	238	.276	.342	.317	.242	34	

While millions of kids on the planet spent the '80s and '90s wanting to be like Mike, Tyner decided to be like Brett—Butler, that is. A speedy center fielder, Tyner hits line singles, bloop singles, bunt singles, Kraft singles and singles bars, but only gets an extra-base hit when an outfielder has to go to his left or right. He never, ever hits the ball over an outfielder's head.

Robin Ventura — 3B — Bats L — Age 32

YEAR	TEAM	LGE	AB	H	DB	TP	HR	BB/SO	R	RBI	SB	CS	OUT	BA	OBP	SLG	EQA	EQR	DEFENSE
1997	ChiSox	AL	183	50	12	1	6	33/20	27	26	0	0	133	.273	.384	.448	.284	29	53-3B 106
1998	ChiSox	AL	589	157	31	4	21	77/109	81	88	1	1	433	.267	.352	.440	.267	80	157-3B 115
1999	NY Mets	NL	592	180	32	0	34	67/108	84	117	1	1	413	.304	.378	.530	.298	100	151-3B 114
2000	NY Mets	NL	487	136	23	1	25	72/89	82	96	0	0	351	.279	.372	.485	.290	79	

He bounced back nicely from a sub-par 1998 to be the highest-ranking Met in the MVP voting, nosing out Piazza and Alfonzo. He enjoyed the highest RBI total of his career, thanks in part to a raft of opportunities courtesy of Piazza and Olerud. The offensive surge of the late 1990s masks the fact that this season was essentially the equal of his 1992, 1995 and 1996 seasons, all of which were between a .298 and a .303 EqA.

Ty Wigginton — 2B — Bats R — Age 22

YEAR	TEAM	LGE	AB	H	DB	TP	HR	BB/SO	R	RBI	SB	CS	OUT	BA	OBP	SLG	EQA	EQR	DEFENSE
1998	Pittsfld	NYP	279	62	11	2	9	11/74	28	23	4	1	218	.222	.253	.373	.207	21	50-2B 89
1999	St Lucie	Fla	464	121	21	3	21	48/90	57	59	5	6	349	.261	.333	.455	.260	60	117-2B 98
2000	NY Mets	NL	301	77	14	2	14	27/72	40	49	4	2	226	.256	.317	.455	.259	39	

He learned this year that the rules don't require him to swing at every pitch. At the same time, he skipped a level, hit for very good power and played a solid second base, leading the Florida State League in putouts and fielding percentage.

Vance Wilson   C   Bats   R Age 27

YEAR	TEAM	LGE	AB	H	DB	TP	HR	BB/SO	R	RBI	SB	CS	OUT	BA	OBP	SLG	EQA	EQR	DEFENSE
1997	Binghmtn	Eas	321	73	13	0	11	12/52	32	28	1	2	250	.227	.263	.371	.207	24	
1998	Norfolk	Int	154	35	3	0	3	6/32	15	13	0	2	121	.227	.260	.305	.180	8	45-C 93
1999	Norfolk	Int	53	12	1	0	3	3/9	8	4	1	0	41	.226	.278	.415	.233	5	
2000	NY Mets	NL	113	27	3	0	4	6/21	10	13	0	0	86	.239	.277	.372	.217	9	

His last two years have been ruined by broken arms. Wilson is a defense guy—he certainly cannot hit—and the Mets think enough of him to keep him on the 40-man roster, ready in case Piazza or Pratt goes down.

PITCHERS (Averages: ERA: 4.50 / H/9: 9.00 / HR/9: 1.00 / BB/9: 3.50 / K/9: 6.50 / KWH: 1.00)

Armando Benitez   Throws R   Age 27

YEAR	TEAM	LGE	IP	H	ER	HR	BB	K	ERA	W	L	H/9	HR/9	BB/9	K/9	KWH	PERA
1997	Baltimor	AL	73.7	48	20	7	43	107	2.44	6	2	5.86	0.86	5.25	13.07	4.14	3.30
1998	Baltimor	AL	67.7	48	27	9	40	88	3.59	5	3	6.38	1.20	5.32	11.70	3.01	3.99
1999	NY Mets	NL	77.0	42	17	4	40	123	1.99	8	1	4.91	0.47	4.68	14.38	6.73	2.34

Franco's injury propelled him into the closer role, and he grabbed it with both hands. He's ideally suited for the role, not only because of his 100-mph fastball, but also because he lacks stamina and needs a long time to warm up. Give him that time, and he can shut anybody down for an inning.

Lesli Brea   Throws R   Age 21

YEAR	TEAM	LGE	IP	H	ER	HR	BB	K	ERA	W	L	H/9	HR/9	BB/9	K/9	KWH	PERA
1997	Everett	Nwn	29.7	43	32	3	35	28	9.71	1	2	13.04	0.91	10.62	8.49	0.39	10.01
1998	Wisconsn	Mid	55.3	58	32	2	52	60	5.20	3	3	9.43	0.33	8.46	9.76	0.89	6.02
1999	St Lucie	Fla	112.3	113	77	6	84	110	6.17	4	8	9.05	0.48	6.73	8.81	0.95	5.29

Brea has similarities to Benitez in that he's a right-handed, flamethrowing Dominican. The big difference is that Brea is five inches and 50 pounds smaller and hasn't yet found a semblance of control. He did start 18 games this year, but that was strictly an effort to get him more innings; his future is in relief.

Eric Cammack   Throws R   Age 24

YEAR	TEAM	LGE	IP	H	ER	HR	BB	K	ERA	W	L	H/9	HR/9	BB/9	K/9	KWH	PERA
1997	Pittsfld	NYP	28.7	14	7	2	20	20	2.20	2	1	4.40	0.63	6.28	6.28	1.07	2.83
1998	Columbia	SAL	30.0	22	17	3	18	30	5.10	1	2	6.60	0.90	5.40	9.00	1.70	3.90
1998	St Lucie	Fla	33.7	28	16	3	18	40	4.28	2	2	7.49	0.80	4.81	10.69	2.37	4.01
1999	Binghmtn	Eas	56.0	32	18	2	42	67	2.89	4	2	5.14	0.32	6.75	10.77	2.50	3.05
1999	Norfolk	Int	8.7	7	3	1	1	15	3.12	1	0	7.27	1.04	1.04	15.58	24.02	3.12

Cammack wasn't that highly regarded out of college, being drafted in the 13th round. He's done nothing since then but rack up saves—eight in 1997, 19 in 1998 and 19 more last year. He doesn't have a great fastball, especially by closer standards, but he can also hit you with a change-up and slider. The Mets don't think he has the stuff to dominate in the majors the way he did in the minors, but they do think he has the ideal makeup for a reliever.

Dennis Cook   Throws L   Age 37

YEAR	TEAM	LGE	IP	H	ER	HR	BB	K	ERA	W	L	H/9	HR/9	BB/9	K/9	KWH	PERA
1997	Florida	NL	61.7	66	28	4	29	59	4.09	4	3	9.63	0.58	4.23	8.61	1.36	4.67
1998	NY Mets	NL	67.3	62	21	5	29	75	2.81	5	2	8.29	0.67	3.88	10.02	2.34	3.88
1999	NY Mets	NL	61.7	53	26	10	25	65	3.79	4	3	7.74	1.46	3.65	9.49	2.38	4.38

His outstanding first half was followed by a truly rotten second half. He denied repeatedly that there was any injury involved, but it looks suspicious. Cook is signed for two more years at an untradeable salary, so he'll be back. Though one of the best-hitting active pitchers, with a career .236 EqA, he only got one at-bat last year.

Octavio Dotel　　　Throws R　　　Age 24

YEAR	TEAM	LGE	IP	H	ER	HR	BB	K	ERA	W	L	H/9	HR/9	BB/9	K/9	KWH	PERA
1997	St Lucie	Fla	47.0	54	22	3	30	31	4.21	3	2	10.34	0.57	5.74	5.94	0.44	5.74
1997	Binghmtn	Eas	54.3	72	51	4	41	33	8.45	1	5	11.93	0.66	6.79	5.47	0.28	7.29
1998	Binghmtn	Eas	66.7	48	23	4	27	66	3.11	5	2	6.48	0.54	3.65	8.91	2.51	2.83
1998	Norfolk	Int	99.0	83	44	8	45	105	4.00	6	5	7.55	0.73	4.09	9.55	2.21	3.64
1999	Norfolk	Int	70.0	52	30	9	35	81	3.86	5	3	6.69	1.16	4.50	10.41	2.69	3.73
1999	NY Mets	NL	84.0	71	50	11	47	82	5.36	4	5	7.61	1.18	5.04	8.79	1.51	4.50

A slender Dominican, Dotel has evolved from a thrower into a pitcher, one who still has a great fastball but also has three other good pitches in his arsenal. A deceptively easy motion contributes to his success. The only thing holding him back right now is his command. He's in Larry Dierker's hands now, and should be very good starting right now.

John Franco　　　Throws L　　　Age 39

YEAR	TEAM	LGE	IP	H	ER	HR	BB	K	ERA	W	L	H/9	HR/9	BB/9	K/9	KWH	PERA
1997	NY Mets	NL	59.3	51	19	3	21	49	2.88	5	2	7.74	0.46	3.19	7.43	1.68	3.19
1998	NY Mets	NL	64.0	69	29	4	30	56	4.08	4	3	9.70	0.56	4.22	7.88	1.13	4.78
1999	NY Mets	NL	39.7	42	14	1	18	39	3.18	3	1	9.53	0.23	4.08	8.85	1.50	4.31

Franco was hindered by injuries last year, but he's still effective when healthy. He wants to remain a closer, which isn't going to happen with the Mets. He'll need to be handled carefully for the rest of his career. He's a hothouse flower at this point: if they try using him as a situational left-hander, it will backfire, and if they try using him as they use Turk Wendell, he'll be back on the disabled list by June.

Dickey Gonzalez　　　Throws R　　　Age 21

YEAR	TEAM	LGE	IP	H	ER	HR	BB	K	ERA	W	L	H/9	HR/9	BB/9	K/9	KWH	PERA
1997	Kingsprt	App	59.3	96	46	7	14	41	6.98	2	5	14.56	1.06	2.12	6.22	0.93	7.43
1997	Columbia	SAL	43.0	69	38	10	21	34	7.95	1	4	14.44	2.09	4.40	7.12	0.60	9.63
1998	Columbia	SAL	104.0	135	73	11	20	69	6.32	4	8	11.68	0.95	1.73	5.97	1.32	5.28
1998	St Lucie	Fla	42.7	59	28	9	17	18	5.91	2	3	12.45	1.90	3.59	3.80	0.24	7.80
1999	St Lucie	Fla	158.0	188	80	15	38	115	4.56	9	9	10.71	0.85	2.16	6.55	1.38	4.78

A control specialist, his stock climbed greatly this year when his fastball improved from 85 mph to 90 mph without costing him any control. I'd like to have seen that translate into more strikeouts, but it's a good sign even without them.

Orel Hershiser　　　Throws R　　　Age 41

YEAR	TEAM	LGE	IP	H	ER	HR	BB	K	ERA	W	L	H/9	HR/9	BB/9	K/9	KWH	PERA
1997	Clevelnd	AL	195.7	192	97	24	69	108	4.46	11	11	8.83	1.10	3.17	4.97	0.66	4.37
1998	San Fran	NL	198.0	212	111	22	90	120	5.05	10	12	9.64	1.00	4.09	5.45	0.56	5.09
1999	NY Mets	NL	175.0	180	91	13	74	86	4.68	9	10	9.26	0.67	3.81	4.42	0.41	4.42

Hershiser was basically a league-average pitcher last season, but even that isn't likely to last much longer, not the way his strikeout rate and KWH are falling. Everything about him now says "crafty left-hander," except for his handedness. The Dodgers have signed him to be the #5 starter and score points with the *Los Angeles Times*.

Bobby Jones　　　Throws R　　　Age 30

YEAR	TEAM	LGE	IP	H	ER	HR	BB	K	ERA	W	L	H/9	HR/9	BB/9	K/9	KWH	PERA
1997	NY Mets	NL	189.3	188	93	25	66	116	4.42	11	10	8.94	1.19	3.14	5.51	0.81	4.52
1998	NY Mets	NL	192.7	200	97	24	56	109	4.53	10	11	9.34	1.12	2.62	5.09	0.79	4.48
1999	NY Mets	NL	58.0	71	37	3	10	30	5.74	2	4	11.02	0.47	1.55	4.66	0.95	4.34

Injuries cost him almost the entire season, and he didn't pitch that well when he finally got back, although he seemed to be close to his old self when he got a chance to pitch some relief late in September. If healthy, Jones will have a spot in the rotation.

Al Leiter   Throws L   Age 34

YEAR	TEAM	LGE	IP	H	ER	HR	BB	K	ERA	W	L	H/9	HR/9	BB/9	K/9	KWH	PERA
1997	Florida	NL	150.0	136	79	14	95	123	4.74	8	9	8.16	0.84	5.70	7.38	0.87	4.74
1998	NY Mets	NL	191.3	155	55	8	75	165	2.59	16	5	7.29	0.38	3.53	7.76	1.75	3.01
1999	NY Mets	NL	209.0	214	105	18	89	156	4.52	11	12	9.22	0.78	3.83	6.72	0.95	4.52

Leiter came into the season with a sore knee that never really healed, and he finally went under the arthroscope in October. The knee threw his mechanics off, making him far more hittable than usual, especially early in the year. His return to form—15 consecutive quality starts from June 6 to August 23—coincided with the Mets' surge to contention. He'll be back at full strength in the spring. With this most erratic of pitchers, I'm making no predictions.

Pat Mahomes   Throws R   Age 29

YEAR	TEAM	LGE	IP	H	ER	HR	BB	K	ERA	W	L	H/9	HR/9	BB/9	K/9	KWH	PERA
1997	Pawtuckt	Int	30.7	26	12	2	18	33	3.52	2	1	7.63	0.59	5.28	9.68	1.74	4.11
1997	Boston	AL	10.3	14	9	2	11	5	7.84	0	1	12.19	1.74	9.58	4.35	0.12	10.45
1999	Norfolk	Int	37.3	41	17	6	13	21	4.10	2	2	9.88	1.45	3.13	5.06	0.62	5.30
1999	NY Mets	NL	62.7	45	25	7	36	49	3.59	4	3	6.46	1.01	5.17	7.04	1.11	3.73

He went 8-0 in part because he usually came in with the Mets losing. If he pitched badly, the guy before him would take the loss; if he pitched well and the Mets came back, he got the win. 1999 was by far the most success he'd ever had in the majors. Mahomes is a poor bet to repeat his performance.

Chuck McElroy   Throws L   Age 32

YEAR	TEAM	LGE	IP	H	ER	HR	BB	K	ERA	W	L	H/9	HR/9	BB/9	K/9	KWH	PERA
1997	Anaheim	AL	15.7	17	6	2	3	18	3.45	1	1	9.77	1.15	1.72	10.34	4.75	4.60
1997	ChiSox	AL	60.0	53	26	3	19	44	3.90	4	3	7.95	0.45	2.85	6.60	1.44	3.15
1998	Colorado	NL	73.7	64	19	3	26	60	2.32	6	2	7.82	0.37	3.18	7.33	1.62	3.18
1999	Colorado	NL	45.7	42	22	8	28	37	4.34	3	2	8.28	1.58	5.52	7.29	0.87	5.52
1999	NY Mets	NL	13.0	12	5	0	8	7	3.46	1	0	8.31	0.00	5.54	4.85	0.38	4.15

McElroy was paroled from Denver in the same deal that brought Darryl Hamilton to the Mets. He was effective as a one-inning left-hander; his platoon split is too small for him to be a specialist, while he doesn't have the stamina to face more than about five hitters. He was sent to Baltimore after the season for Jesse Orosco, part of the Orioles' youth movement.

Rick Reed   Throws R   Age 35

YEAR	TEAM	LGE	IP	H	ER	HR	BB	K	ERA	W	L	H/9	HR/9	BB/9	K/9	KWH	PERA
1997	NY Mets	NL	204.0	197	81	20	33	105	3.57	14	9	8.69	0.88	1.46	4.63	1.27	3.44
1998	NY Mets	NL	209.7	217	86	31	30	145	3.69	14	9	9.31	1.33	1.29	6.22	2.41	4.16
1999	NY Mets	NL	146.0	167	75	21	45	100	4.62	8	8	10.29	1.29	2.77	6.16	0.99	5.30

A succession of injuries, among them a torn calf muscle, a sprained finger, a urinary infection—hell, everything but cholera—kept him from finding any groove until the tail end of the season. There were too many times when his control, while still good by general standards, wasn't as razor-sharp as he requires. He was hit hard on those occasions. Reed seemed to put everything back together towards the end of the season and should be the Mets' best starter in 2000.

Grant Roberts   Throws R   Age 22

YEAR	TEAM	LGE	IP	H	ER	HR	BB	K	ERA	W	L	H/9	HR/9	BB/9	K/9	KWH	PERA
1997	Columbia	SAL	121.0	132	53	2	62	83	3.94	7	6	9.82	0.15	4.61	6.17	0.63	4.54
1998	St Lucie	Fla	66.3	91	46	12	48	55	6.24	2	5	12.35	1.63	6.51	7.46	0.52	8.68
1999	Binghmtn	Eas	130.0	148	84	9	54	78	5.82	5	9	10.25	0.62	3.74	5.40	0.57	4.92
1999	Norfolk	Int	28.0	32	13	1	11	27	4.18	2	1	10.29	0.32	3.54	8.68	1.55	4.50

One of the Mets' most-touted prospects, he showed that he has completely recovered from the elbow surgery that shortened his '98 season. He didn't, however, show that he has advanced as a pitcher, continuing to post only moderate strikeout numbers and yielding far too many hits for a top prospect, all despite a fastball that reaches the mid-90s.

Kenny Rogers — Throws L — Age 35

YEAR	TEAM	LGE	IP	H	ER	HR	BB	K	ERA	W	L	H/9	HR/9	BB/9	K/9	KWH	PERA
1997	NY Yanks	AL	145.3	155	93	17	62	78	5.76	6	10	9.60	1.05	3.84	4.83	0.47	5.02
1998	Oakland	AL	238.3	208	87	18	69	139	3.29	17	9	7.85	0.68	2.61	5.25	1.01	3.25
1999	Oakland	AL	120.3	127	57	7	39	70	4.26	7	6	9.50	0.52	2.92	5.24	0.74	4.04
1999	NY Mets	NL	74.3	73	34	7	27	56	4.12	4	4	8.84	0.85	3.27	6.78	1.19	4.12

Rogers provided significant help to the Mets' rotation in the second half, but his refusal to admit when he was injured or had lost his stuff cost the Mets several key games down the stretch and in the postseason. Rogers pitched all season with a bone spur in his elbow and back problems, and at various times had hamstring problems in both legs. He can still be effective when he's healthy, especially for a team with an infield defense as good as the Mets'. His lack of forthrightness limits his value more than his fragility. Rogers signed a three-year deal with the Rangers and will be their #1 starter.

Glendon Rusch — Throws L — Age 25

YEAR	TEAM	LGE	IP	H	ER	HR	BB	K	ERA	W	L	H/9	HR/9	BB/9	K/9	KWH	PERA
1997	KansasCy	AL	173.3	201	102	26	53	118	5.30	8	11	10.44	1.35	2.75	6.13	0.98	5.40
1998	KansasCy	AL	160.0	180	90	20	52	96	5.06	8	10	10.13	1.13	2.93	5.40	0.74	5.06
1999	Omaha	PCL	106.7	152	71	9	38	82	5.99	4	8	12.83	0.76	3.21	6.92	0.87	6.41

Was Glendon rushed? After a strong 1995 in the Carolina League, he was double-jumped to Triple-A the next year and thrown to the wolves in Kansas City the year after that. Three seasons later, he has yet to make the transition to Successful Major Leaguer. Look for him in Norfolk, where he can be called up for emergency starts. He's still very young for a left-hander and will eventually be a major-league #3 starter.

Jae Weong Seo — Throws R — Age 23

YEAR	TEAM	LGE	IP	H	ER	HR	BB	K	ERA	W	L	H/9	HR/9	BB/9	K/9	KWH	PERA
1998	St Lucie	Fla	33.7	33	17	3	13	29	4.54	2	2	8.82	0.80	3.48	7.75	1.46	4.28
1999	St Lucie	Fla	14.0	10	4	0	2	11	2.57	2	0	6.43	0.00	1.29	7.07	4.52	1.93

A South Korean with a delivery as funky as any of the Asian imports, Seo has been sidelined by elbow problems the last two years and had to have surgery last season. He had a good mix of pitches before the arm problems and was an important part of Korea winning the Asian Games' gold medal last winter.

Jeff Tam — Throws R — Age 29

YEAR	TEAM	LGE	IP	H	ER	HR	BB	K	ERA	W	L	H/9	HR/9	BB/9	K/9	KWH	PERA
1997	Norfolk	Int	107.3	153	79	9	15	54	6.62	4	8	12.83	0.75	1.26	4.53	0.95	5.53
1998	Norfolk	Int	63.3	44	14	3	7	45	1.99	6	1	6.25	0.43	0.99	6.39	4.91	1.85
1999	Norfolk	Int	19.7	25	6	1	3	8	2.75	1	1	11.44	0.46	1.37	3.66	0.64	4.58
1999	Buffalo	Int	24.7	26	10	2	9	11	3.65	2	1	9.49	0.73	3.28	4.01	0.39	4.38
1999	NY Mets	NL	11.3	6	4	3	3	8	3.18	1	0	4.76	2.38	2.38	6.35	2.66	3.18

Started and finished the year in the Mets' organization; in between, he was waived by the Mets, claimed by Cleveland, sent to Buffalo, called up to Cleveland, waived by them and claimed by the Mets. Signed with the A's, where he has a great shot at being an original Sacramento River Cat.

Billy Taylor — Throws R — Age 38

YEAR	TEAM	LGE	IP	H	ER	HR	BB	K	ERA	W	L	H/9	HR/9	BB/9	K/9	KWH	PERA
1997	Oakland	AL	75.7	63	27	3	37	67	3.21	5	3	7.49	0.36	4.40	7.97	1.44	3.45
1998	Oakland	AL	73.0	69	34	7	23	58	4.19	4	4	8.51	0.86	2.84	7.15	1.58	3.82
1999	Oakland	AL	43.3	45	20	3	14	39	4.15	3	2	9.35	0.62	2.91	8.10	1.80	4.15
1999	NY Mets	NL	13.0	21	12	2	8	13	8.31	0	1	14.54	1.38	5.54	9.00	0.75	9.00

Sure, he was a closer in Oakland. He wasn't much of a pitcher, though, regardless of having the glory role. And he was terrible from just before the trade (10 hits and six runs in his final four AL appearances) until mid-September. By then he wasn't trusted in any important situations, like the postseason.

Turk Wendell Throws R Age 33

YEAR	TEAM	LGE	IP	H	ER	HR	BB	K	ERA	W	L	H/9	HR/9	BB/9	K/9	KWH	PERA
1997	ChiCubs	NL	61.3	52	30	4	42	51	4.40	4	3	7.63	0.59	6.16	7.48	0.89	4.40
1997	NY Mets	NL	16.0	16	10	3	15	9	5.63	1	1	9.00	1.69	8.44	5.06	0.25	7.31
1998	NY Mets	NL	75.7	64	25	4	35	55	2.97	6	2	7.61	0.48	4.16	6.54	1.01	3.45
1999	NY Mets	NL	84.3	82	30	8	35	74	3.20	6	3	8.75	0.85	3.74	7.90	1.43	4.27

He wasn't quite as dominant as he was in 1998, but he still pitched a ton of key innings and did it well. The secret for him would seem to be frequent use; he complained loudly whenever Valentine gave him more than a day or two off, and his ERA was almost 6.00 on two or more days of rest.

Masato Yoshii Throws R Age 35

YEAR	TEAM	LGE	IP	H	ER	HR	BB	K	ERA	W	L	H/9	HR/9	BB/9	K/9	KWH	PERA
1998	NY Mets	NL	170.0	171	80	23	56	111	4.24	10	9	9.05	1.22	2.96	5.88	0.96	4.55
1999	NY Mets	NL	170.3	172	85	23	56	101	4.49	10	9	9.09	1.22	2.96	5.34	0.79	4.54

Yoshii was either on or off last season, with very little in-between. He had 20 quality starts, second to Leiter on the staff, but he also had seven "disaster starts" of fewer than five innings pitched while allowing five or more earned runs. That matched the combined total of any other two Mets' starters. Yoshii had only three starts that didn't fall into one of the two categories.

Support-Neutral Records — NEW YORK METS — Park Effect: -6.9%

PITCHER	GS	IP	R	SNW	SNL	SNPCT	W	L	RA	APW	SNVA	SNWAR
Octavio Dotel	14	79.0	48	4.9	5.2	.484	7	2	5.47	-0.48	-0.19	0.59
Orel Hershiser	32	179.0	92	11.4	9.3	.550	13	12	4.63	0.51	0.89	2.58
Jason Isringhausen	5	24.7	20	1.1	2.1	.329	1	2	7.30	-0.63	-0.53	-0.31
Bobby Jones	9	52.7	34	2.8	3.5	.449	3	3	5.81	-0.51	-0.30	0.15
Al Leiter	32	213.0	107	12.2	10.9	.529	13	12	4.52	0.84	0.55	2.40
Rick Reed	26	149.3	77	9.3	7.5	.555	11	5	4.64	0.40	0.74	2.17
Kenny Rogers	12	76.0	35	4.7	4.0	.541	5	1	4.14	0.61	0.37	1.00
Allen Watson	4	20.3	8	1.3	0.9	.588	1	2	3.54	0.29	0.21	0.36
Masato Yoshii	29	170.0	81	11.8	8.5	.580	12	8	4.29	1.10	1.48	3.15
TOTALS	163	964.0	502	59.4	51.9	.534	66	47	4.69	2.12	3.22	12.09

The Bulldog just keeps rolling along. After three years of gradual decline, Orel Hershiser bounced back to have the 17th-best season by a starter in the National League last year. He's looking more like a Hall of Famer each year. Among pitchers who debuted in 1980 or later, you could make a strong case that he's the third-best behind Clemens and Maddux. Of course, he may be caught soon by Pedro Martinez and some others. He crossed the 200-win barrier in 1999, which will get him a few dozen extra votes, and he now has very similar numbers to Hall of Famer Bob Lemon.

Pitcher Abuse Points

PITCHER	AGE	GS	PAP	PAP/S	WKLD	MAX	1-90	91-100	101-110	111-120	121-130	131-140	141+
Octavio Dotel	23	14	66	4.7	11.8	120	4	4	4	2	0	0	0
Orel Hershiser	40	32	22	0.7	0.7	110	18	11	3	0	0	0	0
Jason Isringhausen	26	5	0	0.0	0.0	100	1	4	0	0	0	0	0
Bobby Jones	29	9	34	3.8	5.7	121	3	4	1	0	1	0	0
Al Leiter	33	32	761	23.8	23.8	135	3	2	9	7	7	4	0
Rick Reed	33	26	58	2.2	2.2	113	8	8	9	1	0	0	0
Kenny Rogers	34	12	101	8.4	8.4	131	4	2	4	1	0	1	0
Allen Watson	28	4	0	0.0	0.0	97	3	1	0	0	0	0	0
Masato Yoshii	34	29	139	4.8	4.8	120	12	8	4	5	0	0	0
NEW YORK		163	1181	7.2	8.0	135	56	44	34	16	8	5	0
Ranking (NL)				9	15								

The Mets have one of the oldest rotations in baseball, a deep bullpen and no obvious #1 starter to abuse, so it's not surprising that they would rank next-to-last in the NL in workload. The closest thing they have to an ace is Al Leiter, but as we predicted last year, his heavy workload in 1998 (26.9) caught up with him.... It is worth pointing out that Octavio Dotel, the best pitching prospect the Mets have had since the Young Guns flamed out, was handled with considerably more care than Bill Pulsipher, Jason Isringhausen and Paul Wilson ever were. Give me an arrogant SOB of a manager over Dallas Green any day.

Philadelphia Phillies

For the second year in a row, the Phillies came charging out of the gate and could claim to be in wild-card contention in late July. Heady talk swirled about how they might just be a solid #2 starter away from being a legitimate contender, and rumors of a trade with the Yankees for Andy Pettitte spurred dreams of October baseball for Philadelphia fans.

Then, just as in 1998, the roof collapsed in August and the team finished with a losing record. Predictably, the local media and fans turned and declared that the team was a disaster, the management was incompetent and they had no hope of reaching the postseason in the near future. While it doesn't make nearly as good newspaper copy, the truth isn't nearly as dire.

The biggest improvement in the organization is one that will not satisfy the impatient but is the most important in the long run: the improvement in the farm system. For years, the Phillies' minors had been regarded as a safe haven for organizational soldiers, with many of the same names floating from team to team for years on end, regardless of coaching ability. The results were horrific. Scott Rolen managed to survive the process, but any team that depends on finding players who already have that level of talent and that work ethic is going to be in for some wretched seasons.

Far more common were players like Mike Grace, who managed to reach Philadelphia with pitching mechanics so poor, it's a miracle he ever made it through a season without injury. Or someone like Wendell Magee, who said that the biggest benefit of being in the majors was being able to get real hitting instruction. Many players never even made it that far because they weren't pushed to work, instead treating their time in the minors as a giant fraternity party.

The turnaround in the farm system started with the rehiring of several old faces in Paul Owens, Lee Elia and Dallas Green. After the 1998 season they sent many coaches packing and then helped to put together the "Phillies Way" for minor-league instruction. The fine points of the Phillies

Way are not profound, and tend to focus too much on little-ball techniques. That puts too much emphasis on always hustling and not enough on using the walk as an offensive weapon. Still, much of the program emphasizes good coaching, and that alone can lift the farm system out of the ranks of the wretched.

So far, the results have been encouraging; the Phillies had an overall farm-system winning percentage of .523 last year. Several players in the lower levels of the system showed legitimate development, as opposed to the "great tools and potential" announcements that previous years had produced.

In addition to the developments in the farm system, some less recent changes in the areas of scouting and signing players are beginning to produce results. While the failure to sign J.D. Drew has gotten considerable attention and likely will wind up being regarded as a monumental blunder, there have been some less-remarked-upon but very positive moves. The draft class of 1998 is showing signs of being one of the best in team history. Taking Pat Burrell with the first pick didn't require much genius, but other high draft picks such as Eric Valent, Brad Baisley and Jason Michaels are panning out well, while some sleeper picks from the lower rounds, such as Nick Punto, are also developing. It's possible that by 2002 the Phillies will have three good position players and one or two starting pitchers from the '98 draft. The team also recognized the need for heavy recruiting in Latin America and has taken steps to improve its presence there. So far, the results have been less impressive.

Considerable progress has been made at the major-league level as well. Two years ago, there were two reasons to watch the Phillies, namely Curt Schilling and Scott Rolen. While those two are still crucial to any success the team might have—illustrated by the team's record once both players were done for the 1999 season—the Phillies have added several championship-caliber players. Bobby Abreu is a dominant offensive player, Doug Glanville seems intent on

Phillies Prospectus

1999 record: 77-85; Third place, NL East

Pythagorean W/L: 81-81

Runs scored: 841 (6th in NL)

Runs allowed: 846 (11th in NL)

Team EQA: .263 (8th in NL)

1999 team age: 28.2 (5th-youngest in NL)

1999 park: Veterans Stadium; slight hitters' park, increased run scoring by 3%.

1999: 1998 redux, as the Phillies couldn't survive August in the race.

2000: They're trying really hard; without Schilling until June, it looks bad.

thumbing his nose at analysts by increasing his on-base percentage and Mike Lieberthal had a monster season in 1999. More help for the lineup is on the way, as Burrell should arrive at some point this year. While that does leave some gaps, most notably in the middle infield, that prevent the team from being an offensive juggernaut, some combination of Valent, Punto, Jason Michaels and Jimmy Rollins could fill those holes to create a powerful lineup by 2002.

On the other hand, the pitching is an open question, with the team's refusal to acknowledge the importance of pitch counts a frustrating and befuddling problem. The overwhelming concern has to be the state of Curt Schilling's arm. It's disappointing that the Phillies continue to insist that his injury was something that just happens, not anything that was caused by how they use their pitching staff. There's hard evidence that suggests this is wishful thinking.

In Schilling's six May starts, he averaged 121 pitches per game, finishing the month with outings of 138 and 135 pitches. In his first two starts in June, he struggled through seven and six innings, giving up five runs in each game and topping 100 pitches both times. While warming up for his next start, he started feeling the shoulder pain that will ultimately keep him sidelined until sometime this May.

On May 4, Carlton Loewer threw a 129-pitch complete-game shutout, then struggled through six games in which he gave up 28 runs in 36 innings, topping 110 pitches in four of those six starts. He finally admitted that his arm had been hurting since early May—which certainly sounds like "since the complete game"—and an MRI revealed that he had a stress fracture in his arm.

Robert Person's first five starts in August averaged 117 pitches, including 130-pitch and 144-pitch outings. In the two starts that followed, he was lit up for 12 runs in eight innings, his worst outings of the second half.

The Phillies have several pitchers who have shown they can pitch effectively, including an ace most teams would love to have. But all the pitchers in the world won't do them a bit of good if they don't use them properly, and Terry Francona has yet to demonstrate an understanding of how to manage for a full season. Too often he talks about how throwing a complete game is a great emotional boost for a pitcher. Whatever psychological benefit there might be in pitching a complete game is more than offset by the wear and tear on the pitcher's arm if he throws 140 pitches in the process. If the Phillies blow out their pitching staff, no amount of offense is going to get them very far in October.

Compounding the problems of the rotation is the handling of the bullpen by Francona and pitching coach Galen Cisco. It takes a certain type of skill to burn out both a rotation and a bullpen in the same season, but they managed the feat in 1999. As with the rotation, the primary failure was an inability to manage for the long haul; Francona and Cisco treated each month as if it were October. If a pitcher showed signs of effectiveness out of the pen he would be ridden hard, appearing in several games in a row while others rusted in the bullpen. In addition to the innings they logged in the game, some pitchers would warm up multiple times before entering a game, adding a lot of hidden wear to their arms. Thus, it's hardly surprising that the pitching staff wore out in August, taking the team down with it.

One final piece of the Phillies' future is still up in the air. They have been lobbying for several years for a new baseball-only stadium and have finally secured state funding. However, in a move that reminds Philadelphia fans all too much of past problems the team has had, there was no master plan in place when the funding was delivered. So now the team is arguing with the city over the location of the park and what funding the city will provide. At this point, the hoped-for 2002 opening date will be almost impossible to achieve, and it's quite possible that the project will get tied up in bureaucratic red tape, pushing it back even further.

While the importance of a new ballpark in building a winning team is vastly overstated, the new stadium is important to the Phillies for another reason. The artificial turf at the Vet is widely regarded as one of the worst playing surfaces in professional sports, and by 2001 the Vet will be one of just two outdoor stadiums in baseball with turf. That may do more to hamper efforts to sign free agents and keep their own players than any cash-flow issues.

The next couple of years will be key to the Phillies' development. They have made considerable strides in the past few years, but those strides have merely taken them from wretched to mediocre. They have a core that could become a playoff team if handled correctly and if supplemented by the right additional players. However, if the team continues its current approach, there is a distinct possibility of a repeat of the pattern of the early '90s. Back then, a solid core of players was dogged by pitching injuries and a management that was too fond of some of its players to make the team a repeat contender. That team at least had one season when everything worked. The current version might not be so lucky.

HITTERS (Averages: BA: .270 / OBP: .340 / SLG: .430 / EQA: .260)

Bob Abreu   RF   Bats L   Age 26

YEAR	TEAM	LGE	AB	H	DB	TP	HR	BB/SO	R	RBI	SB	CS	OUT	BA	OBP	SLG	EQA	EQR	DEFENSE
1997	New Orln	AA	199	54	10	4	2	19/50	24	22	6	3	148	.271	.335	.392	.249	23	44-OF 107
1997	Houston	NL	191	49	13	2	3	21/47	23	27	6	2	144	.257	.333	.393	.250	23	43-OF 100
1998	Philadel	NL	500	154	28	6	18	83/129	67	73	20	11	357	.308	.407	.496	.302	89	141-OF 100
1999	Philadel	NL	542	178	36	11	18	101/112	108	85	23	9	373	.328	.437	.535	.325	112	143-RF 87
2000	Philadel	NL	504	152	31	7	17	90/114	116	93	24	12	364	.302	.407	.492	.300	90	

If there was any thought that 1998 was a career year, 1999 put an end to it. Abreu is probably the best player you hear nothing about. He hits for a very high average, knows the difference between a ball and a strike, has good power and uses his speed intelligently. The poor defensive numbers this year may just be a fluke, since he looks solid but not spectacular, in line with the numbers from previous years.

Marlon Anderson   2B   Bats L   Age 26

YEAR	TEAM	LGE	AB	H	DB	TP	HR	BB/SO	R	RBI	SB	CS	OUT	BA	OBP	SLG	EQA	EQR	DEFENSE
1997	Reading	Eas	550	126	16	5	7	28/82	62	46	16	8	432	.229	.275	.315	.200	39	136-2B 99
1998	Scran-WB	Int	579	167	31	11	14	19/81	86	74	15	9	420	.288	.318	.453	.255	69	135-2B 94
1999	Philadel	NL	454	113	25	4	5	18/60	44	51	11	2	343	.249	.281	.355	.216	37	104-2B 97
2000	Philadel	NL	457	118	24	6	10	27/64	58	56	13	4	343	.258	.300	.403	.235	46	

Despite the hype, Anderson has never been that great a prospect. His on-base percentage has always been low, so it wasn't surprising when major-league pitchers discovered that he couldn't lay off pitches low and away. His strong finish means he'll go into the season as the Phillies' second baseman.

Alex Arias   IF   Bats R   Age 32

YEAR	TEAM	LGE	AB	H	DB	TP	HR	BB/SO	R	RBI	SB	CS	OUT	BA	OBP	SLG	EQA	EQR	DEFENSE
1997	Florida	NL	94	24	2	0	1	12/12	13	11	0	1	71	.255	.358	.309	.235	9	18-3B 75
1998	Philadel	NL	134	40	5	0	2	12/18	16	17	2	0	94	.299	.361	.381	.259	16	29-SS 97
1999	Philadel	NL	347	103	19	1	4	31/31	40	45	2	2	246	.297	.362	.392	.259	42	86-SS 88
2000	Philadel	NL	197	59	6	0	3	24/19	29	28	1	1	139	.299	.376	.376	.260	24	

He's not a long-term solution as a starter, but he's been effective as a pinch-hitter for two years and acquitted himself admirably as a replacement while Relaford was injured. If the Phillies decide to give up on Relaford and trade him, Arias could hold the spot until Jimmy Rollins or Nick Punto is ready.

Tom Batson   2B/3B   Bats R   Age 23

YEAR	TEAM	LGE	AB	H	DB	TP	HR	BB/SO	R	RBI	SB	CS	OUT	BA	OBP	SLG	EQA	EQR	DEFENSE	
1999	Batavia	NYP	256	64	10	2	7	27/38	38	24	3	2	194	.250	.325	.387	.242	28	31-2B 98	30-3B 79
2000	Philadel	NL	129	35	7	1	4	17/38	20	21	1	1	95	.271	.356	.434	.265	17		

You have to go all the way down to short-season ball to find a legitimate second-base prospect in the organization. This may give Anderson some job security, unfortunately. Batson had a solid year; if he can build on it next year, he'll work his way into the ranks of prospects to keep an eye on.

Gary Bennett   C   Bats R   Age 28

YEAR	TEAM	LGE	AB	H	DB	TP	HR	BB/SO	R	RBI	SB	CS	OUT	BA	OBP	SLG	EQA	EQR	DEFENSE
1997	Pawtuckt	Int	226	45	7	1	3	13/42	13	18	1	1	182	.199	.248	.279	.169	11	
1998	Scran-WB	Int	285	66	12	0	9	19/46	27	33	0	0	219	.232	.284	.368	.218	24	68-C 102
1999	Philadel	NL	88	24	3	0	1	3/11	6	16	0	0	64	.273	.297	.341	.213	7	21-C 86
2000	Philadel	NL	120	27	2	0	4	9/19	9	13	0	0	93	.225	.279	.342	.205	9	

Bennett is a career minor leaguer who finally got a chance to be a regular backup catcher and demonstrated how easy it is to find a replacement-level player. Now that he has the magic "major league" label, he's likely to spend the next seven or eight years bouncing from team to team.

Rico Brogna 1B Bats L Age 30

YEAR	TEAM	LGE	AB	H	DB	TP	HR	BB/SO	R	RBI	SB	CS	OUT	BA	OBP	SLG	EQA	EQR	DEFENSE
1997	Philadel	NL	549	141	36	1	22	32/115	68	83	10	3	411	.257	.298	.446	.247	62	142-1B 111
1998	Philadel	NL	568	150	37	3	21	48/122	77	104	7	8	426	.264	.321	.451	.254	69	144-1B 111
1999	Philadel	NL	619	169	31	4	22	46/131	83	94	6	5	455	.273	.326	.443	.255	75	152-1B 117
2000	Philadel	NL	578	158	32	2	21	53/124	83	92	9	4	424	.273	.334	.445	.259	73	

You can make a case for a Brogna at first base while you're rebuilding and breaking in young infielders who might need a reliable glove at first. However, you cannot afford to have his bat in the lineup if you expect to compete for a playoff spot. He's an out machine, and his power is poor for a first baseman. If the Phillies wise up, they'll trade Brogna by July 31 and install Burrell at first base.

Pat Burrell 1B/LF Bats R Age 23

YEAR	TEAM	LGE	AB	H	DB	TP	HR	BB/SO	R	RBI	SB	CS	OUT	BA	OBP	SLG	EQA	EQR	DEFENSE	
1998	Clearwtr	Fla	134	34	6	1	6	22/24	23	23	1	0	100	.254	.359	.448	.274	20	20-1B 90	
1999	Reading	Eas	424	129	27	5	25	66/106	73	75	2	2	297	.304	.398	.568	.314	82	82-1B 93	23-OF 99
1999	Scran-WB	Int	33	5	0	0	1	4/8	4	4	0	1	29	.152	.261	.242	.159	1		
2000	Philadel	NL	274	87	17	1	20	52/76	61	74	1	1	188	.318	.426	.606	.332	60		

Until he started swinging from his heels late in the season, he looked like he was ready for the majors offensively. Before that, he was hitting for power and showing good plate discipline during an outstanding year for Reading. He was still finding his way around first base defensively, but showed signs of progress and looked to be developing into a decent defensive player. He's got a lot of work to do in the outfield, so the Phillies had better decide where they want him to play and leave him at that position.

David Doster IF Bats R Age 29

YEAR	TEAM	LGE	AB	H	DB	TP	HR	BB/SO	R	RBI	SB	CS	OUT	BA	OBP	SLG	EQA	EQR	DEFENSE	
1997	Scran-WB	Int	414	116	26	2	13	21/64	56	63	3	3	301	.280	.326	.447	.256	50	73-2B 93	33-3B 70
1998	Scran-WB	Int	585	146	35	3	12	38/89	62	68	13	4	443	.250	.299	.381	.231	57	134-3B 101	
1999	Philadel	NL	97	19	1	0	3	11/23	8	9	1	0	78	.196	.278	.299	.198	7	24-2B 104	
2000	Philadel	NL	216	57	9	0	8	18/37	27	32	2	1	160	.264	.321	.417	.246	24		

After years of being stuck in Triple-A, Doster finally got a chance to sit on a major-league bench this year. He didn't do much in his limited at-bats, but he was a good defensive replacement. If he gets another chance, his offensive numbers should improve some. He'd make a good platoon partner for Anderson.

Rob Ducey OF Bats L Age 35

YEAR	TEAM	LGE	AB	H	DB	TP	HR	BB/SO	R	RBI	SB	CS	OUT	BA	OBP	SLG	EQA	EQR	DEFENSE
1997	Tacoma	PCL	72	19	5	0	0	6/17	5	7	0	0	53	.264	.341	.333	.235	7	21-OF 103
1997	Seattle	AL	143	41	16	2	5	5/30	24	12	3	3	105	.287	.311	.531	.268	20	53-OF 80
1998	Seattle	AL	217	52	19	2	5	22/60	29	22	3	3	168	.240	.336	.415	.253	27	60-OF 97
1999	Philadel	NL	187	47	12	2	7	36/56	27	30	2	1	141	.251	.372	.449	.279	29	23-LF 113
2000	Philadel	NL	143	35	11	1	4	22/40	23	21	1	1	109	.245	.345	.420	.257	18	

He served very nicely as a fourth outfielder/pinch-hitter. Regardless, the decision to re-sign him to a two-year contract is a little puzzling, especially with cheaper alternatives available within the system, guys like Wendell Magee and Billy McMillon. Furthermore, Ducey's chance of maintaining his performance is going to decline every year.

Carlos Duncan IF Bats R Age 23

YEAR	TEAM	LGE	AB	H	DB	TP	HR	BB/SO	R	RBI	SB	CS	OUT	BA	OBP	SLG	EQA	EQR	DEFENSE	
1997	Martnsvl	App	206	43	8	2	8	8/67	20	19	3	2	165	.209	.242	.383	.204	15	54-SS 88	
1998	Piedmont	SAL	114	21	2	2	3	12/47	14	10	3	1	94	.184	.266	.316	.199	8	27-3B 91	
1998	Batavia	NYP	284	66	23	2	5	22/104	39	32	4	2	220	.232	.295	.380	.228	27	70-3B 101	
1999	Piedmont	SAL	282	56	15	2	9	15/92	30	32	5	2	228	.199	.250	.362	.203	21	43-3B 94	30-SS 93
2000	Philadel	NL	289	65	15	2	9	24/102	33	33	7	3	227	.225	.284	.384	.223	27		

His season was wretched enough to justify his being released, yet he has inexplicably remained on the 40-man roster. The fact that the Phillies are worried about a horrendous low-A player being taken in the Rule 5 draft says a lot about their talent-evaluation skills.

Nate Espy — 1B — Bats R — Age 22

YEAR	TEAM	LGE	AB	H	DB	TP	HR	BB/SO	R	RBI	SB	CS	OUT	BA	OBP	SLG	EQA	EQR	DEFENSE
1998	Martnsvl	App	231	64	15	1	9	37/60	32	34	1	1	168	.277	.382	.468	.286	37	56-1B 98
1999	Piedmont	SAL	307	69	19	1	9	40/57	31	30	1	0	238	.225	.315	.381	.238	33	74-1B 107
2000	Philadel	NL	219	60	12	0	11	37/52	40	43	1	0	159	.274	.379	.479	.287	35	

It's looking like the age advantage he had in 1998 played a non-trivial role in his outstanding rookie-ball season. He missed the last six weeks of 1999 with a broken foot, which certainly didn't help matters. The team loves his work ethic, but he's going to have to produce a lot more this year.

Bobby Estalella — C — Bats R — Age 25

YEAR	TEAM	LGE	AB	H	DB	TP	HR	BB/SO	R	RBI	SB	CS	OUT	BA	OBP	SLG	EQA	EQR	DEFENSE
1997	Scran-WB	Int	440	102	25	0	18	47/106	57	62	2	0	338	.232	.318	.411	.247	51	
1998	Scran-WB	Int	246	67	15	1	15	59/50	44	43	0	0	179	.272	.417	.524	.314	49	68-C 99
1998	Philadel	NL	166	32	7	1	8	12/48	16	20	0	0	134	.193	.252	.392	.211	14	44-C 89
1999	Scran-WB	Int	388	83	23	2	12	47/103	48	50	3	1	306	.214	.306	.376	.233	40	101-C 104
1999	Philadel	NL	18	3	0	0	0	4/7	2	1	0	1	16	.167	.318	.167	.162	1	
2000	San Fran	NL	373	83	19	1	17	60/97	54	57	1	0	290	.223	.330	.416	.259	50	

Any way you look at it, last year was a major step back for him. He may regain some strength as he recovers further from his shoulder surgery, but he's reverted to a "pull everything" approach that hurt his performance. He's been traded to the Giants, where he should, at worst, split time with Doug Mirabelli.

Ron Gant — LF — Bats R — Age 35

YEAR	TEAM	LGE	AB	H	DB	TP	HR	BB/SO	R	RBI	SB	CS	OUT	BA	OBP	SLG	EQA	EQR	DEFENSE
1997	St Louis	NL	509	120	23	4	18	57/160	68	63	11	6	395	.236	.314	.403	.242	57	125-OF 97
1998	St Louis	NL	386	94	18	1	27	51/90	61	67	9	0	292	.244	.335	.505	.279	60	93-OF 90
1999	Philadel	NL	515	131	27	5	16	78/111	99	71	11	3	387	.254	.354	.419	.266	70	126-LF 108
2000	Philadel	NL	369	86	14	1	14	62/88	60	52	9	2	285	.233	.343	.390	.253	46	

The combination of the drop in power and the career-high in walks is a warning sign that he's on the verge of a complete offensive collapse. At this point he's probably a decent spare outfielder for a couple of years; as a $6.5 million starter, he's a significant liability.

Doug Glanville — CF — Bats R — Age 29

YEAR	TEAM	LGE	AB	H	DB	TP	HR	BB/SO	R	RBI	SB	CS	OUT	BA	OBP	SLG	EQA	EQR	DEFENSE
1997	ChiCubs	NL	475	139	23	5	4	23/46	74	34	14	11	347	.293	.327	.387	.240	49	130-OF 93
1998	Philadel	NL	682	191	30	7	8	40/87	106	48	24	7	498	.280	.326	.380	.244	73	153-OF 111
1999	Philadel	NL	627	200	39	6	10	40/81	93	68	30	2	429	.319	.366	.448	.282	91	143-CF 107
2000	Philadel	NL	560	164	27	5	11	46/71	92	77	25	6	402	.293	.347	.418	.262	70	

Aside from the disastrous last two months of 1998, he's been an improved hitter who has enough discipline to post an acceptable on-base percentage. If he keeps it up, and I have a hunch that he will, that improvement combines with his excellent defense to make him an above-average player, although not quite as good as the hype.

Kevin Jordan — IF — Bats R — Age 30

YEAR	TEAM	LGE	AB	H	DB	TP	HR	BB/SO	R	RBI	SB	CS	OUT	BA	OBP	SLG	EQA	EQR	DEFENSE	
1997	Philadel	NL	179	49	6	0	7	2/26	19	31	0	1	131	.274	.282	.425	.230	17	15-1B 99	
1998	Philadel	NL	251	70	7	0	4	8/29	22	28	0	0	181	.279	.307	.355	.223	21		
1999	Philadel	NL	347	97	16	3	4	20/34	34	48	0	0	250	.280	.331	.378	.242	36	51-3B 96	20-2B 108
2000	Philadel	NL	275	77	11	1	5	17/29	30	36	0	0	198	.280	.322	.382	.236	27		

He tried hard, but he couldn't come close to filling the hole at third base after Scott Rolen went down for the season. On the other hand, he'd be a better starting second baseman than what the Phillies have now. He's a useful player in the role he's in as long as his salary doesn't get too inflated by arbitration.

Mike Lieberthal   C   Bats R   Age 28

YEAR	TEAM	LGE	AB	H	DB	TP	HR	BB/SO	R	RBI	SB	CS	OUT	BA	OBP	SLG	EQA	EQR	DEFENSE
1997	Philadel	NL	461	115	27	1	22	43/75	60	79	2	4	350	.249	.319	.456	.255	57	
1998	Philadel	NL	315	81	17	3	8	16/43	39	45	2	1	235	.257	.309	.406	.240	33	82-C 102
1999	Philadel	NL	510	150	30	1	31	37/85	79	90	0	0	360	.294	.356	.539	.292	83	134-C 103
2000	Philadel	NL	421	112	20	1	22	43/69	59	76	1	1	310	.266	.334	.475	.266	56	

The big question is whether his performance represented a breakthrough caused by finally being healthy or if it was simply a career year. Given his age, it was most likely a career year. Even if the projection is accurate and he slides most of the way back to his earlier level, his defensive skills are enough for him to be useful in a strong lineup. Unfortunately for the Phillies, they aren't quite there yet.

Wendell Magee   OF   Bats R   Age 27

YEAR	TEAM	LGE	AB	H	DB	TP	HR	BB/SO	R	RBI	SB	CS	OUT	BA	OBP	SLG	EQA	EQR	DEFENSE
1997	Philadel	NL	116	24	2	0	2	9/20	7	10	0	4	96	.207	.264	.276	.166	5	32-OF 116
1997	Scran-WB	Int	298	69	19	1	9	24/56	34	34	3	5	234	.232	.289	.393	.224	28	80-OF 100
1998	Scran-WB	Int	512	131	29	5	18	34/113	69	56	4	4	385	.256	.305	.438	.245	57	126-OF 100
1998	Philadel	NL	75	22	6	1	1	7/11	9	11	0	0	53	.293	.354	.440	.268	10	
1999	Scran-WB	Int	567	141	27	2	15	42/136	71	60	6	6	432	.249	.302	.383	.229	54	139-OF 97
1999	Philadel	NL	14	5	0	0	2	1/4	3	4	0	0	9	.357	.400	.786	.357	3	
2000	Philadel	NL	506	128	26	2	18	53/116	66	75	4	4	382	.253	.324	.419	.247	58	

He had very little organized baseball experience before being drafted by the Phillies, so he suffered from the wretched excuse for coaching in the lower ranks of the farm system in the mid-1990s. He's managed to turn enough of the raw talent into hitting ability to make himself useful as a reserve outfielder or cheap platoon starter. He's not going to reach the level he could have if he had received good coaching five years ago.

Billy McMillon   OF   Bats L   Age 28

YEAR	TEAM	LGE	AB	H	DB	TP	HR	BB/SO	R	RBI	SB	CS	OUT	BA	OBP	SLG	EQA	EQR	DEFENSE
1997	Charlott	Int	205	49	12	0	7	25/54	25	20	5	0	156	.239	.324	.400	.251	24	51-OF 91
1997	Scran-WB	Int	93	24	7	1	3	10/26	14	16	1	0	69	.258	.330	.452	.263	12	22-OF 105
1997	Philadel	NL	73	22	4	1	2	6/17	10	13	2	1	52	.301	.354	.466	.274	10	15-OF 112
1998	Scran-WB	Int	271	63	14	1	10	26/66	33	30	3	2	210	.232	.306	.402	.238	29	68-OF 94
1999	Scran-WB	Int	465	123	33	3	11	52/87	73	63	7	2	344	.265	.345	.419	.261	60	126-OF 87
2000	Detroit	AL	329	80	18	1	10	41/68	50	45	5	1	250	.243	.327	.395	.249	39	

Not to repeat ourselves too much, but this is a player who is far more deserving of a major-league roster spot than many others. He had yet another strong year in Triple-A but can't get even a fourth outfielder job in the majors. McMillon is too old ever to be a star, but he could be a solid left fielder for someone for a few years.

Jason Michaels   OF   Bats R   Age 24

YEAR	TEAM	LGE	AB	H	DB	TP	HR	BB/SO	R	RBI	SB	CS	OUT	BA	OBP	SLG	EQA	EQR	DEFENSE
1998	Batavia	NYP	245	55	11	1	10	30/73	32	34	1	1	191	.224	.314	.400	.241	27	65-OF 89
1999	Clearwtr	Fla	452	106	27	3	11	52/124	64	44	4	3	349	.235	.316	.381	.237	48	92-OF 108
2000	Philadel	NL	280	65	12	1	10	36/89	36	38	1	1	216	.232	.320	.389	.239	30	

The last month of his 1998 season suggested he was capable of the year he had in 1999. What was unexpected was his ability to play a solid center field, which makes his already interesting offensive numbers that much more appealing.

Josue Perez   OF   Bats B   Age 22

YEAR	TEAM	LGE	AB	H	DB	TP	HR	BB/SO	R	RBI	SB	CS	OUT	BA	OBP	SLG	EQA	EQR	DEFENSE
1999	Vero Bch	Fla	201	48	12	1	2	17/32	18	17	7	5	158	.239	.302	.338	.218	18	64-OF 95
1999	Clearwtr	Fla	93	22	2	0	0	5/19	11	5	3	1	72	.237	.280	.258	.183	5	23-OF 99
2000	Philadel	NL	141	34	5	0	2	11/53	16	12	6	3	110	.241	.296	.319	.209	11	

The Phillies trumpeted Perez's signing as evidence that they were willing to spend money and that they were pursuing talent in Latin America. It's also evidence that they focus too much on tools and not enough on performance and baseball ability.

Tom Prince   C   Bats R   Age 35

YEAR	TEAM	LGE	AB	H	DB	TP	HR	BB/SO	R	RBI	SB	CS	OUT	BA	OBP	SLG	EQA	EQR	DEFENSE
1997	LosAngls	NL	101	23	4	0	4	5/15	18	15	0	0	78	.228	.285	.386	.224	9	
1998	LosAngls	NL	82	17	5	1	0	7/23	7	5	0	0	65	.207	.287	.293	.197	6	23-C 114
1999	Clearwtr	Fla	33	9	1	0	1	2/4	3	5	0	0	24	.273	.324	.394	.243	3	
1999	Scran-WB	Int	22	2	0	0	1	3/5	2	1	1	0	20	.091	.226	.227	.159	1	
2000	Philadel	NL	50	9	2	0	1	5/10	4	3	0	0	41	.180	.255	.280	.171	2	

The Phillies have had an experience fetish for years; Prince is just the latest manifestation of it. He's the spitting image of a replacement-level catcher, as was proved when Gary Bennett filled his spot for five months. The Phillies signed him for two years, so they're stuck with his anemic bat in 2000.

Nick Punto   SS   Bats B   Age 22

YEAR	TEAM	LGE	AB	H	DB	TP	HR	BB/SO	R	RBI	SB	CS	OUT	BA	OBP	SLG	EQA	EQR	DEFENSE
1998	Batavia	NYP	289	64	11	3	1	33/50	35	15	7	3	228	.221	.302	.291	.207	22	70-SS 86
1999	Clearwtr	Fla	400	104	19	5	1	56/58	49	37	7	3	299	.260	.353	.340	.245	44	107-SS 105
2000	Philadel	NL	279	74	14	2	1	44/46	49	30	8	2	207	.265	.365	.341	.251	33	

Punto had a solid season that got a lot of people's attention. Not only can he hit, he has good range at shortstop. He's probably a couple years away from the majors, but his development this year makes him a name to watch.

Desi Relaford   SS   Bats B   Age 26

YEAR	TEAM	LGE	AB	H	DB	TP	HR	BB/SO	R	RBI	SB	CS	OUT	BA	OBP	SLG	EQA	EQR	DEFENSE
1997	Scran-WB	Int	524	138	35	3	9	34/75	72	49	22	6	392	.263	.316	.393	.244	58	130-SS 104
1998	Philadel	NL	496	122	27	3	5	32/85	45	41	9	6	380	.246	.296	.343	.216	41	133-SS 92
1999	Philadel	NL	211	49	11	2	1	17/34	29	24	3	3	165	.232	.310	.318	.215	18	58-SS 98
2000	Philadel	NL	319	79	18	2	4	29/53	41	33	10	4	244	.248	.310	.354	.227	30	

He rushed back from his hand injury and consequently was not very effective in September. Of course, his production wasn't that spectacular before he was injured. He walks enough to be not completely useless as a #8 hitter, but the Phillies shouldn't hesitate to replace him if a better option comes along.

Scott Rolen   3B   Bats R   Age 25

YEAR	TEAM	LGE	AB	H	DB	TP	HR	BB/SO	R	RBI	SB	CS	OUT	BA	OBP	SLG	EQA	EQR	DEFENSE
1997	Philadel	NL	570	164	38	3	22	75/137	93	93	13	6	412	.288	.383	.481	.290	93	154-3B 105
1998	Philadel	NL	605	174	45	4	32	92/137	119	109	14	8	439	.288	.392	.534	.304	112	159-3B 104
1999	Philadel	NL	420	110	25	1	26	62/113	69	72	11	2	312	.262	.361	.512	.290	70	108-3B 105
2000	Philadel	NL	494	144	29	2	31	85/124	111	108	21	4	354	.291	.396	.547	.311	95	

He came out of spring training looking like he had a large red "S" on the front of his uniform, playing like a serious MVP candidate in April before going into a prolonged slump in May and June. He appeared to be coming out of it when he suffered the back strain that ended his season six weeks early. Watch out for him this year.

Jimmy Rollins   SS   Bats B   Age 21

YEAR	TEAM	LGE	AB	H	DB	TP	HR	BB/SO	R	RBI	SB	CS	OUT	BA	OBP	SLG	EQA	EQR	DEFENSE
1997	Piedmont	SAL	576	147	24	6	7	46/81	71	51	18	4	433	.255	.310	.354	.231	55	136-SS 101
1998	Clearwtr	Fla	498	109	19	6	7	33/69	54	28	9	4	393	.219	.271	.323	.200	35	118-SS 98
1999	Reading	Eas	539	138	22	7	10	39/48	67	48	13	7	408	.256	.307	.378	.232	53	132-SS 101
2000	Philadel	NL	555	146	22	6	10	51/62	78	67	18	5	414	.263	.325	.378	.241	59	

At 20, he was young for Double-A and hopelessly overmatched early in the season. He managed to turn it around somewhat in the second half, but he needs more time at Reading. There are some reports that the Phillies are considering moving him to second base, which wouldn't be the worst idea in the world.

Kevin Sefcik   UT   Bats R   Age 29

YEAR	TEAM	LGE	AB	H	DB	TP	HR	BB/SO	R	RBI	SB	CS	OUT	BA	OBP	SLG	EQA	EQR	DEFENSE
1997	Scran-WB	Int	124	37	10	1	1	6/12	15	7	3	1	88	.298	.331	.419	.254	14	
1997	Philadel	NL	120	33	3	0	2	4/9	11	6	1	2	89	.275	.304	.350	.217	10	16-2B 98
1998	Philadel	NL	170	53	7	2	3	25/31	27	19	4	2	119	.312	.423	.429	.297	29	39-OF 107
1999	Philadel	NL	209	57	14	3	1	26/24	26	11	8	4	156	.273	.356	.383	.256	26	
2000	*Philadel*	*NL*	*207*	*61*	*13*	*2*	*3*	*25/26*	*36*	*30*	*6*	*4*	*150*	*.295*	*.371*	*.420*	*.268*	*28*	

He has developed into a very nice utility player who can pinch-hit or fill in for a few days at multiple positions. Unless he starts getting large salary increases via arbitration, he's worth keeping around for a while.

Reggie Taylor   CF   Bats L   Age 23

YEAR	TEAM	LGE	AB	H	DB	TP	HR	BB/SO	R	RBI	SB	CS	OUT	BA	OBP	SLG	EQA	EQR	DEFENSE
1997	Clearwtr	Fla	550	123	17	4	14	25/143	56	41	17	10	437	.224	.261	.345	.202	40	133-OF 112
1998	Reading	Eas	339	88	15	5	5	8/71	41	20	14	6	258	.260	.280	.378	.221	30	78-OF 98
1999	Reading	Eas	531	133	18	7	15	9/81	60	53	20	12	410	.250	.266	.395	.218	46	123-OF 105
2000	*Philadel*	*NL*	*518*	*131*	*18*	*5*	*17*	*25/96*	*61*	*64*	*23*	*11*	*398*	*.253*	*.287*	*.405*	*.230*	*50*	

1999 was supposedly Taylor's breakthrough year, the one in which he started to make good use of his tools. It came in his second year at Double-A, though, and it still wasn't that good. At this point, he's probably most useful to the Phillies as over-hyped trade bait.

Eric Valent   OF   Bats L   Age 23

YEAR	TEAM	LGE	AB	H	DB	TP	HR	BB/SO	R	RBI	SB	CS	OUT	BA	OBP	SLG	EQA	EQR	DEFENSE
1998	Piedmont	SAL	91	32	8	0	7	12/19	18	21	0	0	59	.352	.427	.670	.347	21	18-OF 99
1998	Clearwtr	Fla	126	29	7	1	4	13/32	19	19	0	1	98	.230	.312	.397	.237	13	30-OF 96
1999	Clearwtr	Fla	519	124	26	5	19	46/124	69	79	2	1	396	.239	.304	.418	.242	57	131-OF 93
2000	*Philadel*	*NL*	*286*	*73*	*13*	*1*	*13*	*32/83*	*40*	*47*	*1*	*0*	*213*	*.255*	*.330*	*.444*	*.258*	*36*	

The dip in his walk rate is a little alarming, but the best coaches in the system are supposedly at the upper levels, so he may turn that around when he hits Reading. Even so, he may have fallen behind Jason Michaels on the depth chart in left field.

Jon Zuber   1B/OF   Bats L   Age 30

YEAR	TEAM	LGE	AB	H	DB	TP	HR	BB/SO	R	RBI	SB	CS	OUT	BA	OBP	SLG	EQA	EQR	DEFENSE	
1997	Scran-WB	Int	443	123	33	2	4	64/57	70	51	2	2	322	.278	.372	.388	.264	58	75-OF 85	20-1B 108
1998	Scran-WB	Int	284	81	19	3	3	36/38	38	45	0	0	203	.285	.369	.405	.267	37	44-OF 91	28-1B 99
1999	Scran-WB	Int	390	99	21	1	4	71/53	52	40	4	1	292	.254	.370	.344	.255	48	72-1B 115	
2000	*Philadel*	*NL*	*321*	*86*	*21*	*1*	*3*	*58/43*	*59*	*41*	*2*	*1*	*236*	*.268*	*.380*	*.368*	*.262*	*41*		

He doesn't have enough power to be a major-league starter, but if Orlando Merced can collect major-league paychecks, there really should be room for Zuber on someone's bench.

PITCHERS (Averages: ERA: 4.50 / H/9: 9.00 / HR/9: 1.00 / BB/9: 3.50 / K/9: 6.50 / KWH: 1.00)

Scott Aldred   Throws L   Age 32

YEAR	TEAM	LGE	IP	H	ER	HR	BB	K	ERA	W	L	H/9	HR/9	BB/9	K/9	KWH	PERA
1997	SaltLake	PCL	37.7	55	36	4	17	19	8.60	1	3	13.14	0.96	4.06	4.54	0.29	7.17
1997	Minnesot	AL	78.3	99	61	19	28	33	7.01	3	6	11.37	2.18	3.22	3.79	0.29	7.24
1998	Durham	Int	33.3	49	29	3	16	16	7.83	1	3	13.23	0.81	4.32	4.32	0.24	7.29
1998	TampaBay	AL	31.7	33	13	1	12	21	3.69	2	2	9.38	0.28	3.41	5.97	0.83	3.98
1999	TampaBay	AL	24.3	25	13	1	13	22	4.81	1	2	9.25	0.37	4.81	8.14	1.11	4.44
1999	Philadel	NL	32.3	33	14	1	14	18	3.90	2	2	9.19	0.28	3.90	5.01	0.52	3.90

As they did with Yorkis Perez in 1998, the Phillies used Aldred for longer than one left-handed batter, and initially he responded fairly well. However, like the rest of the bullpen, he collapsed over the last few weeks of the season.

Brad Baisley   Throws R   Age 20

YEAR	TEAM	LGE	IP	H	ER	HR	BB	K	ERA	W	L	H/9	HR/9	BB/9	K/9	KWH	PERA
1998	Martnsvl	App	24.7	36	15	3	5	8	5.47	1	2	13.14	1.09	1.82	2.92	0.27	6.20
1999	Piedmont	SAL	139.7	146	71	6	77	71	4.58	8	8	9.41	0.39	4.96	4.58	0.34	4.64

Once again, the Phillies had a very effective rotation at Piedmont. Once again, it was overworked. Baisley was the star of the lot, throwing a no-hitter late in the year. He fits the mold of a Prototypical Phillies Pitcher: a big kid who throws hard. The question is whether he'll avoid the usual fate of the breed, blowing out his arm after a few years.

Ryan Brannan   Throws R   Age 25

YEAR	TEAM	LGE	IP	H	ER	HR	BB	K	ERA	W	L	H/9	HR/9	BB/9	K/9	KWH	PERA
1997	Clearwtr	Fla	26.0	25	3	0	11	19	1.04	3	0	8.65	0.00	3.81	6.58	0.98	3.46
1997	Reading	Eas	51.3	57	19	2	22	32	3.33	4	2	9.99	0.35	3.86	5.61	0.61	4.56
1998	Scran-WB	Int	15.7	22	19	0	14	11	10.91	0	2	12.64	0.00	8.04	6.32	0.29	7.47
1998	Reading	Eas	54.3	61	34	5	33	33	5.63	2	4	10.10	0.83	5.47	5.47	0.40	5.80
1999	Clearwtr	Fla	68.0	115	89	10	60	28	11.78	1	7	15.22	1.32	7.94	3.71	0.08	10.85

His early success may have been due to a bizarre windup that makes him look like a drunk falling down stairs. After teams started to figure out the motion his effectiveness dropped sharply. Needless to say, with the record he's put up, he's no longer referred to as the "closer of the future."

Jeff Brantley   Throws R   Age 36

YEAR	TEAM	LGE	IP	H	ER	HR	BB	K	ERA	W	L	H/9	HR/9	BB/9	K/9	KWH	PERA
1997	Cincnnti	NL	11.7	9	5	2	8	15	3.86	1	0	6.94	1.54	6.17	11.57	2.34	4.63
1998	St Louis	NL	50.7	41	25	12	19	46	4.44	3	3	7.28	2.13	3.38	8.17	2.03	4.62
1999	Philadel	NL	8.7	5	5	0	8	11	5.19	0	1	5.19	0.00	8.31	11.42	2.26	3.12

After a very effective first month, he ripped up a rotator cuff. His attempt to pitch through that was—surprise!—unsuccessful. He'll try to make yet another comeback, this time as a non-roster invitee. You have to wonder how many times he can come back.

Jason Brester   Throws L   Age 23

YEAR	TEAM	LGE	IP	H	ER	HR	BB	K	ERA	W	L	H/9	HR/9	BB/9	K/9	KWH	PERA
1997	San Jose	Cal	133.3	186	87	5	58	122	5.87	6	9	12.56	0.34	3.92	8.24	1.03	6.01
1998	Shrevprt	Tex	102.3	136	67	11	50	64	5.89	4	7	11.96	0.97	4.40	5.63	0.45	6.60
1998	New Havn	Eas	22.0	24	7	0	8	12	2.86	1	1	9.82	0.00	3.27	4.91	0.56	3.68
1999	Carolina	Sou	56.7	78	47	9	28	36	7.46	2	4	12.39	1.43	4.45	5.72	0.44	7.46
1999	Reading	Eas	99.3	123	56	8	29	71	5.07	5	6	11.14	0.72	2.63	6.43	1.06	5.07

Brester was picked up off waivers in the middle of the year and turned into a decent pitcher for Reading. If he keeps it up at Triple-A this year he may find himself in a long-relief/fifth-starter role once the injuries start setting in for the Phillies.

Billy Brewer   Throws L   Age 32

YEAR	TEAM	LGE	IP	H	ER	HR	BB	K	ERA	W	L	H/9	HR/9	BB/9	K/9	KWH	PERA
1997	Philadel	NL	21.3	16	8	2	12	15	3.38	1	1	6.75	0.84	5.06	6.33	0.88	3.80
1999	Scran-WB	Int	66.3	64	33	5	31	49	4.48	4	3	8.68	0.68	4.21	6.65	0.90	4.21
1999	Philadel	NL	25.7	30	18	4	14	27	6.31	1	2	10.52	1.40	4.91	9.47	1.30	6.31

"Can you get batters out?" "More than half of them." "Can you throw strikes?" "If Eric Gregg is the umpire." "Are you healthy?" "No problems since my last surgery." "What hand do you throw with?" "Left." "In that case, I think we can give you a major-league contract. Sign here."

Rob Burger   Throws R   Age 24

YEAR	TEAM	LGE	IP	H	ER	HR	BB	K	ERA	W	L	H/9	HR/9	BB/9	K/9	KWH	PERA
1997	Clearwtr	Fla	150.3	164	100	11	120	122	5.99	6	11	9.82	0.66	7.18	7.30	0.57	6.11
1998	Reading	Eas	112.3	131	94	22	78	83	7.53	3	9	10.50	1.76	6.25	6.65	0.50	7.45
1999	Reading	Eas	25.3	35	47	5	50	19	16.70	0	3	12.43	1.78	17.76	6.75	0.15	14.21
1999	Clearwtr	Fla	22.3	18	13	2	32	18	5.24	1	1	7.25	0.81	12.90	7.25	0.42	7.25

(Rob Burger *continued*)

Burger suffered a catastrophic attack of Blass/Wohlers Disease at the start of the year at Reading, with multiple starts in which he walked or hit virtually every batter he faced. He was sent back to rookie ball to try to regain his form, with very slight success. He's probably done.

Paul Byrd — Throws R — Age 29

YEAR	TEAM	LGE	IP	H	ER	HR	BB	K	ERA	W	L	H/9	HR/9	BB/9	K/9	KWH	PERA
1997	Richmond	Int	16.0	17	7	2	1	11	3.94	1	1	9.56	1.13	0.56	6.19	5.32	3.94
1997	Atlanta	NL	51.7	51	36	6	29	34	6.27	2	4	8.88	1.05	5.05	5.92	0.58	5.05
1998	Richmond	Int	100.0	100	46	8	40	71	4.14	6	5	9.00	0.72	3.60	6.39	0.94	4.23
1998	Philadel	NL	55.3	42	16	6	18	36	2.60	4	2	6.83	0.98	2.93	5.86	1.28	3.09
1999	Philadel	NL	199.3	205	111	31	67	103	5.01	10	12	9.26	1.40	3.03	4.65	0.58	4.88

He's not as good as he looked before the All-Star break, but he should be a solid bottom-of-the-rotation pitcher if he's handled properly. Like the entire rotation, he was overworked early in the season and wore out by mid-August.

David Coggin — Throws R — Age 23

YEAR	TEAM	LGE	IP	H	ER	HR	BB	K	ERA	W	L	H/9	HR/9	BB/9	K/9	KWH	PERA
1997	Clearwtr	Fla	144.0	199	121	16	113	88	7.56	4	12	12.44	1.00	7.06	5.50	0.26	8.12
1998	Reading	Eas	106.7	114	61	9	70	53	5.15	5	7	9.62	0.76	5.91	4.47	0.26	5.57
1999	Reading	Eas	39.0	65	43	9	22	17	9.92	1	3	15.00	2.08	5.08	3.92	0.15	10.38

Coggin is another example of the Phillies' problems with mismanagement in the minor league system. Brief stretches of promising pitching by Coggin were always followed by struggles and arm problems. Finally in 1999, a bone spur was found that had been growing for years and causing muscle damage. The spur is gone now; if no lasting harm was done, Coggin may be a sleeper candidate for sudden development.

Robert Dodd — Throws L — Age 27

YEAR	TEAM	LGE	IP	H	ER	HR	BB	K	ERA	W	L	H/9	HR/9	BB/9	K/9	KWH	PERA
1997	Reading	Eas	77.0	73	34	7	25	71	3.97	5	4	8.53	0.82	2.92	8.30	2.06	3.86
1998	Scran-WB	Int	39.3	42	17	4	21	34	3.89	2	2	9.61	0.92	4.81	7.78	0.98	5.26
1999	Reading	Eas	72.7	100	51	8	28	59	6.32	3	5	12.39	0.99	3.47	7.31	0.93	6.44
1999	Scran-WB	Int	28.7	21	5	1	6	20	1.57	3	0	6.59	0.31	1.88	6.28	2.37	2.20

His record at Double-A illustrates why wins are a terrible statistic, especially for relievers. He picked up several wins after allowing the tying run to score. After a promotion to Triple-A he was pressed into service as an emergency starter. Dodd pitched well in that role, so the Phillies are considering converting him to a starter, which is what he was a few years ago. Decisiveness is not always the organization's strongest point.

Adam Eaton — Throws R — Age 22

YEAR	TEAM	LGE	IP	H	ER	HR	BB	K	ERA	W	L	H/9	HR/9	BB/9	K/9	KWH	PERA
1997	Piedmont	SAL	63.3	113	55	3	43	40	7.82	2	5	16.06	0.43	6.11	5.68	0.25	9.38
1998	Clearwtr	Fla	119.7	192	88	11	61	69	6.62	4	9	14.44	0.83	4.59	5.19	0.30	8.12
1999	Clearwtr	Fla	66.0	96	45	3	30	41	6.14	2	5	13.09	0.41	4.09	5.59	0.44	6.55
1999	Reading	Eas	73.0	71	35	10	31	55	4.32	4	4	8.75	1.23	3.82	6.78	1.03	4.68
1999	Scran-WB	Int	20.3	18	10	1	6	9	4.43	1	1	7.97	0.44	2.66	3.98	0.56	3.10

After two-plus uninspiring years in A-ball, he moved up to Double-A during the season and suddenly looked like a legitimate prospect. He still needs some work to pick up consistency and to see how he reacts when hitters adjust to him, so he likely won't reach the majors until at least 2001. That supposes he stays healthy, which is far from certain; he's had nagging injury problems in his first two years, then had a heavy workload in 1999. Eaton was traded to San Diego in the Ashby deal.

Geoff Geary — Throws R — Age 23

YEAR	TEAM	LGE	IP	H	ER	HR	BB	K	ERA	W	L	H/9	HR/9	BB/9	K/9	KWH	PERA
1998	Batavia	NYP	87.3	112	29	9	19	62	2.99	7	3	11.54	0.93	1.96	6.39	1.35	5.26
1999	Clearwtr	Fla	131.3	213	93	14	41	62	6.37	5	10	14.60	0.96	2.81	4.25	0.33	7.61

He threw more than 200 innings between college and short-season ball in 1998 and was on a pace to have a similar workload last year when he suddenly became a lot less effective. It must be a coincidence.

Wayne Gomes — Throws R — Age 27

YEAR	TEAM	LGE	IP	H	ER	HR	BB	K	ERA	W	L	H/9	HR/9	BB/9	K/9	KWH	PERA
1997	Scran-WB	Int	36.3	35	11	2	25	30	2.72	3	1	8.67	0.50	6.19	7.43	0.77	4.95
1997	Philadel	NL	42.0	47	27	4	25	22	5.79	2	3	10.07	0.86	5.36	4.71	0.31	5.79
1998	Philadel	NL	94.7	95	47	9	38	83	4.47	6	5	9.03	0.86	3.61	7.89	1.43	4.37
1999	Philadel	NL	74.3	70	36	5	54	56	4.36	4	4	8.48	0.61	6.54	6.78	0.62	4.96

After looking like he had suddenly found the strike zone in 1998 and early in 1999, his control deserted him over the last three months and he reverted to the grisly walk rate of his early years. The team's theory is that the pressure of closing got to him, and that putting him back in a setup role will build up his confidence. Skepticism is a wise idea.

Mike Grace — Throws R — Age 30

YEAR	TEAM	LGE	IP	H	ER	HR	BB	K	ERA	W	L	H/9	HR/9	BB/9	K/9	KWH	PERA
1997	Reading	Eas	18.7	34	20	4	8	8	9.64	0	2	16.39	1.93	3.86	3.86	0.18	10.61
1997	Scran-WB	Int	71.3	94	48	1	29	45	6.06	3	5	11.86	0.13	3.66	5.68	0.56	5.30
1997	Philadel	NL	38.3	33	16	3	11	24	3.76	2	2	7.75	0.70	2.58	5.63	1.19	3.29
1998	Philadel	NL	91.7	119	60	10	32	44	5.89	4	6	11.68	0.98	3.14	4.32	0.38	5.89
1998	Scran-WB	Int	69.7	104	50	8	20	32	6.46	3	5	13.44	1.03	2.58	4.13	0.37	6.85
1999	Scran-WB	Int	44.0	58	27	6	19	23	5.52	2	3	11.86	1.23	3.89	4.70	0.36	6.55
1999	Philadel	NL	55.0	80	45	4	29	27	7.36	2	4	13.09	0.65	4.75	4.42	0.23	7.04

Grace has had two choices the past couple of years. He could throw with bad mechanics and be effective for a month until he strained yet another muscle, or he could pitch in a way that kept him healthy but ineffective. He's running out of time to put it all together and will likely will wind up as yet another victim of the inept coaching in the Phillies' system.

Jason Kershner — Throws L — Age 23

YEAR	TEAM	LGE	IP	H	ER	HR	BB	K	ERA	W	L	H/9	HR/9	BB/9	K/9	KWH	PERA
1997	Clearwtr	Fla	92.7	143	63	12	28	40	6.12	4	6	13.89	1.17	2.72	3.88	0.30	7.38
1998	Clearwtr	Fla	86.0	138	73	10	32	50	7.64	3	7	14.44	1.05	3.35	5.23	0.42	7.85
1999	Reading	Eas	86.3	118	77	15	44	71	8.03	2	8	12.30	1.56	4.59	7.40	0.73	7.61

The last member of the 1996 Piedmont "Four Aces" rotation left standing, Kershner is barely doing so after being mishandled over the past few years. He's a left-hander, so he'll get plenty of chances. His strikeout rate is improving, but he still has a way to go.

Carlton Loewer — Throws R — Age 26

YEAR	TEAM	LGE	IP	H	ER	HR	BB	K	ERA	W	L	H/9	HR/9	BB/9	K/9	KWH	PERA
1997	Scran-WB	Int	178.0	215	125	20	52	129	6.32	7	13	10.87	1.01	2.63	6.52	1.11	5.26
1998	Scran-WB	Int	88.3	102	40	5	23	59	4.08	5	5	10.39	0.51	2.34	6.01	1.11	4.28
1998	Philadel	NL	124.7	158	85	18	41	56	6.14	5	9	11.41	1.30	2.96	4.04	0.36	6.06
1999	Philadel	NL	89.7	100	51	8	25	47	5.12	4	6	10.04	0.80	2.51	4.72	0.66	4.52

Early in the season, he had a few outstanding starts and it looked like he might be on the verge of developing into a solid pitcher. After a couple of high-pitch outings, he started struggling and eventually wound up on the disabled list with a stress fracture of his arm. He should be able to bounce back to full strength. Loewer was traded to the Padres as part of the Andy Ashby deal, and was set to be the their #3 starter before breaking his leg in a hunting accident. He's out until midseason.

Steve Montgomery — Throws R — Age 29

YEAR	TEAM	LGE	IP	H	ER	HR	BB	K	ERA	W	L	H/9	HR/9	BB/9	K/9	KWH	PERA
1997	Edmonton	PCL	43.7	63	29	5	19	31	5.98	2	3	12.98	1.03	3.92	6.39	0.60	7.21
1998	Rochestr	Int	81.7	94	59	13	27	55	6.50	3	6	10.36	1.43	2.98	6.06	0.89	5.51
1999	Scran-WB	Int	12.7	18	9	0	12	11	6.39	0	1	12.79	0.00	8.53	7.82	0.42	7.82
1999	Philadel	NL	64.7	54	23	9	30	53	3.20	5	2	7.52	1.25	4.18	7.38	1.30	4.18

Montgomery is another example of how decent relievers can be found among the ranks of the minor-league free agents. There's nothing spectacular about his repertoire and he'll never be overpowering, but he showed this year that if he's used sensibly, he can be an effective short reliever for a while. Pitcher #3 in the Ashby trade, he'll have a chance to replace Dan Miceli as Trevor Hoffman's setup man.

Doug Nickle · Throws R · Age 25

YEAR	TEAM	LGE	IP	H	ER	HR	BB	K	ERA	W	L	H/9	HR/9	BB/9	K/9	KWH	PERA
1997	Boise	Nwn	17.0	36	21	4	10	12	11.12	0	2	19.06	2.12	5.29	6.35	0.30	13.76
1998	CedarRpd	Mid	61.7	94	46	3	29	38	6.71	2	5	13.72	0.44	4.23	5.55	0.40	7.01
1998	Lk Elsin	Cal	59.0	89	55	4	34	44	8.39	2	5	13.58	0.61	5.19	6.71	0.48	7.47
1999	Clearwtr	Fla	64.7	80	36	1	34	50	5.01	3	4	11.13	0.14	4.73	6.96	0.69	5.29

I was all set to make jokes about the Phillies having traded Gregg Jefferies for a wooden Nickle. Then he went out and had a good season. Nickle was 24, which is old for the Florida State League and explains why his translations don't look so great. His performance may suffer at higher levels.

Chad Ogea · Throws R · Age 29

YEAR	TEAM	LGE	IP	H	ER	HR	BB	K	ERA	W	L	H/9	HR/9	BB/9	K/9	KWH	PERA
1997	Buffalo	AmA	19.3	28	13	2	8	9	6.05	1	1	13.03	0.93	3.72	4.19	0.27	6.98
1997	Clevelnd	AL	126.7	134	73	12	47	80	5.19	6	8	9.52	0.85	3.34	5.68	0.76	4.55
1998	Clevelnd	AL	71.0	70	38	8	27	44	4.82	4	4	8.87	1.01	3.42	5.58	0.77	4.44
1998	Buffalo	Int	40.3	47	21	2	6	29	4.69	2	2	10.49	0.45	1.34	6.47	2.23	4.02
1999	Philadel	NL	167.7	192	103	33	59	75	5.53	8	11	10.31	1.77	3.17	4.03	0.37	6.01

The Phillies cut him loose after the season, and it's probably just as well. The constant turning around to watch the screaming line-drive home runs couldn't have helped Scott Rolen's back. Ogea was waived, claimed by the Tigers, then taken by the Devil Rays in the Rule 5 draft. The Trop won't help him much.

Robert Person · Throws R · Age 30

YEAR	TEAM	LGE	IP	H	ER	HR	BB	K	ERA	W	L	H/9	HR/9	BB/9	K/9	KWH	PERA
1999	Toronto	AL	11.0	9	10	1	14	12	8.18	0	1	7.36	0.82	11.45	9.82	0.85	6.55
1999	Philadel	NL	137.3	130	66	21	67	123	4.33	8	7	8.52	1.38	4.39	8.06	1.30	4.98

After years of scouts raving about his high-90s fastball while he had an ERA around 6.00 or 7.00, he finally put together a solid half-season. As it turns out, velocity wasn't his key to success, but the obstacle. When he started sacrificing a little speed to improve his location and using a variety of pitches, including a nasty curve ball, the results improved. As long as he doesn't go back to trying to blow everyone away, he should be a solid starter. Any success he has makes him a candidate for overwork, as we saw in August.

Cliff Politte · Throws R · Age 26

YEAR	TEAM	LGE	IP	H	ER	HR	BB	K	ERA	W	L	H/9	HR/9	BB/9	K/9	KWH	PERA
1997	Pr Willm	Car	111.0	120	50	12	37	80	4.05	7	5	9.73	0.97	3.00	6.49	1.08	4.70
1997	Arkansas	Tex	34.0	42	18	3	11	22	4.76	2	2	11.12	0.79	2.91	5.82	0.78	5.29
1998	St Louis	NL	37.7	45	31	7	19	21	7.41	1	3	10.75	1.67	4.54	5.02	0.39	6.69
1998	Memphis	PCL	46.3	78	49	9	27	35	9.52	1	4	15.15	1.75	5.24	6.80	0.43	10.10
1998	Arkansas	Tex	60.3	72	33	5	20	47	4.92	3	4	10.74	0.75	2.98	7.01	1.15	5.07
1999	Reading	Eas	98.0	145	60	12	40	72	5.51	4	7	13.32	1.10	3.67	6.61	0.67	7.35
1999	Philadel	NL	18.0	19	13	2	14	14	6.50	1	1	9.50	1.00	7.00	7.00	0.55	6.00

If his career is to be salvaged, the Phillies need to figure out what his role will be, send him to Triple-A to work on it and leave him there. He's been jerked back and forth between the minors and the majors, as well as between starting and short relief. This is not the ideal plan for developing a pitcher.

Curt Schilling · Throws R · Age 33

YEAR	TEAM	LGE	IP	H	ER	HR	BB	K	ERA	W	L	H/9	HR/9	BB/9	K/9	KWH	PERA
1997	Philadel	NL	252.7	214	96	26	61	296	3.42	18	10	7.62	0.93	2.17	10.54	5.02	3.21
1998	Philadel	NL	271.7	239	98	23	65	287	3.25	20	10	7.92	0.76	2.15	9.51	3.96	3.18
1999	Philadel	NL	180.0	158	69	23	43	147	3.45	13	7	7.90	1.15	2.15	7.35	2.38	3.55

The workload finally caught up to him last year. The team claims that the shoulder surgery he underwent in the offseason was minor, and that he should be back in mid-May. If the Phillies don't change how they use him, though, he may be back on the disabled list by September. Since his effectiveness frequently drops off sharply after 120 pitches anyway, there's really no reason not to change.

Steve Schrenk　　　Throws R　　　Age 31

YEAR	TEAM	LGE	IP	H	ER	HR	BB	K	ERA	W	L	H/9	HR/9	BB/9	K/9	KWH	PERA
1997	Rochestr	Int	120.7	144	80	21	40	81	5.97	5	8	10.74	1.57	2.98	6.04	0.85	5.97
1998	Pawtuckt	Int	58.7	65	28	7	26	38	4.30	4	3	9.97	1.07	3.99	5.83	0.64	5.37
1999	Scran-WB	Int	41.0	42	18	2	23	29	3.95	3	2	9.22	0.44	5.05	6.37	0.65	4.61
1999	Philadel	NL	50.3	41	22	6	13	35	3.93	3	3	7.33	1.07	2.32	6.26	1.72	3.22

After nearly having his career ended by numerous injuries, Schrenk made it to the majors as a long reliever/spot starter. He pitches well often enough to make him useful in the role. He also gets hit hard on enough occasions to prevent the Phillies from putting him in the rotation.

Anthony Shumaker　　　Throws L　　　Age 27

YEAR	TEAM	LGE	IP	H	ER	HR	BB	K	ERA	W	L	H/9	HR/9	BB/9	K/9	KWH	PERA
1997	Clearwtr	Fla	64.7	89	35	2	27	52	4.87	3	4	12.39	0.28	3.76	7.24	0.84	5.85
1998	Reading	Eas	157.3	182	91	20	56	95	5.21	7	10	10.41	1.14	3.20	5.43	0.66	5.38
1999	Reading	Eas	55.7	62	24	3	21	44	3.88	3	3	10.02	0.49	3.40	7.11	1.11	4.53
1999	Scran-WB	Int	84.3	132	62	13	35	42	6.62	3	6	14.09	1.39	3.74	4.48	0.29	8.22
1999	Philadel	NL	22.7	23	15	3	13	16	5.96	1	2	9.13	1.19	5.16	6.35	0.64	5.56

He pitched well in Double-A but ran into problems in Triple-A and the majors. He doesn't throw hard, relying on location and mixing up his pitches, so it's not too surprising that the more experienced hitters were able to wait him out and take advantage of his mistakes. He could make the adjustments needed to be effective in the majors, but he has no margin for error.

Amaury Telemaco　　　Throws R　　　Age 26

YEAR	TEAM	LGE	IP	H	ER	HR	BB	K	ERA	W	L	H/9	HR/9	BB/9	K/9	KWH	PERA
1997	Iowa	AmA	107.7	141	83	20	42	67	6.94	4	8	11.79	1.67	3.51	5.60	0.57	6.94
1997	ChiCubs	NL	39.0	47	25	4	11	27	5.77	2	2	10.85	0.92	2.54	6.23	1.05	5.08
1998	ChiCubs	NL	27.7	23	12	5	14	17	3.90	2	1	7.48	1.63	4.55	5.53	0.67	4.55
1998	Arizona	NL	119.7	135	66	13	35	57	4.96	6	7	10.15	0.98	2.63	4.29	0.51	4.81
1999	Tucson	PCL	17.7	21	10	1	7	14	5.09	1	1	10.70	0.51	3.57	7.13	1.00	5.09
1999	Philadel	NL	47.3	44	26	8	20	40	4.94	2	3	8.37	1.52	3.80	7.61	1.36	4.75

Telemaco was perhaps the worst victim of Francona's bullpen-management style, never getting a defined role. He alternated periods of inactivity with periods of heavy use. Initially he was able to handle it and pitch well, but around the middle of August he fell apart, which certainly suggests that he was hiding an injury. This wouldn't be surprising under the circumstances.

Evan Thomas　　　Throws R　　　Age 26

YEAR	TEAM	LGE	IP	H	ER	HR	BB	K	ERA	W	L	H/9	HR/9	BB/9	K/9	KWH	PERA
1997	Clearwtr	Fla	77.7	92	43	9	33	65	4.98	4	5	10.66	1.04	3.82	7.53	1.04	5.68
1997	Reading	Eas	80.3	112	54	9	36	67	6.05	3	6	12.55	1.01	4.03	7.51	0.83	6.83
1998	Reading	Eas	151.0	209	76	13	54	101	4.53	8	9	12.46	0.77	3.22	6.02	0.68	6.20
1999	Reading	Eas	115.7	157	71	8	60	94	5.52	5	8	12.22	0.62	4.67	7.31	0.70	6.46

Here's a pitcher who gets results with good control most of the time, a solid low-90s fastball, a nasty curve and a healthy arm that wasn't abused last year. Nevertheless, he's stuck in Double-A. The reason seems to be that he's only 5'10" and "short right-handers can't make it in the majors." Tell that to Pedro Martinez. Once some team gives him a chance, they should get a solid #4 starter.

Randy Wolf　　　Throws L　　　Age 23

YEAR	TEAM	LGE	IP	H	ER	HR	BB	K	ERA	W	L	H/9	HR/9	BB/9	K/9	KWH	PERA
1997	Batavia	NYP	36.3	43	13	2	12	33	3.22	3	1	10.65	0.50	2.97	8.17	1.58	4.71
1998	Reading	Eas	24.7	16	4	0	5	27	1.46	3	0	5.84	0.00	1.82	9.85	6.81	1.46
1998	Scran-WB	Int	140.3	182	94	15	50	103	6.03	6	10	11.67	0.96	3.21	6.61	0.87	5.90
1999	Scran-WB	Int	75.3	77	35	7	30	65	4.18	4	4	9.20	0.84	3.58	7.77	1.37	4.42
1999	Philadel	NL	122.3	126	72	18	64	112	5.30	6	8	9.27	1.32	4.71	8.24	1.16	5.52

Here's the perfect example of how not to handle a young pitcher. Wolf was still working on polishing his curve at Triple-A when injuries forced the Phillies to call him up to the majors. They then rode him hard, frequently letting him throw well over 100 pitches. If he doesn't burn out and gets enough experience to sharpen his control, he's going to be an outstanding pitcher. Unless the team changes its approach to handling pitchers, that's not going to happen.

Support-Neutral Records — PHILADELPHIA PHILLIES — Park Effect: +8.3%

PITCHER	GS	IP	R	SNW	SNL	SNPCT	W	L	RA	APW	SNVA	SNWAR
Joel Bennett	3	13.7	13	0.7	1.3	.355	1	1	8.56	-0.46	-0.30	-0.14
Paul Byrd	32	199.7	119	12.0	11.3	.515	15	11	5.36	-0.19	0.34	2.10
Mike Grace	5	23.3	21	0.9	2.2	.293	0	3	8.10	-0.68	-0.68	-0.42
Joe Grahe	5	23.3	16	1.7	1.7	.495	1	4	6.17	-0.22	-0.05	0.24
Carlton Loewer	13	82.0	49	4.4	4.9	.471	2	5	5.38	-0.09	-0.18	0.43
Chad Ogea	28	153.0	102	8.9	10.3	.461	6	12	6.00	-1.14	-0.76	0.70
Robert Person	22	126.0	65	8.3	6.9	.546	10	5	4.64	0.81	0.55	1.85
Curt Schilling	24	180.3	74	12.2	6.5	.654	15	6	3.69	2.92	2.86	4.25
Steve Schrenk	2	8.3	6	0.7	0.8	.468	1	1	6.48	-0.10	-0.03	0.07
Anthony Shumaker	4	19.3	15	1.3	1.6	.444	0	3	6.98	-0.34	-0.17	0.06
Paul Spoljaric	3	7.7	23	0.0	2.5	.009	0	3	27.00	-1.71	-1.22	-1.06
Randy Wolf	21	120.7	76	6.5	7.9	.450	6	9	5.67	-0.49	-0.69	0.36
TOTALS	162	957.3	579	57.6	58.1	.498	57	63	5.44	-1.68	-0.33	8.44

It's no exaggeration to say that the Philadelphia rotation has been a one-man show the past few years, but that may be starting to change. Last year, Paul Byrd became the first Phillies' 10-game SN Winner other than Curt Schilling since 1994. For comparison, during that same span the Yankees have had 19 10-SNW seasons from 11 different pitchers. The much-maligned Indians have had 15 10-SNW seasons from six different pitchers, and even the Expos have had eight such seasons from four different pitchers.

Pitcher Abuse Points

PITCHER	AGE	GS	PAP	PAP/S	WKLD	MAX	1-90	91-100	101-110	111-120	121-130	131-140	141+
Joel Bennett	29	3	0	0.0	0.0	97	1	2	0	0	0	0	0
Paul Byrd	28	32	273	8.5	14.2	131	8	9	6	6	2	1	0
Mike Grace	29	5	9	1.8	2.7	105	1	1	3	0	0	0	0
Joe Grahe	31	5	10	2.0	2.3	110	3	1	1	0	0	0	0
Carlton Loewer	25	13	147	11.3	24.5	129	4	2	1	5	1	0	0
Chad Ogea	28	28	57	2.0	3.4	119	11	12	4	1	0	0	0
Robert Person	29	22	303	13.8	20.7	144	6	5	4	5	1	0	1
Curt Schilling	32	24	557	23.2	23.2	138	3	2	6	7	3	3	0
Steve Schrenk	30	2	0	0.0	0.0	64	2	0	0	0	0	0	0
Anthony Shumaker	26	4	17	4.3	8.5	109	2	0	2	0	0	0	0
Paul Spoljaric	28	3	0	0.0	0.0	69	3	0	0	0	0	0	0
Randy Wolf	22	21	332	15.8	42.2	134	4	0	9	5	2	1	0
PHILADELPHIA		162	1705	10.5	17.4	144	48	34	36	29	9	5	1
Ranking (NL)				4	3								

Terry Francona's recklessness with the Phillies may have set back their rebuilding process indefinitely. Let's start with Curt Schilling, who despite his spotty health record racked up 1331 PAPs for a team going nowhere in 1998. We said he was a serious injury risk then, and after his celebrated 138-pitch outing last year, in which he was left in to blow a 4-0 lead in the ninth inning, everything went downhill. He is expected to return in May, but his days of dominance may be over. . . . That's not all: Carlton Loewer was pushed too hard for 13 starts before a stress fracture in his arm—picked up before the bone could crack completely, a la Tony Saunders—shut him down. . . . Randy Wolf, who flashed one of the most dominant arms in baseball when he first came up, threw more than 100 pitches in 17 of his 21 starts, and went 2-9, 6.51 after the break. The most egregious case of pitcher abuse on this slope of Mt. Piniella could not, and did not, go unpunished.

Pittsburgh Pirates

Be careful what you wish for. The Pirates loosened their purse strings for 1999, allowing General Manager Cam Bonifay to boost the team's payroll above $20 million for the first time since 1996. Although the rising payroll coincided with an improvement in the team's record, the two events aren't necessarily related. In fact, the moves that increased the Pirates' payroll may have hurt the team's chances of fielding a winner when PNC Park opens in 2001.

Some of those moves even had Bonifay abandoning the Bucs' long-held game plan of building from within. A two-year period of penury had allowed Bonifay to develop one of the game's better farm systems through trades, drafts and relationships with Mexican League teams. These strategies, necessary without the financial safety net of a free-agent budget, had been the foundation of the team's success in 1997.

Admittedly, the rise in the team's 1999 budget was an inevitable reaction to the team's stunning collapse in September of 1998, when the Pirates fell from the edge of the wild-card race to the bottom of the division by going 5-22. The culprit, according to the team, the press and armchair analysts, was the team's force-fed youth movement that had rookies at third base, shortstop and in the outfield for much of the season's final month.

The Pirates' front office chose to read more into that final month than the blue period warranted. Instead of seeing it as an aberration caused by the fatigue that many young players experience at the end of a long season, management saw an inexpensive team's limitations. It ignored the fact that the $9 million wonderboys had stayed within shouting distance of .500 for the previous 300 games.

As a result, Bonifay went on the biggest shopping spree of his tenure as the Pirates' GM, and the spending produced decidedly mixed results. Bonifay's best deal sent one of the team's top relievers, Ricardo Rincon, to Cleveland for outfielder Brian Giles. Giles had the breakout season that many analysts anticipated, while Rincon struggled through injuries and was ineffective for most of the season. Yet, however lopsided the deal may look now, remember that, going

into 1999, Giles hadn't slugged .500 in any season, while Rincon was coming off a year in which he was arguably among baseball's top five relievers through August. It's a steal now, but it wasn't then.

Bonifay also brought in Pat Meares to fill the team's shortstop hole. Of the team's prospects, shortstop Abraham Nunez may have been the least-prepared for a major-league job. In that respect, bringing in a veteran at just $1 million was a good stopgap move. However, Meares was a replacement-level player in Minnesota, so he provided scant benefit above Nunez.

An argument could be made that trading Jon Lieber, a workhorse whose stellar 1998 was overshadowed by a September injury, to the Cubs for Brant Brown was the team's worst move of the offseason. Brown was coming off a flukish '98, a season out of line with his prior performance, and he still had no ability whatsoever to play the field. The result was predictable: though Lieber didn't break out, he was effective for Chicago, while Brown played himself off the field twice while struggling at the plate.

If you don't feel that trade was so bad, you could nominate the signing of first baseman Kevin Young to a four-year extension as the team's worst move of the offseason. Young had a disappointing sophomore campaign as the Bucs' first baseman, but his RBIs were up substantially, thanks to Jason Kendall, so the team decided to reward him. Of course, first basemen with good pop can be found quite easily on the same scrap heap where the Pirates had found Young in the first place. The move effectively buried a number of first-base prospects in their system, including Garrett Long, Ed Furniss and perhaps Ron Wright.

Add to that the signing of Meares to a four-year extension before he had even two dozen Pirate at-bats, and suddenly the team had locked up a first baseman and shortstop who would likely be below average for the lives of their contracts.

That's still not as bad as it got for Pirate fans. Bonifay's worst move of the offseason, easily, was the signing of gymnast's husband Ed Sprague. Sure, at one year and chump

Pirates Prospectus

1999 record: 78-83; Third place, NL Central

Pythagorean W/L: 80-82

Runs scored: 775 (12th in NL)

Runs allowed: 782 (7th in NL)

Team EQA: .254 (11th in NL)

1999 team age: 27.6 (3rd-youngest in NL)

1999 park: Three Rivers Stadium; neutral park, decreased run scoring by less than 1%.

1999: Horrible player-personnel management held them back again.

2000: The same decision-makers making the same bad decisions. Wil Cordero?

change, the move seemed relatively minor, and Pittsburgh radio listeners regularly repeated the newspaper columnists' refrain that Aramis Ramirez wasn't ready. However, Ramirez had performed adequately in the majors at an age when his peers were either in A-ball or playing stooge to the AFL-CIO by holding campus protests against "sweatshop" conditions in Guatemala. Ramirez was going to improve in his second year, probably to a level well above what Sprague had provided in 1998—a performance so bad that no team but the Pirates pursued him seriously.

All of this maneuvering did little to improve the team's fortunes. The Pirates' final record in 1999—78-83—was essentially the same as it had been in 1997 and was on par with the team's pre-September performance in 1998. But the Pittsburgh press and fans consider this a step forward, given the blame that the youth movement took for the team's 1998 collapse, and believe that another year of "improvements" will put the team into wild-card contention.

While enjoying the defensive stylings of Sprague and watching Meares count his money, the organization lost valuable developmental time for a few prospects and suspects, while failing to use the July trading orgy to help the team in the long term. In particular, the glaring failure to promote Aramis Ramirez to the majors until September calls the entire organization's credibility into question.

The Pacific Coast League fought Ramirez, and Ramirez won, running roughshod over opposing pitchers as if they were innocent bystanders caught between Robert Downey Jr. and his pharmaceutical distributor. Ramirez's throwing troubles intensified, but his bat was clearly ready for the majors. Whether the Pirates brought him up to play third base or left field was irrelevant; he had nothing left to prove in Triple-A by June 1, and letting him rot there for three more months just to make Ed Sprague feel good about his implosion was irresponsible. Emil Brown's situation, while less extreme, was similar.

The problem is further exacerbated by the Pirates' Triple-A affiliate's emphasis on "aggressive" hitting—in other words, ignoring plate discipline. In recent years, Ron Wright, T.J.

Staton, Freddy Garcia, Chad Hermansen and others have reached Triple-A with good or acceptable strike-zone judgment, only to lose it at that level. Continuing to send top hitting youngsters to the team's prospect graveyard threatens to undo much of the good done at lower levels of the organization.

The team made just one move in July to either bring in young talent or clear space for the young talent already in the organization. But while Humberto Cota is indeed a fine prospect, the Pirates already had a lot of catching talent in the organization. Giving up the talented, if enigmatic, Jose Guillen for Cota and reported mammal Joe Oliver is hardly the type of move Bonifay needed to make. Clearing out Sprague, Brant Brown and Al Martin would have started a process that will only get more difficult as the obstacle players age and decline.

The Pirates did manage to break in three notable young players this year, though two of them were unintended promotions. Meares's multiple injuries gave Warren Morris a chance to seize the second-base job and hold it; the stability let his bat do the talking, and it said that he's capable of holding the job for the next five years. Rotation injuries and a stellar spring sent Kris Benson north with the Bucs, and he showed that the apparent step forward he took in the spring was legitimate. The Pirates' third prominent rookie, left-hander Scott Sauerbeck, was excellent in short relief. He doesn't project to anything more than that role in the future.

While breaking in three rookies may sound like a good year, it is hardly enough for a team that hopes to contend for the playoffs in 2001. Most young players take two to three years to adjust completely to the majors, and retarding that process in the name of short-term "respectability" puts the team behind its own aggressive schedule.

The Pirates have already announced that their payroll will increase to $32 million in 2000 and $40 million in 2001. Not all of that will go toward retaining current players. Given the organization's recent history, Pirate fans should be concerned about their team's chronic bouts with veteranereal disease.

HITTERS (Averages: BA: .270 / OBP: .340 / SLG: .430 / EQA: .260)

Antonio Alvarez   3B/2B   Bats R   Age 21

YEAR	TEAM	LGE	AB	H	DB	TP	HR	BB/SO	R	RBI	SB	CS	OUT	BA	OBP	SLG	EQA	EQR	DEFENSE
1999	Willmspt	NYP	201	55	11	1	6	16/37	25	33	11	4	150	.274	.351	.428	.267	28	33-3B 86
2000	Pittsbrg	NL	113	35	5	0	6	10/40	23	21	10	2	80	.310	.366	.513	.296	19	

After two years of doing nothing low in the Pirates' farm system, Alvarez busted out like Jennifer Love Hewitt in a slasher film, finding power and the strike zone (but no hook-handed maniacs). Alvarez wins points for his aggressiveness and has a very high offensive ceiling. However, his position is still open to question; while he played mostly third base and second base this year for Williamsport, he's playing the outfield in the Instructional League and may wind up a center fielder.

Mike Benjamin   IF   Bats R   Age 34

YEAR	TEAM	LGE	AB	H	DB	TP	HR	BB/SO	R	RBI	SB	CS	OUT	BA	OBP	SLG	EQA	EQR	DEFENSE
1997	Pawtuckt	Int	106	24	4	1	3	5/21	9	10	2	1	83	.226	.273	.368	.214	9	27-SS 100
1997	Boston	AL	116	27	10	1	0	3/26	12	7	2	3	92	.233	.259	.336	.191	7	
1998	Boston	AL	348	95	15	1	6	14/71	43	39	3	0	253	.273	.313	.374	.234	33	73-2B 97
1999	Pittsbrg	NL	370	92	25	7	1	15/89	39	35	9	1	279	.249	.282	.362	.219	31	82-SS 118
2000	Pittsbrg	NL	257	60	14	2	2	15/60	25	21	5	1	198	.233	.276	.327	.202	18	

The Peter Principle in action. He's had one barely-adequate year with the bat, for which the Bucs signed him to a two-year deal and decided to start him and stick Warren Morris back in the minors. Then Benjamin goes out and hits like Mike Benjamin—somewhere between Rey Ordonez and Ozzie Guillen—and everyone is appalled. If Meares is healthy this year, Benjamin rots on the bench, where he belongs.

Adrian Brown   OF   Bats B   Age 26

YEAR	TEAM	LGE	AB	H	DB	TP	HR	BB/SO	R	RBI	SB	CS	OUT	BA	OBP	SLG	EQA	EQR	DEFENSE
1997	Carolina	Sou	144	37	3	4	1	14/13	20	11	5	3	110	.257	.329	.354	.236	15	34-OF 94
1997	Calgary	PCL	237	63	7	1	1	20/39	36	14	14	3	177	.266	.323	.316	.230	22	63-OF 102
1997	Pittsbrg	NL	148	28	4	0	2	13/18	16	11	7	4	124	.189	.273	.257	.183	9	28-OF 120
1998	Nashvill	PCL	311	83	12	4	2	23/39	45	22	18	5	233	.267	.317	.350	.235	31	81-OF 112
1998	Pittsbrg	NL	153	44	3	2	0	9/18	20	7	4	0	109	.288	.327	.333	.232	14	33-OF 108
1999	Pittsbrg	NL	226	60	5	2	4	31/39	32	16	4	3	169	.265	.357	.358	.249	26	41-RF 101
2000	Pittsbrg	NL	382	100	12	4	3	45/57	60	39	18	5	287	.262	.340	.338	.240	40	

Defensive replacement/pinch-runner who really turned up the walk engine a few notches this year, drastically increasing his value. Brown should be good for 200 at-bats each year and could steal 10 to 15 bases, given the opportunity.

Brant Brown   "RF"   Bats L   Age 29

YEAR	TEAM	LGE	AB	H	DB	TP	HR	BB/SO	R	RBI	SB	CS	OUT	BA	OBP	SLG	EQA	EQR	DEFENSE
1997	Iowa	AA	261	69	19	3	11	26/49	42	41	4	4	196	.264	.336	.487	.269	37	44-OF 88
1997	ChiCubs	NL	137	31	7	1	5	7/28	15	14	2	1	107	.226	.279	.401	.226	13	17-OF 114
1998	ChiCubs	NL	351	104	18	7	15	29/92	57	49	4	6	253	.296	.352	.516	.280	53	78-OF 100
1999	Pittsbrg	NL	343	79	22	3	15	18/113	46	54	2	4	268	.230	.278	.443	.234	35	47-RF 123
2000	Florida	NL	303	74	16	2	13	29/89	40	45	5	4	233	.244	.310	.439	.253	37	

Brown is proof that you might want to scout players before you acquire them. The Bucs expected Brown to boost their offense, without realizing that he's got some pop and little else. They expected him to play center field, but his defense was so bad he was shifted to right field and then lost his job. Twice. Add to that the fact that he is one of the more boneheaded baserunners around, and you have a real turkey of a deal. He's been traded to the Marlins, a team with about a dozen guys better than he is. Eleven, since they were nice enough to send one, Bruce Aven, back to the Pirates in the deal.

Emil Brown   OF   Bats R   Age 25

YEAR	TEAM	LGE	AB	H	DB	TP	HR	BB/SO	R	RBI	SB	CS	OUT	BA	OBP	SLG	EQA	EQR	DEFENSE
1997	Pittsbrg	NL	96	18	2	1	2	9/32	15	6	4	1	79	.188	.304	.292	.215	8	28-OF 98
1998	Carolina	Sou	461	131	23	1	13	32/76	61	49	12	4	334	.284	.342	.423	.260	58	107-OF 96
1999	Nashvill	PCL	426	117	18	4	14	29/81	74	47	11	4	313	.275	.329	.434	.257	53	104-OF 90
2000	Pittsbrg	NL	477	136	21	2	18	41/91	76	76	18	5	346	.285	.342	.451	.267	64	

He reached Triple-A this year and continued to hit, although the loss of plate discipline is typical of Pirate prospects at that level. He has also gotten a bit of a reputation as a dim bulb. Alex Hernandez's emergence, if real, buries him, but Brown could start in center field for about a dozen teams and put up nice roto numbers doing it.

Humberto Cota   C   Bats R   Age 21

YEAR	TEAM	LGE	AB	H	DB	TP	HR	BB/SO	R	RBI	SB	CS	OUT	BA	OBP	SLG	EQA	EQR	DEFENSE
1998	Princetn	App	246	59	12	2	10	22/65	29	36	1	2	188	.240	.311	.427	.245	28	50-C 98
1999	Charl-SC	SAL	343	85	18	1	8	17/52	35	49	0	0	258	.248	.286	.376	.220	29	60-C 95
1999	Hickory	SAL	138	33	10	1	2	18/20	23	16	1	0	105	.239	.327	.370	.241	15	30-C 102
2000	Pittsbrg	NL	306	81	15	1	11	27/58	39	47	1	0	225	.265	.324	.428	.252	36	

Cota is an outstanding defensive catcher who has a lot of work to do with the bat. He more than doubled his walk rate after the trade, which could manifest itself in improved offensive production this year. For now, the Pirates view him as their best long-term catching prospect, although that seems optimistic and ignores the presence of Rico Washington and perhaps Craig Wilson.

Ivan Cruz   1B   Bats L   Age 32

YEAR	TEAM	LGE	AB	H	DB	TP	HR	BB/SO	R	RBI	SB	CS	OUT	BA	OBP	SLG	EQA	EQR	DEFENSE
1997	Columbus	Int	423	111	28	1	19	51/83	55	74	3	3	315	.262	.355	.468	.274	62	113-1B 98
1998	Columbus	Int	204	45	7	0	10	23/49	26	27	0	0	159	.221	.305	.402	.238	22	51-1B 101
1999	Nashvill	PCL	270	74	16	1	17	16/61	40	56	0	1	197	.274	.316	.530	.272	38	63-1B 94
2000	Pittsbrg	NL	240	58	9	0	14	29/58	31	42	0	1	183	.242	.323	.454	.256	30	

He's no different from Brian Daubach, Matt Stairs or, for that matter, Roberto Petagine. Cruz is another minor-league slugger merely an opportunity away from putting up some good numbers in the majors. After a 1999 ruined by injuries, he's not likely to get another chance in Pittsburgh.

J.J. Davis   1B   Bats R   Age 21

YEAR	TEAM	LGE	AB	H	DB	TP	HR	BB/SO	R	RBI	SB	CS	OUT	BA	OBP	SLG	EQA	EQR	DEFENSE
1998	Erie	NYP	200	45	8	1	8	15/56	18	28	1	0	155	.225	.283	.395	.227	19	49-OF 89
1998	Augusta	SAL	107	20	5	0	4	2/24	9	9	0	0	87	.187	.202	.346	.169	5	19-OF 97
1999	Hickory	SAL	329	76	20	1	16	36/100	47	51	1	2	255	.231	.311	.444	.250	40	48-OF 85
2000	Pittsbrg	NL	246	57	12	0	16	28/83	31	44	0	1	190	.232	.310	.476	.256	31	

He showed his first real power between injuries at Hickory, where elbow surgery ended his season in August. His fans in the front office rejoiced, as the breakout followed two unproductive years in the bowels of the farm system. While Davis still has a high power ceiling, his command of the strike zone remains tenuous, and he has to prove he can stay healthy for a full season.

Kory DeHaan   CF   Bats L   Age 23

YEAR	TEAM	LGE	AB	H	DB	TP	HR	BB/SO	R	RBI	SB	CS	OUT	BA	OBP	SLG	EQA	EQR	DEFENSE
1997	Erie	NYP	212	41	10	4	1	29/49	28	13	5	4	175	.193	.294	.292	.203	16	53-OF 99
1998	Augusta	SAL	492	135	39	6	7	56/115	62	59	12	6	363	.274	.355	.421	.264	65	127-OF 102
1999	Lynchbrg	Car	301	87	18	3	8	28/63	40	34	14	5	219	.289	.355	.449	.273	42	77-OF 98
1999	Altoona	Eas	194	51	14	2	3	8/47	22	22	8	4	147	.263	.297	.402	.235	20	47-OF 95
2000	San Dieg	NL	513	139	33	6	9	60/119	91	66	25	9	384	.271	.347	.411	.269	72	

Talented but raw, DeHaan is the organization's fastest player. He completely lost the strike zone when he reached Double-A, and had a hard time catching up to the faster stuff of Eastern League pitchers. His defense is similar: great range, poor jumps. The Pirates tend to ram the tools guys up the ladder too quickly, while leaving polished guys like Paul Ah Yat at one level too long. Picked by the Padres in the Rule 5 draft, where he may stick.

Eddy Furniss   1B   Bats L   Age 24

YEAR	TEAM	LGE	AB	H	DB	TP	HR	BB/SO	R	RBI	SB	CS	OUT	BA	OBP	SLG	EQA	EQR	DEFENSE	
1998	Augusta	SAL	91	34	4	0	8	20/21	24	23	0	0	57	.374	.486	.681	.374	24		
1998	Lynchbrg	Car	113	22	4	0	3	15/38	6	11	0	0	91	.195	.293	.310	.207	9	28-1B 85	
1999	Lynchbrg	Car	459	100	22	1	20	73/120	73	64	2	2	361	.218	.330	.401	.249	56	86-1B 98	
2000	Pittsbrg	NL	274	68	12	0	16	55/85	49	54	1	1	207	.248	.374	.467	.282	44		

The good news is that he's turning into a real slugger, hitting with increasing power to all fields while drawing scads of walks. The bad news is that his defense at first prompted one insider to call him "an AL type player," which ranks slightly above mercury and below arsenic on the Pirates' toxic materials list. Furniss's bat is for real, so the Pirates will have to either fix him or trade him.

Brian Giles   CF/RF   Bats L   Age 29

YEAR	TEAM	LGE	AB	H	DB	TP	HR	BB/SO	R	RBI	SB	CS	OUT	BA	OBP	SLG	EQA	EQR	DEFENSE	
1997	Clevelnd	AL	378	106	17	3	18	61/48	62	62	13	3	275	.280	.382	.484	.293	64	106-OF 94	
1998	Clevelnd	AL	344	89	14	0	16	71/73	51	60	9	5	260	.259	.390	.439	.284	56	96-OF 99	
1999	Pittsbrg	NL	521	163	35	3	37	88/79	103	107	5	2	360	.313	.415	.605	.329	112	104-CF 97	23-RF 108
2000	Pittsbrg	NL	423	124	24	1	27	84/69	94	98	9	3	302	.293	.410	.546	.315	84		

A Bonifay deal that worked out spectacularly, as Ricardo Rincon spent much of the year hurt for Cleveland. Giles blossomed with the full-time opportunity, drawing walks as if he didn't play for Pittsburgh, while providing the Bucs with their first legitimate power threat since Barry Bonds left. He has at least four more years at this level, and could go slightly higher. He was arguably the worst defensive center fielder in the league; he and the team will be better off if he's in right field in 2000.

Yamid Haad   C   Bats R   Age 22

YEAR	TEAM	LGE	AB	H	DB	TP	HR	BB/SO	R	RBI	SB	CS	OUT	BA	OBP	SLG	EQA	EQR	DEFENSE
1997	Erie	NYP	156	37	7	2	1	5/31	19	13	1	1	120	.237	.261	.327	.191	10	
1998	Lynchbrg	Car	305	75	7	1	6	12/52	32	32	1	3	233	.246	.279	.334	.201	21	83-C 98
1999	Lynchbrg	Car	214	51	11	1	5	27/41	26	28	2	1	164	.238	.326	.369	.239	23	31-C 93
1999	Altoona	Eas	141	26	4	0	6	16/33	18	9	4	2	117	.184	.268	.340	.206	11	42-C 92
2000	Pittsbrg	NL	307	74	13	1	9	31/62	37	38	4	2	235	.241	.311	.378	.232	31	

Haad is a defensive standout who just started to show some signs of life with the bat, drawing walks and hitting for power, but with a Double-A average below .200. The Bucs also questioned his attitude after he got his first taste of the majors this summer. If he can boost his average a bit, he'll get to the majors on his cannon arm.

Kevin Haverbusch   3B   Bats R   Age 24

YEAR	TEAM	LGE	AB	H	DB	TP	HR	BB/SO	R	RBI	SB	CS	OUT	BA	OBP	SLG	EQA	EQR	DEFENSE
1997	Erie	NYP	242	60	12	1	8	10/42	25	36	1	2	184	.248	.284	.405	.226	22	50-SS 79
1998	Lynchbrg	Car	186	56	9	1	8	8/33	22	34	2	1	131	.301	.342	.489	.275	26	31-SS 92
1998	Carolina	Sou	165	55	5	0	4	7/21	21	23	1	2	112	.333	.369	.436	.270	21	39-3B 96
1999	Altoona	Eas	338	92	23	1	13	7/64	49	53	3	2	248	.272	.313	.462	.255	41	80-3B 85
2000	Pittsbrg	NL	309	91	11	0	14	16/56	38	54	2	1	219	.294	.329	.466	.262	39	

He's been plagued by injuries and a fatal allergy to walks. Haverbusch has a quick stroke that generates adequate, but not outstanding, power that might have been more appropriate for a shortstop. He also still hasn't adjusted to the position switch, showing great range but overthrowing everything. Even if he gets healthy, he needs to find the strike zone to develop.

Chad Hermansen   CF   Bats R   Age 22

YEAR	TEAM	LGE	AB	H	DB	TP	HR	BB/SO	R	RBI	SB	CS	OUT	BA	OBP	SLG	EQA	EQR	DEFENSE	
1997	Carolina	Sou	486	118	28	3	16	54/145	63	52	11	4	372	.243	.328	.412	.252	59	59-OF 94	32-SS 70
1998	Nashvill	PCL	458	111	24	4	25	44/152	67	66	17	3	350	.242	.313	.476	.264	62	111-OF 91	
1999	Nashvill	PCL	492	121	25	3	26	30/117	70	78	14	7	378	.246	.294	.467	.250	59	119-OF 105	
1999	Pittsbrg	NL	60	13	3	0	1	7/19	5	3	2	2	49	.217	.310	.317	.215	5		
2000	Pittsbrg	NL	517	135	25	3	27	56/143	83	89	19	8	390	.261	.333	.478	.268	73		

(Chad Hermansen *continued*)

He's the new enigma now that Guillen's gone. Hermansen has tremendous power and put up a generally strong performance for a 22-year-old at Triple-A. He's finally found a defensive home in center field and is as good or better with the glove as many of the Pirates' major-league outfielders. However, his plate discipline has gotten worse, prompting concern. A large part of his woes must be attributed to the Nashville coaching staff, which has screwed up a number of Pirate hitting prospects in the last three years. Given his age and previous history of drawing walks, I'd bet on Hermansen's finding the strike zone after some initial struggles, and fulfilling his promise as an All-Star hitter.

Alex Hernandez   **CF**   **Bats L**   **Age 23**

YEAR	TEAM	LGE	AB	H	DB	TP	HR	BB/SO	R	RBI	SB	CS	OUT	BA	OBP	SLG	EQA	EQR	DEFENSE
1997	Lynchbrg	Car	529	144	34	3	5	16/139	62	57	7	4	389	.272	.295	.376	.225	47	129-OF 96
1998	Carolina	Sou	452	106	20	5	8	26/84	47	37	6	2	348	.235	.276	.354	.211	36	110-OF 99
1999	Altoona	Eas	488	123	28	2	15	43/113	69	57	6	5	370	.252	.314	.410	.243	54	106-OF 94
2000	*Pittsbrg*	*NL*	*460*	*121*	*27*	*2*	*11*	*39/105*	*61*	*61*	*8*	*4*	*343*	*.263*	*.321*	*.402*	*.243*	*50*	

A defense/power prospect who finally discovered the strike zone this year as a Double-A repeater, Hernandez may finally be living up to the hype that had the Pirates talking about him as their center fielder of the future. He's still raw, but young enough to improve dramatically, and his defensive ceiling is quite high as well.

Jason Kendall   **C**   **Bats R**   **Age 26**

YEAR	TEAM	LGE	AB	H	DB	TP	HR	BB/SO	R	RBI	SB	CS	OUT	BA	OBP	SLG	EQA	EQR	DEFENSE
1997	Pittsbrg	NL	490	143	39	4	8	48/52	69	48	14	6	353	.292	.391	.437	.284	76	
1998	Pittsbrg	NL	541	179	38	3	13	51/50	98	76	28	6	368	.331	.422	.484	.312	100	143-C 99
1999	Pittsbrg	NL	280	92	19	3	8	34/32	57	39	20	3	191	.329	.426	.504	.320	55	73-C 108
2000	*Pittsbrg*	*NL*	*367*	*121*	*25*	*2*	*11*	*43/38*	*82*	*66*	*22*	*5*	*251*	*.330*	*.400*	*.499*	*.305*	*64*	

Kendall was on pace for a career year in all categories when his foot fell off in a freak play in early July. He took the brace off in mid-September and is expected to be at full strength by the start of spring training, but his days as a prolific and high-percentage basestealer may be over.

Tim Laker   **C**   **Bats R**   **Age 30**

YEAR	TEAM	LGE	AB	H	DB	TP	HR	BB/SO	R	RBI	SB	CS	OUT	BA	OBP	SLG	EQA	EQR	DEFENSE
1997	Rochestr	Int	293	67	11	1	8	26/52	36	29	1	1	227	.229	.301	.355	.223	27	
1998	Durham	Int	136	28	6	0	8	23/36	28	19	1	1	109	.206	.324	.426	.252	17	27-C 97
1998	Nashvill	PCL	152	46	12	1	8	17/28	22	25	1	0	106	.303	.381	.553	.305	27	26-C 86
1999	Nashvill	PCL	402	92	25	2	8	23/74	35	47	2	0	310	.229	.276	.361	.213	32	92-C 92
2000	*Pittsbrg*	*NL*	*317*	*76*	*15*	*1*	*10*	*31/62*	*37*	*41*	*1*	*0*	*241*	*.240*	*.307*	*.388*	*.234*	*32*	

He did a good enough job catching the Bucs' prospects in Triple-A that they refused to promote him when they needed a catcher in July and August. Isn't that a fine how-do-you-do?

Jason Landreth   **OF/1B**   **Bats R**   **Age 24**

YEAR	TEAM	LGE	AB	H	DB	TP	HR	BB/SO	R	RBI	SB	CS	OUT	BA	OBP	SLG	EQA	EQR	DEFENSE	
1999	Willmspt	NYP	217	51	10	0	5	25/39	24	24	1	2	168	.235	.317	.350	.227	21	23-OF 87	23-1B 98
2000	*Pittsbrg*	*NL*	*97*	*25*	*2*	*0*	*5*	*14/28*	*13*	*17*	*0*	*1*	*73*	*.258*	*.351*	*.433*	*.261*	*13*		

The Bucs signed Landreth out of the Texas-Louisiana League before the season, and he responded with a strong showing against mostly younger competition. In fact, he was the oldest player on the Crosscutters this year. Landreth needs another good year to move himself out of the "organization player" category.

Garrett Long   **1B/LF**   **Bats R**   **Age 23**

YEAR	TEAM	LGE	AB	H	DB	TP	HR	BB/SO	R	RBI	SB	CS	OUT	BA	OBP	SLG	EQA	EQR	DEFENSE	
1997	Augusta	SAL	298	81	10	1	8	55/79	44	36	2	1	218	.272	.387	.393	.273	42	29-1B 91	19-OF 91
1998	Lynchbrg	Car	322	86	26	1	8	45/80	43	40	3	1	237	.267	.360	.429	.269	45	62-1B 90	
1998	Carolina	Sou	97	26	2	0	0	8/28	11	6	1	0	71	.268	.329	.289	.217	8	22-OF 93	
1999	Altoona	Eas	367	88	13	3	18	53/103	55	51	3	3	282	.240	.344	.439	.263	50	47-OF 89	47-1B 109
2000	*Pittsbrg*	*NL*	*386*	*103*	*17*	*1*	*16*	*61/106*	*65*	*67*	*4*	*2*	*285*	*.267*	*.367*	*.440*	*.273*	*56*		

Altoona may be small, but hey, it beats New Haven. Long showed increased power this year, along with the plate discipline that makes him something of a leper in this organization, leading the team in walks with just 63. First base is his best position, but it's occupied in Pittsburgh, so he'll need a trade to get his chance. He played well in the Arizona Fall League.

Al Martin LF Bats L Age 32

YEAR	TEAM	LGE	AB	H	DB	TP	HR	BB/SO	R	RBI	SB	CS	OUT	BA	OBP	SLG	EQA	EQR	DEFENSE
1997	Pittsbrg	NL	427	123	24	7	14	44/82	62	59	19	7	311	.288	.359	.475	.280	64	100-OF 83
1998	Pittsbrg	NL	444	109	16	2	13	31/89	59	48	21	3	338	.245	.303	.378	.237	46	105-OF 95
1999	Pittsbrg	NL	543	150	38	8	23	42/118	91	59	17	3	396	.276	.329	.503	.276	79	125-LF 90
2000	*Pittsbrg*	*NL*	*461*	*121*	*20*	*4*	*18*	*42/98*	*68*	*70*	*14*	*4*	*344*	*.262*	*.324*	*.440*	*.257*	*57*	

He bailed out the Pirates by posting one of his best seasons, so apparently the eye surgery worked. That said, he's little more than a stopgap in this organization, with his putrid defense and inability to hit left-handers. Martin is an excellent bit player on a contender, but a luxury for a team like Pittsburgh, so expect the Bucs to try to honor his request for a trade.

Pat Meares SS Bats R Age 31

YEAR	TEAM	LGE	AB	H	DB	TP	HR	BB/SO	R	RBI	SB	CS	OUT	BA	OBP	SLG	EQA	EQR	DEFENSE
1997	Minnesot	AL	438	120	23	3	10	16/83	61	58	7	7	325	.274	.327	.409	.246	49	128-SS 104
1998	Minnesot	AL	542	141	26	3	9	22/84	53	67	6	4	405	.260	.297	.369	.223	48	145-SS 99
1999	Pittsbrg	NL	91	28	3	0	0	8/20	14	6	0	0	63	.308	.378	.341	.254	10	21-SS 105
2000	*Pittsbrg*	*NL*	*211*	*59*	*11*	*1*	*5*	*14/37*	*28*	*29*	*3*	*1*	*153*	*.280*	*.324*	*.412*	*.248*	*23*	

Signing him to a one-year deal on the cheap was smart; signing him for four more years before he'd actually done anything for the team was dumb. Not just any dumb—UPN dumb. Meares has some power and is adequate with the leather. He's also old and will never be more than a #7 hitter on this team, and weak-hitting shortstops are relatively easy to find. Why, there's one just past Warren Morris....

Warren Morris 2B Bats L Age 26

YEAR	TEAM	LGE	AB	H	DB	TP	HR	BB/SO	R	RBI	SB	CS	OUT	BA	OBP	SLG	EQA	EQR	DEFENSE
1997	Charlott	Fla	510	130	26	6	11	49/120	59	58	6	2	382	.255	.326	.394	.246	57	97-2B 87
1998	Carolina	Sou	149	40	8	2	3	16/38	18	19	2	1	110	.268	.342	.409	.256	18	40-2B 92
1998	Tulsa	Tex	389	103	21	2	9	31/77	39	48	5	3	289	.265	.323	.398	.244	43	88-2B 93
1999	Pittsbrg	NL	512	145	22	3	14	53/87	61	68	2	7	374	.283	.353	.420	.259	64	137-2B 98
2000	*Pittsbrg*	*NL*	*495*	*132*	*19*	*3*	*13*	*58/96*	*69*	*71*	*5*	*4*	*367*	*.267*	*.344*	*.396*	*.251*	*58*	

Morris is a fan favorite who wasn't even supposed to make the team, let alone finish third in the Rookie of the Year balloting. A dismal September slump dragged his numbers down, but this was in fact his first season playing this far into the year, so we can't be shocked. At his age, Morris isn't likely to improve significantly on his 1999 season, but he should peak in the .300/.400/.500 range, starting in the next two years.

Abraham Nunez SS Bats B Age 24

YEAR	TEAM	LGE	AB	H	DB	TP	HR	BB/SO	R	RBI	SB	CS	OUT	BA	OBP	SLG	EQA	EQR	DEFENSE
1997	Lynchbrg	Car	310	77	9	3	3	16/47	34	27	15	8	241	.248	.287	.326	.209	24	74-SS 99
1997	Carolina	Sou	196	56	5	1	1	15/30	22	11	6	3	143	.286	.336	.337	.234	19	48-SS 83
1998	Nashvill	PCL	366	85	12	2	3	35/73	42	28	13	6	287	.232	.306	.301	.212	30	94-SS 96
1999	Nashvill	PCL	57	16	0	0	0	5/8	10	2	1	0	41	.281	.339	.281	.221	5	
1999	Pittsbrg	NL	260	57	8	0	0	25/53	23	16	8	1	204	.219	.291	.250	.191	16	56-SS 105
2000	*Pittsbrg*	*NL*	*305*	*77*	*10*	*1*	*1*	*34/58*	*43*	*25*	*14*	*4*	*232*	*.252*	*.327*	*.302*	*.224*	*28*	

He must have made an obscene gesture at Kevin McClatchy, because Nunez is so buried in Pittsburgh that he'd have to dig six feet up just to be six feet under. He can draw some walks, runs well and has shown a good glove in the minors, but has no power and can't seem to handle defense on turf. If he gets his defense together, he'll be a good defensive replacement/pinch-runner for the next few years.

Joe Oliver　　　　　　C　　　　　Bats R　Age 34

YEAR	TEAM	LGE	AB	H	DB	TP	HR	BB/SO	R	RBI	SB	CS	OUT	BA	OBP	SLG	EQA	EQR	DEFENSE
1997	Cincnnti	NL	351	89	12	0	15	24/57	27	43	0	3	265	.254	.311	.416	.241	38	
1998	Detroit	AL	155	35	5	0	5	6/32	7	22	0	1	121	.226	.255	.355	.197	10	43-C 103
1998	Seattle	AL	85	19	3	0	2	10/15	12	10	1	0	66	.224	.305	.329	.220	8	24-C 95
1999	Durham	Int	218	58	14	1	5	4/55	20	32	1	0	160	.266	.285	.408	.230	20	55-C 89
1999	Pittsbrg	NL	135	27	6	0	2	8/33	9	14	2	0	108	.200	.245	.289	.176	7	40-C 97
2000	*Pittsbrg*	*NL*	*286*	*70*	*9*	*0*	*10*	*21/65*	*29*	*36*	*1*	*1*	*217*	*.245*	*.296*	*.381*	*.225*	*26*	

Injuries to Kendall and Keith Osik provided a convenient excuse to throw Jose Guillen down the garbage disposal, fetching Oliver as the main return. Oliver has little to recommend him offensively, and his defensive reputation is that he's a catcher. No future here when Kendall returns, and little future elsewhere.

Keith Osik　　　　　　C　　　　　Bats R　Age 31

YEAR	TEAM	LGE	AB	H	DB	TP	HR	BB/SO	R	RBI	SB	CS	OUT	BA	OBP	SLG	EQA	EQR	DEFENSE
1997	Pittsbrg	NL	106	27	10	1	0	9/21	10	7	0	1	80	.255	.319	.368	.231	10	
1998	Pittsbrg	NL	99	22	4	0	0	13/16	8	7	1	2	79	.222	.326	.263	.205	8	19-C 102
1999	Pittsbrg	NL	168	31	3	1	2	9/30	11	12	0	0	137	.185	.231	.250	.145	5	43-C 103
2000	*Pittsbrg*	*NL*	*129*	*26*	*4*	*0*	*1*	*11/23*	*8*	*7*	*0*	*1*	*104*	*.202*	*.264*	*.256*	*.163*	*6*	

Osik had his chance to make a career for himself when Kendall lost his footing, but he hit like Mickey Rooney on Valium and lost his opportunity. He should play out his contract in Pittsburgh and spend the next few years as a NRI. In the dark of night, when no one is around, he aspires to be Joe Oliver.

Aramis Ramirez　　　　3B　　　　Bats R　Age 22

YEAR	TEAM	LGE	AB	H	DB	TP	HR	BB/SO	R	RBI	SB	CS	OUT	BA	OBP	SLG	EQA	EQR	DEFENSE
1997	Lynchbrg	Car	495	127	22	1	26	65/102	71	93	2	2	370	.257	.353	.463	.273	72	129-3B 91
1998	Nashvill	PCL	168	43	5	0	6	21/28	16	16	0	2	127	.256	.349	.393	.252	20	45-3B 93
1998	Pittsbrg	NL	253	61	11	1	6	18/70	24	24	0	1	193	.241	.303	.364	.224	23	68-3B 87
1999	Nashvill	PCL	455	135	28	1	18	65/55	73	60	4	2	322	.297	.393	.481	.295	76	123-3B 90
1999	Pittsbrg	NL	56	10	1	1	0	6/9	2	6	0	1	46	.179	.258	.232	.158	2	
2000	*Pittsbrg*	*NL*	*470*	*139*	*22*	*1*	*22*	*65/78*	*81*	*94*	*3*	*2*	*333*	*.296*	*.381*	*.487*	*.290*	*75*	

He obliterated Triple-A pitching at age 21 in his first extended trial, making the Bucs' failure to deal Ed Sprague in July all the more perplexing. The knock on Ramirez is his defense. He made 42 errors this year, but most scouts believe his troubles are fixable and that a move to left field won't be necessary. Regardless of where he plays, he's a potential superstar with the stick. If the Pirates don't start him at third base in April, all Pirate fans should report to the Fort Pitt Bridge.

Julian Redman　　　　CF　　　　Bats L　Age 23

YEAR	TEAM	LGE	AB	H	DB	TP	HR	BB/SO	R	RBI	SB	CS	OUT	BA	OBP	SLG	EQA	EQR	DEFENSE
1997	Lynchbrg	Car	425	102	18	4	4	34/82	44	39	11	4	327	.240	.304	.329	.219	37	124-OF 100
1998	Lynchbrg	Car	537	133	27	8	8	30/70	61	44	17	7	411	.248	.288	.372	.224	49	132-OF 99
1999	Altoona	Eas	546	144	23	11	3	41/54	72	55	16	9	411	.264	.318	.363	.233	54	136-OF 104
2000	*Pittsbrg*	*NL*	*543*	*141*	*27*	*9*	*7*	*50/66*	*78*	*63*	*19*	*7*	*409*	*.260*	*.322*	*.381*	*.241*	*58*	

The Pirates' standard-bearer for center-field defense, Redman seems like he's been around forever, but was just 22 this year in his first Double-A campaign. He improved dramatically at the plate after June 1, which coaches credited to a change in his mental approach. Unfortunately, he still doesn't produce enough power to be more than an Adrian Brown-type. The Pirates, never short on scrubby players, already have one of those.

Ed Sprague　　　　　　3B　　　　Bats R　Age 32

YEAR	TEAM	LGE	AB	H	DB	TP	HR	BB/SO	R	RBI	SB	CS	OUT	BA	OBP	SLG	EQA	EQR	DEFENSE
1997	Toronto	AL	506	120	30	5	14	48/98	63	48	0	1	387	.237	.312	.399	.239	54	126-3B 88
1998	Toronto	AL	381	91	16	0	18	23/71	46	49	0	2	292	.239	.302	.423	.240	41	104-3B 90
1998	Oakland	AL	87	13	6	0	3	2/17	8	7	1	0	74	.149	.187	.322	.157	4	22-3B 93
1999	Pittsbrg	NL	492	129	28	2	21	44/92	67	75	2	6	369	.262	.346	.455	.265	67	129-3B 88
2000	*Pittsbrg*	*NL*	*432*	*103*	*21*	*1*	*19*	*41/83*	*50*	*64*	*1*	*2*	*331*	*.238*	*.304*	*.424*	*.240*	*47*	

A Pyrrhic victory: Sprague seemed to be the majors' biggest bargain after his .300/.402/.545 first half, but it was just a small-sample-size fluke. He hit .220/.260/.350 in the second half before breaking his hand. His defense—already atrocious—got even worse, as only the injury spared him the ignominy of committing 30 errors. The Pirates tried to sign him to a two-year extension in July but couldn't come to an agreement, then failed to trade him. Meanwhile, Ramirez destroyed Triple-A while likely wondering what he had to do to get another shot at the major-league job. Sprague was through last winter, and he's through now.

Dale Sveum — UT — Bats B — Age 36

YEAR	TEAM	LGE	AB	H	DB	TP	HR	BB/SO	R	RBI	SB	CS	OUT	BA	OBP	SLG	EQA	EQR	DEFENSE	
1997	Pittsbrg	NL	308	80	18	1	13	27/80	30	47	0	3	231	.260	.319	.451	.253	37	30-3B 105	18-SS 96
1999	Tucson	PCL	66	12	0	0	1	2/25	2	3	0	1	55	.182	.206	.227	.100	1		
1999	Nashvill	PCL	124	35	11	1	2	14/32	18	18	1	0	89	.282	.362	.435	.272	17		
1999	Pittsbrg	NL	71	15	4	1	3	7/28	7	12	0	0	56	.211	.282	.423	.233	7		
2000	*Pittsbrg*	*NL*	*124*	*29*	*5*	*0*	*4*	*14/47*	*14*	*16*	*0*	*0*	*95*	*.234*	*.312*	*.371*	*.231*	*12*		

When he unretired, the media hordes threatened to descend on Three Rivers Stadium in a mob unlike any seen since Michael Jordan unretired. But with a wave of the hand, the ever-modest Sveum told arriving reporters eager for a glimpse of the legend that he didn't want to be a distraction or take away attention from his teammates.

Rico Washington — C/3B/2B — Bats L — Age 22

YEAR	TEAM	LGE	AB	H	DB	TP	HR	BB/SO	R	RBI	SB	CS	OUT	BA	OBP	SLG	EQA	EQR	DEFENSE
1998	Erie	NYP	200	54	11	1	6	12/34	22	22	0	1	147	.270	.323	.425	.249	23	43-3B 107
1999	Hickory	SAL	301	92	12	1	12	40/45	56	41	2	1	210	.306	.395	.472	.293	49	55-C 86
1999	Lynchbrg	Car	210	56	4	0	8	24/44	26	28	2	1	155	.267	.349	.400	.257	26	30-3B 103
2000	*Pittsbrg*	*NL*	*331*	*104*	*11*	*1*	*16*	*44/64*	*58*	*70*	*1*	*1*	*228*	*.314*	*.395*	*.498*	*.298*	*55*	

A catcher at Hickory, where he scorched the ball, Washington shifted to third base at Lynchburg after he hurt his hand, then shifted to second base when the team had an emergency and acquitted himself well. His Hickory manager, Tracy Woodson, said that Washington "may be the best hitting prospect I've ever seen." Washington isn't big, but he has good line-drive power and excellent command of the strike zone, and could finally be the antibiotic that rids Pittsburgh of its chronic infield infections.

Paul Weichard — OF — Bats B — Age 20

YEAR	TEAM	LGE	AB	H	DB	TP	HR	BB/SO	R	RBI	SB	CS	OUT	BA	OBP	SLG	EQA	EQR	DEFENSE
1998	Lethbrid	Pio	186	41	8	1	0	23/52	17	15	6	2	147	.220	.306	.274	.206	14	54-OF 104
1999	Hickory	SAL	324	69	8	2	5	23/93	33	32	9	3	259	.213	.265	.296	.190	20	89-OF 106
2000	*Pittsbrg*	*NL*	*213*	*47*	*5*	*1*	*2*	*22/65*	*24*	*15*	*9*	*2*	*168*	*.221*	*.294*	*.282*	*.202*	*15*	

Weichard is a top-notch Australian Rules football player who actually projects as a power hitter because of his girth. He didn't hit at Hickory, but was just 20 and doesn't have as much baseball experience as his American peers. He also battled a rotator-cuff injury that sapped his power. His outlook is uncertain until he either learns to take a pitch or his power develops, but the team is high on him.

Craig Wilson — DH/C — Bats R — Age 23

YEAR	TEAM	LGE	AB	H	DB	TP	HR	BB/SO	R	RBI	SB	CS	OUT	BA	OBP	SLG	EQA	EQR	DEFENSE
1997	Lynchbrg	Car	410	101	20	1	18	29/98	45	58	3	3	312	.246	.313	.432	.248	48	
1998	Lynchbrg	Car	226	58	11	0	13	20/51	24	41	1	0	168	.257	.326	.478	.266	31	40-C 96
1998	Carolina	Sou	146	43	8	0	5	9/33	15	16	2	1	104	.295	.349	.452	.269	19	29-C 91
1999	Altoona	Eas	372	98	22	2	20	32/107	53	63	1	2	276	.263	.344	.495	.275	55	35-C 83
2000	*Pittsbrg*	*NL*	*361*	*103*	*18*	*1*	*22*	*41/96*	*58*	*76*	*2*	*1*	*259*	*.285*	*.358*	*.524*	*.288*	*58*	

Wilson returned from Tommy John surgery to find most of his offense intact, but most of his defense still unavailable. By the end of the season, his arm strength was still not what it had been before the injury, which isn't a surprise given the injury's severity. The Pirates do expect him to catch again; if he can, he's one of their better prospects because of his power.

Ron Wright   DH   Bats R   Age 24

YEAR	TEAM	LGE	AB	H	DB	TP	HR	BB/SO	R	RBI	SB	CS	OUT	BA	OBP	SLG	EQA	EQR	DEFENSE
1997	Calgary	PCL	323	81	17	0	14	17/83	34	45	0	1	243	.251	.292	.433	.238	34	78-1B 105
1999	Altoona	Eas	82	17	7	0	0	7/29	4	4	0	0	65	.207	.275	.293	.190	5	
2000	*Cincnnti*	*NL*	*117*	*30*	*5*	*0*	*5*	*10/45*	*14*	*18*	*0*	*0*	*87*	*.256*	*.315*	*.427*	*.247*	*13*	

Scar tissue from his 1998 disc operation began pressing on a spinal nerve this year, causing him tremendous pain and robbing him of his calling-card power. The Pirates are still talking bravely about how he's in their plans; the Kevin Young contract indicates otherwise. Wright's future is dependent on his health: if he is healthy, he has enough sock to get a number of chances with other clubs. Wright has been claimed on waivers by the Reds.

Kevin Young   1B   Bats R   Age 31

YEAR	TEAM	LGE	AB	H	DB	TP	HR	BB/SO	R	RBI	SB	CS	OUT	BA	OBP	SLG	EQA	EQR	DEFENSE
1997	Pittsbrg	NL	335	100	19	3	18	16/88	57	72	9	2	237	.299	.338	.534	.285	51	70-1B 101
1998	Pittsbrg	NL	598	164	41	2	29	43/124	90	110	16	8	442	.274	.335	.495	.273	86	153-1B 85
1999	Pittsbrg	NL	585	172	43	6	24	68/123	96	98	19	10	423	.294	.380	.511	.294	99	153-1B 88
2000	*Pittsbrg*	*NL*	*522*	*145*	*31*	*3*	*25*	*57/113*	*88*	*95*	*15*	*6*	*383*	*.278*	*.349*	*.492*	*.278*	*78*	

Young turned his game around, confounding many—including us—who had predicted a decline. Young started drawing walks for the first time as a Pirate, and as a result started hitting for more power. If he can maintain this level for the rest of his contract, he'll justify it. However, at 31 Young is approaching the natural decline phase. This would be an ideal time to trade him. His 23 errors are a huge cause for concern, although much of the trouble may have come from the uncertain infielders he played with most of the year.

PITCHERS (Averages: ERA: 4.50 / H/9: 9.00 / HR/9: 1.00 / BB/9: 3.50 / K/9: 6.50 / KWH: 1.00)

Paul Ah Yat   Throws L   Age 25

YEAR	TEAM	LGE	IP	H	ER	HR	BB	K	ERA	W	L	H/9	HR/9	BB/9	K/9	KWH	PERA
1997	Augusta	SAL	83.3	110	46	9	23	78	4.97	4	5	11.88	0.97	2.48	8.42	1.80	5.72
1997	Lynchbrg	Car	45.7	46	10	3	5	27	1.97	4	1	9.07	0.59	0.99	5.32	2.37	3.15
1998	Lynchbrg	Car	93.7	128	57	12	20	51	5.48	4	6	12.30	1.15	1.92	4.90	0.76	5.96
1998	Carolina	Sou	82.0	90	41	10	21	49	4.50	5	4	9.88	1.10	2.30	5.38	0.95	4.61
1999	Altoona	Eas	87.7	104	52	7	35	68	5.34	4	6	10.68	0.72	3.59	6.98	0.95	5.24
1999	Nashvill	PCL	61.0	77	45	9	28	33	6.64	2	5	11.36	1.33	4.13	4.87	0.38	6.49

Ah Yat is a control artist who struggled on his promotion to Triple-A, but who has adjusted to every promotion so far. As these guys go, Ah Yat has good odds of finding a role in the majors; unfortunately, the Pirates have never given any indication that they see Ah Yat as more than an organizational player. He'll be a Rule 5 gem for a team that needs pitching.

Jimmy Anderson   Throws L   Age 24

YEAR	TEAM	LGE	IP	H	ER	HR	BB	K	ERA	W	L	H/9	HR/9	BB/9	K/9	KWH	PERA
1997	Carolina	Sou	24.3	17	5	1	9	19	1.85	3	0	6.29	0.37	3.33	7.03	1.76	2.59
1997	Calgary	PCL	106.7	102	57	8	66	62	4.81	6	6	8.61	0.68	5.57	5.23	0.43	4.72
1998	Nashvill	PCL	117.7	145	86	7	80	53	6.58	4	9	11.09	0.54	6.12	4.05	0.18	6.27
1999	Nashvill	PCL	129.7	149	62	5	47	77	4.30	7	7	10.34	0.35	3.26	5.34	0.63	4.51
1999	Pittsbrg	NL	29.7	24	13	2	15	13	3.94	2	1	7.28	0.61	4.55	3.94	0.35	3.64

He's a statistical fraud whose bubblegum-card stats don't tell the whole story. The ERAs and won/lost records are nice, but no pitcher survives in the majors with strikeout-to-walk ratios like that. Anderson hasn't been a truly effective pitcher since 1997, and there's no sign that he's going to start now.

Bronson Arroyo — Throws R — Age 23

YEAR	TEAM	LGE	IP	H	ER	HR	BB	K	ERA	W	L	H/9	HR/9	BB/9	K/9	KWH	PERA
1997	Lynchbrg	Car	151.3	190	82	19	37	89	4.88	8	9	11.30	1.13	2.20	5.29	0.84	5.47
1998	Carolina	Sou	124.7	165	85	19	50	75	6.14	5	9	11.91	1.37	3.61	5.41	0.51	6.71
1999	Altoona	Eas	142.3	191	81	17	62	81	5.12	7	9	12.08	1.07	3.92	5.12	0.41	6.58
1999	Nashvill	PCL	12.3	21	14	1	11	9	10.22	0	1	15.32	0.73	8.03	6.57	0.26	10.22

The Pirates change Double-A cities more often than Arroyo changes levels. He's the poor man's Jimmy Anderson: great record, good ERA, lousy peripherals and mediocre stuff. Despite a change in mechanics midseason that pumped his velocity back up over 90 mph, he still didn't return to the performance level that made him a prospect in '97, and is a long shot to do so now.

Kris Benson — Throws R — Age 25

YEAR	TEAM	LGE	IP	H	ER	HR	BB	K	ERA	W	L	H/9	HR/9	BB/9	K/9	KWH	PERA
1997	Lynchbrg	Car	56.3	61	25	1	15	51	3.99	3	3	9.75	0.16	2.40	8.15	2.12	3.67
1997	Carolina	Sou	66.7	85	46	11	34	54	6.21	2	5	11.48	1.49	4.59	7.29	0.75	7.02
1998	Nashvill	PCL	149.0	168	101	24	56	110	6.10	6	11	10.15	1.45	3.38	6.64	0.96	5.62
1999	Pittsbrg	NL	199.0	175	93	15	80	134	4.21	12	10	7.91	0.68	3.62	6.06	0.96	3.62

He showed up at spring training with the command he lacked in 1998, made the team and became its second-best starter despite some wild stretches. Benson adjusted frequently during the season, improving his control dramatically after a rough stretch in mid-May when he lost the strike zone. Everything is back on track for him to assume the #1 role by the end of 2000.

Jason Boyd — Throws R — Age 27

YEAR	TEAM	LGE	IP	H	ER	HR	BB	K	ERA	W	L	H/9	HR/9	BB/9	K/9	KWH	PERA
1997	Reading	Eas	108.7	137	75	14	75	75	6.21	4	8	11.35	1.16	6.21	6.21	0.41	7.21
1998	Tucson	PCL	22.0	27	20	4	17	11	8.18	0	2	11.05	1.64	6.95	4.50	0.20	7.77
1999	Tucson	PCL	75.7	74	38	5	32	48	4.52	4	4	8.80	0.59	3.81	5.71	0.73	4.04

That the Pirates got something for Womack should alone be cause for celebration; as an added bonus, Boyd looks like he might be useful. He throws hard with good control but doesn't have outstanding stuff, so he's a probable middle reliever in the depleted pen next year.

Bobby Bradley — Throws R — Age 19

The Pirates' #1 pick this year, Bradley handled himself well in the Gulf Coast League, including an outstanding 31-to-4 strike-out-to-walk ratio in his 31 innings there. Still, he's just 19 and straight out of high school, so it's a long way to the majors. Comparisons to Greg Maddux are about as sensible as the idea of electing a pro wrestler to statewide office.

Jason Christiansen — Throws L — Age 30

YEAR	TEAM	LGE	IP	H	ER	HR	BB	K	ERA	W	L	H/9	HR/9	BB/9	K/9	KWH	PERA
1997	Pittsbrg	NL	34.7	36	9	2	18	35	2.34	3	1	9.35	0.52	4.67	9.09	1.41	4.67
1998	Pittsbrg	NL	65.0	51	21	2	29	68	2.91	5	2	7.06	0.28	4.02	9.42	2.34	3.05
1999	Pittsbrg	NL	38.0	25	15	2	21	34	3.55	2	2	5.92	0.47	4.97	8.05	1.65	2.84

He had a clean shot at being the closer until he hurt his neck in July, which nearly knocked him out for the season. When healthy, he's the Pirates' best reliever, with truly electric stuff and great control. Christiansen is always a threat to seize the closer's job.

Brad Clontz — Throws R — Age 29

YEAR	TEAM	LGE	IP	H	ER	HR	BB	K	ERA	W	L	H/9	HR/9	BB/9	K/9	KWH	PERA
1997	Atlanta	NL	47.3	55	25	3	19	39	4.75	2	3	10.46	0.57	3.61	7.42	1.09	4.94
1997	Richmond	Int	21.3	12	2	0	2	19	0.84	2	0	5.06	0.00	0.84	8.02	11.24	0.84
1998	LosAngls	NL	20.0	16	13	3	11	13	5.85	1	1	7.20	1.35	4.95	5.85	0.72	4.50
1998	Norfolk	Int	41.7	45	26	4	18	41	5.62	2	3	9.72	0.86	3.89	8.86	1.55	4.97
1999	Nashvill	PCL	17.0	13	8	3	7	18	4.24	1	1	6.88	1.59	3.71	9.53	2.66	4.24
1999	Pittsbrg	NL	49.7	47	18	6	23	39	3.26	4	2	8.52	1.09	4.17	7.07	1.05	4.53

(Brad Clontz *continued*)

Clontz is a submariner whose statistics tell a slightly untrue tale: the 2.74 ERA would be 3.83 if the six unearned runs were charged as earned. He also put far too many baserunners on and was a flyball pitcher, odd for a sidearmer. Clontz has his uses at the back of a pen, but Lamont's reliance on him in important situations merely underscored the problems with the lack of bullpen depth in Triple-A.

Francisco Cordova Throws R Age 28

YEAR	TEAM	LGE	IP	H	ER	HR	BB	K	ERA	W	L	H/9	HR/9	BB/9	K/9	KWH	PERA
1997	Pittsbrg	NL	183.7	163	68	14	51	113	3.33	13	7	7.99	0.69	2.50	5.54	1.15	3.28
1998	Pittsbrg	NL	221.7	206	89	22	73	150	3.61	15	10	8.36	0.89	2.96	6.09	1.12	3.86
1999	Pittsbrg	NL	162.3	159	73	15	56	95	4.05	10	8	8.82	0.83	3.10	5.27	0.76	4.05

The fragile ace is breaking down, apparently: note the dramatically lower strikeout rate. Cordova's velocity was down in April, prompting the team to shut him down for a few weeks. It never came back entirely, and he found himself more vulnerable to extra-base hits. Four months off might help; if they don't, he's headed for the knife.

David Daniels Throws R Age 26

YEAR	TEAM	LGE	IP	H	ER	HR	BB	K	ERA	W	L	H/9	HR/9	BB/9	K/9	KWH	PERA
1997	Augusta	SAL	49.3	72	33	1	19	32	6.02	2	3	13.14	0.18	3.47	5.84	0.56	6.02
1998	Lynchbrg	Car	16.3	14	5	2	5	12	2.76	1	1	7.71	1.10	2.76	6.61	1.54	3.86
1998	Carolina	Sou	38.3	37	15	0	17	29	3.52	2	2	8.69	0.00	3.99	6.81	1.00	3.52
1999	Altoona	Eas	61.3	69	27	7	23	46	3.96	4	3	10.13	1.03	3.38	6.75	1.00	5.14

He's more of a project than prospect. Daniels pitched for the Johnstown Johnnies of the Frontier League, in what happens to be pitching coach Pete Vukovich's hometown. Vukovich liked Daniels's sidearm delivery and sinking action, and converted him to a straight submarine style, which has obviously worked well for him through Double-A. The Pirates see him as a situational reliever who could come in when they need a ground ball; so far, they have to be pleased with his progress.

Mike Garcia Throws R Age 32

YEAR	TEAM	LGE	IP	H	ER	HR	BB	K	ERA	W	L	H/9	HR/9	BB/9	K/9	KWH	PERA
1999	Nashvill	PCL	26.0	25	12	3	11	27	4.15	2	1	8.65	1.04	3.81	9.35	1.98	4.50
1999	Pittsbrg	NL	7.0	2	1	1	3	9	1.29	1	0	2.57	1.29	3.86	11.57	10.09	1.29

Garcia is a journeyman who bounced around Mexico and Taiwan for a few years before the Pirates signed him last winter. After pitching very well with Nashville early on, he returned to Mexico City and impressed the scouts with a fastball around 95 or 96 mph. Garcia is a complete wild card; he could easily take advantage of the Bucs' bullpen brouhaha and turn into the next Billy Taylor.

Greg Hansell Throws R Age 29

YEAR	TEAM	LGE	IP	H	ER	HR	BB	K	ERA	W	L	H/9	HR/9	BB/9	K/9	KWH	PERA
1997	Tucson	PCL	81.3	102	51	14	29	62	5.64	3	6	11.29	1.55	3.21	6.86	0.97	6.31
1998	Omaha	PCL	65.3	70	27	5	17	48	3.72	4	3	9.64	0.69	2.34	6.61	1.45	4.13
1999	Nashvill	PCL	26.0	18	8	2	11	28	2.77	2	1	6.23	0.69	3.81	9.69	2.96	2.77
1999	Pittsbrg	NL	39.7	41	18	5	10	33	4.08	2	2	9.30	1.13	2.27	7.49	1.98	4.31

Will pitch for food. Hansell spent about a month as the Bucs' best reliever, then slowly declined in effectiveness through the rest of the summer. Like Clontz, he's not a bad 11th reliever, sort of like saying that a woman is an OK 11th wife.

Clinton Johnston Throws L Age 22

YEAR	TEAM	LGE	IP	H	ER	HR	BB	K	ERA	W	L	H/9	HR/9	BB/9	K/9	KWH	PERA
1998	Augusta	SAL	54.3	53	25	5	43	44	4.14	3	3	8.78	0.83	7.12	7.29	0.63	5.63
1999	Hickory	SAL	84.0	127	87	14	69	62	9.32	2	7	13.61	1.50	7.39	6.64	0.33	9.75

The Pirates are concerned about their 1998 #1 pick, and with good reason: his low-90s fastball is down in the mid-80s, possibly a result of the sudden increase in workload for this former outfielder. Without the heater, his outstanding change-up barely got low-A hitters out, so he's starting to look like a potential bust. The Pirates could always put him back in the outfield if they want to salvage something from the pick.

Rich Loiselle   Throws R   Age 28

YEAR	TEAM	LGE	IP	H	ER	HR	BB	K	ERA	W	L	H/9	HR/9	BB/9	K/9	KWH	PERA
1997	Pittsbrg	NL	75.0	71	24	7	26	62	2.88	6	2	8.52	0.84	3.12	7.44	1.56	3.96
1998	Pittsbrg	NL	55.7	57	25	2	38	46	4.04	3	3	9.22	0.32	6.14	7.44	0.73	5.01
1999	Pittsbrg	NL	15.3	16	8	2	8	13	4.70	1	1	9.39	1.17	4.70	7.63	0.99	5.28

Loiselle failed to record a save before going down for the year after elbow surgery. He still gets closer consideration because no one else has won the job, but he's not likely to be good enough to pitch effectively until 2001.

Javier Martinez   Throws R   Age 23

YEAR	TEAM	LGE	IP	H	ER	HR	BB	K	ERA	W	L	H/9	HR/9	BB/9	K/9	KWH	PERA
1997	Rockford	Mid	73.7	103	71	9	60	49	8.67	2	6	12.58	1.10	7.33	5.99	0.29	8.43
1997	Daytona	Fla	50.0	75	44	10	35	27	7.92	1	5	13.50	1.80	6.30	4.86	0.21	9.54
1998	Pittsbrg	NL	41.7	39	31	5	37	41	6.70	2	3	8.42	1.08	7.99	8.86	0.87	6.05

The Pirates' apparent Rule 5 success story battled elbow pain most of the year before succumbing to the knife. He may not pitch until 2001, if he's even able to regain his velocity. Check back next fall.

Alex Pena   Throws R   Age 22

YEAR	TEAM	LGE	IP	H	ER	HR	BB	K	ERA	W	L	H/9	HR/9	BB/9	K/9	KWH	PERA
1999	Hickory	SAL	41.3	91	56	7	45	25	12.19	1	4	19.81	1.52	9.80	5.44	0.11	15.46
1999	Altoona	Eas	19.3	26	15	3	10	16	6.98	1	1	12.10	1.40	4.66	7.45	0.74	7.45

Pena is a corner outfielder who converted when the team realized he could light up the radar gun. He gets his fastball up around 95 mph easily, and could go up to 98 if he pushed a little. Pena started to discover his control during a two-week fill-in promotion to Altoona. Curve pitching coach Scott Lovecamp tinkered with his mechanics, and Pena pitched well enough to stay with the team for the duration of the season. A repeat performance in Triple-A will make him a top prospect.

Chris Peters   Throws L   Age 28

YEAR	TEAM	LGE	IP	H	ER	HR	BB	K	ERA	W	L	H/9	HR/9	BB/9	K/9	KWH	PERA
1997	Calgary	PCL	52.0	44	25	4	33	46	4.33	3	3	7.62	0.69	5.71	7.96	1.09	4.33
1997	Pittsbrg	NL	38.3	36	21	6	22	16	4.93	2	2	8.45	1.41	5.17	3.76	0.24	5.40
1998	Pittsbrg	NL	149.0	144	62	13	58	99	3.74	10	7	8.70	0.79	3.50	5.98	0.88	4.11
1999	Pittsbrg	NL	71.7	95	53	16	26	44	6.66	3	5	11.93	2.01	3.27	5.53	0.59	7.41
1999	Nashvill	PCL	47.0	55	18	1	18	27	3.45	3	2	10.53	0.19	3.45	5.17	0.55	4.60

Peters was league-average outside of a horrendous May, when he was pitching with an injured shoulder that nearly ended his season. Like Todd Ritchie, he should be a league-average starter at the back of the rotation.

Todd Ritchie   Throws R   Age 28

YEAR	TEAM	LGE	IP	H	ER	HR	BB	K	ERA	W	L	H/9	HR/9	BB/9	K/9	KWH	PERA
1997	Minnesot	AL	75.7	84	37	10	28	45	4.40	4	4	9.99	1.19	3.33	5.35	0.64	5.23
1998	SaltLake	PCL	60.7	55	36	4	37	51	5.34	3	4	8.16	0.59	5.49	7.57	0.96	4.45
1998	Minnesot	AL	24.3	29	15	1	9	21	5.55	1	2	10.73	0.37	3.33	7.77	1.26	4.81
1999	Pittsbrg	NL	174.3	161	69	15	52	103	3.56	12	7	8.31	0.77	2.68	5.32	0.95	3.61

Here's the nicest revelation in Pittsburgh and another testament to the power of Lamont and Vukovich when it comes to pitching. That said, Ritchie threw more than 2,300 pitches this year, far more than he's thrown in any previous season, leading to shoulder tendinitis and bursitis in September. His poor strikeout rate indicates that he will regress this year. Ritchie is going to disappoint after such a great season, although he should still be a valuable #3 or #4 starter for the team in 2000.

Scott Sauerbeck   Throws L   Age 28

YEAR	TEAM	LGE	IP	H	ER	HR	BB	K	ERA	W	L	H/9	HR/9	BB/9	K/9	KWH	PERA
1997	Binghmtn	Eas	122.3	171	103	13	60	65	7.58	4	10	12.58	0.96	4.41	4.78	0.31	6.99
1998	Norfolk	Int	157.7	186	83	7	76	101	4.74	9	9	10.62	0.40	4.34	5.77	0.54	5.14
1999	Pittsbrg	NL	68.3	51	16	6	36	53	2.11	7	1	6.72	0.79	4.74	6.98	1.14	3.56

(Scott Sauerbeck *continued*)

Cam Bonifay deserves credit for using the Rule 5 draft in a new way: to help his team now, rather than to acquire a prospect for the future. Sauerbeck was well cast as a left-handed reliever who could get right-handed hitters out as well. He tends to pitch around them too much, and is a bit homer-prone against his own kind, so he's unlikely to repeat his 1999 performance. He should still be the #2 left-handed reliever for the Pirates in 2000.

Jason Schmidt   **ThrowsR**   **Age 27**

YEAR	TEAM	LGE	IP	H	ER	HR	BB	K	ERA	W	L	H/9	HR/9	BB/9	K/9	KWH	PERA
1997	Pittsbrg	NL	193.3	180	93	16	81	127	4.33	11	10	8.38	0.74	3.77	5.91	0.83	4.00
1998	Pittsbrg	NL	216.3	231	104	24	75	151	4.33	12	12	9.61	1.00	3.12	6.28	0.98	4.70
1999	Pittsbrg	NL	214.7	210	97	22	82	143	4.07	13	11	8.80	0.92	3.44	6.00	0.89	4.28

The old question was when Schmidt would become an ace. The new question is whether he'll become an ace before his arm blows out. Schmidt had several bouts with "dead arm" syndrome last year, when his top velocity would be 10 mph or more off its norm, and yet he still managed to throw as many pitches in '99 as he did in '98. It's risky, but he still has a high ceiling.

Pete Schourek   **Throws L**   **Age 31**

YEAR	TEAM	LGE	IP	H	ER	HR	BB	K	ERA	W	L	H/9	HR/9	BB/9	K/9	KWH	PERA
1997	Cincnnti	NL	85.7	77	56	18	40	55	5.88	4	6	8.09	1.89	4.20	5.78	0.73	5.25
1998	Houston	NL	79.7	85	44	10	38	56	4.97	4	5	9.60	1.13	4.29	6.33	0.73	5.31
1998	Boston	AL	44.0	44	19	7	15	36	3.89	3	2	9.00	1.43	3.07	7.36	1.47	4.70
1999	Pittsbrg	NL	114.3	123	67	18	48	91	5.27	5	8	9.68	1.42	3.78	7.16	1.05	5.43

He was a worthwhile gamble, as the price wasn't high compared to what worse pitchers (e.g., Willie Blair) have gotten recently, but one that didn't work at all. Schourek could transition to the Greg Swindell role, as he was much more effective his first time through an opposing lineup, but Lamont first needs to accept that Schourek can't start, then go from there.

Jose Silva   **Throws R**   **Age 26**

YEAR	TEAM	LGE	IP	H	ER	HR	BB	K	ERA	W	L	H/9	HR/9	BB/9	K/9	KWH	PERA
1997	Calgary	PCL	68.7	61	18	3	23	47	2.36	6	2	8.00	0.39	3.01	6.16	1.18	3.15
1997	Pittsbrg	NL	37.7	50	23	4	17	28	5.50	2	2	11.95	0.96	4.06	6.69	0.69	6.45
1998	Pittsbrg	NL	101.0	105	54	7	32	61	4.81	5	6	9.36	0.62	2.85	5.44	0.83	4.10
1999	Pittsbrg	NL	98.3	104	62	9	38	74	5.67	4	7	9.52	0.82	3.48	6.77	1.04	4.58

Silva regressed early in the season, becoming more hittable than he had been the previous year, despite no obvious mechanical or physical problems. Once dropped into relief, he looked like the same pitcher he'd been before he broke his arm in 1998, so the Bucs are now thinking "closer." If they keep in mind the possibility that he could return to starting, that's probably a good choice.

Todd Van Poppel   **Throws R**   **Age 28**

YEAR	TEAM	LGE	IP	H	ER	HR	BB	K	ERA	W	L	H/9	HR/9	BB/9	K/9	KWH	PERA
1997	Charlott	Fla	30.3	53	31	4	15	22	9.20	1	2	15.73	1.19	4.45	6.53	0.45	9.49
1997	Tulsa	Tex	37.7	63	32	2	19	20	7.65	1	3	15.05	0.48	4.54	4.78	0.25	8.12
1997	Omaha	AmA	38.3	53	37	9	30	24	8.69	1	3	12.44	2.11	7.04	5.63	0.27	9.63
1998	Oklahoma	PCL	80.0	100	50	10	30	56	5.63	4	5	11.25	1.13	3.38	6.30	0.78	5.96
1998	Pittsbrg	NL	47.3	54	32	4	19	31	6.08	2	3	10.27	0.76	3.61	5.89	0.70	4.94
1999	Nashvill	PCL	154.7	179	96	21	74	123	5.59	7	10	10.42	1.22	4.31	7.16	0.85	5.88

He had a pretty good year in Nashville's rotation, but his Waterloo has been and will remain the majors until he shows he can get people out up there. Vukovich is the right coach for the job, but the Pirates have better and less enigmatic options for their staff. The irony is that Van Poppel originally spurned the Braves the year the A's drafted him, claiming he didn't want to play for a losing organization; had he gone to Atlanta, Leo Mazzone probably would have made him a star by now.

Jeff Wallace — Throws L — Age 24

YEAR	TEAM	LGE	IP	H	ER	HR	BB	K	ERA	W	L	H/9	HR/9	BB/9	K/9	KWH	PERA
1997	Carolina	Sou	42.0	44	36	3	39	32	7.71	1	4	9.43	0.64	8.36	6.86	0.45	6.43
1997	Pittsbrg	NL	12.7	7	1	0	8	13	0.71	1	0	4.97	0.00	5.68	9.24	2.25	2.13
1999	Nashvill	PCL	13.7	18	15	3	9	12	9.88	0	2	11.85	1.98	5.93	7.90	0.66	8.56
1999	Pittsbrg	NL	39.3	25	15	2	37	40	3.43	3	1	5.72	0.46	8.47	9.15	1.29	4.12

Wallace was incredibly wild, but considering that he was coming off major surgery, that's not shocking. He should get back to his '97 level this year, and actually be useful in 2001, assuming he doesn't hurt himself again.

Marc Wilkins — Throws R — Age 29

YEAR	TEAM	LGE	IP	H	ER	HR	BB	K	ERA	W	L	H/9	HR/9	BB/9	K/9	KWH	PERA
1997	Pittsbrg	NL	77.3	60	28	7	35	44	3.26	6	3	6.98	0.81	4.07	5.12	0.69	3.49
1998	Pittsbrg	NL	15.3	13	6	1	10	16	3.52	1	1	7.63	0.59	5.87	9.39	1.47	4.11
1999	Pittsbrg	NL	51.3	47	25	3	25	42	4.38	3	3	8.24	0.53	4.38	7.36	1.12	4.03

He's a tweener reliever who works outside the strike zone too often to be useful; he also needs to stop throwing so many first-pitch fastballs, as opponents torched him for a .656 slugging percentage when they hacked at pitch #1. Filler.

Mike Williams — Throws R — Age 31

YEAR	TEAM	LGE	IP	H	ER	HR	BB	K	ERA	W	L	H/9	HR/9	BB/9	K/9	KWH	PERA
1997	Omaha	AmA	81.0	72	41	9	46	59	4.56	4	5	8.00	1.00	5.11	6.56	0.79	4.56
1998	Nashvill	PCL	34.0	41	26	10	16	27	6.88	1	3	10.85	2.65	4.24	7.15	0.83	7.94
1998	Pittsbrg	NL	51.7	39	11	1	17	56	1.92	5	1	6.79	0.17	2.96	9.75	3.53	2.44
1999	Pittsbrg	NL	59.0	62	32	8	35	73	4.88	3	4	9.46	1.22	5.34	11.14	1.83	5.80

Williams was untouchable in the season's first two months, mediocre in the next two, and so bad in August that he lost the job four months later. The league was bound to catch up to his one pitch (a very good slider) even if he hadn't lost control of it. He's unlikely to see his 1998 level of success again.

Support-Neutral Records — PITTSBURGH PIRATES — Park Effect: +1.8%

PITCHER	GS	IP	R	SNW	SNL	SNPCT	W	L	RA	APW	SNVA	SNWAR
Jimmy Anderson	4	20.3	8	1.4	0.7	.659	2	1	3.54	0.33	0.37	0.51
Kris Benson	31	196.7	105	12.3	10.5	.538	11	14	4.81	0.63	0.86	2.58
Francisco Cordova	27	160.7	83	10.2	8.6	.542	8	10	4.65	0.77	0.77	2.19
Chris Peters	11	55.7	43	2.7	4.3	.385	4	4	6.95	-1.07	-0.83	-0.28
Todd Ritchie	26	170.7	78	11.0	7.6	.592	15	8	4.11	1.78	1.58	3.11
Jason Schmidt	33	212.7	110	12.5	10.8	.538	13	11	4.66	1.01	0.82	2.62
Pete Schourek	17	84.0	58	3.6	6.9	.346	3	7	6.21	-0.97	-1.42	-0.83
Jose Silva	12	65.0	63	1.8	6.7	.207	1	8	8.72	-2.45	-2.38	-1.85
TOTALS	161	965.7	548	55.5	56.1	.497	57	63	5.11	0.05	-0.24	8.04

The Pirates' 1999 rotation is another lesson in replacement value. That is, it shows why league-average starters have enormous value. The top four spots of the rotation—Kris Benson, Francisco Cordova, Todd Ritchie and Jason Schmidt—combined for a fine SNVA of 4.0. If they had just pieced together a league-average performance from fifth starters, that SNVA would have made them the fifth-best rotation in the majors. But of course, league-average starters don't grow on trees, and the 44 starts they got from Jimmy Anderson, Chris Peters, Pete Schourek and Jose Silva were bad enough to drag the Pirates' rotation down to 12th, just behind the disappointing Dodgers. . . . This sort of mediocrity is becoming commonplace for the Pirates. Since 1996, the Pirates' starting rotation has ranked between 12th and 15th in the majors every year, with SNVAs that ranged from a low of -0.78 to a high of 0.88. With no prospect of becoming an offensive powerhouse anytime soon, the Pirates have little hope of getting to the play-offs unless they improve on that consistently average record.

Pitcher Abuse Points

PITCHER	AGE	GS	PAP	PAP/S	WKLD	MAX	1-90	91-100	101-110	111-120	121-130	131-140	141+
Jimmy Anderson	23	4	2	0.5	1.3	102	3	0	1	0	0	0	0
Kris Benson	24	31	346	11.2	26.0	127	11	4	5	7	4	0	0
Francisco Cordova	27	27	225	8.3	15.3	131	14	4	4	1	3	1	0
Chris Peters	27	11	2	0.2	0.3	102	7	3	1	0	0	0	0
Todd Ritchie	27	26	105	4.0	7.4	125	7	10	6	2	1	0	0
Jason Schmidt	26	33	582	17.6	35.3	137	2	9	6	9	5	2	0
Pete Schourek	30	17	7	0.4	0.5	107	12	4	1	0	0	0	0
Jose Silva	25	12	19	1.6	3.4	112	7	3	1	1	0	0	0
PITTSBURGH		161	1288	8.0	16.4	137	63	37	25	20	13	3	0
Ranking (NL)				6	6								

Overall, the Pirates rank near the league average in pitcher workload, but it's not a good sign when the two hardest-worked pitchers on Gene Lamont's staff were also two of the youngest pitchers. . . . Jason Schmidt is no stranger to high pitch counts; his Workload actually dropped from 42.6 to 35.3, and I am extremely dubious about his chances to turn into a #1 pitcher before he gets felled by a lame arm. . . . Kris Benson has very good mechanics and is probably in no imminent danger of injury, but I'd be a little more protective of the best young arm the Pirates have had since Doug Drabek.

Is it possible to be the Cubs without being as cute? Can a team without a superstation get to the point where it forgets that it is a baseball team, and not just a profitable franchise in a semi-feudal entertainment industry? And once it gets there, can it find its way back?

The Cardinals have spent three years in a Big Red blur watching Mark McGwire paste home runs. Despite the team having gone the entire decade without winning 90 games in any season, the turnstiles spun and attendance boomed in 1999. And still, with the benefit of Hollywood-style accounting practices, team owner Bill DeWitt Jr. almost manages to keep a straight face when talking about how much money the Cardinals lost. With fans and cash pouring in, you might lump the Cards with the Cubs and think they're happy, but the Cardinals have more serious problems than anything the Cubs face.

Despite all those fannies in the seats, the organization has slowly withered into the same collection of loyal automatons and joyless martinets who ran the Oakland A's into the ground in a fruitless five-year quest to get one last pennant for a terminally ill team owner. The Cardinals organization has reached a similar point. It isn't that they've finally awakened from a self-indulgent, cash-addled reverie; it's that they're beginning to notice they've been in one and want to fix everything at once before anyone has to take the blame. Fear is a potent motivator, but then, no organization should have expected to live forever off the laurels of a nice little year like 1996.

It's not like General Manager Walt Jocketty hasn't been busy. For this organization, there's no such thing as a small deal. Big-money talent? Not a problem. McGwire and Ray Lankford get what they want, but guys like Gary Gaetti, Eric Davis, Delino DeShields and Donovan Osborne also get multi-year deals. It's the price of business these days—just ask anybody. Blockbuster deals? Jocketty has gone shopping and come back with McGwire, Todd Stottlemyre, Royce Clayton, Fernando Tatis and Edgar Renteria. He's added Dennis Eckersley, Jeff Brantley and Ricky Bottalico to the bullpen. Heck, he'll trade for a new closer every year, because he's on a run, and who would want to bring that wild ride to an end? What other team can't go a year without the thrill of staying up all night haggling with Scott Boras? You want player development, too? Spend more! Not just a little spread around to a half-dozen picks in a single draft, but enough on a really big name or two to make sure everyone knows you're serious.

The Cardinals spend money because that's what they believe a commitment to excellence is supposed to entail. There are plenty of commentators willing to parrot that belief. Following the central concept of American management culture for the second half of the 20th century, the Cardinals have operated under the assumption that spending money produces results. You could compile this sort of litany of short-sighted deals or multi-year contracts for almost any team, but not just any team spends like the Cardinals, not just any team has Tony LaRussa managing it, and not just any team pretends it's a winner with the style that the Cardinals have for the last three seasons.

The Cardinals barely even concede that anything has gone wrong in the first place and scoff at anyone who cares to disagree. They aren't the only team guilty of professional arrogance. Rather than permit the last three years of futility to impact anyone's self-esteem, let alone contribute to an evaluation of the competence of the organization, everyone from DeWitt to Jocketty to LaRussa to the batboys merely talk about "all those injuries." Injuries to lineup regulars, starting pitchers, relievers, utility infielders...you name it. As the story goes, if only they'd stayed healthy, the Cardinals would have been competitive. It's a nice story, because how can you blame management for something they claim is beyond anyone's control?

There are plenty of holes in this fig leaf. First, this is same song and dance LaRussa trotted out during his last three years in Oakland. The rotation fell apart and the lineup got old? All an unfortunate coincidence. The reality is that

---

Cardinals Prospectus

1999 record: 75-86; Fourth place, NL Central

Pythagorean W/L: 78-84

Runs scored: 809 (10th in NL)

Runs allowed: 838 (10th in NL)

Team EQA: .259 (10th in NL)

1999 team age: 28.5 (7th-youngest in NL)

1999 park: Busch Stadium; neutral park, decreased run scoring by less than 1%.

1999: Profitable respectability and a cash cow for the ages.

2000: A push is coming, as they've shored up the rotation. The wild card should be theirs.

nobody's plans work exactly as they expect. Just from among last year's NL playoff teams, the Braves lost half of their starting lineup to injuries and ineffectiveness and suffered through sub-par years from Maddux and Glavine, while the Astros lost a half-dozen regulars and their manager during the year.

Good teams accumulate depth, not only because they might have to trade it during the stretch run, but because they might have to use it. The Cardinals have only themselves to blame if injuries impacted their ability to play .500, let alone contend. Jocketty is guilty of making only the big moves while blowing off the bench. After Eric Davis and Darren Bragg went down, the Cardinals were desperate for outfielders. They were already wasting one roster spot on the third year of Willie McGee's farewell tour, and they hadn't enough sense to sign a few minor-league free agents to play for Memphis to be available just in case something went wrong. Someone like Mark Sweeney would have been extremely handy last year, but he'd already been thrown away in the pointless acquisitions of Fernando Valenzuela and Phil Plantier back in 1997. The Cardinals were so desperate that they resurrected Thomas Howard, even batting him cleanup in defiance of the warning labels.

Unfortunately, that's typical of what happens when the Cardinals need a fill-in or a bench player. They never fish around for someone they can get for the minimum or scare up a minor-league vet or a guy who can contribute if he gets a break. They'll sign major-league veteran stiffs like McGee or Mike Gallego or Carlos Baerga or Eduardo Perez or Shawon Dunston or David Howard or Thomas Howard or Frank Howard or Ron Howard. They don't go spelunking to turn up "unknown" players like Troy O'Leary or Olmedo Saenz.

At the major-league level, a big part of the problem is Tony LaRussa's obvious preference for a veteran team. Larding up your bench with pricey veteran fat reflects a double-edged problem. It means you don't have much on the farm, and it means you don't trust what little you've got. We've chided LaRussa in the past for his failure to develop starting pitchers, but you could argue that Fernando Tatis is the first position player who has developed under LaRussa's tutelage since Walt Weiss in the late 1980s. Even if the Cardinals had young players with talent and a future, it remains to be seen if LaRussa would know how to break them in. Just during his stint with the Cardinals, he has run off Dmitri Young and announced noisily how much J.D. Drew displeases him.

One of the Cardinals' most basic problems is player development. Not everyone has to cherry-pick their support players off the waiver wire or from among minor-league free agents, as relatively cost-effective as that might be. Sometimes an organization is good enough that it doesn't have to go panning for gold in the boondocks because they've already got some in their own farm system. This organization has an uncanny knack for not producing much in the way of quantity and squandering what little it cranks out. The Cardinals throw away guys like Sweeney or Young or Sean Lowe, useful players who give the organization's player-development program some credibility, but who end up more valuable to other teams because the Cardinals got frustrated with what they couldn't do.

As we pointed out last year, the Cardinals could almost do without a farm system, because there probably aren't two dozen players below the major-league level worth paying to develop. When the Cardinals get caught short-handed, as they have time and again over the last few years, they have to find out what Craig Paquette's up to these days. Injuries to pitchers at every level of the system should have the Cardinals reviewing the A's grisly record of developing pitchers was during Jocketty's turn running Oakland's player-development program.

The failure to develop anybody capable of contributing in consecutive seasons was even more apparent on the pitching staff. We could belabor the abuses of the past, such as Alan Benes and Matt Morris being sacrificed for the greater glory of a push for 80 wins in 1997. In 1999, LaRussa and pitching coach Dave Duncan wound up with a staff on which only Kent Bottenfield did his job, but keep in mind that only Bottenfield was asked to do just one job.

The root of the problem was a failure to leave anyone alone. While I'm normally sympathetic to the idea that a pitcher's job is to get people out whenever asked, when a team flip-flops its starters and relievers as much as the Cardinals did, it's hard to believe that they were helping their pitchers. As soon as one starter failed, whether it was Kent Mercker because he's lousy or Donovan Osborne because he can't open a beer bottle without hurting himself, whatever middle reliever was handy got tossed into the rotation. What's the point of stocking your Triple-A affiliate with people like Larry Luebbers or Brian Barnes, who have major-league starting experience, if you instead decide to change gears every other month with Juan Acevedo or Lance Painter? When you treat each week as if you have to win every game, where do you end up when every answer to every problem is barely designed to get you through the week, let alone 162 games? You wind up in an organizational cul-de-sac where Heathcliff Slocumb's agent can ask for (and get) $3.45 million because his client gave you consecutive good months.

So the Cardinals spend money, and Walt Jocketty talks about how it's now all about giving LaRussa "the proper arsenal to go to war with." As long as we're digging up inappropriate military cliches to describe men playing games for money, this statement ranks up there with France's Minister of War declaring, on the eve of the Franco-Prussian War, that the French army would be ready "to the last gaiter button" only weeks before its complete annihilation at the hands of some real professionals. True to Jocketty's word, though, the Cardinals embarked on another big winter bonanza. They snagged two veteran starters in Darryl Kile and Pat Hentgen, plus their fourth closer in four years, Dave Veres.

Will it be enough? Hentgen has been worked hard for the last few years, and while he may or may not be good for 30 starts, he certainly won't be the pitcher who won the Cy Young Award four years ago. Kile might be escaping Colorado, but his one good year in the last six was the year when Larry Dierker was his manager. Veres will be better than Bottalico, but LaRussa's obsession with situational usage patterns means Paul Spoljaric will probably have to pitch in 75 games for about 50 innings, instead of a much more valuable 60 games and 90 innings.

That isn't to say everything is doom and gloom. While they've already wasted two years of their window of opportunity with the McGwire/Lankford power tandem, if Tatis is for real, then along with Drew they have a new righty/lefty power threat. Not too many teams can make that boast. Picking up Edgar Renteria gives them the guy most likely to be the league's best shortstop over the next four or five years. Even if McGwire drops off considerably, they've got a good regular lineup, and chances are that Jocketty will live up to his promise to pick up one more good-hitting outfielder, made all the more necessary given LaRussa's distrust of Drew and the injury problems of Davis and Lankford.

If everything breaks their way, the Cardinals should manage a winning record. If everything breaks their way and the Astros slump, they could even win the division. I'm not enthusiastic about their chances, but there isn't anything else for them to do but to take their chances on winning right now.

HITTERS (Averages: BA: .270 / OBP: .340 / SLG: .430 / EQA: .260)

Darren Bragg — OF — Bats L — Age 30

YEAR	TEAM	LGE	AB	H	DB	TP	HR	BB/SO	R	RBI	SB	CS	OUT	BA	OBP	SLG	EQA	EQR	DEFENSE	
1997	Boston	AL	512	133	37	2	9	58/98	63	56	10	6	385	.260	.339	.393	.250	60	150-OF 103	
1998	Boston	AL	408	114	30	3	8	40/97	49	55	4	3	297	.279	.353	.426	.264	53	111-OF 97	
1999	St Louis	NL	274	71	12	1	6	40/66	36	25	3	0	203	.259	.360	.376	.258	34	33-CF 93	24-RF 102
2000	St Louis	NL	290	76	17	1	8	42/68	47	43	4	2	216	.262	.355	.410	.263	38		

Bragg is your typical stretch outfielder. It's a stretch to play him in center field regularly because he can't field the position, and it's a stretch to play him regularly in either outfield corner because he isn't enough of a hitter. He has plenty of value as a fourth outfielder, but Eric Davis's fragile existence pushed Bragg into too-regular playing time before he blew out his knee in August.

Brent Butler — IF — Bats R — Age 22

YEAR	TEAM	LGE	AB	H	DB	TP	HR	BB/SO	R	RBI	SB	CS	OUT	BA	OBP	SLG	EQA	EQR	DEFENSE	
1997	Peoria	Mid	489	130	29	1	15	47/72	62	55	3	2	361	.266	.334	.421	.255	59	123-SS 99	
1998	Pr Willm	Car	490	134	26	2	12	37/71	61	72	1	2	358	.273	.332	.408	.249	56	112-SS 95	
1999	Arkansas	Tex	529	128	16	1	12	19/51	56	44	0	2	403	.242	.274	.344	.204	38	58-SS 93	45-3B 101
2000	Colorado	NL	480	146	20	1	16	34/56	65	83	1	1	335	.304	.350	.450	.245	50		

We flog scouts as a group for some of their more toolsy biases, but so far, it looks like their reservations about Butler were on target. It doesn't look like he'll be a regular at shortstop, and he has been tried at both second base and third base. Butler has been called a smart player, but how smart was it give up walks for Lent two years ago? He's still young enough to recover from such a bad introduction to Double-A.

Butler was traded to the Rockies in the Kile deal. It's interesting that the new Tribe-flavored Rockies management picked him up, since they're some of the same people who developed Jay Bell and the less-fortunate Mark Lewis. For all three, there were warnings that they'd have to move off shortstop, which was true for Lewis and false for Bell. In Colorado, he could fail to progress as a hitter and still end up looking like Bell because of the park.

Alberto Castillo — C — Bats R — Age 30

YEAR	TEAM	LGE	AB	H	DB	TP	HR	BB/SO	R	RBI	SB	CS	OUT	BA	OBP	SLG	EQA	EQR	DEFENSE
1997	Norfolk	Int	85	17	1	0	1	13/17	4	7	1	0	68	.200	.306	.247	.197	6	
1998	NY Mets	NL	84	18	2	0	3	9/17	13	8	0	2	68	.214	.299	.345	.212	7	28-C 116
1999	St Louis	NL	256	67	5	0	5	21/48	20	30	0	0	189	.262	.323	.340	.228	23	74-C 113
2000	Toronto	AL	180	43	2	0	5	20/35	18	22	0	1	138	.239	.315	.333	.221	16	

(Alberto Castillo *continued*)

Though he's one of the best-throwing catchers around and LaRussa was determined to stop the running game, Castillo's defense drew fire because of some indifferent plate blocking. His hitting was better than anyone should ever expect it to be again, and after snagging him in the Rule 5 draft, the Cards were smart to cash out by shipping him off to the Blue Jays in the Hentgen deal.

Stubby Clapp   UT   Bats L   Age 27

YEAR	TEAM	LGE	AB	H	DB	TP	HR	BB/SO	R	RBI	SB	CS	OUT	BA	OBP	SLG	EQA	EQR	DEFENSE	
1997	Pr Willm	Car	278	69	17	5	2	37/48	35	31	3	2	211	.248	.345	.367	.247	32	40-2B 90	24-OF 95
1998	Arkansas	Tex	516	110	23	4	8	62/125	71	37	7	5	411	.213	.304	.320	.215	44	136-2B 99	
1999	Memphis	PCL	389	81	22	1	9	42/104	50	42	4	4	312	.208	.289	.339	.213	33	63-2B 86	32-OF 91
2000	St Louis	NL	399	89	24	3	10	52/101	54	47	6	4	314	.223	.313	.373	.234	42		

The left-handed version of Joe McEwing, even playing with the same sort of manic hyperactivity, except that he's Canadian. Maybe this is what happens when they get too much sunlight. Despite his small stature (he's 5'8″ in press guides, shorter in reality), he gets good power out of an exaggerated Charlie Lau top-hand-release swing. He doesn't have a position he's good at, but he'll play anywhere his weak arm permits. Clapp is probably not cut out for a grumpy LaRussa outfit: he enjoys himself way too much to be another one of the angry dwarves.

Eric Davis   OF   Bats R   Age 38

YEAR	TEAM	LGE	AB	H	DB	TP	HR	BB/SO	R	RBI	SB	CS	OUT	BA	OBP	SLG	EQA	EQR	DEFENSE
1997	Baltimor	AL	158	49	9	0	9	13/45	28	25	6	0	109	.310	.367	.538	.301	27	17-OF 103
1998	Baltimor	AL	454	153	27	1	30	43/106	79	89	6	6	307	.337	.401	.599	.319	88	66-OF 96
1999	St Louis	NL	192	49	8	2	5	27/49	25	28	4	4	147	.255	.350	.396	.254	24	45-RF 96
2000	St Louis	NL	211	61	9	0	10	28/53	36	40	4	2	152	.289	.372	.474	.285	33	

Over the last four years, Davis has been alternating good seasons with ones lost to injuries. He must be taking career tips from John Travolta. First, it was "he'll be one of the game's greatest center fielders." Then it was "the other guy besides Strawberry who shouldn't have joined the Dodgers." Then it was "the player who came back from cancer." Now it's "the gamer who blew out his shoulder making diving catches to preserve a no-hitter." While Congress wastes its time on "what could have been" for a guy who betrayed the game like Shoeless Joe Jackson, and while fans pretend Pete Rose is a victim of something other than his own vices, why don't we hear more about what Eric Davis could have been? Similar to Fred Lynn, Davis has been a victim of his body's limits, something that actually was beyond his control. It should be a lot more compelling to talk about how good Davis was when healthy than it is to talk about forgiving dumb men for making evil choices.

J.D. Drew   CF   Bats L   Age 24

YEAR	TEAM	LGE	AB	H	DB	TP	HR	BB/SO	R	RBI	SB	CS	OUT	BA	OBP	SLG	EQA	EQR	DEFENSE
1998	Arkansas	Tex	67	19	2	1	4	10/17	13	8	1	1	49	.284	.382	.522	.296	12	
1998	Memphis	PCL	79	23	5	1	2	20/18	12	11	1	2	58	.291	.439	.456	.304	15	21-OF 121
1999	St Louis	NL	369	89	17	6	12	46/76	67	36	17	3	283	.241	.336	.417	.261	49	90-CF 96
1999	Memphis	PCL	85	23	2	1	2	7/20	8	12	5	1	63	.271	.338	.388	.255	10	20-OF 110
2000	St Louis	NL	279	72	12	5	12	46/79	55	48	14	3	210	.258	.363	.466	.283	45	

Though Drew struggled relative to the expectations of instant greatness (promoted by us, among others), once he was healthy he showed power, patience, a great arm and good speed. Because of his limited pro experience, he made a lot of mental mistakes, especially throwing to the wrong base. LaRussa spent the last few months of the season harping on Drew's shortcomings and threatening that he'll have to improve or play in Memphis. For whose benefit does an established manager say that stuff in public? Scott Boras's? To show everyone that Tony LaRussa's famed communication skills are as dead as Elvis? Drew is going to draw fire just for being Drew, so the Cardinals need to end this sort of grandstanding, pronto. It doesn't pay to run down an extremely talented young player just because the manager is cranky that the kid wasn't Instant Cup-o-Mantle.

Cordell Farley   OF   Bats R   Age 27

YEAR	TEAM	LGE	AB	H	DB	TP	HR	BB/SO	R	RBI	SB	CS	OUT	BA	OBP	SLG	EQA	EQR	DEFENSE
1997	Pr Willm	Car	215	48	9	2	2	9/53	21	24	9	3	171	.223	.257	.312	.192	14	54-OF 95
1998	Pr Willm	Car	558	137	25	8	9	22/163	64	46	17	7	428	.246	.279	.367	.218	47	129-OF 88
1999	Arkansas	Tex	421	90	13	5	6	12/119	28	29	10	7	338	.214	.238	.311	.177	22	113-OF 88
2000	St Louis	NL	426	97	16	4	7	25/123	43	37	17	7	336	.228	.271	.333	.205	32	

Farley was an All-Star in the Carolina League in 1998 when he was 25. He was a college pick from the 1996 draft who has only just played his first season in Double-A. Like Scarborough Green, he may get to pinch-run once in a while, but he's about as much of a prospect as Steven Seagal would be on your kid's Little League team.

Chris Haas   3B/1B   Bats L   Age 23

YEAR	TEAM	LGE	AB	H	DB	TP	HR	BB/SO	R	RBI	SB	CS	OUT	BA	OBP	SLG	EQA	EQR	DEFENSE	
1997	Peoria	Mid	118	32	7	0	5	17/40	17	17	1	0	86	.271	.374	.458	.283	18	20-3B 113	
1997	Pr Willm	Car	371	85	9	2	13	32/143	51	46	1	1	287	.229	.295	.369	.224	34	97-3B 100	
1998	Arkansas	Tex	445	105	23	2	16	59/143	57	61	1	1	341	.236	.333	.404	.251	54	104-3B 92	
1999	Memphis	PCL	392	79	15	2	14	58/153	48	56	3	3	316	.202	.307	.357	.227	39	82-3B 96	24-1B 101
2000	*St Louis*	*NL*	*341*	*78*	*12*	*1*	*13*	*45/127*	*42*	*47*	*2*	*1*	*264*	*.229*	*.319*	*.384*	*.240*	*37*		

Potentially a nice spare part, in that he's got a strong arm at third base and can play well at either infield corner, where both Cardinals major-league starters bat right-handed. Bringing him up certainly makes more sense that trying to make John Mabry into a third baseman. A bad year at Memphis looks worse because he struggled after getting hurt in a collision with Eduardo Perez while chasing down a pop-up in June. He'll be much better in his second year at Memphis.

Thomas Howard   OF   Bats B   Age 35

YEAR	TEAM	LGE	AB	H	DB	TP	HR	BB/SO	R	RBI	SB	CS	OUT	BA	OBP	SLG	EQA	EQR	DEFENSE
1997	Houston	NL	259	66	19	1	3	26/47	25	23	1	2	195	.255	.330	.371	.239	27	54-OF 102
1998	LosAngls	NL	77	15	3	0	3	3/15	10	5	1	0	62	.195	.225	.351	.187	5	
1999	Memphis	PCL	116	34	8	1	1	10/23	17	14	1	1	83	.293	.353	.405	.258	14	29-OF 97
1999	St Louis	NL	196	57	7	0	7	14/26	15	27	1	1	140	.291	.345	.434	.262	25	35-RF 96
2000	*St Louis*	*NL*	*208*	*55*	*7*	*0*	*6*	*22/34*	*26*	*29*	*1*	*1*	*154*	*.264*	*.335*	*.385*	*.246*	*23*	

If you're trying to run a team in a four-horse town too small to have its own salt lick, and your starting outfield was wiped out by injuries or somebody's wedding, and your regular fill-in guy couldn't find a sitter, and you've got that big matchup with Shelbyville coming up, THEN you might think about digging up Thomas Howard. That's if you run a responsible organization and don't want to lose a couple dozen paying customers on the nights when you aren't raffling off a toaster oven.

Marcus Jensen   C   Bats B   Age 27

YEAR	TEAM	LGE	AB	H	DB	TP	HR	BB/SO	R	RBI	SB	CS	OUT	BA	OBP	SLG	EQA	EQR	DEFENSE
1997	San Fran	NL	75	12	2	0	1	7/23	5	3	0	0	63	.160	.232	.227	.137	2	
1997	Toledo	Int	82	15	6	0	0	7/25	5	9	0	0	67	.183	.247	.256	.160	3	
1998	Louisvil	Int	233	46	11	0	8	26/71	23	26	0	2	189	.197	.280	.348	.209	19	65-C 98
1999	Memphis	PCL	233	55	14	3	5	24/64	26	30	0	0	178	.236	.315	.386	.238	25	58-C 98
1999	St Louis	NL	34	8	4	0	1	6/12	5	2	0	0	26	.235	.350	.441	.268	5	
2000	*Minnesot*	*AL*	*214*	*47*	*11*	*1*	*7*	*27/62*	*27*	*28*	*0*	*0*	*167*	*.220*	*.307*	*.379*	*.230*	*21*	

He had some time away as Team USA's starting catcher in the Pan Am Games. That plus Eli Marrero's struggles got him back to the majors. He's always been a solid defensive catcher, but at the plate, he's had problems with anything with a wiggle in it. Jensen is a perfectly acceptable backup catcher.

Adam Kennedy   IF   Bats L   Age 24

YEAR	TEAM	LGE	AB	H	DB	TP	HR	BB/SO	R	RBI	SB	CS	OUT	BA	OBP	SLG	EQA	EQR	DEFENSE	
1997	New Jrsy	NYP	117	33	6	2	0	10/11	12	13	3	1	85	.282	.344	.368	.247	13	26-SS 106	
1997	Pr Willm	Car	157	46	10	2	1	3/17	20	23	2	2	113	.293	.313	.401	.237	15	35-SS 91	
1998	Pr Willm	Car	71	18	6	0	0	4/12	7	6	2	1	54	.254	.293	.338	.215	6		
1998	Arkansas	Tex	204	50	10	1	5	5/23	26	18	3	1	155	.245	.268	.377	.214	16	50-SS 94	
1998	Memphis	PCL	303	87	21	6	3	10/42	30	34	12	3	219	.287	.312	.426	.250	34	60-SS 92	
1999	Memphis	PCL	359	104	19	3	8	24/36	52	49	14	4	259	.290	.340	.426	.262	45	48-2B 89	19-SS 101
1999	St Louis	NL	103	26	11	1	1	1/8	12	16	0	1	78	.252	.275	.408	.222	9	25-2B 94	
2000	*St Louis*	*NL*	*452*	*127*	*32*	*5*	*9*	*27/50*	*66*	*62*	*14*	*4*	*329*	*.281*	*.322*	*.434*	*.255*	*54*		

Much could be made of the fact that Kennedy was the only prospect to play in the Futures Game, the Triple-A All-Star Game, the Pan Am Games and the major leagues. However, he's older than Andruw Jones and has more in common with Jim

(Adam Kennedy *continued*)

Gantner than Craig Biggio. Kennedy can spray the ball to all fields and has decent power for a middle infielder, but he could learn a thing or two about taking pitches. He's not a burner on the bases and has work to do on his fielding. His chance to start 2000 as the Cards' second baseman died when the team picked up Fernando Vina.

David Kim — OF — Bats R — Age 24

YEAR	TEAM	LGE	AB	H	DB	TP	HR	BB/SO	R	RBI	SB	CS	OUT	BA	OBP	SLG	EQA	EQR	DEFENSE
1997	New Jrsy	NYP	209	48	13	1	5	13/44	26	25	2	1	162	.230	.293	.373	.225	19	44-OF 98
1998	Peoria	Mid	476	125	28	1	14	41/82	60	72	1	3	354	.263	.331	.414	.250	55	109-OF 87
1999	Potomac	Car	446	97	16	2	16	30/113	51	53	3	3	352	.217	.272	.370	.213	37	110-OF 86
2000	St Louis	NL	425	108	18	1	18	38/97	52	65	3	2	319	.254	.315	.428	.249	49	

A Korean-American out of Seton Hall, Kim's best position is probably DH. He gets a terrible jump on the ball in the field, and his strong arm is wildly inaccurate. The Cardinals don't have much in the way of outfield prospects, so Kim has a career where other organizations wouldn't give him much thought. He could grow up to be the next Ty Van Burkleo if the California League puts a franchise in Seoul.

Ray Lankford — OF — Bats L — Age 33

YEAR	TEAM	LGE	AB	H	DB	TP	HR	BB/SO	R	RBI	SB	CS	OUT	BA	OBP	SLG	EQA	EQR	DEFENSE
1997	St Louis	NL	475	140	37	3	33	95/124	93	99	17	11	346	.295	.412	.594	.321	101	133-OF 100
1998	St Louis	NL	539	160	33	2	34	85/147	95	108	28	6	385	.297	.396	.555	.314	106	132-OF 108
1999	St Louis	NL	423	128	31	1	15	44/109	72	59	12	4	299	.303	.373	.487	.288	67	98-LF 104
2000	St Louis	NL	359	103	18	0	21	63/95	76	74	13	4	260	.287	.393	.513	.304	66	

From weak knees that required surgery and hadn't healed by Opening Day to the world's slowest-healing rib-cage injury, Lankford's extended absences might have been the critical difference between fourth place and leaving the Pirates in the dust while claiming third. The knees are a concern: not only will he never be a regular center fielder again, he may not hit for the same kind of power.

Jason Lariviere — OF — Bats R — Age 26

YEAR	TEAM	LGE	AB	H	DB	TP	HR	BB/SO	R	RBI	SB	CS	OUT	BA	OBP	SLG	EQA	EQR	DEFENSE
1997	Arkansas	Tex	370	88	21	4	5	25/80	37	44	2	2	284	.238	.286	.357	.215	30	57-OF 99
1998	Arkansas	Tex	435	90	24	3	5	36/70	46	39	6	3	348	.207	.270	.310	.195	29	127-OF 93
1999	Memphis	PCL	489	113	27	2	6	37/69	62	33	11	3	379	.231	.292	.331	.215	40	135-OF 98
2000	St Louis	NL	385	86	22	1	4	38/61	42	33	7	2	301	.223	.293	.317	.210	30	

Maybe too much time gets spent asking farm directors about their players, because the Cardinals have called Lariviere a lead-off type. While he could lead you off the beaten track or into the woods or down the primrose path, leading him off in a major-league lineup is more likely to lead you into last place. The Cardinals were terrible against left-handed pitching—only the Padres were worse—and Lariviere isn't the worst guy to carry around as a fifth outfielder to help against southpaws. However, it would mean carrying one less infield/outfield guy, as well as no more goofing around with 12 pitchers.

Jose Leon — 3B — Bats R — Age 23

YEAR	TEAM	LGE	AB	H	DB	TP	HR	BB/SO	R	RBI	SB	CS	OUT	BA	OBP	SLG	EQA	EQR	DEFENSE
1997	Peoria	Mid	405	83	18	1	18	23/127	39	41	3	2	324	.205	.260	.388	.214	34	101-3B 87
1998	Pr Willm	Car	453	125	27	2	22	50/132	72	68	2	1	329	.276	.355	.490	.280	68	117-3B 106
1999	Arkansas	Tex	337	71	12	0	16	19/124	29	43	2	2	268	.211	.263	.389	.214	28	74-3B 99
2000	St Louis	NL	387	94	14	0	19	36/131	45	59	2	1	294	.243	.307	.426	.245	44	

Adjusting to Double-A is still the biggest leap between two rungs in the ladder from the minors to the majors, and in Leon's case it showed. His borderline command of the strike zone took a turn for the worse, and he lost playing time when the organization decided to give Butler experience at third. Haas is probably stuck in Memphis for 2000, which means Leon may have a season that looks like a breakout while repenting at Arkansas, especially if he goes back to taking as many pitches as he did in 1998.

Eli Marrero   C   Bats R   Age 26

YEAR	TEAM	LGE	AB	H	DB	TP	HR	BB/SO	R	RBI	SB	CS	OUT	BA	OBP	SLG	EQA	EQR	DEFENSE
1997	Louisvil	AA	398	104	21	8	17	22/54	55	62	3	3	297	.261	.305	.482	.257	50	
1998	Memphis	PCL	130	28	4	0	6	11/24	18	17	4	3	105	.215	.277	.385	.220	12	25-C 106
1998	St Louis	NL	256	64	19	1	4	28/41	28	20	6	2	194	.250	.324	.379	.242	28	69-C 105
1999	St Louis	NL	319	62	12	1	6	14/55	30	32	10	2	259	.194	.231	.295	.174	16	78-C 108
2000	St Louis	NL	315	69	15	2	7	24/53	32	30	8	3	249	.219	.274	.346	.210	25	

Finding the right level of medication after having your thyroid gland removed takes time and usually leaves you battling fatigue problems in the meantime. The Cardinals seemed only dimly aware of this. In camp, LaRussa claimed he only wanted to see Marrero play good defense, and that any hitting would be a bonus. Marrero wore out quickly and wasn't able to contribute anything on offense. If he's finally healthy, that projection is low. In terms of what to expect, I'd lean more towards what he did in 1997 than anything since.

Joe McEwing   UT   Bats R   Age 27

YEAR	TEAM	LGE	AB	H	DB	TP	HR	BB/SO	R	RBI	SB	CS	OUT	BA	OBP	SLG	EQA	EQR	DEFENSE
1997	Arkansas	Tex	262	57	7	2	3	13/48	24	25	1	2	207	.218	.257	.294	.177	14	56-OF 99
1998	Arkansas	Tex	220	59	17	2	5	14/23	28	28	2	1	162	.268	.314	.432	.249	25	48-OF 109
1998	Memphis	PCL	326	92	24	5	4	17/43	37	34	7	7	241	.282	.322	.423	.247	36	75-OF 102
1999	St Louis	NL	515	141	29	4	8	35/86	61	41	6	4	378	.274	.328	.392	.244	56	82-2B 102
2000	St Louis	NL	391	104	22	3	8	36/61	53	52	6	4	291	.266	.328	.399	.246	44	

McEwing's approach is to volunteer for everything (he offered to be the team's emergency catcher in camp) and never sit still. That attitude is exactly what impresses Tony LaRussa, and it's a sound approach for every minor-league second baseman with moderate talent. Like Mike Hargrove before him, he goes through a lengthy ritual of gyrations and adjustments before every pitch. Maybe some people think it's cute, but if I'm the umpire, I tell him to stand in. If I'm the pitcher, I dust him for wasting so much time that my arm stiffens up between pitches.

Willie McGee   PH   Bats B   Age 41

YEAR	TEAM	LGE	AB	H	DB	TP	HR	BB/SO	R	RBI	SB	CS	OUT	BA	OBP	SLG	EQA	EQR	DEFENSE
1997	St Louis	NL	304	93	22	4	3	22/58	30	38	7	2	213	.306	.353	.434	.268	39	61-OF 90
1998	St Louis	NL	271	70	12	1	3	13/48	28	34	7	2	203	.258	.292	.343	.217	22	54-OF 92
1999	St Louis	NL	273	69	6	0	0	13/59	23	19	6	4	208	.253	.287	.275	.188	16	25-RF 88

If baseball is entertainment, the final two years of Willie McGee's career were reruns. Not the funny reruns, like the *Simpsons* episode you've seen a dozen times and still glance at for a dry chuckle during a couch-surfing session. More like a Dick Van Patten marathon. If you make yourself think about it, there was a time when Dick Van Patten was a star and people enjoyed watching him. No, I don't know anybody like that either, but we can infer their existence from *People* magazine. McGee has retired.

Mark McGwire   1B   Bats R   Age 36

YEAR	TEAM	LGE	AB	H	DB	TP	HR	BB/SO	R	RBI	SB	CS	OUT	BA	OBP	SLG	EQA	EQR	DEFENSE
1997	Oakland	AL	363	103	22	0	35	56/94	46	79	1	0	260	.284	.386	.634	.322	76	97-1B 102
1997	St Louis	NL	178	46	7	0	24	42/60	39	42	2	0	132	.258	.414	.702	.344	46	42-1B 98
1998	St Louis	NL	516	156	27	0	71	163/151	133	147	1	0	360	.302	.475	.767	.381	161	149-1B 95
1999	St Louis	NL	520	144	24	1	62	127/140	112	136	0	0	376	.277	.421	.685	.344	131	141-1B 90
2000	St Louis	NL	482	131	21	0	54	140/135	121	150	0	0	351	.272	.436	.651	.346	124	

No presidents or czars at his birthday parties, no snit fits over having his music played in the clubhouse, no crowd of flunkies following him around. He just plays baseball, and while Sammy Sosa gets headlines and invitations, Big Red can settle for being the better player.

One of last summer's activities was naming All-Century teams, and while Lou Gehrig has been a no-brainer selection for all-time teams for 60 years, McGwire's claim on a spot is pretty strong. While everyone rallying to the Iron Horse's defense will cry about expansion pitching or live balls or other half-baked theories to trash the modern player, keep in mind that Gehrig played in a smaller league drawing on a smaller national population, smaller still because Gehrig didn't have to hit off talented pitchers if they happened to be black or Hispanic. In an eight-team league, Gehrig never had to hit against one of the

(Mark McGwire *continued*)

league's best pitching staffs (his Yankees teammates), and when half of the other teams in the league are worse than some of the better independent minor-league teams, that means long summers spent hitting off of bad pitching. While Gehrig was one of the dominant players of his day, I don't think we need to wrestle too long or too hard with his halo to come to the conclusion that after the last three years, McGwire has staked a legitimate claim as the best first baseman of all time.

Luis Ordaz   SS   Bats R   Age 24

YEAR	TEAM	LGE	AB	H	DB	TP	HR	BB/SO	R	RBI	SB	CS	OUT	BA	OBP	SLG	EQA	EQR	DEFENSE
1997	Arkansas	Tex	387	98	18	4	4	16/44	33	44	7	6	295	.253	.286	.351	.212	31	105-SS 93
1998	Memphis	PCL	213	57	9	2	5	14/20	24	30	2	2	158	.268	.315	.399	.239	22	57-SS 90
1998	St Louis	NL	154	32	6	0	0	12/18	9	8	2	0	122	.208	.265	.247	.170	7	44-SS 110
1999	Memphis	PCL	356	90	20	3	1	20/39	24	36	2	3	269	.253	.299	.334	.213	28	105-SS 96
2000	Arizona	NL	375	95	18	2	5	28/41	41	40	5	3	283	.253	.305	.352	.221	32	

A good old-fashioned 1970s shortstop. You remember—those guys with the slick gloves who could smack a half-dozen singles a week. Davey Concepcion was the best of them, back before Alan Trammell and Robin Yount and Cal Ripken changed expectations of what shortstops could and couldn't do. Some managers might make room for a guy like Ordaz, but Bob Boone isn't running a team into the ground at the moment.

Bill Ortega   CF   Bats R   Age 24

YEAR	TEAM	LGE	AB	H	DB	TP	HR	BB/SO	R	RBI	SB	CS	OUT	BA	OBP	SLG	EQA	EQR	DEFENSE
1997	Pr Willm	Car	255	58	11	0	1	15/42	21	14	1	1	198	.227	.270	.282	.182	14	49-OF 93
1998	Peoria	Mid	407	99	23	1	2	30/73	47	47	1	3	311	.243	.300	.319	.209	31	44-OF 93
1999	Potomac	Car	426	108	25	2	8	26/73	51	54	3	3	321	.254	.300	.378	.227	40	108-OF 102
1999	Arkansas	Tex	69	22	6	0	2	8/10	8	8	0	0	47	.319	.390	.493	.296	11	18-OF 111
2000	St Louis	NL	441	112	23	1	6	34/77	47	48	1	2	331	.254	.307	.351	.222	39	

The organization's indifferent approach to drafting offensive talent creates opportunities for guys like this Cuban defector. The Cardinals are ecstatic with what they're calling a year of major improvement, and he's proved he has the range to play center field. In almost any other organization, he isn't a prospect, but with the Cardinals he's one of the guys who shows up because there isn't anyone else.

Craig Paquette   UT   Bats R   Age 31

YEAR	TEAM	LGE	AB	H	DB	TP	HR	BB/SO	R	RBI	SB	CS	OUT	BA	OBP	SLG	EQA	EQR	DEFENSE
1997	KansasCy	AL	251	57	15	1	8	9/55	25	32	2	2	196	.227	.260	.390	.213	20	70-3B 93
1997	Omaha	AA	90	23	2	0	3	4/29	7	16	0	1	68	.256	.287	.378	.218	8	
1999	Norfolk	Int	282	68	19	2	11	6/52	30	40	2	0	214	.241	.263	.440	.230	27	38-3B 95
1999	St Louis	NL	158	45	6	0	10	4/38	20	35	1	0	113	.285	.302	.513	.265	20	20-RF 92
2000	St Louis	NL	283	68	16	1	11	13/97	28	37	2	1	216	.240	.274	.420	.228	27	

Paquette enjoyed a little bit of everything last year: a virus left him underweight and weak at Norfolk, followed by a stint as the starting first baseman for Team USA in the Pan Am Games. The Cardinals couldn't resist those credentials on top of his being another former LaRussian, trading Shawon Dunston to get him. In late August, he won three straight games with late-inning hits, and faster than you can say "Wonder Dog" a cult hero was born. The Cardinals goofed off with having Paquette work at second base in the instructional league. While he's a better bench player than McGee, if the Cards hand him 300 at-bats, they're in trouble.

Eduardro Perez   1B   Bats R   Age 30

YEAR	TEAM	LGE	AB	H	DB	TP	HR	BB/SO	R	RBI	SB	CS	OUT	BA	OBP	SLG	EQA	EQR	DEFENSE
1997	Cincnnti	NL	299	75	16	0	17	28/75	43	52	4	1	225	.251	.319	.475	.263	40	65-1B 91
1998	Cincnnti	NL	174	43	2	0	5	21/44	20	32	0	1	132	.247	.336	.345	.235	18	39-1B 116
1999	Memphis	PCL	407	104	18	1	13	36/100	45	57	4	5	308	.256	.323	.400	.243	45	90-1B 101
1999	St Louis	NL	32	11	2	0	1	6/6	6	9	0	0	21	.344	.447	.500	.323	6	
2000	St Louis	NL	275	72	8	0	11	33/68	36	43	1	2	205	.262	.341	.411	.254	33	

Because he did not play for the 1995 Oakland A's, he will not get a shot at Craig Paquette's roster spot. That's no reason to feel sorry for him. Consider how many children of the Big Red Machine are hanging around baseball. Ken Griffey Jr. doesn't owe anything to his old man, but Brian McRae got his big break thanks to his manager, Papa Hal. Lee May's son Derrick is still puttering around a good five years after anyone should have considered him useful. Ed Sprague's son Ed Jr. keeps getting opportunities ahead of better players like Tom Evans and Aramis Ramirez. Perez can't hit well enough to be a first baseman and can't handle third base or left field, but he is Tony Perez's kid, so he gets to hang around.

Placido Polanco		**2B/SS**				**Bats R**		**Age 24**										
YEAR	TEAM	LGE	AB	H	DB	TP	HR	BB/SO	R	RBI	SB	CS	OUT	BA	OBP	SLG	EQA	EQR	DEFENSE
1997	Arkansas	Tex	503	132	16	2	2	22/57	52	40	11	3	374	.262	.297	.314	.209	37	126-2B 104
1998	Memphis	PCL	245	64	17	1	1	14/15	30	18	5	2	183	.261	.307	.351	.225	22	55-2B 99
1998	St Louis	NL	115	30	3	2	1	5/9	10	11	2	0	85	.261	.298	.348	.221	10	22-SS 114
1999	Memphis	PCL	118	29	4	1	0	2/11	14	8	1	0	89	.246	.263	.297	.183	6	17-2B 111
1999	St Louis	NL	221	61	8	3	1	12/24	22	18	1	3	163	.276	.313	.353	.222	19	44-2B 99
2000	St Louis	NL	409	111	17	3	2	23/39	45	41	8	4	302	.271	.310	.342	.222	35	

Polanco was supposed to win the second-base job in camp, but a broken fingertip in the first practice game opened the door for McEwing, and now Kennedy is ready and Vina is in town, so it doesn't look like Polanco is going to get his day in the sun. He can pick it at short or second, and managed to get on LaRussa's good side for his work ethic, launching a career as a good utility infielder.

Edgar Renteria		**SS**				**Bats R**		**Age 24**										
YEAR	TEAM	LGE	AB	H	DB	TP	HR	BB/SO	R	RBI	SB	CS	OUT	BA	OBP	SLG	EQA	EQR	DEFENSE
1997	Florida	NL	626	178	23	3	4	44/107	87	52	26	15	463	.284	.335	.350	.237	63	149-SS 100
1998	Florida	NL	526	154	21	2	3	47/76	82	32	44	25	397	.293	.356	.357	.248	61	129-SS 98
1999	St Louis	NL	587	161	35	2	11	46/81	85	60	32	8	434	.274	.329	.397	.252	69	140-SS 95
2000	St Louis	NL	578	169	31	2	11	61/85	111	74	43	15	424	.292	.360	.410	.268	79	

Picking up Renteria was brilliant: ideally, you want to get young players just about to enter the best years of their careers, because they'll not only help the team right now, but into the future. His improved power is more than just getting out of the thick air of the Miami swamplands. He's slowly entering what should be at least a very good five- or six-year stretch, and that's without considering that he's probably a year younger than listed here. Good comparisons would be Barry Larkin or Alan Trammell: the power should keep getting better; he'll take a few more walks and have a shot at an MVP award someday. While he isn't an ideal leadoff man, the Cardinals don't have many alternatives.

Chris Richard		**1B**				**Bats L**		**Age 26**										
YEAR	TEAM	LGE	AB	H	DB	TP	HR	BB/SO	R	RBI	SB	CS	OUT	BA	OBP	SLG	EQA	EQR	DEFENSE
1997	Arkansas	Tex	389	89	22	2	9	48/68	45	42	3	2	302	.229	.320	.365	.235	40	104-1B 86
1998	Arkansas	Tex	89	15	4	1	1	7/12	5	11	0	0	74	.169	.235	.270	.159	4	19-1B 73
1999	Arkansas	Tex	444	103	21	2	18	30/92	52	60	3	3	344	.232	.289	.410	.232	44	127-1B 81
2000	St Louis	NL	299	68	15	1	11	30/60	34	39	2	2	233	.227	.298	.395	.232	30	

Richard missed 1998 after a home-plate collision in winter ball in 1997 caused a bone spur to tear through his rotator cuff. He has bounced back to about where he was before the injury, which is non-prospectdom. He's a big athletic guy whose defense gets rave reviews, and the Cardinals want to see if he can play in the outfield corners. He can't really hit left-handers but started against them anyway. Richard might grow up to be a major-league pinch-hitter, but it's a long shot.

Luis Saturria		**OF**				**Bats R**		**Age 23**										
YEAR	TEAM	LGE	AB	H	DB	TP	HR	BB/SO	R	RBI	SB	CS	OUT	BA	OBP	SLG	EQA	EQR	DEFENSE
1997	Peoria	Mid	452	110	18	3	11	32/99	59	40	10	5	347	.243	.297	.369	.226	42	109-OF 96
1998	Pr Willm	Car	475	132	25	7	13	27/100	62	67	12	7	350	.278	.324	.442	.255	57	126-OF 95
1999	Arkansas	Tex	486	107	27	3	13	28/146	51	48	9	4	383	.220	.268	.368	.213	40	139-OF 99
2000	St Louis	NL	455	115	22	3	16	36/122	59	63	12	5	345	.253	.308	.420	.245	51	

Among the organization's collection of tools players, Saturria might be its best outfield prospect. He runs like the wind, glides in the outfield, has a great arm and, like Butler, his first experience above Double-A was rough going at the plate. He didn't have a good grasp of the strike zone at lower levels, and he was picked apart in the Texas League. He's very raw, and the organization does not have a good record of helping players turn tools into performance.

Fernando Tatis · 3B · Bats R · Age 25

YEAR	TEAM	LGE	AB	H	DB	TP	HR	BB/SO	R	RBI	SB	CS	OUT	BA	OBP	SLG	EQA	EQR	DEFENSE
1997	Tulsa	Tex	378	104	18	1	21	37/81	52	45	10	5	279	.275	.344	.495	.276	56	99-3B 102
1997	Texas	AL	223	58	7	0	9	12/40	28	29	3	0	165	.260	.298	.413	.239	23	58-3B 85
1998	Texas	AL	327	86	15	2	3	11/65	37	30	5	2	243	.263	.296	.349	.218	27	93-3B 105
1998	St Louis	NL	204	59	18	2	8	24/55	28	26	7	3	148	.289	.370	.515	.292	34	53-3B 94
1999	St Louis	NL	538	158	31	3	32	75/127	97	99	18	9	389	.294	.398	.541	.308	102	143-3B 100
2000	*St Louis*	*NL*	*591*	*170*	*30*	*2*	*33*	*69/136*	*105*	*116*	*19*	*8*	*429*	*.288*	*.362*	*.513*	*.289*	*96*	

We copped out last year by saying we didn't know what to expect, projecting him to hit .290 with 20 home runs, while giving that projection a less-than-ringing endorsement. Tatis ended up having the kind of year that should remind all of us that when a player explodes through the minors to reach the majors by 22, he might struggle with adjustments for a year or two, but the talent is going to emerge. What was amazing about Tatis is that there wasn't a phase of the game in which he didn't improve, and it's especially interesting how quickly he went from being an impatient hitter to having a good walk rate. I think the improvement is real.

Ron Warner · 3B/OF · Bats R · Age 31

YEAR	TEAM	LGE	AB	H	DB	TP	HR	BB/SO	R	RBI	SB	CS	OUT	BA	OBP	SLG	EQA	EQR	DEFENSE	
1997	Louisvil	AA	281	59	10	0	7	35/50	36	27	3	1	223	.210	.300	.320	.215	24	23-OF 91	18-1B 98
1998	Memphis	PCL	371	87	23	1	5	33/74	43	29	2	3	287	.235	.302	.342	.218	32	36-3B 102	34-OF 93
1999	Memphis	PCL	241	56	10	1	7	26/76	24	22	5	1	186	.232	.313	.369	.236	25	20-3B 96	17-OF 98
2000	*St Louis*	*NL*	*220*	*50*	*6*	*0*	*7*	*27/57*	*26*	*26*	*4*	*1*	*171*	*.227*	*.312*	*.350*	*.229*	*22*		

He's hanging around waiting for his chance after putting in nine years with the organization. Warner was the shortstop on the same Wyoming team that featured the best player in the Western Athletic Conference back in 1991, two-way star—and fellow Cardinal draft pick—Rigo Beltran. I guess if you pay a scout to watch WAC games, you better get something out of it.

Jack Wilson · SS · Bats R · Age 22

YEAR	TEAM	LGE	AB	H	DB	TP	HR	BB/SO	R	RBI	SB	CS	OUT	BA	OBP	SLG	EQA	EQR	DEFENSE
1998	JohnsnCy	App	239	70	15	2	3	10/33	27	18	6	3	172	.293	.326	.410	.248	26	58-SS 90
1999	Peoria	Mid	255	78	21	3	3	9/24	35	22	5	2	179	.306	.333	.447	.261	31	62-SS 95
1999	Potomac	Car	260	71	10	1	2	14/30	36	15	3	2	191	.273	.312	.342	.222	22	63-SS 94
2000	*St Louis*	*NL*	*305*	*94*	*19*	*2*	*4*	*17/39*	*44*	*43*	*5*	*2*	*213*	*.308*	*.345*	*.423*	*.260*	*37*	

The Cardinals like to find good athletes to play shortstop, and Wilson played a lot of soccer. That probably helps explain the 60 times he booted the ball in 1998. Nevertheless, the Cardinals believe he will turn into a good shortstop. Like Butler before him, he hit well at Peoria, just not as well. He's more of a high-average hitter, with little patience or power. While anyone who translates this well this young bears watching, wait to see if he survives Double-A before getting excited. Wilson struggled in the California Fall League.

Jason Woolf · SS · Bats B · Age 23

YEAR	TEAM	LGE	AB	H	DB	TP	HR	BB/SO	R	RBI	SB	CS	OUT	BA	OBP	SLG	EQA	EQR	DEFENSE
1997	Pr Willm	Car	260	62	11	2	6	46/75	45	16	13	3	201	.238	.361	.365	.260	35	70-SS 97
1998	Arkansas	Tex	293	69	21	3	3	27/93	44	14	15	3	227	.235	.314	.358	.237	31	74-SS 101
1999	Arkansas	Tex	321	78	16	3	7	23/94	36	18	6	2	245	.243	.306	.377	.233	32	73-SS 92
2000	*St Louis*	*NL*	*313*	*78*	*18*	*3*	*7*	*39/95*	*52*	*39*	*14*	*3*	*238*	*.249*	*.332*	*.393*	*.253*	*38*	

Woolf exemplifies just about everything you could say about the Cardinals' player-development program when the player isn't someone like J.D. Drew. He's athletic, runs well and has a strong arm, but hasn't coverted those tools into performance. Part of the problem is that he's injury-prone, missing time to broken fingers, strained quads, strained hamstrings, back spasms and a wonky elbow. There's talk of moving him to the outfield; he could hit well enough to be a useful fourth outfielder, but expectations were higher than that.

PITCHERS (Averages: ERA: 4.50 / H/9: 9.00 / HR/9: 1.00 / BB/9: 3.50 / K/9: 6.50 / KWH: 1.00)

Juan Acevedo   Throws R   Age 30

YEAR	TEAM	LGE	IP	H	ER	HR	BB	K	ERA	W	L	H/9	HR/9	BB/9	K/9	KWH	PERA
1997	Norfolk	Int	112.7	124	60	7	37	80	4.79	6	7	9.91	0.56	2.96	6.39	1.04	4.31
1997	NY Mets	NL	46.7	55	25	6	23	31	4.82	2	3	10.61	1.16	4.44	5.98	0.57	5.98
1998	St Louis	NL	99.0	83	29	7	31	54	2.64	8	3	7.55	0.64	2.82	4.91	0.85	3.09
1999	St Louis	NL	102.0	114	66	16	46	50	5.82	4	7	10.06	1.41	4.06	4.41	0.36	5.82

What went wrong? The easiest explanation is that he was a victim of the general confusion about what to do with the pitching staff. Closing allowed his breaking stuff to get stale, so that when they bumped him back into the rotation a month into the season, he didn't have command of his curve, slider or change, and he's never been overpowering. Traded to Milwaukee for Fernando Vina, there's a rotation spot waiting for him.

John Ambrose   Throws R   Age 25

YEAR	TEAM	LGE	IP	H	ER	HR	BB	K	ERA	W	L	H/9	HR/9	BB/9	K/9	KWH	PERA
1997	WnstnSlm	Car	140.0	176	124	19	136	100	7.97	4	12	11.31	1.22	8.74	6.43	0.31	8.42
1998	Birmnghm	Sou	133.0	174	91	19	68	83	6.16	5	10	11.77	1.29	4.60	5.62	0.44	6.97
1999	Arkansas	Tex	94.3	134	84	11	88	58	8.01	2	8	12.78	1.05	8.40	5.53	0.21	9.06

Ambrose is a big guy who throws in the 90s with zero command. Having already gotten burned by giving up Sean Lowe to get him, the Cards are talking about making him a closer because he throws hard and he's big, and that's what closers are supposed to look like. While I'm in favor of making a silk purse out of a sow's ear, eventually you'll notice the smell.

Rick Ankiel   Throws L   Age 20

YEAR	TEAM	LGE	IP	H	ER	HR	BB	K	ERA	W	L	H/9	HR/9	BB/9	K/9	KWH	PERA
1998	Peoria	Mid	33.3	20	11	0	16	28	2.97	3	1	5.40	0.00	4.32	7.56	1.83	2.16
1998	Pr Willm	Car	117.3	121	66	11	52	130	5.06	6	7	9.28	0.84	3.99	9.97	2.01	4.68
1999	Arkansas	Tex	47.0	30	7	2	19	60	1.34	5	0	5.74	0.38	3.64	11.49	4.72	2.30
1999	Memphis	PCL	86.7	71	34	6	52	99	3.53	6	4	7.37	0.62	5.40	10.28	1.98	3.95
1999	St Louis	NL	33.0	26	11	2	13	38	3.00	3	1	7.09	0.55	3.55	10.36	3.19	3.00

He's as good a pitching prospect as you're going to find. Ankiel can throw into the mid-90s, but he doesn't do it very consistently. His out pitch is a hammer curve. His problem so far is that he hasn't learned how to put batters away quickly, so that he runs through his 110-pitch limit early in games. They say he's coachable and will iron that out in time, but what pitching prospect has time working under LaRussa? After the winter shopping spree, Ankiel isn't guaranteed to be in the rotation but should win the fourth spot. Between his youth and the LaRussa/Duncan track record, you can't help but worry.

Manny Aybar   Throws R   Age 25

YEAR	TEAM	LGE	IP	H	ER	HR	BB	K	ERA	W	L	H/9	HR/9	BB/9	K/9	KWH	PERA
1997	Louisvil	AmA	135.0	142	64	9	50	102	4.27	8	7	9.47	0.60	3.33	6.80	1.09	4.27
1997	St Louis	NL	67.7	66	33	9	31	38	4.39	4	4	8.78	1.20	4.12	5.05	0.53	4.79
1998	St Louis	NL	82.7	91	57	6	44	55	6.21	3	6	9.91	0.65	4.79	5.99	0.56	5.12
1998	Memphis	PCL	78.7	69	27	7	19	54	3.09	6	3	7.89	0.80	2.17	6.18	1.66	3.20
1999	St Louis	NL	97.3	102	62	12	35	72	5.73	4	7	9.43	1.11	3.24	6.66	1.09	4.72

It says something about their year that the Cardinals did the right thing by letting Aybar get experience in middle relief, and it still turned out badly. As the season went on, he lost confidence in his slider, which only made things worse because his fastball lacks movement and his change-up is a work in progress. He gives up a lot of fly balls, so his trade to the Rockies in the Kile deal is the sort of thing that will hurt his career even more than you'd normally expect.

Alan Benes   Throws R   Age 28

YEAR	TEAM	LGE	IP	H	ER	HR	BB	K	ERA	W	L	H/9	HR/9	BB/9	K/9	KWH	PERA
1996	St Louis	NL	186.0	210	129	27	96	123	6.24	7	14	10.16	1.31	4.65	5.95	0.56	6.00
1997	St Louis	NL	160.7	129	58	13	72	149	3.25	12	6	7.23	0.73	4.03	8.35	1.79	3.47

(Alan Benes *continued*)

He's never going to be the same pitcher again. While the Cardinals are talking about his revamped delivery in which he isn't throwing across his body, he showed very little velocity during his rehabilitation work last year. He may reclaim some sort of career in the bullpen, and he might even have a nice run in the rotation this year. Wish him well, but don't bet on his being much more than a reminder of what they shouldn't do with Ankiel.

Ricky Bottalico		**Throws R**					**Age 30**									
YEAR	TEAM	LGE	IP	H	ER	HR	BB	K	ERA	W	L	H/9	HR/9	BB/9	K/9	KWH	PERA
1997	Philadel	NL	73.7	69	31	7	45	83	3.79	5	3	8.43	0.86	5.50	10.14	1.66	4.76
1998	Philadel	NL	44.3	55	30	7	27	26	6.09	2	3	11.17	1.42	5.48	5.28	0.34	7.11
1999	St Louis	NL	73.3	82	41	7	48	64	5.03	4	4	10.06	0.86	5.89	7.85	0.78	5.89

Physically, he's supposedly fine, but his 1999 gave no reason to believe he's going to get back to where he was. While you could say the Cardinals got the better part of the deal with the Phillies because Bottalico pitched and Brantley didn't, he was probably the majors' worst closer. It seems obvious he's pressing, and LaRussa isn't the type of steady hand who will make it easier for him to settle down. He's been non-tendered by the Cardinals, making him a free agent.

Kent Bottenfield		**Throws R**					**Age 31**									
YEAR	TEAM	LGE	IP	H	ER	HR	BB	K	ERA	W	L	H/9	HR/9	BB/9	K/9	KWH	PERA
1997	ChiCubs	NL	85.3	82	37	13	37	70	3.90	5	4	8.65	1.37	3.90	7.38	1.21	4.85
1998	St Louis	NL	135.3	129	70	13	60	94	4.66	7	8	8.58	0.86	3.99	6.25	0.85	4.32
1999	St Louis	NL	190.3	194	84	19	86	120	3.97	12	9	9.17	0.90	4.07	5.67	0.64	4.73

A good example of what happens when you give a utility pitcher a regular job: he's helpful until he wears down. The Cardinals shut him down a week early, squelching a possible bid for 20 wins. LaRussa had been careful to keep him around six innings per start for most of the season, but pushed him hard in late August, when the bullpen's collapse was in full bloom. While Duncan is being credited with turning Bottenfield around, Bottenfield has credited Rick Adair for teaching him the mental side of pitching in 1995 at Toledo. The Cardinals deserve credit for using him.

Justin Brunette		**Throws L**					**Age 24**									
YEAR	TEAM	LGE	IP	H	ER	HR	BB	K	ERA	W	L	H/9	HR/9	BB/9	K/9	KWH	PERA
1999	Peoria	Mid	39.7	47	13	3	20	29	2.95	3	1	10.66	0.68	4.54	6.58	0.67	5.45
1999	Arkansas	Tex	16.3	26	14	3	9	18	7.71	1	1	14.33	1.65	4.96	9.92	1.03	9.37

Brunette blew out his elbow in 1997, but surgery gave his fastball better life and velocity, and now the Cardinals have a left-hander who gets it up into the 90s with good control. He's just a name to remember in case anything bad happens to Paul Spoljaric or if Scott Radinsky isn't healthy.

Rich Croushore		**Throws R**					**Age 29**									
YEAR	TEAM	LGE	IP	H	ER	HR	BB	K	ERA	W	L	H/9	HR/9	BB/9	K/9	KWH	PERA
1997	Arkansas	Tex	79.0	140	69	8	47	52	7.86	2	7	15.95	0.91	5.35	5.92	0.31	9.57
1997	Louisvil	AmA	42.3	42	16	3	15	35	3.40	3	2	8.93	0.64	3.19	7.44	1.45	4.04
1998	Memphis	PCL	27.0	24	18	3	10	32	6.00	1	2	8.00	1.00	3.33	10.67	3.19	4.00
1998	St Louis	NL	54.7	45	30	6	30	45	4.94	3	3	7.41	0.99	4.94	7.41	1.12	4.12
1999	St Louis	NL	72.0	68	38	8	41	85	4.75	4	4	8.50	1.00	5.13	10.63	1.94	4.87

An owner of the rarely seen right-handed screwball, which means his manager has to pick his spots. If he's brought in for innings with plenty of left-handed batters due up, he'll be more effective. If he's put into a closer's role and asked to get Sammy Sosa or Jeff Bagwell or Mike Piazza with the game on the line, expect more game-losing shots to the deepest recesses of the left field grandstand. Croushore was traded to the Rockies in the Kile deal, so there isn't a lot of reason to be optimistic about his future.

Matt DeWitt		**Throws R**					**Age 22**									
YEAR	TEAM	LGE	IP	H	ER	HR	BB	K	ERA	W	L	H/9	HR/9	BB/9	K/9	KWH	PERA
1997	Peoria	Mid	145.0	198	107	20	70	85	6.64	5	11	12.29	1.24	4.34	5.28	0.39	7.14
1998	Pr Willm	Car	135.7	180	94	17	24	84	6.24	5	10	11.94	1.13	1.59	5.57	1.22	5.57
1999	Arkansas	Tex	136.3	182	102	21	71	86	6.73	5	10	12.01	1.39	4.69	5.68	0.43	7.26

Although he had a rough first year in Double-A, he throws hard and has a good slider. The curve and change-up aren't there yet, which is another way of saying he's probably better off as a reliever. DeWitt was traded to the Blue Jays in the Hentgen deal.

Chad Hutchinson — Throws R — Age 23

YEAR	TEAM	LGE	IP	H	ER	HR	BB	K	ERA	W	L	H/9	HR/9	BB/9	K/9	KWH	PERA
1998	New Jrsy	NYP	14.0	21	10	0	5	12	6.43	1	1	13.50	0.00	3.21	7.71	1.02	5.79
1998	Pr Willm	Car	26.7	27	17	5	15	22	5.74	1	2	9.11	1.69	5.06	7.43	0.89	6.07
1999	Arkansas	Tex	130.3	150	93	12	101	121	6.42	5	9	10.36	0.83	6.97	8.36	0.72	6.56
1999	Memphis	PCL	11.3	5	3	1	9	13	2.38	1	0	3.97	0.79	7.15	10.32	2.81	3.18

He fell into the second round in the 1998 draft because of his potential football career, but the Cardinals pulled him away from the NFL with a $3.4 million major-league deal. Not bad for Stanford's #2 starter behind the Royals' Jeff Austin. Hutchinson does things you have to like: his fastball is heavy with great movement, which gets plenty of grounders, and his curve has bite. He's towards the back of the line in the fight for the fifth spot in the Cardinals' rotation.

Tris Jerue — Throws R — Age 24

YEAR	TEAM	LGE	IP	H	ER	HR	BB	K	ERA	W	L	H/9	HR/9	BB/9	K/9	KWH	PERA
1997	New Jrsy	NYP	63.7	104	51	5	32	35	7.21	2	5	14.70	0.71	4.52	4.95	0.28	8.06
1998	Peoria	Mid	120.0	147	68	11	63	68	5.10	6	7	11.03	0.82	4.73	5.10	0.37	6.00
1998	Pr Willm	Car	39.0	42	20	0	16	24	4.62	2	2	9.69	0.00	3.69	5.54	0.64	3.92
1999	Potomac	Car	13.3	24	16	0	10	6	10.80	0	1	16.20	0.00	6.75	4.05	0.11	9.45

He's an object lesson in why we really shouldn't talk about A-ball pitchers. Like Aybar, he was a converted infielder with a good fastball and effective slider, but his fastball has better movement than Aybar's and he was even making progress on his change-up. But we're talking about pitchers, and aptitude and talent take a backseat to the ability to stay healthy, and Jerue blew out his arm in 1999.

Jose Jimenez — Throws R — Age 26

YEAR	TEAM	LGE	IP	H	ER	HR	BB	K	ERA	W	L	H/9	HR/9	BB/9	K/9	KWH	PERA
1997	Pr Willm	Car	133.0	169	99	14	51	55	6.70	5	10	11.44	0.95	3.45	3.72	0.26	5.82
1998	Arkansas	Tex	160.3	196	95	9	85	67	5.33	7	11	11.00	0.51	4.77	3.76	0.20	5.67
1998	St Louis	NL	21.3	22	8	0	9	12	3.38	1	1	9.28	0.00	3.80	5.06	0.54	3.80
1999	St Louis	NL	163.3	170	105	15	68	109	5.79	7	11	9.37	0.83	3.75	6.01	0.77	4.63
1999	Memphis	PCL	25.7	31	10	0	10	14	3.51	2	1	10.87	0.00	3.51	4.91	0.47	4.56

His amazing sinker makes him the ultimate one-trick pony, but mechanical problems kept even that from working consistently, as he'd leave it up where it could get hammered. When it does work, he can post stretches like the one in which he had five quality starts in six games, starting with the no-hitter. He's still learning to change speeds and get his slider working, and if he masters either, he'll stop redefining "maddening inconsistency." Moving to Coors, he'll be an interesting test case for how well an extreme groundball pitcher can succeed a mile up. I'm still optimistic about him, for no good reason.

Kevin Lovingier — Throws L — Age 28

YEAR	TEAM	LGE	IP	H	ER	HR	BB	K	ERA	W	L	H/9	HR/9	BB/9	K/9	KWH	PERA
1997	Arkansas	Tex	65.3	87	36	4	33	64	4.96	3	4	11.98	0.55	4.55	8.82	1.07	6.20
1998	Arkansas	Tex	21.3	25	12	2	17	19	5.06	1	1	10.55	0.84	7.17	8.02	0.63	6.75
1998	Memphis	PCL	55.0	43	25	7	38	51	4.09	3	3	7.04	1.15	6.22	8.35	1.19	4.58
1999	Memphis	PCL	74.3	68	44	7	47	52	5.33	3	5	8.23	0.85	5.69	6.30	0.63	4.72

Lovingier throws hard and has a good split-fingered fastball, but he's not being groomed for a setup role. He has the misfortune of not being an ex-Athletic, so he doesn't get the same opportunities as Mike Mohler. If he keeps at it long enough, he could still have a career.

Larry Luebbers — Throws R — Age 30

YEAR	TEAM	LGE	IP	H	ER	HR	BB	K	ERA	W	L	H/9	HR/9	BB/9	K/9	KWH	PERA
1997	Richmond	Int	134.7	210	115	20	48	74	7.69	4	11	14.03	1.34	3.21	4.95	0.41	7.89
1998	Memphis	PCL	159.0	209	104	22	55	89	5.89	7	11	11.83	1.25	3.11	5.04	0.51	6.28
1999	Memphis	PCL	123.7	142	62	13	39	66	4.51	7	7	10.33	0.95	2.84	4.80	0.59	4.95
1999	St Louis	NL	45.7	45	25	8	15	15	4.93	2	3	8.87	1.58	2.96	2.96	0.25	4.73

(Larry Luebbers *continued*)

It had been five years since Luebbers last got a shot at the majors (with the Reds in 1993), but he was smart enough to re-sign as a minor-league free agent with the Cardinals. He said he had a feeling he'd get an opportunity, but he had clues: all the guys coming through Memphis on rehab assignments, or perhaps all the scar tissue he could spot in the locker room. Luebbers is a better alternative to the usual Steve Ontiveros signing to give you somebody at Triple-A who can pitch if you lose a starter: he doesn't throw hard, but he throws strikes and stays healthy.

Mike Mohler　　Throws L　　Age 31

YEAR	TEAM	LGE	IP	H	ER	HR	BB	K	ERA	W	L	H/9	HR/9	BB/9	K/9	KWH	PERA
1997	Oakland	AL	105.7	106	55	10	55	67	4.68	6	6	9.03	0.85	4.68	5.71	0.58	4.85
1998	Oakland	AL	60.7	68	35	6	27	42	5.19	3	4	10.09	0.89	4.01	6.23	0.72	5.19
1999	Memphis	PCL	14.3	16	5	0	6	13	3.14	1	1	10.05	0.00	3.77	8.16	1.32	4.40
1999	St Louis	NL	49.3	46	24	3	22	30	4.38	3	2	8.39	0.55	4.01	5.47	0.66	3.83

Another somebody who played for LaRussa in Oakland, so he was bound to be a Cardinal someday. He was the Cardinals' best reliever down the stretch, doing a good job preventing inherited runners from scoring and getting left-handed batters out. He and Paul Spoljaric will battle for the second left-hander job behind Radinsky.

Matt Morris　　Throws R　　Age 25

YEAR	TEAM	LGE	IP	H	ER	HR	BB	K	ERA	W	L	H/9	HR/9	BB/9	K/9	KWH	PERA
1996	Arkansas	Tex	157.0	203	91	16	59	110	5.22	7	10	11.64	0.92	3.38	6.31	0.75	5.90
1997	St Louis	NL	215.7	210	86	12	73	138	3.59	15	9	8.76	0.50	3.05	5.76	0.93	3.71
1998	St Louis	NL	115.0	101	35	8	44	76	2.74	9	4	7.90	0.63	3.44	5.95	0.97	3.52

He was good, wasn't he? Maybe he'll change his last name to Forsch to make his comeback seem all the more impressive. It might at least make Duncan and LaRussa listen if they think he's 50 and he says he's tired.

Darren Oliver　　Throws L　　Age 29

YEAR	TEAM	LGE	IP	H	ER	HR	BB	K	ERA	W	L	H/9	HR/9	BB/9	K/9	KWH	PERA
1997	Texas	AL	206.3	199	97	27	83	105	4.23	12	11	8.68	1.18	3.62	4.58	0.50	4.54
1998	Texas	AL	109.3	128	71	10	46	60	5.84	4	8	10.54	0.82	3.79	4.94	0.46	5.35
1998	St Louis	NL	57.7	65	31	7	25	28	4.84	3	3	10.14	1.09	3.90	4.37	0.36	5.46
1999	St Louis	NL	196.0	194	89	15	71	115	4.09	12	10	8.91	0.69	3.26	5.28	0.72	4.04

Oliver strengthened his free agency case with a 3.35 ERA after the All-Star break. Since coming over from Texas, he's improved both his curve and his change-up. More than anyone else on the staff, Duncan and LaRussa can point to him as an example of someone they helped. He'll make big money, but he's a bad risk.

Donovan Osborne　　Throws L　　Age 31

YEAR	TEAM	LGE	IP	H	ER	HR	BB	K	ERA	W	L	H/9	HR/9	BB/9	K/9	KWH	PERA
1997	St Louis	NL	80.0	85	46	11	24	47	5.18	4	5	9.56	1.24	2.70	5.29	0.81	4.72
1998	St Louis	NL	84.7	84	41	11	24	57	4.36	5	4	8.93	1.17	2.55	6.06	1.20	4.25
1999	St Louis	NL	29.0	34	17	4	10	20	5.28	1	2	10.55	1.24	3.10	6.21	0.88	5.59

He started off as the Opening Day starter and blew out his shoulder by the first week of May. This completed the guaranteed portion of the contract Jocketty gave him after his first (and only) 30-start season, in 1996; while the Cardinals claim he was just unlucky to miss most of the last three years, they elected to not pick up their option for 2000.

Lance Painter　　Throws L　　Age 32

YEAR	TEAM	LGE	IP	H	ER	HR	BB	K	ERA	W	L	H/9	HR/9	BB/9	K/9	KWH	PERA
1997	Louisvil	AmA	20.3	20	16	2	5	19	7.08	1	1	8.85	0.89	2.21	8.41	2.70	3.98
1997	St Louis	NL	17.0	13	9	1	8	10	4.76	1	1	6.88	0.53	4.24	5.29	0.72	3.18
1998	St Louis	NL	47.7	43	23	5	29	37	4.34	3	2	8.12	0.94	5.48	6.99	0.82	4.72
1999	St Louis	NL	63.0	63	34	5	24	54	4.86	3	4	9.00	0.71	3.43	7.71	1.44	4.14

Some people just don't learn. When LaRussa started juggling his rotation randomly, he decided to make Painter a starter, sort of like the previous summer's decision to make the equally fragile Mike Busby a starter. Busby lasted two starts, while Painter made it all the way to four before going to the DL with a strained shoulder. After he healed he went back to the pen, where his soft slop has its situational uses. Like DeWitt, Painter was traded to the Jays in the Hentgen deal.

Scott Radinsky   Throws L   Age 32

YEAR	TEAM	LGE	IP	H	ER	HR	BB	K	ERA	W	L	H/9	HR/9	BB/9	K/9	KWH	PERA
1997	LosAngls	NL	60.0	58	24	4	22	41	3.60	4	3	8.70	0.60	3.30	6.15	0.98	3.90
1998	LosAngls	NL	60.0	67	22	5	21	43	3.30	5	2	10.05	0.75	3.15	6.45	0.98	4.65
1999	St Louis	NL	27.3	27	15	2	18	16	4.94	1	2	8.89	0.66	5.93	5.27	0.39	4.94

Radinsky was a poor risk when the Cardinals signed him because he was coming off a year when he had Chavez Ravine going for him and still managed to let a lot of inherited runners score. He did the same with the Cardinals before having surgery to clean up his elbow. He has two more guaranteed years, so he's the bullpen's version of Donovan Osborne.

Britt Reames   Throws R   Age 26

YEAR	TEAM	LGE	IP	H	ER	HR	BB	K	ERA	W	L	H/9	HR/9	BB/9	K/9	KWH	PERA
1996	Peoria	Mid	149.0	137	63	8	50	116	3.81	10	7	8.28	0.48	3.02	7.01	1.47	3.44
1999	Potomac	Car	33.0	48	31	3	28	14	8.45	1	3	13.09	0.82	7.64	3.82	0.11	8.45

He's just now pitching following one of the slowest recoveries ever from Tommy John elbow ligament transplant surgery. They didn't find the tear until 1998, and his elbow was still sore at the start of the year. Not really a prospect, but he did have an amazing 1996. Reames didn't throw hard before the injury: he was a short curveball pitcher. He's someone to remember as an explanation of why scouts get creeped out by short right-handers.

Heathcliff Slocumb   Throws R   Age 34

YEAR	TEAM	LGE	IP	H	ER	HR	BB	K	ERA	W	L	H/9	HR/9	BB/9	K/9	KWH	PERA
1997	Boston	AL	48.0	54	28	4	35	37	5.25	2	3	10.13	0.75	6.56	6.94	0.54	6.19
1997	Seattle	AL	29.0	24	11	2	15	28	3.41	2	1	7.45	0.62	4.66	8.69	1.63	3.72
1998	Seattle	AL	69.0	67	35	5	46	52	4.57	4	4	8.74	0.65	6.00	6.78	0.66	4.96
1999	Baltimor	AL	8.7	15	11	2	8	12	11.42	0	1	15.58	2.08	8.31	12.46	0.90	12.46
1999	St Louis	NL	53.7	48	14	3	29	46	2.35	5	1	8.05	0.50	4.86	7.71	1.14	4.02

Slocumb's career ought to set off alarms every time some general manager has the great idea of giving him a multi-year contract, like the Cardinals just did. There's no doubt that he can be a useful major-league reliever. The problem is that lots of people can be good major-league relievers and not all of them are as inconsistent as Slocumb. Why tie yourself down, and why spend much to keep him?

Robert "Bud" Smith   Throws L   Age 20

YEAR	TEAM	LGE	IP	H	ER	HR	BB	K	ERA	W	L	H/9	HR/9	BB/9	K/9	KWH	PERA
1998	JohnsnCy	App	55.3	112	56	10	44	40	9.11	1	5	18.22	1.63	7.16	6.51	0.24	13.17
1999	Peoria	Mid	49.0	68	25	5	18	42	4.59	2	3	12.49	0.92	3.31	7.71	1.08	6.43
1999	Potomac	Car	99.7	113	57	3	37	69	5.15	5	6	10.20	0.27	3.34	6.23	0.85	4.33

The organization's best pitching prospect behind Ankiel, Smith mixes a good fastball, curve and change-up. Despite being drafted in 1998 out of junior-college ball, he's probably ready for Double-A, which means he could be in the majors for a cup of coffee by season's end. He's extremely young, so he'll need to have his workload watched closely.

Clint Sodowsky   Throws R   Age 27

YEAR	TEAM	LGE	IP	H	ER	HR	BB	K	ERA	W	L	H/9	HR/9	BB/9	K/9	KWH	PERA
1997	Calgary	PCL	14.0	16	7	1	7	8	4.50	1	1	10.29	0.64	4.50	5.14	0.43	5.14
1997	Pittsbrg	NL	53.3	46	19	6	36	48	3.21	4	2	7.76	1.01	6.08	8.10	1.04	4.89
1998	Arizona	NL	77.3	91	58	5	42	40	6.75	3	6	10.59	0.58	4.89	4.66	0.31	5.59
1999	Memphis	PCL	75.7	90	56	12	38	41	6.66	3	5	10.70	1.43	4.52	4.88	0.37	6.42
1999	St Louis	NL	6.3	15	11	1	6	2	15.63	0	1	21.32	1.42	8.53	2.84	0.03	15.63

He was picked up for John Frascatore, a useful right-handed reliever, because the Cards were out of roster spots and needed someone with options. Sodowsky had one, and now it's gone and he's a minor-league free agent. Along with the Ambrose/Lowe swap, another move that left the Cards short of pitchers. Sodowsky still has a nice sinker and could be useful somewhere.

Gene Stechschulte   Throws R   Age 26

YEAR	TEAM	LGE	IP	H	ER	HR	BB	K	ERA	W	L	H/9	HR/9	BB/9	K/9	KWH	PERA
1997	New Jrsy	NYP	30.0	67	25	3	27	17	7.50	1	2	20.10	0.90	8.10	5.10	0.12	13.80
1998	Peoria	Mid	57.0	88	44	1	32	42	6.95	2	4	13.89	0.16	5.05	6.63	0.47	7.11
1999	Arkansas	Tex	37.3	52	35	4	27	30	8.44	1	3	12.54	0.96	6.51	7.23	0.48	7.96

The latest model off of the Cardinals' line of minor-league closers. What, you've forgotten Eric Miller, Jeff Matulevich, Craig Grasser, Steve Montgomery, Travis Welch, Curtis King, Kevin Crafton and Armando Almanza already? These guys all logged 30-save seasons in the Cardinal farm system over the years. Montgomery has made it in the majors, and Almanza should. Stechshulte doesn't have their talent. For both of you playing PCL rotisserie baseball and looking for a guy to give you a bunch of saves, this is probably your man.

Garrett Stephenson   Throws R   Age 28

YEAR	TEAM	LGE	IP	H	ER	HR	BB	K	ERA	W	L	H/9	HR/9	BB/9	K/9	KWH	PERA
1997	Scran-WB	Int	27.3	32	21	6	13	22	6.91	1	2	10.54	1.98	4.28	7.24	0.87	6.91
1997	Philadel	NL	116.0	106	45	12	40	75	3.49	8	5	8.22	0.93	3.10	5.82	0.99	3.88
1998	Philadel	NL	23.7	32	24	3	21	17	9.13	1	2	12.17	1.14	7.99	6.46	0.32	8.37
1998	Scran-WB	Int	68.3	93	56	14	18	40	7.38	2	6	12.25	1.84	2.37	5.27	0.71	6.98
1999	Memphis	PCL	24.7	23	9	2	9	15	3.28	2	1	8.39	0.73	3.28	5.47	0.81	3.65
1999	St Louis	NL	85.0	89	40	10	28	57	4.24	5	4	9.42	1.06	2.96	6.04	0.97	4.55

One of the fun things that's developed over the last two years is the rivalry between the Cardinals and the Phillies, not just because of Drew but also because of the guys they've swapped. Bottalico has his beef with Terry Francona, and LaRussa has his problems with Ron Gant. But the best part is Stephenson, who clearly detests the Phillies organization for mishandling an injured ankle and shoulder in 1998, a dispute that ended up in a grievance hearing, which he won. He's also had a war of words with Curt Schilling, one he might win since he's the healthy one now. While he'll never have a year as good as his partial season in 1997, he can be a good fifth starter.

Mark Thompson   Throws R   Age 29

YEAR	TEAM	LGE	IP	H	ER	HR	BB	K	ERA	W	L	H/9	HR/9	BB/9	K/9	KWH	PERA
1997	Colorado	NL	31.7	38	24	8	14	9	6.82	1	3	10.80	2.27	3.98	2.56	0.11	7.39
1998	Colorado	NL	26.0	35	19	8	14	14	6.58	1	2	12.12	2.77	4.85	4.85	0.30	9.35
1999	Indianap	Int	51.0	56	34	5	32	24	6.00	2	4	9.88	0.88	5.65	4.24	0.24	5.82
1999	Memphis	PCL	50.0	51	23	3	24	21	4.14	3	3	9.18	0.54	4.32	3.78	0.27	4.50
1999	St Louis	NL	29.0	26	11	1	17	21	3.41	2	1	8.07	0.31	5.28	6.52	0.75	4.03

He's slowly adapting to life without his fastball after two major surgeries. Thompson was pitching in the Reds' organization until Bowden had too many guys trying to rehab at Indianapolis at once, and Thompson complained about not getting enough innings. Picked up by the Cards when they started running out of people at both the major- and minor-league levels, he's just roster filler.

Support-Neutral Records — ST. LOUIS CARDINALS — Park Effect: -5.7%

PITCHER	GS	IP	R	SNW	SNL	SNPCT	W	L	RA	APW	SNVA	SNWAR
Juan Acevedo	12	59.7	46	2.5	5.4	.312	2	3	6.94	-1.28	-1.39	-0.90
Rick Ankiel	5	28.0	12	1.9	1.1	.629	0	1	3.86	0.32	0.32	0.62
Manny Aybar	1	3.7	9	0.0	0.9	.002	0	1	22.09	-0.67	-0.45	-0.39
Kent Bottenfield	31	190.3	91	11.2	9.8	.531	18	7	4.30	1.26	0.54	2.23
Jose Jimenez	28	161.0	110	8.8	11.4	.435	5	13	6.15	-2.09	-1.28	0.21
Larry Luebbers	8	45.7	27	2.4	2.9	.461	3	3	5.32	-0.19	-0.16	0.19
Kent Mercker	18	91.3	58	4.9	6.7	.424	6	5	5.72	-0.77	-0.83	-0.01
Darren Oliver	30	196.3	96	12.2	9.2	.569	9	9	4.40	1.09	1.27	3.09
Donovan Osborne	6	29.3	18	1.3	2.2	.373	1	3	5.52	-0.19	-0.42	-0.18
Lance Painter	4	18.0	11	1.1	1.1	.507	0	2	5.50	-0.11	-0.05	0.18
Clint Sodowsky	1	3.3	8	0.0	0.9	.010	0	1	21.60	-0.59	-0.43	-0.36
Garrett Stephenson	12	75.0	35	4.6	3.6	.557	5	3	4.20	0.58	0.44	1.08
Mark Thompson	5	29.3	12	1.9	1.4	.581	1	3	3.68	0.39	0.22	0.52
TOTALS	161	931.0	533	52.8	56.7	.482	50	54	5.15	-2.25	-2.22	6.28

The LaRussa/Duncan partnership's reputation for successful pitching reclamation projects is intact. While they haven't had any cases in St. Louis as spectacular as Dave Stewart or Dennis Eckersley, there have been a number of more recent pitchers who have done their best work under LaRussa/Duncan. Since 1992, Andy Benes's Support-Neutral Winning Percentage (SNPct) under LaRussa/Duncan was .598; under other managers, it was .515. Todd Stottlemyre under LaRussa/Duncan was .514; under others he was .483. Kent Bottenfield under LaRussa/Duncan was .506; under others he was .466. Darren Oliver under LaRussa/Duncan was .543; under others he was .506. Benes and Oliver had been in decline before joining the Cardinals. And all four improved markedly from their first year with LaRussa/Duncan to their second. . . . Jose Jimenez's season certainly wasn't very good, but it was still better than his 6.15 runs allowed average (RA) would have you believe. That's because he received the majors' worst bullpen support. He turned 20 runners over to his relievers during 1999. Given the bases those runners occupied and the number of outs when he left, those runners would have been expected to score 7.1 runs. 15 of the 20 actually did score, adding almost eight runs to Jimenez's runs-allowed total over what he could have expected, and adding .45 to his RA.

Pitcher Abuse Points

PITCHER	AGE	GS	PAP	PAP/S	WKLD	MAX	1-90	91-100	101-110	111-120	121-130	131-140	141+
Juan Acevedo	29	12	3	0.3	0.4	103	9	2	1	0	0	0	0
Rick Ankiel	19	5	17	3.4	10.8	109	3	0	2	0	0	0	0
Manny Aybar	24	1	0	0.0	0.0	88	1	0	0	0	0	0	0
Kent Bottenfield	30	31	406	13.1	17.5	142	6	9	6	5	4	0	1
Jose Jimenez	25	28	110	3.9	8.5	121	10	6	10	1	1	0	0
Larry Luebbers	29	8	24	3.0	4.5	114	5	1	1	1	0	0	0
Kent Mercker	31	18	89	4.9	5.8	121	9	3	4	1	1	0	0
Darren Oliver	28	30	291	9.7	16.2	126	2	11	8	6	3	0	0
Donovan Osborne	30	6	10	1.7	2.2	106	4	0	2	0	0	0	0
Lance Painter	31	4	0	0.0	0.0	85	4	0	0	0	0	0	0
Clint Sodowsky	26	1	0	0.0	0.0	83	1	0	0	0	0	0	0
Garrett Stephenson	27	12	154	12.8	23.5	123	2	1	5	1	3	0	0
Mark Thompson	28	5	3	0.6	1.0	103	2	2	1	0	0	0	0
ST. LOUIS		161	1107	6.9	11.0	142	58	35	40	15	12	0	1
Ranking (NL)				10	9								

Tony LaRussa committed few sins last year, but until September he didn't have any temptations either. Since Rick Ankiel's arm is the most delicate commodity in the game right now, how LaRussa handles him is the single most important question facing the Cardinals in 2000. The warning signs are there: LaRussa blew out Alan Benes in 1997 with a heavy second-half workload, lost Matt Morris for the first half of 1998, and when Morris came back, showed he hadn't learned anything from either experience. The Cardinals kept Ankiel on a strict 110-pitch limit all season and LaRussa stuck to that, but in two of Ankiel's five starts, LaRussa sent him out to pitch the seventh inning despite obvious signs of fatigue. I hope I'm wrong, but if Ankiel pitches as well as Wood did in 1998, I think LaRussa will work him just as hard as Jim Riggleman worked Wood, perhaps harder.

San Diego Padres

Leave it to the national media to screw everything up. The Padres finished 1998 as an old NL Champion faced with the prospect of either re-signing thirty-somethings Ken Caminiti, Steve Finley and Kevin Brown, or letting them walk. The decision was made tougher by extenuating circumstances such as Brown's postseason dominance and owner John Moores's affection for Caminiti and Finley. In spite of all this, General Manager Kevin Towers made the right choice in letting the stars join other teams for tons of money or, in Caminiti's case, an easier commute from home to work.

With the Padres having bit the bullet on their stars, you could have made a case for Towers's being completely ruthless: he could have let first baseman Wally Joyner find another team to play for, and he could have traded Andy Ashby, Joey Hamilton, Greg Vaughn and Quilvio Veras for whatever prospects he could get. After losing Brown, nobody really thought the Padres had what it took to contend for another title in 1999, and if you're not contending, you're wasting both your veterans' time and your money by keeping them around. San Diego would have stumbled to a 100-loss season; while the fans wouldn't have been happy, the minor-league system would have received a shot in the arm, and the additional prospects would have come in handy when the team moves into its new digs in 2002.

There's one thing we tend to overlook in baseball analysis, and that's what the fans are going to think of a move. We do so with good reason. Over time, winning tends to heal all wounds, but it isn't realistic to expect every general manager to sack veterans at the first sign of decline. In today's short-term-oriented baseball atmosphere, many GMs don't have the job security to ride out the rough period that follows such moves. Outside influences, from know-nothing owners to influential columnists to, yes, the fans, will have an impact on any general manager's decisions. Otherwise, the GM risks looking like Dan Duquette, whom most analysts like but whom many fans believe to be a heartless, stat-drunk robot for running Red Sox legends Mike Greenwell, Roger Clemens

and Mo Vaughn out of town. And that's despite the franchise's success on his watch. Making fan-unfriendly decisions in front of two years of .425 baseball is a hard road to travel.

Towers ended up doing the decent thing as far as giving people baseball to watch in 1999. He brought Joyner back, and while he traded major-league players Joey Hamilton and Greg Vaughn, part of the booty was a replacement for each departed player, in the form of Woody Williams and Reggie Sanders. Towers kept Ashby and Sterling Hitchcock in the fold and signed closer Trevor Hoffman to a long-term deal. The Padres entered 1999 with a payroll that was actually higher than it had been in 1998. Without shelling out tens of millions to sign a free agent, the front office gave fans a team that had a good chance of winning more games than it lost.

Of course, things didn't work out that way. The injury bug bit early and often, and other than a 13-game winning streak in June and Tony Gwynn's 3000th hit, the fans didn't have much to cheer. Beyond that, the national media was throwing around terms like "Fire Sale, Part Two" all summer. Articles that were otherwise completely rational made noises about the Padres front office mercilessly dumping now that Proposition C had passed and the East Village ballpark was on the way. According to this line of thinking, once the Padres got what they wanted, any plans they had of putting a good product on the field disintegrated. "They screwed us" was a mantra repeated daily on talk radio in San Diego. Never mind that letting the scandalously recompensed Brown and the aging duo of Finley and Caminiti walk—while collecting the compensatory draft picks—was much, much different from dealing Fred McGriff and a 23-year-old Gary Sheffield for squid scraps.

The Padres went further than they needed to in order to put a major-league-caliber team on the field, and they played Tinky Winky to the public's Jerry Falwell for their trouble.

If anything good can come of this nonsense, we'll see it the next time a team that has been classified as "small market" is coming off a good season and has a bunch of old, expensive free agents to consider. Hopefully, that team's

Padres Prospectus

1999 record: 74-88; Fourth place, NL West

Pythagorean W/L: 74-88

Runs scored: 710 (15th in NL)

Runs allowed: 781 (6th in NL)

Team EQA: .253 (12th in NL)

1999 team age: 29.3 (5th-oldest in NL)

1999 park: Qualcomm Stadium; moderate pitchers' park, decreased run scoring by 9%.

1999: Everything was being done with an eye towards 2002.

2000: They're not a terrible team, and should hover around 90 losses.

management will see the job that the media and many of the fans did on the Padres and consider the possibility that they're damned if they do and damned if they don't. We'll see a scorched-earth campaign that most analysts would probably approve of, and the team and its fans will probably end up better in the long run because of it. It's tough love, but considering the alternative, it makes a lot of sense.

Of course, the Padres didn't help themselves when it came to giving the impression they were serious about the 1999 season. If the reports coming out of the Cactus League—that an outfielder by the name of Garth Brooks was getting action with the Padres—weren't a harbinger of doom, I don't know what would be. There hasn't been such a waste of organized baseball's time since Michael Jordan soaked up a year of minor-league at-bats, and at least Jordan was an athlete. Brooks, to paraphrase Don Sutton, looked like he went to fantasy camp and decided to stay.

Cost/benefit analysis time: is the ink the organization gets for a stunt like this really worth the roster spot? The team missed a chance to look at one minor leaguer because of the Brooks situation, and they didn't do themselves any favors in terms of relations with the guys who were passed up in the process. "To suggest that a 37-year-old country singer could make one of our minor-league clubs insults not only everyone who's playing in the minors, but everyone who's sat there on draft day by a phone that didn't ring," noted Brendan Sullivan, a Padre prospect, at the time of the circus.

You almost wish that the Padres would have at least wasted a roster spot on someone amusing. Who wouldn't want to see the Undertaker giving some pencil-necked Double-A pitcher the bum's rush after an inside pitch? How about Junior Seau sliding hard into second, or Ryan Leaf getting plunked by a karmic purpose pitch? If the team was going to turn spring training into some sort of MTV Rock 'n' Jock extravaganza, they could have at least tailored it towards the local fans.

Maybe an attempt at attracting a younger demographic would have worked. Britney Spears is pretty athletic: why not see if she can turn a pivot? How about an all-Korn infield? Matt Damon pitching to Ben Affleck? (They're everywhere *else*, for crying out loud.) Next time the marketing department gets a bad idea, hopefully they'll at least execute it well.

Generally, Brooks and the Padre brass had a love-fest during the whole affair. One member of the front office who expressed some reservations about it was Director of Player Development Jim Skaalen, so it wasn't a complete surprise when Skaalen was fired towards the end of 1999 and replaced with Ted Simmons. Simmons, a former special assistant to Cleveland Indians General Manager John Hart, was given the newly created title of Vice President of Player Development and Scouting. He will play a large part in the future of this club. Most of Skaalen's cronies in the minor-league system have been reassigned or fired, and when the dust settles, the organization will look completely different.

Simmons has been given one assignment: bring a Cleveland-style renaissance to the San Diego Padres. The excellent Padre farm system of the late 1980s and early 1990s, which produced the Alomar brothers, Carlos Baerga, Benito Santiago, John Kruk, Shane Mack and Dave Hollins, is a memory. Lately, the system has been all but useless at producing position players, so Simmons has been given an unprecedented amount of power to right the ship.

Ironically, Skaalen's efforts in player development were starting to bear fruit by the end of the season. Due in large part to the windfall of draft picks the team got for losing its free agents, the 1999 draft already looks like a great one, with left-hander Mike Bynum, right-hander Jacob Peavy and first-round outfielder/track star Vince Faison all experiencing success in their first minor-league seasons. Third baseman Sean Burroughs, the team's first-round pick in 1998, had a season for the ages as an 18-year-old in the Midwest League. For the first time in years, the Padres have some depth in the minors; they have just one sure blue-chip prospect in Burroughs, but at least a few of the crop of current Padres prospects should be useful major-league players. The system has plenty of pitchers that could turn into solid major-league starters.

With the new tack management is taking on player development and scouting, the future of this franchise looks considerably brighter than it did at this time last year. Many current Padres properties (pitchers Matt Clement and Buddy Carlyle; Burroughs; outfielders Mike Darr, Gary Matthews and Ruben Rivera; shortstop Kevin Nicholson; catchers Ben Davis, Wiki Gonzalez and Wilbert Nieves) have a good chance of being major-league regulars or better in 2002.

The Padres were again aggressive in the trade market this offseason. In addition to the Ashby deal, in which they picked up Carlton Loewer, Adam Eaton and Steve Montgomery, the team swapped setup man Dan Miceli to Florida for #4 starter Brian Meadows. Meadows and Eaton will be in the mix for rotation slots, while Loewer will have one when he returns from an offseason hunting injury. Montgomery will replace Miceli in the pen. Just before Christmas, San Diego traded three regulars—Quilvio Veras, Reggie Sanders and Wally Joyner—to the Braves for Ryan Klesko, Bret Boone and pitching prospect Jason Shiell.

Klesko gives the Padres a left-handed power source they had lacked, but in reality none of these deals has brought in the kind of prospects the Padres need. They actually look a lot like last winter's efforts, the moves of a team afraid to throw itself whole-hog into a rebuilding process, and more concerned with the upcoming season than with the next good team. Continuing to think that way will keep the team from experiencing the highs of 1998 again, while doing nothing to prevent a repeat of the backlash of 1999.

HITTERS (Averages: BA: .270 / OBP: .340 / SLG: .430 / EQA: .260)

Dusty Allen　　　　OF/1B　　Bats R　Age 27

YEAR	TEAM	LGE	AB	H	DB	TP	HR	BB/SO	R	RBI	SB	CS	OUT	BA	OBP	SLG	EQA	EQR	DEFENSE	
1997	Mobile	Sou	478	98	24	2	12	59/136	58	51	1	2	382	.205	.292	.339	.214	41	76-1B 100	54-OF 76
1998	Mobile	Sou	156	32	10	2	4	23/30	20	27	0	0	124	.205	.310	.372	.233	16	33-OF 86	
1998	LasVegas	PCL	289	64	16	1	11	24/87	30	32	0	1	226	.221	.288	.398	.228	28	41-OF 79	33-1B 95
1999	LasVegas	PCL	446	95	24	2	11	63/155	46	58	2	3	354	.213	.311	.350	.226	43	66-1B 89	51-OF 85
2000	San Dieg	NL	333	71	15	1	11	44/107	38	41	0	1	263	.213	.305	.363	.235	35		

He didn't get anything done this year at Las Vegas and should consider pursuing another line of work. Normally I'm as dismissive of strikeouts as anyone, but Allen really racks them up; even with his good plate discipline, his strikeout-to-walk ratio is poor.

George Arias　　　　3B　　　　Bats R　Age 28

YEAR	TEAM	LGE	AB	H	DB	TP	HR	BB/SO	R	RBI	SB	CS	OUT	BA	OBP	SLG	EQA	EQR	DEFENSE
1997	Vancouvr	PCL	397	94	22	3	7	28/57	49	41	2	3	306	.237	.292	.360	.218	34	99-3B 110
1998	LasVegas	PCL	427	108	27	3	24	29/118	51	81	0	1	320	.253	.306	.499	.261	56	107-3B 104
1999	San Dieg	NL	166	41	6	0	8	4/53	19	20	0	0	125	.247	.265	.428	.226	15	43-3B 105
1999	LasVegas	PCL	93	20	5	2	6	14/30	20	19	1	0	73	.215	.322	.505	.272	14	24-3B 89
2000	San Dieg	NL	291	65	13	1	14	28/84	31	42	0	1	227	.223	.292	.419	.243	33	

Sometimes, minor-league power hitters—the guys who take huge cuts—seem to be lost at the major-league level. Arias, the heir apparent to Ken Caminiti, looked that way this year; again, he crushed Triple-A pitching, and again he was ineffective with the big club. Now a minor-league free agent, he could still help someone with his glove as a backup for a year or two. He's probably headed to Japan.

Sean Burroughs　　　3B　　　　Bats R　Age 19

YEAR	TEAM	LGE	AB	H	DB	TP	HR	BB/SO	R	RBI	SB	CS	OUT	BA	OBP	SLG	EQA	EQR	DEFENSE
1999	Ft Wayne	Mid	428	129	26	3	4	55/62	46	57	7	7	306	.301	.392	.404	.274	60	117-3B 94
1999	R Cucmng	Cal	22	8	1	0	1	3/3	2	3	0	0	14	.364	.453	.545	.334	5	
2000	San Dieg	NL	224	73	12	1	3	38/64	46	37	4	3	154	.326	.424	.429	.304	39	

In the vernacular of those crazy kids these days, Burroughs is the Shiznit. He had an incredible season between Fort Wayne and Rancho Cucamonga in 1999 and is the best hitting prospect the Padres have had since Roberto Alomar. The power will come, and the rest of his offensive game is already major-league caliber. Will start the season in the California League this year, and will probably be there for about 100 at-bats.

Mike Darr　　　　　OF　　　　Bats L　Age 24

YEAR	TEAM	LGE	AB	H	DB	TP	HR	BB/SO	R	RBI	SB	CS	OUT	BA	OBP	SLG	EQA	EQR	DEFENSE
1997	R Cucmng	Cal	520	155	29	7	13	43/88	75	71	11	3	368	.298	.355	.456	.274	72	130-OF 92
1998	Mobile	Sou	524	151	38	3	6	42/82	79	72	16	5	378	.288	.346	.406	.258	64	129-OF 100
1999	LasVegas	PCL	373	95	19	0	10	43/102	41	48	7	2	280	.255	.337	.386	.250	44	91-OF 96
2000	San Dieg	NL	428	118	22	2	8	46/99	68	55	15	4	314	.276	.346	.393	.265	57	

He's still on track for a decent peak at the major-league level, but it's more a function of how bad the Padres were this year than anything Darr did that he got some time in the majors. He isn't particularly slow, yet his defense looks poor as he gets a late jump quite often. He's got a cannon for an arm.

Ben Davis　　　　　C　　　　　Bats B　Age 23

YEAR	TEAM	LGE	AB	H	DB	TP	HR	BB/SO	R	RBI	SB	CS	OUT	BA	OBP	SLG	EQA	EQR	DEFENSE
1997	R Cucmng	Cal	475	119	20	1	16	18/104	51	61	1	1	357	.251	.280	.398	.224	42	
1998	Mobile	Sou	435	115	25	1	14	27/62	51	60	2	1	321	.264	.315	.423	.247	49	116-C 108
1999	LasVegas	PCL	196	52	16	1	5	20/40	20	33	3	1	145	.265	.338	.434	.261	25	58-C 97
1999	San Dieg	NL	268	66	15	1	5	22/69	28	29	2	1	203	.246	.303	.366	.227	25	72-C 101
2000	San Dieg	NL	446	117	25	1	16	39/95	58	67	4	1	330	.262	.322	.430	.261	57	

Davis made the majors to stay at age 22. Everyone knows he's got all the tools to be an All-World defensive catcher, including Davis himself. He allowed quite a few more passed balls than a guy with his skills should, because he's in love with the flashy glove stop. His swing looked pretty slow, and a good curveball abuses him, but the improving patience is a good sign. I wouldn't trade him for Travis Lee.

Kevin Eberwein   3B   Bats R   Age 23

YEAR	TEAM	LGE	AB	H	DB	TP	HR	BB/SO	R	RBI	SB	CS	OUT	BA	OBP	SLG	EQA	EQR	DEFENSE
1998	Clinton	Mid	253	66	15	2	11	21/68	34	31	2	1	188	.261	.326	.466	.263	33	52-3B 101
1999	R Cucmng	Cal	417	94	26	2	16	31/139	50	51	3	2	325	.225	.290	.412	.234	43	91-3B 101
2000	San Dieg	NL	265	61	15	1	12	25/100	32	38	1	1	205	.230	.297	.430	.248	32	

His elbow held together, so he turned in a full season at Rancho Cucamonga. Eberwein might be the best power prospect in the Padres system. He has the glove to play third base in the majors, but the presence of Burroughs means Eberwein may be moved over to first base. He might make good trade bait for some help at a position where the Padres are in more immediate need of an upgrade. He'll be in Mobile this year.

Ethan Faggett   OF   Bats L   Age 25

YEAR	TEAM	LGE	AB	H	DB	TP	HR	BB/SO	R	RBI	SB	CS	OUT	BA	OBP	SLG	EQA	EQR	DEFENSE
1997	Sarasota	Fla	415	105	21	7	3	35/98	42	37	9	5	315	.253	.319	.359	.233	41	99-OF 88
1998	Sarasota	Fla	234	52	10	1	3	19/67	27	17	4	2	184	.222	.286	.312	.204	17	58-OF 87
1998	Mobile	Sou	163	38	1	1	3	10/43	16	20	4	1	126	.233	.287	.307	.205	12	38-OF 89
1999	Mobile	Sou	533	118	16	9	5	37/142	55	34	30	8	423	.221	.278	.313	.208	42	126-OF 99
2000	San Dieg	NL	491	110	15	5	5	43/133	56	39	22	7	388	.224	.287	.305	.214	41	

Faggett led the BayBears in triples and stolen bases, but if he can't do better than a .244 batting average at Mobile, he doesn't have much chance to make the majors. Due to the speed, he'll probably make the move to Las Vegas next season, but since he doesn't really do anything with the bat that Garth Brooks doesn't, he isn't going to do much there, either.

Vince Faison   OF   Bats L   Age 19

YEAR	TEAM	LGE	AB	H	DB	TP	HR	BB/SO	R	RBI	SB	CS	OUT	BA	OBP	SLG	EQA	EQR	DEFENSE
1999	Ft Wayne	Mid	49	10	3	0	0	4/19	6	2	3	1	40	.204	.273	.265	.190	3	
2000	San Dieg	NL	23	5	1	0	0	2/18	3	1	2	0	18	.217	.280	.261	.212	2	

Drafted 20th overall by San Diego in 1999; he was expected to go higher. Faison was the fastest man in the draft. He doesn't have the size of most star outfielders (6'0", 177 pounds) but he's got the arm and wheels to play a mean center field. He's not unusually polished for a young player, and has a lot to learn, as you can see from the performance at Fort Wayne. He'll spend 2000 with the Wizards.

Chris Gomez   SS   Bats R   Age 29

YEAR	TEAM	LGE	AB	H	DB	TP	HR	BB/SO	R	RBI	SB	CS	OUT	BA	OBP	SLG	EQA	EQR	DEFENSE
1997	San Dieg	NL	532	142	20	2	6	52/113	63	57	3	8	398	.267	.338	.346	.233	52	145-SS 92
1998	San Dieg	NL	463	136	38	3	5	51/85	61	44	1	4	331	.294	.371	.421	.269	62	134-SS 103
1999	San Dieg	NL	236	60	9	1	1	24/49	19	15	1	2	178	.254	.326	.314	.220	20	72-SS 93
2000	San Dieg	NL	319	82	14	1	4	38/66	40	37	1	3	240	.257	.336	.345	.242	34	

He battled injuries all year and hit like the Chris Gomez of old when he was playing. His range took a big hit due to the foot problems, and his power was nowhere to be found. On the bright side, Juan Melo was traded, and Damian Jackson was even worse, so Gomez's job at shortstop is reasonably safe for 2000.

Wiklenman Gonzalez   C   Bats R   Age 26

YEAR	TEAM	LGE	AB	H	DB	TP	HR	BB/SO	R	RBI	SB	CS	OUT	BA	OBP	SLG	EQA	EQR	DEFENSE
1997	R Cucmng	Cal	110	27	9	0	3	4/27	12	17	0	0	83	.245	.272	.409	.224	10	
1997	Mobile	Sou	143	34	7	1	3	6/13	11	19	1	1	110	.238	.276	.364	.212	11	
1998	R Cucmng	Cal	294	65	18	1	6	16/64	33	36	0	0	229	.221	.264	.350	.203	21	41-C 102
1999	Mobile	Sou	226	62	13	1	7	21/33	27	33	0	0	164	.274	.348	.434	.264	29	52-C 106
1999	San Dieg	NL	84	21	3	1	3	0/8	7	12	0	0	63	.250	.260	.417	.220	7	
2000	San Dieg	NL	370	86	19	1	11	30/57	38	44	0	0	284	.232	.290	.378	.231	37	

(Wiklenman Gonzalez *continued*)

"Wiki" is a crowd favorite who radiates can-do attitude. Guys like this define the word "scrappy." His mechanics are solid; a catching duo of Davis and Gonzalez would be among the majors' best defensively. Of course, he doesn't have Davis's offensive potential, but he's a lot cheaper and more fun to watch than Carlos Hernandez or Greg Myers.

Tony Gwynn — RF — Bats L — Age 40

YEAR	TEAM	LGE	AB	H	DB	TP	HR	BB/SO	R	RBI	SB	CS	OUT	BA	OBP	SLG	EQA	EQR	DEFENSE
1997	San Dieg	NL	608	235	50	3	20	42/28	101	127	10	5	378	.387	.429	.577	.330	118	129-OF 89
1998	San Dieg	NL	477	166	29	0	22	35/18	71	79	4	1	312	.348	.394	.547	.310	83	102-OF 87
1999	San Dieg	NL	414	141	19	0	13	24/14	55	62	6	2	275	.341	.380	.481	.289	62	92-RF 86
2000	San Dieg	NL	338	104	12	0	11	33/13	52	57	5	1	235	.308	.369	.441	.285	51	

Gwynn passed 3,000 hits this season, and while it finally appears that the end may be in sight, he still hit well when he wasn't on the disabled list. He's getting slower every year, and a lot of balls fall in right field that wouldn't with an average fielder out there. The Padres may have to consider a move to first base—something Gwynn is not in favor of—by late this season. He's the best in the league at placing the ball right over the shortstop's head.

Matt Halloran — SS — Bats R — Age 22

YEAR	TEAM	LGE	AB	H	DB	TP	HR	BB/SO	R	RBI	SB	CS	OUT	BA	OBP	SLG	EQA	EQR	DEFENSE
1997	Clinton	Mid	156	31	5	0	2	5/39	14	21	4	2	127	.199	.238	.269	.163	7	46-SS 81
1998	Clinton	Mid	468	102	24	2	1	25/95	38	36	7	6	372	.218	.266	.284	.182	26	123-SS 87
1999	R Cucmng	Cal	310	65	10	2	0	11/73	28	18	7	4	249	.210	.247	.255	.161	13	90-SS 97
2000	San Dieg	NL	299	61	11	1	1	19/69	21	15	8	5	243	.204	.252	.258	.172	15	

Former first-round pick Halloran never caught up with minor-league heat. He was drafted out of high school and wasn't intimately acquainted with the nuances of a wooden bat, so this isn't very surprising. It's good to keep in mind that, for all the advances baseball scouting has made, most first-round picks still end up with career paths like this. The Padres have given up on him; he'll be playing in another system in 2000.

Carlos Hernandez — C/1B — Bats R — Age 33

YEAR	TEAM	LGE	AB	H	DB	TP	HR	BB/SO	R	RBI	SB	CS	OUT	BA	OBP	SLG	EQA	EQR	DEFENSE
1996	Albuquer	PCL	228	44	6	0	5	7/57	13	22	3	2	186	.193	.223	.285	.158	9	
1997	San Dieg	NL	136	44	8	1	3	3/27	16	14	0	2	94	.324	.338	.463	.261	16	
1998	San Dieg	NL	400	114	13	0	12	15/53	37	59	2	2	288	.285	.327	.407	.247	44	105-C 98
2000	San Dieg	NL	118	32	3	0	4	7/17	11	17	0	1	87	.271	.312	.398	.243	13	

Hernandez missed the entire season with a torn ACL; he's supposedly healthy and played first base in winter ball, a position where he'll serve little purpose. At this point, the Padres have many better options than giving Hernandez any playing time. He's very popular with the fans for some reason; maybe because he looks a little like Erik Estrada, everyone's favorite CHiP. That projection looks pretty generous.

Damian Jackson — IF — Bats R — Age 26

YEAR	TEAM	LGE	AB	H	DB	TP	HR	BB/SO	R	RBI	SB	CS	OUT	BA	OBP	SLG	EQA	EQR	DEFENSE
1997	Buffalo	AA	274	80	9	0	5	33/46	47	15	17	6	200	.292	.375	.380	.267	37	66-SS 104
1998	Indianap	Int	520	125	34	8	5	50/131	83	42	15	7	402	.240	.317	.365	.235	54	129-SS 93
1999	San Dieg	NL	391	89	20	2	9	48/104	52	38	30	10	312	.228	.317	.358	.239	44	88-SS 95
2000	San Dieg	NL	386	94	21	4	8	51/99	67	44	23	7	299	.244	.332	.381	.258	50	

Everything broke his way, and he did nothing with the opportunity. Jackson is one of those obviously talented players who has a heartbreaking habit of making the hard look easy... and the easy look hard. His range is excellent at shortstop, and his tendency to muff the easy play is extraordinary. He won't likely get another chance like last year's.

Wally Joyner — 1B — Bats L — Age 38

YEAR	TEAM	LGE	AB	H	DB	TP	HR	BB/SO	R	RBI	SB	CS	OUT	BA	OBP	SLG	EQA	EQR	DEFENSE
1997	San Dieg	NL	466	159	33	2	14	51/50	62	87	2	5	312	.341	.409	.511	.304	80	116-1B 102
1998	San Dieg	NL	454	148	31	1	15	52/43	63	90	1	2	308	.326	.397	.498	.299	75	115-1B 92
1999	San Dieg	NL	325	82	14	2	5	54/53	33	42	0	1	244	.252	.363	.354	.251	39	88-1B 108
2000	Atlanta	NL	285	80	9	0	9	46/37	46	47	0	1	206	.281	.381	.407	.275	41	

It was a lost season for Joyner, who had vision-correction surgery early in the season and played with a bone chip in his shoulder for most of the year. His power took a nosedive, but he'll probably be back to normal in 2000 with injury woes as well documented as his. Traded to the Braves, he'll act as Andres Galarraga insurance. Even if the Big Cat is healthy, he's probably going to be limited to 100 games or so, so Joyner will get some playing time.

Dave Magadan 3B/1B Bats L Age 37

YEAR	TEAM	LGE	AB	H	DB	TP	HR	BB/SO	R	RBI	SB	CS	OUT	BA	OBP	SLG	EQA	EQR	DEFENSE	
1997	Oakland	AL	268	81	11	1	4	48/38	37	29	1	0	187	.302	.413	.396	.286	41	28-3B 97	17-1B 107
1998	Oakland	AL	110	37	5	0	2	12/12	11	14	0	1	74	.336	.402	.436	.285	16	23-3B 108	
1999	San Dieg	NL	249	68	12	1	2	43/36	19	29	1	3	184	.273	.380	.353	.257	31	40-3B 95	20-1B 103
2000	San Dieg	NL	127	32	3	0	3	25/18	20	17	0	1	96	.252	.375	.346	.263	17		

One of the best bench players in baseball year after year, Magadan was asked to be more than that after Arias failed at third base. He delivered slap hits to left field, lots of walks and no speed; it isn't his fault that the Padres needed more than that from their third baseman in 1999. He'll be Phil Nevin's backup at third base in 2000.

Gary Matthews CF Bats B Age 25

YEAR	TEAM	LGE	AB	H	DB	TP	HR	BB/SO	R	RBI	SB	CS	OUT	BA	OBP	SLG	EQA	EQR	DEFENSE
1997	R Cucmng	Cal	270	69	14	2	6	38/57	46	29	4	2	203	.256	.352	.389	.256	34	67-OF 100
1998	Mobile	Sou	254	69	14	3	6	42/53	45	38	6	1	186	.272	.377	.421	.277	38	69-OF 115
1999	LasVegas	PCL	414	88	18	3	6	49/106	41	38	11	4	330	.213	.304	.314	.217	36	119-OF 103
1999	San Dieg	NL	36	8	0	0	0	9/9	4	4	2	0	28	.222	.378	.222	.240	4	
2000	San Dieg	NL	365	81	15	2	6	50/92	48	36	10	3	287	.222	.316	.323	.233	37	

Like Darr, Matthews had a disappointing campaign. He has immediate value as an outfielder with a good glove at all three positions. His path to real playing time in the majors is through Ruben Rivera, and he's going to have to do quite a bit better than he did in 1999 to make that jump. He's become much more selective at the plate as he's moved up through the system.

Phil Nevin 3B/C Bats R Age 29

YEAR	TEAM	LGE	AB	H	DB	TP	HR	BB/SO	R	RBI	SB	CS	OUT	BA	OBP	SLG	EQA	EQR	DEFENSE	
1997	Detroit	AL	251	60	17	1	9	23/65	31	34	0	1	192	.239	.306	.422	.242	28	30-OF 101	
1998	Anaheim	AL	238	56	9	1	8	16/66	27	27	0	0	182	.235	.298	.382	.229	23	62-C 93	
1999	San Dieg	NL	386	105	25	0	25	46/81	50	83	1	0	281	.272	.351	.531	.288	62	60-3B 107	21-C 97
2000	San Dieg	NL	349	86	16	0	19	40/82	47	59	0	0	263	.246	.324	.456	.267	49		

He took a circuitous route, but nevertheless provided an able replacement for the departed Ken Caminiti, which is exactly what the Astros drafted him to be in 1993. Nevin's got a great swing, and now that he's finally getting to play at his natural position shows a good glove as well. His ability to play catcher makes him very valuable to a creative manager. Signed through 2002 with an option, he'll play third base for the Padres in 2000.

David Newhan 2B Bats L Age 26

YEAR	TEAM	LGE	AB	H	DB	TP	HR	BB/SO	R	RBI	SB	CS	OUT	BA	OBP	SLG	EQA	EQR	DEFENSE
1997	Visalia	Cal	242	53	13	1	4	33/62	33	31	3	1	190	.219	.318	.331	.226	23	57-2B 91
1997	Huntsvil	Sou	211	57	11	1	4	21/65	28	25	3	3	157	.270	.340	.389	.248	24	45-2B 88
1998	Mobile	Sou	495	110	21	2	10	45/124	60	32	13	4	389	.222	.289	.333	.214	41	111-2B 92
1999	LasVegas	PCL	366	84	18	1	9	23/91	32	33	13	3	285	.230	.278	.358	.218	32	93-2B 91
1999	San Dieg	NL	43	6	1	0	2	1/11	7	6	2	1	38	.140	.159	.302	.136	1	
2000	San Dieg	NL	391	84	13	1	10	37/102	46	36	17	3	310	.215	.283	.330	.222	36	

Newhan has kicked around the minors for a few years now, and there isn't really a compelling reason to keep him on a roster. That said, if the Padres do move Veras, they could do much worse than a Jackson/Newhan platoon at second base in 2000. He's got speed on the bases, and his eye is OK, but he needs a defensive caddy. His pivot move is especially weak.

Kevin Nicholson SS Bats B Age 24

YEAR	TEAM	LGE	AB	H	DB	TP	HR	BB/SO	R	RBI	SB	CS	OUT	BA	OBP	SLG	EQA	EQR	DEFENSE
1998	Mobile	Sou	494	102	28	2	5	30/118	51	43	5	3	395	.206	.255	.302	.183	28	129-SS 90
1999	Mobile	Sou	493	129	34	2	12	34/98	66	65	8	3	367	.262	.314	.412	.245	54	126-SS 104
2000	San Dieg	NL	321	74	19	1	8	23/86	33	35	3	1	248	.231	.282	.371	.226	30	

(Kevin Nicholson *continued*)

He resurrected his flagging career with a nice season, but keep in mind it was his second time around at Mobile and he's no longer particularly young for the league. He'll move up to Las Vegas in 2000; if he does well, he doesn't have much in his way in this organization. Nicholson's defense is already major-league quality.

Wilbert Nieves		**C**					**Bats R**		**Age 22**									
YEAR	TEAM	LGE	AB	H	DB	TP	HR	BB/SO	R	RBI	SB	CS	OUT	BA	OBP	SLG	EQA	EQR	DEFENSE
1998	Clinton	Mid	391	91	13	0	6	38/71	38	49	3	4	304	.233	.307	.312	.212	31	91-C 99
1999	R Cucmng	Cal	424	123	24	1	7	29/52	45	47	1	3	304	.290	.340	.401	.250	47	117-C 104
2000	*San Dieg*	*NL*	*301*	*79*	*9*	*0*	*8*	*26/49*	*33*	*39*	*1*	*2*	*224*	*.262*	*.321*	*.372*	*.242*	*32*	

Keep an eye on this guy. Nieves put up All-Star numbers at Rancho Cucamonga in 1999, and he's turned himself into a legitimate prospect. He made the jump from Clinton without a hitch and will be tried at Las Vegas next season. If he's for real, the Padres might want to think about trading Davis; Nieves was *that* good in 1999. Pitchers like working with him.

Eric Owens		**UT**					**Bats R**		**Age 29**									
YEAR	TEAM	LGE	AB	H	DB	TP	HR	BB/SO	R	RBI	SB	CS	OUT	BA	OBP	SLG	EQA	EQR	DEFENSE	
1997	Indianap	AA	399	103	14	3	9	34/62	46	38	16	7	303	.258	.321	.376	.240	43	82-2B 95	
1998	Louisvil	Int	255	73	11	3	3	26/33	34	30	11	4	186	.286	.352	.388	.257	31	35-OF 99	26-3B 89
1999	San Dieg	NL	444	120	22	3	9	32/49	51	59	29	7	331	.270	.324	.394	.251	52	44-LF 103	31-CF 109
2000	*San Dieg*	*NL*	*342*	*87*	*13*	*2*	*8*	*33/42*	*49*	*40*	*17*	*6*	*261*	*.254*	*.320*	*.374*	*.249*	*40*		

Another scrappy player. Owens is a great bench guy, especially because he wants so badly to play, and will play so many positions, that he'll keep your starters on their toes. He's one of the best backups in the majors; unfortunately, his speed, defense and patience aren't enough to make him a reasonable starter anywhere on the field.

Jeremey Owens		**OF**					**Bats R**		**Age 23**									
YEAR	TEAM	LGE	AB	H	DB	TP	HR	BB/SO	R	RBI	SB	CS	OUT	BA	OBP	SLG	EQA	EQR	DEFENSE
1998	IdahoFls	Pio	282	60	13	2	6	18/94	28	29	9	3	225	.213	.269	.337	.206	22	65-OF 103
1999	Ft Wayne	Mid	518	123	24	7	9	44/165	67	47	25	7	402	.237	.304	.363	.232	52	127-OF 104
1999	R Cucmng	Cal	38	6	1	0	0	1/13	1	1	1	1	33	.158	.192	.184	.051	0	
2000	*San Dieg*	*NL*	*336*	*75*	*13*	*3*	*6*	*29/125*	*42*	*30*	*17*	*3*	*264*	*.223*	*.285*	*.333*	*.225*	*32*	

He's a speedy outfield prospect taken in the eighth round of the 1998 draft. Owens didn't have a tough time with the Midwest League in 1999, and will start the season with Rancho Cucamonga this year. He's got the mix of speed and power that had everyone so excited about Ray McDavid a few years back; let's hope he's less subject to the fits of swinging at anything. He sure has the strikeouts to be the new McDavid.

Ruben Rivera		**CF**					**Bats R**		**Age 26**									
YEAR	TEAM	LGE	AB	H	DB	TP	HR	BB/SO	R	RBI	SB	CS	OUT	BA	OBP	SLG	EQA	EQR	DEFENSE
1998	LasVegas	PCL	104	14	1	0	3	9/43	7	9	3	0	90	.135	.204	.231	.133	3	28-OF 105
1998	San Dieg	NL	177	41	8	3	7	28/51	34	33	5	1	137	.232	.344	.429	.265	25	54-OF 100
1999	San Dieg	NL	414	81	16	1	23	51/142	62	46	16	7	340	.196	.292	.406	.236	46	116-CF 109
2000	*San Dieg*	*NL*	*284*	*54*	*10*	*1*	*16*	*43/105*	*38*	*39*	*9*	*3*	*233*	*.190*	*.297*	*.401*	*.246*	*35*	

Rivera will go through streaks when he puts it all together, and he just takes your breath away. He's got a beautiful swing and is second only to Andruw Jones in center field, but he endured long dry spells at the plate in 1999. He's worth keeping an eye on.

Reggie Sanders		**LF**					**Bats R**		**Age 32**									
YEAR	TEAM	LGE	AB	H	DB	TP	HR	BB/SO	R	RBI	SB	CS	OUT	BA	OBP	SLG	EQA	EQR	DEFENSE	
1997	Cincnnti	NL	314	78	20	2	19	41/92	50	54	10	7	243	.248	.341	.506	.275	48	84-OF 101	
1998	Cincnnti	NL	486	132	20	6	15	51/133	85	60	21	10	364	.272	.350	.430	.265	66	117-OF 101	
1999	San Dieg	NL	481	137	25	7	25	59/107	86	68	31	13	357	.285	.371	.522	.294	83	81-LF 101	29-RF 103
2000	*Atlanta*	*NL*	*411*	*106*	*17*	*3*	*20*	*60/102*	*72*	*69*	*18*	*10*	*315*	*.258*	*.352*	*.460*	*.274*	*62*		

Some guys were just born brittle. Sanders is in great shape and doesn't take boneheaded risks, but he always seems to visit the disabled list at least once a season, as well as fight the kind of nagging injuries that make him a four-day-a-week player. Despite that, he outplayed Greg Vaughn, and his skill set is less likely to disappear overnight. Maybe moving to left field will help him stay healthy long-term. He'll be the Braves' left fielder in 2000.

Troy Schader   3B   Bats R   Age 23

YEAR	TEAM	LGE	AB	H	DB	TP	HR	BB/SO	R	RBI	SB	CS	OUT	BA	OBP	SLG	EQA	EQR	DEFENSE
1999	IdahoFls	Pio	265	64	13	3	11	21/89	32	34	0	1	202	.242	.301	.438	.244	30	34-3B 76
2000	San Dieg	NL	126	30	3	1	9	12/84	16	23	0	0	96	.238	.304	.492	.268	18	

The 21st-round pick out of Oregon State had a good first year with the bat in Idaho Falls in 1999 and flashed an unexpected power stroke, leading the Pioneer League in home runs and driving the ball to all fields. Schader was a shortstop in college and is still adjusting to the hot corner; with the glut of third basemen in the system, he could move back to shortstop.

Pete Tucci   OF   Bats R   Age 24

YEAR	TEAM	LGE	AB	H	DB	TP	HR	BB/SO	R	RBI	SB	CS	OUT	BA	OBP	SLG	EQA	EQR	DEFENSE
1997	Hagerstn	SAL	475	112	28	3	10	30/96	50	61	3	2	365	.236	.286	.371	.220	41	108-OF 87
1998	Dunedin	Fla	355	94	24	2	18	22/111	52	52	3	2	263	.265	.314	.496	.264	47	90-OF 91
1998	Knoxvill	Sou	140	36	6	3	6	8/30	19	26	2	1	105	.257	.305	.471	.255	17	33-OF 93
1999	Mobile	Sou	315	72	10	0	11	19/88	35	29	6	3	246	.229	.279	.365	.216	27	75-OF 93
2000	San Dieg	NL	372	94	16	2	16	35/102	48	57	5	2	280	.253	.317	.435	.260	48	

Tucci possesses a vicious uppercut swing that didn't go over very well in his first full season in the Southern League. He's a free swinger who has a chance at a major-league career solely due to the power he generates. It's about all he has to offer; his on-base skills are poor and he's a threat to himself and his team defensively. He'll get some hacks in at Las Vegas next year and should find Pacific Coast League park dimensions to his liking.

John Vanderwal   OF/1B   Bats L   Age 34

YEAR	TEAM	LGE	AB	H	DB	TP	HR	BB/SO	R	RBI	SB	CS	OUT	BA	OBP	SLG	EQA	EQR	DEFENSE
1997	Colorado	NL	92	15	0	0	2	9/33	7	12	1	1	78	.163	.238	.228	.143	3	
1998	Colorado	NL	102	27	7	1	5	15/28	16	18	0	0	75	.265	.359	.500	.284	16	
1999	San Dieg	NL	248	68	13	0	8	34/58	25	42	2	1	181	.274	.367	.423	.270	34	32-LF 112
2000	San Dieg	NL	176	42	4	0	6	27/45	24	24	1	0	134	.239	.340	.364	.253	22	

It's kind of surprising that San Diego didn't use Vanderwal more than they did in 1999; he was usually their best bat off the bench against right-handed pitching, so with the team's injury problems in the outfield, you'd think he'd get more than 250 at-bats. He didn't have his usual success as a pinch-hitter, as measured by performance or theatrics: no pinch-hit home runs in 52 at-bats.

Quilvio Veras   2B   Bats B   Age 29

YEAR	TEAM	LGE	AB	H	DB	TP	HR	BB/SO	R	RBI	SB	CS	OUT	BA	OBP	SLG	EQA	EQR	DEFENSE
1997	San Dieg	NL	551	154	24	1	4	71/83	73	48	28	13	410	.279	.369	.348	.255	67	136-2B 98
1998	San Dieg	NL	535	163	31	2	7	85/76	89	52	27	11	383	.305	.406	.409	.286	84	128-2B 108
1999	San Dieg	NL	478	133	25	2	6	60/87	87	39	25	17	362	.278	.361	.377	.254	59	114-2B 103
2000	Atlanta	NL	393	105	21	1	4	62/66	73	43	20	11	299	.267	.367	.356	.257	50	

"Q" was not done recovering from offseason shoulder surgery when he put up woeful numbers in April (.192/.291/.274), but he hit well after that and ended up with another good season. Look for him to steal more bags next year; he stole 18 after the break as his health returned. Now a Brave, he fits their desperate need for a leadoff hitter who can get on base, and should have his best season since 1995.

PITCHERS (Averages: ERA: 4.50 / H/9: 9.00 / HR/9: 1.00 / BB/9: 3.50 / K/9: 6.50 / KWH: 1.00)

Carlos Almanzar   Throws R   Age 26

YEAR	TEAM	LGE	IP	H	ER	HR	BB	K	ERA	W	L	H/9	HR/9	BB/9	K/9	KWH	PERA
1997	Knoxvill	Sou	25.3	32	14	2	6	20	4.97	1	2	11.37	0.71	2.13	7.11	1.56	4.97
1997	Syracuse	Int	49.7	33	9	2	8	40	1.63	5	1	5.98	0.36	1.45	7.25	4.53	1.81
1998	Syracuse	Int	48.3	51	24	7	14	46	4.47	3	2	9.50	1.30	2.61	8.57	2.21	4.66
1998	Toronto	AL	29.0	33	16	4	8	20	4.97	1	2	10.24	1.24	2.48	6.21	1.13	4.97
1999	San Dieg	NL	36.7	48	30	5	15	29	7.36	1	3	11.78	1.23	3.68	7.12	0.87	6.38

Almanzar looked like a future closer after his big half-season at Syracuse in 1997; since then, he's been a solid but unspectacular member of the pen in Toronto and San Diego. He didn't help his cause in 1999, pitching ineffectively after returning from a strained back. I like his chances to have a long career. With the bullpen shaping up to be relatively deep in San Diego in 2000, however, Almanzar may be scrapping for a spot.

Andy Ashby   Throws R   Age 32

YEAR	TEAM	LGE	IP	H	ER	HR	BB	K	ERA	W	L	H/9	HR/9	BB/9	K/9	KWH	PERA
1997	San Dieg	NL	198.0	211	108	17	51	133	4.91	10	12	9.59	0.77	2.32	6.05	1.23	4.14
1998	San Dieg	NL	218.3	239	98	24	61	142	4.04	13	11	9.85	0.99	2.51	5.85	1.03	4.58
1999	San Dieg	NL	203.7	203	89	24	52	127	3.93	13	10	8.97	1.06	2.30	5.61	1.14	4.07

Whenever your favorite team picks up a pitcher with great stuff who can't seem to keep the ball in the strike zone, just keep in mind that Andy Ashby is the upside. It isn't a good percentage move, but nobody can keep their system full of genuine pitching prospects, so it's better than nothing. Ashby has been a quality pitcher since 1994, and the declining peripherals aren't anything to worry about yet. Traded for three cheap arms, he'll start the year as the Phillies' #1 starter, waiting for Curt Schilling to return.

Brian Boehringer   Throws R   Age 31

YEAR	TEAM	LGE	IP	H	ER	HR	BB	K	ERA	W	L	H/9	HR/9	BB/9	K/9	KWH	PERA
1997	NY Yanks	AL	48.0	38	14	4	32	53	2.63	4	1	7.13	0.75	6.00	9.94	1.73	4.12
1998	San Dieg	NL	73.3	80	41	11	47	63	5.03	4	4	9.82	1.35	5.77	7.73	0.79	6.26
1999	San Dieg	NL	93.0	97	36	9	34	62	3.48	6	4	9.39	0.87	3.29	6.00	0.87	4.55

Boehringer started the season strong out of the bullpen, then moved to the rotation in June and got even stronger. His 3.21 ERA through 11 starts was a sign that he'd finally shaken off 1998's malaise, and his control returned to normal. Arthroscopic shoulder surgery in August shelved him for the season; he's reportedly recovering quickly and should be ready for 2000.

Mike Bynum   Throws L   Age 22

YEAR	TEAM	LGE	IP	H	ER	HR	BB	K	ERA	W	L	H/9	HR/9	BB/9	K/9	KWH	PERA
1999	IdahoFls	Pio	16.0	9	0	0	5	13	0.00	2	0	5.06	0.00	2.81	7.31	2.81	1.69
1999	R Cucmng	Cal	36.0	40	19	1	9	32	4.75	2	2	10.00	0.25	2.25	8.00	2.13	3.75

One of San Diego's supplemental picks in the 1999 draft, Bynum was signed quickly and cruised through Idaho Falls and Rancho Cucamonga. Bynum is that rarest of pitchers, a strikeout left-hander who doesn't need to rely on his placement to sit batters down. He probably won't get more than four or five starts at Rancho Cucamonga next season before moving on to Mobile.

Buddy Carlyle   Throws R   Age 22

YEAR	TEAM	LGE	IP	H	ER	HR	BB	K	ERA	W	L	H/9	HR/9	BB/9	K/9	KWH	PERA
1997	Charl-WV	SAL	133.7	170	67	12	39	75	4.51	7	8	11.45	0.81	2.63	5.05	0.63	5.39
1998	Mobile	Sou	170.3	210	88	15	44	80	4.65	9	10	11.10	0.79	2.32	4.23	0.52	5.02
1999	LasVegas	PCL	159.3	175	87	22	48	115	4.91	8	10	9.88	1.24	2.71	6.50	1.18	4.97
1999	San Dieg	NL	36.7	37	26	6	17	28	6.38	1	3	9.08	1.47	4.17	6.87	0.93	5.40

He made it to the majors this season and wasn't embarrassed. His strikeout rate has increased and his control is as solid as ever. With Ashby gone, Carlyle has a chance to make the staff in 2000. He wouldn't disappoint as a bottom-of-the-rotation starter.

Matt Clement   Throws R   Age 25

YEAR	TEAM	LGE	IP	H	ER	HR	BB	K	ERA	W	L	H/9	HR/9	BB/9	K/9	KWH	PERA
1997	R Cucmng	Cal	96.7	85	33	3	36	76	3.07	8	3	7.91	0.28	3.35	7.08	1.41	3.17
1997	Mobile	Sou	84.7	90	37	4	35	75	3.93	5	4	9.57	0.43	3.72	7.97	1.33	4.36
1998	LasVegas	PCL	172.0	147	83	11	95	137	4.34	10	9	7.69	0.58	4.97	7.17	1.00	3.92
1999	San Dieg	NL	179.0	190	100	17	82	130	5.03	9	11	9.55	0.85	4.12	6.54	0.81	4.93

He got his 30 starts as a member of the San Diego rotation in 1999, and the results were uneven but promising. Early in the season, Bochy left Clement in games too long, and Clement got his bell rung, but by September he was cruising and ended the month with a 4-0 record and an ERA in the low 2.00s. Look for improved control and more success next season.

Will Cunnane   Throws R   Age 26

YEAR	TEAM	LGE	IP	H	ER	HR	BB	K	ERA	W	L	H/9	HR/9	BB/9	K/9	KWH	PERA
1997	San Dieg	NL	89.7	117	70	11	52	73	7.03	3	7	11.74	1.10	5.22	7.33	0.65	7.03
1998	LasVegas	PCL	36.3	43	24	1	22	25	5.94	1	3	10.65	0.25	5.45	6.19	0.49	5.45
1999	LasVegas	PCL	36.3	28	4	0	20	43	0.99	4	0	6.94	0.00	4.95	10.65	2.47	2.97
1999	San Dieg	NL	30.3	35	18	7	12	21	5.34	1	2	10.38	2.08	3.56	6.23	0.78	6.53

Cunnane posted a microscopic 0.98 ERA as the closer for Las Vegas in 1999. No, he wasn't really that good, but his strikeout rate skyrocketed and he's in the Padres' plans for 2000. He's always had good stuff, but his 95 mph heater started getting more press this year after his early success.

Rickey Guttormson   Throws R   Age 23

YEAR	TEAM	LGE	IP	H	ER	HR	BB	K	ERA	W	L	H/9	HR/9	BB/9	K/9	KWH	PERA
1998	Clinton	Mid	148.0	199	83	13	54	98	5.05	7	9	12.10	0.79	3.28	5.96	0.67	6.02
1999	R Cucmng	Cal	160.3	196	96	17	41	90	5.39	7	11	11.00	0.95	2.30	5.05	0.75	5.11

The organization's minor-league pitcher of the year in 1999 after tying for the California League lead in wins. I really like the control trend; Guttormson doesn't have overpowering stuff, so he's going to have to work the strike zone well to make it to the majors, and he's doing a better job of that every year.

Junior Herndon   Throws R   Age 21

YEAR	TEAM	LGE	IP	H	ER	HR	BB	K	ERA	W	L	H/9	HR/9	BB/9	K/9	KWH	PERA
1998	Clinton	Mid	124.0	152	76	5	44	70	5.52	6	8	11.03	0.36	3.19	5.08	0.55	4.86
1998	R Cucmng	Cal	36.3	48	23	6	16	20	5.70	2	2	11.89	1.49	3.96	4.95	0.39	6.94
1999	Mobile	Sou	155.3	192	101	25	56	72	5.85	6	11	11.12	1.45	3.24	4.17	0.36	6.14

Baseball America loves Herndon, whom they rate as the top Padre pitching prospect. That's kind of silly; he's no Buddy Carlyle. He pitched all season at Mobile, and didn't do terribly, but a player with Herndon's repertoire should be getting more strikeouts. He still has a big problem with the long ball.

Sterling Hitchcock   Throws L   Age 29

YEAR	TEAM	LGE	IP	H	ER	HR	BB	K	ERA	W	L	H/9	HR/9	BB/9	K/9	KWH	PERA
1997	San Dieg	NL	158.7	175	103	25	57	98	5.84	7	11	9.93	1.42	3.23	5.56	0.72	5.39
1998	San Dieg	NL	170.0	181	90	31	51	149	4.76	9	10	9.58	1.64	2.70	7.89	1.80	5.19
1999	San Dieg	NL	203.7	202	93	27	73	187	4.11	13	10	8.93	1.19	3.23	8.26	1.77	4.55

Both the strikeouts and the walks have increased to the point that he should be considered a strikeout pitcher. Though the trend makes for more exciting games, it's worked for him; Hitchcock is more effective than ever. He'll probably be the ace in San Diego this year.

Trevor Hoffman   Throws R   Age 32

YEAR	TEAM	LGE	IP	H	ER	HR	BB	K	ERA	W	L	H/9	HR/9	BB/9	K/9	KWH	PERA
1997	San Dieg	NL	80.3	60	24	10	25	102	2.69	7	2	6.72	1.12	2.80	11.43	5.18	3.14
1998	San Dieg	NL	71.0	45	13	2	22	81	1.65	7	1	5.70	0.25	2.79	10.27	4.95	1.90
1999	San Dieg	NL	67.0	47	21	5	15	70	2.82	5	2	6.31	0.67	2.01	9.40	5.19	2.28

(Trevor Hoffman *continued*)

There's no end in sight for Hoffman, whose 1999 was his usual solid work. Having to face a guy who has command of four pitches is a hard road to travel for opposing hitters. He signed a four-year, $32 million contract to keep him in San Diego until 2002, and he and Tony Gwynn are the only untouchables on the Padres roster. He might be the most marketable Padre. Expect him to have continued success next year.

Dan Miceli — Throws R — Age 29

YEAR	TEAM	LGE	IP	H	ER	HR	BB	K	ERA	W	L	H/9	HR/9	BB/9	K/9	KWH	PERA
1997	Detroit	AL	82.7	77	46	12	38	80	5.01	4	5	8.38	1.31	4.14	8.71	1.63	4.68
1998	San Dieg	NL	70.3	69	30	6	28	66	3.84	5	3	8.83	0.77	3.58	8.45	1.68	4.22
1999	San Dieg	NL	68.3	67	37	7	34	57	4.87	4	4	8.82	0.92	4.48	7.51	1.07	4.74

Miceli lost somewhere between 25 and 50 pounds after the 1998 season. From a health standpoint, that's great, and there are several Padres on the roster who could stand to do likewise, but Miceli's fastball wasn't snapping in 1999 like it was in 1998. He started overthrowing as a result, and the balls he left up in the zone were souvenirs. He's been traded to Florida for Brian Meadows. The Marlins have no dominant closer, so while Miceli is slated as the setup man for Antonio Alfonseca, there's a good chance he'll pick up five to 10 saves, and could get more.

Jason Middlebrook — Throws R — Age 25

YEAR	TEAM	LGE	IP	H	ER	HR	BB	K	ERA	W	L	H/9	HR/9	BB/9	K/9	KWH	PERA
1997	Clinton	Mid	75.7	95	56	5	48	59	6.66	3	5	11.30	0.59	5.71	7.02	0.57	6.30
1998	R Cucmng	Cal	131.7	218	136	12	85	84	9.30	3	12	14.90	0.82	5.81	5.74	0.28	8.95
1999	Mobile	Sou	58.3	93	69	9	35	29	10.65	1	5	14.35	1.39	5.40	4.47	0.19	9.10

With all that the Padres have invested in Middlebrook, they have no choice but to let him try to pitch through what ails him. Unquestionably talented, but he's had serious control problems ever since his elbow injury in college. He'll start the season at Mobile again.

Heath Murray — Throws L — Age 27

YEAR	TEAM	LGE	IP	H	ER	HR	BB	K	ERA	W	L	H/9	HR/9	BB/9	K/9	KWH	PERA
1997	LasVegas	PCL	106.7	134	62	9	43	84	5.23	5	7	11.31	0.76	3.63	7.09	0.92	5.65
1998	LasVegas	PCL	160.0	190	98	11	74	99	5.51	7	11	10.69	0.62	4.16	5.57	0.52	5.34
1999	LasVegas	PCL	80.7	99	43	4	38	52	4.80	4	5	11.05	0.45	4.24	5.80	0.54	5.36
1999	San Dieg	NL	49.0	61	31	6	25	24	5.69	2	3	11.20	1.10	4.59	4.41	0.28	6.43

He reportedly added a few feet to his fastball in the 1998-99 offseason and came into 1999 looking for a spot with the big club. He got a tryout as emergency starter and later, in the bullpen, but was rocked in both roles. Placed on waivers after the season ended and claimed by Cincinnati, where his prospects don't look any rosier.

Randy Myers — Throws L — Age 37

YEAR	TEAM	LGE	IP	H	ER	HR	BB	K	ERA	W	L	H/9	HR/9	BB/9	K/9	KWH	PERA
1996	Baltimor	AL	58.3	58	21	6	27	76	3.24	4	2	8.95	0.93	4.17	11.73	2.76	4.63
1997	Baltimor	AL	59.3	47	12	2	22	56	1.82	6	1	7.13	0.30	3.34	8.49	2.27	2.88
1998	Toronto	AL	42.7	42	19	4	20	32	4.01	3	2	8.86	0.84	4.22	6.75	0.91	4.64
1998	San Dieg	NL	13.7	16	11	3	7	8	7.24	1	1	10.54	1.98	4.61	5.27	0.43	7.24

The boondoggle. What to do with a player like Myers, who has obviously reached the end of his rope and who didn't even play in 1999 due to "shoulder weakness"? Peddling him to Woody Woodward won't be so easy now that Woodward is not a general manager anymore. The Padres will reportedly look to insurance to cover Myers's contract and set him free. His chance of pitching well in 2000 is worse than Ben Davis's taste in music, and that's saying something.

Jacob Peavy — Throws R — Age 19

YEAR	TEAM	LGE	IP	H	ER	HR	BB	K	ERA	W	L	H/9	HR/9	BB/9	K/9	KWH	PERA
1999	IdahoFls	Pio	10.7	6	0	0	2	8	0.00	1	0	5.06	0.00	1.69	6.75	3.99	0.84

The team signed Peavy, their 15th-round pick in 1999, away from a full ride at Auburn. After a banner Arizona League campaign, including a 1.34 ERA and 90 strikeouts in 74 innings, Peavy was promoted to Idaho Falls. So far, there isn't a lot that can be said about him; he's got an excellent arm and hasn't had any trouble getting hitters out. Check back next year.

Carlos Reyes　　Throws R　　Age 31

YEAR	TEAM	LGE	IP	H	ER	HR	BB	K	ERA	W	L	H/9	HR/9	BB/9	K/9	KWH	PERA
1997	Edmonton	PCL	29.7	32	14	2	3	19	4.25	2	1	9.71	0.61	0.91	5.76	2.81	3.64
1997	Oakland	AL	80.3	93	44	12	25	44	4.93	4	5	10.42	1.34	2.80	4.93	0.62	5.38
1998	Boston	AL	38.3	34	14	2	15	23	3.29	3	1	7.98	0.47	3.52	5.40	0.78	3.52
1998	San Dieg	NL	26.7	25	12	4	7	23	4.05	2	1	8.44	1.35	2.36	7.76	2.26	4.05
1999	San Dieg	NL	76.7	76	36	10	23	55	4.23	5	4	8.92	1.17	2.70	6.46	1.29	4.34

Following two seasons of good work, Reyes was inexplicably put on waivers and claimed by the Phillies. Reyes is very fun to watch; he doesn't throw hard, but he changes speeds well and occasionally he'll make a batter look very silly. With guys like this available on the waiver wire every year, a major-league team has little excuse for assembling a weak bullpen.

Jim Sak　　Throws R　　Age 26

YEAR	TEAM	LGE	IP	H	ER	HR	BB	K	ERA	W	L	H/9	HR/9	BB/9	K/9	KWH	PERA
1997	R Cucmng	Cal	66.7	52	34	5	36	75	4.59	3	4	7.02	0.68	4.86	10.13	2.25	3.64
1998	Mobile	Sou	45.0	43	34	3	37	43	6.80	2	3	8.60	0.60	7.40	8.60	0.87	5.40
1999	Mobile	Sou	25.0	19	14	1	17	28	5.04	1	2	6.84	0.36	6.12	10.08	1.81	3.60
1999	LasVegas	PCL	26.7	23	10	4	20	25	3.38	2	1	7.76	1.35	6.75	8.44	1.02	5.40

Sak has been a closer in the system since 1997 and took over that function for the Stars after Cunnane was called up to the big club. He makes things interesting with the walks, but gives batters fits when he is on and is ready for the major leagues right now. Expect him to compete for a job in the Padres bullpen in 2000.

Wascar Serrano　　Throws R　　Age 21

YEAR	TEAM	LGE	IP	H	ER	HR	BB	K	ERA	W	L	H/9	HR/9	BB/9	K/9	KWH	PERA
1998	Clinton	Mid	145.7	192	94	9	70	99	5.81	6	10	11.86	0.56	4.32	6.12	0.54	6.05
1999	R Cucmng	Cal	123.3	128	63	11	47	95	4.60	7	7	9.34	0.80	3.43	6.93	1.12	4.45
1999	Mobile	Sou	40.3	53	28	5	18	24	6.25	1	3	11.83	1.12	4.02	5.36	0.45	6.47

He breezed through Rancho Cucamonga and confounded California League batters, leading the circuit in strikeouts at the time of his call-up to Mobile. Serrano was named to the Futures Game world team and the California League All-Star team last year. He'll start next season in Mobile, where he'll get a better chance to flash his great fastball. His slight build may push him into the bullpen at some point, but he's had no injury problems yet.

Stan Spencer　　Throws R　　Age 30

YEAR	TEAM	LGE	IP	H	ER	HR	BB	K	ERA	W	L	H/9	HR/9	BB/9	K/9	KWH	PERA
1997	R Cucmng	Cal	36.3	49	23	6	7	28	5.70	2	2	12.14	1.49	1.73	6.94	1.71	6.19
1997	LasVegas	PCL	46.3	47	20	4	20	39	3.88	3	2	9.13	0.78	3.88	7.58	1.21	4.47
1998	LasVegas	PCL	134.7	122	64	15	49	111	4.28	8	7	8.15	1.00	3.27	7.42	1.54	3.94
1998	San Dieg	NL	29.3	32	17	5	4	29	5.22	1	2	9.82	1.53	1.23	8.90	4.91	4.60
1999	San Dieg	NL	37.7	56	41	10	11	35	9.80	1	3	13.38	2.39	2.63	8.36	1.49	8.60
1999	LasVegas	PCL	53.0	71	34	5	18	40	5.77	2	4	12.06	0.85	3.06	6.79	0.94	5.94

What happened? After a solid 1998, Spencer was clueless everywhere he pitched in 1999. He entered the season as the Padres' fourth starter, but that experiment failed after he allowed a very generous 51 baserunners in only 32⅔ innings. Las Vegas wasn't much kinder to him, and as a minor-league free agent, he'll be plying his trade elsewhere this year. If there's a silver lining, it's that Spencer has been healthy for two years after having more health problems than Liz Taylor earlier in his career.

Brendan Sullivan　　Throws R　　Age 25

YEAR	TEAM	LGE	IP	H	ER	HR	BB	K	ERA	W	L	H/9	HR/9	BB/9	K/9	KWH	PERA
1997	Clinton	Mid	57.7	69	40	1	42	37	6.24	2	4	10.77	0.16	6.55	5.77	0.35	5.77
1998	R Cucmng	Cal	38.3	31	11	0	25	23	2.58	3	1	7.28	0.00	5.87	5.40	0.51	3.52
1998	Mobile	Sou	36.0	35	10	1	16	19	2.50	3	1	8.75	0.25	4.00	4.75	0.48	3.75
1999	LasVegas	PCL	65.3	85	55	5	45	41	7.58	2	5	11.71	0.69	6.20	5.65	0.33	6.89

Sullivan may have gone as far as his poor fastball will take him. He was hit hard for the first time in his career in Las Vegas in 1999; his deceptive delivery and formidable off-speed stuff had been enough while he was lower in the system, but Pacific Coast League hitters had little trouble with him. He'll be back for more of the same in 2000.

Donne Wall   Throws R   Age 32

YEAR	TEAM	LGE	IP	H	ER	HR	BB	K	ERA	W	L	H/9	HR/9	BB/9	K/9	KWH	PERA
1997	New Orln	AmA	102.3	131	62	13	28	71	5.45	4	7	11.52	1.14	2.46	6.24	1.03	5.72
1997	Houston	NL	41.0	55	32	9	17	23	7.02	1	4	12.07	1.98	3.73	5.05	0.42	7.68
1998	San Dieg	NL	67.7	55	22	7	33	53	2.93	6	2	7.32	0.93	4.39	7.05	1.16	3.86
1999	San Dieg	NL	69.0	59	29	10	22	51	3.78	5	3	7.70	1.30	2.87	6.65	1.50	3.78

Wall had another fine season in the Padres bullpen in 1999. It's as if a switch snapped on after 1997; it isn't often you see a performance like you see in Wall's career before and after that year. He's probably underrated, due to the home run rate; the rest of his game is setup-man quality. Day in and day out, only Trevor Hoffman is more reliable out of the San Diego pen; expect Wall to play a large part in any success the Padres have in 2000.

Matt Whisenant   Throws L   Age 29

YEAR	TEAM	LGE	IP	H	ER	HR	BB	K	ERA	W	L	H/9	HR/9	BB/9	K/9	KWH	PERA
1998	KansasCy	AL	62.7	56	32	3	35	46	4.60	3	4	8.04	0.43	5.03	6.61	0.81	4.02
1999	KansasCy	AL	40.0	38	24	3	26	28	5.40	2	2	8.55	0.68	5.85	6.30	0.59	4.72
1999	San Dieg	NL	14.7	10	6	0	9	10	3.68	1	1	6.14	0.00	5.52	6.14	0.83	3.07

The Padres may finally have found a left-handed reliever they can live with. Whisenant displays all the control of a rampaging independent counsel, but he's useful as a strictly monitored lefty-killer. If he cuts down those walks, he'll be well equipped to go Grape Ape on the NL at a moment's notice.

Woody Williams   Throws R   Age 33

YEAR	TEAM	LGE	IP	H	ER	HR	BB	K	ERA	W	L	H/9	HR/9	BB/9	K/9	KWH	PERA
1997	Toronto	AL	194.7	196	91	29	66	125	4.21	12	10	9.06	1.34	3.05	5.78	0.90	4.72
1998	Toronto	AL	212.0	188	100	33	85	153	4.25	13	11	7.98	1.40	3.61	6.50	1.09	4.37
1999	San Dieg	NL	206.0	213	100	31	69	132	4.37	12	11	9.31	1.35	3.01	5.77	0.89	4.85

Originally, there were questions about Williams's being able to throw 200 innings, but he's averaged that over the last three years. He enjoyed his first full season in the NL, especially at the plate. It's refreshing to see a pitcher who really seems to like to hit, though Williams isn't very good at it. He'd probably hit a home run off himself; as you can see, he gives up a load of them.

Bryan Wolff   Throws R   Age 28

YEAR	TEAM	LGE	IP	H	ER	HR	BB	K	ERA	W	L	H/9	HR/9	BB/9	K/9	KWH	PERA
1997	R Cucmng	Cal	31.3	25	8	2	8	24	2.30	2	1	7.18	0.57	2.30	6.89	2.15	2.59
1998	Mobile	Sou	122.3	119	54	8	46	100	3.97	8	6	8.75	0.59	3.38	7.36	1.37	3.90
1999	LasVegas	PCL	174.0	201	94	19	68	120	4.86	9	10	10.40	0.98	3.52	6.21	0.79	5.28

Wolff has breathed new life into his career prospects his second time around the Padres system. He and Buddy Carlyle were Las Vegas' most consistent starters this season, and with Carlyle in the majors, Wolff will be the Stars' ace in 2000. For a guy who was released by Kansas City three years ago, that's progress. If Wolff improves on his performance next year, he'll be an excellent cheap option for the back of someone's rotation.

Support-Neutral Records — SAN DIEGO PADRES — Park Effect: -27.2%

PITCHER	GS	IP	R	SNW	SNL	SNPCT	W	L	RA	APW	SNVA	SNWAR
Andy Ashby	31	206.0	95	11.6	12.0	.492	14	10	4.15	0.55	-0.34	1.57
Brian Boehringer	11	61.7	25	3.7	3.2	.536	4	4	3.65	0.51	0.18	0.76
Buddy Carlyle	7	37.7	28	1.3	3.7	.256	1	3	6.69	-0.98	-1.18	-0.85
Matt Clement	31	180.7	106	8.6	12.3	.412	10	12	5.28	-1.82	-1.75	-0.27
Sterling Hitchcock	33	205.7	99	11.3	11.8	.490	12	14	4.33	0.13	-0.31	1.51
Heath Murray	8	39.3	28	1.5	3.7	.294	0	4	6.41	-0.89	-1.02	-0.69
Stan Spencer	8	36.3	43	1.2	4.9	.191	0	7	10.65	-2.56	-1.78	-1.41
Woody Williams	33	208.3	106	11.6	11.4	.504	12	12	4.58	-0.45	-0.22	1.81
TOTALS	162	975.7	530	50.8	63.0	.446	53	66	4.89	-5.50	-6.41	2.43

The San Diego Padres' 1999 provides yet another lesson in just how much difference a top starter can make. If Kevin Brown had stayed with the Padres in 1999, it's very reasonable to expect he would have taken most of the 34 starts made by the Padres' rag-tag collection of fifth starters: Brian Boehringer, Buddy Carlyle, Heath Murray and Stan Spencer. According to SNVA, Brown was worth almost four games above average for the Dodgers, while the Padre quartet was worth almost four games below average for the Padres. Eight extra wins wouldn't have meant the NL West crown, and paying Kevin Brown $100 million probably doesn't make sense for the Padres. But this shows how replacing the chaff that almost every team has in its rotation with one reliable top-of-the-league player can mean a huge improvement in the standings.

Pitcher Abuse Points

PITCHER	AGE	GS	PAP	PAP/S	WKLD	MAX	1-90	91-100	101-110	111-120	121-130	131-140	141+
Andy Ashby	31	31	218	7.0	8.2	131	8	6	12	4	0	1	0
Brian Boehringer	29	11	0	0.0	0.0	98	7	4	0	0	0	0	0
Buddy Carlyle	21	7	0	0.0	0.0	91	6	1	0	0	0	0	0
Matt Clement	24	31	109	3.5	8.2	124	11	12	5	2	1	0	0
Sterling Hitchcock	28	33	398	12.1	20.1	140	3	9	7	12	1	1	0
Heath Murray	26	8	8	1.0	2.0	106	4	2	2	0	0	0	0
Stan Spencer	29	8	0	0.0	0.0	96	6	2	0	0	0	0	0
Woody Williams	32	33	169	5.1	5.1	119	5	8	15	5	0	0	0
SAN DIEGO		162	902	5.6	8.4	140	50	44	41	23	2	2	0
Ranking (NL)				14	13								

Bruce Bochy has a national reputation as a sort of shiftless, anonymous manager who doesn't do anything particularly dramatic to either help or hurt his team. But when handling his starters, it is precisely something he doesn't do that makes him such a good handler of pitchers. Matt Clement had the classic profile for a potential abuse victim: a young power pitcher with severe control problems. Freddy Garcia, the same style of pitcher, was ridden hard by Lou Piniella, but Bochy handled Clement beautifully.... Sterling Hitchcock's 140-pitch outing aside, Bochy gave his three veteran starters reasonable workloads as well.... Brian Boehringer was given a nice orientation to the rigors of starting, and the way Bochy handled 21-year-old Buddy Carlyle, never letting him throw more than 91 pitches, is a very good sign that Bochy will do what it takes to keep his starters healthy and effective.

San Francisco Giants

It is a mark of the relative stability of the Giants' franchise as they move into their new ballpark that the primary topics of discussion have been the same for a few seasons now: General Manager Brian Sabean, Manager Dusty Baker and future Hall of Famer Barry Bonds.

Regarding Sabean, it might finally be time to just agree to disagree. Sabean is very highly regarded by the local media. He is a good interview. He is not afraid to make a move, which means he's often in the news. He is perceived as working at a disadvantage, as the Giants' payroll is not as high as some of the other teams in the NL West, so Sabean looks good when the team plays well. To his credit, he has made some very good moves, notably acquiring Jeff Kent.

Furthermore, Sabean's predilection for Proven Veterans™ means that he always seems to be making a trade in which the Giants get someone with a high profile while giving up young guys who no one knows. The best example of this in 1999 was the acquisition of Clutch Performer Livan Hernandez for a couple of minor-league pitchers. Sabean will cut a deal if he thinks the Giants have a chance to win, and he always thinks they have a chance to win.

It's not the worst strategy in the world as long as you've got Barry Bonds in left field and plenty of talent in the farm system. Bonds alone makes an average team a contender, and if you've got lots of prospects, you can afford to give up a few for immediate success. Unfortunately, Bonds missed 60 games last year, so the team wasn't quite the contender they thought they'd be, and the farm system isn't as deep as Sabean seems to think.

A closer examination of Sabean's most lauded moves shows that he has an uncanny knack for acquiring precisely the players serious analysts would avoid at all costs. J.T. Snow, Jose Vizcaino, Charlie Hayes, Joe Carter, Livan Hernandez...it's a remarkable list, one that suggests Sabean lives in an alternate universe. Sometimes these guys work out: Hayes had a nice 1998 before crapping out last year and Carter had a couple of key hits in 1998. More often they just get in the way of team development. Proven Veterans like Vizcaino keep fresh blood like Rich Aurilia on the bench, and with the ungodly extension of J.T. Snow's contract well into the 21st century, the Giants have doomed themselves to years of mediocre first-base play.

It's not entirely clear just how successful the team has been using this strategy. That reflects upon Dusty Baker, since Dusty, like Sabean, gets credit for doing well with limited resources. For all the praise bestowed on these two team leaders, the fact is the Giants haven't won anything but a divisional crown in 1997 (after which they were immediately swept by the Marlins). The pseudo-excitement over the 1998 wild-card race hid the fact they ended the season 9½ games out of first place; last year, the margin was 14 games.

Even when Sabean gets a younger player, he does it the wrong way. Livan Hernandez's right arm has been treated so badly by his managers that the Pitching Abuse Points award should be named in his honor. Hernandez, despite his youth, had Proven Veteran credentials thanks to his 1997 World Series MVP award, an honor he earned with a 5.27 ERA in the Series. He had been mediocre ever since, which would seem to be a warning sign given his overworked arm. Yet this was Sabean's answer to the Giants' rotation problems. And what did he give up to get Hernandez? The team's best pitching prospect, Jason Grilli, and another top pitching prospect, Nate Bump.

One must feel sorry for Hernandez, who might have thought his arm was getting a reprieve after Jim Leyland left the Marlins. He ended up under the care of Dusty Baker, who has also shown a marked tendency to overwork his pitchers. Dusty was delighted to add Hernandez to his rotation, not because he looked forward to taking special care of Livan's arm, but rather because Livan had "proven" he could go deep into a ballgame, which would help save the overworked bullpen. Baker went right to work: in his second start with the club, Hernandez threw 128 pitches, then followed that outing with a 139-pitch monster. After seven innings of that game, Livan had thrown 128 pitches and had a four-run lead.

Giants Prospectus

1999 record: 86-76; Second place, NL West

Pythagorean W/L: 85-77

Runs scored: 872 (3rd in NL)

Runs allowed: 831 (9th in NL)

Team EQA: .277 (1st in NL)

1999 team age: 29.4 (4th oldest in NL)

1999 park: 3Com Park; extreme pitchers' park, decreased run scoring by 22%. Moving to Pac Bell Park for 2000 season.

1999: Another Baker production; good enough to hang around.

2000: New park, same cast: a problem for an old team that hasn't won much.

He talked Baker into letting him pitch the eighth, loaded the bases, the bullpen gave up a grand slam and the Giants lost the game. Four starts later, Dusty left Hernandez in for 138 pitches. He was pulled after two innings in his next start with "tightness in his side" and made just two starts over the last few weeks of the season.

Hernandez was hardly Baker's only victim in 1999. Russ Ortiz, a 25-year-old right-hander in his first full season in the majors, led the team in innings pitched, topping his previous high by 65 innings. Ortiz threw 130 or more pitches seven times during the season, twice reaching 140 pitches. When a team is trading away its best pitching prospects, it behooves them to take care of the young arms that remain. Unfortunately for Ortiz, the Giants and their fans, Dusty Baker is clearly not the man for that job.

What's odd about Baker's handling of the pitching staff is that he manages to overwork both his starters *and* his relievers. The starters have too many high-pitch outings; the relievers suffer from less identifiable maladies related, in part, to Baker's willingness to use them for three or more days in a row. This pattern first manifested itself during the magnificent Last Real Pennant Race between the Giants and Braves in 1993, when he sent Rod Beck out to the mound for something like 23 days in a row. Beck hasn't been the same since then. Robb Nen, to take a more recent example, last year pitched three days in succession on five different occasions, four days in a row once, and at four different times pitched five times in six days. His ERA in the second half of the season was a run higher than it was in the first half, and he had elbow surgery at season's end.

Baker at least has many other qualities that make him a good manager. As we have noted in the past, Baker seems to shine in "intangible" areas, like leadership, that we dismiss in player evaluation but which are very important when evaluating the team's leader. Players enjoy coming to the Giants because of Baker's reputation, a crucial component for a team that wants to build a winner without spending top dollar. There is plenty to like about Baker as a manager, but the same could have been said about Jim Leyland, another armslagger with a good reputation who suffered burnout during his season as resident genius in Colorado.

Baker may also be the wrong man for the 2000 Giants, a team that is going to rely heavily on young arms in the rotation. The Giants are happy, perhaps justifiably, with the current batch of newcomers to their pitching staff, but several warning signs exist. The most obvious has been pointed out a number of times: Livan Hernandez is a prime candidate for a long stay on the disabled list. Russ Ortiz is in the same boat. Also, Ortiz is not as good as last year's 18-9 record would sug-

gest; if he doesn't cut down on his walks, he could have a long season. Meanwhile, Shawn Estes is maddeningly inconsistent, while Kirk Rueter is far more lucky than effective. Finally, Joe Nathan pitched well for a former shortstop, and his future looks bright, but like too many of these guys, his control is a problem. Giants' starters walked more batters in 1999 than any NL rotation except Colorado's. The triumvirate of Ortiz/Estes/Nathan looks like a break-even crew: one will probably have a fine year, one will have an average year and one will crap out. If Hernandez gets injured and Kirk Rueter continues to be a below-average starter, the Giants will be lucky to reach .500. If the starting pitching doesn't hold up, the Giants will have precious little to celebrate as they open their new stadium.

Of course, there's always Barry Bonds, and that is saying a lot. But even Bonds missed 60 games last year and is not getting any younger. All of the Giants' best hitters are in their thirties, not only Bonds but Jeff Kent and Ellis Burks as well. While the team has some potentially good minor-league pitchers, particularly Jake Esteves and Kurt Ainsworth, the hitters in the farm system are less impressive, mostly fourth outfielders like Calvin Murray and utility infielders like Ramon Martinez. But what else can you expect from a front office that values Proven Veterans over youth and potential?

The Giants are staking a lot of their future on Pac Bell Park. The novelty of a new ballpark will bring in plenty of fans for a few years; the Giants may benefit even more than usual from this novelty because their old park was so hated by so many fans. However, Bay Area sports fans are famously fickle, and novelty isn't going to be enough to get people out to the park on a cool April night in 2004 with the Expos in town unless the Giants have a good team on the field. Even the innovative financing of the park could ultimately hurt the team: they built it "without public funds." While this is a good thing for baseball in general—and for other communities that house baseball teams—the vast assemblage of Giants' owners are said to be concerned about the debt the park has incurred. So despite record-setting season-ticket sales for 2000, Giants' management was quick to announce that the player payroll would not go up significantly for this season.

That throws everything back on the shoulders of Brian Sabean, who will have to do what he can with a mid-sized wallet, one already depleted by silly long-term contracts to players like J.T. Snow. San Francisco fans who have waited since their team's arrival in California in 1958 for a championship will be staking their hopes on the very person who thinks J.T. Snow at first base for a long time is a good idea. That's not a pretty picture.

HITTERS (Averages: BA: .270 / OBP: .340 / SLG: .430 / EQA: .260)

Jeff Allen — OF — Bats R — Age 24

YEAR	TEAM	LGE	AB	H	DB	TP	HR	BB/SO	R	RBI	SB	CS	OUT	BA	OBP	SLG	EQA	EQR	DEFENSE
1998	Salem OR	Nwn	217	49	8	3	8	21/74	27	28	3	2	170	.226	.302	.401	.236	23	55-OF 105
1999	Bakrsfld	Cal	479	106	27	2	8	32/138	51	45	9	2	375	.221	.278	.336	.209	38	120-OF 98
2000	San Fran	NL	278	60	12	1	7	25/101	30	27	6	1	219	.216	.281	.342	.218	24	

Allen led Bakersfield in doubles and was among the team leaders in both home runs and stolen bases. He struck out 130 times in A ball, and his EqAs are less than impressive. Like the majority of the minor leaguers on the following pages, Allen could eventually be a decent extra outfielder.

Rich Aurilia — SS — Bats R — Age 28

YEAR	TEAM	LGE	AB	H	DB	TP	HR	BB/SO	R	RBI	SB	CS	OUT	BA	OBP	SLG	EQA	EQR	DEFENSE
1997	San Fran	NL	103	29	6	0	6	8/15	16	20	1	1	75	.282	.333	.515	.275	15	24-SS 114
1998	San Fran	NL	420	117	30	2	10	30/60	57	52	3	3	306	.279	.330	.431	.254	50	102-SS 100
1999	San Fran	NL	567	165	24	1	23	36/70	68	80	2	3	405	.291	.340	.459	.265	73	142-SS 101
2000	San Fran	NL	429	116	20	1	15	36/57	54	65	2	2	315	.270	.327	.427	.258	53	

Aurilia finally got a full shot after several years of watching the likes of Jose Vizcaino and Shawon Dunston play ahead of him. He set a San Francisco record for home runs by a shortstop and should have the job for a few more years. Aurilia's defense was acceptable, despite the 28 errors. Given the relatively weak competition, Aurilia is one of the best shortstops in the National League.

Marvin Benard — CF — Bats L — Age 29

YEAR	TEAM	LGE	AB	H	DB	TP	HR	BB/SO	R	RBI	SB	CS	OUT	BA	OBP	SLG	EQA	EQR	DEFENSE
1997	San Fran	NL	116	28	2	0	2	12/29	13	15	3	1	89	.241	.323	.310	.224	11	17-OF 88
1998	San Fran	NL	292	100	24	1	3	34/38	44	38	12	5	197	.342	.415	.462	.300	49	60-OF 94
1999	San Fran	NL	571	171	40	5	16	48/96	97	63	23	14	414	.299	.361	.471	.276	83	117-CF 93
2000	San Fran	NL	439	130	27	2	13	49/74	78	70	17	10	319	.296	.367	.456	.282	67	

Benard's power increased with regular playing time, as he hit 16 home runs after totalling just 10 in 350 games prior to 1999. He led the team in stolen bases but was thrown out more than a third of the time, so he wasn't helping the Giants. Benard would be better as a platoon left fielder: he can't hit left-handers or play a major-league center field. Obviously, he's not going to play left field on this team, but the Giants need to find someone to help him out against left-handers and in the late innings.

Barry Bonds — LF — Bats L — Age 35

YEAR	TEAM	LGE	AB	H	DB	TP	HR	BB/SO	R	RBI	SB	CS	OUT	BA	OBP	SLG	EQA	EQR	DEFENSE
1997	San Fran	NL	545	162	30	5	42	145/86	123	103	31	8	391	.297	.451	.602	.344	136	145-OF 96
1998	San Fran	NL	566	180	49	7	41	132/90	127	130	30	14	400	.318	.454	.647	.349	144	147-OF 99
1999	San Fran	NL	360	98	23	2	35	70/61	91	82	14	2	264	.272	.395	.639	.328	82	88-LF 104
2000	San Fran	NL	425	115	23	2	34	112/71	108	104	16	5	315	.271	.423	.574	.333	101	

He had elbow surgery early in the season, then knee surgery at the end of the campaign. Bonds came back too soon from the first injury and hit .227 in his first six weeks back, resulting in his lowest batting average in 10 years. Still, he had his highest slugging percentage since 1994 and the rest of his game was intact. Bonds is the greatest Giant since Willie Mays and the most underappreciated Giant since the team came to San Francisco.

Ellis Burks — RF — Bats R — Age 35

YEAR	TEAM	LGE	AB	H	DB	TP	HR	BB/SO	R	RBI	SB	CS	OUT	BA	OBP	SLG	EQA	EQR	DEFENSE
1997	Colorado	NL	421	115	20	2	30	45/74	85	75	5	2	308	.273	.348	.544	.289	69	96-OF 101
1998	Colorado	NL	350	90	20	4	15	37/78	48	47	3	7	267	.257	.332	.466	.260	46	90-OF 97
1998	San Fran	NL	150	48	5	1	6	19/30	23	23	9	1	103	.320	.408	.487	.309	27	39-OF 107
1999	San Fran	NL	396	117	17	0	33	65/85	72	96	6	5	284	.295	.404	.588	.318	81	96-RF 103
2000	San Fran	NL	343	85	13	1	19	55/74	55	61	5	3	261	.248	.352	.458	.277	53	

Burks can still play, both at the plate and in the field, but he missed 42 games last season, faded in September and underwent offseason knee surgery. He's 35 years old, so he isn't going to improve. Burks has hit much better on the road than at home the last two years and may find the new park more to his liking.

Michael Byas   CF   Bats B   Age 24

YEAR	TEAM	LGE	AB	H	DB	TP	HR	BB/SO	R	RBI	SB	CS	OUT	BA	OBP	SLG	EQA	EQR	DEFENSE
1997	Salem OR	Nwn	293	67	6	1	0	30/47	31	11	15	6	232	.229	.303	.256	.200	21	71-OF 109
1998	San Jose	Cal	534	119	11	1	1	63/103	62	29	14	10	425	.223	.305	.253	.195	36	135-OF 101
1999	Shrevprt	Tex	492	118	6	0	1	55/89	55	34	16	8	382	.240	.317	.258	.204	36	129-OF 111
2000	San Fran	NL	541	124	9	1	1	64/101	63	35	21	10	427	.229	.311	.255	.206	41	

Byas has a terrific glove and is very fast, although he is not a particularly effective base stealer. He's also a slap hitter with absolutely no power who could only manage a .271 average in Double-A. The Giants sent him to the Arizona Fall League, where he hit .183 with a double—yes, just one—in 83 at-bats.

Jay Canizaro   2B   Bats R   Age 26

YEAR	TEAM	LGE	AB	H	DB	TP	HR	BB/SO	R	RBI	SB	CS	OUT	BA	OBP	SLG	EQA	EQR	DEFENSE
1997	Shrevprt	Tex	177	39	5	0	10	21/51	26	29	1	1	139	.220	.309	.418	.243	20	31-2B 88
1997	Phoenix	PCL	80	14	4	0	2	7/25	9	9	2	2	67	.175	.241	.300	.177	4	
1998	Shrevprt	Tex	287	54	7	1	8	40/56	33	22	2	1	234	.188	.293	.303	.207	23	79-2B 100
1998	Fresno	PCL	105	21	5	1	5	15/24	18	11	0	1	85	.200	.304	.410	.237	12	21-2B 102
1999	Fresno	PCL	357	78	15	1	17	38/85	50	51	9	3	282	.218	.298	.409	.239	39	98-2B 94
2000	San Fran	NL	369	82	14	1	17	54/87	51	53	6	3	290	.222	.322	.404	.252	46	

He returned to the big club for the first time since 1996, picking up a few at-bats and hopefully impressing someone. Canizaro has a little pop in his bat and isn't the worst defensive second baseman around, so he might be a decent backup.

Giuseppe Chiaramonte C   Bats R   Age 24

YEAR	TEAM	LGE	AB	H	DB	TP	HR	BB/SO	R	RBI	SB	CS	OUT	BA	OBP	SLG	EQA	EQR	DEFENSE
1997	San Jose	Cal	226	48	9	0	11	20/57	23	35	0	0	178	.212	.284	.398	.228	22	
1998	San Jose	Cal	510	120	26	2	19	35/145	65	65	2	1	391	.235	.288	.406	.231	50	105-C 96
1999	Shrevprt	Tex	403	87	18	1	15	32/99	42	56	2	1	317	.216	.281	.377	.220	36	88-C 86
2000	San Fran	NL	447	102	18	1	20	42/119	49	62	2	1	346	.228	.294	.407	.240	49	

He's making a good impression on the right people, it would seem: he was selected to play in the Futures Game. Chiaramonte hit well in the California Fall League; the only caveat is that he was fairly old for that circuit. His EqAs suggest he'll hit .230 in the majors, which is good enough to make him Scott Servais.

Doug Clark   OF   Bats L   Age 24

YEAR	TEAM	LGE	AB	H	DB	TP	HR	BB/SO	R	RBI	SB	CS	OUT	BA	OBP	SLG	EQA	EQR	DEFENSE
1998	Salem OR	Nwn	228	59	8	3	3	19/36	28	26	3	3	172	.259	.320	.360	.231	22	53-OF 79
1999	Bakrsfld	Cal	417	110	15	1	8	42/95	43	38	6	4	311	.264	.335	.362	.240	44	104-OF 91
1999	Shrevprt	Tex	50	10	2	0	1	3/10	5	5	0	0	40	.200	.245	.300	.175	3	
2000	San Fran	NL	284	66	8	1	5	31/66	31	28	4	2	220	.232	.308	.320	.222	26	

Clark is the latest in the Giants' line of left-handed-hitting corner outfielders who can hit . . . just not enough to earn a job in San Francisco. It's as if the organization decided that Luis Gonzalez was its idea of the perfect player. Jacob Cruz and Armando Rios came before him and were ignored, and Clark isn't as good as either of them.

Wilson Delgado   SS/2B   Bats B   Age 24

YEAR	TEAM	LGE	AB	H	DB	TP	HR	BB/SO	R	RBI	SB	CS	OUT	BA	OBP	SLG	EQA	EQR	DEFENSE
1997	Phoenix	PCL	405	102	18	3	7	17/72	34	43	7	2	305	.252	.283	.363	.218	34	110-SS 103
1998	Fresno	PCL	506	127	18	2	10	45/92	69	51	7	4	383	.251	.315	.354	.229	48	126-SS 101
1999	Fresno	PCL	208	54	8	2	1	15/35	21	26	3	1	155	.260	.309	.332	.220	18	55-SS 95
1999	San Fran	NL	72	19	2	1	0	4/9	7	3	1	0	53	.264	.313	.319	.219	6	
2000	San Fran	NL	311	79	10	1	5	27/55	37	33	8	2	234	.254	.314	.341	.233	31	

(Wilson Delgado *continued*)

Delgado has been in Triple-A for three years now posting superficially decent numbers, but he still can't hit. An adequate glove and his ability to switch-hit make him a possible 25th man, but nothing more.

Pedro Feliz   3B   Bats R   Age 23

YEAR	TEAM	LGE	AB	H	DB	TP	HR	BB/SO	R	RBI	SB	CS	OUT	BA	OBP	SLG	EQA	EQR	DEFENSE
1998	Shrevprt	Tex	364	88	20	1	10	5/69	31	39	0	1	277	.242	.255	.385	.207	27	96-3B 95
1999	Shrevprt	Tex	492	114	23	4	11	13/98	42	62	2	1	379	.232	.255	.362	.202	35	129-3B 104
2000	San Fran	NL	306	74	16	1	9	11/73	27	35	0	0	232	.242	.268	.389	.221	27	

He spent a second year in Double-A with no change in performance. Feliz has a good glove at third base and can hit the occasional home run. Ultimately, though, all you need to know about Feliz is this: in two years at Shreveport, he's had 855 at-bats and walked 28 times.

Tim Flaherty   1B   Bats R   Age 23

YEAR	TEAM	LGE	AB	H	DB	TP	HR	BB/SO	R	RBI	SB	CS	OUT	BA	OBP	SLG	EQA	EQR	DEFENSE
1997	Salem OR	Nwn	112	21	4	0	3	9/47	10	11	0	0	91	.188	.251	.304	.182	6	
1998	Bakrsfld	Cal	483	100	18	0	22	30/173	55	69	0	0	383	.207	.261	.381	.212	39	78-C 90
1999	San Jose	Cal	491	115	28	2	21	53/168	59	64	5	1	377	.234	.316	.428	.250	59	126-1B 94
2000	San Fran	NL	405	89	16	1	19	47/144	48	57	2	0	316	.220	.301	.405	.243	46	

Flaherty was a power-hitting catcher with an awful glove. Now he's a power-hitting first baseman with a poor glove. With Chiaramonte ahead of him, he's unlikely to move back behind the plate, so he'll need to have a massive year at Shreveport to carve out a future.

Edwards Guzman   3B/C   Bats L   Age 23

YEAR	TEAM	LGE	AB	H	DB	TP	HR	BB/SO	R	RBI	SB	CS	OUT	BA	OBP	SLG	EQA	EQR	DEFENSE	
1997	Shrevprt	Tex	379	98	14	3	3	26/64	41	33	2	1	282	.259	.308	.335	.219	32	109-3B 82	
1998	Fresno	PCL	320	88	10	0	9	21/47	40	40	1	0	232	.275	.324	.391	.243	34	74-3B 90	
1999	Fresno	PCL	350	83	6	0	7	14/49	35	38	4	4	271	.237	.271	.314	.193	22	57-3B 99	27-C 82
2000	San Fran	NL	313	79	7	0	9	24/47	32	38	2	1	235	.252	.306	.361	.231	30		

Third basemen who can also play behind the plate are valuable to managers who want the luxury of three catchers without actually carrying three on the roster. Guzman is young and at one point looked like he might hit enough to play, but his walk rate went into free-fall last year, and he doesn't have much margin for error.

Charlie Hayes   3B/1B   Bats R   Age 35

YEAR	TEAM	LGE	AB	H	DB	TP	HR	BB/SO	R	RBI	SB	CS	OUT	BA	OBP	SLG	EQA	EQR	DEFENSE	
1997	NY Yanks	AL	355	96	13	0	13	38/63	39	55	3	2	261	.270	.343	.417	.258	44	89-3B 99	
1998	San Fran	NL	335	97	7	0	14	34/59	41	66	2	1	239	.290	.355	.436	.268	44	37-1B 106	35-3B 100
1999	San Fran	NL	268	57	11	1	6	30/41	33	48	3	1	212	.213	.295	.328	.214	22	49-3B 91	
2000	San Fran	NL	218	49	5	0	7	25/36	23	25	1	1	170	.225	.305	.344	.226	21		

A nice surprise in 1998 went sour in 1999. His main value had been his hitting against lefties; last year he had a 597 OPS against them. He managed to accumulate 48 RBI on only 54 hits, courtesy of Barry Bonds, and he hit better in the second half, so he may show up on a roster this year. Just hope it's not the one of your favorite team.

Jeff Kent   2B   Bats R   Age 32

YEAR	TEAM	LGE	AB	H	DB	TP	HR	BB/SO	R	RBI	SB	CS	OUT	BA	OBP	SLG	EQA	EQR	DEFENSE
1997	San Fran	NL	588	151	37	2	32	47/132	91	125	9	3	440	.257	.326	.490	.269	82	142-2B 99
1998	San Fran	NL	536	168	41	3	34	48/107	100	136	10	5	373	.313	.380	.591	.311	101	131-2B 98
1999	San Fran	NL	519	157	42	2	24	55/111	85	101	11	6	368	.303	.376	.530	.296	88	125-2B 93
2000	San Fran	NL	519	141	31	1	30	56/112	83	99	9	3	381	.272	.343	.509	.286	83	

He is perhaps the best evidence in favor of Brian Sabean's competence. Kent is good for an injury per season, and his defense in 1999 was subpar due to his playing through foot and toe owies. But he's a second baseman who has put up consecutive .290 EqAs, and guys like that don't grow on trees. To most of the nation, he's underrated. In the Bay Area, they think he's better than Bonds. And they wonder why the rest of the country thinks they're weird.

Ramon Martinez IF Bats R Age 27

YEAR	TEAM	LGE	AB	H	DB	TP	HR	BB/SO	R	RBI	SB	CS	OUT	BA	OBP	SLG	EQA	EQR	DEFENSE
1997	Shrevprt	Tex	402	105	27	2	4	29/59	50	37	2	2	299	.261	.315	.368	.231	38	104-SS 110
1998	Fresno	PCL	359	93	17	1	10	30/46	42	43	0	2	268	.259	.319	.396	.240	38	97-2B 100
1999	Fresno	PCL	111	29	6	1	1	7/18	9	12	1	0	82	.261	.305	.360	.227	10	22-SS 96
1999	San Fran	NL	146	40	4	0	6	13/17	21	20	1	2	108	.274	.333	.425	.252	17	
2000	*San Fran*	*NL*	*267*	*69*	*14*	*1*	*6*	*26/37*	*33*	*35*	*1*	*1*	*199*	*.258*	*.324*	*.386*	*.246*	*30*	

He's hitting for a little more power than he used to, and his glove is good enough for his versatility to give him some value as an extra infielder. No star potential, but a good player for a budget-conscious club like the Giants.

Brent Mayne C Bats L Age 32

YEAR	TEAM	LGE	AB	H	DB	TP	HR	BB/SO	R	RBI	SB	CS	OUT	BA	OBP	SLG	EQA	EQR	DEFENSE
1997	Oakland	AL	255	74	10	0	7	16/32	28	22	1	0	181	.290	.343	.412	.257	30	
1998	San Fran	NL	280	80	12	0	5	37/46	27	35	2	2	202	.286	.371	.382	.261	35	73-C 94
1999	San Fran	NL	327	102	22	0	6	39/64	38	42	2	2	227	.312	.395	.434	.284	49	86-C 103
2000	*Colorado*	*NL*	*240*	*81*	*11*	*0*	*8*	*34/42*	*46*	*51*	*1*	*1*	*160*	*.338*	*.420*	*.483*	*.283*	*34*	

Mayne hit .300 for the first time in his career, on his way to becoming a free agent. He is a decent half of a catching platoon. He even reads books. Mayne hit the jackpot, signing a three-year deal with the Rockies to impede Ben Petrick's progress. The move added 134 points of OPS to that Wilton.

Damon Minor 1B Bats L Age 26

YEAR	TEAM	LGE	AB	H	DB	TP	HR	BB/SO	R	RBI	SB	CS	OUT	BA	OBP	SLG	EQA	EQR	DEFENSE
1997	Bakrsfld	Cal	537	125	22	1	22	64/153	67	66	1	0	412	.233	.318	.400	.244	60	129-1B 81
1998	San Jose	Cal	181	39	8	0	5	19/47	17	23	0	0	142	.215	.295	.343	.217	16	44-1B 91
1998	Shrevprt	Tex	292	60	9	2	9	21/62	27	36	0	0	232	.205	.268	.342	.204	22	71-1B 84
1999	Shrevprt	Tex	481	103	27	2	13	60/141	53	54	0	0	378	.214	.309	.360	.229	47	130-1B 102
2000	*San Fran*	*NL*	*443*	*95*	*20*	*1*	*14*	*58/124*	*51*	*53*	*0*	*0*	*348*	*.214*	*.305*	*.359*	*.232*	*45*	

His walk rate jumped back up to go with a .273 average, 20 home runs and 33 doubles. He's 26 years old and hasn't played above Double-A. It's entirely possible that Minor will have a Rookie of the Year season in 2002, followed by several years of mediocrity. At this point, that's the best he can hope for.

Doug Mirabelli C Bats R Age 29

YEAR	TEAM	LGE	AB	H	DB	TP	HR	BB/SO	R	RBI	SB	CS	OUT	BA	OBP	SLG	EQA	EQR	DEFENSE
1997	Phoenix	PCL	324	66	18	1	5	44/77	33	30	1	1	259	.204	.309	.312	.216	28	
1998	Fresno	PCL	264	56	11	1	9	42/60	32	37	1	0	208	.212	.325	.364	.239	29	84-C 105
1999	Fresno	PCL	312	76	16	1	9	38/61	42	34	5	1	237	.244	.327	.388	.246	36	65-C 99
1999	San Fran	NL	88	23	4	0	2	8/25	10	11	0	0	65	.261	.331	.375	.242	9	24-C 110
2000	*San Fran*	*NL*	*338*	*73*	*14*	*1*	*10*	*52/76*	*43*	*41*	*2*	*1*	*266*	*.216*	*.321*	*.352*	*.238*	*37*	

He's 29 years old now, and the Giants have never really given him a chance. He isn't good enough to be a regular at the major-league level, but he could be one of the best #2 catchers in the game, which is higher praise than it sounds. Mirabelli will split the Giants' catching job with Bobby Estalella—picked up from the Phillies for an old whirlpool and some sunflower seeds—and should play less than that projection indicates.

Bill Mueller 3B Bats B Age 29

YEAR	TEAM	LGE	AB	H	DB	TP	HR	BB/SO	R	RBI	SB	CS	OUT	BA	OBP	SLG	EQA	EQR	DEFENSE
1997	San Fran	NL	397	119	28	3	8	47/70	52	46	3	3	281	.300	.378	.446	.279	58	112-3B 95
1998	San Fran	NL	545	169	20	0	13	80/81	96	64	3	4	380	.310	.399	.418	.282	80	128-3B 103
1999	San Fran	NL	420	126	14	1	5	61/51	59	38	4	2	296	.300	.393	.374	.271	56	102-3B 99
2000	*San Fran*	*NL*	*377*	*107*	*9*	*0*	*10*	*56/53*	*58*	*58*	*2*	*1*	*271*	*.284*	*.376*	*.387*	*.272*	*52*	

The Giants want a new third baseman, apparently because Mueller doesn't hit for power. He has a career OBP of .383 and a decent glove at third base; combine his performance with Jeff Kent's and you have a good situation at second and third base. Mueller isn't Vinny Castilla, which bothers Brian Sabean a lot more than it should, especially since Mueller is better.

Calvin Murray — CF — Bats R — Age 28

YEAR	TEAM	LGE	AB	H	DB	TP	HR	BB/SO	R	RBI	SB	CS	OUT	BA	OBP	SLG	EQA	EQR	DEFENSE
1997	Shrevprt	Tex	422	92	20	3	7	49/93	49	38	24	4	334	.218	.304	.329	.227	41	104-OF 98
1998	Shrevprt	Tex	341	82	19	2	5	42/56	38	26	14	7	266	.240	.330	.352	.238	37	89-OF 103
1998	Fresno	PCL	90	18	3	1	2	9/20	12	4	2	1	73	.200	.273	.322	.202	7	
1999	Fresno	PCL	531	140	24	6	14	38/95	78	48	24	9	400	.264	.315	.411	.247	61	129-OF 106
2000	San Fran	NL	475	113	22	3	9	51/89	65	50	19	6	368	.238	.312	.354	.237	50	

A Giants' first-round draft pick back when a Republican was president, Murray hit .334 with 23 homers and 42 steals in the Pacific Coast League, finally getting his first cup of coffee in the majors. He's 28 years old and has been bouncing around the upper minors for several years without showing much. He could help the Giants as a dance partner for Benard in center field.

Armando Rios — OF — Bats L — Age 28

YEAR	TEAM	LGE	AB	H	DB	TP	HR	BB/SO	R	RBI	SB	CS	OUT	BA	OBP	SLG	EQA	EQR	DEFENSE
1997	Shrevprt	Tex	462	106	26	3	10	46/108	56	52	8	4	360	.229	.299	.364	.226	44	112-OF 92
1998	Fresno	PCL	440	108	17	2	18	44/80	59	73	11	4	336	.245	.317	.416	.248	52	114-OF 88
1999	Fresno	PCL	107	24	1	0	3	8/24	16	15	2	1	84	.224	.296	.318	.211	9	16-OF 94
1999	San Fran	NL	152	51	6	0	8	23/35	30	29	6	4	105	.336	.427	.533	.316	29	23-RF 109
2000	San Fran	NL	324	78	10	1	13	44/70	46	46	7	4	250	.241	.332	.398	.255	41	

Rios struggled with some personal difficulties early in the year, then had his season ended by rotator-cuff surgery at midseason. He's not a bad player, but he gets more attention here than he might in an organization with a better farm system. He and Murray are the best extra outfielders the Giants have.

F.P. Santangelo — UT — Bats B — Age 32

YEAR	TEAM	LGE	AB	H	DB	TP	HR	BB/SO	R	RBI	SB	CS	OUT	BA	OBP	SLG	EQA	EQR	DEFENSE	
1997	Montreal	NL	353	87	21	5	5	49/72	55	30	6	5	271	.246	.378	.377	.264	49	80-OF 98	22-3B 103
1998	Montreal	NL	391	92	13	0	7	44/70	56	27	8	4	303	.235	.351	.322	.240	43	27-2B 98	75-OF 100
1999	San Fran	NL	258	70	19	3	3	50/53	48	26	11	4	192	.271	.413	.403	.289	43	38-CF 93	
2000	LosAngls	NL	263	62	11	2	5	44/53	42	30	8	4	205	.236	.345	.350	.251	32		

The likable utility player had his best season since 1996. A fine player to have on a roster: versatile, inexpensive and productive. Having said that, he is 32 years old with bad knees and will decline over the next few years.

Scott Servais — C — Bats R — Age 33

YEAR	TEAM	LGE	AB	H	DB	TP	HR	BB/SO	R	RBI	SB	CS	OUT	BA	OBP	SLG	EQA	EQR	DEFENSE
1997	ChiCubs	NL	386	98	16	0	8	23/55	35	45	0	1	289	.254	.306	.358	.224	34	
1998	ChiCubs	NL	328	75	15	1	8	25/50	36	37	1	0	253	.229	.294	.354	.220	29	91-C 99
1999	San Fran	NL	201	57	7	0	6	11/31	20	21	0	0	144	.284	.331	.408	.250	22	51-C 94
2000	Colorado	NL	234	67	7	0	8	19/34	29	37	0	0	167	.286	.340	.419	.233	22	

Servais is a generic backup catcher who hits left-handers and whose defense is all reputation. On the long list of Dan O'Dowd's moves since taking over in Colorado, acquiring the Giants' catching platoon to block Ben Petrick is one of the dumbest.

J.T. Snow — 1B — Bats L — Age 32

YEAR	TEAM	LGE	AB	H	DB	TP	HR	BB/SO	R	RBI	SB	CS	OUT	BA	OBP	SLG	EQA	EQR	DEFENSE
1997	San Fran	NL	541	155	36	1	31	96/123	83	108	5	4	390	.287	.395	.529	.304	99	151-1B 98
1998	San Fran	NL	443	116	30	1	17	58/82	68	84	1	2	329	.262	.347	.449	.267	60	116-1B 103
1999	San Fran	NL	579	164	29	2	24	80/120	93	97	0	4	419	.283	.376	.465	.281	88	149-1B 117
2000	San Fran	NL	454	117	24	1	20	71/95	72	79	1	2	339	.258	.358	.447	.277	69	

Snow had a decent season at the plate, helped by giving up switch-hitting. While the move was deemed a success by Snow's millions of fans, he had a 644 OPS against left-handers. His defense at first base is catching up with his reputation. J.T. Snow is a 32-year-old average first baseman to whom the Giants gave a four-year contract extension. Yes, Mr. Sabean, you are an idiot.

Tony Torcato 3B Bats L Age 20

YEAR	TEAM	LGE	AB	H	DB	TP	HR	BB/SO	R	RBI	SB	CS	OUT	BA	OBP	SLG	EQA	EQR	DEFENSE
1998	Salem OR	Nwn	221	54	15	1	2	6/43	20	28	1	1	168	.244	.269	.348	.203	16	52-3B 100
1999	Bakrsfld	Cal	419	110	13	0	7	21/65	38	47	1	0	309	.263	.301	.344	.218	34	77-3B 92
2000	*San Fran*	*NL*	*245*	*63*	*5*	*0*	*6*	*14/43*	*22*	*28*	*1*	*0*	*182*	*.257*	*.297*	*.351*	*.224*	*22*	

He was the Giants' first-round pick in the 1998 draft. Torcato is very young, and as a first-round pick, he'll be given every opportunity to succeed. Early returns are less than inspiring. He hit .291 last season, but with just four home runs and 30 walks in 422 at-bats. Check back next year.

Yorvit Torrealba C Bats R Age 21

YEAR	TEAM	LGE	AB	H	DB	TP	HR	BB/SO	R	RBI	SB	CS	OUT	BA	OBP	SLG	EQA	EQR	DEFENSE
1997	Bakrsfld	Cal	447	111	16	2	3	22/57	41	32	2	1	337	.248	.289	.313	.202	31	
1998	Shrevprt	Tex	197	42	7	0	0	14/33	15	11	0	3	158	.213	.275	.249	.168	9	58-C 101
1999	San Jose	Cal	73	21	2	0	2	4/15	8	11	0	0	52	.288	.330	.397	.246	8	
1999	Shrevprt	Tex	217	49	9	1	3	7/37	21	15	0	1	169	.226	.255	.318	.185	12	48-C 99
1999	Fresno	PCL	62	14	0	0	2	3/11	6	8	0	1	49	.226	.279	.323	.196	4	
2000	*San Fran*	*NL*	*355*	*86*	*14*	*1*	*7*	*23/61*	*32*	*37*	*1*	*2*	*271*	*.242*	*.288*	*.346*	*.217*	*30*	

Perhaps the closest thing the Giants have to a sleeper, Torrealba hit .315 in A ball before struggling at both Double- and Triple-A. He's a 21-year-old catcher with a very nice upside. Given the Giants' recent track record with young talent, that probably means he's the next Doug Mirabelli.

Travis Young 2B Bats R Age 25

YEAR	TEAM	LGE	AB	H	DB	TP	HR	BB/SO	R	RBI	SB	CS	OUT	BA	OBP	SLG	EQA	EQR	DEFENSE
1997	Salem OR	Nwn	318	82	10	3	1	15/55	37	21	10	4	240	.258	.297	.318	.211	25	76-2B 90
1998	San Jose	Cal	528	111	18	2	3	44/112	53	47	11	6	423	.210	.278	.269	.186	32	133-2B 94
1999	Shrevprt	Tex	418	93	24	1	3	24/89	48	28	7	5	330	.222	.274	.306	.194	28	108-2B 93
1999	Fresno	PCL	90	18	2	1	1	8/23	11	8	2	1	73	.200	.282	.278	.193	6	26-2B 103
2000	*San Fran*	*NL*	*494*	*108*	*22*	*2*	*3*	*42/108*	*50*	*34*	*16*	*7*	*393*	*.219*	*.280*	*.289*	*.200*	*35*	

You like to think when a team sends a player to the Arizona Fall League, they believe that player has a future. Travis Young is a 25-year-old second baseman who has struggled offensively at every level he has played. The Giants sent him to the AFL where he camped out under the Mendoza Line for much of the season. He has no future.

PITCHERS (Averages: ERA: 4.50 / H/9: 9.00 / HR/9: 1.00 / BB/9: 3.50 / K/9: 6.50 / KWH: 1.00)

Kurt Ainsworth Throws R Age 21

YEAR	TEAM	LGE	IP	H	ER	HR	BB	K	ERA	W	L	H/9	HR/9	BB/9	K/9	KWH	PERA
1999	Salem OR	Nwn	42.3	42	20	1	21	43	4.25	3	2	8.93	0.21	4.46	9.14	1.57	4.04

One of many fine pitching prospects in the Giants' system, Ainsworth had Tommy John surgery a few years ago, but pitched well in the Northwest League. He's only 21 years old, and even with the worrisome injury history, early reports are very positive.

Jeff Andra Throws L Age 24

YEAR	TEAM	LGE	IP	H	ER	HR	BB	K	ERA	W	L	H/9	HR/9	BB/9	K/9	KWH	PERA
1997	Salem OR	Nwn	40.7	52	27	4	12	32	5.98	2	3	11.51	0.89	2.66	7.08	1.23	5.53
1997	San Jose	Cal	27.3	42	27	2	12	21	8.89	1	2	13.83	0.66	3.95	6.91	0.65	7.24
1998	San Jose	Cal	77.3	101	51	3	35	53	5.94	3	6	11.75	0.35	4.07	6.17	0.59	5.59
1999	San Jose	Cal	43.7	68	36	4	23	37	7.42	1	4	14.02	0.82	4.74	7.63	0.65	7.83

Andra has been stuck in the California League for a few years, thanks largely to injuries. Last season marked the first step back, and it wasn't a great success. His future might be in the bullpen.

Chris Brock   Throws R   Age 30

YEAR	TEAM	LGE	IP	H	ER	HR	BB	K	ERA	W	L	H/9	HR/9	BB/9	K/9	KWH	PERA
1997	Richmond	Int	112.7	114	58	9	55	67	4.63	6	7	9.11	0.72	4.39	5.35	0.53	4.63
1997	Atlanta	NL	29.7	37	25	2	20	15	7.58	1	2	11.22	0.61	6.07	4.55	0.23	6.37
1998	Fresno	PCL	110.3	120	50	10	39	91	4.08	7	5	9.79	0.82	3.18	7.42	1.32	4.65
1998	San Fran	NL	27.0	33	14	3	8	18	4.67	1	2	11.00	1.00	2.67	6.00	0.92	5.33
1999	San Fran	NL	104.0	125	67	17	39	72	5.80	5	7	10.82	1.47	3.38	6.23	0.79	6.06

Brock began the 1999 season well for the Giants, then lost five of six decisions and saw his ERA rise by almost two runs in June and July before his season ended due to a torn knee ligament. It's hard to know what to make of his future; he has been effective at times, but is 30 years old and coming off an injury, with not much more than Minor League Journeyman written across his jersey. He was traded to the Phillies for Bobby Estalella, his signature contribution to the Giants' franchise.

Miguel del Toro   Throws R   Age 28

YEAR	TEAM	LGE	IP	H	ER	HR	BB	K	ERA	W	L	H/9	HR/9	BB/9	K/9	KWH	PERA
1999	Fresno	PCL	69.3	77	39	9	35	57	5.06	4	4	10.00	1.17	4.54	7.40	0.90	5.71
1999	San Fran	NL	23.0	24	10	5	11	19	3.91	2	1	9.39	1.96	4.30	7.43	1.02	6.26

The non-roster invitee from the Mexican League made for a nice human interest story, and he pitched fairly well in Triple-A and the majors, although his peripheral numbers suggest he was more than a little lucky. He allowed five home runs in only 23⅔ innings with the Giants.

Alan Embree   Throws L   Age 30

YEAR	TEAM	LGE	IP	H	ER	HR	BB	K	ERA	W	L	H/9	HR/9	BB/9	K/9	KWH	PERA
1997	Atlanta	NL	45.0	39	14	1	20	42	2.80	4	1	7.80	0.20	4.00	8.40	1.69	3.20
1998	Atlanta	NL	18.3	25	14	2	10	18	6.87	1	1	12.27	0.98	4.91	8.84	0.97	6.87
1998	Arizona	NL	34.3	36	19	5	14	23	4.98	2	2	9.44	1.31	3.67	6.03	0.78	5.24
1999	San Fran	NL	57.3	43	21	6	25	51	3.30	4	2	6.75	0.94	3.92	8.01	1.81	3.45

He did a good job in the specialist role, partly because he was effective against right-handed hitters. Guys like this often have careers that last into their forties. Embree's good strikeout rates make him a strong candidate for just that.

Shawn Estes   Throws L   Age 27

YEAR	TEAM	LGE	IP	H	ER	HR	BB	K	ERA	W	L	H/9	HR/9	BB/9	K/9	KWH	PERA
1997	San Fran	NL	199.0	165	79	12	105	168	3.57	13	9	7.46	0.54	4.75	7.60	1.22	3.71
1998	San Fran	NL	146.7	159	93	14	85	130	5.71	6	10	9.76	0.86	5.22	7.98	0.93	5.46
1999	San Fran	NL	197.3	214	118	20	106	152	5.38	9	13	9.76	0.91	4.83	6.93	0.76	5.38

His up-and-down season earned him the nickname "Sybil" among some Giants' fans. Estes put together a fine run from late July through mid-September, culminating in a four-hit shutout of the Marlins, then ruined it with a 10.20 ERA in his last three starts. Estes will never have consistent success until he eliminates at least one walk per nine innings.

Jake Esteves   Throws R   Age 24

YEAR	TEAM	LGE	IP	H	ER	HR	BB	K	ERA	W	L	H/9	HR/9	BB/9	K/9	KWH	PERA
1998	Bakrsfld	Cal	32.3	54	36	8	15	16	10.02	1	3	15.03	2.23	4.18	4.45	0.24	10.30
1999	San Jose	Cal	66.7	70	26	2	20	38	3.51	4	3	9.45	0.27	2.70	5.13	0.77	3.78
1999	Shrevprt	Tex	83.0	99	55	7	28	41	5.96	3	6	10.73	0.76	3.04	4.45	0.45	5.10

Another decent Giants' pitching prospect, Esteves pitched very well for San Jose, something he didn't do for Shreveport. By season's end, he was suffering from a tired arm. Esteves doesn't have the strikeout rate of a top-tier prospect, and his status as one has more to do with the trade of Grilli and Bump than his performance.

Aaron Fultz   Throws L   Age 26

YEAR	TEAM	LGE	IP	H	ER	HR	BB	K	ERA	W	L	H/9	HR/9	BB/9	K/9	KWH	PERA
1997	Shrevprt	Tex	63.0	78	37	7	22	50	5.29	3	4	11.14	1.00	3.14	7.14	1.09	5.57
1998	Shrevprt	Tex	54.7	72	51	4	35	46	8.40	1	5	11.85	0.66	5.76	7.57	0.63	6.75
1998	Fresno	PCL	15.3	23	10	2	3	11	5.87	1	1	13.50	1.17	1.76	6.46	1.31	6.46
1999	Fresno	PCL	133.3	145	82	27	62	120	5.54	6	9	9.79	1.82	4.19	8.10	1.20	6.14

The Giants liked what they saw of Fultz last season, adding him to the 40-man roster in October. It's easy to see what they liked: a left-handed starter/reliever who struck out 151 in 137 innings in Triple-A. If he has just one good season in middle relief for a major-league team, he'll play in the bigs for a decade. Of course, he may never get that chance.

Mark Gardner   Throws R   Age 38

YEAR	TEAM	LGE	IP	H	ER	HR	BB	K	ERA	W	L	H/9	HR/9	BB/9	K/9	KWH	PERA
1997	San Fran	NL	179.0	191	91	29	60	126	4.58	10	10	9.60	1.46	3.02	6.34	1.04	5.13
1998	San Fran	NL	208.3	214	112	30	69	143	4.84	11	12	9.24	1.30	2.98	6.18	1.03	4.75
1999	San Jose	Cal	8.7	13	7	0	4	8	7.27	0	1	13.50	0.00	4.15	8.31	0.92	6.23
1999	San Fran	NL	135.7	144	100	26	54	82	6.63	5	10	9.55	1.72	3.58	5.44	0.65	5.64

For many years, Mark Gardner was a fine addition to a roster, an underrated and thus bargain-priced starting pitcher who filled a mid-rotation slot. Those years are gone. His peripheral numbers weren't too bad, but there aren't many jobs for a 38-year-old journeyman right-hander coming off a 6.47 ERA.

Livan Hernandez   Throws R   Age 25

YEAR	TEAM	LGE	IP	H	ER	HR	BB	K	ERA	W	L	H/9	HR/9	BB/9	K/9	KWH	PERA
1997	Charlott	Int	81.3	79	38	5	40	50	4.20	5	4	8.74	0.55	4.43	5.53	0.59	4.32
1997	Florida	NL	95.7	82	39	5	40	67	3.67	7	4	7.71	0.47	3.76	6.30	1.02	3.39
1998	Florida	NL	233.7	270	133	38	111	155	5.12	11	15	10.40	1.46	4.28	5.97	0.60	6.16
1999	Florida	NL	132.3	164	77	16	53	93	5.24	6	9	11.15	1.09	3.60	6.32	0.74	5.92
1999	San Fran	NL	62.0	67	31	6	20	45	4.50	4	3	9.73	0.87	2.90	6.53	1.13	4.50

Out of the frying pan and into the fire as Hernandez, only a few months free from the notorious Jim Leyland, got to pitch for Dusty Baker. He was again the most abused pitcher in baseball. The chances of his having a better 21st century than the combination of Jason Grilli and Nate Bump are very small.

Ryan Jensen   Throws R   Age 24

YEAR	TEAM	LGE	IP	H	ER	HR	BB	K	ERA	W	L	H/9	HR/9	BB/9	K/9	KWH	PERA
1997	Salem OR	Nwn	71.3	116	68	12	39	38	8.58	2	6	14.64	1.51	4.92	4.79	0.24	9.34
1998	Bakrsfld	Cal	156.0	200	109	18	78	109	6.29	6	11	11.54	1.04	4.50	6.29	0.57	6.46
1999	Fresno	PCL	155.7	153	85	15	77	125	4.91	8	9	8.85	0.87	4.45	7.23	0.99	4.63

Jensen made the leap from A ball to Triple-A and improved in virtually every area. If he continues to improve, he's going to surprise a lot of people very soon. On the other hand, the end result of last year's improvement was only a 5.12 ERA.

John Johnstone   Throws R   Age 31

YEAR	TEAM	LGE	IP	H	ER	HR	BB	K	ERA	W	L	H/9	HR/9	BB/9	K/9	KWH	PERA
1997	Phoenix	PCL	35.3	36	18	3	16	25	4.58	2	2	9.17	0.76	4.08	6.37	0.81	4.58
1997	San Fran	NL	18.7	15	7	1	7	14	3.38	1	1	7.23	0.48	3.38	6.75	1.39	2.89
1998	San Fran	NL	86.7	76	34	10	40	82	3.53	6	4	7.89	1.04	4.15	8.52	1.65	4.15
1999	San Fran	NL	64.3	49	23	8	19	54	3.22	5	2	6.85	1.12	2.66	7.55	2.34	3.22

Johnstone was rolling along nicely with another fine season in middle relief when suddenly he started to stink on a regular basis. After a few weeks, he admitted to having been in a car accident about the time his pitching went in the toilet. He should be fine in 2000.

Kevin Joseph   Throws R   Age 23

YEAR	TEAM	LGE	IP	H	ER	HR	BB	K	ERA	W	L	H/9	HR/9	BB/9	K/9	KWH	PERA
1997	Salem OR	Nwn	40.0	59	43	5	31	25	9.68	1	3	13.28	1.13	6.98	5.63	0.26	8.77
1998	Salem OR	Nwn	38.7	50	31	3	31	25	7.22	1	3	11.64	0.70	7.22	5.82	0.30	7.22
1998	Bakrsfld	Cal	17.7	45	34	4	25	12	17.32	0	2	22.92	2.04	12.74	6.11	0.10	20.38
1999	San Jose	Cal	28.7	20	10	1	15	22	3.14	2	1	6.28	0.31	4.71	6.91	1.21	2.83
1999	Shrevprt	Tex	11.7	10	5	0	6	13	3.86	1	0	7.71	0.00	4.63	10.03	2.10	3.09

He pitched very well in relief at two levels, earning a brief, ugly trip to the California Fall League. It's too soon to predict future success, but the name is worth filing away for later.

Scott Linebrink   Throws R   Age 23

YEAR	TEAM	LGE	IP	H	ER	HR	BB	K	ERA	W	L	H/9	HR/9	BB/9	K/9	KWH	PERA
1997	San Jose	Cal	26.7	33	12	3	11	28	4.05	2	1	11.14	1.01	3.71	9.45	1.61	5.74
1998	Shrevprt	Tex	103.3	117	75	12	66	104	6.53	4	7	10.19	1.05	5.75	9.06	1.05	6.18
1999	Shrevprt	Tex	38.7	60	38	7	17	26	8.84	1	3	13.97	1.63	3.96	6.05	0.50	8.61

A couple of years ago, Linebrink was one of the best pitching prospects in the Giants' organization. Now he's just another struggling young pitcher working his way back from injury problems. Last season's performance in Shreveport wasn't encouraging. His strikeout rates have been impressive in the past; if he gets them back up again, his future could be bright.

Joe Nathan   Throws R   Age 25

YEAR	TEAM	LGE	IP	H	ER	HR	BB	K	ERA	W	L	H/9	HR/9	BB/9	K/9	KWH	PERA
1997	Salem OR	Nwn	56.0	72	27	8	32	24	4.34	3	3	11.57	1.29	5.14	3.86	0.19	7.07
1998	San Jose	Cal	105.7	143	76	16	63	74	6.47	4	8	12.18	1.36	5.37	6.30	0.45	7.67
1999	Fresno	PCL	73.3	67	40	9	42	67	4.91	4	4	8.22	1.10	5.15	8.22	1.19	4.79
1999	San Fran	NL	88.0	85	43	16	44	52	4.40	5	5	8.69	1.64	4.50	5.32	0.54	5.42

Nathan is an ex-shortstop who has developed rapidly since moving to the mound. Last year he didn't even appear in the *Prospectus;* he ended up spending half the season with the Giants and was effective. The peripheral numbers are not as impressive, particularly the strikeout rate. Nathan does throw hard, which is why he was moved to the mound in the first place. He's a nice surprise with an uncertain future.

Robb Nen   Throws R   Age 30

YEAR	TEAM	LGE	IP	H	ER	HR	BB	K	ERA	W	L	H/9	HR/9	BB/9	K/9	KWH	PERA
1997	Florida	NL	73.7	73	34	7	42	75	4.15	4	4	8.92	0.86	5.13	9.16	1.37	4.89
1998	San Fran	NL	87.7	62	22	4	27	104	2.26	8	2	6.37	0.41	2.77	10.68	4.83	2.36
1999	San Fran	NL	70.7	80	34	8	25	73	4.33	4	4	10.19	1.02	3.18	9.30	1.99	5.09

1999 was something of a disaster for Nen. His ERA was its highest since his rookie year, he blew nine saves and the league hit 95 points higher against him than in 1998. He still throws hard with decent control; the difference last year was that he was no longer unhittable. Nen had elbow surgery in the offseason; a recovery from the surgery, and perhaps a change in approach, could lead to a comeback for Nen. He wouldn't be the first closer to lose it after a nice run, though.

Russ Ortiz   Throws R   Age 26

YEAR	TEAM	LGE	IP	H	ER	HR	BB	K	ERA	W	L	H/9	HR/9	BB/9	K/9	KWH	PERA
1997	Shrevprt	Tex	50.0	62	33	3	43	42	5.94	2	4	11.16	0.54	7.74	7.56	0.49	7.02
1997	Phoenix	PCL	80.3	96	53	10	35	60	5.94	3	6	10.76	1.12	3.92	6.72	0.80	5.83
1998	Fresno	PCL	49.3	36	10	3	26	49	1.82	4	1	6.57	0.55	4.74	8.94	1.92	3.28
1998	San Fran	NL	87.0	95	53	11	49	71	5.48	4	6	9.83	1.14	5.07	7.34	0.81	5.79
1999	San Fran	NL	203.0	192	105	23	119	157	4.66	11	12	8.51	1.02	5.28	6.96	0.81	4.97

The good news is very good. Ortiz improved in most areas, winning 18 games in his first full season in the majors and holding opposing hitters to a .244 batting average. The bad news is ominous, though. He threw 207⅔ innings, up from his previous seasonal high of 141⅔. They were tough innings, putting Ortiz among the league leaders in Pitcher Abuse Points. Ortiz is simultaneously the team's rotation ace, a pitcher with major control problems and a significant injury risk. All of that could have been said about Shawn Estes two years ago: he's gone 18-22 with an 4.98 ERA since then.

Bronswell Patrick   Throws R   Age 29

YEAR	TEAM	LGE	IP	H	ER	HR	BB	K	ERA	W	L	H/9	HR/9	BB/9	K/9	KWH	PERA
1997	New Orln	AmA	93.3	129	57	9	35	74	5.50	4	6	12.44	0.87	3.38	7.14	0.91	6.36
1998	Louisvil	Int	35.0	50	24	6	10	24	6.17	1	3	12.86	1.54	2.57	6.17	0.86	7.20
1998	Milwauke	NL	80.3	82	41	9	31	47	4.59	4	5	9.19	1.01	3.47	5.27	0.65	4.59
1999	Fresno	PCL	159.3	201	110	28	51	113	6.21	6	12	11.35	1.58	2.88	6.38	0.93	6.27

Patrick was a nice story in 1998, making the majors after more than 10 years in the minor leagues and pitching well for Milwaukee. This year he picked up his first major-league save, but did little else for the Giants. He won 14 games at Triple-A and will likely show up with some team in 2000, but one suspects his glory days are behind him.

Felix Rodriguez   Throws R   Age 27

YEAR	TEAM	LGE	IP	H	ER	HR	BB	K	ERA	W	L	H/9	HR/9	BB/9	K/9	KWH	PERA
1997	Indianap	AmA	25.7	25	12	0	18	23	4.21	2	1	8.77	0.00	6.31	8.06	0.88	4.56
1997	Cincnnti	NL	46.7	48	22	2	29	32	4.24	3	2	9.26	0.39	5.59	6.17	0.55	4.82
1998	Arizona	NL	44.0	46	32	6	31	35	6.55	2	3	9.41	1.23	6.34	7.16	0.64	6.14
1999	San Fran	NL	64.7	68	31	6	27	52	4.31	4	3	9.46	0.84	3.76	7.24	1.10	4.73

Dusty Baker and Ron Perranoski saw something in Rodriguez that made them think they could get his walks under control. Just about all of his other numbers were the same in 1999 as in earlier years, but he cut his walk rate by almost half, and ended up with a very nice season. If he really has turned a corner, he should have a long career, as a setup man if not a closer.

Rich Rodriguez   Throws L   Age 37

YEAR	TEAM	LGE	IP	H	ER	HR	BB	K	ERA	W	L	H/9	HR/9	BB/9	K/9	KWH	PERA
1997	San Fran	NL	64.7	66	23	7	22	30	3.20	5	2	9.19	0.97	3.06	4.18	0.46	4.45
1998	San Fran	NL	64.3	73	30	7	22	42	4.20	4	3	10.21	0.98	3.08	5.88	0.82	5.04
1999	San Fran	NL	55.0	61	32	8	27	42	5.24	3	3	9.98	1.31	4.42	6.87	0.80	5.73

Rodriguez pitched well for the Giants in 1997, but he's been in decline ever since. He's left-handed, which means he'll get more chances if he wants them, even at the age of 37. Prospective buyers will want to note that left-handed hitters slugged .490 against him last year.

Kirk Rueter   Throws L   Age 29

YEAR	TEAM	LGE	IP	H	ER	HR	BB	K	ERA	W	L	H/9	HR/9	BB/9	K/9	KWH	PERA
1997	San Fran	NL	189.3	197	82	18	53	107	3.90	12	9	9.36	0.86	2.52	5.09	0.82	4.18
1998	San Fran	NL	183.3	206	107	28	60	97	5.25	8	12	10.11	1.37	2.95	4.76	0.57	5.30
1999	San Fran	NL	179.7	221	114	26	52	90	5.71	8	12	11.07	1.30	2.60	4.51	0.53	5.66

The luckiest man in a Giants uniform. To look at the adjusted records above for 1998 and 1999, you'd think Rueter was a #5 starter at best, perhaps a journeyman. His actual record during that time is 31-19, thanks to stupendous run support. Rueter's real-life records are a joke; he is not a very good pitcher. Over the past two years his ERA has jumped from 3.45 to 5.41, a much better reflection of his contribution to the Giants. If they were smart, they'd trade Rueter and his 70-39 career record for a good pitcher. Unfortunately, the Giants think Rueter is a good pitcher.

Jerry Spradlin   Throws R   Age 33

YEAR	TEAM	LGE	IP	H	ER	HR	BB	K	ERA	W	L	H/9	HR/9	BB/9	K/9	KWH	PERA
1997	Philadel	NL	81.3	87	45	9	29	62	4.98	4	5	9.63	1.00	3.21	6.86	1.14	4.76
1998	Philadel	NL	82.3	64	33	9	21	73	3.61	5	4	7.00	0.98	2.30	7.98	2.96	2.95
1999	Clevelnd	AL	3.0	5	5	1	3	2	15.00	0	0	15.00	3.00	9.00	6.00	0.20	15.00
1999	San Fran	NL	56.7	60	30	4	27	50	4.76	3	3	9.53	0.64	4.29	7.94	1.15	4.76

The tall drink of water joined the Giants early in the year after getting himself run out of Cleveland and was a serviceable reliever. His control was off, not a good sign at his age. If he were left-handed, he'd probably stick around another five years. He's not. Traded to the Royals, where he might get a save or two.

Julian Tavarez   Throws R   Age 27

YEAR	TEAM	LGE	IP	H	ER	HR	BB	K	ERA	W	L	H/9	HR/9	BB/9	K/9	KWH	PERA
1997	San Fran	NL	87.7	92	42	6	35	35	4.31	5	5	9.44	0.62	3.59	3.59	0.28	4.41
1998	San Fran	NL	83.7	101	43	5	38	49	4.63	4	5	10.86	0.54	4.09	5.27	0.47	5.27
1999	San Fran	NL	53.0	66	37	7	24	32	6.28	2	4	11.21	1.19	4.08	5.43	0.48	6.28

Never as good as his reputation, Tavarez remains nothing more than the Jose Bautista of the second half of the decade. For his first two seasons with the Giants, he blinded fans with his 90-mph fastball, so much that they didn't notice his poor peripherals. Last season it all caught up with him. He's still young and throws hard, so he'll find someone else he can blind. Reunited with Dan O'Dowd in Colorado.

Jason Verdugo — Throws R — Age 25

YEAR	TEAM	LGE	IP	H	ER	HR	BB	K	ERA	W	L	H/9	HR/9	BB/9	K/9	KWH	PERA
1997	Salem OR	Nwn	69.3	115	61	9	31	45	7.92	2	6	14.93	1.17	4.02	5.84	0.42	8.57
1998	Bakrsfld	Cal	73.7	101	45	5	20	37	5.50	3	5	12.34	0.61	2.44	4.52	0.51	5.62
1998	Shrevprt	Tex	17.3	21	10	4	7	21	5.19	1	1	10.90	2.08	3.63	10.90	2.24	6.75
1999	Shrevprt	Tex	55.7	78	48	7	16	34	7.76	2	4	12.61	1.13	2.59	5.50	0.69	6.47
1999	Fresno	PCL	19.7	19	12	4	11	24	5.49	1	1	8.69	1.83	5.03	10.98	2.06	5.95

The Giants sent him to the Arizona Fall League after he posted decent numbers as a sometime closer in Double- and Triple-A, and he was lit up. He's a football player turned baseball player and so will get extra time to develop. His future is in middle relief.

Ryan Vogelsong — Throws R — Age 22

YEAR	TEAM	LGE	IP	H	ER	HR	BB	K	ERA	W	L	H/9	HR/9	BB/9	K/9	KWH	PERA
1998	Salem OR	Nwn	51.0	53	21	6	19	44	3.71	4	2	9.35	1.06	3.35	7.76	1.44	4.76
1998	San Jose	Cal	16.7	30	20	4	5	18	10.80	0	2	16.20	2.16	2.70	9.72	1.61	10.26
1999	San Jose	Cal	66.7	42	28	4	30	63	3.78	4	3	5.67	0.54	4.05	8.51	2.35	2.56
1999	Shrevprt	Tex	24.7	50	31	7	18	19	11.31	0	3	18.24	2.55	6.57	6.93	0.30	14.23

Vogelsong was even better than Esteves when the two were at San Jose last year, but he was obliterated at Shreveport. Nonetheless, Vogelsong is almost the equal of Esteves as a pitching prospect; he's two years younger with a higher upside.

Ben Weber — Throws R — Age 30

YEAR	TEAM	LGE	IP	H	ER	HR	BB	K	ERA	W	L	H/9	HR/9	BB/9	K/9	KWH	PERA
1999	Fresno	PCL	84.3	78	32	5	34	53	3.42	6	3	8.32	0.53	3.63	5.66	0.79	3.74

Weber has bounced around forever, even spending time pitching in Taiwan. After a nice season for Fresno, the Giants rewarded him with a promotion to their 40-man roster. The chances of Weber's making the team are slim, but he's pitched well enough, never striking out a lot of guys but somehow sticking with the program. The Giants could be in line for a lot of pitcher injuries in 2000, which would help his cause.

Support-Neutral Records — SAN FRANCISCO GIANTS — Park Effect: -15.9%

PITCHER	GS	IP	R	SNW	SNL	SNPCT	W	L	RA	APW	SNVA	SNWAR
Chris Brock	19	106.7	69	4.5	8.2	.354	6	8	5.82	-1.34	-1.68	-0.91
Shawn Estes	32	203.0	121	10.4	13.3	.440	11	11	5.36	-1.54	-1.35	0.35
Mark Gardner	21	122.3	94	5.3	10.0	.344	4	10	6.92	-3.00	-2.37	-1.24
Livan Hernandez	10	63.7	32	4.0	3.3	.543	3	3	4.52	0.10	0.22	0.86
Joe Nathan	14	81.3	40	4.8	4.5	.514	7	3	4.43	0.22	0.05	0.83
Russ Ortiz	33	207.7	109	11.9	11.8	.501	18	9	4.72	-0.12	0.05	1.81
Kirk Rueter	33	184.7	118	10.3	13.2	.438	15	10	5.75	-2.18	-1.57	0.29
TOTALS	162	969.3	583	51.0	64.4	.442	64	54	5.41	-7.85	-6.64	2.00

I've frequently used this space to extoll the virtues of reliability and health in starting pitchers. So often, the performance of a team's rotation is brought down by a handful of awful spot starts made by fill-ins when a regular gets hurt. Examples from 1999 are the Orioles, Royals and Blue Jays. Simply finding starters who will show up for work every five days and not be brutal will often be enough to ensure the staff will at least be decent. But the Giants are an exception to that rule. For the second year in a row, the San Francisco rotation was one of the most durable in the majors, and for the second year in a row, it was one of the worst. Despite using only six starters all year in 1998 and only seven in 1999, the Giants have been undone by a combination of age (Danny Darwin in 1998, Mark Gardner in 1999), youngsters taking their lumps (Russ Ortiz in '98, Chris Brock in '99) and a pitcher who hasn't lived up to the promise he showed in his first two seasons (Shawn Estes).... Another thing the 1999 Giants had in common with previous staffs is starters with good won/lost records due to luck. In four of the last eight years, the luckiest starter in the National League, as measured by the difference between actual record and Support-Neutral W/L record, has been a Giant: John Burkett in 1992 and 1993, Gardner in 1996 and Estes in 1997. While no Giant could beat Kent Bottenfield's good fortune to claim the NL crown in 1999, they did have the third- and fourth-luckiest records in Ortiz and Kirk Reuter, and collectively they had the luckiest rotation in the majors.

Pitcher Abuse Points

PITCHER	AGE	GS	PAP	PAP/S	WKLD	MAX	1-90	91-100	101-110	111-120	121-130	131-140	141+
Chris Brock	29	19	111	5.8	8.8	121	4	5	6	3	1	0	0
Shawn Estes	26	32	496	15.5	31.0	128	1	4	12	10	5	0	0
Mark Gardner	37	21	304	14.5	14.5	130	4	2	7	4	4	0	0
Livan Hernandez	24	10	280	28.0	65.3	141	1	2	2	2	1	1	1
Joe Nathan	24	14	93	6.6	15.5	122	4	2	5	2	1	0	0
Russ Ortiz	25	33	932	28.2	61.2	141	3	3	7	8	8	3	1
Kirk Rueter	28	33	268	8.1	13.5	125	9	8	7	8	1	0	0
SAN FRANCISCO		162	2484	15.3	29.6	141	26	26	46	37	21	4	2
Ranking (NL)				1	1								

We have a new champion! Dusty Baker has deservedly wrested the crown from Tim Johnson as the World's Most Abusive Manager, and he did so without dressing in fatigues or regaling his charges with fiction. If we are to credit Baker for motivating the Giants into being perennial wild-card contenders, shouldn't we also criticize him for their collapse in September last year, as Russ Ortiz (4.83 ERA after July 31) fell off and the already-abused Shawn Estes (5.97 ERA in September) continued to scuffle?... And you, Mr. Sabean: what the hell were you thinking? Pity poor Livan, who escapes from one abusive situation, only to land with the new Monarch of Misuse. Once overachieving, the Giants are now simply overused.

Baseball's Hilbert Problems

by Keith Woolner

"Who of us would not be glad to lift the veil behind which the future lies hidden, to cast a glance at the next advances of our science and at the secrets of its development during future years? What particular goals will there be toward which the leading sabermetric spirits of coming generations will strive? What new methods and new facts in the wide and rich field of sabermetric thought will the new years disclose?"

Here at *Baseball Prospectus*, we're not completely immune to the general fascination with the recent turn of the world's odometer. So, with this edition marking the final year of the second millennium, let's take a look forward at what the third holds for us seamheads.

Our inspiration comes from a similar effort nearly 100 years ago. In 1900, a mathematician named David Hilbert addressed the International Congress of Mathematicians in Paris and delivered what was to become history's most influential speech about mathematics. Hilbert outlined 23 major problems to be studied in the coming century. In doing so he expressed optimism about the field, sharing his feeling that unsolved problems were a sign of vitality, encouraging more people to do more research.

The above quote is, in fact, a bastardization of the opening statements of Hilbert's speech. Hilbert referred to mathematics instead of sabermetrics and spoke in terms of "centuries" instead of "years." Given the relative youth of sabermetrics and baseball analysis compared to math, it's appropriate to use a period of smaller scope than Hilbert. The quotes that appear periodically throughout this essay are similarly taken from Hilbert's speech and altered to refer to baseball analysis.

Hilbert's address was much more than a collection of problems. It outlined a philosophy of mathematics, and the problems put forth were ones relevant to that philosophy. By putting forth our own "Hilbert problems" for baseball analysts of the future, *Baseball Prospectus* is outlining our philosophy for how and why this kind of work ought to be done—our attempt to provide inspiration and guidance to the baseball community at large.

"It is difficult and often impossible to judge the value of a problem correctly in advance; for the final award depends upon the gain which science obtains from the problem. Nevertheless we can ask whether there are general criteria which mark a good sabermetric problem."

We used the following criteria to guide our selection of the baseball research problems for the future.

1. To be relevant, sabermetrics must inform a decision: data for data's sake is not useful. Bill James once defined sabermetrics as the search for objective knowledge about baseball. While this is still true, it doesn't cut to the heart of the matter. A list of players, cross-referenced by preferred breakfast cereal and astrological sign, is objective knowledge, but it isn't what anyone would call useful information. There is already too much irrelevant data clogging up the airwaves and the Web. Baseball analysis must focus on knowledge that can lead to an action or a commitment of resources (time, effort, money) by someone who wants to study the game. The decision can be anything from in-game tactical moves to judging player acquisitions. It can be prospect evaluation or an MVP or Hall of Fame ballot. It can even be some personal idiosyncratic award for things you might think are important. But, in order to produce useful information, you have to start with a relevant question that needs answering.

2. The industry of baseball encompasses more than just the action on the field. To be relevant to the sport as it's practiced today, baseball analysis must expand to explicitly consider the economic, social, technological, competitive and governmental contexts in which the game operates.

3. The amount of potential information is larger than the amount of information that is available today. In raising some of these research questions, we acknowledge that the resources to answer them may not yet be available. It may be years or decades before there's sufficient effort, technology or understanding to create a systematic collection of observations needed to resolve some of these issues. However, by recognizing the importance of the problem itself, we can hope to guide the efforts to acquire new information in a manner that is consistent with the problems we want to solve.

4. Numbers alone are not data, and solving equations is not analysis. Some data can be expressed as numbers, and judicious use of mathematics can yield analytical insights, but we should not abandon a line of reasoning for lack of quantification or a failure to find a tidy formula.

"If we would obtain an idea of the probable development of sabermetric knowledge in the immediate future, we must

let the unsettled questions pass before our minds and look over the problems which the science of today sets and whose solution we expect from the future. To such a review of problems the present day, lying at the meeting of the centuries, seems to me well adapted. For the close of a great epoch not only invites us to look back into the past but also directs our thoughts to the unknown future."

Baseball Prospectus's Hilbert Problems for the Next Century

Defense

1. **Separating defense into pitching and fielding.** – This is one of the oldest and most vexing problems in baseball analysis. Pitching and fielding are so intertwined that they seem impossible to separate. That doesn't mean we shouldn't try.

2. **Evaluating interrelationships among teammates' defensive performances.** – Does having a good shortstop make the second baseman or third baseman better? Does it show up in the numbers? Does a Gold Glove center fielder cut into the apparent defensive performance of a corner outfielder? Can a poor defensive player's shortcomings be covered for by pairing him with a stellar glove man at an adjacent position?

3. **Measuring the catcher's role in run prevention.** – In *Baseball Prospectus 1999*, Keith Woolner presented a compelling case that catchers do not have a noticeable effect on a pitcher's performance. If there is no "game-calling" effect, what impact does a catcher have? Is it primarily controlling the running game? If so, how much of that is attributable to the pitching staff? Is it in preventing wild pitches and passed balls, thus giving the pitcher more confidence to keep the ball low? What about reading a pitcher's physical state and helping to keep his pitch count low? We've made some important first steps, but there's still a lot we don't know about evaluating catcher defense.

4. **Mapping career trajectories for defensive performance.** – The phenomenon of the "Age 27" peak for offensive performance is well documented. However, while we still struggle with developing a reliable assessment of defensive performance, little attention has been paid to how a player's defensive skills change as he ages. Do a player's defensive skills peak earlier in his career? Later? Do strong arms last longer than quick feet? Does defensive longevity vary by position, or by the particular mix of skills a player has? Do difficult positions such as shortstop and catcher wear a player out faster?

5. **Making an assessment of relative positional difficulties.** – Much is made of the "defensive spectrum," where posi-

tions are thought of as if they were laid out on a ruler, with shortstop at the high/difficult end of the spectrum and first base at the low end. This makes intuitive sense and matches well with the observed differences in offensive performance: generally, there are fewer good-hitting shortstops from which to choose, which implies a lower average offensive performance level for all shortstops. That also means that first basemen generally out-hit shortstops.

6. **Quantifying the value of positional flexibility.** – A player who plays two positions at a league-average level gives his manager of flexibility, both in setting up the team's roster and using in-game strategies. Positional value methods that are based on playing time at a position are inadequate because they would penalize a player for time spent at the lesser position, even if a comparable offensive player who plays full-time at the more difficult position was unable to play the easier position. Because roster spots are scarce, a team gets value from a player's ability to play multiple positions, but we do not yet have an understanding of how much value there is to having a Mark Loretta or Jose Hernandez on your roster.

7. **Measuring the value of non-range-based aspects of defense.** – This means measuring skills like an outfielder's arm, a middle infielder's ability to hang in while turning the double play or a first baseman's ability to scoop low throws. To date, the effort spent on assessing defensive performance has focused on converting batted balls into outs, essentially measuring a player's range and sure-handedness. Fielding percentage, range factor, Sherri Nichols' Defensive Average, STATS, Inc.'s Zone Rating—these all focus on opportunities to turn batted balls into outs. While important, there are other, less-studied aspects to baseball defense.

We'd want to start measuring the impact of an outfielder's arm, both in terms of cutting down baserunners and whether an outfielder with a cannon-arm reputation intimidates runners. We'd like to establish ways to determine a middle infielder's ability to turn the double play, a first baseman's ability to handle poor throws, an outfielder's reliability in hitting the cutoff man and a catcher's success in blocking the plate. These are all non-range-based factors in defense, they're all important skills and they've all been ignored, for the most part.

Offense

8. **Evaluating the impact on offensive performance of changing defensive positions up/down the defensive spectrum.** – This is the flip side to understanding the defensive spectrum. Here, we ask whether a player's expected offensive production is influenced by the position he's asked to play, and whether changing his position would alter his performance. Would Jeff Bagwell be the

same hitter had he stayed at third base? Or Matt Williams at shortstop? Ron Gant at second base? How much is a player helped by moving to an easier position?

9. **Predicting the impact on career length from changing positions.** – How much longer are players effective after changing positions, particularly if they're moved to an easier position? Is the trade-off in preventing an offensive decline worth the sacrifices you might be making on defense? Do you burn a productive catcher out by leaving him behind the plate and having him retire with knee problems at 32, or are you better off moving him to first base and keeping his bat on the team until he approaches 40? Mike Piazza would like to know the answer, and so would we.

Pitching

10. **Projecting-minor league pitchers accurately.** – One of the holy grails of sabermetrics is creating useful projections of major-league pitcher performance based on minor-league performance. While strikeout-to-walk ratios and other means of assessment can give us rough guides to good and bad young pitchers, we're nowhere near the level of certainty we want to achieve. Given the lack of progress from purely statistical approaches, this would be an ideal place to marry the analysis of player-development professionals with sabermetric methods to develop a more powerful predictor than either approach has produced alone.

11. **Creating a way to better analyze mechanics.** – The precision and consistency needed to be an effective major-league pitcher is exceptional. Minute variations in a pitcher's release point, arm angle and body position make the difference between Cy Young and Matt Young. While game film and frame analysis help capture nuances in a pitcher's delivery that escape the naked eye, there's much more that could be done. Advances in data storage make it possible to record and analyze every pitch thrown in every game by a pitcher. Cataloging this information, and measuring the angles, velocities and timing of movements could open up new worlds to help instructors improving pitching. Computer-aided analysis could measure consistency in release points. You could help improve a young pitcher's consistency by having him throw 100 fastballs to the same place, and measure the variance around his optimal release point. Pitchers with greater command should see a smaller standard deviation than someone as wild as Brad Pennington. Lessons gained from biomechanics could suggest new delivery methods that improve effectiveness while reducing strain on a pitcher's arm. These kinds of approaches may help identify pitchers who should be converted to knuckleballers, submariners, or other non-traditional delivery styles.

Developmental Strategies

12. **Identifying and quantifying good coaching.** – Most of sabermetrics focuses on the players, and the largest portion of any remaining attention goes to managers. But a team's coaches influence the game as well, and they have rarely been studied in any systematic way. Hitting and pitching coaches affect the development of young players and may help avoid prolonged slumps for all players. Pitching coaches often influence a manager's use (or abuse) of his pitching staff. Coaches at third base make split-second calls on whether to send a runner home or hold him up. Are they doing a good job? Frankly, we have no evidence on which to base useful assessments yet. We all think Leo Mazzone is doing a great job with the Braves, but how great?

13. **Assessing the "coachability" of players.** – Professional baseball players, both in the majors and the minors, possess tremendous physical gifts. However, not every "five-tool" player matures into an effective ballplayer. Is the difference in the quality of his talent, his ability to learn, or both? How much patience can be taught to a free-swinger like Garret Anderson? Can you train any player with blazing speed to read pitchers well enough to become a base-stealing threat? Do draft picks who sign late diminish their peak value by missing out on a season's worth of instruction?

14. **Assessing developmental strategies for minor-league pitchers.** – What is the optimal strategy for developing young pitching? What kind of usage pattern and what quantity of work balances the need for experience against the possibility of physical damage? Some teams have studied the issue and come up with innovative approaches; at A-ball, the A's use eight-man rotations, where matched pairs of pitchers pitch every four days with low pitch counts. By contrast, some teams still think young pitchers need to get as many innings as possible. Should a team try to expose a prospect to as many different hitters and parks as possible? Is that good for development, or bad? Was folding the American Association into the Pacific Coast League and the International League good, because it gave Triple-A pitchers more potential opponents and parks to work in, or was it more important to hone their skills against the same seven or nine opposing teams? Are the competitive structures of the minors good for player development or not? What are some potential improvements?

Economics

15. **Clarifying the win/dollar trade-off preferences for major-league decision-makers.** – Winning has never been the only thing in baseball. The fact that baseball is a business is not news to anyone reading this book—in fact, it

hasn't been news for the last 125 years. As the ultimate decision-maker for a franchise, the owner of a team values two types of outcomes: on-field success and profitability. The relationship of one to the other isn't objectively knowable, as it comes from the personal—or professional— preferences of the owner. It's perfectly rational for an owner to refuse to risk an $80 million payroll for a 10% chance at a World Series, while another would spend $90 million for a 7% chance. The second owner has a higher win-per-dollar trade-off preference than the former, or you could say he's more willing to take risks. For baseball analysis to move to the next level of relevancy for baseball teams, it must be ready to deal with varying preferences and tolerances and account for them rationally in assessing desirable trades, transactions and contracts.

16. **Creating a framework for evaluating trades.** – Whether a trades is a good or bad decision is something that should be assessed based on the information known (or that should have been known) at the time of the trade. Analyzing trades with any consistency is difficult, as there are always several reasons and factors that go into every trade. Salary dumps, stretch-drive pickups, overcoming key injuries, getting rid of a troublemaker or somebody the manager just can't stand, exchanging excess talent at one position to fill some other hole on the team—these have all motivated transactions of various kinds over the years. To be successful, a framework for evaluating trades must be ready to consider financial factors (including the overall health of the club), current and future expected production from the players involved, the team's current and future competitive situation, and the premium ownership places on winning.

17. **Determining the value of draft picks, Rule 5 picks, player-to-be-named-later arrangements, and other nonspecific forms of compensation in transactions.** – The more esoteric forms of compensation in trades are usually ignored, but they must have some real value if teams continue to exchange talent for them. What does a team give up when it signs a Type A free agent? How much is that draft pick worth? Is a typical Rule 5 pick worth the $50,000 and the roster spot? Are teams taking full advantage of the Rule 5 draft? What kinds of PTBNL deals make sense for both teams?

18. **Evaluating the effect of short- and long-term competitiveness on attendance and demand elasticity.** – Scholars like Andrew Zimbalist and Gerald Scully have done pioneering work in measuring the relationship between on-field success and attendance. Building on that work, we should study second-order effects in more detail, such as the impact of five or more losing seasons on long-term attendance trends. How long does it take attendance to recover from a bunch of lousy seasons in a row? How quickly will fickle fans abandon a former champion?

Does fan apathy catch up with a team that consistently contends year after year, but never quite wins the pennant? Is it worth overspending in the short term to build long-term fan loyalty, thus ensuring greater financial resources to devote to the team in the future?

19. **Optimizing the competitive ecology of the game.** – Some issues are bigger than any single team's problems. The long-term survivability of "small-market" clubs has made headlines in the past couple of years. One theory is that "small-market" teams can't hold onto their own farm-developed talent, which supposedly departs through free agency for major media markets like New York and Los Angeles. The current argument is that the Minnesotas of the world can never retain the players produced by their farm system long enough to contend. However, if we went back to making it easier for teams to retain their own players, you risk creating long-term dynasties like the Yankees of the 1950s, which diminishes interest in baseball in the cities without the dynasty. So what's the best way to achieve league-wide competitiveness?

Strategic Decisions

20. **Determining optimal pitcher usage strategies.** – Ideally, a manager wants his best pitchers to throw the most and most important (or highest-leverage) innings. However, he also doesn't want to abuse his pitchers' arms, risking short-term fatigue and long-term injury. There's uncertainty about when high-leverage opportunities will present themselves, yet a regular and tolerable workload is necessary to keep any pitcher sharp. Would a return to four-man rotations with stricter pitch counts lead to greater success? Should teams use a designated closer, or use their best reliever in game-critical situations even if they aren't save situations? Does Tony LaRussa's ill-fated experiment with the three-inning starter warrant a longer trial? Should relievers throw fewer, longer appearances, or should they be mixed and matched as platoon differentials dictate?

21. **Determining optimal roster design.** – Any team's range of in-game strategic options originates with the decisions about which players are on the roster, yet the strategies for constructing a roster have undergone little scrutiny. During the season, a team has many objectives that sometimes conflict with one another. Winning the division or qualifying for the postseason is the ultimate goal, but throughout the season there are other smaller goals: seasoning a rookie, sorting out bullpen roles, assessing a player's readiness after an injury. If a team finds itself in contention, should it ignore potential future payoffs and focus on using established veterans deemed most likely to contribute this year? How would the failure to play that rookie impact the team's competitiveness next year or the year after? Is it worthwhile to

carry a player whose primary talent is pinch-running? How important is a third-string catcher? Or a second left-handed specialist out of the bullpen?

Tactical Decisions

22. **Quantifying the manager's impact on winning.** – Bill James published his *Guide to Baseball Managers* in 1997, and in it set forth some nifty tools for estimating a manager's effectiveness based on seasonal statistics. Careful observation and recording of managerial moves (e.g., roster management, in-game tactics, pitcher usage) set the stage for a detailed assessment of a manager's impact on his team. Unifying this data into a coherent whole is a challenge, but the payoff would be a much better understanding of the value of a manager's contributions to his team.

23. **Developing a game-theoretic framework for analyzing elective strategies.** – In the offense-crazed world of the late 1990s, it seems quaint to concern ourselves with little-ball strategies like the sacrifice bunt and the hit-and-run. These strategies are widely derided in sabermetrics, largely on the basis of expected-run analysis. Tables, indexed by the number of outs and the location of baserunners, give an expected number of runs scored for the rest of the inning, based on the results of actual games. If expected run scoring declines after a player bats, or given a typical success rate for a play, then the strategy is deemed to be bad. While this approach was an important and useful first step, there are two major problems with it: first, this method yields an answer for a league-average team because it's based on the results of the league as a whole, and second, it ignores the changes in shape of run scoring that can be important for many game contexts.

To truly understand where and when to use these strategies, they must be studied not just with an expected-run analysis, but with a true assessment of how much more likely the game is to be won using such a strategy. There is a branch of mathematics called game theory which is ideally suited for studying not only the direct impact of little-ball strategies on the outcome of games, but the move-countermove nature of two managers trying to gain whatever advantages they can against one another. An in-depth treatment of little-ball strategies that recognizes the true richness of managerial decisions and counter-decisions should be welcomed.

"The deep significance of certain problems for the advance of sabermetric science in general and the important role which they play in the work of the individual investigator are not to be denied. As long as a branch of science offers an abundance of problems, so long is it alive; a lack of problems foreshadows extinction or the cessation of independent development. Just as every human undertaking pursues certain objects, so also sabermetric research requires its problems. It is by the solution of problems that the investigator tests the temper of his steel; he finds new methods and new outlooks, and gains a wider and freer horizon."

The range of interesting avenues of exploration is larger than a single publication—even *Baseball Prospectus*—can possibly hope to explore. Fortunately, the community of interested and knowledgeable baseball fans and analysts is large and getting larger, and many of these Hilbert problems will be solved by researchers nobody has even heard of yet. We look forward to seeing the solutions, and with them the posing of more interesting questions, in the century to come.

Top 40 Prospects

by Rany Jazayerli

Our society is obsessed with youth. You can't buy groceries without walking past dozens of magazine covers featuring 19-year-old "women" wearing outfits that could be packed in a thermos. Advertisers cater to the 18-to-24 demographic as if every college senior has already made millions investing in dot-com IPOs. Veterans of the corporate workplace are told their experience is an asset, then laid off in favor of young bucks who don't have families that suck up valuable time. In women's tennis, players turn pro at 13, are washed up at 17 and make a miraculous comeback at 21. Life no longer ends at 30, it's usually over by 25.

At *Baseball Prospectus*, we have our own fascination with youth. (Don't call, Woody. We don't mean it that way.) Young players are cheaper, as even the best rarely make more than a million dollars in their first three seasons combined, and only then when their team signs them to a long-term deal that keeps them locked below market value for even longer. Compared to older players, they have far greater potential for improvement. They generally have more speed and play positions where range is more important, which generally translates into better defense.

The chance to employ Nomar Garciaparra or Scott Rolen cheaply isn't the only reason teams should share our love of youth. Knowing that average or slightly-below-average talent can be found in your farm system, or another team's system, gives a franchise the leverage it needs to avoid blowing money on replaceable talent. A year ago, the Padres gave Carlos Hernandez a three-year deal worth more than $6 million because they did not appreciate that Hernandez's skills were hardly distinguishable from those of dozens of Triple-A catchers, or even those of Ben Davis, their own prize prospect. Now, Davis is the Padres' starter, and Hernandez's contract is an albatross they'd like to unload.

But our passion for young players is focused primarily on great ones, the ones at the core of almost every successful team, the ones whose importance rises along with team payrolls. In an era when Shawn Green commands $14 million a year, the presence of a young star, a Bobby Abreu or a Tim Hudson or a Sean Casey, means a team can be competitive by using the money saved to bring in other good players at market price.

What follows are *Baseball Prospectus*'s Top 40 Prospects, those players most likely to develop into the stars of the next generation. For hitters, we list translated average, on-base percentage and slugging average for the last two seasons, along with EqAs. For pitchers, you'll find translated hits,

walks and strikeouts per nine innings, along with DT-ERA. Ages are as of July 1, 2000.

In an era of stratified salaries and massive payroll imbalances, the cheap superstar is the low-revenue team's primary weapon in the fight to keep up with teams like the Yankees. The poor-cousin teams will not be happy, then, to read that the *Baseball Prospectus* Prospect of the Year is . . .

1. Nick Johnson   1B   New York (AL)   Age 21

	BA	OBP	SLG	EQA
1998:	.269	.404	.460	.293
1999:	.321	.481	.507	.340

He's been described as a souped-up Jim Thome, a left-handed Jeff Bagwell and Don Mattingly with an extra 100 walks a year. But to best express how historic Johnson's talents are, take Frank Thomas—back when he was *Frank Thomas*—and throw in a Gold Glove, a little speed, make him a left-handed hitter and put him in Yankee Stadium. Oh, and imagine he was ready for the major leagues at 21, not 22. Now you've got a good picture of why Nick Johnson is the best prospect in the minor leagues.

When it comes to getting on base, Johnson knows every trick in the book: he won the Eastern League batting title with a .345 average and led all minor leaguers in both walks (123) and times hit-by-pitch (37!). His .525 OBP is the highest of any player, at any level, in recent history. His power is not quite as developed as his plate discipline, but he's got a stroke that's just waiting to take on the Stadium's short porch in right field. Tino Martinez still has another year on his contract, so Johnson may have to wait until 2001 for a full-time job. Then again, he may not. Hall of Fame talent has a way of forcing its way into lineups.

2. Rick Ankiel   LHP   St. Louis   Age 20

	H/9	BB/9	K/9	DT-ERA
1998:	8.42	4.06	9.44	4.60
1999:	6.86	4.54	10.64	2.81

You've heard all the hype about Ankiel, and we're here to tell you it's all warranted. At the age of 20, he has one of the five best fastballs of any left-hander in baseball, and his breaking stuff may be better than his fastball. His control is just poor enough to keep hitters from getting too comfortable at the plate. Let's put it this way: Ankiel is a better prospect, at a younger age, than Kerry Wood was two years ago. Unfortunately, that's a potential problem: Ankiel is so good, so young, that he's at an enormous risk to blow out his arm in the next three years. Until and unless that happens, though, he should be an above-average starter as soon as this year. Expect a fine rookie season, and expect Tony LaRussa to show that he's learned nothing from the ruined careers of Alan Benes and Matt Morris.

3. Pat Burrell   1B/LF   Philadelphia   Age 23

	BA	OBP	SLG	EQA
1998:	.254	.359	.448	.274
1999:	.293	.388	.545	.304

The City of Brotherly Love should be ready to welcome Burrell, the #1 pick in the 1998 draft, with open arms. After posting the second-highest career slugging average in NCAA history, Burrell put on the same power display in Double-A and showed he could take a pitch as well, drawing 83 walks in just 127 games. Those lovable Phillies have moved Burrell to left field to avoid displacing the indispensible Rico Brogna. While Burrell is still adapting to left field, the early returns are that his defense isn't bad enough to keep him out of the Phillies' lineup. Word out of Philadelphia is that they plan to have him start the year in Triple-A, which is about the only thing that's going to keep him from being Rookie of the Year.

4. Sean Burroughs   3B   San Diego   Age 19

	BA	OBP	SLG	EQA
1999:	.304	.395	.411	.277

Along with Nick Johnson, Burroughs is one of only two prospects in baseball who have yet to firmly establish limits on what they can do. Burroughs, the son of 1974 AL MVP Jeff, first rose to national prominence as the pudgy slugging star of the Long Beach team that won the Little League World Series in back-to-back seasons. Six years later, he posted a .471 OBP in the Midwest League, reaching base in his last 54 games of the season, in the most polished season by an 18-year-old hitter since Ken Griffey Jr. tore through the minor leagues in 1988. Unlike Griffey, Burroughs isn't expected to be in the major leagues at 19, but if he shows at Double-A what he showed in the low minors, the Padres might be forced to call him up before he turns 20 in September. What's really frightening about Burroughs is that he hit only six home runs last year. If history—and his physique—are any guide, that could change in a hurry.

5. Vernon Wells   CF   Toronto   Age 21

	BA	OBP	SLG	EQA
1998:	.241	.295	.361	.221
1999:	.295	.344	.457	.269

When the Blue Jays selected Wells with the #5 pick in the 1997 draft, the talk from insiders was that he was a "signability" pick who didn't deserve to go that high on merit. Those insiders have chosen to remain anonymous, and with good reason—Wells now has the best mix of athleticism and performance of any prospect in the game. He pulled off the unprecedented trick of being named the #1 prospect in three different leagues by *Baseball America* last year, but he struggled a little bit in his September call-up. So did the last hitter to burn through four levels in one year, Andruw Jones. Wells might be well served by another half-season in Triple-A; by July, the Blue Jays will be well served if his name is in their lineup every day.

6. Rafael Furcal   SS   Atlanta   Age 19

	BA	OBP	SLG	EQA
1998:	.260	.325	.327	.231
1999:	.299	.356	.362	.253

The bad news: in 242 minor-league games, Furcal has only two career home runs. The good news: just about everything else. Start with the stolen bases for which he has received so much attention. Furcal stole 96 bases in 1999, the most by any player in a single season in the 1990s, after swiping 60 in just 66 games in 1998. Furcal is more than a track star; he's a switch-hitting shortstop who hit .322 and had a .392 OBP while moving from the South Atlantic League up to the tougher Carolina League. Furcal did all that despite not turning 19 until August, and while successfully making the transition from second base to shortstop. The Braves, as you know, need a shortstop badly, and they're not at all afraid of moving a true phenom through the system in one year. Furcal is just that sort of phenom and will probably see some time in Atlanta this year. He's already the top candidate to lead the majors in stolen bases in the 2000s. As with Rickey Henderson before him, the steals may only be a fraction of his real value.

7. Ruben Mateo   OF   Texas   Age 22

	BA	OBP	SLG	EQA
1998:	.273	.324	.445	.257
1999:	.280	.320	.499	.269

We already got a good look at Mateo's five-tool talent last summer, when he all but took away Tom Goodwin's job before going down with an injury that kept his rookie eligibility intact for 2000. Mateo has a skill set similar to Wells's, and while Wells has the higher upside by virtue of being younger, Mateo is more likely to make an impact this season. He completely dominated Triple-A and he does side work as a nifty glove man in center field. Mateo has to be considered the favorite for the AL Rookie of the Year.

8. Ben Petrick   C   Colorado   Age 23

	BA	OBP	SLG	EQA
1998:	.230	.327	.451	.258
1999:	.269	.360	.501	.284

In an environment that makes boys look like men and men look like supermen, Petrick is the best hitting prospect the Rockies have ever produced. That's not really saying much; the only other hitting prospect the Rockies have developed is Todd Helton. Helton, of course, has put up great numbers in his first two seasons without really improving on his minor-league performance. Petrick has the credentials Helton had two years ago, and is nearly 18 months younger than Helton was when he got a job. Petrick has also shown he likes hitting at altitude: after a mid-season promotion to Colorado Springs last year, he had an OBP over .400 and slugged over .600, and had an OPS just under 1000 during his September with the Rockies. The signing of Brent Mayne means that Petrick's not going to be given more than a platoon/backup job, at least at the start of the season.

9. Corey Patterson   CF   Chicago (NL)   Age 20

	BA	OBP	SLG	EQA
1999:	.267	.291	.483	.254

Patterson, the third pick in the 1998 draft, was everything the Cubs hoped he would be in his first full pro season: he hit for average (.320) and power (20 home runs, 35 doubles) and showed off his speed (33 stolen bases, 17 triples). He didn't turn 20 until August, and after playing in the Midwest League all summer, he hit .368 with a .581 slugging average in the Arizona Fall League, which usually features Double- and Triple-A players. The only reason Patterson ranks as low as he does is that while he's everything the Cubs hoped for, the Cubs don't hope for ball four. Patterson drew just 25 walks, and unless he starts hanging out with Mark Grace while shunning just about everyone else in the organization, that isn't going to improve. If it doesn't, he will remain something less than a complete prospect.

10. Michael Cuddyer   3B   Minnesota   Age 21

	BA	OBP	SLG	EQA
1998:	.250	.323	.413	.249
1999:	.278	.371	.449	.279

Scott Rolen Lite. When a young hitter shows preternatural ability to hit for average and power, draw walks and play defense, the chances increase that at least one of those talents will develop into a dominant one. Cuddyer improved every facet of his game while jumping a level last season. Now that a position switch has changed him from an error-prone shortstop to a gifted third baseman, the questions are less about whether his weaknesses will prevent him from becoming a good player, and more about whether his strengths will help him become a great player. Expect his arrival next April, and don't expect it to be a quiet one.

11. Dee Brown   OF   Kansas City   Age 22

	BA	OBP	SLG	EQA
1998:	.253	.330	.397	.249
1999:	.284	.376	.480	.285

In an organization so philosophically opposed to power hitters that they're still waiting for their first-ever 40-home-run hitter, Dee Brown has a chance to be something special. He won't win any awards with his glove, but with a bat in his hand no award is out of his reach. He hit .308/.431/.548 in one of the toughest hitters' parks in the minor leagues, then hit .353/.440/.591 in Double-A. Brown, a former running-back recruit in high school, is also a good bet for 30 to 40 stolen bases a year, which may be just the selling point he needs to find a way into the Royals' crowded outfield. Unless Johnny Damon is traded, Brown is ticketed for Triple-A, which means there could be some historic numbers coming out of Omaha until Brown forces the Royals to find a spot for the most potent bat they've developed in 25 years.

12. Kip Wells   RHP   Chicago (AL)   Age 23

	H/9	BB/9	K/9	DT-ERA
1999:	9.00	4.23	6.52	4.28

In his first pro season—he didn't sign with the White Sox until well into the 1998 offseason—Wells pitched his way to Comiskey Park, winning four games in September in the most impressive pro debut by a Sox pitcher since Jack McDowell in 1987. His strikeout-to-walk ratio tumbled a little as he moved from A ball to Double-A, suggesting he wouldn't be hurt by a few more months in the minor leagues. Otherwise, there's no reason to think he won't be an above-average starting pitcher by the end of the year. Standard health disclaimers apply.

13. Jack Cust   OF/1B   Arizona   Age 21

	BA	OBP	SLG	EQA
1998:	.229	.368	.357	.256
1999:	.262	.372	.501	.289

Purely in terms of offense, Cust is nearly as unstoppable as Nick Johnson. Cust's career OBP in the minors is .463, and he has hit for substantially more power (77 extra-base hits last year) than Johnson has. There are several mitigating factors: Cust has played one classification below Johnson at the same age in excellent hitters' parks, and he has nowhere near Johnson's defensive value. The Diamondbacks already have two excellent young first basemen in the major leagues, so Cust is desperately trying to learn left field. The results are mixed so far, but given that Arizona had a starting outfield of Luis Gonzalez, Steve Finley and Tony Womack in 1999, there's going to be a job available for Cust by 2001.

14. Tony Armas Jr. RHP Montreal Age 22

	H/9	BB/9	K/9	DT-ERA
1998:	12.04	4.94	6.83	4.60
1999:	9.16	3.71	5.39	4.31

It's not going to make anyone think the Red Sox got hosed when they traded for Pedro Martinez, but when you consider that Armas was the lesser of the two prospects acquired by the Expos, you have to admit the Sox gave up some good pitchers. Armas has been handled with kid gloves by Montreal, treatment that is likely to continue under Felipe Alou. In the short term, this means that Armas will probably spend 2000 as a five-inning starter, if not in the bullpen or Triple-A, but it improves his chances of making a long-term impact. If form holds, most of that success will be with another organization, but that's an issue for another chapter.

15. D'Angelo Jimenez SS New York (AL) Age 22

	BA	OBP	SLG	EQA
1998:	.241	.327	.359	.235
1999:	.319	.380	.468	.284

At this writing, he doesn't have a job, and there doesn't appear to be an opening for him any time soon. Attention, major-league GMs: this makes him the single most enticing young player on the trade market today. Jimenez is an inordinately talented player with a ridiculous lack of hype, especially given that he's a Yankee and therefore divinely ordained to attract media attention. You'd think a 21-year-old switch-hitting shortstop who hit .327 with 15 home runs and 26 stolen bases in Triple-A would get some attention, instead of a polite nod as Alfonso Soriano's teammate.

16. Peter Bergeron CF Montreal Age 22

	BA	OBP	SLG	EQA
1998:	.277	.353	.392	.259
1999:	.279	.355	.407	.259

Bergeron has every chance to be the prototypical leadoff hitter for the new millenium, a Brett Butler for his era. He bats left-handed, hits .300 every year, will work the pitcher for a walk every other game, steals bases frequently and efficiently and covers a lot of ground in center field. His performance was even more impressive given that shoulder tendinitis hampered him both at the plate and on the base paths, preventing him from sliding headfirst. The only cause for concern is that the Expo organization has no patience for patience; Bergeron's walk totals dropped from 78 to 56 in his first full season in their system. If he ignores Felipe Alou on this point, Bergeron is going to make Tommy Lasorda look stupid for the next 10 years.

17. Chin-Feng Chen RF Los Angeles Age 22

	BA	OBP	SLG	EQA
1999:	.281	.360	.512	.288

The Dodgers are an incredibly frustrating organization, and we're not just talking about the post-O'Malley years. Every year, their international division opens up a new market for baseball talent in the Far East, with a Hideo Nomo here and a Chan Ho Park there, while the domestic scouts dilute the gravy train with #1 picks like Bill Bene and David Yocum. The Dodgers' newest find is the best hitter in Taiwan, and the first significant hitting prospect ever developed from Asia. Chen had a phenomenal American debut, becoming the first 30/30 player in California League history, before heading back to serve out part of his military obligation. He's more than a gimmick stat; with 75 walks, 10 triples and impressive corner-outfield defense, he should have no problem living up to the hype while helping to convert yet another nation to Dodger Blue.

18. Esteban German 2B Oakland Age 21

	BA	OBP	SLG	EQA
1999:	.272	.380	.367	.265

The crown jewel in an impressive tiara of prospects proudly worn by the A's, who are currently the best-run organization in baseball. From a distance, German is just a speedy, slap-hitting middle infielder. As a 20-year-old second baseman, German hit .311 with 12 triples and stole 40 bases. But he embodies the essence of the A's philosophy: he has made a weapon out of the ability to get on base, leading their minor leaguers with 102 walks. Randy Velarde isn't going to last forever, or even another year, so be prepared to talk German soon.

19. Matt Riley LHP Baltimore Age 20

	H/9	BB/9	K/9	DT-ERA
1998:	6.63	6.87	10.12	3.14
1999:	9.67	3.71	7.76	4.61

Ed Sprague Sr., one of the best baseball scouts in the world, insisted that the Orioles take Riley with their third-round pick in 1997. Riley didn't sign until the following spring, then reached the major leagues in less than two years armed with an amazing curveball and a 95-mph fastball. He finished 1999 with 189 strikeouts in 177 innings, allowing just 147 hits, but most impressive was the improvement in his control. After walking nearly five men per nine innings in 1998, he cut his walk rate to under three a game in 1999. This is not the organization to be in if you're a top prospect, and the Orioles took a terrible risk by giving a clearly-worn-out

Riley three starts in Baltimore in September. In those, he pitched a total of 11 innings and gave up 30 baserunners. Riley is a gem; he just needs to be polished a little more. Right now, the Orioles have a number of butchers and few stone-cutters working with him.

20. Lance Berkman   LF   Houston   Age 24

	BA	OBP	SLG	EQA
1998:	.263	.372	.477	.285
1999:	.285	.374	.448	.282

Some organizations are too successful for their own good. The Astros have more outfielders than Jordan has Muslims, or that other Jordan has endorsements. Berkman was the obvious choice to replace Moises Alou after the infamous Night of the Living Treadmill, but he was busy rehabbing his own knee injury. He returned to do what he always does: beat the cow right out of the cowhide from both sides of the plate. His home-run total dropped as he regained his leg strength, but he had 20 doubles, which is a strong hint that his power didn't leave town, it just went next door. I expect that he'll get a starting job and play 130 games this year, even if I don't know exactly how.

21. Brad Penny   RHP   Florida   Age 22

	H/9	BB/9	K/9	DT-ERA
1998:	9.24	2.48	8.00	4.00
1999:	10.64	3.38	8.14	5.14

Right now, the Diamondbacks are basking in the glow of their 100-win season, a glow so bright that it makes even the trade for Matt Mantei look good. If Brad Penny becomes the pitcher we think he can become, that glow is going to fade faster than the Spice Girls. A year ago, Penny was arguably the best right-handed pitching prospect in baseball. He didn't hurt his arm last year, or suddenly walk every hitter in the ballpark; he simply had some mechanical inconsistencies that made his transition to Double-A a little rocky. He still had a strikeout-to-walk ratio of 135/39, and a nagging mid-season injury kept him from throwing more than 122 innings. In the long run, it may be the best thing that could have happened for his career, and it was definitely the best thing for the Marlins. Matt Mantei may be worth millions of dollars, but he's not worth a Penny.

22. Milton Bradley   CF   Montreal   Age 22

	BA	OBP	SLG	EQA
1998:	.255	.316	.383	.236
1999:	.290	.342	.458	.264

From the makers of such wonderful board games as Monopoly, Life and Chutes and Ladders, comes their latest creation, Tools. Tools is a former #1 draft pick and a switch-hitting outfielder, but lately Tools has become Performance,

hitting .329/.391/.526 in Double-A last season. Bradley then went to the Arizona Fall League and was one of the best play-ers there, hitting .352 and even drawing a fair amount of walks. The Expos will cure him of that annoying habit soon; what they're more concerned about is a temper that has resulted in annual run-ins with umpires, coaches and those vendors who can throw a bag of peanuts across three sec-tions. The word on the street is that his attitude is reminis-cent of Albert Belle. If I'm riding buses for $1,600/month, any comparison to Albert Belle works for me. Look for him in 2001, or sooner if Rondell White is traded.

23. Chad Hermansen   CF   Pittsburgh   Age 22

	BA	OBP	SLG	EQA
1998:	.242	.313	.476	.264
1999:	.243	.296	.451	.246

Hermansen's major-league debut finally happened last September. It was time: following a second straight year in Triple-A, Hermansen appears to have settled at a position—center field—and his power continues to develop. He's still only 22, and still has the base of skills that made him one of the five best prospects in the game just three years ago. The Pirates have imparted to him their own bizarre sense of offensive aggressiveness, as his walks have dropped from 69 to 50 to 35 over the last two years. His ranking is probably the least stable of any hitter on this list. He could hit 400 homers in the new decade, or he could be Cory Snyder with a little more melanin.

24. Ryan Anderson   LHP   Seattle   Age 20

	H/9	BB/9	K/9	DT-ERA
1998:	9.14	7.26	9.06	4.78
1999:	10.27	6.52	9.30	5.83

In terms of predictability, Hermansen is the sunrise when compared to "The Space Needle." Ryan Anderson is, without question, the most intriguing prospect in baseball. He's just a week older than Ankiel, and his stuff, on a good day, makes Ankiel's look positively pedestrian. Only Anderson's idol, Randy Johnson, can match him in both velocity and movement. But Anderson is flaky, arrogant and has a reputation for being hard to coach. He's also just 20, and while he might anger a lot of people, he did hold his own in Double-A last year. There was some talk that he turned a corner in the Arizona Fall League, and he did show the best control of his career—34 innings, nine walks—there. You know Lou Piniella can't wait to bring him up, and while Piniella has destroyed the careers of some fine pitching prospects with his impatience, he has never had a young pitcher this talented. Anderson is either going to be an instant star or an instant flop; either way, he's going to make a big splash, and it should be fun to watch. Unless you're a Mariner fan.

25. Eric Gagne RHP Los Angeles Age 24

	H/9	BB/9	K/9	DT-ERA
1998:	9.50	4.27	7.33	5.36
1999:	8.17	4.50	8.41	3.67

He pronounces it GAHN-yay, not GAG-nee, and yes, he's from Quebec. As John Sickels pointed out last year, Tommy Lasorda must have gotten Gagne confused with the former Dodger shortstop, because this Gagne was spared during the Prospect Pogrom of 1998. Gagne had Tommy John surgery and missed the entire 1997 season, but in the last two years has averaged well over a strikeout per inning while going 21-11 with a 3.13 ERA in the minors. Burn this into your skull: Tommy John surgery, if the new ligament takes to the elbow, can restore the arm as good as new. In some cases, better. Gagne had the most impressive September call-up of any pitcher, allowing just 18 hits in 30 innings with a 2.10 ERA. He's in a great park, and Davey Johnson has a long history of success with rookie pitchers.

26. Aubrey Huff 3B Tampa Bay Age 23

	BA	OBP	SLG	EQA
1998:	.270	.318	.459	.258
1999:	.277	.348	.480	.274

For Devil Ray fans—both of them—there has been little hope that the team is ever going to put together a lineup with hitters more potent than Miguel Cairo and John Flaherty. Huff is the first sign that the Rays may be capable of producing good position players. Huff went straight to a full-season league after he was drafted in 1998, and immediately hit .321 with power and good defense. The Devil Rays challenged him again in 1999, pushing him to Double-A, and he again hit over .300, this time with 65 extra-base hits and more patience. Without yet developing a seminal skill, Huff still has such an impressive overall game that, as a left-handed-hitting third baseman, comparisons to Robin Ventura are not only inevitable, but warranted.

27. Matt LeCroy C Minnesota Age 24

	BA	OBP	SLG	EQA
1998:	.251	.328	.442	.258
1999:	.239	.301	.450	.247

After losing the rights to Travis Lee in the famous draft loophole fiasco of 1997, the Twins drafted LeCroy with the compensation pick, and right now you could argue that they benefited from the exchange. LeCroy was so impressive in his 1998 that he briefly touched down in Triple-A, but was sent back to the Florida State League in 1999. Even for a player with his experience, to hit 20 homers in 89 games in the FSL is impressive stuff, especially for a catcher. LeCroy spent the final month of the season in Triple-A and slugged over

.600, which adds bite to the argument that he could be the best power-hitting catcher in the league by 2001. He should be up by June if not sooner; if he's the Twins' Opening Day catcher, he has a good shot at Jackie Robinson honors.

28. Ed Yarnall LHP New York (AL) Age 24

	H/9	BB/9	K/9	DT-ERA
1998:	7.93	4.52	6.68	4.87
1999:	8.72	3.96	8.09	3.62

When Brian Cashman can make Dave Dombrowski look like Lou Gorman, you know he's good. Cashman turned Mike Lowell, who had absolutely no hope of playing for the Yankees in 1999, into Yarnall and two other former #1 picks (Mark Johnson and Todd Noel). Yarnall was on this list last year, and while the Yankees' depth trapped him in Triple-A for most of 1999, he used his time wisely, improving his control and refining a repertoire that is equal parts power and guile. For a rookie pitcher, he's about as low-risk as they come: he'll be in the low-pressure role of the #5 starter for one of the best-run organizations in baseball.

29. Marcus Giles 2B Atlanta Age 22

	BA	OBP	SLG	EQA
1998:	.267	.361	.503	.285
1999:	.302	.359	.484	.280

After a 1998 season that seemed too good to be true (.329, 37 home runs, 85 walks), Giles's performance in 1999 looks like someone let all the air out of the balloon. That's not the case: Giles was facing a much tougher brand of competition in the Carolina League, and while his homers dropped from 37 to 13, he still hit 40 doubles and had a .326 batting average. The pivotal skill for Giles isn't his power, which is still there, but his defense. He was, by most accounts, an improved second baseman last year. Whether he improved enough to make it to the major leagues at the position is an open question. I think his bat will carry him to a starting job no matter where he plays, but the difference between a league-average left fielder and Jeff Kent is not a trivial one.

30. Michael Restovich OF Minnesota Age 21

	BA	OBP	SLG	EQA
1998:	.289	.386	.467	.288
1999:	.275	.357	.448	.270

The last of the Twins' troika of outstanding young hitters, Restovich is a Minnesota native who "slumped" to a .312/.412/.513 performance in the Midwest League last year, after hitting .369/.489/.613 in his 1998 debut. There were several players who hit as well as Restovich did in the low-A leagues, but few of them were as young and multi-talented as Restovich, and none of them could claim that they were having an off season. Restovich is probably two years away. The

Twins are already pestering the commissioner's office for permission to print 2002 playoff tickets.

31. Jon Garland — RHP — Chicago (AL) — Age 20

	H/9	BB/9	K/9	DT-ERA
1998:	16.09	5.79	4.66	9.03
1999:	10.12	3.76	4.94	5.06

While other big-market teams invest most of their resources towards building great teams, the Cubs and White Sox amuse themselves with games of chicken, trading their brightest prospects to each other for shiny tokens and Pokémon cards. Eight years ago, the White Sox acquired George Bell, who would hit 38 homers on the South Side, for Sammy Sosa, who's at 307 and counting. The Cubs re-upped the ante in 1998, trading Garland, their #1 pick just the year before, for Matt Karchner, who hadn't been picked first since his best friend's dad nabbed him in Pony League. Garland was scuffling a bit when the Cubs traded him, but 18-year-old pitchers usually do. In 1999, Garland moved all the way to Triple-A, throwing one of the most impressive outings of the Triple-A World Series, something 19-year-old pitchers don't usually do. He's a high-risk commodity, both because he's so young and because the light switch turned on awfully abruptly.

32. Adam Piatt — 3B — Oakland — Age 24

	BA	OBP	SLG	EQA
1998:	.245	.325	.415	.251
1999:	.275	.382	.520	.298

Piatt got all the hype for winning the first Texas League Triple Crown since 1922, but more impressively, he won the Quadruple Crown by tying for the league lead in walks. Make all the cracks you want about Midland's ballpark, but if you hit .345/.451/.704 on the moon, you're a prospect. He's not going to move Eric Chavez off third base, but his bat and batting eye should get him to the major leagues in some capacity. Oakland's ability to find him a new position—or organization—quickly will determine just what kind of a contribution he'll make.

33. Alfonso Soriano — SS — New York (AL) — Age 22

	BA	OBP	SLG	EQA
1999:	.260	.307	.435	.245

In a perfect world, D'Angelo Jimenez would have Soriano's hype, and vice versa. Not that Soriano isn't a good prospect, but Jimenez may still be getting invitations to All-Star Games after Soriano has retired, assuming he isn't still being blocked by Derek Jeter 10 years from now. Soriano has a slight edge in power, slugging over .500 in Double-A in his first year on American soil, but his poor showing in Triple-A

(.183 average in 20 games) shows that Soriano still has some things on which to work. Jimenez, in all honesty, doesn't. There's talk that Soriano could move to the outfield, which seems like a waste, especially if it's to a corner spot. He needs a full year in Triple-A to silence the doubts about his plate discipline and his defense. If he manages that, then all he'll need is a new organization.

34. Mike Meyers — RHP — Chicago (NL) — Age 22

	H/9	BB/9	K/9	DT-ERA
1998:	11.72	4.71	6.89	5.97
1999:	7.14	4.04	9.49	2.69

Meyers led the baseball world with a 1.73 ERA last season, but ranks this low on our list because the scouts are skeptical that he has much mojo. Most finesse prospects hit the wall at Double-A; in five starts in the Southern League at the end of the year, Meyers struck out 51 men in 33 innings with a 1.09 ERA. Frankly, his numbers last year were so good that they're hard to take seriously. Kerry Wood's return should get all the headlines in Chicago, but don't let that distract you from keeping up with Meyers, because his performance last year was just too phenomenal to ignore.

35. Jayson Werth — C — Baltimore — Age 21

	BA	OBP	SLG	EQA
1998:	.232	.314	.339	.227
1999:	.285	.367	.375	.262

Werth is not a power hitter (13 homers in three seasons), and his .278 career average evokes more comparisons to Chris Gwynn than Tony. But he has three lines on his resume that most don't: 1) he plays a key defensive position well; 2) he knows the strike zone; 3) he has been much younger than most of his competition, reaching Double-A at 20. His final numbers were brought down by playing through a late-season wrist injury. At 6'6", he's got the frame to add power as he matures. The flip side is that tall catchers don't develop very well, probably because the biomechanics of squatting and standing takes a lot out of their knees. Werth moves well for a lanky catcher, stealing 23 bases last year. Right now, he looks like a knockoff of Jason Kendall, which isn't bad if you can't find the original.

36. Jason Romano — 2B — Texas — Age 21

	BA	OBP	SLG	EQA
1998:	.245	.301	.329	.216
1999:	.279	.335	.473	.268

The Quiet Prospect. Romano does nothing spectacularly but everything well, and plays a key defensive position. It is quite impressive for such a young player to hit .312 with 13 homers and 14 triples in the Florida State League, a notoriously difficult league for power. Romano's one weakness is his mediocre strike zone judgment (39 walks, 72 strikeouts), which is the only reason to be cautious in predicting future greatness. If those numbers converge, he'll be in our Top 10 next year and in Arlington the year after that.

37. Ramon Ortiz   RHP   Anaheim   Age 24

	H/9	BB/9	K/9	DT-ERA
1998:	10.72	3.77	8.74	5.96
1990:	9.31	4.17	7.66	4.68

Fine prospect that Ortiz is, he has the battle scars that come with being an Angels' pitching prospect. The Angels have a philosophy for raising minor-league pitchers that lies somewhere between reckless endangerment and aggravated assault: six of the top 12 innings-pitched totals in the minor leagues last year were compiled by Angel farmhands. After completing eight games as a 21-year-old in 1997, Ortiz missed almost all of 1998 with a tender elbow. He returned last year and pitched very well in Double- and Triple-A. He struggled in September with the Angels, but still finished with 44 strikeouts in 48 innings. His pitching style reminds many of Pedro Martinez, but that refers to his build and his heritage as much as his repertoire. How well Ortiz pitches is almost entirely dependent on how close he is to complete health.

38. Dernell Stenson   1B   Boston   Age 22

	BA	OBP	SLG	EQA
1998:	.247	.355	.426	.266
1999:	.252	.332	.423	.254

He regressed some from his breakthrough 1998 season but still has a bright future. The Red Sox moved him to first base in anticipation of making him Mo Vaughn's successor, but he made 30 errors last year. His offense picked up after a horrible first half, and he still has the power-and-walks package that made him so enticing a year ago. Stenson needs another year in Triple-A, or at least that's what the Red Sox should be telling him. He's quite capable of roaring out of the gate and turning Brian Daubach into yesterday's news.

39. Travis Dawkins   SS   Cincinnati   Age 21

	BA	OBP	SLG	EQA
1998:	.247	.304	.306	.214
1999:	.266	.322	.385	.244

There are some who doubt his bat; Dawkins hit just .272 in the Midwest League for the first half of the season. Few doubt his glove, which is already considered major-league caliber, or his speed, which helped him steal 53 bases last year. What makes Dawkins a Top 40 Prospect is the way he responded when the Reds promoted him all the way to Double-A in August. He hit .364 the rest of the season, a remarkable performance for a 20-year-old at that level. He's not Rey Ordonez, as he chipped in 10 homers and 49 walks. He just needs to fill out his offensive profile, and he'll be in line to succeed Barry Larkin in 2001 or 2002.

40. Mario Encarnacion   OF   Oakland   Age 22

	BA	OBP	SLG	EQA
1998:	.254	.342	.420	.257
1999:	.247	.310	.399	.238

Encarnacion is more tools than performance, which makes him an aberration in the Oakland organization. He's talented enough to beat up Double-A pitchers at the age of 21, but his rawness was exploited after he was promoted to Triple-A late in the year, where he hit just .241 with a strikeout-to-walk ratio of 44/6. Under most circumstances, that would be enough to keep him off this list, but the A's are the one organization in baseball that will not rest until his knowledge of the strike zone improves. The value of a toolsy speed-and-defense player who can still hit, like Encarnacion, increases on a team full of productive, but less athletic, hitters.

Honorable Mention

The 15 best, most exciting, intriguing or just plain *People*-magazine-worthy prospects that we couldn't fit on our list:

Rob Bell: The linchpin of the Bret Boone trade for the Reds, Bell missed half the season with arm problems, but in the second half showed why the Braves made such a mistake in trading him.

Ben Broussard: Another Red prospect, Broussard was the organization's second-round pick last year, and in the span of four months he posted an OPS above 1200 in the Pioneer, Midwest and California Fall Leagues.

Morgan Burkhart: The best hitter ever to come out of the Independent Leagues, Burkhart was signed by the Red Sox after hitting .404/.557/.861—really—for Richmond in 1998. In his first year of organized ball, he hit .298 with 35 homers between A ball and Double-A. He's 28, but so is Brian Daubach.

Scott Comer: Comer makes Bret Saberhagen look like Brad Pennington: in 130 innings last year, he walked fewer hitters (five) than Russ Ortiz did in the time it took to write this. He still has to make the jump to Double-A, and the recent history of extreme control pitchers is not good. Then again, no one in recent history has shown control quite this extreme.

Steve Cox: The International League MVP (.341/.415/.588) plays for an organization that thinks a bat is just something players swing when they're not stealing bases or wearing a glove. With Paul Sorrento gone and Wade Boggs in the front office, Cox may get a chance to play, anyway.

Junior Guerrero: The best of the Royals' many pitching prospects, Guerrero struck out 181 men in just 155 innings and improved as the season went on. He's got an outside shot at a September call-up, which isn't bad for a 20-year-old.

Josh Hamilton: Last year's #1 overall pick has done everything to live up to his reputation, as he was probably the best player in the Appalachian League at the age of 18. He needs to lay off bad pitches more. Hamilton won't be Ken Griffey Jr., but he could arrive awfully fast, like sometime in 2001.

Drew Henson: What's missed in the story of Drew Henson, Yankee farmhand by day and Michigan Wolverine quarterback by night, is just how remarkable it is for any 19-year-old, let alone one who plays baseball only half-time, to hit .280 with 13 homers in half a season in the Florida State League. Forget Josh Booty: Henson holds national high-school records in home runs and RBIs, and if he wants to try, he could become the best two-sport star since Bo Jackson.

Chad Hutchinson: Another former college quarterback, Hutchinson now throws from the mound for the Cardinals, and the inexperience shows: he walked 93 men in 153 innings last year. He's a year away, with tremendous upside.

Josh Kalinowski: A 2.11 ERA and 176 strikeouts in 162 innings, allowing just 119 hits, should get him on the big boys' list, but Kalinowski pitches for the Rockies. Tough break, kid. He's talented enough to survive the environment and pitch well, which sounds a lot like what we said about Jamey Wright.

Steve Lomasney: Young, power-hitting Red Sox catcher who drew 57 walks in just 102 games last year. Jason Varitek sleeps peacefully at night, so Lomasney's future best lies somewhere else.

Mark Mulder: Picked second overall in 1998, Mulder went straight to Triple-A and was effective, if not particularly exciting. A lot of college pitchers take a big jump forward in their second year; if Mulder does, he's the new Jamie Moyer, and the A's are in the playoffs.

John Patterson: No longer Brad Penny's sidekick, Patterson is a fine prospect in his own right and wowed observers in the Arizona Fall League. There's little danger he'll be rushed—the Diamondbacks can't even find room for Brian Anderson in their rotation—so this curveball specialist will get plenty of practice getting his ball to break in Tucson's thin air.

Wilfredo Rodriguez: Rodriguez, Eric Ireland, Tony McKnight—pick an Astro. Rodriguez gets the nod because he's the youngest, least-abused and most left-handed. It doesn't hurt that he has nasty stuff, or that hitters batted just .199 against him last year.

Rico Washington: Washington has played behind the plate, as well as some second base and third base, holding his own at all three spots. He can hit at any position (.325, 20 home runs, 78 walks), but since the Pirates have Aramis Ramirez at third base and Jason Kendall behind the plate, maybe the move Washington needs is to another organization.

Reliever Evaluation Tools

by Michael Wolverton

Back in my college days, when I was spending too much of my time at the Astrodome instead of studying for finals, my friends and I used to cringe whenever Astro reliever Dave Smith was brought into a game with runners on base. Our expectation—admittedly based on a small sample—was that Smith was liable to allow all the runners he was inheriting to score, racking up runs that would be charged to his predecessors. He would then finish the inning before any of his own runners crossed the plate, keeping his own "R" and "ER" columns pristine. Our nickname for him at the time? Dave "Hey, it's not my ERA" Smith.

Regardless of whether or not my friends and I were right about Smith, it is widely understood that the traditional way of assigning runs to pitchers—if a runner scores, the pitcher who let him reach base is charged with the run—doesn't always work well, especially with relievers. A reliever who comes in with the bases loaded and two out and gives up a triple before getting out of the inning has hurt his team plenty, but he has helped his ERA. On the other hand, a reliever in the same situation who strands all three runners by getting the first batter out has done far more to prevent runs than a pitcher who gets that same first batter out with two outs and the bases empty. A metric for evaluating relievers should do a better job of allocating credit for runs prevented and blame for runs scored than the traditional run assignment method.

Gary Skoog came up with a technique for doing this with his Value Added approach, described in an article in the 1987 Bill James *Baseball Abstract*. His idea—applied to all players, not just relievers—was to measure the quality of each appearance by a player in terms of how it changed run expectation. He used a situational scoring table from *The Hidden Game of Baseball*, by John Thorn and Pete Palmer, to map each of the 24 possible base/out states into the expected number of runs that would score in the remainder of the inning starting from that state. According to *Hidden Game*'s table, an average team with one out and runners at second and third would expect to score 1.37 runs in the remainder of the inning; with two outs and a runner on second, a team would expect to score 0.35 runs. Skoog then calculated the value of an appearance as the difference between the expected runs when the appearance started and the expected runs when the appearance ended, plus the number of runs that scored during the appearance itself.

For example, if a reliever entered a game with one out and runners on second and third and was pulled after getting

a strikeout and surrendering a double that scored both runners, his Value Added for that appearance would be 1.37 – 0.35 – 2 = – 0.98 runs. A player's Value Added for the season is the sum of the Value Added results for each appearance in the season. Steve Schulman has extended this system to remove expected runs due to errors. (Skoog had this basic error-removing idea as well, but he wasn't explicit about how to remove them with pitchers.) Schulman has applied his version under another name—Runs Prevented—to evaluate relievers in the past few editions of the STATS, Inc. *Baseball Scoreboard*.

A Better Mousetrap

This system offers a good solution to the run-assignment problem inherent in traditional pitching statistics. Unfortunately, Skoog's and Schulman's realizations of the system do not address some other well-known problems in baseball analysis. In particular, the ratings they produce are not adjusted for park, league or era. For this article, we'll make a few changes to Skoog's and Schulman's calculations, listed here in rough order of importance:

1. The numbers here are adjusted for park and league. For any given appearance by a reliever, we will evaluate that appearance using a situational scoring table for the park and league in which the appearance took place.

2. Instead of using the situational scoring table published in *The Hidden Game of Baseball*, which is based on a computer simulation using data from 1961 to 1977, the numbers here use the actual scoring frequencies for the major leagues in 1999.

3. We will not try to solve the problem of separating pitching from fielding by making any special adjustments for errors.

We'll call our rating Adjusted Runs Prevented (ARP), adopting Schulman's name for the method but adding the "Adjusted" to make it clear we're doing things differently. A reliever's ARP is the number of runs that he prevented over an average pitcher, given the base/out situation when he entered and left each game, adjusted for league and park. The exact formula for a reliever's ARP for a game is

$$ ARP = \frac{ER(sS,P) - ER(sF,P) + IF\left[ER(sO,P) - R\right]}{pe(P)} $$

where

ER(s,P) = the expected number of runs that will score in the remainder of an inning starting in base/out state s in park P,

sS,P = the base/out state when the reliever entered the game in park P,

sF,P = the base/out state when the reliever left the game in park P,

IF = the number of innings the reliever finished,

s0,P = a special state for the beginning of an inning in park P. Note that this state is different from the state for no outs, none on. Using this state instead of the no-out/none-on state once per inning ensures that ARP has the following desirable property: the total ARP for all relievers in that inning will be equal to the league average runs-per-inning minus the number of runs that scored in the inning (park adjusted). This is another way that ARP differs from Skoog's or Schulman's measures.

R = the number of runs that scored while the reliever was in the game, and

pe(P) = the park effect for park P.

ARP represents a reliever's cumulative run prevention above average over the course of a season. We would also like to have a measure of a reliever's rate of run prevention using the same basic approach. We'll do this by making this observation: like ARP, Pete Palmer's Adjusted Pitching Runs (APR) measures production in terms of runs prevented above average. APR is based on the pitcher's rate of runs allowed: Palmer's version is based on park-adjusted ERA, but for this article, we'll use adjusted RA, or ARA. It's easy to compute a pitcher's ARA from his APR by applying the APR formula "backwards":

$$ARA = \frac{LgRA - 9\,(APR)}{IP}$$

If we apply this same "backwards" formula, substituting ARP for APR, we can get a rate stat based on ARP that is directly comparable to adjusted RA. The idea of the stat is to measure runs per 9 innings like RA, but to do a better job of assigning responsibility for runs when two or more pitchers play a role (i.e., inherited-runner situations). This "Runs Allowed Average" derived from ARP, which we'll call Runs Responsible Average (RRA), is calculated as:

$$RRA = \frac{LgRA - 9\,(ARP)}{IP}$$

If a player has an RRA of 3.00, I read it that he prevented runs like a "full-inning pitcher" with a 3.00 RA, where a full-inning pitcher is a pitcher who never enters or leaves a game in the middle of an inning. Starters are usually pretty good approximations to full-inning pitchers, since the vast majority of their innings are full innings. Note that in extreme cases, a reliever's RRA can be negative. For example, if a reliever enters a game with bases loaded and nobody out, and he gets out of the inning with nobody scoring, he'll have a negative RRA for the game. That actually makes a certain amount of sense: that reliever has done even more to prevent runs than a pitcher who came in with nobody on and no one out and pitched a scoreless inning.

1999 Leaders

Here are the top 30 relievers in the majors in 1999, ranked by Adjusted Runs Prevented:

Pitcher	Team	IP	R	ARA	APR	RRA	ARP
Keith Foulke	CHW	105.3	28	2.37	1.4	2.15	35.0
Danny Graves	CIN	111.0	42	3.44	-2.0	2.64	30.9
Jeff Zimmerman	TEX	87.7	24	2.27	-0.2	2.03	30.3
Armando Benitez	NYM	78.0	18	2.18	0.6	1.78	29.1
Billy Wagner	HOU	74.7	14	1.82	-1.5	1.78	27.9
Derek Lowe	BOS	109.3	35	2.72	1.3	2.86	27.8
Scott Sullivan	CIN	113.7	41	3.28	-0.2	3.02	26.8
Mike Remlinger	ATL	83.7	24	2.76	0.0	2.28	26.6
Doug Brocail	DET	82.0	23	2.45	1.1	2.27	26.2
Mariano Rivera	NYY	69.0	15	2.01	0.4	1.95	24.5
Scott Williamson	CIN	93.3	29	2.83	1.1	3.12	21.0
Jerry DiPoto	COL	86.7	44	3.68	3.6	3.19	18.8
Greg Swindell	ARI	64.7	19	2.63	1.6	2.67	17.8
Turk Wendell	NYM	85.7	31	3.42	1.8	3.34	17.2
Scott Sauerbeck	PIT	67.7	19	2.54	2.2	2.97	16.4
Rich Garces	BOS	40.7	9	1.88	-0.0	1.60	16.0
Doug Jones	OAK	104.0	43	3.61	-0.9	3.76	15.9
Matt Mantei	F/A	65.3	21	3.2	0.4	2.98	15.7
Sean Lowe	CHW	95.7	39	3.63	-0.9	3.69	15.4
Steve Montgomery	PHI	64.7	25	3.39	2.0	3.01	15.3
Steve Karsay	CLE	65.7	23	2.91	0.6	3.10	14.9
Steve Kline	MON	69.7	32	4.21	-1.3	3.23	14.8
Trevor Hoffman	SDP	67.3	23	3.60	0.0	3.20	14.6
John Rocker	ATL	72.3	24	3.19	1.7	3.34	14.5
John Johnstone	SFG	65.7	24	3.62	-3.3	3.20	14.2
Mike Venafro	TEX	68.3	29	3.51	-2.1	3.32	13.8
Antonio Alfonseca	FLA	77.7	28	3.63	0.5	3.54	13.8
David Lee	COL	49.0	21	3.11	2.4	2.63	13.7
Roberto Hernandez	TAM	73.3	27	3.20	-1.1	3.48	13.5
Rudy Seanez	ATL	53.7	21	3.76	-1.9	2.96	13.0

1999 was a good year for relievers; the top five relievers from last year each had a better ARP total than 1998's champion, Trevor Hoffman. Keith Foulke blew past Jeff Zimmerman with a strong late-season push to finish first in the majors. Danny Graves, who was outstanding at handling not only his own runners but also those he inherited, finished second to Foulke and first in the National League. Forget the Nasty Boys: the 1999 Reds' 1-2-3 punch of Graves, Scott Sullivan and Scott Williamson was almost certainly a more effective run-prevention team than 1990's Rob Dibble/Randy Myers/Norm Charlton combination.

At the other extreme, here are the worst 10 relievers from 1999, ranked by ARP:

Pitcher	Team	IP	R	ARA	APR	RRA	ARP
Vic Darensbourg	FLA	34.7	36	10.47	-1.0	12.60	-28.7
Mel Rojas	L/D	14.0	28	18.3	0.4	18.67	-21.0
Brian Edmondson	FLA	94.0	65	6.97	-4.9	6.93	-18.6
Carlos Almanzar	SDP	37.3	32	9.04	-3.4	8.97	-15.9
Dan Serafini	CHC	43.3	37	7.87	0.8	8.30	-15.2
Paul Assenmacher	CLE	33.0	32	8.06	-0.7	9.11	-14.5
John Hudek	C/A	21.3	22	9.0	2.1	10.91	-13.7
Joe Mays	MIN	52.3	38	6.49	3.6	7.46	-13.5
Mike DeJean	COL	61.0	61	7.26	0.7	7.12	-13.4
Ricky Bottalico	STL	73.3	45	5.77	6.5	6.79	-13.4

What a disastrous year for the Marlins' bullpen. Vic Darensbourg, who had the majors' 17th-best ARP total in 1998, couldn't have been more disappointing. He was charged with more than a run per inning, and to add insult to injury, he was one of the league's worst at preventing inherited runners from scoring. Brian Edmondson's performance was a letdown as well, although not quite the magnitude of Darensbourg's. Edmondson was only a little worse than average in 1998, but his run prevention declined as his innings total went up in 1999. Mike DeJean was yet another flop. He was a key member of the league-best Rockies' bullpen in 1998 with the 24th-best ARP in the majors. He slumped in a big way in 1999, taking the Rockies' bullpen down with him.

Here are the team numbers from 1999, with bullpens ranked best to worst in ARP:

Team	IP	R	ARA	APR	RRA	ARP
Cincinnati	530.3	216	3.71	84.5	3.70	84.8
Boston	542.3	265	4.15	59.9	4.15	59.9
New York Mets	492.7	209	4.01	61.8	4.07	58.8
Texas	523.3	267	4.22	53.4	4.27	50.5
Atlanta	419.3	184	4.22	43.1	4.12	47.5
New York Yankees	437.0	203	4.29	41.3	4.30	40.7
Arizona	410.7	189	4.13	46.4	4.32	37.3
Houston	403.0	182	4.39	33.7	4.35	35.4
Anaheim	496.3	249	4.50	35.4	4.51	34.7
Pittsburgh	467.7	234	4.53	31.8	4.69	23.7
Chicago White Sox	505.7	266	4.69	25.5	4.76	21.3
Cleveland	511.7	282	4.58	31.9	4.89	14.3
Minnesota	524.7	284	4.84	17.7	4.92	13.2
Philadelphia	481.0	267	4.87	14.4	4.93	11.5
Oakland	502.3	265	4.60	30.2	4.94	11.4
Colorado	493.7	337	4.95	10.4	4.95	10.7
Detroit	492.0	272	4.83	17.1	5.00	7.9
Toronto	473.3	267	4.88	13.6	5.04	5.4
San Francisco	487.0	248	5.05	5.2	5.11	1.8
Milwaukee	523.0	292	5.07	4.2	5.23	-5.0
Los Angeles	450.7	243	5.26	-5.9	5.42	-13.9
Baltimore	441.7	263	5.43	-13.9	5.49	-16.9
Tampa Bay	556.3	325	5.07	4.5	5.42	-17.1
Montreal	504.3	284	5.16	-1.2	5.47	-18.1
San Diego	444.7	251	5.95	-40.1	5.98	-41.3
St. Louis	514.3	305	5.57	-24.6	5.92	-44.6
Chicago Cubs	495.3	314	5.84	-38.5	6.04	-49.3
Kansas City	485.3	336	5.97	-44.4	6.25	-59.6
Seattle	471.0	337	6.08	-49.2	6.37	-64.1
Florida	490.7	302	6.20	-57.9	6.45	-71.2
ML	14571.2	7938	4.90	390.3	5.04	169.5

On a team level, ARP adds less to traditional run assignment methods (e.g., APR) than it does for individuals. The only major difference between ARP and APR for teams is that ARP takes into account how the bullpen handles the runners that the starters leave on base. As a result, you'd expect a team's ARP to be close to its APR, and in general that holds true in the table above. Nevertheless, there are a few teams that the two methods rate differently. The A's and Devil Rays had bullpens that were much worse than you'd expect given the number of runs charged to them. On the other hand, the Braves were somewhat better than their APR and ARA indicated. The best bullpen in the league last year belonged to the Reds, who not only had the Nastier Boys, but who also got good innings out of Dennis Reyes, Ron Villone and Brett Tomko.

Beyond the "R" Column

There are two major reasons that a reliever's "R" column in a box score does a poor job of measuring his performance in that game: (1) it doesn't reflect how well he dealt with the runners he inherited, and (2) it does reflect how well the reliever's successors dealt with the runners he turned over to them. It's interesting to break down these two aspects of performance individually, to see who gave and received the most and least help.

Performance in handling inherited runners can be measured analogously to ARP: for each appearance by the reliever, look at the situation when the reliever entered each game and how that compares to the situation when he left the game. For this, we consider only the runners that the reliever inherited. We figure the number of those inherited runners that would be expected to score, given where they were on the bases and how many outs there were when the reliever entered. We compare that total to the number who actually did score while the reliever was in the game, plus, of any who were still on base when the reliever left the game, how many would have been expected to score from that ending base/out state.

The end result is a number called Inherited Runs Prevented (IRP). If this number is positive, it means that the reliever is chopping runs off his teammates' totals; if it's negative, it means the reliever is adding runs to his teammates. Below are the best and worst relievers of 1999 in this measure. "IRnr" is the number of runners the reliever inherited; "EIRs" is the expected number of those inherited runners to score, "IR" is the number who actually did score while the reliever was in the game; and "EIRf" is the expected number of inherited runners left on base when the reliever left his games.

Here are the best (Table 1) and worst (Table 2) at handling inherited runners in 1999.

The second table shows another aspect of the catastrophe that was the 1999 Florida bullpen: three of the five worst relievers at handling inherited runners were Marlins. For example, Vic Darensbourg inherited 52 runners. Given the bases those runners occupied and how many outs there were, they would have been expected to score 16.3 runs. Darensbourg watched from the mound as 20 of those runners crossed the plate, and he left another 4.4 expected runs worth of those runners on base for others to deal with. The result is that Darensbourg cost his teammates nine runs beyond what they could expect from an average pitcher. On the other end of the spectrum, Danny Graves chopped nine runs off his teammates' ledgers.

The other effect we want to isolate is how much help the reliever got from his successors when he turned runners over to them. This is measured similarly to IRP. For this measure, we consider only those runners who are on base when the reliever left his games; Mike Emeigh calls these "bequeathed runners." Actually, we'll be more restrictive than that: we'll consider only the bequeathed runners who are the reliever's responsibility (i.e., those who will be charged to him if they score). We'll call these "Own Bequeathed Runners" (OBRnr). We figure out the expected number of Own Bequeathed Runners to score given where they were on the bases and how many outs there were when the reliever left the game, and subtract from that total the number who actually did score. The result is Bequeathed Runs Saved (BRS). If it's positive, the reliever's successors bailed him out by chopping runs off his R total; if it's negative, his successors have added runs to his ledger compared to what he could have expected from average bullpen support. In Table 3 and Table 4 are the top 10 and bottom 10 by this measure. OBRnr is the number of the reliever's Own Bequeathed Runners turned over to other relievers during the year; EBR is the expected number of those runners to score; and BR is the number who actually did score.

Table 1

Pitcher	Team	IRnr	EIRs	IR	EIRf	IRP
Danny Graves	CIN	44	18.2	9	0.0	9.0
Jerry DiPoto	COL	32	15.5	4	0.0	8.9
Ricardo Rincon	CLE	42	17.9	5	5.5	6.9
Steve Kline	MON	65	22.0	11	5.2	6.5
Jason Grimsley	NYY	43	17.2	11	0.4	6.1
Shigetoshi Hasegawa	ANA	51	18.9	11	2.0	5.8
Travis Miller	MIN	41	17.1	7	4.6	5.6
Steve Montgomery	PHI	21	7.4	2	0.0	5.6
Keith Foulke	CHW	23	8.5	3	0.0	5.5
Trevor Hoffman	SDP	22	7.1	3	0.0	5.1

Table 2

Pitcher	Team	IRnr	EIRs	IR	EIRf	IRP
Tim Worrell	OAK	49	16.2	25	1.5	-10.0
Vic Darensbourg	FLA	52	16.3	20	4.4	-9.0
Jesus Sanchez	FLA	44	12.4	19	1.3	-8.9
Chuck McElroy	C/N	39	15.1	23	0.5	-8.5
Braden Looper	FLA	51	16.8	23	0.0	-7.0
Rick White	TAM	62	22.8	30	0.0	-7.0
Bobby Ayala	M/C	40	13.9	20	0.6	-6.5
Tim Byrdak	KCR	29	13.2	17	1.7	-5.1
Carlos Reyes	SDP	41	14.7	20	0.0	-5.1
Robb Nen	SFG	15	4.4	8	0.5	-4.7

Table 3

Pitcher	Team	OBRnr	EBR	BR	BRS
Ricky Bottalico	STL	27	10.1	3	6.5
Travis Miller	MIN	29	12.6	6	6.5
Dave Veres	COL	14	8.0	0	6.3
Mike Duvall	TAM	27	8.0	2	5.9
Bill Simas	CHW	19	7.5	2	5.6
Scott Service	KCR	30	10.3	5	5.3
Steve Reed	CLE	21	7.6	2	5.2
Al Reyes	M/B	19	5.9	1	4.9
Brian Williams	HOU	17	7.5	3	4.8
Tim Crabtree	TEX	19	8.1	4	3.7

Table 4

Pitcher	Team	OBRnr	EBR	BR	BRS
Buddy Groom	OAK	44	15.1	22	-7.4
Rheal Cormier	BOS	30	10.5	17	-6.2
Benj Sampson	MIN	20	6.0	12	-6.1
Hector Carrasco	MIN	15	5.8	12	-6.1
Brian Edmondson	FLA	31	10.9	15	-4.9
Bryan Ward	CHW	14	5.3	10	-4.8
Matt Whisenant	K/S	34	13.7	18	-4.1
Scott Sanders	CHC	33	10.2	13	-3.6
Mike Holtz	ANA	15	4.7	8	-3.4
Danny Kolb	TEX	15	5.5	9	-3.4

Ricky Bottalico turned 27 of his runners over to other Cardinal relievers, and they did not let him down. Only three of those 27 runners scored, saving Bottalico an expected 6.5 park-adjusted runs. It's not surprising that the reliever most victimized by his successors, Buddy Groom, would play for the same team as the reliever who was worst in the league at handling inherited runners, Tim Worrell. Groom must have been before Worrell in the standard A's bullpen rotation, and when Groom turned over runners, Worrell usually let them score. The result was that Groom had an expected 7.4 bequeathed runs charged that wouldn't have scored if he'd gotten league-average support.

The previous four tables isolated some interesting components of relief performance not measured by traditional run assignment (or, in the case of bequeathed runners, measured when it should not be). But what about putting those components all together to find out how badly traditional run assignment can underrate or overrate a reliever's contribution? Measuring this is easy. As we mentioned above, ARP and Palmer's Adjusted Pitching Runs are each attempting to measure the same thing—runs prevented above an average pitcher. APR represents the traditional run assignment approach, comparing the league-average run scoring to the number of runs charged to the pitcher. ARP represents the run expectation approach, and, for the reasons we've argued

in this article, should give a more accurate picture of a reliever's performance. The amount that traditional run assignment overrates or underrates a reliever, then, is the difference between those two measures. In Tables 5 and 6 are the lists for 1999.

Table 5

Pitcher	Team	EIRP	EBRS	ARA	RRA	APR	ARP	Diff.
Danny Graves	CIN	9.0	-2.0	3.44	2.64	20.9	30.9	9.9
Rheal Cormier	BOS	2.3	-6.2	4.56	3.40	4.1	12.3	8.2
Steve Kline	MON	6.5	-1.3	4.21	3.23	7.2	14.8	7.6
Mike Myers	MIL	2.5	-3.2	5.27	3.86	-0.6	5.9	6.5
Vladimir Nunez	A/F	4.9	-0.8	4.05	2.75	4.9	10.8	5.9
Bryan Ward	CHW	1.1	-4.8	8.16	6.92	-13.2	-7.8	5.4
Archie Corbin	FLA	1.7	-1.5	9.60	7.34	-10.4	-5.1	5.3
Ricardo Rincon	CLE	6.9	1.4	4.09	3.06	5.2	10.4	5.2
Chris Holt	HOU	1.8	-2.8	9.72	2.01	-3.1	2.1	5.1
Shigetoshi Hasegawa	ANA	5.8	-0.9	4.93	4.33	1.8	6.8	5.0

Table 6

Pitcher	Team	EIRP	EBRS	ARA	RRA	APR	ARP	Diff.
Chuck McElroy	C/N	-8.5	1.6	4.77	6.94	2.2	-10.8	-13.0
Mike Duvall	TAM	-4.7	5.9	4.56	7.10	2.6	-8.7	-11.3
Jesus Sanchez	FLA	-8.9	0.5	5.69	8.60	-2.0	-12.9	-10.9
Tim Worrell	OAK	-10.0	-1.2	4.78	6.06	2.8	-7.1	-9.9
Rick White	TAM	-7.0	0.4	4.44	5.20	8.3	-0.7	-9.0
Bobby Ayala	M/C	-6.5	2.5	4.81	5.80	3.0	-6.0	-9.0
Bill Simas	CHW	-2.3	5.6	4.46	5.54	5.5	-3.1	-8.6
Al Reyes	M/B	-3.7	4.9	4.57	5.74	4.2	-4.4	-8.5
Ricky Bottalico	STL	-1.3	6.5	5.77	6.79	-5.1	-13.4	-8.3
Steve Reed	CLE	-2.1	5.2	4.47	5.69	4.6	-3.7	-8.3

There are lots of names here that we've already seen in the tables above that deal with inherited and bequeathed runners. What these tables give you is an idea of how badly traditional run assignment can distort the picture of the reliever's effectiveness. Since relievers pitch relatively few innings, and since a high percentage of those innings deal with inherited and bequeathed runners, the distortion can be pretty bad. Take Chuck McElroy. His 4.77 park-adjusted RA makes him appear to be a better-than-average reliever in 1999. However, when you take into account his near-league-worst handling of inherited runners and the fact that he got above-average support from his successors, you find that his overall contribution to the Rockies and Mets run-prevention efforts was that of a 6.94 RA pitcher, more than two full runs per nine innings worse!

One more point about these tables: if you're really paying attention, you might be wondering why you can't just add up the Expected Inherited Runs Prevented and Expected

Bequeathed Runs Saved columns to get the Diff figure. After all, I've been saying above that the two differences between traditional run assignment and ARP are inherited runners and bequeathed runners. Well, actually what I said is that those are the two major differences. There are also a number of less significant effects captured by ARP but not by other statistics. In no particular order:

- Traditional statistics treat each of the three outs in an inning equally, while ARP recognizes that all outs are not created equal. You prevent more runs by getting the first out of an inning than by getting the third. A reliever that frequently comes in with two outs will tend to be somewhat overrated by traditional run assignment, all else being equal.
- ARP is park-adjusted game by game. Traditional park adjustments generally adjust a player's raw numbers by half of the effect of his home park, making the assumption that he plays roughly half his time there. If a reliever pitches a disproportionate amount of his innings either at home or on the road, or at a particular road park, ARP will compensate for that.
- If a reliever is on the mound when the home team scores the winning run in the ninth or later, and if there are other runners still on base when that winning run scores, ARP includes those runners in the relievers' final base/out state. For traditional run assignment statistics, those runners effectively disappear. (These runners are also treated as "bequeathed" in calculating Expected Bequeathed Runs Saved.)

In no way would I claim that the tools presented here are the final word in reliever evaluation. There are some shortcomings of these measures that are easy to see now, and perhaps others that will come to light as more results become available. What they do is add to the available information that baseball fans can use to form an overall picture of a reliever's performance. And more information should make everyone happy. Everyone, that is, except Chuck "Hey, it's not my ERA" McElroy.

Arizona Diamondbacks — Park Effect: +3.9%

Pitcher	G	IP	R	ARA	APR	IRnr/G	EIRs/G	IRP	BRS	RRA	ARP
Brian Anderson	12	18.3	13	6.36	-2.5	0.17	0.03	0.4	0.6	7.03	-3.9
Andy Benes	1	2.0	1	4.48	0.1	0.00	0.00	0.0	0.0	4.33	0.2
Dan Carlson	2	4.0	4	8.96	-1.7	0.50	0.12	0.2	-1.5	4.80	0.2
Bobby Chouinard	32	40.3	16	3.56	7.1	0.75	0.28	4.0	0.7	2.73	10.8
John Frascatore	26	33.0	16	4.35	2.9	0.54	0.15	-1.2	0.9	5.31	-0.6
Darren Holmes	44	48.7	21	3.87	6.9	0.64	0.23	3.2	3.5	4.08	5.8
Byung-Hyun Kim	25	27.3	15	4.92	0.7	0.52	0.16	-0.9	0.7	5.37	-0.7
Matt Mantei	30	29.0	10	3.09	6.6	0.00	0.00	0.0	0.4	3.17	6.4
Vladimir Nunez	27	34.0	15	3.95	4.5	0.56	0.19	3.9	-0.6	2.85	8.7
Gregg Olson	61	60.7	28	4.14	6.8	0.38	0.11	-2.5	2.1	4.81	2.3
Vincente Padilla	5	2.7	5	16.81	-3.5	1.20	0.27	-2.1	1.2	27.61	-6.7
Dan Plesac	34	21.7	9	3.72	3.4	0.82	0.26	-0.4	2.8	4.94	0.5
Armando Reynoso	4	6.0	4	5.98	-0.6	1.25	0.36	0.0	-1.3	3.56	1.1
Erik Sabe	17	9.7	7	6.49	-1.4	0.57	0.14	1.0	0.1	5.71	-0.6
Greg Swindell	63	64.7	19	2.63	18.0	0.59	0.18	1.6	1.6	2.67	17.8
Amaury Telemaco	5	6.0	5	7.47	-1.6	0.60	0.19	-0.6	-0.5	8.51	-2.2
Ed Vosberg	4	2.7	1	3.36	0.5	0.75	0.20	-0.2	1.9	10.26	-1.5
TOTALS	382	410.7	189	4.13	46.4	0.54	0.17	4.32	37.3		

Atlanta Braves — Park Effect: -10.0%

Pitcher	G	IP	R	ARA	APR	IRnr/G	EIRs/G	IRP	BRS	RRA	ARP
Sean Bergman	6	6.3	2	3.04	1.5	0.00	0.00	0.0	0.3	3.50	1.2
Micah Bowie	3	4.0	6	14.42	-4.1	0.00	0.00	0.0	0.0	14.58	-4.2
Mike Cather	4	2.7	3	10.81	-1.7	0.25	0.06	-0.8	0.7	15.07	-2.9
Bruce Chen	9	11.0	9	7.86	-3.3	0.22	0.09	1.0	-1.1	5.96	-1.0
David Cortes	4	3.7	3	7.86	-1.1	0.75	0.09	0.5	0.0	6.46	-0.5

Atlanta Braves (continued)

Pitcher	G	IP	R	ARA	APR	IRnr/G	EIRs/G	IRP	BRS	RRA	ARP
Derrin Ebert	5	8.0	5	6.01	-0.8	1.00	0.38	2.1	0.1	4.28	0.8
John Hudek	15	16.7	14	8.07	-5.4	0.00	0.00	0.0	0.4	8.37	-6.0
Kevin McGlinchy	64	70.3	25	3.42	13.5	0.58	0.18	0.1	1.8	3.81	10.4
Terry Mulholland	8	8.3	3	3.46	1.6	1.12	0.44	3.7	0.0	-0.35	5.1
Odalis Perez	1	1.0	0	0.00	0.6	0.00	0.00	0.0	0.0	0.00	0.6
Mike Remlinger	73	83.7	24	2.76	22.2	0.37	0.15	4.5	0.0	2.28	26.6
John Rocker	74	72.3	24	3.19	15.7	0.36	0.11	-1.3	1.7	3.34	14.5
Rudy Seanez	56	53.7	21	3.76	8.2	0.57	0.18	2.3	-1.9	2.96	13.0
Justin Speier	19	28.7	18	6.03	-2.8	0.63	0.26	1.0	0.0	6.05	-2.9
Russ Springer	49	47.3	20	4.06	5.7	0.57	0.15	2.4	2.3	4.28	4.5
Everett Stull	1	0.7	3	43.25	-2.8	0.00	0.00	0.0	0.4	59.39	-4.0
Joe Winkelsas	1	0.3	2	57.67	-1.9	0.00	0.00	0.0	1.4	95.11	-3.3
Mark Wohlers	2	0.7	2	28.83	-1.8	0.00	0.00	0.0	2.6	62.76	-4.3
TOTALS	394	419.3	184	4.22	43.1	0.46	0.15	4.12	47.5		

Chicago Cubs   Park Effect: -1.8%

Pitcher	G	IP	R	ARA	APR	IRnr/G	EIRs/G	IRP	BRS	RRA	ARP
Terry Adams	52	65.0	33	4.68	3.3	0.35	0.08	-2.7	1.4	5.43	-2.1
Rick Aguilera	44	46.3	22	4.38	3.9	0.34	0.14	-0.4	0.7	4.79	1.8
Bobby Ayala	13	16.0	7	4.03	2.0	0.38	0.12	-0.4	-0.3	4.22	1.6
Richie Barker	5	5.0	4	7.37	-1.2	0.40	0.12	-0.4	0.0	8.45	-1.8
Rod Beck	31	30.0	26	7.99	-9.5	0.26	0.11	0.5	0.0	7.83	-8.9
Doug Creek	3	6.0	7	10.75	-3.7	0.00	0.00	0.0	0.0	11.58	-4.3
Kyle Farnsworth	6	13.3	5	3.46	2.5	0.33	0.22	-0.7	0.3	3.96	1.8
Gary Gaetti	1	1.0	2	18.43	-1.5	0.00	0.00	0.0	0.0	16.63	-1.3
Mark Guthrie	11	12.3	6	4.48	0.9	0.09	0.03	0.3	-0.6	3.69	2.0
Felix Heredia	69	52.0	35	6.20	-6.1	0.87	0.29	-3.8	-2.6	6.47	-7.6
Matt Karchner	16	18.0	5	2.56	5.2	0.62	0.21	-0.1	0.9	3.15	4.0
Ray King	10	10.7	8	6.91	-2.1	0.70	0.19	-1.3	-1.2	6.68	-1.8
Brian McNichol	2	1.7	0	0.00	1.0	0.00	0.00	0.0	0.4	1.51	0.7
Kurt Miller	4	3.0	6	18.43	-4.4	0.50	0.13	-0.4	-0.1	20.23	-5.0
Terry Mulholland	10	15.7	8	4.71	0.8	0.30	0.09	-0.3	-0.7	4.35	1.4
Rodney Myers	46	63.7	34	4.92	1.6	0.83	0.31	1.9	0.0	4.77	2.6
Steve Rain	16	14.7	17	10.68	-9.0	1.00	0.37	-3.4	-1.4	12.00	-11.2
Scott Sanders	61	73.7	50	6.26	-9.1	0.64	0.19	-0.9	-3.6	5.89	-6.1
Dan Serafini	38	43.3	37	7.87	-13.1	0.61	0.18	-2.6	0.8	8.30	-15.2
Brad Woodall	3	4.0	2	4.61	0.2	0.00	0.00	0.0	0.0	4.58	0.2
TOTALS	441	495.3	314	5.84	-38.5	0.56	0.19	6.04	-49.3		

Cincinnati Reds   Park Effect: +0.7%

Pitcher	G	IP	R	ARA	APR	IRnr/G	EIRs/G	IRP	BRS	RRA	ARP
Stan Belinda	29	42.7	26	5.55	-1.9	0.45	0.18	1.6	0.7	5.25	-0.5
Jason Bere	2	3.0	6	18.21	-4.4	0.00	0.00	0.0	0.5	19.15	-4.7
Danny Graves	75	111.0	42	3.44	20.9	0.59	0.24	9.0	-2.0	2.64	30.9
Rick Greene	1	5.7	4	6.43	-0.8	2.00	1.16	-0.8	0.0	7.64	-1.6

Cincinnati Reds (continued)

Pitcher	G	IP	R	ARA	APR	IRnr/G	EIRs/G	IRP	BRS	RRA	ARP
John Hudek	2	1.0	3	27.31	-2.5	1.00	0.65	-0.8	1.3	44.08	-4.3
Denny Neagle	1	2.3	1	3.90	0.3	3.00	0.70	-0.3	0.0	5.21	0.0
Steve Parris	1	3.3	3	8.19	-1.1	1.00	0.21	0.1	0.0	5.13	0.0
Dennis Reyes	64	59.0	24	3.70	9.4	0.83	0.26	-1.6	0.6	4.10	6.9
B.J. Ryan	1	2.0	1	4.55	0.1	0.00	0.00	0.0	0.0	5.17	0.0
Scott Sullivan	79	113.7	41	3.28	23.5	0.63	0.25	3.3	-0.2	3.02	26.8
Brett Tomko	7	14.7	4	2.48	4.3	0.86	0.21	-0.6	0.7	3.27	3.1
Ron Villone	7	17.7	1	0.52	9.1	0.71	0.15	-1.3	0.1	1.29	7.6
Gabe White	50	61.0	31	4.63	3.5	0.52	0.18	-2.3	2.5	5.17	-0.2
Scott Williamson	62	93.3	29	2.83	24.0	0.44	0.15	0.4	1.1	3.12	21.0
TOTALS	381	530.3	216	3.71	84.5	0.61	0.22	3.70	84.8		

Colorado Rockies   Park Effect: +52.5%

Pitcher	G	IP	R	ARA	APR	IRnr/G	EIRs/G	IRP	BRS	RRA	ARP
Rigo Beltran	12	11.0	9	5.94	-1.0	0.58	0.25	0.3	0.7	6.87	-2.1
Mike DeJean	56	61.0	61	7.26	-14.3	0.43	0.22	4.8	0.7	7.12	-13.4
Jerry DiPoto	63	86.7	44	3.68	14.0	0.51	0.25	8.9	3.6	3.19	18.8
Luther Hackman	2	2.0	2	7.26	-0.5	0.00	0.00	0.0	1.1	10.40	-1.2
Bobby M. Jones	10	12.3	13	7.65	-3.4	0.40	0.16	0.3	0.0	7.88	-3.8
David Lee	36	49.0	21	3.11	11.1	0.67	0.26	3.2	2.4	2.63	13.7
Curtis Leskanic	63	85.0	54	4.61	5.0	0.76	0.43	2.8	1.4	4.51	5.9
Chuck McElroy	41	40.7	29	5.17	-0.1	0.59	0.22	-4.0	2.0	7.04	-8.6
Mike Porzio	16	14.7	14	6.93	-2.9	0.69	0.31	1.4	0.4	5.36	-0.4
Roberto Ramirez	28	23.7	22	6.75	-4.2	0.75	0.34	1.5	2.3	6.67	-4.0
John Thomson	1	2.0	0	0.00	1.1	0.00	0.00	0.0	0.0	0.00	1.1
Dave Veres	73	77.0	46	4.34	6.9	0.22	0.11	2.4	6.3	4.50	5.5
David Wainhouse	19	28.7	22	5.57	-1.4	0.74	0.40	0.2	0.4	5.45	-1.0
TOTALS	420	493.7	337	4.95	10.4	0.54	0.26	4.95	10.7		

Florida Marlins   Park Effect: -19.0%

Pitcher	G	IP	R	ARA	APR	IRnr/G	EIRs/G	IRP	BRS	RRA	ARP
Antonio Alfonseca	73	77.7	28	3.63	13.0	0.34	0.12	2.5	0.5	3.54	13.8
Armando Almanza	14	15.7	4	2.57	4.5	1.21	0.48	4.2	1.3	1.08	7.1
Hector Almonte	15	15.0	7	4.70	0.7	0.27	0.07	-1.3	-0.5	5.02	0.2
Brent Billingsley	8	7.7	14	18.41	-11.3	0.38	0.14	-2.3	-1.8	19.38	-12.1
Archie Corbin	17	21.0	20	9.60	-10.4	0.35	0.10	1.7	-1.5	7.34	-5.1
Reid Cornelius	3	5.7	4	7.12	-1.2	0.67	0.29	-1.3	0.0	8.83	-2.3
Vic Darensbourg	56	34.7	36	10.47	-20.5	0.93	0.29	-9.0	-1.0	12.60	-28.7
Brian Edmondson	68	94.0	65	6.97	-19.1	0.56	0.15	-3.9	-4.9	6.93	-18.6
Braden Looper	72	83.0	43	5.22	-0.7	0.71	0.23	-7.0	0.5	6.10	-8.8
Matt Mantei	35	36.3	11	3.05	8.4	0.11	0.03	-0.2	0.0	2.82	9.4
Rafael Medina	20	23.3	15	6.48	-3.5	0.75	0.26	3.3	-0.8	4.81	0.8

Florida Marlins (continued)

Pitcher	G	IP	R	ARA	APR	IRnr/G	EIRs/G	IRP	BRS	RRA	ARP
Vladimir Nunez	5	6.7	3	4.54	0.4	0.60	0.18	1.0	-0.2	2.26	2.1
Kirt Ojala	7	10.0	11	11.09	-6.6	1.00	0.22	0.7	0.0	11.50	-7.1
Jesus Sanchez	49	33.7	19	5.69	-2.0	0.90	0.25	-8.9	0.5	8.60	-12.9
Dennis Springer	9	22.0	16	7.33	-5.3	0.89	0.42	0.9	0.0	7.63	-6.1
Mike Tejera	2	4.3	6	13.96	-4.2	1.00	0.36	0.7	-0.8	10.88	-2.8
TOTALS	453	490.7	302	6.20	-57.9	0.62	0.20	6.45	-71.2		

Houston Astros   Park Effect: -12.3%

Pitcher	G	IP	R	ARA	APR	IRnr/G	EIRs/G	IRP	BRS	RRA	ARP
Sean Bergman	3	6.0	5	8.10	-2.0	0.00	0.00	0.0	0.0	8.55	-2.3
Jose Cabrera	26	29.3	7	2.32	9.2	0.77	0.43	2.2	1.0	1.76	11.0
Scott Elarton	27	39.3	12	2.97	9.5	0.59	0.24	3.0	0.0	2.42	11.9
Doug Henry	35	40.7	24	5.74	-2.7	0.26	0.05	-0.4	2.1	6.32	-5.3
Chris Holt	6	6.0	6	9.72	-3.1	0.83	0.31	1.8	-2.8	2.01	2.1
Jeff McCurry	5	4.0	8	19.45	-6.4	0.80	0.17	0.8	-0.9	15.13	-4.4
Trever Miller	47	49.7	29	5.68	-3.0	0.83	0.26	-0.6	-0.4	5.79	-3.6
Wade Miller	4	7.3	4	5.30	-0.1	0.50	0.08	0.4	0.0	4.35	0.6
Jay Powell	67	75.0	38	4.93	1.8	0.45	0.16	-0.4	-1.2	4.89	2.1
Joe Slusarski	3	3.7	0	0.00	2.1	0.33	0.10	0.3	0.0	-0.49	2.3
Billy Wagner	66	74.7	14	1.82	27.5	0.27	0.08	0.2	-1.5	1.78	27.9
Brian Williams	50	67.3	35	5.05	0.7	0.64	0.25	-2.5	4.8	6.06	-6.9
TOTALS	339	403.0	182	4.39	33.7	0.52	0.19	4.35	35.4		

Los Angeles Dodgers   Park Effect: -12.9%

Pitcher	G	IP	R	ARA	APR	IRnr/G	EIRs/G	IRP	BRS	RRA	ARP
Jamie Arnold	33	53.7	38	6.91	-10.5	0.82	0.33	-0.8	-1.8	6.76	-9.6
Doug Bochtler	12	13.0	8	6.00	-1.2	0.75	0.21	0.5	-1.5	5.11	0.0
Pedro Borbon	70	50.7	23	4.43	4.0	0.53	0.15	1.1	3.6	4.83	1.8
Robinson Checo	7	10.3	15	14.16	-10.4	0.86	0.25	-2.6	0.0	15.01	-11.3
Darren Dreifort	1	1.7	0	0.00	1.0	2.00	0.84	-1.3	0.0	7.67	-0.5
Matt Herges	17	24.3	13	5.21	-0.2	0.59	0.19	3.5	0.9	4.64	1.4
Mike Judd	3	4.3	4	9.01	-1.9	0.00	0.00	0.0	-0.2	8.97	-1.8
Jeff Kubenka	6	7.7	12	15.27	-8.6	1.17	0.31	2.1	-1.5	10.43	-4.5
Mike Maddux	49	54.7	21	3.75	8.5	0.35	0.12	-3.9	2.2	4.52	3.8
Onan Masaoka	54	66.7	33	4.83	2.3	0.57	0.19	-1.8	2.0	5.40	-1.9
Alan Mills	68	72.3	33	4.45	5.6	0.60	0.21	0.2	1.9	4.76	3.0
Dave Mlicki	2	7.3	4	5.32	-0.1	0.00	0.00	0.0	-0.7	4.02	0.9
Antonio Osuna	5	4.7	5	10.45	-2.8	1.00	0.35	-0.4	-1.6	9.14	-2.1
Carlos Perez	1	4.3	1	2.25	1.4	0.00	0.00	0.0	0.0	2.52	1.3
Mel Rojas	5	5.0	7	13.66	-4.7	0.40	0.07	0.4	0.0	12.18	-3.9
Jeff Shaw	64	68.0	25	3.59	11.8	0.14	0.03	-1.0	0.3	3.87	9.6
Jeff Williams	2	2.0	1	4.88	0.1	0.00	0.00	0.0	0.0	5.17	0.0
TOTALS	399	450.7	243	5.26	-5.9	0.51	0.17	5.42	-13.9		

Milwaukee Brewers — Park Effect: +1.2%

Pitcher	G	IP	R	ARA	APR	IRnr/G	EIRs/G	IRP	BRS	RRA	ARP
Jim Abbott	5	7.0	6	7.78	-2.1	0.20	0.03	0.1	0.8	8.43	-2.6
Jason Bere	1	1.0	0	0.00	0.6	0.00	0.00	0.0	0.0	0.00	0.6
Rocky Coppinger	29	36.7	16	3.96	4.8	0.66	0.23	-1.6	-1.4	4.38	3.1
Jeff D'Amico	1	1.0	0	0.00	0.6	0.00	0.00	0.0	0.0	0.00	0.6
Carl Dale	4	4.0	9	20.43	-6.8	0.00	0.00	0.0	-0.5	14.57	-4.2
Cal Eldred	5	7.3	7	8.67	-2.9	0.40	0.23	1.2	0.0	7.22	-1.7
Horacio Estrada	4	7.3	6	7.43	-1.9	0.75	0.16	-2.5	0.5	11.16	-4.9
Steve Falteisek	10	12.0	10	7.57	-3.2	0.80	0.21	-0.9	-0.8	8.03	-3.8
Chad Fox	6	6.7	8	10.90	-4.3	0.50	0.28	0.8	-0.6	8.89	-2.8
Reggie Harris	8	12.0	4	3.03	2.8	1.00	0.32	-0.4	0.0	3.55	2.1
Mike Myers	71	41.3	24	5.27	-0.6	1.08	0.38	2.5	-3.2	3.86	5.9
Kyle Peterson	5	7.0	7	9.08	-3.1	0.20	0.09	-0.5	-0.6	7.99	-2.2
Jim Pittsley	15	18.7	12	5.84	-1.4	0.87	0.29	0.3	1.9	6.67	-3.2
Eric Plunk	68	75.3	44	5.30	-1.3	0.76	0.30	-1.2	-2.7	5.15	0.0
Bill Pulsipher	3	5.0	2	3.63	0.8	0.00	0.00	0.0	1.1	5.36	-0.1
Hector Ramirez	15	21.0	8	3.46	3.9	1.00	0.42	-0.4	1.2	4.17	2.3
Al Reyes	26	36.0	17	4.29	3.4	1.00	0.34	-2.6	2.8	5.52	-1.5
Rafael Roque	34	45.3	25	5.01	0.7	0.88	0.32	1.0	-1.6	4.35	4.0
Valerio de los Santos	7	8.3	6	6.54	-1.3	0.43	0.10	-1.3	0.7	8.81	-3.4
David Weathers	63	93.0	49	4.78	3.7	0.44	0.15	-2.2	1.9	5.00	1.5
Bob Wickman	71	74.3	31	3.79	11.2	0.21	0.05	-2.4	2.0	4.54	5.0
Steve Woodard	2	2.7	1	3.41	0.5	0.00	0.00	0.0	0.0	3.58	0.5
TOTALS	453	523.0	292	5.07	4.2	0.67	0.24	5.23	-5.0		

Montreal Expos — Park Effect: -0.8%

Pitcher	G	IP	R	ARA	APR	IRnr/G	EIRs/G	IRP	BRS	RRA	ARP
Bobby Ayala	53	66.0	36	5.00	1.0	0.66	0.23	-6.1	2.8	6.18	-7.6
Miguel Batista	22	36.0	26	6.62	-5.9	0.64	0.23	-0.6	0.8	7.07	-7.7
Shayne Bennett	4	7.3	8	10.00	-4.0	0.50	0.09	0.4	0.0	9.55	-3.6
Rick DeHart	3	1.7	4	22.01	-3.1	0.67	0.11	0.4	1.2	27.18	-4.1
Mike Johnson	2	4.0	2	4.58	0.2	0.00	0.00	0.0	0.7	6.10	-0.4
Steve Kline	82	69.7	32	4.21	7.2	0.79	0.27	6.5	-1.3	3.23	14.8
Ted Lilly	6	6.0	11	16.81	-7.8	0.83	0.16	-2.2	0.2	22.99	-11.9
Mike Maddux	4	5.0	5	9.17	-2.2	0.00	0.00	0.0	0.0	8.98	-2.1
Guillermo Mota	51	55.3	24	3.98	7.2	0.55	0.18	0.4	2.9	4.36	4.8
Carl Pavano	1	1.0	1	9.17	-0.4	0.00	0.00	0.0	0.0	10.33	-0.6
Mel Rojas	3	2.7	5	17.19	-3.6	0.33	0.08	0.2	1.4	20.80	-4.6
J.D. Smart	29	52.0	30	5.29	-0.9	0.72	0.28	-3.9	-1.0	5.89	-4.3
Dan Smith	3	6.0	3	4.58	0.4	0.33	0.04	0.1	0.0	4.80	0.2
David Strickland	17	18.0	10	5.09	0.1	0.47	0.17	1.9	-0.2	3.25	3.8
Anthony Telford	79	96.0	52	4.97	1.9	0.56	0.22	0.0	1.5	5.25	-1.1
Mike Thurman	2	2.0	0	0.00	1.1	0.00	0.00	0.0	0.0	0.00	1.1
Ugueth Urbina	71	75.7	35	4.24	7.6	0.51	0.14	-1.2	0.2	4.51	5.3
TOTALS	432	504.3	284	5.16	-1.2	0.61	0.21	5.47	-18.1		

New York Mets — Park Effect: -6.9%

Pitcher	G	IP	R	ARA	APR	IRnr/G	EIRs/G	IRP	BRS	RRA	ARP
Rigo Beltran	21	31.0	14	4.27	3.0	0.57	0.23	-2.5	1.5	5.47	-1.1
Armando Benitez	77	78.0	18	2.18	25.7	0.39	0.14	4.6	0.6	1.78	29.1
Dennis Cook	71	63.0	27	4.05	7.6	0.75	0.22	4.9	2.8	3.87	8.9
Octavio Dotel	5	6.3	4	5.97	-0.6	1.60	0.50	0.4	-1.1	4.24	0.6
John Franco	46	40.7	14	3.26	8.5	0.17	0.06	-2.5	1.9	4.20	4.3
Matt Franco	2	1.3	2	14.19	-1.3	1.00	0.17	-1.8	0.0	27.13	-3.3
Jason Isringhausen	8	14.7	9	5.80	-1.1	0.12	0.03	-0.8	-0.1	5.96	-1.3
Bobby Jones	3	6.7	3	4.26	0.7	0.00	0.00	0.0	0.4	4.16	0.7
Pat Mahomes	39	63.7	26	3.86	9.1	0.64	0.22	3.7	1.0	3.57	11.1
Josias Manzanillo	12	18.7	12	6.08	-1.9	0.42	0.15	-0.2	-0.7	5.78	-1.3
Chuck McElroy	15	13.3	5	3.55	2.4	1.00	0.40	-4.5	-0.3	6.64	-2.2
Greg McMichael	19	18.7	10	5.07	0.2	0.32	0.12	0.4	0.5	5.27	-0.3
Dan Murray	1	2.0	3	14.19	-2.0	0.00	0.00	0.0	0.0	14.51	-2.1
Glendon Rusch	1	1.0	0	0.00	0.6	0.00	0.00	0.0	0.0	0.00	0.6
Jeff Tam	9	11.3	4	3.34	2.3	0.22	0.08	0.1	-0.2	3.23	2.4
Billy Taylor	18	13.3	12	8.51	-5.0	0.28	0.09	-0.4	-2.9	6.77	-2.4
Allen Watson	10	19.3	10	4.89	0.5	0.30	0.16	0.5	0.1	4.75	0.8
Turk Wendell	80	85.7	31	3.42	16.4	0.57	0.20	3.2	1.8	3.34	17.2
Masato Yoshii	2	4.0	5	11.82	-3.0	1.00	0.21	-1.7	-1.8	11.86	-3.0
TOTALS	439	492.7	209	4.01	61.8	0.51	0.17	4.07	58.8		

Philadelphia Phillies — Park Effect: +8.3%

Pitcher	G	IP	R	ARA	APR	IRnr/G	EIRs/G	IRP	BRS	RRA	ARP
Scott Aldred	29	32.3	15	4.07	3.8	0.72	0.32	-0.8	0.1	4.14	3.6
Joel Bennett	2	3.3	4	10.53	-2.0	0.50	0.08	0.1	0.4	11.08	-2.2
Jeff Brantley	10	8.7	6	6.08	-0.9	0.30	0.06	0.7	-0.3	4.98	0.2
Billy Brewer	25	25.7	20	6.84	-4.8	0.56	0.19	1.6	0.9	6.70	-4.5
Wayne Gomes	73	74.0	38	4.51	5.2	0.41	0.13	3.9	2.9	4.66	3.9
Mike Grace	22	31.7	27	7.48	-8.2	0.68	0.30	-1.1	-1.6	7.76	-9.2
Joe Grahe	8	9.3	0	0.00	5.3	0.88	0.18	-1.4	0.0	1.66	3.6
Carlton Loewer	7	7.7	5	5.72	-0.5	0.86	0.29	-2.9	-0.9	8.40	-2.8
Steve Montgomery	53	64.7	25	3.39	12.6	0.40	0.14	5.6	2.0	3.01	15.3
Chad Ogea	8	15.0	8	4.68	0.8	0.25	0.16	-0.7	0.0	5.41	-0.4
Yorkis Perez	35	32.0	15	4.11	3.7	0.63	0.18	-1.7	0.2	4.50	2.3
Robert Person	9	11.0	7	5.59	-0.5	0.56	0.22	0.1	0.1	4.36	1.0
Cliff Politte	13	17.7	14	6.96	-3.6	0.31	0.19	1.4	-0.9	5.72	-1.1
Jim Poole	51	35.3	20	4.97	0.7	0.82	0.30	-1.4	2.2	6.09	-3.7
Ken Ryan	15	15.7	11	6.16	-1.8	0.33	0.18	-0.9	-0.9	5.65	-0.9
Steve Schrenk	30	42.0	18	3.76	6.4	0.40	0.16	3.7	-0.5	3.11	9.5
Anthony Shumaker	4	3.3	2	5.27	0.0	0.50	0.09	0.4	0.0	4.23	0.3
Paul Spoljaric	2	3.7	1	2.39	1.1	0.50	0.16	0.3	0.0	1.78	1.4
Amaury Telemaco	44	47.0	29	5.42	-1.4	0.36	0.16	-0.9	1.1	5.81	-3.5
Randy Wolf	1	1.0	2	17.56	-1.4	0.00	0.00	0.0	0.0	16.63	-1.3
TOTALS	441	481.0	267	4.87	14.4	0.52	0.19	4.93	11.5		

Pittsburgh Pirates — Park Effect: +1.8%

Pitcher	G	IP	R	ARA	APR	IRnr/G	EIRs/G	IRP	BRS	RRA	ARP
Jimmy Anderson	9	9.0	7	7.04	-1.9	0.33	0.05	0.5	-0.3	6.14	-1.0
Jason Boyd	4	5.3	2	3.40	1.0	0.75	0.29	0.1	0.0	3.54	1.0
Jason Christiansen	39	37.7	17	4.09	4.4	0.49	0.18	2.9	-1.6	3.19	8.2
Brad Clontz	56	49.3	21	3.85	7.1	0.66	0.23	2.4	3.2	4.04	6.0
Jim Dougherty	2	2.0	3	13.58	-1.9	1.50	0.36	-0.8	-0.4	15.00	-2.2
Mike Garcia	7	7.0	1	1.29	3.0	0.14	0.02	0.1	0.4	1.63	2.7
Greg Hansell	33	39.3	20	4.60	2.4	0.88	0.36	1.4	2.2	4.89	1.1
Rich Loiselle	13	15.3	9	5.31	-0.3	0.23	0.08	0.0	0.1	5.33	-0.3
Keith Osik	1	1.0	4	36.22	-3.5	0.00	0.00	0.0	0.0	41.03	-4.0
Chris Peters	8	15.3	16	9.45	-7.3	0.75	0.21	-0.4	0.9	11.22	-10.4
Jason Phillips	6	7.0	9	11.64	-5.1	0.67	0.14	-1.5	0.6	14.66	-7.4
Todd Ritchie	2	2.0	1	4.53	0.1	0.00	0.00	0.0	-0.8	-0.02	1.1
Scott Sauerbeck	65	67.7	19	2.54	19.6	0.86	0.29	0.4	2.2	2.97	16.4
Pete Schourek	13	29.0	17	5.31	-0.5	0.31	0.06	-0.3	-1.6	4.98	0.5
Jose Silva	22	32.3	7	1.96	11.4	0.41	0.15	0.4	0.1	1.85	11.8
Jeff Wallace	41	39.0	17	3.95	5.2	0.63	0.18	3.7	1.8	3.28	8.1
Marc Wilkins	46	51.0	28	4.97	1.0	0.26	0.10	-1.8	0.6	5.34	-1.1
Mike Williams	58	58.3	36	5.59	-2.9	0.38	0.14	-2.3	1.9	6.21	-6.9
TOTALS	425	467.7	234	4.53	31.8	0.56	0.19	4.69	23.7		

St. Louis Cardinals — Park Effect: -5.7%

Pitcher	G	IP	R	ARA	APR	IRnr/G	EIRs/G	IRP	BRS	RRA	ARP
Juan Acevedo	38	42.7	25	5.51	-1.7	0.58	0.23	2.9	3.4	5.61	-2.2
Rick Ankiel	4	5.0	0	0.00	2.9	0.75	0.44	0.8	0.0	-1.32	3.6
Manny Aybar	64	93.3	58	5.84	-7.2	0.41	0.17	2.2	2.9	5.73	-6.1
Alan Benes	2	2.0	0	0.00	1.1	0.00	0.00	0.0	0.0	0.00	1.1
Ricky Bottalico	68	73.3	45	5.77	-5.1	0.40	0.14	-1.3	6.5	6.79	-13.4
Mike Busby	15	17.7	15	7.98	-5.6	0.33	0.15	0.2	-1.0	7.61	-4.8
Rich Croushore	59	71.7	42	5.51	-2.9	0.85	0.33	-2.5	2.4	6.13	-7.9
Rick Heiserman	3	4.3	4	8.67	-1.7	1.00	0.26	-0.2	0.0	9.61	-2.2
Jose Jimenez	1	2.0	4	18.80	-3.0	0.00	0.00	0.0	0.0	19.08	-3.1
Curtis King	2	1.0	2	18.80	-1.5	0.00	0.00	0.0	-0.8	12.59	-0.8
Kent Mercker	7	12.3	15	11.43	-8.6	0.57	0.18	-2.9	-0.3	13.55	-11.5
Mike Mohler	48	49.3	26	4.95	1.0	0.75	0.30	2.5	-0.9	4.36	4.3
Lance Painter	52	45.3	26	5.39	-1.2	0.77	0.27	3.2	-1.4	4.86	1.4
Scott Radinsky	43	27.7	16	5.43	-0.9	0.86	0.29	-4.2	-1.8	6.57	-4.4
Heathcliff Slocumb	40	53.3	16	2.82	13.8	0.52	0.17	-3.9	1.0	3.83	7.8
Clint Sodowsky	2	3.0	3	9.40	-1.4	1.50	0.28	-1.5	0.3	15.14	-3.3
Garrett Stephenson	6	10.3	8	7.28	-2.4	0.67	0.14	-0.1	0.1	7.78	-3.0
TOTALS	454	514.3	305	5.57	-24.6	0.62	0.23	5.92	-44.6		

San Diego Padres — Park Effect: -27.2%

Pitcher	G	IP	R	ARA	APR	IRnr/G	EIRs/G	IRP	BRS	RRA	ARP
Carlos Almanzar	28	37.3	32	9.04	-16.2	0.43	0.19	-2.3	-3.4	8.97	-15.9
Brian Boehringer	22	32.7	13	4.20	3.4	0.64	0.22	1.4	0.5	4.26	3.2
Wil Cunnane	24	31.0	19	6.47	-4.6	0.83	0.34	3.8	0.1	5.79	-2.2
Ed Giovanola	1	1.3	0	0.00	0.8	0.00	0.00	0.0	0.0	0.43	0.7
Domingo Guzman	7	5.0	12	25.32	-11.2	0.00	0.00	0.0	0.6	27.07	-12.2
Trevor Hoffman	64	67.3	23	3.60	11.5	0.34	0.11	5.1	0.0	3.20	14.6
Dan Miceli	66	68.7	39	5.99	-6.5	0.42	0.14	-3.2	2.4	6.69	-11.8
Heath Murray	14	10.7	5	4.94	0.2	0.79	0.14	0.0	-0.8	5.07	0.1
Carlos Reyes	65	77.3	38	5.18	-0.4	0.63	0.23	-5.1	-3.4	5.57	-3.6
Roberto Rivera	12	7.0	4	6.03	-0.7	1.08	0.27	-1.4	-0.8	6.44	-1.0
Stan Spencer	1	2.0	1	5.27	0.0	0.00	0.00	0.0	0.0	4.47	0.1
Ed Vosberg	15	8.3	11	13.92	-8.1	1.00	0.38	-2.5	-1.6	14.42	-8.6
Donne Wall	55	70.3	31	4.65	3.9	0.55	0.16	-0.6	3.1	4.97	1.3
Matt Whisenant	20	15.7	8	5.39	-0.4	0.75	0.32	-0.9	-1.9	4.51	1.1
Matt Whiteside	9	10.0	15	15.82	-11.9	0.44	0.18	0.7	-1.1	11.61	-7.2
TOTALS	403	444.7	251	5.95	-40.1	0.56	0.19	5.98	-41.3		

San Francisco Giants — Park Effect: -15.9%

Pitcher	G	IP	R	ARA	APR	IRnr/G	EIRs/G	IRP	BRS	RRA	ARP
Miguel del Toro	14	23.7	11	4.61	1.4	0.36	0.08	-0.8	0.4	5.27	-0.3
Alan Embree	68	58.7	22	3.72	9.3	0.69	0.24	3.3	3.4	3.46	11.0
Mark Gardner	8	16.7	9	5.35	-0.4	0.25	0.07	0.7	0.4	5.15	0.0
Livan Hernandez	1	2.0	4	19.82	-3.3	0.00	0.00	0.0	0.0	17.87	-2.8
John Johnstone	62	65.7	24	3.62	11.1	0.32	0.10	-0.8	-3.3	3.20	14.2
Joe Nathan	5	9.0	5	5.51	-0.4	0.00	0.00	0.0	0.0	5.94	-0.8
Robb Nen	72	72.3	36	4.93	1.7	0.21	0.06	-4.7	0.8	5.63	-3.9
Bronswell Patrick	6	5.3	7	13.01	-4.7	1.33	0.71	2.4	-0.6	10.10	-2.9
Felix Rodriguez	47	66.3	32	4.78	2.7	0.66	0.27	-3.9	1.7	5.43	-2.1
Rich Rodriguez	62	56.7	33	5.77	-4.0	0.89	0.29	3.0	0.4	5.23	-0.6
Jerry Spradlin	59	58.0	31	5.30	-1.0	0.83	0.25	2.4	3.2	5.46	-2.1
Julian Tavarez	46	52.7	34	6.40	-7.3	0.83	0.27	-0.5	-0.3	6.47	-7.8
TOTALS	450	487.0	248	5.05	5.2	0.60	0.20	5.11	1.8		

Anaheim Angels — Park Effect: -2.5%

Pitcher	G	IP	R	ARA	APR	IRnr/G	EIRs/G	IRP	BRS	RRA	ARP
Juan Alvarez	8	3.0	1	2.99	0.7	1.00	0.22	-0.2	0.2	4.27	0.3
Mike Fyhrie	9	18.0	7	3.49	3.3	0.89	0.26	-3.7	0.7	5.76	-1.2
Shigetoshi Hasegawa	63	74.7	41	4.93	1.8	0.81	0.30	5.8	-0.9	4.33	6.8
Ken Hill	4	4.7	2	3.85	0.7	0.25	0.07	0.3	-0.3	2.66	1.3
Mike Holtz	28	22.3	20	8.03	-7.2	0.61	0.24	0.2	-3.4	6.79	-4.1
Al Levine	49	81.0	40	4.43	6.4	0.90	0.41	3.6	-1.6	3.98	10.5
Mike Magnante	53	69.3	30	3.88	9.7	0.91	0.39	1.1	-0.4	3.71	11.1
Steve Mintz	3	5.0	2	3.59	0.9	0.67	0.38	1.1	0.5	2.46	1.5
Troy Percival	60	57.0	24	3.78	8.6	0.42	0.10	-4.4	0.7	4.70	2.8
Mark Petkovsek	64	83.0	37	4.00	10.5	0.91	0.32	-3.3	1.3	4.61	4.9

Anaheim Angels (continued)

Pitcher	G	IP	R	ARA	APR	IRnr/G	EIRs/G	IRP	BRS	RRA	ARP
Lou Pote	20	29.3	9	2.75	7.8	0.75	0.26	1.6	-0.6	2.25	9.4
Scott Schoeneweis	31	39.3	27	6.16	-4.4	0.81	0.29	-0.2	-0.1	6.55	-6.1
Steve Sparks	2	2.7	3	10.09	-1.5	0.00	0.00	0.0	-0.8	7.51	-0.7
Jarrod Washburn	6	7.0	6	7.69	-2.0	1.17	0.44	2.2	1.6	7.25	-1.6
TOTALS	400	496.3	249	4.50	35.4	0.77	0.29	4.51	34.7		

Baltimore Orioles   Park Effect: -5.5%

Pitcher	G	IP	R	ARA	APR	IRnr/G	EIRs/G	IRP	BRS	RRA	ARP
Ricky Bones	28	37.3	23	5.61	-2.0	0.82	0.29	-0.7	-0.5	5.70	-2.3
Rocky Coppinger	9	15.0	11	6.68	-2.6	0.33	0.15	0.3	0.7	7.14	-3.3
Jim Corsi	13	13.3	4	2.73	3.6	0.62	0.12	1.6	1.5	2.81	3.5
Brian Falkenborg	2	3.0	0	0.00	1.7	0.00	0.00	0.0	0.0	0.00	1.7
Mike Fetters	27	31.0	24	7.05	-6.6	0.56	0.25	-2.3	0.1	7.70	-8.8
Doug Johns	27	53.7	31	5.26	-0.7	0.81	0.26	-1.0	-0.4	5.42	-1.6
Jason Johnson	1	0.7	1	13.67	-0.6	0.00	0.00	0.0	0.5	17.60	-0.9
Scott Kamieniecki	40	48.0	18	3.42	9.2	0.68	0.22	3.1	0.3	3.15	10.6
Doug Linton	6	12.0	11	8.35	-4.3	1.00	0.26	-1.3	-0.5	8.88	-5.0
Gabe Molina	20	23.0	19	7.53	-6.1	0.65	0.24	0.6	-0.1	7.26	-5.4
Jesse Orosco	65	32.0	21	5.98	-3.0	1.12	0.40	3.5	2.4	5.93	-2.8
Al Reyes	27	29.7	16	4.91	0.8	0.56	0.19	-1.1	2.1	6.00	-2.8
Arthur Rhodes	43	53.0	37	6.36	-7.2	0.44	0.19	3.2	-1.2	5.67	-3.1
B.J. Ryan	13	18.3	5	2.48	5.4	1.00	0.42	1.0	1.7	3.14	4.1
Heathcliff Slocumb	10	8.7	12	12.62	-7.2	0.60	0.19	1.0	0.1	12.34	-6.9
Mike Timlin	62	63.0	30	4.34	5.6	0.48	0.20	0.8	-0.8	4.25	6.3
TOTALS	393	441.7	263	5.43	-13.9	0.69	0.25	5.49	-16.9		

Boston Red Sox   Park Effect: +8.5%

Pitcher	G	IP	R	ARA	APR	IRnr/G	EIRs/G	IRP	BRS	RRA	ARP
Rod Beck	12	14.0	3	1.82	5.2	0.08	0.01	0.1	0.0	1.78	5.2
Kirk Bullinger	4	2.0	1	4.25	0.2	0.50	0.14	0.3	-0.2	1.75	0.8
Jin Ho Cho	2	3.3	3	7.64	-0.9	1.00	0.63	-0.7	0.7	11.13	-2.2
Rheal Cormier	60	63.3	34	4.56	4.1	0.85	0.37	2.3	-6.2	3.40	12.3
Jim Corsi	23	24.0	15	5.31	-0.4	0.57	0.24	-2.5	-1.3	5.98	-2.2
Bryce Florie	12	22.3	17	6.46	-3.3	1.00	0.48	0.8	0.5	6.35	-3.0
Rich Garces	30	40.7	9	1.88	14.7	0.57	0.16	1.4	0.0	1.60	16.0
Tom Gordon	21	17.7	11	5.29	-0.3	0.38	0.13	0.6	0.5	5.61	-0.9
Kip Gross	10	9.7	6	5.27	-0.1	0.70	0.27	0.6	0.1	5.05	0.1
Mark Guthrie	46	46.3	32	5.86	-3.7	0.67	0.27	-2.8	-2.3	6.29	-5.9
Tim Harikkala	7	13.0	9	5.88	-1.1	1.29	0.62	-0.4	-0.9	5.71	-0.8
Derek Lowe	74	109.3	35	2.72	29.5	0.61	0.22	2.0	1.3	2.86	27.8
Pedro Martinez	2	5.0	1	1.70	1.9	0.00	0.00	0.0	0.0	1.66	1.9
Tomokazu Ohka	6	7.3	0	0.00	4.2	0.33	0.09	-1.3	0.0	1.69	2.8
Mark Portugal	4	6.7	6	7.64	-1.9	0.00	0.00	0.0	-1.8	5.17	0.0
Pat Rapp	11	20.3	7	2.92	5.0	0.64	0.21	0.3	-0.1	2.83	5.2

Boston Red Sox *(continued)*

Pitcher	G	IP	R	ARA	APR	IRnr/G	EIRs/G	IRP	BRS	RRA	ARP
Brian Rose	4	6.0	3	4.25	0.6	0.00	0.00	0.0	0.0	4.28	0.6
Santana,M	3	4.0	7	14.86	-4.3	0.33	0.15	-0.5	0.0	16.74	-5.2
Tim Wakefield	32	46.3	22	4.03	5.7	0.19	0.09	2.6	0.1	3.63	7.8
John Wasdin	45	74.3	38	4.34	6.6	0.73	0.29	-1.2	2.8	4.99	1.3
Bob Wolcott	4	6.7	6	7.64	-1.9	0.50	0.37	-0.5	-0.4	7.23	-1.5
TOTALS	412	542.3	265	4.15	59.9	0.60	0.24	4.15	59.9		

Chicago White Sox   Park Effect: -1.2%

Pitcher	G	IP	R	ARA	APR	IRnr/G	EIRs/G	IRP	BRS	RRA	ARP
James Baldwin	2	2.7	3	10.03	-1.4	0.00	0.00	0.0	0.0	9.58	-1.3
Chad Bradford	3	3.7	8	19.45	-5.8	1.33	0.37	0.1	-0.6	17.82	-5.2
Carlos Castillo	16	32.7	17	4.64	1.8	0.75	0.21	-1.8	-0.5	5.04	0.4
Pat Daneker	1	3.0	0	0.00	1.7	0.00	0.00	0.0	0.0	0.00	1.7
Joe Davenport	3	1.7	0	0.00	1.0	1.33	0.30	0.9	0.5	-1.94	1.3
Scott Eyre	21	25.0	22	7.84	-7.5	0.67	0.24	-2.6	0.9	8.92	-10.5
Keith Foulke	67	105.3	28	2.37	32.5	0.34	0.13	5.5	1.4	2.15	35.0
Bob Howry	69	67.7	34	4.48	5.0	0.19	0.07	2.7	-1.8	4.03	8.4
Sean Lowe	64	95.7	39	3.63	16.0	0.92	0.33	0.2	-0.9	3.69	15.4
David Lundquist	17	22.0	21	8.51	-8.2	0.59	0.22	-0.4	-1.4	8.28	-7.7
Aaron Myette	1	2.0	1	4.46	0.2	0.00	0.00	0.0	0.0	4.62	0.1
Jaime Navarro	5	8.3	3	3.21	1.8	0.00	0.00	0.0	1.0	4.36	0.7
Jim Parque	1	3.0	1	2.97	0.7	0.00	0.00	0.0	0.0	3.04	0.7
Jesus Pena	26	20.3	15	6.58	-3.2	0.88	0.30	-1.8	-0.8	7.10	-4.4
Todd Rizzo	3	1.3	2	13.37	-1.2	0.33	0.05	0.1	1.5	22.00	-2.5
Bill Simas	70	72.0	36	4.46	5.5	0.81	0.33	-2.3	5.6	5.54	-3.1
Bryan Ward	40	39.3	36	8.16	-13.2	0.98	0.34	1.1	-4.8	6.92	-7.8
TOTALS	409	505.7	266	4.69	25.5	0.63	0.23	4.76	21.3		

Cleveland Indians   Park Effect: +12.9%

Pitcher	G	IP	R	ARA	APR	IRnr/G	EIRs/G	IRP	BRS	RRA	ARP
Paul Assenmacher	55	33.0	32	8.06	-10.7	0.78	0.26	-2.0	-0.7	9.11	-14.5
Jim Brower	7	16.3	3	1.53	6.6	1.00	0.44	0.7	0.4	1.47	6.7
Tom Candiotti	5	10.3	6	4.83	0.4	0.20	0.03	-0.9	2.3	8.41	-3.7
Rich DeLucia	6	9.3	7	6.23	-1.1	0.33	0.08	-1.3	3.1	10.34	-5.4
Sean DePaula	11	11.7	6	4.28	1.1	0.73	0.16	1.6	-1.1	2.31	3.7
Dwight Gooden	4	8.3	4	3.99	1.1	0.75	0.25	0.0	0.0	4.18	0.9
Chris Haney	9	19.0	6	2.63	5.3	0.56	0.17	-1.5	0.2	3.53	3.4
Mike Jackson	72	68.7	32	3.87	9.7	0.21	0.08	0.6	-0.5	3.85	9.8
Steve Karsay	47	65.7	23	2.91	16.3	0.62	0.22	0.3	0.6	3.10	14.9
Mark Langston	21	37.7	18	3.97	4.9	1.38	0.53	0.9	0.4	3.94	5.0
Tom Martin	6	9.3	9	8.02	-3.0	0.17	0.16	0.0	-0.5	7.42	-2.4
Charles Nagy	1	1.0	3	24.94	-2.2	0.00	0.00	0.0	0.0	23.92	-2.1
Jim Poole	3	1.0	2	16.63	-1.3	1.33	0.63	-1.3	-0.6	22.31	-1.9
Jason Rakers	1	2.0	1	4.16	0.2	0.00	0.00	0.0	0.0	4.37	0.2

Cleveland Indians (continued)

Pitcher	G	IP	R	ARA	APR	IRnr/G	EIRs/G	IRP	BRS	RRA	ARP
Steve Reed	62	61.3	33	4.47	4.6	0.68	0.28	-2.1	5.2	5.69	-3.7
Ricardo Rincon	59	44.7	22	4.09	5.2	0.71	0.30	6.9	1.4	3.06	10.4
David Riske	12	14.0	15	8.91	-5.9	0.50	0.25	-1.0	0.0	9.48	-6.7
Paul Shuey	72	81.7	37	3.77	12.5	0.43	0.16	-3.5	0.1	4.13	9.2
Jerry Spradlin	4	3.0	6	16.63	-3.8	0.00	0.00	0.0	0.0	15.94	-3.6
Dave Stevens	5	9.0	10	9.24	-4.1	0.60	0.30	1.5	0.4	7.93	-2.8
Jeff Tam	1	0.3	3	74.82	-2.6	0.00	0.00	0.0	-1.3	35.08	-1.1
Paul Wagner	3	4.3	4	7.67	-1.2	1.67	0.44	-0.6	0.1	9.08	-1.9
TOTALS	466	511.7	282	4.58	31.9	0.59	0.22	4.89	14.3		

Detroit Tigers   Park Effect: +2.8%

Pitcher	G	IP	R	ARA	APR	IRnr/G	EIRs/G	IRP	BRS	RRA	ARP
Matt Anderson	37	38.0	27	6.21	-4.5	0.70	0.25	-4.0	-0.1	7.16	-8.5
Willie Blair	23	52.7	28	4.64	2.9	0.52	0.16	1.8	-1.7	4.10	6.1
Dave Borkowski	5	10.3	2	1.69	4.0	1.80	0.80	0.0	0.0	1.96	3.7
Doug Brocail	70	82.0	23	2.45	24.5	0.43	0.16	3.9	1.1	2.27	26.2
Will Brunson	17	12.0	9	6.55	-1.9	0.71	0.33	-1.5	2.6	9.44	-5.7
Francisco Cordero	20	19.0	7	3.22	4.1	0.70	0.29	0.8	2.4	4.19	2.0
Nelson Cruz	23	35.3	16	3.96	4.7	1.04	0.51	-1.1	-0.3	4.18	3.8
Bryce Florie	24	36.0	23	5.58	-1.8	0.50	0.22	0.1	0.1	5.61	-1.9
Erik Hiljus	6	8.7	5	5.04	0.1	1.33	0.55	-0.7	0.2	6.28	-1.1
Todd Jones	65	66.3	30	3.95	8.8	0.17	0.07	2.3	0.7	3.77	10.1
Masao Kida	49	64.7	48	6.48	-9.6	0.76	0.25	4.2	0.6	6.08	-6.8
Felipe Lira	2	3.3	5	13.10	-2.9	1.50	0.32	-2.6	-0.2	20.06	-5.5
C.J. Nitkowski	61	44.3	25	4.93	1.1	0.82	0.34	0.2	0.0	4.84	1.5
Willis Roberts	1	1.3	4	26.21	-3.1	1.00	0.14	0.1	0.0	27.03	-3.2
Mel Rojas	5	6.3	16	22.07	-11.9	1.20	0.59	-1.9	-1.0	22.89	-12.5
Sean Runyan	12	10.7	4	3.28	2.2	0.75	0.43	-1.8	1.1	5.84	-0.8
Jeff Weaver	1	1.0	0	0.00	0.6	0.00	0.00	0.0	0.0	0.00	0.6
TOTALS	421	492.0	272	4.83	17.1	0.63	0.25	5.00	7.9		

Kansas City Royals   Park Effect: +5.5%

Pitcher	G	IP	R	ARA	APR	IRnr/G	EIRs/G	IRP	BRS	RRA	ARP
Brian Barber	5	8.7	5	4.97	0.2	1.00	0.53	-1.3	0.7	7.32	-2.1
Tim Byrdak	33	24.7	24	8.38	-8.9	0.88	0.40	-5.1	-0.7	9.92	-13.1
Lance Carter	6	5.3	3	4.85	0.2	0.50	0.22	1.3	0.0	3.06	1.2
Chad Durbin	1	2.3	0	0.00	1.3	0.00	0.00	0.0	0.0	0.25	1.3
Chris Fussell	9	18.0	14	6.70	-3.1	0.56	0.17	1.4	-1.1	5.43	-0.6
Terry Mathews	23	34.3	17	4.27	3.3	0.52	0.29	-3.0	0.9	5.34	-0.7
Jeff Montgomery	49	51.3	40	6.71	-9.0	0.51	0.22	-1.6	0.1	7.08	-11.0
Orber Moreno	7	8.0	5	5.39	-0.2	0.00	0.00	0.0	-1.2	3.98	1.0
Alvin Morman	49	53.3	27	4.36	4.6	1.00	0.39	1.8	-0.3	4.05	6.5
Dan Murray	4	8.3	8	8.27	-2.9	0.75	0.36	-1.5	-0.5	9.56	-4.1
Marc Pisciotta	8	8.3	8	8.27	-2.9	0.00	0.00	0.0	-2.9	4.98	0.2
Ken Ray	13	11.3	12	9.12	-5.0	0.69	0.18	-0.5	0.0	9.61	-5.6
Brad Rigby	20	21.3	20	8.08	-7.0	0.90	0.34	-1.0	0.9	9.08	-9.3

Kansas City Royals *(continued)*

Pitcher	G	IP	R	ARA	APR	IRnr/G	EIRs/G	IRP	BRS	RRA	ARP
Glendon Rusch	3	4.0	7	15.08	-4.4	0.67	0.27	-1.1	0.0	17.06	-5.3
Jose Santiago	34	47.3	23	4.19	5.0	1.09	0.50	-0.2	0.8	4.51	3.3
Scott Service	68	75.3	51	5.83	-5.8	0.74	0.29	0.9	5.3	6.34	-10.0
Blake Stein	1	3.0	3	8.62	-1.2	2.00	1.70	-0.3	0.0	8.53	-1.1
Mac Suzuki	13	25.7	14	4.70	1.3	0.77	0.37	-0.2	-0.7	4.57	1.6
Derek Wallace	8	8.3	4	4.14	0.9	0.62	0.22	0.7	0.3	3.96	1.1
Don Wengert	10	19.3	18	8.02	-6.2	0.90	0.42	-1.8	-0.2	8.71	-7.7
Matt Whisenant	48	39.7	28	6.08	-4.1	0.81	0.27	-0.4	-2.2	5.71	-2.5
Jay Witasick	4	7.3	5	5.87	-0.6	0.50	0.13	-1.3	0.6	8.41	-2.7
TOTALS	416	485.3	336	5.97	-44.4	0.75	0.31	6.25	-59.6		

Minnesota Twins   Park Effect: -1.8%

Pitcher	G	IP	R	ARA	APR	IRnr/G	EIRs/G	IRP	BRS	RRA	ARP
Rick Aguilera	17	21.3	3	1.26	9.2	0.18	0.03	-0.5	0.0	1.55	8.5
Hector Carrasco	40	49.0	29	5.29	-0.8	0.65	0.26	-2.6	-6.1	4.79	1.9
Eddie Guardado	63	48.0	25	4.66	2.6	0.86	0.29	4.2	1.0	4.30	4.5
Mike Lincoln	3	6.7	2	2.68	1.8	0.00	0.00	0.0	1.2	4.10	0.8
Joe Mays	29	52.3	38	6.49	-7.8	0.59	0.18	-2.4	3.6	7.46	-13.5
Travis Miller	52	49.7	18	3.24	10.5	0.79	0.33	5.6	6.5	3.37	9.8
Dan Perkins	17	33.0	15	4.06	4.0	1.29	0.56	0.8	0.9	4.22	3.4
Rob Radlosky	7	8.7	12	12.38	-7.0	1.14	0.63	-0.6	0.6	13.84	-8.4
Gary Rath	4	1.7	1	5.36	0.0	0.75	0.31	-0.2	-0.2	5.80	-0.1
Mark Redman	4	8.0	10	11.17	-5.4	0.25	0.03	0.1	0.4	11.67	-5.8
J.C. Romero	5	9.7	4	3.70	1.6	0.40	0.07	0.4	0.7	3.83	1.4
Benj Sampson	26	62.0	44	6.34	-8.3	0.88	0.29	-2.5	-6.1	5.96	-5.6
Mike Trombley	75	87.3	42	4.30	8.2	0.53	0.19	-0.5	2.5	4.75	3.8
Bob Wells	76	87.3	41	4.20	9.2	0.88	0.34	2.5	-1.8	3.85	12.5
TOTALS	418	524.7	284	4.84	17.7	0.73	0.27	4.92	13.2		

New York Yankees   Park Effect: -8.1%

Pitcher	G	IP	R	ARA	APR	IRnr/G	EIRs/G	IRP	BRS	RRA	ARP
Mike Buddie	2	2.0	1	4.62	0.1	0.00	0.00	0.0	0.4	6.44	-0.3
Todd Erdos	4	7.0	4	5.28	-0.1	0.75	0.20	-0.5	0.6	7.07	-1.5
Tony Fossas	5	1.0	4	36.96	-3.5	1.20	0.38	-1.9	0.6	55.55	-5.6
Jason Grimsley	55	75.0	39	4.80	2.8	0.78	0.31	6.1	3.0	4.54	5.1
Hideki Irabu	5	11.3	6	4.89	0.3	0.00	0.00	0.0	0.0	4.96	0.2
Jeff Juden	1	2.0	3	13.86	-1.9	0.00	0.00	0.0	0.0	14.70	-2.1
Ramiro Mendoza	47	84.0	44	4.84	2.8	0.55	0.16	3.6	2.2	4.80	3.2
Dan Naulty	33	49.3	24	4.50	3.5	0.88	0.28	1.5	0.0	4.33	4.4
Jeff Nelson	39	30.3	14	4.26	3.0	0.92	0.28	1.4	3.5	5.08	0.2
Mariano Rivera	66	69.0	15	2.01	24.0	0.41	0.11	2.5	0.4	1.95	24.5
Mike Stanton	72	58.3	30	4.75	2.5	0.88	0.29	2.4	0.0	4.27	5.7
Jay Tessmer	6	6.7	11	15.25	-7.5	0.67	0.20	0.2	2.2	18.68	-10.0
Allen Watson	21	34.3	8	2.15	11.4	0.76	0.26	4.4	2.3	1.70	13.1
Ed Yarnall	3	6.7	0	0.00	3.8	0.00	0.00	0.0	0.0	-0.01	3.8
TOTALS	359	437.0	203	4.29	41.3	0.70	0.23	4.30	40.7		

Oakland Athletics — Park Effect: +3.0%

Pitcher	G	IP	R	ARA	APR	IRnr/G	EIRs/G	IRP	BRS	RRA	ARP
Buddy Groom	76	46.0	29	5.50	-1.8	0.91	0.33	-1.9	-7.4	4.74	2.1
Chad Harville	15	14.3	11	6.69	-2.5	0.53	0.15	-0.3	0.0	6.97	-2.9
Jimmy Haynes	5	7.0	14	17.45	-9.6	0.40	0.07	-1.8	0.5	21.27	-12.5
Jason Isringhausen	20	25.3	6	2.07	8.7	0.70	0.24	1.6	0.0	1.71	9.7
Kevin Jarvis	3	9.7	13	11.73	-7.1	1.00	0.34	-1.9	0.0	13.77	-9.3
Doug Jones	70	104.0	43	3.61	17.7	0.79	0.31	-1.7	-0.9	3.76	15.9
Tim Kubinski	14	12.3	8	5.66	-0.7	1.07	0.48	-0.9	0.6	6.58	-2.0
Brett Laxton	1	1.7	1	5.23	0.0	2.00	1.18	-0.8	0.0	9.56	-0.8
Ron Mahay	5	14.3	3	1.83	5.3	0.20	0.08	0.4	-0.4	1.43	5.9
T.J. Mathews	50	59.0	28	4.14	6.6	0.82	0.30	-0.8	-0.5	4.38	5.0
Greg McMichael	16	14.0	9	5.61	-0.7	1.06	0.43	0.7	-1.0	4.72	0.7
Mike Oquist	5	16.7	6	3.14	3.7	1.60	0.64	-1.7	0.4	4.41	1.4
Brad Rigby	29	62.3	31	4.34	5.6	1.03	0.39	-1.0	-0.5	4.46	4.7
Billy Taylor	43	43.0	23	4.67	2.3	0.40	0.17	0.1	2.0	5.13	0.1
Luis Vizcaino	1	3.3	2	5.23	0.0	3.00	0.73	0.7	0.0	3.41	0.6
Tim Worrell	53	69.3	38	4.78	2.8	0.92	0.31	-10.0	-1.2	6.06	-7.1
TOTALS	406	502.3	265	4.60	30.2	0.82	0.31	4.94	11.4		

Seattle Mariners — Park Effect: +8.2%

Pitcher	G	IP	R	ARA	APR	IRnr/G	EIRs/G	IRP	BRS	RRA	ARP
Paul Abbott	18	29.0	9	2.64	8.1	1.00	0.39	0.2	0.0	2.84	7.4
Mel Bunch	4	7.3	10	11.59	-5.3	1.00	0.19	-2.1	0.0	14.14	-7.3
Rafael Carmona	9	11.3	11	8.25	-3.9	0.56	0.25	2.1	2.3	7.12	-2.5
Ken Cloude	25	49.3	38	6.55	-7.7	1.08	0.45	-1.3	0.5	6.77	-8.9
Tom Davey	16	21.0	13	5.26	-0.3	0.62	0.18	1.9	1.7	5.32	-0.4
Jeff Fassero	6	8.0	10	10.63	-4.9	0.83	0.49	0.0	0.3	10.60	-4.9
Ryan Franklin	6	11.3	6	4.50	0.8	0.17	0.07	0.4	0.1	4.32	1.0
John Halama	14	27.0	13	4.09	3.1	0.50	0.19	0.6	0.4	4.05	3.3
Butch Henry	3	1.7	2	10.20	-0.9	0.33	0.10	0.3	-0.6	6.07	-0.2
Brett Hinchliffe	7	16.3	11	5.73	-1.1	0.86	0.36	1.4	-1.0	4.40	1.3
Mark Leiter	2	1.3	1	6.38	-0.2	1.50	0.75	-0.7	-0.7	6.85	-0.3
Damaso Marte	5	8.7	9	8.83	-3.5	0.60	0.15	-0.1	1.4	10.31	-5.0
Gil Meche	1	1.7	3	15.30	-1.9	1.00	0.39	0.5	-0.8	11.75	-1.2
Jose Mesa	68	68.7	42	5.20	-0.4	0.47	0.19	3.6	2.0	5.02	0.9
Jose Paniagua	59	77.7	38	4.16	8.5	0.98	0.38	0.5	3.3	4.67	4.1
Robert Ramsay	3	3.7	3	6.96	-0.7	1.00	0.40	-1.8	0.0	12.33	-2.9
Frankie Rodriguez	23	47.3	32	5.75	-3.2	0.96	0.35	-1.9	-0.9	6.36	-6.4
Aaron Scheffer	4	4.7	5	9.11	-2.1	0.00	0.00	0.0	0.4	9.15	-2.1
Steve Sinclair	18	13.7	8	4.98	0.3	0.94	0.34	2.1	0.4	4.12	1.6
Sean Spencer	2	1.7	4	20.40	-2.8	0.50	0.11	0.2	-0.7	16.57	-2.1
Dennis Stark	5	6.3	7	9.40	-3.0	0.40	0.08	0.4	-0.6	7.65	-1.8
Mac Suzuki	12	23.3	28	10.20	-13.1	0.75	0.26	-0.8	-2.1	9.32	-10.8
Allen Watson	3	3.0	9	25.50	-6.8	1.00	0.22	-2.1	-0.2	30.14	-8.3

Seattle Mariners *(continued)*

Pitcher	G	IP	R	ARA	APR	IRnr/G	EIRs/G	IRP	BRS	RRA	ARP
Eric Weaver	8	9.3	12	10.93	-6.0	0.88	0.46	-3.4	0.0	14.13	-9.3
Todd Williams	13	9.7	5	4.40	0.8	0.62	0.31	-1.6	0.7	6.80	-1.8
Jordan Zimmerman	12	8.0	8	8.50	-3.0	1.17	0.52	-3.3	1.0	13.59	-7.5
TOTALS	346	471.0	337	6.08	-49.2	0.77	0.30	6.37	-64.1		

Tampa Bay Devil Rays   Park Effect: +4.1%

Pitcher	G	IP	R	ARA	APR	IRnr/G	EIRs/G	IRP	BRS	RRA	ARP
Scott Aldred	37	24.3	15	5.35	-0.6	0.68	0.25	-1.9	0.7	6.55	-3.8
Wade Boggs	1	1.3	1	6.51	-0.2	3.00	0.72	0.7	0.0	2.21	0.4
Mickey Callaway	1	4.0	6	13.02	-3.5	2.00	0.74	0.7	-0.5	10.22	-2.3
Norm Charlton	42	50.7	29	4.97	1.0	0.64	0.29	-2.5	0.6	5.69	-3.1
Mike Duvall	40	40.0	21	4.56	2.6	1.12	0.41	-4.7	5.9	7.10	-8.7
Dave Eiland	6	12.3	14	9.85	-6.5	0.83	0.37	0.2	-2.2	7.98	-3.9
Eddie Gaillard	8	8.7	9	9.01	-3.7	1.12	0.29	0.2	-0.5	8.00	-2.7
Roberto Hernandez	72	73.3	27	3.20	15.9	0.26	0.07	-2.0	-1.1	3.48	13.5
Cory Lidle	4	3.0	2	5.79	-0.2	0.50	0.16	0.7	-1.4	-0.76	2.0
Albie Lopez	51	64.0	40	5.42	-2.0	0.53	0.19	2.9	-0.9	5.10	0.3
Jim Mecir	17	20.7	7	2.94	5.1	0.59	0.16	-1.1	-0.8	3.26	4.3
Jim Morris	5	4.7	3	5.58	-0.2	0.40	0.06	0.3	0.0	5.30	-0.1
Alan Newman	18	15.7	12	6.65	-2.6	0.83	0.24	-2.7	0.6	8.90	-6.5
Bryan Rekar	15	31.7	20	5.48	-1.2	1.00	0.42	-0.4	-0.6	5.61	-1.6
Julio Santana	17	29.3	21	6.21	-3.5	0.71	0.24	1.1	-2.2	5.49	-1.1
Jeff Sparks	8	10.0	6	5.21	-0.1	0.62	0.14	1.1	1.7	5.91	-0.9
Rick White	62	105.7	54	4.44	8.3	1.00	0.37	-7.0	0.4	5.20	-0.7
Esteban Yan	49	57.0	38	5.79	-4.1	0.63	0.26	5.0	3.0	5.50	-2.3
TOTALS	453	556.3	325	5.07	4.5	0.70	0.25	5.42	-17.1		

Texas Rangers   Park Effect: +13.7%

Pitcher	G	IP	R	ARA	APR	IRnr/G	EIRs/G	IRP	BRS	RRA	ARP
John Burkett	5	18.0	6	2.76	4.8	1.00	0.38	-1.3	0.4	4.00	2.3
Tim Crabtree	68	65.0	26	3.31	13.2	0.93	0.30	1.1	3.7	3.96	8.6
Doug Davis	2	2.7	10	31.05	-7.7	1.50	0.53	-1.8	-0.7	33.62	-8.4
Jeff Fassero	4	3.3	7	17.39	-4.5	1.00	0.66	-1.2	0.0	21.07	-5.9
Ryan Glynn	3	4.3	4	7.64	-1.2	0.00	0.00	0.0	0.3	7.72	-1.2
Eric Gunderson	11	10.0	8	6.62	-1.6	0.73	0.26	-2.1	0.4	8.87	-4.1
Jonathan Johnson	1	3.0	5	13.80	-2.9	2.00	1.70	-0.3	1.4	18.00	-4.3
Danny Kolb	16	31.0	18	4.81	1.2	0.56	0.18	0.9	-3.4	3.62	5.3
Corey Lee	1	1.0	3	24.84	-2.2	0.00	0.00	0.0	0.0	23.74	-2.1
Esteban Loaiza	15	28.7	24	6.93	-5.7	1.27	0.55	2.3	-2.8	5.74	-1.9
Mike Morgan	9	17.0	8	3.90	2.4	1.00	0.52	0.8	1.0	4.03	2.1
Mike Munoz	56	52.7	24	3.77	8.0	0.70	0.29	2.9	0.4	3.42	10.1
Danny Patterson	53	60.3	38	5.21	-0.5	0.77	0.26	-4.3	-3.2	5.57	-2.9

Texas Rangers *(continued)*

Pitcher	G	IP	R	ARA	APR	IRnr/G	EIRs/G	IRP	BRS	RRA	ARP
Matt Perisho	3	4.3	3	5.73	-0.3	0.00	0.00	0.0	0.0	5.61	-0.2
Mike Venafro	65	68.3	29	3.51	12.4	1.06	0.47	0.6	-2.1	3.32	13.8
John Wetteland	62	66.0	30	3.76	10.1	0.19	0.07	0.3	-0.2	3.89	9.2
Jeff Zimmerman	65	87.7	24	2.27	28.0	0.62	0.26	4.4	-0.2	2.03	30.3
TOTALS	439	523.3	267	4.22	53.4	0.74	0.29	4.27	50.5		

Toronto Blue Jays   Park Effect: +4.5%

Pitcher	G	IP	R	ARA	APR	IRnr/G	EIRs/G	IRP	BRS	RRA	ARP
John Bale	1	2.0	3	12.99	-1.7	0.00	0.00	0.0	0.0	11.96	-1.5
Tom Davey	29	44.0	28	5.51	-1.8	0.83	0.40	-2.8	-2.0	5.77	-3.0
Kelvim Escobar	3	6.0	2	2.89	1.5	0.00	0.00	0.0	0.0	2.89	1.5
John Frascatore	33	37.0	16	3.74	5.8	0.97	0.37	1.2	2.3	4.29	3.5
Gary Glover	1	1.0	0	0.00	0.6	0.00	0.00	0.0	0.0	0.00	0.6
Roy Halladay	18	45.0	22	4.23	4.5	0.94	0.34	-1.7	0.4	4.78	1.8
Joey Hamilton	4	3.3	4	10.39	-1.9	0.75	0.31	0.2	0.4	11.08	-2.2
John Hudek	3	3.7	5	11.81	-2.7	1.00	0.59	-0.2	0.4	13.43	-3.4
Billy Koch	56	63.7	26	3.54	11.4	0.21	0.06	-3.9	-1.9	3.82	9.4
Graeme Lloyd	74	72.0	36	4.33	6.5	0.68	0.22	2.4	-0.2	4.17	7.8
Eric Ludwick	1	1.0	3	25.97	-2.3	1.00	0.41	0.4	-0.6	17.64	-1.4
Peter Munro	29	47.3	25	4.57	3.0	1.00	0.37	-0.1	2.0	5.15	0.0
Robert Person	11	11.0	12	9.44	-5.3	0.64	0.25	-0.3	-1.4	8.66	-4.3
Dan Plesac	30	22.7	21	8.02	-7.2	1.13	0.42	-0.1	-4.6	6.55	-3.5
Paul Quantrill	41	48.7	19	3.38	9.5	0.73	0.25	-2.5	2.9	4.47	3.7
Nerio Rodriguez	2	2.0	3	12.99	-1.7	0.00	0.00	0.0	0.0	13.22	-1.8
Mike Romano	3	5.3	8	12.99	-4.6	1.33	0.72	0.1	0.0	12.70	-4.5
Steve Sinclair	3	5.7	8	12.22	-4.5	0.00	0.00	0.0	-0.8	11.37	-3.9
Paul Spoljaric	35	52.0	26	4.33	4.7	0.94	0.42	3.5	1.1	3.96	6.9
TOTALS	377	473.3	267	4.88	13.6	0.74	0.28	5.04	5.4		

DT Leaderboards

Top Eqas By Position (50 Games Minimum)

First Base (Position Average=.281)

1.	Mark McGwire	St Louis	0.344
2.	Jeff Bagwell	Houston	0.341
3.	Jason Giambi	Oakland	0.321
4.	Jim Thome	Clevelnd	0.315
5.	Fred McGriff	TampaBay	0.311
6.	John Olerud	NY Mets	0.308
7.	Sean Casey	Cincnnti	0.305
8.	Ryan Klesko	Atlanta	0.302
9.	Carlos Delgado	Toronto	0.301
10.	Mike Sweeney	KansasCy	0.296
11.	Kevin Young	Pittsbrg	0.294
12.	Will Clark	Baltimor	0.292
13.	Eric Karros	LosAngls	0.292
14.	Brian Daubach	Boston	0.288
15.	Mike Stanley	Boston	0.285
16.	Mark Grace	ChiCubs	0.283
17.	Todd Helton	Colorado	0.283
18.	Paul Konerko	ChiSox	0.282
19.	Mo Vaughn	Anaheim	0.281
20.	J.T. Snow	San Fran	0.281
21.	Tony Clark	Detroit	0.281
22.	Randall Simon	Atlanta	0.278
23.	Kevin Millar	Florida	0.277
24.	Tino Martinez	NY Yanks	0.273
25.	Lee Stevens	Texas	0.265
26.	David Segui	Seattle	0.260
27.	Jeff Conine	Baltimor	0.258
28.	Richie Sexson	Clevelnd	0.258
29.	Rico Brogna	Philadel	0.255
30.	Wally Joyner	San Dieg	0.251

Second Base (Position Average=.260)

1.	Roberto Alomar	Clevelnd	0.319
2.	Jay Bell	Arizona	0.300
3.	Chuck Knoblauch	NY Yanks	0.298
4.	Edgardo Alfonzo	NY Mets	0.298
5.	Jeff Kent	San Fran	0.296
6.	Randy Velarde	Oakland	0.294
7.	Craig Biggio	Houston	0.284
8.	Randy Velarde	Anaheim	0.277
9.	Ray Durham	ChiSox	0.274
10.	Jose Offerman	Boston	0.273
11.	Luis Castillo	Florida	0.269
12.	Ron Belliard	Milwauke	0.269
13.	Tony Phillips	Oakland	0.269
14.	Jose Vidro	Montreal	0.261
15.	Homer Bush	Toronto	0.261
16.	Warren Morris	Pittsbrg	0.259
17.	Damion Easley	Detroit	0.259
18.	Pokey Reese	Cincnnti	0.255
19.	Quilvio Veras	San Dieg	0.254
20.	Eric Young	LosAngls	0.254
21.	Carlos Febles	KansasCy	0.252
22.	David Bell	Seattle	0.248
23.	Mark McLemore	Texas	0.246
24.	Joe McEwing	St Louis	0.244
25.	Bret Boone	Atlanta	0.242
26.	Todd Walker	Minnesot	0.241
27.	Miguel Cairo	TampaBay	0.239
28.	Delino DeShields	Baltimor	0.234
29.	Marlon Anderson	Philadel	0.216
30.	Kurt Abbott	Colorado	0.213

Third Base (Position Average=.262)

1.	Chipper Jones	Atlanta	0.352
2.	Fernando Tatis	St Louis	0.308
3.	Cal Ripken	Baltimor	0.303
4.	Robin Ventura	NY Mets	0.298
5.	Ken Caminiti	Houston	0.295
6.	Tony Fernandez	Toronto	0.293
7.	Scott Rolen	Philadel	0.290
8.	Phil Nevin	San Dieg	0.288
9.	Jeff Cirillo	Milwauke	0.288
10.	Matt Williams	Arizona	0.285
11.	Corey Koskie	Minnesot	0.277
12.	Joe Randa	KansasCy	0.273
13.	Dean Palmer	Detroit	0.273
14.	Todd Zeile	Texas	0.271
15.	Bill Mueller	San Fran	0.271
16.	Ed Sprague	Pittsbrg	0.265
17.	Adrian Beltre	LosAngls	0.263
18.	Greg Norton	ChiSox	0.262
19.	Wade Boggs	TampaBay	0.260

Third Base (continued)

20.	Bill Spiers	Houston	0.260
21.	Troy Glaus	Anaheim	0.257
22.	Aaron Boone	Cincnnti	0.256
23.	Eric Chavez	Oakland	0.252
24.	Michael Barrett	Montreal	0.252
25.	Mike Lowell	Florida	0.251
26.	Scott Brosius	NY Yanks	0.249
27.	Kevin Orie	Florida	0.247
28.	Kevin Jordan	Philadel	0.242
29.	Russ Davis	Seattle	0.235
30.	Vinny Castilla	Colorado	0.234

Catcher (Position Average=.247)

1.	Jason Kendall	Pittsbrg	0.320
2.	Dave Nilsson	Milwauke	0.306
3.	Mike Piazza	NY Mets	0.301
4.	Javy Lopez	Atlanta	0.294
5.	Mike Lieberthal	Philadel	0.292
6.	Ivan Rodriguez	Texas	0.285
7.	Brent Mayne	San Fran	0.284
8.	Eddie Taubensee	Cincnnti	0.283
9.	Darrin Fletcher	Toronto	0.267
10.	Mike Difelice	TampaBay	0.267
11.	Brook Fordyce	ChiSox	0.267
12.	Mike Redmond	Florida	0.261
13.	Jorge Posada	NY Yanks	0.259
14.	Jason Varitek	Boston	0.259
15.	Brad Ausmus	Detroit	0.256
16.	Charles Johnson	Baltimor	0.253
17.	Damian Miller	Arizona	0.251
18.	Scott Servais	San Fran	0.250
19.	Tim Spehr	KansasCy	0.248
20.	Tony Eusebio	Houston	0.247
21.	Terry Steinbach	Minnesot	0.247
22.	Chris Widger	Montreal	0.243
23.	Todd Hundley	LosAngls	0.242
24.	Paul Bako	Houston	0.241
25.	Kelly Stinnett	Arizona	0.241
26.	Mark Johnson	ChiSox	0.240
27.	John Flaherty	TampaBay	0.237
28.	Einar Diaz	Clevelnd	0.230
29.	Dan Wilson	Seattle	0.229
30.	Berto Castillo	St Louis	0.228

Center Field (Position Average=.264)

1.	Brian Giles	Pittsbrg	0.329
2.	Bernie Williams	NY Yanks	0.327
3.	Carl Everett	Houston	0.318
4.	Ken Griffey Jr	Seattle	0.302
5.	Brady Anderson	Baltimor	0.300
6.	Kenny Lofton	Clevelnd	0.287
7.	Preston Wilson	Florida	0.286
8.	Doug Glanville	Philadel	0.282
9.	Andruw Jones	Atlanta	0.281
10.	Steve Finley	Arizona	0.277
11.	Marvin Benard	San Fran	0.276
12.	Mike Cameron	Cincnnti	0.274
13.	Chris Singleton	ChiSox	0.270
14.	Jose Cruz	Toronto	0.263
15.	Garrett Anderson	Anaheim	0.261
16.	Carlos Beltran	KansasCy	0.261
17.	J.D. Drew	St Louis	0.261
18.	Devon White	LosAngls	0.253
19.	Jacque Jones	Minnesot	0.249
20.	Gabe Kapler	Detroit	0.247
21.	Marquis Grissom	Milwauke	0.245
22.	Ruben Rivera	San Dieg	0.236
23.	Darryl Hamilton	Colorado	0.229
24.	Tom Goodwin	Texas	0.229
25.	Lance Johnson	ChiCubs	0.226
26.	Torii Hunter	Minnesot	0.224
27.	Brian McRae	NY Mets	0.224
28.	Damon Buford	Boston	0.218
29.	Randy Winn	TampaBay	0.216
30.	Ryan Christenson	Oakland	0.208

Left Field (Position Average=.273)

1.	Barry Bonds	San Fran	0.328
2.	Luis Gonzalez	Arizona	0.310
3.	Gary Sheffield	LosAngls	0.308
4.	Rickey Henderson	NY Mets	0.301
5.	Geoff Jenkins	Milwauke	0.298
6.	Rusty Greer	Texas	0.295
7.	Dave Justice	Clevelnd	0.295
8.	Reggie Sanders	San Dieg	0.294
9.	Cliff Floyd	Florida	0.291
10.	Bubba Trammell	TampaBay	0.288
11.	Ray Lankford	St Louis	0.288
12.	Henry Rodriguez	ChiCubs	0.288
13.	Johnny Damon	KansasCy	0.287
14.	Greg Vaughn	Cincnnti	0.286
15.	Bruce Aven	Florida	0.283
16.	Ben Grieve	Oakland	0.278
17.	Ricky Ledee	NY Yanks	0.278
18.	Chad Curtis	NY Yanks	0.278
19.	Al Martin	Pittsbrg	0.276
20.	B.J. Surhoff	Baltimor	0.276
21.	Rondell White	Montreal	0.275
22.	Troy O'leary	Boston	0.268
23.	Ron Gant	Philadel	0.266

24. Shannon Stewart	Toronto	0.262
25. Gerald Williams	Atlanta	0.261
26. Dante Bichette	Colorado	0.258
27. Carlos Lee	ChiSox	0.255
28. Richard Hidalgo	Houston	0.254
29. Paul Sorrento	TampaBay	0.253
30. Juan Encarnacion	Detroit	0.238

Right Field (Position Average=.279)

1. Manny Ramirez	Cleveind	0.344
2. Larry Walker	Colorado	0.331
3. Bob Abreu	Philadel	0.325
4. Ellis Burks	San Fran	0.318
5. Albert Belle	Baltimor	0.309
6. Jeromy Burnitz	Milwauke	0.309
7. Juan Gonzalez	Texas	0.307
8. Shawn Green	Toronto	0.306
9. Vladimir Guerrero	Montreal	0.302
10. Sammy Sosa	ChiCubs	0.300
11. Tony Gwynn	San Dieg	0.289
12. Matt Stairs	Oakland	0.285
13. Tim Salmon	Anaheim	0.285
14. Roger Cedeno	NY Mets	0.284
15. Jermaine Dye	KansasCy	0.281
16. Dmitri Young	Cincnnti	0.280
17. Magglio Ordonez	ChiSox	0.279
18. Paul O'neill	NY Yanks	0.276
19. Jay Buhner	Seattle	0.273
20. Trot Nixon	Boston	0.271
21. Brian Jordan	Atlanta	0.271
22. Raul Mondesi	LosAngls	0.270
23. Dave Martinez	TampaBay	0.255
24. Tony Womack	Arizona	0.253
25. Matt Lawton	Minnesot	0.247
26. Bob Higginson	Detroit	0.243

| 27. Mark Kotsay | Florida | 0.240 |
| 28. Derek Bell | Houston | 0.228 |

Shortstop (Position Average=.246)

1. Derek Jeter	NY Yanks	0.336
2. Nomar Garciaparra	Boston	0.326
3. Alex Rodriguez	Seattle	0.293
4. Omar Vizquel	Clevelnd	0.285
5. Tony Batista	Toronto	0.282
6. Barry Larkin	Cincnnti	0.279
7. Mark Grudzielanek	LosAngls	0.271
8. Rich Aurilia	San Fran	0.265
9. Jose Hernandez	ChiCubs	0.262
10. Alex Arias	Philadel	0.259
11. Jose Valentin	Milwauke	0.257
12. Royce Clayton	Texas	0.255
13. Andy Fox	Arizona	0.253
14. Edgar Renteria	St Louis	0.252
15. Mark Loretta	Milwauke	0.251
16. Mike Bordick	Baltimor	0.250
17. Miguel Tejada	Oakland	0.247
18. Alex Gonzalez	Florida	0.246
19. Kevin Stocker	TampaBay	0.246
20. Damian Jackson	San Dieg	0.239
21. Ricky Gutierrez	Houston	0.238
22. Deivi Cruz	Detroit	0.233
23. Rey Sanchez	KansasCy	0.232
24. Tim Bogar	Houston	0.229
25. Walt Weiss	Atlanta	0.224
26. Orlando Cabrera	Montreal	0.221
27. Chris Gomez	San Dieg	0.220
28. Rey Ordonez	NY Mets	0.220
29. Mike Benjamin	Pittsbrg	0.219
30. Desi Relaford	Philadel	0.215

Minor League Top Ten Eqas By Position

First Base

1. Nick Johnson	Norwich	0.340
2. Daryle Ward	New Orln	0.323
3. Pat Burrell	Reading	0.314
4. Jeff Manto	Buffalo	0.313
5. Steve Cox	Durham	0.298
6. Morgan Burkhart	Sarasota	0.286
7. Erubiel Durazo	El Paso	0.286
8. David Ortiz	SaltLake	0.279
9. Hee Choi	Lansing	0.277
10. Calvin Pickering	Rochestr	0.275

Second Base

1. Marcus Giles	Myrtle B	0.280
2. Trace Coquillette	Ottawa	0.275
3. Jason Romano	Charlott	0.268
4. Esteban German	Modesto	0.265
5. Scott Sheldon	Oklahoma	0.262
6. Elvis Pena	Carolina	0.262
7. Jason Hardtke	Indianap	0.260
8. Ty Wigginton	St Lucie	0.260
9. William Otero	San Jose	0.260
10. Brian Raabe	Columbus	0.259

Third Base

1.	Adam Piatt	Midland	0.299
2.	Aramis Ramirez	Nashvill	0.295
3.	Bobby Smith	Durham	0.286
4.	Mike Cuddyer	Ft Myers	0.279
5.	Scott Kirby	Beloit	0.278
6.	Aubrey Huff	Orlando	0.274
7.	Sean Burroughs	Ft Wayne	0.274
8.	Mike Edwards	Kinston	0.273
9.	Jarrod Patterson	El Paso	0.267
10.	Eric Hinske	Daytona	0.266

Shortstop

1.	D'angelo Jimenez	Columbus	0.281
2.	Rafael Furcal	Macon	0.262
3.	Jack Wilson	Peoria	0.261
4.	Alfonso Soriano	Norwich	0.260
5.	Jose Ortiz	Vancouvr	0.252
6.	Mendy Lopez	Omaha	0.251
7.	Eddy Martinez	Frederck	0.250
8.	Chris Woodward	Syracuse	0.249
9.	Kevin Nicholson	Mobile	0.245
10.	Danny Solano	Charlott	0.245
11.	Nick Punto	Clearwtr	0.245

Outfield

1.	Roosevelt Brown	Iowa	0.315
2.	Dee Brown	Wilmngtn	0.301
3.	Lyle Mouton	Louisvil	0.298
4.	Lance Berkman	New Orln	0.295
5.	Chin-Feng Chen	San Bern	0.289
6.	Jack Cust	High Des	0.289
7.	Ruben Mateo	Oklahoma	0.287
8.	Valentino Pascucci	Vermont	0.286
9.	Dee Brown	Wichita	0.286
10.	Vernon Wells	Dunedin	0.285
11.	Terrell Lowery	Durham	0.284
12.	Bubba Carpenter	Columbus	0.283
13.	Tony Mota	SanAnton	0.282
14.	Brent Cookson	Albuquer	0.279
15.	Kory Dehaan	Lynchbrg	0.273
16.	Michael Restovich	Quad Cit	0.270
17.	Terrence Long	Norfolk	0.270
18.	Mark Quinn	Omaha	0.268
19.	Chris Wakeland	Jacksnvl	0.268
20.	Rusty Keith	Visalia	0.268
21.	Andy Tomberlin	Norfolk	0.268
22.	Adam Hyzdu	Altoona	0.267
23.	Ray Montgomery	Nashvill	0.266
24.	Bobby Kielty	Quad Cit	0.265
25.	Milton Bradley	Harrisbg	0.264
26.	John Rodriguez	Tampa	0.262
27.	Terrell Merriman	Burlingt	0.262
28.	Matt Watson	Vermont	0.262
29.	Tony Tarasco	Columbus	0.262
30.	D.T. Cromer	Indianap	0.262
31.	Richard Gomez	W Michgn	0.262

Catcher

1.	Rico Washington	Hickory	0.293
2.	Ben Petrick	ColSprin	0.281
3.	Javier Cardona	Jacksnvl	0.276
4.	Thomas Wilson	Durham	0.275
5.	Jason Dewey	Lk Elsin	0.272
6.	Jayson Werth	Frederck	0.271
7.	Wiklenman Gonzalez	Mobile	0.264
8.	Sal Fasano	Omaha	0.264
9.	Randy Knorr	New Orln	0.262
10.	Jon Schaeffer	Quad Cit	0.261
11.	Ben Davis	LasVegas	0.261

Defense

First Base

1.	Tino Martinez	NY Yanks	118
2.	Rico Brogna	Philadel	117
3.	J.T. Snow	San Fran	117
4.	Richie Sexson	Clevelnd	117
5.	David Segui	Seattle	115
6.	Jim Thome	Clevelnd	113
7.	Ron Coomer	Minnesot	112
8.	Eric Karros	LosAngls	111
9.	Wally Joyner	San Dieg	108
10.	Paul Konerko	ChiSox	108
11.	Brian Daubach	Boston	107
12.	Derrek Lee	Florida	106
13.	Jeff Bagwell	Houston	106
14.	Mike Stanley	Boston	106
15.	Todd Helton	Colorado	103
16.	Fred Mcgriff	TampaBay	103
17.	Travis Lee	Arizona	102
18.	Will Clark	Baltimor	101
19.	Tony Clark	Detroit	101
20.	John Olerud	NY Mets	100
21.	Doug Mientkiewicz	Minnesot	99
22.	Mark Grace	ChiCubs	98
23.	Kevin Millar	Florida	98

24.	Darin Erstad	Anaheim	97
25.	Brad Fullmer	Montreal	96
26.	Jeff Conine	Baltimor	95
27.	Sean Berry	Milwauke	94
28.	Mo Vaughn	Anaheim	93
29.	Carlos Delgado	Toronto	91
30.	Mark McGwire	St Louis	90
31.	Mike Sweeney	KansasCy	89
32.	Kevin Young	Pittsbrg	88
33.	Randall Simon	Atlanta	87
34.	Lee Stevens	Texas	87
35.	Ryan Klesko	Atlanta	85
36.	Jason Giambi	Oakland	79
37.	Sean Casey	Cincnnti	76

Second Base

1.	Pokey Reese	Cincnnti	112
2.	Randy Velarde	Oakland	108
3.	Bret Boone	Atlanta	108
4.	Ron Belliard	Milwauke	107
5.	Randy Velarde	Anaheim	107
6.	Tony Phillips	Oakland	106
7.	Mark Mclemore	Texas	105
8.	Miguel Cairo	TampaBay	105
9.	Eric Young	LosAngls	103
10.	Homer Bush	Toronto	103
11.	Quilvio Veras	San Dieg	103
12.	Joe Mcewing	St Louis	102
13.	Luis Castillo	Florida	102
14.	Jose Vidro	Montreal	102
15.	Damion Easley	Detroit	102
16.	Mickey Morandini	ChiCubs	101
17.	Ray Durham	ChiSox	100
18.	Roberto Alomar	Clevelnd	100
19.	Warren Morris	Pittsbrg	98
20.	Craig Biggio	Houston	98
21.	Marlon Anderson	Philadel	97
22.	Todd Walker	Minnesot	97
23.	Chuck Knoblauch	NY Yanks	96
24.	David Bell	Seattle	96
25.	Delino Deshields	Baltimor	95
26.	Carlos Febles	KansasCy	95
27.	Jose Offerman	Boston	94
28.	Kurt Abbott	Colorado	93
29.	Jeff Kent	San Fran	93
30.	Edgardo Alfonzo	NY Mets	93
31.	Jay Bell	Arizona	85

Third Base

1.	Craig Wilson	ChiSox	118
2.	Corey Koskie	Minnesot	115
3.	Scott Brosius	NY Yanks	114

4.	Robin Ventura	NY Mets	114
5.	Aaron Boone	Cincnnti	113
6.	Matt Williams	Arizona	112
7.	John Valentin	Boston	110
8.	Jeff Cirillo	Milwauke	108
9.	Bill Spiers	Houston	107
10.	Phil Nevin	San Dieg	107
11.	Travis Fryman	Clevelnd	106
12.	Scott Rolen	Philadel	105
13.	Greg Norton	ChiSox	105
14.	Kevin Orie	Florida	103
15.	Troy Glaus	Anaheim	103
16.	Joe Randa	KansasCy	102
17.	Gary Gaetti	ChiCubs	102
18.	Shane Andrews	Montreal	101
19.	Fernando Tatis	St Louis	100
20.	Bill Mueller	San Fran	99
21.	Michael Barrett	Montreal	98
22.	Mike Lowell	Florida	97
23.	Kevin Jordan	Philadel	96
24.	Adrian Beltre	LosAngls	96
25.	Vinny Castilla	Colorado	95
26.	Todd Zeile	Texas	94
27.	Dean Palmer	Detroit	94
28.	Ken Caminiti	Houston	93
29.	Russ Davis	Seattle	93
30.	Tony Fernandez	Toronto	92
31.	Eric Chavez	Oakland	89
32.	Cal Ripken	Baltimor	88
33.	Ed Sprague	Pittsbrg	88
34.	Wade Boggs	TampaBay	88
35.	Chipper Jones	Atlanta	88

Catcher

1.	Alberto Castillo	St Louis	113
2.	Jorge Fabregas	Florida	110
3.	Ivan Rodriguez	Texas	110
4.	Eli Marrero	St Louis	108
5.	Henry Blanco	Colorado	108
6.	Jason Kendall	Pittsbrg	108
7.	Javier Valentin	Minnesot	107
8.	John Flaherty	TampaBay	107
9.	Mike Redmond	Florida	106
10.	Mike Macfarlane	Oakland	106
11.	Charles Johnson	Baltimor	104
12.	Brad Ausmus	Detroit	104
13.	Tony Eusebio	Houston	104
14.	Benito Santiago	ChiCubs	104
15.	Mike Difelice	TampaBay	103
16.	Brent Mayne	San Fran	103
17.	Mike Lieberthal	Philadel	103
18.	Damian Miller	Arizona	103

Catcher (continued)

19.	Paul Bako	Houston	103
20.	Chad Kreuter	KansasCy	102
21.	Eddie Perez	Atlanta	102
22.	Mike Matheny	Toronto	102
23.	Einar Diaz	Clevelnd	102
24.	Matt Walbeck	Anaheim	101
25.	Ben Davis	San Dieg	101
26.	Kelly Stinnett	Arizona	101
27.	Mark Johnson	ChiSox	100
28.	Brook Fordyce	ChiSox	99
29.	Dan Wilson	Seattle	97
30.	Terry Steinbach	Minnesot	97
31.	Darrin Fletcher	Toronto	97
32.	Mike Piazza	NY Mets	96
33.	Javy Lopez	Atlanta	96
34.	Jorge Posada	NY Yanks	95
35.	A.J. Hinch	Oakland	94
36.	Joe Girardi	NY Yanks	94
37.	Chris Widger	Montreal	94
38.	Scott Servais	San Fran	94
39.	Tim Spehr	KansasCy	93
40.	Dave Nilsson	Milwauke	92
41.	Todd Hundley	LosAngls	92
42.	Jason Varitek	Boston	92
43.	Eddie Taubensee	Cincnnti	91

Center Field

1.	Andruw Jones	Atlanta	119
2.	Darren Lewis	Boston	109
3.	Ruben Rivera	San Dieg	109
4.	Jacque Jones	Minnesot	109
5.	Doug Glanville	Philadel	107
6.	Chris Singleton	ChiSox	107
7.	Lance Johnson	ChiCubs	107
8.	Torii Hunter	Minnesot	106
9.	Darryl Hamilton	Colorado	106
10.	Damon Buford	Boston	106
11.	Garrett Anderson	Anaheim	104
12.	Ryan Christenson	Oakland	104
13.	Manny Martinez	Montreal	102
14.	Jose Cruz	Toronto	102
15.	Bernie Williams	NY Yanks	101
16.	Randy Winn	TampaBay	101
17.	Steve Finley	Arizona	101
18.	Kenny Lofton	Clevelnd	99
19.	Marquis Grissom	Milwauke	98
20.	Tom Goodwin	Texas	98
21.	Carl Everett	Houston	98
22.	Mike Cameron	Cincnnti	97
23.	Brian Giles	Pittsbrg	97
24.	Ken Griffey Jr	Seattle	96

25.	Brady Anderson	Baltimor	96
26.	J.D. Drew	St Louis	96
27.	Gabe Kapler	Detroit	96
28.	Devon White	LosAngls	96
29.	Preston Wilson	Florida	94
30.	Marvin Benard	San Fran	93
31.	Carlos Beltran	KansasCy	89
32.	Brian Mcrae	NY Mets	87

Left Field

1.	Richard Hidalgo	Houston	117
2.	Geoff Jenkins	Milwauke	111
3.	B.J. Surhoff	Baltimor	110
4.	Brian Hunter	Seattle	110
5.	Ron Gant	Philadel	108
6.	Bubba Trammell	TampaBay	106
7.	Ricky Ledee	NY Yanks	105
8.	Bruce Aven	Florida	105
9.	Barry Bonds	San Fran	104
10.	Troy O'leary	Boston	104
11.	Ray Lankford	St Louis	104
12.	Rondell White	Montreal	102
13.	Johnny Damon	KansasCy	102
14.	Greg Vaughn	Cincnnti	102
15.	Reggie Sanders	San Dieg	101
16.	Rusty Greer	Texas	101
17.	Juan Encarnacion	Detroit	100
18.	Gary Sheffield	LosAngls	99
19.	Ben Grieve	Oakland	99
20.	Cliff Floyd	Florida	99
21.	Paul Sorrento	TampaBay	98
22.	Chad Allen	Minnesot	96
23.	Luis Gonzalez	Arizona	94
24.	Henry Rodriguez	ChiCubs	94
25.	Chad Curtis	NY Yanks	94
26.	Rickey Henderson	NY Mets	94
27.	Dave Justice	Clevelnd	94
28.	Dante Bichette	Colorado	93
29.	Carlos Lee	ChiSox	92
30.	Gerald Williams	Atlanta	90
31.	Al Martin	Pittsbrg	90
32.	Shannon Stewart	Toronto	88

Right Field

1.	Roger Cedeno	NY Mets	120
2.	Jermaine Dye	KansasCy	115
3.	Tony Womack	Arizona	111
4.	Shawn Green	Toronto	108
5.	Dmitri Young	Cincnnti	107
6.	Ellis Burks	San Fran	103
7.	Manny Ramirez	Clevelnd	102
8.	Tim Salmon	Anaheim	101

9.	Raul Mondesi	LosAngls	101		9.	Neifi Perez	Colorado	106
10.	Sammy Sosa	ChiCubs	101		10.	Abraham Nunez	Pittsbrg	105
11.	Paul O'Neill	NY Yanks	101		11.	Miguel Tejada	Oakland	105
12.	Magglio Ordonez	ChiSox	99		12.	Walt Weiss	Atlanta	103
13.	Larry Walker	Colorado	99		13.	Alex Rodriguez	Seattle	102
14.	Mark Kotsay	Florida	99		14.	Tim Bogar	Houston	102
15.	Albert Belle	Baltimor	98		15.	Rey Ordonez	NY Mets	101
16.	Dave Martinez	TampaBay	97		16.	Rich Aurilia	San Fran	101
17.	Vladimir Guerrero	Montreal	97		17.	Nomar Garciaparra	Boston	100
18.	Bob Higginson	Detroit	97		18.	Gary Disarcina	Anaheim	99
19.	Jeromy Burnitz	Milwauke	97		19.	Barry Larkin	Cincnnti	99
20.	Trot Nixon	Boston	97		20.	Andy Fox	Arizona	99
21.	Juan Gonzalez	Texas	95		21.	Royce Clayton	Texas	98
22.	Brian Jordan	Atlanta	95		22.	Desi Relaford	Philadel	98
23.	Matt Lawton	Minnesot	94		23.	Omar Vizquel	Clevelnd	97
24.	Matt Stairs	Oakland	93		24.	Mark Grudzielanek	LosAngls	96
25.	Jay Buhner	Seattle	89		25.	Mike Caruso	ChiSox	96
26.	Derek Bell	Houston	88		26.	Jose Valentin	Milwauke	96
27.	Bob Abreu	Philadel	87		27.	Mark Loretta	Milwauke	96
28.	Tony Gwynn	San Dieg	86		28.	Damian Jackson	San Dieg	95
					29.	Cristian Guzman	Minnesot	95
					30.	Edgar Renteria	St Louis	95

Shortstop

					31.	Chris Gomez	San Dieg	93
1.	Mike Benjamin	Pittsbrg	118		32.	Derek Jeter	NY Yanks	92
2.	Rey Sanchez	KansasCy	113		33.	Kevin Stocker	TampaBay	92
3.	Jose Hernandez	ChiCubs	112		34.	Alex Gonzalez	Florida	90
4.	Tony Batista	Toronto	111		35.	Ricky Gutierrez	Houston	90
5.	Jose Nieves	ChiCubs	109		36.	Andy Sheets	Anaheim	89
6.	Orlando Cabrera	Montreal	108		37.	Alex Arias	Philadel	88
7.	Deivi Cruz	Detroit	107					
8.	Mike Bordick	Baltimor	107					

Minor League Defensive Top Tens

First Base

					5.	Luis Rodriguez	Quad Cit	104
1.	Jeff Leaumont	StatenIs	145		6.	Edwin Diaz	Tucson	104
2.	Robb Gorr	San Bern	131		7.	Kevin Hooper	Utica	104
3.	Aaron Mcneal	Michigan	121		8.	Dustin Carr	Orlando	103
4.	Leo Daigle	W Michgn	117		9.	Alex Garcia	Ft Wayne	103
5.	Nick Crocker	Danville	115		10.	Keith Luuloa	Edmonton	103
6.	Jon Zuber	Scran-Wb	115					
7.	J.R. Phillips	ColSprin	114					
8.	Steve Neal	Sth Bend	113		### Third Base			
9.	Lyle Overbay	Missoula	112					
10.	Allen Butler	Ft Myers	111		1.	Orlando Hudson	Hagerstn	122
					2.	Rob Sasser	Jacksnvl	115
					3.	Asdrubal Oropeza	Jamestwn	115
### Second Base					4.	Andrew Beinbrink	HudsnVal	113
					5.	Carlos Villalobos	New Orln	113
1.	Derek Mann	Charl-Sc	110		6.	Lou Lucca	Scran-Wb	111
2.	Scott Sheldon	Oklahoma	107		7.	Aubrey Huff	Orlando	111
3.	Marty Malloy	Richmond	106		8.	Tom Quinlan	Iowa	109
4.	Jamey Carroll	Harrisbg	105		9.	Wilton Veras	Trenton	109
					10.	Kevin Hodge	Quad Cit	108

Shortstop

1.	Nate Frese	Lansing	120
2.	Brian Shipp	Pittsfld	111
3.	Danny Klassen	Tucson	108
4.	Mark Ellis	Spokane	107
5.	Erick Almonte	Tampa	107
6.	Aaron Capista	Sarasota	106
7.	Nick Punto	Clearwtr	105
8.	Mike Metcalfe	SanAnton	105
9.	Luis Ugueto	Utica	105
10.	Pablo Martinez	Greenvil	104
11.	Ramon Vazquez	New Havn	104
12.	Zach Sorensen	Kinston	104
13.	David Matranga	Kissimme	104
14.	Kevin Nicholson	Mobile	104

Outfield

1.	Ron Calloway	Jupiter	121
2.	Shane Victorino	GreatFls	119
3.	Michael Rosamond	Auburn	118
4.	Tarrik Brock	WestTenn	116
5.	Alejandro Diaz	Chattang	114
6.	Mckay Christensen	Birmnghm	113
7.	Jacque Jones	SaltLake	113
8.	Adam Neubart	High Des	112
9.	Jesus Lebron	St Cath	111
10.	Kurt Airoso	Jacksnvl	111
11.	Bobby Kielty	Quad Cit	111
12.	Esix Snead	Peoria	111
13.	Michael Byas	Shrevprt	111

14.	Wilken Ruan	CapeFear	110
15.	Chris Latham	SaltLake	110
16.	Julio Ramirez	Portland	109
17.	Esix Snead	Potomac	109
18.	Chris Snelling	Everett	109
19.	Jason Michaels	Clearwtr	108
20.	Kenny James	Jupiter	108
21.	Danny Ramirez	WnstnSlm	108
22.	Goefrey Tomlinson	Wichita	108
23.	Gene Kingsale	Bowie	108
24.	Michael Coleman	Pawtuckt	108
25.	Alejandro Diaz	Clinton	108
26.	Stewart Smothers	Myrtle B	108
27.	David Roberts	Buffalo	108
28.	Lou Frazier	Scran-Wb	108
29.	Dewayne Wise	Rockford	108

Catcher

1.	Ben Molina	Edmonton	108
2.	Mark Strittmatter	ColSprin	107
3.	Wiklenman Gonzalez	Mobile	106
4.	Danny Ardoin	Vancouvr	105
5.	Pee Wee Lopez	Lancastr	105
6.	Brian Moon	Stockton	105
7.	Bobby Estalella	Scran-Wb	104
8.	Brandon Inge	W Michgn	104
9.	Wilbert Nieves	R Cucmng	104
10.	Eric Christopherson	Charlott	104
11.	Brian Schneider	Harrisbg	104

Strikeouts (Per 500. Ab)

Majors, Hardest

1.	Tony Gwynn	San Dieg	17
2.	Eric Young	LosAngls	28
3.	Lance Johnson	ChiCubs	30
4.	Darryl Hamilton	Colorado	32
5.	Mike Caruso	ChiSox	34
6.	Nomar Garciaparra	Boston	37
7.	Mark Grace	ChiCubs	37
8.	Neifi Perez	Colorado	39
9.	Wade Boggs	TampaBay	40
10.	Mike Sweeney	KansasCy	42

Minors, Hardest

1.	Brian Raabe	Columbus	21
2.	Juan Pierre	Ashevlle	31
3.	Jesus Ametller	Arkansas	32
4.	Matt Howard	Nashvill	33

5.	Ben Molina	Edmonton	36
6.	Jesus Azuaje	Huntsvil	38
7.	Aaron Miles	Michigan	39
8.	Chris Walther	Lk Elsin	41
9.	Brent Abernathy	Knoxvill	41
10.	Dave Hajek	ColSprin	43

Majors, Easiest

1.	Jay Buhner	Seattle	191
2.	Jim Thome	Clevelnd	177
3.	Paul Sorrento	TampaBay	173
4.	Ruben Rivera	San Dieg	171
5.	Preston Wilson	Florida	158
6.	Derrek Lee	Florida	156
7.	Shane Andrews	Montreal	155
8.	Tim Spehr	KansasCy	153
9.	Todd Hundley	LosAngls	148
10.	Jose Hernandez	Atlanta	147

Minors, Easiest

1.	Tal Light	Carolina	269
2.	Russ Branyan	Buffalo	237
3.	Corey Pointer	Lynchbrg	232
4.	Andy Brown	StatenIs	225

5.	Justin Lincoln	Portland	218
6.	Jason Bass	New Havn	212
7.	Alvin Morrow	Beloit	211
8.	George Lombard	Richmond	209
9.	Skip Kiil	Clearwtr	209
10.	Brandon Folkers	Peoria	207

Best HR Hitters (Per 500. Ab)

Majors

1.	Mark McGwire	St Louis	60
2.	Barry Bonds	San Fran	49
3.	Sammy Sosa	ChiCubs	48
4.	Ellis Burks	San Fran	42
5.	Chipper Jones	Atlanta	41
6.	Manny Ramirez	Clevelnd	40
7.	Greg Vaughn	Cincnnti	40
8.	Alex Rodriguez	Seattle	39
9.	Mike Piazza	NY Mets	38
10.	Jeff Bagwell	Houston	38

Minors

1.	Daryle Ward	New Orln	46
2.	Jeff Manto	Buffalo	41
3.	Roosevelt Brown	Iowa	34
4.	Russ Branyan	Buffalo	34
5.	Morgan Burkhart	Sarasota	34
6.	Brent Cookson	Albuquer	33
7.	Ivan Cruz	Nashvill	31
8.	Mike Hessman	Myrtle B	31
9.	Dee Brown	Wilmngtn	30
10.	Ruben Mateo	Oklahoma	30

Best Double Rate, Players 22. And Under (Future HR Potential)

1.	Domingo Estevez	St Cath	46
2.	Rodney Nye	Pittsfld	43
3.	Jack Wilson	Peoria	41
4.	Ben Davis	LasVegas	41
5.	Andy Burress	Rockford	40
6.	Tony Mota	SanAnton	40
7.	Nick Johnson	Norwich	38
8.	Jose Ortiz	Vancouvr	38
9.	Marcus Giles	Myrtle B	38
10.	Michael Barrett	Montreal	38

11.	Austin Kearns	Rockford	38
12.	Omar Moraga	MahngVal	37
13.	Darren Blakely	Lk Elsin	37
14.	Jim Terrell	WnstnSlm	37
15.	Rafael Alvarez	Ft Myers	37
16.	Aubrey Huff	Orlando	36
17.	Rodney Clifton	Visalia	36
18.	Leo Daigle	W Michgn	36
19.	Brian Cole	Columbia	36
20.	Mike Young	Dunedin	36

Pitching (100 I Minimum)

Best KWH, Majors

1.	Pedro Martinez	Boston	14.930
2.	Keith Foulke	ChiSox	8.720
3.	Randy Johnson	Arizona	6.510
4.	Bret Saberhagen	Boston	4.360
5.	Shane Reynolds	Houston	3.110
6.	Kevin Millwood	Atlanta	2.930
7.	Kevin Brown	LosAngls	2.870
8.	Derek Lowe	Boston	2.820
9.	Jon Lieber	ChiCubs	2.550
10.	John Smoltz	Atlanta	2.530

Best KWH, Minors

1.	Scott Comer	Brevard	3.670
2.	Mike Meyers	Daytona	1.850
3.	Tanyon Sturtze	Charlott	1.670
4.	Randey Dorame	San Bern	1.630
5.	Mike Tejera	Portland	1.610
6.	Ed Yarnall	Columbus	1.530
7.	John Stephens	Delmarva	1.470
8.	Dan Reichert	Omaha	1.430
9.	Matt Riley	Bowie	1.400
10.	Brian Cooper	Erie	1.400

Strikeouts (Per 9 Innings)

Majors

1. Pedro Martinez — Boston — 13.360
2. Randy Johnson — Arizona — 11.760
3. Keith Foulke — ChiSox — 10.730
4. Tim Hudson — Oakland — 8.870
5. Chuck Finley — Anaheim — 8.730
6. David Cone — NY Yanks — 8.560
7. Scott Elarton — Houston — 8.460
8. Sterling Hitchcock — San Dieg — 8.260
9. Randy Wolf — Philadel — 8.240
10. Aaron Sele — Texas — 8.200

Minors

1. Ryan Anderson — New Havn — 9.300
2. Tim Redding — Michigan — 9.150
3. Lesli Brea — St Lucie — 8.810
4. Mike Meyers — Daytona — 8.710
5. Cedrick Bowers — Orlando — 8.650
6. Dan Reichert — Omaha — 8.550
7. John Sneed — Dunedin — 8.500
8. Eric Gagne — SanAnton — 8.360
9. Chad Hutchinson — Arkansas — 8.360
10. Mike Judd — Albuquer — 8.280

Wildest Men (Most Bb/9)

Majors

1. Ryan Dempster — Florida — 5.600
2. Bobby Jones — Colorado — 5.530
3. Russ Ortiz — San Fran — 5.280
4. Ken Hill — Anaheim — 5.240
5. Dwight Gooden — Clevelnd — 5.090
6. Steve Sparks — Anaheim — 4.930
7. Jaret Wright — Clevelnd — 4.910
8. Jimmy Haynes — Oakland — 4.850
9. Shawn Estes — San Fran — 4.830
10. Jamey Wright — Colorado — 4.730

Minors

1. Lance Caraccioli — San Bern — 9.690
2. Ben Howard — Ft Wayne — 8.640
3. Todd Cutchins — St Lucie — 8.610
4. Tim Redding — Michigan — 7.890
5. Jeremy Affeldt — Charl-Wv — 7.770
6. Derrick Lewis — Myrtle B — 7.620
7. Jason Saenz — Columbia — 7.540
8. Cristobal Rodriguez — CapeFear — 7.540
9. Matthew Bruback — Lansing — 7.270
10. Chris Jones — San Jose — 7.010

Control Men (Fewest Bb/9)

Majors

1. Bret Saberhagen — Boston — 0.810
2. Shane Reynolds — Houston — 1.370
3. Gil Heredia — Oakland — 1.470
4. Greg Maddux — Atlanta — 1.480
5. Pedro Martinez — Boston — 1.490
6. Jose Lima — Houston — 1.510
7. Steve Woodard — Milwauke — 1.630
8. Keith Foulke — ChiSox — 1.700
9. Brad Radke — Minnesot — 1.740
10. Jamie Moyer — Seattle — 1.820

Minors

1. Scott Comer — Brevard — 0.450
2. Mike Holmes — Modesto — 1.200
3. Josh Towers — Bowie — 1.420
4. Keith Dunn — Greensbr — 1.650
5. Keith Evans — Ottawa — 1.760
6. Brian Lawrence — R Cucmng — 2.040
7. Dave Telgheder — Buffalo — 2.040
8. Brian Cooper — Erie — 2.090
9. Brett Jodie — Greensbr — 2.130
10. Dickey Gonzalez — St Lucie — 2.160

Gopher Balls

Most HR/9, Majors

1.	Jeff Fassero	Seattle	1.900
2.	Chad Ogea	Philadel	1.770
3.	Denny Neagle	Cincnnti	1.740
4.	Mark Gardner	San Fran	1.720
5.	Kyle Farnsworth	ChiCubs	1.700
6.	John Snyder	ChiSox	1.670
7.	Willie Blair	Detroit	1.670
8.	Tim Belcher	Anaheim	1.660
9.	Brett Tomko	Cincnnti	1.560
10.	Brian Meadows	Florida	1.510
11.	Brian Rose	Boston	1.510

Fewest HR/9, Majors

1.	Pedro Martinez	Boston	0.330
2.	Mike Hampton	Houston	0.420
3.	Ron Villone	Cincnnti	0.450
4.	Tim Hudson	Oakland	0.460
5.	Derek Lowe	Boston	0.480
6.	Scott Elarton	Houston	0.510
7.	Kenny Rogers	Oakland	0.520
8.	Miguel Batista	Montreal	0.580
9.	Rick White	TampaBay	0.580
10.	Alex Fernandez	Florida	0.590
11.	Carl Pavano	Montreal	0.590

Most HR/9, Minors

1.	Ruben Quevedo	Richmond	2.100
2.	Chris Tynan	Savannah	2.050
3.	Felipe Lira	Toledo	1.950
4.	Mark Brownson	ColSprin	1.840
5.	Aaron Fultz	Fresno	1.820
6.	Tom Fordham	Charlott	1.780
7.	John Stewart	Savannah	1.730
8.	Scott Mullen	Omaha	1.720
9.	Jason Grilli	Fresno	1.710
10.	Ryan Bradley	Columbus	1.670
11.	Thomas Jacquez	Reading	1.670

Fewest HR/9, Minors

1.	Josh Kalinowski	Salem Va	0.230
2.	Robert Averette	Rockford	0.230
3.	Greg Kubes	Piedmont	0.290
4.	Pat Strange	Columbia	0.310
5.	Ed Yarnall	Columbus	0.320
6.	Nate Cornejo	W Michgn	0.340
7.	Jeremy Affeldt	Charl-Wv	0.350
8.	Jimmy Anderson	Nashvill	0.350
9.	Mike Maroth	Sarasota	0.350
10.	Joshua Fogg	WnstnSlm	0.360

Best Peripheral Era (PERA)

Majors

1.	Pedro Martinez	Boston	1.74
2.	Derek Lowe	Boston	2.01
3.	Keith Foulke	Chisox	2.13
4.	Bret Saberhagen	Boston	2.72
5.	Kevin Brown	LosAngls	2.76
6.	Randy Johnson	Arizona	2.95
7.	Kevin Millwood	Atlanta	2.96
8.	Mike Hampton	Houston	3.26
9.	Scott Elarton	Houston	3.28
10.	Tim Hudson	Oakland	3.35

Minors

1.	Tanyon Sturtze	Charlott	3.28
2.	Mike Fyhrie	Edmonton	3.53
3.	Jin Cho	Pawtuckt	3.53
4.	Scott Comer	Brevard	3.78
5.	Mike Meyers	Daytona	3.78
6.	Ed Yarnall	Columbus	3.79
7.	Mike Tejera	Portland	3.81
8.	Kyle Peterson	Louisvil	3.83
9.	Josh Kalinowski	Salem Va	3.91
10.	Randey Dorame	San Bern	4.13

Team Name and Ballpark Factors
Index

Team	Full Name	Nickname	League	1999 Park Factor
Akron	Akron, OH	Aeros	Eastern	974
Albuquer	Albuquerque, NM	Dukes	Pacific Coast	1023
Altoona	Altoona, PA	Curve	Eastern	892
Anaheim	Anaheim, CA	Angels	American	1009
Arizona	Arizona (Phoenix)	Diamondbacks	National	974
Arkansas	Arkansas (Little Rock)	Travelers	Texas	972
Ashevlle	Asheville, NC	Tourists	South Atlantic	1100
Atlanta	Atlanta, GA	Braves	National	942
Auburn	Auburn, NY	Doubledays	New York-Penn	1042
Augusta	Augusta, GA	GreenJackets	South Atlantic	950
Bakrsfld	Bakersfield, CA	Blaze	California	982
Baltimor	Baltimore, MD	Orioles	American	992
Batavia	Batavia, NY	Muckdogs	New York-Penn	960
Beloit	Beloit, WI	Snappers	Midwest	1014
Billings	Billings, MT	Mustangs	Pioneer	968
Binghmtn	Binghamton, NY	Mets	Eastern	1099
Birmnghm	Birmingham, AL	Barons	Southern	975
BlngtnNC	Burlington, NC	Indians	Appalach	949
Bluefld	Bluefield, WV	Orioles	Appalach	1121
Boise	Boise, ID	Hawks	Northwest	1021
Boston	Boston, MA	Red Sox	American	1045
Bowie	Bowie, MD	Baysox	Eastern	988
Brevard	Brevard County, FL	Manatees	Florida	938
Bristol	Bristol, TN	White Sox	Appalach	1026
Buffalo	Buffalo, NY	Bisons	International	996
Burlingt	Burlington, IA	Bees	Midwest	1105
Butte	Butte, MT	Copper Kings	Pioneer	1103
Calgary	Calgary, AB	Cannons	Pacific Coast	1114
CapeFear	Cape Fear (Fayetteville, NC)	Crocs	South Atlantic	1000
Carolina	(Zebulon, NC)	Mudcats	Southern	961
CedarRpd	Cedar Rapids, IA	Kernels	Midwest	979
Charl-SC	Charleston, SC	River Dogs	South Atlantic	1000
Charl-WV	Charleston, WV	Alley Cats	South Atlantic	980
Charlott	Charlotte, FL	Rangers	Florida	991
Charlott	Charlotte, NC	Knights	International	1080
Chattang	Chattanooga, TN	Lookouts	Southern	1030
ChiCubs	Chicago, IL	Cubs	National	1055
ChiSox	Chicago, IL	White Sox	American	980
Cincnnti	Cincinnati, OH	Reds	National	987
Clearwtr	Clearwater, FL	Phillies	Florida	1106
Clevelnd	Cleveland, OH	Indians	American	1029
Clinton	Clinton, IA	LumberKings	Midwest	1066
ColSprin	Colorado Springs, CO	Sky Sox	Pacific Coast	1091
Colorado	Colorado (Denver)	Rockies	National	1291
Columbia	Columbia, SC	Bombers	South Atlantic	1020

Team	Full Name	Nickname	League	1999 Park Factor
Columbus	Columbus, OH	Clippers	International	939
Columbus	Columbus, GA	RedStixx	South Atlantic	1060
Danville	Danville, VA	Braves	Appalach	989
Daytona	Daytona, FL	Cubs	Florida	1023
Delmarva	Delmarva (Salisbury, MD)	Shorebirds	South Atlantic	1000
Detroit	Detroit, MI	Tigers	American	1018
Dunedin	Dunedin, FL	Blue Jays	Florida	998
Durham	Durham, NC	Bulls	International	1000
Edmonton	Edmonton, AB	Trappers	Pacific Coast	1018
El Paso	El Paso, TX	Diablos	Texas	1122
Elizbthn	Elizabethton, TN	Twins	Appalach	961
Erie	Erie, PA	SeaWolves	Eastern	1040
Eugene	Eugene, OR	Emeralds	Northwest	1015
Everett	Everett, WA	AquaSox	Northwest	968
Florida	Florida (Miami)	Marlins	National	928
Frederck	Frederick, MD	Keys	Carolina	971
Fresno	Fresno, CA	Grizzlies	Pacific Coast	1068
Ft Myers	Fort Myers, FL	Miracle	Florida	931
Ft Wayne	Fort Wayne, IN	Wizards	Midwest	1026
GreatFls	Great Falls, MT	Dodgers	Pioneer	1030
Greensbr	Greensboro, NC	Bats	South Atlantic	980
Greenvil	Greenville, SC	Braves	Southern	1197
Hagerstn	Hagerstown, MD	Suns	South Atlantic	1050
Harrisbg	Harrisburg, PA	Senators	Eastern	1087
Helena	Helena, MT	Brewers	Pioneer	927
Hickory	Hickory, NC	Crawdads	South Atlantic	1000
High Des	High Desert (Adelanto, CA)	Mavericks	California	1196
Houston	Houston, TX	Astros	National	944
HudsnVal	Hudson Valley (Fishkill, NY)	Renegades	New York-Penn	1030
Huntsvil	Huntsville, AL	Stars	Southern	1018
IdahoFls	Idaho Falls, ID	Padres	Pioneer	970
Indianap	Indianapolis, IN	Indians	International	940
Iowa	Iowa (Des Moines)	Cubs	Pacific Coast	947
Jacksnvl	Jacksonville, FL	Suns	Southern	968
Jackson	Jackson, MS	Generals	Texas	985
Jamestwn	Jamestown, NY	Jammers	New York-Penn	1049
JohnsnCy	Johnson City, TN	Cardinals	Appalach	1114
Jupiter	Jupiter, FL	Hammerheads	Florida	985
KaneCnty	Kane County, IL	Cougars	Midwest	1010
KansasCy	Kansas City, MO	Royals	American	1020
Kingsprt	Kingsport, TN	Mets	Appalach	992
Kinston	Kinston, NC	Indians	Carolina	1017
Kissimme	Kissimmee, FL	Cobras	Florida	987
Knoxvill	Knoxville, TN	Smokies	Southern	1010
Lakeland	Lakeland, FL	Tigers	Florida	1093
Lancastr	Lancaster, CA	JetHawks	California	1126
Lansing	Lansing, MI	Lugnuts	Midwest	1086
LasVegas	Las Vegas, NV	Stars	Pacific Coast	1064
Lk Elsin	Lake Elsinore, CA	Storm	California	918
LosAngls	Los Angeles, CA	Dodgers	National	972

Team	Full Name	Nickname	League	1999 Park Factor
Louisvil	Louisville, KY	RiverBats	International	1027
Lowell	Lowell, MA	Spinners	New York-Penn	939
Lynchbrg	Lynchburg, VA	Hillcats	Carolina	1044
Macon	Macon, GA	Braves	South Atlantic	1000
MahngVal	Mahoning Valley (Niles, OH)	Scrappers	New York-Penn	946
Martnsvl	Martinsville, VA	Astros	Appalach	897
Med Hat	Medicine Hat, AB	Blue Jays	Pioneer	1004
Memphis	Memphis, TN	Redbirds	Pacific Coast	1015
Michigan	Michigan (Battle Creek)	Battle Cats	Midwest	1086
Midland	Midland, TX	RockHounds	Texas	1087
Milwauke	Milwaukee, WI	Brewers	National	1007
Minnesot	Minnesota (Minneapolis)	Twins	American	1059
Missoula	Missoula, MT	Osprey	Pioneer	946
Mobile	Mobile, AL	BayBears	Southern	984
Modesto	Modesto, CA	A's	California	998
Montreal	Montreal, QB	Expos	National	1036
Myrtle B	Myrtle Beach, SC	Pelicans	Carolina	1000
NY Mets	New York, NY	Mets	National	962
NY Yanks	New York, NY	Yankees	American	914
Nashvill	Nashville, TN	Sounds	Pacific Coast	938
New Brit	New Britain, CT	Rock Cats	Eastern	992
New Havn	New Haven, CT	Ravens	Eastern	1025
New Jrsy	New Jersey (Augusta)	Cardinals	New York-Penn	963
New Orln	New Orleans, LA	Zephyrs	Pacific Coast	923
Norfolk	Norfolk, VA	Tides	International	986
Norwich	Norwich, CT	Navigators	Eastern	969
Oakland	Oakland, CA	A's	American	989
Ogden	Ogden, UT	Raptors	Pioneer	1009
Oklahoma	Oklahoma (Oklahoma City)	RedHawks	Pacific Coast	958
Omaha	Omaha, NE	Golden Spikes	Pacific Coast	954
Oneonta	Oneonta, NY	Tigers	New York-Penn	951
Orlando	Orlando, FL	Rays	Southern	993
Ottawa	Ottawa, ON	Lynx	International	1084
Pawtuckt	Pawtucket, RI	Red Sox	International	1046
Peoria	Peoria, IL	Chiefs	Midwest	920
Philadel	Philadelphia, PA	Phillies	National	1019
Piedmont	Piedmont (Kannapolis, NC)	Boll Weevils	South Atlantic	1000
Pittsbrg	Pittsburgh, PA	Pirates	National	993
Pittsfld	Pittsfield, MA	Mets	New York-Penn	969
Portland	Portland, ME	Sea Dogs	Eastern	1088
Portland	Portland, OR	Rockies	Northwest	988
Potomac	Potomac (Woodbridge, VA)	Cannons	Carolina	1092
Princetn	Princeton, WV	Devil Rays	Appalach	1022
Pulaski	Pulaski, VA	Rangers	Appalach	981
Quad Cit	Quad Cities (Davenport, IA)	River Bandits	Midwest	929
R Cucmng	Rancho Cucamonga, CA	Quakes	California	965
Reading	Reading, PA	Phillies	Eastern	985
Richmond	Richmond, VA	Braves	International	980
Rochestr	Rochester, NY	Red Wings	International	984
Rockford	Rockford, IL	—	Midwest	986

Team	Full Name	Nickname	League	1999 Park Factor
Salem OR	Salem-Keizer, OR	Volcanoes	Northwest	1075
Salem VA	Salem, VA	Avalanche	Carolina	1045
SaltLake	Salt Lake City, UT	Buzz	Pacific Coast	1112
SanAnton	San Antonio, TX	Missions	Texas	895
San Bern	San Bernardino, CA	Stampede	California	957
San Dieg	San Diego, CA	Padres	National	960
San Fran	San Francisco, CA	Giants	National	906
San Jose	San Jose, CA	Giants	California	954
Sarasota	Sarasota, FL	Red Sox	Florida	958
Savannah	Savannah, GA	Sand Gnats	South Atlantic	960
Scran-WB	Scranton/Wilkes-Barre, PA	Red Barons	International	983
Seattle	Seattle, WA	Mariners	American	1046
Shrevprt	Shreveport, LA	Captains	Texas	964
So Oregn	Southern Oregon (Medford)	Timberjacks	Northwest	1032
Spokane	Spokane, WA	Indians	Northwest	935
St Cath	St Catherines, ON	Stompers	New York-Penn	996
St Louis	St Louis, MO	Cardinals	National	990
St Lucie	St Lucie, FL	Mets	Florida	959
St Pete	St Petersburg, FL	Devil Rays	Florida	1021
StatenIs	Staten Island, NY		New York-Penn	1077
Sth Bend	South Bend, IN	Silver Hawks	Midwest	944
Stockton	Stockton, CA	Ports	California	981
Syracuse	Syracuse, NY	SkyChiefs	International	1028
Tacoma	Tacoma, WA	Rainiers	Pacific Coast	877
TampaBay	Tampa Bay (St Petersburg, FL)	Devil Rays	American	1006
Tampa	Tampa, FL	Yankees	Florida	1003
Texas	Texas (Arlington)	Rangers	American	1043
Toledo	Toledo, OH	Mud Hens	International	981
Toronto	Toronto, ON	Blue Jays	American	1023
Trenton	Trenton, NJ	Thunder	Eastern	988
Tucson	Tucson, AZ	Sidewinders	Pacific Coast	1129
Tulsa	Tulsa, OK	Drillers	Texas	987
Utica	Utica, NY	Blue Sox	New York-Penn	981
Vancouvr	Vancouver, BC	Canadians	Pacific Coast	865
Vermont	Vermont (Winooski)	Expos	New York-Penn	1115
Vero Bch	Vero Beach, FL	Dodgers	Florida	1085
Visalia	Visalia, CA	Oaks	California	968
W Michgn	West Michigan (Grand Rapids)	Whitecaps	Midwest	919
WestTenn	West Tennessee (Jackson)	Diamond Jaxx	Southern	940
Wichita	Wichita, KS	Wranglers	Texas	1026
Willmspt	Williamsport, PA	Crosscutters	New York-Penn	1046
Wilmngtn	Wilmington, DE	Blue Rocks	Carolina	954
Wisconsn	Wisconsin (Madison)	Timber Rattlers	Midwest	990
WnstnSlm	Winston-Salem, NC	Warthogs	Carolina	1047
Yakima	Yakima, WA	Bears	Northwest	967

Biographies

Jeff Bower has been addicted to baseball ever since he snookered his dad out of a buck by picking the Tigers to win the 1968 World Series . . . *after* they were down three games to one. He works as an engineer for an airplane manufacturer in the Northwest and lives in Seattle with his wife, Vivian, and their children, Mercedes and Harrison.

Clay Davenport got hooked on baseball analysis in the mid-1980s by Bill James's *Baseball Abstracts* and Pete Palmer's *Hidden Game of Baseball*. Since then he's spent too much time, in the opinion of his family and friends, doing baseball analysis instead of real work. He currently resides in Washington D.C. and writes computer routines for weather forecasting at NOAA.

Jeff Hildebrand will escape from the University of Wisconsin-Madison this year with his Ph.D. in mathematics. He is currently trying to convince a college or university to trust him with young, impressionable minds. He is a long-suffering Phillies fan who still curses the name of Joe Carter.

Rany Jazayerli is completing his medical internship at Oakwood Hospital in Dearborn, Michigan. This July, he plans to start his residency in dermatology at Henry Ford Hospital in lovely downtown Detroit. His career as a baseball writer is only the start of what he hopes will be a lifelong campaign to rid the world of ignorance, narrow-mindedness and xenophobia. Oh, and skin cancer. On that note: wear sunscreen.

Chris Kahrl is a founding member of the *Baseball Prospectus* team. He now works for the Oriental Institute at the University of Chicago, which some of you archaeology types might recognize as Indiana Jones's place of employment had he existed.

Keith Law is the lead author of *Fantasy Baseball Index,* an annual magazine for fantasy and rotisserie players, and has contributed to *Baseball Prospectus* for four years. He works in product marketing for a Boston technology startup and holds a master's degree in industrial administration from Carnegie Mellon University.

Dave Pease attends school and works for a wireless-communications company in San Diego. He's also working on a pilot for an animated series, and in his free time enjoys working on his darts game with his limited edition Rupert Murdoch dart board.

Steven Rubio is a lecturer in American Studies at the University of California at Berkeley. He has been a Giants fan since 1958.

Joseph S. Sheehan is a founding member of *Baseball Prospectus*. In addition to playing far too much Strat-O-Matic Baseball, he enjoys spending time with his wife, Sophia, and plotting ways to move out of California.

Michael Wolverton has been writing about baseball since the age of seven, when he wrote a fan letter to Tony Oliva. He's still waiting for a reply. He works as a research scientist in the San Francisco Bay Area, where he lives with his wife, Cindy, and sons, Scott, 3, and Mark, 0.

Keith Woolner lives in the Silicon Valley and is director of marketing for Lumina Decision Systems. He also maintains Stathead.com, a website dedicated to baseball research, and manages the Boston Red Sox mailing list. He double-majored at M.I.T., and holds a master's degree from Stanford University. Sadly, he wasn't able to attend the All Star Game at Fenway Park in 1999, nor was he named to baseball's All-Century Team.

Dedications

Jeff Bower: To Jake Kuhn, who over the last 30 years has evolved from the father of a grade-school pal into a special friend. Thanks for piloting us kids around to different cities to watch baseball games and for letting us have Wiffle-ball marathons in your driveway.

Jeff Hildebrand: To the memory of my father David, who passed away last summer at far too young an age. He passed on to me his love of the game and taught me that it's not enough to compute the statistics—you must also explain them correctly.

Rany Jazayerli: To Drs. Aronson, Johnson, Sweeney and Victor for their support, and to Dr. Lim and the Dermatology faculty at Henry Ford Hospital for the opportunity. To Gary Huckabay, for the vision which created this book. And to my wife Belsam, who makes me a better man whenever she is with me.

Chris Kahrl: To my late great-grandmother Rose, an original flapper and a gloriously wonderful woman with a great outlook on life. It has been my honor to know members of four previous generations of my family, and what Rose, and her children, and her mother, taught me about life in this country in good times and bad could fill its own book. I can only hope to have the good fortune to entertain future generations with equally engaging stories about the wonders I have seen and have yet to see.

Keith Law: To my wife, Christa, for putting up with my baseball pursuits; my parents, for cultivating my love of the game; and my colleagues at the *Prospectus*, for bringing me on board in the first place.

Dave Pease: To the Middle East peace process; the work of the driven folks at Greenpeace, Farm Aid and the Red Cross; and the possibility of a better tomorrow for everyone.

Steven Rubio: To Neal and Sara.

Joseph S. Sheehan: To Rany Jazayerli, Chris Kahrl, Clay Davenport and Gary Huckabay. Few things in my life have been more rewarding than this project, and I'm glad to have been involved from the start. Thanks for a great ride, guys.

Michael Wolverton: To my wife, Cindy, for being supportive of a husband who spends far too much time working on baseball projects. My three-year-old son Scott helped me with in-game analysis many times during 1999; he's especially good at identifying balls and strikes. And a special tip of the cap to Mark Daniel Wolverton, born October 20, 1999. The passion and enthusiasm he showed during the 1999 World Series telecasts inspired me during the writing of this book. At least I think it was passion—it could've been gas.

Keith Woolner: Posthumously, to David Hilbert, inspiration for our look to the future of baseball analysis, and non-posthumously, to my wife, Kathy, for letting me watch all the postseason games, even when they conflicted with *ER*.

Index

The following is an alphabetical index of all 1,634 players in Baseball Prospectus 2000. Davenport Translations for players not listed here can be found at http://www.baseballprospectus.com.